FOREWORD

This dictionary has been designed to provide detailed coverage of the central areas of modern English and German. The user will see that, instead of merely giving *lists* of various possible but different translations, entries are divided up to give more precise information. For example, where a headword has several different meanings the relevant translations for each meaning are marked off by explanatory words in italics. Thus: **disagree** *vi* nicht übereinstimmen; (*quarrel*) (sich) streiten; (*food*) nicht bekommen (*with dat*). Of these explanatory words some act as definitions – (*quarrel*) – and some are typical subjects – (*food*). So if the user wants to know the translation for 'disagree' in the sense of 'quarrel' the dictionary tells him the correct German expression; if it is something that somebody has eaten that 'disagrees' with him then the dictionary gives the proper German equivalent. Again where a headword can be used together with other words in various ways these possibilities are indicated. For example: **abhören** *vt Vokabeln* test; *Telefongespräch* tap; *Tonband etc* listen to. The translations here are related each to a particular context, and by this means confusion and error are avoided. The user will also see that in many cases where a one-word translation is not possible whole phrases have been included, making the dictionary even more useful.

The editors are confident that with its precise analytical treatment and up-to-date wordlist this dictionary will serve the user as a most informative and reliable guide.

VORWORT

Dieses Wörterbuch hat sich eine detaillierte Behandlung der wichtigsten Bereiche der modernen englischen und deutschen Sprache zum Ziel gesetzt. Anstatt mehrere mögliche, aber in der Bedeutung verschiedene Übersetzungen nur einfach aneinanderzureihen, werden dem Benutzer anhand einer Aufgliederung des Eintrags genauere Auskünfte über Sinn und Gebrauch des Wortes gegeben. Wenn zum Beispiel ein Stichwort unterschiedliche Bedeutungen hat, werden die entsprechenden Übersetzungen mit kursiv gedruckten, erklärenden Bezeichnungen voneinander abgegrenzt. So zum Beispiel: **aufsteigen** *vi irreg* (*auf etw*) get onto; (*hochsteigen*) climb; (*Rauch*) rise. Von diesen erklärenden Bezeichnungen sind manche Definitionen oder Quasisynonyme – (*hochsteigen*) – und manche typische Subjekte – (*Rauch*). Wenn also der Benutzer die Entsprechung für ‚aufsteigen‘ in der Bedeutung von ‚hochsteigen‘ sucht, zum Beispiel im Zusammenhang mit Bergsteigern, findet er hier auf Anhieb die

... sich um Rauch, weiß er, daß 'rise' das ... darür ist. Auch wo ein Stichwort je nach korrekte Überset... unterschiedlich angewendet und übersetzt wird, richtige engl. Möglichkeiten aufgezeigt. Zum Beispiel: **abhören** vt Satzzus... werden test; *Telefongespräch* tap; *Tonband etc* listen to. Die Übersetzungen beziehen sich auf den genannten Zusammenhang, und dadurch werden Verwirrung und Fehler vermieden. Außerdem werden in Fällen, in denen eine Übersetzung durch ein einziges entsprechendes Wort nicht möglich ist, ganze Satzkonstruktionen aufgeführt, was den praktischen Wert des Wörterbuchs noch um ein weiteres erhöht.

Die Herausgeber sind der Überzeugung, daß sich dem Benutzer auf Grund dieser detaillierten Aufgliederung der Einträge und der zeitgemäßen Auswahl der Stichwörter ein aufschlußreiches und zuverlässiges Wörterbuch bietet.

editors
Veronika Calderwood-Schnorr
Ute Nicol
Peter Terrell

assistant editor
Anne Dickinson

Regular German noun endings
Regelmäßige Endungen

nom	gen	pl	nom	gen	pl
-ant	m -anten	-anten	-ion	f -ion	-ionen
-anz	f -anz	-anzen	-ist	m -isten	-isten
-ar	m -ar(e)s	-are	-ium	nt -iums	-ien
-chen	nt -chens	-chen	-ius	m -ius	-iusse
-ei	f -ei	-eien	-ive	f -ive	-iven
-elle	f -elle	-ellen	-keit	f -keit	-keiten
-ent	m -enten	-enten	-lein	nt -leins	-lein
-enz	f -enz	-enzen	-ling	m -lings	-linge
-ette	f -ette	-etten	-ment	nt -ments	-mente
-eur	m -eurs	-eure	-mus	m -mus	-men
-euse	f -euse	-eusen	-schaft	f -schaft	-schaften
-heit	f -heit	-heiten	-tät	f -tät	-täten
-ie	f -ie	-ien	-tor	m -tors	-toren
-ik	f -ik	-iken	-ung	f -ung	-ungen
-in	f -in	-innen	-ur	f -ur	-uren
-ine	f -ine	-inen			

Phonetic symbols
Lautschrift

[ː] *length mark* Längezeichen   ['] *stress mark* Betonung
['] *glottal stop* Knacklaut

all vowel sounds are approximate only
alle Vokallaute sind nur ungefähre Entsprechungen

lie	[aɪ]	weit		day	[eɪ]	
now	[aʊ]	Haut		girl	[əː]	
above	[ə]	bitte		board	[ɔː]	
green	[iː]	viel		root	[uː]	Hut
pity	[ɪ]	Bischof		come	[ʌ]	Butler
rot	[ɔ,ɒ]	Post		salon	[ʒ]	Champignon
full	[ʊ]	Pult		avant (garde)	[ɑ̃]	Ensemble
				fair	[ɛə]	mehr
bet	[b]	Ball		beer	[ɪə]	Bier
dim	[d]	dann		toy	[ɔɪ]	Heu
face	[f]	Faß		pure	[ʊə]	
go	[g]	Gast		wine	[w]	
hit	[h]	Herr		thin	[θ]	
you	[j]	ja		this	[ð]	
cat	[k]	kalt				
lick	[l]	Last		Hast	[a]	mash
must	[m]	Mast		Ensemble	[ã]	avant (garde)
nut	[n]	Nuß		Metall	[e]	meths
bang	[ŋ]	lang		häßlich	[ɛ]	
pepper	[p]	Pakt		Cousin	[ɛ̃]	
sit	[s]	Rasse		vital	[i]	
shame	[ʃ]	Schal		Moral	[o]	
tell	[t]	Tal		Champignon	[õ]	salon
vine	[v]	was		ökonomisch	[ɔ̃]	
loch	[x]	Bach		gönnen	[œ]	
zero	[z]	Hase		Heu	[ɔy]	toy
leisure	[ʒ]	Genie		kulant	[u]	
				physisch	[y]	
bat	[æ]			Müll	[ʏ]	
farm	[ɑː]	Bahn		ich	[ç]	
set	[e]	Kette				

[*]   r *can be pronounced before a vowel;* Bindungs-R

Abbreviations used in text
Im Text verwendete Abkürzungen

a	adjective	Adjektiv		Astrol	astrology	Astrologie
abbr	abbreviation	Abkürzung		Astron	astronomy	Astronomie
acc	accusative	Akkusativ		attr	attributive	attributiv
ad	adverb	Adverb		Aut	automobiles	Kraftfahr-
Agr	agriculture	Landwirt-				zeuge
		schaft		aux	auxiliary	Hilfsverb
Anat	anatomy	Anatomie		Aviat	aviation	Luftfahrt
Archit	architecture	Architektur		Biol	biology	Biologie
art	article	Artikel		Bot	botany	Botanik
Art	art	Kunst		Brit	British	britisch

Cards		Kartenspiel		old		veraltet
Chem	chemistry	Chemie		o.s.	oneself	sich
Cine	cinema	Film		Parl	parliament	Parlament
cj	conjunction	Konjunktion		pej	pejorative	abschätzig
col	colloquial	umgangs-sprachlich		Phot	photography	Photographie
Comm	commerce	Handel		Phys	physics	Physik
comp	comparative	Komparativ		pl	plural	Plural
Cook	cooking	Kochen und Backen		Pol	politics	Politik
				poss	possessive	besitzan-zeigend
cpd	compound	zusammen-gesetztes Wort		pref	prefix	Präfix, Vorsilbe
dat	dative	Dativ		prep	preposition	Präposition
Eccl	ecclesiastical	kirchlich		Press		Presse
Elec	electricity	Elektrizität		Print	printing	Typographie
esp	especially	besonders		pron	pronoun	Pronomen, Fürwort
etc	et cetera	und so weiter		Psych	psychology	Psychologie
etw	something	etwas		pt	past	1. Vergangenheit, Imperfekt
euph	euphemism	Euphemismus, Hüllwort		ptp	past participle	Partizip Perfekt
f	feminine	Femininum		Rad	radio	Radio
fig	figurative	übertragen		Rail	railways	Eisenbahn
Fin	finance	Finanzwesen		rel	relative	Relativ-
gen	genitive	Genitiv		Rel	religion	Religion
Geog	geography	Geographie		sb	someone, somebody	jemand (—en, —em)
gram	grammar	Grammatik				
Hist	history	Geschichte		Sch	school	Schulwesen
impers	impersonal	unpersönlich		Sci	science	Naturwissen-schaft
indef	indefinite	unbestimmt				
insep	inseparable	nicht getrennt gebraucht		Scot	Scottish	schottisch
				sing	singular	Singular, Einzahl
interj	interjection	Interjektion, Ausruf		Ski	skiing	Skisport
interrog	interrogative	interrogativ, fragend		sth	something	etwas
				suff	suffix	Suffix, Nachsilbe
inv	invariable	unveränderlich		superl	superlative	Superlativ
irreg	irregular	unregelmäßig		Tech	technology	Technik
jd	somebody	jemand		Tel	telecommun-ications	Nachrichten-technik
jdm	(to) some-body	jemandem				
				Theat	theatre	Theater
jdn	somebody	jemanden		TV	television	Fernsehen
jds	somebody's	jemandes		Univ	university	Hochschul-wesen
Jur	law	Rechtswesen				
Ling	linguistics	Sprachwissen-schaft		US	(North) America	(nord)-amerikanisch
				usu	usually	gewöhnlich
lit	literal	wörtlich		v	verb	Verb
liter	literary	literarisch		vi	intransitive verb	intransitives Verb
Liter	of literature	Literatur				
m	masculine	Maskulinum		vr	reflexive verb	reflexives Verb
Math	mathematics	Mathematik				
Med	medicine	Medizin		vt	transitive verb	transitives Verb
Met	meteorology	Meteorologie				
Mil	military	militärisch		Zool	zoology	Zoologie
Min	mining	Bergbau		~	change of speaker	zwischen zwei Sprechern
Mus	music	Musik				
n	noun	Substantiv, Hauptwort		≈	cultural equivalent	ungefähre Entsprechung
Naut	nautical, naval	nautisch, Seefahrt		®	registered trademark	eingetragenes Warenzeichen
nom	nominative	Nominativ				
nt	neuter	Neutrum				
num	numeral	Zahlwort				
obj	object	Objekt				

A

A, a [a:] *nt* A, a.

Aal [a:l] *m* -(e)s, -e eel.

Aas [a:s] *nt* -es, -e *or* **Äser** carrion; **—geier** *m* vulture.

ab [ap] *prep* +*dat* from; *ad* off; links — to the left; — und zu *or* an now and then *or* again; von da — from then on; der Knopf ist — the button has come off.

Abänderung [ʹapʹɛndərʊŋ] *f* alteration.

abarbeiten [ʹapʹarbaɪtən] *vr* wear o.s. out, slave away.

Abart [ʹapʹa:rt] *f* (*Biol*) variety; **a—ig** *a* abnormal.

Abbau [ʹapbaʊ] *m* -(e)s dismantling; (*Verminderung*) reduction (*gen* in); (*Verfall*) decline (*gen* in); (*Min*) mining; quarrying; (*Chem*) decomposition; **a—en** *vt* dismantle; (*Min*) mine; quarry; (*verringern*) reduce; (*Chem*) break down.

abbeißen [ʹapbaɪsən] *vt irreg* bite off.

abberufen [ʹapbəru:fən] *vt irreg* recall.

Abberufung *f* recall.

abbestellen [ʹapbəʃtɛlən] *vt* cancel.

abbezahlen [ʹapbətsa:lən] *vt* pay off.

abbiegen [ʹapbi:gən] *irreg vi* turn off; (*Straße*) bend; *vt* bend; (*verhindern*) ward off.

Abbild [ʹapbɪlt] *nt* portrayal; (*einer Person*) image, likeness; **a—en**

[ʹapbɪldən] *vt* portray; **—ung** *f* illustration.

Abbitte [ʹapbɪtə] *f*: — leisten *or* tun make one's apologies (*bei* to).

abblasen [ʹapbla:zən] *vt irreg* blow off; (*fig*) call off.

abblenden [ʹapblɛndən] *vti* (*Aut*) dip, dim (*US*).

Abblendlicht *nt* dipped *or* dimmed (*US*) headlights *pl*.

abbrechen [ʹapbrɛçən] *vti irreg* break off; *Gebäude* pull down; *Zelt* take down; (*aufhören*) stop.

abbrennen [ʹapbrɛnən] *irreg vt* burn off; *Feuerwerk* let off; *vi* (*aux sein*) burn down; abgebrannt sein (*col*) be broke.

abbringen [ʹapbrɪŋən] *vt irreg*: jdn von etw — dissuade sb from sth; jdn vom Weg — divert sb; ich bringe den Verschluß nicht ab (*col*) I can't get the top off.

abbröckeln [ʹapbrœkəln] *vti* crumble off *or* away.

Abbruch [ʹapbrʊx] *m* (*von Verhandlungen etc*) breaking off; (*von Haus*) demolition; jdm/etw — tun harm sb/sth; **a—reif** *a* only fit for demolition.

abbrühen [ʹapbry:ən] *vt* scald; abgebrüht (*col*) hard-boiled.

abbuchen [ʹapbu:xən] *vt* debit.

abbürsten [ʹapbyrstən] *vt* brush off.

abdanken [ʹapdaŋkən] *vi* resign; (*König*) abdicate.

Abdankung *f* **resignation;** abdication.

abdecken ['apdɛkən] vt uncover; Tisch clear; Loch cover.

abdichten ['apdɪçtən] vt seal; (Naut) caulk.

abdrängen ['apdrɛŋən] vt push off.

abdrehen ['apdreːən] vt Gas turn off; Licht switch off; Film shoot; jdm den Hals — wring sb's neck; vi (Schiff) change course.

abdrosseln ['apdrɔsəln] vt throttle; (Aut) stall; Produktion cut back.

Abdruck ['apdrʊk] m (Nachdrucken) reprinting; (Gedrucktes) reprint; (Gips—, Wachs—) impression; (Finger—) print; a—en vt print, publish.

abdrücken ['apdrʏkən] vt make an impression of; Waffe fire; Person hug, squeeze; jdm die Luft — squeeze all the breath out of sb; vr leave imprints; (abstoßen) push o.s. away.

abebben ['ap'ɛbən] vi ebb away.

Abend ['aːbənt] m -s, -e evening; zu — essen have dinner or supper; a— ad evening; —brot nt, —essen nt supper; a—füllend taking up the whole evening; —kurs m evening classes pl; —land nt West; a—lich a evening; —mahl nt Holy Communion; —rot nt sunset; a—s ad in the evening.

Abenteuer ['aːbəntɔyər] nt -s, - adventure; a—lich a adventurous.

Abenteurer m -s, - adventurer; —in f adventuress.

aber ['aːbər] cj but; (jedoch) however; das ist — schön that's really nice; nun ist — Schluß! now that's enough! ad tausend und — tausend thousands upon thousands; A— nt but; A—glaube m superstition; —gläubig a superstitious.

aberkennen ['ap'ɛrkɛnən] vt irreg: jdm etw — deprive sb of sth, take sth (away) from sb.

Aberkennung f taking away.

aber- cpd: —malig a repeated; —mals ad once again.

abfahren ['apfaːrən] irreg vi leave, depart; vt take or cart away; Strecke drive; Reifen wear; Fahrkarte use.

Abfahrt ['apfaːrt] f departure; (Ski) descent; (Piste) run; —slauf m (Ski) descent, run down; —(s)tag m day of departure; —szeit f departure time.

Abfall ['apfal] m waste; (von Speisen etc) rubbish, garbage (US); (Neigung) slope; (Verschlechterung) decline; —eimer m rubbish bin, garbage can (US); a—en vi irreg (lit, fig) fall or drop off; (Pol, vom Glauben) break away; (sich neigen) fall or drop away.

abfällig ['apfɛlɪç] a disparaging, deprecatory.

abfangen ['apfaŋən] vt irreg intercept; Person catch; (unter Kontrolle bringen) check.

abfärben ['apfɛrbən] vi (lit) lose its colour; (Wäsche) run; (fig) rub off.

abfassen ['apfasən] vt write, draft.

abfertigen ['apfɛrtɪgən] vt prepare for dispatch, process; (an der Grenze) clear; Kundschaft attend to; jdn kurz — give sb short shrift.

Abfertigung f preparing for dispatch, processing; clearance.

abfeuern ['apfɔyərn] vt fire.

abfinden ['apfɪndən] irreg vt pay off; vr come to terms; sich mit jdm —/nicht — put up with/not get on with sb.

Abfindung f (von Gläubigern) payment; (Geld) sum in settlement.

abflauen ['ap-flauən] vi (Wind, Erregung) die away, subside; (Nachfrage, Geschäft) fall or drop off.

abfliegen ['ap-fli:gən] irreg vi (Flugzeug) take off; (Passagier auch) fly; vt Gebiet fly over.

abfließen ['ap-fli:sən] vi irreg drain away.

Abflug ['ap-flu:k] m departure; (Start) take-off; —zeit f departure time.

Abfluß ['ap-flʊs] m draining away; (Öffnung) outlet.

abfragen ['ap-fra:gən] vt test; jdn or jdm etw — question sb on sth.

Abfuhr ['ap-fu:r] f ⁊, -en removal; (fig) snub, rebuff.

Abführ- ['ap-fy:r] cpd: a—en vt lead away; Gelder, Steuern pay; vi (Med) have a laxative effect; —mittel nt laxative, purgative.

abfüllen ['ap-fʏlən] vt draw off; (in Flaschen) bottle.

Abgabe ['apga:bə] f handing in; (von Ball) pass; (Steuer) tax; (eines Amtes) giving up; (einer Erklärung) giving; a—nfrei a tax-free; a—npflichtig a liable to tax.

Abgang ['apgaŋ] m (von Schule) leaving; (Theat) exit; (Med: Ausscheiden) passing; (Fehlgeburt) miscarriage; (Abfahrt) departure; (der Post, von Waren) dispatch.

Abgas ['apga:s] nt waste gas; (Aut) exhaust.

abgeben ['apge:bən] irreg vt Gegenstand hand or give in; Ball pass; Wärme give off; Amt hand over; Schuß fire; Erklärung, Urteil give; (darstellen, sein) make; jdm etw — (überlassen) let sb have sth; vr:

sich mit jdm/etw — associate with sb/bother with sth.

abgedroschen ['apgədroʃən] a hackneyed; Witz corny.

abgefeimt ['apgəfaimt] a cunning.

abgegriffen ['apgəgrifən] a Buch well-thumbed; Redensart hackneyed.

abgehen ['apge:ən] irreg vi go away, leave; (Theat) exit; (Post) go; (Med: be passed; (Baby) die; (Knopf etc) come off; (abgezogen werden) be taken off; (Straße) branch off; etw geht jdm ab (fehlt) sb lacks sth; vt Strecke go or walk along.

abgelegen ['apgəle:gən] a remote.

abgemacht ['apgəmaxt] a fixed; —! done.

abgeneigt ['apgənaikt] a averse to, disinclined.

Abgeordnete(r) ['apgə'ɔrdnətə(r)] mf member of parliament; elected representative.

Abgesandte(r) ['apgəzantə(r)] mf delegate; (Pol) envoy.

abgeschmackt ['apgəʃmakt] a tasteless; A—heit f lack of taste; (Bemerkung) tasteless remark.

abgesehen ['apgəze:ən] a: es auf jdn/etw —.haben be after sb/sth; — von... apart from...

abgespannt ['apgəʃpant] a tired out.

abgestanden ['apgəʃtandən] a stale; Bier auch flat.

abgestorben ['apgəʃtɔrbən] a numb; (Biol, Med) dead.

abgetakelt ['apgətakəlt] a (col) decrepit, past it.

abgetragen ['apgətra:gən] a shabby, worn out.

abgewinnen ['apgəvinən] vt irreg: jdm Geld — win money from sb einer Sache etw/Geschmack — get sth/pleasure from sth.

abgewöhnen ['apgəvøːnən] vt: jdm/sich etw — cure sb of sth/give sth up.

abgleiten ['apglaɪtən] vi irreg. slip, slide.

Abgott ['apgɔt] m idol.

abgöttisch ['apgœtɪʃ] a: — lieben idolize.

abgrenzen ['apgrɛntsən] vt (lit, fig) mark off; fence off.

Abgrund ['apgrʊnt] m (lit, fig) abyss.

abgründig ['apgrʏndɪç] a unfathomable; Lächeln cryptic.

abhacken ['aphakən] vt chop off.

abhaken ['aphaːkən] vt tick off.

abhalten ['aphaltən] vt irreg Versammlung hold; jdn von etw — (fernhalten) keep sb away from sth; (hindern) keep sb from sth.

abhandeln ['aphandəln] vt Thema deal with; jdm die Waren/8 Mark — do a deal with sb for the goods/beat sb down 8 marks.

abhanden [ap'handən] a: — kommen get lost.

Abhandlung ['aphandlʊŋ] f treatise, discourse.

Abhang ['aphaŋ] m slope.

abhängen ['aphɛŋən] vt irreg Bild take down; Anhänger uncouple; Verfolger shake off; vi (Fleisch) hang; von jdm/etw — depend on sb/sth.

abhängig ['aphɛŋɪç] a dependent (von on); A—keit f dependence (von on).

abhärten ['aphɛrtən] vtr toughen (o.s.) up; sich gegen etw — inure o.s. to sth.

abhauen ['aphaʊən] irreg vt cut

off; Baum cut down; vi (col) clear off or out.

abheben ['apheːbən] irreg vt lift (up); Karten cut; Masche slip; Geld withdraw, take out; vi (Flugzeug) take off; (Rakete) lift off; (Cards) cut; vr stand out (von from), contrast (von with).

abhelfen ['aphɛlfən] vi irreg (+ dat) remedy.

abhetzen ['aphɛtsən] vr wear or tire o.s. out.

Abhilfe ['aphɪlfə] f remedy; — schaffen put things right.

abholen ['aphoːlən] vt Gegenstand fetch, collect; Person call for; (am Bahnhof etc) pick up, meet.

abhorchen ['aphɔrçən] vt (Med) auscultate, sound.

abhören ['aphøːrən] vt Vokabeln test; Telefongespräch tap; Tonband etc listen to.

Abhörgerät nt bug.

Abitur [abi'tuːr] nt -s, -e German school leaving examination; —i'ent(in f) m candidate for school leaving certificate.

abkämmen ['apkɛmən] vt Gegend comb, scour.

abkanzeln ['apkantsəln] vt (col) bawl out.

abkapseln ['apkapsəln] vr shut or cut o.s. off.

abkaufen ['apkaʊfən] vt: jdm etw — buy sth from sb.

abkehren ['apkeːrən] vt Blick avert, turn away; vr turn away.

Abklatsch ['apklatʃ] m -es, -e (fig) (poor) copy.

abklingen ['apklɪŋən] vi irreg die away; (Radio) fade out.

abknöpfen ['apknœpfən] vt unbutton; jdm etw — (col) get sth off sb.

abkochen   5   abmelden

abkochen ['apkɔxən] vt boil.

abkommen ['apkɔmən] vi irreg get away; von der Straße/von einem Plan — leave the road/give up a plan; A— nt -s, - agreement.

abkömmlich ['apkœmliç] a available, free.

abkratzen ['apkratsən] vt scrape off; vi (col) kick the bucket.

abkühlen ['apky:lən] vt cool down; vr (Mensch) cool down or off; (Wetter) get cool; (Zuneigung) cool.

Abkunft ['apkunft] f - origin, birth.

abkürzen ['apkYrtsən] vt shorten; Wort auch abbreviate; den Weg — take a short cut.

Abkürzung f (Wort) abbreviation; (Weg) short cut.

abladen ['apla:dən] vt irreg unload.

Ablage ['apla:gə] f -, -n (für Akten) tray; (für Kleider) cloakroom; a—rn vt deposit; vr be deposited; vi mature.

ablassen ['aplasən] irreg vt Wasser, Dampf let off; (vom Preis) knock off; vi: von etw — give sth up, abandon sth.

Ablauf ['aplauf] m (Abfluß) drain; (von Ereignissen) course; (einer Frist, Zeit) expiry; a—en irreg vi (abfließen) drain away; (Ereignisse) happen; (Frist, Zeit, Paß) expire; vt Sohlen wear (down or out); jdm den Rang a—en steal a march on sb.

ablegen ['aple:gən] vt put or lay down; Kleider take off; Gewohnheit get rid of; Prüfung sit, take; Zeugnis give.

Ableger m -s, - layer; (fig) branch, offshoot.

ablehnen ['aple:nən] vt reject; Einladung decline, refuse; vi decline, refuse.

Ablehnung f rejection; refusal.

ableiten ['aplaitən] vt Wasser divert; (deduzieren) deduce; Wort derive.

Ableitung f diversion; deduction; derivation; (Wort) derivative.

ablenken ['aplɛŋkən] vt turn away, deflect; (zerstreuen) distract; vi change the subject.

Ablenkung f distraction.

ablesen ['aple:zən] vt irreg read out; Meßgeräte read.

ableugnen ['aplɔygnən] vt deny.

ablichten ['apliçtən] vt photocopy; photograph.

abliefern ['apli:fərn] vt deliver; etw bei jdm/einer Dienststelle — hand sth over to sb/in at an office.

Ablieferung f delivery; —sschein m delivery note.

abliegen ['apli:gən] vi irreg be some distance away; (fig) be far removed.

ablisten ['aplɪstən] vt: jdm etw — trick or con sb out of sth.

ablösen ['aplø:zən] vt (abtrennen) take off, remove; (in Amt) take over from; Wache relieve.

Ablösung f removal; relieving.

abmachen ['apmaxən] vt take off; (vereinbaren) agree.

Abmachung f agreement.

abmagern ['apma:gərn] vi get thinner.

Abmagerungskur f diet; eine — machen go on a diet.

Abmarsch ['apmarʃ] m departure; a—bereit a ready to start; a—ieren vi march off.

abmelden ['apmɛldən] vt Zeitungen cancel; Auto take off the road; jdn bei der Polizei — register sb's departure with the police; vr give notice of one's departure; (*im Hotel*) check out.

abmessen ['apmɛsən] *vt irreg* measure.

Abmessung *f* measurement.

abmontieren ['apmɔnti:rən] *vt* take off.

abmühen ['apmy:ən] *vr* wear o.s. out.

Abnäher ['apnɛ:ər] *m* -s, - dart.

Abnahme ['apna:mə] *f* -, -n removal; (*Comm*) buying; (*Verringerung*) decrease (*gen* in).

abnehmen ['apne:mən] *irreg vt* take off, remove; (*Führerschein*) take away; *Geld* get (*jdm* out of sb); (*kaufen, col*: *glauben*) buy (*jdm* from sb); *Prüfung* hold; *Maschen* decrease; **jdm Arbeit —** take work off sb's shoulders; *vi* decrease; (*schlanker werden*) lose weight.

Abnehmer *m* -s, - purchaser, customer.

Abneigung ['apnaigʊŋ] *f* aversion, dislike.

abnorm [ap'nɔrm] *a* abnormal.

abnötigen ['apnø:tigən] *vt:* **jdm etw/Respekt —** force sth from sb/gain sb's respect.

abnutzen ['apnʊtsən] *vt* wear out.

Abnutzung *f* wear (and tear).

Abonnement [abɔn(e)'mãː] *nt* -s, -s subscription.

Abonnent(in *f*) [abɔ'nɛnt(ɪn)] *m* subscriber.

abonnieren [abɔ'ni:rən] *vt* subscribe to.

abordnen ['ap'ɔrdnən] *vt* delegate.

Abordnung *f* delegation.

Abort [a'bɔrt] *m* -(e)s, -e lavatory.

abpacken ['appakən] *vt* pack.

abpassen ['appasən] *vt Person,*

Gelegenheit wait for; (*in Größe*) *Stoff etc* adjust.

abpfeifen ['appfaifən] *vti irreg* (*Sport*) (**das Spiel**) — blow the whistle (for the end of the game).

Abpfiff ['appfif] *m* final whistle.

abplagen ['appla:gən] *vr* wear o.s. out.

Abprall ['appral] *m* rebound; (*von Kugel*) ricochet; **a—en** *vi* bounce off; ricochet.

abputzen ['apputsən] *vt* clean.

abquälen ['ap-kvɛ:lən] *vr* drive o.s. frantic; **sich mit etw —** struggle with sth.

abraten ['apra:tən] *vi irreg* advise, warn (*jdm von etw* sb against sth).

abräumen ['aprɔʏmən] *vt* clear up or away.

abreagieren ['apreagi:rən] *vt Zorn* work off (*an* +*dat* on); *vr* calm down.

abrechnen ['aprɛçnən] *vt* deduct, take off; *vi* (*lit*) settle up; (*fig*) get even.

Abrechnung *f* settlement; (*Rechnung*) bill.

Abrede ['apre:də] *f*: **etw in —** stellen deny or dispute sth.

abregen ['apre:gən] *vr* (*col*) calm or cool down.

abreiben ['apraibən] *vtr irreg* rub off; (*säubern*) wipe; **jdn mit einem Handtuch —** towel sb down.

Abreise ['apraizə] *f* departure; **a—n** *vi* leave, set off.

abreißen ['aprasən] *vt irreg Haus* tear down; *Blatt* tear off.

abrichten ['apriçtən] *vt* train.

abriegeln ['apri:gəln] *vt Tür* bolt; *Straße, Gebiet* seal off.

Abriß ['aprɪs] *m* -sses, -sse (*Übersicht*) outline.

Abruf ['apru:f] *m*: auf — on call; a—en *vt irreg* Mensch call away; (*Comm*) Ware request delivery of.

abrunden ['aprʊndən] *vt* round off.

abrüsten ['aprʏstən] *vi* disarm.

Abrüstung *f* disarmament.

abrutschen ['aprʊtʃən] *vi* slip; (*Aviat*) sideslip.

Absage ['apza:gə] *f* -, -n refusal; a—n *vt* cancel, call off; Einladung turn down; *vi* cry off; (*ablehnen*) decline.

absägen ['apzɛ:gən] *vt* saw off.

absahnen ['apza:nən] *vt* (*lit*) skim; das beste für **sich** — take the cream.

Absatz ['apzats] *m* (*Comm*) sales *pl*; (*Bodensatz*) deposit; (*neuer Abschnitt*) paragraph; (*Treppen—*) landing; (*Schuh—*) heel; —flaute *f* slump in the market; —gebiet *nt* (*Comm*) market.

abschaben ['ap-ʃa:bən] *vt* scrape off; Möhren scrape.

abschaffen ['ap-ʃafən] *vt* abolish, do away with.

Abschaffung *f* abolition.

abschalten ['ap-ʃaltən] *vti* (*lit, col*) switch off.

abschattieren ['ap-ʃati:rən] *vt* shade.

abschätzen ['ap-ʃɛtsən] *vt* estimate; Lage assess; Person size up.

abschätzig ['ap-ʃɛtsɪç] *a* disparaging, derogatory.

Abschaum ['ap-ʃaum] *m* -(e)s scum.

Abscheu ['ap-ʃɔy] *m* -(e)s loathing, repugnance; a—erregend *a* repulsive, loathsome; a—lich [ap'ʃɔylɪç] *a* abominable.

abschicken ['ap-ʃikən] *vt* send off.

abschieben ['ap-ʃi:bən] *vt irreg* push away; Person pack off.

Abschied ['ap-ʃi:t] *m* -(e)s, -e parting; (*von Armee*) discharge; — nehmen say good-bye (*von jdm* to sb), take one's leave (*von jdm* of sb); seinen — nehmen (*Mil*) apply for discharge; zum — on parting; —sbrief *m* farewell letter; —sfeier *f* farewell party.

abschießen [ap-ʃi:sən] *vt irreg* Flugzeug shoot down; Geschoß fire; (*col*) Minister get rid of.

abschirmen ['ap-ʃirmən] *vt* screen.

abschlagen ['ap-ʃla:gən] *vt irreg* (*abhacken*, *Comm*) knock off; (*ablehnen*) refuse; (*Mil*) repel.

abschlägig ['ap-ʃlɛ:gɪç] *a* negative.

Abschlagszahlung *f* interim payment.

abschleifen ['ap-ʃlaifən] *irreg vt* grind down; Rost polish off; *vr* wear off.

Abschlepp- ['ap-ʃlep] *cpd*: —dienst *m* (*Aut*) breakdown service; a—en *vt* take in tow; —seil *nt* towrope.

abschließen ['ap-ʃli:sən] *irreg vt* Tür lock; (*beenden*) conclude, finish; Vertrag, Handel conclude; *vr* (*sich isolieren*) cut o.s. off.

Abschluß ['ap-ʃlus] *m* (*Beendigung*) close, conclusion; (*Comm: Bilanz*) balancing; (*von Vertrag, Handel*) conclusion; zum — in conclusion; —feier *f* end-of-term party; —rechnung *f* final account.

abschmieren ['ap-ʃmi:rən] *vt* (*Aut*) grease, lubricate.

abschneiden ['ap-ʃnaidən] *irreg vt* cut off; *vi* do, come off.

Abschnitt ['ap-ʃnit] *m* section; (*Mil*) sector; (*Kontroll—*) counterfoil; (*Math*) segment; (*Zeit—*) period.

abschnüren ['ap-ʃny:rən] *vt* constrict.

abschöpfen ['ap-ʃœpfən] vt skim off.

abschrauben ['ap-ʃraubən] vt un-.screw.

abschrecken ['ap-ʃrɛkən] vt deter, put off; (mit kaltem Wasser) plunge in cold water; **—d** a deterrent; **—des Beispiel** warning.

abschreiben ['ap-ʃraibən] vt irreg copy; (verlorengeben) write off; (Comm) deduct.

Abschreibung f (Comm) deduction; (Wertverminderung) depreciation.

Abschrift ['ap-ʃrift]√ f copy.

abschürfen ['ap-ʃyrfən] vt graze.

Abschuß ['ap-ʃus] m (eines Geschützes) firing; (Herunterschießen) shooting down; (Tötung) shooting.

abschüssig ['ap-ʃysɪç] a steep.

abschütteln ['ap-ʃytəln] vt shake off.

abschwächen ['ap-ʃvɛçən] vt lessen; Behauptung, Kritik tone down; vr lessen.

abschweifen ['ap-ʃvaifən] vi wander.

Abschweifung f digression.

abschwellen ['ap-ʃvɛlən] vi irreg (Geschwulst) go down; (Lärm) die down.

abschwenken ['ap-ʃvɛŋkən] vi turn away.

abschwören ['ap-ʃvøːrən] vi irreg (+dat) renounce.

abseh- ['apze:] cpd: **—bar** a foreseeable; **in —barer Zeit** in the foreseeable future; **das Ende ist —bar** the end is in sight; **—en** irreg vt Ende, Folgen foresee; **jdm etw —en** (erlernen) copy sth from sb; vi: **von etw —en** refrain from sth;

(nicht berücksichtigen) leave sth out of consideration.

abseits ['apzaits] ad out of the way; prep +gen away from; A—nt (Sport) offside; **im A— stehen** be offside.

Absend- ['apzɛnd] cpd: **a—en** vt irreg send off, dispatch; **er** m **-s**, - sender; **—ung** f dispatch.

absetz- ['apzɛts] cpd: **—bar** a Beamter dismissible; Waren saleable; (von Steuer) deductible; **—en** vt (niederstellen, aussteigen lassen) put down; (abnehmen) take off; (Comm: verkaufen) sell; (Fin: abziehen) deduct; (entlassen) dismiss; König depose; (streichen) drop; (hervorheben) pick out; vr (sich entfernen) clear off; (sich ablagern) be deposited; A—ung f (Fin: Abzug) deduction; (Entlassung) dismissal; (von König) deposing; (Streichung) dropping.

absichern ['apzɪçərn] vtr make safe; (schützen) safeguard.

Absicht ['apzɪçt] f intention; **mit —** on purpose; **a—lich** a intentional, deliberate; **a—slos** a unintentional.

absinken ['apzɪŋkən] vi irreg sink; (Temperatur, Geschwindigkeit) decrease.

absitzen ['apzɪtsən] irreg vi dismount; vt Strafe serve.

absolut [apzɔ'luːt] a absolute; A—ismus [-'tɪsmus] m absolutism.

absolvieren [apzɔl'viːrən] vt (Sch) complete.

absonder- ['apzɔndər] cpd: **—lich** [ap'zɔndərlɪç] a odd, strange; **—n** vt separate; (ausscheiden) give off, secrete; vr cut o.s. off; A—ung f separation; (Med) secretion.

abspalten ['ap-ʃpaltən] vt split off.

Abspannung ['ap-ʃpanʊŋ] f (Ermüdung) exhaustion.

absparen ['ap-ʃpa:rən] vt: sich (dat) etw — scrimp and save for sth.

abspeisen ['ap-ʃpaizən] vt (fig) fob off.

abspenstig ['ap-ʃpɛnstɪç]: — machen lure away (jdm from sb).

absperren ['ap-ʃpɛrən] vt block or close off; Tür lock.

Absperrung f (Vorgang) blocking or closing off; (Sperre) barricade.

abspielen ['ap-ʃpi:lən] vt Platte, Tonband play; **vom Blatt** — (Mus) sight-read; vr happen.

absplittern ['ap-ʃplɪtərn] vt chip off.

Absprache ['ap-ʃpra:xə] f arrangement.

absprechen ['ap-ʃprɛçən] vt irreg (vereinbaren) arrange; jdm etw — deny sb sth.

abspringen ['ap-ʃprɪŋən] vi irreg jump down/off; (Farbe, Lack) flake off; (Aviat) bale out; (sich distanzieren) back out.

Absprung ['ap-ʃprʊŋ] m jump.

abspülen ['ap-ʃpy:lən] vt rinse; Geschirr wash up.

abstammen ['ap-ʃtamən] vi be descended; (Wort) be derived.

Abstammung f descent; derivation.

Abstand ['ap-ʃtant] m distance; (zeitlich) interval; davon — nehmen, etw zu tun refrain from doing sth; — halten (Aut) keep one's distance; mit — der beste by far the best; —ssumme f compensation.

abstatten ['ap-ʃtatən] vt Dank give; Besuch pay.

abstauben ['ap-ʃtaubən] vti dust;

(col: stehlen) pinch; (den Ball) — (Sport) tuck the ball away.

abstechen ['ap-ʃtɛçən] irreg vt cut; Tier cut the throat of; vi contrast (gegen, von with).

Abstecher m -s, - detour.

abstecken ['ap-ʃtɛkən] vt (losmachen) unpin; Fläche mark out.

abstehen ['ap-ʃte:ən] vi irreg (Ohren, Haare) stick out; (entfernt sein) stand away.

absteigen ['ap-ʃtaigən] vi irreg (vom Rad etc) get off, dismount; (in Gasthof) put up (in +dat at); (Sport) be relegated (in +acc to).

abstellen ['ap-ʃtɛlən] vt (niederstellen) put down; (entfernt stellen) pull out; (hinstellen) Auto park; (ausschalten) turn or switch off; Mißstand, Unsitte stop; (ausrichten) gear (auf +acc to).

Abstellgleis nt siding.

abstempeln ['ap-ʃtɛmpəln] vt stamp.

absterben ['ap-ʃtɛrbən] vi irreg die; (Körperteil) go numb.

Abstieg ['ap-ʃti:k] m -(e)s, -e descent; (Sport) relegation; (fig) decline.

abstimmen ['ap-ʃtɪmən] vi vote; vt Instrument tune (auf +acc to); Interessen match (auf +acc with); Termine, Ziele fit in (auf +acc with); vr agree.

Abstimmung f vote.

abstinent [apsti'nɛnt] a abstemious; (von Alkohol) teetotal.

Abstinenz [apsti'nɛnts] f abstinence; teetotalism; **—ler** m -s, - teetotaller.

abstoßen ['ap-ʃto:sən] vt irreg push off or away; (verkaufen) unload; (anekeln) repel, repulse; **—d** a repulsive.

abstrahieren [apstra'hi:rən] *vti* abstract.

abstrakt [ap'strakt] *a* abstract; *ad* abstractly, in the abstract; A—ion [apstraktsi'oːn] *f* abstraction; A—um *nt* -s, -kta abstract concept/noun.

abstreiten ['ap-ʃtraitən] *vt Irreg* deny.

Abstrich ['ap-ʃtrɪç] *m* (*Abzug*) cut; (*Med*) smear; **—e machen** lower one's sights.

abstufen ['ap-ʃtuːfən] *vt Hang* terrace; *Farben* shade; *Gehälter* grade.

abstumpfen ['ap-ʃtumpfən] *vt* (*lit, fig*) dull, blunt; *vi* (*lit, fig*) become dulled.

Absturz ['ap-ʃtʊrts] *m* fall; (*Aviat*) crash.

abstürzen ['ap-ʃtʏrtsən] *vi* fall; (*Aviat*) crash.

absuchen [apzuːxən] *vt* scour, search.

absurd [ap'zʊrt] *a* absurd.

Abszeß [aps'tsɛs] *m* -sses, -sse abscess.

Abt [apt] *m* -(e)s, ⁼e abbot.

abtasten [aptastən] *vt* feel, probe.

abtauen ['aptauən] *vti* thaw.

Abtei [ap'tai] *f* ⁓, -en abbey.

Abteil [ap'tail] *nt* -(e)s, -e compartment; **a—en** *vt* divide up; (*abtrennen*) divide off; **—ung** *f* (*in Firma, Kaufhaus*) department; (*Mil*) unit; **—ungsleiter** *m* head of department.

abtönen ['aptøːnən] *vt* (*Phot*) tone down.

abtragen ['aptraːgən] *vt Irreg Hügel, Erde* level down; *Essen* clear away; *Kleider* wear out; *Schulden* pay off.

abträglich ['aptrɛːklɪç] *a* harmful (*dat* to).

abtransportieren ['aptransportiːrən] *vt* take away, remove.

abtreiben ['aptraibən] *Irreg vt Boot, Flugzeug* drive off course; *Kind* abort; *vi* be driven off course; abort.

Abtreibung *f* abortion; **—sversuch** *m* attempted abortion.

abtrennen ['aptrɛnən] *vt* (*lostrennen*) detach; (*entfernen*) take off; (*abteilen*) separate off.

abtreten ['aptreːtən] *Irreg vt* wear out; (*überlassen*) hand over, cede (*jdm* to *sb*); *vi* go off; (*zurücktreten*) step down.

Abtritt ['aptrɪt] *m* resignation.

abtrocknen ['aptrɔknən] *vti* dry.

abtrünnig ['aptrʏnɪç] *a* renegade.

abtun ['aptuːn] *vt Irreg* take off; (*fig*) dismiss.

aburteilen ['ap'urtailən] *vt* condemn.

abverlangen ['ap-fɛrlaŋən] *vt*: **jdm etw —** demand *sth* from *sb*.

abwägen ['apvɛːgən] *vt Irreg* weigh up.

abwählen ['apvɛːlən] *vt* vote out (of office).

abwandeln ['apvandəln] *vt* adapt.

abwandern ['apvandərn] *vi* move away.

abwarten ['apvartən] *vt* wait for; *vi* wait.

abwärts ['apvɛrts] *ad* down.

Abwasch ['apvaʃ] *m* -(e)s wash-ing-up; **a—en** *vt Irreg Schmutz* wash off; *Geschirr* wash (up).

Abwasser ['apvasər] *nt* -s, -wässer sewage.

abwechseln ['apvɛksəln] *vir* alternate; (*Personen*) take turns; **—d** *a* alternate.

Abweg ['apveːk] *m*: auf —e geraten/führen go/lead astray; a—ig ['apveːgɪç] *a* wrong.

Abwehr ['apveːr] *f* - defence; (*Schutz*) .protection; (—dienst) counter-intelligence (service); a—en *vt* ward off; *Ball* stop; a—ende Geste dismissive gesture.

abweichen ['apvaɪçən] *vi irreg* deviate; (*Meinung*) differ; —d *a* deviant; differing.

abweisen ['apvaɪzən] *vt irreg* turn away; *Antrag* turn down; —d *a* (*Haltung*) cold.

abwenden ['apvɛndən] *irreg vt* avert; *vr* turn away.

abwerben ['apvɛrbən] *vt irreg* woo away (*jdm* from sb).

abwerfen ['apvɛrfən] *vt irreg* throw off; *Profit* yield; (*aus Flugzeug*) drop; *Spielkarte* discard.

abwerten ['apvɛrtən] *vt* (*Fin*) devalue.

abwesend ['apveːzənt] *a* absent.

Abwesenheit ['apveːzənhaɪt] *f* absence.

abwickeln ['apvɪkəln] *vt* unwind; *Geschäft* wind up.

abwiegen ['apviːgən] *vt irreg* weigh out.

abwimmeln ['apvɪməln] *vt* (*col*) *Person* get rid of; *Auftrag* get out of.

abwinken ['apvɪŋkən] *vi* wave it/him *etc* aside.

abwirtschaften ['apvɪrtʃaftən] *vi* go downhill.

abwischen ['apvɪʃən] *vt* wipe off or away; (*putzen*) wipe.

abwracken ['apvrakən] *vt* *Schiff* break (up); **abgewrackter Mensch** wreck of a person.

Abwurf ['apvʊrf] *m* throwing off;

(*von Bomben etc*) dropping; (*von Reiter, Sport*) throw.

abwürgen ['apvʏrgən] *vt* (*col*) scotch; *Motor* stall.

abzahlen ['aptsaːlən] *vt* pay off.

abzählen ['aptsɛːlən] *vti* count (up).

Abzahlung *f* repayment; auf — kaufen buy on hire purchase.

abzapfen ['aptsapfən] *vt* draw off; **jdm Blut/Geld** — take blood from sb/bleed sb.

abzäunen ['aptsɔʏnən] *vt* fence off.

Abzeichen ['aptsaɪçən] *nt* badge; (*Orden*) decoration.

abzeichnen ['aptsaɪçnən] *vt* draw, copy; *Dokument* initial; *vr* stand out; (*fig: bevorstehen*) loom.

Abziehbild *nt* transfer.

abziehen ['aptsiːən] *irreg vt* take off; *Tier* skin; *Bett* strip; *Truppen* withdraw; (*subtrahieren*) take away, subtract; (*kopieren*) run off; *vi* go away; (*Truppen*) withdraw.

abzielen ['aptsiːlən] *vi* be aimed (*auf +acc* at).

Abzug ['aptsuːk] *m* departure; (*von Truppen*) withdrawal; (*Kopie*) copy; (*Subtraktion*) subtraction; (*Betrag*) deduction; (*Rauch—*) flue; (*von Waffen*) trigger.

abzüglich ['aptsyːklɪç] *prep +gen* less.

abzweigen ['aptsvaɪgən] *vi* branch off; *vt* set aside.

Abzweigung *f* junction.

Accessoires [aksɛsoˈaːrs] *pl* accessories *pl*.

ach [ax] *interj* oh; **mit A— und Krach** by the skin of one's teeth.

Achse ['aksə] *f* -, -n axis; (*Aut*) axle; auf — sein be on the move.

Achsel ['aksəl] *f* -, -n shoulder;

—höhle f armpit; —zucken nt shrug (of one's shoulders).

Achsenbruch m (Aut) broken axle.

Acht [axt] f - attention; (Hist) proscription; **sich in — nehmen** be careful (vor + dat of), watch out (vor + dat for); **etw außer a— lassen** disregard sth; **~** f —, -en, **a—** num eight; **a— Tage** a week; **a—bar** a novelty; **a—e(r,s)** a eighth; **—el** num eighth; **a—en** vt respect; vi pay attention (auf + acc to); **darauf a—en, daß ...** be careful that ...

ächten ['ɛçtən] vt outlaw, ban.

Achter- cpd: —bahn f big dipper, roller coaster; —deck nt (Naut) afterdeck.

acht- cpd: —fach a eightfold; —geben vi irreg take care (auf + acc of); —los a careless; —mal ad eight times; —sam a attentive.

Achtung ['axtuŋ] f attention; (Ehrfurcht) respect; interj look out!; (Mil) attention!; — Lebensgefahr/Stufe! danger/mind the step!

acht- cpd: —zehn num eighteen; —zig num eighty; A—ziger(in f) m -s, - octogenarian; A—zigerjahre pl eighties pl.

ächzen ['ɛçtsən] vi groan (vor + dat with).

Acker ['akər] m -s, ˙̈ field; —bau m agriculture; a—n vti plough; (col) slog away.

addieren [a'diːrən] vt add (up).

Addition [aditsi'oːn] f addition.

Ade [a'deː] nt -s, -s, a— interj farewell, adieu.

Adel ['aːdəl] m -s nobility; a—ig, adlig a noble.

Ader ['aːdər] f —, -n vein.

Adjektiv ['atjɛktiːf] nt -s, -e adjective.

Adler ['aːdlər] m -s, - eagle.

Admiral [atmi'raːl] m -s, -e admiral; —ität f admiralty.

adopt- cpd: —ieren [adɔp'tiːrən] vt adopt; A—ion [adɔptsi'oːn] f adoption; A—iveltern [adɔp'tiːf-] pl adoptive parents pl; A—ivkind nt adopted child.

Adress- cpd: —ant [adrɛ'sant] m sender; —at [adrɛ'saːt] m -en, -en addressee; —e [a'drɛsə] f -, -n address; a—ieren [adrɛ'siːrən] vt address (an + acc to).

Advent [at'vɛnt] m -(e)s, -e Advent; —skranz m Advent wreath.

Adverb [at'vɛrp] nt adverb; a—ial [atvɛrbi'aːl] a adverbial.

aero- [aero] pref aero-.

Affäre [a'fɛːrə] f -, -n affair.

Affe ['afə] m -n, -n monkey.

affektiert [afɛk'tiːrt] a affected.

Affen- cpd: a—artig a like a monkey; **mit a—artiger Geschwindigkeit** like a flash; —hitze f (col) incredible heat; —schande f (col) crying shame.

affig ['afɪç] a affected.

After ['aftər] m -s, - anus.

Agent [a'gɛnt] m agent; —ur [-'tuːr] f agency.

Aggregat [agre'gaːt] nt -(e)s, -e aggregate; (Tech) unit; —zustand m (Phys) state.

Aggress- cpd: —ion [agrɛsi'oːn] f aggression; a—iv [agrɛ'siːf] a aggressive; —ivität [agrɛsivi'tɛːt] f aggressiveness.

Agitation [agitatsi'oːn] f agitation.

Agrar- [a'graːr] cpd: —politik f agricultural policy; —staat m agrarian state.

aha [a'haː] interj aha.

Ahn [aːn] m -en, -en forebear.

ähneln ['ɛ:nəln] *vi* (+ *dat*) be like, resemble; *vr* be alike *or* similar.

ahnen ['a:nən] *vt* suspect; *Tod, Gefahr* have a presentiment of; **du ahnst es nicht** you have no idea.

ähnlich ['ɛ:nlɪç] *a* similar (*dat* to); **Ä—keit** *f* similarity.

Ahnung ['a:nʊŋ] *f* idea, suspicion; presentiment; **a—slos** a unsuspecting.

Ahorn ['a:hɔrn] *m* -s, -e maple.

Ähre ['ɛ:rə] *f* -, -n ear.

Akademie [akade'mi:] *f* academy.

Akademiker(in *f)* [aka'de:mikər(ɪn)] *m* -s, - university graduate.

akademisch a academic.

akklimatisieren [aklimati'zi:rən] *vr* become acclimatized.

Akkord [a'kɔrt] *m* -(e)s, -e (*Mus*) chord; **im —** arbeiten do piecework; **—arbeit** *f* piecework; **—eon** [a'kɔrdeɔn] *nt* -s, -s accordion.

Akkusativ ['akuzati:f] *m* -s, -e accusative (case).

Akrobat(in *f)* [akro'ba:t(m)] *m* -en, -en acrobat.

Akt [akt] *m* -(e)s, -e act; (*Art*) nude.

Akte ['aktə] *f* -, -n file; **etw zu den —n legen** (*lit, fig*) file sth away; **a—nkundig** a on the files; **—nschrank** *m* filing cabinet; **—ntasche** *f* briefcase.

Aktie ['aktsiə] *f* -, -n share; **—ngesellschaft** *f* joint-stock company; **—nkurs** *m* share price.

Aktion [aktsi'o:n] *f* campaign; (*Polizei—, Such—*) action; **—är** ['nɛ:r] *m* -s, -e shareholder.

aktiv [ak'ti:f] *a* active; (*Mil*) regular; **A—** *nt* -s (*Gram*) active (voice); **A—a** [ak'ti:va] *pl* assets *pl*; **—ieren** [-'vi:rən] *vt* activate;

A—ität *f* activity; **A—saldo** *m* (*Comm*) credit balance.

Aktualität [aktuali'tɛ:t] *f* topicality; (*einer Mode*) up-to-dateness.

aktuell [aktu'ɛl] a topical; up-to-date.

Akustik [a'kʊstik] *f* acoustics *pl*.

akut [a'ku:t] a acute.

Akzent [ak'tsɛnt] *m* accent; (*Betonung*) stress.

akzeptieren [aktsep'ti:rən] *vt* accept.

Alarm [a'larm] *m* -(e)s, -e alarm; **a—bereit** a standing by; **—bereitschaft** *f* stand-by; **a—ieren** [-'mi:rən] *vt* alarm.

albern ['albərn] a silly.

Album ['album] *nt* -s, **Alben** album.

Algebra ['algebra] *f* - algebra.

alias ['a:lias] *ad* alias.

Alibi ['a:libi] *nt* -s, -s alibi.

Alimente [ali'mɛntə] *pl* alimony.

Alkohol ['alkohɔl] *m* -s, -e alcohol **a—frei** a non-alcoholic; **—lker(in** *f)* [alko'ho:likər(ɪn)] *m* -s, - alcoholic; **a—isch** a alcoholic; **—verbot** *nt* ban on alcohol.

All [al] *nt* -s universe; **a—'abendlich** a every evening; **a—bekannt** a universally known; **a—e(r,s)** just, all; **wir a—e** all of us; **a—e beide** both of us/you *etc*; **a—e vier Jahre** every four years; *ad* (*col: zu Ende*) finished; **etw a—e machen** finish sth up.

Allee [a'le:] *f* -, -n avenue.

allein [a'lam] *ad* alone; (*ohne Hilfe*) on one's own, by oneself; **nicht —** (*nicht nur*) not only; *cj* but, only; **A—gang** *m*: **im A—gang** on one's own; **A—herrscher** *m* autocrat; **A—hersteller** *m* sole manufacturer; **—stehend** a single.

alle- cpd: **—mal** ad (jedesmal) always; (ohne weiteres) with no bother; **ein für —mal** once and for all; **—nfalls** ad at all events; (höchstens) at most; **—rbeste(r,s)** a very best; **—rdings** ad (zwar) admittedly; (gewiß) certainly.

allerg- cpd: **—isch** [a'lɛrgɪʃ] a allergic; **A—ie** [-'giː] f allergy.

aller- ['alər] cpd: **—hand** a inv (col) all sorts of; **das ist doch —hand!** that's a bit thick; **—hand!** (lobend) good show!; **A—'heiligen** nt All Saints' Day; **—höchste(r,s)** a very highest; **—höchstens** ad at the very most; **—lei** a inv all sorts of; **—letzte(r,s)** a very last; **—seits** ad on all sides; **prost —seits!** cheers everyone!; **—wenigste(r,s)** a very least.

alles pron everything; **— in allem** all in all.

allgemein ['algə'maɪn] a general; **—gültig** a generally accepted; **A—heit** f (Menschen) general public; (pl: Redensarten) general remarks pl.

Alliierte(r) [ali'iːrtə(r)] m ally.

all- cpd: **—jährlich** a annual; **—mählich** a gradual; **A—tag** m everyday life; **—täglich** a,ad daily; (gewöhnlich) commonplace; **—tags** ad on weekdays; **—'wissend** a omniscient; **—zu** ad all too; **—zuoft** ad all too often; **—zuviel** ad too much.

Almosen ['almoːzən] nt -s, - alms pl.

Alpen ['alpən] pl Alps pl; **—blume** f alpine flower.

Alphabet [alfa'beːt] nt -(e)s, -e alphabet; **a—isch** a alphabetical.

Alptraum ['alptraum] m nightmare.

als [als] cj (zeitlich) when; (comp)

than; (Gleichheit) as; **nichts —** nothing but; **— ob** as if.

also ['alzo] cj so; (folglich) therefore; **ich komme — morgen** so I'll come tomorrow; **— gut** or **schön!** okay then; **—, so was!** well really!; **na —!** there you are then!

alt [alt] a old; **ich bin nicht mehr der —e** I am not the man I was; **alles beim —en lassen** leave everything as it was; **A— m -s, -e** (Mus) alto; **A—ar** [al'taːr] m -(e)s, -äre altar; **—bekannt** a long-known; **A—eisen** nt scrap iron.

Alter ['altər] nt -s, - age; (hohes) old age; **im — von** at the age of; **a—n** vi grow old, age; **—na'tive** f alternative; **—sgrenze** f age limit; **—sheim** nt old people's home; **—sversorgung** f old age pension; **—tum** nt antiquity.

alt- cpd: **—'hergebracht** a traditional; **—klug** a precocious; **—modisch** a old-fashioned; **A—papier** nt waste paper; **A—stadt** f old town; **A—stimme** f alto; **A—'weibersommer** m Indian summer.

Aluminium [alu'miːnium] nt -s aluminium, aluminum (US); **—folie** f tinfoil.

am [am] = **an dem**; **— Sterben** on the point of dying; **— 15. März** on March 15th; **— besten/schönsten** best/most beautiful.

Amalgam [amal'gaːm] nt -s, -e amalgam.

Amateur [ama'tøːr] m amateur.

Amboß ['ambɔs] m -sses, -sse. anvil.

ambulant [ambu'lant] a outpatient.

Ameise ['aːmaɪzə] f -, -n ant.

Ampel ['ampəl] f -, -n traffic lights pl.

amphibisch [am'fi:bɪʃ] *a* amphibious.
amputieren [ampu'ti:rən] *vt* amputate.
Amsel ['amzəl] *f* **-, -n** blackbird.
Amt [amt] *nt* **-(e)s, ⁻er** office; (*Pflicht*) duty; (*Tel*) exchange; **a—ieren** [am'ti:rən] *vi* hold office; **a—lich** *a* official; **—sperson** *f* official; **—srichter** *m* district judge; **—sstunden** *pl* office hours *pl*; **—szeit** *f* period of office.
amüsant [amy'zant] *a* amusing.
Amüsement [amyzə'mã:] *nt* amusement.
amüsieren [amy'zi:rən] *vt* amuse; *vr* enjoy o.s.
an [an] *prep* + *dat* (*räumlich*) at; (*auf, bei*) on; (*nahe bei*) near; (*zeitlich*) on; + *acc* (*räumlich*) (on)to; **— Ostern** at Easter; **— diesem Ort/Tag** at this place/on this day; **— und für sich** actually; *ad*: **von ... —** from ... on; **— die 5 DM** around 5 marks; **das Licht ist —** the light is on.
analog [ana'lo:k] *a* analogous; **A—ie** [-'gi:] *f* analogy.
Analyse [ana'ly:zə] *f* **-, -n** analysis.
analysieren [analy'zi:rən] *vt* analyse.
Ananas ['ananas] *f* **-, -** *or* **-se** pineapple.
Anarchie [anar'çi:] *f* anarchy.
Anatomie [anato'mi:] *f* anatomy.
anbahnen ['anba:nən] *vtr* open up.
anbändeln ['anbɛndəln] *vi* (*col*) flirt.
Anbau ['anbaʊ] *m* (*Agr*) cultivation; (*Gebäude*) extension; **a—en** *vt* (*Agr*) cultivate; *Gebäudeteil* build on.
anbehalten ['anbəhaltən] *vt irreg* keep on.
anbei [an'baɪ] *ad* enclosed.
anbeißen ['anbaɪsən] *irreg vt* bite into; *vi* (*lit*) bite; (*fig*) swallow the bait; **zum A—** (*col*) good enough to eat.
anbelangen ['anbəlaŋən] *vt* concern; **was mich anbelangt** as far as I am concerned.
anberaumen ['anbəraʊmən] *vt* fix.
anbeten ['anbe:tən] *vt* worship.
Anbetracht ['anbətraxt] *m*: **in —** (+ *gen*) in view of.
Anbetung *f* worship.
anbiedern ['anbi:dərn] *vr* make up (*bei* to).
anbieten ['anbi:tən] *irreg vt* offer; *vr* volunteer.
anbinden ['anbɪndən] *irreg vt* tie up; *vi*: **mit jdm —** start something with sb; **kurz angebunden** (*fig*) curt.
Anblick ['anblɪk] *m* sight; **a—en** *vt* look at.
anbrechen ['anbrɛçən] *irreg vt* start; *Vorräte* break into; *vi* start; (*Tag*) break; (*Nacht*) fall.
anbrennen ['anbrɛnən] *vi irreg* catch fire; (*Cook*) burn.
anbringen ['anbrɪŋən] *vt irreg* bring; *Ware* sell; (*festmachen*) fasten.
Anbruch ['anbrʊx] *m* beginning; **— des Tages/der Nacht** dawn/nightfall.
anbrüllen ['anbrʏlən] *vt* roar at.
Andacht ['andaxt] *f* **-, -en** devotion; (*Gottesdienst*) prayers *pl*.
andächtig ['andɛçtɪç] *a* devout.
andauern ['andaʊərn] *vi* last, go on; **—d** *a* continual.
Andenken ['andɛŋkən] *nt* **-s, -** memory; souvenir.

andere(r,s) ['andərə(r,z)] a other; (verschieden) different; am —n Tage the next day; ein —s Mal another time; kein —r nobody else; von etw —m sprechen talk about sth else;'—nteils, —rseits ad on the other hand.

ändern ['ɛndərn] vt alter, change; vr change.

ander- cpd: —nfalls ad otherwise; —s ad differently (als from); wer —s? who else?; jd/irgendwo —s sb/somewhere else; —s ausse-hen/klingen look/sound different; —sartig a different; —seits ad on the other hand; —sfarbig a of a different colour; —sgläubig a of a different faith; —sherum ad the other way round; —swo ad else-where; —swoher ad from else-where; —swohin ad elsewhere.

anderthalb ['andərt'halp] a one and a half.

Änderung ['ɛndəruŋ] f alteration, change.

anderweitig ['andər'vaıtıç] a other; ad otherwise; (anderswo) elsewhere.

andeuten ['andɔytən] vt indicate; (Wink geben) hint at.

Andeutung f indication; hint.

Andrang ['andraŋ] m crush.

andrehen ['andre:ən] vt turn or switch on; (col) jdm etw — unload sth onto sb.

androhen ['andro:ən] vt: jdm etw — threaten sb with sth.

aneignen ['an'aıgnən] vt: sich (dat) etw — acquire sth; (widerrecht-lich) appropriate sth.

aneinander [an'aı'nandər] ad at/on/to etc one another or each other; —fügen vt put together; —geraten vi irreg clash; —legen vt put together.

anekeln ['an'e:kəln] vt disgust.

Anemone [ane'mo:nə] f -, -n anemone.

anerkannt ['an'ɛrkant] a recog-nized, acknowledged.

anerkennen ['an'ɛrkɛnən] vt irreg recognize, acknowledge; (wür-digen) appreciate; —d a appreci-ative; —swert a praiseworthy.

Anerkennung f recognition, ac-knowledgement; appreciation.

anfachen ['anfaxən] vt (lit) fan into flame; (fig) kindle.

anfahren ['anfa:rən] irreg vt de-liver; (fahren gegen) hit; Hafen put into; (fig) bawl out; vi drive up; (losfahren) drive off.

Anfall ['anfal] m (Med) attack; a—en irreg vt attack; (fig) over-come; vi (Arbeit) come up; (Produkt) be obtained.

anfällig ['anfɛlıç] a delicate; — für etw prone to sth.

Anfang ['anfaŋ] m -(e)s, -fänge beginning, start; von — an right from the beginning; zu — at the beginning; — Mai at the beginning of May; a—en vti irreg begin, start; (machen) do.

Anfänger(in f) ['anfɛŋər(m)] m -s, - beginner.

anfänglich ['anfɛŋlıç] a initial.

anfangs ad at first; A—buchstabe m initial or first letter; A—stadium nt initial stages pl.

anfassen ['anfasən] vt handle; (berühren) touch; vi lend a hand; vr feel.

anfechten ['anfɛçtən] vt irreg dispute; (beunruhigen) trouble.

anfertigen ['anfɛrtıgən] vt make.

anfeuern ['anfɔyərn] vt (fig) spur on.

anflehen ['anfle:ən] vt implore.

anfliegen ['anfli:gən] irreg vt fly to; vi fly up.

Anflug ['anflu:k] m (Aviat) approach; (Spur) trace.

anfordern ['anfordərn] vt demand.

Anforderung f demand (gen for).

Anfrage ['anfra:gə] f inquiry; a—n vi inquire.

anfreunden ['anfrɔyndən] vr make friends.

anfügen ['anfy:gən] vt add; (beifügen) enclose.

anfühlen ['anfy:lən] vtr feel.

anführen ['anfy:rən] vt lead; (zitieren) quote; (col: betrügen) lead up the garden path.

Anführer m leader.

Anführung f leadership; (Zitat) quotation; —sstriche, —szeichen pl quotation marks pl, inverted commas pl.

Angabe ['anga:bə] f statement; (Tech) specification; (col: Prahlerei) boasting; (Sport) service; —n pl (Auskunft) particulars pl.

angeben ['ange:bən] irreg vt give; (anzeigen) inform on; (bestimmen) set; vi (col) boast; (Sport) serve.

Angeber m -s, - (col) show-off; —ei [-'rai] f (col) showing off.

angeblich ['ange:plɪç] a alleged.

angeboren ['angəbo:rən] a inborn, innate (jdm in sb).

Angebot ['angəbo:t] nt offer; (Comm) supply (an + dat of).

angebracht ['angəbraxt] a appropriate, in order.

angegriffen ['angəgrɪfən] a exhausted.

angeheitert ['angəhaɪtərt] a tipsy.

angehen ['ange:ən] irreg vt concern; (angreifen) attack; (bitten) approach (um for); vi (Feuer)

light; (col: beginnen) begin; —d a prospective; er ist ein —der Vierziger he is approaching forty.

angehören ['angəhø:rən] vi belong (dat to).

Angehörige(r) mf relative.

Angeklagte(r) ['angəkla:ktə(r)] mf accused.

Angel ['aŋəl] f -, -n fishing rod; (Tür—) hinge.

Angelegenheit ['aŋələgənhaɪt] f affair, matter.

Angel- cpd: —haken m fish hook; a—n vt catch; vi fish; —n nt -s angling, fishing; —rute f fishing rod.

angemessen ['angəmɛsən] a appropriate, suitable.

angenehm ['angəne:m] a pleasant; —! (bei Vorstellung) pleased to meet you; jdm — sein be welcome.

angenommen ['angənɔmən] a assumed; —, wir ... assuming we...

angesehen ['angəze:ən] a respected.

angesichts ['angəzɪçts] prep +gen in view of, considering.

angespannt ['angəʃpant] a Aufmerksamkeit close; Arbeit hard.

Angestellte(r) ['angəʃtɛltə(r)] mf employee.

angetan ['angəta:n] a: von jdm/etw — sein be impressed by sb/sth; es jdm — haben appeal to sb.

angewiesen ['angəvi:zən] a: auf jdn/etw — sein be dependent on sb/sth.

angewöhnen ['angəvø:nən] vt: jdm/sich etw — get sb/become accustomed to sth.

Angewohnheit ['angəvo:nhaɪt] f habit.

angleichen ['anglaɪçən] vtr irreg adjust (dat to).

Angler ['aŋlər] m -s, - angler.

angreifen ['angraɪfən] vt irreg attack; (anfassen) touch; Arbeit tackle; (beschädigen) damage.

Angreifer m -s, - attacker.

Angriff ['angrɪf] m attack; etw in — nehmen make a start on sth.

Angst [aŋst] f -, ̈-e fear; — haben be afraid or scared (vor +dat of); — haben um jdn/etw be worried about sb/sth; nur keine —! don't be scared; a— a: jdm. ist a— sb is afraid or scared; jdm a— machen scare sb; ̈-hase m (col) chicken, scaredy-cat.

ängst- [εŋst] cpd: ̈-igen vt frighten; vr worry (o.s.) (vor +dat, um about); ̈-lich a nervous; (besorgt) worried; Ä̈-lichkeit f nervousness.

anhaben ['anha:bən] vt irreg have on; er kann mir nichts — he can't hurt me.

anhalt- ['anhalt] cpd: ̈-en irreg vt stop; (gegen etw halten) hold up (jdm against sb); jdn zur Arbeit/Höflichkeit ̈-en make sb work/be polite; vi stop; (andauern) persist; ̈-end a persistent; Ä-er m -s, - hitch-hiker; per Ä-er fahren hitch-hike; Ä-spunkt m clue.

anhand [an'hant] prep +gen with.

Anhang ['anhaŋ] m appendix; (Leute) family; supporters pl.

anhäng- ['anhεŋ] cpd: ̈-en vt irreg hang up; Wagen couple up; Zusatz add (an); sich an jdn ̈-en attach o.s. to sb; Ä-er m -s, - supporter; (Aut) trailer; (am Koffer) tag; (Schmuck) pendant; Ä-erschaft f supporters pl; Ä-eschloß nt padlock; ̈-ig a (Jur) sub judice; ̈-ig machen Prozeß bring; ̈-lich a devoted; Ä-lichkeit f devotion; Ä-sel nt -s, - appendage.

Anhäufung ['anhɔyfuŋ] f accumulation.

anheben ['anhe:bən] vt irreg lift up; Preise raise.

anheimelnd ['anhaɪməlnt] a comfortable, cosy.

anheimstellen [an'haɪmʃtɛlən] vt: jdm etw — leave sth up to sb.

Anhieb ['anhi:b] m: auf — at the very first go; (kurz entschlossen) on the spur of the moment.

Anhöhe ['anhø:ə] f hill.

anhören ['anhø:rən] vt listen to; (anmerken) hear; vr sound.

animieren [ani'mi:rən] vt encourage, urge on.

Anis [a'ni:s] m -es, -e aniseed.

ankaufen ['ankaufən] vt purchase, buy.

Anker ['aŋkər] m -s, - anchor; vor — gehen drop anchor; ä-n vti anchor; ̈-platz m anchorage.

Anklage ['ankla:gə] f accusation; (Jur) charge; ̈-bank f dock; ä-n vt accuse; (Jur) charge (gen with).

Ankläger ['anklε:gər] m accuser.

Anklang ['anklaŋ] m: bei jdm — finden meet with sb's approval.

Ankleide- ['anklaɪdə] cpd: ̈-kabine f changing cubicle; ä-n vtr dress.

anklopfen ['anklɔpfən] vi knock.

anknüpfen ['anknypfən] vt fasten or tie on; (fig) start; vi (anschließen) refer (an +acc to).

ankommen ['ankɔmən] vi irreg arrive; (näherkommen) approach; (Anklang finden) go down (bei with); es kommt darauf an it depends; (wichtig sein) that (is what) matters; es kommt auf ihn an it depends on him; es darauf — lassen let things take their course; **gegen jdn/etw —** cope with sb/sth.

ankündigen ['ankʏndɪgən] *vt* announce.

Ankündigung *f* announcement.

Ankunft ['ankʊnft] *f* -, **-künfte** arrival; **—szeit** *f* time of arrival.

ankurbeln ['ankʊrbəln] *vt* (*Aut*) crank; (*fig*) boost.

Anlage ['anla:gə] *f* disposition; (*Begabung*) talent; (*Park*) gardens *pl*; (*Beilage*) enclosure; (*Tech*) plant; (*Fin*) investment; (*Entwurf*) layout.

anlangen ['anlaŋən] *vi* arrive.

Anlaß ['anlas] *m* **-sses, -lässe** cause (*zu* for); (*Ereignis*) occasion; **aus —** (+gen) on the occasion of; **— zu etw geben** give rise to sth; **etw zum — nehmen** take the opportunity of sth.

anlassen *irreg vt* leave on; *Motor* start; *vr* (*col*) start off.

Anlasser *m* -s, - (*Aut*) starter.

anläßlich ['anlɛslɪç] *prep* +gen on the occasion of.

Anlauf ['anlaʊf] *m* run-up; **a—en** *irreg vi* begin; (*Film*) show; (*Sport*) run up; (*Fenster*) mist up; (*Metall*) tarnish; **rot a—en** colour; **gegen etw a—en** run into *or* up against sth; **angelaufen kommen** come running up; **vt** call at.

anläuten ['anlɔʏtən] *vi* ring.

anlegen ['anle:gən] *vt* put (*an* +acc against/on); (*anziehen*) put on; (*gestalten*) lay out; *Geld* invest; *Gewehr* aim (*auf* +acc at); **es auf etw** (*acc*) **—** be out for sth/to do sth; **sich mit jdm —** (*col*) quarrel with sb; *vi* dock.

Anlegestelle *f*, **Anlegeplatz** *m* landing place.

anlehnen ['anle:nən] *vt* lean (*an* +acc against); *Tür* leave ajar; **vr** lean (*an* +acc on).

anleiten ['anlaɪtən] *vt* instruct.

Anleitung *f* instructions *pl*.

anlernen ['anlɛrnən] *vt* teach, instruct.

anliegen ['anli:gən] *vi irreg* (*Kleidung*) cling; **A— nt** -s, - matter; (*Wunsch*) wish; **-d a** adjacent; (*beigefügt*) enclosed.

Anlieger *m* -s, - resident.

anlügen ['anly:gən] *vt irreg* lie to.

anmachen ['anmaxən] *vt* attach; *Elektrisches* put on; *Salat* dress.

anmaßen ['anma:sən] *vt*: **sich** (*dat*) **etw —** lay claim to sth; **-d a** arrogant.

Anmaßung *f* presumption.

Anmeld- ['anmɛld] *cpd*: **—eform-** ular *nt* registration form; **a—en** *vt* announce; **vr** (*sich ankündigen*) make an appointment; (*polizeilich, für Kurs etc*) register; **—ung** *f* announcement; appointment; registration.

anmerken ['anmɛrkən] *vt* observe; (*anstreichen*) mark; **jdm etw —** notice sb's sth; **sich** (*dat*) **nichts — lassen** not give anything away.

Anmerkung *f* note.

Anmut ['anmu:t] *f* - grace; **a—en** *vt* give a feeling; **a—ig a** charming.

annähen ['annɛ:ən] *vt* sew on.

annähern ['annɛ:ərn] *vr* get closer; **-d a** approximate.

Annäherung *f* approach; **—sver-** such *m* advances *pl*.

Annahme ['anna:mə] *f* -, **-n** acceptance; (*Vermutung*) assumption.

annehm- ['anne:m] *cpd*: **—bar a** acceptable; **—en** *irreg vt* accept; *Namen* take; *Kind* adopt; (*vermuten*) suppose, assume; **angenom-**

men, das ist so assuming that is
so; **vr** take care (gen of);
A—lichkeit f comfort.

annektieren [anɛk'tiːrən] vt annex.

Annonce [a'nõːsə] f -, -n advertisement.

annoncieren [anõ'siːrən] vti advertise.

annullieren [anʊ'liːrən] vt annul.

Anode [a'noːdə] f -, -n anode.

anöden ['anˈøːdən] vt (col) bore
stiff.

anonym [ano'nyːm] a anonymous.

Anorak ['anorak] m -s, -s anorak.

anordnen ['anˈɔrdnən] vt arrange;
(befehlen) order.

Anordnung f arrangement; order.

anorganisch ['anˈɔrgaːnɪʃ] a inorganic.

anpacken ['anpakən] vt grasp;
(fig) tackle; **mit —** lend a hand.

anpassen ['anpasən] vt fit (jdm to
sb); (fig) adapt (dat to); vr adapt.

Anpassung f fitting; adaptation;
a—sfähig a adaptable.

Anpfiff ['anpfɪf] m (Sport) (starting) whistle; kick-off; (col) rocket.

anpöbeln ['anpøːbəln] vt abuse.

Anprall ['anpral] m collision
(gegen, an +acc with).

anprangern ['anpraŋərn] vt denounce.

anpreisen ['anpraɪzən] vt irreg ex-
tol.

Anprobe ['anproːbə] f trying on.

anprobieren ['anproːbiːrən] vt try
on.

anrechnen ['anrɛçnən] vt charge;
(fig) count; jdm etw hoch — value
sb's sth greatly.

Anrecht ['anrɛçt] nt right (auf
+acc to).

Anrede ['anreːdə] f form of ad-

dress; **a—n** vt address; (belästigen) accost.

anregen ['anreːgən] vt stimulate;
angeregte Unterhaltung lively discussion; **—d** a stimulating.

Anregung f stimulation; (Vorschlag) suggestion.

anreichern ['anraɪçərn] vt enrich.

Anreise ['anraɪzə] f journey; **a—n**
vi arrive.

Anreiz ['anraɪts] m incentive.

Anrichte ['anrɪçtə] f -, -n sideboard; **a—n** vt serve up; **Unheil
a—n** make mischief.

anrüchig ['anryçɪç] a dubious.

anrücken ['anrʏkən] vi approach;
(Mil) advance.

Anruf ['anruːf] m call; **a—en** vt
irreg call out to; (bitten) call on;
(Tel) ring up, phone, call.

anrühren ['anryːrən] vt touch;
(mischen) mix.

ans [ans] **= an das.**

Ansage ['anzaːgə] f -, -n announcement; **a—n** vt announce; vr say
one will come; **—r(in** f) m -s, **—**
announcer.

ansammeln ['anzaməln] vtr collect.

Ansammlung f collection; (Leute)
crowd.

ansässig ['anzɛsɪç] a resident.

Ansatz ['anzats] m start; (Haar—)
hairline; (Hals—) base; (Ver-
längerungsstück) extension; (Ver-
anschlagung) estimate; **die ersten
Ansätze zu etw** the beginnings of
sth; **—punkt** m starting point.

anschaffen ['anʃafən] vt buy,
purchase.

Anschaffung f purchase.

anschalten ['anʃaltən] vt switch on.

anschau- ['anʃau] cpd: **—en** vt
look at; **—lich** a illustrative;
A—ung f (Meinung) view; (aus

eigener A—ung from one's own experience; A—ungsmaterial *nt* illustrative material.

Anschein ['anʃain] *m* appearance; allem — nach to all appearances; den — haben seem, appear; a—end *a* apparent.

Anschlag ['anʃla:k] *m* notice; (*Attentat*) attack; (*Comm*) estimate; (*auf Klavier*) touch; (*Schreibmaschine*) character; a—en ['anʃla:gən] *irreg vt* put up; (*beschädigen*) chip; *Akkord* strike; *Kosten* estimate; *vi* hit (*an* +acc against); (*wirken*) have an effect; (*Glocke*) ring; (*Hund*) bark; —zettel *m* notice.

anschließen ['anʃli:sən] *irreg vt* connect up; *Sender* link up; *vr*: (sich) an etw (acc) — adjoin sth; (*zeitlich*) follow sth; *vr* join (*jdm/etw* sb/sth); (*beipflichten*) agree (*jdm/etw* with sb/sth); —d *a* adjacent; (*zeitlich*) subsequent; *ad* afterwards; —d an etw (acc) following.

Anschluß ['anʃlus] *m* (*Elec, Rail*) connection; (*von Wasser etc*) supply; im — an (+acc) following; — finden make friends.

anschmiegsam ['anʃmi:kza:m] *a* affectionate.

anschmieren ['anʃmi:rən] *vt* smear; (*col*) take in.

anschnallen ['anʃnalən] *vt* buckle on; *vr* fasten one's seat belt.

anschneiden ['anʃnaidən] *vt irreg* cut into; *Thema* broach.

Anschnitt ['anʃnit] *m* first slice.

anschreiben ['anʃraibən] *vt irreg* write (up); (*Comm*) charge up; (*benachrichtigen*) write to; bei jdm gut/schlecht angeschrieben sein be well/badly thought of by sb, be in sb's good/bad books.

anschreien ['anʃraiən] *vt irreg* shout at.

Anschrift ['anʃrift] *f* address.

Anschuldigung ['anʃuldigʊŋ] *f* accusation.

anschwellen ['anʃvɛlən] *vi irreg* swell (up).

anschwemmen ['anʃvɛmən] *vt* wash ashore.

anschwindeln ['anʃvindəln] *vt* lie to.

ansehen ['anze:ən] *vt irreg* look at; jdm etw — see sth (from sb's face); jdn/etw als etw — look on sb/sth as sth; — für consider; A— *nt* -s respect; (*Ruf*) reputation.

ansehnlich ['anze:nliç] *a* fine-looking; (*beträchtlich*) considerable.

ansein ['anzain] *vi irreg* (*col*) be on.

ansetzen ['anzɛtsən] *vt* (*anfügen*) fix on (*an* +acc to); (*anlegen, an Mund etc*) put (*an* +acc to); (*festlegen*) fix; (*entwickeln*) develop; *Fett* put on; *Blätter* grow; (*zubereiten*) prepare; jdn/etw auf jdn/etw — set sb/sth on sb/sth; *vi* (*anfangen*) start, begin; (*Entwicklung*) set in; (*dick werden*) put on weight; zu etw — prepare to do sth; *vr* (*Rost etc*) start to develop.

Ansicht ['anziçt] *f* (*Anblick*) sight; (*Meinung*) view, opinion; zur — on approval; meiner — nach in my opinion; —skarte *f* picture postcard; —ssache *f* matter of opinion.

anspannen ['anʃpanən] *vt* harness; *Muskel* strain.

Anspannung *f* strain.

Anspiel ['anʃpi:l] *nt* (*Sport*) start; a—en *vi* (*Sport*) start play; auf etw (acc) a—en refer *or* allude to sth'; —ung *f* reference, allusion (*auf* +acc to).

Ansporn ['anʃpɔrn] *m* -(e)s
incentive.

Ansprache ['anʃpraːxə] *f* address.

ansprechen ['anʃpreçən] *irreg vt*
speak to; (*bitten, gefallen*) appeal
to; **jdn auf etw** (*acc*) (hin) — ask
sb about sth; **etw als etw** — regard
sth as sth; *vi* react (*auf* + *acc* to);
—**d** *a* attractive.

anspringen ['anʃprɪŋən] *vi irreg*
(*Aut*) start.

Anspruch ['anʃprʊx] *m* (*Recht*)
claim (*auf* + *acc* to); **hohe An-
sprüche stellen/haben** demand/
expect a lot; **jdn/etw in** — **nehmen**
occupy sb/take up sth; **a—slos** *a*
undemanding; **a—svoll** *a* demand-
ing.

anspucken ['anʃpukən] *vt* spit at.

anstacheln ['anʃtaxəln] *vt* spur on.

Anstalt ['anʃtalt] *f* -, -en institution; **—en machen, etw zu tun**
prepare to do sth.

Anstand ['anʃtant] *m* decency.

anständig ['anʃtɛndɪç] *a* decent;
(*col*) proper; (*groß*) considerable;
A—keit *f* propriety, decency.

anstandslos *ad* without any ado.

anstarren ['anʃtarən] *vt* stare at.

anstatt [an'ʃtat] *prep* + *gen* instead
of; *cj*: — **etw zu tun** instead of
doing sth.

anstecken ['anʃtɛkən] *cpd*: **a—en** *vt*
pin on; (*Med*) infect; *Pfeife* light;
Haus set fire to; *vr*: **ich habe mich
bei ihm angesteckt** I caught it from
him; *vi* (*fig*) be infectious; **a—end**
a infectious; —**ung** *f* infection.

anstehen ['anʃteːən] *vi irreg* queue
(up), line up (*US*).

anstelle [an'ʃtɛlə] *prep* + *gen* in
place of; —**n** [an-] *vt* (*einschalten*)

turn on; (*Arbeit geben*) employ;
(*machen*) do; *vr* queue (up), line
up (*US*); (*col*) act.

Anstellung *f* employment; (*Posten*) post, position.

Anstieg ['anʃtiːk] *m* -(e)s, -**e**
climb; (*fig: von Preisen etc*)
increase (*gen* in).

anstift- ['anʃtɪft] *cpd*: **—en** *vt*
Unglück cause; **jdn zu etw** —**en**
put sb up to sth; **A—er** *m* -s,
-, **—instigator**.

anstimmen ['anʃtɪmən] *vt* *Lied*
strike up with; *Geschrei* set up;
vi strike up.

Anstoß ['anʃtoːs] *m* impetus;
(*Ärgernis*) offence; (*Sport*) kick-
off; **der erste** — the initiative; —
nehmen an (+ *dat*) take offence at;
a—en *irreg vt* push; (*mit Fuß*)
kick; *vi* knock, bump; (*mit der
Zunge*) lisp; (*mit Gläsern*) drink (a
toast) (*auf* + *acc* to); **an etw** (*acc*)
a—en (*angrenzen*) adjoin sth.

anstößig ['anʃtøːsɪç] *a* offensive,
indecent; **A—keit** *f* indecency,
offensiveness.

anstreben ['anʃtreːbən] *vt* strive
for.

anstreichen ['anʃtraɪçən] *vt irreg*
paint.

Anstreicher *m* -s, - painter.

anstrengen ['anʃtrɛŋən] *vt* strain;
(*Jur*) bring; *vr* make an effort;
angestrengt *ad* as hard as one can;
—**d** *a* tiring.

Anstrengung *f* effort.

Anstrich ['anʃtrɪç] *m* coat of paint.

Ansturm ['anʃturm] *m* rush; (*Mil*)
attack.

ansuchen ['anzuːxən] *vi*: **um etw**
— apply for sth; **A—** *nt* -s,- request.

Antagonismus [antago'nɪsmus] *m*
antagonism.

antasten ['antastən] vt touch;
Recht infringe upon; *Ehre* question.
Anteil ['antail] m -s, -e share (*an*
+*dat* in); (*Mitgefühl*) sympathy;
— **nehmen** an (+*dat*) share in;
(*sich interessieren*) take an interest
in; —**nahme** f - sympathy.
Antenne [an'tɛnə] f -, -n aerial;
(*Zool*) antenna.
Anthrazit [antra'tsɛ̈t] m -s, -e
anthracite.
Anti- ['anti] *in cpds* anti-;
—**alko'holiker** m teetotaller;
a—**autori'tär** a anti-authoritarian;
—**biotikum** [antibi'o:tikum] nt -s,
-ka antibiotic.
antik [an'ti:k] a antique; **A—e** f -,
-n (*Zeitalter*) ancient world;
(*Kunstgegenstand*) antique.
Antikörper m antibody.
Antilope [anti'lo:pə] f -, -n
antelope.
Antipathie [antipa'ti:] f antipathy.
Antiquariat [antikvari'a:t] nt
-(e)s, -e secondhand bookshop.
Antiquitäten [antikvi'tɛ:tən] pl
antiques pl; —**handel** m antique
business; —**händler** m antique
dealer.
Antrag ['antra:k] m -(e)s, -träge
proposal; (*Parl*) motion; (*Gesuch*)
application.
antreffen ['antrɛfən] vt irreg meet.
antreiben ['antraibən] irreg vt
drive on; *Motor* drive; (*anschwemmen*) wash up; vi be washed up.
antreten ['antre:tən] irreg vt *Amt*
take up; *Erbschaft* come into;
Beweis offer; *Reise* start, begin; vi
(*Mil*) fall in; (*Sport*) line up; **gegen
jdn —** play/fight against sb.
Antrieb ['antri:p] m (*lit,fig*) drive;
aus eigenem — of one's own accord.

antrinken ['antrɪŋkən] vt irreg
Flasche, Glas start to drink from;
sich (*dat*) **Mut/einen Rausch —**
give oneself Dutch courage/get
drunk; **angetrunken sein** to be tipsy.
Antritt ['antrɪt] m beginning,
commencement; (*eines Amts*)
taking up.
antun ['antu:n] vt irreg: **jdm etw
—** do sth to sb; **sich** (*dat*) **Zwang
—** force o.s.
Antwort ['antvɔrt] f -, -en answer,
reply; **um — wird gebeten** RSVP;
a—en vi answer, reply.
anvertrauen ['anfɛrtrauən] vt: **jdm
etw —** entrust sb with sth; **sich**
jdm — confide in sb.
anwachsen ['anvaksən] vi irreg
grow; (*Pflanze*) take root.
Anwalt ['anvalt] m -(e)s, -wälte,
Anwältin ['anvɛltɪn] f solicitor;
lawyer; (*fig*) champion.
Anwandlung ['anvandluŋ] f caprice; (*von etw a fit of sth.*)
Anwärter ['anvɛrtər] m candidate.
anweisen ['anvaizən] vt irreg
instruct; (*zuteilen*) assign (*jdm etw
sth to sb*).
Anweisung f instruction; (*Comm*)
remittance; (*Post—, Zahlungs—*)
money order.
anwend- ['anvɛnd] cpd: —**bar** ['an-
vɛnt-] a practicable, applicable;
—**en** vt irreg use, employ; *Gesetz,
Regel* apply; **A—ung** f use; application.
Anwesen- ['anve:zən] cpd: **a—d** a
present; **die —den** those present;
—**heit** f presence; —**heitsliste** f
attendance register.
anwidern ['anvi:dərn] vt disgust.
Anwuchs ['anvu:ks] m growth.
Anzahl ['antsa:l] f number (*an*
+*dat* of); **a—en** vt pay on

account; —ung f deposit, payment on account.

anzapfen ['antsapfən] vt tap; Person (um Geld) touch.

Anzeichen ['antsaıçən] nt sign, indication.

Anzeige ['antsaıgə] f -, -n (Zeitungs—) announcement; (Werbung) advertisement; (bei Polizei) report; — erstatten gegen jdn report sb (to the police); a—n vt (zu erkennen geben) show; (bekanntgeben) announce; (bei Polizei) report; —nteil m advertisements pl; —r m indicator.

anzetteln ['antstəln] vt (col) instigate.

anziehen ['antsi:ən] irreg vt attract; Kleidung put on; Mensch dress; Schraube, Seil pull tight; Knie draw up; Feuchtigkeit absorb; vr get dressed; —d a attractive.

Anziehung f (Reiz) attraction; —skraft f power of attraction; (Phys) force of gravitation.

Anzug ['antsu:k] m suit; im — sein be approaching.

anzüglich ['antsy:klıç] a personal; (anstößig) offensive; A—keit f offensiveness; (Bemerkung) personal remark.

anzünden ['antsyndən] vt light.

Anzünder m lighter.

anzweifeln ['antsvaıfəln] vt doubt.

apart [a'part] a distinctive.

Apathie [apa'ti:] f apathy.

apathisch [a'pa:tıʃ] a apathetic.

Apfel ['apfəl] m -s, :- apple; —saft m apple juice; —sine [apfəl'zi:nə] f -, -n orange; —wein m cider.

Apostel [a'pɔstəl] m -s, - apostle.

Apostroph [apo'stro:f] m -s, -e apostrophe.

Apotheke [apo'te:kə] f -, -n chemist's (shop), drugstore (US); —r(in f) m -s, - chemist, druggist (US).

Apparat [apa'ra:t] m -(e)s, -e piece of apparatus; camera; telephone; (Rad, TV) set; am — bleiben hold the line; —ur [-'tu:r] f apparatus.

Appartement [apart[ə]'mã:] nt -s, -s flat.

Appell [a'pɛl] m -s, -e (Mil) muster, parade; (fig) appeal; a—ieren [apɛ'li:rən] vi appeal (an + acc to).

Appetit [ape'ti:t] m -(e)s, -e appetite; guten — enjoy your meal; a—lich a appetizing; —losigkeit f lack of appetite.

Applaus [a'plaus] m -es, -e applause.

Appretur [apre'tu:r] f finish.

Aprikose [apri'ko:zə] f -, -n apricot.

April [a'prıl] m -(s), -e April; —wetter nt April showers pl.

Aquaplaning [akva'pla:nıŋ] nt -(s) aquaplaning.

Aquarell [akva'rɛl] nt -s, -e watercolour.

Aquarium [a'kva:rıum] nt aquarium.

Äquator [ɛ'kva:tor] m -s equator.

Arbeit ['arbaıt] f -, -en work (no art); (Stelle) job; (Erzeugnis) piece of work; (wissenschaftliche) dissertation; (Klassen—) test; das war eine — that was a hard job; a—en vi work; vt work, make; —er(in f) m -s, - worker; (ungelernt) labourer; —erschaft f workers pl, labour force; —geber m -s, - employer; —nehmer m -s, - employee; a—sam a industrious.

Arbeits- *in cpds* labour; **—amt** *nt* employment exchange; **a—fähig** *a* a fit for work, able-bodied; **—gang** *m* operation; **—gemeinschaft** *f* study group; **—kräfte** *pl* workers *pl, labour*; **a—los** *a* unemployed, out-of-work; **—losigkeit** *f* unemployment; **—platz** *m* job; place of work; **a—scheu** a work-shy; **—tag** *m* work(ing) day; **—teilung** *f* division of labour; **a—unfähig** a unfit for work; **—zeit** *f* working hours *pl.*

Archäologe [arçɛo'lo:gə] *m* **-n,** **-n** archaeologist.

Architekt(in *f)* [arçi'tɛkt(ɪn)] *m* **-en, -en** architect; **—ur** ['-'tu:r] *f* architecture.

Archiv [ar'çi:f] *nt* **-s, -e** archive.

arg [ark] *a* bad, awful; *ad* awfully, very.

Ärger ['ɛrgər] *m* **-s** (*Wut*) anger; (*Unannehmlichkeit*) trouble; **ä—lich** *a* (*zornig*) angry; (*lästig*) annoying, aggravating; **ä—n** *vt* annoy; *vr* get annoyed; **—nis** *nt* **-ses, -se** annoyance; **öffentliches —nis erregen** be a public nuisance.

arg- *cpd:* **—listig** a cunning, insidious; **—los** a guileless, innocent; **A—losigkeit** *f* guilelessness, innocence; **A—ument** [argu'mɛnt] *nt* argument; **A—wohn** *m* suspicion; **—wöhnisch** a suspicious.

Arie ['a:riə] *f* **-, -n** aria.

Aristokrat [arɪsto'kra:t] *m* **-en,-en** aristocrat **—ie** ['-'ti:] *f* aristocracy; **a—isch** a aristocratic.

arithmetisch [arɪt'me:tɪʃ] a arithmetical.

arm [arm] a poor; **A—** *m* **-(e)s, -e** arm; (*Fluß—*) branch; (*Elec*) armature; **A—a'turenbrett** *nt* instrument panel; (*Aut*) dashboard; **A—band** *nt* bracelet;

A—banduhr *f* (wrist) watch; **A—e(r)** *mf* poor man/woman; **die A—en** the poor; **A—ee** [ar'me:] *f* **-, -n** army; **A—eekorps** *nt* army corps.

Ärmel ['ɛrmal] *m* **-s,** - sleeve; **etw aus dem — schütteln** (*fig*) produce sth just like that.

ärmlich ['ɛrmlɪç] a poor.

armselig a wretched, miserable.

Armut ['armu:t] *f* - poverty.

Aroma [a'ro:ma] *nt* **-s, Aromen** aroma; **a—tisch** [aro'ma:tɪʃ] a aromatic.

arrangieren [arã'ʒi:rən] *vt* arrange; *vr* come to an arrangement.

Arrest [a'rɛst] *m* **-(e)s, -e** detention.

arrogant [aro'gant] a arrogant.

Arroganz *f* arrogance.

Arsch [arʃ] *m* **-es, ⁻e** (col) arse, bum.

Art [a:rt] *f* **-, -en** (*Weise*) way; (*Sorte*) kind, sort; (*Biol*) species; **eine — (von) Frucht** a kind of fruit; **Häuser aller —** houses of all kinds; **es ist nicht seine —, das zu tun** it's not like him to do that; **ich mache das auf meine —** I do that my (own) way; **nach — des Hauses** à la maison; **a—en** *vi* **: nach jdm a—en** take after sb; **der Mensch ist so geartet, daß ... human nature** is such that ...

Arterie [ar'te:riə] *f* artery; **—nver-kalkung** *f* arteriosclerosis.

artig ['a:rtɪç] a good, well-behaved.

Artikel [ar'ti:kəl] *m* **-s,** - article.

Artillerie [artɪlə'ri:] *f* artillery.

Arznei [a:rts'naɪ] *f* medicine; **—mittel** *nt* medicine, medicament.

Arzt [a:rtst] *m* **-es, ⁻e, Ärztin** ['ɛːrtstɪn] *f* doctor.

ärztlich ['ɛːrtstlıç] a medical.

As [as] nt -ses, -se ace.

Asbest [as'bɛst] m -(e)s, -e asbestos.

Asche ['aʃə] f -, -n ash, cinder; —bahn f cinder track; —becher m ashtray; —nbrödel nt Cinderella; —rmittwoch m Ash Wednesday.

asozial ['azotsiaːl] a antisocial; Familien: asocial.

Aspekt [as'pɛkt] m -(e)s, -e aspect.

Asphalt [as'falt] m -(e)s, -e asphalt; a—ieren [-'tiːrən] vt asphalt; —straße f asphalt road.

Assistent(in f) [asɪs'tɛnt(ɪn)] m assistant.

Assoziation [asotsiatsi'oːn] f association.

Ast [ast] m -(e)s, ⁻e bough, branch; —er f -, -n aster.

ästhetisch [ɛs'teːtıʃ] a aesthetic.

Asthma ['astma] nt -s asthma; —tiker(in f) [ast'maːtikər(ın)] m -s, - asthmatic.

Astro- [astro] cpd: —'loge m -n, -n astrologer; —lo'gie f astrology; —'naut m -en, -en astronaut; —'nautik f astronautics; —'nom m -en, -en astronomer; —no'mie f astronomy.

Asyl [a'zyːl] nt -s, -e asylum; (Heim) home; (Obdachlosen—) shelter.

Atelier [atəli'eː] nt -s, -s studio.

Atem ['aːtəm] m -s breath; den —anhalten hold one's breath; außer — out of breath; a—beraubend a breath-taking; a—los a breathless; —pause f breather; —zug m breath.

Atheismus [ate'ısmʊs] m atheism.

Atheist m atheist; a—isch a atheistic.

Äther ['ɛːtər] m -s, - ether.

Athlet [at'leːt] m -en, -en athlete; —ik f athletics.

Atlas ['atlas] m - or -ses, -se or At'lanten atlas.

atmen ['aːtmən] vti breathe.

Atmosphäre [atmo'sfɛːrə] f -, -n atmosphere.

atmosphärisch a atmospheric.

Atmung ['aːtmʊŋ] f respiration.

Atom [a'toːm] nt -s, -e atom; a—ar [ato'maːr] a atomic; —bombe f atom bomb; —energie f atomic or nuclear energy; —kern m atomic nucleus; —kernforschung f nuclear research; —kraftwerk nt nuclear power station; —krieg m nuclear or atomic war; —macht f nuclear or atomic power; —müll m atomic waste; —sperrvertrag m (Pol) nuclear nonproliferation treaty; —versuch m atomic test; —waffen pl atomic weapons pl; —zeitalter nt atomic age.

Attentat [atɛn'taːt] nt -(e)s, -e (attempted) assassination. (auf +acc of).

Attentäter [atɛn'tɛːtər] m (wouldbe) assassin.

Attest [a'tɛst] nt -(e)s, -e certificate.

attraktiv [atrak'tiːf] a attractive.

Attrappe [a'trapə] f -, -n dummy.

Attribut [atri'buːt] nt -(e)s, -e (Gram) attribute.

ätzen ['ɛtsən] vi be caustic.

auch [aux] cj also, too, as well; (selbst, sogar) even; (wirklich) really; oder — or; — das ist schön that's nice too or as well; das habe ich — nicht gemacht I don't do it either; ich — nicht nor I, me neither; — wenn das Wetter schlecht ist even if the weather is bad; wer/was — whoever/whatever; so sieht es — aus it looks like it too; — das noch! not that as well!

auf [auf] prep +acc or dat (räumlich) on; (hinauf: +acc) up; (in Richtung: +acc) to; (nach) after; — der Reise on the way; — der Post/dem Fest at the post office/party; — das Land into the country; — der Straße on the road; — dem Land/der ganzen Welt in the country/the whole world; — deutsch in German; — Lebenszeit for sb's lifetime; bis — ihn except for him; — einmal at once; ad: — und ab up and down; — und davon up and away; —! (los) come on!; — sein (col) (Person) be up; (Tür) be open; von Kindheit — from childhood onwards; — daß so that.

aufatmen ['auf'a:tmən] vi heave a sigh of relief.

aufbahren ['aufba:rən] vt lay out.

Aufbau ['aufbau] m (Bauen) building, construction; (Struktur) structure; (aufgebautes Teil) superstructure; a—en vt erect, build (up); Existenz base; (gestalten) construct; (gründen) found, base (auf + dat on).

aufbäumen ['aufbɔymən] vr rear; (fig) revolt, rebel.

aufbauschen ['aufbauʃən] vt puff out; (fig) exaggerate.

aufbehalten ['aufbəhaltən] vt irreg keep on.

aufbekommen ['aufbəkɔmən] vt irreg (öffnen) get open; Hausaufgaben be given.

aufbessern ['aufbɛsərn] vt Gehalt increase.

aufbewahren ['aufbəva:rən] vt

keep; Gepäck put in the left-luggage office.

Aufbewahrung f (safe)keeping; (Gepäck—) left-luggage office; jdm etw zur — geben give sth for safekeeping; —sort m storage place.

aufbieten ['aufbi:tən] vt irreg Kraft summon (up), exert; Armee, Polizei mobilize; Brautpaar publish the banns of.

aufblasen ['aufbla:zən] irreg vt blow up, inflate; vr (col) become big-headed.

aufbleiben ['aufblaibən] vi irreg (Laden) remain open; (Person) stay up.

aufblenden ['aufblɛndən] vt Scheinwerfer turn on full beam.

aufblicken ['aufblikən] vi (lit, fig) look up (zu (lit, fig) to).

aufblühen ['aufbly:ən] vi blossom, flourish.

aufbrauchen ['aufbrauxən] vt use up.

aufbrausen ['aufbrauzən] vi (fig) flare up; —d a hot-tempered.

aufbrechen ['aufbrɛçən] irreg vt break or prize open; vi burst open; (gehen) start, set off.

aufbringen ['aufbrɪŋən] vt irreg (öffnen) open; (in Mode) bring into fashion; (beschaffen) procure; (Fin) raise; (ärgern) irritate; Verständnis für etw — be able to understand sth.

Aufbruch ['aufbrux] m departure.

aufbrühen ['aufbry:ən] vt Tee make.

aufbürden ['aufbyrdən] vt burden (jdm etw sb with sth).

aufdecken ['aufdɛkən] vt uncover.

aufdrängen ['aufdrɛŋən] vt force (jdm on sb); vr intrude (jdm on sb).

aufdringlich ['aufdrıŋlıç] a pushy.

aufeinander [auf'ai'nandər] ad achten after each other; schießen at each other; vertrauen each other; A—folge f succession, series; —folgen vi follow one another; —folgend a consecutive; —legen vt lay on top of one another; —prallen vi hit one another.

Aufenthalt ['auf'enthalt] m stay; (Verzögerung) delay; (Rail: Halten) stop; (Ort) haunt; —sgenehmigung f residence permit.

auferlegen ['auf'erle:gən] vt impose (jdm etw sth upon sb).

Auferstehung · ['auf'ersteːuŋ] f resurrection.

aufessen ['auf'esən] vt irreg eat up.

auffahr- ['auffa:r] cpd: **—en** irreg vi (Auto) run, crash (auf +acc into); (herankommen) draw up; (hochfahren) jump up; (wütend werden) flare up; (in den Himmel) ascend; vt Kanonen, Geschütz bring up; **—end** a hot-tempered; **A—t** f (Haus—) drive; (Autobahn—) slip road; **A—unfall** m pile-up.

auffallen ['auffalən] vi irreg be noticeable; jdm — strike sb; **—d** a striking.

auffällig ['auffɛlıç] a conspicuous, striking.

auffang- ['auffaŋ] cpd: **—en** vt irreg catch; Funkspruch intercept; Preise peg; **A—lager** nt refugee camp.

auffassen ['auffasən] vt understand, comprehend; (auslegen) see, view.

Auffassung f (Meinung) opinion; (Auslegung) view, concept; (also **—sgabe**) grasp.

auffindbar ['auffintba:r] a to be found.

auffordern ['auffordərn] vt (befehlen) call upon, order; (bitten) ask.

Aufforderung f (Befehl) order; (Einladung) invitation.

auffrischen ['auffrıʃən] vt freshen up; Kenntnisse brush up; Erinnerungen reawaken; vi (Wind) freshen.

aufführen ['auffyːrən] vt (Theat) perform; (in einem Verzeichnis) list, specify; vr (sich benehmen) behave.

Aufführung f (Theat) performance; (Liste) specification.

Aufgabe ['aufga:bə] f **-, -n** task; (Sch) exercise; (Haus—) homework; (Verzicht) giving up; (von Gepäck) registration; (von Post) posting; (von Inserat) insertion.

Aufgang ['aufgaŋ] m ascent; (Sonnen—) rise; (Treppe) staircase.

aufgeben ['aufge:bən] irreg vt (verzichten) give up; Paket send, post; Gepäck register; Bestellung give; Inserat insert; Rätsel, Problem set; vi give up.

Aufgebot ['aufgəboːt] nt supply; (von Kräften) utilization; (Ehe—) banns pl.

aufgedreht ['aufgədreːt] a (col) excited.

aufgedunsen ['aufgedʊnzən] a swollen, puffed up.

aufgehen ['aufge:ən] vi irreg (Sonne, Teig) rise; (sich öffnen) open; (klarwerden) become clear (jdm to sb); (Math) come out exactly; (sich widmen) be absorbed (in +dat in); in Rauch/Flammen — go up in smoke/flames.

aufgeklärt ['aufgəklɛːrt] a enlightened; (sexuell) knowing the facts of life.

aufgelegt ['aufgəleːkt] a: gut/schlecht — sein be in a good/bad mood; zu etw — sein be in the mood for sth.

aufgeregt ['aufgəreːkt] a excited.

aufgeschlossen ['aufgəʃlɔsən] a open, open-minded.

aufgeweckt ['aufgəvɛkt] a bright, intelligent.

aufgießen ['aufgiːsən] vt irreg Wasser pour over; Tee infuse.

aufgreifen ['aufgraifən] vt irreg Thema take up; Verdächtige pick up, seize.

aufgrund [auf'grunt] prep +gen on the basis of; (wegen) because of.

aufhaben ['aufhaːbən] vt irreg have on; Arbeit have to do.

aufhalsen ['aufhalzən] vt (col) jdm etw — saddle or lumber sb with sth.

aufhalten ['aufhaltən] irreg vt Person detain; Entwicklung check; Tür, Hand hold open; Augen keep open; vr (wohnen) live; (bleiben) stay; sich über etw/jdn — go on about sth/sb; sich mit etw — waste time over.

aufhängen ['aufhɛŋən] irreg vt Wäsche hang up; Menschen hang; vr hang o.s.

Aufhänger m -s, - (am Mantel) hook; (fig) peg.

aufheben ['aufheːbən] irreg vt (hochheben) raise, lift; Sitzung wind up; Urteil annul; Gesetz repeal, abolish; (aufbewahren) keep; bei jdm gut aufgehoben sein be well looked after at sb's; vr cancel o.s. out; viel A—(s) machen make a fuss (von about).

aufheitern ['aufhaitərn] vtr (Him-

mel, Miene) brighten; Mensch cheer up.

aufhellen ['aufhɛlən] vtr clear up; Farbe, Haare lighten.

aufhetzen ['aufhɛtsən] vt stir up (gegen against).

aufholen ['aufhoːlən] vt make up; vi catch up.

aufhorchen ['aufhɔrçən] vi prick up one's ears.

aufhören ['aufhøːrən] vi stop; — etw zu tun stop doing sth.

aufklappen ['aufklapən] vt open.

aufklären ['aufklɛːrən] vt Geheimnis etc clear up; Person enlighten; (sexuell) tell the facts of life to; (Mil) reconnoitre; vr clear up.

Aufklärung f (von Geheimnis) clearing up; (Unterrichtung, Zeitalter) enlightenment; (sexuell) sex education; (Mil, Aviat) reconnaissance.

aufkleben ['aufkleːbən] vt stick on.

Aufkleber m -s, - sticker.

aufknöpfen ['aufknœpfən] vt unbutton.

aufkommen ['aufkɔmən] vi irreg (Wind) come up; (Zweifel, Gefühl) arise; (Mode) start; für jdn/etw — be liable or responsible for sb/sth.

aufladen ['auflaːdən] vt irreg load.

Auflage ['auflaːgə] f edition; (Zeitung) circulation; (Bedingung) condition; jdm etw zur — machen make sth a condition for sb.

auflassen ['auflasən] vt irreg (offen) leave open; (aufgesetzt) leave on.

auflauern ['auflauərn] vi: jdm — lie in wait for sb.

Auflauf ['auflauf] m (Cook) pudding; (Menschen—) crowd.

aufleben ['aufleːbən] vi revive.

auflegen ['aufle:gən] *vt* put on; *Telefon* hang up; *(Print)* print.

auflehnen ['aufle:nən] *vt* lean on; *vr* rebel *(gegen* against).

Auflehnung *f* rebellion.

auflesen ['aufle:zən] *vt irreg* pick up.

aufleuchten ['auflɔʏçtən] *vi* light up.

aufliegen ['aufli:gən] *vi irreg* lie on; *(Comm)* be available.

auflockern ['auflɔkərn] *vt* loosen; *(fig)* Eintönigkeit *etc* liven up.

auflösen ['auflø:zən] *vtr* dissolve; *Haare etc* loosen; *Mißverständnis* sort out; *(in Tränen)* aufgelöst sein be in tears.

Auflösung *f* dissolving; *(fig)* solution.

aufmachen ['aufmaxən] *vt* open; *Kleidung* undo; *(zurechtmachen)* do up; *vr* set out.

Aufmachung *f (Kleidung)* outfit, get-up; *(Gestaltung)* format.

aufmerksam ['aufmɛrkza:m] *a* attentive; jdn auf etw *(acc)* — machen point sth out to sb; A—keit *f* attention, attentiveness.

aufmuntern ['aufmuntərn] *vt (ermutigen)* encourage; *(erheitern)* cheer up.

Aufnahme ['aufna:mə] *f* -, -n reception; *(Beginn)* beginning; *(in Verein etc)* admission; *(in Liste etc)* inclusion; *(Notieren)* taking down; *(Phot)* shot; *(auf Tonband etc)* recording; a—fähig *a* receptive; —prüfung *f* entrance test.

aufnehmen ['aufne:mən] *vt irreg* receive; *(hochheben)* pick up; *(beginnen)* take up; *(in Verein etc)* admit; *(in Liste etc)* include; *(fassen)* hold; *(notieren)* take down; *(photographieren)* photo-

graph; *(auf Tonband, Platte)* record; *(Fin: leihen)* take out; es mit jdm — können be able to compete with sb.

aufopfern ['auf'ɔpfərn] *vtr* sacrifice; —d *a* selfless.

aufpassen ['aufpasən] *vi (aufmerksam sein)* pay attention; auf jdn/etw — look after or watch sb/sth; aufgepaßt! look out!

Aufprall ['aufpral] *m* -s, -e impact; a—en *vi* hit, strike.

Aufpreis ['aufprais] *m* extra charge.

aufpumpen ['aufpumpən] *vt* pump up.

aufputschen ['aufputʃən] *vt (aufhetzen)* inflame; *(erregen)* stimulate.

aufraffen ['aufrafən] *vr* rouse o.s.

aufräumen ['aufrɔʏmən] *vti* Dinge clear away; Zimmer tidy up.

aufrecht ['aufrɛçt] *a (lit, fig)* upright; —erhalten *vt irreg* maintain.

aufreg- ['aufre:g] *cpd:* —en *vt* excite; *vr* get excited; —end *a* exciting; A—ung *f* excitement.

aufreiben ['aufraibən] *vt irreg* Haut rub open; *(erschöpfen)* exhaust; —d *a* strenuous.

aufreißen ['aufraisən] *vt irreg* Umschlag tear open; Augen open wide; Tür tear open; Straße take up.

aufreizen ['aufraitsən] *vt* incite, stir up; —d *a* exciting, stimulating.

aufrichten ['aufriçtən] *vt* put up, erect; *(moralisch)* console; *vr* rise; *(moralisch)* take heart *(an* +*dat* from).

aufrichtig ['aufriçtıç] *a* sincere, honest; A—keit *f* sincerity.

aufrücken ['aufrʏkən] *vi* move up; *(beruflich)* be promoted.

Aufruf ['aufruːf] *m* summons ; (*zur Hilfe*) call ; (*des Namens*) calling out ; **a—en** *vt irreg* (*auffordern*) call upon (*zu* for) ; *Namen* call out.

Aufruhr ['aufruːr] *m* -(e)s, -e uprising, revolt ; **in — sein** be in uproar.

aufrührerisch ['aufryːrərɪʃ] *a* rebellious.

aufrunden ['aufrʊndən] *vt Summe* round up.

Aufrüstung ['aufrʏstʊŋ] *f* rearmament.

aufrütteln ['aufrʏtəln] *vt* (*lit, fig*) shake up.

aufs [aufs] = **auf das**.

aufsagen ['aufzaːgən] *vt Gedicht* recite ; *Freundschaft* put an end to.

aufsammeln ['aufzaməln] *vt* gather up.

aufsässig ['aufzɛsɪç] *a* rebellious.

Aufsatz ['aufzats] *m* (*Geschriebenes*) essay ; (*auf Schrank etc*) top.

aufsaugen ['aufzaugən] *vt irreg* soak up.

aufschauen ['aufʃauən] *vi* look up.

aufscheuchen ['aufʃɔyçən] *vt* scare *or* frighten away.

aufschieben ['aufʃiːbən] *vt irreg* push open ; (*verzögern*) put off, postpone.

Aufschlag ['aufʃlaːk] *m* (*Ärmel—*) cuff ; (*Jacken—*) lapel ; (*Hosen—*) turn-up ; (*Aufprall*) impact ; (*Preis—*) surcharge ; (*Tennis*) service ; **a—en** *irreg vt* (*öffnen*) open ; (*verwunden*) cut ; (*hochschlagen*) turn up ; (*aufbauen*) *Zelt, Lager* pitch, erect ; *Wohnsitz* take up ; *vi* (*aufprallen*) hit ; (*teurer werden*) go up ; (*Tennis*) serve.

aufschließen ['aufʃliːsən] *irreg vt* open up, unlock ; *vi* (*aufrücken*) close up.

Aufschluß ['aufʃlʊs] *m* information ; **a—reich** *a* informative, illuminating.

aufschnappen ['aufʃnapən] *vt* (*col*) pick up ; *vi* fly open.

aufschneiden ['aufʃnaidən] *irreg vt Geschwür* cut open ; *Brot* cut up ; (*Med*) lance ; *vi* brag.

Aufschneider *m* -s, - boaster, braggart.

Aufschnitt ['aufʃnɪt] *m* (slices of) cold meat.

aufschnüren ['aufʃnyːrən] *vt* unlace ; *Paket* untie.

aufschrauben ['aufʃraubən] *vt* (*fest—*) screw on ; (*lösen*) unscrew.

aufschrecken ['aufʃrɛkən] *vt* startle ; *vi irreg* start up.

Aufschrei ['aufʃrai] *m* cry ; **a—en** *vi irreg* cry out.

aufschreiben ['aufʃraibən] *vt irreg* write down.

Aufschrift ['aufʃrɪft] *f* (*Inschrift*) inscription ; (*auf Etikett*) label.

Aufschub ['aufʃuːp] *m* -(e)s, -schübe delay, postponement.

aufschwatzen ['aufʃvatsən] *vt*: **jdm etw —** talk sb into (getting/having etc) sth.

Aufschwung ['aufʃvʊŋ] *m* (*Elan*) boost ; (*wirtschaftlich*) upturn, boom ; (*Sport*) circle.

aufsehen ['aufzeːən] *vi irreg* (*lit, fig*) look up (*zu* lit at, fig fig) ; **A— nt -s** sensation, stir ; **—erregend** *a* sensational.

Aufseher(in *f*) *m* -s, - guard ; (*im Betrieb*) supervisor ; (*Museums—*) attendant ; (*Park—*) keeper.

aufsein ['aufzain] *vi irreg* (*col*) be open ; (*Person*) be up.

aufsetzen ['aufzɛtsən] *vt* put on ; *Flugzeug* put down ; *Dokument* draw up; *vr* sit upright; *vi* (*Flugzeug*) touch down.

Aufsicht ['aufzɪçt] *f* supervision; die — haben be in charge.

aufsitzen ['aufzɪtsən] *vi irreg* (*aufrecht hinsitzen*) sit up; (*aufs Pferd, Motorrad*) mount, get on; (*Schiff*) run aground; **jdn — lassen** (*col*) stand sb up; **jdm — (col**) be taken in by sb.

aufspalten ['aufʃpaltən] *vt* split.

aufsparen ['aufʃpaːrən] *vt* save (up).

aufsperren ['aufʃpɛrən] *vt* unlock; *Mund* open wide.

aufspielen ['aufʃpiːlən] *vr* show off; **sich als etw —** try to come on as sb.

aufspießen ['aufʃpiːsən] *vt* spear.

aufspringen ['aufʃprɪŋən] *vi irreg* jump (*auf +acc* onto); (*hochspringen*) jump up; (*sich öffnen*) spring open; (*Hände, Lippen*) become chapped.

aufspüren ['aufʃpyːrən] *vt* track down; trace.

aufstacheln ['aufʃtaxəln] *vt* incite.

Aufstand ['aufʃtant] *m* insurrection, rebellion.

aufständisch ['aufʃtɛndɪʃ] *a* rebellious, mutinous.

aufstechen ['aufʃtɛçən] *vt irreg* prick open, puncture.

aufstecken ['aufʃtɛkən] *vt* stick on, pin up; (*col*) give up.

aufstehen ['aufʃteːən] *vi irreg* get up; (*Tür*) be open.

aufsteigen ['aufʃtaɪgən] *vi irreg* (*auf etw*) get onto; (*hochsteigen*) climb; (*Rauch*) rise.

aufstellen ['aufʃtɛlən] *vt* (*aufrecht stellen*) put up; (*aufreihen*) line up; (*nominieren*) put up; (*formu-*

lieren) *Programm etc* draw up; (*leisten*) *Rekord* set up.

Aufstellung *f* (*Sport*) line-up; (*Liste*) list.

Aufstieg ['aufʃtiːk] *m -(e)s, -e* (*auf Berg*) ascent; (*Fortschritt*) rise; (*beruflich, Sport*) promotion.

aufstoßen ['aufʃtoːsən] *irreg vt* push open; *vi* belch.

aufstrebend ['aufʃtreːbənt] *a* ambitious; *Land* up-and-coming.

Aufstrich ['aufʃtrɪç] *m* spread.

aufstülpen ['aufʃtʏlpən] *vt Ärmel* turn up; *Hut* put on.

aufstützen ['aufʃtʏtsən] *vr* lean (*auf +acc on*); *vt Körperteil* prop, lean; *Person* prop up.

aufsuchen ['aufzuːxən] *vt* (*besuchen*) visit; (*konsultieren*) consult.

auftakeln ['auftaːkəln] *vt* (*Naut*) rig (out); *vr* (*col*) deck o.s. out.

Auftakt ['auftakt] *m* (*Mus*) upbeat; (*fig*) prelude.

auftanken ['auftaŋkən] *vi* get petrol; *vt* refuel.

auftauchen ['auftauxən] *vi* appear; (*aus Wasser etc*) emerge; (*U-Boot*) surface; (*Zweifel*) arise.

auftauen ['auftauən] *vti* thaw; (*fig*) relax.

aufteilen ['auftaɪlən] *vt* divide up; *Raum* partition.

Aufteilung *f* division; partition.

auftischen ['auftɪʃən] *vt* serve (up); (*fig*) tell.

Auftrag ['auftraːk] *m -(e)s, -träge* order; (*Anweisung*) commission; (*Aufgabe*) mission; **im — von** on behalf of; **a—en** [-gan] *irreg vt Essen* serve; *Farbe* put on; *Kleidung* wear out; **jdm etw a—en** tell sb sth; **jdm/mir etc look fat; dick a—en** (*fig*) exaggerate; **—geber** *m -s, -*

(*Comm*) purchaser, customer.

auftreiben ['aʊftraɪbən] *vt irreg* (*col: beschaffen*) raise.

auftreten ['aʊftre:tən] *irreg vt* kick open; *vi* appear; (*mit Füßen*) tread; (*sich verhalten*) behave; A— *nt -s* (*Vorkommen*) appearance; (*Benehmen*) behaviour.

Auftrieb ['aʊftri:p] *m* (*Phys*) buoyancy, lift; (*fig*) impetus.

Auftritt ['aʊftrɪt] *m* (*des Schauspielers*) entrance; (*lit, fig: Szene*) scene.

auftun ['aʊftu:n] *irreg vt* open; *vr* open up. .

aufwachen ['aʊfvaxən] *vi* wake up.

aufwachsen ['aʊfvaksən] *vi irreg* grow up.

Aufwand ['aʊfvant] *m -(e)s* expenditure, (*Kosten auch*) expense; (*Luxus*) show; bitte, keinen —! please don't go out of your way.

aufwärmen ['aʊfvɛrmən] *vt* warm up; *alte Geschichten* rake up.

aufwärts ['aʊfvɛrts] *ad* upwards; A—entwicklung *f* upward trend; —gehen *vi irreg* look up.

aufwecken ['aʊfvɛkən] *vt* wake(n) up.

aufweichen ['aʊfvaɪçən] *vt* soften, soak.

aufweisen ['aʊfvaɪzən] *vt irreg* show.

aufwenden ['aʊfvɛndən] *vt* expend; *Geld spend*; *Sorgfalt* devote.

aufwendig *a* costly.

aufwerfen ['aʊfvɛrfən] *irreg vt* *Fenster etc* throw open; *Probleme* throw up, raise; *vr*: sich zu etw — make o.s. out to be sth.

aufwerten ['aʊfvɛrtən] *vt* (*Fin*) revalue; (*fig*) raise in value.

aufwiegeln ['aʊfvi:gəln] *vt* stir up, incite.

aufwiegen ['aʊfvi:gən] *vt irreg* make up for.

Aufwind ['aʊfvɪnt] *m* up-current.

aufwirbeln ['aʊfvɪrbəln] *vt* whirl up; *Staub* — (*fig*) create a stir.

aufwischen ['aʊfvɪʃən] *vt* wipe up.

aufzählen ['aʊftsɛ:lən] *vt* count out.

aufzeichnen ['aʊftsaɪçnən] *vt* sketch; (*schriftlich*) jot down; (*auf Band*) record.

Aufzeichnung *f* (*schriftlich*) note; (*Tonband—*) recording; (*Film—*) record.

aufzeigen ['aʊftsaɪgən] *vt* show, demonstrate.

aufziehen ['aʊftsi:ən] *vt irreg* (*hochziehen*) raise, draw up; (*öffnen*) pull open; *Uhr* wind up; (*col: necken*) tease; (*großziehen*) *Kinder* raise, bring up; *Tiere* rear.

Aufzug ['aʊftsu:k] *m* (*Fahrstuhl*) lift, elevator; (*Aufmarsch*) procession, parade; (*Kleidung*) getup; (*Theat*) act.

aufzwingen ['aʊftsvɪŋən] *vt irreg*: jdm etw — force sth upon sb.

Aug- ['aʊg] *cpd*: —apfel *m* eyeball; (*fig*) apple of one's eye; —e *nt -s, -n* eye; (*Fett—*) globule of fat; unter vier —en in private; —enblick *m* moment; im —enblick at the moment; —enblicklich *a* (*sofort*) instantaneous; (*gegenwärtig*) present; —enbraue *f* eyebrow; a—enscheinlich *a* obvious; —enweide *f* sight for sore eyes; —enzeuge *m* eye witness.

August [aʊˈgʊst] *m -(e)s or -, -e* August.

Auktion [aʊktsiˈo:n] *f* auction; —ator [-ˈna:tor] *m* auctioneer.

Aula ['aʊla] *f -, Aulen or -s* assembly hall.

aus [aʊs] *prep* + *dat* out of; (*von...her*) from; (*Material*) made of; — **ihr wird nie etwas** she'll never get anywhere; *ad* out; (*beendet*) finished, over; (*ausgezogen*) off; — **und ein gehen** come and go; (*bei jdm*) visit frequently; **weder — noch ein wissen** be at sixes and sevens; **auf etw** (*acc*) — **sein** be after sth; **vom Fenster** — out of the window; **vom Rom** — from Rome; **von sich** — of one's own accord; **A— nt** - outfield; **ins A—** gehen go out.

ausarbeiten ['aʊsʔarbaɪtən] *vt* work out.

ausarten ['aʊsʔartən] *vi* degenerate; (*Kind*) become overexcited.

ausatmen ['aʊsʔaːtmən] *vi* breathe out.

ausbaden ['aʊsbaːdən] *vt*: **etw** — **müssen** (*col*) carry the can for sth.

Ausbau ['aʊsbaʊ] *m* extension, expansion; removal; **a—en** *vt* extend, expand; (*herausnehmen*) take out, remove; **a—fähig** *a* (*fig*) worth developing.

ausbedingen ['aʊsbədɪŋən] *vt irreg*: **sich** (*dat*) **etw** — insist on sth.

ausbessern ['aʊsbɛsərn] *vt* mend, repair.

ausbeulen ['aʊsbɔʏlən] *vt* beat out.

Ausbeute ['aʊsbɔʏtə]. *f* yield; (*Fische*) catch; **a—n** *vt* exploit; (*Min*) work.

ausbild- ['aʊsbɪld] *cpd*: **—en** *vt* educate; *Lehrling, Soldat* instruct, train; *Fähigkeiten* develop; *Geschmack* cultivate;. **A—er** *m* **-s,** - instructor; **A—ung** *f* education; training, instruction; development, cultivation.

ausbitten.['aʊsbɪtən] *vt irreg*: **sich**

(*dat*) **etw** — (*erbitten*) ask for sth; (*verlangen*) insist on sth.

ausbleiben ['aʊsblaɪbən] *vi irreg* (*Personen*) stay away, not come; (*Ereignisse*) fail to happen, not happen.

Ausblick ['aʊsblɪk] *m* (*lit, fig*) prospect, outlook, view.

ausbomben ['aʊsbɔmbən] *vt* bomb out.

ausbrechen ['aʊsbrɛçən] *irreg vi* break out; **in Tränen/Gelächter** — burst into tears/out laughing; *vt* break off.

ausbreiten ['aʊsbraɪtən] *vt* spread (out); *Arme* stretch out; *vr* spread; (*über Thema*) expand, enlarge (*über* + *acc* on).

ausbrennen ['aʊsbrɛnən] *irreg vt* scorch; *Wunde* cauterize; *vi* burn out.

ausbringen ['aʊsbrɪŋən] *vt irreg* **ein Hoch** propose.

Ausbruch ['aʊsbrʊx] *m* outbreak; (*von Vulkan*) eruption; (*Gefühls—*) outburst; (*von Gefangenen*) escape.

ausbrüten ['aʊsbryːtən] *vt* (*lit, fig*) hatch.

Ausbuchtung ['aʊsbʊxtʊŋ] *f* bulge; (*Küste*) projection, protuberance.

ausbuhen ['aʊsbuːən] *vt* boo.

ausbürsten ['aʊsbʏrstən] *vt* brush out.

Ausdauer ['aʊsdaʊər] *f* perseverance, stamina; **a—nd** *a* persevering.

ausdehnen ['aʊsdeːnən] *vtr* (*räumlich*) expand; *Gummi* stretch; (*Nebel*) extend; (*zeitlich*) stretch; (*fig*) *Macht* extend.

ausdenken ['aʊsdɛŋkən] *vt irreg* (*zu Ende denken*) think through; **sich** (*dat*) **etw** — think sth up.

ausdiskutieren ['ausdɪskuti:rən]
vt talk out.
ausdrehen ['ausdre:ən] vt turn or
switch off; Licht auch turn out.
Ausdruck ['ausdruk] m
expression, phrase; (Kundgabe,
Gesichts—) expression.
ausdrücken ['ausdrykən] vt (also
vr: formulieren, zeigen) express;
Zigarette put out; Zitrone squeeze.
ausdrücklich a express, explicit.
ausdrucks- cpd:—los a ex-
pressionless, blank; —voll a ex-
pressive; A—weise f mode of expression.
auseinander [aus'aɪ'nandər] ad (getrennt) apart; — schreiben write as
separate words; —bringen vt irreg
separate; —fallen vi irreg fall
apart; —gehen vi irreg (Menschen)
separate; (Meinungen) differ;
(Gegenstand) fall apart; (col: dick
werden) put on weight; —halten vt
irreg tell apart; —nehmen vt irreg
take to pieces, dismantle; —setzen
vt (erklären) set forth, explain; vr
(sich verständigen) come to terms,
settle; (sich befassen) concern
o.s.; A—setzung f argument.
auserlesen ['aus'erle:zən] a select,
choice.
ausfahren ['ausfa:rən] irreg vi
drive out; (Naut) put out (to sea);
vt take out; (Tech) Fahrwerk drive
out; ausgefahrene Wege rutted
roads.
Ausfahrt f (des Zuges etc) leaving,
departure; (Autobahn—, Gara-
gen—) exit, way out; (Spazierfahrt) drive, excursion.
Ausfall ['ausfal] m loss;
(Nichtstattfinden) cancellation;
(Mil) sortie; (Fechten) lunge;
(radioaktiv) fall-out; a—en vi irreg
(Zähne, Haare) fall or come out;

(nicht stattfinden) be cancelled;
(wegbleiben) be omitted; (Person)
drop out; (Lohn) be stopped;
(nicht funktionieren) break down;
(Resultat haben) turn out; wie ist
das Spiel ausgefallen? what was the
result of the game?; a—end a impertinent; —straße f arterial road.
ausfegen ['ausfe:gən] vt sweep out.
ausfeilen ['ausfaɪlən] vt file out;
Stil polish up.
ausfertigen ['ausfertɪgən] vt draw
up; Rechnung make out; doppelt
— duplicate.
Ausfertigung f drawing up;
making out; (Exemplar) copy.
ausfindig machen ['ausfɪndɪç
maxən] vt discover.
ausfliegen ['ausfli:gən] vti irreg fly
away; sie sind ausgeflogen (col)
they're out.
ausflippen ['ausflɪpən] vi (col)
freak out.
Ausflucht ['ausfluxt] f -, -flüchte
excuse.
Ausflug ['ausflu:k] m excursion,
outing.
Ausflügler ['ausfly:klər] m -s, -
tripper.
Ausfluß ['ausflus] m outlet; (Med)
discharge.
ausfragen ['ausfra:gən] vt interrogate, question.
ausfransen ['ausfranzən] vi fray.
ausfressen ['ausfresən] vt irreg eat
up; (aushöhlen) corrode; (col: anstellen) be up to.
Ausfuhr ['ausfu:r] f -, -en export,
exportation; in cpds export.
ausführ- ['ausfy:r] cpd: —bar a
feasible; (Comm) exportable; —en
vt (verwirklichen) carry out;
Person take out; Hund take for a
walk; (Comm) export; (erklären)

give details of; **—lich** _a_ detailed;
_ad_ in detail; **A—lichkeit** _f_ detail;
A—ung _f_ execution, performance;
(Durchführung) completion; _(Her-
stellungsart)_ version; _(Erklärung)_
explanation.

ausfüllen ['ausfʏlən] _vt_ fill up;
Fragebogen etc fill in; _(Beruf)_ be
fulfilling for.

Ausgabe ['ausgaːbə] _f_ _(Geld)_
expenditure, outlay; _(Aushändi-
gung)_ giving out; _(Gepäck—)_ left-
luggage office; _(Buch)_ edition; _(Nummer)_ issue.

Ausgang ['ausgaŋ] _m_ way out,
exit; _(Ende)_ end; _(Ausgangspunkt)_
starting point; _(Ergebnis)_ result;
(Ausgehtag) free time, time off;
kein — no · exit; **—sbasis** _f_,
—spunkt _m_ starting point; **—s-
sperre** _f_ curfew.

ausgeben ['ausgeːbən] _irreg vt Geld_
spend; _(austeilen)_ issue, distribute; _vr:_ **sich für etw/jdn —**
pass o.s. off as sth/sb.

ausgebucht ['ausgəbuːxt] _a_ fully
booked.

ausgedient ['ausgədiːnt] _a Soldat_
discharged; _(verbraucht)_ no longer
in use; **— haben** have done good
service.

ausgefallen ['ausgəfalən] _a_ _(ungewöhnlich)_ exceptional.

ausgeglichen ['ausgəglɪçən] _a_
(well-)balanced; **A—heit** _f_ balance;
(von Mensch) even-temperedness.

Ausgeh- ['ausgeː] _cpd:_ **—anzug** _m_
good suit; **a—en** _vi irreg_ go out;
(zu Ende gehen) come to an end;
(Benzin) run out; _(Haare, Zähne)_
fall or come out; _(Feuer, Ofen,
Licht)_ go out; _(Strom)_ go off;
(Resultat haben) turn out; **mir ging
das Benzin aus** I ran out of petrol;
auf etw _(acc)_ **a—en** aim at sth; **von**

etw a—en _(wegführen)_ lead away
from sth; _(herrühren)_ come from
sth; _(zugrunde legen)_ proceed from
sth; **wir können davon a—en, daß
...** we can proceed from the
assumption that ..., we can take
as our starting point that ...; **leer.
a—en** get nothing; **schlecht a—en**
turn out badly; **—verbot** _nt_ curfew.

ausgelassen ['ausgəlasən] _a_
boisterous, high-spirited; **A—heit** _f_
boisterousness, high spirits _pl,_
exuberance.

ausgelastet ['ausgəlastət] _a_ fully
occupied.

ausgelernt ['ausgəlɛrnt] _a_ trained,
qualified.

ausgemacht ['ausgəmaxt] _a_ _(col)_
settled; _Dummkopf etc_ out-and-
out, downright; **es gilt als —, daß
...** it is settled that ...; **es war
eine —e Sache, daß ...** it was a
foregone conclusion that ...

ausgenommen ['ausgənɔmən]
prep +gen _or_ dat, _cj_ except; **An-
wesende sind —** present company
excepted.

ausgeprägt ['ausgəprɛːkt] _a_ prominent.

ausgerechnet ['ausgəreçnət] _ad_
just, precisely; **— du/heute** you of
all people/today of all days.

ausgeschlossen ['ausgəʃlɔsən] _a_
(unmöglich) impossible, out of the
question; **es ist nicht —, daß ...**
it cannot be ruled out that ...

ausgeschnitten ['ausgəʃnɪtən] _a_
Kleid low-necked.

ausgesprochen ['ausgəʃprɔxən] _a_
.Faulheit, Lüge etc out-and-out;
(unverkennbar) marked; _ad_
decidedly.

ausgezeichnet ['ausgətsaiçnət] _a_
excellent.

ausgiebig ['ausgi:bɪç] a Gebrauch thorough, good; Essen generous, lavish; — schlafen have a good sleep.

Ausgleich ['ausglaɪç] m -(e)s, -e balance; (Vermittlung) reconciliation; (Sport) equalization; zum — (+ gen) in order to offset; das ist ein guter — that's very relaxing; a— in irreg vt balance (out); reconcile; Höhe even up; vi (Sport) equalize; —stor nt equalizer.

ausgraben ['ausgra:bən] vt irreg dig up; Leichen exhume; (fig) unearth.

Ausgrabung f excavation; (Ausgraben auch) digging up.

Ausguß ['ausgus] m (Spüle) sink; (Abfluß) outlet; (Tülle) spout.

aushaben ['ausha:bən] vt irreg (col) Kleidung have taken off; Buch have finished.

aushalten ['aushaltən] irreg vt bear, stand; Geliebte keep; vi hold out; das ist nicht zum — that is unbearable.

aushandeln ['aushandəln] vt negotiate.

aushändigen ['aushɛndɪgən] vt: jdm etw — hand sth over to sb.

Aushang ['aushaŋ] m notice.

aushängen ['aushɛŋən] irreg vt Meldung put up; Fenster take off its hinges; vi be displayed; vr hang out.

Aushängeschild nt (shop) sign.

ausharren ['ausharən] vi hold out.

ausheben ['aushe:bən] vt irreg Erde lift out; Grube hollow out; Tür take off its hinges; Diebesnest clear out; (Mil) enlist.

aushecken ['aushɛkən] vt (col) concoct, think up.

aushelfen ['aushɛlfən] vi irreg: jdm — help sb out.

Aushilfe ['aushɪlfə] f help, assistance; (Person) (temporary) worker.

Aushilfs- cpd: —kraft f temporary worker; a—weise ad temporarily, as a stopgap.

ausholen ['ausho:lən] vi swing one's arm back; (zur Ohrfeige) raise one's hand; (beim Gehen) take long strides; weit — (fig) be expansive.

aushorchen ['aushɔrçən] vt sound out, pump.

aushungern ['aushuŋərn] vt starve out.

auskennen ['auskɛnən] vr irreg know thoroughly; (an einem Ort) know one's way about; (in Fragen etc) be knowledgeable.

auskippen ['auskɪpən] vt empty.

ausklammern ['ausklamərn] vt Thema exclude, leave out.

Ausklang ['ausklaŋ] m end.

auskleiden ['ausklaɪdən] vr undress; vt Wand line.

ausklingen ['ausklɪŋən] vi irreg (Ton, Lied) die away; (Fest) peter out.

ausklopfen ['ausklɔpfən] vt Teppich beat; Pfeife knock out.

auskochen ['auskɔxən] vt boil; (Med) sterilize; ausgekocht (fig) out-and-out.

auskommen ['auskɔmən] vi irreg: mit jdm — get on with sb; mit etw — get by with sth; A— nt -s: sein A— haben get by.

auskosten ['auskɔstən] vt enjoy to the full.

auskugeln ['ausku:gəln] vt (col) Arm dislocate.

auskundschaften ['aʊs-kʊnt-ʃaftən] vt spy out; Gebiet reconnoitre.

Auskunft ['aʊskʊnft] f -, -künfte information; (nähere) details pl, particulars pl; (Stelle) information office; (Tel) inquiries'; jdm — erteilen give sb information.

auskuppeln ['aʊskʊpəln] vi disengage the clutch.

auslachen ['aʊslaxən] vt laugh at, mock.

ausladen ['aʊsla:dən] irreg vt unload; (col) Gäste cancel an invitation to; vi stick out.

Auslage ['aʊsla:gə] f shop window (display); —n pl outlay, expenditure.

Ausland ['aʊslant] nt foreign countries pl; im/ins — abroad.

Ausländer(in f) ['aʊslɛndər(ɪn)] m -s, - foreigner.

ausländisch a foreign.

Auslands- cpd: —gespräch nt international call; —korrespondent(in f) m foreign correspondent; —reise f trip abroad.

auslassen ['aʊslasən] irreg vt leave out; Wort etc auch omit; Fett melt; Kleidungsstück let out; Wut, Ärger vent (an + dat on); vr: sich über etw (acc) — speak one's mind about sth.

Auslassung f omission; —zeichen nt apostrophe.

Auslauf ['aʊslaʊf] m (für Tiere) run; (Ausfluß) outflow, outlet; a—en vi irreg run out; (Behälter) leak; (Naut) put out (to sea); (langsam aufhören) run down.

Ausläufer ['aʊslɔyfər] m (von Gebirge) spur; (Pflanze) runner; (Met) (von Hoch) ridge; (von Tief) trough.

ausleeren ['aʊsle:rən] vt empty.

auslegen ['aʊsle:gən] vt Waren lay out; Köder put down; Geld lend; (bedecken) cover; Text etc interpret.

Auslegung f interpretation.

Ausleihe ['aʊslaɪə] f -, -n issuing; (Stelle) issue desk; a—n vt irreg (verleihen) lend; sich (dat) etw a—en borrow sth.

Auslese ['aʊsle:zə] f -, -n selection; (Elite) elite; (Wein) choice wine; a—n vt irreg select; (col: zu Ende lesen) finish.

ausliefern ['aʊsli:fərn] vt deliver (up), hand over; (Comm) deliver; jdm/etw ausgeliefert sein be at the mercy of sb/sth; vr: sich jdm — give o.s. up to sb.

auslöschen ['aʊslœʃən] vt extinguish; (fig) wipe out, obliterate.

auslosen ['aʊslo:zən] vt draw lots for.

auslösen ['aʊslø:zən] vt Explosion, Schuß set off; (hervorrufen) cause, produce; Gefangene ransom; Pfand redeem.

Auslöser m -s, - (Phot) release.

ausmachen ['aʊsmaxən] vt Licht, Radio turn off; Feuer put out; (entdecken) make out; (vereinbaren) agree; (beilegen) settle; (Anteil darstellen, betragen) represent; (bedeuten) matter; das macht ihm nichts aus it doesn't matter to him; macht es Ihnen etwas aus, wenn …? would you mind if …?

ausmalen ['aʊsma:lən] vt paint; (fig) describe; sich (dat) etw — imagine sth.

Ausmaß ['aʊsma:s] nt dimension; (fig auch) scale.

ausmerzen ['aʊsmɛrtsən] vt eliminate.

ausmessen ['ausmɛsən] vt irreg measure.

Ausnahme ['ausnaːmə] f -, -n exception; **eine — machen** make an exception; **—fall** m exceptional case; **—zustand** m state of emergency.

ausnahms- cpd: **—los** ad without exception; **—weise** ad by way of exception, for once.

ausnehmen ['ausneːmən] irreg vt take out, remove; Tier gut; Nest rob; (col: Geld abnehmen) clean out; (ausschließen) make an exception; vr look, appear; **—d** a exceptional.

ausnützen ['ausnytsən] vt Zeit, Gelegenheit use, turn to good account; Einfluß use; Mensch, Gutmütigkeit exploit.

auspacken ['auspakən] vt unpack.

auspfeifen ['auspfaɪfən] vt irreg hiss/boo at.

ausplaudern ['ausplaudərn] vt Geheimnis blab.

ausprobieren ['ausprobiːrən] vt try (out).

Auspuff ['auspuf] m -(e)s, -e (Tech) exhaust; **—rohr** nt exhaust (pipe); **—topf** m (Aut) silencer.

ausradieren ['ausradiːrən] vt erase, rub out.

ausrangieren ['ausrãʒiːrən] vt (col) chuck out.

ausrauben ['ausraubən] vt rob.

ausräumen ['ausrɔymən] vt Dinge clear away; Schrank, Zimmer empty; Bedenken put aside.

ausrechnen ['ausrɛçnən] vt calculate, reckon.

Ausrechnung f calculation, reckoning.

Ausrede ['ausreːdə] f excuse; **a—n**

vi have one's say; vt: **jdm etw a—n** talk sb out of sth.

ausreichen ['ausraɪçən] vi suffice, be enough; **—d** a sufficient, adequate; (Sch) adequate.

Ausreise ['ausraɪzə] f departure; **bei der —** when leaving the country; **—erlaubnis** f exit visa; **a—n** vi leave the country.

ausreißen ['ausraɪsən] irreg vt tear or pull out; vi (Riß bekommen) tear; (col) make off, scram.

ausrenken ['ausrɛŋkən] vt dislocate.

ausrichten ['ausrɪçtən] vt Botschaft deliver; Gruß pass on; Hochzeit etc arrange; (erreichen) get anywhere (bei with); (in gerade Linie bringen) get in a straight line; (angleichen) bring into line; **jdm etw —** take a message for sb; **ich werde es ihm —** I'll tell him.

ausrotten ['ausrotən] vt stamp out, exterminate.

ausrücken ['ausrykən] vi (Mil) move off; (Feuerwehr, Polizei) be called out; (col: weglaufen) run away.

Ausruf ['ausruːf] m (Schrei) cry, exclamation; (Verkünden) proclamation; **a—en** vt irreg cry out, exclaim; call out; **—ezeichen** nt exclamation mark.

ausruhen ['ausruːən] vtr rest.

ausrüsten ['ausrystən] vt equip, fit out.

Ausrüstung f equipment.

ausrutschen ['ausrutʃən] vi slip.

Aussage ['ausaːgə] f -, -n (Jur) statement; **a—n** vt say, state; vi (Jur) give evidence.

ausschalten ['ausʃaltən] vt switch off; (fig) eliminate.

Ausschank ['ausʃaŋk] m -(e)s,

-schänke dispensing, giving out; (*Comm*) selling; (*Theke*) bar.

Ausschau ['aʊsʃaʊ] *f:* — **halten** look out, watch (*nach* for); a—en *vi* look out (*nach* for), be on the look-out.

ausscheiden ['aʊsʃaɪdən] *irreg vt* separate; (*Med*) give off, secrete; *vi* leave (*aus etw* sth); (*Sport*) be eliminated or knocked out; **er scheidet für den Posten aus** he can't be considered for the job.

Ausscheidung *f* separation; retiral; elimination.

ausschenken ['aʊsʃɛŋkən] *vt* pour out; (*Comm*) sell.

ausschimpfen ['aʊsʃɪmpfən] *vt* scold, tell off.

ausschlachten ['aʊsʃlaxtən] *vt Auto* cannibalize; (*fig*) make a meal of.

ausschlafen ['aʊsʃlaːfən] *irreg vir* have a long lie (in); *vt* sleep off; **ich bin nicht ausgeschlafen** I don't have or get enough sleep.

Ausschlag ['aʊsʃlaːk] *m* (*Med*) rash; (*Pendel*—) swing; (*Nadel*) deflection; **den** — **geben** (*fig*) tip the balance; a—en [-gən] *irreg vt* knock out; (*auskleiden*) deck out; (*verweigern*) decline; *vi* (*Pferd*) kick out; (*Bot*) sprout; (*Zeiger*) be deflected; a—**gebend** *a* decisive.

ausschließen ['aʊsʃliːsən] *vt irreg* shut or lock out; (*fig*) exclude; **ich will mich nicht** — myself not excepted.

ausschließlich *a, ad* exclusive(ly); *prep* +*gen* excluding, exclusive of.

Ausschluß ['aʊsʃlʊs] *m* exclusion.

ausschmücken ['aʊsʃmʏkən] *vt* decorate; (*fig*) embellish.

ausschneiden ['aʊsʃnaɪdən] *vt irreg* cut out; *Büsche* trim.

Ausschnitt ['aʊsʃnɪt] *m* (*Teil*) section; (*von Kleid*) neckline; (*Zeitungs*—) cutting; (*aus Film etc*) excerpt.

ausschreiben ['aʊsʃraɪbən] *vt irreg* (*ganz schreiben*) write out (in full); (*ausstellen*) write (out); *Stelle, Wettbewerb etc* announce, advertise.

Ausschreitung ['aʊsʃraɪtʊŋ] *f* excess.

Ausschuß ['aʊsʃʊs] *m* committee, board; (*Abfall*) waste, scraps *pl*; (*Comm: also* —**ware** *f*) reject.

ausschütten ['aʊsʃʏtən] *vt* pour out; *Eimer* empty; *Geld* pay; *vr* shake (with laughter).

ausschweifend ['aʊsʃvaɪfənt] *a Leben* dissipated, debauched; *Phantasie* extravagant.

Ausschweifung *f* excess.

ausschweigen ['aʊsʃvaɪgən] *vr irreg* keep silent.

ausschwitzen ['aʊsʃvɪtsən] *vt* exude; (*Mensch*) sweat out.

aussehen ['aʊszeːən] *vi irreg* look; **das sieht nach nichts aus** that doesn't look anything special; **es sieht nach Regen aus** it looks like rain; **es sieht schlecht aus** things look bad; **A—** *nt* -s appearance.

aussein ['aʊszaɪn] *vi irreg* (*col*) be out; (*zu Ende*) be over.

außen ['aʊsən] *ad* outside; (*nach* —) outwards; — **ist es rot** it's red (on the) outside; A—**antenne** *f* outside aerial; A—**bordmotor** *m* outboard motor.

aussenden ['aʊszɛndən] *vt irreg* send out, emit.

Außen- *cpd:* —**dienst** *m* outside or field service; (*von Diplomat*) foreign service; —**handel** *m* foreign trade; —**minister** *m* foreign minister; —**ministerium** *nt* foreign office; —politik f foreign policy; —seite f outside; —seiter m -s, -, —stehende(r) mf outsider; —welt f outside world.

außer ['ausər] prep +dat (räumlich) out of; (abgesehen von) except; — Gefahr sein be out of danger; — Zweifel beyond any doubt; — Betrieb out of order; — sich (dat) sein/geraten be beside o.s.; — Dienst retired; — Landes abroad; cj (ausgenommen) except; — wenn unless; — daß except; —amtlich a unofficial, private; —dem cj besides, in addition; —dienstlich a unofficial.

äußere(r,s) ['ɔysərə(r,z)] a outer, external.

außer- cpd: —ehelich a extramarital; —gewöhnlich a unusual; —halb prep +gen, ad outside; A—kraftsetzung f putting out of action.

äußer- cpd: —lich a, ad external; —n vt utter, express; (zeigen) show; vr give one's opinion; (sich zeigen) show itself.

außer- cpd: —ordentlich a extraordinary; —planmäßig a unscheduled; —'stande ad not in a position, unable.

äußerst ['ɔysərst] ad extremely, most; —e(r,s) a utmost; (räumlich) farthest; Termin last possible; Preis highest; —enfalls ad if the worst comes to the worst.

aussetzen ['auszɛtsən] vt Kind, Tier abandon; Boote lower; Belohnung offer; Urteil, Verfahren postpone; jdn/sich etw (dat) — lay sb/o.s. open to sth; jdm/etw ausgesetzt sein be exposed to sb/sth; an jdm/etw etwas — find fault with sb/sth; vi (aufhören) stop; (Pause machen) drop out.

Aussicht ['auszɪçt] f view; (in Zukunft) prospect; in — sein be in view; etw in — haben have sth in view; a—slos a hopeless; —spunkt m viewpoint; a—sreich a promising; —sturm m observation tower.

aussöhnen ['auszøːnən] vt reconcile; vr reconcile o.s., become reconciled.

Aussöhnung f reconciliation.

aussondern ['auszɔndərn] vt separate, select.

aussortieren ['auszɔrtiːrən] vt sort out.

ausspannen ['ausʃpanən] vt spread or stretch out; Pferd unharness; (col) Mädchen. steal (jdm from sb); vi relax.

aussparen ['ausʃpaːrən] vt leave open.

aussperren ['ausʃpɛrən] vt lock out.

ausspielen ['ausʃpiːlən] vt Karte lead; Geldprämie offer as a prize; jdn gegen jdn — play sb off against sb; vi (Cards) lead; ausgespielt haben be finished.

Aussprache ['ausʃpraːxə] f pronunciation; (Unterredung) (frank) discussion.

aussprechen ['ausʃprɛçən] irreg vt pronounce; (zu Ende sprechen) speak; (äußern) say, express; vr (sich äußern) speak (über +acc about); (sich anvertrauen) unburden o.s. (diskutieren) discuss; vi (zu Ende sprechen) finish speaking.

Ausspruch ['ausʃprux] m saying, remark.

ausspülen ['ausʃpyːlən] vt wash out; Mund rinse.

ausstaffieren ['ausʃtafiːrən] vt equip, kit out; Zimmer furnish.

Ausstand ['aʊsʃtant] *m* strike; **in den — treten** go on strike.

ausstatten ['aʊsʃtatən] *vt Zimmer etc* furnish; **jdn mit etw —** equip sb *or* kit sb out with sth.

Ausstattung *f* (*Ausstatten*) provision; (*Kleidung*) outfit; (*Aussteuer*) dowry; (*Aufmachung*) make-up; (*Einrichtung*) furnishing.

ausstechen ['aʊsʃtɛçən] *vt irreg Augen, Rasen, Graben* dig out; *Kekse* cut out; (*übertreffen*) outshine.

ausstehen ['aʊsʃteːən] *irreg vt* stand, endure; *vi* (*noch nicht dasein*) be outstanding.

aussteigen ['aʊsʃtaɪgən] *vi irreg* get out, alight.

ausstellen ['aʊsʃtɛlən] *vt* exhibit, display; (*col: ausschalten*) switch off; *Rechnung etc* make out; *Paß, Zeugnis* issue.

Ausstellung *f* exhibition; (*Fin*) drawing up; (*einer Rechnung*) making out; (*eines Passes etc*) issuing.

aussterben ['aʊsʃtɛrbən] *vi irreg* die out.

Aussteuer ['aʊsʃtɔʏər] *f* dowry.

ausstopfen ['aʊsʃtɔpfən] *vt* stuff.

ausstoßen ['aʊsʃtoːsən] *vt irreg Luft, Rauch* give off, emit; (*aus Verein etc*) expel, exclude; *Auge* poke out.

ausstrahlen ['aʊsʃtraːlən] *vti* radiate; (*Rad*) broadcast.

Ausstrahlung *f* radiation; (*fig*) charisma.

ausstrecken ['aʊsʃtrɛkən] *vtr* stretch out.

ausstreichen ['aʊsʃtraɪçən] *vt irreg* cross out; (*glätten*) smooth out.

ausströmen ['aʊsʃtrøːmən] *vi* (*Gas*) pour out, escape; *vt* give off; (*fig*) radiate.

aussuchen ['aʊszuːxən] *vt* select, pick out.

Austausch ['aʊstaʊʃ] *m* exchange; **a—bar** a exchangeable; **a—en** *vt* exchange, swop; **—motor** *m* reconditioned engine.

austeilen ['aʊstaɪlən] *vt* distribute, give out.

Auster ['aʊstər] *f* -, -n oyster.

austoben ['aʊstoːbən] *vr* (*Kind*) run wild; (*Erwachsene*) sow one's wild oats.

austragen ['aʊstraːgən] *vt irreg Post* deliver; *Streit etc* decide; *Wettkämpfe* hold.

Austräger ['aʊstrɛːgər] *m* delivery boy; (*Zeitungs—*) newspaper boy.

austreiben ['aʊstraɪbən] *vt irreg* drive out, expel; *Geister* exorcize.

austreten ['aʊstreːtən] *irreg vt* (*zur Toilette*) be excused; **aus etw —** leave sth; *vt Feuer* tread out, trample; *Schuhe* wear out; *Treppe* wear down.

austrinken ['aʊstrɪŋkən] *irreg vt Glas* drain; *Getränk* drink up; *vi* finish one's drink, drink up.

Austritt ['aʊstrɪt] *m* emission; (*aus Verein, Partei etc*) retirement, withdrawal.

austrocknen ['aʊstrɔknən] *vti* dry up.

ausüben ['aʊsˈyːbən] *vt Beruf* practise, carry out; *Funktion* perform; *Einfluß* exert; *Reiz, Wirkung* exercise, have (*auf jdn* on sb).

Ausübung *f* practice, exercise.

Ausverkauf ['aʊsfɛrkaʊf] *m* sale; **a—en** *vt* sell out; *Geschäft* sell up; **a—t** *a Karten, Artikel* sold out; (*Theat*) *Haus* full.

Auswahl ['ausvaːl] f selection, choice (an + dat of).

auswählen ['ausvɛːlən] vt select, choose.

Auswander- ['ausvandər] cpd: **—er** m emigrant; **a—n** vi emigrate; **—ung** f emigration.

auswärtig ['ausvɛrtɪç] a (nicht am/vom Ort) out-of-town; (ausländisch) foreign; **A—e(s)** Amt nt Foreign Office, State Department (US).

auswärts ['ausvɛrts] ad outside; (nach ·außen) outwards; **—** essen eat out; **A—spiel** nt away game.

auswechseln ['ausvɛksəln] vt change, substitute.

Ausweg ['ausveːk] m way out; **a—los** a hopeless.

ausweichen ['ausvaɪçən] vi irreg: jdm/etw **—** (lit) make aside or make way for sb/sth; (fig) sidestep sb/sth; **—d** a evasive.

ausweinen ['ausvaɪnən] vr have a (good) cry.

Ausweis ['ausvaɪs] m **-es, -e** identity card, passport; (Mitglieds—, Bibliotheks— etc) card; **a—en** [-zən] irreg vt expel, banish; vr prove one's identity; **—karte** f, **—papiere** pl identity papers pl; **—ung** f expulsion.

ausweiten ['ausvaɪtən] vt stretch.

auswendig ['ausvɛndɪç] ad by heart; **—** lernen vt learn by heart.

auswert- ['ausveːrt] cpd: **—en** vt evaluate; **A—ung** f evaluation, analysis; (Nutzung) utilization.

auswirk- ['ausvɪrk] cpd: **—en** vr have an effect; **A—ung** f effect.

auswischen ['ausvɪʃən] vt wipe out; jdm eins **—** (col) put one over on sb.

Auswuchs ['ausvuːks] m (out)-growth; ·(fig) product.

auswuchten ['ausvuxtən] vt (Aut) balance.

auszacken ['austsakən] vt Stoff etc pink.

auszahlen ['austsaːlən] vt Lohn, Summe pay out; Arbeiter pay off; Miterbe buy out; vr (sich lohnen) pay.

auszählen ['austsɛːlən] vt Stimmen count; (Boxen) count out.

auszeichnen ['austsaɪçnən] vt honour; (Mil) decorate; (Comm) price; vr distinguish o.s.

Auszeichnung f distinction; (Comm) pricing; (Ehrung) awarding of decoration; (Ehre) honour; (Orden) decoration; mit **—** with distinction.

ausziehen ['austsiːən] irreg vt Kleidung take off; Haare, Zähne, Tisch etc pull out; (nachmalen) trace; vr undress; vi (aufbrechen) leave; (aus ·Wohnung) move out.

Auszug ['austsuːk] m (aus Wohnung) removal; (aus Buch etc) extract; (Konto—) statement; (Ausmarsch) departure.

Auto ['auto] nt **-s, -s** (motor-)car; **—** fahren drive; **—bahn** f motorway; **—fahrer(in** f) m motorist, driver; **—fahrt** f drive; **a—gen** [-'geːn] a autogenous; **—'gramm** nt autograph; **—'mat** m **-en, -en** machine; **a—'matisch** a automatic; **a—'nom** [-'noːm] a autonomous.

Autopsie [auto'psiː] f post-mortem, autopsy.

Autor ['autor] m **-s, -en, Autorin** [au'toːrɪn] f author.

Auto- cpd: **—radio** nt car radio; **—reifen** m car tyre; **—rennen** nt motor racing.

autoritär [autori'tɛːr] a authoritarian.

Autorität f authority.
Auto- cpd: —unfall m car or motor accident; —verleih m car hire.
Axt [akst] f -, ⸚e axe.

B

B, b [be:] nt B, b.
Baby ['be:bi] nt -s, -s baby;
—ausstattung f layette; -sitter ['be:bizitər] m -s, - baby-sitter.
Bach [bax] m -(e)s, ⸚e stream, brook.
Back- [bak] cpd: —blech nt baking tray; —bord nt -(e)s, -e (Naut) port; —e f -, -n cheek; b—en vti irreg bake; —enbart m sideboards pl; —enzahn m molar.
Bäcker ['bɛkər] m -s, - baker; —ei [-'rai] f bakery; (—laden) baker's (shop).
Back- cpd: —form f baking tin; —hähnchen nt roast chicken; —obst nt dried fruit; —ofen m oven; —pflaume f prune; —pulver nt baking powder; —stein m brick.
Bad [ba:t] nt -(e)s, ⸚er bath; (Schwimmen) bathe; (Ort) spa.
Bade- ['ba:də] cpd: —anstalt f (swimming) baths pl; —anzug m bathing suit; —hose f bathing or swimming trunks pl; —kappe f bathing cap; —mantel m bath(ing) robe; —meister m baths attendant; b—n vi bathe, have a bath; vt bath; —ort m spa; —tuch nt bath towel; —wanne f bath (tub); —zimmer nt bathroom.
baff [baf] a: — sein (col) be flabbergasted.
Bagatelle [baga'tɛlə] f -, -n trifle.
Bagger ['bagər] m -s, - excavator; (Naut) dredger; b—n vti excavate;

(Naut) dredge.
Bahn [ba:n] f -, -en railway, railroad (US); (Weg) road, way; (Spur) lane; (Renn—) track; (Astron) orbit; (Stoff—) length; b—brechend a pioneering; —damm m railway embankment; b—en vt: sich/jdm einen Weg b—en clear a way/a way for sb; —fahrt f railway journey; —hof m station; auf dem —hof at the station; —hofshalle f station concourse; -hofsvorsteher m stationmaster; —hofswirtschaft f station restaurant; —linie f (railway) line; —steig m platform; —steigkarte f platform ticket; —strecke f (railway) line; —übergang m level crossing, grade crossing (US); —wärter m signalman.
Bahre ['ba:rə] f -, -n stretcher.
Bajonett [bajo'nɛt] nt -(e)s, -e bayonet.
Bakelit® [bake'li:t] nt -s Bakelite®.
Bakterien [bak'te:riən] pl bacteria pl.
Balance [ba'lãːsə] f -, -n balance, equilibrium.
balan'cieren vti balance.
bald [balt] ad (zeitlich) soon; (beinahe) almost; —...-... now...now...; —ig ['baldiç] a early, speedy; —möglichst ad as soon as possible.
Baldrian ['baldria:n] m -s, -e valerian.
Balken ['balkən] m -s, - beam; (Trag—) girder; (Stütz—) prop.

Balkon [bal'kõ:] *m* -s, -s *or* -e balcony; (*Theat*) (dress) circle.

Ball [bal] *m* -(e)s, ⁼e ball; (*Tanz*) dance, ball.

Ballade [ba'la:də] *f* -, -n ballad.

Ballast ['balast] *m* -(e)s, -e ballast; (*fig*) weight, burden.

Ballen ['balən] *m* -s, - bale; (*Anat*) ball; **b—** *vt* (*formen*) make into a ball; *Faust* clench; *vr* build up; (*Menschen*) gather.

Ballett [ba'lɛt] *nt* -(e)s, -e ballet; —(t)änzer(in *f*) *m* ballet dancer.

Ball- *cpd*: —junge *m* ball boy; —kleid *nt* evening dress.

Ballon [ba'lõ:] *m* -s, -s *or* -e balloon.

Ballspiel *nt* ball game.

Ballung ['balʊŋ] *f* concentration; (*von Energie*) build-up; —sgebiet *nt* conurbation.

Bambus ['bambʊs] *m* -ses, -se bamboo; —rohr *nt* bamboo cane.

Bammel ['baməl] *m* -s (*col*) (einen) — haben vor jdm/etw be scared of sb/sth.

banal [ba'na:l] *a* banal; **B—ität** [banali'tɛ:t] *f* banality.

Banane [ba'na:nə] *f* -, -n banana.

Banause [ba'nauzə] *m* -n, -n philistine.

Band [bant] *m* -(e)s, ⁼e (*Buch-*) volume; *nt* -(e)s, ⁼er (*Stoff-*) ribbon, tape; (*Fließ-*) production line; (*Faß-*) hoop; (*Ton-*) tape; (*Anat*) ligament; etw 'auf — aufnehmen tape sth; am laufenden — (*col*) non-stop; *nt* -(e)s, -e (*Freundschafts- etc*) bond; [bɛnt] *f* -, -s band, group.

Bandage [ban'da:ʒə] *f* -, -n bandage.

banda'gieren *vt* bandage.

Bande ['bandə] *f* -, -n band; (*Straßen—*) gang.

bändigen ['bɛndɪgən] *vt Tier* tame; *Trieb, Leidenschaft* control, restrain.

Bandit [ban'di:t] *m* -en, -en bandit.

Band- *cpd*: —maß *nt* tape measure; —säge *f* band saw; —scheibe *f* (*Anat*) disc; —wurm *m* tapeworm.

bange ['baŋə] *a* scared; (*besorgt*) anxious; jdm wird es — sb is becoming·scared; jdm — machen scare sb; **B—macher** *m* -s, - scaremonger; **—n** *vi*: um jdn/etw — be anxious *or* worried about sb/sth.

Banjo ['banjo, 'bɛndʒo] *nt* -s, -s banjo.

Bank [baŋk] *f* -, ⁼e (*Sitz—*) bench; (*Sand—* etc) (sand)bank *or* -bar; *f* -, -en (*Geld—*) bank; —anweisung *f* banker's order; —beamte(r) *m* bank clerk.

Bankett [ban'kɛt] *nt* -(e)s, -e (*Essen*) banquet; (*Straßenrand*) verge.

Bankier [baŋki'e:] *m* -s, -s banker.

Bank- *cpd*: —konto *m* bank account; —note *f* banknote; —raub *m* bank robbery.

Bankrott [baŋ'krɔt] *m* -(e)s, -e bankruptcy; — machen go bankrupt; **b—** *a* bankrupt.

Bann [ban] *m* -(e)s, -e (*Hist*) ban; (*Kirchen—*) excommunication; (*fig: Zauber*) spell; **b—en** *vt Geister* exorcise; *Gefahr* avert; (*bezaubern*) enchant; (*Hist*) banish; **—er** *nt* -s, - banner, flag.

bar [ba:r] *a* (*unbedeckt*) bare; (*frei von*) lacking (*gen* in); (*offenkundig*) utter, sheer; —es Geld cash; etw_(in) — bezahlen pay sth (in) cash; etw für —e Münze nehmen (fig) take sth at its face value; B— f -, -s bar.

Bär [bɛːr] m -en, -en bear.

Baracke [ba'rakə] f -, -n hut, barrack.

barbarisch [bar'baːrɪʃ] a barbaric, barbarous.

Bar- cpd: —bestand m money in hand; b—fuß a barefoot; —geld nt cash, ready money; b—geldlos a non-cash; b—häuptig a bareheaded; —hocker m bar stool; —kauf m cash purchase; —keeper ['baːrkiːpər] m -s, -; —mann m barman, bartender.

barmherzig [barm'hɛrtsɪç] a merciful, compassionate; B—keit f mercy, compassion.

Barometer [baro'meːtər] nt -s, - barometer.

Baron [ba'roːn] m -s, -e baron; —esse [baro'nɛsə] f -, -n, —in f baroness.

Barren ['barən] m -s, - parallel bars pl; (Gold—) ingot.

Barriere [bari'ɛːrə] f -, -n barrier.

Barrikade [bari'kaːdə] f -, -n barricade.

Barsch [barʃ] m -(e)s, -e perch; b— [barʃ] a brusque, gruff.

Bar- cpd: —schaft f ready money; —scheck m open or uncrossed cheque.

Bart [baːrt] m -(e)s, ²e beard; (Schlüssel—) bit.

bärtig ['bɛːrtɪç] a bearded.

Barzahlung f cash payment.

Base ['baːzə] f -, -n (Chem) base; (Kusine) cousin.

basieren [ba'ziːrən] vt base; vi be based.

Basis ['baːzɪs] f -, Basen basis.

basisch ['baːzɪʃ] a (Chem) alkaline.

Baß [bas] m Basses, Bässe bass; —schlüssel m bass clef; —stimme f bass voice.

Bassin [ba'sɛ̃ː] nt -s, -s pool.

Bassist [ba'sɪst] m bass.

Bast [bast] m -(e)s, -e raffia; b—eln vt make; vi do handicrafts.

Bataillon [batal'joːn] nt -s, -e battalion.

Batist [ba'tɪst] m -(e)s, -e batiste.

Batterie [batə'riː] f battery.

Bau [bau] m -(e)s (Bauen) building, construction; (Aufbau) structure; (Körper—) frame; (Baustelle) building site; pl -e (Tier—) hole, burrow; (Min) working(s); pl -ten (Gebäude) building; sich im — befinden be under construction; —arbeiter m building worker.

Bauch [baux] m -(e)s, Bäuche belly; (Anat auch) stomach, abdomen; —fell nt peritoneum; b—ig a bulging; —muskel m abdominal muscle; —redner m ventriloquist; —tanz m belly dance; belly dancing; —schmerzen pl, —weh nt stomach-ache.

bauen ['bauən] vti build; (Tech) construct; auf jdn/etw — depend or count upon sb/sth.

Bauer ['bauər] m -n or -s, -n farmer; (Schach) pawn; nt or m -s, - (Vogel—) cage.

Bäuerin ['bɔyərɪn] f farmer; (Frau des Bauers) farmer's wife.

bäuerlich a rustic.

Bauern- cpd: —brot nt black bread; —fängerei f deception; —haus nt farmhouse; —hof m farm(yard); —schaft f farming community.

Bau- cpd: b—fällig a dilapidated; —fälligkeit f dilapidation; —firma f construction firm; —führer m foreman; —**gelände** f building site; —**genehmigung** f building permit; —**herr** m purchaser; —**kosten** pl construction costs pl; —**land** nt building land; —**leute** pl building workers pl; **b—lich** a structural.

Baum [baum] m -(e)s, **Bäume** tree.

baumeln ['bauməln] vi dangle.

bäumen ['bɔymən] vr rear (up).

Baum- cpd: —**schule** f nursery; —**stamm** m tree trunk; —**stumpf** m tree stump; —**wolle** f cotton.

Bau- cpd: —**plan** m architect's plan; —**platz** m building site.

Bausch [bauʃ] m -(e)s, **Bäusche** (Watte—) ball, wad; **in — und Bogen** (fig) lock, stock and barrel; **b—en** vtir puff out; **b—ig** a baggy, wide.

Bau- cpd: **b—sparen** vi insep save with a building society; —**sparkasse** f building society; —**stein** m building stone, freestone; —**stelle** f building site; —**teil** nt prefabricated part (of building); —**unternehmer** m contractor, builder; —**weise** f (method of) construction; —**werk** nt building; —**zaun** m hoarding.

Bazillus [ba'tsɪlus] m -, **Bazillen** bacillus.

beabsichtigen [bə'apzɪçtɪgən] vt intend.

beachten [bə'axtən] vt take note of; Vorschrift obey; Vorfahrt observe; —**swert** a noteworthy.

beachtlich a considerable.

Beachtung f notice, attention, observation.

Beamte(r) [bə'amtə(r)] m -n, -n, **Beamtin** f official, civil servant; (Bank— etc) employee.

beängstigend [bə'ɛŋstɪgənt] a alarming.

beanspruchen [bə'anʃpruxən] vt claim; Zeit, Platz take up, occupy; Mensch take up sb's time.

beanstanden [bə'anʃtandən] vt complain about, object to.

Beanstandung f complaint.

beantragen [bə'antra:gən] vt apply for, ask for.

beantworten [bə'antvɔrtən] vt answer.

Beantwortung f reply (gen to).

bearbeiten [bə'arbaitən] vt work; Material process; Thema deal with; Land cultivate; (Chem) treat; Buch revise; (col: beeinflussen wollen) work on.

Bearbeitung f processing; treatment; cultivation; revision.

Beatmung [bə'a:tmuŋ] f respiration.

beaufsichtigen [bə'aufzɪçtɪgən] vt supervise.

Beaufsichtigung f supervision.

beauftragen [bə'auftra:gən] vt instruct; **jdn mit etw —** entrust sb with sth.

bebauen [bə'bauən] vt build on; (Agr) cultivate.

beben [be:bən] vi tremble, shake; **B—** nt -s - earthquake.

bebildern [bə'bɪldərn] vt illustrate.

Becher ['bɛçər] nt -s, - mug; (ohne Henkel) tumbler.

Becken ['bɛkən] nt -s, - basin; (Mus) cymbal; (Anat) pelvis.

bedacht [bə'daxt] a thoughtful, careful; **auf etw** (acc) **— sein** be concerned about sth.

bedächtig [bə'dɛçtɪç] a (umsichtig) thoughtful, reflective; (langsam) slow, deliberate.

bedanken [bə'daŋkən] vr say thank you (bei jdm to sb).

Bedarf [bə'darf] m -(e)s need, requirement; (Comm) demand; supply; **je nach —** according to demand; **bei —** if necessary; **— an etw** (dat) **haben** be in need of sth; **—sartikel** m requisite; **—sfall** m case of need; **—shaltestelle** f request stop.

bedauerlich [bə'dauɐlɪç] a regrettable.

bedauern [bə'dauɐn] vt be sorry for; (bemitleiden) pity; B— nt -s regret; **—swert** a Zustände regrettable; Mensch pitiable, unfortunate.

bedecken [bə'dɛkən] vt cover.

bedeckt a covered; Himmel overcast.

bedenken [bə'dɛŋkən] vt irreg think (over), consider; B— nt -s, - (Überlegen) consideration; (Zweifel) doubt; (Skrupel) scruple.

bedenklich a doubtful; (bedrohlich) dangerous, risky.

Bedenkzeit f time for reflection.

bedeuten [bə'dɔytən] vt mean; signify; (wichtig sein) be of importance; **—d** a important; (beträchtlich) considerable.

Bedeutung f meaning; significance; (Wichtigkeit) importance; b—slos a insignificant, unimportant; b—svoll a momentous, significant.

bedienen [bə'di:nən] vt serve; Maschine work, operate; vr (beim Essen) help o.s.; (gebrauchen) make use (gen of).

Bedienung f service; (Kellnerin) waitress; (Verkäuferin) shop assistant; (Zuschlag) service (charge).

bedingen [bə'dɪŋən] vt (voraussetzen) demand, involve; (verursachen) cause, occasion.

bedingt a limited, conditional; Reflex conditioned.

Bedingung f condition; (Voraussetzung) stipulation; **—sform** f (Gram) conditional; b—slos a unconditional.

bedrängen [bə'drɛŋən] vt pester, harass.

Bedrängnis f trouble.

bedrohen [bə'dro:ən] vt threaten.

bedrohlich a ominous, threatening.

Bedrohung f threat, menace.

bedrucken [bə'drʊkən] vt print on.

bedrücken [bə'drʏkən] vt oppress, trouble.

bedürf- [bə'dʏrf] cpd: **—en** vi irreg +gen need, require; B—nis nt -ses, -se need; B—nis nach etw haben need sth; B—nisanstalt f public convenience, comfort station (US); **—nislos** a frugal, modest; **—tig** a in need (gen of), poor, needy.

beehren [bə'e:rən] vt honour; **wir — uns** we have pleasure in.

beeilen [bə'ailən] vt hurry.

beeindrucken [bə'aindrʊkən] vt impress, make an impression on.

beeinflussen [bə'ainflʊsən] vt influence.

Beeinflussung f influence.

beeinträchtigen [bə'aintrɛçtigən] vt affect adversely; Freiheit infringe upon.

beend(ig)en [bə'ɛnd(ɪg)ən] vt end, finish, terminate.

Beend(ig)ung f end(ing), finish(ing).

beengen [bə'ɛŋən] vt cramp; (fig) hamper, oppress.

beerben [bə'ɛrbən] vt inherit from.

beerdigen [bə'e:rdigən] vt bury.

Beerdigung f funeral, burial; **—sunternehmer** m undertaker.

Beere ['beːrə] f -, -n berry; (Trauben—) grape.
Beet [beːt] nt -(e)s, -e bed.
befähigen [bə'fɛːɪgən] vt enable.
befähigt a (begabt) talented; (fähig) capable (für of).
Befähigung f capability; (Begabung) talent, aptitude.
befahrbar [bə'faːrbaːr] a passable; (Naut) navigable.
befahren [bə'faːrən] vt irreg use, drive over; (Naut) navigate; a used.
befallen [bə'falən] vt irreg come over.
befangen [bə'faŋən] a (schüchtern) shy, self-conscious; (voreingenommen) biased; **B—heit** f shyness; bias.
befassen [bə'fasən] vr concern o.s.
Befehl [bə'feːl] m -(e)s, -e command, order; b—en irreg vt order; jdm etw b—en order sb to do sth; vi give orders; b—igen vt be in command of; —sempfänger m subordinate; —sform f (Gram) imperative; —shaber m -s, -commanding officer; —sverweigerung f insubordination.
befestigen [bə'fɛstɪgən] vt fasten (an +dat to); (stärken) strengthen; (Mil) fortify.
Befestigung f fastening; strengthening; (Mil) fortification.
befeuchten [bə'fɔʏçtən] vt dampen (en), moisten.
befinden [bə'fɪndən] irreg vr be; (sich fühlen) feel; vt: jdn/etw für or als etw — deem sb/sth to be sth; vi decide (über +acc on), adjudicate; **B—** nt -s health, condition; (Meinung) view, opinion.
befliegen [bə'fliːgən] vt irreg fly to.

befolgen [bə'fɔlgən] vt comply with, follow.
befördern [bə'fœrdərn] vt (senden) transport, send; (beruflich) promote.
Beförderung f transport, conveyance; promotion; —skosten pl transport costs pl.
befragen [bə'fraːgən] vt question.
befreien [bə'fraɪən] vt set free; (erlassen) exempt.
Befreier m -s, - liberator.
Befreiung f liberation, release; (Erlassen) exemption.
befremden [bə'frɛmdən] vt surprise, disturb; **B—** nt -s surprise, astonishment.
befreunden [bə'frɔʏndən] vr make friends; (mit Idee etc) acquaint o.s.
befreundet a friendly.
befriedigen [bə'friːdɪgən] vt satisfy; —d a satisfactory.
Befriedigung f satisfaction, gratification.
befristet [bə'frɪstət] a limited.
befruchten [bə'frʊxtən] vt fertilize; (fig) stimulate.
Befugnis [bə'fuːknɪs] f -, -se authorization, powers pl.
befugt a authorized, entitled.
befühlen [bə'fyːlən] vt feel, touch.
Befund [bə'fʊnt] m -(e)s, -e findings pl; (Med) diagnosis.
befürchten [bə'fʏrçtən] vt fear.
Befürchtung f fear, apprehension.
befürwort- [bə'fyːrvɔrt] cpd: —en vt support, speak in favour of; **B—er** m -s, - supporter, advocate; **B—ung** f support(ing), favouring.
begabt [bə'gaːpt] a gifted.
Begabung [bə'gaːbʊŋ] f talent, gift.
begatten [bə'gatən] vr mate; vt mate or pair (with).

begeben [bə'ge:bən] *vr irreg* (*gehen*) proceed (*zu, nach* to); (*geschehen*) occur; **B—heit** *f* occurrence.

begegnen [bə'ge:gnən] *vi* meet (*jdm* sb); meet with (*etw* (*dat*) sth); (*behandeln*) treat (*jdm* sb); Blicke — sich eyes meet.

Begegnung *f* meeting.

begehen [bə'ge:ən] *vt irreg* Straftat commit; (*beschreiten*) cover; *Straße etc* use, negotiate; *Feier* celebrate.

begehren [bə'ge:rən] *vt* desire; **—swert** *a* desirable.

begehrt *a* in demand; *Junggeselle* eligible.

begeistern [bə'gaistərn] *vt* fill with enthusiasm, inspire; *vr*: sich für *etw* — get enthusiastic about sth.

begeistert *a* enthusiastic.

Begeisterung *f* enthusiasm.

Begierde [bə'gi:rdə] *f* -, -n desire, passion.

begierig [bə'gi:rɪç] *a* eager, keen.

begießen [bə'gi:sən] *vt irreg* water; (*mit Alkohol*) drink to.

Beginn [bə'gɪn] *m* -(e)s beginning; zu — at the beginning; **b—en** *vti irreg* start, begin.

beglaubigen [bə'glaubɪgən] *vt* countersign.

Beglaubigung *f* countersignature; **—sschreiben** *nt* credentials *pl*.

begleichen [bə'glaiçən] *vt irreg* settle, pay.

Begleit- [bə'glait] *cpd*: **b—en** *vt* accompany; (*Mil*) escort; **—er** *m* **-s, -** companion; (*Freund*) escort; (*Mus*) accompanist; **—erscheinung** *f* concomitant (occurrence); **—musik** *f* accompaniment; **—schiff** *nt* escort vessel; **—schreiben** *nt* covering letter; **—umstände** *pl* concomit-

ant circumstances *pl*; **—ung** *f* company; (*Mil*) escort; (*Mus*) accompaniment.

beglücken [bə'glʏkən] *vt* make happy, delight.

beglückwünschen [bə'glʏk-vʏnʃən] *vt* congratulate (*zu* on).

Beglückwünschung *f* congratulation, good wishes *pl*.

begnadigen [bə'gna:dɪgən] *vt* pardon.

Begnadigung *f* pardon, amnesty.

begnügen [bə'gny:gən] *vr* be satisfied, content o.s.

Begonie [bə'go:niə] *f* begonia.

begraben [bə'gra:bən] *vt irreg* bury.

Begräbnis [bə'grɛ:pnɪs] *nt* -ses, -se burial, funeral.

begradigen [bə'gra:dɪgən] *vt* straighten (out).

begreifen [bə'graifən] *vt irreg* understand, comprehend.

begreiflich [bə'graifliç] *a* understandable.

Begrenztheit [bə'grɛntsthait] *f* limitation, restriction; (*fig*) narrowness.

Begriff [bə'grɪf] *m* -(e)s, -e concept, idea; im — sein, etw zu tun be about to do sth; schwer von — (*col*) slow, dense; **—sbestimmung** *f* definition; **b—sstutzig** *a* dense, slow.

begründ- [bə'grʏnd] *cpd*: **—en** *vt* (*Gründe geben*) justify; **—et** *a* well-founded, justified; **B—ung** *f* justification, reason.

begrüßen [bə'gry:sən] *vt* greet, welcome; **—swert** *a* welcome.

Begrüßung *f* greeting, welcome.

begünstigen [bə'gʏnstɪgən] *vt* *Person* favour; *Sache* further, promote.

begutachten [bə'guːt'axtən] *vt* assess.

begütert [bə'gyːtərt] *a* wealthy, well-to-do.

behaart [bə'haːrt] *a* hairy.

behäbig [bə'hɛːbɪç] *a* (*dick*) portly, stout ; (*geruhsam*) comfortable.

behaftet [bə'haftət] *a*: mit etw — sein be afflicted by sth.

behagen [bə'haːgən] *vi*: das behagt ihm nicht he does not like it ; B— *nt* -s comfort, ease.

behaglich [bə'haːklɪç] *a* comfortable, cosy ; B—keit *f* comfort, cosiness.

behalten [bə'haltən] *vt irreg* keep, retain ; (*im Gedächtnis*) remember.

Behälter [bə'hɛltər] *m* -s, - container, receptacle.

behandeln [bə'handəln] *vt* treat ; *Thema* deal with ; *Maschine* handle. **Behandlung** *f* treatment ; (*von Maschine*) handling.

beharren [bə'harən] *vi*: auf etw (*dat*) — stick or keep to sth.

beharrlich [bə'harlɪç] *a* (*ausdauernd*) steadfast, unwavering ; (*hartnäckig*) tenacious, dogged ; B—keit *f* steadfastness ; tenacity.

behaupten [bə'hauptən] *vt* claim, assert, maintain ; *sein Recht* defend ; *vr* assert o.s.

Behauptung *f* claim, assertion.

Behausung [bə'hauzʊŋ] *f* dwelling, abode, (*armselig*) hovel.

beheimatet [bə'haimaːtət] *a* domiciled ; *Tier, Pflanze* with its habitat in.

beheizen [bə'haitsən] *vt* heat.

Behelf [bə'hɛlf] *m* -(e)s, -e expedient, makeshift ; b—en *vr irreg*: sich mit etw b—en make do with sth ; b—smäßig *a* improvised,

makeshift ; (*vorübergehend*) temporary.

behelligen [bə'hɛlɪgən] *vt* trouble, bother.

Behendigkeit [bə'hɛndɪçkait] *f* agility, quickness.

beherbergen [bə'hɛrbɛrgən] *vt* put up, house.

beherrschen [bə'hɛrʃən] *vt Volk* rule, govern ; *Situation* control ; *Sprache, Gefühle* master ; *vr* control o.s.

beherrscht *a* controlled ; B—heit *f* self-control.

Beherrschung *f* rule ; control ; mastery.

beherzigen [bə'hɛrtsɪgən] *vt* take to heart.

beherzt *a* spirited, brave.

behilflich [bə'hɪlflɪç] *a* helpful ; jdm — sein help sb (*bei* with).

behindern [bə'hɪndərn] *vt* hinder, impede.

Behinderte(r) *mf* disabled person.

Behinderung *f* hindrance ; (*Körper*—) handicap.

Behörde [bə'høːrdə] *f* -, -n authorities *pl*.

behördlich [bə'høːrtlɪç] *a* official.

behüten [bə'hyːtən] *vt* guard ; jdn vor etw (*dat*) — preserve sb from sth.

behutsam [bə'huːtzaːm] *a* cautious, careful ; B—keit *f* caution, carefulness.

bei [bai] *prep* +*dat* (*örtlich*) near, by ; (*zeitlich*) at, on ; (*während*) during ; —m Friseur at the hairdresser's ; — uns at our place ; — einer Firma arbeiten work for a firm ; — Nacht at night ; — Nebel in fog ; — Regen if it rains ; etw — sich haben have sth on one ; jdn — sich haben have sb with one ;

— Goethe in Goethe; —m Militär in the army; —m Fahren while driving.

beibehalten ['baɪbəhaltən] vt irreg keep, retain.

Beibehaltung f keeping, retaining.

Beiblatt ['baɪblat] nt supplement.

beibringen ['baɪbrɪŋən] vt irreg Beweis, Zeugen bring forward; Gründe adduce; jdm etw — (zufügen) inflict sth on sb; (zu verstehen geben) make sb understand sth; (lehren) teach sb sth.

Beichte ['baɪçtə] f -, -n confession; b—n vt confess; vi go to confession.

Beicht- cpd: —geheimnis nt secret of the confessional; —stuhl m confessional.

beide(s) ['baɪdə(z)] pron, a both; meine —n Brüder my two brothers, both my brothers; die ersten —n the first two; wir — we two; einer von —n one of the two; alles —s both (of them); —mal ad both times; —rlei a of both; —rseitig a mutual, reciprocal; —rseits ad mutually; prep +gen on both sides of.

beidrehen [baɪdre:ən] vi heave to.

beieinander [baɪ'aɪ'nandər] ad together.

Beifahrer ['baɪfa:rər] m passenger; —sitz m passenger seat.

Beifall ['baɪfal] m -(e)s applause; (Zustimmung) approval.

beifällig ['baɪfelɪç] a approving; Kommentar favourable.

Beifilm ['baɪfilm] m supporting film.

beifügen ['baɪfy:gən] vt enclose.

beige ['be:ʒə] a beige, fawn.

beigeben ['baɪge:bən] irreg vt (zufügen) add; (mitgeben) give; vi (nachgeben) give in (dat to).

Beigeschmack ['baɪgeʃmak] m aftertaste.

Beihilfe ['baɪhilfə] f aid, assistance; (Studien—) grant; (Jur) aiding and abetting.

beikommen ['baɪkɔmən] vi irreg (+dat) get at; (einem Problem) deal with.

Beil [baɪl] nt -(e)s, -e axe, hatchet.

Beilage [baɪla:gə] f (Buch— etc) supplement; (Cook) vegetables and potatoes pl.

beiläufig ['baɪlɔyfɪç] a casual, incidental; ad casually, by the way.

beilegen ['baɪle:gən] vt (hinzufügen) enclose, add; (beimessen) attribute, ascribe; Streit settle.

beileibe [baɪ'laɪbə] : — nicht ad by no means.

Beileid ['baɪlaɪt] nt condolence, sympathy; herzliches — deepest sympathy.

beiliegend ['baɪli:gənt] a (Comm) enclosed.

beim [baɪm] = bei dem.

beimessen ['baɪmesən] vt irreg attribute, ascribe (dat to).

Bein [baɪn] nt -(e)s, -e leg; —bruch m fracture of the leg.

beinah(e) ['baɪna:(ə)] ad almost, nearly.

beinhalten [bə'ɪnhaltən] vt contain.

beipflichten ['baɪpflɪçtən] vi: jdm/etw — agree with sb/sth.

Beirat ['baɪra:t] m legal adviser; (Körperschaft) advisory council; (Eltern—) parents' council.

beirren [bə'ɪrən] vt confuse, muddle; sich nicht — lassen not let o.s. be confused.

beisammen [baɪ'zamən] ad together; B—sein nt -s get-together.

Beischlaf ['baɪʃla:f] m sexual intercourse.

Beisein ['baɪzaɪn] nt **-s** presence.

beiseite [baɪ'zaɪtə] ad to one side, aside; stehen on one side, aside; etw — legen (sparen) put sth by; jdn/etw — schaffen put sb/get sth out of the way.

beisetzen ['baɪzɛtsən] vt bury.

Beisetzung f funeral.

Beisitzer ['baɪzɪtsər] m **-s**, **-** (bei Prüfung) assessor.

Beispiel ['baɪʃpiːl] nt **-(e)s**, **-e** example; sich jdm ein — nehmen take sb as an example; zum — for example; b—haft a exemplary; b—los a unprecedented, unexampled; b—sweise ad for instance or example.

beispringen ['baɪʃprɪŋən] vi irreg: jdm — come to the aid of sb.

beißen ['baɪsən] irreg vti bite; (stechen: Rauch, Säure) burn; vr (Farben) clash; —d a biting, caustic; (fig auch) sarcastic.

Beißzange ['baɪs-tsaŋə] f pliers pl.

Beistand ['baɪʃtant] m **-(e)s**, ̈e support, help; (Jur) adviser.

beistehen ['baɪʃteːən] vi irreg: jdm — stand by sb.

beisteuern ['baɪʃtɔʏərn] vt contribute.

beistimmen ['baɪʃtɪmən] vi (+ dat) agree with.

Beistrich ['baɪʃtrɪç] m comma.

Beitrag ['baɪtraːk] m **-(e)s**, ̈e contribution; (Zahlung) fee, subscription; (Versicherungs—) premium; b—en ['baɪtraːgən] vt irreg contribute (zu to); (mithelfen) help (zu with); —szahlende/r mf fee-paying member.

beitreten ['baɪtreːtən] vi irreg join (einem Verein a club).

Beitritt ['baɪtrɪt] m joining, mem-bership; —serklärung f declaration of membership.

Beiwagen ['baɪvaːgən] m (Motorrad—) sidecar; (Straßenbahn—) extra carriage.

beiwohnen ['baɪvoːnən] vi: einer Sache (dat) — attend or be present at sth.

Beiwort ['baɪvɔrt] nt adjective.

Beize ['baɪtsə] f **-**, **-n** (Holz—) stain; (Cook) marinade.

beizeiten [baɪ'tsaɪtən] ad in time.

bejahen [bə'jaːən] vt Frage say yes to, answer in the affirmative; (gutheißen) agree with.

bejahrt [bə'jaːrt] a aged, elderly.

bejammern [bə'jamərn] vt lament, bewail; —swert a lamentable.

bekämpfen [bə'kɛmpfən] vt Gegner fight; Seuche combat; vr fight.

Bekämpfung f fight or struggle against.

bekannt [bə'kant] a (well-)known; (nicht fremd) familiar; mit jdm — sein know sb; jdn mit jdm — machen introduce sb to sb; sich mit etw — machen familiarize o.s. with sth; das ist mir — I know that; es/sie kommt mir — vor it/she seems familiar; durch etw — werden become famous because of sth; —e(r) mf friend, acquaintance; B—enkreis m circle of friends; B—gabe f announcement; —geben vt irreg announce publicly; —lich ad as is well known, as you know; —machen vt announce; B—machung f publication; announcement; B—schaft f acquaintance.

bekehren [bə'keːrən] vt convert; vr become converted.

Bekehrung f conversion.

bekennen [bə'kɛnən] vt irreg confess; Glauben profess; Farbe

— (col) show where one stands.

Bekenntnis [bə'kɛntnɪs] nt -ses, -se admission, confession; (Religion) confession, denomination; —schule f denominational school.

beklagen [bə'kla:gən] vt deplore, lament; vr complain; —swert a lamentable, pathetic.

beklatschen [bə'klatʃən] vt applaud, clap.

bekleben [bə'kle:bən] vt: etw mit Bildern — stick pictures onto sth.

bekleiden [bə'klaɪdən] vt clothe; Amt occupy, fill.

Bekleidung f clothing; —sindustrie f clothing industry, rag trade.

beklemmen [bə'klɛmən] vt oppress.

beklommen [bə'klɔmən] a anxious, uneasy; B—heit f anxiety, uneasiness.

bekommen [bə'kɔmən] irreg vt get, receive; Kind have; Zug catch, get; vi: jdm — agree with sb.

bekömmlich [bə'kœmlɪç] a wholesome, easily digestible.

bekräftigen [bə'krɛftɪgən] vt confirm, corroborate.

Bekräftigung f corroboration.

bekreuzigen [bə'krɔytsɪgən] vr cross o.s.

bekritteln [bə'krɪtəln] vt criticize, pick holes in.

bekümmern [bə'kymərn] vt worry, trouble.

bekunden [bə'kundən] vt (sagen) state; (zeigen) show.

belächeln [bə'lɛçəln] vt laugh at.

beladen [bə'la:dən] vt irreg load.

Belag [bə'la:k] m -(e)s, -̶e covering, coating; (Brot—) spread; (Zahn—) tartar; (auf Zunge) fur; (Brems—) lining.

belagern [bə'la:gərn] vt besiege.

Belagerung f siege; —szustand m state of siege.

Belang [bə'laŋ] m -(e)s importance; —e pl interests pl, concerns pl; b—en vt (Jur) take to court; b—los a trivial, unimportant; —losigkeit f triviality.

belassen [bə'lasən] vt irreg (in Zustand, Glauben) leave; (in Stellung) retain; es dabei — leave it at that.

belasten [bə'lastən] vt (lit) burden; (fig: bedrücken) trouble, worry; (Comm) Konto debit; (Jur) incriminate; vr weigh o.s. down; (Jur) incriminate o.s.; —d a (Jur) incriminating.

belästigen [bə'lɛstɪgən] vt annoy, pester.

Belästigung f annoyance, pestering.

Belastung [bə'lastuŋ] f (lit) load; (fig: Sorge etc) weight; (Comm) charge, debit(ing); (Jur) incriminatory evidence; —sprobe f capacity test; (fig) test; —szeuge m witness for prosecution.

belaufen [bə'laufən] vr irreg amount (auf +acc to).

belauschen [bə'lauʃən] vt eavesdrop on.

belebt [bə'le:pt] a Straße crowded.

Beleg [bə'le:k] m -(e)s, -e (Comm) receipt; (Beweis) documentary evidence, proof; (Beispiel) example; b—en vt (Jur) cover; Kuchen, Brot spread; Platz reserve, book; Kurs, Vorlesung register for; (beweisen) verify, prove; (Mil: mit Bomben) bomb; —schaft f personnel, staff.

belehren [bə'le:rən] vt instruct, teach; jdn eines Besseren — teach sb better.

Belehrung f instruction.

beleibt [bə'laɪpt] a stout, corpulent.

beleidigen [bə'laɪdɪgən] vt insult, offend.

Beleidigung f insult ; (Jur) slander, libel.

belesen [bə'le:zən] a well-read.

beleuchten [bə'lɔʏçtən] vt light, illuminate ; (fig) throw light on.

Beleuchtung f lighting, illumination.

belichten [bə'lɪçtən] vt expose.

Belichtung f exposure ; **—smesser** m exposure meter.

Belieben [bə'li:bən] nt: (ganz) nach — (just) as you wish.

beliebig [bə'li:bɪç] a any you like, as you like ; — viel as many as you like ; ein —es Thema any subject you like or want.

beliebt [bə'li:pt] a popular ; sich bei jdm — machen make o.s. popular with sb ; **B—heit** f popularity.

beliefern [bə'li:fərn] vt supply.

bellen ['bɛlən] vi bark.

belohnen [bə'lo:nən] vt reward.

Belohnung f reward.

belügen [bə'ly:gən] vt irreg lie to, deceive.

belustigen [bə'lʊstɪgən] vt amuse.

Belustigung f amusement.

bemächtigen [bə'mɛçtɪgən] vr: sich einer Sache (gen) — take possession of sth, seize sth.

bemalen [bə'ma:lən] vt paint.

bemängeln [bə'mɛŋəln] vt criticize.

bemannen [bə'manən] vt man.

Bemannung f manning ; (Naut, Aviat etc) crew.

bemänteln [bə'mɛntəln] vt cloak, hide.

bemerk- [bə'mɛrk] cpd: **—bar** a perceptible, noticeable ; sich **—bar** machen (Person) make or get o.s.

noticed ; (Unruhe) become noticeable ; **—en** vt (wahrnehmen) notice, observe ; (sagen) say, mention ; **—enswert** a remarkable, noteworthy ; **B—ung** f remark ; (schriftlich auch) note.

bemitleiden [bə'mɪtlaɪdən] vt pity.

bemühen [bə'my:ən] vr take trouble or pains.

Bemühung f trouble, pains pl, effort.

bemuttern [bə'mʊtərn] vt mother.

benachbart [bə'naxba:rt] a neighbouring.

benachrichtigen [bə'na:xrɪçtɪgən] vt inform.

Benachrichtigung f notification, information.

benachteiligen [bə'na:xtaɪlɪgən] vt (put at a) disadvantage, victimize.

benehmen [bə'ne:mən] vr irreg behave ; **B— nt -s** behaviour.

beneiden [bə'naɪdən] vt envy ; **—swert** a enviable.

benennen [bə'nɛnən] vt irreg name.

Bengel ['bɛŋəl] m -s, - (little) rascal or rogue.

benommen [bə'nɔmən] a dazed.

benötigen [bə'nø:tɪgən] vt need.

benutzen [bə'nʊtsən], **benützen** [bə'nʏtsən] vt use.

Benutzer m -s, - user.

Benutzung f utilization, use.

Benzin [bɛnt'si:n] nt -s, -e (Aut) petrol, gas(oline) (US) ; **—kanister** m petrol can ; **—tank** m petrol tank ; **—uhr** f petrol gauge.

beobacht- [bə'o:baxt] cpd: **—en** vt observe ; **B—er m -s, -** observer ; (eines Unfalls) witness ; (Press, TV) correspondent ; **B—ung** f observation.

bepacken [bə'pakən] vt load, pack.

bepflanzen [bə'pflantsən] vt plant.

bequem [bə'kve:m] a comfortable; *Ausrede* convenient; *Person* lazy, indolent; **—en** vr condescend (zu to); **B—lichkeit** f convenience, comfort; (*Faulheit*) laziness, indolence.

beraten [bə'ra:tən] irreg vt advise; (*besprechen*) discuss, debate; vr consult; *gut/schlecht —* sein be well/ill advised; *sich — lassen* get advice.

Berater m **-s, -** adviser.

beratschlagen [bə'ra:t-ʃla:gən] vti deliberate (on), confer (about).

Beratung f advice, consultation; (*Besprechung*) consultation; **—s- stelle** f advice centre.

berauben [bə'raubən] vt rob.

berechenbar [bə'rɛçənba:r] a calculable.

berechnen [bə'rɛçnən] vt calculate; (*Comm: anrechnen*) charge; **—d** a *Mensch* calculating, scheming; **B—ung** f calculation; (*Comm*) charge.

berechtig- [bə'rɛçtıç] cpd: **—en** vt entitle, authorize; (*fig*) justify; **—t** [bə'rɛçtıçt] a justifiable, justified; **B—ung** f authorization; (*fig*) justification.

bereden [bə're:dən] vtr (*besprechen*) discuss; (*überreden*) persuade.

beredt [bə're:t] a eloquent.

Bereich [bə'raıç] m **-(e)s, -e** (*Bezirk*) area; (*Phys*) range; (*Ressort, Gebiet*) sphere.

bereichern [bə'raıçərn] vt enrich; vr get rich.

Bereifung [bə'raıfuŋ] f (set of) tyres pl; (*Vorgang*) fitting with tyres.

bereinigen [bə'raınıgən] vt settle.

bereisen [bə'raızən] vt travel through.

bereit [bə'raıt] a ready, prepared; *zu etw —* sein be ready for sth; *sich — erklären* declare o.s. willing; **—en** vt prepare, make ready; *Kummer, Freude* cause; **—halten** vt irreg keep in readiness; **—legen** vt lay out; **—machen** vtr prepare, get ready; **—s** ad already; **B—schaft** f readiness; (*Polizei*) alert; *in B—schaft sein* be on the alert or on stand-by; **B—schafts- dienst** m emergency service; **—stehen** vi irreg (*Person*) be prepared; (*Ding*) be ready; **—stellen** vt *Kisten, Pakete etc* put ready; *Geld etc* make available; *Truppen, Maschinen* put at the ready; **B—ung** f preparation; **—willig** a willing, ready; **B—willigkeit** f willingness, readiness.

bereuen [bə'rɔyən] vt regret.

Berg [bɛrk] m **-(e)s, -e** mountain, hill; **b—ab** ad downhill; **b—an, b—auf** ad uphill; **—arbeiter** m miner; **—bahn** f mountain railway; **—bau** m mining; **b—en** ['bɛrgən] vt irreg (*retten*) rescue; *Ladung* salvage; (*enthalten*) contain; **—führer** m mountain guide; **—gipfel** m mountain top, peak, summit; **b—ig** [bɛrgıç] a mountainous, hilly; **—kamm** m crest, ridge; **—kette** f mountain range; **—mann** m, pl **—leute** miner; **—rutsch** m landslide; **—schuh** m walking boot; **—steigen** nt mountaineering; **—steiger(in** f) m **-s, -** mountaineer, climber; **—ung** ['bɛrguŋ] f (*von Menschen*) rescue; (*von Material*) recovery; (*Naut*) salvage; **—wacht** f mountain rescue service; **—werk** nt mine.

Bericht [bə'rɪçt] *m* -(e)s, -e report, account; **b—en** *vti* report; **—erstatter** *m* -s, - reporter, (newspaper) correspondent; **—erstattung** *f* reporting.

berichtigen [bə'rɪçtɪgən] *vt* correct.

Berichtigung *f* correction.

beritten [bə'rɪtən] *a* mounted.

Bernstein ['bɛrnʃtaɪn] *m* amber.

bersten ['bɛrstən] *vi irreg* burst, split.

berüchtigt [bə'rʏçtɪçt] *a* notorious, infamous.

berücksichtigen [bə'rʏkzɪçtɪgən] *vt* consider, bear in mind.

Berücksichtigung *f* consideration.

Beruf [bə'ru:f] *m* -(e)s, -e occupation, profession; (*Gewerbe*) trade; **b—en** *irreg vt* (*in Amt*) appoint (*in +acc* to; *zu* as); *vr*: **sich auf jdn/etw b—en** refer or appeal to sb/sth; **b—en** *a* competent, qualified; **b—lich** *a* professional; **—sausbildung** *f* vocational *or* professional training; **—sberater** *m* careers adviser; **—sberatung** *f* vocational guidance; **—sbezeichnung** *f* job description; **—sgeheimnis** *nt* professional secret; **—skrankheit** *f* occupational disease; **—sleben** *nt* professional life; **b—smäßig** *a* professional; **—srisiko** *nt* occupational hazard; **—sschule** *f* vocational *or* trade school; **—ssoldat** *m* professional soldier, regular; **—ssportler** *m* professional (sportsman); **b—stätig** *a* employed; **—sverkehr** *m* commuter traffic; **—swahl** *f* choice of a job; **—ung** *f* vocation, calling; (*Ernennung*) appointment; (*Jur*) appeal; **—ung einlegen** appeal.

beruhen [bə'ru:ən] *vi*: **auf etw** (*dat*) **— be based on sth; etw auf sich — lassen** leave sth at that.

beruhigen [bə'ru:ɪgən] *vt* calm, pacify, soothe; *vr* (*Mensch*) calm (o.s.) down; (*Situation*) calm down.

Beruhigung *f* reassurance; (*der Nerven*) calming; **zu jds — to reassure sb**; **—smittel** *nt* sedative; **—spille** *f* tranquillizer.

berühmt [bə'ry:mt] *a* famous; **B— heit** *f* (*Ruf*) fame; (*Mensch*) celebrity.

berühren [bə'ry:rən] *vt* touch; (*gefühlsmäßig bewegen*) affect; (*flüchtig erwähnen*) mention, touch on; *vr* meet, touch.

Berührung *f* contact; **—spunkt** *m* point of contact.

besagen [bə'za:gən] *vt* mean.

besagt *a* **Tag** etc in question.

besänftig- [bə'zɛnftɪg] *cpd*: **—en** *vt* soothe, calm; **—end** *a* soothing; **B—ung** *f* soothing, calming.

Besatz [bə'zats] *m* -es, ⁺e trimming, edging; **—ung** *f* garrison; (*Naut, Aviat*) crew; **—ungsmacht** *f* occupying power.

besaufen [bə'zaʊfən] *vr irreg* (*col*) get drunk *or* stoned.

beschädig- [bə'ʃɛ:dɪg] *cpd*: **—en** *vt* damage; **B—ung** *f* damage; (*Stelle*) damaged spot.

beschaffen [bə'ʃafən] *vt* get, acquire; *a* constituted; **B—heit** *f* constitution, nature.

Beschaffung *f* acquisition.

beschäftigen [bə'ʃɛftɪgən] *vt* occupy; (*beruflich*) employ; *vr* occupy or concern o.s.

beschäftigt *a* busy, occupied.

Beschäftigung *f* (*Beruf*) employment; (*Tätigkeit*) occupation; (*Befassen*) concern.

beschämen [bə'ʃɛ:mən] *vt* put to shame; **—d** *a* shameful; **Hilfsbereitschaft** shaming.

beschämt a ashamed.

beschatten [bə'ʃatən] vt shade; _Verdächtige_ shadow.

beschaulich [bə'ʃaʊlɪç] a contemplative.

Bescheid [bə'ʃaɪt] m -(e)s, -e information; _(Weisung)_ directions pl; — wissen be well-informed _(über + acc_ about); ich weiß — I know; jdm — geben or sagen let sb know.

bescheiden [bə'ʃaɪdən] vr irreg content o.s.; a modest; **B—heit** f modesty.

bescheinen [bə'ʃaɪnən] vt irreg shine on.

bescheinigen [bə'ʃaɪnɪgən] vt certify; _(bestätigen)_ acknowledge. **Bescheinigung** f certificate; _(Quittung)_ receipt.

bescheißen [bə'ʃaɪsən] vt irreg (col) cheat.

beschenken [bə'ʃɛŋkən] vt give presents to.

bescheren [bə'ʃeːrən] vt: jdm etw — give sb sth as a present; jdn — give presents to sb. **Bescherung** f giving of presents; (col) mess.

beschildern [bə'ʃɪldərn] vt signpost.

beschimpfen [bə'ʃɪmpfən] vt abuse. **Beschimpfung** f abuse, insult.

Beschiß [bə'ʃɪs] m -sses (col) das ist ⊹ that is a swizz or a cheat.

Beschlag [bə'ʃlaːk] m -(e)s, -e _(Metallband)_ fitting; _(auf Fenster)_ condensation; _(auf Metall)_ tarnish; _.finish;_ _(Hufeisen)_ horseshoe; jdn/etw in — nehmen or mit — belegen monopolize sb/sth; b—en [bə'ʃlaːgən]. irreg vt cover; _Pferd_ shoe; _Fenster, Metall_ cover; b—en

sein be well versed _(in_ or _auf + dat_ in); vir _(Fenster etc)_ mist over; b—nahmen vt seize, confiscate; requisition; **—nahmung** f confiscation, sequestration.

beschleunigen [bə'ʃlɔʏnɪgən] vt accelerate, speed up; vi (Aut) accelerate. **Beschleunigung** f acceleration.

beschließen [bə'ʃliːsən] vt irreg decide on; _(beenden)_ end, close.

Beschluß [bə'ʃlʊs] m -sses, -schlüsse decision, conclusion; _(Ende)_ close, end.

beschmutzen [bə'ʃmʊtsən] vt dirty, soil.

beschneiden [bə'ʃnaɪdən] vt irreg cut, prune, trim; _(Rel)_ circumcise.

beschönigen [bə'ʃøːnɪgən] vt gloss over.

beschränken [bə'ʃrɛŋkən] vt limit, restrict _(auf + acc_ to); vr restrict o.s.

beschrankt [bə'ʃraŋkt] a _Bahnübergang_ with barrier. **beschränk-** [bə'ʃrɛŋk] cpd: **—t** a confined, narrow; _Mensch_ limited, narrow-minded; **B—theit** f narrowness; **B—ung** f limitation.

beschreiben [bə'ʃraɪbən] vt irreg describe; _Papier_ write on. **Beschreibung** f description.

beschriften [bə'ʃrɪftən] vt mark, label. **Beschriftung** f lettering.

beschuldigen [bə'ʃʊldɪgən] vt accuse. **Beschuldigung** f accusation.

beschummeln [bə'ʃʊməln] vti (col) cheat.

beschütz- [bə'ʃʏts] cpd: **—en** vt protect _(vor + dat_ from); **B—er** m -s, - protector **B—ung** f protection.

Beschwerde [bə'ʃveːrdə] *f* -, -n complaint; (*Mühe*) hardship; (*pl: Leiden*) pain.

beschweren [bə'ʃveːrən] *vt* weight down; (*fig*) burden; *vr* complain.

beschwerlich *a* tiring, exhausting.

beschwichtigen [bə'ʃvɪçtɪgən] *vt* soothe, pacify.

Beschwichtigung *f* soothing, calming.

beschwindeln [bə'ʃvɪndəln] *vt* (*betrügen*) cheat; (*belügen*) fib to.

beschwingt [bə'ʃvɪŋt] *a* cheery, in high spirits.

beschwipst [bə'ʃvɪpst] *a* tipsy.

beschwören [bə'ʃvøːrən] *vt irreg Aussage* swear to; (*anflehen*) implore; *Geister* conjure up.

beseelen [bə'zeːlən] *vt* inspire.

besehen [bə'zeːən] *vt irreg* look at; *genau* — examine closely.

beseitigen [bə'zaɪtɪgən] *vt* remove.

Beseitigung *f* removal.

Besen [ˈbeːzən] *m* -s, - broom; —stiel *m* broomstick.

besessen [bə'zɛsən] *a* possessed.

besetz- [bə'zɛts] *cpd:* —en *vt Haus, Land* occupy; *Platz* take, fill; *Posten* fill; *Rolle* cast; (*mit Edelsteinen*) set; —t *a* full; (*Tel*) engaged, busy; *Platz* taken; *WC* engaged; **B—tzeichen** *nt* engaged tone; **B—ung** *f* occupation; filling; (*von Rolle*) casting; (*die Schauspieler*) cast.

besichtigen [bə'zɪçtɪgən] *vt* visit, look at.

Besichtigung *f* visit.

Besied(e)lung [bə'ziːd(ə)luŋ] *f* population.

besiegeln [bə'ziːgəln] *vt* seal.

besiegen [bə'ziːgən] *vt* defeat, overcome.

Besiegte(r) [bə'ziːçtə(r)] *m* loser.

besinnen [bə'zɪnən] *vr irreg* (*nachdenken*) think, reflect; (*erinnern*) remember; **sich anders —** change one's mind.

besinnlich *a* contemplative.

Besinnung *f* consciousness; **zur — kommen** recover consciousness; (*fig*) come to one's senses; **b—slos** *a* unconscious.

Besitz [bə'zɪts] *m* -es possession; (*Eigentum*) property; **b—anzeigend** *a* (*Gram*) possessive; **b—en** *vt irreg* possess, own; *Eigenschaft* have; —**er(in** *f*) *m* -s, - owner, proprietor; —**ergreifung** *f*, —**nahme** *f* occupation, seizure.

besoffen [bə'zɔfən] *a* (*col*) drunk, pissed.

besohlen [bə'zoːlən] *vt* sole.

Besoldung [bə'zɔldun] *f* salary, pay.

besondere(r,s) [bə'zɔndərə(r,z)] *a* special; (*eigen*) particular; (*gesondert*) separate; (*eigentümlich*) peculiar.

Besonderheit [bə'zɔndərhaɪt] *f* peculiarity.

besonders [bə'zɔndərs] *ad* especially, particularly; (*getrennt*) separately.

besonnen [bə'zɔnən] *a* sensible, level-headed; **B—heit** *f* prudence.

besorg- [bə'zɔrg] *cpd:* —en *vt* (*beschaffen*) acquire; (*kaufen auch*) purchase; (*erledigen*) Geschäfte deal with; (*sich kümmern um*) take care of; **es jdm —** (*col*) show sb what for; **B—nis** *f* -, -se anxiety, concern; —t [bə'zɔrçt] *a* anxious, worried; **B—theit** *f* anxiety, worry; **B—ung** *f* acquisition; (*Kauf*) purchase.

bespielen [bə'ʃpiːlən] *vt* record.

bespitzeln [bə'ʃpɪtsəln] *vt* spy on.

besprechen [bəˈʃprɛçən] *irreg vt* discuss ; *Tonband etc* record, speak onto ; *Buch* review ; *vr* discuss, consult.

Besprechung *f* meeting, discussion ; *(von Buch)* review.

besser [ˈbɛsər] *a* better ; **nur ein —er ...** just a glorified ... ; **—gehen** *vi irreg impers:* **es geht ihm** — he feels better ; **—n** *vt* make better, improve ; *vr* improve ; *Menschen* reform ; **B—ung** *f* improvement ; **gute B—ung!** get well soon ; **B—wisser** *m* -s, - know-all.

Bestand [bəˈʃtant] *m* -(e)s, ⸚e *(Fortbestehen)* duration, stability ; *(Kassen—)* amount, balance ; *(Vorrat)* stock ; **eiserne(r)** — iron rations *pl* ; — **haben, von** — **sein** last long, endure.

beständig [bəˈʃtɛndiç] *a (ausdauernd)* constant *(auch fig)* ; *Wetter* settled ; *Stoffe* resistant ; *Klagen etc* continual.

Bestand- *cpd:* **—saufnahme** *f* stocktaking ; **—teil** *m* part, component ; *(Zutat)* ingredient.

bestärken [bəˈʃtɛrkən] *vt:* **jdn in etw** *(dat)* — strengthen *or* confirm sb in sth.

bestätigen [bəˈʃtɛːtɪgən] *vt* confirm ; *(anerkennen, Comm)* acknowledge.

Bestätigung *f* confirmation ; acknowledgement.

bestatt- [bəˈʃtat] *cpd:* **—en** *vt* bury ; **B—er** *m* -s, - undertaker ; **B—ung** *f* funeral.

bestäuben [bəˈʃtɔybən] *vt* powder, dust ; *Pflanze* pollinate.

beste(r,s) [ˈbɛstə(r,z)] *a* best ; **sie singt am —n** she sings best ; **so ist es am —n** it's best that way ; **am —n gehst du gleich** you'd better go

at once ; **jdn zum —n haben** pull sb's leg ; **etw zum —n geben** tell a joke/story *etc* ; **aufs** — in the best possible way ; **zu jds B—n** for the benefit of sb.

bestechen [bəˈʃtɛçən] *vt irreg* bribe.

bestechlich *a* corruptible ; **B—keit** *f* corruptibility.

Bestechung *f* bribery, corruption.

Besteck [bəˈʃtɛk] *nt* -(e)s, -e knife, fork and spoon, cutlery ; *(Med)* set of instruments.

bestehen [bəˈʃteːən] *irreg vi* be ; exist ; *(andauern)* last ; *vt Kampf, Probe, Prüfung* pass ; — **auf** (+ *dat)* insist on ; — **aus** consist of.

bestehlen [bəˈʃteːlən] *vt irreg* rob.

besteigen [bəˈʃtaɪgən] *vt irreg* climb, ascend ; *Pferd* mount ; *Thron* ascend.

Bestell- [bəˈʃtɛl] *cpd:* **—buch** *nt* order book ; **b—en** *vt* order ; *(kommen lassen)* arrange to see ; *(nominieren)* name ; *Acker* cultivate ; *Grüße, Auftrag* pass on ; **—schein** *m* order coupon ; **—ung** *f (Comm)* order ; *(Bestellen)* ordering.

bestenfalls [ˈbɛstənˈfals] *ad* at best.

bestens [ˈbɛstəns] *ad* very well.

besteuern [bəˈʃtɔʏərn] *vt* tax.

Bestie [ˈbɛstiə] *f (lit, fig)* beast.

bestimm- [bəˈʃtɪm] *cpd:* **—en** *vt Regeln* lay down ; *Tag, Ort* fix ; *(beherrschen)* characterize ; *(aussehen)* mean ; *(ernennen)* appoint ; *(definieren)* define ; *(veranlassen)* induce ; **—t** *a (entschlossen)* firm ; *(gewiß)* certain, definite ; *Artikel* definite ; *ad (gewiß)* definitely, for sure ; **B—theit** *f* certainty ; **B—ung** *f (Verordnung)* regulation ; *(Festsetzen)* determining ; *(Verwendungszweck)* purpose ; *(Schicksal)* fate ; *(Definition)*

definition ; **B—ungsort** *m* destination.

Best- *cpd*: **—leistung** *f* best performance ; **b—möglich** *a* best possible.

bestrafen [bə'ʃtraːfən] *vt* punish.

Bestrafung *f* punishment.

bestrahlen [bə'ʃtraːlən] *vt* shine on ; (*Med*) treat with X-rays.

Bestrahlung *f* (*Med*) X-ray treatment, radiotherapy.

Bestreben [bə'ʃtreːbən] *nt* **-s**, **Bestrebung** [bə'ʃtreːbʊŋ] *f* endeavour, effort.

bestreichen [bə'ʃtraɪçən] *vt irreg Brot* spread.

bestreiten [bə'ʃtraɪtən] *vt irreg* (*abstreiten*) dispute ; (*finanzieren*) pay for, finance.

bestreuen [bə'ʃtrɔyən] *vt* sprinkle, dust ; *Straße* (spread with) grit.

bestürmen [bə'ʃtʏrmən] *vt* (*mit Fragen, Bitten etc*) overwhelm, swamp.

bestürzen [bə'ʃtʏrtsən] *vt* dismay.

bestürzt *a* dismayed.

Bestürzung *f* consternation.

Besuch [bə'zuːx] *m* **-(e)s**, **-e** visit ; (*Person*) visitor ; **einen — machen bei jdm** pay sb a visit or call ; **— haben** have visitors ; **bei jdm auf or zu — sein** be visiting sb ; **b—en** *vt* visit ; (*Sch etc*) attend ; **gut —t** well-attended ; **—er(in** *f*) *m* **-s,** **-** visitor, guest ; **—serlaubnis** *f* permission to visit ; **—szeit** *f* visiting hours *pl*.

betagt [bə'taːkt] *a* aged.

betasten [bə'tastən] *vt* touch, feel.

betätigen [bə'tɛːtɪɡən] *vt* (*bedienen*) work, operate ; *vr* involve o.s. ; **sich politisch —** be involved in politics ; **sich als etw —** work as sth.

Betätigung *f* activity ; (*beruflich*) occupation ; (*Tech*) operation.

betäuben [bə'tɔybən] *vt* stun ; (*fig*) *Gewissen* still ; (*Med*) anaesthetize.

Betäubungsmittel *nt* anaesthetic.

Bete ['beːtə] *f* **-, -n**: **rote —** beetroot.

beteiligen [bə'taɪlɪɡən] *vr* (*an* + *dat* in) take part or participate, share ; (*an* *Geschäft: finanziell*) have a share ; *vt*: **jdn —** give sb a share or interest (*an* + *dat* in).

Beteiligung *f* participation ; (*Anteil*) share, interest ; (*Besucherzahl*) attendance.

beten ['beːtən] *vti* pray.

beteuern [bə'tɔyərn] *vt* assert ; *Unschuld* protest ; **jdm etw —** assure sb of sth.

Beteuerung *f* assertion, protest(ation), assurance.

Beton [be'tõː] *m* **-s, -s** concrete.

betonen [be'toːnən] *vt* stress.

betonieren [beto'niːrən] *vt* concrete.

Betonung *f* stress, emphasis.

betören [bə'tøːrən] *vt* beguile.

Betracht [bə'traxt] *m*: **in — kommen** be concerned or relevant ; **nicht in — kommen** be out of the question ; **etw in — ziehen** consider sth ; **außer — bleiben** not be considered ; **b—en** *vt* look at ; (*fig auch*) consider ; **—er(in** *f*) *m* **-s, -** onlooker.

beträchtlich [bə'trɛçtlɪç] *a* considerable.

Betrachtung *f* (*Ansehen*) examination ; (*Erwägung*) consideration.

Betrag [bə'traːk] *m* **-(e)s, ⁻e** amount ; **b—en** [bə'traːɡən] *irreg vt* amount to ; *vr* behave ; **—en** *nt* **-s** behaviour.

betrauen [bə'trauən] *vt*: **jdn mit etw —** entrust sb with sth.

betreffen [bə'trɛfən] vt irreg concern, affect; **was mich betrifft** as for me; **—d** a relevant, in question.

betreffs [bə'trɛfs] prep +gen concerning, regarding.

betreiben [bə'traibən] vt irreg (ausüben) practise; Politik follow; Studien pursue; (vorantreiben) push ahead; (Tech: antreiben) drive.

betreten [bə'tre:tən] vt irreg enter; Bühne etc step onto; **B—** verboten keep off/out; a embarrassed.

Betrieb [bə'tri:p] m -(e)s, -e (Firma) firm, concern; (Anlage) plant; (Tätigkeit) operation; (Treiben) traffic; **außer — sein** be out of order; **in — sein** be in operation; **—sausflug** m firm's outing; **b—sfähig** a in working order; **—sferien** pl company holidays pl; **—sklima** nt (working) atmosphere; **—skosten** pl running costs pl; **—srat** m workers' council; **b—ssicher** a safe, reliable; **—sstoff** m fuel; **—störung** f breakdown; **—sunfall** m industrial accident; **—swirtschaft** f economics.

betrinken [bə'triŋkən] vr irreg get drunk.

betroffen [bə'trɔfən] a (bestürzt) amazed, perplexed; **von etw — werden** or **sein** be affected by sth.

betrüben [bə'try:bən] vt grieve.

betrübt [bə'try:pt] a sorrowful, grieved.

Betrug [bə'tru:k] m -(e)s deception; (Jur) fraud.

betrügen [bə'try:gən] irreg vt cheat; (Jur) defraud; Ehepartner be unfaithful to; vr deceive o.s.

Betrüger m -s, - cheat, deceiver; **b—isch** a deceitful; (Jur) fraudulent.

betrunken [bə'truŋkən] a drunk.

Bett [bɛt] nt -(e)s, -en bed; **ins** or **zu — gehen** go to bed; **—bezug** m duvet cover; **—decke** f blanket; (Daunen—) quilt; (Überwurf) bedspread.

Bettel- ['bɛtəl] cpd: **b—arm** a very poor, destitute; **—ei** [bɛtə'lai] f begging; **b—n** vi beg.

Bett- cpd: **b—en** vt make a bed for; **b—lägerig** a bedridden; **—laken** nt sheet.

Bettler(in f) ['bɛtlər(m)] m -s, - beggar.

Bett- cpd: **—nässer** m -s, - bedwetter; **—vorleger** m bedside rug; **—wäsche** f, **—zeug** nt bedclothes pl, bedding.

beugen ['bɔygən] vt bend; (Gram) inflect; vr (sich fügen) bow (dat to).

Beule ['bɔylə] f -, -n bump, swelling.

beunruhigen [bə''unru:igən] vt disturb, alarm; vr become worried.

Beunruhigung f worry, alarm.

beurkunden [bə''u:rkundən] vt attest, verify.

beurlauben [bə''u:rlaubən] vt give leave or holiday to.

beurteilen [bə''urtailən] vt judge; Buch etc review.

Beurteilung f judgement; review; (Note) mark.

Beute ['bɔytə] f - booty, loot; **—l** m -s, - bag; (Geld—) purse; (Tabak—) pouch.

bevölkern [bə'fœlkərn] vt populate.

Bevölkerung f population.

bevollmächtigen [bə'fɔlmɛçtigən] vt authorize.

Bevollmächtigte(r) mf authorized agent.

Bevollmächtigung f authorization.

bevor [bə'fo:r] cj before; **—munden** vt insep dominate; **—stehen** vi *irreg* be in store (*dat* for); —stehend *a* imminent, approaching; —zugen *vt insep* prefer; B—zugung *f* preference.

bewachen [bə'vaxən] *vt* watch, guard.

Bewachung *f* (*Bewachen*) guarding; (*Leute*) guard, watch.

bewaffnen [bə'vafnən] *vt* arming;

Bewaffnung *f* (*Vorgang*) arming; (*Ausrüstung*) armament, arms *pl*.

bewahren [bə'va:rən] *vt* keep; **jdn vor jdm/etw** — save sb from sb/sth.

bewähren [bə'vɛ:rən] *vr* prove o.s.; (*Maschine*) prove its worth.

bewahrheiten [bə'va:rhaitən] *vr* come true.

bewährt *a* reliable.

Bewährung *f* (*Jur*) probation; —sfrist *f* (period of) probation.

bewaldet [bə'valdət] *a* wooded.

bewältigen [bə'vɛltigən] *vt* overcome; *Arbeit* finish; *Portion* manage.

bewandert [bə'vandərt] *a* expert, knowledgeable.

bewässern [bə'vɛsərn] *vt* irrigate.

Bewässerung *f* irrigation.

Beweg- [bə've:g] *cpd:* **b—en** *vtr* move; **jdn zu etw b—en** induce sb to (do) sth; **—grund** [bə've:k-] *m* motive; **b—lich** *a* movable, mobile; (*flink*) quick; **b—t** *a* *Leben* eventful; *Meer* rough; (*ergriffen*) touched; **—ung** *f* movement, motion; (*innere*) emotion; (*körperlich*) exercise; **sich** (*dat*) **—ung machen** take exercise; **—ungsfreiheit** *f* freedom of movement or action; **b—ungslos** *a* motionless.

Beweis [bə'vais] *m* **-es, -e** proof; (*Zeichen*) sign; **b—bar** [bə'vaiz-] *a* provable; **b—en** *vt irreg* prove;

(*zeigen*) show; **—führung** *f* reasoning; **—kraft** *f* weight, conclusiveness; **b—kräftig** *a* convincing, conclusive; **—mittel** *nt* evidence.

bewenden [bə'vɛndən] *vi:* **etw dabei — lassen** leave sth at that.

Bewerb- [bə'vɛrb] *cpd:* **b—en** *vr irreg* apply (um for); **—er(in f)** *m* **-s, -** applicant; **—ung** *f* application.

bewerkstelligen [bə'vɛrkʃtɛligən] *vt* manage, accomplish.

bewerten [bə've:rtən] *vt* assess.

bewilligen [bə'viligən] *vt* grant, allow.

Bewilligung *f* granting.

bewirken [bə'virkən] *vt* cause, bring about.

bewirten [bə'virtən] *vt* entertain.

bewirtschaften [bə'virt-ʃaftən] *vt* manage.

Bewirtung *f* hospitality.

bewohn- [bə'vo:n] *cpd:* **—bar** *a* inhabitable; **—en** *vt* inhabit, live in; **B—er(in f)** *m* **-s, -** inhabitant; (*von Haus*) resident.

bewölkt [bə'vœlkt] *a* cloudy, overcast.

Bewölkung *f* clouds *pl*.

Bewunder- [bə'vundər] *cpd:* **—er** *m* **-s, -** admirer; **b—n** *vt* admire; **b—nswert** *a* admirable, wonderful; **—ung** *f* admiration.

bewußt [bə'vust] *a* conscious; (*absichtlich*) deliberate; **sich** (*dat*) **einer Sache — sein** be aware of sth; **—los** *a* unconscious; **B—losigkeit** *f* unconsciousness; **—machen** *vt:* **jdm/sich etw —machen** make sb/o.s. aware of sth; **B—sein** *nt* consciousness; **bei B—sein** conscious.

bezahlen [bə'tsa:lən] *vt* pay (for); **es macht sich bezahlt** it will pay.

Bezahlung f payment.

bezaubern [bəˈtsaubərn] vt enchant, charm.

bezeichnen [bəˈtsaiçnən] vt (kennzeichnen) mark; (nennen) call; (beschreiben) describe; (zeigen) show, indicate; —d·a characteristic, typical (für of).

Bezeichnung f (Zeichen) mark, sign; (Beschreibung) description.

bezeugen [bəˈtsɔygən] vt testify to.

Bezichtigung [bəˈtsɪçtɪgυŋ] f accusation.

beziehen [bəˈtsiːən] irreg vt (mit Überzug) cover; Bett make; Haus, Position move into; Standpunkt take up; (erhalten) receive; Zeitung subscribe to, take; etw auf jdn/etw — relate sth to sb/sth; vr refer (auf + acc to); (Himmel) cloud over.

Beziehung f (Verbindung) connection; (Zusammenhang) relation; (Verhältnis) relationship; (Hinsicht) respect; —en haben (vorteilhaft) have connections or contacts; b—sweise ad or; (genauer gesagt auch) that is, or rather.

Bezirk [bəˈtsɪrk] m -(e)s, -e district.

Bezug [bəˈtsuːk] m -(e)s, ⸚e (Hülle) covering; (Comm) ordering; (Gehalt) income, salary; (Beziehung) relationship (zu to); in b— auf (+ acc) with reference to; — nehmen auf (+ acc) refer to.

bezüglich [bəˈtsyːklɪç] prep + gen concerning, referring to; a concerning; (Gram) relative.

Bezugs- cpd: —nahme f reference (auf + acc to); —spreis m retail price; —squelle f source of supply.

bezwecken [bəˈtsvɛkn̩] vt aim at.

bezweifeln [bəˈtsvaifəln] vt doubt, query.

Bibel [ˈbiːbəl] f -, -n Bible.

Biber [ˈbiːbər] m -s, - beaver.

Biblio- cpd: —graphie [bibliograˈfiː] f bibliography; —thek [biblioˈteːk] f -, -en library; —thekar(in f) [biblioteˈkaːr(ɪn)] m -s, -e librarian.

biblisch [ˈbiːblɪʃ] a biblical.

bieder [ˈbiːdər] a upright, worthy; Kleid etc plain.

bieg- [biːg] cpd: —bar a flexible; —en irreg vtr bend; vi turn; —sam [ˈbiːk-] a supple; B—ung f bend, curve.

Biene [ˈbiːnə] f -, -n bee; —nhonig m honey; —nkorb m beehive; —nwachs nt beeswax.

Bier [biːr] nt -(e)s, -e beer; —brauer m brewer; —deckel m, —filz m beer mat; —krug m, —seidel m beer mug.

bieten [ˈbiːtən] irreg vt offer; (bei Versteigerung) bid; vr (Gelegenheit) be open (dat to); sich (dat) etw — lassen put up with sth.

Bikini [biˈkiːni] m -s, -s bikini.

Bilanz [biˈlants] f balance; (fig) outcome; — ziehen take stock (aus of).

Bild [bɪlt] nt -(e)s, -er (lit, fig) picture; photo; (Spiegel—) reflection; —bericht m pictorial report.

bilden [ˈbɪldən] vt form; (erziehen) educate; (ausmachen) constitute; vr arise; (erziehen) educate o.s.

Bilder- [ˈbɪldər] cpd: —buch nt picture book; —rahmen m picture frame.

Bild- cpd: —fläche f screen; (fig) scene; —hauer m -s, - sculptor; b—hübsch a lovely, pretty as a picture; b—lich a figurative; pictorial; —schirm m television screen; b—schön a lovely; —ung ['bɪldʊŋ] f formation; (Wissen, Benehmen) education; —ungslücke f gap in one's education; —ungspolitik f educational policy; —weite f (Phot) distance.

Billard ['bɪljart] nt -s, -e billiards; —ball m, —kugel f billiard ball.

billig ['bɪlɪç] a cheap; (gerecht) fair, reasonable; —en ['bɪlɪgən] vt approve of; **B—ung** f approval.

Billion [bɪli'oːn] f billion, trillion (US).

bimmeln ['bɪməln] vi tinkle.

Binde ['bɪndə] f -, -n bandage; (Arm—) band; (Med) sanitary towel; —glied nt connecting link; b—n vt irreg bind, tie; —strich m hyphen; —wort nt conjunction.

Bind- cpd: —faden m string; —ung f bond, tie; (Ski—) binding.

binnen ['bɪnən] prep +dat or gen within; **B—hafen** m inland harbour; **B—handel** m internal trade.

Binse ['bɪnzə] f -, -n rush, reed; —nwahrheit f truism.

Bio- [bio] cpd bio-; —graphie [gra'fiː] f biography; —loge ['loːgə] m -n, -n biologist; —logie [lo'giː] f biology; b—logisch ['loːgɪʃ] a biological.

Birke ['bɪrkə] f -, -n birch.

Birnbaum m pear tree.

Birne ['bɪrnə] f -, -n pear; (Elec) · (light) bulb.

bis [bɪs] ad, prep +acc (räumlich: — zu/an +acc) to, as far as; (zeitlich) till, until; Sie haben — Dienstag Zeit you have until or till Tuesday; — Dienstag muß es fertig sein it must be ready by Tuesday; — hierher this far; — in die Nacht into the night; — auf weiteres until further notice; —bald/gleich see you later/soon; — auf etw (acc) (einschließlich) including sth; (aus-

geschlossen) except sth; — zu up to; cj ·(mit Zahlen) to; (zeitlich) until, till; von ... — ... from ...to...

Bischof ['bɪʃɔf] m -s, ⁼e bishop.
bischöflich [bɪʃøːflɪç] a episcopal.
bisher [bɪs'heːr] ad, —ig a till now, hitherto.

Biskuit [bɪs'kviːt] m or nt -(e)s, -s or -e biscuit; —teig m sponge mixture.

bislang [bɪs'laŋ] ad hitherto.

Biß [bɪs] m -sses, -sse bite.
bißchen ['bɪsçən] a, ad bit.
Bissen ['bɪsən] m -s, - bite, morsel.
bissig ['bɪsɪç] a Hund snappy; Bemerkung cutting, biting.

Bistum ['bɪstuːm] nt bishopric.

bisweilen [bɪs'vaɪlən] ad at times, occasionally.

Bitte ['bɪtə] f -, -n request; b— interj please; (wie b—?) (I beg your) pardon; (als Antwort auf Dank) you're welcome; b— schön! it was a pleasure; b—n vti irreg ask (um for); b—nd a pleading, imploring.

bitter ['bɪtər] a bitter; —böse a very angry; **B—keit** f bitterness; —lich a bitter.

blähen ['blɛːən] vtr swell, blow out.
Blähungen pl (Med) wind.

blam- cpd: —abel [bla'maːbəl] a disgraceful; **B—age** [bla'maːʒə] f -, -n disgrace; —ieren [bla'miːrən] vr make a fool of o.s., disgrace o.s.; vt let down, disgrace.

blank [blaŋk] a bright; (unbedeckt) bare; (sauber) clean, polished; (col: ohne Geld) broke; (offensichtlich) blatant.

blanko ['blaŋko] ad blank; **B—scheck** m blank cheque.

Bläschen ['blɛːsçən] *nt* bubble; (*Med*) spot, blister.

Blase ['blaːzə] *f* -, -n bubble; (*Med*) blister; (*Anat*) bladder; —balg *m* bellows *pl*; **b—n** *vti irreg* blow.

Blas- *cpd*: —instrument *nt* brass or wind instrument; —kapelle *f* brass band.

blaß [blas] *a* pale.

Blässe ['blɛsə] *f* - paleness, palour.

Blatt [blat] *nt* -(e)s, "er leaf; newspaper; (*von Papier*) sheet; (*Cards*) hand; **vom — singen/spielen** sight-read.

blättern ['blɛtərn] *vi*: **in etw** (*dat*) — leaf through sth.

Blätterteig *m* flaky or puff pastry.

blau [blau] *a* blue; (*col*) drunk, stoned; (*Cook*) boiled; *Auge* black; —er Fleck bruise; Fahrt ins B—e mystery tour; —äugig *a* blue-eyed; **B—licht** *nt* flashing blue light; —**machen** *vi* (*col*) skive off work; **B—strumpf** *m* (*fig*) blue-stocking.

Blech [blɛç] *nt* -(e)s, -e sheet metal; (*Back—*) baking tray; —**büchse** *f*, —**dose** *f* tin, can; **b—en** *vti* (*col*) pay; —**schaden** *m* (*Aut*) damage to bodywork.

Blei [blai] *nt* -(e)s, -e lead; —**be** *f* -, -n roof over one's head; **b—ben** *vi irreg* stay, remain, **b—benlassen** *vt irreg* leave (alone).

bleich [blaiç] *a* faded, pale; —**en** *vt* bleach.

Blei- *cpd*: **b—ern** *a* leaden; —**stift** *m* pencil; —**stiftspitzer** *m* pencil sharpener.

Blende ['blɛndə] *f* -, -n (*Phot*) aperture; **b—n** *vt* blind, dazzle; (*fig*) hoodwink; **b—nd** *a* (*col*) grand; **b—nd aussehen** look smashing.

Blick [blik] *m* -(e)s, -e (*kurz*) glance, glimpse; (*Anschauen*) look, gaze; (*Aussicht*) view; **b—en** *vi* look; **sich b—en lassen** put in an appearance; —**fang** *m* eye-catching object; —**feld** *nt* range of vision (*auch fig*).

blind [blint] *a* blind; *Glas etc* dull; —**er Passagier** stowaway; **B—darm** *m* appendix; **B—darmentzündung** *f* appendicitis; **B—enschrift** ['blindən-] *f* braille; **B—heit** *f* blindness; —**lings** *ad* blindly; **B—schleiche** *f* slow worm; —**schreiben** *vi irreg* touch-type.

blink- [blink] *cpd*: —**en** *vi* twinkle, sparkle; (*Licht*) flash, signal; (*Aut*) indicate; *vt* flash, signal; **B—er** *m* -s, -, **B—licht** *nt* (*Aut*) indicator.

blinzeln ['blintsəln] *vi* blink, wink.

Blitz [blits] *m* -es, -e (*flash of*) lightning; —**ableiter** *m* lightning conductor; **b—en** *vi* (*aufleuchten*) glint, shine; **es blitzt** (*Met*) there's a flash of lightning; —**licht** *nt* flashlight; **b—schnell** *a*, *ad* as quick as a flash.

Block [blɔk] *m* -(e)s, "e (*lit, fig*) block; (*von Papier*) pad; —**ade** [blɔˈkaːdə] *f* -, -n blockade; —**flöte** *f* recorder; **b—frei** *a* (*Pol*) unaligned; **b—ieren** [blɔˈkiːrən] *vt* block; *vi* (*Räder*) jam; —**schrift** *f* block letters *pl*.

blöd [bløːt] *a* silly, stupid; —**eln** ['bløːdəln] *vi* (*col*) fool around; **B—heit** *f* stupidity; **B—sinn** *m* nonsense; —**sinnig** *a* silly, idiotic.

blond [blɔnt] *a* blond, fair-haired.

bloß [bloːs] *a* (*unbedeckt*) bare; (*nackt*) naked; (*nur*) mere; *ad* only, merely; **laß das —!** just don't do that!

Blöße ['blø:sə] *f* -, **-n** bareness; nakedness; *(fig)* weakness; **sich** *(dat)* **eine — geben** *(fig)* lay o.s. open to attack.

bloß- *cpd:* **—legen** *vt* expose; **—stellen** *vt* show up.

blühen ['bly:ən] *vi (lit)* bloom, be in bloom; *(fig)* flourish.

Blume ['blu:mə] *f* -, **-n** flower; *(von Wein)* bouquet; **—nkohl** *m* cauliflower; **—ntopf** *m* flowerpot; **—nzwiebel** *f* bulb.

Bluse ['blu:zə] *f* -, **-n** blouse.

Blut [blu:t] *nt* **-(e)s** blood; **b—arm** *a* anaemic; *(fig)* penniless; **b—befleckt** *a* bloodstained; **—buche** *f* copper beech; **—druck** *m* blood pressure.

Blüte ['bly:tə] *f* -, **-n** blossom; *(fig)* prime; **—zeit** *f* flowering period; *(fig)* prime.

Blut- *cpd:* **—egel** *m* leech; **b—en** *vi* bleed.

Blütenstaub *m* pollen.

Blut- *cpd:* **—er** *m* -s, - *(Med)* haemophiliac; **—erguß** *m* haemorrhage; *(auf Haut)* bruise; **—gruppe** *f* blood group; **b—ig** *a* bloody; **b—jung** *a* very young; **—probe** *f* blood test; **—schande** *f* incest; **—spender** *m* blood donor; **—übertragung** *f* blood transfusion; **—ung** *f* bleeding, haemorrhage; **—vergiftung** *f* blood poisoning; **—wurst** *f* black pudding.

Bö(e) ['bø:(ə)] *f* -, **-en** squall.

Bock [bɔk] *m* **-(e)s, ¨e** buck, ram; *(Gestell)* trestle, support; *(Sport)* buck.

Boden ['bo:dən] *m* **-s, ¨** ground; *(Fuß—)* floor; *(Meeres—, Faß—)* bottom; *(Speicher)* attic; **b—los** *a* bottomless; *(col)* incredible; **—satz** *m* dregs *pl,* sediment; **—schätze** *pl* mineral wealth; **—turnen** *nt* floor exercises *pl.*

Bogen ['bo:gən] *m* -s, - *(Biegung)* curve; *(Archit)* arch; *(Waffe, Mus)* bow; *(Papier)* sheet; **—gang** *m* arcade; **—schütze** *m* archer.

Bohle ['bo:lə] *f* -, **-n** plank.

Bohne ['bo:nə] *f* -, **-n** bean; **—nkaffee** *m* pure coffee; **b—rn** *vt* wax, polish; **—rwachs** *nt* floor polish.

Bohr- ['bo:r] *cpd:* **b—en** *vt* bore; **—er** *m* -s, - drill; **—insel** *f* oil rig; **—maschine** *f* drill; **—turm** *m* derrick.

Boje ['bo:jə] *f* -, **-n** buoy.

Bolzen ['bɔltsən] *m* -s, - bolt.

Bomb- *cpd:* **b—ardieren** [bɔmbar'di:rən] *vt* bombard; *(aus der Luft)* bomb; **—e** ['bɔmbə] *f* -, **-n** bomb; **—enangriff** *m* bombing raid; **—enerfolg** *m (col)* huge success.

Bonbon [bõ'bõ:] *m* or *nt* **-s, -s** sweet.

Boot [bo:t] *nt* **-(e)s, -e** boat.

Bord [bɔrt] *m* **-(e)s, -e** *(Aviat, Naut)* board; *(an — gehen)* board; *(Brett)* shelf; **—ell** [bɔr'dɛl] *nt* -s, **-e** brothel; **—funkanlage** *f* radio; **—stein** *m* kerb(stone).

borgen ['bɔrgən] *vt* borrow; **jdm etw —** lend sb sth.

borniert [bɔr'ni:rt] *a* narrow-minded.

Börse ['bö:rzə] *f* -, **-n** stock exchange; *(Geld—)* purse.

Borste ['bɔrstə] *f* -, **-n** bristle.

Borte ['bɔrtə] *f* -, **-n** edging; *(Band)* trimming.

bös [bø:s] *a* bad, evil; *(zornig)* angry; **—artig** ['bø:z-] *a* malicious.

Böschung ['bœʃʊŋ] *f* slope; *(Ufer— etc)* embankment.

bos- ['bo:s] *cpd:* **—haft** *a* malicious, spiteful; **B—heit** *f* malice, spite.

böswillig ['bø:svɪlɪç] a malicious.
Botanik [bo'ta:nɪk] f botany.
botanisch [bo'ta:nɪʃ] a botanical.
Bot- ['bo:t] cpd: —e m -n, -n messenger; —enjunge m errand boy; —schaft f message, news; (Pol) embassy; —schafter m -s, - ambassador.
Bottich ['bɔtɪç] m -(e)s, -e vat, tub.
Bouillon [bu'ljõ:] f -, -s consommé.
Bowle ['bo:lə] f -, -n punch.
Box- ['bɔks] cpd: **b—en** vi box; **—er** m -s, - boxer; **—handschuh** m boxing glove; **—kampf** m boxing match.
boykottieren [bɔykɔ'ti:rən] vt boycott.
Branche ['brã:ʃə] f -, -n line of business; **—nverzeichnis** nt yellow pages pl.
Brand [brant] m -(e)s, ²e fire; (Med) gangrene; **b—en** [brandən] vi surge; (Meer) break; **b—marken** vt brand; (fig) stigmatize; **—salbe** f ointment for burns; **—stifter** m arsonist, fire-raiser; **—stiftung** f arson; **—ung** f surf; **—wunde** f burn.
Branntwein ['brantvaɪn] m brandy.
Brat- ['bra:t] cpd: **—apfel** m baked apple; **b—en** vt irreg roast, fry; **—en** m -s, - roast, joint; **—huhn** nt roast chicken; **—kartoffeln** pl fried or roast potatoes pl; **—pfanne** f frying pan; **—rost** m grill.
Bratsche ['bra:tʃə] f -, -n viola.
Brat- cpd: **—spieß** m spit; **—wurst** f grilled sausage.
Brauch [braux] m -(e)s, Bräuche custom; **b—bar** a usable, serviceable; Person capable; **b—en** vt (bedürfen) need; (müssen) have to; (verwenden) use.

Braue ['brauə] f -, -n brow; **b—n** vt brew; **—'rei** f brewery.
braun [braun] a brown; (von Sonne auch) tanned.
Bräune ['brɔynə] f -, -n brownness; (Sonnen—) tan; **b—n** vt make brown; (Sonne) tan.
braungebrannt a tanned.
Brause ['brauzə] f -, -n shower bath; (von Gießkanne) rose; (Getränk) lemonade; **b—n** vi roar; (auch vr: duschen) take a shower; **—pulver** nt lemonade powder.
Braut [braut] f -, Bräute bride; (Verlobte) fiancée.
Bräutigam ['brɔytɪgam] m -s, -e bridegroom; fiancé.
Braut- cpd: **—jungfer** f bridesmaid; **—paar** nt bride and bridegroom, bridal pair.
brav [bra:f] a (artig) good; (ehrenhaft) worthy, honest.
Brech- ['brɛç] cpd: **—eisen** nt crowbar; **b—en** vti irreg break; Licht refract; (fig) Mensch crush; (speien) vomit; **die Ehe b—en** commit adultery; **—reiz** m nausea, retching.
Brei [braɪ] m -(e)s, -e (Masse) pulp; (Cook) gruel; (Hafer—) porridge.
breit [braɪt] a wide, broad; **B—e** f -, -n width; breadth; (Geog) latitude; **b—en** vt: etw über etw (acc) **—en** spread sth over sth; **B—engrad** m degree of latitude; **—machen** vr spread o.s. out; **—schult(e)rig** a broad-shouldered; **—treten** vt irreg (col) enlarge upon; **B—wandfilm** m wide-screen film.
Brems- ['brɛmz] cpd: **—belag** m brake lining; **—e** f -, -n brake; (Zool) horsefly; **b—en** vi brake, apply the brakes; vt Auto brake; (fig) slow down; **—licht** nt brake

light; **—pedal** nt brake pedal; **—schuh** m brake shoe; **—spur** f tyre marks pl; **—weg** m braking distance.

Brenn- ['brɛn] cpd: **b—bar** a inflammable; **b—en** irreg vi burn, be on fire; (Licht, Kerze etc) burn; vt Holz etc burn; (Ziegel, Ton fire; Kaffee roast; darauf **b—en**, etw **zu tun** be dying to do sth; **—material** nt fuel; **—(n)essel** f nettle; **—spiritus** m methylated spirits; **—stoff** m liquid fuel.

brenzlig ['brɛntsliç] a smelling of burning, burnt; (fig) precarious.

Brett [brɛt] nt -(e)s, -er board, plank; (Bord) shelf; (Spiel—) board; **Schwarze(s)** —, notice board; **—er** pl (Ski) skis pl; (Theat) boards pl; **—erzaun** m wooden fence.

Brezel ['bre:tsəl] f -, -n bretzel, pretzel.

Brief [bri:f] m -(e)s, -e letter; **—beschwerer** m -s, - paperweight; **—kasten** m letterbox; **b—lich** a,ad by letter; **—marke** f postage stamp; **—öffner** m letter opener; **—papier** nt notepaper; **—tasche** f wallet; **—träger** m postman; **—umschlag** m envelope; **—wechsel** m correspondence.

Brikett [bri'kɛt] nt -s, -s briquette.

brillant [bril'jant] a (fig) sparkling, brilliant; **B—** m -en, -en brilliant, diamond.

Brille ['brilə] f -, -n spectacles pl; (Schutz—) goggles pl; (Toiletten—) (toilet) seat.

bringen ['brɪŋən] vt irreg bring; (mitnehmen, begleiten) take; (einbringen) Profit bring in; (veröffentlichen) publish; (Theat, Cine) show; (Rad, TV) broadcast; (in einen Zustand versetzen) get; (col:

tun können) manage; jdn dazu —, etw zu tun make sb do sth; jdn nach Hause — take sb home; jdn um etw — make sb lose sth; jdn auf eine Idee — give sb an idea.

Brise ['bri:zə] f -, -n breeze.

bröckelig ['brœkəliç] a crumbly.

Brocken ['brɔkən] m -s, - piece, bit; (Fels—) lump of rock.

brodeln ['bro:dəln] vi bubble.

Brokat [bro'ka:t] m -(e)s, -e brocade.

Brombeere ['brombe:rə] f blackberry, bramble.

bronchial [brɔnçi'a:l] a bronchial.

Bronchien ['brɔnçiən] pl bronchia(l tubes) pl.

Bronze ['brõ:sə] f -, -n bronze.

Brosame ['bro:za:mə] f -, -n crumb.

Brosche ['brɔʃə] f -, -n brooch.

Broschüre [brɔ'ʃy:rə] f -, -n pamphlet.

Brot [bro:t] nt -(e)s, -e bread; (—laib) loaf.

Brötchen ['brø:tçən] nt roll.

brotlos ['bro:tlo:s] a (Person unemployed; Arbeit etc unprofitable.

Bruch [brux] m -(e)s, ˉe breakage; (zerbrochene Stelle) break; (fig) split, breach; (Med: Eingeweide—) rupture, hernia; (Bein— etc) fracture; (Math) fraction; **—bude** f (col) shack.

brüchig ['bryçiç] a brittle, fragile; Haus dilapidated.

Bruch- cpd: **—landung** f crash landing; **—strich** m (Math) line; **—stück** nt fragment; **—teil** m fraction.

Brücke ['brykə] f -, -n bridge; (Teppich) rug.

Bruder ['bru:dər] m -s, ˉ brother.

Brüder- ['bry:dər] cpd: **b—lich** a brotherly; **—lichkeit** f fraternity;

—**schaft** f brotherhood, fellowship;
—**schaft trinken** fraternize, address
each other as 'du'.

Brühe ['bry:ə] f -, -n broth, stock;
(pej) muck.

brüllen ['brylən] vi bellow, scream.

Brumm- ['brum] cpd:—**bär** m
grumbler; **b—eln** vti mumble;
b—en vi (Bär, Mensch etc) growl;
(Insekt, Radio) buzz; (Motoren)
roar; (murren) grumble; vt growl;
jdm brummt der Kopf sb's head is
buzzing.

brünett [bry'nɛt] a brunette, dark-
haired.

Brunnen ['brunən] m -s, - fountain; (tief) well; (natürlich)
spring; —**kresse** f watercress.

brüsk [brysk] a abrupt, brusque.

Brust [brust] f -, ̈-e breast;
(Männer—) chest.

brüsten ['brystən] vr boast.

Brust- cpd:—**fellentzündung** f
pleurisy; —**kasten** m chest;
—**schwimmen** nt breast-stroke;
—**warze** f nipple.

Brüstung ['brystuŋ] f parapet.

Brut [bru:t] f -, -en brood;
(Brüten) hatching; —**al** [bru'ta:l]
a brutal; —**ali'tät** f brutality;
—**apparat** m, —**kasten** m incubator.

brüten ['bry:tən] vi hatch, brood
(auch fig).

brutto ['bruto] ad gross; **B—einkommen** nt, **B—gehalt** nt gross
salary; **B—gewicht** nt gross
weight; **B—lohn** m gross wages pl.

Bub [bu:p] m -en, -en boy, lad;
—**e** [bu:bə] m -n, -n (Schurke)
rogue; (Cards) jack;—**ikopf** m
bobbed hair, shingle.

Buch [bu:x] nt -(e)s, ̈-er book;
(Comm) account book; —**binder** m
bookbinder; —**drucker** m printer;

—**e** f -, -n beech tree; **b—en** vt
book; Betrag enter.

Bücher- ['by:çər] cpd:—**brett** nt
bookshelf; —**ei** [-'raɪ] f library;
—**regal** nt bookshelves pl, bookcase; —**schrank** m bookcase.

Buch- cpd:—**fink** m chaffinch;
—**führung** f book-keeping, account-
ing; —**halter(in** f) m -s, - book-
keeper; —**handel** m book trade;
—**händler(in** f) m bookseller;
—**handlung** f bookshop.

Büchse ['byksə] f -, -n tin, can;
(Holz—) box; (Gewehr) rifle; —n-
fleisch nt tinned meat; —**nöffner** m
tin or can opener.

Buch- cpd:—**stabe** m -ns, -n letter
(of the alphabet); **b—stabieren**
[bu:xʃta'bi:rən] vt spell; **b—stäb-
lich** ['bu:xʃtɛ:plɪç] a literal.

Bucht [buxt] f -, -en bay.

Buchung ['bu:xuŋ] f booking;
(Comm) entry.

Buckel ['bukəl] m -s, - hump.

bücken ['bykən] vr bend.

Bückling ['byklɪŋ] m (Fisch) kipper; (Verbeugung) bow.

Bude ['bu:də] f -, -n booth, stall;
(col) digs pl.

Budget [by'dʒe:] nt -s, -s budget.

Büffel ['byfəl] m -s, - buffalo.

Büf(f)ett [by'fe:] nt -s, -s (Anrichte) sideboard; (Geschirrschrank) dresser; **kaltes —** cold
buffet.

Bug [bu:k] m -(e)s, -e (Naut) bow;
(Aviat) nose.

Bügel ['by:gəl] m -s, - (Kleider—)
hanger; (Steig—) stirrup; (Bril-
len—) arm; —**brett** nt ironing
board; —**eisen** nt iron; —**falte** f
crease; **b—n** vti iron.

Bühne ['by:nə] f -, -n stage;
—**nbild** nt set, scenery.

Buhruf ['buːruːf] *m* boo.

Bulette [bu'lɛtə] *f* meatball.

Bull- ['bʊl] *cpd:* —**dogge** *f* bulldog; —**dozer** ['buldoːzər] *m* -s, - bulldozer; —**e** *m* -n, -n bull.

Bummel ['buməl] *m* -s, - stroll; (*Schaufenster—*) window-shopping; —**ant** [-'lant] *m* slowcoach; —**ei** [-'laɪ] *f* wandering; dawdling; skiving; **b—n** *vi* wander, stroll; (*trödeln*) dawdle; (*faulenzen*) skive, loaf around; —**streik** *m* go-slow; —**zug** *m* slow train.

Bummler(in *f*) ['bumlər(ɪn)] *m* -s, - (*langsamer Mensch*) dawdler; (*Faulenzer*) idler, loafer.

Bund [bunt] *m* -(e)s, -̈e (*Freundschafts—* etc) bond; (*Organisation*) union; (*Pol*) confederacy; (*Hosen—*, *Rock—*) waistband; *nt* -(e)s, -e bunch; (*Stroh—*) bundle.

Bünd- ['bʏnd] *cpd:* —**chen** *nt* ribbing; (*Ärmel—*) cuff; —**el** *nt* -s, -n bundle, bale; **b—eln** *vt* bundle.

Bundes- ['bundəs] *in cpds* Federal (*esp West German*): —**bahn** *f* Federal Railways *pl*; —**hauptstadt** *f* Federal capital; —**kanzler** *m* Federal Chancellor; —**land** *nt* Land; —**präsident** *m* Federal President; —**rat** *m* upper house of West German Parliament; —**republik** *f* Federal Republic (of West Germany); —**staat** *m* Federal state; —**straße** *f* Federal Highway, 'A' road; —**tag** *m* West German Parliament; —**verfassungsgericht** *nt* Federal Constitutional Court; —**wehr** *f* West German Armed Forces *pl*.

Bünd- *cpd:* **b—ig** *a* (*kurz*) concise; —**nis** *nt* -ses, -se alliance.

Bunker ['buŋkər] *m* -s, - bunker.

bunt [bunt] *a* coloured; (*gemischt*) mixed; **jdm wird es zu — ** it's

getting too much for sb; **B—stift** *m* coloured pencil, crayon.

Burg [burk] *f* -, -en castle, fort.

Bürge ['bʏrgə] *m* -n, -n guarantor; **b—n** *vi* vouch; —**r**(in *f*) *m* -s, - citizen; member of the middle class; —**rkrieg** *m* civil war; **b—rlich** *a* Rechte civil; Klasse middle-class; (*pej*) bourgeois; gut **b—rliche Küche** good home cooking; —**rmeister** *m* mayor; —**recht** *nt* civil rights *pl*; —**rschaft** *f* population, citizens *pl*; —**rsteig** *m* pavement; —**rtum** *nt* citizens *pl*.

Bürg- *cpd:* —**in** *f* see Bürge; —**schaft** *f* surety; —**schaft leisten** give security.

Büro [by'roː] *nt* -s, -s office; —**angestellte**(r) *mf* office worker; —**klammer** *f* paper clip; —**krat** [byro'kraːt] *m* -en, -en bureaucrat; —**kra'tie** *f* bureaucracy; **b—'kratisch** *a* bureaucratic; —**kra'tismus** *m* red tape; —**schluß** *m* office closing time.

Bursch(e) ['burʃ(ə)] *m* -en, -en lad, fellow; (*Diener*) servant.

Bürste ['bʏrstə] *f* -, -n brush; **b—n** *vt* brush.

Bus [bus] *m* -ses, -se bus.

Busch [buʃ] *m* -(e)s, -̈e bush, shrub.

Büschel ['bʏʃəl] *nt* -s, - tuft.

buschig *a* bushy.

Busen ['buːzən] *m* -s, - bosom; (*Meer—*) inlet, bay; —**freund**(in *f*) *m* bosom friend.

Buße ['buːsə] *f* -, -n atonement, penance; (*Geld*) fine.

büßen ['byːsən] *vti* do penance (for), atone (for).

Büste ['bʏstə] *f* -, -n bust; —**nhalter** *m* bra.

Butter ['butər] *f* - butter; —**blume** *f* buttercup; —**brot** *nt* (piece of)

bread and butter; —**brotpapier** nt
greaseproof paper; —**dose** f butter
dish; b—**weich** a soft as butter;

(fig,col) soft.

Butzen ['butsən] m -s, - core.

C

*(see also under Ǩ and Z; CH under
SCH)*

C, c [tse:] nt C, c.

Café [ka'fe:] nt -s, -s café.

Cafeteria [kafete'ri:a] f -, -s
cafeteria.

Camp- [kɛmp] cpd: c—**en** vi camp;
—**er(in** f) m -s, - camper; —**ing** nt
-s camping; —**ingplatz** m camp-
(ing) site.

Caravan ['kɛravɛn] m -s, -s
caravan.

Cellist [tʃɛ'lıst] m cellist.

Cello ['tʃɛlo] nt -s, -s or Celli cello.

Chamäleon [ka'mɛ:leon] nt -s, -s
chameleon.

Champagner [ʃam'panjər] m -s, -
champagne.

Champignon ['ʃampinjo] m -s, -s
button mushroom.

Chance ['ʃã:s(ə)] f -, -n chance,
opportunity.

Chaos ['ka:ɔs] nt -s, - chaos.

chaotisch [ka'o:tıʃ] a chaotic.

Charakter [ka'raktər] m -s, -e
[karak'te:rə] character; c—**fest** a of
firm character; c—**i'sieren** vt
characterize; —**istik** [karak-
te'rıstık] f characterization;
c—**istisch** [karakte'rıstıʃ] a
characteristic, typical (für of);
c—**los** a unprincipled; —**losigkeit** f
lack of principle; —**schwäche** f
weakness of character; —**stärke** f
strength of character; —**zug** m
characteristic, trait.

charmant [ʃar'mant] a charming.

Charme [ʃarm] m -s charm.

Chassis [ʃa'si:] nt -, - chassis.

Chauffeur [ʃo'fø:r] m chauffeur.

Chauvinismus [ʃovi'nısmus] m
chauvinism, jingoism.

Chauvinist [ʃovi'nıst] m
chauvinist, jingoist.

Chef [ʃɛf] m -s, -s head; (col)
boss; —**arzt** m head physician;
—**in** f (col) boss.

Chemie [çe'mi:] f - chemistry;
—**faser** f man-made fibre.

Chemikalie [çemi'ka:liə] f -, -n
chemical.

Chemiker(in f) ['çe:mikər(ın)] m
-s, -(industrial) chemist.

chemisch ['çe:mıʃ] a chemical; —**e**
Reinigung dry cleaning.

Chiffre ['ʃıfər] f -, -n (Geheim-
zeichen) cipher; (in Zeitung) box
number.

Chiffriermaschine [ʃıfri:rma'ʃi:nə]
f cipher machine.

Chips [tʃıps] pl crisps pl, chips pl
(US).

Chirurg [çi'rurk] m -en, -en
surgeon; —**ie** [-'gi:] f surgery;
c—**isch** a surgical.

Chlor [klo:r] nt -s chlorine;
—**o'form** nt -s chloroform;
c—**ofor'mieren** vt chloroform;
—**ophyll** [kloro'fyl] nt -s
chlorophyll.

Cholera ['ko:lera] f - cholera.

cholerisch [ko'le:rıʃ] a choleric.

Chor [ko:r] *m* -(e), -e *or* ⸚e choir;
(*Musikstück*, *Theat*) chorus; —al
[ko'ra:l] *m* -s, -äle chorale.

Choreograph [koreo'gra:f] *m* -en,
-en choreographer; —ie [-'fi:] *f*
choreography.

Chor- *cpd*: —gestühl *nt* choir stalls
pl; —knabe *m* choirboy.

Christ ['krist] *m* -en, -en
Christian; —baum *m* Christmas
tree; —enheit *f* Christendom;
—entum *nt* Christianity; —in *f*
Christian; —kind *nt* ≈ Father
Christmas; (*Jesus*) baby Jesus;
c—lich a Christian; —us *m* - Christ.

Chrom [kro:m] *nt* -s (*Chem*)
chromium; chrome; —osom
[kromo'zo:m] *nt* -s, -en (*Biol*)
chromosome.

Chron- ['kro:n] *cpd*: —ik *f*
chronicle; c—isch a chronic;
—ologie [-lo'gi:] *f* chronology;
c—ologisch [-'lo:gɪʃ] a chronological.

Chrysantheme [kryzan'te:mə] *f* -,
-n chrysanthemum.

circa ['tsırka] *ad* about,
approximately.

Clown [klaun] *m* -s, -s clown.

Computer [kɔm'pju:tər] *m* -s, -
computer.

Conférencier [kõferãsi'e:] *m* -s, -s
compère.

Coupé [ku'pe:] *nt* -s, -s (*Aut*)
coupé, sports version.

Coupon [ku'põ:] *m* -s, -s coupon;
(*Stoff*—) length of cloth.

Cousin [ku'zɛ̃:] *m* -s, -s cousin; —e
[ku'zi:nə] *f* -, -n cousin.

Creme [krɛ:m] *f* -, -s (*lit*, *fig*)
cream; (*Schuh*—) polish; (*Speise*—)
paste; (*Cook*) mousse; c—farben a
cream(-coloured).

Curry(pulver *nt*) ['kari(pulfər] *m*
or nt -s curry powder.

Cutter(in *f*) ['katər(ın)] *m* -s, -
(*Cine*) editor.

D

D, d [de:] *nt* D, d.

da [da:] *ad* (*dort*) there; (*hier*)
here; (*dann*) then; —, wo where;
cj as; —behalten *vt irreg* keep.

dabei [da'bai] *ad* (*räumlich*) close
to it; (*noch dazu*) besides; (*zusammen mit*) with them; (*zeitlich*)
during this; (*obwohl doch*) but,
however; was ist schon —? what
of it?; es ist doch nichts —, wenn
... it doesn't matter if ...; bleiben
wir — let's leave it at that; es soll
nicht — bleiben this isn't the end
of it; es bleibt — — that's settled;
das Dumme/Schwierige — the
stupid/difficult part of it; er war

gerade —, zu gehen he was just
leaving; —sein *vi irreg* (*anwesend*)
be present; (*beteiligt*) be involved;
—stehen *vi irreg* stand around.

Dach [dax] *nt* -(e)s, ⸚er roof;
—boden *m* attic, loft; —decker *m*
-s, - slater, tiler; —fenster *nt*,
—luke *f* skylight; —pappe *f* roofing
felt; —rinne *f* gutter; —ziegel *m*
roof tile.

Dachs [daks] *m* -es, -e badger.

Dackel ['dakəl] *m* -s, - dachshund.

dadurch [da'durç] *ad* (*räumlich*)
through it; (*durch diesen
Umstand*) thereby, in that way;

(*deshalb*) because of that, for that reason; *cj*: —, daß because.

dafür [da'fy:r] *ad* for it; (*anstatt*) instead; **er kann nichts** — he can't help it; **er ist bekannt** — he is well-known for that; **was bekomme ich** —? what will I get for it?; **D—halten** *nt* -s: **nach meinem D—halten** in my opinion.

dagegen [da'ge:gən] *ad* against it; (*im Vergleich damit*) in comparison with it; (*bei Tausch*) for it; **ich habe nichts** — I don't mind; **ich war** — I was against it; — **kann man nichts tun** one can't do anything about it; *cj* however; **—halten** *vt irreg* (*vergleichen*), compare with it; (*entgegnen*) object to it.

daheim [da'haɪm] *ad* at home; **D—** *nt* -s home.

daher [da'he:r] *ad* (*räumlich*) from there; (*Ursache*) from that; — **kommt er auch** that's where he comes from too; *cj* (*deshalb*) that's why; — **die Schwierigkeiten** that's what is causing the difficulties.

dahin [da'hɪn] *ad* (*räumlich*) there; (*zeitlich*) then; (*vergangen*) gone; **das tendiert** — it is tending towards that; **er bringt es noch** —, **daß ich** ... he'll make me ...; — **gegen** *cj* on the other hand; **—gehend** *ad* on this matter; **—gestellt** *ad*: **—gestellt bleiben** remain to be seen; **—gestellt sein lassen** leave sth open *or* undecided.

dahinten [da'hɪntən] *ad* over there.

dahinter [da'hɪntər] *ad* behind it; **—kommen** *vi irreg* get to the bottom of sth.

Dahlie ['da:liə] *f* -, -n dahlia.

dalassen ['da:lasən] *vt irreg* leave (behind).

damalig ['da:ma:lɪç] *a* of that time, then.

damals ['da:ma:ls] *ad* at that time, then.

Damast [da'mast] *m* -(e)s, -e damask.

Dame ['da:mə] *f* -, -n lady; (*Schach, Cards*) queen; (*Spiel*) draughts; **d—haft** a ladylike; **—wahl** *f* ladies' excuse-me; **—spiel** *nt* draughts.

damit [da'mɪt] *ad* with it; (*begründend*) by that; **was meint er** —? what does he mean by that?; **genug** —! that's enough; — **basta!** and that's that; — **eilt es nicht** there's no hurry; *cj* in order that *or* to.

dämlich ['dɛ:mlɪç] a (*col*) \silly, stupid.

Damm [dam] *m* -(e)s, ⸚e dyke; (*Stau—*) dam; (*Hafen—*) mole; (*Bahn—, Straßen—*) embankment.

Dämm— ['dɛm] *cpd*: **d—en** *vt Wasser* dam up; *Schmerzen* keep back; **d—erig** a dim, faint; **d—ern** *vi* (*Tag*) dawn; (*Abend*) fall; **—erung** *f* twilight; (*Morgen—*) dawn; (*Abend—*) dusk.

Dämon ['dɛ:mən] *m* -s, -en [dɛ'mo:nən] demon; **d—isch** [dɛ'mo:nɪʃ] a demoniacal.

Dampf [dampf] *m* -(e)s, ⸚e steam; (*Dunst*) vapour; **d—en** *vi* steam.

dämpfen ['dɛmpfən] * vt* (*Cook*) steam; (*bügeln auch*) iron with a damp cloth; (*fig*) dampen, subdue.

Dampf— *cpd*: **—er** *m* -s, - steamer; **—kochtopf** *m* pressure cooker; **—maschine** *f* steam engine; **—schiff** *nt* steamship; **—walze** *f* steamroller.

danach [da'na:x] *ad* after that; (*zeitlich auch*) afterwards; (*gemäß*) accordingly; according to which *or* that; **er sieht** — **aus** he looks it.

daneben [da'ne:bən] ad ·beside it;
(*im Vergleich*) in comparison;
—benehmen vr *irreg* misbehave;
—gehen vi *irreg* miss; (*Plan*) fail.

Dank [daŋk] m -(e)s thanks pl;
vielen or schönen — many thanks;
jdm — sagen thank sb; d— prep
+dat or gen thanks to; d—bar a
grateful; *Aufgabe* rewarding;
—barkeit f gratitude; d—e *interj*
thank you, thanks; d—en vi (+dat)
thank; d—enswert a *Arbeit* worthwhile; rewarding; *Bemühung*
kind; d—sagen vi express one's
thanks.

dann [dan] ad then; — und wann
now and then.

daran [da'ran] ad on it; stoßen
against it; es liegt —, daß ... the
cause of it is that ...; gut/schlecht
— sein be well/badly off; das
Beste/Dümmste — the best/stupid-
est thing about it; ich war nahe —,
zu ... I was on the point of ...;
er ist — gestorben he died from
or of it; —gehen vi *irreg* start;
—setzen vt stake; er hat alles
—gesetzt, von Glasgow wegzu-
kommen he has done his utmost to
get away from Glasgow.

darauf [da'rauf] ad (*räumlich*) on
it; (*zielgerichtet*) towards it;
(*danach*) afterwards; es kommt
ganz — an, ob ... it depends
whether ...; die Tage — the days
following or thereafter; am Tag —
the next day; —folgend a Tag, Jahr
next, following; —hin [-'hin] ad (*im
Hinblick darauf*) in this respect;
(*aus diesem Grund*) as a result;
—legen vt lay or put on top.

daraus [da'raus] ad from it; was
ist — geworden? what became of
it?; — geht hervor, daß ... this
means that ...

Darbietung [da:r'bi:tuŋ] f performance.

darin [da'rın] ad in (there), in it.

Dar- [da:r] cpd: d—legen vt
explain, expound, set forth; —le-
gung f explanation; —leh(e)n nt -s,
• loan.

Darm [darm] m -(e)s, ⸚e intestine;
(*Wurst—*) skin; —saite f gut string.

Darstell- [da:r'ftɛl] cpd: d—en vt
(*abbilden, bedeuten*) represent;
(*Theat*) act; (*beschreiben*) describe; vr appear to be; —er(in f)
m -s, - actor/actress; —ung f portrayal, depiction.

darüber [da'ry:bər] ad (*räumlich*)
over/above it; *fahren* over it;
(*mehr*) more; (*währenddessen*)
meanwhile; *sprechen, streiten*
about it; — geht nichts there's
nothing like it; seine Gedanken —
his thoughts about or on it.

darum [da'rum] ad (*räumlich*)
round it; — herum round about
(it); er bittet — he is pleading for
it; es geht —, daß ... the thing
is that ...; er würde viel — geben,
wenn ... he would give a lot to
...; cj that's why; ich tue es —,
weil ... I am doing it because ...

darunter [da'runtər] ad (*räumlich*)
under it; (*dazwischen*) among
them; (*weniger*) less; ein Stockwerk — one floor below (it); was
verstehen Sie —? what do you
understand by that?; —fallen vi
irreg be included; —mischen vt
Mehl mix in; vr mingle.

das [das] def art the; pron that;
— heißt that is.

Dasein [da:zam] nt -s (*Leben*) life;
(*Anwesenheit*) presence; (*Bestehen*) existence; d— vi *irreg* be
there.

daß [das] *cj* that.

dasselbe [das'zɛlbə] *art, pron* the same.

dastehen ['da:ʃteːən] *vi irreg* stand there.

Datenverarbeitung ['da:tənfɛr'arbaɪtʊŋ] *f* data processing.

datieren [da'ti:rən] *vt* date.

Dativ ['da:ti:f] *m* -s, -e dative.

Dattel ['datəl] *f* -, -n date.

Datum ['da:tʊm] *nt* -s, **Daten** date; (*pl: Angaben*) data *pl*; das heutige — today's date.

Dauer ['daʊər] *f* -, -n duration; (*gewisse Zeitspanne*) length; (*Bestand, Fortbestehen*) permanence; es war nur von kurzer — it didn't last long; auf die — in the long run; (*auf längere Zeit*) indefinitely; —auftrag *m* standing order; d—haft a lasting, durable; —haftigkeit *f* durability; —karte *f* season ticket; —lauf *m* long-distance run; d—n *vi* last; es hat sehr lang gedauert, bis er ... it took him a long time to ...; d—nd a constant; —regen *m* continuous rain; —welle *f* perm(anent wave); —wurst *f* German salami; —zustand *m* permanent condition.

Daumen ['daʊmən] *m* -s, - thumb; —lutscher *m* thumb-sucker.

Daune ['daʊnə] *f* -, -n down; —ndecke *f* down duvet or quilt.

davon [da'fɔn] *ad* of it; (*räumlich*) away; (*weg von*) from it; (*Grund*) because of it; das kommt —! that's what you get; — abgesehen apart from that; — sprechen/wissen talk/know of or about it; was habe ich —? what's the point?; —gehen *vi irreg* leave, go away; —kommen *vi irreg* escape; —laufen *vi irreg* run away; —tragen *vt irreg* carry off; *Verletzung* receive.

davor [da'fo:r] *ad* (*räumlich*) in front of it; (*zeitlich*) before (that); — warnen warn about it.

dazu [da'tsu:] *ad* legen, stellen by it; essen, singen with it; und — noch an in addition; ein Beispiel/seine Gedanken — one example for/his thoughts on this; wie kommt ich denn —? why should I?; — fähig sein to be capable of it; sich — äußern say sth on it; —gehören *vi* belong to it; —gehörig a appropriate; —kommen *vi irreg* (*Ereignisse*) happen too; (*an einen Ort*) come along; —mal [da:tsuma:l] *ad* in those days.

dazwischen [da'tsvɪʃən] *ad* in between; (*räumlich auch*) among (them); (*zusammen mit*) among them; der Unterschied — the difference between them; —kommen *vi irreg* (*hineingeraten*) get caught in it; es ist etwas —gekommen something cropped up; —reden *vi* (*unterbrechen*) interrupt; (*sich einmischen*) interfere; —treten *vi irreg* intervene.

Debatte [de'batə] *f* -, -n debate.

Deck [dɛk] *nt* -(e)s, -s or -e deck; an — gehen go on deck; —e *f* -, -n cover; (*Bett—*) blanket; (*Tisch—*) tablecloth; (*Zimmer—*) ceiling; unter einer — stecken be hand in glove; —el *m* -s, - lid; d—en *vt* cover; *vr* coincide; *vi* lay the table; —mantel *m*: unter dem —mantel von under the guise of; —name *m* assumed name; —ung *f* (*Schützen*) covering; (*Schutz*) cover; (*Sport*) defence; (*Übereinstimmen*) agreement; d—ungsgleich a congruent.

Defekt [de'fɛkt] *m* -(e)s, -e fault, defect; d— a faulty.

defensiv [defen'si:f] a defensive.

definieren [defi'ni:rən] vt define.

Definition [definitsi'o:n] f definition.

definitiv [defini'ti:f] a definite.

Defizit ['de:fitsit] nt -s, -e deficit.

deftig ['deftiç] a Essen large; Witz coarse.

Degen ['de:gən] m -s, - sword.

degenerieren [degene'ri:rən] vi degenerate.

degradieren [degra'di:rən] vt degrade.

Dehn- ['de:n] cpd: d—bar a elastic; (fig) Begriff loose; —barkeit f elasticity; looseness; d—en vtr stretch; —ung f stretching.

Deich [daiç] m -(e)s, -e dyke.

Deichsel ['daiksəl] f -, -n shaft; d—n vt (fig, col) wangle.

dein [dain] pron (D— in Briefen) your; —e(r,s) yours; —er pron gen of du of you; —erseits ad on your part; —esgleichen pron people like you; —etwegen, —etwillen ad (für dich) for your sake; (wegen dir) on your account; —ige pron: der/die/das —ige yours.

dekadent [deka'dent] a decadent.

Dekadenz f decadence.

Dekan [de'ka:n] m -s, -e dean.

Deklination [deklinatsi'o:n] f declension.

deklinieren [dekli'ni:rən] vt decline.

Dekolleté [dekol'te:] nt -s, -s low neckline.

Deko- [deko] cpd: —rateur[-ra'tö:r] m window dresser; —ration [-ratsi'o:n] f decoration; (in Laden) window dressing; d—rativ [-ra'ti:f] a decorative; d—rieren [-'ri:rən] vt decorate; Schaufenster dress.

Delegation [delegatsi'o:n] f delegation.

delikat [deli'ka:t] a (zart, heikel) delicate; (köstlich) delicious.

Delikatesse [delika'tesə] f -, -n delicacy; (pl: Feinkost) delicatessen pl; —ngeschäft nt delicatessen (shop).

Delikt [de'likt] nt -(e)s, -e (Jur) offence.

Delle ['delə] f -, -n (col) dent.

Delphin [del'fi:n] m -s, -e dolphin.

Delta ['delta] nt -s, -s delta.

dem [de:m] art der of der.

Demagoge [dema'go:gə] m -n, -n demagogue.

Demarkationslinie [demarkatsi'o:nzli:niə] f demarcation line.

dementieren [demen'ti:rən] vt deny.

dem- cpd: —gemäß, —nach ad accordingly; —nächst ad shortly.

Demokrat [demo'kra:t] m -en, -en democrat; —ie [-'ti:] f democracy; d—isch a democratic; d—isieren [-i'si:rən] vt democratize.

demolieren [demo'li:rən] vt demolish.

Demon- [demon] cpd: —strant(in f) [-'strant(in)] m demonstrator; —stration [-stratsi'o:n] f demonstration; d—strativ [-stra'ti:f] a demonstrative; Protest pointed; d—strieren [-'stri:rən] vi demonstrate.

Demoskopie [demosko'pi:] f public opinion research.

Demut ['de:mu:t] f - humility.

demütig ['de:my:tiç] a humble; —en ['de:my:tigən] vt humiliate; D—ung f humiliation.

demzufolge ['de:mtsu'folgə] ad accordingly.

den [de:n] art acc of der.

denen [de:nən] pron dat of diese.

Denk- [deŋk] cpd: —art f mentality; d—bar a conceivable; d—en *vti irreg* think; **—en** *nt* -s thinking; **—er** *m* -s, - thinker; **—fähigkeit** *f* intelligence; **d—faul** *a* lazy; **—fehler** *m* logical error; **—mal** *nt* -s, **—er** monument; **d—würdig** *a* memorable; **—zettel** *m*: jdm einen **—zettel verpassen** teach sb a lesson.

denn [dɛn] *cj* for; *ad* then; *(nach Komparativ)* than.

dennoch ['dɛn'nɔx] *cj* nevertheless.

Denunziant [denuntsi'ant] *m* informer.

deponieren [depo'ni:rən] *vt (Comm)* deposit.

Depot [de'po:] *nt* -s, -s warehouse; *(Bus—, Rail)* depot; *(Bank—)* strongroom.

Depression [depresi'o:n] *f* depression.

deprimieren [depri'mi:rən] *vt* depress.

der [de(:)r] *def art* the; *rel pron* that, which; *(jemand)* who; *demon pron* this one; **—art** *ad* so; *(solcher Art)* such; **—artig** *a* such, this sort of.

derb [dɛrp] *a* sturdy; *Kost* solid; *(grob)* coarse; **D—heit** *f* sturdiness; solidity; coarseness.

der- *cpd:* **'—gleichen** *pron* such; **'—jenige** *pron* he; she; it; *(rel)* the one (who); that (which); **'—maßen** *ad* to such an extent, so; **'—selbe** *art, pron* the same; **'—weil(en)** *ad* in the meantime; **'—zeitig** *a* present, current; *(damalig)* then.

des [dɛs] *art 'gen of* der.

Deserteur [dezɛr'tø:r] *m* deserter.

desertieren [dezɛr'ti:rən] *vi* desert.

desgleichen ['dɛs'glaiçən] *pron* the same.

deshalb ['dɛs'halp] *ad* therefore, that's why.

Desinfektion [dezɪnfɛktsi'o:n] *f* disinfection; **—smittel** *nt* disinfectant.

desinfizieren [dezɪnfi'tsi:rən] *vt* disinfect.

dessen ['dɛsən] *pron gen of* der, das; **—ungeachtet** *ad* nevertheless, regardless.

Dessert [dɛ'sɛ:r] *nt* -s, -s dessert.

Destillation [dɛstilatsi'o:n] *f* distillation.

destillieren [dɛsti'li:rən] *vt* distil.

desto ['dɛsto] *ad* all or so much the; **—** **besser** all the better.

deswegen ['dɛs've:gən] *cj* therefore, hence.

Detail [de'tai] *nt* -s, -s detail; **—lieren** [deta'ji:rən] *vt* specify, give details of.

Detektiv [detɛk'ti:f] *m* -s, -e detective.

Detektor [de'tɛktɔr] *m (Tech)* detector.

deut- ['dɔyt] *cpd:* **—en** *vt* interpret, explain; *vi* point *(auf +acc* to or at); **—lich** *a* clear; *Unterschied* distinct; **D—lichkeit** *f* clarity; distinctness; **D—ung** *f* interpretation.

Devise [de'vi:zə] *f* -, -n motto, device; *(pl: Fin)* foreign currency or exchange.

Dezember [de'tsɛmbər] *m* -(s), - December.

dezent [de'tsɛnt] *a* discreet.

dezimal [detsi'ma:l] *a* decimal; **D—bruch** *m* decimal (fraction); **D—system** *nt* decimal system.

Dia ['di:a] *nt* -s, -s *see* **Diapositiv**; **—betes** [dia'be:tɛs] *m* -, - *(Med)* diabetes; **—gnose** [dia'gno:zə] *f* -, -n diagnosis; **d—gonal** [diago'na:l] *a* diagonal; **—gonale** *f* -, -n diagonal.

Dialekt [dia'lɛkt] *m* -(e)s, -e
dialect; —ausdruck *m* dialect
expression/word; —frei *a* pure,
standard; d—isch *a* dialectal,
Logic dialectical.

Dialog [dia'lo:k] *m* -(e)s, -e
dialogue.

Diamant [dia'mant] *m* diamond.

Diapositiv [diapozi'ti:f] *nt* -s, -e
(*Phot*) slide, transparency.

Diät [di'ɛ:t] *f*,- diet; —en *pl* (*Pol*)
allowance. :

dich [dɪç] *pron acc of* du you;
yourself.

dicht [dɪçt] *a* dense; *Nebel* thick;
Gewebe close; (*undurchlässig*)
(water)tight; (*fig*) concise; *ad*: —
an/bei close to; —bevölkert *a*
densely *or* heavily populated; D—e
f -, -n density; thickness; closeness; (water)tightness; (*fig*) conciseness; —en *vt* (*dicht machen*)
make watertight; seal; (*Naut*)
caulk; *vti* (*Liter*) compose, write;
D—er(in *f*) *m* -s, - poet; (*Autor*)
writer; —erisch *a* poetical;
—halten *vi irreg* (*col*) keep mum;
D—ung *f* (*Tech*) washer; (*Aut*)
gasket; (*Gedichte*) poetry; (*Prosa*)
(piece of) writing.

dick [dɪk] *a* thick; (*fett*) fat; *durch*
— *und dünn* through thick and
thin; D—e *f* -, -n thickness;
fatness; —fellig *a* thickskinned;
—flüssig *a* viscous; D—icht *nt* -s,
-e thicket; D—kopf *m* mule;
D—milch *f* soured milk.

die [di:] *def art see* der.

Dieb(in *f*) [di:p/di:bɪn] *m* -(e)s, -e
thief; d—isch *a* thieving; (*col*)
immense; —stahl *m* -(e)s, ⁺e theft.

Diele ['di:lə] *f* -, -n (*Brett*) board;
(*Flur*) hall, lobby; (*Eis*—) ice-
cream parlour; (*Tanz*—) dance-hall.

dienen ['di:nən] *vi* serve (*jdm* sb).

Diener *m* -s, - servant; —in *f*
(maid)servant; —schaft *f* servants
pl.

Dienst [di:nst] *m* -(e)s, -e service;
außer — retired; — haben be on
duty; *der* öffentliche — the civil
service; —ag *m* Tuesday; d—ags
ad on Tuesdays; —bote *m* servant;
d—eifrig *a* zealous; d—frei *a* off
duty; —geheimnis *nt* professional
secret; —gespräch *nt* business
call; —grad *m* rank; d—habend *a*
Arzt on duty; d—lich *a* official;
—mädchen *nt* domestic servant;
—reise *f* business trip; —stelle *f*
office; d—tuend *a* on duty;
—vorschrift *f* service regulations
pl; —weg *m* official channels *pl*;
—zeit *f* office hours *pl*; (*Mil*)
period of service.

dies- [di:s] *cpd*: —bezüglich *a* *Frage*
on this matter; —e(r,s) [di:zə(r,z)]
pron this (one); —elbe [di:'zɛlbə]
pron, are the same; D—elöl *nt*
diesel oil; —ig *a* drizzly; —jährig
a this year's; —mal *ad* this time;
—seits *prep* +*gen* on this side;
D—seits *nt* - this life.

Dietrich ['di:trɪç] *m* -s, -e picklock.

differential [diferɛntsi'a:l] *a* differential; D—getriebe *nt* differential
gear; D—rechnung *f* differential
calculus.

differenzieren [diferɛn'tsi:rən] *vt*
make differences in, differentiate;
complex.

Dikt- [dɪkt] *cpd*: —aphon -a'fo:n]
nt dictaphone; —at [-'ta:t] *nt* -(e)s,
-e dictation; —ator [-'ta:tɔr] *m* dictator; d—atorisch [-a'to:rɪʃ] *a* dic-
tatorial; —atur [-a'tu:r] *f* dictatorship; d—ieren [-'ti:rən] *vt* dictate.

Dilemma [di'lɛma] *nt* -s, -s *or* -ta
dilemma.

Dilettant [dile'tant] *m* dilettante, amateur; **d—isch** *a* amateurish, dilettante.

Dimension [dimεnzi'o:n] *f* dimension.

Ding [dɪŋ] *nt* -(e)s, -e thing, object; **d—lich** *a* real, concrete; **—sbums** ['dɪŋksbums] *nt* - (col) thingummybob.

Diözese [diö'tse:zə] *f* -, -n diocese.

Diphtherie [dɪfte'ri:] *f* diphtheria.

Diplom [di'plo:m] *nt* -(e)s, -e diploma, certificate; **—at** [-'ma:t] *m* -en, -en diplomat; **—atie** [-a'ti:] *f* diplomacy; **d—atisch** [-'ma:tɪʃ] *a* diplomatic; **—ingenieur** *m* qualified engineer.

dir [di:r] *pron dat of* **du** (to) you.

direkt [di'rεkt] *a* direct; **D—or** *m* director; (*Sch*) principal, headmaster; **D—orium** [-'to:rium] *nt* board of directors; **D—übertragung** *f* live broadcast.

Dirigent [diri'gεnt] *m* conductor.

dirigieren [diri'gi:rən] *vt* direct; (*Mus*) conduct.

Dirne ['dɪrnə] *f* -, -n prostitute.

Diskont [dɪs'kɔnt] *m* -s, -e discount; **—satz** *m* rate of discount.

Diskothek [dɪsko'te:k] *f* -, -en disco(theque).

Diskrepanz [dɪskre'pants] *f* discrepancy.

diskret [dɪs'kre:t] *a* discreet; **D—ion** [-tsi'o:n] *f* discretion.

Diskussion [dɪskusi'o:n] *f* discussion; debate; **zur — stehen** be under discussion.

diskutabel [dɪsku'ta:bəl] *a* debatable.

diskutieren [dɪsku'ti:rən] *vti* discuss; debate.

Dissertation [dɪsεrtatsi'o:n] *f* dissertation, doctoral thesis.

Distanz [dɪs'tants] *f* distance.

Distel ['dɪstəl] *f* -, -n thistle.

Disziplin [dɪstsi'pli:n] *f* discipline.

divers [di'vεrs] *a* various.

Dividende [divi'dεndə] *f* -, **-n** dividend.

dividieren [divi'di:rən] *vt* divide (*durch* by).

doch [dɔx] *ad:* das ist nicht wahr! ~ —! that's not true! ~ yes it is!; nicht —! oh no!; er kam — noch he came after all; *cj* (*aber*) but; (*trotzdem*) all the same.

Docht [dɔxt] *m* -(e)s, -e wick.

Dock [dɔk] *nt* -s, -s *or* -e dock.

Dogge ['dɔgə] *f* -, -n bulldog.

Dogma ['dɔgma] *nt* -s, **men** dogma; **d—tisch** [dɔ'gma:tɪʃ] *a* dogmatic.

Doktor ['dɔktɔr] *m* -s, -en [-'to:rən] doctor; **—and** [-'rant] *m* -en, -en candidate for a doctorate; **—arbeit** *f* doctoral thesis; **—titel** *m* doctorate.

Dokument [doku'mεnt] *nt* document; **—arbericht** [-'ta:rbərɪçt] *m* documentary; **—arfilm** *m* documentary (film); **d—arisch** *a* documentary.

dolmetschen ['dɔlmεtʃən] *vti* interpret.

Dolmetscher(in *f*) *m* -s, - interpreter.

Dom [do:m] *m* -(e)s, -e cathedral.

dominieren [domi'ni:rən] *vt* dominate; *vi* predominate.

Dompfaff ['do:mpfaf] *m* bullfinch.

Dompteur [dɔmp'tö:r] *m*, **Dompteuse** [dɔmp'tö:zə] *f* (*Zirkus*) trainer.

Donner ['dɔnər] *m* -s, - thunder; **d—n** *vi impers* thunder; **—stag** *m* Thursday; **—wetter** *nt* thunderstorm; *(fig)* dressing-down; *interj* good heavens!

doof [do:f] *a (col)* daft, stupid.

Doppel ['dɔpəl] *nt* -s, - duplicate; *(Sport)* doubles; **—bett** *nt* double bed; **—fenster** *nt* double glazing; **—gänger** *m* -s, - double; **—punkt** *m* colon; **—stecker** *m* two-way adaptor; **d—t** a double; **in d—ter Ausführung** in duplicate; **—verdiener** *pl* two-income family; **—zentner** *m* 100 kilograms; **—zimmer** *nt* double room.

Dorf [dɔrf] *nt* -(e)s, ⁻er village; **—bewohner** *m* villager.

Dorn [dɔrn] *m* -(e)s, -en *(Bot)* thorn; *pl* -e *(Schnallen—)* tongue, pin; **d—ig** a thorny; **—röschen** *nt* Sleeping Beauty.

dörren ['dœrən] *vt* dry.

Dörrobst ['dœro:pst] *nt* dried fruit.

Dorsch [dɔrʃ] *m* -(e)s, -e cod.

dort [dɔrt] *ad* there; **— drüben** over there; **—her** from there; **—hin** *(to)* there; **—ig** a of that place; **in that town.**

Dose ['do:zə] *f* -, -n box; *(Blech—)* tin, can; **—nöffner** *m* tin or can opener.

dösen ['dø:zən] *vi (col)* doze.

Dosis ['do:zɪs] *f* -, Dosen dose.

Dotter ['dɔtər] *m* -s, - egg yolk.

Dozent [do'tsɛnt] *m* university lecturer.

Drache ['draxə] *m* -n, -n *(Tier)* dragon; **—n** *m* -s, - kite.

Draht [dra:t] *m* -(e)s, ⁻e wire; **auf — sein** to be on the ball; **—gitter** *nt* wire grating; **—seil** *nt* cable; **—seilbahn** *f* cable railway, funicular; **—zange** *f* pliers *pl*.

drall [dral] *a* strapping; **Frau** buxom.

Drama ['dra:ma] *nt* -s, Dramen drama, play; **—tiker** [-'ma:tikər] *m* -s, - dramatist; **d—tisch** [-'ma:tɪʃ] a dramatic.

dran [dran] *ad (col)* see daran.

Drang [draŋ] *m* -(e)s, ⁻e *(Trieb)* impulse, urge, desire *(nach* for); *(Druck)* pressure.

drängeln ['drɛŋəln] *vti* push, jostle.

drängen ['drɛŋən] *vt (schieben)* push, press; *(antreiben)* urge; *vi (eilig sein)* be urgent; *(Zeit)* press; **auf etw** *(acc)* **—** press for sth.

drastisch ['drastɪʃ] a drastic.

drauf [drauf] *ad (col)* see darauf; **D—gänger** *m* -s, - daredevil.

draußen ['drausən] *ad* outside, out-of-doors.

Dreck [drɛk] *m* -(e)s mud, dirt; **d—ig** a dirty, filthy.

Dreh- ['dre:] *cpd:* **—achse** *f* axis of rotation; **—arbeiten** *pl (Cine)* shooting; **—bank** *f* lathe; **d—bar** a revolving; **—buch** *nt (Cine)* script; *Film* shooting; **—en** *vti* turn, rotate; *Zigaretten* roll; *Film* shoot; **vr turn;** *(handeln von)* be *(um* about); **—orgel** *f* barrel organ; **—tür** *f* revolving door; **—ung** *f (Rotation)* rotation; *(Um—, Wendung)* turn; **—wurm** *m (col)* **den —wurm haben/bekommen** be/become dizzy; **—zahl** *f* rate of revolutions; **—zahlmesser** *m* rev(olution) counter.

drei [drai] *num* three; **D—eck** *nt* triangle; **—eckig** a triangular; **—einhalb** *num* three and a half; **D—einigkeit** *f* [-'amɪçkait] *f* ... ; **D—faltigkeit** *f*-'faltɪçkait] *f* Trinity; **—erlei** a *inv* of three kinds; **—fach** a,*ad* triple, treble; **—hundert** *num* three hundred; **D—königsfest** *nt* Epiphany; **—mal** *ad* three times, thrice; **—malig** a three times..

dreinreden ['draɪnreːdən] vi: jdm — (dazwischenreden) interrupt sb; (sich einmischen) interfere with sb.

dreißig ['draɪsɪç] num thirty.

dreist [draɪst] a bold, audacious; D—igkeit f boldness, audacity.

drei- cpd: —viertel num three-quarters; D—viertelstunde f three-quarters of an hour; —zehn num thirteen.

dreschen ['drɛʃən] vt irreg thresh.

dressieren [drɛ'siːrən] vt train.

Drill- ['drɪl] cpd: —bohrer m light drill; d—en vt (bohren) drill, bore; (Mil) drill; (fig) train; —ing m triplet.

drin [drɪn] ad (col) see darin.

dringen ['drɪŋən] vi irreg (Wasser, Licht, Kälte) penetrate (durch through); in +acc into); auf etw (acc) — insist on sth; in jdn — entreat sb.

dringend ['drɪŋənt], **dringlich** ['drɪŋlɪç] a urgent.

Dringlichkeit f urgency.

drinnen ['drɪnən] ad inside, indoors.

dritte(r,s) ['drɪtə(r,z)] a third; D—l nt -s, - third; —ns ad thirdly.

droben ['droːbən] ad above, up there.

Droge ['droːgə] f -, -n drug; d—nabhängig a addicted to drugs; —rie [-'riː] f chemist's shop.

Drogist [dro'gɪst] m pharmacist, chemist.

drohen ['droːən] vi threaten (jdm sb).

dröhnen ['dʀøːnən] vi (Motor) roar; (Stimme, Musik) ring, resound.

Drohung ['droːʊŋ] f threat.

drollig ['drɔlɪç] a droll.

Droschke ['drɔʃkə] f -, -n cab; —nkutscher m cabman.

Drossel ['drɔsəl] f -, -n thrush.

drüben ['dryːbən] ad over there, on the other side.

drüber ['dryːbər] ad (col) see darüber.

Druck [drʊk] m -(e)s, -e (Phys, Zwang) pressure; (Print) (Vorgang) printing; (Produkt) print; (fig: Belastung) burden, weight; —buchstabe m block letter.

Drück- ['drʏk] cpd: —eberger m -s, - shirker, dodger; d—en vti Knopf, Hand press; (zu eng sein) pinch; (fig) Preise keep down; (fig: belasten) oppress, weigh down; jdm etw in die Hand d—en press sth into sb's hand; vr: sich vor etw (dat) d—en get out of (doing) sth; d—end a oppressive; —er m -s, - button; (Tür—) handle; (Gewehr—) trigger.

Druck- cpd: —er m -s, - printer; —e'rei f printing works, press; —erschwärze f printer's ink; —fehler m misprint; —knopf m press stud, snap fastener; —mittel nt leverage; —sache f printed matter; —schrift f block or printed letters pl.

drunten ['drʊntən] ad below, down there.

Drüse ['dryːzə] f -, -n gland.

Dschungel ['dʒʊŋəl] m -s, - jungle.

du [duː] pron (D— in Briefen) you.

ducken ['dʊkən] vt Kopf, Person duck; (fig) take down a peg or two; vr duck.

Duckmäuser ['dʊkmɔʏzər] m -s, - yes-man.

Dudelsack ['duːdəlzak] m bagpipes pl.

Duell [du'ɛl] nt -s, -e duel.

Duett [du'ɛt] nt -(e)s, -e duet.

Duft [dʊft] m -(e)s, ⁼e scent, odour; d—en vi smell, be fragrant;

d—ig a *Stoff, Kleid* delicate, diaphanous; *Muster* fine.

duld- ['duld] *cpd:* **—en** *vti* suffer; (*zulassen*) tolerate; **—sam** a tolerant.

dumm [dum] a stupid; das wird mir zu — that's just too much; der D—e sein be the loser; **—dreist** a impudent; **—erweise** *ad* stupidly; **D—heit** *f* stupidity; (*Tat*) blunder, stupid mistake; **D—kopf** *m* blockhead.

dumpf [dumpf] a *Ton* hollow, dull; *Luft* close; *Erinnerung, Schmerz* vague; **D—heit** *f* hollowness, dullness; closeness; vagueness; **—ig** a musty.

Düne ['dy:nə] *f* -, -n dune.

Dung [dun] *m* -(e)s *see* Dünger.

düngen ['dyŋən] *vt* manure.

Dünger *m* -s, - dung, manure; (*künstlich*) fertilizer.

dunkel ['dunkəl] a dark; *Stimme* deep; *Ahnung* vague; (*rätselhaft*) obscure; (*verdächtig*) dubious, shady; im **—n tappen** (*fig*) grope in the dark.

Dünkel ['dyŋkəl] *m* -s self-conceit; **d—haft** a conceited.

Dunkel- *cpd:* **—heit** *f* darkness; (*fig*) obscurity; **—kammer** *f* (*Phot*) dark room; **d—n** *vi impers* grow dark; **—ziffer** *f* estimated number of unnotified cases.

dünn [dyn] a thin; **—flüssig** a watery, thin; **—gesät** a scarce; **D—heit** *f* thinness.

Dunst [dunst] *m* -es, ꞏe vapour; (*Wetter*) haze.

dünsten ['dynstən] *vt* ꞏsteam.

dunstig [dunstiç] a vaporous; *Wetter* hazy, misty.

Duplikat [dupli'ka:t] *nt* -(e)s, -e duplicate.

Dur [du:r] *nt* -, - (*Mus*) major.

durch [durç] *prep* +*acc* through; (*Mittel, Ursache*) by; (*Zeit*) during; den Sommer — during the summer; 8 Uhr — past 8 o'clock; — und — completely; **—arbeiten** *vti* work through; *vr* work one's way through; **—'aus** *ad* completely; (*unbedingt*) definitely; **—beißen** *irreg vt* bite through; *vr* (*fig*) battle on; **—blättern** *vt* leaf through.

Durchblick ['durçblik] *m* view; (*fig*) comprehension; **d—en** *vi* look through; (*col: verstehen*) understand (*bei etw* sth); etw d—en lassen (*fig*) hint at sth.

durch'bohren *vt insep* bore through, pierce.

durchbrechen ['durçbreçən] *vti irreg* break; [durç'breçən] *vt irreg insep Schranken* break through; *Schallmauer* break; *Gewohnheit* break free from.

durch- ['durç] *cpd:* **—brennen** *vi irreg* (*Draht, Sicherung*) burn through; (*col*) run away; **—bringen** *irreg vt* get through; *Geld* squander; *vr* make a living.

Durchbruch ['durçbrux] *m* (*Öffnung*) opening; (*Mil*) breach; (*von Gefühlen etc*) eruption; (*der Zähne*) cutting; (*fig*) breakthrough; **zum — kommen** break through.

durch- *cpd:* **—diskutieren** *vt* talk over, discuss; **—drängen** *vr* force one's way through; **—drehen** *vt Fleisch* mince; *vi* (*col*) crack up.

durchdringen ['durçdriŋən] *vi irreg* penetrate, get through; mit etw — get one's way with sth;

[dʊrç'drɪnən] vt irreg insep penetrate.

durcheinander [dʊrç'aɪ'nandər] ad in a mess, in confusion; (col: verwirrt) confused; — trinken mix one's drinks; D— nt -s (Verwirrung) confusion; (Unordnung) mess; —bringen vt irreg mess up; (verwirren) confuse; —reden vi talk at the same time.

durch- [dʊrç] cpd: D—fahrt f transit; (Verkehr) thoroughfare; D—fall m (Med) diarrhoea; —fallen vi irreg fall through; (in Prüfung) fail; —finden vr irreg find one's way through.

durch'forschen vt insep explore.

durch- [dʊrç] cpd: —fressen vr irreg eat through; —fragen vr find one's way by asking.

durchführ- [dʊrçfyːr] cpd: —bar a feasible, practicable; —en vt carry out; D—ung f execution, performance.

Durchgang [dʊrçgaŋ] m passage(way); (bei Produktion, Versuch) run; (Sport) round; (bei Wahl) ballot; — verboten no thoroughfare; —handel m transit trade; —slager nt transit camp; —sstadium nt transitory stage; —sverkehr m through traffic.

durchgefroren [dʊrçgefroːrən] a See completely frozen; Mensch frozen stiff.

durchgehen [dʊrçgeːən] irreg vt (behandeln) go over; vi go through; (ausreißen: Pferd) break loose; (Mensch) run away; mein Temperament ging mit mir durch my temper got the better of me; jdm etw — lassen let sb get away with sth; —d a Zug through; Öffnungszeiten continuous.

durch- [dʊrç] cpd: —greifen vi irreg take strong action; —halten irreg vi last out; vt keep up; —hecheln vt (col) gossip about; —kommen vi irreg get through; (überleben) pull through.

durch'kreuzen vt insep thwart, frustrate.

durch [dʊrç] cpd: —lassen vt irreg Person let through; Wasser let in; —lässig a leaky; D—lauf(wasser)-erhitzer m -s, - (hot water) geyser.

durch- cpd: —'leben vt insep live or go through, experience; '—lesen vt irreg read through; —'leuchten vt insep X-ray; —löchern [-'lœçərn] vt insep perforate; (mit Löchern) punch holes in; (mit Kugeln) riddle; '—machen vt go through; die Nacht —machen make a night of it.

Durch- [dʊrç] cpd: —marsch m march through; —messer m -s, - diameter.

durch'nässen vt insep soak (through).

durch- [dʊrç] cpd: —nehmen vt irreg go over; —numerieren vt number consecutively; —pausen vt trace; —peitschen vt (lit) whip soundly; (fig) Gesetzentwurf, Reform force through.

durchqueren [dʊrç'kveːrən] vt insep cross.

durch- [dʊrç] cpd: D—reiche f -, -n (serving) hatch; D—reise f transit; auf der D—reise passing through; Güter in transit; —ringen vr irreg reach after a long struggle; —rosten vi rust through.

durchs [dʊrçs] = durch das.

Durchsage [dʊrçzaːgə] f -, -n intercom or radio announcement.

durchschauen [dʊrç'ʃaʊən] vi (lit) look or see through; [dʊrç'ʃaʊən] vt insep Person, Lüge see through.

durchscheinen ['durçʃaɪnən] vi irreg shine through; —d a translucent.

Durchschlag ['durçʃlaːk] m (Doppel) carbon copy; (Sieb) strainer; d—en irreg vt (entzweischlagen) split (in two); (sieben) sieve; vi (zum Vorschein kommen) emerge, come out; vr get by; d—end a resounding.

durch ['durç] cpd: —schlüpfen vi slip through; —schneiden vt irreg cut through.

Durchschnitt ['durçʃnɪt] m (Mittelwert) average; über/unter dem — above/below average; im — on average; d—lich a average; ad on average; —sgeschwindigkeit f average speed; —smensch m average man, man in the street; —swert m average.

durch- cpd: 'D—schrift f copy; —'schwimmen vt irreg insep swim across; .'—sehen vt irreg look through.

durchsetzen ['durçzɛtsən] vt enforce; seinen Kopf — get one's own way; vr (Erfolg haben) succeed; (sich behaupten) get one's way; [durç'zɛtsən] vt insep mix.

Durchsicht ['durçzɪçt] f looking through, checking; d—ig a transparent; —igkeit f transparence.

durch- cpd: '—sickern vi seep through; (fig) leak out; '—sieben vt sieve; —'sprechen vt irreg talk over; —'stehen vt irreg live through; —stöbern [-'ʃtøːbərn] vt insep ransack, search through; '—streichen vt irreg cross out; —'suchen vt insep search; D—'suchung f search; —'tränken vt insep soak; —trieben [-'triːbən] a cunning, wily; —'wachsen a (lit)

Speck streaky; (fig: mittelmäßig) so-so.

durch- ['durç] cpd: —weg ad throughout, completely; —zählen vt count; vi count off; —ziehen irreg vt Faden draw through; vi pass through.

durch- cpd: —'zucken vt insep shoot or flash through; 'D—zug m (Luft) draught; (von Truppen, Vögeln) passage; '—zwängen vtr squeeze or force through.

dürfen ['dyrfən] vi irreg be allowed; darf ich? may I?; es darf geraucht werden you may smoke; was darf es sein? what can I do for you?; das darf nicht geschehen that must not happen; das — Sie mir glauben you can believe me; es dürfte Ihnen bekannt sein, daß ... as you will probably know ...

dürftig ['dyrftɪç] a (ärmlich) needy, poor; (unzulänglich) inadequate.

dürr [dyr] a dried-up; Land arid; (mager) skinny, gaunt; D—e f -, -n aridity; (Zeit) drought; (Magerkeit) skinniness.

Durst [durst] m -(e)s thirst; — haben be thirsty; d—ig a thirsty.

Dusche ['duʃə] f -, -n shower; d—n vir have a shower.

Düse ['dyːzə] f -, -n nozzle; (Flugzeug—) jet; —nantrieb m jet propulsion; —nflugzeug m jet (plane); —njäger m jet fighter.

Dussel ['dusəl] m -s, - (col) twit.

düster ['dyːstər] a dark; Gedanken, Zukunft gloomy; D—keit f darkness, gloom; gloominess.

Dutzend ['dutsənt] nt -s, -e dozen; d—(e)mal ad a dozen times; —mensch m man in the street; d—weise ad by the dozen.

duzen ['duːtsən] vtr use the familiar

form of address or 'du' (*jdn to or*
with sb).
Dynamik [dy'na:mɪk] *f* (*Phys*) dynamics; (*fig: Schwung*) momentum; (*von Mensch*) dynamism.
dynamisch [dy'na:mɪʃ] *a* (*lit, fig*)

dynamic.
Dynamit [dyna'mi:t] *nt* -s dynamite.
Dynamo [dy'na:mo] *m* -s, -s dynamo.
D-Zug ['de:tsu:k] *m* through train.

E

E, e [e:] *nt* E, e.
Ebbe ['ɛbə] *f* -, -n low tide.
eben ['e:bən] *a* level; . (*glatt*)
smooth; *ad* just; (*bestätigend*)
exactly; — **deswegen** just because
of that; —**bürtig** *a*: **jdm** —**bürtig**
sein to be sb's peer; **E—e** *f* -, -n plain;
—**erdig** *a* at ground level; —**falls**
ad likewise; **E—heit** *f* levelness;
smoothness; —**so** *ad* just as;
—**sogut** *ad* just as well; —**sooft** *ad*
just as often; —**soviel** *ad* just as
much; —**soweit** *ad* just as far;
—**sowenig** *ad* just as little.
Eber ['e:bar] *m* -s, - boar; —**esche**
f mountain ash, rowan.
ebnen ['e:bnən] *vt* level.
Echo ['ɛço] *nt* -s, -s echo.
echt [ɛçt] *a* genuine; (*typisch*)
typical; **E—heit** *f* genuineness.
Eck- ['ɛk] *cpd*: —**ball** *m* corner
(kick); —**e** *f* -, -n corner; (*Math*)
angle; —**ig** *a* angular; —**zahn** *m*
eye tooth.
edel ['e:dəl] *a* noble; **E—metall** *nt*
rare metal; **E—stein** *m* precious
stone.
Efeu ['e:fɔy] *m* -s ivy.
Effekt- [ɛ'fɛkt] *cpd*: —**en** *pl* stocks
pl; —**enbörse** *f* Stock Exchange;
—**hasche'rei** *f* sensationalism;
e—iv [-'ti:f] *a* effective, actual.
egal [e'ga:l] *a* all the same.

Ego- [ego] *cpd*: —**ismus** [-'ɪsmʊs]
m selfishness, egoism; —**ist** [-'ɪst]
m egoist; **e—istisch** *a* selfish, egoistic; **e—zentrisch** [-'tsɛntrɪʃ] *a* egocentric, self-centred.
Ehe [e:ə] *f* -, -n marriage; **e—** *cf*
before; —**brecher** *m* -s, - adulterer;
—**brecherin** *f* adulteress; —**bruch**
m adultery; —**frau** *f* married
woman; wife; —**leute** *pl* married
people *pl*; **e—lich** *a* matrimonial;
Kind legitimate; **e—malig** *a* former; **e—mals** *ad* formerly; —**mann**
m married man; husband; —**paar**
nt married couple.
eher ['e:ar] *ad* (*früher*) sooner;
(*lieber*) rather, sooner; (*mehr*)
more.
Ehe- *cpd*: —**ring** *m* wedding ring;
—**scheidung** *f* divorce; —**schließung** *f* marriage.
eheste(r,s) ['e:astə(r,z)] *a* (*frü-
heste*) first, earliest; **am —n**
(*liebsten*) soonest; (*meist*) most;
(*wahrscheinlichst*) most probably.
Ehr- ['e:r] *cpd*: **e—bar** *a*
honourable, respectable; **—e** *f* -, -n
honour; **e—en** *vt* honour; —**engast**
m guest of honour; **e—enhaft** *a*
honourable; —**enmann** *m* man of
honour; —**enmitglied** *nt* honorary
member; —**enplatz** *m* place of
honour; —**enrechte** *pl* civic rights
pl; **e—enrührig** *a* defamatory;

—enrunde f lap of honour; —en-
sache f point of honour; —envoll
a honourable; —enwort nt word of
honour; e—erbietig a respectful;
—furcht f awe, deep respect;
—gefühl nt sense of honour; —geiz
m ambition; e—geizig a ambitious;
e—lich a honest; —lichkeit f
honesty; e—los a dishonourable;
—ung f honour(ing); e—würdig a
venerable.

Ei [ai] nt -(e)s, -er egg; e— interj
well, well; (beschwichtigend) now,
now.

Eich- ['aiç] cpd: —amt nt Office of
Weights and Measures; —e f -, -n
oak (tree); —el f -, -n acorn;
(Cards) club; e—en vt standardize; —hörnchen nt squirrel; —maß
nt standard; —ung f standardiza-
tion.

Eid ['ait] m -(e)s, -e oath; —echse
['aidɛksə] f -, -n lizard; e—esstatt-
liche Erklärung affidavit;
—genosse m Swiss; e—lich a
(sworn) upon oath.

Ei- cpd: —dotter nt egg yolk;
—erbecher m eggcup; —erkuchen
m omelette; pancake; —erschale f
eggshell; —erstock m ovary;
—eruhr f egg timer.

Eifer ['aifər] m -s zeal, enthusiasm;
—sucht f jealousy; e—süchtig a
jealous (auf +acc of).

eifrig ['aifriç] a zealous, enthusiastic.

Eigelb ['aigɛlp] nt -(e)s, - egg yolk.

eigen ['aigən] a own; (—artig)
peculiar; mit der/dem ihm —en ...
with that ... peculiar to him; sich
(dat) etw zu — machen make sth
one's own; E—art f peculiarity;
characteristic; —artig a peculiar;
E—bedarf m one's own require-
ments pl; E—gewicht nt dead

weight; —händig a with one's own
hand; E—heim nt owner-occupied
house; E—heit f peculiarity;
E—lob nt self-praise; —mächtig a
high-handed; E—name m proper
name; —s ad expressly, on purpose; E—schaft f quality, property,
attribute; E—schaftswort nt adjective; E—sinn m obstinacy;
—sinnig a obstinate; —tlich a
actual, real; ad actually, really;
E—tor nt own goal; E—tum nt
property; E—tümer(in f) m -s,
owner, proprietor; —tümlich a
peculiar; E—tümlichkeit f peculiarity; E—tumswohnung f freehold
flat.

eignen ['aignən] vr be suited.
Eignung f suitability.

Eil- ['ail] cpd: —bote m courier;
—brief m express letter; —e f
haste; es hat keine —e there's no
hurry; e—en vi (Mensch) hurry;
(dringend sein) be urgent; —ends
ad hastily; e—fertig a eager, soli-
citous; —gut nt express goods pl,
fast freight (US); e—ig a hasty,
hurried; (dringlich) urgent; es
e—ig haben be in a hurry; —zug
m semi-fast train, limited stop train.

Eimer ['aimər] m -s, - bucket, pail.

ein(e) [ain(ə)] num one; indef art
a, an; ad: nicht — noch aus wissen
not know what to do; —e(r,s) pron
one; (jemand) someone.

einander [ai'nandər] pron one
another, each other.

einarbeiten [ainarbaitən] vr familiarize o.s. (in +acc with).

einarmig ['ain'armiç] a one-armed.

einatmen ['ain:atmən] vti inhale,
breathe in.

einäugig [ain'ɔygiç] a one-eyed.

Einbahnstraße ['ainba:nʃtra:sə] f
one-way street.

Einband ['aınbant] *m* binding, cover.

einbändig ['aınbɛndiç] *a* one-volume.

einbau- ['aınbau] *cpd:* **—en** *vt* build in; *Motor* install, fit; **E—möbel** *pl* built-in furniture.

einbe- ['aınbə] *cpd:* **—griffen** *a* included, inclusive; **—rufen** *vt irreg* convene; (*Mil*) call up; **E—rufung** *f* convocation; call-up.

einbett- ['aınbɛt] *cpd:* **—en** *vt* embed; **E—zimmer** *nt* single room.

einbeziehen ['aınbətsi:ən] *vt irreg* include.

einbiegen ['aınbi:gən] *vi irreg* turn.

einbilden ['aınbıldən] *vt:* sich (*dat*) etw **—** imagine sth.

Einbildung *f* imagination; (*Dünkel*) conceit; **—skraft** *f* imagination.

einbinden ['aınbındən] *vt irreg* bind (up).

einblenden ['aınblɛndən] *vt* fade in.

einbleuen ['aınbløyən] *vt* (*col*) jdm etw **—** hammer sth into sb.

Einblick ['aınblık] *m* insight.

einbrechen ['aınbrɛçən] *vi irreg* (*in Haus*) break in; (*in Land etc*) invade; (*Nacht*) fall; (*Winter*) set in; (*durchbrechen*) break.

Einbrecher *m* **-s**, **-** burglar.

einbringen ['aınbrıŋən] *vt irreg* bring in; *Geld, Vorteil* yield; (*mitbringen*) contribute.

Einbruch ['aınbrux] *m* (*Haus—*) break-in, burglary; (*Eindringen*) invasion; (*des Winters*) onset; (*Durchbrechen*) break; (*Met*) approach; (*Mil*) penetration; **—** *der Nacht* nightfall; **e—ssicher** *a* burglar-proof.

einbürgern ['aınbʏrgərn] *vt* naturalize; *vr* become adopted; *das hat* sich so eingebürgert that's become a custom.

Einbuße ['aınbu:sə] *f* loss, forfeiture.

einbüßen ['aınby:sən] *vt* lose, forfeit.

eindecken ['aındɛkən] *vr* lay in stocks (*mit* of).

eindeutig ['aındɔytıç] *a* unequivocal.

eindring- ['aındrıŋ] *cpd:* **—en** *vi irreg* (*in* +*acc*) force one's way in(to); (*in Haus*) break in(to); (*in Land*) invade; (*Gas, Wasser*) penetrate; (*mit Bitten*) pester (*auf jdn* sb); **—lich** *a* forcible, urgent; **E—ling** *m* intruder.

Eindruck ['aındrʊk] *m* impression; **e—sfähig** *a* impressionable; **e—svoll** *a* impressive.

eindrücken ['aındrʏkən] *vt* press in.

eineiig ['aın'aıç] *a* Zwillinge identical.

eineinhalb ['aın'aın'halp] *num* one and a half.

einengen ['aın'ɛŋən] *vt* confine, restrict.

einer- ['aınər] *cpd:* 'E—'lei *nt* **-s** sameness; **—lei** *a* (*gleichartig*) the same kind of; *es ist mir* **—lei** it is all the same to me; **—seits** *ad* on one hand.

einfach ['aınfax] *a* simple; (*nicht mehrfach*) single; *ad* simply; **E—heit** *f* simplicity.

einfädeln ['aınfɛːdəln] *vt* Nadel thread; (*fig*) contrive.

einfahren ['aınfaːrən] *irreg vt* bring in; *Barriere* knock down; *Auto* run in; *vi* (*Zug*) pull in; (*Min*) go down.

Einfahrt *f* (*Vorgang*) driving in; pulling in; (*Min*) descent; (*Ort*) entrance.

Einfall ['aɪnfal] m (Idee) idea, notion; (Licht—) incidence; (Mil) raid; e—en vi irreg (Licht) fall; (Mil) raid; (einstimmen) join in (in +acc with); (einstürzen) fall in, collapse; etw fällt jdm ein sth occurs to sb; das fällt mir gar nicht ein I wouldn't dream of it; sich (dat) etwas e—en lassen have a good idea.

einfältig ['aɪnfɛltɪç] a simple(-minded).

Einfamilienhaus [aɪnfa'miːlɪənhaus] nt detached house.

einfangen ['aɪnfaŋən] vt irreg catch.

einfarbig ['aɪnfarbɪç] a all one colour; Stoff etc self-coloured.

einfass- ['aɪnfas] cpd: e—en vt set; Beet enclose; Stoff edge, border; Bier barrel; E—ung f setting; enclosure; barrelling.

einfetten ['aɪnfɛtən] vt grease.

einfinden ['aɪnfɪndən] vr irreg come, turn up.

einfliegen ['aɪnfliːgən] vt irreg fly in.

einfließen ['aɪnfliːsən] vi irreg flow in.

einflößen ['aɪnfløːsən] vt: jdm etw — (lit) give sb sth; (fig) instil sth in sb.

Einfluß ['aɪnflus] m influence; —bereich m sphere of influence; e—reich a influential.

einförmig ['aɪnfœrmɪç] a uniform; E—keit f uniformity.

einfrieren ['aɪnfriːrən] irreg vi freeze (in); vt freeze.

einfügen ['aɪnfyːgən] vt fit in; (zusätzlich) add.

Einfuhr ['aɪnfuːr] f — import; —artikel m imported article.

einführ- ['aɪnfyːr] cpd: —en vt bring in; Mensch, Sitten introduce;

Ware import; E—ung f introduction; E—ungspreis m introductory price.

Eingabe ['aɪngaːbə] f petition; (Daten—) input.

Eingang ['aɪngaŋ] m entrance; (Comm: Ankunft) arrival; (Sendung) post; e—s ad, prep +gen at the outset (of); —sbestätigung f acknowledgement of receipt; —shalle f entrance hall.

eingeben ['aɪngeːbən] vt irreg Arznei give; Daten etc feed; Gedanken inspire.

eingebildet ['aɪngəbɪldət] a imaginary; (eitel) conceited.

Eingeborene(r) ['aɪngəboːrənə(r)] mf native.

Eingebung f inspiration.

einge- ['aɪngə] cpd: —denk prep +gen bearing in mind; —fallen a Gesicht gaunt; —fleischt a inveterate; —fleischter Junggeselle confirmed bachelor; —froren a frozen.

eingehen ['aɪngeːən] irreg vi (Aufnahme finden) come in; (verständlich sein) be comprehensible (jdm to sb); (Sendung, Geld) be received; (Tier, Pflanze) die; (Firma) fold; (schrumpfen) shrink; auf etw (acc) — go into sth; auf jdn — respond to sb; vt enter into; Wette make; —d a exhaustive, thorough.

einge- ['aɪngə] cpd: E—machte(s) nt preserves pl; —meinden vt incorporate; —nommen a (von) fond (of), partial (to); (gegen) prejudiced; —schrieben a registered; —sessen a old-established; —spielt a: aufeinander —spielt sein be in tune with each other; E—ständnis nt -ses, -se admission, confession; —stehen vt irreg confess; —tragen

a (*Comm*) registered; E—weide *nt*
-s, - innards *pl*, intestines *pl*;
E—weihte(r) *mf* initiate; —wöhnen
vt accustom.

eingießen ['aıngi:sən] *vt irreg* pour
(out).

eingleisig ['aınglaızıç] *a* single-
track.

eingraben ['aıngra:bən] *irreg vt* dig
in; *vr* dig o.s. in.

eingreifen ['aıngraıfən] *vi irreg* Intervene, interfere; (*Zahnrad*) mesh.
Eingriff ['aıngrıf] *m* intervention,
interference; (*Operation*) operation.

einhaken ['aınha:kən] *vt* hook in;
vr: sich bei jdm — link arms with
sb; *vi* (*sich einmischen*) intervene.
Einhalt ['aınhalt] *m*: — gebieten
(+*dat*) put a stop to; **e—en** *irreg*
vt Regel keep; *vi* stop.

einhändig ['aınhendıç] *a* one-
handed; —en' [-dıgən] *vt* hand in.

einhängen ['aınheŋən] *vt* hang;
Telefon (*auch vi*) hang up; **sich bei**
jdm — link arms with sb.

einheim- ['aınhaım] *cpd*: —isch *a*
native; —sen *vt* (*col*) bring home.
Einheit ['aınhaıt] *f* unity; (*Maß,
Mil*) unit; **e—lich** *a* uniform;
—spreis *m* uniform price.

einhellig ['aınhelıç] *a,ad* unanimous.

einholen ['aınho:lən] *vt Tau* haul
in; *Fahne, Segel* lower; (*Vorsprung aufholen*) catch up with;
Verspätung make up; *Rat,
Erlaubnis* ask; *vi* (*einkaufen*) buy,
shop.

Einhorn ['aınhorn] *nt* unicorn.

einhüllen ['aınhylən] *vt* wrap up.

einig ['aınıç] *a* (*vereint*) united; **sich**
(*dat*) — sein be in agreement; —
werden agree; —e ['aınıgə] *pl*
some; (*mehrere*) several; —e(r,s)
a some; —**emal** *ad* a few times;

—en *vt* unite; *vr* agree (*auf +acc*
on); —**ermaßen** *ad* somewhat;
(*leidlich*) reasonably; —es *pron*
something; —**gehen** *vi irreg* agree;
E—**keit** *f* unity; (*Übereinstimmung*) agreement; E—**ung** *f*
agreement; (*Vereinigung*) unification.

einimpfen ['aınımpfən] *vt* inoculate
(*jdm etw sb* with sth); (*fig*)
impress (*jdm etw sb* upon sb).

einjährig ['aınje:rıç] *a* of or for one
year; (*Alter*) one-year-old; *Pflanze*
annual.

einkalkulieren ['aınkalkuli:rən] *vt*
take into account, allow for.

Einkauf ['aınkaof] *m* purchase;
e—en *vt* buy; *vi* go shopping;
—**summel** *m* shopping spree;
—**snetz** *nt* string bag; —**spreis** *m*
cost price.

Einklang ['aınklaŋ] *m* harmony.

einkleiden ['aınklaıdən] *vt* clothe;
(*fig*) express.

einklemmen ['aınklɛmən] *vt* jam.

einknicken ['aınknıkən] *vt* bend
in; *Papier* fold; *vi* give way.

einkochen ['aınkoxən] *vt* boil
down; *Obst* preserve, bottle.

Einkommen ['aınkomən] *nt* -s, -
income; —(s)**steuer** *f* income tax,
einkreisen ['aınkraızən] *vt* encircle.

Einkünfte ['aınkynftə] *pl* income,
revenue.

einlad- ['aınla:d] *cpd*: —**en** *vt irreg
Person* invite; *Gegenstände* load;
jdn ins Kino —**en** take sb to the
cinema; E—**ung** *f* invitation.

Einlage ['aınla:gə] *f* (*Programm—*)
interlude; (*Spar—*) deposit;
(*Schuh—*) insole; (*Fußstütze*) sup-

port; (Zahn—) temporary filling;
(Cook) noodles pl, vegetables pl etc
in soup; e—rn vt store.

Einlaß ['ainlas] m -sses, -lässe
admission.

einlassen irreg vt let in; (einsetzen) set in; vr: sich mit jdm/auf
etw (acc) — get involved with
sb/sth.

Einlauf ['ainlauf] m arrival; (von
Pferden) finish; (Med) enema;
e—en irreg vi arrive, come in; (in
Hafen) enter; (Sport) finish;
(Wasser) run in; (Stoff) shrink; vt
Schuhe break in; jdm das Haus
e—en invade sb's house; vr (Sport)
warm up; (Motor, Maschine) run
in.

einleben ['ainle:bən] vr settle down.

Einlege- ['ainle:gə] cpd: —arbeit f
inlay; e—n vt (einfügen) Blatt,
Sohle insert; (Cook) pickle; (in
Holz etc) inlay; Geld deposit;
Pause make; Protest make; Veto
use; Berufung lodge; ein gutes
Wort bei jdm e—n put in a good
word with sb; —sohle f insole.

einleiten ['ainlaitən] vt introduce,
start; Geburt induce.

Einleitung f introduction;
induction.

einleuchten ['ainlɔyçtən] vi be
clear or evident (jdm to sb); —d
a clear.

einliefern ['ainli:fərn] vt take (in
+acc into).

einlösen ['ainlø:zən] vt Scheck
cash; Schuldschein, Pfand redeem;
Versprechen keep.

einmachen ['ainmaxən] vt preserve.

einmal ['ainma:l] ad once;
(erstens) first; (zukünftig) sometime; nehmen wir — 就 just let's
suppose; noch — once more; nicht

— not even; auf — all at once;
es war — once upon a time there
was/were; E—'eins nt multiplication tables pl; —ig a unique;
(einmal geschehend) single;
(prima) fantastic.

Einmann- ['ainˈman] cpd: —betrieb
m one-man business; —bus m one-
man-operated bus.

Einmarsch ['ainmarʃ] m entry;
(Mil) invasion; e—ieren vi march
in.

einmengen ['ainmɛŋən], **einmischen** ['ainmiʃən] vr interfere
(in +acc with).

einmünden ['ainmyndən] vi run (in
+acc into), join.

einmütig ['ainmy:tiç] a unanimous.

Einnahme ['ainna:mə] f -, -n
(Geld) takings pl, revenue; (von
Medizin) taking; (Mil) capture,
taking; —quelle f source of income.

einnehmen ['ainne:mən] irreg vt
take; Stellung, Raum take up; —
für/gegen · persuade\ in favour
of/against; —d a charming.

einnicken ['ainnikən] vi nod off.

einnisten ['ainnistən] vr nest; (fig)
settle o.s.

Einöde ['ainˈø:də] f -, -n desert,
wilderness.

einordnen ['ainˈɔrdnən] vt arrange,
fit in; vr adapt; (Aut) get into lane.

einpacken ['ainpakən] vt pack (up).

einparken ['ainparkən] vt park.

einpendeln ['ainpɛndəln] vr even
out.

einpferchen ['ainpferçən] vt pen
in, coop up.

einpflanzen ['ainpflantsən] vt
plant; (Med) implant.

einplanen ['ainpla:nən] vt plan for.

einpräg- ['ainprɛ:g] cpd: —en vt
impress, imprint; (beibringen)

impress (jdm on sb); sich (dat) etw —en memorize sth.; —sam a easy to remember; Melodie catchy.

einrahmen ['aınra:mən] vt frame.

einrasten ['aınrastən] vi engage.

einräumen ['aınrɔymən] vt (ordnend) put away; (überlassen) Platz give up; (zugestehen) admit, concede.

einrechnen ['aınrεçnən] vt include; (berücksichtigen) take into account.

einreden ['aınre:dən] vt: jdm/sich etw — talk sb/o.s. into believing sth.

einreiben ['aınraıbən] vt irreg rub in.

einreichen ['aınraıçən] vt hand in; Antrag submit.

Einreise ['aınraızə] f entry; —bestimmungen pl entry regulations pl; —erlaubnis f, —genehmigung f entry permit; e—n vi enter (in ein Land a country).

einreißen ['aınraısən] vt irreg Papier tear; Gebäude pull down; vi tear; (Gewohnheit werden) catch on.

einrichten ['aınrıçtən] vt Haus furnish; (schaffen) establish, set up; (arrangieren) arrange; (möglich machen) manage; vr (in Haus) furnish one's house; (sich vorbereiten) prepare, o.s. (auf +acc for); (sich anpassen) adapt (auf +acc to).

Einrichtung f (Wohnungs—) furnishings pl; (öffentliche Anstalt) organization; (Dienste) service.

einrosten ['aınrostən] vi get rusty.

einrücken ['aınrʏkən] vi (Soldat) join up; (in Land) move in; vt Anzeige insert; Zeile indent.

Eins [aıns] f -, -en one; e— num one'; es ist mir alles e— it's all one to me.

einsalzen ['aınzaltsən] vt salt.

einsam ['aınza:m] a lonely, solitary; E—keit f loneliness, solitude.

einsammeln ['aınzaməln] vt collect.

Einsatz ['aınzats] m (Teil) inset; (an Kleid) insertion; (Tisch) leaf; (Verwendung) use, employment; (Spiel—) stake; (Risiko) risk; (Mil) operation; (Mus) entry; im — in action; e—bereit a ready for action.

einschalten ['aınʃaltən] vt (einfügen) insert; Pause make; (Elec) switch on; (Aut) Gang engage; Anwalt bring in; vr (dazwischentreten) intervene.

einschärfen ['aınʃεrfən] vt impress (jdm etw sth on sb).

einschätzen ['aınʃεtsən] vt estimate, assess; vr rate o.s.

einschenken ['aınʃεŋkən] vt pour out.

einschicken ['aınʃıkən] vt send in.

einschieben ['aınʃi:bən] vt irreg push in; (zusätzlich) insert.

einschiffen ['aınʃıfən] vt take on board; vr embark, go on board.

einschläfern ['aınʃlɛ:fərn] vt (Med) soporific; (langweilig) boring; Stimme lulling.

einschlafen ['aınʃla:fən] vi irreg fall asleep, go to sleep.

Einschlag ['aınʃla:k] m impact; (Aut) lock; (fig: Beimischung) touch, hint; e—en irreg vt knock in; Fenster smash, break; Zähne, Schädel smash in; Steuer turn; (kürzer machen) take up; Ware pack, wrap up; Weg, Richtung take; vi hit (in etw (acc) sth, auf jdn sb); (sich einigen) agree; (Anklang finden) work, succeed.

einschlägig ['aɪnʃlɛːgɪç] a relevant.

einschleichen ['aɪnʃlaɪçən] vr irreg (in Haus, Fehler) creep in, steal in; (in Vertrauen) worm one's way in.

einschließen ['aɪnʃliːsən] irreg vt Kind lock in; Häftling lock up; Gegenstand lock away; Bergleute cut off; (umgeben) surround; (Mil) encircle; (fig) include, comprise; vr lock o.s. in.

einschließlich ad inclusive; prep + gen inclusive of, including.

einschmeicheln ['aɪnʃmaɪçəln] vr ingratiate o.s. (bei with).

einschnappen ['aɪnʃnapən] vi (Tür) click to; (fig) be touchy; eingeschnappt sein be in a huff.

einschneidend ['aɪnʃnaɪdənt] a incisive.

Einschnitt ['aɪnʃnɪt] m cutting; (Med) incision; (Ereignis) incident.

einschränken ['aɪnʃrɛŋkən] vt limit, restrict; Kosten cut down, reduce; vr cut down on (expenditure); —d a restrictive.

Einschränkung f restriction, limitation; reduction; (von Behauptung) qualification.

Einschreib- ['aɪnʃraɪb] cpd: —e-brief m recorded delivery letter; e—en irreg vt write in; Post send recorded delivery; vr register; (Univ) enrol; —en nt recorded delivery letter; —(e)sendung f recorded delivery packet.

einschreiten ['aɪnʃraɪtən] vi irreg step in, intervene; — gegen take action against.

Einschub ['aɪnʃuːp] m -s, ⁺e insertion.

einschüchtern ['aɪnʃʏçtərn] vt intimidate.

einsehen ['aɪnzeːən] vt irreg (hineinsehen in) realize; Akten have a look at; (verstehen) see; E— nt -s

understanding; ein E— haben show understanding.

einseifen ['aɪnzaɪfən] vt soap, lather; (fig) take in, cheat.

einseitig ['aɪnzaɪtɪç] a one-sided; E—keit f one-sidedness.

Einsend- ['aɪnzɛnd] cpd: e—en vt irreg send in; —er m -s, - sender, contributor; —ung f sending in.

einsetzen ['aɪnzɛtsən] vt put (in); (in Amt) appoint, install; Geld stake; (verwenden) use; (Mil) employ; vi (beginnen) set in; (Mus) enter, come in; vr work hard; sich für jdn/etw — support sb/sth.

Einsicht ['aɪnzɪçt] f insight; (in Akten) look, inspection; zu der — kommen, daß ... come to the conclusion that ...; e—ig a' Mensch judicious; —nahme f -, -n examination; e—slos a unreasonable; e—svoll a understanding.

Einsiedler ['aɪnziːdlər] m hermit.

einsilbig ['aɪnzɪlbɪç] a (lit,fig) monosyllabic; E—keit f (fig) taciturnity.

einsinken ['aɪnzɪŋkən] vi irreg sink in.

Einsitzer ['aɪnzɪtsər] m -s, - single-seater.

einspannen ['aɪnʃpanən] vt Werkstück, Papier put (in), insert; Pferde harness; (col) Person rope in.

einsperren ['aɪnʃpɛrən] vt lock up.

einspielen ['aɪnʃpiːlən] vr (Sport) warm up; sich aufeinander — become attuned to each other; vt (Film) Geld bring in; Instrument play in; gut eingespielt smoothly running.

einspringen ['aɪnʃprɪŋən] vi irreg (aushelfen) help out, step into the breach.

einspritzen ['aɪnʃprɪtsən] vt inject.

Einspruch ['aɪnʃprux] m protest, objection; —srecht nt veto.

einspurig ['aɪnʃpuːrɪç] a single-line.

einst [aɪnst] ad once; (zukünftig) one or some day.

Einstand ['aɪnʃtant] m (Tennis) deuce; (Antritt) entrance (to office).

einstechen ['aɪnʃtɛçən] vt irreg stick in.

einstecken ['aɪnʃtɛkən] vt stick in, insert; Brief post; (Elec) Stecker plug in; Geld pocket; (mitnehmen) take; (überlegen sein) put in the shade; (hinnehmen) swallow.

einstehen ['aɪnʃteːən] vi irreg guarantee (für jdn/etw sb/sth); (verantworten) answer (für for).

einsteigen ['aɪnʃtaɪgən] vi irreg get in or on; (in Schiff) go on board; (sich beteiligen) come in; (hineinklettern) climb in.

einstell- ['aɪnʃtɛl] cpd: —bar a adjustable; —en vti (aufhören) stop; Geräte adjust; Kamera etc focus; Sender, Radio tune in; (unterstellen) put; (in Firma) employ, take on; vr (anfangen) set in; (kommen) arrive; sich auf jdn/etw —en adapt to sb/prepare o.s. for sth; E—ung f (Aufhören) suspension, cessation; adjustment; focusing; (von Arbeiter etc) appointment; (Haltung) attitude.

Einstieg ['aɪnʃtiːk] m -(e)s, -e entry; (fig) approach.

einstig ['aɪnstɪç] a former.

einstimm- ['aɪnʃtɪm] cpd: —en vi join in; vt (Mus) tune; (in Stimmung bringen) put in the mood; —ig a unanimous; (Mus) for one voice; E—igkeit f unanimity.

einst- [aɪnst] cpd: —malig a former; —mals ad once, formerly.

einstöckig ['aɪnʃtœkɪç] a single-storeyed.

einstudieren ['aɪnʃtudiːrən] vt study, rehearse.

einstündig ['aɪnʃtyndɪç] a one-hour.

einstürmen ['aɪnʃtʏrmən] vi: auf jdn — rush at sb; (Eindrücke) overwhelm sb.

Einsturz ['aɪnʃtʊrts] m collapse; —gefahr f danger of collapse.

einstürzen ['aɪnʃtʏrtsən] vi fall in, collapse.

einst- ['aɪnst] cpd: —weilen ad meanwhile; (vorläufig) temporarily, for the time being; —weilig a temporary.

eintägig ['aɪntɛːgɪç] a one-day.

eintauchen ['aɪntauxən] vt immerse, dip in; vi dive.

eintauschen ['aɪntauʃən] vt exchange.

eintausend ['aɪntauzənt] num one thousand.

einteil- ['aɪntaɪl] cpd: —en vt (in Teile) divide (up); Menschen assign; —ig a one-piece.

eintönig ['aɪntøːnɪç] a monotonous; E—keit f monotony.

Eintopf(gericht nt) ['aɪntɔpf(gərɪçt)] m stew.

Eintracht ['aɪntraxt] f: concord, harmony.

einträchtig ['aɪntrɛçtɪç] a harmonious.

Eintrag ['aɪntraːk] m -(e)s, -e entry; amtlicher — entry in the register; —en irreg vt (in Buch) enter; Profit yield; jdm etw —en bring sb sth; vr put one's name down.

einträglich ['aɪntrɛːklɪç] a profitable.

eintreffen ['aɪntrɛfən] vi irreg happen; (ankommen) arrive.

eintreten ['aɪntreːtən] *irreg vi* occur; *(hineingehen)* enter (*in etw* (acc) sth); *(sich einsetzen)* intercede; *(in Club, Partei)* join (*in etw* (acc) sth); *(in Stadium etc)* enter; *vt Tür* kick open.

Eintritt ['aɪntrɪt] *m (Betreten)* entrance; *(Anfang)* commencement; *(in Club etc)* joining; **—geld** *nt,* **—spreis** *m* charge for admission; **—skarte** *f* admission ticket.

eintrocknen ['aɪntrɔknən] *vi* dry up.

einüben ['aɪn'yːbən] *vt* practise, drill.

einver- ['aɪnfɛr] *cpd:* **—leiben** *vt* incorporate; *Gebiet* annex; *sich* (dat) *etw* **—leiben** *(fig: geistig)* acquire; **E—nehmen** *nt* **-s, -** agreement, understanding; **—standen** *interj* agreed; **a:** **—standen sein** agree, be agreed; **E—ständnis** *nt* understanding; *(gleiche Meinung)* agreement.

Einwand ['aɪnvant] *m* **-(e)s, -̈e** objection; **—erer** ['aɪnvandərər] *m* immigrant; **e—ern** *vi* immigrate; **—erung** *f* immigration; **e—frei** *a* perfect; *ad* absolutely.

einwärts ['aɪnvɛrts] *ad* inwards.

einwecken ['aɪnvɛkən] *vt* bottle, preserve.

Einwegflasche ['aɪnveːgflaʃə] *f* nodeposit bottle.

einweichen ['aɪnvaɪçən] *vt* soak.

einweih- ['aɪnvaɪ] *cpd:* **—en** *vt Kirche* consecrate; *Brücke* open; *Gebäude* inaugurate; *Person* initiate (*in* + acc in); **E—ung** *f* consecration; opening; inauguration; initiation.

einweis- ['aɪnvaɪz] *cpd:* **—en** *vt irreg (in Amt)* install; *(in Arbeit)* introduce; *(in Anstalt)* send;

E—ung *f* installation; introduction; sending:

einwenden ['aɪnvɛndən] *vt irreg* object, oppose *(gegen* to).

einwerfen ['aɪnvɛrfən] *vt irreg* throw in; *Brief* post; *Geld* put in, insert; *Fenster* smash; *(äußern)* interpose.

einwickeln ['aɪnvɪkəln] *vt* wrap up; *(fig col)* outsmart.

einwillig- ['aɪnvɪlɪg] *cpd:* **—en** *vi* consent, agree (*in* + acc to); **E—ung** *f* consent.

einwirk- ['aɪnvɪrk] *cpd:* **—en** *vi:* auf jdn/etw **—en** influence sb/sth; **E—ung** *f* influence.

Einwohner ['aɪnvoːnər] *m* **-s, -** inhabitant; **—'meldeamt** *nt* registration office; **—schaft** *f* population, inhabitants *pl.*

Einwurf ['aɪnvʊrf] *m (Öffnung)* slot; *(Einwand)* objection; *(Sport)* throw-in.

Einzahl ['aɪntsaːl] *f* singular; **e—en** *vt* pay in; **—ung** *f* paying in.

einzäunen ['aɪntsɔʏnən] *vt* fence in.

einzeichnen ['aɪntsaɪçnən] *vt* draw in.

Einzel ['aɪntsəl] *nt* **-s, -** *(Tennis)* singles; *in cpds* individual; single; **—bett** *nt* single bed; **—fall** *m* single instance, individual case; **—haft** *f* solitary confinement; **—heit** *f* particular, detail; **e—n** *a* single; *(vereinzelt)* the odd; *ad* singly; **e—n angeben** specify; **der/die e—ne** the individual; **das e—ne** the particular; **ins e—ne gehen** go into detail(s); **—teil** *nt* component (part); **—zimmer** *nt* single room.

einziehen ['aɪntsiːən] *irreg vt* draw in, take in; *Kopf* duck; *Fühler, Antenne, Fahrgestell* retract; *Steuern, Erkundigungen* collect; *(Mil)* draft, call up; *(aus dem Verkehr* *ziehen*) withdraw; (*konfiszieren*) confiscate; *vi* move in(to); (*Friede*, *Ruhe*) come; (*Flüssigkeit*) penetrate.

einzig ['aintsɪç] *a* only; (*ohnegleichen*) unique; **das —e** the only thing; **der/die —e** the only one; **—artig** *a* unique.

Einzug ['aintsuːk] *m* entry, moving in.

Eis [ais] **-es, -** ice; (*Speise-*) ice cream; **—bahn** *f* ice *or* skating rink; **—bär** *m* polar bear; **—becher** *m* sundae; **—bein** *nt* pig's trotters *pl*; **—berg** *m* iceberg; **—blumen** *pl* ice fern; **—decke** *f* sheet of ice; **—diele** *f* ice-cream parlour.

Eisen ['aizən] *nt* **-s, -** iron; **—bahn** *f* railway, railroad (*US*); **—bahner** *m* **-s, -** railwayman, railway employee, railroader (*US*); **—bahnschaffner** *m* railway guard; **—bahnübergang** *m* level crossing, grade crossing (*US*); **—bahnwagen** *m* railway carriage; **—erz** *nt* iron ore; **e—haltig** a containing iron.

eisern ['aizərn] *a* iron; *Gesundheit* robust; *Energie* unrelenting; *Reserve* emergency.

Eis- cpd: e—frei *a* clear of ice; **—hockey** *nt* ice hockey; **e—ig** ['aizɪç] *a* icy; **e—kalt** *a* icy cold; **—kunstlauf** *m* figure skating; **—laufen** *nt* ice skating; **—läufer** (*in* f) *m* ice-skater; **—pickel** *m* ice-axe; **e—schießen** *nt* ≈ curling; **—schrank** *m* fridge, ice-box (*US*); **—zapfen** *m* icicle; **—zeit** *f* ice age.

eitel ['aitəl] *a* vain; **E—keit** *f* vanity.

Eiter ['aitər] *m* **-s** pus; **e—ig** *a* suppurating; **e—n** *vi* suppurate.

Ei- cpd: [ai] **—weiß** *nt* **-es, -e** white of an egg; **—zelle** *f* ovum.

Ekel ['eːkəl] *m* **-s** nausea, disgust; *nt* **-s, -** (*col: Mensch*) nauseating

person; **e—erregend**, **e—haft**, **ek(e)lig** a nauseating, disgusting; **e—n** *vt* disgust; **es ekelt jdn** *or* **jdm sb** is disgusted; *vr* loathe, be disgusted (*vor + dat* at).

Ekstase [ɛk'staːzə] *f* **-, -n** ecstasy.

Ekzem [ɛk'tseːm] *nt* **-s, -e** (*Med*) eczema.

Elan [e'lãː] *m* **-s** elan.

elastisch [e'lastɪʃ] *a* elastic.

Elastizität [elastitsiˈtɛːt] *f* elasticity.

Elch [ɛlç] *m* **-(e)s, -e** elk.

Elefant [ele'fant] *m* elephant.

elegant [ele'gant] *a* elegant.

Eleganz [ele'gants] *f* elegance.

Elek- cpd: [e'lek] **—trifizierung** [-trifitsiːˈrʊŋ] *f* electrification; **—triker** [-trikər] *m* **-s, -** electrician; **e—trisch** [-trɪʃ] *a* electric; **e—trisieren** [-triˈziːrən] *vt* (*lit, fig*) electrify; **Mensch** give an electric shock to; *vr* get an electric shock; **e—trizität** [-tritsiˈtɛːt] *f* electricity; **—trizitätswerk** *nt* electricity works, power plant.

Elektro- [e'lektro] **cpd: —de** [elɛk'troːdə] *f* **-, -n** electrode; **—herd** *m* electric cooker; **—lyse** [-'lyːzə] *f* **-, -n** electrolysis; **—n** [-ɔn] *nt* **-s, -en** electron; **—nen(ge)hirn** [elɛk'troːnən-] *nt* electronic brain; **—nenrechner** *m* computer; **e—nisch** a electronic; **—rasierer** *m* **-s, -** electric razor.

Element [ele'mɛnt] *nt* **-s, -e** element; (*Elec*) cell, battery; **e—ar** ['taːr] *a* elementary; (*naturhaft*) elemental.

Elend ['eːlɛnt] *nt* **-(e)s** misery; **e—a** miserable; **e—iglich** [eːlɛnd-] *ad* miserably; **—sviertel** *nt* slum.

elf [ɛlf] *num* eleven; **E—** *f* **-, -en** (*Sport*) eleven; **E—e** *f* **-, -n** elf; **E—enbein** *nt* ivory; **E—meter** *m* (*Sport*) penalty (kick).

eliminieren [elimi'ni:rən] *vt* eliminate.

Elite [e'li:tə] *f* -, -n elite.

Elixier [eli'ksi:r] *nt* -s, -e elixir.

Ell- *cpd:* —e ['ɛlə] *f* -, -n ell; (*Maß*) yard; —(en)bogen *m* elbow; —ipse ['ɛ'lɪpsə] *f* -, -n ellipse.

Elster ['ɛlstər] *f* -, -n magpie.

Elter- ['ɛltər] *cpd:* —lich *a* parental; —n *pl* parents *pl*; —nhaus *nt* home; e—nlos *a* parentless.

Email [e'ma:j] *nt* -s, -s enamel; e—lieren [ema'ji:rən] *vt* enamel.

Emanzipation [emantsipatsi'o:n] *f* emancipation.

emanzi'pieren *vt* emancipate.

Embryo ['ɛmbryo] *m* -s, -s *or* -nen embryo.

Emi- [emi] *cpd:* —grant ['grant] *m* emigrant; —gration [-gratsi'o:n] *f* emigration; e—grieren [-'gri:rən] *vi* emigrate.

Empfang [ɛm'pfaŋ] *m* -(e)s, ⁻e reception; (*Erhalten*) receipt; in —nehmen receive; e—en *irreg vt* receive; *vi* (*schwanger werden*) conceive.

Empfäng- [ɛm'pfɛŋ] *cpd:* —er *m* -s, - receiver; (*Comm*) addressee, consignee; e—lich *a* receptive, susceptible; —nis *f* -, -se conception; —nisverhütung *f* contraception.

Empfangs- *cpd:* —bestätigung *f* acknowledgement; —dame *f* receptionist; —schein *m* receipt; —zimmer *nt* reception room.

empfehlen [ɛm'pfe:lən] *irreg vt* recommend; *vr* take one's leave; —swert *a* recommendable.

Empfehlung *f* recommendation; —sschreiben *nt* letter of recommendation.

empfind- [ɛm'pfɪnt] *cpd:* —en [ɛm'pfɪndən] *vt irreg* feel; —lich *a* sensitive; *Stelle* sore; (*reizbar*) touchy; **E**—lichkeit *f* sensitiveness; (*Reizbarkeit*) touchiness; —sam *a* sentimental; **E**—ung *f* feeling, sentiment; —ungslos *a* unfeeling, insensitive.

empor [ɛm'po:r] *ad* up, upwards.

empören [ɛm'pø:rən] *vt* make indignant; shock; *vr* become indignant; —d *a* outrageous.

empor- *cpd:* —kommen *vi irreg* rise; succeed; **E**—kömmling *m* upstart, parvenu.

Empörung *f* indignation.

emsig ['ɛmzɪç] *a* diligent, busy.

End- ['ɛnt] *in cpds* final; —auswertung *f* final analysis; —bahnhof ['ɛnt-] *m* terminus; e—e *nt* -s, -n end; am — at the end; (*schließlich*) in the end; am —e sein to be at the end of one's tether; —e Dezember at the end of December; zu —e sein to be finished; e—en *vi* end; e—gültig *a* final, definite; —ivie [ɛn'di:viə] *f* endive; e—lich *a* final; (*Math*) finite; *ad* finally; e—lich! at last!; e—los *a* endless, infinite; —spiel *nt* final(s); —spurt *m* (*Sport*) final spurt; —station *f* terminus; —ung *f* ending.

Energie [enɛr'gi:] *f* energy; e—los *a* lacking in energy, weak; —wirtschaft *f* energy industry.

energisch [e'nɛrgɪʃ] *a* energetic.

eng [ɛŋ] *a* narrow; *Kleidung* tight; (*fig*) Horizont *auch* limited; *Freundschaft, Verhältnis* close; — an etw (*dat*) close to sth.

Engagement [ãɡaʒə'mãː] *nt* -s, -s engagement; (*Verpflichtung*) commitment.

engagieren [ãɡa'ʒi:rən] *vt* engage; ein engagierter Schriftsteller a committed writer; *vr* commit o.s.

Enge ['ɛŋə] f -, -n (lit,fig) narrowness; (Land—) defile; (Meer—) straits pl; jdn in die — treiben drive sb into a corner.

Engel ['ɛŋəl] m -s, - angel; e—haft a angelic; —macher m -s, - (col) backstreet abortionist.

eng- cpd: —herzig a petty; E—paß m defile, pass; (fig, Verkehr) bottleneck.

en gros [ã'gro] ad wholesale.

engstirnig ['ɛŋʃtırnıç] a narrowminded.

Enkel ['ɛŋkəl] m -s, - grandson; —in f granddaughter; —kind nt grandchild.

en masse [ã'mas] ad en masse.

enorm [e'nɔrm] a enormous.

Ensemble [ã'sãbəl] nt -s, -s company, ensemble.

entarten [ɛnt''a:rtən] vi degenerate.

entbehr- [ɛnt'be:r] cpd: —en vt do without, dispense with; —lich a superfluous. E—ung f privation.

entbinden [ɛnt'bındən] irreg vt release (gen from); (Med) deliver; vi (Med) give birth.

Entbindung f release; (Med) confinement; —sheim nt maternity hospital.

entblößen [ɛnt'blø:sən] vt denude, uncover; (berauben) deprive (gen of).

entdeck- [ɛnt'dɛk] cpd: —en vt discover; jdm etw —en disclose sth to sb; E—er m -s, - discoverer; E—ung f discovery.

Ente ['ɛntə] f -, -n duck; (fig) canard, false report.

entehren [ɛnt''e:rən] vt dishonour, disgrace.

enteignen [ɛnt''aıgnən] vt expropriate; Besitzer dispossess.

enteisen [ɛnt''aızən] vt de-ice, defrost.

enterben [ɛnt''ɛrbən] vt disinherit.

entfachen [ɛnt'faxən] vt kindle.

entfallen [ɛnt'falən] vi irreg drop, fall; (wegfallen) be dropped; jdm — (vergessen) slip sb's memory; auf jdn — be allotted to sb.

entfalten [ɛnt'faltən] vt unfold; Talente develop; vr open; (Mensch) develop one's potential.

Entfaltung f unfolding; (von Talenten) development.

entfern- [ɛnt'fɛrn] cpd: —en vt remove; (hinauswerfen) expel; vr go away, retire, withdraw; —t a distant; weit davon —t sein, etw zu tun be far from doing sth; E—ung f distance; (Wegschaffen) removal; E—ungsmesser m -s, - (Phot) rangefinder.

entfesseln [ɛnt'fɛsəln] vt (fig) arouse.

entfetten [ɛnt'fɛtən] vt take the fat from.

entfremd- [ɛnt'frɛmd] cpd: —en vt estrange, alienate; E—ung f alienation, estrangement.

entfrost- [ɛnt'frɔst] cpd: —en vt defrost; E—er m -s, - (Aut) defroster.

entführ- [ɛnt'fy:r] cpd: —en vt carry off, abduct; kidnap; E—er m kidnapper; E—ung f abduction; kidnapping.

entgegen [ɛnt'ge:gən] prep +dat contrary to, against; ad towards; —bringen vt irreg bring; (fig) show (jdm etw sb sth); —gehen vi irreg (+dat) go to meet, go towards; —gesetzt a opposite; (widersprechend) opposed; —halten vt irreg (fig) object; —kommen vi irreg approach; meet (jdm sb); (fig) accommodate (jdm sb); E—kommen nt obligingness; —kommend a obliging; —laufen vi irreg (+dat) run towards or to meet; (fig) run counter to; —nehmen vt irreg receive, accept; —sehen vi irreg (+dat) await; —setzen vt oppose (dat to); —treten vi irreg (+dat) (lit) step up to; (fig) oppose, counter; —wirken vi (+dat) counteract.

entgegnen [ɛnt'ge:gnən] vt reply, retort.

Entgegnung f reply, retort.

entgehen [ɛnt'ge:ən] vi irreg (fig) jdm — escape sb's notice; sich (dat) etw — lassen miss sth.

entgeistert [ɛnt'gaɪstərt] a thunderstruck.

Entgelt [ɛnt'gɛlt] nt -(e)s, -e compensation, remuneration; e—en vt irreg: jdm etw e—en repay sb for sth.

entgleisen [ɛnt'glaɪzən] vi (Rail) be derailed; (fig: Person) misbehave; — lassen derail.

Entgleisung f derailment; (fig) faux pas, gaffe.

entgleiten [ɛnt'glaɪtən] vi irreg slip (jdm from sb's hand).

entgräten [ɛnt'grɛ:tən] vt fillet, bone.

Enthaarungsmittel [ɛnt'ha:ruŋsmɪtəl] nt depilatory.

enthalten [ɛnt'haltən] irreg vt contain; vr abstain, refrain (gen from).

enthaltsam [ɛnt'haltza:m] a abstinent, abstemious; E—keit f abstinence.

enthemmen [ɛnt'hɛmən] vt: jdn — free sb from his. inhibitions.

enthüllen [ɛnt'hYlən] vt reveal, unveil.

Enthusiasmus [ɛntuzi'asmʊs] m enthusiasm.

entkernen [ɛnt'kɛrnən] vt stone; core.

entkommen [ɛnt'kɔmən] vi irreg get away, escape (dat, aus from).

entkorken [ɛnt'kɔrkən] vt uncork.

entkräften [ɛnt'krɛftən] vt weaken, exhaust; Argument refute.

entladen [ɛnt'la:dən] irreg vt unload; (Elec) discharge; vr (Elec, Gewehr) discharge; (Ärger etc) vent itself.

entlang [ɛnt'laŋ] prep + acc or dat, ad along; — dem Fluß, den Fluß — along the river; —gehen vi irreg walk along.

entlarven [ɛnt'larfən] vt unmask, expose.

entlassen [ɛnt'lasən] vt irreg discharge; Arbeiter dismiss.

Entlassung f discharge; dismissal.

entlasten [ɛnt'lastən] vt relieve; Achse relieve the load on; Angeklagte exonerate; Konto clear.

Entlastung f relief; (Comm) crediting; —szeuge m defence witness.

entledigen [ɛnt'le:dɪgən] vr: sich jds/einer Sache — rid o.s. of sb/sth.

entleeren [ɛnt'le:rən] vt empty; evacuate.

entlegen [ɛnt'le:gən] a remote.

entlocken [ɛnt'lɔkən] vt elicit (jdm etw sth from sb).

entlüften [ɛnt'lʏftən] vt ventilate.

entmachten [ɛnt'maxtən] vt deprive of power.

entmenscht [ɛnt'mɛnʃt] a inhuman, bestial.

entmilitarisiert [ɛntmilitari'zi:rt] a demilitarized.

entmündigen [ɛnt'mʏndɪgən] vt certify.

entmutigen [ɛnt'mu:tɪgən] vt discourage.

Entnahme [εnt'naːmə] f -, -n removal, withdrawal.

entnehmen [εnt'neːmən] vt irreg (+ dat) take out (of), take (from); (folgern) infer (from).

entpuppen [εnt'pupən] vr (fig) reveal o.s., turn out (als to be).

entrahmen [εnt'raːmən] vt skim.

entreißen [εnt'raɪsən] vt irreg snatch (away) (jdm etw sth from sb).

entrichten [εnt'rɪçtən] vt pay.

entrosten [εnt'rɔstən] vt derust.

entrüst- [εnt'rʏst] cpd: **—en** vt incense, outrage; vr be filled with indignation; **—et** a indignant, outraged; **E—ung** f indignation.

entsagen [εnt'zaːgən] vi renounce (dat sth).

entschädigen [εnt'ʃεːdɪgən] vt compensate.

Entschädigung f compensation.

entschärfen [εnt'ʃεrfən] vt defuse; Kritik tone down.

Entscheid [εnt'ʃaɪt] m -(e)s, -e decision; **e—en** vtir irreg decide; **e—end** a decisive; Stimme casting; **—ung** f decision; **—ungsspiel** nt play-off.

entschieden [εnt'ʃiːdən] a decided; (entschlossen) resolute; **E—heit** f firmness, determination.

entschließen [εnt'ʃliːsən] vr irreg decide.

entschlossen [εnt'ʃlɔsən] a determined, resolute; **E—heit** f determination.

Entschluß [εnt'ʃlʊs] m decision; **e—freudig** a decisive; **—kraft** f determination, decisiveness.

entschuld- [εnt'ʃʊld] cpd: **—bar** a excusable; **—igen** vt excuse; vr apologize; **E—igung** f apology; (Grund) excuse; jdn um **E—igung**

bitten apologize to sb; **E—igung!** excuse me; (Verzeihung) sorry.

entschwinden [εnt'ʃvɪndən] vi irreg disappear.

entsetz- [εnt'zεts] cpd: **—en** vt horrify; (Mil) relieve; vr be horrified or appalled; **E—en** nt -s horror, dismay; **—lich** a dreadful, appalling; **—t** a horrified.

entsichern [εnt'zɪçərn] vt release the safety catch of.

entsinnen [εnt'zɪnən] vr irreg remember (gen sth).

entspannen [εnt'ʃpanən] vtr Körper relax; (Pol) Lage ease.

Entspannung f relaxation, rest; (Pol) détente; **—spolitik** f policy of détente; **—sübungen** pl relaxation exercises pl.

entsprechen [εnt'ʃprεçən] vi irreg (+ dat) correspond to; Anforderungen, Wünschen meet, comply with; **—d** a appropriate; ad accordingly.

entspringen [εnt'ʃprɪŋən] vi irreg spring (from).

entstehen [εnt'ʃteːən] vi irreg arise, result.

Entstehung f genesis, origin.

entstellen [εnt'ʃtεlən] vt disfigure; Wahrheit distort.

entstören [εnt'ʃtøːrən] vt (Rad) eliminate interference from; (Aut) suppress.

enttäuschen [εnt'tɔʏʃən] vt disappoint.

Enttäuschung f disappointment.

entwaffnen [εnt'vafnən] vt (lit,fig) disarm.

Entwarnung [εnt'varnʊŋ] f all clear (signal).

entwässer- [εnt'vεsər] cpd: **—n** vt drain; **E—ung** f drainage.

entweder ['ɛntveːdər] cj either.

entweichen [ɛnt'vaɪçən] vi irreg escape.

entweihen [ɛnt'vaɪən] vt irreg desecrate.

entwenden [ɛnt'vɛndən] vt irreg purloin, steal.

entwerfen [ɛnt'vɛrfən] vt irreg Zeichnung sketch; Modell design; Vortrag, Gesetz etc draft.

entwerten [ɛnt'veːrtən] vt devalue; (stempeln) cancel.

entwickeln [ɛnt'vɪkəln] vtr develop (auch Phot); Mut, Energie show, display.

Entwickler m -s, - developer.
Entwicklung [ɛnt'vɪklʊŋ] f development; (Phot) developing; —sabschnitt m stage of development; —shilfe f aid for developing countries; —sjahre pl adolescence sing; —sland nt developing country.

entwirren [ɛnt'vɪrən] vt disentangle.

entwischen [ɛnt'vɪʃən] vi escape.

entwöhnen [ɛnt'vøːnən] vt wean; Süchtige cure (dat, von of).

Entwöhnung f weaning; cure, curing.

entwürdigend [ɛnt'vʏrdɪgənt] a degrading.

Entwurf [ɛnt'vʊrf] m outline, design; (Vertrags—, Konzept) draft.

entwurzeln [ɛnt'vʊrtsəln] vt uproot.

entziehen [ɛnt'tsiːən] irreg vt withdraw, take away (dat from); Flüssigkeit draw, extract; vr escape (dat from); (jds Kenntnis) be outside; (der Pflicht) shirk.

Entziehung f withdrawal; —sanstalt f drug addiction/alcoholism treatment centre; —skur f treat-

ment for drug addiction/alcoholism.

entziffern [ɛnt'tsɪfərn] vt decipher; decode.

entzücken [ɛnt'tsʏkən] vt delight; E— nt -s delight; —d a delightful, charming.

entzünden [ɛnt'tsʏndən] vt light, set light to; (fig, Med) inflame; Streit spark off; vr (lit, fig) catch fire; (Streit) start; (Med) become inflamed.

Entzündung f (Med) inflammation.

entzwei [ɛnt'tsvaɪ] ad broken; in two; —brechen vtl irreg break in two; —en vt set at odds; vr fall out; —gehen vi irreg break (in two).

Enzian ['ɛntsiaːn] m -s, -e gentian.

Enzym [ɛn'tsyːm] nt -s, -e enzyme.

Epidemie [epide'miː] f epidemic.

Epilepsie [epilɛp'siː] f epilepsy.

episch ['eːpɪʃ] a epic.

Episode [epi'zoːdə] f -, -n episode.

Epoche [e'pɔxə] f -, -n epoch; e—machend a epoch-making.

Epos ['eːpɔs] nt -s, Epen epic (poem).

er [eːr] pron he; it.

erachten [ɛr'axtən] vt: — für or als consider (to be); meines E—s in my opinion.

erarbeiten [ɛr'arbaɪtən] vt (auch sich (dat) —) work for, acquire; Theorie work out.

erbarmen [ɛr'barmən] vr have pity or mercy (gen on); E— nt -s pity.

erbärmlich [ɛr'bɛrmlɪç] a wretched, pitiful; E—keit f wretchedness.

erbarmungs- [ɛr'barmʊŋs] cpd: —los a pitiless, merciless; —voll a compassionate; —würdig a pitiable, wretched.

erbau- [ɛr'bau] cpd: —en vt build, erect; (fig) edify; E—er m -s, •

builder; —lich a edifying; E—ung f construction; (fig) edification.

Erbe ['ɛrbə] m -n, -n heir; nt -s inheritance; (fig) heritage; e—n vt inherit.

erbeuten [ɛr'bɔytən] vt carry off; (Mil) capture.

Erb- [ɛrb] cpd: —faktor m gene; —fehler m hereditary defect; —folge f (line of) succession; —in f heiress.

erbittern [ɛr'bɪtərn] vt embitter; (erzürnen) incense.

erbittert [ɛr'bɪtərt] a Kampf fierce, bitter.

erblassen [ɛr'blasən] vi, **erbleichen** [ɛr'blaɪçən] vi irreg (turn) pale.

erblich ['ɛrplɪç] a hereditary.

Erbmasse ['ɛrbmasə] f estate; (Biol) genotype.

erbosen [ɛr'boːzən] vt anger; **sich ~** grow angry.

erbrechen [ɛr'brɛçən] vtr irreg vomit.

Erb- cpd: —recht nt right of succession, hereditary right; law of inheritance; —schaft f inheritance, legacy.

Erbse ['ɛrpsə] f -, -n pea.

Erb- cpd: —stück nt heirloom; —teil nt inherited trait; (portion of) inheritance.

Erd- ['eːrd] cpd: —achse f earth's axis; —atmosphäre f earth's atmosphere; —bahn f orbit of the earth; —beben nt earthquake; —beere f strawberry; —boden m ground; —e f ~, -n earth; zu ebener ~ at ground level; e—en vt (Elec) earth.

erdenkbar [ɛr'dɛŋkbaːr], **erdenklich** [-lɪç] a conceivable.

Erd- cpd: —gas nt natural gas; —geschoß nt ground floor;

—kunde f geography; —nuß f peanut; —oberfläche f surface of the earth; —öl nt (mineral), oil.

erdreisten [ɛr'draɪstən] vr dare, have the audacity (to do sth).

erdrosseln [ɛr'drɔsəln] vt strangle, throttle.

erdrücken [ɛr'drykən] vt crush.

Erd- cpd: —rutsch m landslide; —teil m continent.

erdulden [ɛr'dʊldən] vt endure, suffer.

ereifern [ɛr'aɪfərn] vr get excited.

ereignen [ɛr'aɪgnən] vr happen.

Ereignis [ɛr'aɪgnɪs] nt -ses, -se event; e—reich a eventful.

erfahren [ɛr'faːrən] vt irreg learn, find out; (erleben) experience; a experienced.

Erfahrung f experience; e—s-gemäß ad according to experience.

erfassen [ɛr'fasən] vt seize; (fig) (einbeziehen) include, register; (verstehen) grasp.

erfind- [ɛr'fɪnd] cpd: —en vt irreg invent; E—er m -s, - inventor; —erisch a inventive; E—ung f invention; E—ungsgabe f inventiveness.

Erfolg [ɛr'fɔlk] m -(e)s, -e success; (Folge) result; (sich ergeben) follow; (stattfinden) take place; (Zahlung) be effected; e—en vi follow; (sich ergeben) result; (stattfinden) take place; (Zahlung) be effected; e—los a unsuccessful; —losigkeit f lack of success; e—reich a successful; e—versprechend a promising.

erforder- [ɛr'fɔrdər] cpd: —lich a requisite, necessary; —n vt require, demand; E—nis nt -ses,-se requirement; prerequisite.

erforsch- [ɛr'fɔrʃ] cpd: —en vt Land explore; Problem investigate; Gewissen search; E—er m -s, - explorer; investigator; E—ung f exploration; investigation; searching.

erfragen [ɛrˈfraːgən] *vt* inquire after, ascertain.

erfreuen [ɛrˈfrɔyən] *vr*: sich — an (+*dat*) enjoy; sich einer Sache (*gen*) — enjoy sth; *vt* delight.

erfreulich [ɛrˈfrɔylɪç] *a* pleasing, gratifying; —**erweise** *ad* happily, luckily.

erfrieren [ɛrˈfriːrən] *vi irreg* freeze (to death); (Glieder) get frostbitten; (Pflanzen) be killed by frost.

erfrischen [ɛrˈfrɪʃən] *vt* refresh.

Erfrischung *f* refreshment; —**sraum** *m* snack bar, cafeteria.

erfüllen [ɛrˈfylən] *vt* Raum etc fill; (*fig*) Bitte etc fulfil; *vr* come true.

ergänzen [ɛrˈgɛntsən] *vt* supplement, complete; *vr* complement one another.

Ergänzung *f* completion; (*Zusatz*) supplement. ·

ergattern [ɛrˈgatərn] *vt* (*col*) get hold of, hunt up.

ergaunern [ɛrˈgaunərn] *vt* (*col*) sich (*dat*) etw — get hold of sth by underhand methods.

ergeben [ɛrˈgeːbən] *irreg vt* yield, produce; *vr* surrender; (sich hingeben) give o.s. up, yield (*dat* to); (folgen) result; a devoted, humble; (dem Trunk) addicted (to); **E—heit** *f* devotion, humility.

Ergebnis [ɛrˈgeːpnɪs] *nt* —ses, -se result; e—los *a* without result, fruitless.

ergehen [ɛrˈgeːən] *irreg vi* be issued, go out; etw über sich — lassen put up with sth; *vi impers*: es ergeht ihm gut/schlecht he's faring or getting on well/badly; *vr* sich in etw (*dat*) — indulge in sth.

ergiebig [ɛrˈgiːbɪç] *a* productive.

ergötzen [ɛrˈgœtsən] *vt* amuse, delight.

ergreifen [ɛrˈgraifən] *vt irreg* (*lit, fig*) seize; Beruf take up; Maßnahmen resort to; (rühren) move; —d *a* moving, affecting.

ergriffen [ɛrˈgrɪfən] *a* deeply moved.

Erguß [ɛrˈgus] *m* discharge; (*fig*) outpouring, effusion.

erhaben [ɛrˈhaːbən] *a* (*lit*) raised, embossed; (*fig*) exalted, lofty; über etw (*acc*) — sein be above sth.

erhalten [ɛrˈhaltən] *vt irreg* receive; (bewahren) preserve, maintain; gut — in good condition.

erhältlich [ɛrˈhɛltlɪç] *a* obtainable, available.

Erhaltung *f* maintenance, preservation.

erhängen [ɛrˈhɛŋən] *vtr* hang.

erhärten [ɛrˈhɛrtən] *vt* harden; These substantiate, corroborate.

erhaschen [ɛrˈhaʃən] *vt* catch.

erheben [ɛrˈheːbən] *irreg vt* raise; Protest, Forderungen make; Fakten ascertain, establish; *vr* rise (up); sich über etw (*acc*) — rise above sth.

erheblich [ɛrˈheːplɪç] *a* considerable.

erheitern [ɛrˈhaitərn] *vt* amuse, cheer (up).

Erheiterung *f* exhilaration; zur allgemeinen — to everybody's amusement.

erhellen [ɛrˈhɛlən] *vt* (*lit, fig*) illuminate; Geheimnis shed light on; *vr* brighten, light up.

erhitzen [ɛrˈhitsən] *vt* heat; *vr* heat up; (*fig*) become heated or aroused.

erhoffen [ɛrˈhofən] *vt* hope for.

erhöhen [ɛrˈhøːən] *vt* raise; (verstärken) increase.

erhol- [ɛr'hoːl] *cpd:* **—en** *vr* recover; (*entspannen*) have a rest; **—sam** a restful; **E—ung** f recovery; relaxation, rest; **—ungsbedürftig** a in need of a rest, rundown; **E—ungsheim** *nt* convalescent/rest home.

erhören [ɛr'høːrən] *vt* Gebet etc hear; Bitte etc yield to.

Erika ['eːrika] ka] f -, **Eriken** heather.

erinnern [ɛr'ɪnərn] *vt* remind (an +acc of); *vr* remember (an etw (acc) sth).

Erinnerung f memory; (*Andenken*) reminder; **—stafel** f commemorative plaque.

erkalten [ɛr'kaltən] *vi* go cold, cool (down).

erkält- [ɛr'kɛlt] *cpd:* **—en** *vr* catch cold; **—et a** with a cold; **—et sein** have a cold; **E—ung** f cold.

erkenn- [ɛr'kɛn] *cpd:* **—bar a** recognizable; **—en** *vt irreg* recognize; (*sehen, verstehen*) see; **—tlich a: sich —tlich zeigen** show one's appreciation; **E—tlichkeit** f gratitude; (*Geschenk*) token of one's gratitude; **E—tnis** f -, **-se** knowledge; (*das Erkennen*) recognition; (*Einsicht*) insight; **zur E—tnis kommen** realize; **E—ung** f recognition; **E—ungsmarke** f identity disc.

Erker ['ɛrkər] *m* **-s**, **-** bay; **—fenster** *nt* bay window.

erklär- [ɛr'klɛːr] *cpd:* **—bar a** explicable; **—en** *vt* explain; **—lich a** explicable; (*verständlich*) understandable; **E—ung** f explanation; (*Aussage*) declaration.

erklecklich [ɛr'klɛklɪç] a considerable.

erklingen [ɛr'klɪŋən] *vi irreg* resound, ring out.

Erkrankung [ɛr'kraŋkʊŋ] f illness.

erkund- [ɛr'kʊnd] *cpd:* **—en** *vt* find out, ascertain; (*esp Mil*) reconnoitre, scout; **—igen** *vr* inquire (*nach* about); **E—igung** f inquiry; **E—ung** f reconnaissance, scouting.

erlahmen [ɛr'laːmən] *vi* tire; (*nachlassen*) flag, wane.

erlangen [ɛr'laŋən] *vt* attain, achieve.

Erlaß [ɛr'las] *m* **-sses**, **-lässe** decree; (*Aufhebung*) remission.

erlassen *vt irreg* Verfügung issue; Gesetz enact; Strafe remit; jdm etw — release sb from sth.

erlauben [ɛr'laubən] *vt* allow, permit (*jdm etw* sb to do sth); *vr* permit o.s., venture.

Erlaubnis [ɛr'laupnɪs] f -, **-se** permission.

erläutern [ɛr'lɔʏtərn] *vt* explain.
Erläuterung f explanation.

Erle ['ɛrlə] f -, **-n** alder.

erleben [ɛr'leːbən] *vt* experience; Zeit live through; (*mit—*) witness; (*noch mit—*) live to see.

Erlebnis [ɛr'leːpnɪs] *nt* **-ses**, **-se** experience.

erledigen [ɛr'leːdɪgən] *vt* take care of, deal with; Antrag etc process; (*col: erschöpfen*) wear out; (*col: ruinieren*) finish; (*col: umbringen*) do in.

erlegen [ɛr'leːgən] *vt* kill.

erleichter- [ɛr'laiçtər] *cpd:* **—n** *vt* make easier; (*fig*) Last lighten; (*lindern, beruhigen*) relieve; **—t a** relieved; **E—ung** f facilitation; lightening; relief.

erleiden [ɛr'laidən] *vt irreg* suffer, endure.

erlernbar a learnable.

erlernen [ɛr'lɛrnən] *vt* learn, acquire.

erlesen [ɛr'le:zən] a select, choice.
erleuchten [ɛr'lɔʏçtən] vt illuminate; (fig) inspire.
Erleuchtung f (Einfall) inspiration.
erlogen [ɛr'lo:gən] a untrue, made-up.
Erlös [ɛr'lø:s] m -es, -e proceeds pl.
erlöschen [ɛr'lœʃən] vi (Feuer) go out; (Interesse) cease, die; (Vertrag, Recht) expire.
erlösen [ɛr'lø:zən] vt redeem, save.
Erlösung f release; (Rel) redemption.
ermächtigen [ɛr'mɛçtigən] vt authorize, empower.
Ermächtigung f authorization; authority.
ermahnen [ɛr'ma:nən] vt exhort, admonish.
Ermahnung f admonition, exhortation.
ermäßigen [ɛr'mɛsigən] vt reduce.
Ermäßigung f reduction.
ermessen [ɛr'mɛsən] vt irreg estimate, gauge; **E— nt -s** estimation; discretion; **in jds E—** liegen lie within sb's discretion.
ermitteln [ɛr'mɪtəln] vt determine; Täter trace; vi: gegen jdn — investigate sb.
Ermittlung f [ɛr'mɪtluŋ] f determination; (Polizei—) investigation.
ermöglichen [ɛr'mø:klɪçən] vt make possible (dat for).
ermord- [ɛr'mɔrd] cpd: **—en** vt murder; **E—ung** f murder.
ermüden [ɛr'my:dən] vti tire; **—d** a tiring; (Tech) fatigue; (fig) wearisome.
Ermüdung f fatigue; **—serscheinung** f sign of fatigue.
ermuntern [ɛr'muntərn] vt rouse; (ermutigen) encourage; (beleben)

liven up; (aufmuntern) cheer up.
ermutigen [ɛr'mu:tigən] vt encourage.
ernähr- [ɛr'nɛ:r] cpd: **—en** vt feed, nourish; Familie support; vr support o.s., earn a living; sich **—en** von live on; **E—er** m -s, - breadwinner; **E—ung** f nourishment; nutrition; (Unterhalt) maintenance.
ernennen [ɛr'nɛnən] vt irreg appoint.
Ernennung f appointment.
erneu- [ɛr'nɔʏ] cpd: **—ern** vt renew; restore; renovate; **E—erung** f renewal; restoration; renovation; **—t** a renewed, fresh; ad once more.
erniedrigen [ɛr'ni:drigən] vt humiliate, degrade.
Ernst [ɛrnst] m -es seriousness; das ist mein — I'm quite serious; im — in earnest; — machen mit etw put sth into practice; **e— a** serious; **—fall** m emergency; **e—gemeint** a meant in earnest, serious; **e—haft** a serious; **—haftigkeit** f seriousness; **e—lich** a serious.
Ernte ['ɛrntə] f -, -n harvest; **—dankfest** nt harvest festival; **e—n** vt harvest; Lob etc earn.
ernüchtern [ɛr'nʏçtərn] vt sober up; (fig) bring down to earth.
Ernüchterung f sobering up; (fig) disillusionment.
Erober- [ɛr'o:bər] cpd: **—er** m -s, - conqueror; **e—n** vt conquer; **—ung** f conquest.
eröffnen [ɛr'ʔœfnən] vt open; jdm etw — disclose sth to sb; vr present itself.
Eröffnung f opening; **—sansprache** f inaugural or opening address.

erogen [εro'geːn] a erogenous.

erörtern [εr''œrtərn] vt discuss.

Erörterung f discussion.

Erotik [e'roːtik] f eroticism.

erotisch a erotic. .

erpicht [εr'piçt] a eager, keen (auf +acc on).

erpress- [εr'prεs] cpd: —en vt Geld etc extort; Mensch blackmail; E—er m -s, • blackmailer; E—ung f blackmail; extortion.

erproben [εr'proːbən] vt test.

erraten [εr'raːtən] vt irreg guess.

erreg- [εr'reːk] cpd: —bar a excitable; (reizbar) irritable; E—barkeit f excitability; irritability; —en vt excite; (ärgern) infuriate; (hervorrufen) arouse, provoke; vr get excited or worked up; E—er m -s, • causative agent; E—theit f excitement; (Beunruhigung) agitation; E—ung f excitement.

erreichbar a accessible, within reach.

erreichen [εr'raiçən] vt reach; Zweck achieve; Zug catch.

errichten [εr'riçtən] vt erect, put up; (gründen) establish, set up.

erringen [εr'riŋən] vt irreg gain, win.

erröten [εr'røːtən] vi blush, flush.

Errungenschaft [εr'ruŋənʃaft] f achievement; (col: Anschaffung) acquisition.

Ersatz [εr'zats] m -es substitute; replacement; (Schaden—) compensation; (Mil) reinforcements pl; —befriedigung f vicarious satisfaction; —dienst m (Mil) alternative service; —mann m replacement; (Sport) substitute; e—pflichtig a liable to pay compensation; —reifen m (Aut) spare tyre; —teil nt spare (part).

ersaufen [εr'zaufən] vi irreg (col) drown.

ersäufen [εr'zɔyfən] vt drown.

erschaffen [εr'ʃafən] vt irreg create.

erscheinen [εr'ʃaınən] vi irreg appear.

Erscheinung f appearance; (Geist) apparition; (Gegebenheit) phenomenon; (Gestalt) figure.

erschießen [εr'ʃiːsən] vt irreg .shoot (dead).

erschlaffen [εr'ʃlafən] vi go limp; (Mensch) become' exhausted.

erschlagen [εr'ʃlaːgən] vt irreg strike · dead.

erschleichen [εr'ʃlaıçən] vt irreg obtain by stealth or dubious methods.

erschöpf- [εr'ʃœpf] cpd: —en vt exhaust; —end a exhaustive, thorough; —t a exhausted; E—ung f exhaustion.

erschrecken [εr'ʃrεkən] vt startle, frighten; vi irreg be frightened or startled; —d a alarming, frightening.

erschrocken [εr'ʃrɔkən] a fright- ened, startled.

erschüttern [εr'ʃytərn] vt shake; (ergreifen) move deeply.

Erschütterung f shaking; shock.

erschweren [εr'ʃveːrən] vt complicate.

erschwingen [εr'ʃviŋən] vt irreg afford.

erschwinglich a within one's means.

ersehen [εr'zeːən] vt irreg: aus etw —, daß gather from sth that.

ersetz- [εr'zεts] cpd: —bar a replaceable; —en vt replace; jdm Unkosten etc —en pay sb's expenses etc.

ersichtlich [ɛr'zɪçtlɪç] a evident, obvious.

erspar- [ɛr'ʃpa:r] cpd: **—en** vt Ärger etc spare; Geld save: E**—nis** f -, -se saving.

ersprießlich [ɛr'ʃpri:slɪç] a profitable, useful; (angenehm) pleasant.

erst [e:rst] ad (at) first; (nicht früher, nur) only; (nicht bis) not till; — einmal first.

erstarren [ɛr'ʃtarən] vi stiffen; (vor Furcht) grow rigid; (Materie) solidify.

erstatten [ɛr'ʃtatən] vt Kosten (re)pay; Anzeige etc — report sb; Bericht — make a report.

Erstaufführung ['e:rstauffy:rʊŋ] f first performance.

erstaunen [ɛr'ʃtaunən] vt astonish; vi be astonished; E— nt -s astonishment.

erstaunlich a astonishing.

erst- ['e:rst] cpd: E-ausgabe f first edition; **—beste(r,s)** a first that comes along; **—e(r,s)** a first.

erstechen [ɛr'ʃtɛçən] vt irreg stab (to death).

erstehen [ɛr'ʃte:ən] vt irreg buy; vi (a)rise.

ersteigen [ɛr'ʃtaɪgən] vt irreg climb, ascend.

erstellen [ɛr'ʃtɛlən] vt erect, build.

erst- cpd: **—emal** ad (the) first time; **—ens** ad firstly, in the first place; **—ere(r,s)** pron (the) former.

ersticken [ɛr'ʃtɪkən] vt (lit, fig) stifle; Mensch suffocate; Flammen smother; vi (Mensch) suffocate; (Feuer) be smothered; in Arbeit — be snowed under with work.

Erstickung f suffocation.

erst- cpd: **—klassig** a first-class; E**—kommunion** f first communion;

—malig a first; **—mals** ad for the first time.

erstrebenswert [ɛr'ʃtre:bənsve:rt] a desirable, worthwhile.

erstrecken [ɛr'ʃtrɛkən] vr extend, stretch.

Ersttags- [e:rsta:gz] cpd: **—brief** m first-day cover; **—stempel** m first-day (date) stamp.

ersuchen [ɛr'zu:xən] vt request.

ertappen [ɛr'tapən] vt catch, detect.

erteilen [ɛr'taɪlən] vt give.

ertönen [ɛr'tø:nən] vi sound, ring out.

Ertrag [ɛr'tra:k] m -(e)s, ⸚e yield; (Gewinn) proceeds pl; e**—en** vt irreg bear, stand.

erträglich [ɛr'trɛ:klɪç] a tolerable, bearable.

ertränken [ɛr'trɛŋkən] vt drown.

erträumen [ɛr'trɔymən] vt: sich (dat) etw — dream of sth, imagine sth.

ertrinken [ɛr'trɪŋkən] vi irreg drown; E— nt -s drowning.

erübrigen [ɛr'y:brɪgən] vt spare; vr be unnecessary.

erwachen [ɛr'vaxən] vi awake.

erwachsen [ɛr'vaksən] a grown-up; E**—e(r)** mf adult; E**—en-bildung** f adult education.

erwägen [ɛr'vɛ:gən] vt irreg consider.

Erwägung f consideration.

erwähn- [ɛr've:n] cpd: **—en** vt mention; **—enswert** a worth mentioning; E**—ung** f mention.

erwärmen [ɛr'vɛrmən] vt warm, heat; vr get warm, warm up; sich — für warm to.

erwarten [ɛr'vartən] vt expect; (warten auf) wait for; etw kaum — können hardly be able to wait for sth.

Erwartung f expectation; e—sgemäß ad as expected; e—svoll a expectant.

erwecken ['ɛr'vɛkən] vt rouse, awake; den Anschein — give the impression.

erwehren [ɛr'veːrən] vr fend, ward (gen off); (des Lachens etc) refrain (gen from).

erweichen [ɛr'vaiçən] vti soften.

Erweis [ɛr'vais] m -es, -e proof; e—en irreg vt prove; Ehre, Dienst do (jdm sb); vr prove (als to be).

Erwerb [ɛr'vɛrp] m -(e)s, -e acquisition; (Beruf) trade; e—en vt irreg acquire; e—slos a unemployed; —squelle f source of income; e—stätig a (gainfully) employed; e—sunfähig a unemployable.

erwidern ['ɛr'viːdərn] vt reply; (vergelten) return.

erwiesen [ɛr'viːzən] a proven.

erwischen [ɛr'vɪʃən] vt (col) catch, get.

erwünscht [ɛr'vynʃt] a desired.

erwürgen [ɛr'vyrgən] vt strangle.

Erz [ɛːrts] nt -es, -e ore.

erzähl- [ɛr'tsɛːl] cpd: —en vt tell; E—er m -s, - narrator; E—ung f story, tale.

Erz- cpd: —bischof m archbishop; —engel m archangel.

érzeug- [ɛr'tsɔyg] cpd: —en vt produce; Strom generate; E—erpreis m producer's price; E—nis nt -ses, -se product, produce; E—ung f production; generation.

erziehen [ɛr'tsiːən] vt irreg bring up; (bilden) educate, train.

Erziehung f bringing up; (Bildung) education; —sbeihilfe f educational grant; —sberechtigte(r) mf parent,

guardian; —sheim nt approved school.

erzielen [ɛr'tsiːlən] vt achieve, obtain; Tor score.

erzwingen [ɛr'tsvɪŋən] vt irreg force, obtain by force.

es [ɛs] pron nom, acc it.

Esche ['ɛʃə] f -, -n ash.

Esel ['eːzəl] m -s, - donkey, ass; —sohr nt dog-ear.

Eskalation [ɛskalatsi'oːn] f escalation.

eßbar ['ɛsbaːr] a eatable, edible.

essen ['ɛsən] vti irreg eat; E— nt -s, - meal; food; E—szeit f mealtime; dinner time.

Essig ['ɛsɪç] m -s, -e vinegar; —gurke f gherkin.

Eß- ['ɛs] cpd: —kastanie f sweet chestnut; —löffel m tablespoon; —tisch m dining table; —waren pl victuals pl, food provisions pl; —zimmer nt dining room.

etablieren [eta'bliːrən] vr become established; set up business.

Etage [e'taːʒə] f -, -n floor, storey; —nbetten pl bunk beds pl; —nwohnung f flat.

Etappe [e'tapə] f -, -n stage.

Etat [e'ta] m -s, -s budget; —jahr nt financial year; —posten m budget item.

etepetete [eːtəpe'teːtə] a (col) fussy.

Ethik ['eːtɪk] f ethics sing.

ethisch ['eːtɪʃ] a ethical.

Etikett [eti'kɛt] nt -(e)s, -e label; tag; —e f etiquette, manners pl; e—ieren [-'tiːrən] vt label; tag.

etliche ['ɛtlɪçə] pron pl some, quite a few; —s a thing or two.

Etui [ɛt'viː] nt -s, -s case.

etwa ['ɛtva] ad (ungefähr) about; (vielleicht) perhaps; (beispielsweise) for instance; nicht — by no means; —ig ['ɛtva-ɪç] a possible; —s pron something; anything; (ein wenig) a little; ad a little.

Etymologie [etymolo'gi:] f etymology.

euch [ɔʏç] pron acc of ihr you; yourselves; dat of ihr (to) you.

euer ['ɔʏər] pron gen of ihr of you; pron your; —e(r,s) yours.

Eule ['ɔʏlə] f -, -n owl.

eure(r,s) ['ɔʏrə(r,z)] pron your; yours; -rseits ad on your part; —sgleichen pron people like you; —twegen, —twillen ad (für euch) for your sakes; (wegen euch) on your account.

eurige pron: der/die/das — yours.

Euro- [ɔʏro] cpd: —krat [-'kra:t] m -en, -en eurocrat; —pameister [ɔʏ'ro:pa-] m European champion.

Euter ['ɔʏtər] nt -s, - udder.

evakuieren [evaku'i:rən] vt evacuate.

evangelisch [evaŋ'ge:lɪʃ] a Protestant.

Evangelium [evaŋ'ge:lɪʊm] nt gospel.

Eva(s)kostüm ['e:fa(s)kɔsty:m] nt: im — in one's birthday suit.

eventuell [evɛntu'ɛl] a possible; ad possibly, perhaps.

EWG [e:ve:'ge:] f - EEC, Common Market.

ewig ['e:vɪç] a eternal; E—keit f eternity.

exakt [ɛ'ksakt] a exact.

Examen [ɛ'ksa:mən] nt -s, - or Examina examination.

Exempel [ɛ'ksɛmpəl] nt -s, - example.

Exemplar [ɛksɛm'pla:r] nt -s, -e specimen; (Buch—) copy; e—isch a exemplary.

exerzieren [ɛksɛr'tsi:rən] vi drill.

Exil [ɛ'ksi:l] nt -s, -e exile.

Existenz [ɛksɪs'tɛnts] f existence; (Unterhalt) livelihood, living; (pej: Mensch) character; —kampf m struggle for existence; —minimum nt -s subsistence level.

existieren [ɛksɪs'ti:rən] vi exist.

exklusiv [ɛksklu'zi:f] a exclusive; —e [-'zi:və] ad, prep +gen exclusive of, not including.

exorzieren [ɛksɔr'tsi:rən] vt exorcize.

exotisch [ɛ'kso:tɪʃ] a exotic.

Expansion [ɛkspanzi'o:n] f expansion.

Expedition [ɛkspediʦi'o:n] f expedition; (Comm) forwarding department.

Experiment [ɛksperi'mɛnt] nt experiment; e—ell [-'tɛl] a experimental; e—ieren [-'ti:rən] vi experiment.

Experte [ɛks'pɛrtə] m -n, -n expert, specialist.

explo- [ɛksplo] cpd: —dieren [-'di:rən] vi explode; E—sion [ɛksplozi'o:n] f explosion; —siv [-'zi:f] a explosive.

Exponent [ɛkspo'nɛnt] m exponent.

Export [ɛks'pɔrt] m -(e)s, -e export; —eur [-'tø:r] m exporter; —handel m export trade; e—ieren [-'ti:rən] vt export; —land nt exporting country.

Expreß- [ɛks'prɛs] cpd: —gut nt express goods pl or freight; —zug m express (train).

extra ['ɛkstra] a inv (col: gesondert) separate; (besondere) extra; ad (gesondert) separately; (speziell) specially; (absichtlich) on purpose; (vor Adjektiven, zusätzlich) extra; E— nt -s, -s extra; E—ausgabe f, E—blatt nt special edition.

Extrakt [εks'trakt] m -(e)s, -e extract.

extrem [εks'tre:m] a extreme; —istisch [-'mistɪʃ] a (Pol) extremist; E—itäten [-'tɛ:tən] pl

extremities pl.

Exzellenz [εkstsε'lεnts] f excellency.

exzentrisch [εks'tsεntrɪʃ] a eccentric.

Exzeß [εks'tsεs] m -sses, -sse excess.

F

F, f [εf] nt F, f.

Fabel ['fa:bəl] f -, -n fable; f—haft a fabulous, marvellous.

Fabrik [fa'bri:k] f factory; —ant [-'kant] m (Hersteller) manufacturer; (Besitzer) industrialist; —arbeiter m factory worker; —at [-'ka:t] nt -(e)s, -e manufacture, product; —ation [-atsi'o:n] f manufacture, production; —besitzer m factory owner; —gelände nt factory premises pl.

Fach [fax] nt -(e)s, ⁻er compartment; (Sachgebiet) subject; im Mann vom — an expert; —arbeiter m skilled worker; —arzt m (medical) specialist; —ausdruck m technical term.

Fächer ['fεçər] m -s, - fan.

Fach- cpd: f—kundig a expert, specialist; f—lich a professional; expert; —mann m, pl -leute specialist; —schule f technical college; f—simpeln vi talk ‹shop›; —werk nt timber frame.

Fackel ['fakəl] f -, -n torch; f—n vi (col) dither.

fad(e) ['fa:t, fa:də] a insipid; (langweilig) dull.

Faden ['fa:dən] m -s, ⁼ thread; —nudeln pl vermicelli pl; f—scheinig a (lit, fig) threadbare.

fähig ['fɛ:ɪç] a capable (zu, gen of); able; F—keit f ability.

Fähnchen ['fɛ:nçən] nt pennon, streamer.

fahnden ['fa:ndən] vi: — nach search for.

Fahndung f search; —sliste f list of wanted criminals, wanted list.

Fahne ['fa:nə] f -, -n flag, standard; eine — haben (col) smell of drink; —nflucht f desertion.

Fahrbahn f carriageway (Brit), roadway.

Fähre ['fɛ:rə] f -, -n ferry.

fahren ['fa:rən] irreg vt drive; Rad ride; (befördern) drive, take; Rennen drive in; vi (sich bewegen) go; (Schiff) sail; (abfahren) leave; mit dem Auto/Zug — go or travel by car/train; mit der Hand — über (+acc) pass one's hand over.

Fahr- cpd: —er m -s, - driver; —erflucht f hit-and-run; —gast m passenger; —geld nt fare; —gestell nt chassis; (Aviat) undercarriage; —karte f. ticket; —kartenausgabe f, —kartenschalter m ticket office; f—lässig a negligent; f—lässige Tötung manslaughter; —lässigkeit f negligence; —lehrer m driving instructor; —plan m timetable;

f—planmäßig a (Rail) scheduled; —preis m fare; —prüfung f driving test; —rad nt bicycle; —schein m ticket; —schule f driving school; —schüler(in f) m learner (driver); —stuhl m lift, elevator (US).

Fahrt [faːrt] f -, -en journey; (kurz) trip; (Aut) drive; (Geschwindigkeit) speed.

Fährte ['fɛːrtə] f -, -n track, trail.

Fahrt- cpd: —kosten pl travelling expenses pl; —richtung f course, direction.

Fahr- cpd: —zeug nt vehicle; —zeughalter m -s, - owner of a vehicle.

Fak- [fak] cpd: f—tisch a actual; —tor m factor; —tum nt -s, -ten fact; —ul'tät f faculty.

Falke ['falkə] m -n, -n falcon.

Fall [fal] m -(e)s, ⸚e (Sturz) fall; (Sachverhalt, Jur, Gram) case; auf jeden —, auf alle ⸚e in any case; (bestimmt) definitely; —e f -, -n trap; f—en vi irreg fall; etw f—en lassen drop sth.

fällen ['fɛlən] vt Baum fell; Urteil pass.

fallenlassen vt irreg Bemerkung make; Plan abandon, drop.

fällig ['fɛlɪç] a due; F—keit f (Comm) maturity.

Fall- cpd: —obst nt fallen fruit, windfall; f—s adv in case, if; —schirm m parachute; —schirmjäger m parachute troops pl; —schirmspringer m parachutist; —tür f trap door.

falsch [falʃ] a false; (unrichtig) wrong.

fälschen ['fɛlʃən] vt forge.

Fälscher m -s, - forger.

Falsch- cpd: —geld nt counterfeit money; —heit f falsity, falseness; (Unrichtigkeit) wrongness.

fälsch- cpd: —lich a false; —licherweise ad mistakenly; F—ung f forgery.

Fältchen ['fɛltçən] nt crease, wrinkle.

Falte ['faltə] f -, -n (Knick) fold, crease; (Haut—) wrinkle; (Rock—) pleat; f—n vt fold; Stirn wrinkle; f—nlos a without folds; without wrinkles.

familiär [famili'ɛːr] a familiar.

Familie [fa'miːliə] f family; —ähnlichkeit f family resemblance; —nkreis m family circle; —nname m surname; —nstand m marital status; —nvater m head of the family.

Fanatiker [fa'naːtikər] m -s, - fanatic.

fanatisch a fanatical.

Fanatismus [fana'tɪsmʊs] m fanaticism.

Fang [faŋ] m -(e)s, ⸚e catch; (Jagen) hunting; (Kralle) talon, claw; f—en irreg vt catch; vr get caught; (Flugzeug) level out; (Mensch: nicht fallen) steady o.s.; (fig) compose o.s.; (in Leistung) get back on form.

Farb- ['farb] cpd: —abzug m coloured print; —aufnahme f colour photograph; —band m typewriter ribbon; —e f -, -n colour; (zum Malen etc) paint; (Stoff—) dye; f—echt a colourfast.

färben ['fɛrbən] vt colour; Stoff, Haar dye.

farben- ['farbən] cpd: —blind a colour-blind; —froh a prächtig a colourful, gay.

Farb- cpd: —fernsehen nt colour television; —film m colour film; f—ig a coloured; —ige(r) mf coloured; —kasten m paint-box; f—los a colourless; —photographie

f colour photography; —stift m
coloured pencil; —stoff m dye;
—ton m hue, tone.

Färbung ['fɛrbuŋ] f colouring;
(Tendenz) bias.

Farn [farn] m -(e)s, -e, —kraut
nt fern; bracken.

Fasan [fa'za:n] m -(e)s, -e(n)
pheasant.

Fasching ['faʃɪŋ] m -s, -e or -s
carnival.

Faschismus [fa'ʃɪsmʊs] m fascism.
Faschist m fascist.

faseln ['fa:zəln] vi talk nonsense,
drivel.

Faser ['fa:zər] f -, -n fibre; f—n
vi fray.

Faß [fas] nt -sses, Fässer vat,
barrel; (Öl) drum; Bier vom —
draught beer; f—bar a comprehensible; —bier nt draught beer.

fassen ['fasən] vt (ergreifen) grasp,
take; (inhaltlich) hold; Entschluß
etc take; (verstehen) understand;
Ring etc set; (formulieren)
formulate, phrase; nicht zu —
unbelievable; vr calm down.

faßlich ['faslıç] a intelligible.

Fassung ['fasuŋ] f (Umrahmung)
mounting; (Lampen—) socket;
(Wortlaut) version;
(Beherrschung) composure; jdn
aus der — bringen upset sb;
f—slos a speechless; —svermögen
nt capacity; (Verständnis) comprehension.

fast [fast] ad almost, nearly.

fasten ['fastən] vi fast; F— nt -s
fasting; —zeit f Lent.

Fastnacht f Shrove Tuesday;
carnival.

fatal [fa'ta:l] a fatal; (peinlich)
embarrassing.

faul [faul] a rotten; Person lazy;
Ausreden lame; daran ist etwas —
there's sth fishy about it; —en vi
rot; —enzen vi idle; F—enzer m
-s, - idler, loafer; F—heit f
laziness; —ig a putrid.

Fäulnis ['fɔylnıs] f - decay, putre-
faction.

Faust ['faust] f -, Fäuste fist;
—handschuh m mitten.

Favorit [favo'ri:t] m -en, -en
favourite.

Februar ['fe:brua:r] m -(s), -e
February.

fechten ['fɛçtən] vi irreg fence.

Feder ['fe:dər] f -, -n feather;
(Schreib—) pen nib; (Tech)
spring; —ball m shuttlecock;
—ballspiel nt badminton; —bett nt
continental quilt; —halter m pen-
holder, pen; f—leicht a light as a
feather; f—n vi (nachgeben) be
springy; (sich bewegen) bounce;
vt spring; —ung f suspension;
—vieh nt poultry.

Fee [fe:] f -, -n fairy; f—nhaft
['fe:ən-] a fairylike.

Fege- ['fe:gə] cpd: —feuer nt
purgatory; f—n vt sweep.

fehl [fe:l] a: — am Platz or Ort out
of place; —en vi be wanting or
missing; (abwesend sein) be
absent; etw fehlt jdm sb lacks sth;
du fehlst mir I miss you; was fehlt
ihm? what's wrong with him?
F—er m -s, - mistake, error;
(Mangel, Schwäche) fault; —erfrei
a faultless; without any mistakes;
—erhaft a incorrect; faulty;
F—geburt f miscarriage; —gehen
vi irreg go astray; F—griff m
blunder; F—konstruktion f badly
designed thing; F—schlag m
failure; —schlagen vi irreg fail;
F—schluß m wrong conclusion;

F—start m (Sport) false start;
F—tritt m false move; (fig)
blunder, slip; F—zündung f (Aut)
misfire, backfire.

Feier ['faɪər] f -, -n celebration;
—abend m time to stop work;
—abend machen stop, knock off;
was machst du am —abend? what
are you doing after work?; jetzt ist
—abend! that's enough!; f—lich a
solemn; —lichkeit f solemnity; pl
festivities (pl); f—n vti celebrate;
—tag m holiday.

feig(e) ['faɪg(ə)] a cowardly; F—e
f -, -n fig; F—heit f cowardice;
F—ling m coward.

Feil- [faɪl] cpd: —e f -, -n file; f—en
vti file; f—schen vi haggle.

fein [faɪn] a fine; (vornehm)
refined; Gehör etc keen; —! great!

Feind [faɪnt] m -(e)s, -e enemy;
f—lich a hostile; —schaft f
enmity; f—selig a hostile;
—seligkeit f hostility.

Fein- cpd: f—fühlend, f—fühlig a
sensitive; —gefühl nt delicacy,
tact; —heit f fineness; refinement;
keenness; —kostgeschäft nt
delicatessen (shop); —schmecker
m -s, - gourmet.

feist [faɪst] a fat.

Feld [fɛlt] nt -(e)s, -er field;
(Schach) square; (Sport) pitch;
—blume f wild flower; —herr m
commander; —webel m -s, -
sergeant; —weg m path; —zug m
(lit, fig) campaign.

Felge ['fɛlgə] f -, -n (wheel) rim;
—nbremse f caliper brake.

Fell [fɛl] nt -(e)s, -e fur; coat;
(von Schaf) fleece; (von toten
Tieren) skin.

Fels [fɛls] m -en, -en, **Felsen**
['fɛlzən] m -s, - rock; (von Dover
etc) cliff; f—enfest a firm;

—envorsprung m ledge; f—ig a
rocky; —spalte f crevice.

feminin [femiˈniːn] a feminine;
(pej) effeminate.

Fenster ['fɛnstər] nt -, - window;
—brett nt windowsill; —laden m
shutter; —putzer m -s, - window
cleaner; —scheibe f windowpane;
—sims m windowsill.

Ferien ['feːriən] pl holidays pl,
vacation (US); — haben be on
holiday; —kurs m holiday course;
—reise f holiday; —zeit f holiday
period.

Ferkel ['fɛrkəl] nt -s, - piglet.

fern [fɛrn] a,ad far-off, distant;
von hier a long way (away) from
here; F—amt nt (Tel) exchange;
F—bedienung f remote control;
F—e f -, -n distance; —er a,ad
further; (weiterhin) in future;
F—flug m long-distance flight;
F—gespräch nt trunk call; F—glas
nt binoculars pl; —halten vtr irreg
keep away; F—lenkung f remote
control; —liegen vi irreg; jdm
—liegen be far from sb's mind;
F—rohr nt telescope; F—schreiber
m teleprinter; —schriftlich a by
telex; F—sehapparat m television
set; —sehen vi irreg watch television; F—sehen nt -s television;
im F—sehen on television;
F—seher m television; F—sprecher
m telephone; F—sprechzelle f telephone box or booth (US).

Ferse ['fɛrzə] f -, -n heel.

fertig ['fɛrtɪç] a (bereit) ready;
(beendet) finished; (gebrauchs—)
ready-made; F—bau m prefab-
(ricated house); —bringen vt irreg
(fähig sein) manage, be capable of;
(beenden) finish; —keit f skill;
—machen vt (beenden) finish;
(col) Person finish; (körperlich)

exhaust; (moralisch) get down; vr get ready; **—stellen** vt complete; **F—ware** f finished product.

Fessel ['fɛsəl] f -, -n fetter; **f—n** vt bind; (mit Fesseln) fetter; (fig) spellbind; **f—nd** a fascinating, captivating.

fest [fɛst] a firm; Nahrung solid; Gehalt regular; ad schlafen soundly; **F—** nt -(e)s, -e party; festival; **—angestellt** a permanently employed; **F—beleuchtung** f illumination; **—binden** vt irreg tie, fasten; **—bleiben** vi irreg stand firm; **F—essen** nt banquet; **—fahren** vr irreg get stuck; **—halten** irreg vt seize, hold fast; Ereignis record; vr hold on (an + dat to); **—igen** vt strengthen; **F—igkeit** f strength; **—klammern** vr cling on (an + dat to); **F—land** nt mainland; **—legen** vt fix; vr commit o.s.; **—lich** a festive; **—machen** vt fasten; Termin etc fix; **F—nahme** f -, -n capture; **—nehmen** vt irreg capture, arrest; **F—rede** f address; **—schnallen** vt strap down; vr fasten one's seat belt; **—setzen** vt fix, settle; **F—spiel** nt festival; **—stehen** vi irreg be certain; **—stellen** vt establish; (sagen) remark; **F—ung** f fortress.

Fett [fɛt] nt -(e)s, -e fat, grease; **f—** a fat; Essen etc greasy; **f—arm** a low fat; **f—en** vt grease; **—fleck** m grease spot or stain; **f—gedruckt** a bold-type; **—gehalt** m fat content; **f—ig** a greasy, fatty; **—näpfchen** nt: ins —näpfchen treten put one's foot in it.

Fetzen ['fɛtsən] m -s, - scrap.

feucht [fɔʏçt] a damp; Luft humid; **F—igkeit** f dampness; humidity.

Feuer ['fɔʏər] nt -s, - fire; (zum Rauchen) a light; (fig: Schwung) spirit; **—alarm** m fire alarm; **—eifer** m zeal; **f—fest** a fireproof; **—gefahr** f danger of fire; **f—gefährlich** a inflammable; **—leiter** f fire escape ladder; **—löscher** m -s, - fire extinguisher; **—melder** m -s, - fire alarm; **f—n** vti (lit, fig) fire; **f—sicher** a fireproof; **—stein** m flint; **—wehr** f -, -en fire brigade; **—werk** nt fireworks pl; **—zeug** nt (cigarette) lighter.

Fichte ['fɪçtə] f -, -n spruce, pine.

fidel [fi'de:l] a jolly.

Fieber ['fi:bər] nt -s, - fever, temperature; **f—haft** a feverish; **—messer** m, **—thermometer** nt thermometer.

fies [fi:s] a (col) nasty.

Figur [fi'gu:r] f -, -en figure; (Schach—) chessman, chess piece.

Filiale [fili'a:lə] f -, -n (Comm) branch.

Film [fɪlm] m -(e)s, -e film; **—aufnahme** f shooting; **f—en** vti film; **—kamera** f cine-camera; **—vorführgerät** nt cine-projector.

Filter ['fɪltər] m -s, - filter; **f—n** vt filter; **—mundstück** nt filter tip; **—papier** nt filter paper; **—zigarette** f tipped cigarette.

Filz [fɪlts] m -es, -e felt; **f—en** vt (col) frisk; vi (Wolle) mat.

Finale [fi'na:lə] nt -s, -(s) finale; (Sport) final(s).

Finanz [fi'nants] f finance; **—amt** nt Inland Revenue Office; **—beamte(r)** m revenue officer; **f—iell** [-tsi'ɛl] a financial; **f—ieren** [-tsi:rən] vt finance; **—minister** m Chancellor of the Exchequer (Brit), Minister of Finance.

Find- ['find] cpd: **f—en** irreg vt find; (meinen) think; vr · be (found); (sich fassen) compose o.s.; **ich finde nichts dabei, wenn ...** I don't see what's wrong if ...; **das wird sich f—en** things will work out; **—er** m -s, - finder; **—erlohn** m reward; **f—ig** a resourceful.

Finger ['fiŋər] m -s, - finger.; **—abdruck** m fingerprint; **—handschuh** m glove; **—hut** m thimble; (Bot) foxglove; **—ring** m ring; **—spitze** f fingertip; **—zeig** m -(e)s, -e hint, pointer.

fingieren [fiŋ'gi:rən] vt feign.

fingiert a made-up, fictitious.

Fink. ['fiŋk] m -en, -en finch.

finster ['finstər] a dark, gloomy; (verdächtig) dubious; (verdrossen) grim; **Gedanke** dark; **F—nis** f - darkness, gloom.

Finte ['fintə] f -, -n feint, trick.

firm [firm] a well-up; **F—a** f -, **-men** firm; **F—einhaber** m owner of firm; **F—enschild** nt (shop) sign; **F—enzeichen** nt registered trademark.

Firnis ['firnis] m -ses, -se varnish.

Fisch [fiʃ] m -(e)s, -e fish; pl (Astrol) Pisces; **f—en** vti fish; **—er** m -s, - fisherman; **—e'rei** f fishing, fishery; **—fang** m fishing; **—geschäft** nt fishmonger's (shop); **—gräte** f fishbone; **—zug** m catch or draught of fish.

fix [fiks] a fixed; Person alert, smart; **— und fertig** finished; (erschöpft) done in; **—ieren** [fi'ksi:rən] vt fix; (anstarren) stare at.

flach [flax] a flat; Gefäß shallow.

Fläche ['flɛçə] f -, -n area; (Ober—) surface; **—ninhalt** m surface area.

Flach- cpd: **—heit** f flatness; shallowness; **—land** nt lowland.

flackern ['flakərn] vi flare, flicker.

Flagge ['flagə] f -, -n flag.

flagrant [fla'grant] a flagrant; **in —i** red-handed.

Flamme ['flamə] f -, -n flame.

Flanell [fla'nɛl] m -s, -e flannel.

Flanke ['flaŋkə] f -, -n flank; (Sport: Seite) wing.

Flasche ['flaʃə] f -, -n bottle (col: Versager) wash-out; **—nbier** nt bottled beer; **—nöffner** m bottle opener; **—nzug** m pulley.

flatterhaft a flighty, fickle.

flattern ['flatərn] vi flutter.

flau [flau] a weak, listless; Nachfrage slack; **jdm ist — sb feels** queasy.

Flaum [flaum] m -(e)s (Feder) down; (Haare) fluff.

flauschig ['flauʃiç] a fluffy.

Flausen ['flauzən] pl silly ideas pl; (Ausflüchte) weak excuses pl.

Flaute ['flautə] f -, -n calm; (Comm) recession.

Flechte ['flɛçtə] f -, -n plait; (Med) dry scab; (Bot) lichen; **f—n** vt irreg plait; Kranz twine.

Fleck [flɛk] m -(e)s, -e, **Flecken** m -s, - spot; (Schmutz—) stain; (Stoff—) patch; (Makel) blemish; **nicht vom — kommen** (lit, fig) not get any further; **vom — weg** straight away; **f—enlos** a spotless; **—enmittel** nt, **—enwasser** nt stain remover; **f—ig** a spotted; stained.

Fledermaus ['fle:dərmaus] f bat.

Flegel ['fle:gəl] m -s, - flail; (Person) lout; **f—haft** a loutish, un-mannerly; **—jahre** pl adolescence; **f—n** vr lounge about.

flehen ['fle:ən] vi implore; **—tlich** a imploring.

Fleisch [flaɪʃ] nt -(e)s flesh;
(Essen) meat; —brühe f beef tea,
stock; —er m -s, - butcher; —e'rei
f butcher's (shop); f—ig a fleshy;
f—lich a carnal; —pastete f meat
pie; —wolf m mincer; —wunde f
flesh wound.

Fleiß [flaɪs] m -es diligence,
industry; f—ig a diligent, industrious.

flektieren [flɛk'tiːrən] vt inflect.

flennen ['flɛnən] vi (col) cry,
blubber.

fletschen ['flɛtʃən] vt Zähne show.

flexibel [flɛ'ksiːbəl] a flexible.

Flicken ['flɪkən] m -s, - patch; f—
vt mend.

Flieder ['fliːdər] m -s, - lilac.

Fliege ['fliːgə] f -, -n fly;
(Kleidung) bow tie; f—n vti irreg
fly; auf jdn/etw f—en (col) to be mad
about sb/sth; —npilz m toadstool;
—r m -s, - flier, airman; —ralarm
m air-raid warning.

fliehen ['fliːən] vi irreg flee.

Fliese ['fliːzə] f -, -n tile.

Fließ- ['fliːs] cpd: —arbeit f pro-
duction-line work; —band nt production or assembly line; f—en vi
irreg flow; f—end a flowing; Rede,
Deutsch fluent; Übergänge
smooth; —heck nt fastback; —
papier nt blotting paper.

flimmern ['flɪmərn] vi glimmer.

flink [flɪŋk] a nimble, lively;
F—heit f nimbleness, liveliness.

Flinte ['flɪntə] f-, -n rifle; shotgun.

Flitter ['flɪtər] m -s, - spangle,
tinsel; —wochen pl honeymoon.

flitzen ['flɪtsən] vi flit.

Flocke ['flɔkə] f -, -n flake.

flockig a flaky.

Floh [floː] m -(e)s, ∸e flea.

florieren [flo'riːrən] vi flourish.

Floskel ['flɔskəl] f -, -n empty
phrase.

Floß [floːs] nt -es, ∸e raft, float.

Flosse ['flɔsə] f -, -n fin.

Flöte ['fløːtə] f -, -n flute;
(Block-) recorder.

Flötist(in f) [fløː'tɪst(ɪn)] m flautist.

flott [flɔt] a lively; (elegant) smart;
(Naut) afloat; F—e f -, -n fleet,
navy.

Flöz [fløːts] nt -es, -e layer, seam.

Fluch [fluːx] m -(e)s, ∸e curse;
f—en vi curse, swear.

Flucht [fluxt] f -, -en flight;
(Fenster-) row; (Reihe) range;
(Zimmer-) suite; f—artig a hasty.

flüchten ['flʏçt] cpd: —en vir flee,
escape; f—ig a fugitive; (Chem)
volatile; (vergänglich) transitory;
(oberflächlich) superficial; (eilig)
fleeting; F—igkeit f transitoriness,
volatility; superficiality; f—ig-
keitsfehler m careless slip; F—ling
m fugitive, refugee.

Flug [fluːk] m -(e)s, ∸e flight; im
— airborne, in flight; —abwehr
['fluːg-] f anti-aircraft defence;
—blatt nt pamphlet.

Flügel ['flyːgəl] m -s, - wing;
(Mus) grand piano.

Fluggast m airline passenger.

flügge ['flʏgə] a (fully-)fledged.

Flug- cpd: —geschwindigkeit f
flying or air speed; —gesellschaft
f airline (company); —hafen m airport; —höhe f altitude (of flight);
—plan m flight schedule; —platz
m airport; (klein) airfield; —post
f airmail; f—s [fluks] ad speedily;
—schrift f pamphlet; —strecke f
air route; —verkehr m air traffic;
—wesen nt aviation; —zeug nt
(aero)plane, airplane (US);
—zeugentführung f hijacking of a

plane; —**zeughalle** f hangar; —**zeugträger** m aircraft carrier.

Flunder ['flʊndər] f -, -n flounder.

flunkern ['flʊŋkərn] vi fib, tell stories.

Fluor ['fluːɔr] nt -s fluorine.

Flur [fluːr] m -(e)s, -e hall; (Treppen—) staircase.

Fluß [flʊs] m -sses, ⸗sse river; (Fließen) flow; im — sein (fig) be in a state of flux.

flüssig ['flʏsɪç] a liquid; — machen vt Geld make available; **F-keit** f liquid; (Zustand) liquidity.

flüster- ['flʏstər] cpd: —n vti whisper; **F-propaganda** f whispering campaign.

Flut [fluːt] f -, -en (lit, fig) flood; (Gezeiten) high tide; **f-en** vi flood; —**licht** nt floodlight.

Fohlen ['foːlən] nt -s, - foal.

Föhn [føːn] m -(e)s, -e foehn, warm south wind.

Föhre ['føːrə] f -, -n Scots pine.

Folge ['fɔlgə] f -, -n series, sequence; (Fortsetzung) instalment; (Auswirkung) result; in rascher — in quick succession; etw zur — haben result in sth; — haben have consequences; einer Sache — leisten comply with sth; **f—n** vi follow (jdm sb); (gehorchen) obey (jdm sb); jdm **f—n können** (fig) follow or understand sb; —**nd** a following; **f—ndermaßen** ad as follows, in the following way; **f—nreich, f—nschwer** a momentous; **f—richtig** a logical; **f—rn**, tr conclude (aus + dat from); —**rung** f conclusion; **f—widrig** a illogical;

folg- cpd: —**lich** ad consequently; —**sam** a obedient.

Folie ['foːliə] f -, -n foil.

Folter ['fɔltər] f -, -n torture; (Gerät) rack; **f—n** vt torture.

Fön® [føːn] m -(e)s, -e hair-dryer; **f—en** vt (blow) dry.

Fontäne [fɔn'tɛːnə] f -, -n fountain.

foppen ['fɔpən] vt tease.

Förder- ['fœrdər] cpd: —**band** nt conveyor belt; —**korb** m pit cage; **f—lich** a beneficial.

fordern ['fɔrdərn] vt demand.

Förder- cpd: **f—n** vt promote; (unterstützen) help; (Kohle extract; —**ung** f promotion; help; extraction.

Forderung ['fɔrdərʊŋ] f demand.

Forelle [fo'rɛlə] f -, -n trout.

Form [fɔrm] f -, -en shape; (Gestaltung) form; (Guß—) mould; (Back—) baking tin; in — sein be in good form or shape; in — von in the shape of; **f—ali'sieren** vt formalize; —**ali'tät** f formality; —**at** [-'maːt] nt -(e)s, -e format; (fig) distinction; —**ati'on** f formation; **f—bar** a malleable; —**el** f -, -n formula; **f—ell** [-'mɛl] a formal; **f—en** vt form, shape; —**fehler** m faux-pas, gaffe; (Jur) irregularity; **f—ieren** [-'miːrən] vt form; vr form up.

förmlich ['fœrmlɪç] a formal; (col) real; **F—keit** f formality.

Form- cpd: **f—los** a shapeless; Benehmen etc informal; —**u'lar** nt -s, -e form; **f—u'lieren** vt formulate.

forsch [fɔrʃ] a energetic, vigorous; —**en** vt search (nach for); vi (wissenschaftlich) (do) research; —**end** a searching; **F—er** m -s, - research scientist; (Natur—) explorer.

Forschung ['fɔrʃʊŋ] f research; —**sreise** f scientific expedition.

Forst [fɔrst] m -(e)s, -e forest; —**arbeiter** m forestry worker;

—wesen nt, —wirtschaft f forestry.

Förster ['fœrstər] m -s, - forester; (für Wild) gamekeeper.

fort [fɔrt] ad away; (verschwunden) gone; (vorwärts) on; und so — and so on; in einem — on and on; —bestehen vi irreg survive; —bewegen vtr move away; —bilden vr continue one's education; —bleiben vi irreg stay away; —bringen vt irreg take away; F—dauer f continuance; —fahren vi irreg depart; (fortsetzen) go on, continue; —führen vt continue, carry on; —gehen vi irreg go away; —geschritten a advance; —kommen vi irreg get on; (wegkommen) get away; —können vi irreg be able to get away; —müssen vi irreg have to go; —pflanzen vr reproduce; F—pflanzung f reproduction; —schaffen vt remove; —schreiten vi irreg advance.

Fortschritt ['fɔrt-ʃrɪt] m advance; —e machen make progress; f—lich ad progressive.

fort- cpd: —setzen vt continue; F—setzung f continuation; (folgender Teil) instalment; F—setzung folgt to be continued; —während a incessant; continual; —ziehen irreg vt pull away; vi move on; (umziehen) move away.

Foto ['fo:to] nt -s, -s photo(graph); m -s, -s (—apparat) camera; —'graf m photographer; —'graphie f photography; (Bild) photograph; f—gra'phieren vt photograph; vi take photographs.

Foul nt -s, -s foul.

Fracht [fraxt] f -, -en freight; (Naut) cargo; (Preis) carriage; —er m -s, - freighter, cargo boat; —gut nt freight.

Frack [frak] m -(e)s, -̈e tails pl.

Frage ['fra:gə] f -, -n question; etw in — stellen question sth; jdm eine — stellen ask sb a question, put a question to sb; nicht in — kommen be out of the question; —bogen m questionnaire; f—n vti ask; —zeichen nt question mark.

frag- cpd: —lich a questionable, doubtful; —los ad unquestionably.

Fragment [fra'gmɛnt] nt fragment; f—arisch [-'ta:rɪʃ] a fragmentary.

fragwürdig ['fra:kvʏrdɪç] a questionable, dubious.

Fraktion [fraktsi'o:n] f parliamentary party.

frank- ['fraŋk] a frank, candid; —ieren [-'ki:rən] vt stamp, frank; —o ad post-paid; carriage paid.

Franse ['franzə] f -, -n fringe; f—n vi fray.

Fratze ['fratsə] f -, -n grimace.

Frau [frau] f -, -en woman; (Ehe—) wife; (Anrede) Mrs; — Doktor Doctor; —enarzt m gynaecologist; —enbewegung f feminist movement; —enzimmer nt female, broad (US).

Fräulein ['frɔylaɪn] nt young lady; (Anrede) Miss.

fraulich ['fraulɪç] a womanly.

frech [frɛç] a cheeky, impudent; F—dachs m cheeky monkey; F—heit f cheek, impudence.

Fregatte [fre'gatə] f frigate.

frei [fraɪ] a free; Stelle, Sitzplatz auch vacant; Mitarbeiter freelance; Geld available; (unbekleidet) bare; sich (dat) einen Tag — nehmen take a day off; von etw — sein be free of sth; im F—en in the open air; — sprechen talk without notes; F—bad nt open-air swimming pool; —bekommen vt *irreg:* jdn/einen Tag —bekommen get sb freed/get a day off; **F—er** *m* -s, - suitor; —gebig *a* generous; **F—gebigkeit** *f* generosity; —halten *vt irreg* keep free; —händig *ad* fahren with no hands; **F—heit** *f* freedom; —heitlich *a* liberal; **F—heitsstrafe** *f* prison sentence; —heraus *ad* frankly; **F—karte** *f* free ticket; —kommen *vi irreg* get free; —lassen *vt irreg* (set) free; **F—lauf** *m* freewheeling; —legen *vt* expose; —lich *ad* certainly, admittedly; ja —lich yes of course; **F—lichtbühne** *f* open-air theatre; —machen *vt* Post frank; Tage —machen take days off; *vr* arrange to be free; —sinnig *a* liberal; —sprechen *vt irreg* acquit (von of); **F—spruch** *m* acquittal; —stellen *vt:* jdm etw —stellen leave sth (up) to sb; **F—stoß** *m* free kick; —tag *m* Friday; —tags *ad* on Fridays; **F—übungen** *pl* (physical) exercises *pl*; —willig *a* voluntary; **F—willige(r)** *mf* volunteer; **F—zeit** *f* spare or free time; —zügig *a* liberal, broad-minded; (mit Geld) generous.

fremd [fremt] *a* (unvertraut) strange; (ausländisch) foreign; (nicht eigen) someone else's; etw ist jdm — sth is foreign to sb; —artig *a* strange; **F—e(r)** [ˈfrɛmdə(r)] *mf* stranger; (Ausländer) foreigner; **F—enführer** *m* (tourist) guide; **F—enlegion** *f* foreign legion; **F—enverkehr** *m* tourism; **F—enzimmer** *nt* guest room; **F—körper** *m* foreign body; —ländisch *a* foreign; **F—ling** *m* stranger; **F—sprache** *f* foreign language; —sprachig *a* foreign-language; **F—wort** *nt* foreign word.

Frequenz [freˈkvɛnts] *f* (Rad) frequency.

fressen [ˈfrɛsən] *vti irreg* eat.

Freude [ˈfrɔydə] *f* -, -n joy, delight.

freudig *a* joyful, happy.

freudlos *a* joyless.

freuen [ˈfrɔyən] *vt impers* make happy or pleased; *vr* be glad or happy; sich auf etw (acc) — look forward to sth; sich über etw (acc) — be pleased about sth.

Freund [frɔynt] *m* -(e)s, -e friend; boyfriend; —in [-din] *f* friend; girlfriend; **f—lich** *a* kind, friendly; **f—licherweise** *ad* kindly; —lichkeit *f* friendliness, kindness; —schaft *f* friendship; **f—schaftlich** *a* friendly.

Frevel [ˈfreːfəl] *m* -s, - crime, offence (an +dat against); **f—haft** *a* wicked.

Frieden [ˈfriːdən] *m* -s, - peace; im — in peacetime; —sschluß *m* peace agreement; —verhandlungen *pl* peace negotiations *pl*; —svertrag *m* peace treaty; —szeit *f* peacetime.

fried- [ˈfriːt] *cpd:* —fertig *a* peaceable; **F—hof** *m* cemetery; —lich *a* peaceful.

frieren [ˈfriːrən] *vti irreg* freeze; ich friere, es friert mich I am freezing, I'm cold.

Fries [friːs] *m* -es, -e (Archit) frieze.

frigid(e) [friˈɡiːt, friˈɡiːdə] *a* frigid.

Frikadelle [frikaˈdɛlə] *f* meatball.

frisch [frɪʃ] *a* fresh; (lebhaft) lively; — gestrichen! wet paint!; sich — machen freshen (o.s.) up; **F—e** *f* freshness; liveliness.

Friseur [friˈzøːr] *m*, **Friseuse** [friˈzøːzə] *f* hairdresser.

Frisier- [fri'zi:r] cpd: **f—en** vtr do (one's hair); (fig) Abrechnung fiddle, doctor; **—salon** m hairdressing salon; **—tisch** m dressing table.

Frisör [fri'zø:r] m -s, e hairdresser.

Frist [frist] f -, -en period; (Termin) deadline; **f—en** vt Dasein lead; (kümmerlich) eke out; **f—los** a Entlassung instant.

Frisur [fri'zu:r] f hairdo, hairstyle.

fritieren [fri'ti:rən] vt deep fry.

frivol [fri'vo:l] a frivolous.

froh [fro:] a happy, cheerful; **ich bin —, daß ...** I'm glad that ...

fröhlich ['frø:lıç] a merry, happy; **F—keit** f merriness, gaiety.

froh- cpd: **—'locken** vi exult; (pej) gloat; **F—sinn** m cheerfulness.

fromm [from] a pious, good; Wunsch idle.

Frömm- ['frœm] cpd: **—e'lei** f false piety; **—igkeit** f piety.

frönen ['frø:nən] vi indulge (etw (dat) in sth).

Fronleichnam [fro:n'laıçna:m] m -(e)s Corpus Christi.

Front [front] f -, -en front; **f—al** [fron'ta:l] a frontal.

Frosch [frɔʃ] m -(e)s, ⁺e frog; (Feuerwerk) squib; **—mann** m frogman; **—schenkel** m frog's leg.

Frost [frɔst] m -(e)s, ⁺e frost; **—beule** f chilblain.

frösteln ['frœstəln] vi shiver.

Frost- cpd: **f—ig** a frosty; **—schutzmittel** nt anti-freeze.

Frottee [frɔ'te:] nt or m -(s), -s towelling.

frottieren [frɔ'ti:rən] vt rub, towel.

Frottier(hand)tuch nt towel.

Frucht [fruxt] f -, ⁺e (lit, fig) fruit; (Getreide) corn; **f—bar,** **f—bringend** a fruitful, fertile; **—barkeit** f fertility; **f—en** vi be of use; **f—los**

a fruitless; **—saft** m fruit juice.

früh [fry:] a,ad early; **heute —** this morning; **F—aufsteher** m -s, - early riser; **F—e** f - early morning; **—er** a earlier; (ehemalig) former; ad formerly; **—er war das anders** that used to be different; **—estens** ad at the earliest; **F—geburt** f premature birth/baby; **F—jahr** nt, **F—ling** m spring; **—reif** a precocious; **F—stück** nt breakfast; **—stücken** vi (have) breakfast; **—zeitig** a early; (pej) untimely.

frustrieren [frus'tri:rən] vt frustrate.

Fuchs [fuks] m -es, ⁺e fox; **f—en** (col) vt rile, annoy; vr be annoyed; **f—teufelswild** a hopping mad.

Füchsin ['fyksın] f vixen.

fuchteln ['fuxtəln] vi gesticulate wildly.

Fuge ['fu:gə] f -, -n joint; (Mus) fugue.

fügen ['fy:gən] vt place, join; vr be obedient (in +acc to); (anpassen) adapt oneself (in +acc to); impers happen.

fügsam ['fy:kza:m] a obedient.

fühl- ['fy:l] cpd: **—bar** a perceptible, noticeable; **—en** vtir feel; **F—er** m -s, -feeler.

führen ['fy:rən] vt lead; Geschäft run; Name bear; Buch keep; vi lead; vr behave.

Führer ['fy:rər] m -s, - leader; (Fremden-) guide; **—schein** m driving licence.

Fuhrmann ['fu:rman] m, pl -leute carter.

Führung ['fy:rʊŋ] f leadership; (eines Unternehmens) management; (Mil) command; (Benehmen) conduct; (Museums-) conducted tour; **—szeugnis** nt certificate of good conduct.

Fuhrwerk ['fu:rvɛrk] *nt* cart.

Fülle ['fylə] *f* - wealth, abundance; **f—n** *vtr* fill; (*Cook*) stuff; **—n** *nt* -s, - foal; **—r** *m* -s, -, **Füllfederhalter** *m* fountain pen.

Füllung *f* filling; (*Holz—*) panel.

fummeln ['fuməln] *vi* (*col*) fumble.

Fund [funt] *m* -(e)s, -e find; **—ament** [-da'mɛnt] *nt* foundation; **f—amen'tal** a fundamental; **—büro** *nt* lost property office, lost and found; **—grube** *f* (*fig*) treasure trove; **f—ieren** [-'di:rən] *vt* back up; **f—iert** a sound.

fünf [fynf] *num* five; **—hundert** *num* five hundred; **—tel** *nt* -s, - fifth; **—zehn** *num* fifteen; **—zig** *num* fifty.

fungieren [fuŋ'gi:rən] *vi* function; (*Person*) act.

Funk [fuŋk] *m* -s radio, wireless; **—e(n)** *m* -ns, -n (*lit, fig*) spark; **f—eln** *vi* sparkle; **f—en** *vt* radio; **—er** *m* -s, - radio operator; **—gerät** *nt* radio set; **—haus** *nt* broadcasting centre; **—spruch** *m* radio signal; **—station** *f* radio station.

Funktion [fuŋktsi'o:n] *f* function; **f—ieren** [-'ni:rən] *vi* work, function.

für [fy:r] *prep* +acc for; was — what kind of sort of; das F— und Wider the pros and cons *pl*; Schritt — Schritt step by step; F—bitte *f* intercession.

Furche ['furçə] *f*-, -n furrow; **f—n** *vt* furrow.

Furcht [furçt] *f*- fear; **f—bar** a terrible, frightful.

fürcht- ['fyrçt] *cpd*: **—en** *vt* be afraid of, fear; *vr* be afraid (*vor* +dat of); **—erlich** a awful.

furcht- *cpd*: **—los** a fearless; **—sam** a timid.

füreinander [fy:r'aɪ'nandər] *ad* for each other.

Furnier [fur'ni:r] *nt* -s, -e veneer.

fürs [fy:rs] = **für das.**

Fürsorge ['fy:rzɔrgə] *f* care; (*Sozial—*) welfare; **—amt** *nt* welfare office; **—r(in** *f*) *m* -s, - welfare worker; **—unterstützung** *f* social security, welfare benefit (*US*).

Für- *cpd*: **—sprache** *f* recommendation; (*um Gnade*) intercession; **—sprecher** *m* advocate.

Fürst [fyrst] *m* -en, -en prince; **—in** *f* princess; **—entum** *nt* principality; **f—lich** a princely.

Furt [furt] *f* -, -en ford.

Fürwort ['fy:rvɔrt] *nt* pronoun.

Fuß [fu:s] *m* -es, ⁼e foot; (*von Glas, Säule etc*) base; (*von Möbel*) leg; **zu** — on foot; **—ball** *m* football; **—ballspiel** *nt* football match; **—ballspieler** *m* footballer; **—boden** *m* floor; **—bremse** *f* (*Aut*) footbrake; **f—en** *vi* rest, be based (*auf* +dat on); **—ende** *nt* foot; **—gänger(in** *f*) *m* -s, - pedestrian; **—gängerzone** *f* pedestrian precinct; **—note** *f* footnote; **—pfleger(in** *f*) *m* chiropodist; **—spur** *f* footprint; **—tritt** *m* kick; (*Spur*) footstep; **—weg** *m* footpath.

Futter ['futər] *nt* -s, - fodder, feed; (*Stoff*) lining; **—al** [-'ra:l] *nt* -s, -e case.

füttern ['fytərn] *vt* feed; *Kleidung* line.

Futur [fu'tu:r] *nt* -s, -e future.

G

G, g [ge:] *nt* G, g.

Gabe ['ga:bə] *f* -, -n gift.

Gabel ['ga:bəl] *f* -, -n fork; —frühstück *nt* mid-morning snack; —ung *f* fork.

gackern ['gakərn] *vi* cackle.

gaffen ['gafən] *vi* gape.

Gage ['ga:ʒə] *f* -, -n fee; salary.

gähnen ['gɛ:nən] *vi* yawn.

Gala ['gala] *f* - formal dress; —vorstellung *f* (Theat) gala performance.

galant [ga'lant] a gallant, courteous.

Galerie [galə'ri:] *f* gallery.

Galgen ['galgən] *m* -s, - gallows *pl*; —frist *f* respite; —humor *m* macabre humour.

Galle ['galə] *f* -, -n gall; (Organ) gall-bladder.

Galopp [ga'lɔp] *m* -s, -s *or* -e gallop; g—ieren [-'pi:rən] *vi* gallop.

galvanisieren [galvani'zi:rən] *vt* galvanize.

Gamasche [ga'maʃə] *f* -, -n gaiter; (kurz) spat.

Gammler ['gamlər] *m* -s, - loafer, layabout.

Gang [gaŋ] *m* -(e)s, ≃e walk; (Boten—) errand; (—art) gait; (Abschnitt eines Vorgangs) operation; (Essens—, Ablauf) course; (Flur etc) corridor; (Durch—) passage; (Tech) gear; **in — bringen** start up; (fig) get off the ground; **in — sein** be in operation; (fig) be under way; [gɛŋ] *f* -, ≃s gang; g— a: g— und gäbe usual, normal; g—bar a passable; Methode practicable.

Gängel- ['gɛŋəl] *cpd*: —band *nt*: jdn am —band halten (fig) spoonfeed sb; g—n *vt* spoonfeed.

gängig ['gɛŋɪç] a common, current; Ware in demand, selling well.

Ganove [ga'no:və] *m* -n, -n (col) crook.

Gans [gans] *f* -, ≃e goose.

Gänse- ['gɛnzə] *cpd*: —blümchen *nt* daisy; —braten *m* roast goose; —füßchen *pl* (col) inverted commas *pl* (Brit), quotes *pl*; —haut *f* goose pimples *pl*; —marsch *m*: im —marsch in single file; —rich *m* -s, -e gander.

ganz [gants] a whole; (vollständig) complete; **— Europa** all Europe; **sein —es Geld** all his money; a*d* quite; (völlig) completely; **— und gar nicht** not at all; **es sieht — so aus it really looks like it; aufs G—e gehen go for the lot.**

gänzlich ['gɛntslɪç] a,ad complete(ly), entire(ly).

gar [ga:r] a cooked, done; ad quite; **— nicht/nichts/keiner** not/nothing/nobody at all; **— nicht schlecht** not bad at all.

Garage [ga'ra:ʒə] *f* -, -n garage.

Garantie [garan'ti:] *f* guarantee; g—ren *vt* guarantee.

Garbe ['garbə] *f* -, -n sheaf; (Mil) burst of fire.

Garde ['gardə] *f* -, -n guard(s); **die alte —** the old guard; —'robe *f* -, -n wardrobe; (Abgabe) cloakroom; —'robenfrau *f* cloakroom attendant; —'robenständer *m* hallstand.

Gardine [gar'di:nə] f curtain;

gären ['gɛ:rən] vi irreg ferment.

Garn [garn] nt -(e)s, -e thread; yarn (auch fig).

Garnele [gar'ne:lə] f -, -n shrimp, prawn.

garnieren [gar'ni:rən] vt decorate; Speisen garnish.

Garnison [garni'zo:n] f -, -en garrison.

Garnitur [garni'tu:r] f (Satz) set; (Unterwäsche) set of (matching) underwear; (fig) erste — top rank; zweite — second rate.

garstig ['garstɪç] a nasty, horrid.

Garten ['gartən] m -s, = garden; —arbeit f gardening; —bau m horticulture; —fest nt garden party; —gerät nt gardening tool; —haus nt summerhouse; —kresse f cress; —lokal nt beer garden; —schere f pruning shears pl; —tür f garden gate.

Gärtner(in f) ['gɛrtnər(ɪn)] m -s, - gardener; —ei [-'raɪ] f nursery; (Gemüse-) market garden (Brit), truck farm (US); g—n vi garden.

Gärung ['gɛ:rʊŋ] f fermentation.

Gas [ga:s] nt -es, -e gas; — geben (Aut) accelerate, step on the gas; g—förmig a gaseous; —herd m, —kocher m gas cooker; —leitung f gas pipeline; —maske f gasmask; —pedal nt accelerator, gas pedal.

Gasse ['gasə] f -, -n lane, alley; —njunge m street urchin.

Gast [gast] m -es, =e guest; —arbeiter(in f) m foreign worker;

Gästebuch ['gɛstəbu:x] nt visitors' book, guest book.

Gast- cpd: g—freundlich a hospitable; —geber m -s, - host; —geberin f hostess; —haus nt, —hof m hotel, inn; g—ieren [-'ti:rən] vi (Theat) (appear as a)

G.G.D.—C

guest; g—lich a hospitable; —lichkeit f hospitality; —rolle f guest role.

gastronomisch [gastro'no:mɪʃ] a gastronomic(al).

Gast- cpd: —spiel nt (Sport) away game; —stätte f restaurant; pub; —wirt m innkeeper; —wirtschaft f hotel, inn; —zimmer nt (guest) room.

Gas- cpd: —vergiftung f gas poisoning; —werk nt gasworks sing or pl; —zähler m gas meter.

Gatte ['gatə] m -n, -n husband, spouse; die —n husband and wife.

Gatter ['gatər] nt -s, - railing, grating; (Eingang) gate.

Gattin f wife, spouse.

Gattung ['gatʊŋ] f genus; kind.

Gaukler ['gaʊklər] m -s, - juggler, conjurer.

Gaul [gaʊl] m -(e)s, Gäule horse, nag.

Gaumen ['gaʊmən] m -s, - palate.

Gauner ['gaʊnər] m -s, - rogue; —ei [-'raɪ] f swindle.

Gaze ['ga:zə] f -, -n gauze.

Gebäck [gə'bɛk] nt -(e)s, -e pastry.

Gebälk [gə'bɛlk] nt -(e)s timberwork.

Gebärde [gə'bɛ:rdə] f -, -n gesture; g—n vi behave.

gebären [gə'bɛ:rən] vt irreg give birth to, bear.

Gebärmutter f uterus, womb.

Gebäude [gə'bɔydə] nt -s, - building; —komplex m (building) complex.

Gebein [gə'baɪn] nt -(e)s, -e bones pl.

Gebell [gə'bɛl] nt -(e)s barking.

geben ['ge:bən] irreg vti (jdm etw) give (sb sth or sth to sb); Karten deal; ein Wort gab das andere one angry word led to another; **v impers es gibt** there is/are; **there will be**; **gegeben** given; **zu gegebener Zeit** in good time; **vr** (*sich verhalten*) behave, act; (*aufhören*) abate; **sich geschlagen — admit** defeat; **das wird sich schon —** that'll soon sort itself out.

Gebet [gə'be:t] *nt* -(e)s, -e prayer.

Gebiet [gə'bi:t] *nt* -(e)s, -e area; (*Hoheits—*) territory; (*fig*) field; **g—en** *vt irreg* command, demand; **—er** *m* -s, - master; (*Herrscher*) ruler; **g—erisch** *a* imperious.

Gebilde [gə'bildə] *nt* -s, - object, structure; **g—t** *a* cultured, educated.

Gebimmel [gə'bıməl] *nt* -s (continual) ringing.

Gebirge [gə'bırgə] *nt* -s, - mountain chain.

gebirgig *a* mountainous.

Gebirgszug [gə'bırkstsu:k] *m* mountain range.

Gebiß [gə'bıs] *nt* -sses, -sse teeth *pl*; (*künstlich*) dentures *pl*.

geblümt [gə'bly:mt] *a* flowery.

Geblüt [gə'bly:t] *nt* -(e)s blood, race.

geboren [gə'bo:rən] *a* born; **Frau** née.

geborgen [gə'bɔrgən] *a* secure, safe.

Gebot [gə'bo:t] *nt* -(e)s, -e command(ment *Bibl*); (*bei Auktion*) bid.

Gebräu [gə'brɔy] *nt* -(e)s, -e brew, concoction.

Gebrauch [gə'braux] *m* -(e)s, **Gebräuche** use; (*Sitte*) custom; **g—en** *vt* use.

gebräuchlich [gə'brɔyçlıç] *a* usual, customary.

Gebrauchs- *cpd:* **—anweisung** *f* directions *pl* for use; **—artikel** *m* article of everyday use; **g—fertig** *a* ready for use; **—gegenstand** *m* commodity.

gebraucht [gə'brauxt] *a* used; **G—wagen** *m* secondhand or used car.

gebrechlich [gə'breçlıç] *a* frail; **G—keit** *f* frailty.

Gebrüder [gə'bry:dər] *pl* brothers *pl*.

Gebrüll [gə'bryl] *nt* -(e)s roaring.

Gebühr [gə'by:r] *f* -, -en charge, fee; **nach —** fittingly; **über —** unduly; **g—en** *vi:* **jdm g—en be** sb's due or due to sb; *vr* be fitting; **g—end** *a,ad* fitting(ly), appropriate(ly); **—enfrei** *a* free of charge; **—enpflichtig** *a* subject to charges.

Geburt [gə'bu:rt] *f* -, -en birth; **—enbeschränkung** *f,* **—enkontrolle** *f,* **—enregelung** *f* birth control; **—enziffer** *f* birth-rate.

gebürtig [gə'byrtıç] *a* born in, native of; **—e Schweizerin** native of Switzerland, Swiss-born.

Geburts- *cpd:* **—anzeige** *f* birth notice; **—datum** *nt* date of birth; **—jahr** *nt* year of birth; **—ort** *m* birthplace; **—tag** *m* birthday; **—urkunde** *f* birth certificate.

Gebüsch [gə'byʃ] *nt* -(e)s, -e bushes *pl*.

Gedächtnis [gə'dɛçtnıs] *nt* -ses,-se memory; **—feier** *f* commemoration; **—schwund** *m* loss of memory, failing memory; **—verlust** *m* amnesia.

Gedanke [gə'daŋkə] *m* -ns, -n thought; **sich über etw** (*acc*) **—n machen** think about sth; **—naustausch** *m* exchange of ideas; **g—nlos** *a* thoughtless; **—nlosigkeit**

f thoughtlessness; **—nstrich** m
dash; **—nübertragung** f thought
transference, telepathy; **g—nver-**
loren a lost in thought; **g—nvoll** a
thoughtful.
Gedärm [gə'dɛrm] nt -(e)s, -e
intestines pl, bowels pl.
Gedeck [gə'dɛk] nt -(e)s, -e
cover(ing); (Speisenfolge) menu;
ein — auflegen lay a place.
gedeihen [gə'daɪən] vi irreg thrive,
prosper.
gedenken [gə'dɛŋkən] vi irreg (sich
erinnern) (+gen) remember;
(beabsichtigen) intend.
Gedenk- cpd: **—feier** f
commemoration; **—minute** f
minute's silence; **—tag** m remembrance day.
Gedicht [gə'dɪçt] nt -(e)s, -e poem.
gediegen [gə'di:gən] a (good) quality; Mensch reliable, honest;
G—heit f quality; reliability,
honesty.
Gedränge [gə'drɛŋə] nt -s crush,
crowd; **ins — kommen** (fig) get
into difficulties.
gedrängt a compressed; **— voll**
packed.
gedrungen [gə'drʊŋən] a thickset,
stocky.
Geduld [gə'dʊlt] f - patience;
g—en [gə'dʊldən] vr be patient;
g—ig a patient, forbearing;
—sprobe f trial of (one's) patience.
gedunsen [gə'dʊnzən] a bloated.
geeignet [gə'aɪgnət] a suitable.
Gefahr [gə'fa:r] f-, -en danger; —
laufen, etw zu tun run the risk of
doing sth; **auf eigene —** at one's
own risk.
gefährden [gə'fɛ:rdən] vt endanger.
Gefahren- cpd: **—quelle** f source

of danger; **—zulage** f danger
money.
gefährlich [gə'fɛ:rlɪç] a dangerous.
Gefährte [gə'fɛ:rtə] m -n, -n,
Gefährtin f companion.
Gefälle [gə'fɛlə] nt -s, - gradient,
incline.
gefallen [gə'falən] m -s, - favour;
nt -s pleasure; **an etw** (dat) —
finden derive pleasure from sth;
jdm etw zu — tun do sth to please
sb; **g—** vi irreg: **jdm g—** please
sb; **er/es gefällt mir** I like him/it;
das gefällt mir an ihm that's one
thing I like about him; **sich** (dat)
etw g— lassen put up with sth;
ptp of **fallen.**
gefällig [gə'fɛlɪç] a (hilfsbereit)
obliging; (erfreulich) pleasant;
G—keit f favour; helpfulness; **etw**
aus G—keit tun do sth as a favour.
gefälligst ad kindly.
gefallsüchtig a eager to please.
gefangen [gə'faŋən] a captured;
(fig) captivated; **G—e(r)** m
prisoner, captive; **G—enlager** nt
prisoner-of-war camp; **—halten** vt
irreg keep prisoner; **G—nahme** f-,
-n capture; **G—schaft** f captivity.
Gefängnis [gə'fɛŋnɪs] nt -ses, -se
prison; **—strafe** f prison sentence;
—wärter m prison warder.
Gefasel [gə'fa:zəl] nt -s twaddle,
drivel.
Gefäß [gə'fɛ:s] nt -es, -e vessel
(auch Anat), container.
gefaßt [gə'fast] a composed, calm;
auf etw (acc) **— sein** be prepared
or ready for sth.
Gefecht [gə'fɛçt] nt -(e)s, -e fight;
(Mil) engagement.
gefeit [gə'faɪt] a: **gegen etw — sein**
be immune to sth.
Gefieder [gə'fi:dər] nt -s, ▪

plumage, feathers pl; **g—t** a feathered.

gefleckt [gə'flɛkt] a spotted, mottled.

geflissentlich [gə'flɪsəntlɪç] a,ad intentional(ly).

Geflügel [gə'fly:gəl] nt -s poultry.

Gefolge [gə'fɔlgə] nt -s, - retinue.

Gefolg- cpd: **—schaft** f following; (Arbeiter) personnel; **—smann** m follower.

gefragt [ge'fra:kt] a in demand.

gefräßig [gə'frɛ:sɪç] a voracious.

Gefreite(r) [gə'fraɪtə(r)] m -n, -n lance corporal; (Naut) able seaman; (Aviat) aircraftman.

gefrieren [gə'fri:rən] vi irreg freeze.

Gefrier- cpd: **—fach** nt icebox; **—fleisch** nt frozen meat; **g—getrocknet** a freeze-dried; **—punkt** m freezing point; **—schutzmittel** nt antifreeze; **—truhe** f deep-freeze.

Gefüge [gə'fy:gə] nt -s, - structure.

gefügig [gə'fy:gɪç] a pliant; Mensch obedient.

Gefühl [gə'fy:l] nt -(e)s, -e feeling; etw im **—** haben have a feel for sth; **g—los** a unfeeling; **—sbetont** a emotional; **—sduselei** [-zdu:zə'laɪ] f emotionalism; **g—smäßig** a instinctive.

gegebenenfalls [ga'ge:bənənfals] ad if need be.

gegen ['ge:gən] prep +acc against; (in Richtung auf, jdn betreffend, kurz vor) towards; (im Austausch für) (in return) for; (ungefähr) round about; (im Angriff m counterattack; **G—beweis** m counterevidence.

Gegend ['ge:gənt] f -, -en area, district.

Gegen- cpd: **g—ei'nander** ad against one another; **—fahrbahn** f oncoming carriageway; **—frage** f counter-question; **—gewicht** nt counterbalance; **—gift** nt antidote; **—leistung** f service in return; **—lichtaufnahme** f contre-jour photograph; **—maßnahme** f counter-measure; **—probe** f crosscheck; **—satz** m contrast; **—sätze** überbrücken overcome differences; **g—sätzlich** a contrary, opposite; (widersprüchlich) contradictory; **—schlag** m counter attack; **—seite** f opposite side; (Rückseite) reverse; **g—seitig** a mutual, reciprocal; **sich g—seitig helfen** help each other; **—seitigkeit** f reciprocity; **—spieler** m opponent; **—stand** m object; **g—ständlich** a objective, concrete; **—stimme** f vote against; **—stoß** m counterblow; **—stück** nt counterpart; **—teil** nt opposite; **im —teil** on the contrary; **ins —teil umschlagen** swing to the other extreme; **g—teilig** a opposite, contrary.

gegenüber [ge:gən'y:bər] prep +dat opposite; (zu) to(wards); (angesichts) in the face of; (als) opposite; **G—** nt -s, - person opposite; **g—liegen** vr irreg face each other; **—stehen** vr irreg be opposed (to each other); **—stellen** vt confront; (fig) contrast; **G—stellung** f confrontation; (fig) contrast; **—treten** vi irreg (+dat) face.

Gegen- cpd: **—verkehr** m oncoming traffic; **—vorschlag** m counterproposal; **—wart** f present; **g—wärtig** a present; **das ist mir nicht mehr g—wärtig** that has slipped my mind; ad at present; **—wert** m equivalent; **—wind** m headwind; **—wirkung** f reaction; **g—zeichnen** vti countersign; **—zug** m *m* counter-move; (*Rail*) corresponding train in the other direction.

Gegner ['gɛgnər] *m* -s, - opponent; **g—isch** *a* opposing; **—schaft** *f* opposition.

Gehackte(s) [gə'haktə(z)] *nt* mince(d meat).

Gehalt [gə'halt] *m* -(e)s, -e content; *nt* -(e)s, ¨er salary; **—sempfänger** *m* salary earner; **—serhöhung** *f* salary increase; **—szulage** *f* salary increment.

geharnischt [gə'harnɪʃt] *a* (*fig*) forceful, angry.

gehässig [gə'hɛsɪç] *a* spiteful, nasty; **G—keit** *f* spite(fulness).

Gehäuse [gə'hɔʏzə] *nt* -s, - case; casing; (*von Apfel etc*) core.

Gehege [gə'he:gə] *nt* -s, - enclosure, preserve; **jdm ins — kommen** (*fig*) poach on sb's preserve.

geheim [gə'haim] *a* secret; **G—dienst** *m* secret service, intelligence service; **—halten** *vt irreg* keep secret; **G—nis** *nt* -ses, -se secret; mystery; **G—niskrämer** *m* secretive type; **—nisvoll** *a* mysterious; **G—polizei** *f* secret police; **G—schrift** *f* code, secret writing.

Geheiß [gə'hais] *nt* -es command; **auf jds —** at sb's behest.

gehen ['ge:ən] *irreg vi* go; (*zu Fuß —*) walk; **— nach** (*Fenster*) face; *v impers*: **wie geht es (dir)?** how are you *or* things?; **mir/ihm geht es gut** I'm/he's (doing) fine; **geht das?** is that possible?; **geht's noch?** can you manage?; **es geht** not too bad, O.K.; **das geht nicht** that's not on; **es geht um etw** sth is concerned, it's about sth.

geheuer [gə'hɔʏər] *a*: **nicht —** eery; (*fragwürdig*) dubious.

Geheul [gə'hɔʏl] *nt* -(e)s howling.

Gehilfe [gə'hɪlfə] *m* -n, **-n**, **Gehilfin** *f* assistant.

Gehirn [gə'hɪrn] *nt* -(e)s, -e brain; **—erschütterung** *f* concussion; **—wäsche** *f* brainwashing.

Gehör [gə'hø:r] *nt* -(e)s hearing; **musikalisches —** ear; **— finden** gain a hearing; **jdm — schenken** give sb a hearing.

gehorchen [gə'hɔrçən] *vi* obey (*jdm* sb).

gehören [gə'hø:rən] *vi* belong; *vr impers* be right *or* proper.

gehörig *a* proper; **— zu** *or* **+dat** belonging to; part of.

gehorsam [gə'ho:rza:m] *a* obedient; **G— m** -s obedience.

Gehsteig *m*, **Gehweg** *m* ['ge:-] pavement, sidewalk (*US*).

Geier ['gaiər] *m* -s, - vulture.

geifern ['gaifərn] *vi* salivate; (*fig*) bitch.

Geige ['gaigə] *f* -, -n violin; **—r** *m* -s, - violinist; **—rzähler** *m* geiger counter.

geil [gail] *a* randy, horny (*US*).

Geisel ['gaizəl] *f* -, -n hostage.

Geißel ['gaisəl] *f* -, -n scourge, whip; **g—n** *vt* scourge.

Geist [gaist] *m* -(e)s, -er spirit; (*Gespenst*) ghost; (*Verstand*) mind; **g—erhaft** *a* ghostly; **—esabwesend** *a* absent-minded; **—esblitz** *m* brainwave; **—esgegenwart** *f* presence of mind; **—eshaltung** *f* mental attitude; **—eskrank** *a* mentally ill; **—eskranke(r)** *mf* mentally ill person; **—eskrankheit** *f* mental illness; **—esstörung** *f* mental disturbance; **—eswissenschaften** *pl* arts (subjects) *pl*; **—eszustand** *m* state of mind; **g—ig** *a* intellectual; mental; *Getränke* alcoholic; **g—ig**

behindert mentally handicapped; **g—lich** a spiritual, religious; clerical; **—liche(r)** m clergyman; **—lichkeit** f clergy; **g—los** a uninspired, dull; **g—reich** a clever; witty; **g—tötend** a soul-destroying; **g—voll** a intellectual; (weise) wise.

Geiz [gaɪts] m **-es** miserliness, meanness; **g—en** vi to be miserly; **—hals** m, **—kragen** m miser; **g—ig** a miserly, mean.

Geklapper [gə'klapər] nt **-s** rattling.

geknickt [gə'knɪkt] a (fig) dejected.

gekonnt [gə'kɔnt] a skilful.

Gekritzel [gə'krɪtsəl] nt **-s** scrawl, scribble.

gekünstelt [gə'kynstəlt] a artificial, affected.

Gelächter [gə'lɛçtər] nt **-s**, **-** laughter.

geladen [gə'la:dən] a loaded; (Elec) live; (fig) furious.

Gelage [gə'la:gə] nt **-s**, **-** feast, banquet.

gelähmt [gə'lɛ:mt] a paralysed.

Gelände [gə'lɛndə] nt **-s**, **-** land, terrain; (von Fabrik, Sport—) grounds pl; (Bau—) site; **g—gängig** a able to go cross-country; **—lauf** m cross-country race.

Geländer [gə'lɛndər] nt **-s**, **-** railing; (Treppen—) banister(s).

gelangen [gə'laŋən] vi (an +acc or zu) reach; (erwerben) attain; in **jds Besitz —** to come into sb's possession.

gelassen [gə'lasən] a calm, composed; **G—heit** f calmness, composure.

Gelatine [ʒela'ti:nə] f gelatine.

geläufig [gə'lɔyfɪç] a (üblich) common; **das ist mir nicht —** I'm

not familiar with that; **G—keit** f commonness; familiarity.

gelaunt [gə'launt] a: **schlecht/gut —** in a bad/good mood; **wie ist er —?** what sort of mood is he in?

Geläut(e) [gə'lɔyt(ə)] nt **-(e)s**, **-(e)** ringing; (Läutwerk) chime.

gelb [gɛlp] a yellow; (Ampellicht) amber; **—lich** a yellowish; **G—sucht** f jaundice.

Geld [gɛlt] nt **-(e)s**, **-er** money; **etw zu — machen** sell sth off; **—anlage** f investment; **—beutel** m, **—börse** f purse; **—einwurf** m slot; **—geber** m **-s**, **-** financial backer; **g—gierig** a avaricious; **—mittel** pl capital, means pl; **—schein** m banknote; **—schrank** m safe, strongbox; **—strafe** f fine; **—stück** nt coin; **—verlegenheit** f: **in —verlegenheit sein/kommen** to be/run short of money; **—verleiher** m **-s**, **-** moneylender; **—wechsel** m exchange (of money).

Gelee [ʒe'le:] nt or m **-s**, **-s** jelly.

gelegen [gə'le:gən] a situated; (passend) convenient, opportune; **etw kommt jdm —** sth is convenient for sb.

Gelegenheit [gə'le:gənhaɪt] f opportunity; (Anlaß) occasion; **bei jeder —** at every opportunity; **—sarbeit** f casual work; **—sarbeiter** m casual worker; **—skauf** m bargain.

gelegentlich [gə'le:gəntlɪç] a occasional; ad occasionally; (bei Gelegenheit) some time (or other); prep +gen on the occasion of.

gelehrig [gə'le:rɪç] a quick to learn, intelligent.

gelehrt a learned; **G—e(r)** mf scholar; **G—heit** f scholarliness.

Geleise [gə'laɪzə] nt **-s**, **-** track; see Gleis.

Geleit [gə'laɪt] *nt* -(e)s, -e escort; g—en *vt* escort; —schutz *m* escort.

Gelenk [gə'lɛŋk] *nt* -(e)s, -e joint; g—ig *a* supple.

gelernt [gə'lɛrnt] *a* skilled.

Geliebte(r) [gə'li:ptə(r)] *mf* sweetheart, beloved.

gelind(e) [gə'lɪnt, gə'lɪndə] *a* mild, light; (*fig*) *Wut* fierce; —e gesagt to put it mildly.

gelingen [gə'lɪŋən] *vi* irreg succeed; **die Arbeit gelingt mir nicht** I'm not being very successful with this piece of work; **es ist mir gelungen, etw zu tun** I succeeded in doing sth.

geilen ['gɛlən] *vi* shrill.

geloben [gə'lo:bən] *vti* vow, swear.

gelten ['gɛltən] *irreg vt* (*wert sein*) be worth; **etw gilt bei jdm viel/wenig** sb values sth highly/sb doesn't value sth very highly; **jdm viel/wenig** — mean a lot/not mean much to sb; **was gilt die Wette?** do you want to bet?; *vi* (*gültig sein*) be valid; (*erlaubt sein*) be allowed; **jdm** — (*gemünzt sein auf*) be meant for or aimed at sb; **etw** —**lassen** accept sth; **als** *or* **für etw** — be considered to be sth; **jdm** *or* **für jdn** — (*betreffen*) apply to, *or* for sb; *v impers* **es gilt, etw zu tun** it is necessary to do sth; **—d** prevailing; **etw** —**d machen** to assert sth; **sich** —**d machen** make itself/o.s. felt. ..

Geltung ['gɛltʊŋ] *f*: — **haben** have validity; **sich/etw** (*dat*) **verschaffen** establish oneself/sth; **etw zur** —**bringen** show sth to its best advantage; **zur** — **kommen** be seen/heard *etc* to its best advantage; —**sbedürfnis** *nt* desire for admiration.

Gelübde [gə'lʏpdə] *nt* -s, - vow.

gelungen [gə'lʊŋən] *a* successful.

gemächlich [gə'mɛ:çlɪç] *a* leisurely.

Gemahl [gə'ma:l] *m* -(e)s, -e husband; —**in** *f* wife.

Gemälde [gə'mɛ:ldə] *nt* -s, - picture, painting.

gemäß [gə'mɛ:s] *prep* +*dat* in accordance with; *a* appropriate (*dat* to); —**igt** *a* moderate; *Klima* temperate.

gemein [gə'maɪn] *a* common; (*niederträchtig*) mean; **etw** — **haben** (**mit**) have sth in common (with).

Gemeinde [gə'maɪndə] *f* -, -n district, community; (*Pfarr*—) parish; (*Kirchen*—) congregation; —**steuer** *f* local rates *pl*; —**verwaltung** *f* local administration; —**vorstand** *m* local council; —**wahl** *f* local election.

Gemein- *cpd*: **g—gefährlich** *a* dangerous to the public; —**gut** *nt* public property; —**heit** *f* commonness; mean thing to do/to say; **g—hin** *ad* generally; —**nutz** *m* public good; —**platz** *m* commonplace, platitude; **g—sam** *a* joint, common (*auch Math*); **g—same Sache mit jdm machen** be in cahoots with sb; *ad* together, jointly; **etw g—sam haben** have sth in common; —**samkeit** *f* community, having in common; —**schaft** *f* community; **in** —**schaft mit** jointly or together with; **g—schaftlich** *a* see **g—sam**; —**schaftsarbeit** *f* teamwork; team effort; —**schaftserziehung** *f* coeducation; —**sinn** *m* public spirit; **g—verständlich** *a* generally comprehensible; —**wohl** *nt* common good.

Gemenge [gə'mɛŋə] *nt* -s, - mixture; (*Hand*—) scuffle.

gemessen [gə'mɛsən] a measured.
Gemetzel [gə'mɛtsəl] nt -s, - slaughter, carnage, butchery.
Gemisch [gə'mɪʃ] nt -es, -e mixture; **g—t** a mixed.
Gemse ['gɛmzə] f -, -n chamois.
Gemunkel [gə'muŋkəl] nt-s gossip.
Gemurmel [gə'murməl] nt -s murmur(ing).
Gemüse [gə'my:zə] nt -s, - vegetables. pl; **—garten** m vegetable garden; **—händler** m greengrocer.
Gemüt [gə'my:t] nt -(e)s, -er disposition, nature; person; sich (dat) etw zu —e führen (col) indulge in sth; die **—er** erregen arouse strong feelings; **g—lich** a comfortable, cosy; Person good-natured; **—lichkeit** f comfortableness, cosiness; amiability; **—bewegung** f emotion; **—smensch** m sentimental person; **—sruhe** f composure; **—szustand** m state of mind; **g—voll** a warm, tender.

genau [gə'nau] a,ad exact(ly), precise(ly); etw **—** nehmen take sth seriously; **—genommen** ad strictly speaking; **G—igkeit** f exactness, accuracy.
genehm [gə'ne:m] a agreeable, acceptable; **—igen** vt approve, authorize; sich (dat) etw **—igen** indulge in sth; **G—igung** f approval, authorization.
geneigt [gə'naikt] a well-disposed, willing; **—** sein, etw zu tun be inclined to do sth.
General [gene'ra:l] m -s, -e or ¨e general; **—direktor** m director general; **—konsulat** nt consulate general; **—probe** f dress rehearsal; **—stabskarte** f ordnance survey map; **—streik** m general strike;

g—überholen vt thoroughly overhaul.
Generation [generatsi'o:n] f generation; **—skonflikt** m generation gap.
Generator [gene'ra:tor] m generator, dynamo.
genesen [ge'ne:zən] vi irreg convalesce, recover, get well; **G—de(r)** mf convalescent.
Genesung f recovery, convalescence.
genetisch [ge'ne:tɪʃ] a genetic.
genial [geni'a:l] a brilliant; **G—ität** f brilliance, genius.
Genick [gə'nik] nt -(e)s, -e (back of the) neck; **—starre** f stiff neck.
Genie [ʒe'ni:] nt -s, -s genius.
genieren [ʒe'ni:rən] vt bother; geniert es Sie, wenn ...? do you mind if ...?; vr feel awkward or self-conscious.
genießbar a edible; drinkable.
genießen [gə'ni:sən] vt irreg enjoy; eat; drink.
Genießer m -s, - epicure; pleasure lover; **g—isch** a appreciative; ad with relish.
Genosse [gə'nosə] m -n, -n, **Genossin** f comrade (esp Pol), companion; **—nschaft** f cooperative (association).
genug [gə'nu:k] ad enough.
Genüge [gə'ny:gə] f -: jdm/etw **—** tun or leisten satisfy sb/sth; **g—n** vi be enough, suffice; (+dat) satisfied; **g—nd** a sufficient.
genügsam [gə'ny:kza:m] a modest, easily satisfied; **G—keit** f moderation.
Genugtuung [gə'nu:ktu:uŋ] f satisfaction.
Genuß [gə'nus] m -sses, ¨sse pleasure; (Zunehmen) con-

sumption; **in den — von etw kommen** receive the benefit of sth; **—mittel** pl (semi-)luxury items pl.
genüßlich [gəˈnʏslɪç] ad with relish.

Geograph [geoˈgraːf] m -en, -en geographer; **—ie** [-ˈfiː] f geography; **g—isch** a geographical.

Geologe [geoˈloːgə] m -n, -n geologist; **—gie** [-ˈgiː] f geology.

Geometrie [geomeˈtriː] f geometry.

Gepäck [gəˈpɛk] nt -(e)s luggage, baggage; **—abfertigung** f, **—annahme** f, **—ausgabe** f luggage desk/office; **—aufbewahrung** f left-luggage office, checkroom (US); **—netz** nt luggage-rack; **—träger** m porter; (Fahrrad) carrier; **—wagen** m luggage van, baggage car (US).

gepflegt [gəˈpfleːkt] a well-groomed; Park etc well looked after.

Gepflogenheit [gəˈpfloːganhait] f custom.

Geplapper [gəˈplapər] nt -s chatter.

Geplauder [gəˈplaudər] nt -s chat(ting).

Gepolter [gəˈpɔltər] nt -s din.

gerade [gəˈraːdə] a straight; Zahl even; ad (genau) exactly; (örtlich) straight; (eben) just; **warum — ich?** why me?; **— weil** just or precisely because; **nicht — schön** not exactly nice; **das ist es ja —** that's just it; **jetzt — nicht!** not now!; **— noch** just; **— neben** right next to by; **G— f-,-n, -n** straight line; **—aus** ad straight ahead; **—heraus** ad straight out, bluntly; **—so** ad just so; **—so dumm** etc just as stupid etc; **—so wie** just as; **—zu** ad (beinahe) virtually, almost.

geradlinig a rectilinear.

Gerät [gəˈrɛːt] nt -(e)s, -e device; (Werkzeug) tool; (Sport)

apparatus; (Zubehör) equipment no pl.

geraten [gəˈraːtən] vi irreg (gelingen) turn out well (jdm for sb); ... (gedeihen) thrive; **gut/schlecht — turn out** well/badly; **an jdn — come across** sb; **in etw** (acc) **— get into sth;** **in Angst — get frightened; nach jdm — take after sb.**

Geratewohl [garaːtəˈvoːl] nt: **aufs — on the off chance**; (bei Wahl) at random.

geraum [gəˈraum] a: **seit —er Zeit** for some considerable time.

geräumig [gəˈrɔymɪç] a roomy.

Geräusch [gəˈrɔyʃ] nt -(e)s, -e sound, noise; **g—los** a silent; **g—voll** a noisy.

gerben [ˈgɛrbən] vt tan.

Gerber m -s, - tanner; **—ei** [-ˈrai] f tannery.

gerecht [gəˈrɛçt] a just, fair; **jdm/etw — werden** do justice to sb/sth; **G—igkeit** f justice, fairness.

Gerede [gəˈreːdə] nt -s talk, gossip.

gereizt [gəˈraitst] a irritable; **G—heit** f irritation.

Gericht [gəˈrɪçt] nt -(e)s, -e court; (Essen) dish; **mit jdm ins — gehen** (fig) judge sb harshly; **über jdn zu — sitzen** sit in judgement on sb; **das Letzte — the Last Judgement;** **g—lich** a,ad judicial(ly), legal(ly); **—sbarkeit** f jurisdiction; **—shof** m court (of law); **—skosten** pl (legal) costs pl; **—ssaal** m courtroom; **—sverfahren** nt legal proceedings pl; **—sverhandlung** f court proceedings pl; **—svollzieher** m bailiff.

gerieben [gəˈriːbən] a grated; (col: schlau) smart, wily.

gering [gəˈrɪŋ] a slight, small; (niedrig) low; Zeit short; **—achten** vt think little of; **—fügig** a slight,

trivial; —schätzig a disparaging;
G—schätzung f disdain; —ste(r,s)
a slightest, least; —stenfalls ad at
the very least.

gerinnen [gə'rınən] vi irreg congeal; (Blut) clot; (Milch) curdle.

Gerinnsel [gə'rınzəl] nt -s, - clot.

Gerippe [gə'rıpə] nt -s, - skeleton.

gerissen [gə'rısən] a wily, smart.

gern(e) ['gern(ə)] ad willingly,
gladly; — haben, — mögen like;
etwas — tun like doing something;
G—egroß m -, -e show-off.

Geröll [gə'rœl] nt -(e)s, -e scree.

Gerste ['gerstə] f -, -n barley;
—nkorn nt (im Auge) stye.

Gerte ['gertə] f -, -n switch, rod;
g—nschlank a willowy.

Geruch [gə'rux] m -(e)s, ⁻e smell,
odour; g—los a odourless;
g—tilgend a deodorant.

Gerücht [gə'rʏçt] nt -(e)s, -e
. rumour.

geruhen [gə'ru:ən] vi deign.

Gerümpel [gə'rʏmpəl] nt -s junk.

Gerüst [gə'rʏst] nt -(e)s, -e
(Bau—) scaffold(ing); frame.

gesamt [gə'zamt] a whole, entire;
Kosten total; Werke complete; im
—en all in all; G—ausgabe f complete edition; G—deutsch a all-
German; G—eindruck m general
impression; G—heit f totality,
whole.

Gesandte(r) [gə'zantə(r)] m envoy.

Gesandtschaft [gə'zant-ʃaft] f
legation.

Gesang [gə'zaŋ] m -(e)s, ⁻e song;
(Singen) singing; —buch nt (Rel)
hymn book; —verein m choral
society.

Gesäß [gə'zɛ:s] nt -es, -e seat,
bottom.

Geschäft [gə'ʃɛft] nt -(e)s, -e
business; (Laden) shop;
(—sabschluß) deal; —emacher m
-s, - profiteer; g—ig a active, busy;
(pej) officious; g—lich a commercial; ad on business;
—sbericht m financial report;
—sführer m manager; (Klub)
secretary; —sjahr nt financial
year; —slage f business conditions
pl; —smann m businessman;
g—smäßig a businesslike; —sreise
f business trip; —sschluß m closing
time; —ssinn m business sense;
—sstelle f office, place of business;
g—stüchtig a efficient; —sviertel
nt business quarter; —swagen m
company car; —szweig m branch (of a business).

geschehen [gə'ʃe:ən] vi irreg
happen; es war um ihn — that was
the end of him.

gescheit [gə'ʃaıt] a clever.

Geschenk [gə'ʃɛŋk] nt -(e)s, -e
present, gift; —packung f gift pack.

Geschicht- [gə'ʃıçt] cpd: —e f -,
-n story; (Sache) affair; (Historie)
history; —enerzähler m storyteller; g—lich a historical;
—sschreiber m historian.

Geschick [gə'ʃık] nt -(e)s, -e
aptitude; (Schicksal) fate;
—lichkeit f skill, dexterity; g—t a
skilful.

geschieden [gə'ʃi:dən] a divorced.

Geschirr [gə'ʃır] nt -(e)s, -e
crockery; pots and pans pl;
(Pferd) harness; —spülmaschine f
dishwashing machine; —tuch nt
dish cloth.

Geschlecht [gə'ʃlɛçt] nt -(e)s, -er
sex; (Gram) gender; (Art)
species; family; g—lich a sexual;
—skrankheit f venereal disease;
—steil nt or m genitals pl;

—sverkehr m sexual intercourse;
—swort nt (Gram) article.

Geschmack [gəˈʃmak] m -(e)s, -̈e
taste; **nach jds —** to sb's taste;
— finden an etw (dat) (come to)
like sth; **g—los** a tasteless; (fig) in
bad taste; —(s)sache f matter of
taste; —sinn m sense of taste;
g—voll a tasteful.

Geschmeide [gəˈʃmaidə] nt -s, -
jewellery.

geschmeidig a supple; (formbar)
malleable.

Geschmeiß [gəˈʃmais] nt vermin pl.

Geschmiere [gəˈʃmiːrə] nt -s
scrawl; (Bild) daub.

Geschöpf [gəˈʃœpf] nt -(e)s, -e
creature.

Geschoß [gəˈʃos] nt -sses, -sse
(Mil) projectile, missile; (Stockwerk) floor.

geschraubt [gəˈʃraupt] a stilted,
artificial.

Geschrei [gəˈʃrai] nt -s cries pl,
shouting; (fig: Aufhebens) noise,
fuss.

Geschütz [gəˈʃyts] nt -es, -e gun,
cannon; **ein schweres — auffahren**
(fig) bring out the big guns;
—feuer nt artillery fire, gunfire;
g—t a protected.

Geschwader [gəˈʃvaːdər] nt -s, -
(Naut) squadron; (Aviat) group.

Geschwafel [gəˈʃvaːfəl] nt -s silly
talk.

Geschwätz [gəˈʃvɛts] nt -es
chatter, gossip; **g—ig** a talkative;
—igkeit f talkativeness.

geschweige [gəˈʃvaigə] ad: —
(denn) let alone, not to mention.

geschwind [gəˈʃvint] a quick,
swift; **G—igkeit** [-dɪçkait] f speed,
velocity; **G—igkeitsbegrenzung** f
speed limit; **G—igkeitsmesser** m
(Aut) speedometer;

G—igkeitsüberschreitung f
exceeding the speed limit.

Geschwister [gəˈʃvistər] pl
brothers and sisters pl.

geschwollen [gəˈʃvɔlən] a
pompous.

Geschworene(r) [gəˈʃvoːrənə(r)]
mf juror; pl jury.

Geschwulst [gəˈʃvulst] f -, -̈e
swelling; growth, tumour.

Geschwür [gəˈʃvyːr] nt -(e)s, -e
ulcer.

Gesell- [gəˈzɛl] cpd: **—e** m -n, -n
fellow; (Handwerk—) journey-
man; **g—ig** a sociable; —**igkeit** f
sociability; —**schaft** f society;
(Begleitung, Comm) company;
(Abend—schaft etc) party;
g—schaftlich a social;
—**schaftsanzug** m evening dress;
g—schaftsfähig a socially
acceptable; —**schaftsordnung** f
social structure; —**schaftsreise** f
group tour; —**schaftsschicht** f
social stratum.

Gesetz [gəˈzɛts] nt -es, -e law;
—**buch** nt statute book; —**entwurf**
m, —**esvorlage** f legislative;
g—gebend a legislative; —**geber** m -s, -
legislator; —**gebung** f legislation; **g—lich**
a legal, lawful; —**lichkeit** f legality,
lawfulness; **g—los** a lawless;
g—mäßig a lawful; **g—t** a Mensch
sedate; **g—tenfalls** ad supposing
(that); **g—widrig** a illegal, unlawful.

Gesicht [gəˈzɪçt] nt -(e)s, -er face;
das zweite — second sight; **das ist
mir nie zu — gekommen** I've never
laid eyes on that; —**sausdruck** m
(facial) expression; —**sfarbe** f complexion; —**spunkt** m point of view;
—**szüge** pl features pl.

Gesindel [gəˈzɪndəl] nt -s rabble.
gesinnt [gəˈzɪnt] a disposed,
minded.

Gesinnung [gəˈzɪnʊŋ] f disposition; (*Ansicht*) views pl; —sgenosse m like-minded person; —slosigkeit f lack of conviction; —swandel m change of opinion, volte-face.

gesittet [gəˈzɪtət] a well-mannered.

Gespann [gəˈʃpan] nt -(e)s, -e team; (col) couple; **g—t** a tense, strained; (*begierig*) eager; **ich bin g—t, ob** I wonder if or whether; **auf etw/jdn g—t sein** look forward to sth/meeting sb.

Gespenst [gəˈʃpɛnst] nt -(e)s, -er ghost, spectre; **g—isch** a ghostly.

Gespiele [gəˈʃpiːlə] m -n, -n, **Gespielin** f playmate.

Gespött [gəˈʃpœt] nt -(e)s mockery; **zum — werden** become a laughing stock.

Gespräch [gəˈʃprɛːç] nt -(e)s, -e conversation; discussion(s); (*Anruf*) call; **zum — werden** become a topic of conversation; **g—ig** a talkative; **—igkeit** f talkativeness; **—sthema** nt subject or topic (of conversation).

Gespür [gəˈʃpyːr] nt -s feeling.

Gestalt [gəˈʃtalt] f -, -en form, shape; (*Person*) figure; **in — von** in the form of; **— annehmen** take shape; **g—en** vt (*formen*) shape, form; (*organisieren*) arrange, organize; vr turn out (zu to be); **—ung** f formation; organization.

geständig [gəˈʃtɛndɪç] a: **— sein** have confessed.

Geständnis [gəˈʃtɛntnɪs] nt -ses, -se confession.

Gestank [gəˈʃtaŋk] m -(e)s stench.

gestatten [gəˈʃtatən] vt permit, allow; **— Sie?** may I?; **sich** (dat) **—, etw zu tun** take the liberty of doing sth.

Geste [ˈɡɛstə] f -, -n gesture.

gestehen [gəˈʃteːən] vt irreg confess.

Gestein [gəˈʃtain] nt -(e)s, -e rock.

Gestell [gəˈʃtɛl] nt -(e)s, -e frame; (*Regal*) rack, stand.

gestern [ˈɡɛstərn] ad yesterday; **— abend/morgen** yesterday evening/morning.

gestikulieren [ɡɛstikuˈliːrən] vi gesticulate.

Gestirn [gəˈʃtɪrn] nt -(e)s, -e star; (*Sternbild*) constellation.

Gestöber [gəˈʃtøːbər] nt -s, - flurry, blizzard.

Gesträuch [gəˈʃtrɔʏç] nt -(e)s, -e shrubbery, bushes pl.

gestreift [gəˈʃtraift] a striped.

gestrig [ˈɡɛstrɪç] a yesterday's.

Gestrüpp [gəˈʃtrʏp] nt -(e)s, -e undergrowth.

Gestüt [gəˈʃtyːt] nt -(e)s, -e stud farm.

Gesuch [gəˈzuːx] nt -(e)s, -e petition; (*Antrag*) application; **g—t** a (*Comm*) in demand; wanted; (fig) contrived.

gesund [gəˈzʊnt] a healthy; **wieder — werden** get better; **G—heit** f health(iness); **G—heit!** bless you!; **—heitlich** a,ad health attr, physical; **wie geht es Ihnen —heitlich?** how's your health?; **—heitsschädlich** a unhealthy; **G—heitswesen** nt health service; **G—heitszustand** m state of health.

Getöse [gəˈtøːzə] nt -s din, racket.

Getränk [gəˈtrɛŋk] nt -(e)s, -e drink.

getrauen [gəˈtrauən] vr dare, venture.

Getreide [gəˈtraidə] nt·-s, - cereals pl, grain; **—speicher** m granary.

getrennt [gə'trɛnt] a separate.

getreu [gə'trɔy] a faithful.

Getriebe [gə'tri:bə] nt -s, - (Leute) bustle; (Aut) gearbox; —öl nt transmission oil.

getrost [gə'tro:st] ad without any ·bother; — sterben die in peace.

Getue [gə'tu:ə] nt -s fuss.

geübt [gəy:pt] a experienced.

Gewächs [gə'vɛks] nt -es, -e growth; (Pflanze) plant.

gewachsen [gə'vaksən] a: jdm/etw — sein to be sb's equal/equal to sth.

Gewächshaus nt greenhouse.

gewagt [gə'va:kt] a daring, risky.

gewählt [gə've:lt] .a Sprache refined, elegant.

Gewähr [gə've:r] f - guarantee; keine — übernehmen für accept no responsibility for; g—en vt grant; (geben) provide; g—leisten vt guarantee.

Gewahrsam [gə'va:rza:m] m -s, -e safekeeping; (Polizei—) custody.

Gewähr- cpd: —smann m informant, source; —ung f granting.

Gewalt [gə'valt] f -, -en power; (große Kraft) force; (—taten) violence; mit aller — with all one's might; —anwendung f use of force; —herrschaft f tyranny; g—ig a tremendous; (Irrtum huge; —marsch m forced march; g—sam a forcible; g—tätig a violent.

Gewand [gə'vant] nt -(e)s, ⁻er garment.

gewandt [gə'vant] a deft, skilful; (erfahren) experienced; G—heit f dexterity, skill.

Gewässer [gə'vɛsər] nt -s, - waters pl.

Gewebe [gə've:bə] nt -s, - (Stoff) fabric; (Biol) tissue.

Gewehr [gə've:r] nt -(e)s, -e gun; rifle; —lauf m rifle barrel.

Geweih [gə'vai] nt -(e)s, -e antlers pl.

Gewerb- [gə'vɛrb] cpd: -e nt -s, - trade, occupation; Handel und —e trade and industry; —eschule f technical school; g—etreibend a carrying on a trade; industrial; g—lich a industrial; trade attr; g—smäßig a professional; —szweig m line of trade.

Gewerkschaft [gə'vɛrkʃaft] f trade union; —ler m -s, - trade unionist; —sbund m trade unions federation.

Gewicht [gə'vıçt] nt -(e)s, -e weight; (fig) importance; g—ig a weighty.

gewieft [gə'vi:ft] a, **gewiegt** [gə'vi:kt] a shrewd, cunning.

gewillt [gə'vılt] a willing, prepared.

Gewimmel [gə'vıməl] nt -s swarm.

Gewinde [gə'vındə] nt -s, - (Kranz) wreath; (von Schraube) thread.

Gewinn [gə'vın] m -(e)s, -e profit; (bei Spiel) winnings pl; etw mit — verkaufen sell sth at a profit; —beteiligung f profit-sharing; g—bringend a profitable; g—en vt irreg win; (erwerben) gain; Kohle, Öl ·extract; vi win; (profitieren) gain; an etw (dat) g—en gain in sth; g—end a winning, attractive; —er(in f) m -s, - winner; —spanne f profit margin; —sucht f love of gain; —(n)ummer f winning number; —ung f winning, gaining; (von Kohle etc) extraction.

Gewirr [gə'vır] nt -(e)s, -e tangle; (von Straßen) maze.

gewiß [gə'vıs] a,ad certain(ly).

Gewissen [gə'vısən] nt -s, ⁻ conscience; g—haft a conscientious; —haftigkeit f conscientiousness; g—los a unscrupulous; —sbisse pl pangs of conscience, qualms pl; —sfrage f matter of conscience; —sfreiheit f freedom of conscience; —skonflikt m moral conflict.

gewissermaßen [gəvɪsər'ma:sən] ad more or less, in a way.

Gewiß- cpd: —heit f certainty; g—lich ad surely.

Gewitter [gə'vɪtər] nt -s, - thunderstorm; g—n vi impers: es gewittert there's a thunderstorm; g—schwül a sultry and thundery.

gewitzigt [gə'vɪtsɪçt] a: — sein have learned by experience.

gewitzt [gə'vɪtst] a shrewd, cunning.

gewogen [gə'vo:gən] a well-disposed (+dat towards).

gewöhnen [gə'vø:nən] vt: jdn an etw (acc) — accustom sb to sth; (erziehen zu) teach sb sth; vr: sich an etw (acc) — get used or accustomed to sth.

Gewohnheit [gə'vo:nhaɪt] f habit; (Brauch) custom; aus — from habit; zur — werden become a habit; —s- in cpds habitual; —smensch m creature of habit; —srecht nt common law; —stier nt (col) creature of habit.

gewöhnlich [gə'vø:nlɪç] a usual, ordinary; (pej) common; wie — as usual.

gewohnt [gə'vo:nt] a usual; etw — sein be used to sth.

Gewöhnung f getting accustomed (an +acc to).

Gewölbe [gə'vœlbə] nt -s, - vault.

Gewühl [gə'vy:l] nt -(e)s throng.

Gewürz [gə'vvrts] nt -es, -e spice, seasoning; —nelke f clove.

gezähnt [gə'tsɛ:nt] a serrated, toothed.

Gezeiten [gə'tsaɪtən] pl tides pl.

Gezeter [gə'tse:tər] nt -s clamour, yelling.

gezielt [gə'tsi:lt] a with a particular aim in mind, purposeful; Kritik pointed.

geziemen [gə'tsi:mən] vr impers be fitting; —d a proper.

geziert [gə'tsi:rt] a affected; G—heit f affectation.

Gezwitscher [gə'tsvɪtʃər] nt -s twitter(ing), chirping.

gezwungen [gə'tsvʊŋən] a forced; —ermaßen ad of necessity.

Gicht [ɡɪçt] f - gout; g—isch a gouty.

Giebel ['ɡi:bəl] m -s, - gable; —dach nt gable(d) roof; —fenster nt gable window.

Gier [ɡi:r] f- greed; g—ig a greedy.

Gieß- ['ɡi:s] cpd: —bach m torrent; g—en vt irreg pour; Blumen water; Metall cast; Wachs mould; —e'rei f foundry; —kanne f watering can.

Gift [ɡɪft] nt -(e)s, -e poison; g—ig a poisonous; (fig: boshaft) venomous; —zahn m fang.

Gilde ['ɡɪldə] f -, -n guild.

Ginster ['ɡɪnstər] m -s, - broom.

Gipfel ['ɡɪpfəl] m -s, - summit, peak; (fig) height; g—n vi culminate; —treffen nt summit (meeting).

Gips [ɡɪps] m -es, -e plaster; (Med) plaster of Paris); —abdruck m plaster cast; g—en vt plaster; —figur f plaster figure; —verband m plaster (cast).

Giraffe [ɡi'rafə] f -, -n giraffe.

Girlande [ɡɪr'landə] f -, -n garland.

Giro ['ʒi:ro] nt -s, -s giro; —konto nt current account.

girren ['gɪrən] vi coo.

Gischt [gɪʃt] m -(e)s, -e spray, foam.

Gitarre [gi'tarə] f -, -n guitar.

Gitter ['gɪtər] nt -s, - grating, bars pl; (für Pflanzen) trellis; (Zaun) railing(s); —bett nt cot; —fenster nt barred window; —zaun m railing(s).

Glacéhandschuh [gla'se:hant-ʃu:] m kid glove.

Gladiole [gladi'o:lə] f -, -n gladiolus.

Glanz [glants] m -es shine, lustre, (fig) splendour.

glänzen ['glɛntsən] vi shine (also fig), gleam; vt polish; —d a shining; (fig) brilliant.

Glanz— cpd: —leistung f brilliant achievement; —los a dull; —zeit f heyday.

Glas [gla:s] nt -es, ⁒er glass; —bläser m -s, - glass blower; —er m -s, - glazier; g—ieren [gla'zi:rən] vt glaze; g—ig a glassy; —scheibe f pane; —ur [gla'zu:r] f glaze; (Cook) icing.

glatt [glat] a smooth; (rutschig) slippery; Absage flat; Lüge downright; G—eis nt (black) ice; jdn aufs G—eis führen (fig) take sb for a ride.

Glätte ['glɛtə] f -, -n smoothness, slipperiness; g—n vt smooth out.

Glatze ['glatsə] f -, -n bald head; eine — bekommen go bald.

glatzköpfig a bald.

Glaube ['glaubə] m -ns, -n faith (an + acc in); belief (an + acc in); g—n vti believe (an + acc in, jdm sb); think; —nsbekenntnis nt creed.

glaubhaft ['glaubhaft] a credible; G—igkeit f credibility.

gläubig ['glɔybɪç] a (Rel) devout; (vertrauensvoll) trustful; G—e(r) mf believer; die G—en the faithful; G—er m -s, - creditor.

glaubwürdig ['glaubvʏrdɪç] a credible; Mensch trustworthy; G—keit f credibility; trustworthiness.

gleich [glaiç] a equal; (identisch) (the) same, identical; es ist mir — it's all the same to me; 2 mal 2 — 4 2 times 2 is or equals 4; ad equally; (sofort) straight away; (bald) in a minute; — groß the same size; — nach/an right after/at; —altrig a of the same age; —artig a similar; —bedeutend a synonymous; —berechtigt a having equal rights; G—berechtigung f equal rights pl; —bleibend a constant; — en vi irreg: jdm/etw — be like sb/sth; vr be alike; —ermaßen ad equally; —falls ad likewise; danke —falls! the same to you; G—förmigkeit f uniformity; —gesinnt a likeminded; G—gewicht nt equilibrium, balance; —gültig a indifferent; (unbedeutend) unimportant; G—gültigkeit f indifference; G—heit f equality; —kommen vi irreg + dat be equal to; G—mache'rei f egalitarianism; —mäßig a even, equal; G—mut m equanimity; G—nis nt -ses, -se parable; —sam ad as it were; —sehen vi irreg (jdm) be or look like (sb); G—strom m (Elec) direct current; —tun vi irreg: es jdm —tun match sb; G—ung f equation; —viel ad no matter; —wohl ad nevertheless; —zeitig a simultaneous.

Gleis [glais] nt -es, -e track, rails pl; (Bahnsteig) platform.

Gleit- ['glaɪt] cpd: gliding ; sliding ; **g—en** vi irreg glide ; (rutschen) slide ; **—flug** m glide ; gliding.

Gletscher ['glɛtʃər] m -s, - glacier ; **—spalte** f crevasse.

Glied [gliːt] nt -(e)s, -er member ; (Arm, Bein) limb ; (von Kette) link ; (Mil) rank(s) ; **g—ern** vt organize, structure ; **—erung** f structure, organization ; **—maßen** pl limbs pl.

Glimm- ['glɪm] cpd: **g—en** vi irreg glow, gleam ; **—er** m -s, - glow, gleam ; (Mineral) mica ; **—stengel** m (col) fag.

glimpflich ['glɪmpflɪç] a mild, lenient ; **— davonkommen** get off lightly.

glitzern ['glɪtsərn] vi glitter, twinkle.

Globus ['gloːbus] m - or -ses, **Globen** or -se globe.

Glöckchen ['glœkçən] nt (little) bell.

Glocke ['glɔkə] f -, -n bell ; etw an die große — hängen (fig) shout sth from the rooftops ; **—ngeläut** nt peal of bells ; **—nspiel** nt chime(s) ; (Mus) glockenspiel.

Glorie ['gloːriə] f -, -n glory ; (von Heiligen) halo.

Glosse ['glɔsə] f -, -n comment.

glotzen ['glɔtsən] vi (col) stare.

Glück [glyk] nt -(e)s luck, fortune ; (Freude) happiness ; **— haben** be lucky ; **viel —** good luck ; **zum —** fortunately ; **g—en** vi succeed ; **es glückte ihm, es zu bekommen** he succeeded in getting it.

gluckern ['glukərn] vi glug.

Glück- cpd: **g—lich** a fortunate ; (froh) happy ; **g—licherweise** ad fortunately ; **—sbringer** m -s, - lucky charm ; **g—'selig** a blissful ; **—sfall** m stroke of luck ; **—skind** nt lucky person ; **—ssache** f matter

of luck ; **—sspiel** nt game of chance ; **—sstern** m lucky star ; **g—strahlend** a radiant (with happiness) ; **—wunsch** m congratulations pl, best wishes pl.

Glüh- ['glyː] cpd: **—birne** f light bulb ; **g—en** vi glow ; **—wein** m mulled wine ; **—würmchen** nt glowworm.

Glut [gluːt] f -, -en (Röte) glow ; (Feuers—) fire ; (Hitze) heat ; (fig) ardour.

Gnade ['gnaːdə] f -, -n (Gunst) favour ; (Erbarmen) mercy ; (Milde) clemency ; **—nfrist** f reprieve, respite ; **—ngesuch** nt petition for clemency ; **—nstoß** m coup de grâce.

gnädig ['gnɛːdɪç] a gracious ; (voll Erbarmen) merciful.

Gold [gɔlt] nt -(e)s gold ; **g—en** a golden ; **—fisch** m goldfish ; **—grube** f goldmine ; **—regen** m laburnum ; **—schnitt** m gilt edging ; **—während** f gold standard.

Golf [gɔlf] m -(e)s, -e gulf ; nt -s golf ; **—platz** m golf course ; **—schläger** m golf club ; **—spieler** m golfer ; **—strom** m Gulf Stream.

Gondel ['gɔndəl] f -, -n gondola ; (Seilbahn) cable-car.

gönnen ['gœnən] vt: **jdm etw —** not begrudge sb sth ; **sich** (dat) **etw —** allow oneself sth.

Gönner m -s, - patron ; **g—haft** a patronizing ; **—miene** f patronizing air.

Gosse ['gɔsə] f -, -n gutter.

Gott [gɔt] m -es, **-er** god ; **um —es Willen!** for heaven's sake! ; **— sei Dank!** thank God! ; **—esdienst** m service ; **—eshaus** nt place of worship ; **—heit** f deity.

Gött- [gœt] cpd: **—in** f goddess ; **g—lich** a divine.

Gott- *cpd:* **g—los** a godless;
—**vertrauen** *nt* trust in God.

Götze ['gœtsə] *m* -n, -n idol.

Grab [gra:p] *nt* -(e)s, ⁼er grave;
g—en ['gra:bən] *vt irreg* dig; —**en**
m -s, ⁼ ditch; (Mil) trench; —**rede**
f funeral oration; —**stein** *m* gravestone.

Grad [gra:t] *m* -(e)s, -e degree;
—**einteilung** *f* graduation;
g—weise *ad* gradually.

Graf [gra:f] *m* -en̄, -en count, earl;
—**schaft** *f* county.

Gräfin ['grɛ:fɪn] *f* countess.

Gram [gra:m] *m* -(e)s, grief, sorrow.

grämen ['grɛ:mən] *vr* grieve.

Gramm [gram] *nt* -s, -e gram(me);
—**atik·** ['matɪk] *f* grammar;
g—atisch a grammatical; —**o'phon**
nt -s, -e gramophone.

Granat [gra'na:t] *m* -(e)s, -e
(Stein) garnet; —**apfel** *m* pome-
granate; —**e** *f* -, -n (Mil) shell;
(Hand—) grenade.

Granit [gra'ni:t] *m* -s, -e granite.

graphisch ['gra:fɪʃ] a graphic; —**e**
Darstellung graph.

Gras [gra:s] *nt* -es, ⁼er grass;
g—en *vi* graze; —**halm** *m* blade of
grass; **g—ig** a grassy; —**narbe** *f*
turf.

grassieren [gra'si:rən] *vi* be
rampant, rage.

gräßlich ['grɛslɪç] a horrible.

Grat [gra:t] *m* -(e)s, -e ridge.

Gräte ['grɛ:tə] *f* -, -n fishbone.

gratis ['gra:tɪs] a,ad free (of
charge); **G—probe** *f* free sample.

Gratulation [gratulatsi'o:n] *f* con-
gratulation(s).

gratulieren [gratu'li:rən] *vi:* **jdm —**
(zu etw) congratulate sb (on sth);
(ich) **gratuliere!** congratulations!

grau [grau] a grey; —**en** *vi* (Tag)
dawn; *vi impers:* **es graut jdm vor**
etw sb dreads sth, sb is afraid of
sth; *vr:* **sich —en vor** dread, have
a horror of; **G—en** *nt* -s horror;
—**enhaft** a horrible; —**haarig** a
grey-haired; —**meliert** a grey-
flecked.

grausam ['grauza:m] a cruel;
G—keit *f* cruelty.

Grausen ['grauzən] *nt* -s horror;
g— *vi impers, vr* see grauen.

gravieren [gra'vi:rən] *vt* engrave;
—**d** a grave.

Grazie ['gra:tsiə] *f* -, -n grace.

graziös [gratsi'ø:s] a graceful.

greif- [graɪf] *cpd:* —**bar** a tangible,
concrete; **in —barer Nähe** within
reach; —**en** *vt irreg* seize; grip;
nach etw '—en reach for sth; **um**
sich —en (fig) spread; **zu etw —en**
(fig) turn to sth.

Greis [graɪs] *m* -es, -e old man;
—**enalter** *nt* old age; **g—enhaft** a
senile.

grell [grɛl] a harsh.

Grenz- ['grɛnts] *cpd:* —**beamte(r)**
m frontier official; —**e** *f* -, -n
boundary; (Staats—) frontier;
(Schranke) limit; **g—en** *vi* border
(an +acc on); **g—enlos** a boundless; —**fall** *m* borderline case;
—**linie** *f* boundary; —**übergang** *m*
frontier crossing.

Greuel ['grɔʏəl] *m* -s, - horror,
revulsion; **etw ist jdm ein — sb**
loathes sth; —**tat** *f* atrocity.

greulich ['grɔʏlɪç] a horrible.

griesgrämig ['gri:sgrɛ:mɪç] a
grumpy.

Grieß [gri:s] *m* -es, -e (Cook)
semolina.

Griff [grɪf] *m* -(e)s, -e grip;
(Vorrichtung) handle; **g—bereit** a
handy.

Griffel ['grɪfəl] m -s, - slate pencil; (Bot) style.·

Grille ['grɪlə] f -, -n cricket; (fig) whim; **g~n** vt grill.

Grimasse [gri'masə] f -, -n grimace.

Grimm [grɪm] m -(e)s fury; **g~ig** a furious; (heftig) fierce, severe.

grinsen ['grɪnzən] vi grin.

Grippe ['grɪpə] f-, -n influenza, flu.

grob [grɔːp] a coarse, gross; Fehler, Verstoß bad; **G~heit** f coarseness; coarse expression; **G~ian** ['groːbiaːn] m -s, -e ruffian; **~knochig** a large-boned.

Groll [grɔl] m -(e)s resentment; **g~en** vi bear ill will (+dat or mit towards); (Donner) rumble.

groß [groːs] a big, large; (hoch) tall; (fig) great; im —en und ganzen on the whole; ad greatly; —artig a great, splendid; **G~aufnahme** f (Cine) close-up.

Größe ['gröːsə] f -, -n size; (fig) greatness; (Länge) height.

Groß- cpd: —einkauf m bulk purchase; **g~eltern** pl grandparents pl; **g~enteils** ad mostly.

Größen- cpd: —unterschied m difference in size; —wahn m megalomania.

Groß- cpd: —format nt large size; —handel m wholesale trade; —händler m wholesaler; **g~herzig** a generous; —macht f great power; —maul m braggart; —mut f· magnanimity; **g~mütig** a magnanimous; —mutter f grandmother; **g~spurig** a pompous; —stadt f city, large town.

größte(r,s) ['gröːstə(r,z)] a superl of groß; —nteils ad for the most part.

Groß- cpd: —tuer m -s, - boaster; **g~tun** vi irreg boast; —vater m

grandfather; **g~ziehen** vt irreg raise; **g~zügig** a generous; Planung on a large scale.

grotesk [gro'tɛsk] a grotesque.

Grotte ['grɔtə] f -,· -n grotto.

Grübchen ['gryːpçən] nt dimple.

Grube ['gruːbə] f -, -n pit; mine; —narbeiter m miner; —ngas nt firedamp.

grübeln ['gryːbəln] vi brood.

Grübler ['gryːblar] m -s, - brooder; **g~isch** a brooding, pensive.

Gruft [gruft] f -, ₌e tomb, vault.

grün [gryːn] a green; **G~anlage** f park.

Grund [grʊnt] m ground; (von See, Gefäß) bottom; (fig) reason; im —e genommen basically; —ausbildung f basic training; —bedeutung f basic meaning; —bedingung f fundamental condition; —besitz m land(ed property), real estate; —buch nt land register; **g~ehrlich** a thoroughly honest.

gründ- [grynd] cpd: —en vt found; —en auf (+acc) base on; vr be based (auf+dat on); **G~er** m -s, - founder; —lich a thorough; **G~ung** f foundation.

Grund- cpd: **g~falsch** a utterly wrong; —gebühr f basic charge; —gedanke m basic idea; —gesetz nt constitution; —lage f foundation; —legend a fundamental; **g~los** a groundless; —mauer f foundation wall; —regel f basic rule; —riß m plan; (fig) outline; —satz m principle; **g~sätzlich** a, ad fundamental(ly); Frage of principle; (prinzipiell) on principle; —schule f elementary school; —stein m foundation stone; —steuer f rates pl; —stück nt estate; plot; **g~verschieden**

utterly different; **—zug** *m* characteristic.

Grün- *cpd:* **—e** *nt* **-n:** im **—en** in the open air; **—kohl** *m* kale; **—schnabel** *m* greenhorn; **—span** *m* verdigris; **—streifen** *m* central reservation.

grunzen ['gruntsən] *vi* grunt.

Gruppe ['grupə] *f* -, -n group; **g—nweise** *ad* in groups.

gruppieren [gru'pi:rən] *vtr* group.

gruselig *a* creepy.

gruseln ['gru:zəln] *vi impers:* es gruselt jdm vor etw sth gives sb the creeps; *vr* have the creeps.

Gruß [gru:s] *m* **-es,** **ⁱe** greeting; (*Mil*) salute; viele **ⁱe** best wishes; **ⁱe an** (+*acc*) regards to.

grüßen ['gry:sən] *vt* greet; (*Mil*) salute; jdn von jdm **—** give sb sb's regards; jdn **—** lassen send sb one's regards.

gucken ['gukən] *vi* look.

Gulasch ['gu:laʃ] *nt* -(e)s, -e goulash.

gültig ['gyltiç] *a* valid; **G—keit** *f* validity; **G—keitsdauer** *f* period of validity.

Gummi ['gumi] *nt or m* -s, -s rubber; (**—harze**) gum; (**—band** *nt*) rubber or elastic band; (*Hosen—*) elastic; **g—eren** [gu'mi:rən] *vt* gum; **—knüppel** *m* rubber truncheon; **—strumpf** *m* elastic stocking.

Gunst [gunst] *f* **-** favour.

günstig ['gynstiç] *a* favourable.

Gurgel ['gurgəl] *f* -, -n throat; **g—n** *vi* gurgle; (im *Mund*) gargle.

Gurke ['gurkə] *f* -, -n cucumber; saure **—** pickled cucumber, gherkin.

Gurt [gurt] *m* -(e)s, -e belt.

Gürtel ['gyrtəl] *m* -s, - belt; (*Geog*) zone; **—reifen** *m* radial tyre.

Guß [gus] *m* **-sses, Güsse** casting; (*Regen—*) downpour; (*Cook*) glazing; **—eisen** *nt* cast iron.

Gut [gu:t] *nt* -(e)s, **ⁱer** (*Besitz*) possession; (*pl:* Waren) goods *pl*; **g—** *a* good; *ad* well; laß es **g—** sein that'll do; **—achten** *nt* -s, **-** (expert) opinion; **—achter** *m* -s, **-** expert; **g—artig** *a* good-natured; (*Med*) benign; **g—bürgerlich** *a* Küche (good) plain; **—dünken** *nt:* nach **—dünken** at one's discretion.

Güte ['gy:tə] *f* - goodness, kindness; (*Qualität*) quality.

Güter- *cpd:* **—abfertigung** *f* (*Rail*) goods office; **—bahnhof** *m* goods station; **—wagen** *m* goods waggon, freight car (*US*); **— zug** *m* goods train, freight train (*US*).

Gut- *cpd:* **g—gehen** *v impers irreg* work, come off; es geht jdm **g—** sb's doing fine; **g—gelaunt** *a* good-humoured, in a good mood; **g—gemeint** *a* well meant; **g—gläubig** *a* trusting; **—haben** *nt* -s credit; **g—heißen** *vt irreg* approve (of); **g—herzig** *a* kind(-hearted).

gütig ['gy:tiç] *a* kind.

gütlich ['gy:tliç] *a* amicable.

Gut- *cpd:* **g—mütig** *a* good-natured; **—mütigkeit** *f* good nature; **—sbesitzer** *m* landowner; **—schein** *m* voucher; **g—schreiben** *vt irreg* credit; **—schrift** *f* credit; **—sherr** *m* squire; **g—tun** *vi irreg:* jdm **g—tun** do sb good; **g—willig** *a* willing.

Gymnasium [gym'na:ziʊm] *nt* grammar school (*Brit*), high school (*US*).

Gymnastik [gym'nastɪk] *f* exercises *pl*, keep fit.

H

H, h [ha:] *nt* H, h.
Haar [ha:r] *nt* -(e)s, -e hair; **um ein —** nearly; **—bürste** *f* hairbrush; **h—en** *vir* lose hair; **—esbreite** *f*: **um —esbreite** by a hair's-breadth; **h—genau** *ad* precisely; **h—ig** *a* hairy; (fig) nasty; **—klemme** *f* hair grip; **h—los** *a* hairless; **—nadel** *f* hairpin; **h—scharf** *ad* beobachten very sharply; *daneben* by a hair's breadth; **—schnitt** *m* haircut; **—schopf** *m* head of hair; **—spalte'rei** *f* hair-splitting; **—spange** *f* hair slide; **h—sträubend** *a* hair-raising; **—teil** *nt* hairpiece; **—waschmittel** *nt* shampoo.
Habe ['ha:bə] *f* - property.
haben ['ha:bən] *vt, v aux irreg* have; **Hunger/Angst —** be hungry/afraid; **woher hast du das?** where did you get that from?; **was hast du denn?** what's the matter (with you)?; **H—** *nt* -s, - credit.
Habgier *f* avarice; **h—ig** *a* avaricious.
Habicht ['ha:bɪçt] *m* -(e)s, -e hawk.
Habseligkeiten *pl* belongings *pl*.
Hachse ['haksə] *f* -, -n (Cook) knuckle.
Hacke ['hakə] *f* -, -n hoe; (Ferse) heel; **h—n** *vt* hack, chop; *Erde* hoe.
Hackfleisch *nt* mince, minced meat.
Häcksel ['heksəl] *m or nt* -s chopped straw, chaff.
hadern ['ha:dərn] *vi* quarrel.

Hafen ['ha:fən] *m* -s, = harbour, port; **—arbeiter** *m* docker; **—damm** *m* jetty, mole; **—stadt** *f* port.
Hafer ['ha:fər] *m* -s, - oats *pl*; **—brei** *m* porridge; **—flocken** *pl* porridge oats *pl*; **—schleim** *m* gruel.
Haft [haft] *f* - custody; **h—bar** *a* liable, responsible; **—befehl** *m* warrant (of arrest); **h—en** *vi* stick, cling; **h—en für** be liable or responsible for; **h—enbleiben** *vi irreg* stick (*an* + *dat* to); **—pflicht** *f* liability; **—pflichtversicherung** *f* third party insurance; **—schalen** *pl* contact lenses *pl*; **—ung** *f* liability.
Hage- ['ha:gə] *cpd*: **—butte** *f* -, **-n** rose hip; **—dorn** *m* hawthorn.
Hagel ['ha:gəl] *m* -s hail; **h—n** *vi impers* hail.
hager ['ha:gər] *a* gaunt.
Häher ['hɛ:ər] *m* -s, - jay.
Hahn [ha:n] *m* -(e)s, =e cock; (Wasser—) tap, faucet (US).
Hähnchen ['hɛ:nçən] *nt* cockerel; (Cook) chicken.
Hai(fisch) ['haɪ(fɪʃ)] *m* -(e)s, -e shark.
Häkchen ['hɛ:kçən] *nt* small hook.
Häkel- ['hɛ:kəl] *cpd*: **—arbeit** *f* crochet work; **h—n** *vt* crochet; **—nadel** *f* crochet hook.
Haken ['ha:kən] *m* -s, - hook; (fig) catch; **—kreuz** *nt* swastika; **—nase** *f* hooked nose.
halb [halp] *a* half; **— eins** half past twelve; **ein —es Dutzend** half a

dozen; H—**dunkel** nt semi-darkness.

halber ['halbər] prep +gen (wegen) on account of; (für) for the sake of.

Halb- cpd: —**heit** f half-measure; h—**ieren** vt halve; —**insel** f peninsula; h—**jährlich** ½ half-yearly; —**kreis** m semicircle; —**kugel** f hemisphere; h—**laut** a in an undertone; —**links** m -, - (Sport) inside-left; —**mond** m half-moon; (fig) crescent; h—**offen** a half-open; —**rechts** m -, - (Sport) inside-right; —**schuh** m shoe; —**tagsarbeit** f part-time work; h—**wegs** ad halfway; h—**wegs besser** more or less better; —**wüchsige(r)** mf adolescent; —**zeit** f (Sport) half; (Pause) half-time.

Halde ['haldə] f -, -n tip; (Schlacken—) slag heap.

Hälfte ['hɛlftə] -, -n f half.

Halfter ['halftər] f -, -n, or nt -s, - halter; (Pistolen—) holster.

Hall [hal] m -(e)s, -e sound.

Halle ['halə] f -, -n hall; (Aviat) hangar; h—**n** vi echo, resound; —**nbad** nt indoor swimming pool.

hallo [ha'lo:] interj hallo.

Halluzination [halutsinatsi'o:n] f hallucination.

Halm [halm] m -(e)s, -e blade, stalk.

Hals [hals] m -es, ¨e neck; (Kehle) throat; — **über Kopf** in a rush; —**kette** f necklace; —**krause** f ruff; —**Nasen-Ohren-Arzt** m ear nose and throat specialist; —**schlagader** f carotid artery; —**schmerzen** pl sore throat; h—**starrig** a stubborn, obstinate; —**tuch** nt scarf; —**weh** nt sore throat; —**wirbel** m cervical vertebra.

Halt [halt] m -(e)s, -e stop; (fester —) hold; (innerer —) stability; h—! stop!, halt!; h—**bar** a durable; **Lebensmittel** non-perishable; (Mil, fig) tenable; —**barkeit** f durability; (non-)perishability; tenability.

halten, ['haltən] irreg vt keep; (fest—) hold; — **für** regard as; — **von** think of; vi hold; (frisch bleiben) keep; (stoppen) stop; **an sich — restrain** oneself; vr (frisch bleiben) keep; (sich behaupten) hold out; **sich rechts/links —** keep to the right/left.

Halt- cpd: —**estelle** f stop; h—**los** a unstable; —**losigkeit** f instability; h—**machen** vi stop; —**ung** f posture; (fig) attitude; (Selbstbeherrschung) composure; —**verbot** nt ban on stopping.

Halunke [ha'luŋkə] m -n, -n rascal.

hämisch ['hɛ:mɪʃ] a malicious.

Hammel ['haməl] m -s, ¨ or - wether; —**fleisch** nt mutton; —**keule** f leg of mutton.

Hammer ['hamər] m -s, ¨ hammer.

hämmern ['hɛmərn] vti hammer.

Hampelmann ['hampəlman] m (lit, fig) puppet.

Hamster ['hamstər] m -s, - hamster; —**ei** [-'rai] f hoarding; —**er** m -s, - hoarder; h—**n** vi hoard.

Hand [hant] f -, ¨e hand; —**arbeit** f manual work; (Nadelarbeit) needlework; —**arbeiter** m manual worker; —**besen** m brush; —**bremse** f handbrake; —**buch** nt handbook, manual.

Hände- ['hɛndə] cpd: —**druck** m handshake; —**klatschen** nt clapping, applause.

Handel ['handəl] m -s trade; (Geschäft) transaction; — **haben** quarrel.

handeln ['handəln] vi trade; act; — von be about; vr impers: sich — um be a question of, be about; H— nt -s action.

Handels- cpd: —bilanz f balance of trade; h—einig a: mit jdm h—einig werden conclude a deal with sb; —kammer f chamber of commerce; —marine f merchant navy; —recht nt commercial law; —reisende(r) m commercial traveller; —schule f business school; —vertreter m sales representative.

Hand- cpd: —feger m -s, - brush; h—fest a hefty; h—gearbeitet a handmade; —gelenk nt wrist; —gemenge nt scuffle; —gepäck nt hand-luggage; h—geschrieben a handwritten; h—greiflich a palpable; h—greiflich werden become violent; —griff m flick of the wrist; h—haben vt irreg insep handle; —karren m handcart; —kuß m kiss on the hand.

Händler ['hɛndlər] m -s, - trader, dealer.

handlich ['handlɪç] a handy.

Handlung ['handluŋ] f -, -en act(ion); (in Buch) plot; (Geschäft) shop; —sbevollmächtigte(r) mf authorized agent; —sweise f manner of dealing.

Hand- cpd: —pflege f manicure; —schelle f handcuff; —schlag m handshake; —schrift f handwriting; (Text) manuscript; —schuh m glove; —tasche f handbag; —tuch nt towel; —werk nt trade, craft; —werker m -s - craftsman, artisan; —werkzeug nt tools pl.

Hanf [hanf] m -(e)s hemp.

Hang [haŋ] m -(e)s, ⁻e inclination; (Ab-) slope.

Hänge- ['hɛŋə] in cpds hanging; —brücke f suspension bridge; —matte f hammock.

hängen ['hɛŋən] irreg vi hang; — an (fig) be attached to; vt hang (an + acc on(to)); sich — an (+ acc) hang on to, cling to; —bleiben vi irreg be caught (an + dat on); (fig) remain, stick.

Hängeschloß nt padlock.

hänseln ['hɛnzəln] vt tease.

hantieren [han'ti:rən] vi work, be busy; mit etw — handle sth.

hapern ['ha:pərn] vi impers: es hapert an etw (dat) sth leaves something to be desired.

Happen ['hapən] m -s, - mouthful.

Harfe ['harfə] f -, -n harp.

Harke ['harkə] f -, -n rake; h—n vti rake.

harmlos ['harmlo:s] a harmless; H—igkeit f harmlessness.

Harmonie [harmo'ni:] f harmony; h—ren vi harmonize.

Harmonika [har'mo:nika] f -, -s (Zieh-) concertina.

harmonisch [har'mo:nɪʃ] a harmonious.

Harmonium [har'mo:niʊm] nt -s, -nien or -s harmonium.

Harn [harn] m -(e)s, -e urine; —blase f bladder.

Harnisch ['harnɪʃ] m -(e)s, -e armour; jdn in — bringen infuriate sb; in — geraten become angry.

Harpune [har'pu:nə] f -, -n harpoon.

harren ['harən] vi wait (auf + acc for).

hart [hart] a hard; (fig) harsh.

Härte ['hɛrtə] f -, -n hardness; (fig) harshness; h—n vtr harden.

hart- cpd: —gekocht a hard-boiled; —gesotten a tough, hard-boiled;

—**herzig** a hard-hearted; —**näckig** a stubborn; **H—näckigkeit** f stubbornness.

Harz [ha:rts] nt -es, -e resin.

Haschee [ha'ʃe:] nt -s, -s hash.

haschen ['haʃən] vt catch, snatch; vi (col) smoke hash.

Haschisch ['haʃɪʃ] nt - hashish.

Hase ['ha:zə] m -n, -n hare.

Haselnuß ['ha:zəlnʊs] f hazelnut.

Hasen- cpd: —**fuß** m coward; —**scharte** f harelip.

Haspe ['haspə] f -, -n hinge; —**l** f -, n reel, bobbin; (Winde) winch.

Haß [has] m -sses hate, hatred.

hassen ['hasən] vt hate; —**enswert** a hateful.

häßlich ['hɛslɪç] a ugly; (gemein) nasty; **H—keit** f ugliness; nastiness.

Hast [hast] f - haste; **h—en** vir ·rush; **h—ig** a hasty.

hätscheln ['hɛtʃəln] vt pamper; (zärtlich) cuddle.

Haube ·['haubə] f -, -n hood; (Mütze) cap; (Aut) bonnet, hood (US).

Hauch [haux] m -(e)s, -e breath; (Luft—) breeze; (fig) trace; **h—en** vi breathe; **h—fein** a very fine.

Haue ['hauə] f -, -n hoe, pick; (col) hiding; **h—n** vt irreg hew, cut; (col) thrash.

Haufen ['haufən] m -s, - heap; (Leute) crowd; **ein — (x)** (col) loads or a lot (of x); **auf einem —** in one heap; **h—weise** ad in heaps; in droves; **etw h—weise haben** have piles of sth.

häufen ['hɔyfən] vt pile up; vr accumulate.

häufig ['hɔyfɪç] a,ad frequent(ly); **H—keit** f frequency.

Haupt [haupt] nt -(e)s, **Häupter** head; (Ober—) chief; in cpds main; —**bahnhof** m central station; **h—beruflich** ad as one's main occupation; —**buch** nt (Comm) ledger; —**darsteller(in** f) m leading actor/actress; —**eingang** m main entrance; —**fach** nt main subject; —**film** m main film.

Häuptling ['hɔyptlɪŋ] m chief(tain).

Haupt- cpd: —**mann** m, pl **-leute** (Mil) captain; —**postamt** nt main post office; —**quartier** nt headquarters pl; —**rolle** f leading part; —**sache** f main thing; **h—sächlich** a,ad chief(ly); —**satz** m main clause; —**schlagader** f aorta; —**stadt** f capital; —**straße** f main street; —**wort** nt noun.

Haus [haus] nt -es, **Häuser** house; **nach —e** home; **zu —e** at home; —**angestellte** f domestic servant; —**arbeit** f housework; (Sch) homework; —**arzt** m family doctor; —**aufgabe** f (Sch) homework; —**besitzer(in** f) m, —**eigentümer(in** f) m house-owner.

hausen ['hauzən] vi live· (in poverty); (pej) wreak havoc.

Häuser- ['hɔyzər] cpd: —**block** m block (of houses); —**makler** m estate agent.

Haus- cpd: —**frau** f housewife; —**freund** m family friend; (col) lover; **h—gemacht** a home-made; —**halt** m household; (Pol) budget; **h—halten** vi irreg keep house (sparen) economize; —**hälterin** f housekeeper; —**haltsgeld** nt housekeeping (money); —**haltsgerät** nt domestic appliance; —**haltsplan** m budget; —**haltung** f housekeeping; —**herr** m host; (Vermieter) landlord; **h—hoch** a: **h—hoch verlieren** lose by a mile.

hausieren [hau'zi:rən] *vi* hawk, peddle.

Hausierer *m* -s, - hawker, peddlar.

häuslich ['hɔyslıç] *a* domestic; H—keit *f* domesticity.

Haus- *cpd:* —meister *m* caretaker, janitor; —ordnung *f* house·rules *pl;* —putz *m* ·house cleaning; —schlüssel *m* front-door key; —schuh *m* slipper; —suchung *f* police raid; —tier *nt* domestic animal; —verwalter *m* caretaker; —wirt *m* landlord; —wirtschaft *f* domestic science.

Haut [haut] *f* -,. **Häute** skin; (*Tier*—) hide.

häuten ['hɔytən] *vt* skin; *vr* slough one's skin.

Haut-· *cpd:* h—eng *a* skin-tight; —farbe *f* complexion.

Haxe ['haksə] *f* -,. -n *see* Hachse.

Hebamme ['he:p'amə] *f* -, -n midwife.

Hebel ['he:bəl] *m* -s, - lever.

heben ['he:bən] *vt irreg* raise, lift.

hecheln ['hɛçəln] *vi* (*Hund*) pant.

Hecht [hɛçt] *m* -(e)s, -e pike.

Heck [hɛk] *nt* -(e)s, -e stern; (*von Auto*) rear.

Hecke ['hɛkə] *f* -,. -n hedge; —nrose *f* dog rose; —schütze *m* sniper.

Heer [he:r] *nt* -(e)s, -e army.

Hefe ['he:fə] *f* -,. -n yeast.

Heft ['hɛft] *nt* -(e)s, -e exercise book; (*Zeitschrift*) number; (*von Messer*) haft; h—en *vt* fasten, (*an* + *acc* to); (*nähen*) tack; —er *m* -s, - folder.

heftig *a* fierce, violent; H—keit *f* fierceness, violence.

Heft- *cpd:* —klammer *f* paper clip; —maschine *f* stapling machine;

—pflaster *nt* sticking plaster; —zwecke *f* drawing pin.

hegen ['he:gən] *vt* nurse; (*fig*) harbour, foster.

Hehl [he:l] *m or nt:* kein(en) — aus etw (*dat*) machen make no secret of sth; —er *m* -s, - receiver (of stolen goods), fence.

Heide ['haidə] *f* -, -n heath, moor; (—*kraut*) heather; *m* -n, -n, Heidin *f* heathen, pagan; —kraut *nt* heather; —lbeere *f* bilberry; h—nmäßig *a* (*col*) terrific; —ntum *nt* paganism.

heidnisch ['haidnıʃ] *a* heathen, pagan.

heikel ['haikəl] *a* awkward, thorny; (*wählerisch*) fussy.

Heil [hail] *nt* -(e)s well-being; (*Seelen*—) salvation; h— a in one piece, intact; h— *interj* hail; —and *m* -(e)s, -e saviour; h—bar *a* curable; h—en *vt* cure; *vi* heal; h—froh *a* very relieved; —gymnastin *f* physiotherapist.

heilig ['hailıç] *a* holy; H—abend *m* Christmas Eve; H—e(r) *mf* saint; —en *vt* sanctify, hallow; H—enschein *m* halo; H—keit *f* holiness; —sprechen *vt irreg* canonize; H—tum *nt* shrine; (*Gegenstand*) relic.

Heil- *cpd:* h—los *a* unholy; —mittel *nt* remedy; h—sam *a* (*fig*) salutary; —sarmee *f* Salvation Army; —ung *f* cure.

Heim [haim] *nt* -(e), -e home; h—ad home.

Heimat ['haima:t] *f* -, -en home (town/country *etc*); —land *nt* homeland; h—lich *a* native, home *attr*; *Gefühle* nostalgic; h—los *a* homeless; —ort *m* home town/area; —vertriebene(r) *mf* displaced person.

Heim- cpd: h—**begleiten** vt accompany home; h—**elig** a homely; h—**fahren** vi irreg drive/go home; —**fahrt** f journey home; —**gang** m return home; (Tod) decease; h—**gehen** vi irreg go home; (sterben) pass away; h—**isch** a (gebürtig) native; sich h—**isch fühlen** feel at home; —**kehr** f -, -en homecoming; h—**kehren** vi return home; h—**lich** a secret; —**lichkeit** f secrecy; —**reise** f journey home; h—**suchen** vt afflict; (Geist) haunt; h—**tückisch** a malicious; h—**wärts** ad homewards; —**weg** m way home; —**weh** nt homesickness; —**weh haben** be homesick; h—**zahlen** vt: jdm etw h—**zahlen** pay back sb for sth.

Heirat ['haɪraːt] f -, -en marriage; h—**en** vti marry; —**santrag** m proposal.

heiser ['haɪzər] a hoarse; H—**keit** f hoarseness.

heiß [haɪs] a hot; —**e(r) Draht** hot line; —**blütig** a hot-blooded.

heißen ['haɪsən] irreg vi be called; (bedeuten) mean; vt command; (nennen) name; v impers it says; it is said.

Heiß- cpd: h—**ersehnt** a longed for; —**hunger** m ravenous hunger; h—**laufen** vir irreg overheat.

heiter ['haɪtər] a cheerful; Wetter bright; H—**keit** f cheerfulness; (Belustigung) amusement.

Heiz- ['haɪts] cpd: h—**bar** a heated; Raum with heating; leicht h—**bar** easily heated; —**decke** f electric blanket; h—**en** vt heat; —**er** m -s, - stoker; —**körper** m radiator; —**öl** nt fuel oil; —**sonne** f electric fire; —**ung** f heating; —**ungsanlage** f heating system.

hektisch ['hɛktɪʃ] a hectic.

Held [hɛlt] m -en, -en hero; —**in** f heroine.

helfen ['hɛlfən] irreg vi help (jdm sb, bei with); (nützen) be of use; sich (dat) zu — wissen be resourceful; v impers: es hilft nichts, du mußt ... it's no use, you have to ...

Helfer m -s, - helper, assistant; —**shelfer** m accomplice.

hell [hɛl] a clear, bright; Farbe light; —**blau** a light blue; —**blond** a ash-blond; H—**e** f - clearness, brightness; H—**er** m -s, - farthing; —**hörig** a keen of hearing; Wand poorly soundproofed; H—**igkeit** f clearness, brightness; lightness; H—**seher** m clairvoyant; —**wach** a wide-awake.

Helm ['hɛlm] m -(e)s, -e (auf Kopf) helmet.

Hemd [hɛmt] nt -(e)s, -en shirt; (Unter—) vest; —**bluse** f blouse; —**enknopf** m shirt button.

hemmen ['hɛmən] vt check, hold up; gehemmt sein be inhibited.

Hemmung f (Psych) inhibition; h—**slos** a unrestrained, without restraint.

Hengst [hɛŋst] m -es, -e stallion.

Henkel ['hɛŋkəl] m -s, - handle; —**krug** m jug.

henken ['hɛŋkən] vt hang.

Henker m -s, - hangman.

Henne ['hɛnə] f -, -n hen.

her [heːr] ad here; (Zeit) ago; — damit! hand it over!

herab [hɛ'rap] ad down; —**hängen** vi irreg hang down; —**lassen** irreg vt let down; vr condescend; H—**lassung** f condescension; —**sehen** vi irreg look down (auf +acc on); —**setzen** vt lower, reduce; (fig) belittle, disparage; **H—setzung** f reduction; disparagement; —**würdigen** vt belittle, disparage.

heran [hɛ'ran] ad: näher —! come up closer!; — **zu mir!** come up to me!; —**bilden** vt train; —**bringen** vt irreg bring up (an +acc to); —**fahren** vi irreg drive up (an +acc to); —**kommen** vi irreg (an +acc) approach, come near; —**machen** vr: **sich an jdn —machen** make up to sb; —**wachsen** vi irreg grow up; —**ziehen** vt irreg pull nearer; (aufziehen) raise; (ausbilden) train; **jdn zu etw —ziehen** call upon sb to help in sth.

herauf [hɛ'rauf] ad up(ward(s)), up here; —**beschwören** vt irreg conjure up, evoke; —**bringen** vt irreg bring up; —**ziehen** irreg vt draw or pull up; vi approach; (Sturm) gather.

heraus [hɛ'raus] ad out; outside; from; —**arbeiten** vt work out; —**bekommen** vt irreg get out; (fig) find or figure out; —**bringen** vt irreg bring out; Geheimnis elicit; —**finden** vt irreg find out; —**fordern** vt challenge; **H—forderung** f challenge; provocation; —**geben** vt irreg give up; surrender; Geld give back; Buch edit; (veröffentlichen) publish; —**geber** m -s, - editor; (Verleger) publisher; —**gehen** vi irreg: aus sich (dat) —**gehen** come out of one's shell; —**halten** vr irreg: **sich aus etw —halten** keep out of sth; —**hängen** vti irreg hang out; —**holen** vt get out (aus of); —**kommen** vi irreg come out; dabei **kommt nichts** — nothing will come of it; —**nehmen** vt irreg take out; **sich** (dat) **Freiheiten —nehmen** take liberties; —**reißen** vt irreg tear

out; pull out; —**rücken** vt Geld fork out, hand over; **mit etw —rücken** (fig) come out with sth; —**rutschen** vi slip out; —**schlagen** vt irreg knock out; (fig) obtain; —**stellen** vr turn out (als to be); —**wachsen** vi irreg grow out (aus of); —**ziehen** vt irreg pull out, extract.

herb [hɛrp] a (slightly) bitter, acid; Wein dry; (fig) (schmerzlich) bitter; (streng) stern, austere.

herbei [hɛr'bai] ad (over) here; —**führen** vt bring about; —**lassen** vr irreg: **sich —lassen zu** condescend or deign to; —**schaffen** vt procure.

herbemühen ['hɛrbəmyːən] vr take the trouble to come.

Herberge ['hɛrbɛrgə] f -, -n shelter; hostel, inn.

Herbergsmutter f, **Herbergsvater** m warden.

her- ['hɛr] cpd: —**bitten** vt irreg ask to come (here); —**bringen** vt irreg bring here.

Herbst [hɛrpst] m -(e)s, -e autumn, fall (US); **h—lich** a autumnal.

Herd [hɛrt] m -(e)s, -e cooker; (fig, Med) focus, centre.

Herde ['hɛrdə] f -, -n herd; (Schaf—) flock.

herein [hɛ'rain] ad in (here), here; —**!** come in!; —**bitten** vt irreg ask in; —**brechen** vi irreg set in; —**bringen** vt irreg bring in; —**dürfen** vi irreg have permission to enter; **H—fall** m letdown; —**fallen** vi irreg be caught, taken in; —**fallen auf** (+acc) fall for; —**kommen** vi irreg come in; —**lassen** vt irreg admit; —**legen** vt: **jdn —legen** take sb in; —**platzen** vi burst in.

Her- ['hɛr] *cpd:* **—fahrt** *f* journey here; **h—fallen** *vi irreg:* **h—fallen über** fall upon; **—gang** *m* course of events, circumstances *pl;* **h—geben** *vt irreg* give, hand (over); **sich zu etw h—geben** lend one's name to sth; **h—gehen** *vi irreg:* **hinter jdm h—gehen** follow sb; **es geht hoch h—** there are a lot of goings-on; **h—halten** *vt irreg* hold out; **h—halten müssen** (col) have to suffer; **h—hören** *vi* listen; **hör mal h—!** listen here!

Hering ['heːrɪŋ] *m* **-s, -e** herring.

her- ['hɛr] *cpd:* **—kommen** *vi irreg* come; **komm mal —!** come here!; **—kömmlich** a traditional; **H—kunft** *f* **-, -künfte** origin; **—laufen** *vi irreg:* **—laufen hinter** (+dat) run after; **—leiten** *vr* derive; **—machen** *vr:* **sich —machen über** (+acc) set about or upon.

Hermelin [hɛrmə'liːn] *m* or *nt* **-s, -e** ermine.

hermetisch [hɛr'meːtɪʃ] *a,ad* hermetic(ally).

her- *cpd:* **—'nach** *ad* afterwards; **—'nieder** *ad* down.

heroisch [he'roːɪʃ] a heroic.

Herold ['heːrɔlt] *m* **-(e)s, -e** herald.

Herr [hɛr] *m* **-(e)n, -en** master; (Mann) gentleman; (adliger, Rel.) Lord; (vor Namen) Mr.; **mein —!** sir!; **meine —en!** gentlemen!; **—enbekanntschaft** *f* gentleman friend; **—endoppel** *nt* men's doubles; **—eneinzel** *nt* men's singles; **—enhaus** *nt* mansion; **h—enlos** a ownerless.

herrichten ['heːrɪçtən] *vt* prepare.

Herr- *cpd:* **—in** *f* mistress; **h—isch** a domineering; **h—lich** a marvellous, splendid; **—lichkeit** *f* splendour, magnificence; **—schaft**

f power, rule; (Herr und Herrin) master and mistress; **meine —schaften!** ladies and gentlemen!

herrschen ['hɛrʃən] *vt* rule; (bestehen) prevail, be.

Herrscher(in *f*) *m* **-s, -** ruler.

Herrschsucht *f* domineering behaviour.

her- ['hɛr] *cpd:* **—rühren** *vi* arise, originate; **—sagen** *vt* recite; **—stammen** *vi* descend, come from; **—stellen** *vt* make, manufacture; **H—steller** *m* **-s, -** manufacturer; **H—stellung** *f* manufacture; **H—stellungskosten** *pl* manufacturing costs *pl.*

herüber [hɛ'ryːbər] *ad* over (here), across.

herum [hɛ'rʊm] *ad* about, (a)round; **um etw —** around sth; **—ärgern** *vi* get annoyed (mit with); **—führen** *vt* show around; **—gehen** *vi irreg* walk or go round (um etw sth); walk about; **—irren** *vi* wander about; **—kriegen** *vt* bring or talk around; **—lungern** *vi* lounge about; **—sprechen** *vr irreg* get around, be spread; **—treiben** *vir irreg* drift about; **—ziehen** *vir irreg* wander about.

herunter [hɛ'rʊntər] *ad* downward(s), down (there); **—gekommen** a run-down; **—hängen** *vi irreg* hang down; **—holen** *vt* bring down; **—kommen** *vi* come down in the world; (fig) come down; **—machen** *vt* take down; (schimpfen) abuse, criticise severely.

hervor [hɛr'foːr] *ad* out, forth; **—brechen** *vi irreg* burst forth, break out; **—bringen** *vt irreg* produce; Wort utter; **—gehen** *vi irreg* emerge, result; **—heben** *vt irreg* stress; (als Kontrast) set off;

—ragend *a* excellent; (*lit*) projecting; —rufen *vt irreg* cause, give rise to; —treten *vi irreg* come out.

Herz [hɛrts] *nt* -ens, -en heart; —anfall *m* heart attack; h—en *vt* caress, embrace; —enslust *f*: nach —enslust to one's heart's content; —fehler *m* heart defect; h—haft *a* hearty; —infarkt *m* heart attack; —klopfen *nt* palpitation; h—lich *a* cordial; h—lichen Glückwunsch congratulations *pl*; h—liche Grüße best wishes; —lichkeit *f* cordiality; h—los *a* heartless; —losigkeit *f* heartlessness.

Herzog ['hɛrtsoːk] *m* -(e)s, ⁼e duke; —in *f* duchess; h—lich *a* ducal; —tum *nt* duchy.

Herz- *cpd*: —schlag *m* heartbeat; (*Med*) heart attack; h—zerreißend *a* heartrending.

heterogen [hetero'geːn] *a* heterogeneous.

Hetze ['hɛtsə] *f* -, -n (*Eile*) rush; h—n *vt* hunt; (*verfolgen*) chase; jdn/etw auf jdn/etw — set sb/sth on sb/sth; *vi* (*eilen*) rush; h—n gegen stir up feeling against; h—n zu agitate for; —'rei *f* agitation; (*Eile*) rush.

Heu [hɔy] *nt* -(e)s hay; —boden *m* hayloft.

Heuchelei [hɔyçə'lai] *f* hypocrisy.

heucheln ['hɔyçəln] *vt* pretend, feign; *vi* be hypocritical.

Heuchler(in *f***)** [hɔyçlər(ın)] *m* -s, - hypocrite; h—isch *a* hypocritical.

Heuer ['hɔyər] *f* -, -n (*Naut*) pay; h— *ad* this year.

Heugabel *f* pitchfork.

heulen ['hɔylən] *vi* howl; cry; das —de Elend bekommen get the blues.

heurig ['hɔyrıç] *a* this year's.

Heu- *cpd*: —schnupfen *m* hay

fever; —schrecke *f* grasshopper, locust.

heute ['hɔytə] *ad* today; —abend this evening/morning; das H— today.

heutig ['hɔytıç] *a* today's.

heutzutage ['hɔyttsutaːgə] *ad* nowadays.

Hexe ['hɛksə] *f* -, -n witch; h—n *vi* practise witchcraft; ich kann doch nicht h—n I can't work miracles; —nkessel *m* (*lit, fig*) cauldron; —nmeister *m* wizard; —nschuß *m* lumbago; —'rei *f* witchcraft.

Hieb [hiːp] *m* -(e)s, -e blow; (*Wunde*) cut, gash; (*Stichelei*) cutting remark; —e bekommen get a thrashing.

hier [hiːr] *ad* here; —auf *ad* thereupon; (*danach*) after that; —behalten *vt irreg* keep here; —bei *ad* herewith, enclosed; —bleiben *vi irreg* stay here; —durch *ad* by this means; (*örtlich*) through here; —her *ad* this way, here; —lassen *vt irreg* leave here; —mit *ad* hereby; —nach *ad* hereafter; —von *ad* about this, hereof; —zulande *ad* in this country.

hiesig ['hiːzıç] *a* of this place, local.·

Hilfe ['hɪlfə] *f* -, -n help; aid; Erste — first aid; —! help!.

Hilf- *cpd*: h—los *a* helpless; —losigkeit *f* helplessness; h—reich *a* helpful; —saktion *f* relief measures *pl*; —sarbeiter *m* labourer; h—sbedürftig *a* needy; h—sbereit *a* ready to help; —skraft *f* assistant, helper; —sschule *f* school for backward children; —szeitwort *nt* auxiliary verb.

Himbeere ['hɪmbeːrə] *f* -, -n raspberry.

Himmel ['hɪməl] *m* -s, - sky; (*Rel, liter*) heaven; h—angst *a*: es ist mir h—angst I'm scared to death; h—blau a sky-blue; —fahrt f Ascension; h—schreiend a outrageous; —srichtung f direction.

himmlisch ['hɪmlɪʃ] a heavenly.

hin [hɪn] ad there; — und her to and fro; bis zur Mauer — up to the wall; Geld —, Geld her money or no money; mein Glück ist — my happiness has gone.

hinab [hɪˈnap] ad down; —gehen vi irreg go down; —sehen vi irreg look down.

hinauf [hɪˈnauf] ad up; —arbeiten vr work one's way up; —steigen vi irreg climb.

hinaus [hɪˈnaus] ad out; —befördern vt kick/throw out; —gehen vi irreg go out; —gehen über (+acc) exceed; —laufen vi irreg run out; —laufen auf (+acc) come to, amount to; —schieben vt irreg put off, postpone; —werfen vt irreg throw out; —wollen vi want to .go out; —wollen auf (+acc) drive at, get at; —ziehen irreg vt draw out; vr be protracted.

Hinblick ['hɪnblɪk] m: in or im — auf (+acc) in view of.

hinder- ['hɪndər] cpd: —lich a awkward; —n vt hinder, hamper; jdn an etw (dat) —n prevent sb from doing sth; H—nis nt -ses, -se obstacle.

hindeuten ['hɪndɔʏtən] vi point (auf +acc to).

hindurch [hɪnˈdʊrç] ad through; across; (zeitlich) over.

hinein [hɪˈnaɪn] ad in; —fallen vi irreg fall in; —fallen in (+acc) fall into; —gehen vi irreg go in; —gehen in (+acc) go into, enter; —geraten in irreg: —geraten in (+acc) get into; —passen vi fit in; —passen in (+acc) fit into;

—reden vi: jdm —reden interfere in sb's affairs; —steigern vr get worked up; —versetzen vr: sich —versetzen in (+acc) put oneself in the position of.

hin- ['hɪn] cpd: —fahren irreg vi go; drive; vt take; drive; H—fahrt f journey there; —fallen vi irreg fall down; —fällig a frail, decrepit; Regel etc unnecessary, otiose; H—gabe f devotion; —geben vr irreg +dat give oneself up to, devote oneself to; —gehen vi irreg go; (Zeit) pass; —halten vt irreg hold out; (warten lassen) put off, stall.

hinken ['hɪŋkən] vi limp; (Vergleich) be unconvincing.

hin- ['hɪn] cpd: —legen vt put down; vr lie down; —nehmen vt irreg (fig) put up with, take; —reichen vi be adequate; vt: jdm etw —reichen hand sb sth; H—reise f journey out; —reißen vt irreg carry away, enrapture; sich —reißen lassen, etw zu tun get carried away and do sth; —richten vt execute; H—richtung f execution; —sichtlich prep +gen with regard to; H—spiel nt (Sport) first leg; —stellen vt put (down); vr place o.s.

hintanstellen [hɪntˈanʃtəlsən] vt (fig) ignore.

hinten ['hɪntən] ad at the back; behind; —herum ad round the back; (fig) secretly.

hinter ['hɪntər] prep +dat or acc behind; (nach) after; — jdm hersein be after sb; H—achse f rear axle; H—bein nt hind leg; sich auf die H—beine stellen get tough; H—bliebene(r) mf surviving relative; —drein ad afterwards; —e(r,s) a rear, back; —einander ad one after the other; H—gedanke m ulterior motive; —gehen vt irreg deceive; H—grund m background; H—halt m ambush; —hältig a underhand, sneaky; —her ad afterwards, after; H—hof m backyard; H—kopf m back of one's head; —'lassen vt irreg leave; H—'lassenschaft f (testator's) estate; —'legen vt deposit; H—list f cunning, trickery; (Handlung) trick, dodge; —listig a cunning, crafty; H—mann m, pl —männer person behind; H—rad nt back wheel; H—radantrieb m (Aut) rear wheel drive; —rücks ad from behind; H—teil nt behind; H—treffen nt: ins H—treffen kommen lose ground; —'treiben vt irreg prevent, frustrate; H—tür f back door; (fig: Ausweg) escape, loophole; —'ziehen vt irreg Steuern evade (paying).

hinüber [hr'ny:bər] ad across, over; —gehen vi irreg go over or across.

hinunter [hr'nʊntər] ad down; —bringen vt irreg take down; —schlucken vt (lit, fig) swallow; —steigen vi irreg descend.

hin- ['hɪn] cpd: H—weg m journey out; —'weghelfen vi irreg: jdm über etw (acc) —weghelfen help sb to get over sth; —'wegsetzen vr: sich —wegsetzen über (+acc) disregard; H—weis m -es, -e (Andeutung) hint; (Anweisung) instruction; (Verweis) reference; —weisen vi irreg (auf +acc) (anzeigen) point to; (sagen) point out, refer to; —werfen vt irreg throw down; —ziehen vr irreg (fig) drag on; —zielen vi aim (auf +acc at).

hinzu [hɪn'tsu:] ad in addition; —fügen vt add.

Hirn [hɪrn] nt -(e)s, -e brain(s); —gespinst nt -(e)s, -e fantasy; h—verbrannt a half-baked, crazy.

Hirsch [hɪrʃ] m -(e)s, -e stag.

Hirse ['hɪrzə] f -, -n millet.

Hirt ['hɪrt] m -en, -en herdsman; (Schaf—, fig) shepherd.

hissen ['hɪsən] vt hoist.

Historiker [hɪs'to:rikər] m -s, - historian.

historisch [hɪs'to:rɪʃ] a historical.

Hitze ['hɪtsə] f - heat; h—beständig a heat-resistant; —welle f heatwave.

hitzig a hot-tempered; Debatte heated.

Hitz- cpd: —kopf m hothead; h—köpfig a fiery, hotheaded; —schlag m heatstroke.

Hobel ['ho:bəl] m -s, - plane; —bank f carpenter's bench; h—n vti plane; —späne pl wood shavings pl.

hoch [ho:x] a high; H— nt -s, -s (Ruf) cheer; (Met) anticyclone; —achten vt respect; H—achtung f respect, esteem; —achtungsvoll ad yours faithfully; H—amt nt high mass; —arbeiten vr work one's way up; —begabt a extremely gifted; —betagt a very old, aged; H—betrieb m intense activity; (Comm) peak time; —bringen vt irreg bring up; H—burg f stronghold; H—deutsch nt High German; —dotiert a highly paid; H—druck m high pressure; H—ebene f plateau; —erfreut a highly delighted; —fliegend a (fig) highflown; H—form f top form; —gradig a intense, extreme; —halten vt irreg hold up; (fig) uphold, cherish; H—haus nt multistorey building; —heben vt irreg lift (up); H—konjunktur f boom;

H—land nt highlands pl; —leben
vi: jdn —leben lassen give sb three
cheers; H—mut m pride; —mütig
a proud, haughty; —näsig a stuck-
up, snooty; H—ofen m blast
furnace; —prozentig a Alkohol
strong; H—rechnung f projected
result; H—saison f high season;
H—schätzung f high esteem;
H—schule f college; university;
H—sommer m middle of summer;
H—spannung f high tension;
H—sprache f standard language;
—springen vi high jump up,
H—sprung m high jump.

höchst [höːçst] ad highly,
extremely; —e(r,s) a highest;
(äußerste) extreme.

Hochstapler ['hoːxstaˌplər] m -s, -
swindler.

Höchst- cpd: h—ens ad at the
most; —geschwindigkeit f
maximum speed; h—persönlich ad
in person; —preis m maximum
price; h—wahrscheinlich ad most
probably.

Hoch- cpd h—trabend a pompous;
—verrat m high treason; —wasser
nt high water; (Überschwemmung)
floods pl; h—wertig a high-class,
first-rate; —würden m Reverend;
—zahl f (Math) exponent.

Hochzeit ['hoxtsaɪt] f -, -en
wedding; —sreise f honeymoon.

hocken ['hɔkən] vir squat, crouch.

Hocker m -s, - stool.

Höcker ['hœkər] m -s, - hump.

Hode ['hoːdə] m -n, - testicle.

Hof [hoːf] m -(e)s, ¨e (Hinter—)
yard; (Bauern—) farm; (Königs—)
court.

hoffen ['hɔfən] vi hope (auf +acc
for); —tlich ad I hope, hopefully.

Hoffnung ['hɔfnʊŋ] f hope;
h—slos a hopeless; —slosigkeit f

hopelessness; —sschimmer m
glimmer of hope; h—svoll a
hopeful.

höflich ['höːflɪç] a polite,
courteous; H—keit f courtesy,
politeness.

hohe(r,s) ['hoːə(r,z)] a see hoch.

Höhe ['höːə] f -, -n height; (An—)
hill.

Hoheit ['hoːhaɪt] f (Pol)
sovereignty; (Titel) Highness;
—sgebiet nt sovereign territory;
—sgewässer nt territorial waters
pl; —szeichen nt national emblem.

Höhen- ['höːən] cpd: —angabe f
altitude reading; (auf Karte) height
marking; —messer m -s, - alti-
meter; —sonne f sun lamp;
—unterschied m difference in
altitude; —zug m mountain chain.

Höhepunkt m climax.

höher a,ad higher.

hohl [hoːl] a hollow.

Höhle ['höːlə] f -, -n cave, hole;
(Mund—) cavity; (fig, Zool) den.

Hohl- cpd: h—heit f hollowness;
—maß nt measure of volume;
—saum m hemstitch.

Hohn [hoːn] m -(e)s scorn.

höhnen ['höːnən] vt taunt, scoff at.

höhnisch a scornful, taunting.

hold [hɔlt] a charming, sweet.

holen ['hoːlən] vt get, fetch; Atem
take; jdn/etw — lassen send for
sb/sth.

Hölle ['hœlə] f -, -n hell; —nangst
f: eine —nangst haben be scared
to death.

höllisch ['hœlɪʃ] a hellish, infernal.

holperig ['hɔlpərɪç] a rough, bumpy.

holpern ['hɔlpərn] vi jolt.

Holunder [ho'lʊndər] m -s, - elder.

Holz [hɔlts] nt -es, ¨er wood.

hölzern ['hœltsərn] a (lit, fig) wooden.

Holz- cpd: **—fäller** m -s, - lumberjack, woodcutter; **h—ig** a woody; **—klotz** m wooden block; **—kohle** f charcoal; **—scheit** nt log; **—schuh** m clog; **—weg** m (fig) wrong track; **—wolle** f fine wood shavings pl; **—wurm** m woodworm.

homosexuell [homozɛksu'ɛl] a homosexual.

Honig ['ho:nɪç] m -s, -e honey; **—wabe** f honeycomb.

Honorar [hono'ra:r] nt -s, -e fee. **honorieren** [hono'ri:rən] vt remunerate; Scheck honour.

Hopfen ['hɔpfən] m -s, - hops pl.

hopsen ['hɔpsən] vi hop.

Hör- cpd: **—apparat** m hearing aid; **h—bar** a audible.

horch [hɔrç] interj listen; **—en** vi listen; (pej) eavesdrop; **H—er** m -s, - listener; eavesdropper.

Horde ['hɔrdə] f -, -n horde.

hören ['hø:rən] vti hear; **H—sagen** nt: vom H—sagen from hearsay.

Hörer m -s, - hearer; (Rad) listener; (Univ) student; (Telefon—) receiver.

Horizont [hori'tsɔnt] m -(e)s, -e horizon; **h—al** [-'ta:l] a horizontal.

Hormon [hɔr'mo:n] nt -s, -e hormone.

Hörmuschel f (Tel) earpiece.

Horn [hɔrn] nt -(e)s, ⁻er horn; **—haut** f horny skin.

Hornisse [hɔr'nɪsə] f -, -n hornet.

Horoskop [horo'sko:p] nt -s, -e horoscope.

Hör- cpd: **—rohr** nt ear trumpet; (Med) stethoscope; **—saal** m lecture room; **—spiel** nt radio play.

Hort [hɔrt] m -(e)s, -e hoard;

(Sch) nursery school; **h—en** vt hoard.

Hose ['ho:zə] f -, -n trousers pl, pants (US) pl; **—nanzug** m trouser suit; **—nrock** m culottes pl; **—ntasche** f (trouser) pocket; **—nträger** m braces pl, suspenders (US) pl.

Hostie ['hɔstiə] f (Rel) host.

Hotel [ho'tɛl] nt -s, -s hotel; **—ier** [hotɛli'e:] m -s, -s hotelkeeper, hotelier.

Hub [hu:p] m -(e)s, ⁻e lift; (Tech) stroke.

hüben ['hy:bən] ad on this side, over here.

Hubraum m (Aut) cubic capacity.

hübsch [hypʃ] a pretty, nice.

Hubschrauber m -s, - helicopter.

hudeln ['hu:dəln] vi be sloppy.

Huf [hu:f] m -(e)s, -e hoof; **—eisen** nt horseshoe; **—nagel** m horseshoe nail.

Hüft- ['hyft] cpd: **—e** f -, -n hip; **—gürtel** m, **—halter** m -s, - girdle.

Hügel ['hy:gəl] m -s, - hill; **h—ig** a hilly.

Huhn [hu:n] nt -(e)s, ⁻er hen; (Cook) chicken.

Hühner- ['hy:nər] cpd: **—auge** nt corn; **—brühe** f chicken broth.

Huld [hult] f - favour; **h—igen** ['huldɪgən] vi pay homage (jdm to sb); **—igung** f homage.

Hülle ['hylə] f -, -n cover(ing); wrapping; **in — und Fülle** galore; **h—n** vt cover, wrap (in + acc with)..

Hülse ['hylzə] f -, -n husk, shell; **—nfrucht** f legume.

human [hu'ma:n] a humane; **—i'tär** a humanitarian; **H—i'tät** f humanity.

Hummel ['huməl] f -, -n bumblebee.

Hummer ['hʊmər] m -s, - lobster.

Humor [hu'moːr] m -s, -e humour;
— **haben** have a sense of humour;
—**ist** [-'rɪst] m humorist; **h**—**istisch**
a, **h**—**voll** a humorous.

humpeln ['hʊmpəln] vi hobble.

Humpen ['hʊmpən] m -s, - tankard.

Hund [hʊnt] m dog; —**ehütte** f (dog) kennel; —**ekuchen**
m dog biscuit; **h**—**emüde** a (col)
dog-tired.

hundert ['hʊndərt] num hundred;
H—'**jahrfeier** f centenary;
—**prozentig** a,ad one hundred per
cent.

Hündin ['hʏndɪn] f bitch.

Hunger ['hʊŋər] m -s hunger; —
haben be hungry; —**lohn** m starvation wages pl; **h**—**n** vi starve;
—**snot** f\famine; —**streik** m hunger
strike.

hungrig ['hʊŋrɪç] a hungry.

Hupe ['huːpə] f -, -n horn, hooter;
h—**n** vi hoot, sound one's horn.

hüpfen ['hʏpfən] vi hop, jump.

Hürde ['hʏrdə] f -, -n hurdle; (für
Schafe) pen; —**nlauf** m hurdling.

Hure ['huːrə] f -, -n whore.

hurtig ['hʊrtɪç] a,ad brisk(ly),
quick(ly).

huschen ['hʊʃən] vi flit, scurry.

Husten ['huːstən] m -s cough; **h**—
vi cough; —**anfall** m coughing fit;
—**bonbon** m or nt cough drop;

—**saft** m cough mixture.

Hut [huːt] m -(e)s, ꞊e hat; f - care;
auf der — **sein** be on the lookout; **hüten** ['hyːtən] vt guard; vr watch•
out; **sich** —, **zu** take care not to;
sich — **vor** beware of.

Hütte·['hʏtə] f -, -n hut, cottage;
(Eisen-) forge; —**nwerk** nt
foundry.

hutzelig ['hʊtsəlɪç] a shrivelled.

Hyäne [hy'ɛːnə] f -, -n hyena.

Hyazinthe [hya'tsɪntə] f -, -n
hyacinth.

Hydr- cpd: —**ant** [hy'drant] m
hydrant; **h**—**aulisch** [hy'draulɪ] a
hydraulic; —**ierung** [hy'driːrʊŋ] f
hydrogenation.

Hygiene [hygi'eːnə] f - hygiene.

hygienisch [hygi'eːnɪʃ] a hygienic.

Hymne ['hʏmnə] f -, -n hymn,
anthem.

hyper- ['hyːpər] pref hyper-.

Hypno- [hyp'no] cpd: —**se** f -, -n
hypnosis; **h**—**tisch** a hypnotic;
—**tiseur** [-'tizøːr] m hypnotist;
h—**ti'sieren** vt hypnotize.

Hypothek [hypo'teːk] f -, -en
mortgage.

Hypothese [hypo'teːzə] f -, -n
hypothesis.

hypothetisch [hypo'teːtɪʃ] a hypothetical.

Hysterie [hyste'riː] f hysteria.

hysterisch [hys'teːrɪʃ] a hysterical.

I

I, i [iː] nt I, i.

ich [ɪç] pron I; — **bin's!** it's me!;
I— nt -(s), -(s) self; (Psych) ego.

Ideal [ide'aːl] nt -s, -e ideal; **i—** a

ideal; —**ist** [-'lɪst] m idealist;
i—**istisch** [-'lɪstɪʃ] a idealistic.

Idee [i'deː] f -, -n [i'deːən] idea;
i—**ll** [ide'ɛl] a ideal.

identi- [i'dɛnti] *cpd:* **—fizieren**
[-fi'tsi:rən] *vt* identify; **—sch** *a*
identical; **I—tät** [-'tɛːt] *f* identity.

Ideo- [ideo] *cpd:* **—loge** [-'lo:gə] *m*
-n, -n ideologist; **—logie** [-lo'gi:] *f*
ideology; **i—logisch** [-'lo:gɪʃ] *a*
ideological.

idiomatisch [idio'mɑːtɪʃ] *a*
idiomatic.

Idiot [idi'oːt] *m* **-en, -en** idiot;
i—isch *a* idiotic.

idyllisch [i'dʏlɪʃ] *a* idyllic.

Igel [i'gəl] *m* **-s, -** hedgehog.

ignorieren [ɪgno'riːrən] *vt* ignore.

ihm [iːm] *pron dat of* **er, es** (to)
him, (to) it.

ihn [iːn] *pron acc of* **er** him; it;
—en *pron dat of* **sie** *pl* (to) them;
I—en *pron dat of* **Sie** (to) you.

ihr [iːr] *pron¹ nom pl* you; *dat of*
sie *sing* (to) her; **—(e)** *poss pron*
sing her; its; *pl* their; **I—(e)** *poss*
pron your; **—e(r,s)** *poss pron sing*
hers; its; *pl* theirs; **I—e(r,s)** *poss*
pron yours; **—er** *gen pl of* **sie**
sing/pl of her/them; **I—er** *pron*
gen of **Sie** of you; **—erseits** *ad for*
her/their part; **—esgleichen** *pron*
people like her/them; (*von Dingen*)
others like it; **—etwegen,**
—etwillen *ad* (*für sie*) for
her/its/their sake; (*wegen ihr*) on
her/its/their account; **—ige** *pron:*
der/die/das **—ige** hers; its; theirs.

Ikone [i'koːnə] *f* **-, -n** icon.

illegal [i'legaːl] *a* illegal.

Illusion [iluzi'oːn] *f* illusion.

illusorisch [ilu'zoːrɪʃ] *a* illusory.

illustrieren [ilʊs'triːrən] *vt*
illustrate.

Illustrierte *f* **-n, -n** picture
magazine.

Iltis [i'ltɪs] *m* **-ses, -se** polecat.

im [ɪm] = **in dem.**

imaginär [imagi'nɛːr] *a* imaginary.

Imbiß ['ɪmbɪs] *m* **-sses, -sse**
snack; **—halle** *f,* **—stube** *f* snack
bar.

imitieren [imi'tiːrən] *vt* imitate.

Imker ['ɪmkər] *m* **-s, -** beekeeper.

Immatrikulation [ɪmatrikulat-
si'oːn] *f* (*Univ*) registration.

immatrikulieren [ɪmatriku'liːrən]
vir register.

immer ['ɪmər] *ad* always; **—** wieder
again and again; **—** noch still; **—**
noch nicht still not; **für —** forever;
— wenn ich ... everytime I ...;
— schöner/trauriger more and
more beautiful/sadder and sadder;
was/wer (*auch*) **—** what-
ever/whoever; **—hin** *ad* all the
same; **—zu** *ad* all the time.

Immobilien [ɪmo'biːliən] *pl* real
estate.

immun [i'muːn] *a* immune; **I—ität**
[-i'tɛːt] *f* immunity.

Imperativ ['ɪmperatiːf] *m* **-s, -e**
imperative.

Imperfekt ['ɪmpɛrfɛkt] *nt* **-s, -e**
imperfect (tense).

Imperialist [ɪmperia'lɪst] *m*
imperialist; **i—isch** *a* imperialistic.

Impf- [ɪmpf] *cpd:* **i—en** *vt*
vaccinate; **—stoff** *m* vaccine;
—ung *f* vaccination; **—zwang** *m*
compulsory vaccination.

implizieren [ɪmpli'tsiːrən] *vt* imply
(*mit* by).

imponieren [ɪmpo'niːrən] *vi*
impress (*jdm* sb).

Import [ɪm'pɔrt] *m* **-(e)s, -e**
import; **i—ieren** [-'tiːrən] *vt* import;
imposant [ɪmpo'zant] *a* imposing.

impotent ['ɪmpotɛnt] *a* impotent.

imprägnieren [ɪmprɛ'gniːrən] *vt*
(water)proof.

Improvisation [ɪmprovizatsl'o:n] f
improvization.

improvisieren [ɪmprovi'zi:rən] vti
improvize.

Impuls [ɪm'pʊls] m -es, -e
impulse; **i—iv** ['-zi:f] a impulsive.

imstande [ɪm'ʃtandə] a: — sein be
in a position; (fähig) be able.

in [ɪn] prep + acc in(to); to; + dat
in; — der/die Stadt in/into town;
— der/die Schule at/to school.

Inanspruchnahme [ɪn'anʃprʊx-
na:mə] f -, -n demands pl (gen on).

Inbegriff ['ɪnbəgrɪf] m embodiment,
personification; **i—en** a included.

inbrünstig ['ɪnbrʏnstɪç] a ardent.

indem [ɪn'de:m] cj while; — man
etw macht (dadurch) by doing sth.

indes(sen) [ɪn'dɛs(ən)] ad meanwhile; cj while.

Indianer(in f) [ɪndi'a:nər(ɪn)] m -s,
- Red Indian.

indianisch a Red Indian.

indigniert [ɪndɪ'gni:rt] a indignant.

Indikativ ['ɪndikati:f] m -s, -e
indicative.

indirekt ['ɪndirɛkt] a indirect.

indiskret ['ɪndɪskre:t] a indiscreet;
I—ion [ɪndɪskretsi'o:n] f indiscretion.

indiskutabel ['ɪndɪskuta:bəl] a out
of the question.

Individu— [ɪndividu'] cpd: **—alist**
[-a'lɪst] m individualist; **—alität**
[-ali'tɛt] f individuality; **i—ell** [-'ɛl]
a individual; **—um** [ɪndi'vi:duʊm]
nt -s, -en individual.

Indiz [ɪn'di:ts] nt -es, -ien sign (für
of); (Jur) clue; **—ienbeweis** m cir-
cumstantial evidence.

indoktrinieren [ɪndɔktri'ni:rən] vt
indoctrinate.

industrialisieren [ɪndʊstriali-
'zi:rən] vt industrialize.

Industrie [ɪndʊs'tri:] f industry, in
cpds industrial; **—gebiet** nt
industrial area; **i—ll** [ɪndʊstri'ɛl] a
industrial; **—zweig** m branch of
industry.

ineinander [ɪn'aɪnandər] ad in(to)
one another or each other.

Infanterie [ɪnfantə'ri:] f infantry.

Infarkt [ɪn'farkt] m -(e)s, -e
coronary (thrombosis).

Infektion [ɪnfɛktsi'o:n] f infection;
—skrankheit f infectious disease.

Infinitiv ['ɪnfiniti:f] m -s, -e
infinitive.

infizieren [ɪnfi'tsi:rən] vt infect; vr
be infected (bei by).

Inflation [ɪnflatsi'o:n] f inflation.

inflatorisch [ɪnfla'to:rɪʃ] a
inflationary.

infolge [ɪn'fɔlgə] prep + gen as a
result of, owing to; **—dessen**
[-'dɛsən] ad consequently.

Informatik [ɪnfɔr'ma:tɪk] f information studies pl.

Information [ɪnfɔrmatsi'o:n] f
information no pl.

informieren [ɪnfɔr'mi:rən] vt
inform; vr find out (über + acc
about).

Infusion [ɪnfuzi'o:n] f infusion.

Ingenieur [ɪnʒeni'ø:r] m engineer;
—schule f school of engineering.

Ingwer ['ɪŋvər] m -s ginger.

Inhaber(in f) ['ɪnha:bər(ɪn)] m -s,
- owner; (Haus—) occupier;
(Lizenz—) licensee, holder; (Fin)
bearer.

inhaftieren [ɪnhaf'ti:rən] vt take
into custody.

inhalieren [ɪnha'li:rən] vti inhale.

Inhalt ['ɪnhalt] m -(e)s, -e contents
pl; (eines Buchs etc) content;
(Math) area; volume; **i—lich** a as
regards content; **—sangabe** f

summary; **i—slos** _a_ empty; **i—(s)reich** _a_ full; **—sverzeichnis** _nt_ table of contents.

inhuman ['ɪnhuman] _a_ inhuman.

Initiative [initsia'tiːvə] _f_ initiative.

Injektion [ɪnjɛktsi'oːn] _f_ injection.

inklusive [ɪnklu'ziːvə] _prep, a_ inclusive (_gen_ of).

inkognito [ɪn'kɔgnito] _ad_ incognito.

inkonsequent ['ɪnkɔnzekvɛnt] _a_ inconsistent.

inkorrekt ['ɪnkɔrɛkt] _a_ incorrect.

Inkrafttreten [ɪn'kraftˌtreːtən] _nt_ **-s** coming into force.

Inland ['ɪnlant] _nt_ (_Geog_) inland; (_Pol, Comm_) home (country); **—sporto** _nt_ inland postage.

inmitten [ɪn'mɪtən] _prep_ +_gen_ in the middle of; — von amongst.

innehaben ['ɪnəhaːbən] _vt irreg_ hold.

innen ['ɪnən] _ad_ inside; **I—aufnahme** _f_ indoor photograph; **I—einrichtung** _f_ (interior) furnishings _pl_; **I—minister** _m_ minister of the interior, Home Secretary (_Brit_); **I—politik** _f_ domestic policy; **I—stadt** _f_ town/city centre.

inner- ['ɪnər] _cpd_: **—e(r,s)** _a_ inner; (_im Körper, inländisch_) internal; **I—e(s)** _nt_ inside; (_Mitte_) centre; (_fig_) heart; **I—eien** [-'raɪən] _pl_ innards _pl_; **—halb** _ad, prep_ +_gen_ within; (_räumlich_) inside; **—lich** _a_ internal; (_geistig_) inward; **I—ste(s)** _nt_ heart; **—ste(r,s)** _a_ innermost.

innig ['ɪnɪç] _a_ profound; _Freundschaft_ intimate.

inoffiziell ['ɪnʔofitsiɛl] _a_ unofficial.

ins [ɪns] = **in das**.

Insasse ['ɪnzasə] _m_ **-n, -n** (_Anstalt_) inmate; (_Aut_) passenger.

insbesondere [ɪnsbə'zɔndərə] _ad_ (e)specially.

Inschrift ['ɪnʃrɪft] _f_ inscription.

Insekt [ɪn'zɛkt] _nt_ **-(e)s, -en** insect.

Insel ['ɪnzəl] _f_ **-, -n** island.

Inser- _cpd_: **—at** [ɪnzə'raːt] _nt_ **-(e)s, -e** advertisement; **—ent** [ɪnze'rɛnt] _m_ advertiser; **I—ieren** [ɪnze'riːrən] _vti_ advertise.

insgeheim [ɪnsgə'haɪm] _ad_ secretly.

insgesamt [ɪnsgə'zamt] _ad_ altogether, all in all.

insofern ['ɪnzo'fɛrn] **, insoweit** ['ɪnzo'vaɪt] _ad_ in this respect; — als in so far as; _cj_ if; (_deshalb_) (and) so.

Installateur [ɪnstala'tøːr] _m_ electrician; plumber.

Instand- [ɪn'ʃtant] _cpd_: **—haltung** _f_ maintenance; **—setzung** _f_ overhaul; (_eines Gebäudes_) restoration.

Instanz [ɪn'stants] _f_ authority; (_Jur_) court; **—enweg** _m_ official channels _pl_.

Instinkt [ɪn'stɪŋkt] _m_ **-(e)s, -e** instinct; **i—iv** [-'tiːf] _a_ instinctive.

Institut [ɪnsti'tuːt] _nt_ **-(e)s, -e** institute.

Instrument [ɪnstru'mɛnt] _nt_ instrument.

inszenieren [ɪnstse'niːrən] _vt_ direct; (_fig_) stage-manage.

Intell- [ɪntɛl] _cpd_: **i—ektuell** [-ɛktu'ɛl] _a_ intellectual; **i—igent** [-'gɛnt] _a_ intelligent; **—igenz** [-i'gɛnts] _f_ intelligence; (_Leute_) intelligentsia _pl_.

Intendant [ɪntɛn'dant] _m_ director.

intensiv [ɪntɛn'ziːf] _a_ intensive.

Interess- _cpd_: **i—ant** [ɪntərɛ'sant] _a_ interesting; **i—anterweise** _ad_ interestingly enough; **—e** [ɪntə'rɛsə] _nt_ **-s, -n** interest; **—e haben** be interested (_an_ +_dat_ in).

—ent [ɪntərɛˈsɛnt] *m* interested
party; i—ieren [ɪntərɛˈsiːrən] *vt*
interest; *vr* be interested (*für* in).
Inter- [ɪntər] *cpd:* —nat [-ˈnaːt] *nt*
-(e)s, -e boarding school;
i—national [-natsioˈnaːl] *a* international; i—nieren [-ˈniːrən] *vt*
intern; i—pretieren [-preˈtiːrən] *vt*
interpret; —punktion [-puŋktsioˈoːn]
f punctuation; —vall [-ˈval] *nt* -s,
-e interval; —view [-ˈvjuː] *nt* -s, -s
interview; i—viewen [-ˈvjuːəm] *vt*
interview.

intim [ɪnˈtiːm] *a* intimate; I—ität
[ɪntimiˈtɛːt] *f* intimacy.
intolerant [ˈɪntolerant] *a* intolerant.
intransitiv [ˈɪntranzitiːf] *a* (*Gram*)
intransitive.
Intrige [ɪnˈtriːgə] *f* -, -n intrigue,
plot.
Invasion [ɪnvaziˈoːn] *f* invasion.
Inventar [ɪnvɛnˈtaːr] *nt* -s, -e
inventory.
Inventur [ɪnvɛnˈtuːr] *f* stocktaking;
— machen stocktake.
investieren [ɪnvɛsˈtiːrən] *vt* invest.
inwiefern [ɪnviˈfɛrn], **inwieweit**
[ɪnviˈvaɪt] *ad* how far, to what
extent.
inzwischen [ɪnˈtsvɪʃən] *ad* meanwhile.

irdisch [ˈɪrdɪʃ] *a* earthly.
irgend [ˈɪrgənt] *ad* at all;
wann/was/wer — whenever/what-
ever/whoever; — jemand/etwas
somebody/something; any-
body/anything; —ein(e,s) *a* some,
any; —einmal *ad* sometime or
other; (*fragend*) ever; —wann *ad*
sometime; —wie *ad* somehow;
—wo *ad* somewhere; anywhere.
Ironie [iroˈniː] *f* irony.
ironisch [iˈroːnɪʃ] *a* ironic(al).
irre [ˈɪrə] *a* crazy, mad; I—(r) *mf*
lunatic; —führen *vt* mislead;
—machen *vt* confuse; —n *vir* be
mistaken; (*umher—*) wander,
stray; I—nanstalt *f* lunatic asylum.
irrig [ˈɪrɪç] *a* incorrect, wrong.
Irr- *cpd:* i—sinnig *a* mad, crazy;
(*col*) terrific; —tum *m* -s, -tümer
mistake, error; i—tümlich *a*
mistaken.
Isolation [izolatsiˈoːn] *f* isolation;
(*Elec*) insulation.
Isolator [izoˈlaːtor] *m* insulator.
Isolier- [izoˈliːr] *cpd:* —band *nt*
insulating tape; i—en *vt* isolate;
(*Elec*) insulate; —station *f* (*Med*)
isolation ward; —ung *f* isolation;
(*Elec*) insulation.

J

J, j [jɔt] *nt* J, j.
ja [jaː] *ad* yes; tu das — nicht! don't
do that!
Jacht [jaxt] *f* -, -en yacht.
Jacke [ˈjakə] *f* -, -n jacket;
(*Woll—*) cardigan.
Jackett [ʒaˈkɛt] *nt* -s, -s *or* -e
jacket.

Jagd [jaːkt] *f* -, -en hunt; (*Jagen*)
hunting; —beute *f* kill; —flugzeug
nt fighter; —gewehr *nt* sporting
gun.
jagen [ˈjaːgən] *vi* hunt; (*eilen*)
race; *vt* hunt; (*weg—*) drive (off);
(*verfolgen*) chase.
Jäger [ˈjɛːgər] *m* -s, - hunter.

jäh [jɛ:] *a* sudden, abrupt; *(steil)* steep, precipitous; **—lings** *ad* abruptly.

Jahr [ja:r] *nt* **-(e)s, -e** year; **j—elang** *ad* for years; **'—esabonnement** *nt* annual subscription; **—esabschluß** *m* end of the year; *(Comm)* annual statement of account; **—esbericht** *m* annual report; **—eswechsel** *m* turn of the year; **—eszahl** *f* date, year; **—eszeit** *f* season; **—gang** *m* age group; *(von Wein)* vintage; **—'hundert** *nt* **-s, -e** century; **—'hundertfeier** *f* centenary.

jährlich ['jɛ:rlɪç] *a,ad* yearly.

Jahr- *cpd:* **—markt** *m* fair; **—'zehnt** *nt* decade.

Jähzorn ['jɛ:tsɔrn] *m* sudden anger; hot temper; **j—ig** *a* hot-tempered.

Jalousie [ʒalu'zi:] *f* venetian blind.

Jammer ['jamər] *m* **-s** misery; **es ist ein —, daß ...** it is a crying shame that ...

jämmerlich ['jɛmərlɪç] *a* wretched, pathetic; **J—keit** *f* wretchedness.

jammer- *cpd:* **—n** *vi* wail; *vt impers:* **es jammert ihn** it makes sb feel sorry; **—schade** *a:* **es ist —schade** it is a crying shame.

Januar ['janua:r] *m* **-s, -** January.

Jargon [ʒar'gõ:] *m* **-s, -s** jargon.

jäten ['jɛ:tən] *vt:* Unkraut **—** weed.

jauchzen ['jauxtsən] *vi* rejoice, shout (with joy).

Jauchzer *m* **-s, -** shout for joy.

jaulen ['jaulən] *vi* howl.

ja- *cpd:* **—'wohl** *ad* yes (of course); **J—wort** *nt* consent.

Jazz [dʒɛs] *m* **-** Jazz.

je [je:] *ad* ever; *(jeweils)* each; **—** nach depending on; **—** nachdem it

depends; **—... desto** or **—** the ... the.

jede(r,s) ['je:də(r,s)] *a* every, each; *pron* everybody; (**—** *einzelne*) each; **ohne —** x without any x; **—nfalls** *ad* in any case; **—rmann** *pron* everone; **—rzeit** *ad* at any time; **—smal** *ad* every time, each time.

jedoch [je'dɔx] *ad* however.

jeher [je:he:r] *ad:* **von —** all along.

jemals ['je:ma:ls] *ad* ever.

jemand ['je:mant] *pron* somebody; anybody.

jene(r,z) ['je:nə(r,z)] *a* that; *pron* that one.

jenseits ['je:nzaits] *ad* on the other side; *prep* +*gen* on the other side of, beyond; **das J—** the hereafter, the beyond.

jetzig ['jɛtsɪç] *a* present.

jetzt [jɛtst] *ad* now.

je— *cpd:* **—weilig** *a* respective; **—weils** *ad* —weils zwei zusammen two at a time; **zu —weils 5 DM** at 5 marks each; **—weils das erste** the first each time.

Joch [jɔx] *nt* **-(e)s, -e** yoke.

Jockei ['dʒɔke] *m* **-s, -s** jockey.

Jod [jo:t] *nt* **-(e)s** iodine.

jodeln ['jo:dəln] *vi* yodel.

Joghurt ['jo:gurt] *m* or *nt* **-s, -s** yogurt.

Johannisbeere [jo'hanɪsbe:rə] *f* redcurrant; **schwarze —** black-currant.

johlen ['jo:lən] *vi* yell.

Jolle ['jɔlə] *f* **-, -n** dinghy.

jonglieren [ʒõ'gli:rən] *vi* juggle.

Joppe ['jɔpə] *f* **-, -n** jacket.

Journal- ['ʒur'na:l] *cpd:* **—ismus** ['-lɪsmus] *m* journalism; **—ist(in** *f)* ['-lɪst] *m* journalist; **j—istisch** *a* journalistic.

Jubel ['ju:bəl] *m* **-s** rejoicing; **j—n**
vi rejoice.

Jubiläum [jubi'lɛ:ʊm] *nt* **-s,**
Jubiläen anniversary, jubilee.

jucken ['jʊkən] *vi* itch; *vt* **es juckt**
mich am Arm my arm is itching;
das juckt mich that's itchy.

Juckreiz ['jʊkrats] *m* itch.

Jude ['ju:də] *m* **-n, -n** Jew; **J—ntum**
nt - Judaism; Jewry;
—nverfolgung *f* persecution of the
Jews.

Jüd- ['jy:d] *cpd:* **—in** *f* Jewess; **j—isch** *a* Jewish.

Judo ['ju:do] *nt* **-(s)** judo.

Jugend ['ju:gənt] *f* - youth;
—herberge *f* youth hostel;
—kriminalität *f* juvenile crime;
j—lich *a* youthful; **—liche(r)** *mf*
teenager, young person; **—richter**
m juvenile court judge.

Juli ['ju:li] *m* **-(s), -s** July.

jung [jʊŋ] *a* young; **J—e** *m* **-n, -n**
boy, lad; **J—e(s)** *nt* young animal;

(pl) young *pl.*

Jünger ['jʏŋər] *m* **-s, - disciple; j—**
a younger.

Jung- *cpd:* **—fer** *f* -, **-n: alte —fer**
old maid; **—fernfahrt** *f* maiden
voyage; **—frau** *f* virgin; *(Astrol)*
Virgo; **—geselle** *m* bachelor.

Jüngling ['jʏŋlɪŋ] *m* youth.

jüngst [jʏŋst] *ad* lately, recently;
—e(r,s) *a* youngest; *(neueste)*
latest.

Juni ['ju:ni] *m* **-(s), -s** June.

Junior ['ju:nior] *m* **-s, -en** ['-o:rən]
junior.

Jurist [ju'rɪst] *m* jurist, lawyer;
j—isch *a* legal.

Justiz [jus'ti:ts] *f* - justice;
—beamte(r) *m* judicial officer;
—irrtum *m* miscarriage of justice.

Juwel [ju'veːl] *nt or m* **-s, -en**
jewel; **—ier** *m* ['-'liːr] *m* **-s, -e**
jeweller; **—iergeschäft** *nt* jeweller's
(shop).

Jux [jʊks] *m* **-es, -e** joke, lark.

K

K, k [ka:] *nt* K, k.

Kabarett [kaba'rɛt] *nt* **-s, -e** *or* **-s**
cabaret; **—ist** [-'tɪst] *m* cabaret
artiste.

Kabel ['ka:bəl] *nt* **-s, -** *(Elec)* wire;
(stark) cable; **—jau** [-jau] *m* **-s, -e**
or **-s** cod; **k—n** *vti* cable.

Kabine [ka'bi:nə] *f* cabin; *(Zelle)*
cubicle.

Kabinett [kabi'nɛt] *nt* **-s, -e** *(Pol)*
cabinet; small room.

Kachel ['kaxəl] *f* -, **-n** tile; **k—n**
vt tile; **—ofen** *m* tiled stove.

Kadaver [ka'da:vər] *m* **-s, -**

carcass.

Kadett [ka'dɛt] *m* **-en, -en** cadet.

Käfer ['kɛːfər] *m* **-s, -** beetle.

Kaffee ['kafe] *m* **-s, -s** coffee;
—kanne *f* coffeepot; **—klatsch** *m,*
—kränzchen *nt* hen party; coffee
morning; **—löffel** *m* coffee spoon;
—mühle *f* coffee grinder; **—satz** *m*
coffee grounds *pl.*

Käfig ['kɛːfɪç] *m* **-s, -e** cage.

kahl [ka:l] *a* bald; **—fressen** *vt irreg*
strip bare; **—geschoren** *a* shaven,
shorn; **K—heit** *f* baldness;
—köpfig *a* bald-headed.

Kahn [ka:n] *m* -(e)s, ⸗e boat, barge.

Kai [kai] *m* -s, -e *or* -s quay.

Kaiser [ˈkaizər] *m* -s, - emperor;
—in *f* empress; k—lich *a* imperial;
—reich *nt* empire; —schnitt *m*
(*Med*) Caesarian (section).

Kajüte [kaˈjy:tə] *f* -, -n cabin.

Kakao [kaˈka:o] *m* -s, -s cocoa.

Kaktee [kakˈte:(ə)] *f*-, -n, **Kaktus**
[ˈkaktus] *m* -, -se cactus.

Kalb [kalp] *nt* -(e)s, ⸗er calf;
k—en [ˈkalbən] *vi* calve; —fleisch
nt veal; —sleder *nt* calf(skin).

Kalender [kaˈlɛndər] *m* -s, ⸗
calendar; (*Taschen—*) diary.

Kali [ˈka:li] *nt* -s, -s potash.

Kaliber [kaˈli:bər] *nt* -s, - (*lit, fig*)
calibre.

Kalk [kalk] *m* -(e)s, -e lime; (*Biol*)
calcium; —stein *m* limestone.

Kalkulation [kalkulatsiˈo:n] *f*
calculation.

kalkulieren [kalkuˈli:rən] *vt*
calculate.

Kalorie [kaloˈri:] *f* calorie.

kalt [kalt] *a* cold; **mir ist (es)** —
I am cold; —bleiben *vi irreg* be
unmoved; (*ruhig*) cool; **K—blütigkeit** *f* cold-
bloodedness; coolness.

Kälte [ˈkɛltə] *f* - cold; coldness;
—grad *m* degree of frost or below
zero; —welle *f* cold spell.

kalt- *cpd*: —herzig *a* cold-hearted;
—schnäuzig *a* cold, unfeeling;
—stellen *vt* chill; (*fig*) leave out in
the cold.

Kamel [kaˈme:l] *nt* -(e)s, -e camel.

Kamera [ˈkamera] *f* -, -s camera.

Kamerad [kaməˈra:t] *m* -en, -en
comrade, friend; —schaft *f*
comradeship; k—schaftlich *a*
comradely.

Kamera- *cpd*: —führung *f* camera
work; —mann *m* cameraman.

Kamille [kaˈmilə] *f*-, -n camomile;
—ntee *m* camomile tea.

Kamin [kaˈmi:n] *m* -s, -e (*außen*)
chimney; (*innen*) fireside, fire-
place; —feger, —kehrer *m* -s, -
chimney sweep.

Kamm [kam] *m* -(e)s, ⸗e comb;
(*Berg—*) ridge; (*Hahnen—*) crest.

kämmen [ˈkɛmən] *vt* comb.

Kammer [ˈkamər] *f* -, -n chamber;
small bedroom; —diener *m* valet.

Kampf [kampf] *m* -(e)s, ⸗e fight,
battle; (*Wettbewerb*) contest; (*fig:
Anstrengung*) struggle; k—bereit *a*
ready for action.

kämpfen [ˈkɛmpfən] *vi* fight.

Kämpfer *m* -s, - fighter, com-
batant.

Kampfer [ˈkampfər] *m* -s camphor.

Kampf- *cpd*: —handlung *f* action;
k—los *a* without a fight; k—lustig
a pugnacious; —richter *m* (*Sport*)
referee; (*Tennis*) umpire.

Kanal [kaˈna:l] *m* -s, **Kanäle**
(*Fluß*) canal; (*Rinne, Ärmel—*)
channel; (*für Abfluß*) drain;
—isation [-izatsiˈo:n] *f* sewage
system; k—isieren [-iˈzi:rən] *vt*
provide with a sewage system.

Kanarienvogel [kaˈna:riənfo:gəl]
m canary.

Kandi- [kandi] *cpd*: —dat [-ˈda:t] *m*
-en, -en candidate; —datur
[-daˈtu:r] *f* candidature, candidacy;
k—dieren [-ˈdi:rən] *vi* stand, run.

Kandis(zucker) [ˈkandıs] *m* -
candy.

Känguruh [ˈkɛŋguru] *nt* -s, -s
kangaroo.

Kaninchen [kaˈni:nçən] *nt* rabbit.

Kanister [kaˈnıstər] *m* -s, - can,
canister.

Kanne ['kanə] *f* -, -n (*Krug*) jug; (*Kaffee*—) pot; (*Milch*—) churn; (*Gieß*—) can.

Kanon ['ka:nɔn] *m* -s, -s canon.

Kanone [ka'no:nə] *f* -, -n gun; (*Hist*) cannon; (*fig: Mensch*) ace.

Kantate [kan'ta:tə] *f* -, -n cantata.

Kante ['kantə] *f* -, -n edge.

Kantine [kan'ti:nə] *f* canteen.

Kantor ['kantɔr] *m* choirmaster.

Kanu ['ka:nu] *nt* -s, -s canoe.

Kanzel ['kantsəl] *f* -, -n pulpit.

Kanzlei [kants'laɪ] *f* chancery; (*Büro*) chambers *pl*.

Kanzler ['kantslər] *m* -s, - chancellor.

Kap [kap] *nt* -s, -s cape.

Kapazität [kapatsi'tɛ:t] *f* capacity; (*Fachmann*) authority.

Kapelle [ka'pɛlə] *f* (*Gebäude*) chapel; (*Mus*) band.

Kaper ['ka:pər] *f* -, -n caper; k—n *vt* capture.

kapieren [ka'pi:rən] *vti* (*col*) understand.

Kapital [kapi'ta:l] *nt* -s, -e *or* -ien capital; —anlage *f* investment; —ismus ['-lɪsmʊs] *m* capitalism; —ist ['-lɪst] *m* capitalist; k—kräftig *a* wealthy; —markt *m* money market.

Kapitän [kapi'tɛ:n] *m* -s, -e captain.

Kapitel [ka'pɪtəl] *nt* -s, - chapter.

Kapitulation [kapitulatsi'o:n] *f* capitulation.

kapitulieren [kapitu'li:rən] *vi* capitulate.

Kaplan [ka'pla:n] *m* -s, Kapläne chaplain.

Kappe ['kapə] *f* -, -n cap; (*Kapuze*) hood; k—n *vt* cut.

Kapsel ['kapsəl] *f* -, -n capsule.

kaputt [ka'pʊt] *a* (*col*) smashed, broken; —gehen *vi irreg* break; (*Schuhe*) fall apart; (*Firma*) go bust; (*Stoff*) wear out; (*sterben*) cop it; —lachen *vr* laugh o.s. silly; —machen *vt* break; *Mensch* exhaust, wear out.

Kapuze [ka'pu:tsə] *f* -, -n hood.

Karaffe [ka'rafə] *f* -, -n caraffe (*geschliffen*) decanter.

Karambolage [karambo'la:ʒə] *f* -, -n (*Zusammenstoß*) crash.

Karamel [kara'mɛl] *m* -s caramel; —bonbon *m or nt* toffee.

Karat [ka'ra:t] *nt* -(e)s, -e carat; — *nt* -s karate.

Karawane [kara'va:nə] *f* -, -n caravan.

Kardinal [kardi'na:l] *m* -s, **Kardinäle** cardinal; —zahl *f* cardinal number.

Karfreitag [ka:r'fraita:k] *m* Good Friday.

karg [kark] *a* scanty, poor; *Mahlzeit auch* meagre; — mit *Worten sein use few words*; **K—heit** *f* poverty, scantiness; meagreness.

kärglich ['kɛrklɪç] *a* poor, scanty.

kariert [ka'ri:rt] *a Stoff* checked; *Papier* squared.

Karies ['ka:riɛs] *f* - caries.

Karikatur [karika'tu:r] *f* caricature; —ist ['-rɪst] *m* cartoonist.

karikieren [kari'ki:rən] *vt* caricature.

Karneval ['karnəval] *m* -s, -e *or* -s carnival.

Karo ['ka:ro] *nt* -s, -s square; (*Cards*) diamonds; —**As** *nt* ace of diamonds.

Karosse [ka'rɔsə] f -, -n coach, carriage; --rie [-'ri:] f (Aut) body(work).

Karotte [ka'rɔtə] f -, -n carrot.

Karpfen ['karpfən] m -s, - carp.

Karre ['karə] f -, -n, --n m -s, - cart, barrow; k--n vt cart, transport.

Karriere [kari'e:rə] f -, -n career; -- machen get on, get to the top; --macher m -s, - careerist.

Karte ['kartə] f -, -n card; (Land--) map; (Speise--) menu; (Eintritts--, Fahr--) ticket; alles auf eine -- setzen put all one's eggs in one basket.

Kartei [kar'tai] f card index; --karte f index card.

Kartell [kar'tɛl] nt -s, -e cartel.

Karten- cpd: --haus nt (lit, fig) house of cards; --spiel nt card game; pack of cards.

Kartoffel [kar'tɔfəl] f -, -n potato; --brei m, --püree nt mashed potatoes pl; --salat m potato salad.

Karton [kar'tɔ̃:] m -s, -s cardboard; (Schachtel) cardboard box; k--iert [karto'ni:rt] a hardback.

Karussell [karʊ'sɛl] nt -s, -s roundabout (Brit), merry-go-round.

Karwoche ['ka:rvɔxə] f Holy Week.

Kaschemme [ka'ʃɛmə] f -, -n dive.

Käse ['kɛ:zə] m -s, - cheese; --blatt nt (col) local rag; --kuchen m cheesecake.

Kaserne [ka'zɛrnə] f -, -n barracks pl; --nhof m parade ground.

Kasino [ka'zi:no] nt -s, -s club; (Mil) officers' mess; (Spiel--) casino.

Kasper ['kaspər] m -s, - Punch; (fig) clown.

Kasse ['kasə] f -, -n (Geldkasten) cashbox; (in Geschäft) till, cash register; (Kino--, Theater-- etc) box office; ticket office; (Kranken--) health insurance; (Spar--) savings bank; -- machen count the money; getrennte -- führen pay separately; an der -- (in Geschäft) at the desk; gut bei -- sein to be in the money; --narzt m panel doctor (Brit); --nbestand m cash balance; --npatient m panel patient (Brit); --nprüfung f audit; --nsturz m: --nsturz machen check one's money; --nzettel m receipt.

Kasserolle [kasə'rɔlə] f -, -n casserole.

Kassette [ka'sɛtə] f small box; (Tonband, Phot) cassette; (Bücher--) case; --nrecorder m -s, - cassette recorder.

kassieren [ka'si:rən] vt take; vi: darf ich --? would you like to pay now?

Kassierer [ka'si:rər] m -s, - cashier; (von Klub) treasurer.

Kastanie [kas'ta:niə] f chestnut; --nbaum m chestnut tree.

Kästchen ['kɛstçən] nt small box, casket.

Kaste ['kastə] f -, -n caste.

Kasten ['kastən] m -s, - box (Sport auch), case; (Truhe) chest; --wagen m van.

kastrieren [kas'tri:rən] vt castrate.

Katalog [kata'lo:k] m -(e)s, -e catalogue; k--isieren [katalogi'zi:rən] vt catalogue.

Katapult [kata'pʊlt] m or nt -(e)s, -e catapult.

Katarrh [ka'tar] m -s, -e catarrh.

katastrophal [katastro'fa:l] a catastrophic.

Katastrophe [kata'stro:fə] f -, -n catastrophe, disaster.

Kategorie [katego'riː] *f* category.
kategorisch [kate'goːrɪʃ] *a* categorical.
kategorisieren [kategori'ziːrən] *vt* categorize.
Kater ['kaːtər] *m* -s, - tomcat; (*col*) hangover.
Katheder [ka'teːdər] *nt* -s, - lecture desk.
Kathedrale [kate'draːlə] *f* -, -n cathedral.
Kathode [ka'toːdə] *f* -, -n cathode.
Katholik [kato'liːk] *m* -en, -en Catholic.
katholisch [ka'toːlɪʃ] *a* Catholic.
Katholizismus [katoli'tsɪsmʊs] *m* Catholicism.
Kätzchen ['kɛtsçən] *nt* kitten.
Katze ['katsə] *f* -, -n cat; **für die Katz** (*col*) in vain, for nothing; **—nauge** *nt* cat's eye; (*Fahrrad*) rear light; **—njammer** *m* (*col*) hangover; **—nsprung** *m* (*col*) stone's throw; short journey; **—nwäsche** *f* lick and a promise.
Kauderwelsch ['kaudərvɛlʃ] *nt* -(s) jargon; (*col*) double Dutch.
kauen ['kauən] *vti* chew.
kauern ['kauərn] *vi* crouch.
Kauf [kauf] *m* -(e)s, **Käufe** purchase, buy; (*Kaufen*) buying; **ein guter — a** bargain; **etw in — nehmen** put up with sth; **k—en** *vt* buy.
Käufer(in *f*) ['kɔyfər(m)] *m* -s, - buyer.
Kauf- *cpd:* **—haus** *nt* department store; **—kraft** *f* purchasing power; **—laden** *m* shop, store.
käuflich ['kɔyflɪç] *a,ad* purchasable, for sale; (*pej*) venal; **— erwerben** purchase.
Kauf- *cpd:* **k—lustig** *a* interested in buying; **—mann** *m*, *pl* **-leute**

businessman; shopkeeper; **k—männisch** *a* commercial; **—männischer Angestellter** clerk.
Kaugummi ['kaugumi] *m* chewing gum.
Kaulquappe ['kaulkvapə] *f* -, **-n** tadpole.
kaum [kaum] *ad* hardly, scarcely.
Kaution [kautsi'oːn] *f* deposit; (*Jur*) bail.
Kautschuk ['kautʃuk] *m* -s, **-e** indiarubber.
Kauz [kauts] *m* -es, **Käuze** owl; (*fig*) queer fellow.
Kavalier [kava'liːr] *m* -s, **-e** gentleman, cavalier; **—sdelikt** *nt* peccadillo.
Kavallerie [kavalə'riː] *f* cavalry.
Kavallerist [kavalə'rɪst] *m* trooper, cavalryman.
Kaviar ['kaːviar] *m* caviar.
keck [kɛk] *a* daring, bold; **K—heit** *f* daring, boldness.
Kegel ['keːgəl] *m* -s, - skittle; (*Math*) cone; **—bahn** *f* skittle alley; bowling alley; **k—förmig** *a* conical; **k—n** *vi* play skittles.
Kehle ['keːlə] *f* -, -n throat.
Kehl- *cpd:* **—kopf** *m* larynx; **—laut** *m* guttural.
Kehre ['keːrə] *f* -, -n turn(ing), bend; **k—n** *vti* (*wenden*) turn; (*mit Besen*) sweep; **sich an etw** (*dat*) **nicht k—n** not heed sth.
Kehr- *cpd:* **—icht** *m* -s sweepings *pl*; **—maschine** *f* sweeper; **—reim** *m* refrain; **—seite** *f* reverse, other side; wrong side; bad side; **k—tmachen** *vi* turn about, about-turn.
keifen ['kaifən] *vi* scold, nag.
Keil ['kail] *m* -(e)s, **-e** wedge; (*Mil*) arrowhead; **k—en** *vt* wedge;

vr fight ; **—e'rel** f (col) punch-up ;
—riemen m (Aut) fan belt.

Keim [kaɪm] m **-(e)s, -e** bud ;
(Med, fig) germ ; **etw im —
ersticken** nip sth in the bud ; **k—en**
vi germinate ; **k—frei** a sterile ;
k—tötend a antiseptic, germicidal ;
—zelle f (fig) nucleus.

kein [kaɪn] a no, not any ; **—e(r,s)**
pron no one, nobody ; none ;
—esfalls ad on no account ;
—eswegs ad by no means ; **—mal**
ad not once.

Keks [ke:ks] m or nt **-es, -e** biscuit.

Kelch [kɛlç] m **-(e)s, -e · cup,**
goblet, chalice.

Kelle ['kɛlə] f **-, -n** ladle ;
(Maurer—) trowel.

Keller ['kɛlər] m **-s, - cellar ;
—assel** f **-, -n** woodlouse ;
—wohnung f basement flat.

Kellner ['kɛlnər] m **-s, - waiter ;
—in** f waitress.

keltern ['kɛltərn] vt press.

kennen ['kɛnən] vt irreg know ;
—lernen vt get to know ; **sich
—lernen** get to know each other ;
(zum erstenmal) meet.

Kenn- cpd : **—er m -s, - con-**
noisseur ; **—karte** f identity card ;
k—tlich a distinguishable,
discernible ; **etw k—tlich machen**
mark sth ; **—tnis** f -, -se knowledge
no pl ; **etw zur —tnis nehmen take**
notice of sth ; **von etw —tnis nehmen** take
notice of sth ; **jdn in —tnis setzen**
inform sb ; **—zeichen** nt mark,
characteristic ; **k—zeichnen** vt
insep characterize ; **k—zeichnender-
weise** ad characteristically ;
—ziffer f reference number.

kentern ['kɛntərn] vi capsize.

Keramik [ke'raːmɪk] f **-, -en**
ceramics pl, pottery.

Kerb- [kɛrb] cpd : **—e f -, -n** notch,
groove ; **—el m -s, -** chervil ; **k—en**
vt notch ; **—holz** nt : **etw auf dem
—holz haben** have done sth wrong.

Kerker ['kɛrkər] m **-s, - prison.**

Kerl [kɛrl] m **-s, -e** chap, bloke
(Brit), guy.

Kern [kɛrn] m **-(e)s, -e** (Obst—)
pip, stone ; (Nuß—) kernel ;
(Atom—) nucleus ; (fig) heart,
core ; **—energie** f nuclear energy ;
—forschung f nuclear research ;
—frage f central issue ; **—gehäuse**
nt core ; **k—gesund** a thoroughly
healthy, fit as a fiddle ; **k—ig** a
robust ; Ausspruch pithy ; **—kraftwerk** nt nuclear power station ;
k—los a seedless, pipless ; **—physik**
f nuclear physics ; **—reaktion** f
nuclear reaction ; **—spaltung** f
nuclear fission ; **—waffen** pl
nuclear weapons pl.

Kerze ['kɛrtsə] f **-, -n** candle ;
(Zünd—) plug ; **k—ngerade** a
straight as a die ; **—nständer** m
candle holder.

keß [kɛs] a saucy.

Kessel ['kɛsəl] m **-s, - kettle ;** (von
Lokomotive etc) boiler ; (Geog)
depression ; (Mil) encirclement ;
—treiben nt -s, - (fig) witch hunt.

Kette ['kɛtə] f **-, -n** chain ; **k—n**
vt chain ; **—nhund** m watchdog ;
—nladen m chain store ;
—nrauchen nt chain smoking ;
—nreaktion f chain reaction.

Ketzer ['kɛtsər] m **-s, - heretic ;
k—isch** a heretical.

keuchen ['kɔʏçən] vi pant, gasp.

Keuchhusten m whooping cough.

Keule ['kɔʏlə] f **-, -n** club ; (Cook)
leg.

keusch [kɔʏʃ] a chaste ; **K—heit** f
chastity.

Kfz [kaːɛftsɛt] *abbr of* **Kraftfahrzeug.**

kichern ['kiçərn] *vi* giggle.

kidnappen ['kɪdnæpən] *vt* kidnap.

Kiebitz ['kiːbɪts] *m* -es, -e peewit.

Kiefer ['kiːfər] *m* -s, - jaw; *f* -, -n pine; —zapfen *m* pine cone.

Kiel [kiːl] *m* -(e)s, -e (*Feder*—) quill; (*Naut*) keel; k—holen *vt Person* keelhaul; *Schiff* career; —wasser *nt* wake.

Kieme ['kiːmə] *f* -, -n gill.

Kies [kiːs] *m* -es, -e gravel; —el ['kiːzəl] *m* -s, - pebble; —elstein *m* pebble; —grube *f* gravel pit; —weg *m* gravel path.

Kilo ['kiːlo] kilo; —gramm [kilo'gram] *nt* -s, -e kilogram; —meter [kilo'meːtər] *m* kilometre; —meterzähler *m* ≈ milometer.

Kimme ['kɪmə] *f* -, -n notch; (*Gewehr*) backsight.

Kind [kɪnt] *nt* -(e)s, -er child; von — auf from childhood; sich bei jdm lieb — machen ingratiate o.s. with sb; —erbett ['kɪndərbɛt] *nt* cot; —erei [kɪndə'raɪ] *f* childishness; —ergarten *m* nursery school, playgroup; —ergeld *nt* family allowance; —erlähmung *f* poliomyelitis; k—erleicht *a* childishly easy; k—erlos *a* childless; —ermädchen *nt* nursemaid; k—erreich *a* with a lot of children; —erspiel *nt* child's play; —erstube *f*: eine gute —erstube haben be well-mannered; —erwagen *m* pram, baby carriage (*US*); —erzahl *nt* infancy; —esbeine *pl*: von —esbeinen an from early childhood; —heit *f* childhood; k—isch *a* childish; k—lich *a* childlike; k—sköpfig *a* childish.

Kinn [kɪn] *nt* -(e)s, -e chin; —haken *m* (*Boxen*) uppercut; —lade *f* jaw.

Kino ['kiːno] *nt* -s, -s cinema; —besucher *m* cinema-goer; —programm *nt* film programme.

Kiosk [kiˈɔsk] *m* -(e)s, -e kiosk.

Kipp- ['kɪp] *cpd*: —e *f* -, -n cigarette end; (*col*) fag; auf der —e stehen (*fig*) be touch and go; k—en *vi* topple over, overturn; *vt* tilt.

Kirch- ['kɪrç] *cpd*: —e *f* -, -n church; —endiener *m* churchwarden; —enfest *nt* church festival; —enlied *nt* hymn; —gänger *m* -s, - churchgoer; —hof *m* churchyard; k—lich *a* ecclesiastical; —turm *m* church tower, steeple.

Kirsche ['kɪrʃə] *f* -, -n cherry.

Kissen ['kɪsən] *nt* -s, - cushion; (*Kopf*—).pillow; —bezug *m* pillowslip.

Kiste ['kɪstə] *f* -, -n box; chest.

Kitsch [kɪtʃ] *m* -(e)s trash; k—ig *a* trashy.

Kitt [kɪt] *m* -(e)s, -e putty; —chen *nt* (*col*) clink; —el *m* -s, - overall, smock; k—en *vt* putty; (*fig*) *Ehe etc* cement.

Kitz [kɪts] *nt* -es, -e kid; (*Reh*—) fawn.

kitzel- ['kɪtsəl] *cpd*: —ig *a* (*lit, fig*) ticklish; —n *vt* tickle.

klaffen ['klafən] *vi* gape.

kläffen ['klɛfən] *vi* yelp.

Klage ['klaːgə] *f* -, -n complaint; (*Jur*) action; k—n *vi* (weh—) lament, wail; (*sich beschweren*) complain; (*Jur*) take legal action.

Kläger(in *f*) ['klɛːgər(ɪn)] *m* -s, - plaintiff.

kläglich ['klɛːklɪç] *a* wretched.

Klamm [klam] *f* -, -en ravine; k—*a Finger* numb; (*feucht*) damp.

Klammer ['klamər] *f* -, -n clamp; (*in Text*) bracket; (*Büro*—) clip;

(*Wäsche*—) peg; (*Zahn*—) brace;
k—n *vr* cling (*an* + *acc* to).
Klang [klaŋ] *m* -(e)s, ⁼e sound;
k—voll *a* sonorous.
Klappe ['klapə] *f* -, -n valve;
(*Ofen*—) damper; (*col: Mund*)
trap; k—n *vi* (*Geräusch*) click; *vti*
Sitz etc tip; *v impers* work.
Klapper ['klapər] *f* -, -n rattle;
k—ig *a* run-down, worn-out; k—n
vi clatter, rattle; —schlange *f* rattle-
snake; —storch *m* stork.
Klapp- *cpd*: —messer *nt* jack-
knife; —rad *nt* collapsible bicycle;
—stuhl *m* folding chair.
Klaps [klaps] *m* -es, -e slap; k—en
vt slap.
klar [klɑːr] *a* clear; (*Naut*) ready
for sea; (*Mil*) ready for action; sich
(*dat*) im K—en sein über (+ *acc*)
be clear about; ins K—e kommen
get clear.
Klär- ['klɛːr] *cpd*: —anlage *f* purification plant; k—en *vt* (*Flüßigkeit*)
purify; *Probleme* clarify; *vr* clear
(itself) up.
Klar- *cpd*: —heit *f* clarity.; —inette *f*
[klari'nɛtə] *f* clarinet; k—legen *vt*
clear up, explain; k—machen *vt*
Schiff get ready for sea; jdm etw
k—machen make sth clear to sb;
k—sehen *vi irreg* see clearly;
—sichtfolie *f* transparent film;
k—stellen *vt* clarify.
Klärung ['klɛːruŋ] *f* purification;
clarification.
Klasse ['klasə] *f* -, -n class; (*Sch
auch*) form; k— *a* (*col*) smashing;
—narbeit *f* test; —nbewußtsein *nt*
class consciousness; —ngesellschaft *f* class society; —nkampf *m*
class conflict; —nlehrer *m* form
master; k—nlos *a* classless;
—nsprecher(in *f*) *m* form prefect;
—nzimmer *nt* classroom.

klassifizieren [klasifi'tsiːrən] *vt*
classify.
Klassifizierung *f* classification.
Klassik ['klasɪk] *f* (*Zeit*) classical
period; (*Stil*) classicism; —er *m* -s,
- classic.
klassisch *a* (*lit, fig*) classical. ·
Klatsch [klatʃ] *m* -(e)s, -e smack,
crack; (*Gerede*) gossip; —base *f*
gossip, scandalmonger; —e *f* -, -n
(*col*) crib; k—en *vi* (*Geräusch*)
clash; (*reden*) gossip; (*Beifall*)
applaud, clap; —mohn *m* (*corn*)
poppy; k—naß *a* soaking wet;
—spalte *f* gossip column.
klauben ['klaubən] *vt* pick.
Klaue ['klauə] *f* -, -n claw; (*col:
Schrift*) scrawl; k—n *vt* claw;
(*col*) pinch.
Klause ['klauzə] *f* -, -n cell;
hermitage.
Klausel ['klauzəl] *f* -, -n clause.
Klausur [klau'zuːr] *f* seclusion;
—arbeit *f* examination paper.
Klaviatur [klavia'tuːr] *f* keyboard.
Klavier [kla'viːr] *nt* -s, -e piano.
Kleb- ['kleːb] *cpd*: —emittel *nt*
glue; k—en *vti* stick (*an* + *acc* to);
k—rig *a* sticky; —stoff *m* glue;
—streifen *m* adhesive tape.
kleckern ['klɛkərn] *vi* slobber.
Klecks [klɛks] *m* -es, -e blot,
stain; k—en *vi* blot; (*pej*) daub.
Klee [kleː] *m* -s clover; —blatt *nt*
cloverleaf; (*fig*) trio.
Kleid [klait] *nt* -(e)s, -er garment;
(*Frauen*—) dress; *pl* clothes *pl*;
k—en ['klaidən] *vt* clothe, dress;
(*auch vi*) suit; *vr* dress; —erbügel
m coat hanger; —erbürste *f* clothes
brush; —erschrank *m* wardrobe;
k—sam *a* becoming; —ung *f*
clothing; —ungsstück *nt* garment.

Kleie ['klaɪə] f -, -n bran.

klein [klaɪn] a little, small; K—bürgertum nt petite bourgeoisie; K—e(r,s) little one; K—format nt small size; im K—format small-scale; K—geld nt small change; —gläubig a of little faith; —hacken vt chop up, mince; K—holz nt firewood; K—holz aus jdm machen make mincemeat of sb; K—igkeit f trifle; K—kind nt infant; K—kram m details pl; —laut a dejected, quiet; —lich a petty, paltry; K—lichkeit f pettiness, paltriness; —mütig a faint-hearted; K—od ['klaɪno:t] nt -s, -odien gem, jewel; treasure; —schneiden vt irreg chop up; —städtisch a provincial; —stmöglich a smallest possible.

Kleister ['klaɪstər] m -s, - paste; k—n vt paste.

Klemme ['klɛmə] f -, -n clip; (Med) clamp; (fig) jam; k—n vt (festhalten) jam; (quetschen) pinch, nip; vr catch o.s.; (sich hineinzwängen) squeeze o.s.; sich hinter jdn/etw k—n get on to sb/get down to sth; vi (Tür) stick, jam.

Klempner ['klɛmpnər] m -s, - plumber.

Kleptomanie [klɛptoma'ni:] f kleptomania.

Kleriker ['kle:rɪkər] m -s, - cleric.

Klerus ['kle:rʊs] m - clergy.

Klette ['klɛtə] f -, -n burr.

Kletter- ['klɛtər] cpd: —er m -s, - climber; k—n vi climb; —pflanze f creeper; —seil nt climbing rope.

klicken ['klɪkən] vi click.

Klient(in f) [kli'ɛnt(ɪn)] m client.

Klima ['kli:ma] nt -s, -s or -te [kli'ma:tə] climate; —anlage f air conditioning; k—tisieren [-i'zi:rən]

vt air-condition; —wechsel m change of air.

klimpern ['klɪmpərn] vi tinkle; (mit Gitarre) strum.

Klinge ['klɪŋə] f -, -n blade, sword.

Klingel ['klɪŋəl] f -, -n bell; —beutel m collection bag; k—n vi ring.

klingen ['klɪŋən] vi irreg sound; (Gläser) clink.

Klinik ['kli:nɪk] f hospital, clinic.

klinisch ['kli:nɪʃ] a clinical.

Klinke ['klɪŋkə] f -, -n handle.

Klinker ['klɪŋkər] m -s, - clinker.

Klippe ['klɪpə] f -, -n cliff; (im Meer) reef; (fig) hurdle; k—nreich a rocky.

klipp und klar ['klɪp'ʊntkla:r] a clear and concise.

Klips [klɪps] m -es, -e clip; (Ohr—) earring.

klirren ['klɪrən] vi clank, jangle; (Gläser) clink; —de Kälte biting cold.

Klischee [kli'ʃe:] nt -s, -s (Druckplatte) plate, block; (fig) cliché; —vorstellung f stereotyped idea.

Klo [klo:] nt -s, -s (col) loo.

Kloake [klo'a:kə] f -, -n sewer.

klobig ['klo:bɪç] a clumsy.

klopfen ['klɔpfən] vti knock; (Herz) thump; es klopft sb's knocking; jdm auf die Schulter — tap sb on the shoulder; vt beat.

Klopfer m -s, - (Teppich—) beater; (Tür—) knocker.

Klöppel ['klœpəl] m -s, - (von Glocke) clapper; k—n vi make lace.

Klops [klɔps] m -es, -e meatball.

Klosett [klo'zɛt] nt -s, -e or -s lavatory, toilet; —papier nt toilet paper.

Kloß [klo:s] m -es, ̈-e (Erd—) clod; (im Hals) lump; (Cook) dumpling.

Kloster ['klo:stər] nt -s, - (Männer—) monastery; (Frauen—) convent.

klösterlich ['klø:stərlɪç] a monastic; convent.

Klotz [klɔts] m -es, ⁻e log; (Hack—) block; ein — am Bein (fig) drag, millstone round (sb's) neck.

Klub [klup] m -s, -s club; —sessel m easy chair.

Kluft [kluft] f -, ⁻e cleft, gap; (Geol) gorge, chasm.

klug [klu:k] a clever, intelligent; K—heit f cleverness, intelligence.

Klümpchen ['klympçən] nt clot, blob.

Klumpen ['klumpən] m -s, - (Erd—) clod; (Blut—) lump, clot; (Gold—) nugget; (Cook) lump; k— vi go lumpy, clot.

Klumpfuß ['klump-fu:s] m clubfoot.

knabbern ['knabərn] vti nibble.

Knabe ['kna:bə] m -n, -n boy; k—nhaft a boyish.

Knäckebrot ['knɛkəbro:t] nt crispbread.

knacken ['knakən] vti (lit, fig) crack.

Knall [knal] m -(e)s, -e bang; (Peitschen—) crack; — und Fall (col) unexpectedly; —bonbon m cracker; —effekt m surprise effect, spectacular effect; k—en vi bang; crack; k—rot a bright red.

knapp [knap] a tight; Geld scarce; Sprache concise; K—e m -n, -n (Edelmann) young knight; —halten vt irreg stint; K—heit f tightness; scarcity; conciseness.

knarren ['knarən] vi creak.

knattern ['knatərn] vi rattle; (MG) chatter.

Knäuel ['knɔyəl] m or nt -s, - (Woll—) ball; (Menschen—) knot.

Knauf [knauf] m -(e)s, Knäufe knob; (Schwert—) pommel.

Knauser ['knauzər] m -s, - miser; k—ig a miserly; k—n vi be mean.

knautschen ['knautʃən] vti crumple.

Knebel ['kne:bəl] m -s, - gag; k—n vt gag; (Naut) fasten.

Knecht [knɛçt] m -(e)s, -e farm labourer; servant; k—en vt enslave; —schaft f servitude.

kneifen ['knaifən] vti irreg pinch; (sich drücken) back out; vor etw — dodge sth.

Kneipe ['knaipə] f -, -n (col) pub.

Knet- [kne:t] cpd: k—en vt knead; Wachs mould; —masse f Plasticine.

Knick [knik] m -(e)s, -e (Sprung) crack; (Kurve) bend; (Falte) fold; k—en vti (springen) crack; (brechen) break; Papier fold; geknickt sein be downcast.

Knicks [knɪks] m -es, -e curtsey; k—en vi curtsey.

Knie [kni:] nt -s, - knee; —beuge f -, -n knee bend; k—n vi kneel; —fall m genuflection; —gelenk nt knee joint; —kehle f back of the knee; —scheibe f kneecap; —strumpf m knee-length sock.

Kniff [knif] m -(e)s, -e (Zwicken) pinch; (Falte) fold; (fig) trick, knack; k—elig a tricky.

knipsen ['knɪpsən] vti Fahrkarte punch; (Phot) take a snap (of), snap.

Knirps [knɪrps] m -es, -e little chap; ® (Schirm) telescopic umbrella.

knirschen ['knɪrʃən] vi crunch; mit den Zähnen — grind one's teeth.

knistern ['knɪstərn] vi crackle.

Knitter- ['knɪtər] cpd: —**falte** f crease; **k—frei** a non-crease; **k—n** vi crease.

Knoblauch ['kno:plaux] m -(e)s garlic.

Knöchel ['knœçəl] m -s, - knuckle; (Fuß—) ankle.

Knochen ['knɔxən] m -s, - bone; —**bau** m bone structure; —**bruch** m fracture; —**gerüst** nt skeleton.

knöchern ['knœçərn] a bone.

knochig ['knɔxɪç] a bony.

Knödel ['knø:dəl] m -s, - dumpling.

Knolle ['knɔlə] f -, -n bulb.

Knopf [knɔpf] m -(e)s, ⁺e button; (Kragen—) stud; —**loch** nt buttonhole.

knöpfen ['knœpfən] vt button.

Knorpel ['knɔrpəl] m -s, - cartilage, gristle; **k—ig** a gristly.

knorrig ['knɔrɪç] a gnarled, knotted.

Knospe ['knɔspə] f -, -n bud; **k—n** vi bud.

Knoten ['kno:tən] m -s, - knot; (Bot) node; (Med) lump; **k—** vt knot; —**punkt** m junction.

knuffen ['knʊfən] vt (col) cuff.

Knüller ['knʏlər] m -s, - (col) hit; (Reportage) scoop.

knüpfen ['knʏpfən] vt tie; Teppich knot; Freundschaft form.

Knüppel ['knʏpəl] m -s, - cudgel; (Polizei—) baton, truncheon; (Aviat) (joy)stick; —**schaltung** f (Aut) floor-mounted gear change.

knurren ['knʊrən] vi (Hund) snarl, growl; (Magen) rumble; (Mensch) mutter.

knusperig ['knʊspərɪç] a crisp; Keks crunchy.

Koalition [koalitsi'o:n] f coalition.

Kobalt ['ko:balt] nt -s cobalt.

Kobold ['ko:bɔlt] m -(e)s, -e goblin, imp.

Kobra ['ko:bra] f -, -s cobra.

Koch [kɔx] m -(e)s, ⁺e cook; —**buch** nt cookery book; **k—en** vti cook; Wasser boil; —**er** m -s, - stove, cooker.

Köcher ['kœçər] m -s, - quiver.

Kochgelegenheit ['kɔxgəle:gən- hait] f cooking facilities pl.

Köchin ['kœçɪn] f cook.

Koch- cpd: —**löffel** m kitchen spoon; —**nische** f kitchenette; —**platte** f boiling ring, hotplate; —**salz** nt cooking salt; —**topf** m saucepan, pot.

Köder ['kø:dər] m -s, - bait, lure; **k—n** vt lure, entice.

Koexistenz [kɔɛksɪs'tɛnts] f coexistence.

Koffein [kɔfe'i:n] nt -s caffeine; **k—frei** a decaffeinated.

Koffer ['kɔfər] m -s, - suitcase; (Schrank—) trunk; —**radio** nt portable radio; —**raum** m (Aut) boot, trunk (US).

Kognak ['kɔnjak] m -s, -s brandy, cognac.

Kohl [ko:l] m -(e)s, -e cabbage.

Kohle ['ko:lə] f -, -n coal; (Holz—) charcoal; (Chem) carbon; —**hydrat** nt -(e)s, -e carbohydrate; —**ndioxyd** nt -(e)s, -e carbon dioxide; —**ngrube** f coal pit, mine; —**nhändler** m coal merchant, coalman; —**nsäure** f carbon dioxide; —**nstoff** m carbon; —**npapier** nt carbon paper; —**nstift** m charcoal pencil.

Köhler ['kø:lər] m -s, - charcoal burner.

Kohl- cpd: —**rübe** f turnip; **k—schwarz** a coal-black.

Koje ['ko:jə] f -, -n cabin; (Bett) bunk.

Kokain [koka'i:n] nt -s cocaine.

kokett [ko'kɛt] a coquettish, flirtatious; -ieren [-'ti:rən] vi flirt.

Kokosnuß ['ko:kɔsnus] f coconut.

Koks [ko:ks] m -es, -e coke.

Kolben ['kɔlbən] m -s, - (Gewehr—) rifle butt; (Keule) club; (Chem) flask; (Tech) piston; (Mais—) cob.

Kolchose [kɔl'go:zə] f -, -n collective farm.

Kolik ['ko:lik] f colic, gripe.

Kollaps [kɔ'laps] m -es, -e collapse.

Kolleg [kɔ'le:k] nt -s, -s or -ien lecture course; -e [kɔ'le:gə] m -n, -n, -in f colleague; -ium nt board; (Sch) staff.

Kollekte [kɔ'lɛktə] f -, -n (Rel) collection.

kollektiv [kɔlɛk'ti:f] a collective.

kollidieren [kɔli'di:rən] vi collide; (zeitlich) clash.

Kollision [kɔlizi'o:n] f collision; . (zeitlich) clash.

kolonial [koloni'a:l] a colonial; K—warenhändler m grocer.

Kolonie [kolo'ni:] f colony.

kolonisieren [koloni'zi:rən] vt colonize.

Kolonist [kolo'nist] m colonist.

Kolonne [kɔ'lɔnə] f -, -n column; (von Fahrzeugen) convoy.

Koloß ['ko:lɔs] m -sses, -sse colossus.

kolossal [kolɔ'sa:l] a colossal.

Kombi- ['kɔmbi] cpd: —nation [-natsi'o:n] f combination; (Vermutung) conjecture; (Hemdhose) combinations pl; (Aviat) flying suit; k—nieren [-'ni:rən] vt combine; vi deduce, work out; (vermuten) guess;

—wagen m station wagon; —zange f (pair of) pliers.

Komet [ko'me:t] m -en, -en comet.

Komfort [kɔm'fo:r] m -s luxury.

Komik -, ['ko:mik] f humour, comedy; —er m -s, - comedian.

komisch ['ko:miʃ] a funny.

Komitee [komi'te:] nt -s, -s committee.

Komma ['kɔma] nt -s, -s or -ta comma.

Kommand- [kɔ'mand] cpd: —ant ['-dant] m commander, commanding officer; —eur [-'dø:r] m commanding officer; k—ieren ['di:rən] vti command; —o nt -s, -s command, order; (Truppe) detachment, squad; auf —o to order.

kommen ['kɔmən] vi irreg come; (näher —) approach; (passieren) happen; (gelangen, geraten) get; (Blumen, Zähne, Tränen etc) appear; (in die Schule, das Gymnasium etc) go; — lassen send for; das kommt in den Schrank that goes in the cupboard; zu sich — come round or to; zu etw — acquire sth; um etw — lose sth; nichts auf jdn/etw — lassen have nothing said against sb/sth; jdm frech — get cheeky with sb; auf jeden vierten kommt ein Platz there's one place to every fourth person; wer kommt zuerst? who's first?; unter ein Auto — be run over by a car; wie hoch kommt das? what does that cost?; K— nt -s coming.

Kommentar [kɔmɛn'ta:r] m commentary; kein — no comment; k—los a without comment.

Kommentator [kɔmɛn'ta:tor] m (TV) commentator.

kommentieren [kɔmɛn'ti:rən] *vt* comment on.

kommerziell [kɔmɛrtsi'ɛl] *a* commercial.

Kommilitone [kɔmili'to:nə] *m* -n, -n fellow student.

Kommiß [kɔ'mɪs] *m* -sses (life in the) army; **—brot** *nt* army bread.

Kommissar [kɔmɪ'sa:r] *m* police inspector.

Kommission [kɔmɪsi'o:n] *f* (*Comm*) commission; (*Ausschuß*) committee.

Kommode [kɔ'mo:də] *f* -, -n (chest of) drawers.

Kommune [kɔ'mu:nə] *f* -, -n commune.

Kommunikation [kɔmunikatsi'o:n] *f* communication.

Kommunion [kɔmuni'o:n] *f* communion.

Kommuniqué [kɔmyni'ke:] *nt* -s, -s communiqué.

Kommunismus [kɔmu'nɪsmʊs] *m* communism.

Kommunist [kɔmu'nɪst] *m* communist; **k—isch** *a* communist.

kommunizieren [kɔmuni'tsi:rən] *vi* communicate; (*Eccl*) receive communion.

Komödiant [kɔmödi'ant] *m* comedian; **—in** *f* comedienne.

Komödie [ko'mö:diə] *f* comedy.

Kompagnon [kɔmpan'jõ:] *m* -s, -s (*Comm*) partner.

kompakt [kɔm'pakt] *a* compact.

Kompanie [kɔmpa'ni:] *f* company.

Komparativ ['kɔmparati:f] *m* -s, -e comparative.

Kompaß ['kɔmpas] *m* -sses, -sse compass.

kompetent [kɔmpe'tɛnt] *a* competent.

Kompetenz [kɔmpe'tɛnts] *f* competence, authority.

komplett [kɔm'plɛt] *a* complete.

Komplikation [kɔmplikatsi'o:n] *f* complication.

Kompliment [kɔmpli'mɛnt] *nt* compliment.

Komplize [kɔm'pli:tsə] *m* -n, -n accomplice.

komplizieren [kɔmpli'tsi:rən] *vt* complicate.

Komplott [kɔm'plɔt] *nt* -(e)s, -e plot.

komponieren [kɔmpo'ni:rən] *vt* compose.

Komponist [kɔmpo'nɪst] *m.* composer.

Komposition [kɔmpozitsi'o:n] *f* composition.

Kompost [kɔm'pɔst] *m* -(e)s, -e compost; **—haufen** *m* compost heap.

Kompott [kɔm'pɔt] *nt* -(e)s, -e stewed fruit.

Kompresse [kɔm'prɛsə] *f* -, -n compress.

Kompressor [kɔm'prɛsɔr] *m* compressor.

Kompromiß [kɔmpro'mɪs] *m* -sses, -sse compromise; **k—bereit** *a* willing to compromise; **—lösung** *f* compromise solution.

kompromittieren [kɔmpromɪ'ti:rən] *vt* compromise.

Kondens- [kɔn'dɛns] *cpd:* **—ation** [kɔndɛnzatsi'o:n] *f* condensation; **—ator** [kɔndɛn'za:tɔr] *m* condenser; **k—ieren** [kɔndɛn'zi:rən] *vt* condense; **—milch** *f* condensed milk; **—streifen** *m* vapour trail.

Kondition- [kɔnditsi'o:n] *cpd:* **—alsatz** [kɔnditsio'na:lzats] *m* conditional clause; **—straining** nt fitness training.

Konditor [kɔn'di:tɔr] m pastry-cook; **—ei** [kɔndito'raɪ] f café; cake shop.

kondolieren [kɔndo'li:rən] vi condole (jdm with sb).

Kondom [kɔn'do:m] nt **-s, -e** condom.

Konfektion [kɔnfɛktsi'o:n] f production of ready-made clothing; **—skleidung** f ready-made clothing.

Konferenz [kɔnfe'rɛnts] f conference, meeting.

konferieren [kɔnfe'ri:rən] vi confer, have a meeting.

Konfession [kɔnfɛsi'o:n] f religion; (christlich) denomination; **k—ell** ['-nɛl] a denominational; **k—slos** a non-denominational; **—sschule** f denominational school.

Konfetti [kɔn'fɛti] nt **-(s)** confetti.

Konfirmand [kɔnfɪr'mant] m candidate for confirmation.

Konfirmation [kɔnfɪrmatsi'o:n] f (Eccl) confirmation.

konfirmieren [kɔnfɪr'mi:rən] vt confirm.

konfiszieren [kɔnfɪs'tsi:rən] vt confiscate.

Konfitüre [kɔnfi'ty:rə] f **-, -n** jam.

Konflikt [kɔn'flɪkt] m **-(e)s, -e** conflict.

konform [kɔn'fɔrm] a concurring; **— gehen** be in agreement.

konfrontieren [kɔnfrɔn'ti:rən] vt confront.

konfus [kɔn'fu:s] a confused.

Kongreß [kɔn'grɛs] m **-sses, -sse** congress.

Kongruenz [kɔngru'ɛnts] f agreement, congruence.

König ['kø:nɪç] m **-(e)s, -e** king; **—in** ['kø:nɪgɪn] f queen; **k—lich** a

royal; **—reich** nt kingdom; **—tum** nt **-(e)s, -tümer** kingship.

konisch ['ko:nɪʃ] a conical.

Konjugation [kɔnjugatsi'o:n] f conjugation.

konjugieren [kɔnju'gi:rən] vt conjugate.

Konjunktion [kɔnjuŋktsi'o:n] f conjunction.

Konjunktiv ['kɔnjuŋkti:f] m **-s, -e** subjunctive.

Konjunktur [kɔnjuŋk'tu:r] f economic situation; (Hoch—) boom.

konkav [kɔn'ka:f] a concave.

konkret [kɔn'kre:t] a concrete.

Konkurrent(in f) [kɔnku'rɛnt(ɪn)] m competitor.

Konkurrenz [kɔnku'rɛnts] f competition; **k—fähig** a competitive; **—kampf** m competition; (col) rat race.

konkurrieren [kɔnku'ri:rən] vi compete.

Konkurs [kɔn'kurs] m **-es, -e** bankruptcy.

können ['kœnən] vti irreg be able to, can; (wissen) know; **— Sie Deutsch?** can you speak German? **ich kann nicht ...** I can't or cannot **...; ich kann gehen?** can I go? **das kann sein** that's possible; **das kann nicht mehr** I can't go on; **K—** nt **-s** ability.

konsequent [kɔnze'kvɛnt] a consistent.

Konsequenz [kɔnze'kvɛnts] f consistency; (Folgerung) conclusion.

Konserv- [kɔn'zɛrv] cpd: **k—ativ** [-a'ti:f] a conservative; **—atorium** [-a'to:rium] nt academy of music, conservatory; **—e** f **-, -n** tinned food; **—enbüchse** f tin, can; **k—ieren** [-'vi:rən] vt preserve;

—**ierung** f preservation;
—**ierungsmittel** nt preservative.

Konsonant [kɔnzo'nant] m consonant.

konstant [kɔn'stant] a constant.

Konstitution [kɔnstitutsi'oːn] f constitution; **k—ell** [-'nɛl] a constitutional.

konstruieren [kɔnstru'iːrən] vt construct.

Konstrukteur [kɔnstruk'tøːr] m engineer, designer.

Konstruktion [kɔnstruktsi'oːn] f construction.

konstruktiv [kɔnstruk'tiːf] a constructive.

Konsul ['kɔnzʊl] m -s, -n consul; —**at** [-'laːt] nt consulate.

konsultieren [kɔnzʊl'tiːrən] vt consult.

Konsum [kɔn'zuːm] m -s consumption; —**artikel** m consumer article; —**ent** [-'mɛnt] m consumer; **k—ieren** [-'miːrən] vt consume.

Kontakt [kɔn'takt] m -(e)s, -e contact; **k—arm** a unsociable; **k—freudig** a sociable; —**linsen** pl contact lenses pl.

Konterfei ['kɔntəfai] nt -s, -s picture.

kontern ['kɔntərn] vti counter.

Konterrevolution [kɔntərrevolutsɪoːn] f counter-revolution.

Kontinent ['kɔntinɛnt] m continent.

Kontingent [kɔntiŋ'gɛnt] m -(e)s, -e quota; (Truppen—) contingent.

kontinuierlich [kɔntinu'iːrlɪç] a continuous.

Kontinuität [kɔntinui'tɛːt] f continuity.

Konto ['kɔnto] nt -s, **Konten** account; —**auszug** m statement (of account); —**inhaber(in** f) m

account holder; —**r** [kɔn'toːr] nt -s, -e office; —**rist** [-'rɪst] m clerk, office worker; —**stand** m state of account.

Kontra ['kɔntra] nt -s, -s (Cards) double; **jdm — geben** (fig) contradict sb; —**baß** m double bass; —**hent** [-'hɛnt] m contracting party; —**punkt** m counterpoint.

Kontrast [kɔn'trast] m -(e)s, -e contrast.

Kontroll- [kɔn'trɔl] cpd: —**e** f -, -n control, supervision; (Paß—) passport control; —**eur** [-'løːr] m inspector; **k—ieren** [-'liːrən] vt control, supervise; (nachprüfen) check.

Kontur [kɔn'tuːr] f contour.

Konvention [kɔnvɛntsi'oːn] f convention; **k—ell** [-'nɛl] a conventional.

Konversation [kɔnvɛrzatsi'oːn] f conversation; —**slexikon** nt encyclopaedia.

konvex [kɔn'vɛks] a convex.

Konvoi ['kɔnvɔy] m -s, -e convoy.

Konzentration [kɔntsɛntratsi'oːn] f concentration; —**slager** nt concentration camp.

konzentrieren [kɔntsɛn'triːrən] vtr concentrate.

konzentriert a concentrated; ad zuhören, arbeiten intently.

Konzept [kɔn'tsɛpt] nt -(e)s, -e rough draft; **jdn aus dem —**
bringen confuse sb.

Konzern [kɔn'tsɛrn] m -s, -e combine.

Konzert [kɔn'tsɛrt] nt -(e)s, -e concert; (Stück) concerto; —**saal** m concert hall.

Konzession [kɔntsɛsi'oːn] f licence; (Zugeständnis) concession; **k—ieren** [-'niːrən] vt license.

Konzil [kɔn'tsiːl] *nt* **-s, -e** *or* **-ien** council.

konzipieren [kɔntsi'piːrən] *vt* conceive.

Kopf [kɔpf] *m* **-(e)s, ̈e** head; **—bedeckung** *f* headgear.

köpfen ['kœpfən] *vt* behead; *Baum* lop; *Ei* take the top off; *Ball* head.

Kopf- *cpd:* **—haut** *f* scalp; **—hörer** *m* headphone; **—kissen** *nt* pillow; **k—los** a panic-stricken; **—losigkeit** *f* panic; **k—rechnen** *vi* do mental arithmetic; **—salat** *m* lettuce; **—schmerzen** *pl* headache; **—sprung** *m* header, dive; **—stand** *m* headstand; **—tuch** *nt* headscarf; **k—über** *ad* head over heels; **—weh** *nt* headache; **—zerbrechen** *nt:* jdm **—zerbrechen machen** give sb a lot of headaches.

Kopie [ko'piː] *f* copy; **k—ren** *vt* copy.

Koppel ['kɔpəl] *f* **-, -n** (*Weide*) enclosure; *nt* **-s, -** (*Gürtel*) belt; **k—n** *vt* couple; **—ung** *f* coupling; **—ungsmanöver** *nt* docking manoeuvre.

Koralle [ko'ralə] *f* **-, -n** coral; **—nkette** *f* coral necklace; **—nriff** *nt* coral reef.

Korb [kɔrp] *m* **-(e)s, ̈e** basket; jdm einen **— geben** (*fig*) turn sb down; **—ball** *m* basketball; **—stuhl** *m* wicker chair.

Kord [kɔrt] *m* **-(e)s, -e** corduroy.

Kordel ['kɔrdəl] *f* **-, -n** cord, string.

Kork [kɔrk] *m* **-(e)s, -e** cork; **—en** *m* **-s, -** stopper, cork; **—enzieher** *m* **-s, -** corkscrew.

Korn [kɔrn] *m* **-(e)s, ̈er** corn, grain; (*Gewehr*) sight; **—blume** *f* cornflower; **—kammer** *f* granary.

Körnchen ['kœrnçən] *nt* grain, granule.

Körper ['kœrper] *m* **-s, -** body; **—bau** *m* build; **k—behindert** a disabled; **—gewicht** *nt* weight; **—größe** *f* height; **—haltung** *f* carriage, deportment; **k—lich** a physical; **—pflege** *f* personal hygiene; **—schaft** *f* corporation; **—teil** *m* part of the body.

Korps [kɔːr] *nt* **-, -** (*Mil*) corps; students' club.

korpulent [kɔrpu'lɛnt] a corpulent.

korrekt [kɔ'rɛkt] a correct; **K—heit** *f* correctness; **K—or** *m* proofreader; **K—ur** [-'tuːr] *f* (*eines Textes*) proofreading; (*Text*) proof; (*Sch*) marking, correction.

Korrespondent [kɔrɛspɔn'dɛnt] *cpd:* **—ent(in** *f*) [-'dɛnt(in)] *m* correspondent; **—enz** [-'dɛnts] *f* correspondence; **k—ieren** [-'diːrən] *vi* correspond.

Korridor ['kɔridoːr] *m* **-s, -e** corridor.

korrigieren [kɔri'giːrən] *vt* correct.

korrumpieren [kɔrum'piːrən] *vt* corrupt.

Korruption [kɔruptsi'oːn] *f* corruption.

Korsett [kɔr'zɛt] *nt* **-(e)s, -e** corset.

Kose- ['koːzə] *cpd:* **—form** *f* pet form; **K—n** *vt* caress; *vi* bill and coo; **—name** *m* pet name; **—wort** *nt* term of endearment.

Kosmetik [kɔs'meːtik] *f* cosmetics *pl*; **—erin** *f* beautician.

kosmetisch a cosmetic; *Chirurgie* plastic.

kosmisch ['kɔsmiʃ] a cosmic.

Kosmo- [kɔsmo] *cpd:* **—naut** ['naut] *m* **-en, -en** cosmonaut; **—polit** [-po'liːt] *m* **-en, -en** cosmopolitan; **k—politisch** [-po'liːtiʃ] a cosmopolitan; **—s** *m* **-** cosmos.

Kost [kɔst] *f* **-** (*Nahrung*) food; (*Verpflegung*) board; **k—bar** a precious; *(teuer)* costly, expensive; **—barkeit** f preciousness; costliness, expensiveness; *(Wertstück)* valuable; **—en** pl cost(s); *(Ausgaben)* expenses pl; **auf —** von at the expense of; **k—en** vt cost; vti *(versuchen)* taste; **—enanschlag** m estimate; **k—enlos** a free (of charge); **—geld** nt board.

köstlich ['kœstlɪç] a precious; *Einfall* delightful; *Essen* delicious; **sich — amüsieren** have a marvellous time.

Kost- cpd: **—probe** f taste; *(fig)* sample; **k—spielig** a expensive.

Kostüm [kɔs'ty:m] nt **-s, -e** costume; *(Damen—)* suit; **—fest** nt fancy-dress party; **k—ieren** [kɔsty'mi:rən] vtr dress up; **.—verleih** m costume agency.

Kot [ko:t] m **-(e)s** excrement.

Kotelett [kotə'lɛt] nt **-(e)s, -e** or **-s** cutlet, chop; **—en** pl sideboards pl.

Köter ['kø:tər] m **-s, -** cur.

Kotflügel m *(Aut)* wing.

Krabbe ['krabə] f **-, -n** shrimp; **k—ln** vi crawl.

Krach [krax] m **-(e)s, -s** or **-e** crash; *(andauernd)* noise; *(col: Streit)* quarrel, row; **k—en** vi crash; *(beim Brechen)* crack; vr *(col)* row, quarrel.

krächzen ['krɛçtsən] vi croak.

Kraft [kraft] f **-, -e** strength, power, force; *(Arbeits—)* worker; **in —treten** come into effect; **k—** prep *+gen* by virtue of; **—ausdruck** m swearword; **—fahrer** m motor driver; **—fahrzeug** nt motor vehicle; **—fahrzeugbrief** m logbook; **—fahrzeugsteuer** f ≈ road tax.

kräftig ['krɛftɪç] a strong; **—en** [krɛftɪgən] vt strengthen.

Kraft- cpd: **k—los** a weak; powerless; *(Jur)* invalid; **—probe** f trial of strength; **—rad** nt motorcycle; **k—voll** a vigorous; **—wagen** m motor vehicle; **—werk** nt power station.

Kragen ['kra:gən] m **-s, -** collar; **—weite** f collar size.

Krähe ['krɛ:ə] f **-, -n** crow; **k—n** vi crow.

krakeelen [kra'ke:lən] vi *(col)* make a din.

Kralle ['kralə] f **-, -n** claw; *(Vogel—)* talon; **k—n** vt clutch; *(krampfhaft)* claw.

Kram [kra:m] m **-(e)s** stuff, rubbish; **k—en** vi rummage; **—laden** m *(pej)* small shop.

Krampf [krampf] m **-(e)s, -e** cramp; *(zuckend)* spasm; **—ader** f varicose vein; **k—haft** a convulsive; *(fig)* *Versuche* desperate.

Kran [kra:n] m **-(e)s, -e** crane; *(Wasser—)* tap.

Kranich ['kra:nɪç] m **-s, -e** *(Zool)* crane.

krank [kraŋk] a ill, sick; **K—e(r)** mf sick person; invalid, patient.

kränkeln ['krɛŋkəln] vi be in bad health.

kranken ['kraŋkən] vi: **an etw** *(dat)* **—** *(fig)* suffer from sth.

kränken ['krɛŋkən] vt hurt.

Kranken- cpd: **—bericht** m medical report; **—geld** nt sick pay; **—haus** nt hospital; **—kasse** f health insurance; **—pfleger** m nursing orderly; **—schwester** f nurse; **—versicherung** f health insurance; **—wagen** m ambulance.

Krank- cpd: **k—haft** a diseased; *Angst etc* morbid; **—heit** f illness, disease; **—heitserreger** m disease-carrying agent.

kränk- ['krɛŋk] cpd: **—lich** a sickly; **K—ung** f insult, offence.

Kranz [krants] m -es, ⸚e wreath, garland.

Kränzchen ['krɛntsçən] nt small wreath; ladies' party.

Krapfen ['krapfən] m -s, - fritter; (Berliner) doughnut.

kraß [kras] a crass.

Krater ['kra:tər] m -s, - crater.

Kratz- ['krats] cpd: **—bürste** f (fig) crosspatch; **k—en** vti scratch; **—er** m -s, - scratch; (Werkzeug) scraper.

Kraul(schwimmen) ['kraul(ʃvɪm-en)] nt -s crawl; **k—en** vi (schwimmen) do the crawl; vt (streicheln) tickle.

kraus [kraus] a crinkly; Haar frizzy; Stirn wrinkled; **K—e** ['krauzə] f -, -n frill, ruffle.

kräuseln ['krɔyzəln] vt Haar make frizzy; Stoff gather; Stirn wrinkle; vr (Haar) go frizzy; (Stirn) wrinkle; (Wasser) ripple.

Kraut [kraut] nt -(e)s, Kräuter plant; (Gewürz) herb; (Gemüse) cabbage.

Krawall [kra'val] m -s, -e row, uproar.

Krawatte [kra'vatə] f -, -n tie.

kreativ [krea'ti:f] a creative.

Kreatur [krea'tu:r] f creature.

Krebs ·[kre:ps] m -es, -e crab; (Med, Astrol) cancer.

Kredit [kre'di:t] m -(e)s, -e credit.

Kreide ['kraidə] f -, -n chalk; **k—bleich** a as white as a sheet.

Kreis [krais] m -es, -e circle; (Stadt— etc) district; im — gehen (lit, fig) go round in circles.

kreischen ['kraiʃən] vi shriek, screech.

Kreis- cpd: **—el** ['kraizəl] m -s, - top; (Verkehrs—) roundabout; **k—en** ['kraizən] vi spin; **k—förmig** a circular; **—lauf** m (Physiol) circulation; (fig: der Natur etc) cycle; **—säge** f circular saw; **—stadt** f county town; **—verkehr** m roundabout traffic.

Kreißsaal ['krais-za:l] m delivery room.

Krem [kre:m] f-, -s cream, mousse.

Krematorium [krema'to:riʊm] nt crematorium.

Krempe ['krɛmpə] f-, -n brim; **—l** m -s (col) rubbish.

krepieren [kre'pi:rən] vi (col: sterben) die, kick the bucket.

Krepp [krɛp] m -s, -s or -e crepe; **—papier** nt crepe paper; **—sohle** f crepe sole.

Kresse ['krɛsə] f -, -n cress.

Kreuz [krɔyts] nt -es, -e cross; (Anat) small of the back; (Cards) clubs ; **k—** vtr cross; vi (Naut) cruise; **—er** m -s, - (Schiff) cruiser; **—fahrt** f cruise; **—feuer** nt (fig) im —feuer stehen be caught in the crossfire; **—gang** m cloisters pl; **k—igen** vt crucify; **—igung** f crucifixion; **—otter** f adder; **—ung** f (Verkehrs—) crossing, junction; (Züchten) cross; **—verhör** nt cross-examination; **—weg** m crossroads; (Rel) Way of the Cross; **—worträtsel** nt crossword puzzle; **—zeichen** nt sign of the cross; **—zug** m crusade.

Kriech- ['kri:ç] cpd: **k—en** vi irreg crawl, creep; (pej) grovel, crawl; **—er** m -s, - crawler; **—spur** f crawler lane; **—tier** nt reptile.

Krieg [kri:k] m -(e)s, -e war; **k—en** ['kri:gən] vt (col) get; **—er** m -s, - warrior; **k—erisch** a war-like; **—führung** f warfare;

—sbemalung f war paint;
—serklärung f declaration of war;
—sfuß m: mit jdm/etw auf —sfuß stehen be at loggerheads with sb/not get on with sth;
—sgefangene(r) m prisoner of war;
—sgefangenschaft f captivity;
—sgericht m court-martial;
—sschiff nt warship; —sschuld f war guilt; —sverbrecher m war criminal; —sversehrte(r) m person disabled in the war; —szustand m state of war.

Krimi ['kri:mi] m -s, -s (col) thriller; k—nal [-'na:l] m a criminal; —nalbeamte(r) m detective; —nalität f criminality; —nalpolizei f detective force, CID (Brit); —nalroman m detective story; k—nell [-'nɛl] a criminal; —nelle(r) m criminal.

Krippe ['krɪpə] f -, -n manger, crib; (Kinder—) crèche.

Krise ['kri:zə] f -, -n crisis; k—ln vi: es kriselt there's a crisis; —nherd m trouble spot.

Kristall [krɪs'tal] m -s, -e crystal; nt -s (Glas) crystal.

Kriterium [kri'te:rium] nt criterion.

Kritik [kri'ti:k] f criticism; (Zeitungs—) review, write-up; —er ['kri:tikər] m -s, - critic; k—los a uncritical.

kritisch ['kri:tɪʃ] a critical.

kritisieren [kriti'zi:rən] vti criticize.

kritteln ['krɪtəln] vi find fault, carp.

kritzeln ['krɪtsəln] vti scribble, scrawl.

Krokodil [kroko'di:l] nt -s, -e crocodile.

Krokus ['kro:kus] m -, - or -se crocus.

Krone ['kro:nə] f -, -n crown; (Baum—) top.

krönen ['krø:nən] vt crown.

Kron- cpd: —korken m bottle top; —leuchter m chandelier; —prinz m crown prince.

Krönung ['krø:nʊŋ] f coronation.

Kropf [krɔpf] m -(e)s, -e (Med) goitre; (im Vogel) crop.

Kröte ['krø:tə] f -, -n toad.

Krücke ['krykə] f -, -n crutch.

Krug [kru:k] m -(e)s, -e jug; (Bier—) mug.

Krümel ['kry:məl] m -s, - crumb; k—n vti crumble.

krumm [krʊm] a (lit, fig) crooked; (kurvig) curved; —beinig a bandy-legged.

krümm- ['krym] cpd: —en vtr curve, bend; K—ung f bend, curve.

krumm- cpd: —lachen vr (col) laugh o.s. silly; —nehmen vt irreg (col) jdm etw —nehmen take sth amiss.

Krüppel ['krypəl] m -s, - cripple.

Kruste ['krustə] f -, -n crust.

Kruzifix [krutsi'fɪks] nt -es, -e crucifix.

Kübel ['ky:bəl] m -s, - tub; (Eimer) pail.

Küche ['kyçə] f -, -n kitchen; (Kochen) cooking, cuisine.

Kuchen ['ku:xən] m -s, - cake; —blech nt baking tray; —form f baking tin; —gabel f pastry fork; —teig m cake mixture.

Küchen- cpd: —herd m range; (Gas, Elec) cooker, stove; —schabe f cockroach; —schrank m kitchen cabinet.

Kuckuck ['kʊkʊk] m -s, -e cuckoo.

Kufe [ku:fə] f -, -n (Faß) vat; (Schlitten—) runner; (Aviat) skid.

Kugel ['ku:gəl] f -, -n ball; (Math) sphere; (Mil) bullet; (Erd—) globe; (Sport) shot; k—förmig a spherical; **—lager** nt ball bearing; **k—n** vt roll; (Sport) bowl; vr (vor Lachen) double up; **k—rund** a (Gegenstand round); (col) Person tubby; **—schreiber** m ball-point (pen), biro ®; **k—sicher** a bulletproof; **—stoßen** nt -s shot-put.

Kuh [ku:] f -, ¨e cow.

kühl [ky:l] a (lit, fig) cool; **K—anlage** f refrigerating plant; **K—e** f -coolness; **—en** vt cool; **K—er** m -s, - (Aut) radiator; **K—erhaube** f (Aut) bonnet, hood (US); **K—raum** m cold-storage chamber; **K—schrank** m refrigerator; **K—truhe** f freezer; **K—ung** f cooling; **K—wagen** m (Rail) refrigerator van; **K—wasser** nt cooling water.

kühn [ky:n] a bold, daring; **K—heit** f boldness.

Küken ['ky:kən] nt -s, - chicken.

kulant [ku'lant] a obliging.

Kuli ['ku:li] m -s, -s coolie; (col: Kugelschreiber) biro ®.

Kulisse [ku'lɪsə] f -, -n scene.

kullern ['kulərn] vi roll.

Kult [kult] m -(e)s, -e worship, cult; **mit etw — treiben** make a cult out of sth; **k—ivieren** [-i'vi:rən] vt cultivate; **k—iviert** a cultivated, refined; **—ur** [kul'tu:r] f culture; civilization; (das Boden) cultivation; **k—urell** [-u'rɛl] a cultural; **—urfilm** m documentary film.

Kümmel ['kyməl] m -s, - caraway seed; (Branntwein) kümmel.

Kummer ['kumər] m -s grief, sorrow.

kümmer- ['kymər] cpd: **—lich** a miserable, wretched; **—n** vr: **sich um jdn —n** look after sb; **sich um etw —n** see to sth; vt concern; **das kümmert mich nicht** that doesn't worry me.

Kumpan [kum'pa:n] m -s, -e mate; (pej) accomplice.

Kumpel ['kumpəl] m -s, - (col) mate.

kündbar ['kyntba:r] a redeemable, recallable; Vertrag terminable.

Kunde ['kundə] m -n, -n, **Kundin** f customer; f -, -n (Botschaft) news; **—ndienst** m after-sales service.

Kund- cpd: **—gabe** f announcement; **k—geben** vt irreg announce; **—gebung** f announcement; (Versammlung) rally; **k—ig** a expert, experienced.

Künd- ['kynd] cpd: **k—igen** vi give in one's notice; **jdm k—igen** give sb his notice; vt cancel; (jdm) die Stellung/Wohnung — give (sb) notice; **—igung** f notice; **—igungsfrist** f period of notice.

Kundschaft f customers pl, clientele.

künftig ['kynftɪç] a future; ad in future.

Kunst [kunst] f -, ¨e art; (Können) skill; **das ist doch keine —** it's 'easy'; **—akademie** f academy of art; **—dünger** m artificial manure; **—faser** f synthetic fibre; **—fertigkeit** f skilfulness; **—geschichte** f history of art; **—gewerbe** nt arts and crafts pl; **—griff** m trick, knack; **—händler** m art dealer; **—harz** nt artificial resin.

Künstler(in f) ['kynstlər(ɪn)] m -s, - artist; **k—isch** a artistic; **—name** m stagename; pseudonym.

künstlich ['kynstlɪç] a artificial.

Kunst- cpd: **—sammler** m -s, - art collector; **—seide** f artificial silk; **—stoff** m synthetic material; **—stopfen** nt -s invisible mending; **—stück** nt trick; **—turnen** nt gymnastics; k—voll a ingenious, artistic; —werk nt work of art.

kunterbunt ['kʊntərbʊnt] a higgledy-piggledy.

Kupfer ['kʊpfər] nt -s, - copper; —geld nt coppers pl; k—n a copper; —stich m copperplate engraving.

Kuppe ['kʊpə] f -, -n (Berg—) top; (Finger—) tip; —l f -, -n cupola, dome; —'lei f (Jur) procuring; k—ln vi (Jur) procure; (Aut) declutch; vt join.

Kupp- ['kʊp] cpd: —ler m -s, - pimp; —lerin f matchmaker; —lung f coupling; (Aut) clutch.

Kur [ku:r] f -, -en cure, treatment.

Kür [ky:r] f -, -en (Sport) free skating/exercises pl.

Kurbel ['kʊrbəl] f -, -n crank, winch; (Aut) starting handle; —welle f crankshaft.

Kürbis ['kʏrbɪs] m -ses, -se pumpkin; (exotisch) gourd.

Kur- ['ku:r] cpd: —gast m visitor (to a health resort); k—ieren [ku'ri:rən] vt cure; k—ios [kuri'o:s] a curious, odd; —iosi'tät f curiosity; —ort m health resort; —pfuscher m quack.

Kurs [kʊrs] m -es, -e course; (Fin) rate; hoch im — stehen (fig) be highly thought of; —buch nt timetable; k—ieren [kʊr'zi:rən] vi circulate; k—iv ad in italics; —ive [kʊr'zi:və] f -, -n italics pl; —us ['kʊrzʊs] m -, Kurse course; —wagen m (Rail) through carriage.

Kurve ['kʊrvə] f -, -n curve;

(Straßen— auch) bend; k—nreich, kurvig a Straße bendy.

kurz [kʊrts] a short; zu — kommen come off badly; den — eren ziehen get the worst of it; K—arbeit f short-time work; —ärm(e)lig a short-sleeved.

Kürze ['kʏrtsə] f -, -n shortness, brevity; k—n vt cut short; (in der Länge) shorten; Gehalt reduce.

kurz- cpd: —erhand ad on the spot; K—fassung f shortened version; —fristig a short-term; —gefaßt a concise; K—geschichte f short story; —halten vt irreg keep short; —lebig a shortlived.

kürzlich ['kʏrtslɪç] ad lately, recently.

Kurz- cpd: —schluß m (Elec) short circuit; —schrift f shorthand; k—sichtig a short-sighted; —welle f shortwave.

kuscheln ['kʊʃəln] vr snuggle up.

Kusine [ku'zi:nə] f cousin.

Kuß [kʊs] m -sses, -sse kiss.

küssen ['kʏsən] vtr kiss.

Küste ['kʏstə] f -, -n coast, shore; —nwache f coastguard (station).

Küster ['kʏstər] m -s, - sexton, verger.

Kutsche ['kʊtʃə] f -, -n coach, carriage; —r m -s, - coachman.

Kutte ['kʊtə] f -, -n cowl.

Kuvert [ku'vert] nt -s, -e or -s envelope; cover.

Kybernetik [kybər'ne:tɪk] f cybernetics.

kybernetisch [kybər'ne:tɪʃ] a cybernetic.

L

L, l [ɛl] *nt* L, l.

laben ['la:bən] *vtr* refresh (o.s.); (*fig*) relish (*an etw* (*dat*) sth.).

Labor [la'bo:r] *nt* -s, -e *or* -s lab; —ant(in *f*) [labo'rant(ɪn)] *m* lab(oratory) assistant; —atorium [labora'to:rɪʊm] *nt* laboratory.

Labyrinth [laby'rɪnt] *nt* -s, -e labyrinth.

Lache ['laxə] *f* -, -n (*Wasser*) pool, puddle; (*col: Gelächter*) laugh.

lächeln ['lɛçəln] *vi* smile; L— *nt* -s smile.

lachen ['laxən] *vi* laugh.

lächerlich ['lɛçərlɪç] *a* ridiculous; L—keit *f* absurdity.

Lach- *cpd*: —gas *nt* laughing gas; l—haft *a* laughable.

Lachs [laks] *m* -es, -e salmon.

Lack [lak] *m* -(e)s, -e lacquer, varnish; (*von Auto*) paint; l—ieren [la'ki:rən] *vt* varnish; *Auto* spray; —ierer [la'ki:rər] *m* -s, - varnisher; —leder *nt* patent leather.

Lackmus ['lakmʊs] *m or nt* - litmus.

Lade ['la:də] *f* -, -n box, chest; —baum *m* derrick; —fähigkeit *f* load capacity.

laden ['la:dən] *vt irreg Lasten* load; (*Jur*) summon; (*einladen*) invite.

Laden ['la:dən] *m* -s, - shop; (*Fenster*—) shutter; —besitzer *m* shopkeeper; —dieb *m* shoplifter; —diebstahl *m* shoplifting; —hüter *m* -s, - unsaleable item; —preis *m* retail price; —schluß *m* closing time; —tisch *m* counter.

Laderaum *m* (*Naut*) hold.

Ladung ['la:dʊŋ] *f* (*Last*) cargo, load; (*Beladen*) loading; (*Jur*) summons; (*Einladung*) invitation; (*Spreng*—) charge.

Lage ['la:gə] *f* -, -n position, situation; (*Schicht*) layer; in der — sein be in a position; l—nweise ad in layers.

Lager ['la:gər] *nt* -s, - camp; (*Comm*) warehouse; (*Schlaf*—) bed; (*von Tier*) lair; (*Tech*) bearing; —arbeiter(in *f*) *m* storehand; —bestand *m* stocks *pl*; —geld *nt* storage (charges *pl*); —haus *nt* warehouse, store.

lagern ['la:gərn] *vi* (*Dinge*) be stored; (*Menschen*) camp; (*auch vr: rasten*) lie down; *vt* store; (*betten*) lay down; *Maschine* bed.

Lager- *cpd*: —schuppen *m* storeshed; —stätte *f* resting place; —ung *f* storage.

Lagune [la'gu:nə] *f* -, -n lagoon.

lahm [la:m] *a* lame; —en *vi* be lame, limp.

lähmen ['lɛ:mən] *vt* paralyse.

lahmlegen *vt* paralyse.

Lähmung *f* paralysis.

Laib [laɪp] *m* -s, -e loaf.

Laich [laɪç] *m* -(e)s, -e spawn; l—en *vi* spawn.

Laie ['laɪə] *m* -n, -n layman; l—nhaft *a* amateurish.

Lakai [la'kaɪ] *m* -en, -en lackey.

Laken ['la:kən] *nt* -s, - sheet.

Lakritze [la'krɪtsə] *f* -, -n liquorice.

lallen ['lalən] *vti* slur; (*Baby*) babble.

Lamelle [la'mɛlə] *f* lamella; (*Elec*) lamina; (*Tech*) plate.

lamentieren [lamɛn'ti:rən] *vi* lament.

Lametta [la'mɛta] *nt* -s tinsel.

Lamm [lam] *nt* -(e)s, ⁻er lamb; —**fell** *nt* lambskin; l—**fromm** a like a lamb; —**wolle** *f* lambswool.

Lampe ['lampə] *f* -, -n lamp; —**nfieber** *nt* stage fright; —**nschirm** *m* lampshade.

Lampion [lãpi'õ:] *m* -s, -s Chinese lantern.

Land [lant] *nt* -(e)s, ⁻er land; (*Nation, nicht Stadt*) country; (*Bundes—*) state; auf dem —(e) in the country; —**arbeiter** *m* farm or agricultural worker; —**besitz** *m* landed property; —**besitzer** *m* landowner; —**ebahn** *f* runway; l—**einwärts** *ad* inland; l—**en** ['landən] *vti* land.

Ländereien [lɛndə'raiən] *pl* estates *pl*.

Landes- ['landəs] *cpd:* —**farben** *pl* national colours *pl*; —**innere(s)** *nt* inland region; —**tracht** *f* national costume; l—**üblich** a customary; —**verrat** *m* high treason; —**verweisung** *f* banishment; —**währung** *f* national currency.

Land- *cpd:* —**gut** *nt* estate; —**haus** *nt* country house; —**karte** *f* map; —**kreis** *m* administrative region; l—**läufig** a customary.

ländlich ['lɛntlıç] a rural.

Land- *cpd:* —**schaft** *f* countryside; (*Art*) landscape; l—**schaftlich** a scenic; regional; —**smann** *m*, *pl* —**sleute** compatriot, fellow countryman or countrywoman; —**straße** *f* country road; —**streicher** *m* -s, - tramp; —**strich** *m* region; —**tag** *m* (*Pol*) regional parliament.

Landung ['landʊŋ] *f* landing; —**shoot** *nt* landing craft; —**sbrücke** *f* jetty, pier; —**sstelle** *f* landing place.

Land- *cpd:* —**vermesser** *m* surveyor; —**wirt** *m* farmer; —**wirtschaft** *f* agriculture; —**zunge** *f* spit.

lang [laŋ] a long; *Mensch* tall; —**atmig** a long-winded; —e ad for a long time; *dauern, brauchen* **a** long time.

Länge ['lɛŋə] *f* -, -n length; (*Geog*) longitude; —**ngrad** *m* longitude; —**nmaß** *nt* linear measure.

langen ['laŋən] *vi* (*ausreichen*) do, suffice; (*fassen*) reach (*nach* for); es langt mir I've had enough.

lang- *cpd:* **L—eweile** *f* boredom; —**lebig** a long-lived.

länglich a longish.

lang- *cpd:* **L—mut** *f* forbearance, patience; —**mütig** a forbearing.

längs [lɛŋs] *prep* +*gen* or *dat* along; *ad* lengthwise.

lang- *cpd:* —**sam** a slow; **L—samkeit** *f* slowness; **L—schläfer(in** *f*) *m* late riser; **L—spielplatte** *f* long-playing record.

längst [lɛŋst] *ad* das ist — fertig that was finished a long time ago, that has been finished for a long time; —**e(r,s)** a longest.

lang- *cpd:* —**weilig** a boring, tedious; **L—welle** *f* long wave; —**wierig** a lengthy, long-drawn-out.

Lanze ['lantsə] *f* -, -n lance.

Lanzette [lan'tsɛtə] *f* lancet.

lapidar [lapi'daːr] a terse, pithy.

Lappalie [la'paːliə] *f* trifle.

Lappen ['lapən] *m* -s, - cloth, rag; (*Anat*) lobe.

läppisch ['lɛpɪʃ] a foolish.

Lapsus ['lapsʊs] *m* -, - slip.

Lärche ['lɛrçə] f -, -n larch.

Lärm [lɛrm] m -(e)s noise; l—en vi be noisy, make a noise.

Larve ['larfə] f -, -n mask; (Biol) larva.

lasch [laʃ] a slack; Geschmack tasteless.

Lasche ['laʃə] f -, -n (Schuh—) tongue; (Rail) fishplate.

Laser ['leɪzə] m -s, - laser.

lassen ['lasən] vti irreg leave; (erlauben) let; (aufhören mit) stop; (veranlassen) make; etw machen — to have sth done; es läßt sich machen it can be done; es läßt sich öffnen it can be opened, it opens.

lässig ['lɛsɪç] a casual; L—keit f casualness.

läßlich ['lɛslɪç] a pardonable, venial.

Last [last] f -, -en load, burden; (Naut, Aviat) cargo; (usu pl: Gebühr) charge; jdm zur — fallen be a burden to sb; —auto nt lorry, truck; l—en vi (auf +dat) weigh on.

Laster ['lastər] nt -s, - vice.

Lästerer ['lɛstərər] m -s, - mocker; (Gottes—) blasphemer.

lasterhaft a immoral.

lästerlich a scandalous.

lästern ['lɛstərn] vti Gott blaspheme; (schlecht sprechen) mock.

Lästerung f jibe; (Gottes—) blasphemy.

lästig ['lɛstɪç] a troublesome, tiresome.

Last- cpd: —kahn m barge; —kraftwagen m heavy goods vehicle; —schrift f debiting; debit item; —tier nt beast of burden; —träger m porter; —wagen m lorry, truck.

latent [la'tɛnt] a latent.

Laterne [la'tɛrnə] f -, -n lantern; (Straßen—) lamp, light; —npfahl m lamppost.

Latrine [la'triːnə] f latrine.

Latsche ['latʃə] f -, -n dwarf pine; l—n ['la:tʃən] vi (col) (gehen) wander, go; (lässig) slouch.

Latte ['latə] f -, -n lath; (Sport) goalpost; (quer) crossbar; —nzaun m lattice fence.

Latz [lats] m -es, ⁻e bib; (Hosen—) flies pl.

Lätzchen ['lɛtsçən] nt bib.

Latzhose f dungarees pl.

lau [lau] a Nacht balmy; Wasser lukewarm.

Laub [laup] nt -(e)s foliage; —baum m deciduous tree; —e ['laubə] f -, -n arbour; —frosch m tree frog; —säge f fretsaw.

Lauch [laux] m -(e)s, -e leek.

Lauer ['lauər] f: auf der — sein or liegen, l—n vi lie in wait; (Gefahr) lurk.

Lauf [lauf] m -(e)s, Läufe run; (Wett—) race; (Entwicklung, Astron) course; (Gewehr) barrel; einer Sache ihren — lassen let sth take its course; —bahn f career; —bursche m errand boy.

laufen ['laufən] vti irreg run; (col: gehen) walk; —d a running; Monat, Ausgaben current; auf dem —den sein/halten be/keep up to date; am —den Band (fig) continuously; — lassen vt irreg leave running; —lassen vt irreg Person let go.

Läufer ['lɔyfər] m -s, - (Teppich, Sport) runner; (Fußball) halfback; (Schach) bishop.

Lauf- cpd: —kundschaft f passing trade; —masche f run, ladder (Brit); im —schritt at a run;

—stall *m* playpen; —steg *m* dais; —zettel *m* circular.

Lauge ['lauɡə] *f* -, -n soapy water; (*Chem*) alkaline solution.

Laune ['launə] *f* -, -n mood, humour; (*Einfall*) caprice; (*schlechte*) temper; l—nhaft *a* capricious, changeable.

launisch *a* moody; bad-tempered.

Laus [laus] *f* -, **Läuse** louse; —bub *m* rascal, imp.

lauschen ['lauʃən] *vi* eavesdrop, listen in.

lauschig ['lauʃɪç] *a* snug.

lausen ['lauzən] *vt* delouse.

laut [laut] *a* loud; *ad* loudly; lesen aloud; *prep* +*gen* or *dat* according to; **L**— *m* -(e)s, -e sound.

Laute ['lautə] *f* -, -n lute.

lauten ['lautən] *vi* say; (*Urteil*) be.

läuten ['lɔʏtən] *vti* ring, sound.

lauter ['lautər] *a* Wasser clear, pure; *Wahrheit, Charakter* honest; *inv Freude, Dummheit etc* sheer; (*mit pl*) nothing but, only; **L**—keit *f* purity; honesty, integrity.

läutern ['lɔʏtərn] *vt* purify.

Läuterung *f* purification.

laut- *cpd:* —hals *ad* at the top of one's voice; —los *a* noiseless, silent; —malend *a* onomatopoeic; **L**—schrift *f* phonetics *pl*; **L**—sprecher *m* loudspeaker; **L**—sprecherwagen *m* loudspeaker van; —stark *a* vociferous; **L**—stärke *f* (*Rad*) volume.

lauwarm ['lauvarm] *a* (*lit, fig*) lukewarm.

Lava ['laːva] *f* -, **Laven** lava.

Lavendel [la'vɛndəl] *m* -s, - lavender.

Lawine [la'viːnə] *f* avalanche; —ngefahr *f* danger of avalanches.

lax [laks] *a* lax.

Lazarett [latsa'rɛt] *nt* -(e)s, -e (*Mil*) hospital, infirmary.

Lebe- *cpd:* —hoch *nt* three cheers *pl*; —mann *m, pl* —männer man about town.

leben ['leːbən] *vti* live; **L**— *nt* -s, - life; —d *a* living; —dig [le'bɛndɪç] *a* living, alive; (*lebhaft*) lively; **L**—digkeit *f* liveliness.

Lebens- *cpd:* —alter *nt* age; —art *f* way of life; —erwartung *f* life expectancy; l—fähig *a* able to live; l—froh *a* full of the joys of life; —gefahr *f:* —gefahr! danger!; in —gefahr dangerously ill; l—gefährlich *a* dangerous; *Verletzung* critical; —haltungskosten *f* cost of living *sing*; —jahr *nt* year of life; —lage *f* situation in life; —lauf *m* curriculum vitae; l—lustig *a* cheerful, lively; —mittel *pl* food *sing*; —mittelgeschäft *nt* grocer's; l—müde *a* tired of life; —retter *m* lifesaver; —standard *m* standard of living; —stellung *f* permanent post; —unterhalt *m* livelihood; —versicherung *f* life insurance; —wandel *m* way of life; —weise *f* way of life, habits *pl*; —zeichen *nt* sign of life; —zeit *f* lifetime.

Leber ['leːbər] *f* -, -n liver; —fleck *m* mole; —tran *m* cod-liver oil; —wurst *f* liver sausage.

Lebe- *cpd:* —wesen *nt* creature; —wohl *nt* farewell, goodbye.

leb- ['leːp] *cpd:* —haft *a* lively, vivacious; **L**—haftigkeit *f* liveliness, vivacity; **L**—kuchen *m* gingerbread; —los *a* lifeless.

lechzen ['lɛçtsən] *vi:* nach etw — long for sth.

leck [lɛk] *a* leaky, leaking; **L**— *nt*

-(e)s, -e leak; —en vi (Loch haben) leak; vti (schlecken) lick.

lecker ['lɛkər] a delicious, tasty; L—bissen m dainty morsel; L—maul nt: ein L—maul sein enjoy one's food.

Leder ['le:dər] nt -s, - leather; l—n a leather; —waren pl leather goods pl.

ledig ['le:dɪç] a single; einer Sache — sein be free of sth; —lich ad merely, solely.

leer [le:r] a empty; vacant; L—e f - emptiness; —en vt empty; vr become empty; L—gewicht nt weight when empty; L—lauf m neutral; —stehend a empty; L—ung f emptying; (Post) collection.

legal [le'ga:l] a legal, lawful; —i'sieren vt legalize; L—i'tät f legality.

legen ['le:gən] vt lay, put, place; El lay; vr lie down; (fig) subside.

Legende [le'gɛndə] f -, -n legend.

leger [le'ʒe:r] a casual.

legieren [le'gi:rən] vt alloy.

Legierung f alloy.

Legislative [legɪsla'ti:və] f legislature.

legitim [legi'ti:m] a legitimate; L—ation [-atsi'o:n] f legitimation; —ieren [-'mi:rən] vt legitimate; vr prove one's identity; L—i'tät f legitimacy.

Lehm [le:m] m -(e)s, -e loam; —ig a loamy.

Lehne ['le:nə] f -, -n arm; back; l—n vtr lean.

Lehnstuhl m armchair.

Lehr- cpd: —amt nt teaching profession; —brief m indentures pl; —buch nt textbook.

Lehre ['le:rə] f -, -n teaching, doctrine; (beruflich). apprenticeship; (moralisch) lesson; (Tech) gauge; l—n vt teach; —r(in f) m -s, - teacher.

Lehr- cpd: —gang m course; —jahre pl apprenticeship; —kraft f teacher; —ling m apprentice; —plan m syllabus; l—reich a instructive; —satz m proposition; —stelle f apprenticeship; —stuhl m chair; —zeit f apprenticeship.

Leib [laɪp] m -(e)s, -er body; halt ihn mir vom —! keep him away from me; —eserziehung ['laɪbəs-] f physical education; —esübung f physical exercise; l—haftig a personified; Teufel incarnate; l—lich a bodily; Vater etc own; —wache f bodyguard.

Leiche ['laɪçə] f -, -n corpse; —nbeschauer m -s, - doctor who makes out death certificate; —nhemd nt shroud; —nträger m bearer; —nwagen m hearse.

Leichnam ['laɪçna:m] m -(e)s, -e corpse.

leicht [laɪçt] a light; (einfach) easy; L—athletik f athletics sing; —fallen vi irreg: jdm —fallen be easy for sb; —fertig a frivolous; —gläubig a credible, credulous; L—gläubigkeit f gullibility, credulity; —hin ad lightly; L—igkeit f easiness; mit L—igkeit with ease; —lebig a easy-going; —machen vt: es sich (dat) —machen make things easy for oneself; —nehmen vt irreg take lightly; L—sinn m carelessness; —sinnig a careless.

Leid [laɪt] nt -(e)s grief, sorrow; l—a: etw l— haben or sein be tired of sth; es tut mir/ihm l— I am/he is sorry; er/das tut mir l— I am sorry for him/it; l—en ['laɪdən] irreg vt suffer; (erlauben) permit; jdn/etw nicht l—en können not be able to stand sb/sth; vi suffer; —en nt -s, - suffering; (Krankheit) complaint; —enschaft f passion; l—enschaftlich a passionate.

leider ['laɪdər] ad unfortunately; ja, — yes, I'm afraid so; — nicht I'm afraid not.

leidig ['laɪdɪç] a miserable, tiresome.

leidlich a tolerable; ad tolerably.

Leid- cpd: —tragende(r) mf bereaved; (Benachteiligter) one who suffers; —wesen nt: zu jds —wesen to sb's dismay.

Leier ['laɪər] f -, -n lyre; (fig) old story; —kasten m barrel organ; l—n vti Kurbel turn; (col) Gedicht rattle off.

Leihbibliothek f lending library.

leihen ['laɪən] vt irreg lend; sich (dat) etw — borrow sth.

Leih- cpd: —gebühr f hire charge; —haus nt pawnshop; —schein m pawn ticket; (Buch— etc) borrowing slip; —wagen m hired car.

Leim [laɪm] m -(e)s, -e glue; l—en vt glue.

Leine ['laɪnə] f -, -n line, cord; (Hunde—) leash, lead; —n nt -s, - linen; l—n a linen.

Lein- cpd: —tuch nt (Bett—) sheet; linen cloth; —wand f (Art) canvas; (Cine) screen.

leise ['laɪzə] a quiet; (sanft) soft, gentle.

Leiste ['laɪstə] f -, -n ledge; (Zier—) strip; (Anat) groin.

leisten ['laɪstən] vt Arbeit do; Gesellschaft keep; Ersatz supply; (vollbringen) achieve; sich (dat) etw — können to be able to afford sth.

Leistung f performance; (gute) achievement; —sdruck m

pressure; l—sfähig a efficient; —sfähigkeit f efficiency; —szulage f productivity bonus.

Leit- cpd: —artikel m leading article; —bild nt model.

leiten ['laɪtən] vt lead; Firma manage; (in eine Richtung) direct; (Elec) conduct.

Leiter ['laɪtər] m -s, - leader, head; (Elec) conductor; f -, -n ladder.

Leit- cpd: —faden m guide; —fähigkeit f conductivity; —motiv nt leitmotiv; —planke f -, -n crash barrier.

Leitung f (Führung) direction; (Cine, Theat etc) production; (von Firma) management; directors pl; (Wasser—) pipe; (Kabel) cable; eine lange — haben to be slow on the uptake; —sdraht m wire; —smast m telegraph pole; —srohr nt pipe; —swasser nt tap water.

Lektion [lɛktsi'oːn] f lesson.

Lektor(in f) m ['lɛktor(m)] (Univ) lector; (Verlag) editor.

Lektüre [lɛk'tyːrə] f -, -n (Lesen) reading; (Lesestoff) reading matter.

Lende ['lɛndə] f -, -n loin; —nbraten m roast sirloin; —nstück nt fillet.

lenk- ['lɛŋk] cpd: —bar a Fahrzeug steerable; Kind manageable; —en vt steer; Kind guide; Blick, Aufmerksamkeit direct (auf + acc at); L—rad nt steering wheel; L—stange f handlebars pl.

Lenz [lɛnts] m -es, -e (liter) spring.

Leopard [leo'part] m -en, -en leopard.

Lepra ['leːpra] f -, leprosy.

Lerche ['lɛrçə] f -, -n lark.

lern- [lɛrn] cpd: —begierig a eager to learn; —en vt learn.

lesbar ['le:sba:r] *a* legible.

Lesbierin ['lesbiərin] *f* lesbian.

lesbisch ['lesbiʃ] *a* lesbian.

Lese ['le:zə] *f* -, -n gleaning; (*Wein*) harvest; **—buch** *nt* reading book, reader; **l—n** *vti irreg* read; (*ernten*) gather, pick; **—r(in** *f*) *m* -s, - reader; **—rbrief** *m* reader's letter; **l—rlich** *a* legible; **—saal** *m* reading room; **—zeichen** *nt* bookmark.

Lesung ['le:zuŋ] *f* (*Parl*) reading; (*Eccl*) lesson.

letzte(r, s) ['letstə(r,z)] *a* last; (*neueste*) latest; **zum —nmal** ad for the last time; **—ns** *ad* lately; **—re(r,s)** *a* latter.

Leuchte ['lɔyçtə] *f* -, -n lamp, light; **l—n** *vi* shine, gleam; **—r** *m* -s, - candlestick.

Leucht- *cpd*: **—farbe** *f* fluorescent colour; **—feuer** *nt* beacon; **—käfer** *m* glow-worm; **—kugel** *f*, **—rakete** *f* flare; **—reklame** *f* neon sign; **—röhre** *f* strip light; **—turm** *m* lighthouse; **—zifferblatt** *nt* luminous dial.

leugnen ['lɔygnən] *vti* deny.

Leugnung *f* denial.

Leukämie [lɔykε'mi:] *f* leukaemia.

Leukoplast® [lɔyko'plast] *nt* -(e)s, -e elastoplast ®.

Leumund ['lɔymunt] *m* -(e)s, -e reputation; **—szeugnis** *nt* character reference.

Leute ['lɔytə] *pl* people *pl*.

Leutnant ['lɔytnant] *m* -s, -s *or* -e lieutenant.

leutselig ['lɔytze:liç] *a* affable; **L—keit** *f* affability.

Lexikon ['lεksikon] *nt* -s, Lexiken *or* Lexika dictionary.

Libelle [li'bεlə] *f* -, -n dragonfly; (*Tech*) spirit level.

liberal [libe'ra:l] *a* liberal; **L—ismus** [libera'lismus] *m* liberalism.

Libero ['li:bero] *m* -s, -s (*Fußball*) sweeper.

Licht [liçt] *nt* -(e)s, -er light; **l—** *a* light, bright; **—bild** *nt* photograph; (*Dia*) slide; **—blick** *m* cheering prospect; **l—empfindlich** *a* sensitive to light; **l—en** *vt* clear; *Anker* weigh; *vr* clear up; (*Haar*) thin; **l—erloh** *ad*: **l—erloh brennen** blaze; **—hupe** *f* flashing of headlights; **—jahr** *nt* light year; **—maschine** *f* dynamo; **—meß** *f* Candlemas; **—schalter** *m* light switch.

Lichtung *f* clearing, glade.

Lid [li:t] *nt* -(e)s, -er eyelid; **—schatten** *m* eyeshadow.

lieb [li:p] *a* dear; **—äugeln** *vi insep* ogle (*mit jdm/etw* sb/sth).

Liebe ['li:bə] *f* -, -n love; **l—bedürftig** *a*: **l—bedürftig sein** need love; **—'lei** *f* flirtation; **l—n** *vt* love; like; **l—nswert** *a* lovable; **l—nswürdig** *a* kind; **l—nswürdigerweise** *ad* kindly; **—nswürdigkeit** *f* kindness.

lieber ['li:bər] *ad* rather, preferably; **ich gehe — nicht** I'd rather not go; *see* **gern, lieb.**

Liebes- *cpd*: **—brief** *m* love letter; **—dienst** *m* good turn; **—kummer** *m*: **—kummer haben be** lovesick; **—paar** *nt* courting couple, lovers *pl.*

liebevoll *a* loving.

lieb- ['li:p] *cpd*: **—gewinnen** *vt irreg* get fond of; **—haben** *vt irreg* be fond of; **L—haber** *m* -s, - lover; **L—haberei** *f* hobby; **—kosen** [li:p'ko:zən] *vt insep* caress; **—lich** *a* lovely, charming; **L—ling** *m* darling; **L—lings-** *in cpds*

favourite; **—los** a unloving;
L—schaft f love affair.

Lied [li:t] nt **-(e)s, -er** song; (Eccl)
hymn; **—erbuch** nt songbook;
hymn book.

liederlich ['li:dərlıç] a slovenly;
Lebenswandel loose, immoral;
L—keit f slovenliness; immorality.

Lieferant [lifə'rant] m supplier.

liefern ['li:fərn] vt deliver;
(versorgen mit) supply; Beweis
produce.

Liefer- cpd: **—schein** m delivery
note; **—termin** m delivery date;
—ung f delivery; supply; **—wagen**
m van.

Liege ['li:gə] f **-, -n** bed.

liegen ['li:gən] vi irreg. lie; (sich
befinden) be; mir liegt nichts/viel
daran it doesn't matter to me/it
matters a lot to me; es liegt bei
Ihnen, ob ... it rests with you
whether ...; Sprachen — mir nicht
languages are not my line; woran
liegt es? what's the cause?;
—bleiben vi irreg (Person) stay in
bed; stay lying down; (Ding) be
left (behind); **—lassen** vt irreg
(vergessen) leave behind;
L—schaft f real estate.

Liege- cpd: **—sitz** m (Aut) reclining
seat; **—stuhl** m deck chair;
—wagen m (Rail) couchette.

Lift [lıft] m **-(e)s, -e** or **-s** lift.

Likör [li'kø:r] m **-s, -e** liqueur.

lila ['li:la] a purple, lilac; **L—** nt **-s,
-s** (Farbe) purple, lilac.

Lilie ['li:liə] f lily.

Limonade [limo'na:də] f lemonade.

lind [lınt] a gentle, mild; **L—e**
['lındə] f **-, -n** lime tree, linden;
—ern vt alleviate, soothe;
L—erung f alleviation; **—grün** a
lime green.

Lineal [line'a:l] nt **-s, -e** ruler.

Linie ['li:niə] f line; **—nblatt** nt
ruled sheet; **—nflug** m scheduled
flight; **—nrichter** m linesman.

liniieren [lini'i:rən] vt line.

Linke ['lıŋkə] f **-, -n** left side; left
hand; (Pol) left; **l—(r,s)** a left; **l—
Masche** purl.

linkisch a awkward, gauche.

links [lıŋks] ad left; to or on the
left; **— von mir** on or to my left;
L—außen [lıŋks'ʔausən] m **-s, -**
(Sport) outside left; **L—händer(in
f)** m **-s, -** left-handed person;
L—kurve f left-hand bend;
L—verkehr m traffic on the left.

Linoleum [li'no:leum] nt **-s**
lino(leum).

Linse ['lınzə] f **-, -n** lentil; (optisch)
lens.

Lippe ['lıpə] f **-, -n** lip; **—nstift** m
lipstick.

liquidieren [likvi'di:rən] vt
liquidate.

lispeln ['lıspəln] vi lisp.

List [lıst] f **-, -en** cunning; trick,
ruse.

Liste ['lıstə] f **-, -n** list.

listig ['lıstıç] a cunning, sly.

Litanei [lita'nai] f litany.

Liter ['li:tər] nt or m **-s, -** litre.

literarisch [lite'ra:rıʃ] a literary.

Literatur [litera'tu:r] f literature;
—preis m award for literature.

Litfaßsäule ['lıtfaszɔylə] f
advertising pillar.

Lithographie [litogra'fi:] f
lithography.

Liturgie [litur'gi:] f liturgy.

liturgisch [li'turgıʃ] a liturgical.

Litze ['lıtsə] f **-, -n** braid; (Elec)
flex.

live [laıf] ad (Rad, TV) live.

Livree [li'vre:] *f* -, -n livery.

Lizenz [li'tsɛnts] *f* licence.

Lkw [ɛlka:'ve:] *m* = **Lastkraftwagen.**

Lob [lo:p] *nt* -(e)s praise; **l—en** ['lo:bən] *vt* praise; **l—enswert** *a* praiseworthy.

löblich ['lø:plɪç] *a* praiseworthy, laudable.

Lobrede *f* eulogy.

Loch [lɔx] *nt* -(e)s, ⁻er hole; **l—en** *vt* punch holes in; **—er** *m* -s, - punch.

löcherig ['lœçərɪç] *a* full of holes.

Loch- *cpd*: **—karte** *f* punch card; **—streifen** *m* punch tape.

Locke ['lɔkə] *f* -, -n lock, curl; **l—n** *vt* entice; *Haare* curl; **—nwickler** *m* -s, - curler.

locker ['lɔkər] *a* loose; **l—lassen** *vi irreg*: **nicht l—lassen** not let up; **l—n** *vt* loosen.

lockig ['lɔkɪç] *a* curly.

Lock- *cpd*: **—ruf** *m* call; **—ung** *f* enticement; **—vogel** *m* decoy, bait.

Lodenmantel ['lo:dənmantəl] *m* thick woollen coat.

lodern ['lo:dərn] *vi* blaze.

Löffel ['lœfəl] *m* -s, - spoon; **l—n** *vt* (eat with a) spoon; **l—weise** *ad* by spoonfuls.

Logarithmentafel [loga'rɪt-manta:fəl] *f* log(arithm) tables *pl*.

Logarithmus [loga'rɪtmʊs] *m* logarithm.

Loge ['lo:ʒə] *f* -, -n (*Theat*) box; (*Freimaurer*) (masonic) lodge; (*Pförtner—*) office.

logieren [lo'ʒi:rən] *vi* lodge, stay.

Logik ['lo:gɪk] *f* logic.

logisch ['lo:gɪʃ] *a* logical.

Lohn [lo:n] *m* -(e)s, ⁻e reward; (*Arbeits—*) pay, wages *pl*; **—büro**

nt wages office; **—empfänger** *m* wage earner.

lohnen ['lo:nən] *vt* (*liter*) reward (*jdm etw* sb for sth); *vr impers* be worth it; **—d** *a* worthwhile.

Lohn- *cpd*: **—steuer** *f* income tax; **—streifen** *m* pay slip; **—tüte** *f* pay packet.

lokal [lo'ka:l] *a* local; **L—** *nt* -(e)s, -e pub(lic house); **—isieren** *vt* localize; **L—isierung** *f* localization.

Lokomotive [lokomo'ti:və] *f* -, -n locomotive.

Lokomotivführer *m* engine driver.

Lorbeer ['lɔrbe:r] *m* -s, -en (*lit, fig*) laurel; **—blatt** *nt* (*Cook*) bay leaf.

Lore ['lo:rə] *f* -, -n (*Min*) truck.

Los [lo:s] *nt* -es, -e (*Schicksal*) lot, fate; lottery ticket.

los [lo:s] *a* loose; **—!** go on!; **etw — sein** be rid of sth; **was ist —?** what's the matter?; **dort ist nichts/viel** — there's nothing/a lot going on there; **etw — haben** (*col*) be clever; **—binden** *vt irreg* untie.

löschen ['lœʃən] *vt Feuer, Licht* put out, extinguish; *Durst* quench; (*Comm*) cancel; *Tonband* erase; *Fracht* unload; *vi* (*Feuerwehr*) put out a fire; (*Papier*) blot.

Lösch- *cpd*: **—fahrzeug** *nt* fire engine; fire boat; **—gerät** *nt* fire extinguisher; **—papier** *nt* blotting paper; **—ung** *f* extinguishing; (*Comm*) cancellation; (*Fracht*) unloading.

lose ['lo:zə] *a* loose.

Lösegeld *nt* ransom.

losen ['lo:zən] *vi* draw lots.

lösen ['lø:zən] *vt* loosen; *Rätsel etc* solve; *Verlobung* call off; (*Chem*) dissolve; *Partnerschaft* break up; *Fahrkarte* buy; *vr* (*aufgehen*) come loose; (*Zucker etc*) dissolve;

(Problem, Schwierigkeit) (re)solve itself.

los- *cpd:* **—fahren** *vi irreg* leave; **—gehen** *vi irreg* set out; *(anfangen)* start; *(Bombe)* go off; **auf jdn —gehen** · go for sb; **—kaufen** *vt* Gefangene, Geißeln pay ransom for; **—kommen** *vi irreg:* **von etw —kommen** get away from sth; **—lassen** *vt irreg Seil* let go of; *Schimpfe* let loose; **—laufen** *vi irreg* run off.

löslich [ˈløːslɪç] *a* soluble; **L—keit** *f* solubility.

los- *cpd:* **—lösen** *vtr* free; **—machen** *vt* loosen; *Boot* unmoor; *vr* get free; **—sagen** *vr* renounce *(von jdm/etw* sb/sth); **—schrauben** *vt* unscrew; **—sprechen** *vt irreg* absolve.

Losung [ˈloːzʊŋ] *f* watchword, slogan.

Lösung [ˈløːzʊŋ] *f (Lockermachen)* loosening; *(eines Rätsels, Chem)* solution; **—smittel** *nt* solvent.

los- *cpd:* **—werden** *vt irreg* get rid of; **—ziehen** *vi irreg (inf: aufmachen)* set out; **gegen jdn —ziehen** run sb down.

Lot [loːt] *nt -(e)s, -e* plummet; **im —** vertical; *(fig)* on an even keel; **l—en** *vti* plumb, sound.

löten [ˈløːtən] *vt* solder.

Lötkolben *m* soldering iron.

Lotse [ˈloːtsə] *m -n, -n* pilot; *(Aviat)* air traffic controller; *see* **Schüler—;** **l—n** *vt* pilot; *(col)* lure.

Lotterie [lɔtəˈriː] *f* lottery.

Löwe [ˈløːvə] *m -n, -n* lion; *(Astrol)* Leo; **—nanteil** *m* lion's share; **—nmaul** *nt* snapdragon; **—nzahn** *m* dandelion.

Löwin [ˈløːvɪn] *f* lioness.

loyal [loaˈjaːl] *a* loyal; **L—ität** *f* loyalty.

Luchs [lʊks] *m -es, -e* lynx.

Lücke [ˈlʏkə] *f -, -n* gap; **—nbüßer** *m -s, -* stopgap; **l—nhaft** *a* defective, full of gaps; **l—nlos** *a* complete.

Luder [ˈluːdər] *nt -s, - (pej: Frau)* hussy; *(bedauernswert)* poor wretch.

Luft [lʊft] *f -, =e* air; *(Atem)* breath; **in der —** liegen be in the air; **jdn wie — behandeln** ignore sb; **—angriff** *m* air raid; **—ballon** *m* balloon; **—blase** *f* air bubble; **l—dicht** *a* airtight; **—druck** *m* atmospheric pressure.

lüften [ˈlʏftən] *vti* air; *Hut* lift, raise.

Luft- *cpd:* **—fahrt** *f* aviation; **l—gekühlt** *a* air-cooled; **l—ig** *a Ort* breezy; *Raum* airy; *Kleider* summery; **—kissenfahrzeug** *nt* hovercraft; **—krieg** *m* war in the air; *aerial warfare;* **—kurort** *m* health resort; **l—leer** *a:* **—leerer Raum** vacuum; **l—linie** *f:* in der **—linie** as the crow flies; **—loch** *nt* air-hole; *(Aviat)* air-pocket; **—matratze** *f* lilo ®, air mattress; **—pirat** *m* hijacker; **—post** *f* air-mail; **—röhre** *f (Anat)* wind pipe; **—schlange** *f* streamer; **—schutz** *m* anti-aircraft defence; **—schutzkeller** *m* air-raid shelter; **—sprung** *m: (fig)* einen **—sprung machen** jump for joy.

Lüftung [ˈlʏftʊŋ] *f* ventilation.

Luft- *cpd:* **—verkehr** *m* air traffic; **—waffe** *f* air force; **—zug** *m* draught.

Lüge [ˈlyːgə] *f -, -n* lie; **jdn/etw —n strafen** give the lie to sb/sth; **l—n** *vi irreg* lie.

Lügner(in *f) m -s, -* liar.

Luke [ˈluːkə] *f -, -n* dormer window, hatch.

Lümmel ['lymǝl] *m* -s, - 'lout'; **l—n**
vr lounge. (about).

Lump [lump] *m* -en, -en scamp,
rascal.

Lumpen ['lumpǝn] *m* -s, - rag; **sich
nicht l—** lassen not be mean.

lumpig ['lumpɪç] *a* shabby.

Lunge ['luŋǝ] *f* -, -n lung;
—nentzündung *f* pneumonia;
l—nkrank a consumptive.

lungern ['luŋǝrn] *vi* hang about.

Lunte ['luntǝ] *f* -, -n fuse; **—
riechen** smell a rat.

Lupe ['lu:pǝ] *f* -, -n magnifying
glass; **unter die — nehmen** (fig)
scrutinize.

Lupine [lu'pi:nǝ] *f* lupin.

Lust [lust] *f* -, ̈e joy, delight;
(*Neigung*) desire; **— haben zu or
auf etw** (acc)/**etw zu tun** feel like
sth/doing sth.

lüstern ['lystǝrn] *a* lustful,
lecherous.

Lustgefühl *nt* pleasurable feeling.

lustig ['lustɪç] *a* (*komisch*)
amusing, funny; (*fröhlich*) cheerful.

Lüstling *m* lecher.

Lust- *cpd*: **l—los** a unenthusiastic;
—mord *m* sex(ual) murder; **—spiel**
nt comedy; **l—wandeln** *vi* stroll
about.

lutschen ['lutʃǝn] *vti* suck; **am
Daumen —** suck one's thumb.

Lutscher *m* -s, - lollipop.

luxuriös [luksuri'ø:s] *a* luxurious.

Luxus ['luksus] *m* .- luxury;
—artikel *pl* luxury goods *pl*;
—hotel *nt* luxury hotel; **—steuer** *f*
tax on luxuries.

Lymphe ['lymfǝ] *f* -, -n lymph.

lynchen ['lynçǝn] *vt* lynch.

Lyrik ['ly:rɪk] *f* lyric poetry; **—er**
m -s, - lyric poet.

lyrisch ['ly:rɪʃ] *a* lyrical.

M

M, m [ɛm] *nt* M, m.

Mach- [max] *cpd*: **—art** *f* make;
m—bar a feasible; **—e** *f* ˙- (*col*)
show, sham; *m—en vt* make; (*tun*)
do; (*col: reparieren*) fix;
(*betragen*) be; **das macht nichts**
that doesn't matter; **mach's gut!**
good luck!; **vr** come along (nicely);
sich an etw (acc) **m—en** set about
sth; *vi:* **in etw** (dat) **m—en**
(*Comm*) be or deal in sth.

Macht [maxt] *f* -s, ̈e power;
—haber *m* -s, - ruler.

mächtig ['mɛçtɪç] *a* powerful,
mighty; (*col: ungeheuer*) enormous.

Macht- *cpd*: **m—los** a powerless;
—probe *f* trial of strength;

—stellung *f* position of power;
—wort *nt*: **ein —wort sprechen** lay
down the law.

Machwerk *nt* work; (*schlechte
Arbeit*) botched-up job.

Mädchen ['mɛ:tçǝn] *nt* girl;
m—haft a girlish; **—name** *m*
maiden name.

Made ['ma:dǝ] *f* -, -n maggot.

madig ['ma:dɪç] a maggoty; **jdm
etw — machen** spoil sth for sb.

Magazin [maga'tsi:n] *nt* -s, -e
magazine.

Magd [ma:kt] *f* -, ̈e maid(servant).

Magen ['ma:gǝn] *m* -s, - or ̈-
stomach; **—schmerzen** *pl* stomach-
ache.

mager ['ma:gər] _a_ lean; (_dünn_) thin; M—keit _f_ leanness; thinness.

Magie [ma'gi:] _f_ magic; —r ['ma:giər] _m_ -s, - magician.

magisch ['ma:gɪʃ] _a_ magical.

Magnet [ma'gne:t] _m_ -s _or_ -en, -en magnet; m—isch _a_ magnetic; ℞—i'sieren _vt_ magnetize; —nadel _f_ magnetic needle.

Mahagoni [maha'go:ni] _nt_ -s -s mahogany.

mähen ['mɛ:ən] _vti_ mow.

Mahl [ma:l] _nt_ -(e)s, -e, meal; m—en _vt irreg._ grind; —stein _m_ grindstone; —zeit _f_ meal; _interj_ enjoy your meal.

Mahnbrief _m_ remainder.

Mähne ['mɛ:nə] _f_ -, -n mane.

Mahn- [ma:n] _cpd:_ m—en _vt_ remind; (_warnend_) warn; (_wegen Schuld_) demand payment from; —ung _f_ reminder; admonition, warning.

Mähre ['mɛ:rə] _f_ -, -n mare.

Mai [maɪ] _m_ -(e)s, -e May; —glöckchen _nt_ lily of the valley; —käfer _m_ cockchafer.

Mais [maɪs] _m_ -es, -e maize, corn (_US_); —kolben _m_ corncob.

Majestät [majɛs'tɛ:t] _f_ majesty; m—isch _a_ majestic.

Major [ma'jo:r] _m_ -s, -e (_Mil_) major; (_Aviat_) squadron .leader.

Majoran [majo'ra:n] _m_ ·s, -e marjoram.

makaber [ma'ka:bər] _a_ macabre.

Makel ['ma:kəl] _m_ -s, - blemish; (_moralisch_) stain; m—los _a_ immaculate, spotless.

mäkeln ['mɛ:kəln] _vi_ find fault.

Makkaroni [maka'ro:ni] _pl_ macaroni _sing._

Makler ['ma:klər] _m_ -s, - broker.

Makrele [ma'kre:lə] _f_ -, -n mackerel.

Makrone [ma'kro:nə] _f_ -, -n macaroon.

Mal [ma:l] _nt_ -(e)s, -e mark, sign; (_Zeitpunkt_) time; m— _ad_ times; (_col_) see einmal; -m— _suff_ -times; m—en _vti_ paint; —er _m_ -s, - painter; —e'rei _f_ painting; m—erisch _a_ picturesque; —kasten _m_ paintbox; m—nehmen _vti irreg_ multiply.

Malz [malts] _nt_-es malt; —bonbon _nt_ cough drop; —kaffee _m_ malt coffee.

Mama ['mama:] _f_ -, -s, **Mami** ['mami] _f_ -, -s (_col_) mum(my).

Mammut ['mamut] _nt_ -s, -e _or_ -s mammoth.

man [man] _pron_ one, people _pl_, you.

manche(r,s) ['mançə(r,z)] _a_ many a; (_pl_) a number of; _pron_ some; —rlei _a inv_ various; _pron_ a variety of things.

manchmal _ad_ sometimes.

Mandant(in _f_) [man'dant(m)] _m_ (_Jur_) client.

Mandarine [manda'ri:nə] _f_ mandarin, tangerine.

Mandat [man'da:t] _nt_ -(e)s, -e mandate.

Mandel ['mandəl] _f_ -, -n almond; (_Anat_) tonsil.

Manege [ma'ne:ʒə] _f_ -, -n ring, arena.

Mangel ['maŋəl] _f_ -, -n mangle; _m_ -s, = lack; (_Knappheit_) shortage (_an_ + _dat of_); (_Fehler_) defect, fault; —erscheinung _f_ deficiency symptom; m—haft _a_ poor; (_fehlerhaft_) defective, faulty; m—n _vi impers:_ es mangelt jdm an etw (_dat_) sb lacks sth; _vt_ Wäsche mangle; m—s _prep_ + _gen_ for lack of.

Manie [ma'ni:] f mania.

Manier [ma'ni:r] f – manner ; style ; (pej) mannerism ; **—en** pl manners pl ; m**—iert** [mani'ri:rt] a mannered, affected ; m**—lich** a well-mannered.

Manifest [mani'fɛst] nt **-es, -e** manifesto.

Maniküre [mani'ky:rə] f –, **-n** manicure ; m**—n** vt manicure.

manipulieren [manipu'li:rən] vt manipulate.

Manko ['maŋko] nt **-s, -s** deficiency ; (Comm) deficit.

Mann [man] m **-(e)s, ⁷er** man ; (Ehe—) husband ; (Naut) hand ; **seinen — stehen** hold one's own.

Männchen ['mɛnçən] nt little man ; (Tier) male.

Mannequin [manə'kɛ̃:] nt **-s, -s** fashion model.

mannigfaltig ['manɪçfaltɪç] a various, varied ; **M—keit** f variety.

männlich ['mɛnlɪç] a (Biol) male ; (fig, Gram) masculine.

Mann- cpd: **—schaft** f (Sport, fig) team ; (Naut, Aviat) crew ; (Mil) other ranks pl ; **—sleute** pl (col) menfolk pl ; **—weib** nt (pej) mannish woman.

Manöver [ma'nø:vər] nt **-s, –** manoeuvre.

manövrieren [manø'vri:rən] vti manoeuvre.

Mansarde [man'zardə] f–, **-n** attic.

Manschette [man'ʃɛtə] f cuff ; (Papier—) paper frill ; (Tech) collar ; sleeve ; **—nknopf** m cufflink.

Mantel ['mantəl] m **-s, ⁷** coat ; (Tech) casing, jacket.

Manuskript [manu'skrɪpt] nt **-(e)s, -e** manuscript.

Mappe ['mapə] f **–, -n** briefcase ; (Akten—) folder.

Märchen ['mɛ:rçən] nt fairy tale ; m**—haft** a fabulous ; **—prinz** m prince charming.

Marder ['mardər] m **-s, –** marten.

Margarine [marga'ri:nə] f. margarine.

Marienkäfer [ma'ri:ɔnkɛ:fər] m ladybird.

Marine [ma'ri:nə] f navy ; m**—blau** a navy-blue.

marinieren [mari'ni:rən] vt marinate.

Marionette [mario'nɛtə] f puppet.

Mark [mark] f –, – (Münze) mark ; nt **-(e)s** (Knochen—) marrow ; **durch — und Bein gehen go** right through sb ; m**—ant** [mar'kant] a striking.

Marke ['markə] f –, **-n** mark ; (Warensorte) brand ; (Fabrikat) make ; (Rabatt—, Brief—) stamp ; (Essens—) ticket ; (aus Metall etc) token, disc.

Mark- cpd: m**—ieren** [mar'ki:rən] vt mark ; vti (col) act ; **—ierung** f marking ; m**—ig** ['markɪç] a (fig) pithy ; **—ise** [mar'ki:zə] f –, **-n** awning ; **—stück** nt one-mark piece.

Markt [markt] m **-(e)s, ⁷e** market ; **—forschung** f market research ; **—platz** m market place ; **—wirtschaft** f market economy.

Marmelade [marmə'la:də] f –, **-n** jam.

Marmor ['marmor] m **-s, -e** marble ; m**—ieren** [-'ri:rən] vt marble ; m**—n** a marble.

Marone [ma'ro:nə] f –, **-n** or **Maroni** chestnut.

Marotte [ma'rɔtə] f –, **-n** fad, quirk.

Marsch [marʃ] m **-(e)s, ⁷e** march ; m**—** interj march ; f –, **-en** marsh ; **—befehl** m marching orders pl ; m**—bereit** a ready to move ; m**—ieren** [mar'ʃi:rən] vi march.

Marter ['martər] f -, -n torment;
m—n vt torture.
Märtyrer(in f) ['mɛrtyrər(ın)] m -s,
- martyr.
März [mɛrts] m -(es), -e March.
Marzipan [martsi'pa:n] nt -s, -e
marzipan.
Masche ['maʃə] f -, -n mesh;
(Strick—) stitch; **das ist die
neueste** — that's the latest dodge;
—ndraht m wire mesh; m—nfest
a runproof.
Maschine [ma'ʃi:nə] f machine;
(Motor) engine; —ll [maʃi'nɛl] a
machine(-); mechanical; —nbauer
m mechanical engineer; —ngewehr
nt machine gun; —npistole f sub-
machine gun; —nschaden m
mechanical fault; —nschlosser m
fitter; —nschrift f typescript;
m—schreiben vi irreg type.
Maschinist [maʃi'nɪst] m engineer.
Maser ['ma:zər] f -n grain;
speckle; m pl (Med) measles
sing; —ung f grain(ing).
Maske ['maskə] f -, -n mask;
—nball m fancy-dress ball; —rade
[-'ra:də] f masquerade.
maskieren [mas'ki:rən] vt mask;
(verkleiden) dress up; vr disguise
o.s., dress up.
Maß [ma:s] nt -es, -e measure;
(Mäßigung) moderation; (Grad)
degree, extent; f-, -(e) litre of beer.
Massage [ma'sa:ʒə] f -, -n
massage.
Maß- cpd: —anzug m made-
to-measure suit; —arbeit f (fig)
neat piece of work.
Masse ['masə] f -, -n mass;
—nartikel m mass-produced
article; —ngrab nt mass grave;
m—nhaft a loads of; —nmedien pl
mass media pl.

Mass- cpd: —eur [ma'sö:r] m
masseur; —euse [ma'sö:zə] f
masseuse.
maß- cpd: —gebend a authoritative; —halten vi irreg exercise
moderation.
massieren [ma'si:rən] vt massage;
(Mil) mass.
massig ['masıç] a massive; (col)
massive amount of.
mäßig ['mɛ:sıç] a moderate; —en
['mɛ:sıgən] vt restrain, moderate;
M—keit f moderation.
massiv [ma'si:f] a solid; (fig)
heavy, rough; M— nt -s, -e massif.
Maß- cpd: —krug m tankard;
—los a extreme; —nahme f -, -n
measure, step; m—regeln vt insep
reprimand; —stab m rule,
measure; (fig) standard; (Geog)
scale; m—voll a moderate.
Mast ['mast] m -(e)s, -e(n) mast;
(Elec) pylon.
mästen ['mɛstən] vt fatten.
Material [materi'a:l] nt -s, -ien
material(s); —fehler m material
defect; —ismus ['-lismʊs] m
materialism; —ist [-'lɪst] m
materialist; m—istisch [-'lɪstıʃ] a
materialistic.
Materie [ma'te:rɪə] f matter, substance; m—ll [materi'ɛl] a material.
Mathematik [matema'ti:k] f
mathematics sing; —er(in f)
[mate'ma:tikər(ın)] m -s, - mathematician.
mathematisch [mate'ma:tıʃ] a
mathematical.
Matratze [ma'tratsə] f -, -n
mattress.
Matrize [ma'tri:tsə] f -, -n matrix;
(zum Abziehen) stencil.
Matrose [ma'tro:zə] m -n, -n sailor.

Matsch [matʃ] *m* -(e)s mud; (Schnee—) slush; **m—ig** a muddy; slushy.

matt [mat] a weak; (glanzlos) dull; (Phot) matt; (Schach) mate.

Matte ['matə] *f* -, -n mat.

Matt- cpd: **—igkeit** *f* weakness; dullness; **—scheibe** *f* (TV) screen; **—scheibe haben** (col) be not quite with it.

Mauer ['mauər] *f* -, -n wall; **m—n** *vti* build; lay bricks; **—werk** *nt* brickwork; (Stein) masonry.

Maul [maul] *nt* -(e)s, Mäuler mouth; **m—en** *vi* (col) grumble; **—esel** *m* mule; **—korb** *m* muzzle; **—sperre** *f* lockjaw; **—tier** *nt* mule; **—wurf** *m* mole; **—wurfshaufen** *m* molehill.

Maurer ['maurər] *m* -s, - brick-layer.

Maus [maus] *f* -, Mäuse mouse.

mäuschenstill ['mɔysçən'ʃtıl] a very quiet.

Maus- [mauz] cpd: **—efalle** *f* mousetrap; **m—en** *vt* (col) flinch; *vi* catch mice; **m—ern** *vr* moult; **m—(e)tot** a stone dead.

maximal [maksi'maːl] a maximum.

Maxime [ma'ksiːmə] *f* -, -n maxim.

Mayonnaise [majo'nɛːzə] *f* -, -n mayonnaise.

Mechan- [me'çaːn] cpd: **—ik** *f* mechanics sing; (Getriebe) mechanics pl; **—iker** *m* -s, - mechanic, engineer; **—isch** a mechanical; **m—isieren** *vt* mechanize; **—isierung** *f* mechanization; **—ismus** [meça'nısmus] *m* mechanism.

meckern ['mɛkərn] *vi* bleat; (col) moan.

Medaille [me'daljə] *f* -, -n medal.

Medaillon [medal'jõː] *nt* -s, -s (Schmuck) locket.

Medikament [medika'mɛnt] *nt* medicine.

meditieren [medi'tiːrən] *vi* meditate.

Medizin [medi'tsiːn] *f* -, -en medicine; **m—isch** a medical.

Meer [meːr] *nt* -(e)s, -e sea; **—busen** *m* bay, gulf; **—enge** *f* straits pl; **—esspiegel** *m* sea level; **—rettich** *m* horseradish; **—schweinchen** *nt* guinea-pig.

Megaphon [mega'foːn] *nt* -s, -e megaphone.

Mehl ['meːl] *nt* -(e)s, -e flour; **m—ig** a floury.

mehr [meːr] *a,ad* more; **M—aufwand** *m* additional expenditure; **—deutig** a ambiguous; **—ere** a several; **—eres** *pron* several things; **—fach** a multiple; (wiederholt) repeated; **M—heit** *f* majority; **—malig** a repeated; **—mals** ad repeatedly; **—stimmig** a for several voices; **—stimmig singen** harmonize; **M—wertsteuer** *f* value added tax, VAT; **M—zahl** *f* majority; (Gram) plural.

meiden ['maɪdən] *vt* irreg avoid.

Meile ['maɪlə] *f* -, -n mile; **—nstein** *m* milestone; **m—nweit** a for miles.

mein [maɪn] pron my; **—e(r,s)** mine.

Meineid ['maɪn'aɪt] *m* perjury.

meinen ['maɪnən] *vti* think; (sagen) say; (sagen wollen) mean; **das will ich —** I should think so.

mein- cpd: **—er** *pron gen* of ich of me; **—erseits** ad for my part; **—esgleichen** *pron* people like me; **—etwegen, —etwillen** ad (für mich) for my sake; (wegen mir) on my account; (von mir aus) as far as I'm concerned; **:** I don't care or 'mind; —ige *pron*: der/die/das —ige mine.

Meinung ['maɪnʊŋ] *f* opinion; jdm die — sagen give sb a piece of one's mind; —**saustausch** *m* exchange of views; —**sumfrage** *f* opinion poll; —**sverschiedenheit** *f* difference of opinion.

Meise ['maɪzə] *f* -, -n tit(mouse).

Meißel ['maɪsəl] *m* -s, - chisel; **m**—**n** *vt* chisel.

meist ['maɪst] *a,ad* most(ly); —**ens** *ad* generally, usually.

Meister ['maɪstər] *m* -s, - master; (Sport) champion; —**haft** *a* masterly; **m**—**n** *vt* master; —**schaft** *f* mastery; (Sport) championship; —**stück** *nt*, —**werk** *nt* masterpiece.

Melancholie [melaŋko'li:] *f* melancholy.

melancholisch [melaŋ'ko:lɪʃ] *a* melancholy.

Melde- ['mɛldə] *cpd*: —**frist** *f* registration period; **m**—**n** *vt* report; *vr* report (bei to); (Sch) put one's hand up; (freiwillig) volunteer (auf etw, an Telefon) answer; sich zu Wort **m**—**n** ask to speak; —**pflicht** *f* obligation to register with the police; —**stelle** *f* registration office.

Meldung ['mɛldʊŋ] *f* announcement; (Bericht) report.

meliert [me'li:rt] *a* mottled, speckled.

melken ['mɛlkən] *vt irreg* milk.

Melodie [melo'di:] *f* melody, tune.

melodisch [me'lo:dɪʃ] *a* melodious, tuneful.

Melone [me'lo:nə] *f* -, -n melon; (Hut) bowler (hat).

Membran(e) [mɛm'bra:n(ə)] *f* -, -en (Tech) diaphragm.

Memoiren [memo'a:rən] *pl* memoirs *pl*.

Menge ['mɛŋə] *f* -, *n* quantity; (Menschen—) crowd; (große Anzahl) lot (of); **m**—**n** *vt* mix; *vr*: sich **m**—**n in** (+acc) meddle with; —**nlehre** *f* (Math) set theory; —**nrabatt** *m* bulk discount.

Mensch [mɛnʃ] *m* -en, -en human being, man; person; kein — nobody; *nt* -(e)s, -er hussy; —**enalter** *nt* generation; —**enfeind** *m* misanthrope; —**enfreundlich** *a* philanthropical; —**enkenner** *m* -s, - judge of human nature; —**enliebe** *f* philanthropy; **m**—**enmöglich** *a* humanly possible; —**enrecht** *nt* human rights *pl*; **m**—**enscheu** *a* shy; —**enwürdig** *a* degrading; —**enverstand** *m*: gesunder —**enverstand** common sense; —**heit** *f* humanity, mankind; **m**—**lich** *a* human; (human) humane; —**lichkeit** *f* humanity.

Menstruation [mɛnstruatsi'o:n] *f* menstruation.

Mentalität [mentali'tɛ:t] *f* mentality.

Menü [me'ny:] *nt*- -s, -s menu.

Merk- [mɛrk] *cpd*: —**blatt** *nt* instruction sheet *or* leaflet; **m**—**en** *vt* notice; sich (dat) etw **m**—**en** remember sth; **m**—**lich** *a* noticeable; —**mal** *nt* sign, characteristic; **m**—**würdig** *a* odd.

Meß- [mɛs] *cpd*: **m**—**bar** *a* measurable; —**becher** *m* measuring cup; —**buch** *nt* missal.

Messe ['mɛsə] *f* -, -n fair; (Eccl) mass; (Mil) mess; **m**—**n** *irreg vt* measure; *vr* compete; —**r** *nt* -s, - knife; —**rspitze** *f* knife point; (in Rezept) pinch; —**stand** *m* exhibition stand.

Meß- cpd: **—gerät** nt measuring device, gauge; **—gewand** nt chasuble.

Messing ['mɛsɪŋ] nt **-s** brass.

Metall [me'tal] nt **-s, -e** metal; **m—en, -en,** **—isch** a metallic.

Metaphysik [metafy'zi:k] f metaphysics sing.

Metastase [meta'sta:zə] f **-, -n** (Med) secondary growth.

Meteor [mete'o:r] nt **-s, -e** meteor.

Meter ['me:tər] nt or m **-s, -** metre; **—maß** nt tape measure.

Methode [me'to:də] f **-, -n** method. **methodisch** [me'to:dɪʃ] a methodical.

Metropole [metro'po:lə] f **-, -n** metropolis.

Metzger ['mɛtsgər] m **-s, -** butcher; **—ei** [-'raɪ] f butcher's (shop).

Meuchelmord ['mɔʏçəlmɔrt] m assassination.

Meute ['mɔʏtə] f **-, -n** pack; **—rei** f mutiny; **—rer** m **-s, -** mutineer; **m—rn** vi mutiny.

miauen [mi'auən] vi miaow.

mich [mɪç] pron acc of **ich** me; myself.

Miene ['mi:nə] f **-, -n** look, expression.

mies [mi:s] a (col) lousy.

Miet- ['mi:t] cpd: **—auto** nt hired car; **—e** f **-, -n** rent; **zur —e wohnen** live in rented accommodation; **m—en** vt rent; Auto hire; **—er(in** f) m **-s, -** tenant; **—shaus** nt tenement, block of flats; **—vertrag** m tenancy agreement.

Migräne [mi'grɛ:nə] f **-, -n** migraine.

Mikro- cpd: **—be** [mi'kro:bə] f **-, -n** microbe; **—fon, —phon** [mikro'fo:n] nt **-s, -e** microphone;

—skop [mikro'sko:p] nt **-s, -e** microscope; **m—skopisch** a microscopic.

Milch [mɪlç] f **-** milk; (Fisch—) milt, roe; **—glas** nt frosted glass; **m—ig** a milky; **—kaffee** m white coffee; **—pulver** nt powdered milk; **—straße** f Milky Way; **—zahn** m milk tooth.

mild [mɪlt] a mild; Richter lenient; (freundlich) kind, charitable; **M—e** ['mɪldə] f **-,** in mildness; leniency; **—ern** vt mitigate, soften; Schmerz alleviate; **—ernde Umstände** extenuating circumstances.

Milieu [mili'ø] nt **-s, -s** background, environment; **m—ge-schädigt** a maladjusted.

Mili- [mili] cpd: **m—tant** [-'tant] a militant; **—tär** [-'tɛ:r] nt **-s** military, army; **—'tärgericht** nt military court; **m—'tärisch** a military; **—tarismus** [-ta'rɪsmus] m militarism; **m—ta'ristisch** a militaristic; **—'tärpflicht** f (compulsory) military service.

Milz [mɪlts] f **-, -en** spleen.

Mimik ['mi:mɪk] f mime.

Mimose [mi'mo:zə] f **-, -n** mimosa; (fig) sensitive person.

minder ['mɪndər] a inferior; ad less; **M—heit** f minority; **—jährig** a minor; **M—jährigkeit** f minority; **—n** vtr decrease, diminish; **M—ung** f decrease; **—wertig** a inferior; **M—wertigkeitsgefühl** nt, **M—wertigkeitskomplex** m inferiority complex.

Mindest- ['mɪndəst] cpd: **—alter** nt minimum age; **—betrag** m minimum amount; **m—e** a least; **m—ens, zum m—en** ad at least; **—lohn** m minimum wage; **—maß** nt minimum.

Mine ['mi:nə] f -, -n mine; (Bleistift—) lead; (Kugelschreiber—) refill; **—nfeld** nt minefield.

Mineral [mine'ra:l] nt -s, -e or -ien mineral; **m—isch** a mineral; **—wasser** nt mineral water.

Miniatur [minia'tu:r] f miniature.

minimal [mini'ma:l] a minimal.

Minister [mi'nɪstər] m -s, - minister; **m—iell** [ministeri'ɛl] a ministerial; **—ium** [mins'te:rium] nt ministry; **—präsident** m prime minister.

minus ['mi:nus] ad minus; **M—** nt -, - deficit; **M—pol** m negative pole; **M—zeichen** nt minus sign.

Minute [mi'nu:tə] f -, -n minute; **—nzeiger** m minute hand.

mir [mi:r] pron dat of **ich** (to) me; **— nichts, dir nichts** just like that.

Misch- ['mɪʃ] cpd: **—ehe** f mixed marriage; **m—en** vt mix; **—ling** m half-caste; **—ung** f mixture.

Miß- ['mɪs] cpd: **m—'achten** vt insep disregard; **—'achtung** f disregard; **m—behagen** vt discomfort, uneasiness; **—'bildung** f deformity; **m—'billigen** vt insep disapprove of; **—'billigung** f disapproval; **—brauch** m abuse; (falscher Gebrauch) misuse; **m—'brauchen** vt insep abuse; misuse (zu for); **m—'deuten** vt insep misinterpret; **—erfolg** m failure.

Misse- ['mɪsə] cpd: **—tat** f misdeed; **—täter(in** f) m criminal; (col) scoundrel.

Miß- ['mɪs] cpd: **m—'fallen** vi irreg insep displease (jdm sb); **—fallen** nt -s displeasure; **—geburt** f freak; (fig)

abortion; **—geschick** nt misfortune; **m—glücken** [mɪs'glykn] vi insep fail; **jdm m—glückt etw** sb does not succeed with sth; **—griff** m mistake; **—gunst** f envy; **m—günstig** a envious; **m—'handeln** vt insep ill-treat; **—'handlung** f ill-treatment; **—helligkeit** f: **—helligkeiten haben** be at variance.

Mission [mɪsi'o:n] f mission; **—ar** [mɪsio'na:r] m missionary.

Miß- cpd: **—klang** m discord; **—kredit** m discredit; **m—lingen** [mɪs'lɪŋən] vi irreg insep fail; **—'lingen** nt -s failure; **—mut** nt bad temper; **m—mutig** a cross; **m—'raten** vi irreg insep turn out badly; a ill-bred; **—stand** m state of affairs; abuse; **—stimmung** f ill-humour, discord; **m—'trauen** vi insep mistrust; **—trauen** nt -s distrust, suspicion (of); **—trauensantrag** m (Pol) motion of no confidence; **—trauensvotum** nt -s, -voten (Pol) vote of no confidence; **m—trauisch** a distrustful, suspicious; **—verhältnis** nt disproportion; **—verständnis** nt misunderstanding; **m—verstehen** vt irreg insep misunderstand.

Mist [mɪst] m -(e)s dung; dirt; (col) rubbish; **—el** f -, -n mistletoe; **—haufen** m dungheap.

mit [mɪt] prep + dat with; (mittels) by; **— der Bahn** by train; **'— 10 Jahren** at the age of 10; ad along, too; **wollen Sie —?** do you want to come along?

Mitarbeit ['mit'arbait] f cooperation; **m—en** vi cooperate, collaborate; **—er(in** f) m collaborator; co-worker; pl staff.

Mit- cpd: **—bestimmung** f participation in decision-making; (Pol) determination; m—bringen vt irreg bring along; —bürger(in f) m fellow citizen; —denken vi irreg follow; du hast ja m—gedacht! good thinking!

miteinander [mɪt'aɪ'nandər] ad together, with one another.

Mit- cpd: m—erleben vt see, witness; —esser ['mɪt'ɛsər] m -s, - blackhead; m—geben vt irreg give; —gefühl nt sympathy; m—gehen vi irreg go/come along; m—genommen a done in, in a bad way; —gift f dowry.

Mitglied ['mɪtgliːt] nt member; —sbeitrag m membership fee; —schaft f membership.

Mit- cpd: m—halten vi irreg keep up; —hilfe f help, assistance; m—hören vt listen in to; m—kommen vi irreg come along; (verstehen) keep up, follow; —läufer m hanger-on; (Pol) fellow-traveller.

Mitleid nt sympathy; (Erbarmen) compassion; —enschaft f: in —enschaft ziehen affect; m—ig a sympathetic; m—slos a pitiless, merciless.

Mit- cpd: m—machen vt join in, take part in; —mensch m fellow man; m—nehmen vt irreg take along/away; (anstrengen) wear out, exhaust.

mitsamt [mɪt'zamt] prep +dat together with.

Mitschuld f complicity; m—ig a also guilty (an +dat of); —ige(r) mf accomplice.

Mit- cpd: —schüler(in f) m schoolmate; m—spielen vi join in, take part; —spieler(in f) m partner; —spracherecht ['mɪtʃpraːxərɛçt] nt voice, say.

Mittag ['mɪtaːk] m -(e)s, -e midday, lunchtime; (zu) — essen have lunch; m— a at lunchtime or noon; —essen nt lunch, dinner; m—s ad at lunchtime or noon; —spause f lunch break; —sschlaf m early afternoon nap, siesta.

Mittäter(in f) [mɪttɛ:tər(ɪn)] m accomplice.

Mitte ['mɪtə] f -, -n middle; aus unserer — from our midst.

mitteil- ['mɪttaɪl] cpd: —en vt: jdm etw —en inform sb of sth, communicate sth to sb; —sam a communicative; M—ung f communication.

Mittel ['mɪtəl] nt -s means; method; (Math) average; (Med) medicine; ein — zum Zweck a means to an end; —alter nt Middle Ages pl; m—alterlich a mediaeval; m—bar a indirect; —ding nt cross; m—los a without means; m—mäßig a· mediocre, middling; —mäßigkeit f mediocrity; —punkt m centre; m—s prep +gen by means of; —stand m middle class; —streifen m central reservation; —stürmer m centre-forward; —weg m middle course; —welle f (Rad) medium wave; —wert m average value, mean.

mitten ['mɪtən] ad in the middle; — auf der Straße/in der Nacht in the middle of the street/night; —hindurch ad [-hɪn'dʊrç] through the middle.

Mitternacht ['mɪtərnaxt] f midnight; m—s ad at midnight.

mittlere(r,s) ['mɪtlərə(r,z)] a middle; (durchschnittlich) medium, average.

mittlerweile ['mɪtlər'vaɪlə] ad meanwhile.

Mittwoch [ˈmɪtvɔx] m -(e)s, -e Wednesday; **m—s** ad on Wednesdays.

mitunter [mɪtˈʊntər] ad occasionally, sometimes.

Mit- cpd: **m—verantwortlich** a also responsible; **—verschulden** [ˈmɪtfɛrʃʊldən] nt contributory negligence; **m—wirken** vi contribute (bei to); (Theat) take part (bei in); **—wirkung** f contribution; participation; **—wisser** [ˈmɪtvɪsər] m -s, - sb in the know.

Möbel [ˈmøːbəl] nt -s, - (piece of) furniture; **—wagen** m furniture or removal van.

mobil [moˈbiːl] a mobile; (Mil) mobilized; **M—iar** [mobiˈliːaːr] nt -s, -e movable assets pl; **M—machung** f mobilization.

möblieren [møˈbliːrən] vt furnish; **möbliert wohnen** live in furnished accommodation.

Mode [ˈmoːdə] f -, -n fashion.

Modell [moˈdɛl] nt -s, -e model; **m—ieren** [-ˈliːrən] vt model.

Mode- cpd: **—(n)schau** f fashion show; **m—rn** [moˈdɛrn] a modern; (modisch) fashionable; **m—rni'sieren** vt modernize; **—schmuck** m fashion jewellery; **—wort** nt fashionable word.

modisch [ˈmoːdɪʃ] a fashionable.

mogeln [ˈmoːɡəln] vi (col) cheat.

mögen [ˈmøːɡən] vti irreg like; **ich möchte …** I would like …; **das mag wohl sein** that may well be so.

möglich [ˈmøːklɪç] a possible; **—erweise** ad possibly; **M—keit** f possibility; **nach M—keit** if possible; **—st** ad as … as possible.

Mohn [moːn] m -(e)s, -e (—blume) poppy; (—samen) poppy seed.

Möhre [ˈmøːrə] f -, -n, **Mohrrübe** f carrot.

mokieren [moˈkiːrən] vr make fun (über + acc of).

Mole [ˈmoːlə] f -, -n (harbour) mole; **—kül** [moleˈkyːl] nt -s, -e molecule.

Molkerei [mɔlkəˈrai] f dairy.

Moll [mɔl] nt -, - (Mus) minor (key); **m—ig a** cosy; (dicklich) plump.

Moment [moˈmɛnt] m -(e)s, -e moment; **im —** at the moment; nt factor, element; **m—an** [-ˈtaːn] a momentary; ad at the moment.

Monarch [moˈnarç] m -en, -en monarch; **—ie** [monarˈçiː] f monarchy.

Monat [ˈmoːnat] m -(e)s, -e month; **m—elang** ad for months; **m—lich** a monthly; **—skarte** f monthly ticket.

Mönch [mœnç] m -(e)s, -e monk.

Mond [moːnt] m -(e)s, -e moon; **—fähre** f lunar (excursion) module; **—finsternis** f eclipse of the moon; **m—hell a** moonlit; **—landung** f moon landing; **—schein** m moonlight; **—sonde** f moon probe.

Mono- [mono] in cpds mono; **—log** [-ˈloːk] m -s, -e monologue; **—pol** [-ˈpoːl] nt -s, -e monopoly; **m—polisieren** [-poliˈziːrən] vt monopolize; **m—ton** [-ˈtoːn] a monotonous; **—tonie** [-toˈniː] f monotony.

Monsun [mɔnˈzuːn] m -s, -e monsoon.

Montag [ˈmoːntaːk] m -(e)s, -e Monday; **m—s** ad on Mondays.

Montage [mɔnˈtaːʒə] f -, -n (Phot etc) montage; (Tech) assembly; (Einbauen) fitting.

Monteur [mɔnˈtøːr] m fitter, assembly man.

montieren [mɔnˈtiːrən] vt assemble, set up.

Monument [monu'mɛnt] nt monument; **m—al** ['-'ta:l] a monumental.

Moor [mo:r] nt -(e)s, -e moor.

Moos [mo:s] nt -es, -e moss.

Moped ['mo:pɛt] nt -s, -s moped.

Mops [mɔps] m -es, ⁼e pug.

Moral [mo'ra:l] f -, -en morality; (einer Geschichte) moral; **m—isch** a moral.

Moräne [mo'rɛ:nə] f -, -n moraine.

Morast [mo'rast] m -(e)s, -e morass, mire; **m—ig** a boggy.

Mord [mɔrt] m -(e)s, -e murder; **—anschlag** m murder attempt.

Mörder ['mœrdər] m -s, - murderer; **—in** f murderess.

Mord- cpd: **—kommission** f murder squad; **—sglück** nt (col) amazing luck; **m—smäßig** a (col) terrific, enormous; **—sschreck** m (col) terrible fright; **—verdacht** m suspicion of murder; **—waffe** f murder weapon.

morgen ['mɔrgən] ad, **M—** nt tomorrow; **— früh** tomorrow morning; **M—** m -s, - morning; **M—mantel** m, **M—rock** m dressing gown; **M—röte** f dawn; **—s** ad in the morning.

morgig ['mɔrgɪç] a tomorrow's; der **—e Tag** tomorrow.

Morphium ['mɔrfium] nt morphine.

morsch [mɔrʃ] a rotten.

Morse- ['mɔrzə] cpd: **—alphabet** nt Morse code; **m—n** vi send a message by morse code.

Mörtel ['mœrtəl] m -s, - mortar.

Mosaik [moza'i:k] nt -s, -en or -e mosaic.

Moschee [mɔ'ʃe:] f -, -n [mɔ'ʃe:ən] mosque.

Moskito [mɔs'ki:to] m -s, -s mosquito.

Most [mɔst] m -(e)s, -e (unfermented) fruit juice; (Apfelwein) cider.

Motel [mo'tel] nt -s, -s motel.

Motiv [mo'ti:f] nt -s, -e motive; (Mus) theme; **m—ieren** [moti'vi:rən] vt motivate; **—ierung** f motivation.

Motor ['mo:tor] m -s, -en [mo'to:rən] engine; (esp Elec) motor; **—boot** nt motorboat; **—enöl** nt motor oil; **m—isieren** [motori'zi:rən] vt motorize; **—rad** nt motorcycle; **—roller** m motor scooter; **—schaden** m engine trouble or failure.

Motte ['mɔtə] f -, -n moth; **—nkugel** f, **—npulver** nt mothball(s).

Motto ['mɔto] nt -s, -s motto.

Möwe ['mø:və] f -, -n seagull.

Mucke ['mʊkə] f -, -n (usu pl) caprice; (von Ding) snag, bug; **seine —n haben** be temperamental.

Mücke ['mʏkə] f -, -n midge, gnat; **—nstich** m midge or gnat bite.

mucksen ['mʊksən] vr (col) budge; (Laut geben) open one's mouth.

müde ['my:də] a tired.

Müdigkeit ['my:dɪçkaɪt] f tiredness.

Muff [mʊf] m -(e)s, -e (Handwärmer) muff; **—el** m -s, - (col) killjoy, sourpuss; **m—ig** a (Luft) musty.

Mühe ['my:ə] f -, -n trouble; pains pl; **mit Müh und Not** with great difficulty; **sich** (dat) **— geben** go to a lot of trouble; **m—los** a without trouble, easy.

muhen ['mu:ən] vi low, moo.

mühevoll a laborious, arduous.

Mühle ['my:lə] f -, -n mill; (Kaffee—) grinder.

Müh- cpd: **—sal** f -, -e hardship, tribulation; **m—sam** a arduous, troublesome; **m—selig** a arduous, laborious.

Mulatte [mu'latə] m -n, -n, **Mulattin** f mulatto.

Mulde ['muldə] f -, -n hollow, depression.

Mull [mul] m -(e)s, -e thin muslin; **—binde** f gauze bandage.

Müll [myl] m -(e)s refuse; **—abfuhr** f rubbish disposal; (Leute) dustmen pl; **—abladeplatz** m rubbish dump; **—eimer** m dustbin, garbage can (US); **—er** m -s, - miller; **—haufen** m rubbish heap; **—schlucker** m -s, - garbage disposal unit; **—wagen** m dustcart, garbage truck (US).

mulmig ['mulmiç] a rotten; (col) dodgy; jdm ist — sb feels funny.

multiplizieren [multipli'tsi:rən] vt multiply.

Mumie ['mu:miə] f mummy.

Mumm [mum] m -s (col) gumption, nerve.

Mund [munt] m -(e)s, ⁻er ['myndər] mouth; **—art** f dialect.

Mündel ['myndəl] nt -s, - ward.

münden ['myndən] vi flow (in + acc into).

Mund- cpd: **m—faul** a taciturn; **—fäule** f (Med) ulcerative stomatitis; **—geruch** m bad breath; **—harmonika** f mouth organ.

mündig ['myndiç] a of age; **M—keit** f majority.

mündlich ['myntliç] a oral.

Mund- cpd: **—stück** nt mouthpiece; (Zigaretten—) tip; **m—tot** a: jdn m—tot machen muzzle sb.

Mündung ['mynduŋ] f mouth; (Gewehr) muzzle.

Mund- cpd: **—wasser** nt mouthwash; **—werk** nt: ein großes **—werk** haben have a big mouth; **—winkel** m corner of the mouth.

Munition [munitsi'o:n] f ammunition; **—slager** nt ammunition dump.

munkeln ['munkəln] vi whisper, mutter.

Münster ['mynstər] nt -s, - minster.

munter ['muntər] a lively; **M—keit** f liveliness.

Münze ['myntsə] f -, -n coin; **m—n** vt coin, mint; auf jdn gemünzt sein be aimed at sb.

Münzfernsprecher ['myntsfərnʃprɛçər] m callbox, pay phone (US).

mürb(e) ['myrb(ə)] a Gestein crumbly; Holz rotten; Gebäck crisp; jdn — machen wear sb down; **M—(e)teig** m shortcrust pastry.

murmeln ['murməln] vti murmur, mutter.

Murmeltier ['murməlti:r] nt marmot.

murren ['murən] vi grumble, grouse.

mürrisch ['myrɪʃ] a sullen.

Mus [mu:s] nt -es, -e puree.

Muschel ['muʃəl] f -, -n mussel; (—schale) shell; (Telefon—) receiver.

Muse ['mu:zə] f -, -n muse.

Museum [mu'ze:um] nt -s, Museen museum.

Musik [mu'zi:k] f music; (Kapelle) band; **m—alisch** ['ka:lɪʃ] a musical; **—box** f jukebox; **—er** ['mu:zikər] m -s, - musician; **—hochschule** f music school; **—instrument** nt musical instrument; **—truhe** f radiogram.

musizieren [muzi'tsi:rən] vi make music.

Muskat [mus'ka:t] *m* -(e)s, -e
nutmeg.

Muskel ['muskəl] *m* -s, -n muscle;
—kater *m*: einen —kater haben be
stiff.

Muskulatur [muskula'tu:r] *f*
muscular system.

muskulös [musku'lø:s] *a* muscular.

Muß [mus] *nt* - necessity, must.

Muße ['mu:sə] *f* - leisure.

müssen ['mysən] *vi irreg* must,
have to; er hat gehen — he (has)
had to go.

müßig ['my:siç] *a* idle; M—gang *m*
idleness.

Muster ['mustər] *nt* -s, - model;
(Dessin) pattern; (Probe) sample;
— ohne Wert free sample;
m—gültig *a* exemplary; m—n *vt*
Tapete pattern; (fig, Mil) examine;
Truppen inspect; —schüler *m*
model pupil; —ung *f* (von Stoff)
pattern; (Mil) inspection.

Mut [mu:t] *m* courage; nur —!
cheer up!; jdm — machen
encourage sb; m—ig *a*
courageous; m—los *a* discouraged,
despondent.

mutmaßlich ['mu:tma:sliç] *a*
presumed; *ad* probably.

Mutter ['mutər] *f* -, = mother; *pl*
—n (Schrauben—) nut; —land *nt*
mother country.

mütterlich ['mytərliç] *a* motherly;
—erseits *ad* on the mother's side.

Mutter- *cpd*: —liebe *f* motherly
love; —mal *nt* birthmark, mole;
—schaft *f* motherhood, maternity;
—schutz *m* maternity regulations;
'm—'seelena'llein *a* all alone;
—sprache *f* native language; —tag
m Mother's Day.

mutwillig ['mu:tviliç] *a* malicious,
deliberate.

Mütze ['mytsə] *f* -, -n cap.

mysteriös [mysteri'ø:s] *a*
mysterious.

Mystik ['mystik] *f* mysticism; —er
m -s, - mystic.

Mythos ['my:tɔs] *m* -, **Mythen**
myth.

N

N, n [ɛn] *nt* N, n.

na [na] *interj* well.

Nabel ['na:bəl] *m* -s, - navel;
—schnur *f* umbilical cord.

nach [na:x] *prep* +dat after; (in
Richtung) to; (gemäß) according
to; — oben/hinten up/back; ihm
—! after him!; — wie vor still; —
und — gradually; dem Namen —
judging by his name; —ahmen *vt*
ape; —ahmen *vt* imitate;
N—ahmung *f* imitation.

Nachbar(in *f*) ['naxba:r(m)] *m* -s,

—n neighbour; —haus *nt*: im
—haus next door; n—lich *a*
neighbourly; —schaft *f* neighbourhood; —staat *m* neighbouring state.

nach- *cpd*: —bestellen *vt* order
again; N—bestellung *f* (Comm)
repeat order; —bilden *vt* copy;
N—bildung imitation, copy;
—blicken *vi* look or gaze after;
—datieren *vt* postdate.

nachdem [na:x'de:m] *cj* after;
(weil) since; je — (ob) it depends
(whether).

nach- *cpd*: **—denken** *vi irreg* think (über +*acc* about); **N—denken** *nt* **-s** reflection, meditation; **—denklich** *a* thoughtful, pensive.

Nachdruck ['naːxdrʊk] *m* emphasis; (*Print*) reprint, reproduction.

nachdrücklich ['naːxdrʏklɪç] *a* emphatic.

nacheifern ['naːxaɪfərn] *vi* emulate (*jdm* sb).

nacheinander [naːx'aɪ'nandər] *ad* one after the other.

nachempfinden ['naːxɛmpfɪndən] *vt irreg*: jdm etw — feel with sb.

Nacherzählung ['naːxɛrtsɛːluŋ] *f* reproduction (of a story).

Nachfahr ['naːxfaːr] *m* **-s, -en** descendant.

Nachfolge ['naːxfɔlgə] *f* succession; **n—n** *vi* (*lit*) follow (*jdm/etw* sb/sth); **—r(in** *f*) *m* **-s, -** successor.

nach- *cpd*: **—forschen** *vti* investigate; **N—forschung** *f* investigation.

Nachfrage ['naːxfraːgə] *f* inquiry; (*Comm*) demand; **n—n** *vi* inquire.

nach- *cpd*: **—fühlen** *vt* see **—empfinden**; **—füllen** *vt* refill; **—geben** *vi irreg* give way, yield.

Nach- *cpd*: **—gebühr** *f* surcharge; (*Post*) excess postage; **—geburt** *f* afterbirth.

nachgehen ['naːxgeːən] *vi irreg* follow (*jdm* sb); (*erforschen*) inquire (*einer Sache* into sth); (*Uhr*) be slow.

Nachgeschmack ['naːxgəʃmak] *m* aftertaste.

nachgiebig ['naːxgiːbɪç] *a* soft, accommodating; **N—keit** *f* softness.

Nachhall ['naːxhal] *m* resonance; **n—en** *vi* resound.

nachhaltig ['naːxhaltɪç] *a* lasting; *Widerstand* persistent.

nachhelfen ['naːxhɛlfən] *vi irreg* assist, help (*jdm* sb).

nachher [naːx'heːr] *ad* afterwards.

Nachhilfeunterricht ['naːxhɪlfəʊntərrɪçt] *m* extra tuition.

nachholen ['naːxhoːlən] *vt* catch up with; *Versäumtes* make up for.

Nachkomme ['naːxkɔmə] *m* **-, -n** descendant; **n—n** *vi irreg* follow; *einer Verpflichtung* fulfil; **—nschaft** *f* descendants *pl*.

Nachkriegs- ['naːxkriːks] *in cpds* postwar; **—zeit** *f* postwar period.

Nach- *cpd*: **—laß** *m* **-lasses, -lässe** (*Comm*) discount, rebate; (*Erbe*) estate; **n—lassen** *irreg vt Strafe* remit; *Summe* take off; *Schulden* cancel; *vi* decrease, ease off; (*Sturm auch*) die down; (*schlechter werden*) deteriorate; er hat n—gelassen he has got worse; **n—lässig** *a* negligent, careless; **—lässigkeit** *f* negligence, carelessness.

nachlaufen ['naːxlaʊfən] *vi irreg* run after, chase (*jdm* sb).

nachmachen ['naːxmaxən] *vt* imitate, copy (*jdm etw* sth from sb); (*fälschen*) counterfeit.

Nachmittag ['naːxmɪtaːk] *m* afternoon; **am —, n—s** *ad* in the afternoon.

Nach- *cpd*: **—nahme** *f* **-, -n** cash on delivery; **per —nahme** C.O.D.; **—name** *m* surname; **—porto** *nt* excess postage.

nachprüfen ['naːxpryːfən] *vt* check, verify.

nachrechnen ['naːxrɛçnən] *vt* check.

Nachrede ['naːxreːdə] *f*: **üble —** libel; slander.

Nachricht ['na:xrıçt] *f -, -en* (piece of) news; (*Mitteilung*) message; **—en** *pl* news; **—enagentur** *f* news agency; **—endienst** *m* (*Mil*) intelligence service; **—ensprecher(in** *f*) *m* newsreader; **—entechnik** *f* telecommunications *sing.*

nachrücken ['na:xrykən] *vi* move up.

Nachruf ['na:xru:f] ·*m* obituary (notice).

nachsagen ['na:xza:gən] *vt* repeat; jdm etw — say sth of sb.

nachschicken · ['na:xʃıkən] *vt* forward.

Nachschlag— ['na:xʃla:g] *cpd:* **n—en** *vi irreg* look up; *vi:* jdm **n—en** take after sb; **—ewerk** *nt* reference book.

nachsehen ['na:xze:ən] *irreg vt* (*prüfen*) check; jdm etw — forgive sb sth; *vi* look after (jdm sb); (*erforschen*) look and see; das N— ·haben come off worst.

nachsenden ['na:xzɛndən] *vt irreg* send on, forward.

Nachsicht ['na:xzıçt] *f* · indulgence, leniency; **n—ig** *a* indulgent, lenient.

nachsitzen ['na:xzıtsən] *vi irreg* (*Sch*) be kept in.

Nachspeise ['na:xʃpaızə] *f* dessert, sweet, pudding.

Nachspiel ['na:xʃpi:l] *nt* epilogue; (*fig*) sequel.

nachsprechen ['na:xʃprɛçən] *vt irreg* repeat· (jdm after sb).

nächst [nɛ:çst] · *prep* + *dat* (*räumlich*) next to; (*außer*) apart from; **—beste(r,s** *a* first that ·comes along; (*zweitbeste*) next best; **N—e(r)** *mf* neighbour;

—e(r,s) next; (*nächstgelegen*) nearest; **N—enliebe** *f* love for one's fellow men; **—ens** *ad* shortly, soon; **—liegend** *a* (*lit*) nearest; (*fig*) obvious; **—möglich** *a* next possible.

nachsuchen ['na:xzu:xən] *vi:* um etw — ask or apply for sth.

Nacht [naxt] *f -,* ·e night.

Nachteil ['na:xtaıl] *m* disadvantage; **n—ig** *a* disadvantageous.

Nachthemd *nt* nightshirt; nightdress.

Nachtigall ['naxtıgal] *f -, -en* nightingale.

Nachtisch ['na:xtıʃ] *m see* Nachspeise.

nächtlich ['nɛçtlıç] *a* nightly.

Nach— *cpd:* **—trag** *m* -(e)s, -träge supplement; **n—tragen** *vt irreg* carry (jdm after sb); (*zufügen*) add; jdm etw **n—tragen** hold sth against sb; **n—tragend** *a* resentful; **n—träglich** *a,ad* later, subsequent(ly); ·additional(ly); **n—trauern** *vi:* jdm/etw **n—trauern** mourn the loss of sb/sth.

Nacht— *cpd:* **—ruhe** *f* sleep; **n—s** *ad* by night; **—schicht** *f* nightshift; **n—süber** ·*ad* during the night; **—tarif** *m* off-peak tariff; **—tisch** *m* · bedside table; **—topf** *m* chamberpot; **—wächter** *m* night watchman.

Nach— *cpd:* **—untersuchung** *f* checkup; **n—wachsen** *vi irreg* grow · again; **—wehen** *pl* afterpains *pl*; (*fig*) after-effects *pl*.

Nachweis ['na:xvaıs] *m* -es, -e proof; **n—bar** *a* provable, demonstrable; **n—en** ['na:xvaızən] *vt irreg* prove; jdm etw **n—en** point sth out to sb; **n—lich** *a* evident, demonstrable.

nach- cpd: **—winken** vi wave (jdm after sb); **—wirken** vi have after-effects; **N—wirkung** f after-effect; **N—wort** nt appendix; **N—wuchs** m offspring; (beruflich etc) new recruits pl; **—zahlen** vti pay extra; **N—zahlung** f additional payment; (zurückdatiert) back pay; **—zählen** vt count again; **N—zügler** m -s, - straggler.

Nacken ['nakən] m -s, - nape of the neck.

nackt [nakt] a naked; Tatsachen plain, bare; **N—heit** f nakedness; **N—kultur** f nudism.

Nadel ['naːdəl] f -, -n needle; (Steck-) pin; **—kissen** nt pincushion; **—öhr** nt eye of a needle; **—wald** m coniferous forest.

Nagel ['naːgəl] m -s, ⁻ nail; **—feile** f nailfile; **—haut** f cuticle; **—lack** m nail varnish; **n—n** vti nail; **n—neu** a brand-new; **—schere** f nail scissors pl.

nagen ['naːgən] vti gnaw.

Nagetier ['naːgiːtiːr] nt rodent.

nah(e) ['naː(ə)] a,ad (räumlich) near(by); Verwandte near; Freunde close; (zeitlich) near, close; prep +dat near (to), close to; **N—aufnahme** f close-up.

Nähe ['nɛːə] f - nearness, proximity; (Umgebung) vicinity; in der — close by; at hand; aus der — from close to.

nahe- cpd: **—bei** ad nearby; **—gehen** vi irreg grieve (jdm sb); **—kommen** vi irreg get close (jdm to sb); **—legen** vt: jdm etw **—legen** suggest sth to sb; **—liegen** vi irreg be obvious; **—liegend** a obvious; **—n** vir approach, draw near.

Näh- ['nɛː] cpd: **n—en** vti sew; **n—er** a,ad nearer; Erklärung, Erkundigung more detailed;

—ere(s) nt details pl, particulars pl; **—erei** f sewing, needlework; **—erin** f seamstress; **n—erkommen** vir irreg get closer; **n—ern** vr approach; **—erungswert** m approximate value.

nahe- cpd: **—stehen** vi irreg be close (jdm to sb); einer Sache **—stehen** sympathize with sth; **—stehend** a close; **—treten** vi irreg: jdm (zu) **—treten** offend sb; **—zu** ad nearly.

Näh- cpd: **—garn** nt thread; **—kasten** m workbox; **—maschine** f sewing machine; **—nadel** f needle.

nähren ['nɛːrən] vtr feed.

nahrhaft ['naːrhaft] a nourishing, nutritious.

Nähr- ['nɛːr] cpd: **—gehalt** m nutritional value; **—stoffe** pl nutrients pl.

Nahrung ['naːruŋ] f food; (fig auch) sustenance; **—smittel** nt foodstuffs pl; **—smittelindustrie** f food industry; **—ssuche** f search for food.

Nährwert m nutritional value.

Naht [naːt] f -, ⁻e seam; (Med) suture; (Tech) join; **n—los** a seamless; **n—los ineinander übergehen** follow without a gap.

Nah- cpd: **—verkehr** m local traffic; **—verkehrszug** m local train; **—ziel** nt immediate objective.

naiv [naˈiːf] a naive; **N—ität** [naiviˈtɛːt] f naivety.

Name ['naːmə] m -ns, -n name; im **—n von** on behalf of; **n—ns** ad by the name of; **n—ntlich** a by name; ad particularly, especially.

namhaft ['naːmhaft] a (berühmt) famed, renowned; (beträchtlich) considerable; **— machen** name.

nämlich ['nɛːmlɪç] ad that is to say,

namely; (denn) since; der/die/das
—e the same.

Napf [napf] *m* -(e)s, ˙̈e bowl, dish.

Narbe ['narbə] *f* —, -n scar.

narbig ['narbɪç] *a* scarred.

Narkose [nar'ko:zə] *f* —, -n
anaesthetic.

Narr [nar] *m* -en, -en fool; n—en
vt fool; —heit *f* foolishness.

Närr- ['nɛr] *cpd*: —in *f* fool;
n—isch a foolish, crazy.

Narzisse [nar'tsɪsə] *f* —, -n
narcissus; daffodil.

nasch- ['naʃ] *cpd*: —en *vti* nibble;
eat secretly; —haft *a* sweet-
toothed.

Nase ['na:zə] *f* —, -n nose;
—nbluten *nt* -s nosebleed; —nloch
nt nostril; —nrücken *nt* bridge of
the nose; —ntropfen *pl* nose drops
pl; n—weis *a* pert, cheeky;
(neugierig) nosey.

Nashorn ['na:shɔrn] *nt* rhinoceros.

naß [nas] *a* wet.

Nässe ['nɛsə] *f* - wetness; n—n *vt*
wet.

Naß- *cpd*: n—kalt *a* wet and cold;
—rasur *f* wet shave.

Nation [natsi'o:n] *f* nation.

national [natsio'na:l] *a* national;
N—hymne *f* national anthem;
—isieren [-'zi:rən] *vt* nationalize;
N—i'sierung *f* nationalization;
N—ismus [-'lɪsmus] *m* nationalism;
—istisch [-'lɪstɪʃ] *a* nationalistic;
N—i'tät *f* nationality;
N—mannschaft *f* national team;
N—sozialismus *m* national
socialism.

Natron ['na:trɔn] *nt* -s soda.

Natter ['natər] *f* —, -n adder.

Natur [na'tu:r] *f* nature;
(körperlich) constitution; —alien
[natu'ra:liən] *pl* natural produce; in

—alien in kind; —a'lismus *m*
naturalism; —erscheinung *f*
natural phenomenon or event;
n—farben *a* natural coloured;
n—gemäß *a* natural; —geschichte
f natural history; —gesetz *nt* law
of nature; —katastrophe *f* natural
disaster.

natürlich [na'ty:rlɪç] *a* natural; *ad*
naturally; —erweise *ad* naturally,
of course; N—keit *f* naturalness.

Natur- *cpd*: n—produkt *nt* natural
product; n—rein *a* natural, pure;
—schutzgebiet *nt* nature reserve;
—wissenschaft *f* natural science;
—wissenschaftler(in *f*) *m* scientist;
—zustand *m* natural state.

nautisch ['nautɪʃ] *a* nautical.

Navelorange [na:valorã:ʒə] *f*
navel orange.

Navigation [navigatsi'o:n] *f* navigation; —sfehler *m* navigational
error; —sinstrumente *pl* navigation
instruments *pl*.

Nazi ['na:tsi] *m* -s, -s Nazi.

Nebel ['ne:bəl] *m* -s, - fog, mist;
n—ig *a* foggy, misty;
—scheinwerfer *m* foglamp.

neben ['ne:bən] *prep* +*acc* or *dat*
next to; (außer) apart from,
besides; —an [ne:bən'an] *ad* next
door; N—anschluß *m* (Tel)
extension; —bei [ne:bən'bai] *ad* at
the same time; (außerdem)
additionally; (beiläufig)
incidentally; N—beschäftigung *f*
sideline; N—buhler(in *f*) *m* -s, -
rival; —einander [ne:bən'ai'nandər]
ad side by side; —einanderlegen *vt*
put next to each other; N—eingang
m side entrance; N—erscheinung *f*
side effect; N—fach *nt* subsidiary
subject; N—fluß *m* tributary;
N—geräusch *nt* (Rad)
atmospherics *pl*, interference;

—her [neːbən'heːr] ad (zusätzlich) besides; (gleichzeitig) at the same time; (daneben) alongside; —herfahren vi irreg drive alongside; N—kosten pl extra charges pl, extras pl; N—produkt nt byproduct; N—rolle f minor part; N—sache f trifle, side issue; —sächlich a minor, peripheral; N—straße f side street; N—zimmer nt adjoining room.

Necessaire [nesɛ'sɛːr] nt -s, -s (Näh—) needlework box; (Nagel—) manicure case.

neck- ['nɛk] cpd: —en vt tease; N—e'rei f teasing; —isch a coy; Einfall, Lied amusing.

Neffe ['nɛfə] m -n, -n nephew.

negativ [nega'tiːf] a negative; N— nt -s, -e (Phot) negative.

Neger ['neːgər] m -s, - negro; —in f negress.

negieren [ne'giːrən] vt (bestreiten) deny; (verneinen) negate.

nehmen ['neːmən] vt irreg take; jdn zu sich — take sb in; sich ernst — take o.s. seriously; nimm dir noch einmal help yourself.

Neid [naɪt] m -(e)s envy; —er m -s, - envier; n—isch a envious, jealous.

neigen ['naɪgən] vt incline, lean; Kopf bow; vi: zu etw — tend to sth.

Neigung f (des Geländes) slope; (Tendenz) tendency, inclination; (Vorliebe) liking; (Zuneigung) affection; —swinkel m angle of inclination.

nein [naɪn] ad no.

Nelke ['nɛlkə] f -, -n carnation, pink; (Gewürz) clove.

Nenn- ['nɛn] cpd: n—en vt irreg name; (mit Namen) call; n—enswert a worth mentioning;

—er m -s, - denominator; —ung f naming; —wert m nominal value; (Comm) par.

Neon ['neːɔn] nt -s neon; —licht nt neon light; —röhre f neon tube.

Nerv [nɛrf] m -s, -en nerve; jdm auf die —en gehen get on sb's nerves; n—enaufreibend a nerve-racking; —enbündel nt bundle of nerves; —enheilanstalt f mental home; n—enkrank a mentally ill; —enschwäche f neurasthenia; —ensystem nt nervous system; —enzusammenbruch m nervous breakdown; n—ös [nɛr'vøːs] a nervous; —osi'tät f nervousness; n—ötend a nerve-racking; Arbeit soul-destroying.

Nerz [nɛrts] m -es, -e mink.

Nessel ['nɛsəl] f -, -n nettle.

Nest [nɛst] nt -(e)s, -er nest; (col: Ort) dump; n—eln vi fumble or fiddle about (an + dat with).

nett [nɛt] a nice; (freundlich auch) kind; —erweise ad kindly; —o ad net.

Netz [nɛts] nt -es, -e net; (Gepäck—) rack; (Einkaufs—) string bag; (Spinnen—) web; (System) network; jdm ins — gehen (fig) fall into sb's trap; —anschluß m mains connection; —haut f retina.

neu [nɔʏ] a new; Sprache, Geschichte modern; seit —estem (since) recently; — schreiben rewrite, write again; N—anschaffung f new purchase or acquisition; —artig a new kind of; N—auflage f, N—ausgabe f new edition; N—bau m -s, -ten new building; —erdings ad (kürzlich) (since) recently; (von neuem) again; N—erung f innovation, new departure; N—gier f curiosity;

—**gierig** a curious; N—**heit** f newness; novelty; N—**igkeit** f news; N—**jahr** nt New Year; —**lich** ad recently, the other day; N—**ling** in novice; N—**mond** m new moon.

neun [nɔyn] num nine; —**zehn** num nineteen; —**zig** num ninety.

neureich a nouveau riche; N—**e**(r) mf nouveau riche.

Neur— cpd: —**ose** [nɔy'ro:zə] f —, -n neurosis; —**otiker** [nɔy'ro:tikər] m -s, — neurotic; n—**otisch** a neurotic.

Neutr— cpd: n—**al** [nɔy'tra:l] a neutral; —**alität** f neutrality; n—**alisieren** vt neutralize; —**on** ['nɔytrɔn] nt -s, -en neutron; —**um** ['nɔytrʊm] nt -s, -a or -en neuter.

Neu— cpd: —**wert** m purchase price; —**zeit** f modern age; n—**zeitlich** a modern, recent.

nicht [nɪçt] ad not; pref non—; — wahr? isn't it/he?, don't you etc; — **doch!** don't!; —**berühren!** do not touch! was du — sagst! the things you say!; N—**achtung** f disregard; N—**angriffspakt** m non-aggression pact.

Nichte [ˈnɪçtə] f —, -n niece.

nichtig ['nɪçtɪç] a (ungültig) null, void; (wertlos) futile; N—**keit** f nullity, invalidity; (Sinnlosigkeit) futility.

Nicht— cpd: —**raucher**(in f) m non-smoker; n—**rostend** a stainless.

nichts [nɪçts] pron nothing; für — und wieder — for nothing at all; N— nt -s nothingness; (pej: Person) . nonentity; —**destoweniger** ad nevertheless; N—**nutz** m -es, -e good-for-nothing; —**nutzig** a worthless, useless; —**sagend** a meaningless; N—**tun** nt -s idleness.

Nickel ['nɪkəl] nt -s nickel.

nicken ['nɪkən] vi nod.

Nickerchen ['nɪkərçən] nt nap.

nie [ni:] ad never; — **wieder** or mehr never again; — **und nimmer** never ever.

nieder ['ni:dər] low; (gering) inferior; ad down; N—**gang** m decline; —**gehen** vi irreg descend; (Aviat) come down; (Regen) fall; (Boxer) go down; —**geschlagen** a depressed, dejected; N—**geschlagenheit** f depression, dejection; N—**lage** f defeat; (Lager) depot; (Filiale) branch; —**lassen** vr irreg (sich setzen) sit down; (an Ort) settle (down); (Arzt, Rechtsanwalt) set up a practice; N—**lassung** f settlement; (Comm) branch; —**legen** vt lay down; Arbeit stop; Amt resign; —**machen** vt mow down; N—**schlag** m (Chem) precipitate, sediment; (Met) precipitation; rain-fall; (Boxen) knockdown; —**schlagen** irreg vt Gegner beat down; Gegenstand knock down; Augen lower; (Jur) Prozeß dismiss; Aufstand put down; vr (Chem) precipitate; N—**schrift** f transcription; —**trächtig** a base, mean; N—**trächtigkeit** f meanness, baseness; outrage; N—**ung** f (Geog) depression; flats pl.

niedlich ['ni:tlɪç] a sweet, nice, cute.

niedrig ['ni:drɪç] a low; Stand lowly, humble; Gesinnung mean.

niemals ['ni:ma:ls] ad never.

niemand ['ni:mant] pron nobody, no one; N—**sland** nt no-man's land.

Niere ['ni:rə] f —, -n kidney; —**nentzündung** f kidney infection.

nieseln ['ni:zəln] vi drizzle.

niesen ['ni:zən] vi sneeze.

Niet ['ni:t] m -(e)s, -e & f -, -n (Tech) rivet; (Los) blank; (Reinfall) flop; (Mensch) failure; **n—en** vt rivet.

Nihil- cpd: **—ismus** [nihi'lɪsmʊs] m nihilism; **—ist** [nihi'lɪst] m nihilist; **n—istisch** a nihilistic.

Nikotin [niko'ti:n] nt -s nicotine.

Nilpferd ['ni:lpfe:rt] nt hippopotamus.

nimmersatt ['nɪmɐzat] a insatiable; **N—** m -(e)s, -e glutton.

nippen ['nɪpən] vti sip.

Nippsachen ['nɪpzaxən] pl knick-knacks pl.

nirgends ['nɪrgənts], **nirgendwo** ['nɪrgəntvo:] ad nowhere.

Nische ['ni:ʃə] f -, -n niche.

nisten ['nɪstən] vi nest.

Nitrat [ni'tra:t] nt -(e)s, -e nitrate.

Niveau [ni'vo:] nt -s, -s level.

Nixe ['nɪksə] f -, -n water nymph.

noch [nɔx] ad still; (in Zukunft) still, yet; one day; (außerdem) else; cj nor; — nie never (yet); — nicht not yet; immer — still; — heute today; — vor einer Woche only a week ago; und wenn es — so schwer ist however hard it is; — einmal again; — dreimal three more times; — und — heaps of; (mit Verb) again and again; —mal(s) ad again, once more; —malig a repeated.

Nockenwelle ['nɔkənvɛlə] f camshaft.

Nominativ ['no:minati:f] m -s, -e nominative.

nominell [nomi'nɛl] a nominal.

Nonne ['nɔnə] f -, -n nun; **—nkloster** nt convent.

Nord(en) ['nɔrd(ən)] m -s north; **n—isch** a northern; **n—ische**

Kombination (Skî) nordic combination.

nördlich ['nœrtlɪç] a northerly, northern; — von, — prep +gen (to the) north of.

Nord- cpd: **—pol** m North Pole; **n—wärts** ad northwards.

Nörg- ['nœrg] cpd: **—e'lei** f grumbling; **n—eln** vi grumble; **—ler** m -s, - grumbler.

Norm [nɔrm] f -, -en norm; (Größenvorschrift) standard; **n—al** [nɔr'ma:l] a normal; **n—alerweise** ad normally; **n—ali'sieren** vt normalize; vr return to normal; **n—en** vt standardize.

Not [no:t] f -, ¨e need; (Mangel) want; (Mühe) trouble; (Zwang) necessity; —zur — if necessary; (gerade noch) just about; — ar [no'ta:r] m -s, -e notary; **n—ari'ell** a notarial; **—ausgang** m emergency exit; **—behelf** m -s, -e makeshift; **—bremse** f emergency brake; **n—dürftig** a scanty; (behelfsmäßig) makeshift; sich **n—dürftig verständigen** just about understand each other.

Note ['no:tə] f -, -n note; (Sch) mark; **—nblatt** nt sheet of music; **—nschlüssel** m clef; **—nständer** m music stand.

Not- cpd: **—fall** m (case of) emergency; **n—falls** ad if need be; **n—gedrungen** a necessary, unavoidable; **etw n—gedrungen machen** be forced to do sth.

notieren [no'ti:rən] vt note; (Comm) quote.

Notierung f (Comm) quotation.

nötig ['nø:tɪç] a necessary; etw — haben need sth; **n—en** vt compel, force; **—enfalls** ad if necessary.

Notiz [no'ti:ts] f -, -en note; (Zeitungs—) item; — nehmen take notice; **—buch** nt notebook; **—zettel** m piece of paper.

Not- cpd: **'—lage** f crisis, emergency; **n—landen** vi make a forced or emergency landing; **n—leidend** a needy; **—lösung** f temporary solution; **—lüge** f white lie.

notorisch [no'to:rɪʃ] a notorious.

Not- cpd: **—ruf** m emergency call; **—stand** m state of emergency; **—standsgesetz** nt emergency law; **—unterkunft** f emergency accommodation; **—verband** m emergency dressing; **—wehr** f self-defence; **n—wendig** a necessary; **—wendigkeit** f necessity; **—zucht** f rape.

Novelle [no'vɛlə] f -, **-n** short story; (Jur) amendment.

November [no'vɛmbər] m -(s), - November.

Nu [nu:] m: **im — in** an instant.

Nuance [ny'ã:sə] f -, **-n** nuance.

nüchtern ['nʏçtərn] a sober; Magen empty; Urteil prudent; **N—heit** f sobriety.

Nudel ['nu:dəl] f -, **-n** noodle.

Null [nul] f -, **-en** nought, zero; (pej: Mensch) washout; **n— num** zero; Fehler no; **n— Uhr** midnight; **n— und nichtig** null and

void; **—pünkt** m zero; auf dem **—punkt** at zero.

numerieren [nume'ri:rən] vt number.

numerisch [nu'me:rɪʃ] a numerical.

Nummer ['numər] f -, **-n** number; **—nscheibe** f telephone dial; **—nschild** nt (Aut) number or. license (US) plate.

nun [nu:n] ad now; interj well.

nur [nu:r] ad just, only.

Nuß [nus] f -, **Nüsse** nut; **—baum** m walnut tree; hazelnut tree; **—knacker** m -s, - nutcracker.

Nüster ['nʏstər] f -, **-n** nostril.

Nutte ['nutə] f -, **-n** tart.

nutz [nuts], **nütze** ['nʏtsə] a: zu nichts **— sein** be useless; **—bar** a: **—bar machen** utilize; **N—barmachung** v utilization; **—bringend** a profitable; **—en,** **nützen** vt use (zu etw for sth); vi be of use; was nützt es? what's the use?, what use is it?; **N—en** m usefulness; profit; von **N—en** useful.

nützlich ['nʏtslɪç] a useful; **N—keit** f usefulness.

Nutz- cpd: **n—los** a useless; **—losigkeit** f uselessness; **—nießer** m -s, - beneficiary.

Nymphe ['nʏmfə] f -, **-n** nymph.

O

O, o [o:] nt O, o.

Oase [o'a:zə] f -, **-n** oasis.

ob [ɔp] cj if, whether; **— das wohl wahr ist?** can that be true?; **und —!** you bet!

Obacht ['o:baxt] f: **—geben** pay attention.

Obdach ['ɔpdax] nt -(e)s shelter, lodging; **o—los** a homeless; **—lose(r)** mf homeless person.

Obduktion [ɔpdʊktsi'o:n] f postmortem.

obduzieren [ɔpdu'tsi:rən] vt do a post mortem on.

O-Beine ['o:baɪnə] pl bow or bandy legs pl.

oben ['o:bən] ad above; (*in Haus*) upstairs; nach — up; von — down; — ohne topless; jdn von — bis unten ansehen look sb up and down; Befehl von — orders from above; —an ad at the top; —auf ad up above, on the top; a (*munter*) in form; —drein ad into the bargain; —erwähnt, —genannt a above-mentioned; —hin ad cursorily, superficially.

Ober ['o:bər] m -s, - waiter; —arm m upper arm; —arzt m senior physician; —aufsicht f supervision; —befehl m supreme command; —befehlshaber m commander-in-chief; —begriff m generic term; —bekleidung f outer clothing; —'bürgermeister m lord mayor; —deck nt upper or top deck; o—e(r,s) a upper; die —en the bosses; (*Eccl*) the superiors; —fläche f surface; o—flächlich a superficial; —geschoß nt upper storey; o—halb ad, prep +gen above; —haupt nt head, chief; —haus nt upper house; House of Lords; —hemd nt shirt; —herrschaft f supremacy, sovereignty; —in f matron; (*Eccl*) Mother Superior; o—irdisch a above ground; *Leitung* overhead; —kellner m head waiter; —kiefer m upper jaw; —kommando nt supreme command; —körper m trunk, upper part of body; —leitung f direction; (*Elec*) overhead cable; —licht nt skylight; —lippe f upper lip; —prima f -, -primen final year of secondary school; —schenkel m thigh; —schicht f upper classes pl; —schule f grammar school (*Brit*),

high school (*US*); —schwester f (*Med*) matron; —sekunda f -, -sekunden seventh year of secondary school.

Oberst ['o:bərst] m -en or -s, -en or -e colonel; o—e(r,s) a very top, topmost.

Ober- cpd: —stufe f upper school; —teil m upper part; —tertia ['-tɛrtsia] f -, -tertien fifth year of secondary school; —wasser nt: —wasser haben/bekommen be/get on top (of things); —weite f bust/chest measurement.

obgleich [ɔp'glaɪç] cj although.

Obhut ['ɔphu:t] f - care, protection; in jds — sein be in sb's care.

obig ['o:bɪç] a above.

Objekt [ɔp'jɛkt] nt -(e)s, -e object; —iv [-'ti:f] nt -s, -e lens; o—iv a objective; —ivi'tät f objectivity.

Oblate [o'bla:tə] f -, -n (*Gebäck*) wafer; (*Eccl*) host.

obligatorisch [ɔbliga'to:rɪʃ] a compulsory, obligatory.

Oboe [o'bo:ə] f -, -n oboe.

Obrigkeit ['o:brɪçkaɪt] f (*Behörden*) authorities pl, administration; (*Regierung*) government.

obschon [ɔp'ʃo:n] cj although.

Observatorium [ɔpzɛrva'to:rium] nt observatory.

obskur [ɔps'ku:r] a obscure; (*verdächtig*) dubious.

Obst [o:pst] nt -(e)s fruit; —bau m fruit-growing; —baum m fruit tree; —garten m orchard; —händler m fruiterer, fruit merchant; —kuchen m fruit tart.

obszön [ɔps'tsø:n] a obscene; o—i'tät f obscenity.

obwohl [ɔp'vo:l] cj although.

Ochse ['ɔksə] m -n, -n ox; **o—n** vti (col) cram, swot; **—schwanzsuppe** f oxtail soup; **—nzunge** f oxtongue.

öd(e) ['ø:d(ə)] a Land waste, barren; (fig) dull; **Ö—e** f -, -n desert, waste(land); (fig) tedium.

oder ['o:dər] cj or.

Ofen ['o:fən] m -s, -̈ oven; (Heiz—) fire, heater; (Kohle—) stove; (Hoch—) furnace; (Herd) cooker, stove; **—rohr** nt stovepipe.

offen ['ɔfən] a open; (aufrichtig) frank; Stelle vacant; **— gesagt** to be honest; **—bar** a obvious; **—baren** [ɔfən'ba:rən] vt reveal, manifest; **O—barung** f (Rel) revelation; **—bleiben** vi irreg (Fenster) stay open; (Frage, Entscheidung) remain open; **—halten** vt irreg keep open; **O—heit** f candour, frankness; **—herzig** a candid, frank; Kleid revealing; **O—herzigkeit** f frankness; **—kundig** a well-known; (klar) evident; **—lassen** vt irreg leave open; **—sichtlich** a evident, obvious; **—siv** [ɔfɛn'zi:f] a offensive; **O—sive** f -, -n offensive; **—stehen** vi irreg be open; (Rechnung) be unpaid; es steht Ihnen —, es zu tun you are at liberty to do it.

öffentlich ['œfəntlɪç] a public; **Ö—keit** f (Leute) public; (einer Versammlung etc) public nature; **in aller Ö—keit** in public; **an die Ö—keit dringen** reach the public ear.

offerieren [ɔfe'ri:rən] vt offer.

Offerte [ɔ'fɛrtə] f -, -n offer.

offiziell [ɔfitsi'ɛl] a official.

Offizier [ɔfi'tsi:r] m -s, -e officer; **—skasino** nt officers' mess.

öffnen ['œfnən] vtr open; **jdm die Tür —** open the door for sb.

Öffner ['œfnər] m -s, - opener.

Öffnung ['œfnʊŋ] f opening; **—szeiten** pl opening times pl.

oft [ɔft] ad often.

öfter ['œftər] ad more often or frequently; **—s** ad often, frequently.

oftmals ad often, frequently.

ohne ['o:nə] prep + acc, cj without; **das ist nicht —** (col) it's not bad; **— weiteres** without a second thought; (sofort) immediately; **—dies** [o:nə'di:s] ad anyway; **—einander** [o:nə?aɪ'nandər] ad without each other; **—gleichen** [o:nə'glaɪçən] a unsurpassed, without equal; **—hin** [o:nə'hɪn] ad anyway, in any case.

Ohnmacht ['o:nmaxt] f faint; (fig) impotence; **in —** fallen faint.

ohnmächtig ['o:nmɛçtɪç] a in a faint, unconscious; (fig) weak, impotent; **sie ist —** she has fainted.

Ohr [o:r] nt -(e)s, -en ear; (Gehör) hearing.

Öhr [ø:r] nt -(e)s, -e eye.

Ohr- cpd: —enarzt m ear specialist; **o—enbetäubend** a deafening; **—enschmalz** nt earwax; **—enschmerzen** pl earache; **—enschützer** m -s, - earmuff; **—feige** f slap on the face; box on the ears; **o—feigen** vt slap sb's face; box sb's ears; **—läppchen** nt ear lobe; **—ringe** pl earrings pl; **—wurm** m earwig; (Mus) catchy tune.

okkupieren [ɔku'pi:rən] vt occupy.

ökonomisch [øko'no:mɪʃ] a economical.

Oktanzahl [ɔk'ta:ntsa:l] f (bei Benzin) octane.

Oktave [ɔk'ta:fə] f -, -n octave.

Oktober [ɔk'to:bər] *m* ´ -(s), -
October.

ökumenisch [øku'me:nɪʃ] *a*
ecumenical.

Öl [ø:l] *nt* -(e)s, -e oil; —baum *m*
olive tree; ö—en *vt* oil; (Tech)
lubricate; —farbe *f* oil paint;
—feld *nt* oilfield; —film *m* film of
oil; —heizung *f* oil-fired central
heating; ö—ig *a* oily.

oliv [o'li:f] *a* olive-green; **O—e**
[o'li:və] *f* -, -n olive.

Öl- *cpd:* —meßstab *m* dipstick;
—pest *f* oil pollution; —sardine *f*
sardine; —scheich *m* oil sheik;
—standanzeiger *m* (Aut) oil gauge;
—ung *f* lubrication; oiling; (Eccl)
anointment; die Letzte —ung
Extreme Unction; —wechsel *m* oil
change; —zeug *nt* oilskins *pl*.

Olymp- [o'lymp] *cpd:* —iade
[-ia:də] *f* Olympic Games *pl*;
—iasieger(in *f*) [-iazi:gər(ɪn)] *m*
Olympic champion; —iateil-
nehmer(in *f*) *m*, —ionike [-io'ni:kə]
m, —io'nikin *f* Olympic competitor;
o—isch *a* Olympic.

Oma ['o:ma] *f* -, -s (col) granny.

Omelett [ɔm(ə')'lɛt] *nt* -(e)s, -s,
Omelette *f* omlet(te).

Omen ['o:mən] *nt* -s, - or **Omina**
omen.

Omnibus ['ɔmnibus] *m* (omni)bus.

Onanie [ona'ni:] *f* masturbation;
o—ren *vi* masturbate.

Onkel ['ɔŋkəl] *m* -s, - uncle.

Opa ['o:pa] *m* -s, -s (col) grandpa.

Opal [o'pa:l] *m* -s, -e opal.

Oper ['o:pər] *f* -, -n opera; opera
house; —ation [operatsi'o:n] *f*
operation; —ationssaal *m*
operating theatre; —ette [ope'rɛtə]
f operetta; o—ieren [ope'ri:rən] *vti*
operate; —nglas *nt* opera glasses
pl; —nhaus *nt* opera house;

—nsänger(in *f*) *m* operatic singer.

Opfer ['ɔpfər] *nt* -s, - sacrifice;
(Mensch) victim; o—n *vt* sacrifice;
—stock *m* (Eccl) offertory box;
—ung *f* sacrifice.

Opium ['o:pium] *nt* -s opium.

opponieren [ɔpo'ni:rən] *vi* oppose
(gegen jdn/etw sb/sth).

opportun [ɔpɔr'tu:n] *a* opportune;
O—ismus [-'nɪsmʊs] *m*
opportunism; **O—ist** [-'nɪst] *m*
opportunist.

Opposition [ɔpozitsi'o:n] *f*
opposition; o—ell [-'nɛl] *a*
opposing.

Optik ['ɔptɪk] *f* optics *sing*; —er *m*
-s, - optician.

optimal [ɔpti'ma:l] *a* optimal,
optimum.

Optimismus [ɔpti'mɪsmʊs] *m*
optimism.

Optimist [ɔpti'mɪst] *m* optimist;
o—isch *a* optimistic.

optisch ['ɔptɪʃ] *a* optical.

Orakel [o'ra:kəl] *nt* -s, - oracle.

Orange [o'rɑ̃:ʒə] *f* -, -n orange;
o—e *a* orange; —ade [orɑ̃'ʒa:də] *f*
orangeade; —at [orɑ̃'ʒa:t] *nt* -s, -e
candied peel; —nmarmelade *f*
marmelade; —nschale orange peel.

Orchester [ɔr'kɛstər] *nt* -s, -
orchestra.

Orchidee [ɔrçi'de:ə] *f* -, -n orchid.

Orden ['ɔrdən] *m* -s, - (Eccl) order;
(Mil) decoration; —sschwester *f*
nun.

ordentlich ['ɔrdəntlɪç] *a*
(anständig) decent, respectable;
(geordnet) tidy, neat; (col:
annehmbar) not bad; (col: tüchtig)
real, proper; — er Professor (full)
professor; *ad* properly; **O—keit** *f*
respectability; tidiness, neatness.

Ordinalzahl [ɔrdi'naːltsaːl] *f* ordinal number.

ordinär [ɔrdi'nɛːr] *a* common, vulgar.

ordnen ['ɔrdnən] *vt* order, put in order.

Ordner *m* -s, - steward; (*Comm*) file.

Ordnung *f* order; (*Ordnen*) ordering; (*Geordnetsein*) tidiness; **o—sgemäß** a proper, according to the rules; **o—shalber** ad as a matter of form; **—sliebe** *f* tidiness, .orderliness; **—sstrafe** *f* fine; **o—swidrig** a contrary to the rules, irregular; **—szahl** *f* ordinal number.

Organ [ɔr'gaːn] *nt* -s, -e organ; (*Stimme*) voice; **—isation** [-izatsi'oːn] *f* organisation; **—isationstalent** *nt* organizing ability; (*Person*) good organizer; **—isator** [-i'zaːtor] *m* organizer; **o—isch** a organic; **o—isieren** [-i'ziːrən] *vt* organize, arrange; (*col: beschaffen*) acquire; *vr* organize; **—ismus** ['nismus] *m* organism; **—ist** ['nist] *m* organist; **—verpflanzung** *f* transplantation (of organs).

Orgasmus [ɔr'gasmus] *m* orgasm.

Orgel ['ɔrgəl] *f* -, -n organ; **—pfeife** *f* organ pipe; wie die **—pfeifen** stehen stand in order of height.

Orgie ['ɔrgiə] *f* orgy.

Orient ['oːriɛnt] *m* -s Orient, east; **—ale** [-'taːlə] *m* -n Oriental; **o—alisch** ['taːlɪʃ] a oriental; **o—ieren** [-'tiːrən] *vt* (*örtlich*) locate; (*fig*) inform; *vr* find one's way *or* bearings; inform oneself; **—ierung** [-'tiːruŋ] *f* orientation; (*fig*) information; **—ierungssinn** *m* sense of direction.

original [origi'naːl] a original; **O— nt** -s, -e original; **O—fassung** *f* original version; **O—ität** *f* originality.

originell [origi'nɛl] a original.

Orkan [ɔr'kaːn] *m* -(e)s, -e hurricane.

Ornament [ɔrna'mɛnt] *nt* decoration, ornament; **—al** [-'taːl] a decorative, ornamental.

Ort [ɔrt] *m* -(e)s, -e *or* ¨er place; an — und Stelle on the spot; **o—en** *vt* locate.

ortho- [ɔrto] *cpd:* **—dox** ['dɔks] a orthodox; **O—graphie** [-gra'fiː] *f* spelling, orthography; **—'graphisch** a orthographic; **O—päde** [-'pɛːdə] *m* -n, -n orthopaedic specialist, orthopaedist; **O—pädie** [-pɛ'diː] *f* orthopaedics *sing*; **o—'pädisch** a orthopaedic.

örtlich ['œrtlɪç] a local; **Ö—keit** *f* locality.

Orts- *cpd:* **—sangabe** *f* (name of the) town; **o—sansässig** a local; **—schaft** *f* village, small town; **o—sfremd** a non-local; **—sfremde(r)** *mf* stranger; **—sgespräch** *nt* local (phone)call; **—sname** *m* place-name; **—snetz** *nt* (*Tel*) local telephone exchange area; **—ssinn** *m* sense of direction; **—szeit** *f* local time; **—ung** *f* locating.

Öse ['øːzə] *f* -, -n loop, eye.

Ost- [ɔst] *cpd:* **—block** *m* (*Pol*) Eastern bloc; **o—en** *m* -s east; **o—entativ** [ɔstɛnta'tiːf] a pointed, ostentatious.

Oster- ['oːstər] *cpd:* **—ei** *nt* Easter egg; **—fest** *nt* Easter; **—glocke** *f* daffodil; **—hase** *m* Easter bunny; **—montag** *m* Easter Monday; **—n** *nt* -s, - Easter; **—sonntag** *m* Easter Day *or* Sunday.

östlich ['œstlɪç] a eastern, easterly.

Ost- cpd: —see f Baltic Sea; o—wärts ad eastwards; —wind m east wind.

oszillieren [ɔstsɪˈliːrən] vi oscillate.

Otter [ˈɔtər] m -s, - otter; f -, -n (Schlange) adder.

Ouvertüre [uvɛrˈtyːrə] f -, -n overture.

oval [oˈvaːl] a oval.

Ovation [ovatsiˈoːn] f ovation.

Ovulation [ovulatsiˈoːn] f ovulation.

Oxyd [ɔˈksyːt] nt -(e)s, -e oxide; o—ieren [ɔksyˈdiːrən] vti oxidize; —ierung f oxidization.

Ozean [ˈoːtseaːn] m -s, -e ocean; —dampfer m (ocean-going) liner; o—isch [otseˈaːnɪʃ] a oceanic.

Ozon [oˈtsoːn] nt -s ozone.

P

P, p [peː] nt P, p.

Paar [paːr] nt -(e)s, -e pair; (Ehe—) couple; ein p— a few; p—en vtr couple; Tiere mate; —lauf m pair skating; p—mal ad: ein p—mal a few times; —ung f combination; mating; p—weise ad in pairs; in couples.

Pacht [paxt] f -, -en lease; p—en vt lease.

Pächter [ˈpɛçtər] m -s, - lease-holder, tenant.

Pack [pak] m -(e)s, -e or ⁻e bundle, pack; nt -(e)s (pej) mob, rabble.

Päckchen [ˈpɛkçən] nt small package; (Zigaretten) packet; (Post—) small parcel.

Pack- cpd: p—en vt pack; (fassen) grasp, seize; (col: schaffen) manage; (fig: fesseln) grip; —en m -s, - bundle; (fig: Menge) heaps of; —esel m (lit, fig) packhorse; —papier nt brown paper, wrapping paper; —ung f packet; (Pralinen—) box; (Med) compress.

Pädagog- [pɛdaˈgoːg] cpd: —e m —n, -n teacher; —ik f education; p—isch a educational, pedagogical.

Paddel [ˈpadəl] nt -s, - paddle;

—boot nt canoe; p—n vi paddle.

paffen [ˈpafən] vti puff.

Page [ˈpaːʒə] m -n, -n page; —nkopf m pageboy.

Paillette [parˈjɛtə] f sequin.

Paket [paˈkeːt] nt -(e)s, -e packet; (Post—) parcel; —karte f dispatch note; —post f parcel post; —schalter m parcels counter.

Pakt [pakt] m -(e)s, -e pact.

Palast [paˈlast] m -es, Paläste palace.

Palette [paˈlɛtə] f palette; (Lade—) pallet.

Palme [ˈpalmə] f -, -n palm (tree).

Palmsonntag m Palm Sunday.

Pampelmuse [pampəlmuˈzə] f -, -n grapefruit.

pampig [ˈpampɪç] a (col: frech) fresh.

panieren [paˈniːrən] vt (Cook) coat with egg and breadcrumbs.

Paniermehl [paˈniːrmeːl] nt breadcrumbs pl.

Panik [ˈpaːnɪk] f panic.

panisch [ˈpaːnɪʃ] a panic-stricken.

Panne [ˈpanə] f -, -n (Aut etc) breakdown; (Mißgeschick) slip.

panschen [ˈpanʃən] vi splash about; vt water down.

Panther ['pantər] m -s, - panther.

Pantoffel [pan'tɔfəl] m -s, -n slipper; —held m (col) henpecked husband.

Pantomime [panto'mi:mə] f -, -n mime.

Panzer ['pantsər] m -s, - armour; (Platte) armour plate; (Fahrzeug) tank; —glas nt bulletproof glass; p—n vtr armour; (fig) arm o.s.; —schrank m strongbox.

Papa [pa'pa:] m -s, -s (col) dad, daddy; —gei [-'gai] m -s, -en parrot.

Papier [pa'pi:r] nt -s, -e paper; (Wert—) share; —fabrik f paper mill; —geld nt paper money; —korb m wastepaper basket; —krieg m red tape; angry correspondence; —tüte f paper bag.

Papp- [pap] cpd: —deckel m, —e f -, -n cardboard; —einband m pasteboard; —el f -, -n poplar; p—en vti (col) stick; —enstiel m (col): keinen —enstiel wert sein not be worth a thing; für einen —enstiel bekommen get for a song; p—erlapapp interj rubbish; p—ig a sticky; —maché [-ma'ʃe:] nt -s, -s papier-mâché.

Paprika [paprika] m -s, -s (Gewürz) paprika; (—schote) pepper.

Papst [pa:pst] m -(e)s, ⁀e pope.

päpstlich ['pɛ:pstlɪç] a papal.

Parabel [pa'ra:bəl] f -, -n parable; (Math) parabola.

Parade [pa'ra:də] f (Mil) parade, review; (Sport) parry; —marsch m march-past; —schritt m goose-step.

Paradies [para'di:s] nt -es, -e paradise; p—isch a heavenly.

paradox [para'dɔks] a paradoxical; P— nt -es, -e paradox.

Paragraph [para'gra:f] m -en, -en paragraph; (Jur) section.

parallel [para'le:l] a parallel; P—e f parallel.

paramilitärisch [paramili'tɛ:rɪʃ] a paramilitary.

Paranuß ['pa:ranʊs] f Brazil nut.

paraphieren [para'fi:rən] vt Vertrag initial.

Parasit [para'zi:t] m -en, -en (lit, fig) parasite.

parat [pa'ra:t] a ready.

Pärchen ['pɛːrçən] nt couple.

Parfüm [par'fy:m] nt -s, -s or -e perfume; —erie [-ə'ri:] f perfumery; —flasche f scent bottle; p—ieren [-'mi:rən] vt scent, perfume.

parieren [pa'ri:rən] vt parry; vi (col) obey.

Parität [pari'tɛ:t] f parity.

Park [park] m -s, -s park; —anlage f park; (um Gebäude) grounds pl; p—en vti park; —ett [par'kɛt] nt -(e)s, -e parquet (floor); (Theat) stalls pl; —haus nt multistorey car park; —lücke f parking space; —platz m parking place; car park, parking lot (US); —scheibe f parking disc; —uhr f parking meter; —verbot nt no parking.

Parlament [parla'mɛnt] nt parliament; —arier [-'ta:riər] m -s, - parliamentarian; p—arisch [-'ta:rɪʃ] a parliamentary; —sbeschluß m vote of parliament; —smitglied nt member of parliament; —ssitzung f sitting (of parliament).

Parodie [paro'di:] f parody; p—ren vt parody.

Parole [pa'ro:lə] f -, -n password; (Wahlspruch) motto.

Partei [par'tai] f party; — ergreifen für jdn take sb's side; —führung f party leadership; —genosse m party member; **p—isch** *a* partial, biased; **p—los** *a* neutral; **—nahme** *f* -, -n support, taking the part of; **—tag** *m* party conference.

Parterre [par'tɛr] *nt* -s, -s ground floor; (Theat) stalls *pl.*

Partie [par'ti:] *f* part; (Spiel) game; (Ausflug) outing; (Mann, Frau) catch; (Comm) lot; mit von der — sein join in.

Partikel [par'ti:kəl] *f* -, -n particle.

Partisan [parti'za:n] *m* -s or -en, -en partisan.

Partitur [parti'tu:r] *f* (Mus) score.

Partizip [parti'tsi:p] *nt* -s, -ien participle.

Partner(in *f*) ['partnər] *m* -s, - partner; **p—schaftlich** *a* as partners.

Party ['pa:rti] *f* -, -s or **Parties** party.

Parzelle [par'tsɛlə] *f* plot, allotment.

Paß [pas] *m* -sses, ⁻sse pass; (Ausweis) passport.

Pass- *cpd*: **p—abel** [pa'sa:bəl] *a* passable, reasonable; **—age** [pa'sa:ʒə] *f* -, -n passage; **—agier** [pasa'ʒi:r] *m* -s, -e passenger; **—agierdampfer** *m* passenger steamer; **—agierflugzeug** *nt* airliner; **—ant** [pa'sant] *m* passer-by.

Paß- *cpd*: **—amt** *nt* passport office; **—bild** *nt* passport photograph.

passen ['pasən] *vi* (Farbe) go (zu with); (auf Frage, Cards, Sport) pass; **das paßt mir nicht** that doesn't suit me; **er paßt nicht zu dir** he's not right for you; **—d** *a* suitable; (zusammen-) matching; (angebracht) fitting; **Zeit convenient.**

passier- [pa'si:r] *cpd*: **—bar** *a* passable; **—t** *vt* pass; (durch Sieb) strain; *vi* happen; **P—schein** *m* pass, permit.

Passion [pasi'o:n] *f* passion; **p—iert** [-'i:rt] *a* enthusiastic, passionate; **—sspiel** *nt* Passion Play.

passiv ['pasi:f] *a* passive; **P—** *nt* -s, -e passive; **P—a** *pl* (Comm) liabilities *pl*; **P—ität** *f* passiveness.

Paß- *cpd*: **—kontrolle** *f* passport control; **—stelle** *f* passport office; **—straße** *f* (mountain) pass; **—zwang** *m* requirement to carry a passport.

Paste ['pastə] *f* -, -n paste.

Pastell [pas'tɛl] *nt* -(e)s, -e pastel.

Pastete [pas'te:tə] *f* -, -n pie.

pasteurisieren [pastøri'zi:rən] *vt* pasteurize.

Pastor ['pastor] *m* vicar; pastor, minister.

Pate ['pa:tə] *m* -n, -n godfather; **—nkind** *nt* godchild.

Patent [pa'tɛnt] *nt* -(e)s, -e patent; (Mil) commission; **p—** *a* clever; **—amt** *nt* patent office; **p—ieren** [-'ti:rən] *vt* patent; **—inhaber** *m* patentee; **—schutz** *m* patent right.

Pater ['pa:tər] *m* -s, - or **Patres** (Eccl) Father.

pathetisch [pa'te:tɪʃ] *a* emotional; bombastic.

Pathologe [pato'lo:gə] *m* -n, -n pathologist.

pathologisch *a* pathological.

Pathos ['pa:tɔs] *nt* - emotiveness, emotionalism.

Patient(in *f*) [patsi'ɛnt(m)] *m* patient.

Patin ['pa:tɪn] *f* godmother; **—a** ['pa:tina] *f* - patina.

Patriarch [patri'arç] *m* -en, -en patriarch; **p—alisch** [-'ça:lɪʃ] *a* patriarchal.

Patriot [patri'o:t] *m* **-en, -en**
patriot; **p—isch** *a* patriotic;
—ismus ['-tɪsmʊs] *m* patriotism.
Patron [pa'tro:n] *m* **-s, -e** patron;
(*pej*) beggar; **—e** *f* **-, -n** cartridge;
—enhülse *f* cartridge case; **—in** *f*
patroness.
Patrouille [pa'trʊljə] *f* **-, -n** patrol.
patrouillieren [patrʊl'ji:rən] *vi*
patrol.
patsch [patʃ] *interj* splash; **P—e** *f*
-, -n (*col*: Händchen) paw;
(*Fliegen—*) swat; (*Feuer—*)
beater; (*Bedrängnis*) mess, jam;
—en *vti* smack, slap; (*im Wasser*)
splash; **—naß** a soaking wet.
patzig ['patsɪç] *a* (*col*) cheeky,
saucy.
Pauke ['paʊkə] *f* **-, -n** kettledrum;
auf die — hauen live it up; **p—n**
vti (*Sch*) swot, cram; **—r** *m* **-s, -**
(*col*) teacher.
pausbäckig ['paʊsbɛkɪç] a chubby-
cheeked.
pauschal [paʊ'ʃa:l] a *Kosten*
inclusive; *Urteil* sweeping; **P—e** *f*
-, -n, **P—gebühr** *f* flat rate;
P—preis *m* all-in price; **P—reise** *f*
package tour; **P—summe** *f* lump
sum.
Pause ['paʊzə] *f* **-, -n** break;
(*Theat*) interval; (*Innehalten*)
pause; (*Kopie*) tracing; **p—n** *vt*
trace; **p—nlos** a non-stop;
—nzeichen *nt* call sign; (*Mus*) rest.
pausieren [paʊ'zi:rən] *vi* make a
break.
Pauspapier ['paʊspapi:r] *nt*
tracing paper.
Pavian ['pa:vi̯a:n] *m* **-s, -e** baboon.
Pazifist [patsi'fɪst] *m* pacifist;
p—isch a pacifist.
Pech [pɛç] *nt* **-s, -e** pitch; (*fig*)
bad luck; **— haben** be unlucky;
p—schwarz a pitch-black;

—strähne *m* (*col*) unlucky patch;
—vogel *m* (*col*) unlucky person.
Pedal [pe'da:l] *nt* **-s, -e** pedal.
Pedant [pe'dant] *m* pedant; **—erie**
f pedantry; **p—isch** a pedantic.
Peddigrohr ['pɛdɪçro:r] *nt* cane.
Pegel ['pe:gəl] *m* **-s, -** water gauge;
—stand *m* water level.
peilen ['paɪlən] *vt* get a fix on.
Pein [paɪn] *f* **-** agony, pain; **p—igen**
vt torture; (*plagen*) torment;
p—lich a (*unangenehm*)
embarrassing, awkward, painful;
(*genau*) painstaking; **P—lichkeit** *f*
painfulness, awkwardness;
scrupulousness.
Peitsche ['paɪtʃə] *f* **-, -n** whip;
p—n *vt* whip; (*Regen*) lash.
Pelikan ['pe:likan] *m* **-s, -e** pelican.
Pelle ['pɛlə] *f* **-, -n** skin; **p—n** *vt*
skin, peel.
Pellkartoffeln *pl* jacket potatoes
pl.
Pelz [pɛlts] *m* **-es, -e** fur.
Pendel ['pɛndəl] *nt* **-s, -** pendulum;
—verkehr *m* shuttle traffic; (*für*
Pendler) commuter traffic.
Pendler ['pɛndlər] *m* **-s, -**
commuter.
penetrant [pene'trant] a sharp;
Person pushing.
Penis ['pe:nɪs] *m* **-, -se** penis.
Pension [pɛnzi'o:n] *f* (*Geld*)
pension; (*Ruhestand*) retirement;
(*für Gäste*) boarding or guest-
house; **halbe/volle —** half/full
board; **—är(in** *f*) ['-nɛr(ɪn)] *m* **-e,**
-e pensioner; **—at** [-'na:t] *nt* **-(e)s,**
-e boarding school; **p—ieren**
[-'ni:rən] *vt* pension (off); **—iert**
a retired; **—ierung** *f* retirement;
—sgast *m* boarder, paying guest.
Pensum ['pɛnzʊm] *nt* **-s, Pensen**
quota; (*Sch*) curriculum.

per [pɛr] *prép* +*acc* by, per; (*pro*) per; (*bis*) by.

Perfekt ['pɛrfɛkt] *nt* -(e)s, -e perfect; **p—** [pɛr'fɛkt] *a* perfect; **—ionismus** [pɛrfɛktsio'nɪsmʊs] *m* perfectionism.

perforieren [pɛrfo'riːrən] *vt* perforate.

Pergament [pɛrga'mɛnt] *nt* parchment; **—papier** *nt* greaseproof paper.

Periode [peri'oːdə] *f* -, -n period. **periodisch** [peri'oːdɪʃ] *a* periodic; (*dezimal*) recurring.

Peripherie [perife'riː] *f* periphery; (*um Stadt*) outskirts *pl*; (*Math*) circumference.

Perle ['pɛrlə] *f* -, -n (*lit, fig*) pearl; **p—n** *vi* sparkle; (*Tropfen*) trickle.

Perlmutt ['pɛrlmʊt] *nt* -s mother-of-pearl.

perplex [pɛr'plɛks] *a* dumbfounded.

Persianer [pɛrzi'aːnər] *m* -s, - Persian lamb.

Person [pɛr'zoːn] *f* -, -en person; ich für meine — personally I; klein von — of small build; **—al** [-'naːl] *nt* -s personnel; (*Bedienung*) servants *pl*; **—alausweis** *m* identity card; **—alien** [-'naːliən] *pl* particulars *pl*; **—alität** *f* personality; **—alpronomen** *nt* personal pronoun; **—enaufzug** *m* lift, elevator (*US*); **—enkraftwagen** *m* private motorcar; **—enkreis** *m* group of people; **—enschaden** *m* injury to persons; **—enwaage** *f* scales *pl*; **—enzug** *m* stopping train; passenger train; **p—ifizieren** [-ifi'tsiːrən] *vt* personify.

persönlich [pɛr'zøːnlɪç] *a* personal; *ad* in person; personally; **P—keit** *f* personality.

Perspektive [pɛrspɛk'tiːvə] *f* perspective.

Perücke [pe'rʏkə] *f* -, -n wig.

pervers [pɛr'vɛrs] *a* perverse; **P—ität** *f* perversity.

Pessimismus [pɛsi'mɪsmʊs] *m* pessimism.

Pessimist [pɛsi'mɪst] *m* pessimist; **p—isch** *a* pessimistic.

Pest [pɛst] *f* - plague.

Petersilie [petar'ziːliə] *f* parsley.

Petroleum [pe'troːleʊm] *nt* -s paraffin, kerosene (*US*).

petzen ['pɛtsən] *vi* (*col*) tell tales.

Pfad [pfaːt] *m* -(e)s, -e path; **—finder** *m* -s, - boy scout; **—finderin** *f* girl guide.

Pfahl [pfaːl] *m* -(e)s, ⁼e post, stake; **—bau** *m* pile dwelling.

Pfand [pfant] *nt* -(e)s, ⁼er pledge, security; (*Flaschen—*) deposit; (*im Spiel*) forfeit; (*fig: der Liebe etc*) pledge; **—brief** *m* bond.

pfänden ['pfɛndən] *vt* seize, distrain.

Pfänderspiel *nt* game of forfeits.

Pfand- *cpd*: **—haus** *nt* pawnshop; **—leiher** *m* -s, - pawnbroker; **—schein** *m* pawn ticket.

Pfändung ['pfɛndʊŋ] *f* seizure, distraint.

Pfanne ['pfanə] *f* -, -n (frying) pan.

Pfannkuchen *m* pancake; (*Berliner*) doughnut.

Pfarr- [pfar] *cpd*: **—ei** [-'raɪ] *f* parish; **—er** *m* -s, - priest; (*evangelisch*) vicar; minister; **—haus** *nt* vicarage; manse.

Pfau [pfaʊ] *m* -(e)s, -en peacock; **—enauge** *nt* peacock butterfly.

Pfeffer ['pfɛfər] *m* -s, - pepper; **—korn** *nt* peppercorn; **—kuchen** *m* gingerbread; **—minz** *nt* -es, -e peppermint; **—mühle** *f* pepper-mill; **p—n** *vt* pepper; (*col: werfen*) fling; gepfefferte Preise/Witze steep prices/spicy jokes.

Pfeife ['pfaɪfə] f -, -n whistle; (Tabak—, Orgel—) pipe; p—n vti irreg whistle; —r m -s, - piper.

Pfeil [pfaɪl] m -(e)s, -e arrow.

Pfeiler ['pfaɪlər] m -s, - pillar, prop; (Brücken—) pier.

Pfennig ['pfɛnɪç] m -(e)s, -e pfennig (hundredth part of a mark).

Pferd [pfeːrt] nt -(e)s, -e horse; —erennen nt horse-race; horse-racing; —eschwanz m (Frisur) ponytail; —estall m stable.

Pfiff [pfɪf] m -(e)s, -e whistle; (Kniff) trick; —erling m ['pfɪfərlɪŋ] m yellow chanterelle; keinen —erling wert not worth a thing; p—ig a sly, sharp.

Pfingsten ['pfɪŋstən] nt -, - Whitsun.

Pfingstrose ['pfɪŋstroːzə] f peony.

Pfirsich ['pfɪrzɪç] m -s, -e peach.

Pflanz- ['pflants] cpd: —e f -, -n plant; p—en vt plant; —enfett nt vegetable fat; —er m -s, - planter; —ung f plantation.

Pflaster ['pflastər] nt -s, - plaster; (Straße) pavement; p—müde a dead on one's feet; p—n vt pave; —stein m paving stone.

Pflaume ['pflaʊmə] f -, -n plum.

Pflege ['pfleːgə] f -, -n care; (von Idee) cultivation; (Kranken—) nursing; in — sein (Kind) be fostered out; p—bedürftig a needing care; —eltern pl foster parents pl; —kind nt foster child; p—leicht a easy-care; —mutter f foster mother; p—n vt look after; Kranke nurse; Beziehungen foster; —r m -s, - orderly; male nurse; —rin f nurse, attendant; —vater m foster father.

Pflicht [pflɪçt] f -, -en duty; (Sport) compulsory section; p—bewußt a conscientious; —fach nt (Sch) compulsory subject; —gefühl nt sense of duty; p—gemäß a dutiful; ad as in duty bound; p—vergessen a irresponsible; —versicherung f compulsory insurance.

Pflock [pflɔk] m -(e)s, ᵉe peg; (für Tiere) stake.

pflücken ['pflʏkən] vt pick; Blumen auch pluck.

Pflug [pfluːk] m -(e)s, ᵉe plough.

pflügen ['pflyːgən] vt plough.

Pforte ['pfɔrtə] f -, -n gate; door.

Pförtner ['pfœrtnər] m -s, - porter, doorkeeper, doorman.

Pfosten ['pfɔstən] m -s, - post.

Pfote ['pfoːtə] f -, -n paw; (col: Schrift) scrawl.

Pfropf [pfrɔpf] m -(e)s, -e (Flaschen—) stopper; (Blut—) clot; p—en vt (stopfen) cram; Baum graft; P—en m -s, - see Pfropf.

pfui [pfʊɪ] interj ugh; (na na) tut tut.

Pfund [pfʊnt] nt -(e)s, -e pound; p—ig a (col) great; p—weise ad by the pound.

pfuschen ['pfʊʃən] vi (col) be sloppy; jdm in etw (acc) — interfere in sth.

Pfuscher ['pfʊʃər] m -s, - (col) sloppy worker; (Kur—) quack; —ei ['-raɪ] f (col) sloppy work; (Kur—) quackery.

Pfütze ['pfʏtsə] f -, -n puddle.

Phänomen [fɛnoˈmeːn] nt -s, -e phenomenon; p—al [-ˈnaːl] a phenomenal.

Phantasie [fantaˈziː] f imagination; p—los a unimaginative;

p—ren *vi* fantasize; –p—voll *a* imaginative.

phantastisch [fan'tastɪʃ] *a* fantastic.

Pharisäer [fari'zɛːər] *m* -s, - (*lit, fig*) pharisee.

Pharmazeut(in *f*) [farma'tsɔʏt(ɪn)] *m* -en, -en pharmacist.

Phase ['faːzə] *f* -, -n phase.

Philanthrop [filan'troːp] *m* -en, -en philanthropist; p—isch *a* philanthropic.

Philologe [filo'loːgə] *m* -n, -n philologist.

Philologie [filolo'giː] *f* philology.

Philosoph [filo'zoːf] *m* -en, -en philosopher; –ie [-'fiː] *f* philosophy; p—isch *a* philosophical.

Phlegma ['flɛgma] *nt* -s lethargy; p—tisch [flɛ'gmatɪʃ] *a* lethargic.

Phonet- [fo'neːt] *cpd*: –ik *f* phonetics *sing*; p—isch *a* phonetic.

Phosphor ['fɔsfɔr] *m* -s phosphorus; –p—eszieren [fɔsfɔrɛs'tsiːrən] *vt* phosphoresce.

Photo ['foːto] *nt* -s, -s *etc see* **Foto**.

Phrase ['fraːzə] *f* -, -n phrase; (*pej*) hollow phrase.

Physik [fy'ziːk] *f* physics *sing*; p—alisch [-'kaːlɪʃ] *a* of physics; –er(in *f*) ['fyːzikər(ɪn)] *m* -s, - physicist.

Physiologe [fyzio'loːgə] *m* -n, -n physiologist.

Physiologie [fyzio'giː] *f* physiology.

physisch ['fyːzɪʃ] *a* physical.

Pianist(in *f*) [pia'nɪst(ɪn)] *m* pianist.

picheln ['pɪçəln] *vi* (*col*) booze.

Pickel ['pɪkəl] *m* -s, - pimple; (*Werkzeug*) pickaxe; (*Berg–*) iceaxe; p—ig *a* pimply.

picken ['pɪkən] *vi* pick, peck.

Picknick ['pɪknɪk] *nt* -s, -e *or* -s picnic; — machen have a picnic.

piepen ['piːpən], **piepsen** ['piːpsən] *vi* chirp.

piesacken ['piːzakən] *vt* (*col*) torment.

Pietät [pie'tɛːt] *f* piety, reverence; p—los *a* impious, irreverent.

Pigment [pɪ'gmɛnt] *nt* pigment.

Pik [piːk] *nt* -s, -s (*Cards*) spades; einen — auf jdn haben (*col*) have it in for sb; p—ant [pi'kant] *a* spicy, piquant; (*anzüglich*) suggestive; p—iert [pi'kiːrt] *a* offended.

Pilger ['pɪlgər] *m* -s, - pilgrim; –fahrt *f* pilgrimage.

Pille ['pɪlə] *f* -, -n pill.

Pilot [pi'loːt] *m* -en, -en pilot.

Pilz [pɪlts] *m* -es, -e fungus; (*eßbar*) mushroom; (*giftig*) toadstool; –krankheit *f* fungal disease.

pingelig ['pɪŋəlɪç] *a* (*col*) fussy.

Pinguin ['pɪŋguiːn] *m* -s, -e penguin.

Pinie ['piːniə] *f* pine.

pinkeln ['pɪŋkəln] *vi* (*col*) pee.

Pinsel ['pɪnzəl] *m* -s, - paintbrush.

Pinzette [pɪn'tsɛtə] *f* tweezers *pl*.

Pionier [pio'niːr] *m* -s, -e pioneer; (*Mil*) sapper, engineer.

Pirat [pi'raːt] *m* -en, -en pirate; –ensender *m* pirate radio station.

Pirsch [pɪrʃ] *f* - stalking.

Piste ['pɪstə] *f* -, -n (*Ski*) run, piste; (*Aviat*) runway.

Pistole [pɪs'toːlə] *f* -, -n pistol.

Pizza ['pɪtsa] *f* -, -s pizza.

Pkw [peːkaːveː] *m* -(s), -(s) *see* **Personenkraftwagen.**

Plackerei [plakə'raɪ] *f* drudgery.

plädieren [plɛ'diːrən] *vi* plead.

Plädoyer [plɛdoa'je:] nt -s, -s speech for the defence; (fig) plea.

Plage ['pla:gə] f -, -n plague; (Mühe) nuisance; —geist m pest, nuisance; p—n vt torment; vr toil, slave.

Plakat [pla'ka:t] nt -(e)s, -e placard; poster.

Plan [pla:n] -(e)s, -e plan; (Karte) map; —e f -, -n tarpaulin; p—en vt plan; Mord etc plot; —er m -s, - planner; —et [pla'ne:t] m -en -es planet; —etenbahn f orbit (of a planet); p—gemäß according to schedule or plan; on time; p—ieren [pla'ni:rən] vt plane, level; —ierraupe f bulldozer.

Planke ['plaŋkə] f -, -n plank.

Plänkelei [plɛŋkə'laɪ] f skirmish(ing).

plänkeln ['plɛŋkəln] vi skirmish.

Plankton ['plaŋktɔn] nt -s plankton.

Plan- cpd: p—los a Vorgehen un-systematic; Umherlaufen aimless; p—mäßig a according to plan; systematic; (Rail) scheduled.

Plansch- ['planʃ] cpd: —becken nt paddling pool; p—en vi splash.

Plan- cpd: —soll nt -s output target; —stelle f post.

Plantage [plan'ta:ʒə] f -, -n plantation.

Plan- cpd: —ung f planning; —wagen m covered wagon; —wirt-schaft f planned economy.

plappern ['plapərn] vi chatter.

plärren ['plɛrən] vi (Mensch) cry, whine; (Radio) blare.

Plasma ['plasma] nt -s, Plasmen plasma.

Plastik ['plastɪk] f sculpture; nt -s (Kunststoff) plastic; —folie f plastic film.

Plastilin [plasti'li:n] nt -s plasticine.

plastisch ['plastɪʃ] a plastic; stell dir das — vor! just picture it!

Platane [pla'ta:nə] f -, -n plane (tree).

Platin [pla'ti:n] nt -s platinum.

Platitüde [plati'ty:də] f -, -n platitude.

platonisch [pla'to:nɪʃ] a platonic.

platsch [platʃ] interj splash; —en vi splash; —naß a drenched.

plätschern ['plɛtʃərn] vi babble.

platt [plat] a flat; (col: überrascht) flabbergasted; (fig: geistlos) flat, boring; —deutsch a low German; P—e f -, -n (Speisen—, Phot, Tech) plate; (Stein—) flag; (Kachel) tile; (Schall—) -record. -

Plätt- ['plɛt] cpd: —eisen nt iron; p—en vt iron.

Platt- cpd: —enspieler m record player; —enteller m turntable; —fuß m flat foot; (Reifen) flat tyre.

Platz [plats] m -es, -e place; (Sitz—) seat; (Raum) space, room; (in Stadt) square; (Sport—) playing field; jdm — machen make room for sb; —angst f (Med) agora-phobia; (col) claustrophobia; —anweiser(in f) m -s, - usher(ette).

Plätzchen ['plɛtsçən] nt spot; (Gebäck) biscuit.

Platz- cpd: p—en vi burst; (Bombe) explode; vor Wut p—en (col) be bursting with anger; —karte f seat reservation; —mangel m lack of space; —patrone f blank cartridge; —regen m downpour; —wunde f cut.

Plauderei [plaudə'raɪ] f chat, con-versation; (Rad) talk.

plaudern ['plaudərn] vi chat, talk.

plausibel [plau'zi:bəl] *a* plausible.

plazieren [pla'tsi:rən] *vt* place; *vr* (*Sport*) be placed; (*Tennis*) be seeded.

Plebejer [ple'be:jər] *m* -s, - plebeian.

plebejisch [ple'be:jɪʃ] *a* plebeian.

pleite ['plaɪtə] *a* (*col*) broke; P— *f* -, -n bankruptcy; (*col: Reinfall*) flop; P— machen go bust.

Plenum ['ple:nʊm] *nt* -s plenum.

Pleuelstange ['plɔʏəlʃtaŋə] *f* connecting rod.

Plissee [plɪ'se:] *nt* -s, -s pleat.

Plombe ['plɔmbə] *f* -, -n lead seal; (*Zahn—*) filling.

plombieren [plɔm'bi:rən] *vt* seal; *Zahn* fill.

plötzlich ['plœtslɪç] *a* sudden; *ad* suddenly.

plump [plʊmp] *a* clumsy; *Hände* coarse; *Körper* shapeless; —sen *vi* (*col*) plump down, fall.

Plunder ['plʊndər] *m* -s rubbish.

plündern ['plʏndərn] *vti* plunder; *Stadt* sack.

Plünderung ['plʏndərʊŋ] *f* plundering, sack, pillage.

Plural ['plu:ra:l] *m* -s, -e plural; p—istisch [plura'lɪstɪʃ] *a* pluralistic.

Plus [plʊs] *nt* -, - plus; (*Fin*) profit; (*Vorteil*) advantage; p— *ad* plus.

Plüsch [ply:ʃ] *m* -(e)s, -e plush.

Plus- *cpd*: —pol *m* (*Elec*) positive pole; —punkt *m* point; (*fig*) point in sb's favour; —quamperfekt *nt* -s, -e pluperfect.

Po [po:] *m* -s, -s (*col*) bottom, bum.

Pöbel ['pø:bəl] *m* -s mob, rabble; —ei [-'laɪ] *f* vulgarity; p—haft *a* low, vulgar.

pochen ['pɔxən] *vi* knock; (*Herz*) pound; **auf etw** (*acc*) — (*fig*) insist on sth.

Pocken ['pɔkən] *pl* smallpox.

Podium ['po:diʊm] *nt* podium; —sdiskussion *f* panel discussion.

Poesie [poe'zi:] *f* poetry.

Poet [po'e:t] *m* -en, -en poet; p—isch *a* poetic.

Pointe [po'ɛ̃:tə] *f* -, -n point.

Pokal [po'ka:l] *m* -s, -e goblet; (*Sport*) cup; —spiel *nt* cup-tie.

Pökel- ['pø:kəl] *cpd*: —fleisch *nt* salt meat; p—n *vt* pickle, salt.

Pol [po:l] *m* -s, -e pole; p—ar [po'la:r] *a* polar; —arkreis *m* arctic circle.

Polemik [po'le:mɪk] *f* polemics.

polemisch *a* polemical.

polemisieren [polemi'zi:rən] *vi* polemicize.

Police [po'li:s(ə)] *f* -, -n insurance policy.

Polier [po'li:r] *m* -s, -e foreman; p—en *vt* polish.

Poliklinik [poli'kli:nɪk] *f* out-patients.

Politik [poli'ti:k] *f* politics *sing*; (*eine bestimmte*) policy; —er(in *f*) [po'li:tɪkər(ɪn)] *m* -s, - politician.

politisch [po'li:tɪʃ] *a* political.

politisieren [politi'zi:rən] *vi* talk politics; *vt* politicize.

Politur [poli'tu:r] *f* polish.

Polizei [poli'tsaɪ] *f* police; —beamte(r) *m* police officer; p—lich *a* police; sich p—lich melden register with the police; —revier *nt* police station; —spitzel *m* police spy, informer; —staat *m* police state; —streife *f* police patrol; —stunde *f* closing time; p—widrig *a* illegal.

Polizist [poli'tsɪst] *m* -en, -en policeman; —in *f* policewoman.

Pollen ['pɔlən] *m* -s, - pollen.

Polster ['pɔlstər] nt -s, - cushion; (Polsterung) upholstery; (in Kleidung) padding; (fig: Geld) reserves pl; **—er** m -s, - upholsterer; **—möbel** pl upholstered furniture; **p—n** vt upholster; pad; **—ung** f upholstery.

Polter- ['pɔltər] cpd: **—abend** m party on eve of wedding; **p—n** vi (Krach machen) crash; (schimpfen) rant.

Polygamie [polyga'mi:] f polygamy.

Polyp [po'ly:p] m -en -en polyp; (pl: Med) adenoids pl; (col) cop.

Pomade [po'ma:də] f pomade.

Pommes frites [pɔm'frit] pl chips pl, French fried potatoes pl.

Pomp [pɔmp] m -(e)s pomp.

Pony ['pɔni] m -s, -s (Frisur) fringe; nt -s, -s (Pferd) pony.

Popo [po'po:] m -s, -s bottom, bum.

populär [popu'lɛ:r] a popular.

Popularität [popularitɛ:t] f popularity.

Pore ['po:rə] f -, -n pore.

Pornographie [pɔrnogra'fi:] f pornography.

porös [po'rø:s] a porous.

Porree ['pore] m -s, -s leek.

Portal [pɔr'ta:l] nt -s, -e portal.

Portemonnaie [pɔrtmo'ne:] nt -s, -s purse.

Portier [pɔrti'e:] m -s, -s porter; see Pförtner.

Portion [pɔrtsi'o:n] f portion, helping; (col: Anteil) amount.

Porto ['pɔrto] nt -s, -s postage; **p—frei** a post-free, (postage) prepaid.

Porträt [pɔr'trɛ:] nt -s, -s portrait; **p—ieren** [pɔrtrɛ'ti:rən] vt paint, portray.

Porzellan [pɔrtse'la:n] nt -s, -e china, porcelain; (Geschirr) china.

Posaune [po'zaunə] f -, -n trombone.

Pose ['po:zə] f -, -n pose.

posieren [po'zi:rən] vi pose.

Position [pozitsi'o:n] f position; **—slichter** pl (Aviat) position lights pl.

positiv ['po:ziti:f] a positive; **P—** nt -s, -e (Phot) positive.

Positur [pozi'tu:r] f posture, attitude.

possessiv ['pɔsesi:f] a possessive; **P—(pronomen)** nt -s, -e possessive pronoun.

possierlich [pɔ'si:rlıç] a funny.

Post [pɔst] f -, -en post (office); (Briefe) mail; **—amt** nt post office; **—anweisung** f postal order, money order; **—bote** m postman; **—en** m -s, - post, position; (Comm) item; (auf Liste) entry; (Mil) sentry; (Streik—) picket; **—fach** nt post-office box; **—karte** f postcard; **p—lagernd** ad poste restante; **—leitzahl** f postal code; **—scheckkonto** nt postal giro account; **—sparkasse** f post office savings bank; **—stempel** m postmark; **p—wendend** ad by return (of post).

potent [po'tɛnt] a potent; (fig) high-powered.

Potential [potɛntsi'a:l] nt -s, -e potential.

potentiell [potɛntsi'el] a potential.

Potenz [po'tɛnts] f power; (eines Mannes) potency.

Pracht [praxt] f - splendour, magnificence.

prächtig ['prɛçtıç] a splendid.

Pracht- cpd: **—stück** nt showpiece; **p—voll** a splendid, magnificent.

Prädikat [prɛdi'ka:t] nt -(e)s, -e title; (Gram) predicate; (Zensur) ·distinction.

prägen ['prɛːgən] vt stamp; Münze mint; Ausdruck coin; Charakter form.

prägnant [prɛ'gnant] a precise, terse.

Prägnanz [prɛ'gnants] f conciseness, terseness.

Prägung ['prɛːgʊŋ] f· minting; forming; (Eigenart) character, stamp.

prahlen ['pra:lən] vi boast, brag.

Prahlerei [pra:lə'rai] f boasting.

prahlerisch [pra:lərɪʃ] a boastful.

Praktik ['praktɪk] f practice; p—abel [-'ka:bəl] a practicable; —ant(in f) [-'kant(ɪn)] m trainee; —um nt -s, Praktika or Praktiken practical training.

praktisch [praktɪʃ] a practical, handy; —er Arzt general practitioner.

praktizieren [praktɪ'tsi:rən] vti· practise.

Praline [pra'li:nə] f chocolate.

prall [pral] a firmly rounded; Segel taut; Arme plump; Sonne blazing; —en vi bounce, rebound; (Sonne) blaze.

Prämie [prɛ'miə] f premium; (Belohnung) award, prize; p—ren [prɛ'mi:rən] vt give an award to.

Pranger [praŋər] m -s, - (Hist) pillory; jdn an den — stellen (fig) pillory sb.

Präparat [prɛpa'ra:t] nt -(e)s, -e (Biol) preparation; (Med) medicine.

Präposition [prɛpozitsi'o:n] f preposition.

Prärie [prɛ'ri:] f prairie.

Präsens ['prɛːzɛns] nt · present tense.

präsentieren [prɛzɛn'ti:rən] vt present.

Präservativ [prɛzɛrva'ti:f] nt -s, -e contraceptive.

Präsident(in f) [prɛzi'dɛnt(m)] m president; —schaft f presidency; —schaftskandidat m presidential candidate.

Präsidium [prɛ'zi:diʊm] nt presidency, chair(manship); (Polizei-) police headquarters pl.

prasseln ['prasəln] vi (Feuer) crackle; (Hagel) drum; (Wörter) rain down.

prassen ['prasən] vi· live it up.

Präteritum [prɛ'te:ritʊm] nt -s, Präterita preterite.

Pratze [pratsə] f -, -n paw.

Präventiv- [prɛvɛn'ti:f] in cpds preventive.

Praxis ['praksɪs] f -, Praxen practice; (Behandlungsraum) surgery; (von Anwalt) office.

Präzedenzfall [prɛtse'dɛntsfal] m precedent.

präzis [prɛ'tsi:s] a precise; P—Ion [prɛtsi'zio:n] f precision.

predigen ['pre:digən] vti preach.

Prediger m -s, - preacher.

Predigt [pre:dɪçt] f -, -en sermon.

Preis [prais] m -es, -e price; (Sieges—) prize; um keinen — not at any price; P—elbeere f cranberry; p—en [praizən] vt irreg praise; p—geben vt irreg abandon; (opfern) sacrifice; (zeigen) expose; p—gekrönt a prize-winning; —gericht nt jury; p—günstig a inexpensive; —lage f price range; p—lich a price, in price; —sturz m slump; —träger(in f) m prizewinner; p—wert a inexpensive.

prekär [pre'kɛ:r] a precarious.

Prell- [prɛl] cpd: —bock m buffers pl; p—en vt bump; (fig) cheat, swindle; —ung f bruise.

Premiere [prəmi'ɛ:rə] f ⁓, -n premiere.

Premierminister [prəmr'e:mnister] m prime minister, premier.

Presse ['prɛsə] f ⁓, -n press; —freiheit f freedom of the press; —meldung f press report; p—n vt press.

pressieren [prɛ'si:rən] vi (be in a) hurry.

Preß- [prɛs] cpd: —luft f compressed air; —luftbohrer . m pneumatic drill.

Prestige [prɛs'ti:ʒə] nt -s prestige.

prickeln ['prɪkəln] vti tingle, tickle.

Priester ['pri:star] m -s, - priest.

prima ['pri:ma] a first-class, excellent; P— f ⁓, Primen sixth form, top class.

primär [pri'mɛ:r] a primary.

Primel ['pri:məl] f ⁓, -n primrose.

primitiv [primi'ti:f] a primitive.

Prinz [prɪnts] m -en, -en prince; —essin [prɪn'tsɛsɪn] f princess.

Prinzip [prɪn'tsi:p] nt -s, -ien principle; p—iell [-'ɛl] a,ad on principle; p—ienlos a unprincipled.

Priorität [priori'tɛ:t] f priority.

Prise ['pri:zə] f ⁓, -n pinch.

Prisma ['prɪsma] nt -s, Prismen prism.

privat [pri'va:t] a privat; P— in cpds private.

pro [pro:] prep +acc per; P— nt - pro.

Probe ['pro:bə] f ⁓, -n test; (Teststück) sample; (Theat) rehearsal; jdn auf die — stellen put sb to the test; —exemplar nt specimen copy; —fahrt f test

drive; p—n vt try; (Theat) rehearse; —weise ad on approval; —zeit f probation period.

probieren [pro'bi:rən] vti try; Wein, Speise taste, sample.

Problem [pro'ble:m] nt -s, -e problem; —atik [-'ma:tɪk] f problem; p—atisch [-'ma:tɪʃ] a problematic; p—los a problem-free.

Produkt [pro'dukt] nt -(e)s, -e product; (Agr) produce no pl; —ion [produktsi'o:n] f production; output; p—iv [-'ti:f] a productive; —ivität f productivity.

Produzent [produ'tsɛnt] m manufacturer; (Film) producer.

produzieren [produ'tsi:rən] vt produce.

Professor [pro'fɛsor] m professor.

Professur [profɛ'su:r] f chair.

Profil [pro'fi:l] nt -s, -e profile; (fig) image; p—ieren [profi'li:rən] vr create an image for o.s.

Profit [pro'fi:t] m -(e)s, -e profit; p—ieren [profi'ti:rən] vi profit (von from).

Prognose [pro'gno:zə] f ⁓, -n prediction, prognosis.

Programm [pro'gram] nt -s, -e programme; p—(m)äßig a according to plan; p—ieren [-'mi:rən] vt programme; —ierer(in f) m -s, - programmer.

progressiv [progrɛ'si:f] a progressive.

Projekt [pro'jɛkt] nt -(e)s, -e project; —or [pro'jɛktor] m projector.

projizieren [proji'tsi:rən] vt project.

proklamieren [prokla'mi:rən] vt proclaim.

Prolet [pro'le:t] m -en, -en prole, pleb; —ariat [-ari'a:t] nt -(e)s, -e proletariat; —arier [-'taːriər] *m* -s, - proletarian.

Prolog [pro'loːk] *m* -(e)s, -e prologue.

Promenade [promə'naːdə] *f* promenade.

Promille [pro'milə] *nt* -(s), - alcohol level.

prominent [promi'nɛnt] *a* prominent.

Prominenz [promi'nɛnts] *f* VIPs *pl*.

Promotion [promotsi'oːn] *f* doctorate, Ph.D.

promovieren [promo'viːrən] *vi* do a doctorate or Ph.D.

prompt [prɔmpt] *a* prompt.

Pronomen [pro'noːmɛn] *nt* -s, - pronoun.

Propaganda [propa'ganda] *f* propaganda.

Propeller [pro'pɛlər] *m* -s, - propeller.

Prophet [pro'feːt] *m* -en, -en prophet; —in *f* prophetess.

prophezeien [profe'tsaiən] *vt* prophesy.

Prophezeiung *f* prophecy.

Proportion [proportsi'oːn] *f* proportion; p—al [-'naːl] *a* proportional.

Prosa ['proːza] *f* - prose; p—isch [pro'zaːiʃ] *a* prosaic.

prosit ['proːzit] *interj* cheers.

Prospekt [pro'spɛkt] *m* -(e)s, -e leaflet, brochure.

prost [proːst] *interj* cheers.

Prostituierte [prostitu'iːrtə] *f* -n, -n prostitute.

Prostitution [prostitutsi'oːn] *f* prostitution.

Protest [pro'tɛst] *m* -(e)s, -e protest; —ant(in *f*) [protɛs'tant] *m* Protestant; p—antisch [protɛs'tantiʃ] *a* Protestant; p—ieren [protɛs'tiːrən] *vi* protest;

—kundgebung *f* (protest) rally.

Prothese [pro'teːzə] *f* -, -n artificial limb; (Zahn—) dentures *pl*.

Protokoll [proto'kɔl] *nt* -s, -e register; (von Sitzung) minutes *pl*; (diplomatisch) protocol; (Polizei—) statement; p—ieren [-'liːrən] *vt* take down in the minutes.

Proton ['proːtɔn] *nt* -s, -en proton.

Protz ['prɔts] *m* -en, -e(n) swank; p—en *vi* show off; p—ig *a* ostentatious.

Proviant [provi'ant] *m* -s, -e provisions *pl*, supplies *pl*.

Provinz [pro'vɪnts] *f* -, -en province; p—iell *a* provincial.

Provision [provizi'oːn] *f* (Comm) commission.

provisorisch [provi'zoːriʃ] *a* provisional.

Provokation [provokatsi'oːn] *f* provocation.

provozieren [provo'tsiːrən] *vt* provoke.

Prozedur [protse'duːr] *f* procedure; (pej) carry-on.

Prozent [pro'tsɛnt] *nt* -(e)s, -e per cent, percentage; —rechnung *f* percentage calculation; —satz *m* percentage; p—ual [-'uaːl] *a* percentage; as a percentage.

Prozeß [pro'tsɛs] *m* -sses, -sse trial, case; —kosten *pl* (legal) costs *pl*.

prozessieren [protse'siːrən] *vi* bring an action, go to law (mit against).

Prozession [protsɛsi'oːn] *f* procession.

prüde ['pryːdə] *a* prudish; P—rie ['riː] *f* prudery.

Prüf- ['pryːf] *cpd*: .p—en *vt* examine, test; (nach—) check;

—er *m* -s, - examiner; **—ling** *m*
examinee; **—stein** *m* touchstone;
—ung *f* examination; checking;
—ungsausschuß *m*, **—ungskommission** *f* examining board.

Prügel ['pry:gəl] *m* -s, - cudgel; *pl*
beating; **—ei** [-'lai] *f* fight; **—knabe**
m scapegoat; **p—n** *vt* beat; *vr*
fight; **—strafe** *f* corporal punishment.

Prunk [pruŋk] *m* -(e)s pomp,
show; **p—voll** *a* splendid, magnificent.

Psalm [psalm] *m* -s, **-en** psalm.

pseudo- [psɔydo] *in cpds* pseudo.

Psych- ['psyç] *cpd*: **—iater** [-i'a:tər]
m -s, - psychiatrist; **p—isch** a
psychological; **—oanalyse**
[-o'analy:zə] *f* psychoanalysis;
—ologe [-o'lo:gə] *m* -n, -n
psychologist; **—olo'gie** *f* psychology; **p—ologisch** a psychological.

Pubertät [puber'tɛ:t] *f* puberty.

Publikum ['pu:blikom] *nt* -s
audience; (*Sport*) crowd.

publizieren [publi'tsi:rən] *vt*
publish, publicize.

Pudding ['pudiŋ] *m* -s, -e *or* -s
blancmange.

Pudel ['pu:dəl] *m* -s poodle.

Puder ['pu:dər] *m* -s, - powder;
—dose *f* powder compact; **p—n** *vt*
powder; **—zucker** *m* icing sugar.

Puff [puf] *m* -s, -e (*Wäsche—*)
linen basket; (*Sitz—*) pouf; *pl* -e
(*col: Stoß*) push; *pl* -s (*col:
Bordell*) brothel; **—er** *m* -s, -
buffer; **—erstaat** *m* buffer state.

Pulli ['puli] *m* -s, -s (*col*), **Pullover** [pu'lo:vər] *m* -s, - pullover,
jumper.

Puls [puls] *m* -es, -e pulse; **—ader**
f artery; **p—ieren** [pul'zi:rən] *vi*
throb, pulsate.

Pult [pult] *nt* -(e)s, -e desk.

Pulver ['pulfər] *nt* -s, - powder;
p—ig a powdery; **p—isieren**
[pulveri'zi:rən] *vt* pulverize;
—schnee *m* powdery snow.

pummelig ['puməliç] a chubby.

Pumpe ['pumpə] *f* -, -n pump;
p—n *vt* pump; (*col*) lend, borrow.

Punkt [puŋkt] *m* -(e)s, -e point;
(*bei Muster*) dot; (*Satzzeichen*) full
stop; **p—ieren** [-'ti:rən] *vt* dot;
(*Med*) aspirate.

pünktlich ['pyŋktliç] a punctual;
P—keit *f* punctuality.

Punkt- *cpd*: **—sieg** *m* victory on
points; **—zahl** *f* score.

Punsch [punʃ] *m* -(e)s, -e punch.

Pupille [pu'pilə] *f* -, -n pupil.

Puppe ['pupə] *f* -, -n doll;
(*Marionette*) puppet; (*Insekten—*)
pupa, chrysalis; **—nspieler** *m*
puppeteer; **—nstube** *f* doll's house.

pur [pu:r] a pure; (*völlig*) sheer;
Whisky neat.

Püree [py're:] *nt* -s, -s mashed
potatoes *pl*.

Purzel- ['purtsəl] *cpd*: **—baum** *m*
somersault; **p—n** *vi* tumble.

Puste ['pu:stə] *f* - (*col*) puff; (*fig*)
steam; **—l** ['pustəl] *f* -, -n pustule;
p—n *vi* puff, blow.

Pute ['pu:tə] *f* -, -n turkey-hen; **—r**
m -s, - turkey-cock.

Putsch [putʃ] *m* -(e)s, -e revolt,
putsch; **p—en** *vi* revolt; **—ist**
[pu't ʃist] *m* rebel.

Putz [puts] *m* -es (*Mörtel*) plaster,
roughcast; **p—en** *vt* clean; *Nase*
wipe, blow; *vr* clean oneself; dress
oneself up; **—frau** *f* charwoman;
p—ig a quaint, funny; **—lappen** *m*
cloth; **—tag** *m* cleaning day;
—zeug *nt* cleaning things *pl*.

Puzzle ['pasəl] *nt* -s, -s jigsaw.

Pyjama [pi'dʒa:ma] *m* -s, -s pyjamas *pl.*

Pyramide [pyra'mi:də] *f* -, -n pyramid.

Q

Q, q [ku:] *nt* Q, q.

quabb(e)lig ['kvab(ə)lıç] *a* wobbly; *Frosch* slimy.

Quacksalber ['kvakzalbər] *m* -s, - quack (doctor).

Quader ['kva:dər] *m* -s, - square stone; (*Math*) cuboid.

Quadrat [kva'dra:t] *nt* -(e)s, -e square; **q~isch** *a* square; **—meter** *m* square metre.

quadrieren [kva'dri:rən] *vt* square.

quaken ['kva:kən] *vi* croak, (*Ente*) quack.

quäken ['kvɛ:kən] *vi* screech; **—d** *a* screeching.

Qual [kva:l] *f* -, -en pain, agony; (*seelisch*) anguish.

Quäl- [kvɛ:l] *cpd:* **q~en** *vt* torment; *vr* struggle; (*geistig*) torment oneself; **—erei** [-'ə'raı] *f* torture, torment; **—geist** *m* pest.

qualifizieren [kvalifi'tsi:rən] *vtr* qualify; (*einstufen*) label.

Qualität [kvali'tɛ:t] *f* quality; **—sware** *f* article of high quality.

Qualle ['kvalə] *f* -, -n jellyfish.

Qualm [kvalm] *m* -(e)s thick smoke; **q~en** *vti* smoke.

qualvoll ['kva:lfɔl] *a.* excruciating, painful, agonizing.

Quant- ['kvant] *cpd:* **—entheorie** *f* quantum theory; **—ität** [-i'tɛ:t] *f* quantity; **q~itativ** [-ita'ti:f] *a* quantitative; **—um** *nt* -s, Quanten quantity, amount.

Quarantäne [karan'tɛ:nə] *f* -, -n quarantine.

Quark [kvark] *m* -s curd cheese; (*col*) rubbish.

Quarta ['kvarta] *f* -, **Quarten** third year of secondary school; **—l** [kvar'ta:l] *nt* -s, -e quarter (year).

Quartier [kvar'ti:r] *nt* -s, -e accommodation; (*Mil*) quarters *pl*; (*Stadt—*) district.

Quarz [kva:rts] *m* -es, -e quartz.

quasseln ['kvasəln] *vi* (*col*) natter.

Quatsch [kvatʃ] *m* -es rubbish; **q~en** *vi* chat, natter.

Quecksilber ['kvɛkzılbər] *nt* mercury.

Quelle ['kvɛlə] *f* -, -n spring; (*eines Flusses*) source; **q~n** *vi* (*hervor—*) pour *or* gush forth; (*schwellen*) swell.

quengel- ['kvɛŋəl] *cpd:* **q~el** [-'laı] *f* (*col*) whining; **—ig** *a* (*col*) whining; **—n** *vi* (*col*) whine.

quer ['kve:r] *ad* crossways, diagonally; (*rechtwinklig*) at right angles; **—** auf dem Bett across the bed; **Q~balken** *m* crossbeam; **—feldein** *ad* across country; **Q~flöte** *f* flute; **Q~kopf** *m* awkward customer; **Q~schiff** *nt* transept; **Q~schnitt** *m* cross-section; **—schnittsgelähmt** *a* paralysed below the waist; **Q~straße** *f* intersecting road; **Q~treiber** *m* -s, - obstructionist; **Q~verbindung** *f* connection, link.

quetschen ['kvɛtʃən] *vt* squash, crush; (*Med*) bruise.

Quetschung *f* bruise, contusion.

quieken ['kvi:kən] *vi* squeak.

quietschen ['kvi:tʃən] *vi* squeak.

Quint- ['kvɪnt] *cpd*: —**a** *f* -, -en second form in secondary school; —**essenz** [-'ɛsɛnts] *f* quintessence; —**ett** [-'tɛt] *nt* -(e)s, -e quintet.

Quirl [kvɪrl] *m* -(e)s, -e whisk.

quitt [kvɪt] *a* quits, even; Q—**e** *f* -, -n quince; —**engelb** a sickly yellow; —**ieren** [-'ti:rən] *vt* give a receipt for; *Dienst* leave; Q—**ung** *f* receipt.

Quiz [kvɪs] *nt* -, - quiz.

Quote ['kvo:tə] *f* -, -n number, rate.

R

R, r [ɛr] *nt* R, r.

Rabatt [ra'bat] *m* -(e)s, -e discount; —**e** *f* -, -n flowerbed, border; —**marke** *f* trading stamp.

Rabe ['ra:bə] *m* -n, -n raven; —**nmutter** *f* bad mother.

rabiat [rabi'a:t] *a* furious.

Rache ['raxə] *f* - revenge, vengeance; —**n** *m* -s, - throat.

rächen ['rɛçən] *vt* avenge, revenge; *vr* take (one's) revenge; **das wird sich** — you'll pay for that.

Rach- ['rax] *cpd*: —**itis** [ra'xi:tɪs] *f* - rickets *sing*; —**sucht** *f* vindictiveness; **r**—**süchtig** *a* vindictive.

Racker ['rakər] *m* -s, - rascal, scamp.

Rad [ra:t] *nt* -(e)s, ⸚er wheel; (*Fahr*—) bike; —**ar** [ra:da:r] *m* or *nt* -s radar; —**arkontrolle** *f* radar-controlled speed trap; —**au** [ra'dau] *m* -s (*col*) row; —**dampfer** *m* paddle steamer; **r**—**ebrechen** *vi insep*: **deutsch** *etc* **r**—**ebrechen** speak broken German *etc*; **r**—**eln** *vi*, **r**—**fahren** *vi irreg* cycle; —**fahrer(in** *f*) *m* cyclist; —**fahrweg** *m* cycle track or path.

Radier- [ra'di:r] *cpd*: **r**—**en** *vt* rub out, erase; (*Art*) etch; —**gummi** *m* rubber, eraser; —**ung** *f* etching.

Radieschen [ra'di:sçən] *nt* radish.

radikal [radi'ka:l] *a*, **R**—**e(r)** *mf* radical.

Radio ['ra:dio] *nt* -s, -s radio, wireless; **r**—**aktiv** *a* radioactive; —**aktivität** *f* radioactivity; —**apparat** *m* radio, wireless set.

Radium ['ra:dium] *nt* -s radium.

Radius ['ra:dius] *m* -, **Radien** radius.

Rad- *cpd*: —**kappe** *f* (*Aut*) hub cap; —**ler(in** *f*) *m* -s, - cyclist; —**rennbahn** *f* cycling (race)track; —**rennen** *nt* cycle race; **cycle racing**; —**sport** *m* cycling.

raff- [raf] *cpd*: —**en** *vt* snatch, pick up; *Stoff* gather (up); *Geld* pile up, rake in; **R**—**inade** [-i'na:də] *f* refined sugar; —**inieren** [-i'ni:rən] *vt* refine; —**i'niert** *a* crafty, cunning; *Zucker* refined.

ragen ['ra:gən] *vi* tower, rise.

Rahm [ra:m] *m* -s cream; —**en** *m* -s, - frame(work); **im** —**en des Möglichen** within the bounds of possibility; **r**—**en** *vt* frame; **r**—**ig** *a* creamy.

Rakete [ra'ke:tə] *f* -, -n rocket; **ferngelenkte** — guided missile.

rammen ['ramən] vt ram.

Rampe ['rampə] f -, -n ramp; —nlicht vt (Theat) footlights pl.

ramponieren [rampo'ni:rən] vt (col) damage.

Ramsch [ramʃ] m -(e)s, -e junk.

ran [ran] ad (col) = **heran**.

Rand [rant] m -(e)s, ¨er edge; (von Brille, Tasse etc) rim; (Hut—) brim; (auf Papier) margin; (Schmutz—, unter Augen) ring; (fig) verge, brink; außer ~ und Band wild; am ~ be bemerkt mentioned in passing; r—alieren [randa'li:rən] vi (go on the) rampage; —bemerkung f marginal note; (fig) odd comment; —erscheinung f unimportant side effect, marginal phenomenon.

Rang [raŋ] m -(e)s, ¨e rank; (Stand) standing; (Wert) quality; (Theat) circle; —abzeichen nt badge of rank; —älteste(r) m senior officer.

Rangier- [rãʒi:r] cpd: —bahnhof m marshalling yard; r—en vt (Rail) shunt, switch (US); vi rank, be classed; —gleis nt siding.

Rang- cpd: —ordnung f hierarchy; (Mil) rank; —unterschied m social distinction; (Mil) difference in rank.

Ranke ['raŋkə] f -, -n tendril, shoot.

Ränke ['rɛŋkə] pl intrigues pl; —schmied m intriguer; r—voll a scheming.

Ranzen ['rantsən] m -s, - satchel; (col: Bauch) gut, belly.

ranzig ['rantsɪç] a rancid.

Rappe ['rapə] m -n, -n black horse.

Raps [raps] m -es, -e (Bot) rape.

rar [ra:r] a rare; sich — machen (col) keep oneself to oneself; R—i'tät f rarity; (Sammelobjekt) curio.

rasant [ra'zant] a quick, rapid.

rasch [raʃ] a quick; —eln vi rustle.

Rasen ['ra:zən] m -s, - lawn; grass; r— vi rave; (schnell) race; r—d a furious; r—de Kopfschmerzen m splitting headache; —mäher m -s, -; —mähmaschine f lawnmower; —platz m lawn.

Raserei [ra:zə'raɪ] f raving, ranting; (Schnelle) reckless speeding.

Rasier- [ra'zi:r] cpd: —apparat m shaver; —creme f shaving cream; r—en vtr shave; —klinge f razor blade; —messer nt razor; —pinsel m shaving brush; —seife f shaving soap or stick; —wasser nt shaving lotion.

Rasse ['rasə] f -, -n race; (Tier—) breed; —hund m thoroughbred dog; —l f -, -n rattle; r—ln vi rattle, clatter; —nhaß m race or racial hatred; —ntrennung f racial segregation.

Rast [rast] f -, -en rest; r—en vi rest; —haus nt (Aut) service station; r—los a tireless; (unruhig) restless; —platz m (Aut) layby.

Rasur [ra'zu:r] f shaving; (Radieren) erasure.

Rat [ra:t] m -(e)s, —schläge (piece of) advice; jdn zu —e ziehen consult sb; keinen — wissen not know what to do; —e f -, -n instalment; r—en vti irreg guess; (empfehlen) advise (jdm sb); r—enweise ad by instalments; —enzahlung f hire purchase; —geber m -s, - adviser; —haus nt town hall.

ratifizier- [ratifi'tsi:r] cpd: —en vt ratify; R—ung f ratification.

Ration [ratsi'om] f ration; r—al [-'na:l] a rational; r—ali'sieren vt

rationalize; r—ell ['nɛl] a efficient; r—ieren ['nliːrən] vt ration.
Rat- cpd: r—los a at a loss,
helpless; —losigkeit f helplessness; r—sam' a advisable; —schlag
m (piece of) advice.
Rätsel ['rɛːtsəl] nt -s, - puzzle;
(Wort—) riddle; r—haft a
mysterious; es ist mir r—haft it's
a mystery to me.
Rats- cpd: —herr m councillor;
—keller m town-hall restaurant.
Ratte ['ratə] f -, -n rat; —nfänger
m -s, - ratcatcher.
rattern ['ratərn] vi rattle, clatter.
Raub [raup] m -(e)s robbery;
(Beute) loot, booty; —bau m
ruthless exploitation; r—en
[rauban] vt rob; —Mensch kidnap,
abduct.
Räuber ['rɔybər] m -s, - robber;
r—isch a thieving.
Raub- cpd: r—gierig a rapacious;
—mord m robbery with murder;
—tier nt predator; —überfall m
robbery with violence; —vogel m
bird of prey.
Rauch ['raux] · m -(e)s smoke;
r—en vti smoke; —er m -s, -
smoker; —erabteil nt (Rail)
smoker.
räuchern ['rɔyçərn] vt smoke, cure.
Rauch- cpd: —fahne f smoke trail;
—fleisch nt smoked meat; r—ig a
smoky.
räudig ['rɔydɪç] a mangy.
rauf [rauf] ad (col) = herauf;
R—bold m -(e)s, -e rowdy,
hooligan; —en vt Haare pull out;
vir fight; R—e'rei f brawl, fight;
—lustig a spoiling for a fight,
rowdy.
rauh [rau] a rough, coarse; Wetter
harsh; —haarig a wire-haired;
R—reif m hoarfrost.

Raum [raum] m -(e)s, Räume
space; (Zimmer, Platz) room;
(Gebiet) area; —bild nt 3D picture.
räumen ['rɔymən] vt clear;
Wohnung, Platz vacate; (weg-
bringen) shift, move; (in Schrank
etc) put away.
Raum- cpd: —fahrt f space travel;
—inhalt m cubic capacity, volume.
räumlich ['rɔymlɪç] a spatial;
R—keiten pl premises pl.
·Raum- cpd: —mangel m lack of
space; —meter m. cubic metre;
—pflegerin f cleaner; —schiff. nt
spaceship; —schiffahrt f space
travel; r—sparend a space-saving.
Räumung ['rɔymuŋ] f vacating,
evacuation; clearing (away);
—sverkauf m clearance sale.
raunen ['raunən] vti whisper
mysteriously.
Raupe ['raupə] f -, -n caterpillar;
(—nkette) (caterpillar) track;
—nschlepper m caterpillar tractor.
raus [raus] ad (col) = heraus,
hinaus.
Rausch [rauʃ] m -(e)s, Räusche
intoxication; r—en vi (Wasser)
rush; (Baum) rustle; (Radio etc)
hiss; (Mensch) sweep, sail; r—end
a Beifall thunderous; · Fest
sumptuous; —gift' nt drug;
—giftsüchtige(r) mf drug addict.
räuspern ['rɔyspərn] vr clear one's
throat.
Raute ['rautə] f -, -n diamond;
(Math) rhombus; r—nförmig a
rhombic.
Razzia ['ratsia] f -, Razzien raid.
Reagenzglas [rea'gɛntsglaːs] nt
test tube.
reagieren [rea'giːrən] vi react (auf
+acc to).
Reakt- cpd: —ion [reaktsi'oːn] f
reaction; r—io'när a reactionary;

—ionsgeschwindigkeit *f* speed of reaction; —or [re'aktor] *m* reactor.
real [re'a:l] *a* real, material; R—ismus [-'lɪsmʊs] *m* realism; R—ist [-'lɪst] *m* realist; —istisch *a* realistic.
Rebe ['re:bə] *f* -, -n vine.
Rebell [re'bɛl] *m* -en, -en rebel; —i'on *f* rebellion; r—isch *a* rebellious.
Reb- *cpd:* —ensaft *m* grape juice; —huhn ['rɛphu:n] *nt* partridge; —stock *m* vine.
Rechen ['rɛçən] *m* -s, - rake; r— *vti* rake; —aufgabe *f* sum, mathematical problem; —fehler *m* miscalculation; —maschine *f* calculating machine; —schaft *f* account; —schaftsbericht *m* report; —schieber *m* slide rule.
Rech- ['rɛç] *cpd:* r—nen *vti* calculate; jdn/etw r—nen zu *or* unter (+ *acc*) count sb/sth among; r—nen mit reckon with; r—nen auf (+ *acc*) count on; r—ner *m* -s, - calculator; —nung *f* calculation(s); (*Comm*) bill, check (*US*); jdm/etw —nung tragen take sb/sth into account; —nungsbuch *nt* account book; —nungsjahr *nt* financial year; —nungsprüfer *m* auditor; —nungsprüfung *f* audit(ing).
recht [rɛçt] *a*, *ad* right; (*vor Adjektiv*) really, quite; das ist mir — that suits me; jetzt erst — now more than ever; — haben be right; jdm — geben agree with sb; R— *nt* -(e)s, -e right; (*Jur*) law; R— sprechen administer justice; mit R— rightly, justly; von R—s wegen by rights; R—e *f* -n, -n right (hand); (*Pol*) Right; —e(r,s) *a* right; (*Pol*) right-wing; R—e(r) *mf* right person; R—e(s) *nt* right thing; etwas/nichts R—es

something/nothing proper; R—eck *nt* -s, -e rectangle; —eckig *a* rectangular; —fertigen *vt insep* justify (o.s.); R—fertigung *f* justification; —haberisch *a* dogmatic; —lich *a*, —mäßig *a* legal, lawful.
rechts [rɛçts] *ad* on/to the right; R—anwalt *m*, R—anwältin *f* lawyer, barrister; R—außen *m* -, - (*Sport*) outside right; R—beistand *m* legal adviser.
Recht- *cpd:* r—schaffen *a* upright; —schreibung *f* spelling.
Rechts- *cpd:* —drehung *f* clockwise rotation; —fall *m* (*law*) case; —frage *f* legal question; —händer *m* -s, - right-handed person; r—kräftig *a* valid, legal; —kurve *f* right-hand bend; —pflege *f* administration of justice; r—radikal *a* (*Pol*) extreme right-wing; —spruch *m* verdict; —verkehr *m* driving on the right; r—widrig *a* illegal; —wissenschaft *f* jurisprudence.
recht- *cpd:* —winklig *a* right-angled; —zeitig *a* timely; *ad* in time.
Reck [rɛk] *nt* -(e)s, -e horizontal bar; r—en *vtr* stretch.
Redak- *cpd:* —teur [redak'tø:r] *m* editor; —tion [redaktsi'o:n] *f* editing; (*Leute*) editorial staff; (*Büro*) editorial office(s).
Rede ['re:də] *f* -, -n speech; (*Gespräch*) talk; jdn zur R— stellen take sb to task; —freiheit *f* freedom of speech; r—gewandt *a* eloquent; r—n *vi* talk, speak; *vt* say; *Unsinn etc* talk; —n *nt* -s talking, speech; —nsart *f* set phrase; —wendung *f* expression, idiom.

red- cpd: —**lich** ['re:tliç] a honest;
R—**lichkeit** f honesty; R—**ner** m -s,
• speaker, orator; —**selig**
['re:tze:liç] a talkative, loquacious;
R—**seligkeit** f talkativeness.

reduzieren [redu'tsi:rən] vt reduce.

Reede ['re:də] f -, -n protected
anchorage; —**r** m -s, • shipowner;
—**rei** f shipping line or firm.

reell [re'ɛl] a fair, honest; (Math)
real.

Refer- cpd: —**at** [refe'ra:t] nt -(e)s,
-e report; (Vortrag) paper;
(Gebiet) section; —**ent** [refe'rɛnt]
m speaker; (Berichterstatter)
reporter; (Sachbearbeiter) expert;
—**enz** [refe'rɛnts] f reference;
r—**ieren** [refe'ri:rən] vi: r—ieren
über (+acc) speak or talk on.

reflektieren [reflek'ti:rən] vti
reflect; — **auf** (+acc) to be interested
in.

Reflex [re'flɛks] m -es, -e reflex;
—**bewegung** f reflex action; r—**iv**
['ksi:f] a (Gram) reflexive.

Reform [re'form] f -, -en reform;
—**ati'on** f reformation; —**ator**
['ma:tɔr] m reformer; r—**a'torisch**
a reformatory, reforming; —**haus**
nt health food shop; r—**ieren**
['mi:rən] vt reform.

Refrain [rə'frɛ:] m -s, -s refrain,
chorus.

Regal [re'ga:l] nt -s, -e
.(book)shelves pl, bookcase;. stand,
rack.

rege ['re:gə] a lively, active;
Geschäft brisk.

Regel ['re:gəl] f -, -n rule; (Med)
period; r—**los** a irregular,
unsystematic; r—**mäßig** a regular;
—**mäßigkeit** f regularity; r—**n** vt
regulate, control; Angelegenheit
settle; vr: sich von selbst r—n take
care of itself; r—**recht** a regular,

proper, thorough; —**ung** f
regulation; settlement; r—**widrig** a
irregular, against the rules.

regen ['re:gən] vtr move, stir; R—
m -s, - rain; R—**bogen** m rainbow;
R—**bogenhaut** f (Anat) iris;
R—**guß** m downpour; R—**mantel**
m raincoat, mac(kintosh);
R—**menge** f rainfall; R—**schauer** m
shower (of rain); R—**schirm** m
umbrella.

Regent [re'gɛnt] m regent;
—**schaft** f regency.

Regen- cpd: —**tag** m rainy day;
—**wurm** m earthworm; —**zeit** f
rainy season, rains pl.

Regie [re'ʒi:] f (Film etc) direction;
(Theat) production; r—**ren**
[re'gi:rən] vti govern, rule; —**rung**
f government; (Monarchie) reign;
—**rungswechsel** m change of
government; —**rungszeit** f period
in government; (von König) reign.

Regiment [regi'mɛnt] nt -s, -er
regiment.

Region [regi'o:n] f region.

Regisseur [reʒi'sø:r] m director;
(Theat) (stage) producer.

Register [re'gistər] nt -s, -
register; (in Buch) table of
contents, index.

Registratur [registra'tu:r] f
registry, record office.

registrieren [regis'tri:rən] vt
register.

reg- ['re:g] cpd: R—**ler** m -s, •
regulator, governor; —**los**
['re:klo:s] a motionless; —**nen** vi
impers rain; —**nerisch** a rainy;
—**sam** [re:kza:m] a active.

regulär [regu'lɛ:r] a regular.

regulieren [regu'li:rən] vt regulate;
(Comm) settle.

Regung ['re:guŋ] f motion;

(Gefühl) feeling, impulse; **r—slos** a
motionless.

Reh [re:] nt -(e)s, -e deer, roe;
—bock m roebuck; —kalb nt,
—kitz. nt fawn.

Reib- ['raɪb] cpd: —e f -, -n, —eisen
nt grater; **r—en** vt irreg rub;
(Cook) grate; —e'rei f friction no
pl; —fläche f rough surface; —ung
f friction; **r—ungslos** a smooth.

reich [raɪç] a rich; **R—** nt -(e)s, -e
empire, kingdom; (fig) realm; das
Dritte R— the Third Reich; —en
vi reach; (genügen) be enough or
sufficient (jdm for sb); vt hold out;
(geben) pass, hand; (anbieten)
offer; —haltig a ample, rich; —lich
a ample, plenty of; **R—tum** m -s,
-tümer wealth; **R—weite** f range.

reif [raɪf] a ripe; Mensch, Urteil
mature; **R—** m -(e)s hoarfrost;
-(e)s, -e (Ring) ring, hoop; **R—e** f
- ripeness; maturity; —en vi
mature; ripen; **R—en** m -s, - ring,
hoop; (Fahrzeug—) tyre;
R—enschaden m puncture;
R—eprüfung f school leaving
exam; **R—ezeugnis** nt school
leaving .certificate.

Reihe ['raɪə] f -, -n row; (von
Tagen etc, col: Anzahl) series sing;
der — nach in turn; er ist an der
— it's his turn; **an die — kommen**
have one's turn; **r—n** vt set in a
row; arrange in series; Perlen
string; —nfolge f sequence;
alphabetische —nfolge alphabetical
order; —nhaus nt terraced house;
—r m -s, - heron.

Reim [raɪm] m -(e)s, -e rhyme;
r—en vt rhyme.

rein [raɪn] ad (col) = **herein,
hinein**; a, ad pure(ly); (sauber)
clean; etw ins — schreiben make
a fair copy of sth; etw ins. —e

bringen clear up sth; **R—** in cpds
(Comm) net(t); **R—(e)machefrau** f
charwoman; **R—fall** m (col) letdown; **R—gewinn** m net profit;
R—heit f purity; cleanliness;
—igen vt clean; Wasser purify;
R—igung f cleaning; purification;
(Geschäft) cleaners; chemische
R—igung dry cleaning; dry
cleaners; —lich a clean;
R—lichkeit f cleanliness; —rassig
a pedigree; **R—schrift** f fair copy;
—waschen vr irreg clear oneself.

Reis [raɪ] m -es, -e rice; nt -es,
-er twig, sprig.

Reise ['raɪzə] f -, -n journey;
(Schiff—) voyage; —n pl travels
pl; —andenken nt souvenir;
—büro nt travel agency; **r—fertig**
a ready to start; —führer m
guide(book); (Mensch) travel
guide; —gepäck nt luggage;
—gesellschaft f party of travellers;
—kosten pl travelling expenses pl;
—leiter m courier; —lektüre f
reading matter for the journey;
r—n vi travel; go (nach to);
—nde(r) mf traveller; —paß m
passport; —pläne pl plans pl for
a journey; —proviant m provisions
pl for the journey; —scheck m
traveller's cheque; —tasche f
travelling bag or case; —verkehr
m tourist/holiday traffic; —wetter
nt holiday weather; —ziel nt
destination.

Reisig ['raɪzɪç] nt -s brushwood.

Reiß- [raɪs'] cpd: —aus nehmen run
away, flee; —brett nt drawing
board; **r—en** vti irreg tear;
(ziehen) pull, drag; Witz crack;
etw an sich —en snatch sth up;
(fig) take over sth; sich um etw
r—en scramble for sth; **r—end** a
Fluß torrential; .(Comm) rapid;

—er m -s, - (col) thriller; **r—erisch** a sensationalistic; **—leine** f (Aviat) ripcord; **—nagel** m drawing pin, thumbtack· (US); **—schiene** f drawing rule, square; **—verschluß** m zip(per), zip fastener; **—zeug** nt geometry set; **—zwecke** f = **—nagel**.

Reit- ['raɪt] cpd: **r—en** vti irreg ride; **—er(in** f) m -s, - rider; (Mil) cavalryman, trooper; **—e'rei** f cavalry; **—hose** f riding breeches pl; **—pferd** nt saddle horse; **—stiefel** m riding boot; **—zeug** nt riding outfit.

Reiz [raɪts] m -es, -e stimulus; (angenehm) charm; (Verlockung) attraction; **r—bar** a irritable; **—barkeit** f irritability; **r—en** vt stimulate; (unangenehm) irritate; (verlocken) appeal to, attract; **r—end** a charming; **r—los** a unattractive; **r—voll** a attractive; **—wäsche** f sexy underwear.

rekeln ['re:kəln] vr stretch out; (lümmeln) lounge or loll about.

Reklam- cpd: **—ation** [reklamatsi'o:n] f complaint; **—e** [re'kla:mə] f -, -n advertising; advertisement; **—e machen für etw** advertise sth; **r—ieren** [rekla'mi:rən] vti complain (about); (zurückfordern) reclaim.

rekon- [rekon] cpd: **—struieren** [stru'i:rən] vt reconstruct; **R—valeszenz** [-vales'tsɛnts] f convalescence.

Rekord [re'kort] m -(e)s, -e record; **—leistung** f record performance.

Rekrut [re'kru:t] m -en, -en recruit; **r—ieren** [-'ti:rən] vt recruit; vr be recruited.

Rektor ['rɛktor] m (Univ) rector, vice-chancellor; (Sch) headmaster;

—at ['-'rat] nt -(e)s, -e rectorate, vice-chancellorship; headship; (Zimmer) rector's etc office.

Relais [rə'lɛ:] nt -, - relay.

relativ [rela'ti:f] a relative; **R—ität** [relativi'tɛ:t] f relativity.

relevant [rele'vant] a relevant.

Relief [reli'ɛf] nt -s, -s relief.

Religion [religi'o:n] f religion; **—slehre** f, **—sunterricht** m religious instruction.

religiös [religi'ø:s] a religious.

Relikt [re'likt] nt -(e)s, -e relic.

Reling ['re:lɪŋ] f -, -s (Naut) rail.

Reliquie [re'li:kviə] f relic.

Reminiszenz [reminis'tsɛnts] f reminiscence, recollection.

Remoulade [remu'la:də] f remoulade.

Ren [rɛn] nt -s, -s or -e reindeer.

Rendezvous [rãde'vu:] nt -, - rendezvous.

Renn- ['rɛn] cpd: **—bahn** f racecourse; (Aut) circuit, race track; **r—en** vti irreg run, race; **R—en** nt -s, - running; (Wettbewerb) race; **—fahrer** m racing driver; **—pferd** nt racehorse; **—platz** m racecourse; **—wagen** m racing car.

renovier- [reno'vi:r] cpd: **—en** vt renovate; **R—ung** f renovation.

rentabel [rɛn'ta:bəl] a profitable, lucrative.

Rentabilität [rɛntabili'tɛ:t] f profitability.

Rente ['rɛntə] f -, -n pension; **—nempfänger** m pensioner.

Rentier ['rɛnti:r] nt reindeer.

rentieren [rɛn'ti:rən] vr pay, be profitable.

Rentner(in f) ['rɛntnər(m)] m -s, - pensioner.

Repar- [repa] cpd: **—ation** [-atsi'o:n] f reparation; **—atur**

ad (rundherum) round about; *(überall)* all round.

Rinn- ['rɪn] *cpd:* —**e** *f* -, -n gutter, drain; **r—en** *vi irreg* run, trickle; —**sal** *nt* -s, -e trickle of water; —**stein** *m* gutter.

Rippchen ['rɪpçən] *nt* small rib; cutlet.

Rippe ['rɪpə] *f* -, -n rib; —**nfellentzündung** *f* pleurisy.

Risiko ['riːziko] *nt* -s, -s or **Risiken** risk.

riskant [rɪs'kant] *a* risky, hazardous.

riskieren [rɪs'kiːrən] *vt* risk.

Riß [rɪs] *m* -sses, -sse tear; *(in Mauer, Tasse etc)* crack; *(in Haut)* scratch; *(Tech)* design.

rissig ['rɪsɪç] *a* torn; cracked; scratched.

Ritt [rɪt] *m* -(e)s, -e ride; —**er** *m* -s, - knight; —**erlich** *a* chivalrous; —**erschlag** *m* knighting; —**ertum** *nt* -s chivalry; —**erzeit** *f* age of chivalry; **r—lings** *ad* astride.

Ritus ['riːtus] *m* -, **Riten** rite.

Ritze ['rɪtsə] *f* -, -n crack, chink; **r—n** *vt* scratch.

Rivale [ri'vaːlə] *m* -n, -n rival.

Rivalität [rivali'tɛːt] *f* rivalry.

Rizinusöl ['riːtsinusœːl] *nt* castor oil.

Robbe ['rɔbə] *f* -, -n seal.

Robe ['roːbə] *f* -, -n robe.

Roboter ['rɔbɔtər] *m* -s, - robot.

röcheln ['rœçəln] *vi* wheeze.

Rock [rɔk] *m* -(e)s, ⁼e skirt; *(Jackett)* jacket; *(Uniform—)* tunic.

Rodel ['roːdəl] *m* -s, - toboggan; —**bahn** *f* toboggan run; **r—n** *vi* toboggan.

roden ['roːdən] *vti* clear.

Rogen ['roːgən] *m* -s, - roe, spawn.

Roggen ['rɔgən] *m* -s, - rye; —**brot** *nt* rye bread, black bread.

roh [roː] *a* raw; *Mensch* coarse, crude; **R—bau** *m* shell of a building; **R—eisen** *nt* pig iron; **R—ling** *m* ruffian; **R—material** *nt* raw material; **R—öl** *nt* crude oil.

Rohr [roːr] *nt* -(e)s, -e pipe, tube; *(Bot)* cane; ~ *(Schilf)* reed; *(Gewehr—)* barrel; —**bruch** *m* burst pipe.

Röhre ['røːrə] *f* -, -n tube, pipe; *(Rad etc)* valve; *(Back—)* oven,.

Rohr- *cpd:* —**geflecht** *nt* wickerwork; —**leger** *m* -s, - plumber; —**leitung** *f* pipeline; —**post** *f* pneumatic post; —**stock** *m* cane; —**stuhl** *m* basket chair; —**zucker** *m* cane sugar.

Roh- *cpd:* —**seide** *f* raw silk; —**stoff** *m* raw material.

Rokoko ['rɔkoko] *nt* -s rococo.

Roll- ['rɔl] *cpd:* —**(l)aden** *m* shutter; —**bahn** *f*, —**feld** *nt* (Aviat) runway.

Rolle ['rɔlə] *f* -, -n roll; *(Theat, soziologisch)* role; *(Garn— etc)* reel, spool; *(Walze)* roller; *(Wäsche—)* mangle; **keine —spielen** not matter; **r—n** *vti* roll; *(Aviat)* taxi; *Wäsche* mangle; —**nbesetzung** *f* (Theat) cast; **—r** *m* -s, - scooter; *(Welle)* roller.

Roll- *cpd:* —**mops** *m* pickled herring; —**schuh** *m* roller skate; —**stuhl** *m* wheelchair; —**treppe** *f* escalator.

Roman [ro'maːn] *m* -s, -e novel; —**schreiber** *m*, —**schriftsteller** *m* novelist; —**tik** [ro'mantɪk] *f* romanticism; —**tiker** [ro'mantɪkər] *m* -s, - romanticist; **r—tisch** [ro'mantɪʃ] *a* romantic; —**ze** [ro'mantsə] *f* -, -n romance.

Römer ['røːmər] *m* -s, - wineglass; *(Mensch)* Roman.

röntgen ['rœntgən] vt X-ray;
R—aufnahme f, R—bild nt X-ray;
R—strahlen pl X-rays pl.

rosa ['ro:za] a pink, rose(-coloured).

Rose [ro:zə] f -, -n rose; —nkohl
m Brussels sprouts pl; —nkranz m
rosary; —nmontag m Shrove
Monday.

Rosette [ro'zɛtə] f rosette; rose
window.

rosig ['ro:zɪç] a rosy.

Rosine [ro'zi:nə] f raisin, currant.

Roß [rɔs] nt -sses, -sse horse,
steed; —kastanie f horse chestnut.

Rost [rɔst] m -(e)s, -e rust;
(Gitter) grill, gridiron; (Bett—)
springs pl; —braten m roast(ed)
meat, joint; r— en vi rust.

rösten ['rø:stən] vt roast; toast;
grill.

Rost- cpd: r—frei a rust-free;
rustproof; stainless; r—ig a rusty;
—schutz m rust-proofing.

rot {ro:t] a red; R—ation f
[rotatsi'o:n] f rotation; —bäckig a
red-cheeked; —blond a strawberry
blond.

Röte ['rø:tə] f - redness; —ln pl
German measles sing; r—n vtr
redden.

rot- cpd: —haarig a red-haired;
—ieren [ro'ti:rən] vi rotate;
R—käppchen nt Little Red Riding
Hood; R—kehlchen nt robin;
R—stift m red pencil; R—wein m
red wine.

Rotz [rɔts] m -es, -e (col) snot.

Roulade [ru'la:də] f (Cook) beef
olive.

Route ['ru:tə] f -, -n route.

Routine [ru'ti:nə] f experience;
routine.

Rübe ['ry:bə] f -, -n turnip; gelbe

— carrot; rote — beetroot;
—nzucker m beet sugar.

Rubin [ru'bi:n] m -s, -e ruby.

Rubrik [ru'bri:k] f heading;
(Spalte) column.

Ruck [ruk] m -(e)s, -e jerk, jolt.

Rück- ['rʏk] cpd: —antwort f reply,
answer; r—bezüglich a reflexive;
r—blenden vi flash back;
r—blickend a retrospective; r—en
vti move; —en m -s, - back;
(Berg—) ridge; —endeckung f
backing; —enlehne f back (of
chair); —enmark nt spinal cord;
r—enschwimmen nt backstroke;
r—enwind m following wind;
—erstattung f return, restitution;
—fahrt f return journey; —fall m
relapse; r—fällig a relapsing;
r—fällig werden relapse; —flug m
return flight; —frage f question;
—gabe f return; —gang m decline,
fall; r—gängig a: etw —gängig
machen cancel sth; —grat nt -(e)s,
-e spine, backbone; —griff m
recourse; —halt m backing,
reserve; r—haltlos a unreserved;
—kehr f -, en return; —koppelung
f feedback; —lage f reserve,
savings pl; r—läufig a declining,
falling; —licht nt back light;
r—lings ad from behind,
backwards; —nahme f -, en taking
back; —porto nt return postage;
—reise f return journey; (Naut)
home voyage; —ruf m recall.

Rucksack [ˈrʊkzak] m rucksack.

Rück- cpd: —schau f reflection;
r—schauend a, ad retrospectively, in
retrospect; —schluß m conclusion;
—schritt m retrogression;
r—schrittlich a reactionary; retrograde; —seite f back; (von Münze
etc) reverse; —sicht f
consideration; —sicht nehmen auf

(+acc) show consideration for;
r—sichtslos a inconsiderate;
Fahren reckless; (*unbarmherzig*)
ruthless; **r—sichtsvoll** a con-
siderate; **—sitz** m back seat;
—spiegel m (*Aut*) rear-view
mirror; **—spiel** nt return match;
—sprache f further discussion or
talk; **—stand** m arrears pl;
r—ständig a backward, out-
of-date; *Zahlungen* in arrears;
—stoß m recoil; **—strahler** m -s,
— rear reflector; **—tritt** m
resignation; **—trittbremse** f pedal
brake; **—vergütung** f repayment;
(*Comm*) refund; **—versicherung** f
reinsurance; **r—wärtig** a rear;
r—wärts ad backward(s), back;
—wärtsgang m (*Aut*) reverse gear;
—weg m return journey, way
back; **r—wirkend** a retroactive;
—wirkung f reaction; retrospective
effect; **—zahlung** f repayment;
—zug m retreat.

Rüde ['ry:də] m -n, -n male
dog/fox/wolf; r— a coarse, gruff.

Rudel ['ru:dəl] nt -s, - pack; herd.

Ruder ['ru:dər] nt -s, - oar;
(*Steuer*) rudder; **—boot** nt rowing
boat; **—er** m -s, - rower; **r—n** vti
row.

Ruf [ru:f] m -(e)s, -e call, cry;
(*Ansehen*) reputation; **r—en** vti
irreg call; cry; **—name** m usual
(first) name; **—nummer** f
(tele)phone number; **—zeichen** nt
(*Rad*) call sign; (*Tel*) ringing tone.

Rüge ['ry:gə] f -, -n reprimand,
rebuke; **r—** vt reprimand.

Ruhe ['ru:ə] f - rest;
(*Ungestörtheit*) peace, quiet;
(*Gelassenheit*, *Stille*) calm;
(*Schweigen*) silence; sich· zur —
setzen retire; **—!** be quiet!,
silence!; **r—los** a restless; **r—n** vi

rest; **—pause** f break; **—platz** m
resting place; **—stand** m retirement; letzte **—stätte** f final resting
place; **—störung** f breach of the
peace; **—tag** m closing day.

ruhig ['ru:ɪç] a quiet;
(*bewegungslos*) still; *Hand* steady;
(*gelassen*, *friedlich*) calm;
Gewissen clear; **tu das** — feel free
to do that.

Ruhm [ru:m] m -(e)s fame, glory.

rühm- ['ry:m] cpd: **—en** vt praise;
vr boast; **—lich** a laudable.

ruhm- cpd: **—los** a inglorious;
—reich a glorious.

Ruhr [ru:r] f - dysentery.

Rühr- ['ry:r] cpd: **—ei** nt scrambled
egg; **r—en** vtr (*lit, fig*) move, stir
(*auch Cook*); vi: **r—en** von come
or stem from; **r—en an** (+acc)
touch; (*fig*) touch on; **r—end** a
touching, moving; **r—ig** a active,
lively; **r—selig** a sentimental,
emotional; **—ung** f emotion.

Ruin [ru'i:n] m -s, -e, f -, -n ruin;
r—ieren [rui'ni:rən] vt ruin.

rülpsen ['rylpsən] vi burp, belch.

Rum [rum] m -s, -s rum.

Rummel ['ruməl] m -s (*col*)
hubbub; (*Jahrmarkt*) fair; **—platz**
m fairground, fair.

rumoren [ru'mo:rən] vi be noisy,
make a noise.

Rumpel- ['rumpəl] cpd: **—kammer**
f junk room; **r—n** vi rumble;
(*holpern*) jolt.

Rumpf [rumpf] m -(e)s, ¨e trunk,
torso; (*Aviat*) fuselage; (*Naut*)
hull.

rümpfen ['rympfən] vt *Nase* turn
up.

rund [runt] a round; ad (*etwa*)
around; — **um etw** round sth;
R—bogen m Norman or
Romanesque arch; **R—brief** m

circular; R—e ['rundə] f -, -n round; (in Rennen) lap; (Gesellschaft) circle; —en vt make round; vr (fig) take shape; —erneuert ag Reifen remoulded; R—fahrt f (round) trip.

Rundfunk ['rʊntfʊŋk] m -(e)s broadcasting; (—anstalt) broadcasting service; im — on the radio; —empfang m reception; —gebühr f licence; —gerät nt wireless set; —sendung f broadcast, radio programme.

Rund- cpd: r—heraus ad straight out, bluntly; r—herum ad round about; all round; r—lich a plump, rounded; —reise f round trip; —schreiben nt (Comm) circular; —ung f curve, roundness.

runter ['rʊntər] ad (col) = herunter, hinunter.

Runzel ['rʊntsəl] f -, -n wrinkle; r—ig a wrinkled; r—n vt wrinkle; die Stirn r—n frown.

Rüpel ['ry:pəl] m -s, - lout; r—haft a loutish.

rupfen ['rʊpfən] vt pluck; R— m -s, - sackcloth.

ruppig ['rʊpɪç] a rough, gruff.

Rüsche ['ry:ʃə] f -, -n frill.

Ruß [ru:s] m -es soot; r—en vi smoke; (Ofen) be sooty; r—ig a sooty.

Rüssel ['rysəl] m -s, - snout; (Elefanten-) trunk.

rüsten ['rystən] vtir prepare; (Mil) arm.

rüstig ['rystɪç] a sprightly, vigorous; R—keit f sprightliness, vigour.

Rüstung ['rystʊŋ] f preparation; arming; (Ritter-) armour; (Waffen etc) armaments pl; —skontrolle f armaments control.

Rüstzeug nt tools pl; (fig) capacity.

Rute ['ru:tə] f -, -n rod, switch.

Rutsch [rʊtʃ] m -(e)s, -e slide; (Erd-) landslide; —bahn f slide; r—en vi slide; (ausr—en) slip; r—ig a slippery.

rütteln ['rytəln] vti shake, jolt.

S

S,s [ɛs] nt S,s.

Saal [za:l] m -(e)s, Säle hall; room.

Saat [za:t] f -, -en seed; (Pflanzen) crop; (Säen) sowing.

sabbern ['zabərn] vi (col) dribble.

Säbel ['zɛ:bəl] m -s, - sabre, sword.

Sabotage [zabo'ta:ʒə] f -, -n sabotage.

sabotieren [zabo'ti:rən] vt sabotage.

Sach- [zax] cpd: —bearbeiter m specialist; s—dienlich a relevant,

helpful; —e f -, -n thing; (Angelegenheit) affair, business; (Frage) matter; (Pflicht) task; zur —e to the point; s—gemäß a appropriate, suitable; s—kundig a expert; —lage f situation, state of affairs; s—lich a matter-of-fact, objective; Irrtum, Angabe factual.

sächlich ['zɛxlɪç] a neuter.

Sach- cpd: —schaden m material damage; s—t(e) ad softly, gently; —verständige(r) mf expert.

Sack [zak] m -(e)s, ⸚e sack; **—en** vi sag, sink; **—gasse** f cul-de-sac, dead-end street (US).

Sadismus [za'dısmus] m sadism.

Sadist [za'dıst] m sadist; **—isch** a sadistic.

säen ['zɛːən] vti sow.

Saft [zaft] m -(e)s, ⸚e juice; (Bot) sap; **—ig** a juicy; **—los** a dry.

Sage ['zaːgə] f -, -n saga.

Säge ['zɛːgə] f -, -n saw; **—mehl** nt sawdust; **—n** vti saw.

sagen ['zaːgən] vti say (jdm to sb), tell (jdm sb); **—haft** a legendary; (col) great, smashing.

Sägewerk nt sawmill.

Sahne ['zaːnə] f - cream.

Saison [zɛ'zõː] f -, -s season; **—arbeiter** m seasonal worker.

Saite ['zaɪtə] f -, -n string; **—n-instrument** nt string-instrument.

Sakko ['zako] m or nt -s, -s jacket.

Sakrament [zakrament] nt sacrament.

Sakristei [zakrıs'taɪ] f sacristy.

Salat [za'laːt] m -(e)s, -e salad; (Kopfsalat) lettuce; **—soße** f salad dressing.

Salb- ['zalb] cpd: **—e** f -n ointment; **—ei** [zal'baɪ] m or f -s or -e sage; **s—en** vt anoint; **—ung** f anointing; **s—ungsvoll** a unctuous.

Saldo ['zaldo] m -s, **Salden** balance.

Salmiak [zalmi'ak] m -s sal ammoniac; **—geist** m liquid ammonia.

Salon [za'lõː] m -s, -s salon.

salopp [za'lop] a casual.

Salpeter [zal'peːtər] m -s saltpetre; **—säure** f nitric acid.

Salut [za'luːt] m -(e)s, -e salute; **s—ieren** [-'tiːrən] vi salute.

Salve ['zalvə] f -, -n salvo.

Salz [zalts] nt -es, -e salt; **s—en** vt irreg salt; **s—ig** a salty; **—kartoffeln** pl boiled potatoes pl; **—säure** f hydrochloric acid.

Samen ['zaːmən] m -s, - seed; (Anat) sperm.

Sammel- ['zaməl] cpd: **—band** m anthology; **—becken** nt reservoir; **—bestellung** f collective order; **s—n** vt collect; vr assemble, gather; (konzentrieren) concentrate; **—name** m collective name; **—surium** [-'zuːrium] nt hotchpotch.

Sammlung ['zamluŋ] f collection; assembly, gathering; concentration.

Samstag ['zamstaːk] m Saturday; **s—s** ad (on) Saturdays.

Samt [zamt] m -(e)s, -e velvet; **s—** prep +dat (along) with, together with; **s— und sonders** each and every one (of them).

sämtlich ['zɛmtlıç] a all (the), entire.

Sand [zant] m -(e)s, -e sand; **—ale** [zan'daːlə] f -, -n sandal; **—bank** f sandbank; **s—ig** ['zandıç] a sandy; **—kasten** m sandpit; **—kuchen** m Madeira cake; **—papier** nt sandpaper; **—stein** m sandstone; **—uhr** f hourglass.

sanft [zanft] a soft, gentle; **—mütig** a gentle, meek.

Sänger(in f) ['zɛŋər(ın)] m -s, - singer.

Sani- cpd: **s—eren** [za'niːrən] vt redevelop; (Betrieb) make financially sound; vr line one's pocket; become financially sound; **—erung** f redevelopment; making viable; **s—tär** [zani'tɛːr] a sanitary; **s—täre Anlagen** sanitation; **—täter** [zani'tɛːtər] m -s, - first-aid attendant; (Mil) (medical) orderly.

sanktionieren [zaŋktsio'ni:rən] vt sanction.

Saphir ['za:fi:r] m -s, -e sapphire.

Sardelle [zar'dɛlə] f anchovy.

Sardine [zar'di:nə] f sardine.

Sarg [zark] m -(e)s, ⁻e coffin.

Sarkasmus [zar'kasmus] m sarcasm.

sarkastisch [zar'kastɪʃ] a sarcastic.

Satan ['za:tan] m -s, -e Satan; devil.

Satellit [zatɛ'li:t] m -en, -en satellite.

Satire [za'ti:rə] f -, -n satire.

satirisch [za'ti:rɪʃ] a satirical.

satt [zat] a full; Farbe rich, deep; jdn/etw — sein or haben be fed up with sb/sth; sich — hören/sehen an (+dat) see/hear enough of; sich — essen eat one's fill; — machen be filling.

Sattel ['zatəl] m -s, ⁻ saddle; (Berg) ridge; s⁻fest a (fig) proficient; s—n vt saddle.

sättigen ['zɛtɪgən] vt satisfy; (Chem) saturate.

Satz [zats] m -es, ⁻e (Gram) sentence; (Neben—, Adverbial—) clause; (Theorem) theorem; (Mus) movement; (Tennis, Briefmarken etc) set; (Kaffee) grounds pl; (Sprung) jump; (Comm) rate; —gegenstand m (Gram) subject; —lehre f syntax; —teil m constituent (of a sentence); —ung f statute, rule; s—ungsgemäß a statutory; —zeichen nt punctuation mark.

Sau [zau] f -, ⁻e Säue sow; (col) dirty pig.

sauber ['zaubər] a clean; (ironisch) fine; —halten vt irreg keep clean; S⁻keit f cleanness; (einer Person) cleanliness.

säuber- ['zɔybər] cpd: —lich ad neatly; —n vt clean; (Pol etc) purge; S—ung f cleaning; purge.

Sauce ['zo:sə] f -, -n sauce, gravy.

sauer ['zauər] a sour; (Chem) acid; (col) cross.

Sauerei [zauə'rai] f (col) rotten state of affairs; scandal; (Schmutz etc) mess; (Unanständigkeit) obscenity.

säuerlich ['zɔyərlɪç] a sourish, tart.

Sauer- cpd: —milch f sour milk; —stoff m oxygen; —stoffgerät nt breathing apparatus; —teig m leaven.

saufen ['zaufən] vti irreg (col) drink, booze.

Säufer ['zɔyfər] m -s, - (col) boozer.

Sauferei [zaufə'rai] f drinking, boozing; booze-up.

saugen ['zaugən] vti irreg suck.

säugen ['zɔygən] vt suckle.

Sauger [zaugər] m -s, - dummy, comforter (US); (auf Flasche) teat; (Staub—) vacuum cleaner, hoover ®.

Säug- ['zɔyg] cpd: —etier nt mammal; —ling m infant, baby.

Säule ['zɔylə] f -, -n column, pillar; —ngang m arcade.

Saum [zaum] m -(e)s, Säume hem; (Naht) seam.

säumen ['zɔymən] vt hem; seam; vi delay, hesitate.

Sauna ['zauna] f -, -s sauna.

Säure ['zɔyrə] f -, -n acid; (Geschmack) sourness, acidity; s—beständig a acid-proof; s—haltig a acidic.

säuseln ['zɔyzəln] vti murmur, rustle.

sausen ['zauzən] vi blow; (col: eilen) rush; (Ohren) buzz; etw — lassen (col) give sth a miss.

Saustall ['zauʃtal] *m* (*col*) pigsty.

Saxophon [zakso'foːn] *nt* -s, -e saxophone.

Schabe ['ʃaːbə] *f* -, -n cockroach; **s—n** *vt* scrape; **—rnack** ['ʃaːbərnak] *m* -(e)s, -e trick, prank.

schäbig ['ʃɛːbɪç] *a* shabby; **S—keit** *f* shabbiness.

Schablone [ʃa'bloːnə] *f* -, -n stencil; (*Muster*) pattern; (*fig*) convention; **s—nhaft** *a* stereotyped, conventional.

Schach [ʃax] *nt* -s, -s chess; (*Stellung*) check; **—brett** *nt* chessboard; **—figur** *f* chessman; **'s—'matt** *a* checkmate; **—partie** *f*, —spiel *nt* game of chess.

Schacht [ʃaxt] *m* -(e)s, ⁼e shaft; **—el** *f* -, -n box; (*pej: Frau*) bag, cow.

schade ['ʃaːdə] *a* a pity or shame; **sich** (*dat*) zu — sein für etw consider oneself too good for sth; *interj* (what a) pity or shame.

Schädel ['ʃɛːdəl] *m* -s, - skull; **—bruch** *m* fractured skull.

Schaden ['ʃaːdən] *m* -s, ⁼ damage; (*Verletzung*) injury; (*Nachteil*) disadvantage; **s—** *vi* (*+dat*) hurt; **einer Sache** — damage sth; **—ersatz** *m* compensation, damages *pl*; **s—ersatzpflichtig** *a* liable for damages; **—freude** *f* malicious delight; **s—froh** *a* gloating, with malicious delight.

schadhaft ['ʃaːthaft] *a* faulty, damaged.

schäd- ['ʃɛːt] *cpd:* **—igen** ['ʃɛdɪgən] *vt* damage; *Person* do harm to, harm; **S—igung** *f* damage; harm; **—lich** *a* harmful (*für* to); **S—lichkeit** *f* harmfulness; **S—ling** *m* pest; **S—lingsbekämpfungsmittel** *nt* pesticide.

schadlos ['ʃaːtloːs] *a*: **sich — halten an** (*+dat*) take advantage of.

Schaf [ʃaːf] *nt* -(e)s, -e sheep; **—bock** *m* ram.

Schäfchen ['ʃɛːfçən] *nt* lamb; **—wolken** *pl* cirrus clouds *pl*.

Schäfer ['ʃɛːfər] *m* -s, -e shepherd; **—hund** *m* Alsatian; **—in** *f* shepherdess.

schaffen ['ʃafən] *vt irreg* create; *Platz* make; **sich** (*dat*) **etw** — get o.s. sth; *vt* (*erreichen*) manage, do; (*erledigen*) finish; *Prüfung* pass; (*transportieren*) take; *vi* (*col: arbeiten*) work; **sich an etw** (*dat*) zu — machen busy oneself with sth; **S—** *nt* -s (creative) activity; **S—sdrang** *m* creative urge; energy; **S—skraft** *f* creativity.

Schaffner(in *f*) ['ʃafnər(ɪn)] *m* -s, - (*Bus*) conductor/conductress; (*Rail*) guard.

Schaft [ʃaft] *m* -(e)s, ⁼e shaft; (*von Gewehr*) stock; (*von Stiefel*) leg; (*Bot*) stalk; tree trunk; **—stiefel** *m* high boot.

Schakal [ʃa'kaːl] *m* -s, -e jackal.

Schäker ['ʃɛːkər] *m* -s, - flirt; joker; **s—n** *vi* flirt; joke.

schal [ʃaːl] *a* a flat; (*fig*) insipid; **S—** *m* -s, -e or -s scarf.

Schälchen ['ʃɛːlçən] *nt* cup, bowl.

Schale ['ʃaːlə] *f* -, -n skin; (*abgeschält*) peel; (*Nuß—, Muschel—, Ei—*) shell; (*Geschirr*) dish, bowl.

schälen ['ʃɛːlən] *vt* peel; shell; *vr* peel.

Schall [ʃal] *m* -(e)s, ⁼e sound; **—dämpfer** *m* -s, - (*Aut*) silencer; **s—dicht** *a* soundproof; **s—en** *vi* (re)sound; **s—end** *a* resounding, loud; **—mauer** *f* sound barrier; **—platte** *f* (gramophone) record.

Schalt- [ʃalt] *cpd*: **—bild** *nt* circuit diagram; **—brett** *nt* switchboard; **s—en** *vt* switch, turn; *vi (Aut)* change (gear); *(col: begreifen)* catch on; **s—en und walten** do as one pleases; **—er** *m* -s, - counter; *(an Gerät)* switch; **—erbeamte(r)** *m* counter clerk; **—hebel** *m* switch; *(Aut)* gear-lever; **—jahr** *nt* leap year; **—ung** *f* switching; *(Elec)* circuit; *(Aut)* gear change.

Scham [ʃaːm] *f* - shame; *(—gefühl)* modesty; *(Organe)* private parts *pl*.

schämen [ˈʃɛːmən] *vr* be ashamed.

Scham- *cpd*: **—haare** *pl* pubic hair; **s—haft** a modest, bashful; **s—los** a shameless.

Schande [ˈʃandə] *f* - disgrace.

schändlich [ˈʃɛntlɪç] a disgraceful, shameful; **S—keit** *f* disgracefulness.

Schandtat [ˈʃanttaːt] *f (col)* escapade, shenanigan.

Schändung [ˈʃɛndʊŋ] *f* violation, defilement.

Schank- [ʃaŋk] *cpd*: **—erlaubnis** *f*, **—konzession** *f* (publican's) licence; **—tisch** *m* bar.

Schanze [ˈʃantsə] *f* -, -n *(Mil)* fieldwork, earthworks *pl*; *(Sprung—)* skijump.

Schar [ʃaːr] *f* -, -en band, company; *(Vögel)* flock; *(Menge)* crowd; in -en in droves; **—ade** [ʃaˈraːdə] *f* charade; **s—en** *vr* assemble, rally; **s—enweise** *ad* in droves.

scharf [ʃarf] a sharp; *Essen* hot; *Munition* live; **—nachdenken** think hard; **auf etw** *(acc)* **— sein** *(col)* be keen on sth; **S—blick** *m* (fig) penetration.

Schärf- [ʃɛrf] *cpd*: **—e** *f* -, -n sharpness; *(Strenge)* rigour; **s—en** *vt* sharpen.

Scharf- *cpd*: **s—machen** *vt (col)* stir up; **—richter** *m* executioner; **—schießen** *nt* firing live ammunition; **—schütze** *m* marksman, sharpshooter; **—sinn** *m* penetration, astuteness; **s—sinnig** a astute, shrewd.

Scharmützel [ʃarˈmʏtsəl] *nt* -s, - skirmish.

Scharnier [ʃarˈniːr] *nt* -s, -e hinge.

Schärpe [ˈʃɛrpə] *f* -, -n sash.

scharren [ˈʃarən] *vti* scrape, scratch.

Scharte [ˈʃartə] *f* -, -n notch, nick; *(Berg)* wind gap.

schartig [ˈʃartɪç] a jagged.

Schaschlik [ˈʃaʃlɪk] *m* or *nt* -s, -e (shish) kebab.

Schatten [ˈʃatən] *m* -s, - shadow; **—bild** *nt*, **—riß** *m* silhouette; **—seite** *f* shady side, dark side.

schattieren [ʃaˈtiːrən] *vti* shade.

Schattierung [ʃaˈtiːrʊŋ] *f* shading.

schattig [ˈʃatɪç] a shady.

Schatulle [ʃaˈtʊlə] *f* -, -n casket; *(Geld—)* coffer.

Schatz [ʃats] *m* -es, ⁼e treasure; *(Person)* darling; **—amt** *nt* treasury.

schätz- [ʃɛts] *cpd*: **—bar** a assessable; **S—chen** *nt* darling, love; **—en** *vt (abschätzen)* estimate; *Gegenstand* value; *(würdigen)* value, esteem; *(vermuten)* reckon; **—enlernen** *vt* learn to appreciate; **S—ung** *f* estimate; estimation; valuation; **nach meiner S—ung** ... I reckon that ...; **—ungsweise** *ad* approximately; **it is thought**; **S—wert** *m* estimated value.

Schau [ʃaʊ] *f* - show; *(Ausstellung)* display, exhibition; **etw zur — stellen** make a show of sth, show sth off; **—bild** *nt* diagram.

Schauder ['ʃaʊdər] *m* -s, -s shudder; (*wegen Kälte*) shiver; s—haft *a* horrible; s—n *vi* shudder; shiver.

schauen ['ʃaʊən] *vi* look.

Schauer ['ʃaʊər] *m* -s, - (*Regen—*) shower; (*Schreck*) shudder; —geschichte *f* horror story; s—lich a horrific, spine-chilling.

Schaufel ['ʃaʊfəl] *f* -, -n shovel; (*Naut*) paddle; (*Tech*) scoop; s—n *vt* shovel, scoop.

Schau- *cpd:* —fenster *nt* shop window; —fensterauslage *f* window display; —fensterbummel *m* window shopping (expedition); —fensterdekorateur *m* window, dresser; —geschäft *nt* show business; —kasten *m* showcase.

Schaukel ['ʃaʊkəl] *f* -, -n swing; s—n *vi* swing, rock; —pferd *nt* rocking horse; —stuhl *m* rocking chair.

Schaulustige(r) ['ʃaʊlʊstɪgə(r)] *mf* onlooker.

Schaum [ʃaʊm] *m* -(e)s, Schäume foam; (*Seifen—*) lather.

schäumen ['ʃɔɪmən] *vi* foam.

Schaum- *cpd:* —gummi *m* foam (rubber); s—ig *a* frothy, foamy; —krone *f* white crest; —schläger *m* (*fig*) windbag; —wein *m* sparkling wine.

Schau- *cpd:* —platz *m* scene; s—rig *a* horrific, dreadful; —spiel *nt* spectacle; (*Theat*) play; —spieler *m* actor; —spielerin *f* actress; s—spielern *vi insep* act.

Scheck [ʃɛk] *m* -s, -s cheque; —buch *nt* cheque book; s—ig a dappled, piebald.

scheel [ʃeːl] a (*col*) dirty; jdn — ansehen give sb a dirty look.

scheffeln ['ʃɛfəln] *vt* amass.

Scheibe ['ʃaɪbə] *f* -, -n disc; (*Brot etc*) slice; (*Glas—*) pane (*Mil*) target; —nbremse *f* (*Aut*) disc brake; —nwaschanlage *f* (*Aut*) windscreen washers *pl*; —nwischer *m* (*Aut*) windscreen wiper.

Scheich [ʃaɪç] *m* -s, -e or -s sheik(h).

Scheide ['ʃaɪdə] *f* -, -n sheath; (*Grenze*) boundary; (*Anat*) vagina; s—n *irreg vt* separate; *Ehe* dissolve; sich s—n lassen get a divorce; *vi* (de)part.

Scheidung (*Ehe—*) divorce; —sgrund *m* grounds *pl* for divorce; —sklage *f* divorce suit.

Schein [ʃaɪn] *m* -(e)s, -e light; (*An—*) appearance; (*Geld*) (bank)-note; (*Bescheinigung*) certificate; zum — in pretence; s—bar a apparent; s—en *vi irreg* shine; (*Anschein haben*) seem; s—heilig a hypocritical; —tod *m* apparent death; —werfer *m* -s, - floodlight; spotlight; (*Such—*) searchlight; (*Aut*) headlamp.

Scheiß- [ʃaɪs] *in cpds* (*col*) bloody; —e *f* - (*col*) shit.

Scheit [ʃaɪt] *nt* -(e)s, -e or -er log, billet.

Scheitel ['ʃaɪtəl] *m* -s, - top; (*Haar*) parting; s—n *vt* part; —punkt *m* zenith, apex.

scheitern ['ʃaɪtərn] *vi* fail.

Schelle ['ʃɛlə] *f* -, -n small bell; s—n *vi* ring.

Schellfisch ['ʃɛlfɪʃ] *m* haddock.

Schelm [ʃɛlm] *m* -(e)s, -e rogue; s—isch a mischievous, roguish.

Schelte ['ʃɛltə] *f* -, -n scolding; s—n *vt irreg* scold.

Schema ['ʃeːma] *nt* -s, -s or -ta scheme, plan; (*Darstellung*) schema; **nach** — quite

mechanically; **s—tisch** [ʃeˈmaːtɪʃ] *a* schematic; *(pej)* mechanical.

Schemel [ˈʃeːməl] *m* -s, - (foot‐)stool.

Schenkel [ˈʃɛŋkəl] *m* -s, - thigh.

schenken [ˈʃɛŋkən] *vt (lit, fig)* give; *Getränk* pour; **sich** *(dat)* **etw — (col)** skip sth; **das ist geschenkt!** *(billig)* that's a giveaway!; *(nichts wert)* that's worthless!

Schenkung [ˈʃɛŋkʊŋ] *f* gift; **—sur‐kunde** *f* deed of gift.

Scherbe [ˈʃɛrbə] *f* -, -n broken piece, fragment; *(archäologisch)* potsherd.

Schere [ˈʃeːrə] *f* -, -n scissors *pl*; *(groß)* shears *pl*; **s—n** *vt irreg* cut; *Schaf* shear; *(sich kümmern)* bother; *vr* care; **scher dich (zum Teufel)!** get lost!; **—nschleifer** *m* -s, - knife‐grinder; **—'rei** *f (col)* bother, trouble.

Scherflein [ˈʃɛrflaɪn] *nt* mite, bit.

Scherz [ʃɛrts] *m* -es, -e joke; fun; **—frage** *f* conundrum; **s—haft** *a* joking, jocular.

scheu [ʃɔʏ] *a* shy; **S— f** - shyness; *(Angst)* fear *(vor +dat* of); *(Ehrfurcht)* awe; **S—che f** -, -n scarecrow; **—chen** *vt* scare (off); **—en** *vr*: **sich —en vor** *(+dat)* be afraid of, shrink from; *vt* shun; *vi (Pferd)* shy.

Scheuer- [ˈʃɔʏər] *cpd*: **—bürste f** scrubbing brush; **—lappen** *m* floor‐cloth; **—leiste f** skirting board; **s—n** *vt* scour, scrub.

Scheuklappe f blinker.

Scheune [ˈʃɔʏnə] *f* -, -n barn.

Scheusal [ˈʃɔʏzaːl] *nt* -s, -e monster.

scheußlich [ˈʃɔʏslɪç] *a* dreadful, frightful; **S—keit f** dreadfulness.

Schi [ʃiː] *m see* Ski.

Schicht [ʃɪçt] *f* -, -en layer; *(Klasse)* class, level; *(in Fabrik etc)* shift; **—arbeit f** shift work; **s—en** *vt* layer, stack.

schick [ʃɪk] *a* stylish, chic; **—en** *vt* send; *vr* resign oneself *(in +acc* to); *v impers (anständig sein)* be fitting; **—lich** *a* proper, fitting; **S—sal** *nt* -s, -e fate; **—salsschlag** *m* great misfortune, blow.

Schieb- [ʃiːb] *cpd*: **—edach** *nt (Aut)* sunshine roof; **s—en** *vti irreg* push; *Schuld* put *(auf jdn* on sb); **—er** *m* -s, - slide; *(Besteckteil)* pusher; *(Person)* profiteer; **—etür f** sliding door; **—lehre f** *(Math)* calliper rule; **—ung f** fiddle.

Schieds- [ˈʃiːts] *cpd*: **—gericht** *nt* court of arbitration; **—richter** *m* referee, umpire; *(Schlichter)* arbitrator; **s—richtern** *vti insep* referee, umpire; arbitrate; **—spruch** *m* (arbitration) award.

schief [ʃiːf] *a* crooked; *Ebene* sloping; *Turm* leaning; *Winkel* oblique; *Blick* funny; *Vergleich* distorted; *ad* crooked(ly); **—** **ansehen** askance; **etw — stellen** slope sth.

Schiefer [ˈʃiːfər] *m* -s, - slate; **—dach** *nt* slate roof; **—tafel f** (child's) slate.

schief- *cpd*: **—gehen** *vi irreg (col)* go wrong; **—lachen** *vr (col)* double up with laughter; **—liegen** *vi irreg (col)* be wrong.

schielen [ˈʃiːlən] *vi* squint; **nach etw —** *(fig)* eye sth.

Schienbein *nt* shinbone.

Schiene [ˈʃiːnə] *f* -, -en rail; *(Med)* splint; **s—n** *vt* put in splints; **—nstrang** *m* (Rail etc) (section of) track.

schier [ʃiːr] *a* pure; *Fleisch* lean and boneless; *(fig)* sheer; *ad* nearly, almost.

Schieß- [ʃiːs] cpd: —**bude** f shooting gallery; —**budenfigur** f (col) clown, ludicrous figure; s—**en** vti irreg shoot (auf +acc at); (Salat etc) run to seed; Ball kick; Geschoß fire; —**e'rei** f shooting incident, shoot-up; —**platz** m firing range; —**pulver** nt gunpowder; —**scharte** f embrasure; —**stand** m rifle or shooting range.

Schiff [ʃɪf] nt -(e)s, -e ship, vessel; (Kirchen—) nave; s—**bar** a navigable; —**bau** m shipbuilding; —**bruch** m shipwreck; s—**brüchig** a shipwrecked; —**chen** nt small boat; (Weben) shuttle; (Mütze) forage cap; —**er** m -s, - bargeman, boatman; —(**f**)**ahrt** f shipping; (Reise) voyage; —(**f**)**ahrtslinie** f shipping route; s—**junge** m cabin boy; —**sladung** f cargo, shipload; —**splanke** f gangplank.

Schikane · [ʃi'kaːnə] f -, -n harassment; dirty trick; mit allen —**n** with all the trimmings.

schikanieren [ʃikɑ'niːrən] vt harass, torment.

Schild [ʃɪlt] m -(e)s, -e shield; (Mützen—) peak, visor; etw im —**e führen** be up to sth; nt -(e)s, -er sign; nameplate; (Etikett) label; —**bürger** m duffer, blockhead; —**drüse** f thyroid gland; s—**ern** [ʃɪldərn] vt depict, portray; —**erung** f description, portrayal; —**kröte** f tortoise; (Wasser—) turtle.

Schilf [ʃɪlf] nt -(e)s, -e, —**rohr** nt (Pflanze) reed; (Material) reeds pl, rushes pl.

schillern [ʃɪlərn] vi shimmer; —**d** a iridescent.

Schimmel [ʃɪməl] m -s, - mould; (Pferd) white horse; s—**ig** a mouldy; s—**n** vi get mouldy.

Schimmer [ʃɪmər] m -s glimmer; s—**n** vi glimmer, shimmer.

Schimpanse [ʃɪm'panzə] m -n, -n chimpanzee.

Schimpf [ʃɪmpf] m -(e)s, -e disgrace; s—**en** vti scold; vi curse, complain; —**wort** nt term of abuse.

Schind- [ʃɪnd] cpd: —**el** f -, -n shingle; s—**en** irreg vt maltreat, drive too hard; (col) Eindruck s—**en** create an impression; vr sweat and strain, toil away (mit at); —**er** m -s, - knacker; (fig) slave driver; —**e'rei** f grind, drudgery; —**luder** nt: —**luder treiben mit** muck or mess about; Vorrecht abuse.

Schinken [ʃɪŋkən] m -s, - ham.

Schippe [ʃɪpə] f -, -n shovel; s—**n** vt shovel.

Schirm [ʃɪrm] m -(e)s, -e (Regen—) umbrella; (Sonnen—) parasol, sunshade; (Wand—, Bild—) screen; (Lampen—) (lamp)shade; (Mützen—) peak; (Pilz—) cap; —**bildaufnahme** f X-ray; —**herr** m patron, protector; —**mütze** f peaked cap; —**ständer** m umbrella stand.

schizophren [ʃɪtso'freːn] a schizophrenic.

Schlacht [ʃlaxt] f -, -en battle; s—**en** vt slaughter, kill; —**enbummler** m football supporter; —**er** m -s, - butcher; —**feld** nt battlefield; —**haus** nt, —**hof** m slaughterhouse, abattoir; —**plan** m (lit, fig) battle plan; —**ruf** m battle cry, war cry; —**schiff** nt battle ship; —**vieh** nt animals kept for meat; beef cattle.

Schlacke [ʃlakə] f -, -n slag.

Schlaf [ʃlaːf] m -(e)s sleep; —**anzug** m pyjamas pl.

Schläf- ['ʃlɛ:f] *cpd:* **—chen** *nt* nap; **—e** *f* -, **-n** temple.

schlafen ['ʃa:fən] *vi irreg* sleep; **S—gehen** *nt* -s going to bed; **S—szeit** *f* bedtime.

Schläfer(in *f)* ['ʃlɛ:fər(m)] *m* -s, - sleeper.

schlaff [ʃlaf] *a* slack; *(energielos)* limp; *(erschöpft)* exhausted; **S—heit** *f* slackness; limpness; exhaustion.

Schlaf- *cpd:* **—gelegenheit** *f* sleeping accommodation; **—lied** *nt* lullaby; **—los** *a* sleepless; **—losigkeit** *f* sleeplessness, insomnia; **—mittel** *nt* soporific, sleeping pill.

schläfrig ['ʃlɛ:friç] *a* sleepy.

Schlaf- *cpd:* **—saal** *m* dormitory; **—sack** *m* sleeping bag; **—tablette** *f* sleeping pill; **s—trunken** *a* drowsy, half-asleep; **—wagen** *m* sleeping car, sleeper; **s—wandeln** *vi insep* sleepwalk; **—zimmer** *nt* bedroom.

Schlag [ʃla:k] *m* -(e)s, -̈e *(lit, fig)* blow; stroke *(auch Med)*; *(Puls—, Herz—)* beat; *(pl: Tracht Prügel)* beating; *(Elec)* shock; *(Blitz—)* bolt, stroke; *(Autotür)* car door; *(col: Portion)* helping; *(Art)* kind, type; **mit einem —** all at once; **auf — in** rapid succession; **—ader** *f* artery; **—anfall** *m* stroke; **s—artig** *a* sudden, without warning; **—baum** *m* barrier; **s—en** ['ʃla:gən] *irreg vti* strike, hit; *(wiederholt —, besiegen)* beat; *(Glocke)* ring; *Stunde* strike; *Sahne* whip; *(Schlacht* fight; *(einwickeln)* wrap; **nach jdm s—en** *(fig)* take after sb; **vr** fight; **sich gut s—en** *(fig)* do well; **s—end** *a* Beweis convincing; **s—ende Wetter** *(Min)* firedamp; **—er**

['ʃla:gər] *m* -s, - *(lit, fig)* hit; **—ersänger(in** *f) m* pop singer.

Schläg- ['ʃlɛ:g] *cpd:* **—er** *m* -s, - brawler; *(Sport)* bat; *(Tennis etc)* racket; *(golf)* club; hockey stick; *(Waffe)* rapier; **—e'rei** *f* fight, punch-up.

Schlag- *cpd:* **s—fertig** *a* quickwitted; **—fertigkeit** *f* ready wit, quickness of repartee; **—instrument** *nt* percussion instrument; **—loch** *nt* pothole; **—rahm** *m*, **—sahne** *f* (whipped) cream; **—seite** *f* *(Naut)* list; **—wort** *nt* slogan, catch phrase; **—zeile** *f* headline; **—zeug** *nt* percussion; drums *pl*; **—zeuger** *m* -s, - drummer.

Schlamassel [ʃla'masəl] *m* -s, - *(col)* mess.

Schlamm [ʃlam] *m* -(e)s, -e mud; **s—ig** *a* muddy.

Schlamp- [ʃlamp] *cpd:* **—e** *f* -, **-n** *(col)* slattern, slut; **s—en** *vi (col)* be sloppy; **—e'rei** *f (col)* disorder, untidiness; sloppy work; **s—ig** *a* *(col)* slovenly, sloppy.

Schlange ['ʃlaŋə] *f* -, **-n** snake; *(Menschen—)* queue *(Brit)*, line-up *(US)*; **— stehen** (form a) queue, line up.

schlängeln ['ʃlɛŋəln] *vr* twist, wind; *(Fluß)* meander.

Schlangen- *cpd:* **—biß** *m* snake bite; **—ngift** *nt* snake venom; **—linie** *f* wavy line.

schlank [ʃlaŋk] *a* slim, slender; **S—heit** *f* slimness, slenderness; **S—heitskur** *f* diet.

schlapp [ʃlap] *a* limp; *(locker)* slack; **S—e** *f* -, **-n** *(col)* setback; **S—heit** *f* limpness; slackness; **S—hut** *m* slouch hat; **—machen** *vi (col)* wilt, droop.

Schlaraffenland [ʃla'rafənlant] *nt* land of milk and honey.

schlau [ʃlau] a crafty, cunning.

Schlauch [ʃlaux] m -(e)s, **Schläuche** hose; (in Reifen) inner *tube; (col: Anstrengung) grind; —boot nt rubber dinghy; s—en vt (col) tell on, exhaust; s—los a Reifen tubeless.

Schlau- cpd: —heit f, **Schläue** [ʃlɔʏə] f - cunning; —kopf m clever dick.

schlecht [ʃlɛçt] a bad; — und recht after a fashion; jdm ist — sb feels sick or bad; —erdings ad simply; —gehen vi impers irreg: jdm geht es — sb is in a bad way; S—heit f badness; '—hin ad simply; der Dramatiker —hin THE playwright; S—igkeit f badness; bad deed; —machen vt run down; etw —machen do sth badly; —weg ad simply.

schlecken [ʃlɛkən] vti lick.

Schlegel [ʃleːgəl] m -s, - (drum)-stick; (Hammer) mallet, hammer; (Cook) leg.

Schleie [ʃlaɪə] f -, -n tench.

schleichen [ʃlaɪçən] vi irreg creep, crawl; —d a gradual; creeping.

Schleier [ʃlaɪər] m -s, - veil; s—haft a (col) jdm s—haft sein be a mystery to sb.

Schleif- [ʃlaɪf] cpd: —e f -, -n loop; (Band) bow; s—en vt drag; (Mil) Festung raze; vi drag; s—en vt irreg grind; Edelstein cut; (Mil) Soldaten drill; —stein m grindstone.

Schleim [ʃlaɪm] m -(e)s, -e slime; (Med) mucus; (Cook) gruel; s—ig a slimy.

Schlemm- [ʃlɛm] cpd: s—en vi feast; —er m -s, - gourmet; —e'rei f gluttony, feasting.

schlendern [ʃlɛndərn] vi stroll.

Schlendrian [ʃlɛndriaːn] m -(e)s sloppy way of working.

schlenkern [ʃlɛŋkərn] vti swing, dangle.

Schlepp- [ʃlɛp] cpd: —e f -, -n train; s—en vt drag; Auto, Schiff tow; (tragen) lug; s—end a dragging, slow; —er m -s, - tractor; (Schiff) tug; —tau nt towrope; jdn ins —tau nehmen (fig) take sb in tow.

Schleuder [ʃlɔʏdər] f -, -n catapult; (Wäsche—) spin-drier; (Butter— etc) centrifuge; s—n vt hurl; Wäsche spin-dry; vi (Aut) skid; —preis m give-away price; —sitz m (Aviat) ejector seat; (fig) hot seat; —ware f cheap or cut-price goods pl.

schleunig [ʃlɔʏnɪç] a quick, prompt; —st ad straight away.

Schleuse [ʃlɔʏzə] f -, -n lock; (—ntor) sluice.

Schlich [ʃlɪç] m -(e)s, -e dodge, trick.

schlicht [ʃlɪçt] a simple, plain; —en vt smooth, dress; Streit settle; S—er m -s, - mediator, arbitrator; S—ung f settlement; arbitration.

Schlick [ʃlɪk] m -(e)s, -e mud; (Öl—) slick.

Schließ- [ʃliːs] cpd: —e f -, -n fastener; s—en irreg vtir close, shut; (beenden) close; Freundschaft, Bündnis, Ehe enter into; (folgern) infer (aus + dat from); etw in sich s—en include sth; —fach nt locker; s—lich ad finally; (— doch) after all.

Schliff [ʃlɪf] m -(e)s, -e cut(ting); (fig) polish.

schlimm [ʃlɪm] a bad; —er a worse; —ste(r,s) a worst; —stenfalls ad at (the) worst.

Schling- [ˈʃlɪŋ] cpd: **-e** f **-, -n** loop; (esp Henkers—) noose; (Falle) snare; (Méd) sling; **-el** m **-s, -** rascal; **s—en** irreg vt wind; vti (essen) bolt (one's food), gobble; **s—en** vi roll.

Schlips [ʃlɪps] m **-es, -e** tie.

Schlitten [ˈʃlɪtən] m **-s, -** sledge, sleigh; **-bahn** f toboggan run; **—fahren** nt **-s** tobogganing.

schlittern [ˈʃlɪtɐn] vi slide.

Schlittschuh [ˈʃlɪt.ʃuː] m skate; **— laufen** skate; **-bahn** f skating rink; **—läufer(in** f) m skater.

Schlitz [ʃlɪts] m **-es, -e** slit; (für Münze) slot; (Hosen—) flies pl; **s—äugig** a slant-eyed; **s—en** vt slit.

schlohweiß [ˈʃloːˈvaɪs] a snow-white.

Schloß [ʃlɔs] nt **-sses, =sser** lock; (an Schmuck etc) clasp; (Bau) castle; château.

Schlosser [ˈʃlɔsɐ] m **-s, -** (Auto—) fitter; (für Schlüssel etc) locksmith; **-ei** [-ˈraɪ] f metal (working) shop.

Schlot [ʃloːt] m **-(e)s, -e** chimney; (Naut) funnel.

schlottern [ˈʃlɔtɐn] vi shake, tremble; (Kleidung) be baggy.

Schlucht [ʃlʊxt] f **-, -en** gorge, ravine.

schluchzen [ˈʃlʊxtsən] vi sob.

Schluck [ʃlʊk] m **-(e)s, -e** swallow; (Menge) drop; **—auf** m **-s, —en** m **-s, -** hiccups pl; **s—en** vti swallow.

schludern [ˈʃluːdɐn] vi skimp, do sloppy work.

Schlummer [ˈʃlʊmɐ] m **-s** slumber; **s—n** vi slumber.

Schlund [ʃlʊnt] m **-(e)s, =e** gullet; (fig) jaw.

schlüpfen [ˈʃlʏpfən] vi slip; (Vogel etc) hatch (out).

Schlüpfer [ˈʃlʏpfɐ] m **-s, -** panties pl, knickers pl.

Schlupfloch [ˈʃlʊpflɔx] nt hole; hide-out; (fig) loophole.

schlüpfrig [ˈʃlʏpfrɪç] a slippery; (fig) lewd; **S—keit** f slipperiness; (fig) lewdness.

schlurfen [ˈʃlʊrfən] vi shuffle.

schlürfen [ˈʃlʏrfən] vti slurp.

Schluß [ʃlʊs] m **-sses, =sse** end; (—folgerung) conclusion; **am —** at the end; **— machen** finish with.

Schlüssel [ˈʃlʏsəl] m **-s, -** (lit, fig) key; (Schraub—) spanner, wrench; (Mus) clef; **-bein** nt collarbone; **-blume** f cowslip, primrose; **-bund** m bunch of keys; **-kind** nt latchkey child; **-loch** nt keyhole; **-position** f key position; **-wort** f combination.

schlüssig [ˈʃlʏsɪç] a conclusive.

Schluß- cpd: **-licht** nt taillight; (fig) tailender; **-strich** m (fig) final stroke; **-verkauf** m clearance sale; **-wort** nt concluding words pl.

Schmach [ʃmaːx] f = disgrace, ignominy.

schmachten [ˈʃmaːxtən] vi languish; long (nach for).

schmächtig [ˈʃmɛçtɪç] a slight.

schmachvoll a ignominious, humiliating.

schmackhaft [ˈʃmakhaft] a tasty.

schmäh- [ˈʃmɛː] cpd: **—en** vt abuse, revile; **—lich** a ignominious, shameful; **S—ung** f abuse.

schmal [ʃmaːl] a narrow; Person, Buch etc slender, slim; (karg) meagre.

schmälern [ˈʃmɛːlɐn] vt diminish; (fig) belittle.

Schmal- *cpd:* —film *m* cine film; —spur *f* narrow gauge.

Schmalz [ʃmalts] *nt* -es, -e dripping, lard; *(fig)* sentiment, schmaltz; **s—ig** *a (fig)* schmaltzy, slushy.

schmarotzen [ʃmaˈrɔtsən] *vi* sponge; *(Bot)* be parasitic.

Schmarotzer *m* -s, - parasite; sponger.

Schmarren [ʃmarən] *m* -s, - *(Aus)* small piece of pancake; *(fig)* rubbish, tripe.

schmatzen [ʃmatsən] *vi* smack one's lips; eat noisily.

Schmaus [ʃmaʊs] *m* -es, **Schmäuse** feast; **s—en** *vi* feast.

schmecken [ʃmɛkən] *vti* taste; **es** schmeckt ihm he likes it.

Schmeichel- [ʃmaɪçəl] *cpd:* —ei ·[ˈlaɪ] *f* flattery; **s—haft** *a* flattering; **s—n** *vi* flatter.

schmeißen [ʃmaɪsən] *vt irreg (col)* throw, chuck.

Schmeißfliege *f* bluebottle.

Schmelz [ʃmɛlts] *m* -es, -e enamel; *(Glasur)* glaze; *(von Stimme)* melodiousness; **s—bar** *a* fusible; **s—en** *vti irreg* melt; Erz smelt; —**hütte** *f* smelting works *pl*; —**punkt** *m* melting point; —**wasser** *nt* melted snow.

Schmerz [ʃmɛrts] *m* -es, -en pain; *(Trauer)* grief; **s—empfindlich** *a* sensitive to pain; **s—en** *vti* hurt; —**ensgeld** *nt* compensation; **s—haft, —lich** *a* painful; **s—los** *a* painless; **s—stillend** *a* soothing.

Schmetterling [ʃmɛtərlɪŋ] *m* butterfly.

schmettern [ʃmɛtərn] *vti* smash; Melodie sing loudly, bellow out; *(Trompete)* blare.

Schmied [ʃmiːt] *m* -(e)s, -e blacksmith; —**e** [ʃmiːdə] *f* -, -n smithy,

forge; —**eisen** *nt* wrought iron; **s—en** *vt* forge; Pläne devise, concoct.

schmiegen [ʃmiːɡən] *vt* press, nestle; *vr* cling, nestle (up) (*an* +*acc* to).

schmiegsam [ʃmiːkzaːm] *a* flexible, pliable.

Schmier- [ʃmiːr] *cpd:* —e *f* -, -n grease; *(Theat)* greasepaint, make-up; **s—en** *vt* smear; *(ölen)* lubricate, grease; *(bestechen)* bribe; *vti (schreiben)* scrawl; —**fett** *nt* grease; —**fink** *m* messy person; —**geld** *nt* bribe; **s—ig** *a* greasy; —**mittel** *nt* lubricant; —**seife** *f* soft soap.

Schminke [ʃmɪŋkə] *f* -, -n make-up; **s—n** *vtr* make up.

schmirgel- [ʃmɪrɡəl] *cpd:* —n *vt* sand (down); **S—papier** *nt* emery paper.

Schmöker [ʃmøːkər] *m* -s, - *(col)* (trashy) old book; **s—n** *vi (col)* browse.

schmollen [ʃmɔlən] *vi* sulk, pout; —**d** *a* sulky.

Schmor- [ʃmoːr] *cpd:* —**braten** *m* stewed or braised meat; **s—en** *vt* stew, braise.

Schmuck [ʃmʊk] *m* -(e)s, -e jewellery; *(Verzierung)* decoration.

schmücken [ʃmʏkən] *vt* decorate.

Schmuck- *cpd:* **s—los** *a* unadorned, plain; —**losigkeit** *f* simplicity; —**sachen** *pl* jewels *pl*, jewellery.

Schmuggel [ʃmʊɡəl] *m* -s smuggling; **s—n** *vti* smuggle.

Schmuggler *m* -s, - smuggler.

schmunzeln [ʃmʊntsəln] *vi* smile benignly.

Schmutz [ʃmʊts] *m* -es dirt, filth; **s—en** *vi* get dirty; —**fink** *m* filthy creature; —fleck m stain; s—ig a dirty.

Schnabel ['ʃnɑːbəl] m -s, ⁼ beak, bill; (Ausguß) spout.

Schnake ['ʃnɑːkə] f -, -n cranefly; (Stechmücke) gnat.

Schnalle ['ʃnalə] f -, -n buckle, clasp; s—n vt buckle.

schnalzen ['ʃnaltsən] vi snap; (mit Zunge) click.

Schnapp- ['ʃnap] cpd: s—en vt grab, catch; vi snap; —schloß nt spring lock; —schuß m (Phot) snapshot.

Schnaps [ʃnaps] m -es, ⁼e spirits pl; schnapps.

schnarchen ['ʃnarçən] vi snore.

schnattern ['ʃnatərn] vi chatter; (zittern) shiver.

schnauben ['ʃnaubən] vi snort; vr blow one's nose.

schnaufen ['ʃnaufən] vi puff, pant.

Schnauz- ['ʃnauts] cpd: —bart m moustache; —e f -, -n snout, muzzle; (Ausguß) spout; (col) gob.

Schnecke ['ʃnɛkə] f -, -n snail; —nhaus nt snail's shell.

Schnee [ʃneː] m -s snow; (Ei—) beaten egg white; —ball m snowball; —flocke f snowflake; —gestöber nt snowstorm; —glöckchen nt snowdrop; —kette f (Aut) (snow) chain; —pflug m snowplough; —schmelze f thaw; —wehe f snowdrift; —witchen nt Snow White.

Schneid [ʃnaɪt] m -(e)s (col) pluck; —e f ['ʃnaɪdə] f -, -n edge; (Klinge) blade; s—en vtr irreg cut (o.s.); (kreuzen) cross, intersect; s—end a cutting; —er m -s, ⁼ tailor; —erin f dressmaker; s—ern vt make; vi be a tailor; —ezahn m incisor; s—ig a dashing; (mutig) plucky.

schneien ['ʃnaɪən] vi snow.

Schneise ['ʃnaɪzə] f -, -n clearing.

schnell [ʃnɛl] a,ad quick(ly), fast; —en vi shoot, fly; S—hefter m -s, ⁼ loose-leaf binder; S—igkeit f speed; —stens ad as quickly as possible; S—straße f expressway; S—zug m fast or express train.

schneuzen ['ʃnɔytsən] vr blow one's nose.

schnippisch ['ʃnɪpɪʃ] a sharp-tongued.

Schnitt [ʃnɪt] m -(e)s, -e cut(ting); (—punkt) intersection; (Quer—) (cross) section; (Durch—) average; (an Buch) edge; (col: Gewinn) profit; —blumen pl cut flowers pl; —e f -, -n slice; (belegt) sandwich; —fläche f section; —lauch m chive; —muster nt pattern; —punkt m (point of) intersection; —wunde f cut.

Schnitz- ['ʃnɪts] cpd: —arbeit f wood carving; —el nt -s, - chip; (Cook) escalope; s—en vt carve; —er m -s, - carver; (col) blunder; —erei f carving; carved woodwork.

schnodderig ['ʃnɔdərɪç] a (col) snotty.

schnöde ['ʃnøːdə] a base, mean.

Schnorchel ['ʃnɔrçəl] m -s, - snorkel.

Schnörkel ['ʃnœrkəl] m -s, - flourish; (Archit) scroll.

schnorren ['ʃnɔrən] vti cadge.

schnüffeln ['ʃnʏfəln] vi sniff.

Schnüffler m -s, - snooper.

Schnuller ['ʃnulər] m -s, - dummy, comforter (US).

Schnupfen ['ʃnupfən] m -s, - cold.

schnuppern ['ʃnupərn] vi sniff.

Schnur [ʃnuːr] f -, ⸚e string, cord; (Elec) flex; s— gerade a straight (as a die or arrow).

schnüren [ˈʃnyːrən] vt tie.

Schnurr- [ˈʃnur] cpd: —bart m moustache; s—en vi purr; (Kreisel) hum.

Schnür- [ˈʃnyːr] cpd: —schuh m lace-up (shoe); —senkel m shoelace.

schnurstracks ad straight (away).

Schock [ʃɔk] m -(e)s, -e shock; s—ieren [ʃɔˈkiːrən] vt shock, outrage.

Schöffe [ˈʃœfə] m -n, -n lay magistrate; —ngericht nt magistrates' court.

Schöffin f lay magistrate.

Schokolade [ʃokoˈlaːdə] f -, -n chocolate.

Scholle [ˈʃɔlə] f -, -n clod; (Eis—) ice floe; (Fisch) plaice.

schon [ʃoːn] ad already; (zwar) certainly; warst du — einmal da? have you ever been there?; ich war — einmal da I've been there before; das ist — immer so that has always been the case; das wird — (noch) gut that'll be OK; wenn ich das — höre . . . I only have to hear that . . . ; — der Gedanke the very thought.

schön [ʃøːn] a beautiful; (nett) nice; —e Grüße best wishes; —en Dank (many) thanks.

schonen [ˈʃoːnən] vt look after; vr take it easy; —d a careful, gentle.

Schön- cpd: —geist m cultured person, aesthete; —heit f beauty; —heitsfehler m blemish, flaw; —heitsoperation f cosmetic plastic surgery; s—machen vr make oneself look nice.

Schon- cpd: —ung f good care; (Nachsicht) consideration; (Forst)

plantation of young trees; s—ungslos a unsparing, harsh; —zeit f close season.

Schöpf- [ˈʃœpf] cpd: S—e m vt scoop, ladle; (Mut summon up; Luft breath in; —er m -s, - creator; s—erisch a creative; —kelle f ladle; —löffel m skimmer, scoop; f creation.

Schorf [ʃɔrf] m -(e)s, -e scab.

Schornstein [ˈʃɔrnʃtain] m chimney; (Naut) funnel; —feger m -s, - chimney sweep.

Schoß [ʃoːs] m -es, ⸚e lap; (Rock—) coat tail; —hund m pet dog, lapdog.

Schote [ˈʃoːtə] f -, -n pod.

Schotter [ˈʃɔtər] m -s broken stone, road metal; (Rail) ballast.

schraffieren [ʃraˈfiːrən] vt hatch.

schräg [ʃrɛːk] a slanting, not straight; etw — stellen put sth at an angle; — gegenüber diagonally opposite; S—e f -, -n slant; S—schrift f italics pl; S—streifen m bias binding; S—strich m oblique stroke.

Schramme [ˈʃramə] f -, -n scratch; s—n vt scratch.

Schrank [ʃraŋk] m -(e)s, ⸚e cupboard; (Kleider—) wardrobe; —e f -, -n barrier; s—enlos a boundless; (zügellos) unrestrained; —enwärter m (Rail) level crossing attendant; —koffer m trunk.

Schraube [ˈʃraubə] f -, -n screw; s—n vt screw; —nschlüssel m spanner; —nzieher m -s, - screwdriver.

Schraubstock [ˈʃraubʃtɔk] m (Tech) vice.

Schrebergarten [ˈʃreːbərgartən] m allotment.

Schreck [ʃrɛk] m -(e)s, -e, —en m -s, - terror; fright; s—en vt frighten, scare; **—gespenst** *nt* spectre, nightmare; **s—haft** *a* jumpy, easily frightened; **s—lich** *a* terrible, dreadful; **—schuß** *m* shot fired in the air.

Schrei [ʃraɪ] *m* -(e)s, -e scream; (Ruf) shout.

Schreib- [ʃraɪb] *cpd*: **—block** *m* writing pad; **s—en** *vti irreg* write; (buchstabieren) spell; **—en** *nt* -s, - letter, communication; **—er** *m* -s, - writer; (Büro—) clerk; **s—faul** *a* bad about writing letters; **—fehler** *m* spelling mistake; **—maschine** *f* typewriter; **—papier** *nt* notepaper; **—tisch** *m* desk; **—ung** *f* spelling; **—waren** *pl* stationery; **—weise** *f* spelling; way of writing; **—zeug** *nt* writing materials *pl*.

schreien [ʃraɪən] *vti irreg* scream; (rufen) shout; **—d** *a* (fig) glaring; Farbe loud.

Schreiner [ʃraɪnər] *m* -s, - joiner; (Zimmermann) carpenter; (Möbel—) cabinetmaker; **—ei** [-ʃraɪ] *f* joiner's workshop.

schreiten [ʃraɪtən] *vi irreg* stride.

Schrift [ʃrɪft] *f* -, -en writing; handwriting; (—art) script; (Gedrucktes) pamphlet, work; **—deutsch** *nt* written German; **—führer** *m* secretary; **s—lich** *a* written; *ad* in writing; **—setzer** *m* compositor; **—sprache** *f* written language; **—steller(in** *f*) *m* -s, - writer; **—stück** *nt* document.

schrill [ʃrɪl] *a* shrill; **—en** *vi* sound or ring shrilly.

Schritt [ʃrɪt] *m* -(e)s, -e step; (Gangart) walk; (Tempo) pace; (von Hose) crutch; **—macher** *m* -s, - pacemaker; **—(t)empo** *nt*: im **—(t)empo** at a walking pace.

schroff [ʃrɔf] *a* steep; (zackig)

jagged; (fig) brusque; (ungeduldig) abrupt.

schröpfen [ʃrœpfən] *vt* (fig) fleece.

Schrot [ʃroːt] *m* or *nt* -(e)s, -e (Blei) (small) shot; (Getreide) coarsely ground grain, groats *pl*; **—flinte** *f* shotgun.

Schrott [ʃrɔt] *m* -(e)s, -e scrap metal; **—haufen** *m* scrap heap; **s—reif** *a* ready for the scrap heap.

schrubben [ʃrubən] *vt* scrub.

Schrubber *m* -s, - scrubbing brush.

Schrulle [ʃrulə] *f* -, -n eccentricity, queer idea/habit.

schrumpfen [ʃrumpfən] *vi* shrink; (Apfel) shrivel.

Schub- [ʃuːb] *cpd*: **—fach** *nt* drawer; **—karren** *m* wheelbarrow; **—lade** *f* drawer.

schüchtern [ʃʏçtərn] *a* shy; **S—heit** *f* shyness.

Schuft [ʃuft] *m* -(e)s, -e scoundrel; **s—en** *vi* (col) graft, slave away.

Schuh [ʃuː] *m* -(e)s, -e shoe; **—band** *nt* shoelace; **—creme** *f* shoe polish; **—löffel** *m* shoehorn; **—macher** *m* -s, - shoemaker.

Schul- [ʃuːl] *cpd*: **—aufgaben** *pl* homework; **—besuch** *m* school attendance.

Schuld [ʃult] *f* -, -en guilt; (Fin) debt; (Verschulden) fault; **s— a**: **s—** sein or haben be to blame (an + dat for); er ist or hat **s—** it's his fault; jdm **s—** geben blame sb; **s—en** [ʃɔldən] *vt* owe; **s—enfrei** *a* free from debt; **—gefühl** *nt* feeling of guilt; **s—ig** *a* guilty (an + dat of); (gebührend) due; jdm etw **s—ig** sein owe sb sth; jdm etw **s—ig** bleiben not provide sb with sth; **s—los** *a* innocent, without guilt; **—ner** *m* -s, - debtor;

—schein *m* promissory note, IOU;
—spruch *m* verdict of guilty.

Schule ['ʃuːlə] *f* -, -n school; s—n
vt train, school.

Schüler(in *f*) ['ʃyːlər(ɪn)] *m* -s, —
pupil.

Schul- ['ʃuːl] *cpd:* —ferien *pl* school
holidays *pl;* s—frei *a:* s—freier Tag
holiday; —frei sein be a holiday;
—funk *m* schools' broadcasts *pl;*
—geld *nt* school fees *pl;* —hof *m*
playground; —jahr *nt* school year;
—junge *m* schoolboy; —mädchen
nt schoolgirl; s—pflichtig *a:* of
school age; —schiff *nt* (*Naut*)
training ship; —stunde *f* period,
lesson; —tasche *f* satchel.

Schulter ['ʃʊltər] *f* -, -n shoulder;
—blatt *nt* shoulder blade; s—n *vt*
shoulder.

Schul- *cpd:* —ung *f.* education,
schooling; —wesen *nt* educational
system; —zeugnis *nt* school report.

Schund [ʃʊnt] *m* -(e)s trash,
garbage; —roman *m* trashy novel.

Schuppe ['ʃʊpə] *f* -, -n scale; *pl*
(*Haar—*) dandruff; s—n *vt* scale;
vr peel; —n *m .* s, — shed.

schuppig ['ʃʊpɪç] *a* scaly.

Schur [ʃuːr] *f* -, -en shearing.

Schür- ['ʃyːr] *cpd:* —eisen *nt*
poker; s—en *vt* rake; (*fig*) stir up;
s—fen ['ʃyrfən] *vti* scrape, scratch;
(*Min*) prospect, dig; —fung *f*
abrasion; (*Min*) prospecting;
—haken *m* poker.

Schurke ['ʃʊrkə] *m* -n, -n rogue.

Schurz [ʃʊrts] *m* -es, -e, **Schürze**
['ʃyrtsə] *f* -, -n apron.

Schuß [ʃus] *m* -sses, -̈sse shot;
(*Weben*) woof; —bereich *m*
effective range.

Schüssel ['ʃysəl] *f* -, -n bowl.

Schuß- *cpd:* —linie *f* line of fire;
—verletzung *f* bullet wound;

—waffe *f* firearm; —weite *f* range
(of fire).

Schuster ['ʃuːstər] *m* -s, — cobbler,
shoemaker.

Schutt [ʃʊt] *m* -(e)s rubbish;
(*Bau—*) rubble; —abladeplatz *m*
refuse dump.

Schütt- [ʃʏt] *cpd:* —elfrost *m*
shivering; s—eln *vtr* shake; s—en
vt pour; (*Zucker, Kies etc*) tip;
(*ver—*) spill; *vi* impers pour
(down); s—er *a* (*Haare*) sparse, thin.

Schutt- *cpd:* —halde *f* dump;
—haufen *m* heap of rubble.

Schutz [ʃʊts] *m* -es protection;
(*Unterschlupf*) shelter; jdn in —
nehmen stand up for sb; —anzug
m overalls *pl;* —befohlene(r) *mf*
charge; —blech *nt* mudguard;
—brille *f* goggles *pl.*

Schütze ['ʃytsə] *m* -n, -n gunman;
(*Gewehr—*) rifleman; (*Scharf—
Sport—*) marksman; (*Astrol*)
Sagittarius.

Schutz- *cpd:* —engel *m* guardian
angel; —gebiet *nt* protectorate;
(*Natur—*) reserve; —haft *f*
protective custody; —impfung *f*
immunisation; s—los *a*
defenceless; —mann *m*, *pl* -leute or
-männer policeman; —maßnahme *f*
precaution; —patron *m* patron
saint; —umschlag *m* (*book*)
jacket; —vorrichtung *f* safety
device.

schwach [ʃvax] *a* weak, feeble.

Schwäche ['ʃvɛçə] *f* -, -n
weakness; s—n *vt* weaken.

Schwach- *cpd:* —heit *f* weakness;
s—köpfig *a* silly, lame-brained.

Schwäch- *cpd:* s—lich *a* weakly,
delicate; —ling *m* weakling.

Schwach- *cpd:* —sinn *m*
imbecility; s—sinnig *a* mentally

deficient; **Idee** idiotic; **—strom** m
weak current.
Schwächung ['ʃvɛçʊŋ] f
weakening.
Schwaden ['ʃvaːdən] m -s, - cloud.
schwafeln ['ʃvaːfəln] vti blather,
drivel.
Schwager ['ʃvaːgər] m -s, ≈
brother-in-law.
Schwägerin ['ʃvɛːgərɪn] f sister-
law.
Schwalbe ['ʃvalbə] f -, -n swallow.
Schwall [ʃval] m -(e)s, -e surge;
(Worte) flood, torrent.
Schwamm [ʃvam] m -(e)s, ⁻e
sponge; (Pilz) fungus; **—ig** a
spongy; **Gesicht** puffy.
Schwan [ʃvaːn] m -(e)s, ⁻e swan;
s—en vi impers: jdm schwant etw
sb has a foreboding of sth.
schwanger ['ʃvaŋər] a pregnant.
schwängern ['ʃvɛŋərn] vt make
pregnant.
Schwangerschaft f pregnancy.
Schwank [ʃvaŋk] m -(e)s, ⁻e
funny story; **s—en** vi sway;
(taumeln) stagger, reel; (Preise,
Zahlen) fluctuate; (zögern)
hesitate, vacillate; **—ung** f
fluctuation.
Schwanz [ʃvants] m -es, ⁻e tail.
schwänzen ['ʃvɛntsən] (col) vt
skip, cut; vi play truant.
Schwänzer ['ʃvɛntsər] m -s, - (col)
truant.
Schwarm [ʃvarm] m -(e)s, ⁻e
swarm; (col) heart-throb, idol.
schwärm- ['ʃvɛrm] cpd: **s—en** vi
swarm; **—en·für** be mad or wild
about; **S—erei** f [-əˈraɪ] f
enthusiasm; **—erisch** a
impassioned, effusive.
Schwarte ['ʃvaːrtə] f -, -n hard
skin; (Speck—) rind.

schwarz [ʃvarts] a black; ins S—e
treffen (lit, fig) hit the bull's eye;
S—arbeit f illicit work,
moonlighting; S—brot nt black
bread.
Schwärze ['ʃvɛrtsə] f -, -n
blackness; (Farbe) blacking;
(Drucker—) printer's ink; **s—n** vt
blacken.
Schwarz- cpd: **s—fahren** vi irreg
travel without paying; drive
without a licence; **—handel** m
black-market (trade); **s—hören** vi
listen to the radio without a licence.
schwärzlich ['ʃvɛrtslɪç] a blackish,
darkish.
Schwarz- cpd: **—markt** m black
market; **s—sehen** vi irreg (col) see
the gloomy side of things; (TV)
watch TV without a licence;
—seher m pessimist; (TV) viewer
without a licence; **s—weiß** a black
and white.
schwatzen ['ʃvatsən], **schwätzen**
['ʃvɛtsən] vi chatter.
Schwätzer ['ʃvɛtsər] m -s, -
gasbag; **—in** f chatterbox, gossip.
schwatzhaft a talkative, gossipy.
Schwebe ['ʃveːbə] f: in der — (fig)
in abeyance; **—bahn** f overhead
railway; **—balken** m (Sport) beam;
s—n vi drift, float; (hoch) soar;
(unentschieden sein) be in the
balance.
Schwefel ['ʃveːfəl] m -s sulphur;
s—ig a sulphurous; **—säure** f
sulphuric acid.
Schweif [ʃvaɪf] m -(e)s, -e tail;
s—en vi wander, roam.
Schweig- ['ʃvaɪg] cpd: **—egeld** nt
hush money; **s—en** vi irreg be
silent; stop talking; **—en** nt -s
silence; **s—sam** ['ʃvaɪkzaːm] a
silent, taciturn; **—samkeit** f
taciturnity, quietness.

Schwein [ʃvaɪn] nt -(e)s, -e pig; (fig) (good) luck; —efleisch nt pork; —ehund m (col) stinker, swine; —erei [-ə'raɪ] f mess; (Gemeinheit) dirty trick; —estall m pigsty; s—isch a filthy; —sleder nt pigskin.

Schweiß [ʃvaɪs] m -es sweat, perspiration; s—en vti weld; —er m -s, - welder; —füße pl sweaty feet pl; —naht f weld.

schwelen [ʃveːlən] vi smoulder.

schwelgen [ʃvɛlgən] vi indulge.

Schwelle [ʃvɛlə] f -, -n threshold (auch fig); doorstep; (Rail) sleeper; s—n vi irreg swell.

Schwellung f swelling.

Schwengel [ʃvɛŋəl] m -s, - pump handle; (Glocken-) clapper.

Schwenk- [ʃvɛŋk] cpd: s—bar a swivel-mounted; s—en vt swing; Fahne wave; (abspülen) rinse; vi turn, swivel; (Mil) wheel; —ung f turn; wheel.

schwer [ʃveːr] a heavy; (schwierig) difficult, hard; (schlimm) serious, bad; ad (sehr) very (much); verletzt etc seriously, badly; —arbeiter m manual worker, labourer; S—e f -, -n weight, heaviness; (Phys) gravity; —elos a weightless; Kammer zero-G; S—enöter m -s, - casanova, ladies' man; —erziehbar a difficult (to bring up); —fallen vi irreg: jdm —fallen be difficult for sb; s—fällig a ponderous; S—gewicht nt heavyweight; (fig) emphasis; —hörig a hard of hearing; S—industrie f heavy industry; S—kraft f gravity; S—kranke(r) mf person who is seriously ill; —lich ad hardly; —machen vt: jdm/sich etw —machen make sth difficult for sb/o.s.; S—metall nt

heavy metal; —mütig a melancholy; —nehmen vt irreg take to heart; S—punkt m centre of gravity; (fig) emphasis, crucial point.

Schwert [ʃveːrt] nt -(e)s, -er sword; —lilie f iris.

Schwester [ʃvɛstər] f -, -n sister; (Med) nurse; s—lich a sisterly.

Schwieger- [ʃviːgər] cpd: —eltern pl parents-in-law pl; —mutter f mother-in-law; —sohn m son-in-law; —tochter f daughter-in-law; —vater m father-in-law.

Schwiele [ʃviːlə] f -, -n callus.

schwierig [ʃviːrɪç] a difficult, hard; S—keit f difficulty.

Schwimm- [ʃvɪm] cpd: —bad nt swimming baths pl; —becken nt swimming pool; s—en vi irreg swim; (treiben, nicht sinken) float; (fig: unsicher sein) be all at sea; —er m -s, - swimmer; (Angeln) float; —lehrer m swimming instructor; —sport m swimming; —weste f life jacket.

Schwindel [ʃvɪndəl] m -s giddiness; dizzy spell; (Betrug) swindle, fraud; (Zeug) stuff; s—frei a free from giddiness; s—n vi (col: lügen) fib; jdm schwindelt es sb feels giddy.

schwinden [ʃvɪndən] vi irreg disappear; (sich verringern) decrease; (Kräfte) decline.

Schwind- [ʃvɪnd] cpd: —ler m -s, - swindler; (Lügner) liar; s—lig a giddy; mir ist s—lig I feel giddy.

Schwing- ['ʃvɪŋ] cpd: s—en vti irreg swing; Waffe etc brandish; (vibrieren) vibrate; . (klingen) sound; —er m -s, - (Boxen) swing; —tür f swing door(s); —ung f vibration; (Phys) oscillation.

Schwips [ʃvɪps] m -es, -e: einen . haben be tipsy.

schwirren ['ʃvɪrən] vi buzz.

schwitzen ['ʃvɪtsən] vi sweat, perspire.

schwören ['ʃvø:rən] . vti irreg swear. .

schwul [ʃvu:l] a (col) gay, queer.

schwül [ʃvy:l] a sultry, close; **S—e** f - sultriness, closeness.

Schwulst [ʃvʊlst] f -(e)s, ⸚e bombast.

schwülstig ['ʃvʏlstɪç] a pompous.

Schwund [ʃvʊnt] m -(e)s loss; (Schrumpfen)` shrinkage.

Schwung [ʃvʊŋ] m -(e)s, ⸚e swing; (Triebkraft) momentum; (fig: Energie) verve, energy; (col: Menge) batch; s—haft a brisk, lively; —rad nt flywheel; s—voll a vigorous.

Schwur [ʃvu:r] m -(e)s, ⸚e oath; —gericht nt court with a jury.

sechs [zɛks] num six; —hundert num six hundred; —te(r,s) a sixth; **S—tel** nt -s sixth.

sechzehn ['zɛçtse:n] num sixteen.

sechzig ['zɛçtsɪç] num sixty.

See [ze:] f -, -n sea; m -s, -n lake; —bad nt seaside resort; —fahrt f seafaring; (Reise) voyage; —gang m (motion of the) sea; —gras nt seaweed; —hund m seal; —igel ['ze:'i:gəl] m sea urchin; s—krank a seasick; —krankheit f seasickness; —lachs m rock salmon.

Seel- ['ze:l] cpd: —e f -, -n soul; —enfriede(n) m peace of mind; s—enruhig ad calmly.

Seeleute ['ze:lɔytə] pl seamen pl.

Seel- cpd: s—isch a mental; —sorge f pastoral duties pl; —sorger m -s, - clergyman.

See- cpd: —macht f naval power; —mann m, pl -leute seaman, sailor; —meile. f nautical mile; —not f distress; —pferd(chen) nt sea horse; —räuber m pirate; —rose f water lily; —stern m starfish; s—tüchtig a seaworthy; —weg m sea route; auf dem —weg by sea; —zunge f sole.

Segel ['ze:gəl] nt -s, - sail; —boot nt yacht; —fliegen nt -s gliding; —flieger m glider pilot; —flugzeug nt glider; s—n vti sail; —schiff nt sailing vessel; —sport m sailing; —tuch nt canvas.

Segen ['ze:gən] m -s, - blessing; s—sreich a beneficial.

Segler ['ze:glər] . m -s, - sailor, yachtsman; (Boot) sailing boat.

segnen ['ze:gnən] vt bless.

Seh- [ze:] cpd: s—en vti irreg see; (in bestimmte Richtung) look; s—enswert a worth seeing; —enswürdigkeiten pl sights pl (of a town); —er m -s, - seer; —fehler · m sight defect.

Sehn- ['ze:n] cpd: —e f -, -n sinew; (an Bogen) string; s—en vr long, yearn (nach for); s—ig a sinewy; s—lich a ardent; —sucht f longing; s—süchtig a longing.

sehr [ze:r] ad (vor a,ad) very; (mit Verben) a lot, (very) much; zu — too much.

seicht [zaɪçt] a (lit, fig) shallow.

Seide ['zaɪdə] f -, -n silk; —l nt -s, - tankard, beer mug; s—n a silk; —npapier nt tissue paper.

seidig ['zaɪdɪç] a silky.

Seife ['zaɪfə] f -, -n soap; **—nlauge**
f soapsuds pl; **—nschale** f soap
dish; **—nschaum** m lather.

seifig ['zaɪfɪç] a soapy.

seihen ['zaɪən] vt strain, filter.

Seil [zaɪl] nt -(e)s, -e rope; cable;
—bahn f cable railway; **—hüpfen**
nt -s, **—springen** nt -s skipping;
—tänzer(in f) m tightrope walker;
—zug m tackle.

sein [zaɪn] vi irreg be; **laß das —!**
leave that!; stop that!; **es ist an
dir, zu . . .** it's up to you to . .
•

sein [zaɪn] pron his; its; **—e(r,s)**
his; its; **—er** pron gen of er of
him; **—erseits** ad for his part;
—erzeit ad in those days, formerly;
—esgleichen:pron people like him;
—etwegen, —etwillen ad (für ihn)
for his sake; (wegen ihm) on his
account; (von ihm aus) as far as
he is concerned; **—ige** pron:
der/die/das **—** his.

Seismograph [zaɪsmo'graːf] m
-en, -en seismograph.

seit [zaɪt] prep, cj since; **er ist —
einer Woche hier** he has been here
for a week; **— langem** for a long
time; **—dem** [zaɪt'deːm] ad,cj since.

Seite ['zaɪtə] f -, -n side; (Buch-)
page; (Mil) flank; **—nansicht** f side
view; **—nhieb** m (fig) passing shot,
dig; **—nruder** nt (Aviat) rudder;
s—ns prep +gen on the part of;
—nschiff nt aisle; **—nsprung** m
extramarital escapade; **—nstechen**
nt (a) stitch; **—nstraße** f side road;
—nwagen m sidecar; **—nzahl** f
page number; number of pages.

seit- cpd: **—her** [zaɪt'heːr] ad,cj
since (then); **—lich** a on one or the
side; side; **—wärts** ad sidewards.

Sekretär [zekre'tɛːr] m secretary;
(Möbel) bureau; **—in** f secretary.

Sekretariat [zekretari'aːt] nt
-(e)s, -e secretary's office,
secretariat.

Sekt [zɛkt] m **-(e)s, -e**
champagne; **—e** f -, -n sect.

sekundär [zekun'dɛːr] a secondary.

Sekunde [ze'kundə] f -, -n second.

selber ['zɛlbər] = **selbst.**

selbst [zɛlpst] pron myself; itself;
themselves etc; von **—** by itself
etc; ad even; **S— nt - self;
S—achtung f self-respect;—ändig**
['zɛlpʃtɛndɪç] a independent;
S—ändigkeit f independence;
S—auslöser m (Phot) delayed-
action shutter release;
S—bedienung f self-service;
S—befriedigung f masturbation;
S—beherrschung f self-control;
—bewußt a (self-)confident;
S—bewußtsein nt self-confidence;
S—erhaltung f self-preservation;
S—erkenntnis f self-knowledge;
—gefällig a smug, self-satisfied;
—gemacht a home-made;
S—gespräch nt conversation with
oneself; **S—kostenpreis** m cost
price; **—los** a unselfish, selfless;
S—mord m suicide; **S—mörder(in**
f) m suicide; **—mörderisch** a
suicidal; **—sicher** a self-assured;
—süchtig a selfish; **—tätig** a automatic; **—verständlich** a obvious;
ad naturally; **ich halte das für**
granted; **S—vertrauen** nt self-confidence; **S—verwaltung** f
autonomy, self-government;
S—zweck m end in itself.

selig ['zeːlɪç] a happy, blissful; (Rel)
blessed; (tot) late; **S—keit** f bliss.

Sellerie ['zɛləriː] m -s, -(s) or f -,
-n celery.

selten ['zɛltən] a rare; ad seldom, rarely; **S—heit** f rarity.

Selterswasser ['zɛltərsvasər] nt soda water.

seltsam ['zɛltza:m] a strange, curious; **—erweise** ad curiously, strangely; **S—keit** f strangeness.

Semester [ze'mɛstər] nt -s, - semester.

Semi- [zemi] in cpds semi-; **—kolon** [-'ko:lɔn] nt -s, -s semicolon; **—nar** [-'na:r] nt -s, -e seminary; (Kurs) seminar, (Univ: Ort) department building.

Semmel ['zɛməl] f -, -n roll.

Senat [ze'na:t] m -(e)s, -e senate, council.

Sende- ['zɛndə] cpd: **—bereich** m range of transmission; **—folge** f (Serie) series; **s—n** vt irreg send; vti (Rad, TV) transmit, broadcast; **—r** m -s, - station; (Anlage) transmitter; **—reihe** f series (of broadcasts); **—station** f, **—stelle** f transmitting station.

Sendung ['zɛnduŋ] f consignment; (Aufgabe) mission; (Rad, TV) transmission; (Programm) programme.

Senf [zɛnf] m -(e)s, -e mustard.

sengen ['zɛŋən] vt singe; vi scorch.

Senk- ['zɛŋk] cpd: **—blei** nt plumb; **—e** f -, -n depression; **—el** m -s, - (shoe)lace; **s—en** vt lower; vr sink, drop gradually; **—fuß** m flat foot; **s—recht** a vertical, perpendicular; **—rechte** f -n, -n perpendicular; **—rechtstarter** m (Aviat) vertical take-off plane; (fig) high-flier.

Sensation [zenzatsi'o:n] f sensation; **s—ell** [-'nɛl] a sensational; **—ssucht** f sensationalism.

Sense ['zɛnzə] f -, -n scythe.

sensibel [zɛn'zi:bəl] a sensitive.

Sensibilität [zɛnzibili'tɛ:t] f sensitivity.

sentimental [zentimɛn'ta:l] a sentimental; **S—i'tät** f sentimentality.

separat [zepa'ra:t] a separate.

September [zɛp'ɛmbər] m -(s), • September.

septisch ['zɛptɪʃ] a septic.

Serie ['ze:riə] f series; **—nherstellung** f mass production; **s—nweise** ad in series.

seriös [zeri'ø:s] a serious, bona fide.

Serpentine [zɛrpɛn'ti:n(ə)] f hairpin (bend).

Serum ['ze:rum] nt -s, Seren serum.

Service [zɛr'vi:s] nt -(s), - set, service; ['zœ:rvis] m -, -s service.

servieren [zɛr'vi:rən] vti serve.

Serviette [zɛrvi'ɛtə] f napkin, serviette.

Sessel ['zɛsəl] m -s, - armchair; **—lift** m chairlift.

seßhaft ['zɛshaft] a settled; (ansässig) resident.

Sets [zɛts] pl tablemats pl.

setzen ['zɛtsən] vt put, set; Baum etc plant; Segel, (Print) set; vr settle; (person) sit down; vi leap.

Setz- [zɛts] cpd: **—er** m -s, - (Print) compositor; **—e'rei** f caseroom; **—ling** m young plant; **—maschine** f (Print) typesetting machine.

Seuche ['zɔyçə] f -, -n epidemic; **—ngebiet** nt infected area.

seufzen ['zɔyftsən] vti sigh.

Seufzer ['zɔyftsər] m -s, - sigh.

Sex [zɛks] m -(es) sex; **—ualität** [-uali'tɛt] f sex, sexuality; **s—uell** [-u'el] a sexual.

Sexta ['zɛksta] f -, Sexten first year of secondary school.

sezieren [ze'tsi:rən] *vt* dissect.

sich [zɪç] *pron* himself; herself; itself; oneself; yourself; yourselves; themselves; each other.

Sichel ['zɪçəl] *f* -, -n sickle; (Mond—) crescent.

sicher ['zɪçər] *a* safe (vor +dat from); (gewiß) certain (+gen of); (zuverlässig) secure, reliable, (selbst—) confident; **—gehen** *vi* irreg make sure.

Sicherheit ['zɪçərhait] *f* safety; security (auch Fin); (Gewißheit) certainty; (Selbst—) confidence; **—sabstand** *m* safe distance; **—glas** *nt* safety glass; **—shalber** *ad* for safety; to be on the safe side; **—snadel** *f* safety pin; **—schloß** *nt* safety lock; **—sverschluß** *m* safety clasp; **—svorkehrung** *f* safety precaution.

sicher- *cpd*: **—lich** *ad* certainly, surely; **—n** *vt* secure; (schützen) protect; Waffe put the safety catch on; jdm/sich etw **—n** secure sth for sb/(for o.s.); **—stellen** *vt* impound; **S—ung** *f* (Sichern) securing; (Vorrichtung) safety device; (an Waffen) safety catch; (Elec) fuse.

Sicht [zɪçt] *f* sight (Aus—) view; auf or nach — (Fin) at sight; auf lange — on a long-term basis; **s—bar** *a* visible; **—barkeit** *f* visibility; **s—en** *vt* sight; (auswählen) sort out; **s—lich** *a* evident, obvious; **—verhältnisse** *pl* visibility; **—vermerk** *m* visa; **—weite** *f* visibility.

sickern ['zɪkərn] *vi* trickle, seep.

Sie [zi:] *pron* sing, pl, nom, acc you.

sie [zi:] *pron* sing nom she; acc her; pl nom they; acc them.

Sieb [zi:p] *nt* -(e)s, -e sieve; (Cook) strainer; **s—en** ['zi:bən] *vt* sift; Flüssigkeit strain.

sieben ['zi:bən] *num* seven; **—hundert** *num* seven hundred; **S—sachen** *pl* belongings *pl*.

siebte(r,s) ['zi:ptə(r,z)] *a* seventh; **S—l** *nt* -s, - seventh.

siebzehn ['zi:ptse:n] *num* seventeen.

siebzig ['zi:ptsɪç] *num* seventy.

sied- [zi:d] *cpd*: **—eln** *vi* settle; **—en** *vti* boil, simmer; **S—epunkt** *m* boiling point; **S—ler** *m* -s, - settler; **S—lung** *f* settlement; (Häuser—) housing estate.

Sieg [zi:k] *m* -(e)s, -e victory; **—el** ['zi:gəl] *nt* -s, - seal; **—ellack** *m* sealing wax; **—elring** *m* signet ring; **s—en** *vi* be victorious; (Sport) win; **—er** *m* -s, - victor; (Sport etc) winner; **s—essicher** *a* sure of victory; **—eszug** *m* triumphal procession; **s—reich** *a* victorious.

siehe [zi:ə] (Imperativ) see; (— da) behold.

siezen ['zi:tsən] *vt* address as 'Sie'.

Signal [zɪ'gna:l] *nt* -s, -e signal.

Signatur [zɪgna'tu:r] *f* signature.

Silbe ['zɪlbə] *f* -, -n syllable.

Silber ['zɪlbər] *nt* -s silver; **—bergwerk** *nt* silver mine; **—blick** *m*: einen **—blick** haben have a slight squint; **s—n** *a* silver; **—papier** *nt* silver paper.

Silhouette [zilu'ɛtə] *f* silhouette.

Silo ['zi:lo] *nt* or *m* -s, -s silo.

Silvester(abend *m)* [zɪl'vɛstər(a:bənt)] *nt* -s, - New Year's Eve, Hogmanay (Scot).

simpel ['zɪmpəl] *a* simple; **S—** *m* **-s,** - (col) simpleton.

Sims [zɪms] nt or m -es, -e (Kamin—) mantlepiece; (Fenster—) (window)sill.

simulieren [zimu'li:rən] vti simulate; (vortäuschen) feign.

simultan [zimʊl'ta:n] a simultaneous.

Sinfonie [zɪmfo'ni:] f symphony.

singen ['zɪŋən] vti irreg sing.

Singular ['zɪŋgula:r] m singular.

Singvogel ['zɪŋfo:gəl] m songbird.

sinken ['zɪŋkən] vi irreg sink; (Preise etc) fall, go down.

Sinn [zɪn] m -(e)s, -e mind; (Wahrnehmungs—) sense; (Bedeutung) sense, meaning; — für etw sense of sth; von —en sein be out of one's mind; —bild nt symbol; s—bildlich a symbolic; s—en vi irreg ponder; auf etw (acc) s—en contemplate sth; —enmensch m sensualist; —estäuschung f illusion; s—gemäß a faithful; Wiedergabe in one's own words; s—ig a clever; s—lich a sensual, sensuous; Wahrnehmung sensory; —lichkeit f sensuality; s—los a senseless, meaningless; —losigkeit f senselessness; meaninglessness; s—voll a meaningful; (vernünftig) sensible.

Sintflut ['zɪntflu:t] f Flood.

Sinus ['zi:nʊs] m -, - or -se (Anat) sinus; (Math) sine.

Siphon [zi'fõ:] m -s, -s siphon.

Sippe ['zɪpə] f -, -n clan, kin.

Sippschaft ['zɪpʃaft] f (pej) relations pl, tribe; (Bande) gang.

Sirene [zi're:nə] f -, -n siren.

Sirup ['zi:rʊp] m -s, -e syrup.

Sitt- [zɪt] cpd: -e f -, -n custom; pl morals pl; —enpolizei f vice squad; s—lich a moral; —lichkeit

f morality; —lichkeitsverbrechen nt sex offence; s—sam a modest, demure.

Situation [zituatsi'o:n] f situation.

Sitz [zɪts] m -es, -e seat; der Anzug hat einen guten — the suit is a good fit; s—en vi irreg sit; (Bemerkung, Schlag) strike home, tell; (Gelerntes) have sunk in; s—en bleiben remain seated; s—enbleiben vi irreg (Sch) have to repeat a year; auf etw (dat) s—enbleiben be lumbered with sth; s—end a Tätigkeit sedentary; s—enlassen vt irreg (Sch) make (sb) repeat a year; Mädchen jilt; Wartenden stand up; etw auf sich (dat) s—enlassen take sth lying down; —gelegenheit f place to sit down; —platz m seat; —streik m sit-down strike; —ung f meeting.

Skala ['ska:la] f -, Skalen scale.

Skalpell [skal'pɛl] nt -s, -e scalpel.

Skandal [skan'da:l] m -s, -e scandal; s—ös [skanda'lø:s] a scandalous.

Skelett [ske'lɛt] nt -(e)s, -e skeleton.

Skepsis ['skɛpsɪs] f - scepticism.

skeptisch ['skɛptɪʃ] a sceptical.

Ski, Schi [ʃi:] m -s, -er ski; — laufen or fahren ski; —fahrer m, —läufer m skier; —lehrer m ski instructor; —lift m ski-lift; —springen nt ski-jumping.

Skizze ['skɪtsə] f -, -n sketch.

skizzieren [skɪ'tsi:rən] vti sketch.

Sklave ['skla:və] m -n, -n slave; **Sklavin** f slave; —rei f slavery.

Skonto ['skɔnto] m or nt -s, -s discount.

Skorpion [skɔrpi'o:n] m -s, -e scorpion; (Astrol) Scorpio.

Skrupel ['skru:pəl] m -s, - scruple; s—los a unscrupulous.

Slalom ['sla:lɔm] m -s, -s slalom.

Smaragd [sma'rakt] m -(e)s, -e emerald.

Smoking ['smo:kɪŋ] m -s, -s dinner jacket.

so [zo:] ad so; (auf diese Weise) like this; (etwa) roughly; — ein such a; —, das ist fertig well, that's finished; — etwas! well, well! —, .. wie . .. as . .. as . .. ; — daß so that, with the result that; cj so; (vor a) as.

Socke ['zɔkə] f -, -n sock.

Sockel ['zɔkəl] m -s, - pedestal, base.

Sodawasser ['zo:davasər] nt soda water.

Sodbrennen ['zo:tbrɛnən] nt -s, - heartburn.

soeben [zo''e:bən] ad just (now).

Sofa ['zo:fa] nt -s, -s sofa.

sofern [zo'fɛrn] cj if, provided (that).

sofort [zo'fɔrt] ad immediately, at once; —ig a immediate.

Sog [zo:k] m -(e)s, -e suction.

so- cpd: —gar [zo'ga:r] ad even; —genannt ['zo:gənant] a so-called; —gleich [zo'glaɪç] ad straight away, at once.

Sohle ['zo:lə] f -, -n sole; (Tal— etc) bottom; (Min) level.

Sohn [zo:n] m -(e)s, ⁼e son.

solang(e) [zo'laŋ(ə)] cj as or so long as.

Solbad ['zo:lba:t] nt saltwater bath.

solch [zɔlç] pron such; ein —e(r,s) . .. such a . ..

Sold [zɔlt] m -(e)s, -e pay; —at [zɔl'da:t] m -en, -en soldier; s—atisch a soldierly.

Söldner ['zœldnər] m -s, - mercenary.

solid(e) [zo'li:d(ə)] a solid; Leben, Person staid, respectable; —arisch [zoli'da:rɪʃ] a in/with solidarity; sich —arisch erklären declare one's solidarity.

Solist(in f) [zo'lɪst(ɪn)] m soloist.

Soll [zɔl] nt -s, -(s) (Fin) debit (side); (Arbeitsmenge) quota, target.

sollen ['zɔlən] vi be supposed to; (Verpflichtung) shall, ought to; du hättest nicht gehen — you shouldn't have gone; soll ich? shall I?; was soll das? what's that supposed to mean?

Solo ['zo:lo] nt -s, -s or Soli solo.

somit [zo'mɪt] cj and so, therefore.

Sommer ['zɔmər] m -s, - summer; s—lich a summery; summer; —sprossen pl freckles pl.

Sonate [zo'na:tə] f -, -n sonata.

Sonde ['zɔndə] f -, -n probe.

Sonder- ['zɔndər] in cpds special; —angebot nt special offer; s—bar a strange, odd; —fahrt f special trip; —fall m special case; s—gleichen a inv without parallel, unparalleled; s—lich a particular; (außergewöhnlich) remarkable; (eigenartig) peculiar; —ling m eccentric; s—n cj but; nicht nur .. , s—n auch not only .. , but also; vt separate; —zug m special train.

sondieren [zɔn'di:rən] vt suss out; Gelände sound out.

Sonett [zo'nɛt] nt -(e)s, -e sonnet.

Sonnabend ['zɔn'a:bənt] m Saturday.

Sonne ['zɔnə] f -, -n sun; s—n vt put out in the sun; vr sun oneself; —naufgang m sunrise; s—nbaden vi sunbathe; —nbrand m sunburn; —nbrille f sunglasses pl; —nfinsternis f solar eclipse;

—nschein m sunshine; —nschirm m parasol, sunshade; —nstich m sunstroke; —nuhr f sundial; —nuntergang m sunset; —nwende f solstice.

sonnig ['zɔnɪç] a sunny.

Sonntag ['zɔntɑːk] m Sunday; s—s ad (on) Sundays.

sonst [zɔnst] ad otherwise (auch cj); (mit pron, in Fragen) else; (zu anderer Zeit) at other times, normally; — noch etwas? anything else?; — nichts nothing else; —ig a other; —jemand pron anybody (at all); —wo(hin) ad somewhere else; —woher ad from somewhere else.

sooft [zo'ɔft] cj whenever.

Sopran [zo'prɑːn] m -s, -e, soprano; —istin [zoprɑ'nɪstɪn] f soprano.

Sorge ['zɔrgə] f -, -n care, worry; s—n vi: für jdn s—n look after sb; für etw s—n take care of or see to sth; vr worry (um about); s—nfrei a carefree; —nkind nt problem child; s—nvoll a troubled, worried; —recht nt custody (of a child).

Sorg- [zɔrk] cpd: —falt f care(fulness); s—fältig a careful; s—los a careless; (ohne Sorgen) carefree; s—sam a careful.

Sorte ['zɔrtə] f -, -n sort; (Waren—) brand; —n pl (Fin) foreign currency.

sortieren [zɔr'tiːrən] vt sort (out).

Sortiment [zɔrti'mɛnt] nt assortment.

sosehr [zo'zeːr] cj as much as.

Soße ['zoːsə] f -, -n sauce; (Braten—) gravy.

Souffleur [zu'fløːr] m, **Souffleuse** [zu'fløːzə] f prompter.

soufflieren [zu'fliːrən] vti prompt.

souverän [zuvə'rɛːn] a sovereign; (überlegen) superior.

so- cpd: —viel [zo'fiːl] cj: as far as; pron as much (wie as); tut nicht —viel don't talk so much; —weit [zo'vaɪt] cj: as far as; a: —weit sein be ready; —weit wie or als möglich as far as possible; ich bin —weit zufrieden by and large I'm quite satisfied; —wenig [zo've:nɪç] cj little as; pron as little (wie as); —wie [zo'viː] cj (sobald) as soon as; (ebenso) as well as; —wieso [zovi'zoː] ad anyway; —wohl [zo'voːl] cj: —wohl ... als or wie auch both ... and.

sozial [zotsi'ɑːl] a social; S—abgaben pl national insurance contributions pl; S—demokrat m social democrat; s—isieren vt socialize; S—ismus ['-lɪsmʊs] m socialism; S—ist ['-lɪst] m socialist; s—istisch a socialist; S—politik f social welfare policy; S—produkt nt (gross/net) national product; S—staat m welfare state.

Sozio- [zotsio] cpd: —loge [-'loːgə] m -n, -n sociologist; —logie [-lo'giː] f sociology; s—logisch [-lo'giːʃ] a sociological.

Sozius ['zoːtsiʊs] m -, -se (Comm) partner; (Motorrad) pillion rider; —sitz m pillion (seat).

sozusagen [zotsu'zɑːgən] ad so to speak.

Spachtel ['ʃpaxtəl] m -s, -e spatula.

spähen ['ʃpɛːən] vi peep, peek.

Spalier [ʃpa'liːr] nt -s, -e (Gerüst) trellis; (Leute) guard of honour.

Spalt [ʃpalt] m -(e)s, -e crack; (Tür—) chink; (fig: Kluft) split; —e f -, -n crack, fissure; (Gletscher—) crevasse; (in Text)

column; s—en vtr (lit, fig) split;
—ung f splitting.
Span [ʃpaːn] -(e)s, ̈e shaving;
—ferkel m sucking-pig.
Spange [ʃpaŋə] f -, -n clasp;
(Haar—) hair slide; (Schnalle)
buckle; (Armreif) bangle.
Spann [ʃpan] cpd: —beton m pre-
stressed concrete; —e f -, ̈e
(Zeit—) space; (Differenz) gap;
s—en vt (straffen) tighten, tauten;
(befestigen) brace; vi be tight;
s—end a exciting, gripping; —kraft
f elasticity; (fig) energy; —ung f
tension; (Elec) voltage; (fig)
suspense; (unangenehm) tension.
Spar- [ʃpaːr] cpd: —buch nt
savings book; —büchse f
moneybox; s—en vti save; sich
(dat) etw s—en save oneself sth;
Bemerkung keep sth to oneself; mit
etw (dat) s—en be sparing with
sth; an etw (dat) s—en economize
on sth; —er m -s, - saver.
Spargel [ʃpargəl] m -s, -
asparagus.
Spar- cpd: —kasse f savings bank;
—konto nt savings account.
spärlich [ʃpɛːrlɪç] a meagre;
Bekleidung scanty.
Spar- cpd: —maßnahme f economy
measure, cut; s—sam a
economical, thrifty; —samkeit f
thrift, economizing; s—schwein nt
piggy bank.
Sparte [ʃpartə] f -, -n field; line
of business; (Press) column.
Spaß [ʃpaːs] m -es, ̈e joke;
(Freude) fun; jdm — machen be
fun (for sb); s—en vi joke; mit ihm
ist nicht zu s—en you can't take
liberties with him; s—eshalber ad
for the fun of it; s—haft, s—ig a
funny, droll; —macher m -s, -

joker, funny man; —verderber m
-s, - spoilsport.
spät [ʃpɛːt] a, ad late; —er a, ad
later; —estens ad at the latest.
Spaten [ʃpaːtən] m -s, - spade.
Spatz [ʃpats] m -en, -en sparrow.
spazier- [ʃpaːtsiːr] cpd: —en vi
stroll, walk; —enfahren vi irreg go
for a drive; —engehen vi irreg go
for a walk; S—gang m walk;
S—stock m walking stick; S—weg
m path, walk.
Specht [ʃpɛçt] m -(e)s, -e
woodpecker.
Speck [ʃpɛk] m -(e)s, -e bacon.
Spediteur [ʃpediˈtøːr] m carrier;
(Möbel—) furniture remover.
Spedition [ʃpeditsiˈoːn] f carriage;
(—sfirma) road haulage
contractor; removal firm.
Speer [ʃpeːr] m -(e)s, -e spear;
(Sport) javelin.
Speiche [ʃpaɪçə] f -, -n spoke.
Speichel [ʃpaɪçəl] m -s saliva,
spit(tle).
Speicher [ʃpaɪçər] m -s, -
storehouse; (Dach—) attic, loft;
(Korn—) granary; (Wasser—)
tank; (Tech) store; s—n vt store.
speien [ʃpaɪən] vti irreg spit;
(erbrechen) vomit; (Vulkan) spew.
Speise [ʃpaɪzə] f -, -n food; —eis
[ˈ-ʔaɪs] nt ice-cream; —kammer f
larder, pantry; —karte f menu;
s—n vt feed; eat; vi dine; —röhre
f gullet, oesophagus; —saal m
dining room; —wagen m dining
car; —zettel m menu.
Spektakel [ʃpɛkˈtaːkəl] m -s, -
(col) row; nt -s, - spectacle.
Speku- [ʃpeku] cpd: —lant [-ˈlant]
m speculator; —lation [-latsiˈoːn] f
speculation; s—lieren [-ˈliːrən] vi

(fig) speculate; **auf etw** *(acc)*
s—**lieren** have hopes of sth.
Spelunke·[ʃpeˈluŋkə] *f* -, -**n** dive:
Spende [ˈʃpɛndə] *f* -, -**n** donation;
s—**n** *vt* donate, give; —**r** *m* -s, - donor, donator.
spendieren [ʃpɛnˈdiːrən] *vt* pay
for, buy; **jdm etw** — treat sb to
sth, stand sb sth.
Sperling [ˈʃpɛrlɪŋ] *m* sparrow.
Sperma [ˈʃpɛrma] *nt* -s, **Spermen**
sperm.
Sperr-·[ˈʃpɛr] *cpd* =**angelweit**
[-ˈʔaŋəlˈvait] a wide open; —**e** *f* -,
-**n** barrier; *(Verbot)* ban; **s**—**en** *vt*
block; *(Sport)* suspend, bar; *(vom Ball)* obstruct; *(einschließen)* lock;
(verbieten) ban; *vr* baulk, jib(e);
—**gebiet** *nt* prohibited area; —**holz**
nt plywood; **s**—**ig** a bulky; —**müll**
m bulky refuse; —**sitz** *m (Theat)*
stalls *pl*; —**stunde** *f*; —**zeit** *f*
closing time.
Spesen [ˈʃpeːzən] *pl* expenses *pl*.
Spezial- [ʃpetsiˈaːl] *in cpds* special;
s—**i'sieren** *vr* specialize;
—**i'sierung** *f* specialization; —**ist**
[-ˈlɪst] *m* specialist; —**i'tät** *f*
speciality.
speziell [ʃpetsiˈɛl] a special.·
spezifisch [ʃpeˈtsiːfɪʃ] a specific.·
Sphäre [ˈsfɛːrə] *f* -, -**n** sphere.
spicken [ˈʃpɪkən] *vt* lard; *vi (Sch)*
copy, crib.
Spiegel [ˈʃpiːgəl] *m* -s, - mirror;
(Wasser—) level; *(Mil)* tab; —**bild**
nt reflection; **s**—**bildlich** a
reversed; —**ei** [-ˈai] *nt* fried egg;
—**fechterei** [-fɛçtəˈrai] *f* shadow-
boxing, bluff; **s**—**n** *vt* mirror,
reflect; *vr* be reflected; *vi* gleam;
(wider—) be reflective; —**schrift** *f*
mirror-writing; —**ung** *f* reflection.
Spiel [ʃpiːl] *nt* -(e)s, -**e** game;
(Schau—) play; *(Tätigkeit)*

play(ing); *(Cards)* deck; *(Tech)*
(free) play; **s**—**en** *vti* play; *(um Geld)* gamble; *(Theat)* perform,
act; **s**—**end** ad easily; —**er** *m* -s,
- player; *(um Geld)* gambler;
—**e'rei** *f* trifling pastime; **s**—**erisch** a
playful; *Leichtigkeit* effortless;
s—**erisches Können** skill as a
player; acting ability; —**feld** *nt*
pitch, field; —**film** *m* feature film;
—**plan** *m (Theat)* programme;
—**platz** *m* playground; —**raum** *m*
room to manoeuvre, scope;
—**sachen** *pl* toys *pl*; —**verderber** *m*
-s, - spoilsport; —**waren** *pl*, —**zeug**
nt toys *pl*.
Spieß [ʃpiːs] *m* -es, -**e** spear;
(Brat—) spit; —**bürger** *m*, —**er** *m*
-s, - bourgeois; —**rutenlaufen** *nt*
running the gauntlet.
Spikes [spaiks] *pl* spikes *pl*; *(Aut)*
studs *pl*.
Spinat [ʃpiˈnaːt] *m* -(e)s, -**e**
spinach.
Spind [ʃpɪnt] *m* or *nt* -(e)s, -**e**
locker.
Spinn- [ʃpɪn] *cpd*: —**e** *f* -, -**n**
spider; **s**—**en** *vti irreg* spin; *(col)*
talk rubbish; *(verrückt)* be crazy or
mad; —**e'rei** *f* spinning mill;
—**(en)gewebe** *nt* cobweb; —**rad** *nt*
spinning-wheel; —**webe** *f* cobweb.
Spion [ʃpiˈoːn] *m* -s, -**e** spy; *(in Tür)* spyhole; —**age** [ʃpioˈnaːʒə] *f*
-, -**n** espionage; **s**—**ieren**
[ʃpioˈniːrən] *vi* spy.
Spirale [ʃpiˈraːlə] *f* -, -**n** spiral.
Spirituosen [ʃpirituˈoːzən] *pl*
spirits *pl*.
Spiritus [ˈʃpiːritʊs] *m* -, -**se**
(methylated) spirit.
Spital [ʃpiˈtaːl] *nt* -s, -**er** hospital.
spitz [ʃpɪts] a pointed; *Winkel*
acute; *(fig)* Zunge sharp; *Bemerkung* caustic; **S**—. *m* -es, -**e** spitz

S—bogen m pointed arch; S—bube m rogue; S—e f -, -n point, tip; (Berg—) peak; (Bemerkung) taunt, dig; (erster Platz) lead, top; (usu pl: Gewebe) lace; S—el m -s, - police informer; —en vt sharpen; S—en- in cpds top; S—enleitung f top performance; S—enlohn m top wages pl; S—ensportler m top-class sportsman; —findig a (over)-subtle; —ig a see spitz; S—name m nickname.

Splitter ['ʃplɪtɐ] m -s, - splinter; s—nackt a stark naked.

spontan [ʃpɔn'taːn] a spontaneous.

Sport [ʃpɔrt] m -(e)s, -e sport; (fig) hobby; —lehrer(in f) m games or P.E. teacher; —ler(in f) m -s, - sportsman/woman; —lich a sporting; Mensch sporty; —platz m playing or sports field; —verein m sports club; —wagen m sports car; —zeug nt sports gear.

Spott [ʃpɔt] m -(e)s mockery, ridicule; s—billig a dirt-cheap; s—en vi mock (über +acc at), ridicule.

spöttisch ['ʃpœtɪʃ] a mocking.

Sprach- ['ʃpraːx] cpd: s—begabt a good at languages; —e f -, -n language; —fehler m speech defect; —fertigkeit f fluency; —führer m phrasebook; —gebrauch m (linguistic) usage; —gefühl nt feeling for language; s—lich a linguistic; s—los a speechless; —rohr nt megaphone; (fig) mouthpiece.

Spray [spreː] m or nt -s, -s spray.

Sprech- ['ʃprɛç] cpd: —anlage f intercom; s—en irreg vi speak (mit to); das spricht für ihn that's a point in his favour; vt say; Sprache speak; Person speak to; —er(in f) m -s, - speaker; (für

Gruppe) spokesman; (Rad, TV) announcer; —stunde f consultation (hour); (doctor's) surgery; —stundenhilfe f (doctor's) receptionist; —zimmer nt consulting room, surgery.

spreizen ['ʃpraɪtsən] vt spread; vr put on airs.

Spreng- ['ʃprɛŋ] cpd: —arbeiten pl blasting operations pl; s—en vt sprinkle; (mit Sprengstoff) blow up; Gestein blast; Versammlung break up; —ladung f explosive charge; —stoff m explosive(s).

Spreu [ʃprɔʏ] f - chaff.

Sprich- ['ʃprɪç] cpd: —wort nt proverb; s—wörtlich a proverbial.

Spring- ['ʃprɪŋ] cpd: —brunnen m fountain; s—en vi irreg jump; (Glas) crack; (mit Kopfsprung) dive; —er m -s, - jumper; (Schach) knight.

Sprit [ʃprɪt] m -(e)s, -e (col) petrol, fuel.

Spritz- ['ʃprɪts] cpd: —e f -, -n syringe; injection; (an Schlauch) nozzle; s—en vt spray; (Med) inject; vi splash; (heraus—) spurt; (Med) give injections; —pistole f spray gun.

spröde ['ʃprøːdə] a brittle; Person reserved, coy.

Sproß [ʃprɔs] m -sses, -sse shoot; (Kind) scion.

Sprosse ['ʃprɔsə] f -, -n rung.

Sprößling ['ʃprœslɪŋ] m offspring no pl.

Spruch [ʃprux] m -(e)s, -̈e saying, maxim; (Jur) judgement.

Sprudel ['ʃpruːdəl] m -s, - mineral water; lemonade; s—n vi bubble.

Sprüh- ['ʃpryː] cpd: —dose f aerosol (can); s—en vti spray; (fig) sparkle; —regen m drizzle.

Sprung [ʃprʊŋ] *m* -(e)s, ̈e jump; (*Riß*) crack; —brett *nt* springboard; s—haft *a* erratic; *Aufstieg* rapid; —schanze *f* skijump.

Spucke [ʃpʊkə] *f* - spit; s—en *vti* spit.

Spuk [ʃpuːk] *m* -(e)s, -e haunting; (*fig*) nightmare; s—en *vi* (*Geist*) walk; hier spukt es this place is haunted.

Spule [ʃpuːlə] *f* -, -n spool; (*Elec*) coil.

Spül- [ʃpyːl] *cpd:* —e *f* -, -n (kitchen) sink; s—en *vti* rinse; *Geschirr* wash up; *Toilette* flush; —maschine *f* dishwasher; —stein *m* sink; —ung *f* rinsing; flush; (*Med*) irrigation.

Spur [ʃpuːr] *f* -, -en trace; (*Fuß-, Rad-, Tonband-*) track; (*Fährte*) trail; (*Fahr-*) lane; s—los *ad* without (a) trace.

spür- [ʃpyːr] *cpd:* —bar *a* noticeable, perceptible; —en *vt* feel; S—hund *m* tracker dog; (*fig*) sleuth.

Spurt [ʃpʊrt] *m* -(e)s, -s *or* -e spurt.

sputen [ʃpuːtən] *vr* make haste.

Staat [ʃtaːt] *m* -(e)s, -en state; (*Prunk*) show; (*Kleidung*) finery; mit etw — machen show off *or* parade sth; s—enlos *a* stateless; s—lich *a* state(-); state-run; —sangehörigkeit *f* nationality; —sanwalt *m* public prosecutor; —sbürger *m* citizen; —sdienst *m* civil service; s—seigen *a* stateowned; —sexamen *nt* (*Univ*) degree; s—sfeindlich *a* subversive; —smann *m, pl* -männer statesman; —ssekretär *m* secretary of state.

Stab [ʃtaːp] *m* -(e)s, ̈e rod; (*Gitter—*) bar; (*Menschen*) staff; —hochsprubg *m* pole vault; s—il

[ʃta'biːl] *a* stable; *Möbel* sturdy; s—ilisieren *vt* stabilize; —reim *m* alliteration.

Stachel [ʃtaxəl] *m* -s, -n spike; (*von Tier*) spine; (*von Insekten*) sting; —beere *f* gooseberry; —draht *m* barbed wire; s—ig *a* prickly; —schwein *nt* porcupine.

Stadion [ʃtaːdiɔn] *nt* -s, Stadien stadium.

Stadium [ʃtaːdiʊm] *nt* stage, phase.

Stadt [ʃtat] *f* -, ̈e town.

Städt- [ʃtɛːt] *cpd:* —chen *nt* small town; —ebau *m* town planning; —er(in *f*) *m* -s, - town dweller; s—isch *a* municipal; (*nicht ländlich*) urban.

Stadt- *cpd:* —mauer *f* city wall(s); —plan *m* street map; —rand *m* outskirts *pl*; —teil *m* district, part of town.

Staffel [ʃtafəl] *f* -, -n rung; (*Sport*) relay (team); (*Aviat*) squadron; —ei [-'laɪ] *f* easel; s—n *vt* graduate; —ung *f* graduation.

Stahl [ʃtaːl] *m* -(e)s, ̈e steel; —helm *m* steel helmet.

Stall [ʃtal] *m* -(e)s, ̈e stable; (*Kaninchen—*) hutch; (*Schweine—*) sty; (*Hühner—*) henhouse.

Stamm [ʃtam] *m* -(e)s, ̈e (*Baum—*) trunk; (*Menschen—*) tribe; (*Gram*). stem; —baum *m* family tree; (*von Tier*) pedigree; s—eln *vti* stammer; s—en *vi:* s—en von *aus* come from; —gast *m* regular (customer); s—halter *m* -s, - son and heir.

stämmig [ʃtɛmiç] *a* sturdy; *Mensch* stocky; S—keit *f* sturdiness; stockiness.

stampfen [ʃtampfən] *vti* stamp; (*stapfen*) tramp; (*mit Werkzeug*) pound.

Stand [ʃtant] *m* **-(e)s, ⸚e** position; *(Wasser—, Benzin— etc)* level; *(Stehen)* standing position; *(Zustand)* state; *(Spiel—)* score; *(Messe— etc)* stand; *(Klasse)* class; *(Beruf)* profession.

Standard ['ʃtandart] *m* **-s, -s** standard.

Ständ- ['ʃtɛnd] *cpd:* **—chen** *nt* serenade; **—er** *m* **-s, -** stand.

Stand- ['ʃtand] *cpd:* **—esamt** *nt* registry office; **—esbeamte(r)** *m* registrar; **—esbewußtsein** *nt* status consciousness; **s—esgemäß** *a,ad* according to one's social position; **—esunterschied** *m* social difference; **s—haft** *a* steadfast; **—haftigkeit** *f* steadfastness; **s—halten** *vi irreg* stand firm *(jdm/etw* against sb/sth), resist *(jdm/etw* sb/sth).

ständig ['ʃtɛndɪç] *a* permanent; *(ununterbrochen)* constant, continual.

Stand- *cpd:* **—licht** *nt* sidelights *pl*, parking lights *pl (US)*; **—ort** *m* location; *(Mil)* garrison; **—punkt** *m* standpoint.

Stange ['ʃtaŋə] *f* **-, -n** stick; *(Stab)* pole, bar; rod; *(Zigaretten)* carton; **von der —** *(Comm)* off the peg; **eine — Geld** quite a packet.

Stanniol [ʃtani'o:l] *nt* **-s, -e** tinfoil.

Stanze ['ʃtantsə] *f* **-, -n** stanza; *(Tech)* stamp; **s—n** *vt* stamp.

Stapel ['ʃta:pəl] *m* **-s, -** pile; *(Naut)* stocks *pl*; **—lauf** *m* launch; **s—n** *vt* pile (up).

Star [ʃta:r] *m* **-(e)s, -e** starling; *(Med)* cataract; *m* **-s, -s** *(Film etc)* star.

stark [ʃtark] *a* strong; *(heftig, groß)* heavy; *(Maßangabe)* thick.

Stärke ['ʃtɛrkə] *f* **-, -n** strength; heaviness; thickness; *(Cook, Wäsche—)* starch; **s—n** *vt* strengthen; *Wäsche* starch.

Starkstrom *m* heavy current.

Stärkung ['ʃtɛrkʊŋ] *f* strengthening; *(Essen)* refreshment.

starr [ʃtar] *a* stiff; *(unnachgiebig)* rigid; *Blick* staring; **—en** *vi* stare; **—en vor** *or* **von** be covered in; *Waffen* be bristling with; **S—heit** *f* rigidity; **—köpfig** *a* stubborn; **S—sinn** *m* obstinacy.

Start [ʃtart] *m* **-(e)s, -e** start; *(Aviat)* takeoff; **—automatik** *f* *(Aut)* automatic choke; **—bahn** *f* runway; **s—en** *vti* start; take off; **—er** *m* **-s, -** starter; **—erlaubnis** *f* takeoff clearance; **—zeichen** *nt* start signal.

Station [ʃtatsi'o:n] *f* station; hospital ward; **s—ieren** [-'ni:rən] *vt* station.

Statist [ʃta'tɪst] *m* extra, supernumerary; **—ik** *f* statistics; **—iker** *m* **-s, -** statistician; **s—isch** *a* statistical.

Stativ [ʃta'ti:f] *nt* **-s, -e** tripod.

statt [ʃtat] *cj, prep* +*gen or dat* instead of; **S—** *f* **-** place.

Stätte ['ʃtɛtə] *f* **-, -n** place.

statt- *cpd:* **—finden** *vi irreg* take place; **—haft** *a* admissible; **—lich** *a* imposing, handsome.

Statue ['ʃta:tuə] *f* **-, n** statue.

Statur [ʃta'tu:r] *f* stature.

Status ['ʃta:tʊs] *m* **-, -** status.

Stau [ʃtaʊ] *m* **-(e)s, -e** blockage; *(Verkehrs—)* (traffic) jam.

Staub [ʃtaʊp] *m* **-(e)s** dust; **s—en** ['ʃtaʊbən] *vi* be dusty; **—faden** *m* stamen; **s—ig** *a* dusty; **—sauger** *m* vacuum cleaner; **—tuch** *nt* duster.

Staudamm *m* dam.

Staude ['ʃtaʊdə] *f* **-, -n** shrub.

stauen ['ʃtauən] vt Wasser dam up; Blut stop the flow of; vr (Wasser) become dammed up; (Med, Verkehr) become congested; (Menschen) collect together; (Gefühle) build up.

staunen ['ʃtaunəh] vi be astonished; S— nt -s amazement.

Stauung ['ʃtauʊŋ] f (von Wasser) damming-up; (von Blut, Verkehr) congestion.

Stech- ['ʃtɛç] cpd: —becken nt bed-pan; s—en vt irreg (mit Nadel etc) prick; (mit Messer) stab; (mit Finger) poke; (Biene etc) sting; (Mücke) bite; (Sonne) burn; (Cards) take; (Art) engrave; Torf, Spargel cut; in See s—en put to sea; —en nt -s, - (Sport) play-off; jump-off; s—end a piercing, stabbing; Geruch pungent; —ginster m gorse; —palme f holly; —uhr f time clock.

Steck- ['ʃtɛk] cpd: —brief m 'wanted' poster; —dose f (wall) socket; s—en vt put, insert; Nadel stick; Pflanzen plant; (beim Nähen) pin; vi irreg be; (festsitzen) be stuck; (Nadeln) stick; s—enbleiben vi irreg get stuck; s—enlassen vt irreg leave in; —enpferd nt hobby-horse; —er m -s, - plug; —nadel f pin; —rübe f swede, turnip; —zwiebel f bulb.

Steg [ʃteːk] m -(e)s, -e small bridge; (Anlege—) landing stage; —reif m: aus dem —reif just like that.

stehen ['ʃteːən] irreg vi stand (zu by); (sich befinden) be; (in Zeitung) say; (stillstehen) have stopped; jdm — suit sb; vi impers: es steht schlecht um things are bad for; wie steht's? how are things?; (Sport) what's the score?; —

bleiben remain standing; —bleiben vi irreg (Uhr) stop; (Fehler) stay as it is; —lassen vt irreg leave; Bart grow.

stehlen ['ʃteːlən] vt irreg steal.

steif [ʃtaif] a stiff; S—heit f stiffness.

Steig- [ʃtaik] cpd: —bügel m stirrup; —e f [ʃtaigə] f -, -n (Straße) steep road; (Kiste) crate; —eisen nt crampon; s—en vi irreg rise; (klettern) climb; s—en in (+acc)/auf (+acc)t get in/on; s—en vt raise; (Gram) compare; vi (Auktion) bid; vr increase; —erung f raising; (Gram) comparison; —ung f incline, gradient, rise.

steil [ʃtail] a steep.

Stein [ʃtain] m -(e)s, -e stone; (in Uhr) jewel; s—alt a ancient; —bock m (Astrol) Capricorn; —bruch m quarry; —butt m -s, -e turbot; s—ern a (made of) stone; (fig) stony; —gut nt stoneware; s—hart a hard as stone; s—ig a stony; s—igen vt stone; —kohle f mineral coal; —metz m -es, -e stonemason.

Steiß [ʃtais] m -es, -e rump.

Stell- ['ʃtɛl] cpd: —dichein nt -(s), -(s) rendezvous; —e f -, -n place; (Arbeit) post, job; (Amt) office; s—en vt put; Uhr etc set; (zur Verfügung —) supply; (fassen) Dieb apprehend; vr (sich auf-stellen) stand; . (sich einfinden) present oneself; (bei Polizei) give oneself up; (vorgeben) pretend (to be); sich zu etw s—en have an opinion of sth; —enangebot nt offer of a post; (Zeitung) vacancies; —engesuch nt application for a post; —ennachweis m, —envermittlung f employment agency; **—ung** _f_ position; (Mil) line; **—ung nehmen zu** comment on; **—ungnahme** _f_ **-**, **-n** comment; **s—vertretend** _a_ **-vertreter** _m_ deputy, acting; **-vertreter** _m_ deputy; **—werk** _nt_ (Rail) signal box.

Stelze ['ʃtɛltsə] _f_ **-**, **-n** stilt.

Stemm- ['ʃtɛm] _cpd_: **—bogen** _m_ (Ski) stem turn; **s—en** _vt_ lift (up); (drücken) press; **sich s—en gegen** (fig) resist, oppose.

Stempel ['ʃtɛmpəl] _m_ **-s**, **-** stamp; (Bot) pistil; **—kissen** _nt_ inkpad; **s—n** _vt_ stamp; _Briefmarke_ cancel; **s—n gehen** (col) be/go on the dole.

Stengel ['ʃtɛŋəl] _m_ **-s**, **-** stalk.

Steno- ['ʃteno] _cpd:_ **- —gramm** ['-gram] _nt_ shorthand report; **—graphie** [-gra'fiː] _f_ shorthand; **s—graphieren** [-gra'fiːrən] _vi_ write (in) shorthand; **—typist(in** _f_ [-ty'pɪst(ɪn)] _m_ shorthand typist.

Stepp- ['ʃtɛp] _cpd:_ **—decke** _f_ quilt; **—e** _f_ **-**, **-n** prairie; steppe; **s—en** _vt_ stitch; _vi_ tap-dance.

Sterb- ['ʃtɛrb] _cpd:_ **—ebett** _nt_ deathbed; **—efall** _m_ death; **s—en** _vi irreg_ die; **—eurkunde** _f_ death certificate; **s—lich** ['ʃtɛrplɪç] _a_ mortal; **—lichkeit** _f_ mortality; **—lichkeitsziffer** _f_ death rate.

stereo- ['steːreo] _in cpds_ stereo〈-〉; **—typ** [stereo'tyːp] _a_ stereotype.

steril [ʃte'riːl] _a_ sterile; **—isieren** [-i'siːrən] _vt_ sterilize; **S—isierung** _f_ sterilization.

Stern [ʃtɛrn] _m_ **-(e)s**, **-e** star; **—bild** _nt_ constellation; (Chem _nt_) asterisk; **—schnuppe** _f_ **-**, **-n** meteor, falling star; **—stunde** _f_ historic moment.

stet [ʃteːt] _a_ steady; **—ig** _a_ constant, continual; **—s** _ad_ continually, always.

Steuer ['ʃtɔʏər] _nt_ **-s**, **-** (Naut) helm; **(—ruder)** rudder; (Aut) steering wheel; _f_ **-**, **-n** tax; **—bord** _nt_ starboard; **—erklärung** _f_ tax return; **—klasse** _f_ tax group; **—knüppel** _m_ control column; (Aviat) joystick; **—mann** _m_, _pl_ **-männer** _or_ **-leute** helmsman; **s—n** _vti_ steer; _Flugzeug_ pilot; _Entwicklung, Tonstärke_ control; **s—pflichtig** _a_ taxable; _Person_ liable to pay tax; **—rad** _nt_ steering wheel; **—ung** _f_ steering (auch Aut); piloting; control; (Vorrichtung) controls _pl_; **—zahler** _m_ **-s**, **-** taxpayer; **—zuschlag** _m_ additional tax.

Steward ['stjuːart] _m_ **-s**, **-s** steward; **—eß** ['stjuːərdɛs] _f_ **-**, **-essen** stewardess; air hostess.

stibitzen [ʃti'bɪtsən] _vt_ (col) pilfer, steal.

Stich [ʃtɪç] _m_ **-(e)s**, **-e** (Insekten—) sting; (Messer—) stab; (beim Nähen) stitch; (Färbung) tinge; (Cards) trick; (Art) engraving; **jdn im — lassen** leave sb in the lurch; **—el** _m_ **-s**, **-** engraving tool, style; **—elei** _f_ (fig) jibe, taunt; **s—eln** _vi_ (fig) jibe; **s—haltig** a sound, tenable; **—probe** _f_ spot check; **—wahl** _f_ final ballot; **—wort** _nt_ cue; (in _Wörterbuch_) headword; (für Vortrag) note; **—wortverzeichnis** _nt_ index.

Stick- [ʃtɪk] _cpd:_ **s—en** _vti_ embroider; **—erei** _f_ embroidery; **s—ig** a stuffy, close; **—stoff** _m_ nitrogen.

Stiefel ['ʃtiːfəl] _m_ **-s**, **-** boot.

Stief- ['ʃtiːf] _in cpds_ step; **—kind** _nt_ stepchild; (fig) Cinderella; **—mutter** _f_ stepmother; **—mütterchen** _nt_ pansy.

Stiege ['ʃtiːgə] f -, -n staircase.

Stiel [ʃtiːl] m -(e)s, -e handle; (Bot) stalk.

stier [ʃtiːr] a staring, fixed; **S—** m -(e)s, -e bull; (Astrol) Taurus; **—en** vi stare.

Stift [ʃtift] m -(e)s, -e peg; (Nagel) tack; (Farb—) crayon; (Blei—) pencil; nt -(e)s, -e (charitable) foundation; (Eccl) religious institution; **s—en** vt found; (Unruhe) cause; (spenden) contribute; **—er(in** f) m -s, - founder; **—ung** f donation; (Organisation) foundation; **—zahn** m crown tooth.

Stil [ʃtiːl] m -(e)s, -e style; **—blüte** f howler.

still [ʃtil] a quiet; (unbewegt) still; (heimlich) secret; **S—e** f -, -n stillness, quietness; **in aller S—e** quietly; **—en** vt stop, pause; **s—en** a Säugling breast-feed; (befriedigen) satisfy; **—gestanden** interj attention; **—halten** vi irreg keep still; **—(l)egen** vt close down; **—schweigen** vi irreg be silent; **S—schweigen** nt silence; **—schweigend** a,ad silent(ly); Einverständnis tacit(ly); **S—stand** m standstill; **—stehen** vi irreg stand still.

Stimm- ['ʃtim] cpd: **—abgabe** f voting; **—bänder** pl vocal chords pl; **s—berechtigt** a entitled to vote; **—e** f -, -n voice; (Wahl—) vote; **s—en** vt (Mus) tune; das stimmte ihn traurig that made him feel sad; vi be right; **s—en für/gegen** vote for/against; **—enmehrheit** f majority (of votes); **—enthaltung** f abstention; **—gabel** f tuning fork; **s—haft** a voiced; **—lage** f register; **s—los** a voiceless; **—recht** nt right to vote; **—ung** f mood; atmosphere; **s—ungsvoll** a enjoyable;

full of atmosphere; **—zettel** m ballot paper.

stinken ['ʃtiŋkən] vi irreg stink.

Stipendium [ʃti'pɛndiʊm] nt grant.

Stirn [ʃtirn] f -, -en forehead, brow; (Frechheit) impudence; **—höhle** f sinus; **—runzeln** nt -s frown(ing).

stöbern ['ʃtøːbərn] vi rummage.

stochern ['ʃtɔxərn] vi poke (about).

Stock [ʃtɔk] m -(e)s, ⁼e stick; (Bot) stock; pl **-werke** storey; **s—** in cpds vor a (col) completely; **s—en** vi stop, pause; **s—end** a halting; **s—finster** a (col) pitchdark; **s—taub** a stone-deaf; **—ung** f stoppage; **—werk** nt storey, floor.

Stoff [ʃtɔf] m -(e)s, -e (Gewebe) material, cloth; (Materie) matter; (von Buch etc) subject (matter); **s—lich** a material; with regard to subject matter; **—wechsel** m metabolism.

stöhnen ['ʃtøːnən] vi groan.

stoisch ['ʃtoːiʃ] a stoical.

Stollen ['ʃtɔlən] m -s, - (Min) gallery; (Cook) cake eaten at Christmas; (von Schuhen) stud.

stolpern ['ʃtɔlpərn] vi stumble, trip.

Stolz [ʃtɔlts] m -es pride; **s—** a proud; **s—ieren** [ʃtɔl'tsiːrən] vi strut.

Stopf- ['ʃtɔpf] cpd: **s—en** vt (hinein—) stuff; (voll—) fill (up); (nähen) darn; vi (Med) cause constipation; **—garn** nt darning thread.

Stoppel ['ʃtɔpəl] f -, -n stubble.

Stopp- ['ʃtɔp] cpd: **s—en** vti stop; (mit Uhr) time; **—schild** nt stop sign; **—uhr** f stopwatch.

Stöpsel ['ʃtœpsəl] m -s, - plug; (für Flaschen) stopper.

Stör [ʃtøːr] m -(e)s, -e sturgeon.

Storch m -(e)s, ‥e stork.
Stör- [ʃtøːr] cpd: s—en vt disturb; (behindern, Rad) interfere with; vr sich an etw (dat) s—en let sth bother one; s—end a disturbing, annoying; —enfried m -(e)s, -e troublemaker.

störrig [ˈʃtœrɪç], **störrisch** [ˈʃtœrɪʃ] a stubborn, perverse.

Stör- cpd: —sender m jammer; —ung f disturbance; interference.

Stoß [ʃtoːs] m -es, ‥e (Schub) push; (Schlag) blow; knock; (mit Schwert) thrust; (mit Fuß) kick; (Erd—) shock; (Haufen) pile; —dämpfer m -s, - shock absorber; s—en irreg vt (mit Druck) shove, push; (mit Schlag) knock, bump; (mit Fuß) kick; (Schwert etc) thrust; (an—) 'Kopf etc bump; (zerkleinern) pulverize; vr get a knock; sich an etw (+dat) (fig) take exception to; vi: s—en an or auf (+acc) bump into; (finden) come across; (angrenzen) be next to; —stange f (Aut) bumper.

Stotterer [ˈʃtɔtərər] m -s, - stutterer.

stottern [ˈʃtɔtərn] vti stutter.

stracks [ʃtraks] ad straight.

Straf- [ˈʃtraːf] cpd: —anstalt f penal institution; —arbeit f (Sch) punishment; lines pl; s—bar a punishable; —barkeit f criminal nature; —e f -, -n punishment; (Jur) penalty; (Gefängnis—) sentence; (Geld—) fine; s—en vt punish.

straff [ʃtraf] a tight; (streng) strict; Stil etc concise; Haltung erect; s—en vt tighten, tauten.

Straf- cpd: —gefangene(r) mf prisoner, convict; —gesetzbuch nt penal code; —kolonie f penal colony.

Sträf- [ˈʃtreːf] cpd: s—lich a criminal; —ling m convict.

Straf- cpd: —porto nt excess postage (charge); —predigt f severe lecture; —raum m (Sport) penalty area; —recht nt criminal law; —stoß m (Sport) penalty (kick); —tat f punishable act; —zettel m ticket.

Strahl [ʃtraːl] m -s, -en ray, beam; (Wasser—) jet; s—en vi radiate; (fig) beam; —enbehandlung, —entherapie f radiotherapy; —ung f radiation.

Strähne [ˈʃtrɛːnə] f -, -n strand.

stramm [ʃtram] a tight; Haltung erect; Mensch robust; s—stehen vi irreg (Mil) stand to attention.

strampeln [ˈʃtrampəln] vi kick (about), fidget.

Strand [ʃtrant] m -(e)s, ‥e shore; (mit Sand) beach; —bad nt open-air swimming pool, lido; s—en [ˈʃtrandən] vi run aground; (fig: Mensch) fail; —gut nt flotsam; —korb m beach chair.

Strang [ʃtraŋ] m -(e)s, ‥e cord, rope; (Bündel) skein; (Schienen—) track; über die ‥e schlagen (col) kick over the traces.

Strapaze [ʃtraˈpaːtsə] f -, -n strain, exertion; s—ieren [ʃtrapaˈtsiːrən] vt Material treat roughly, punish; Mensch, Kräfte wear out, exhaust; s—ierfähig a hard-wearing; s—iös [ʃtrapatsiˈøːs] a exhausting, tough.

Straße [ˈʃtraːsə] f -, -n street, road; —nbahn f tram, streetcar (US); —nbeleuchtung f street lighting; —nfeger m; —nkehrer m -s, - roadsweeper; —nsperre f roadblock; —nverkehrsordnung f highway code.

Strateg- [ʃtraˈteːg] cpd: —e m -n, -n. strategist; —ie [ʃtrateˈgiː] f strategy; s—isch a strategic.

Stratosphäre [ʃtratoˈsfɛːrə] f - stratosphere.

sträuben [ˈʃtrɔybən] vt ruffle; vr bristle; (Mensch) resist (gegen etw sth).

Strauch [ʃtraux] m -(e)s, **Sträucher** bush, shrub; s—eln vi stumble, stagger.

Strauß [ʃtraus] m -es, **Sträuße** bunch; bouquet; pl -e ostrich.

Streb- [ˈʃtreːb] cpd: —e f -, -n strut; —ebalken m buttress; s—en vi strive (nach for), endeavour; s—en zu or nach (sich bemühen) make for; —er m -s, - (pej) pusher, climber; (Sch) swot; s—sam a industrious; —samkeit f industry.

Strecke [ˈʃtrɛkə] f -, -n stretch; (Entfernung) distance; (Rail) line; (Math) line; s—n vt stretch; Waffen lay down; (Cook) eke out; vr stretch (oneself); vi (Sch) put one's hand up.

Streich [ʃtraiç] m -(e)s, -e trick, prank; (Hieb) blow; s—eln vt stroke; s—en irreg vt (berühren) stroke; (auftragen) spread; (anmalen) paint; (durch—) delete; (nicht genehmigen) cancel; vi (berühren) brush; (schleichen) prowl; —holz nt match; —instrument nt string instrument.

Streif- [ˈʃtraif] cpd: —band nt wrapper; —e f -, -n patrol; s—en vt (leicht berühren) brush against, graze; (Blick) skim over; Thema, Problem touch on; (ab—) take off; vi (gehen) roam; —en m -s, - (Linie) stripe; (Stück) strip; (Film) film; —endienst m patrol duty; —enwagen m patrol car; —schuß

m graze; grazing shot; —zug m scouting trip.

Streik [ʃtraik] m -(e)s, -s strike; —brecher m -s, - blackleg, strikebreaker; s—en vi strike; —kasse f strike fund; —posten m (strike) picket.

Streit [ʃtrait] m -(e)s, -e argument; dispute; s—en vir irreg argue; dispute; —frage f point at issue; s—ig a: jdm etw s—ig machen dispute sb's right to sth; —igkeiten pl quarrel, dispute; —kräfte pl (Mil) armed forces pl; s—lustig a quarrelsome; —sucht f quarrelsomeness.

streng [ʃtrɛŋ] a (severe; Lehrer, Maßnahme) strict; (Geruch etc) sharp; S—e f - severity; strictness; —genommen ad strictly speaking; —gläubig a orthodox, strict.

Streu [ʃtrɔy] f -, -en litter, bed of straw; s—en vt strew, scatter, spread; —ung f dispersion.

Strich [ʃtriç] m -(e)s, -e (Linie) line; (Feder—, Pinsel—) stroke; (von Geweben) nap; (von Fell) pile; auf den — gehen (col) walk the streets; jdm gegen den — einen rub sb up the wrong way; einen — machen durch (lit) cross out; (fig) foil; —einteilung f calibration; —mädchen nt streetwalker; —punkt m semicolon; s—weise ad here and there.

Strick [ʃtrik] m -(e)s, -e rope; (col: Kind) rascal; s—en vti knit; —jacke f cardigan; —leiter f rope ladder; —nadel f knitting needle; —waren pl knitwear.

Strieme [ˈʃtriːmə] f -, -n, **Striemen** m -s, - weal.

strikt [ˈʃtrikt] a strict.

strittig ['ʃtrɪtɪç] a disputed, in dispute.

Stroh [ʃtroː] nt -(e)s straw; —**blume** f everlasting flower; —**dach** nt thatched roof; —**halm** m (drinking) straw; —**mann** m, pl -**männer** dummy, straw man; —**witwe** f grass widow.

Strolch [ʃtrɔlç] m -(e)s, -e layabout, bum.

Strom [ʃtroːm] m -(e)s, ⁼e river; (fig) stream; (Elec) current; s—**abwärts** [-"apvɛrts] ad downstream; s—**aufwärts** ["aufvɛrts] ad upstream.

strömen ['ʃtrøːmən] vi stream, pour.

Strom- cpd: —**kreis** m circuit; s—**linienförmig** a streamlined; —**rechnung** f electricity bill; —**sperre** f power cut; —**stärke** f amperage.

Strömung ['ʃtrøːmʊŋ] f current.

Strophe ['ʃtroːfə] f -, -n verse.

strotzen ['ʃtrɔtsən] vi: —**vor** or **von** abound in, be full of.

Strudel [ʃtruːdəl] m -s, - whirlpool, vortex; (Cook) strudel; s—n vi swirl, eddy.

Struktur [ʃtrʊk'tuːr] f structure; s—**ell** [-'rɛl] a structural.

Strumpf [ʃtrʊmpf] m -(e)s, ⁼e stocking; —**band** nt garter; —**hose** f (pair of) tights.

Strunk [ʃtrʊŋk] m -(e)s, ⁼e stump.

struppig ['ʃtrʊpɪç] a shaggy, unkempt.

Stube ['ʃtuːbə] f -, -n room; —**narrest** m confinement to one's room; (Mil) confinement to quarters; —**nhocker** m (col) stay-at-home; s—**nrein** a house-trained.

Stuck [ʃtʊk] m -(e)s stucco.

Stück [ʃtyk] nt -(e)s, -e piece; (etwas) bit; (Theat) play; —**arbeit** f piecework; —**chen** nt little piece; —**lohn** m piecework wages pl; s—**weise** ad bit by bit, piecemeal; (Comm) individually; —**werk** nt bits and pieces pl.

Student(in f) [ʃtu'dɛnt(ɪn)] m student; s—**isch** a student, academic.

Studie ['ʃtuːdiə] f study.

studieren [ʃtu'diːrən] vti study.

Studio ['ʃtuːdio] nt -s, -s studio.

Studium ['ʃtuːdiʊm] nt studies pl.

Stufe ['ʃtuːfə] f -, -n step; (Entwicklungs—) stage; —**nleiter** f (fig) ladder; s—**nweise** ad gradually.

Stuhl [ʃtuːl] m -(e)s, ⁼e chair; —**gang** m bowel movement.

stülpen ['ʃtʏlpən] vt (umdrehen) 'turn upside down; (bedecken) put.

stumm [ʃtʊm] a silent; (Med) dumb; S—**el** m -s, - stump; (Zigaretten-) stub; S—**film** m silent film; S—**heit** f silence; dumbness.

Stümper ['ʃtʏmpər] m -s, - incompetent, duffer; s—**haft** a bungling, incompetent; s—**n** vi (col) bungle.

stumpf [ʃtʊmpf] a blunt; (teilnahmslos, glanzlos) dull; Winkel obtuse; S— m -(e)s, ⁼e stump; S—**heit** f bluntness; dullness; S—**sinn** m tediousness; —**sinnig** a dull.

Stunde [ʃtʊndə] f -, -n hour; s—n vt: jdm etw s—en give sb time to pay sth; —**ngeschwindigkeit** f average speed per hour; —**nkilometer** pl kilometres per hour; s—**nlang** a for hours; —**nlohn** m hourly wage; —**nplan** m timetable; s—**nweise** a by the hour; every hour.

stündlich ['ʃtʏntlɪç] a hourly.

Stups [ʃtʊps] m -es, -e (col) push; —nase f snub nose.

stur [ʃtuːr] a obstinate, pigheaded.

Sturm [ʃtʊrm] m -(e)s, ‍̈e storm, gale; (Mil etc) attack, assault.

stürm- ['ʃtʏrm] cpd: —en vi (Wind) blow hard, rage; (rennen) storm; ‍vt (Mil, fig) storm; v impers es —t there's a gale blowing; S—er m -s, - (Sport) forward, striker; —isch a stormy.

Sturm- cpd: —warnung f gale warning; —wind m storm, gale.

Sturz [ʃtʊrts] m -es, ‍̈e fall; (Pol) overthrow.

stürzen ['ʃtʏrtsən] vt (werfen) hurl; (Pol) overthrow; (umkehren) overturn; vr rush; (hinein—) plunge; vi fall; (Aviat) dive; (rennen) dash.

Sturz- cpd: —flug m nose-dive; —helm m crash helmet.

Stute ['ʃtuːtə] f -, -n mare.

Stütz- ['ʃtʏts] cpd: —balken m brace, joist; —e f -, -n support; help; s—en vt (lit, fig) support; Ellbogen etc prop up.

stutz- ['ʃtʊts] cpd: —en vt trim; Ohr, Schwanz dock; Flügel clip; vi hesitate; become suspicious; —ig a perplexed, puzzled; (mißtrauisch) suspicious.

Stütz- cpd: —mauer f·supporting wall; —punkt m point of support; (von Hebel) fulcrum; (Mil, fig) base.

Styropor® ['ʃtyro'poːr] nt -s polystyrene.

Subjekt [zʊp'jɛkt] nt -(e)s, -e subject; s—iv [-'tiːf] a subjective; —ivität f subjectivity.

Substantiv [zʊpstan'tiːf] nt -s, -e noun.

Substanz [zʊp'stants] f substance.

subtil [zʊp'tiːl] a subtle.

subtrahieren [zʊptra'hiːrən] vt subtract.

Subvention [zʊpvɛntsi'oːn] f subsidy; s—ieren [-'niːrən] vt subsidize.

subversiv [zʊpvɛr'ziːf] a subversive.

Such- ['zuːx] cpd: —aktion f search; —e f -, -n search; s—en vti look (for), seek; (ver—) try; —er m -s, - seeker, searcher; (Phot) viewfinder.

Sucht [zʊxt] f -, ‍̈e mania; (Med) addiction, craving.

süchtig ['zʏçtɪç] a ·addicted; S—e(r) mf addict.

Süd- [zyːt] cpd: —en ['zyːdən] m -s south; —früchte pl Mediterranean fruit; s—lich a southern; s—lich von (to the) south of; s—wärts ad southwards.

süff- cpd: —ig ['zʏfɪç] a Wein pleasant to the taste; —isant [zyfi'zant] a smug.

suggerieren [zʊgɛ'riːrən] vt suggest (jdm etw sth to sb).

Sühne ['zyːnə] f -, -n atonement, expiation; s—n vt atone for, expiate.

Sulfonamid [zʊlfona'miːt] nt -(e)s, -e (Med) sulphonamide.

Sultan ['zʊltan] m -s, -e sultan; —ine [zʊlta'niːnə] f sultana.

Sülze ['zʏltsə] f -, -n brawn.

Summ- [zʊm] cpd: s—arisch [zu'maːrɪʃ] a summary; —e f -, -n sum, total; s—en vti buzz; Lied hum; s—ieren [zu'miːrən] vtr add up (to).

Sumpf [zʊmpf] m -(e)s, ‍̈e swamp, marsh; s—ig a marshy.

Sünde ['zyndə] f -, -n sin; —**nbock** m (col) scapegoat; —**nfall** m Fall (of man); —**r(in** f) m -s, - sinner.

Super ['zu:pər] nt -s (Benzin) four star (petrol); —**lativ** [-lati:f] m -s, -e superlative; —**markt** m supermarket.

Suppe ['zupə] f -, -n soup.

surren ['zurən] vi buzz, hum.

Surrogat [zuro'ga:t] nt -(e)s, -e substitute, surrogate.

suspekt [zus'pɛkt] a suspect.

süß [zy:s] a sweet; **S—e** f - sweetness; —**en** vt sweeten; **S—igkeit** f sweetness; (Bonbon etc) sweet, candy (US); —**lich** a sweetish; (fig) sugary; **S—speise** f pudding, sweet; **S—stoff** m sweetening agent; **S—wasser** nt fresh water.

Sylvester [zyl'vɛstər] nt -s, - see **Silvester**.

Symbol [zym'bo:l] nt -s, -e symbol; **s—isch** a symbolic(al).

Symmetrie [zyme'tri:] f symmetry; —**achse** f symmetric axis.

symmetrisch [zy'me:trɪʃ] a symmetrical.

Sympath- cpd: —**ie** [zympa'ti:] f

liking, sympathy; **s—isch** [zym'pa:tɪʃ] a likeable, congenial; **er ist mir s—** I like him; **s—isieren** vi sympathize.

Symptom [zymp'to:m] nt -s, -e symptom; **s—atisch** [zympto-'ma:tɪʃ] a symptomatic.

Synagoge [zyna'go:gə] f -, -n synagogue.

synchron [zyn'kro:n] a synchronous; **S—getriebe** nt synchromesh (gears pl); —**i'sieren** vt synchronize; Film dub.

Syndikat [zyndi'ka:t] nt -(e)s, -e combine, syndicate.

Synonym [zyno'ny:m] nt -s, -e synonym; **s—** a synonymous.

Syntax ['zyntaks] f -, -en syntax.

Synthese [zyn'te:zə] f -, -n synthesis.

synthetisch [zyn'te:tɪʃ] a synthetic.

Syphilis ['zyfilɪs] f - syphilis.

System [zys'te:m] nt -s, -e system; **s—atisch** [zystə'ma:tɪʃ] a systematic; **s—ati'sieren** vt systematize.

Szene ['stse:nə] f -, -n scene; —**rie** [stsenə'ri:] f scenery.

Szepter ['stsɛptər] nt -s, - sceptre.

T

T, t [te:] T, t.

Tabak ['ta:bak] m -s, -e tobacco.

Tabell- [ta'bɛl] cpd: **t—arisch** [tabɛ'la:rɪʃ] a tabular; —**e** f table; —**enführer** m top of the table, league leader.

Tabernakel [tabɛr'na:kəl] m -s, - tabernacle.

Tablette [ta'blɛtə] f tablet, pill.

Tachometer [taxo'me:tər] m -s, -

.(Aut) speedometer.

Tadel ['ta:dəl] m -s, - censure, scolding; (Fehler) fault, blemish; **t—los** a faultless, irreproachable; **t—n** vt scold; **t—nswert** a blameworthy.

Tafel ['ta:fəl] f -, -n table (auch Math); (Anschlag—) board; (Wand—) blackboard; (Schiefer—)

slate; (Gedenk—) plaque; (Illustration) plate; (Schalt—) panel; (Schokolade etc) bar.
Täfel- ['tɛ:fəl] cpd: **t—n** vt panel; **—ung** f panelling.
Taft [taft] m **-(e)s, -e** tafetta.
Tag [ta:k] m **-(e)s, -e** day; daylight; unter/über — (Min) underground/on the surface; **an den — kommen** come to light; **guten —!** good morning/afternoon!; **t—aus, t—ein** ad day in, day out; **—dienst** m day duty; **—ebuch** ['ta:gəbu:x] nt diary, journal; **—edieb** m idler; **—egeld** nt daily allowance; **t—elang** ad for days; **t—en** vi sit, meet; v impers: **es tagt** dawn is breaking; **—esablauf** m course of the day; **—esanbruch** m dawn; **—eslicht** nt daylight; **—esordnung** f agenda; **—essatz** m daily rate; **—eszeit** f time of day; **—eszeitung** f daily (paper).
täglich ['tɛ:klɪç] a,ad daily.
Tag- cpd: **t—süber** ad during the day; **—ung** f conference.
Taille ['taljə] f **-, -n** waist.
Takel ['ta:kəl] nt **-s, -** tackle; **t—n** vt rig.
Takt [takt] m **-(e)s, -e** (Mus) time; **—gefühl** nt tact; **—ik** f tactics pl; **t—isch** a tactical; **t—los** a tactless; **—losigkeit** f tactlessness; **—stock** m (conductor's) baton; **t—voll** a tactful.
Tal [ta:l] nt **-(e)s, ⁼er** valley.
Talar [ta'la:r] m **-s, -e** (Jur) robe; (Univ) gown.
Talent [ta'lɛnt] nt **-(e)s, -e** talent; **t—iert** [talɛn'ti:rt], **t—voll** a talented, gifted.
Taler ['ta:lər] m **-s, -** taler, florin.
Talg [talk] m **-(e)s, -e** tallow; **—drüse** f sebaceous gland.

Talisman ['ta:lɪsman] m **-s, -e** talisman.
Tal- cpd: **—sohle** f bottom of a valley; **—sperre** f dam.
Tamburin [tambu'ri:n] nt **-s, -e** tambourine.
Tampon ['tampɔn] m **-s, -s** tampon.
Tang [taŋ] m **-(e)s, -e** seaweed; **—ente** [taŋ'gɛntə] f **-, -n** tangent; **t—ieren** [taŋ'gi:rən] vt (lit) be tangent to; (fig) affect.
Tank [taŋk] m **-s, -s** tank; **t—en** vi fill up with petrol or gas (US); (Aviat) (re)fuel; **—er** m **-s, -,** **—schiff** nt tanker; **—stelle** f petrol or gas (US) station; **—wart** m petrol pump or gas station (US) attendant.
Tanne ['tanə] f **-, -n** fir; **—nbaum** m fir tree; **—nzapfen** m fir cone.
Tante ['tantə] f **-, -n** aunt.
Tanz [tants] m **-es, -e** dance.
Tänz- ['tɛnts] cpd: **t—eln** vi dance along; **—er(in** f) m **-s, -** dancer.
Tanz- cpd: **t—en** vti dance; **—fläche** f (dance) floor; **—schule** f dancing school.
Tape- cpd: **—te** [ta'pe:tə] f **-, -n** wallpaper; **—tenwechsel** m (fig) change of scenery; **t—zieren** [tape'tsi:rən] vt (wall)paper; **—zierer** [tape'tsi:rər] m **-s, -** (interior) decorator.
tapfer ['tapfər] a brave; **T—keit** f courage, bravery.
tappen ['tapən] vi walk uncertainly or clumsily.
täppisch ['tɛpɪʃ] a clumsy.
Tarif [ta'ri:f] m **-s, -e** tariff, (scale of) fares/charges; **—lohn** m standard wage rate.
Tarn- ['tarn] cpd: **t—en** vt camouflage; Person, Absicht disguise;

—farbe f camouflage paint; —ung f camouflaging; disguising.

Tasche ['taʃə] f -, -n pocket; handbag; —n in cpds pocket; —nbuch nt paperback; —ndieb m pickpocket; —ngeld nt pocket money; —nlampe f (electric) torch, flashlight (US); —nmesser nt penknife; —nspieler m conjurer; —ntuch nt handkerchief.

Tasse ['tasə] f -, -n cup.

Tast- ['tast] cpd: —atur [-a'tu:r] f keyboard; —e f -, -n push-button control; (an Schreibmaschine) key; t—en vt feel, touch; vi feel, grope; vr feel one's way; —sinn m sense of touch.

Tat [ta:t] f -, -en act, deed, action; in der — indeed, as a matter of fact; —bestand m facts pl of the case; t—enlos a inactive.

Tät- ['tɛ:t] cpd: —er(in f) m -s, perpetrator, culprit; —erschaft f guilt; t—ig a active; in einer Firma t—ig sein work for a firm; T—igkeit f activity; (Beruf) occupation; t—lich a violent; —lichkeit f violence; pl blows pl.

tätowieren [tɛto'vi:rən] vt tattoo.

Tat- cpd: —sache f fact; t—sächlich a actual; ad really.

Tatze ['tatsə] f -, -n paw.

Tau [tau] nt -(e)s, -e rope; m -(e)s dew.

taub [taup] a deaf; Nuß hollow; T—heit f deafness; —stumm a deaf-and-dumb.

Taube ['taubə] f -, -n dove; pigeon; —nschlag m dovecote.

Tauch- ['taux] cpd: t—en vt dip; vi dive; (Naut) submerge; —er m -s, - diver; —eranzug m diving suit; —sieder m -s, - portable immersion heater.

tauen ['tauən] vti, v impers thaw.

Tauf- ['tauf] cpd: —becken nt font; —e f -, -n baptism; t—en vt christen, baptize; —name m Christian name; —pate m godfather; —patin f godmother; —schein m certificate of baptism.

Taug- ['taug] cpd: t—en vi be of use; t—en für do or be good for; nicht t—en be no good or useless; —enichts m -es, -e good-for-nothing; t—lich ['tauklıç] a suitable; (Mil) fit (for service); —lichkeit f suitability; fitness.

Taumel ['tauməl] m -s dizziness; (fig) frenzy; t—ig a giddy, reeling; t—n vi reel, stagger.

Tausch [tauʃ] m -(e)s, -e exchange; t—en vt exchange, swap; —handel m barter.

täuschen ['tɔyʃən] vt deceive; vi be deceptive; vr be wrong; —d a deceptive.

Täuschung f deception; (optisch) illusion.

tausend ['tauzənt] num (a) thousand; T—füßler m -s, - centipede; millipede.

Tau- cpd: —tropfen m dew drop; —wetter nt thaw; —ziehen nt -s, tug-of-war.

Taxi ['taksi] nt -(s), -(s) taxi; —fahrer m taxi driver.

Tech- ['tɛç] cpd: —nik f technology; (Methode, Kunstfertigkeit) technique; —niker m -s, - technician; t—nisch a technical; —nolo'gie f technology; t—no'logisch a technological.

Tee [te:] m -s, -s tea; —kanne f teapot; —löffel m teaspoon.

Teer [te:r] m -(e)s, -e tar; t—en vt tar.

Tee- cpd: —sieb nt tea strainer; —wagen m tea trolley.

Teich [taɪç] m -(e)s, -e pond.
Teig [taɪk] m -(e)s, -e dough; t—ig a doughy; —waren pl pasta sing.
Teil [taɪl] m or nt -(e)s, -e part; (An—) share; (Bestand—) component; zum — partly; t—bar a divisible; —betrag m instalment; —chen nt (atomic) particle; t—en vtr divide; (mit jdm) share; t—haben vi irreg share (an +dat in); —haber m -s, - partner; —kaskoversicherung f third party, fire and theft insurance; —nahme f -, -n participation; (Mitleid) sympathy; t—nahmslos a disinterested, apathetic; t—nehmen vi irreg take part (an +dat in); —nehmer m, participant; t—s ad partly; —ung f division; t—weise ad partially, in part; —zahlung f payment by instalments.
Teint [tɛ̃:] m -s, -s complexion.
Telefon [tele'fo:n] nt -s, -e telephone; —amt nt telephone exchange; —anruf m, —at [telefo'na:t] nt -(e)s, -e (tele)phone call; —buch nt telephone directory; t—ieren [telefo'ni:rən] vi telephone; t—isch [-ɪʃ] a telephone; Benachrichtigung by telephone; —ist(in f) [telefo'nɪst(ɪn)] m telephonist; —nummer f (tele)phone number; —verbindung f telephone connection; —zelle f telephone kiosk, callbox; —zentrale f telephone exchange.
Telegraf [tele'gra:f] m -en, -en telegraph; —enleitung f telegraph line; —enmast m telegraph pole; —ie [-'fi:] f telegraphy; t—ieren [-'fi:rən] vti telegraph, wire; t—isch a telegraphic.
Telegramm [tele'gram] nt -s, -e telegram, cable; —adresse f tele-

graphic address; —formular nt telegram form.
Tele- cpd: —graph = —graf; —kolleg ['teleklɛk] nt university of the air; —objektiv ['tele'ɔpjɛkti:f] nt telephoto lens; —pathie [telepa'ti:] f telepathy; t—pathisch [tele'pa:tɪʃ] a telepathic; —phon —fon; —skop [tele'sko:p] nt -s, -e telescope.
Teller ['tɛlər] m -s, - plate.
Tempel ['tempəl] m -s, - temple.
Temperafarbe ['tempərafarbə] f distemper.
Temperament [tempera'mɛnt] nt temperament; (Schwung) vivacity, liveliness; t—los a spiritless; t—voll a high-spirited, lively.
Temperatur [tempera'tu:r] f temperature.
Tempo ['tempo] nt -s, -s speed, pace; pl Tempi (Mus) tempo; —! get a move on!; t—rär [-'rɛ:r] a temporary; —taschentuch ® nt paper handkerchief.
Tendenz [ten'dɛnts] f tendency; (Absicht) intention; t—iös [-'i̯ø:s] a biased, tendentious.
tendieren [tɛn'di:rən] vi show a tendency, incline (zu to(wards)).
Tenne ['tɛnə] f -, -n threshing floor.
Tennis ['tɛnɪs] nt - tennis; —platz m tennis court; —schläger m tennis racket; —spieler(in f) m tennis player.
Tenor [te'no:r] m -s, ⁼e tenor.
Teppich ['tepɪç] m -s, -e carpet; —boden m wall-to-wall carpeting; —kehrmaschine f carpet sweeper; —klopfer m carpet beater.
Termin [tɛr'mi:n] m -s, -e (Zeitpunkt) date; (Frist) time limit, deadline; (Arzt— etc) appointment; —kalender m diary, appoint-

ments book; —ologie [-olo'gi:] f
terminology.

Termite [tɛr'mi:tə] f -, -n termite.

Terpentin [tɛrpɛn'ti:n] nt -s, -e
turpentine, turps sing.

Terrasse [tɛ'rasə] f -, -n terrace.

Terrine [tɛ'ri:nə] f tureen.

territorial [tɛritori'a:l] a territorial.

Territorium [tɛri'to:rium] nt territory.

Terror [tɛror] m -s terror; reign
of terror; **t—isieren** [tɛrori'zi:rən]
vt terrorize; **—ismus** [-'rɪsmʊs] m
terrorism; **—ist** [-'rɪst] m terrorist.

Terz [tɛrts] f -, -en (Mus) third;
—ett [tɛr'tsɛt] nt -(e)s, -e trio.

Tesafilm ® ['te:zafɪlm] m sellotape
®.

Testament [tɛsta'mɛnt] nt will,
testament; (Rel) Testament;
t—arisch [-'ta:rɪʃ] a testamentary;
—svollstrecker m executor (of a
will).

Test- [tɛst] cpd: **—at** [tɛs'ta:t] nt
-(e)s, -e certificate; **—ator**
[tɛs'ta:tor] m testator; **—bild** nt
(TV) test card; **t—en** vt test.

Tetanus ['te:tanus] m - tetanus;
—impfung f (anti-)tetanus injection.

teuer ['tɔyər] a dear, expensive;
T—ung f increase in prices;
T—ungszulage f cost of living
bonus.

Teufel ['tɔyfəl] m -s, - devil; **—el**
[-'lai] f devilry; **—saustreibung** f
exorcism.

teuflisch ['tɔyflɪʃ] a fiendish,
diabolical.

Text [tɛkst] m -(e)s, -e text;
(Lieder—) words pl; **t—en** vi write
the words.

textil [tɛks'ti:l] a textile; **T—ien**
[-iən] pl textiles pl; **T—industrie** f textile
industry; **—waren** pl textiles pl.

Theater [te'a:tər] nt -s, - theatre;
(col) fuss; **—spielen** (lit, fig) play-
act; **—besucher** m playgoer;
—kasse f box office; **—stück** nt
(stage-)play.

theatralisch [tea'tra:lɪʃ] a
theatrical.

Theke ['te:kə] f -, -n (Schanktisch)
bar; (Ladentisch) counter.

Thema ['te:ma] nt -s, Themen or
-ta theme, topic, subject.

Theo- [teo] cpd: **—loge** [-'lo:gə] m
-n, -n theologian; **—logie** [-lo'gi:] f
theology; **t—logisch** [-'lo:gɪʃ] a
theological; **—retiker** [-'re:tikər] m
-s, - theorist; **t—retisch** [-'re:tɪʃ] a
theoretical; **—rie** [-'ri:] f theory.

Thera- [tera] cpd: **—peut** [-'pɔyt] m
-en, -en therapist; **t—peutisch**
[-'pɔytɪʃ] a therapeutic; **—pie** [-'pi:]
f therapy.

Therm- cpd: **—albad** [tɛrm'a:lba:t]
nt thermal bath; thermal spa;
—ometer [tɛrmo'me:tər] nt -s, -
thermometer; **—osflasche**
['tɛrmɔsflaʃə] f Thermos ® flask;
—ostat [tɛrmo'sta:t] m -(e)s or -en,
-e(n) thermostat.

These ['te:zə] f -, -n thesis.

Thrombose [trɔm'bo:zə] f -, -n
thrombosis.

Thron [tro:n] m -(e)s, -e throne;
—besteigung f accession (to the
throne); **—erbe** m heir to the
throne; **—folge** f succession (to the
throne).

Thunfisch ['tu:nfɪʃ] m tuna.

Thymian ['ty:mia:n] m -s, -e
thyme.

Tick [tɪk] m -(e)s, -s tic;
(Eigenart) quirk; (Fimmel) craze;
t—en vi tick.

tief [ti:f] a deep; (tiefsinnig) profound; Ausschnitt, Ton low; **T—**
nt -s, -s (Met) depression;

T—druck *m* low pressure; T—e *f* •, -n depth; T—ebene *f* plain; T—enpsychologie *f* depth psychology; T—enschärfe *f* (Phot) depth of focus; —ernst a very grave or solemn; T—gang *m* (Naut) draught; (geistig) depth; —gekühlt a frozen; —greifend a far-reaching; T—kühlfach *nt* deep-freeze compartment; T—kühltruhe *f* deep-freeze, freezer; T—land *nt* lowlands *pl*; T—punkt *m* low point; (fig) low ebb; T—schlag *m* (Boxen, fig) blow below the belt; —schürfend a profound; T—see *f* deep sea; T—sinn *m* profundity; —sinnig a profound; melancholy; T—stand *m* low level; —stapeln *vi* be overmodest; T—start *m* (Sport) crouch start; T—stwert *m* minimum or lowest value.

Tiegel ['ti:gəl] *m* -s, - saucepan; (Chem) crucible.

Tier [ti:r] *nt* -(e)s, -e animal; —arzt *m* vet(erinary surgeon); —garten *m* zoo(logical gardens *pl*); t—isch a animal; (lit, fig) brutish; (fig) Ernst etc deadly; —kreis *m* zodiac; —kunde *f* zoology; t—liebend a fond of animals; —quälerei [-kvɛ:ləˈraɪ] *f* cruelty to animals; —schutzverein *m* society for the prevention of cruelty to animals.

Tiger ['ti:gər] *m* -s, - tiger; —in *f* tigress.

tilgen ['tɪlgən] *vt* erase, expunge; Sünden expiate; Schulden pay off.

Tilgung *f* erasing, blotting out; expiation; repayment.

Tinktur *f* tincture.

Tinte ['tɪntə] *f* -, -n ink; —nfaß *nt* inkwell; —nfisch *m* cuttlefish; —nfleck *m* ink stain, blot; —nstift *m* copying or indelible pencil.

tippen ['tɪpən] *vti* tap, touch; (col: schreiben) type; (col: raten) tip (auf jdn sb); (im Lotto etc) bet (on).

Tipp- [tɪp] *cpd*: —fehler *m* (col) typing error; —se *f* •, -n (col) typist; t—topp a (col) tip-top; —zettel *m* (pools) coupon.

Tisch [tɪʃ] *m* -(e)s, -e table; bei — at table; vor/nach — before/ after eating; unter den — fallen (fig) be dropped; —decke *f* table-cloth; —ler *m* -s, - carpenter, joiner; —le'rei *f* joiner's workshop; (Arbeit) carpentry, joinery; t—lern *vi* do carpentry etc; —rede *f* after-dinner speech; —tennis *nt* table tennis.

Titel ['ti:təl] *m* -s, - title; —anwärter *m* (Sport) challenger; —bild *nt* cover (picture); (von Buch) frontispiece; —rolle *f* title role; —seite *f* cover; (Buch—) title page; —verteidiger *m* defending champion, title holder.

titulieren [titu'li:rən] *vt* entitle; (anreden) address.

Toast [to:st] *m* -(e)s, -s or -e toast; —er *m* -s, - toaster.

tob- ['to:b] *cpd*: —en *vi* rage; (Kinder) romp about; T—sucht *f* raving madness; —süchtig a maniacal; —suchtsanfall *m* maniacal fit.

Tochter ['tɔxtər] *f* -, = daughter.

Tod [to:t] *m* -(e)s, -e death; t—ernst a (col) deadly serious; ad in dead earnest; —esangst ['to:dəsaŋst] *f* mortal fear; —esanzeige *f* obituary (notice); —esfall *m* death; —eskampf *m* throes *pl* of death; —esstoß *m* death-blow; —esstrafe *f* death penalty; —estag *m* anniversary of death; —esursache *f* cause of death; —esurteil *nt* death sentence; **—esverachtung** f utter disgust; **t—krank** a dangerously ill.

tödlich ['tø:tliç] a deadly, fatal.

tod- cpd: **—müde** a dead tired; **—schick** a (col) smart, classy; **—sicher** a (col) absolutely or dead certain; **T—sünde** f deadly sin.

Toilette [toa'lstə] f toilet, lavatory; (Frisiertisch) dressing table; (Kleidung) outfit; **—nartikel** pl toiletries pl, toilet articles pl; **—npapier** nt toilet paper; **—ntisch** m dressing table.

toi, toi, toi ['tɔy, 'tɔy, 'tɔy] interj touch wood.

tolerant [tole'rant] a tolerant.

Toleranz [tole'rants] f tolerance.

tolerieren [tole'ri:rən] vt tolerate.

toll [tɔl] a mad; Treiben wild; (col) terrific; **—en** vi romp; **T—heit** f madness, wildness; **T—kirsche** f deadly nightshade; **—kühn** a daring; **T—wut** f rabies.

Tölpel ['tœlpəl] m **-s, -** oaf, clod.

Tomate [to'ma:tə] f **-, -n** tomato; **—nmark** nt tomato puree.

Ton [to:n] m **-(e)s, -e** (Erde) clay; pl **⁼e** (Laut) sound; (Mus) note; (Redeweise) tone; (Farb-, Nuance) shade; (Betonung) stress; **—abnehmer** m pick-up; **t—angebend** a leading; **—art** f (musical) key; **—band** nt tape; **—bandgerät** nt tape recorder.

tönen ['tø:nən] vi sound; vt shade; Haare tint.

tönern ['tø:nərn] a clay.

Ton- cpd: **—fall** m intonation; **—film** m sound film; **t—haltig** a clayey; **—höhe** f pitch; **—ika** f **-, -iken** (Mus), **—ikum** nt **-s, -ika** (Med) tonic; **—künstler** m musician; **—leiter** f (Mus) scale; **t—los** a soundless.

Tonne ['tɔnə] f **-, -n** barrel; (Maß) ton.

Ton- cpd: **—spur** f soundtrack; **—taube** f clay pigeon; **—waren** pl pottery, earthenware.

Topf [tɔpf] m **-(e)s, ⁼e** pot; **—blume** f pot plant.

Töpfer ['tœpfər] m **-s, -** potter; **—ei** [-'rai] f piece of pottery; potter's workshop; **—scheibe** f potter's wheel.

topographisch [topo'gra:fɪʃ] a topographic.

topp [tɔp] interj O.K.

Tor [to:r] m **-en, -en** fool; nt **-(e)s, -e** gate; (Sport) goal; **—bogen** m archway.

Torf [tɔrf] m **-(e)s** peat; **—stechen** nt peat-cutting.

Tor- cpd: **—heit** f foolishness; foolish deed; **—hüter** m **-s, -** goalkeeper.

töricht ['tø:rɪçt] a foolish.

torkeln ['tɔrkəln] vi stagger, reel.

torpedieren [tɔrpe'di:rən] vt (lit, fig) torpedo.

Torpedo [tɔr'pe:do] m **-s, -s** torpedo.

Torte ['tɔrtə] f **-, -n** cake; (Obst—) flan, tart.

Tortur [tɔr'tu:r] f ordeal.

Tor- cpd: **—verhältnis** nt goal average; **—wart** m **-(e)s, -e** goalkeeper.

tosen ['to:zən] vi roar.

tot [to:t] a dead; **einen —en Punkt** haben be at one's lowest.

total [to'ta:l] a total; **—itär** [totali'tɛ:r] a totalitarian; **T—schaden** m (Aut) complete write-off.

tot- cpd: **—arbeiten** vr work oneself to death; **—ärgern** vr (col) get really annoyed.

töten ['tø:tən] *vti* kill.

Tot- *cpd:* —**enbett** *nt* death bed; **t—enblaß** a deathly pale, white as a sheet; —**engräber** *m* -s, - grave-digger; —**enhemd** *nt* shroud; —**enkopf** *m* skull; —**enschein** *m* death certificate; —**enstille** *f* deathly silence; —**entanz** *m* danse macabre; —**e(r)** *mf* dead person; **t—fahren** *vt irreg* run over; **t—geboren** a stillborn; **t—lachen** *vr* (*col*) laugh one's head off.

Toto ['to:to] *m or nt* -s, -s pools *pl*; —**schein** *m* pools coupon.

tot- *cpd:* —**sagen** *vt:* **jdn —sagen** say that sb is dead; —**schlagen** *vt irreg* (*lit, fig*) kill; **T—schläger** *m* killer; (*Waffe*) cosh; —**schweigen** *vt irreg* hush up; —**stellen** *vr* pretend to be dead; —**treten** *vt irreg* trample to death.

Tötung ['tø:tʊŋ] *f* killing.

Toupet [tu'pe:] *nt* -s, -s toupee.

toupieren [tu'pi:rən] *vt* back-comb.

Tour [tu:r] *f* -, -en tour, trip; (*Umdrehung*) revolution; (*Verhaltensart*) way; **in einer —** incessantly; —**enzahl** *f* number of revolutions; —**enzähler** *m* rev counter; —**ismus** [tu'rɪsmʊs] *m* tourism; —**ist** [tu'rɪst] *m* tourist; —**istenklasse** *f* tourist class; —**nee** [tur'ne:] *f* -, -n (*Theat etc*) tour; **auf —nee gehen** go on tour.

Trab [tra:p] *m* -(e)s trot; —**ant** [tra'bant] *m* satellite; —**antenstadt** *f* satellite town; **t—en** *vi* trot sb.

Tracht [traxt] *f* -, -en (*Kleidung*) costume, dress; **eine — Prügel** a sound thrashing; **t—en** *vi* strive (*nach* for), endeavour; **jdm nach dem Leben t—en** seek to kill sb.

trächtig ['trɛçtɪç] a *Tier* pregnant; (*fig*). rich, fertile.

Tradition [traditsi'o:n] *f* tradition; **t—ell** [-'nɛl] a traditional.

Trag- [tra:g] *cpd:* —**bahre** *f* stretcher; **t—bar** a *Gerät* portable; *Kleidung* wearable; (*erträglich*) bearable.

träge ['trɛ:gə] a sluggish, slow; (*Phys*) inert.

tragen ['tra:gən] *irreg vt* carry; *Kleidung, Brille* wear; *Namen, Früchte* bear; (*erdulden*) endure; **sich mit einem Gedanken — have** an idea in mind; *vi* (*schwanger sein*) be pregnant; (*Eis*) hold; **zum T— kommen** have an effect.

Träger [trɛ:gər] *m* -s, - carrier; wearer; bearer; (*Ordens—*) holder; (*an Kleidung*) (shoulder) strap; (*Körperschaft etc*) sponsor; —**rakete** *f* launch vehicle; —**rock** *m* skirt with shoulder straps.

Trag- [tra:k] *cpd:* —**fähigkeit** *f* load-carrying capacity; —**fläche** *f* (*Aviat*) wing; —**flügelboot** *nt* hydrofoil.

Trägheit ['trɛ:khait] *f* laziness; (*Phys*) inertia.

Tragi- ['tra:gi] *cpd:* ⅃k *f* tragedy; **t—komisch** a tragi-comic; **t—sch** a tragic.

Tragödie [tra'gö:diə] *f* tragedy.

Trag- ['tra:k] *cpd:* —**weite** *f* range; (*fig*) scope; —**werk** *nt* wing assembly.

Train- [trɛ:n] *cpd:* —**er** *m* -s, - (*Sport*) trainer, coach; (*Fußball*) manager; **t—ieren** [trɛ'ni:rən] *vt* train; *Mensch auch* coach; *Übung* practise; **Fußball t—ieren** do football practice; —**ing** *nt* -s, -s training; —**ingsanzug** *m* track suit.

Traktor ['traktɔr] *m* tractor.

trällern ['trɛlərn] *vti* trill, sing.

trampeln ['trampəln] *vti* trample, stamp.

trampen ['trampən] vi hitch-hike.

Tran [tra:n] m -(e)s, -e train oil, blubber.

tranchieren [trã'ʃi:rən] vt carve.

Tranchierbesteck [trã'ʃi:rbəʃtɛk] nt (pair of) carvers.

Träne ['trɛ:nə] f -, -n tear; t—n vi water; —ngas nt teargas.

Tränke ['trɛŋkə] f -, -n watering place; t—n vt (naß machen) soak; Tiere water.

Trans- cpd: —formator [transfor'ma:tɔr] m transformer; —istor [tran'zistɔr] m transistor; t—itiv [tranzi:tif] a transitive; t—parent [transpa'rɛnt] a transparent; —parent nt -(e)s, -e (Bild) transparency; (Spruchband) banner; t—pirieren [transpi'ri:rən] vi perspire; —plantation [transplantatsi'oːn] f transplantation; (Haut—) graft(ing); —port [trans'pɔrt] m -(e)s, -e transport; t—portieren [transpɔr'ti:rən] vt transport; —portkosten pl transport charges pl, carriage; —portmittel nt means of transportation; —portunternehmen nt carrier.

Trapez [tra'pe:ts] nt -es, -e trapeze; (Math) trapezium.

Traube ['traubə] f -, -n grape; bunch (of grapes); —nlese f vintage; —nzucker m glucose.

trauen ['trauən] vi: jdm/etw trust sb/sth; vr dare; vt marry.

Trauer ['trauər] f - sorrow; (für Verstorbenen) mourning; —fall m death, bereavement; —marsch m funeral march; t—n vi mourn (um for); —rand m black border; —spiel nt tragedy.

Traufe ['traufə] f -, -n eaves pl.

träufeln ['trɔyfəln] vti drip.

traulich ['traulɪç] a cosy, intimate.

Traum [traum] m -(e)s, Träume dream; —a nt -s, -men trauma; —bild nt vision.

träum- ['trɔym] cpd: t—en vti dream; T—er m -s, - dreamer; T—e'rel f dreaming; —erisch a dreamy.

traumhaft a dreamlike; (fig) wonderful.

traurig ['traurɪç] a sad; T—keit f sadness.

Trau- ['trau] cpd: —ring m wedding ring; —schein m marriage certificate; —ung f wedding ceremony; —zeuge m witness (of a marriage).

treffen ['trɛfən] irreg vti strike, hit; (Bemerkung) hurt; (begegnen) meet; Entscheidung etc make; Maßnahmen take; er hat es gut getroffen he did well; — auf (+ acc) come across, meet with; vr meet; es traf sich, daß... it so happened that...; es trifft sich gut it's convenient; wie es so trifft as these things happen; T— nt -s, - meeting; —d a pertinent, apposite.

Treff- cpd: —er m -s, - hit; (Tor) goal; (Los) winner; t—lich a excellent; —punkt m meeting place.

Treib- ['traib] cpd: —eis nt drift ice; t—en irreg vti drive; Studien etc pursue; Sport do, go in for; Unsinn t—en fool around; vi (Schiff etc) drift; (Pflanzen) sprout; (Cook: aufgehen) rise; (Tee, Kaffee) be diuretic; —en nt -s activity; —haus nt hothouse; —stoff m fuel.

trenn- ['trɛn] cpd: —bar a separable; t—en vt separate; (teilen) divide; vr separate; sich —en von part with; T—schärfe f (Rad) selectivity; T—ung f separation; T—wand f partition (wall).

Trepp- [trɛp] *cpd:* t—ab ad downstairs; t—auf ad upstairs; —e f -, -n stair(case); —engeländer nt banister; —enhaus nt staircase.

Tresor [tre'zo:r] *m -s, -e* safe.

treten ['tre:tən] *irreg vi* step; (*Tränen, Schweiß*) appear; — nach kick at; — in (+acc) step in(to); **in Verbindung** — get in contact; **in Erscheinung** — appear; vt (*mit Fußtritt*) kick; (*nieder*—) tread, trample.

treu [trɔy] a faithful, true; T—e f = loyalty, faithfulness; T—händer m -s, = trustee; T—handgesellschaft f trust company; —herzig a innocent; —lich ad faithfully; —los a faithless.

Tribüne [tri'by:nə] f -, -n grandstand; (*Redner*—) platform.

Tribut [tri'bu:t] *nt -(e)s, -e* tribute.

Trichter ['trɪçtər] *m -s, -* funnel; (*in Boden*) crater.

Trick [trɪk] *m -s, -e or -s* trick; —film *m* cartoon.

Trieb [tri:p] *m -(e)s, -e* urge, drive; (*Neigung*) inclination; (*an Baum etc*) shoot; —feder f (fig) motivating force; t—haft a impulsive; —kraft f (fig) drive; —täter *m* sex offender; —wagen *m* (Rail) diesel railcar; —werk nt engine.

triefen ['tri:fən] *vi* drip.

triftig ['trɪftɪç] a good, convincing.

Trigonometrie [trigonome'tri:] f trigonometry.

Trikot [tri'ko:] *nt -s, -s* vest; (*Sport*) shirt; *m -s, -s* (Gewebe) tricot.

Triller ['trɪlər] *m -s, -* (Mus) trill; t—n vi trill, warble; —pfeife f whistle.

Trimester [tri'mɛstər] *nt -s, -* term.

trink- ['trɪŋk] *cpd:* —bar a drinkable; —en vti irreg drink; T—er m -s, - drinker; T—geld nt tip; T—halm m (drinking) straw; T—spruch· m toast; T—wasser nt drinking water.

trippeln ['trɪpəln] *vi* toddle.

Tripper ['trɪpər] *m -s, -* gonorrhoea.

Tritt [trɪt] *m -(e)s, -e* step; (*Fuß*—) kick; —brett nt (Rail) step; (Aut) running-board.

Triumph [tri'umf] *m -(e)s, -e* triumph; —bogen *m* triumphal arch; t—ieren [-'fi:rən] vi triumph; (jubeln) exult.

trivial [trivi'a:l] a trivial.

trocken ['trɔkən] a dry; T—dock nt dry dock; T—element nt dry cell; T—haube f hair-dryer; T—heit f dryness; —legen vt Sumpf drain; Kind put a clean nappy on; T—milch f dried milk.

trocknen ['trɔknən] *vti* dry.

Troddel ['trɔdəl] f -, -n tassel.

Trödel ['trø:dəl] *m -s* (col) junk; t—n vi (col) dawdle.

Trödler ['trø:dlər] *m -s, -* secondhand dealer.

Trog [tro:k] *m -(e)s, -e* trough.

Trommel ['trɔməl] f -, -n drum; —fell nt eardrum; t—n vi irreg drum; —revolver *m* revolver; —waschmaschine f tumble-action washing machine.

Trommler ['trɔmlər] *m -s, -* drummer.

Trompete [trɔm'pe:tə] f -, -n trumpet; —r *m -s, -* trumpeter.

Tropen ['tro:pən] pl tropics pl; t—beständig a suitable for the tropics; —helm *m* topee, sun helmet.

Tropf [trɔpf] m -(e)s, ⁺e (col) rogue; armer — poor devil.

tröpfeln ['trœpfəln] vi drop, trickle.

Tropfen ['trɔpfən] m -s, ~ drop; t— vti drip; v impers: es tröpft a few raindrops are falling; t—weise ad in drops.

Tropfsteinhöhle f stalactite cave.

tropisch ['tro:pɪʃ] a tropical.

Trost [tro:st] m -es consolation, comfort; t—bedürftig a in need of consolation.

tröst- ['trø:st] cpd: —en vt console, comfort; T—er(in f) m -s, ~ comfort(er); —lich a comforting.

trost- cpd: —los a bleak; Verhältnisse wretched; T—preis m consolation prize; —reich a comforting.

Tröstung ['trø:stʊŋ] f comfort; consolation.

Trott [trɔt] m -(e)s, ⁺e trot; (Routine) routine; —el m -s, ~ (col)ˉ fool, dope; t—en vi trot; —oir [trɔto'a:r] nt -s, -s or -e pavement, sidewalk (US).

Trotz [trɔts] m -es pigheadedness; etw aus — tun do sth just to show them; jdm zum — in defiance of sb; t— prep +gen or dat in spite of; —alter nt obstinate phase; t—dem ad nevertheless; cj although; t—ig a defiant, pigheaded; —kopf m obstinate child; —reaktion f fit of pique.

trüb [try:p] a dull; Flüssigkeit, Glas cloudy; (fig) gloomy; —en ['try:bən] vt cloud; vr become clouded; T—heit f cloudiness; cloudiness; gloom; T—sal f -, -e distress; —selig a sad, melancholy; T—sinn m depression; —sinnig a depressed, gloomy.

trudeln ['tru:dəln] vi (Aviat) (go into a) spin.

Trüffel ['tryfəl] f -, -n truffle.

trüg- ['try:g] cpd: —en vt irreg deceive; vi be deceptive; —erisch a deceptive.

Trugschluß ['tru:gʃlʊs] m false conclusion.

Truhe ['tru:ə] f -, -n chest.

Trümmer ['trymər] pl wreckage; (Bau—) ruins pl; —haufen m heap of rubble.

Trumpf [trʊmpf] m -(e)s, ⁺e (lit, fig) trump; t—en vti trump.

Trunk [trʊŋk] m -(e)s, ⁺e drink; t—en a intoxicated; —enbold m -(e)s, -e drunkard; —enheit f intoxication; —enheit am Steuer drunken driving; —sucht f alcoholism.

Trupp [trʊp] m -s, -s troop; —e f -, -n troop; (Waffengattung) force; (Schauspiel—) troupe; —en pl troops pl; —enführer m (military) commander; —enteil m unit; —enübungsplatz m training area.

Truthahn ['tru:tha:n] m turkey.

Tube ['tu:bə] f -, -n tube.

Tuberkulose [tubɛrku'lo:zə] f -, -n tuberculosis.

Tuch [tu:x] nt -(e)s, ⁺er cloth; (Hals—) scarf; (Kopf—) headscarf; (Hand—) towel.

tüchtig ['tyçtɪç] a efficient, (cap)able; (col: kräftig) good, sound; T—keit f efficiency, ability.

Tücke ['tykə] f -, -n (Arglist) malice; (Trick) trick; (Schwierigkeit) difficulty, problem; seine —n haben be temperamental.

tückisch ['tykɪʃ] a treacherous; (böswillig) malicious.

Tugend ['tu:gənt] f -, -en virtue; t—haft a virtuous.

Tüll [tyl] *m* -s, -e tulle; **—e** *f* **—**, -n spout.

Tulpe ['tolpə] *f* -, -n tulip.

tummeln ['toməln] *vr* romp, gambol; *(sich beeilen)* hurry.

Tumor ['tu:mɔr] *m* -s, -e tumour.

Tümpel ['tympəl] *m* -s, - pool, pond.

Tumult [tu'mult] *m* -(e)s, -e tumult.

tun [tu:n] *irreg vt (machen)* do; *(legen)* put; jdm etw — *(antun)* do sth to sb; etw tut es auch sth will do; das tut nichts that doesn't matter; das tut nichts zur Sache that's neither here nor there; *vi* act; so —, als ob act as if; *vr:* es tut sich etwas/viel something/a lot is happening.

Tünche ['tynçə] *f* -, -n whitewash; **t—n** *vt* whitewash.

Tunke ['toŋkə] *f* -, -n sauce; **t—n** *vt* dip, dunk.

tunlichst ['tu:nlıçst] *ad* if at all possible; **—** bald as soon as possible.

Tunnel ['tonəl] *m* -s, -s *or* - tunnel.

Tüpfel ['tyfəl] *m* -s, - dot, spot; **—chen** *nt* (small) dot; **t—n** *vt* dot, spot.

tupfen ['tupfən] *vti* dab; *(mit Farbe)* dot; **T—** *m* -s, - dot, spot.

Tür [ty:r] *f* -, -en door.

Turbine [tur'bi:nə] *f* turbine.

Türkis [tyr'ki:s] *m* -es, -e turquoise; **t—** *a* turquoise.

Turm [torm] *m* -(e)s, -e tower; *(Kirch—)* steeple; *(Sprung—)* diving platform; *(Schach)* castle, rook.

Türm- ['tyrm] *cpd:* **—chen** *nt* turret; **t—en** *vr* tower up; *vt* heap up; *vi (col)* scarper, bolt.

Turn- ['torn] *cpd:* **t—en** *vi* do gymnastic exercises; *vt* perform; **—en** *nt* -s gymnastics; *(Sch)* physical education, P.E.; **—er(in** *f) m* -s, - gymnast; **—halle** *f* gym(nasium); **—hose** *f* gym shorts *pl*.

Turnier [tur'ni:r] *nt* -s, -e tournament.

Turnus ['tornos] *m* **—**, -se rota; im **—** in rotation.

Turn- *cpd:* **—verein** *m* gymnastics club; **—zeug** *nt* gym things *pl*.

Tusche ['tuʃə] *f* -, -n Indian ink.

tuscheln ['tuʃəln] *vti* whisper.

Tuschkasten *m* paintbox.

Tüte ['ty:tə] *f* -, -n bag.

tuten ['tu:tən] *vi (Aut)* hoot.

TÜV [tyf] *m* MOT.

Typ [ty:p] *m* -s, -en type; **—e** *f* -, -n *(Print)* type.

typisch ['ty:pıʃ] *a* typical *(für of)*.

Typhus ['ty:fos] *m* -typhoid (fever).

Tyrann [ty'ran] *m* -en, -en tyrant; **—ei** [-'nai] *f* tyranny; **t—isch** *a* tyrannical; **t—i'sieren** *vt* tyrannize.

U

U, u [u:] *nt* U, u.

U-Bahn [u:ba:n] *f* underground, tube.

übel ['y:bəl] *a* bad; *(moralisch auch)* wicked; jdm ist — sb feels sick; **Ü—** *nt* -s, - evil; *(Krankheit)*

disease; **—gelaunt** a bad-tempered, ill-humoured; **Ü—keit** *f* nausea; **—nehmen** *vt irreg:* jdm eine Bemerkung *etc* **—nehmen** be offended at sb's remark *etc*;

Ü—stand *m* bad state of affairs, abuse; —wollend *a* malevolent.

üben ['y:bən] *vti* exercise, practise.

über ['y:bər] *prep* +*dat* or *acc* over; (hoch — auch) above; (*quer* — auch) across; (*Route*) via; (*betreffend*) about; *ad* over; den ganzen Tag — all day long; jdm in etw (*dat*) — sein (*col*) be superior to sb in sth; — und — all over; —all [y:bər'al] *ad* everywhere.

überanstrengen [y:bər'anʃtrɛŋən] *vtr insep* overexert (o.s.).

überantworten [y:bər'antvɔrtən] *vt insep* hand over, deliver (up).

überarbeiten [y:bər'arbaɪtən] *vt insep* revise, rework; *vr* overwork (o.s.).

überaus ['y:bər'aus] *ad* exceedingly.

überbelichten [y:bərbəliçtən] *vt* (*Phot*) overexpose.

über'bieten *vt irreg insep* outbid; (*übertreffen*) surpass; *Rekord* break.

Überbleibsel [y:bərblaɪpsəl] *nt* -s, - residue, remainder.

Überblick ['y:bərblɪk] *m* view; (*fig*) (*Darstellung*) survey, overview; (*Fähigkeit*) overall view, grasp (*über* +*acc* of); ü—en [-'blɪkən] *vt insep* survey.

überbring- [y:bər'brɪŋ] *cpd:* —en *vt irreg insep* deliver, hand over; Ü—er *m* -s, - bearer; Ü—ung *f* delivery.

überbrücken [y:bər'brʏkən] *vt insep* bridge (over).

über'dauern *vt insep* outlast.

über'denken *vt irreg insep* think over.

überdies [y:bər'di:s] *ad* besides.

überdimensional ['y:bər-dimɛnziona:l] *a* oversize.

Überdruß ['y:bərdrʊs] *m* -sses weariness; bis zum — ad nauseam.

'überdrüssig ['y:bərdrʏsɪç] *a* tired, sick (gen of).

übereifrig ['y:bəraɪfrɪç] *a* overkeen, overzealous.

übereilen [y:bər'aɪlən] *vt insep* hurry.

übereilt *a* (over)hasty, premature.

überein- [y:bər'aɪn] *cpd:* —ander [y:bər'a'nandər] *ad* one upon the other; *sprechen* about each other; —anderschlagen *vt irreg* fold, cross; —kommen *vi irreg* agree; Ü—kunft *f* -, -künfte agreement; —stimmen *vi* agree; Ü—stimmung *f* agreement.

überempfindlich ['y:bər-ɛmpfɪntlɪç] *a* hypersensitive.

überfahren ['y:bərfa:rən] *irreg vt* take across; *vi* (go a)cross; [-'fa:rən] *vt insep* (*Aut*) run over; (*fig*) walk all over.

Überfahrt ['y:bərfa:rt] *f* crossing.

Überfall ['y:bərfal] *m* (*Bank*—, *Mil*) raid; (*auf jdn*) assault; ü—en [-'falən] *vt irreg insep* attack; *Bank* raid; (*besuchen*) surprise.

überfällig ['y:bərfɛlɪç] *a* overdue.

über'fliegen *vt irreg insep* fly over, overfly; *Buch* skim through.

Überfluß ['y:bərflʊs] *m* (super)abundance, excess (*an* +*dat* of).

überflüssig ['y:bərflʏsɪç] *a* superfluous.

über'fordern *vt insep* demand too much of; *Kräfte etc* overtax.

über'führen *vt insep Leiche etc* transport; *Täter* have convicted (gen of).

Über'führung *f* transport; conviction; (*Brücke*) bridge, overpass.

Übergabe ['y:bɐrga:bə] f handing over; (Mil) surrender.

Übergang ['y:bɐrgaŋ] m crossing; (Wandel, Überleitung) transition; —serscheinung f transitory phenomenon; —slösung f provisional solution, stopgap; —sstadium nt state of transition; —szeit f transitional period.

über'geben irreg insep vt hand over; (Mil) surrender; dem Verkehr — open to traffic; vr be sick.

übergehen ['y:bɐrge:ən] irreg vi (Besitz) pass; (zum Feind etc) go over, defect; (überleiten) go on (zu to); (sich verwandeln) turn (in +acc into); [-'ge:ən] vt insep pass over, omit.

Übergewicht ['y:bɐrgəvɪçt] nt excess weight; (fig) preponderance.

überglücklich ['y:bɐrglʏklɪç] a overjoyed.

übergroß ['y:bɐrgro:s] a outsize, huge.

überhaben ['y:bɐrha:bən] vt irreg (col) be fed up with.

überhandnehmen [y:bɐr'hantne:mən] vi irreg gain the ascendancy.

überhängen ['y:bɐrhɛŋən] vi irreg overhang.

überhaupt [y:bɐr'haupt] ad at all; (im allgemeinen) in general; (besonders) especially; — nicht not at all.

überheblich [y:bɐr'he:plɪç] a arrogant; Ü—keit f arrogance.

über'holen vt insep overtake; (Tech) overhaul.

überholt a out-of-date, obsolete.

über'hören vt insep not hear; (absichtlich) ignore.

überirdisch ['y:bɐr'ɪrdɪʃ] a supernatural, unearthly.

überkompensieren ['y:bɐrkɔmpɛnzi:rən] vt insep overcompensate for.

über'laden vt irreg insep overload; a (fig) cluttered.

über'lassen irreg insep vt: jdm etw — leave sth to sb; vr: sich etw (dat) — give o.s. over to sth.

über'lasten vt insep overload; Mensch overtax.

überlaufen [y:bɐr'laufən] irreg vi (Flüssigkeit) flow over; (zum Feind etc) go over, defect; [-'laufən] insep vt (Schauer etc) come over; — sein be inundated or besieged.

Überläufer ['y:bɐrlɔyfɐr] m -s, - deserter.

über'leben vt insep survive; Ü—de(r) mf survivor.

über'legen vt insep consider; a superior; Ü—heit f superiority.

Überlegung f consideration, deliberation.

über'liefern vt insep hand down, transmit.

Überlieferung f tradition.

überlisten [y:bɐr'lɪstən] vt insep outwit.

überm ['y:bɐrm] = über dem.

Übermacht ['y:bɐrmaxt] f superior force, superiority.

übermächtig ['y:bɐrmɛçtɪç] a superior (in strength); Gefühl etc overwhelming.

übermannen [y:bɐr'manən] vt insep overcome.

Übermaß ['y:bɐrma:s] nt excess (an +dat of).

übermäßig ['y:bɐrmɛ:sɪç] a excessive.

Übermensch ['y:bɐrmɛnʃ] m superman; ü—lich a superhuman.

übermitteln [y:bɐr'mɪtəln] vt insep convey.

übermorgen ['y:bərmɔrgən] *ad* the day after tomorrow.

Übermüdung [y:bər'my:duŋ] *f* fatigue, overtiredness.

Übermut ['y:bərmu:t] *m* exuberance.

übermütig ['y:bərmy:tɪç] *a* exuberant, high-spirited; **— werden** get overconfident.

übernachten [y:bər'naxtən] *vi insep* spend the night (*bei jdm* at sb's place).

übernächtigt [y:bər'nɛçtɪçt] *a* tired, sleepy.

Übernahme ['y:bərna:mə] *f* -, -n taking over or on, acceptance.

über'nehmen *irreg insep vt* take on, accept; *Amt, Geschäft* take over; *vr* take on too much.

über'prüfen *vt insep* examine, check.

Überprüfung *f* examination.

überqueren [y:bər'kve:rən] *vt insep* cross.

überragen [y:bər'ra:gən] *vt insep* tower above; (*fig*) surpass; ['y:bərra:gən] *vi* project, stick out.

überraschen [y:bər'raʃən] *vt insep* surprise.

Überraschung *f* surprise.

überreden [y:bər're:dən] *vt insep* persuade.

überreich ['y:bərraɪç] *a* very/too rich; **—en** [-'raɪçən] *vt insep* present, hand over; **—lich** *a, ad* (more than) ample.

überreizt [y:bər'raɪtst] *a* overwrought.

Überreste ['y:bərrɛstə] *pl* remains *pl*, remnants *pl*.

überrumpeln [y:bər'rumpəln] *vt insep* take by surprise.

überrunden [y:bər'rundən] *vt insep* lap.

übers ['y:bərs] = **über das.**

übersättigen [y:bər'zɛtɪgən] *vt insep* satiate.

Überschall- ['y:bərʃal] *cpd:* **—flugzeug** *nt* supersonic jet; **—geschwindigkeit** *f* supersonic speed.

über'schätzen *vtr insep* overestimate.

überschäumen ['y:bərʃɔymən] *vi* froth over; (*fig*) bubble over.

Überschlag ['y:bərʃla:k] *m* (*Fin*) estimate; (*Sport*) somersault; **ü—en** [-'ʃla:gən] *irreg insep vt* (*berechnen*) estimate; (*auslassen*) *Seite* omit; *vr* somersault; (*Stimme*) crack; (*Aviat*) loop the loop; *a* lukewarm, tepid; ['y:bərʃla:gən] *irreg vt Beine* cross; *vi* (*Wellen*) break over; (*Funken*) flash over.

überschnappen ['y:bərʃnapən] *vi* (*Stimme*) crack; (*col: Mensch*) flip one's lid.

über'schneiden *vr irreg insep* (*lit, fig*) overlap; (*Linien*) intersect.

über'schreiben *vt irreg insep* provide with a heading; *jdm etw* **—** transfer or make over sth to sb.

über'schreiten *vt irreg insep* cross over; (*fig*) exceed; (*verletzen*) transgress.

Überschrift ['y:bərʃrɪft] *f* heading, title.

Überschuß ['y:bərʃus] *m* surplus (*an* +*dat* of).

überschüssig ['y:bərʃʏsɪç] *a* surplus, excess.

über'schütten *vt insep jdn/etw mit etw* — (*lit*) pour sth over sb/sth; *jdm mit etw* — (*fig*) shower sb with sth.

Überschwang ['y:bərʃvaŋ] *m* exuberance, excess.

überschwemmen [y:bər'ʃvɛmən] *vt insep* flood.

Überschwemmung f flood.

überschwenglich ['y:bərʃvɛŋliç] a effusive; **Ü—keit** f effusion.

Übersee ['y:bərze:] f nach/in — overseas; **ü—isch** a overseas.

über'sehen vt irreg insep look (out) over; (fig) Folgen see, get an overall view of; (nicht beachten) overlook.

über'senden vt irreg insep send, forward.

übersetz- cpd **—en** [y:bər'zɛtsən] vt insep translate; ['y:bərzɛtsən] vi cross; **Ü—er(in** f) ['zɛtsər(in)] m **-s,** - translator; **Ü—ung** [-zɛtsuŋ] translation; (Tech) gear ratio.

Übersicht ['y:bərzɪçt] f overall view; (Darstellung) survey; **ü—lich** a clear; Gelände open; **—lichkeit** f clarity, lucidity.

übersiedeln ['y:bərzi:dəln] or [y:bər'zi:dəln] vi sep or insep move.

über'spannen vt insep (zu sehr spannen) overstretch; (überdecken) cover.

überspannt a eccentric; Idee wild, crazy; **Ü—keit** f eccentricity.

überspitzt [y:bər'ʃpɪtst] a exaggerated.

über'springen vt irreg insep jump over; (fig) skip.

über'sprudeln ['y:bərʃpru:dəln] vi bubble over.

über'stehen [y:bər'ʃte:ən] irreg vt insep overcome, get over; Winter etc survive, get through; ['y:bərʃte:ən] vi project.

über'steigen vt irreg insep climb over; (fig) exceed.

über'stimmen vt insep outvote.

Überstunden ['y:bərʃtʊndən] pl overtime.

über'stürzen insep vt rush; vr

follow (one another) in rapid succession.

überstürzt a (over)hasty.

übertölpen [y:bər'tœlpən] vt insep dupe.

über'tönen vt insep drown (out).

Übertrag ['y:bərtra:k] m -(e)s, **-träge** ['tra:gə] amount brought forward; **ü—bar** ['tra:kba:r] a transferable; (Med) infectious; **ü—en** ['tra:gən] irreg insep vt transfer (auf + acc to); (Rad) broadcast; (übersetzen) render; Krankheit transmit; jdm etw **ü—en** assign sth to sb; vr spread (auf + acc to); a figurative; **—ung** ['tra:guŋ] f transfer(ence); (Rad) broadcast; rendering; transmission.

über'treffen vt irreg insep surpass.

über'treiben vt irreg insep exaggerate.

Übertreibung f exaggeration.

übertreten [y:bər'tre:tən] irreg vt insep cross; Gebot etc break; ['y:bərtre:tən] vi (über Linie, Gebiet) step (over); (Sport) overstep; (in andere Partei) go over (in + acc to); (zu anderem Glauben) be converted.

Über'tretung f violation, transgression.

übertrieben [y:bər'tri:bən] a exaggerated, excessive.

übertrumpfen [y:bər'trumpfən] vt insep outdo; (Cards) overtrump.

übervölkert [y:bər'fœlkərt] a overpopulated.

übervoll ['y:bərfɔl] a overfull.

übervorteilen [y:bər'fɔrtailən] vt insep dupe, cheat.

über'wachen vt insep supervise; Verdächtigen keep under surveillance.

Überwachung f supervision; surveillance.

überwältigen [y:bər'vɛltɪgən] vt insep overpower; **—d** a overwhelming.

überweisen [y:bər'vaɪzən] vt irreg insep transfer.

Überweisung f transfer.

über'wiegen vi irreg insep predominate; **—d** a predominant.

über'winden irreg insep vt overcome; vr make an effort, bring oneself (to do sth).

Überwindung f effort, strength of mind.

Überwurf ['y:bərvʊrf] m wrap, shawl.

Überzahl ['y:bərtsa:l] f superiority, superior numbers pl; **in der — sein** outnumber sb, be numerically superior.

überzählig ['y:bərtsɛ:lɪç] a surplus.

über'zeugen vt insep convince; **—d** a convincing.

Überzeugung f conviction; **—skraft** f power of persuasion.

überziehen ['y:bərtsi:ən] irreg vt put on [-'tsi:ən] vt insep cover; **Konto** overdraw.

Überzug ['y:bərtsu:k] m cover; (Belag) coating.

üblich ['y:plɪç] a usual.

U-Boot ['u:bo:t] nt submarine.

übrig ['y:brɪç] a remaining; **für jdn etwas — haben** (col) be fond of sb; **die —en** ['y:brɪgən] the others; **das —e** the rest; **im —** besides; **—bleiben** vi irreg remain, be left (over); **—ens** ad besides; (nebenbei bemerkt) by the way; **—lassen** vt irreg leave (over).

Übung ['y:bʊŋ] f practice; (Turn-, Aufgabe etc) exercise; **— macht den Meister** practice makes perfect.

Ufer ['u:far] nt **-s, -** bank; (Meeres—) shore; **—befestigung** f embankment.

Uhr [u:r] f **-, -en** clock; (Armband—) watch; **wieviel — ist es?** what time is it?; **1 — 1** o'clock; **20 — 8** o'clock, 20.00 (twenty hundred) hours; **—band** nt watch strap; **—(en)gehäuse** nt clock/watch case; **—kette** f watch chain; **—macher** m **-s, -** watchmaker; **—werk** nt clockwork; works of a watch; **—zeiger** m hand; **—zeigersinn** m: **im —zeigersinn** clockwise; **entgegen dem —zeigersinn** anticlockwise; **—zeit** f time (of day).

Uhu ['u:hu] m **-s, -s** eagle owl.

UKW [u:ka:'ve:] abbr VHF.

Ulk [ʊlk] m **-s, -e** lark; **u—ig** a funny.

Ulme ['ʊlmə] f **-, -n** elm.

Ultimatum [ʊlti'ma:tʊm] nt **-s, Ultimaten** ultimatum.

Ultra- cpd: **—kurzwellen** [ultra'kʊrtsvɛlən] pl very high frequency; **u—violett** ['ultra-] a ultraviolet.

um [ʊm] prep +acc (a)round; (zeitlich) at; (mit Größenangabe) by; (für) for; **er schlug — sich** hit about him; **Stunde — Stunde** hour after hour; **Auge — Auge** an eye for an eye; **— vieles (besser)** (better) by far; **— nichts besser** not in the least better; **— so besser** so much the better; **— . . . willen** for the sake of; cj (damit) (in order) to; **zu klug, — zu . . .** clever to . . .; ad (ungefähr) about.

umadressieren ['ʊmadrɛsi:rən] vt readdress.

umänder- ['ʊm'ɛndər] cpd: **—n** vt alter; **U—ung** f alteration.

umarbeiten ['ʊm'arbaɪtən] *vt* remodel; '*Buch etc* revise, rework.

umarmen· [ʊm''armən] *vt insep* embrace.

Umbau ['ʊmbaʊ] *m* -(e)s, -e *or* -ten reconstruction, alteration(s); **u—en** *vt* rebuild, reconstruct.

umbenennen ['ʊmbənɛnən] *vt irreg* rename.

umbiegen ['ʊmbiːgən] *vt irreg* bend (over).

umbilden ['ʊmbɪldən] *vt* reorganize; (*Pol*) *Kabinett* reshuffle.

umbinden ['ʊmbɪndən] *vt irreg Krawatte etc* put on; ['ʊmbɪndən] *vt irreg insep* tie (sth) round.

umblättern ['ʊmblɛtərn] *vt* turn over.

umblicken ['ʊmblɪkən] *vr* look around.

umbringen ['ʊmbrɪŋən] *vt irreg* kill.

Umbruch ['ʊmbrʊx] *m* radical change; (*Print*) make-up.

umbuchen ['ʊmbuːxən] *vti* change one's reservation/flight *etc.*

umdenken ['ʊmdɛŋkən] *vi irreg.* adjust one's views.

um'drängen *vt insep* crowd round.

umdrehen ['ʊmdreːən] *vtr* turn (round); *Hals* wring.

Um'drehung *f* revolution; rotation.

umeinander [ʊm'aɪ'nandər] *ad* round one another; (*für einander*) for one another.

umfahren ['ʊmfaːrən] *vt irreg* run over; ['ʊm'faːrən] *insep* drive/sail round.

umfallen ['ʊmfalən] *vi irreg* fall down *or* over.

Umfang ['ʊmfaŋ] *m* extent; (*von Buch*) size; (*Reichweite*) range; (*Fläche*) area; (*Math*) circumference; **u—reich** *a* extensive; *Buch etc* voluminous.

um'fassen *vt insep* embrace; (*umgeben*) surround; (*enthalten*) include; **—d** *a* comprehensive, extensive.

umform- ['ʊmfɔrm] *cpd:* **—en** *vt* transform; **U—er** *m* -s, - (*Elec*) transformer, converter.

Umfrage ['ʊmfraːgə] *f* poll.

umfüllen ['ʊmfʏlən] *vt* transfer; *Wein* decant.

umfunktionieren ['ʊmfʊŋktsioni:rən] *vt* convert, transform.

Umgang ['ʊmgaŋ] *m* company; (*mit jdm*) dealings *pl*; (*Behandlung*) way of behaving.

umgänglich ['ʊmgɛŋlɪç] *a* sociable.

Umgangs- *cpd:* **—formen** *pl* manners *pl*; **—sprache** *f* colloquial language.

umgeb- [ʊm'geːb] *cpd:* **—en** *vt irreg insep* surround; **U—ung** *f* surroundings *pl*; (*Milieu*) environment; (*Personen*) people in one's circle.

umgehen ['ʊmgeːən] *irreg vi* go (a)round; **im Schlosse** — haunt the castle; **mit jdm grob** *etc* — treat sb roughly *etc*; **mit Geld sparsam** — be careful with one's money; ['ʊmge:ən] *vt insep* bypass; (*Mil*) outflank; *Gesetz etc* circumvent; (*vermeiden*) avoid; '**—d** *a* immediate.

Um'gehung *f* bypassing; outflanking; circumvention; avoidance; **—straße** *f* bypass.

umgekehrt ['ʊmgəkeːrt] *a* reverse(d); (*gegenteilig*) opposite; *ad* the other way around; **und** — and vice versa.

umgraben ['ʊmgraːbən] *vt irreg* dig up.

umgruppieren ['ʊmgrupiːrən] *vt* regroup.

Umhang ['umhaŋ] m wrap, cape.
umhängen ['umhɛŋən] vt Bild hang somewhere else; jdm etw — put sth on sb.
umhauen ['umhauən] vt fell; (fig) bowl over.
umher [um'he:r] ad around, about; —gehen vi irreg walk about; —reisen vi travel about; —schweifen vi roam about; —ziehen vi irreg wander from place to place.
umhinkönnen [um'hinkœnən] vi irreg ich kann nicht umhin, das zu tun I can't help doing it.
umhören [um'hø:rən] vr ask around.
Umkehr ['umke:r] f — turning back; (Änderung) change; u—en vi turn back; vt turn round, reverse; Tasche etc turn inside out; Gefäß etc turn upside down.
umkippen ['umkipən] vt tip over; vi overturn; (fig: Meinung ändern) change one's mind; (col: Mensch) keel over.
Umkleideraum ['umklaɪdəraum] m changing- or dressing room.
umkommen ['umkomən] vi irreg die, perish; (Lebensmittel) go bad.
Umkreis ['umkraɪs] m neighbourhood; (Math) circumcircle; im — von within a radius of; u—en [um'kraɪzən] vt insep circle (round); (Satellit) orbit.
umladen ['umla:dən] vt irreg transfer, reload.
Umlage ['umla:gə] f share of the costs.
Umlauf ['umlauf] m (Geld—) circulation; (von Gestirn) revolution; (Schreiben) circular; —bahn f orbit.
Umlaut ['umlaut] m umlaut.
umlegen ['umle:gən] vt put on; (verlegen) move, shift; Kosten

share out; (umkippen) tip over; (col: töten) bump off.
umleiten ['umlaɪtən] vt divert.
Umleitung f diversion.
umlernen ['umlɛrnən] vi learn something new; adjust one's views.
umliegend ['umli:gənt] a surrounding.
Umnachtung [um'naxtuŋ] f (mental) derangement.
um'rahmen vt insep frame.
um'randen vt insep border, edge.
umrechnen ['umrɛçnən] vt convert.
Umrechnung f conversion; —skurs m rate of exchange.
um'reißen vt irreg insep outline, sketch.
um'ringen vt insep surround.
Umriß ['umris] m outline.
umrühren ['umry:rən] vti· stir.
ums [ums] = **um das.**
umsatteln ['umzatəln] vi (col) change one's occupation; switch.
Umsatz ['umzats] m turnover.
umschalten ['umʃaltən] vt switch.
Umschau ['umʃau] f look(ing) round; — halten nach look around for; u—en vr look round.
Umschlag ['umʃla:k] m cover; (Buch— auch) jacket; (Med) compress; (Brief—) envelope; (Wechsel) change; (von Hose) turn-up; u—en ['umʃla:gən] irreg vi change; (Naut) capsize; vt knock over; Ärmel turn up; Seite turn over; Waren transfer; —platz m (Comm) distribution centre.
umschreiben vt irreg ['umʃraɪbən] (neu—) rewrite; (übertragen) transfer (auf +acc to); [-'ʃraɪbən] insep paraphrase; (abgrenzen) circumscribe, define.
umschulen ['umʃu:lən] vt retrain; Kind send to another school.

umschwärmen [umˈʃvɛrmən] vt insep swarm round; (fig) surround, idolize.

Umschweife [ˈumʃvaifə] pl: ohne — without beating about the bush, straight out.

Umschwung [ˈumʃvʊŋ] m change (around), revolution.

umsehen [ˈumzeːən] vr irreg look around or about; (suchen) look out (nach for).

umseitig [ˈumzaitiç] ad overleaf.

Umsicht [ˈumziçt] f prudence, caution; u—ig a cautious, prudent.

umsonst [umˈzɔnst] ad in vain; (gratis) for nothing.

umspringen [ˈumʃpriŋən] vi irreg change; (Wind auch) veer; mit jdm — treat sb badly.

Umstand [ˈumʃtant] m circumstance; Umstände pl (fig: Schwierigkeiten) fuss; in anderen Umständen sein be pregnant; Umstände machen go to a lot of trouble; unter Umständen possibly; mildernde Umstände (Jur) extenuating circumstances.

umständlich [ˈumʃtɛntliç] a ad Methode cumbersome, complicated; Ausdrucksweise, Erklärung auch long-winded; Mensch ponderous.

Umstands- cpd: —kleid nt maternity dress; —wort nt adverb.

Umstehende(n) [ˈumʃteːəndə(n)] pl bystanders pl.

Umsteig- cpd: —ekarte f transfer ticket; u—en vi irreg (Rail) change.

umstellen [ˈumʃtɛlən] vt (an anderen Ort) change round, rearrange; (Tech) convert; vr adapt o.s. (auf +acc to); [umˈʃtɛlən] vt insep surround.

Umstellung [ˈumʃtɛlʊŋ] f change; (Umgewöhnung) adjustment; (Tech) conversion.

umstimmen [ˈumʃtimən] vt (Mus) retune; jdn — make sb change his mind.

umstoßen [ˈumʃtoːsən] vt irreg (lit) overturn; Plan etc change, upset.

umstritten [umˈʃtritən] a disputed.

Umsturz [ˈumʃturts] m overthrow.

umstürzen [ˈumʃtyrtsən] vt (umwerfen) overturn; vi collapse, fall down; Wagen overturn.

umstürzlerisch a revolutionary.

Umtausch [ˈumtauʃ] m exchange; u—en vt exchange.

Umtriebe [ˈumtriːbə] pl machinations pl, intrigues pl.

umtun [ˈumtuːn] vr irreg see; sich nach etw — look for sth.

umwandeln [ˈumvandəln] vt change, convert; (Elec) transform.

umwechseln [ˈumvɛksəln] vt change.

Umweg [ˈumveːk] m detour, roundabout way.

Umwelt [ˈumvɛlt] f environment; —verschmutzung f environmental pollution.

umwenden [ˈumvɛndən] vtr irreg turn (round).

-um'werben vt irreg insep court, woo.

umwerfen [ˈumvɛrfən] vt irreg (lit) upset, overturn; Mantel throw on; (fig: erschüttern) upset, throw.

umziehen [ˈumtsiːən] irreg vtr change; vi move.

umzingeln [ˈumtsiŋəln] vt insep surround, encircle.

Umzug [ˈumtsuːk] m procession; (Wohnungs—) move, removal.

unab- [ˈunʔap] cpd: —'änderlich a irreversible, unalterable; —hängig *a* independent; **U—hängigkeit** *f* independence; **—kömmlich** a indispensable; **zur Zeit —kömmlich** not free at the moment; **—lässig** *a* incessant, constant; **—sehbar** *a* immeasurable; *Folgen* unforeseeable; *Kosten* incalculable; **—sichtlich** *a* unintentional; **—'wendbar** *a* inevitable.

unachtsam ['un'axtza:m] *a* careless; **U—keit** *f* carelessness.

unan- ['un'an] *cpd*: **—'fechtbar** *a* indisputable; **—gebracht** *a* uncalled-for; **—gemessen** *a* inadequate; **—genehm** *a* unpleasant; **U—nehmlichkeit** *f* inconvenience; *pl* trouble; **—sehnlich** *a* unsightly; **—ständig** *a* indecent, improper; **U—ständigkeit** *f* indecency, impropriety.

unappetitlich ['un'apeti:tliç] *a* unsavoury.

Unart ['un'a:rt] *f* bad manners *pl*; (*Angewohnheit*) bad habit; **u—ig** *a* naughty, badly behaved.

unauf- ['un'auf] *cpd*: **—'bleiblich** a inevitable, unavoidable; **—geglichen** *a* volatile; **—'sprechlich** *a* inexpressible; **—'stehlich** *a* intolerable; **—'weichlich** *a* inescapable, ineluctable.

unbändig ['unbɛndıç] *a* extreme, excessive.

unbarmherzig ['unbarmhɛrtsıç] *a* pitiless, merciless.

unbeabsichtigt ['unbə'apzıçtıçt] *a* unintentional.

unbeachtet ['unbə'axtət]   **a** unnoticed, ignored.

unbedenklich ['unbədɛŋklıç] *a* unhesitating; *Plan* unobjectionable; *ad* without hesitation.

unbedeutend ['unbədɔytənt] *a* insignificant, unimportant;. *Fehler* slight.

unbedingt   ['unbədıŋt]   **a** unconditional; *ad* absolutely; **mußt du — gehen?** do you really have to go?

unbefangen ['unbəfaŋən]   **a** impartial, unprejudiced; (*ohne Hemmungen*) uninhibited; **U—heit** *f* impartiality; uninhibitedness.

unbefriedig- ['unbəfri:dıg]   *cpd*: **—end** *a* unsatisfactory; **—t** [-dıçt] *a* unsatisfied, dissatisfied.

unbefugt   ['unbəfu:kt]   **a** unauthorized.

unbegabt ['unbəga:pt] *a* untalented.

unbegreiflich ['unbə'graıflıç] *a* inconceivable.

unbegrenzt ['unbəgrɛntst]   **a** unlimited.

unbegründet ['unbəgryndət] *a* unfounded.

Unbehag- ['unbəha:g] *cpd*: **—en** *nt* discomfort; **u—lich** [-klıç] *a* uncomfortable; *Gefühl* uneasy.

unbeholfen ['unbəhɔlfən]   **a** awkward, clumsy; **U—heit** *f* awkwardness, clumsiness.

unbeirrt ['unbə'ırt] *a* imperturbable.

unbekannt ['unbəkant] *a* unknown.

unbekümmert ['unbəkymərt] *a* unconcerned.

unbeliebt ['unbəli:pt] *a* unpopular; **U—heit** *f* unpopularity.

unbequem ['ʊnbəkveːm] *a Stuhl* uncomfortable; *Mensch* bothersome; *Regelung* inconvenient.

unberech-   cpd: **—enbar** [ʊnbə'rɛçənbaːr] *a* incalculable; *Mensch, Verhalten* unpredictable; **—tigt** ['ʊnbərɛçtɪçt] *a* unjustified; *(nicht erlaubt)* unauthorized.

unberufen [ʊnbə'ruːfən] *interj* touch wood.

unberührt ['ʊnbəryːrt] *a* untouched, intact; **sie ist noch —** she is still a virgin.

unbescheiden [ʊnbə'ʃaɪdən] *a* presumptuous.

unbeschreiblich [ʊnbə'ʃraɪplɪç] *a* indescribable.

unbesonnen [ʊnbəzɔnən] *a* unwise, rash, imprudent.

unbeständig ['ʊnbəʃtɛndɪç] *a Mensch* inconstant; *Wetter* unsettled; *Lage* unstable.

unbestechlich [ʊnbə'ʃtɛçlɪç] *a* incorruptible.

unbestimmt ['ʊnbəʃtɪmt] *a* indefinite; *Zukunft auch* uncertain; **U—heit** *f* vagueness.

unbeteiligt [ʊnbə'taɪlɪçt] *a* unconcerned, indifferent.

unbeugsam ['ʊnbɔykzaːm] *a* inflexible, stubborn; *Wille auch* unbending.

unbewacht ['ʊnbəvaxt] *a* unguarded, unwatched.

unbeweglich ['ʊnbəveːklɪç] *a* immovable.

unbewußt ['ʊnbəvʊst] *a* unconscious.

unbrauchbar ['ʊnbrauxbaːr] *a Arbeit* useless; *Gerät auch* unusable; **U—keit** *f* uselessness.

und [ʊnt] *cj* and; **— so weiter** and so on.

Undank ['ʊdaŋk] *m* ingratitude; **u—bar** *a* ungrateful; **—barkeit** *f* ingratitude.

undefinierbar [ʊndefi'niːrbaːr] *a* indefinable.

undenkbar . [ʊn'dɛŋkbaːr] *a* inconceivable.

undeutlich ['ʊndɔytlɪç] *a* indistinct.

undicht ['ʊndɪçt] *a* leaky.

Unding ['ʊndɪŋ] *nt* absurdity.

unduldsam ['ʊnduldsaːm] *a* intolerant.

undurch- ['ʊndʊrç] cpd: **—führbar** ['fyːrbaːr] *a* impracticable; **—lässig** [-lɛsɪç] *a* waterproof, impermeable; **—sichtig** [-zɪçtɪç] *a* opaque; *(fig)* obscure.

uneben [ʊn'eːbən] *a* uneven.

unehelich ['ʊn'eːəlɪç] *a* illegitimate.

uneigennützig ['ʊn'aɪgənnYtsɪç] *a* unselfish.

uneinig ['ʊn'aɪnɪç] *a* divided; **— sein** disagree; **U—keit** *f* discord, dissension.

uneins ['ʊn'aɪns] *a* at variance, at odds.

unempfindlich ['ʊn'ɛmpfɪntlɪç] *a* insensitive; **U—keit** *f* insensitivity.

unendlich [ʊn'ɛntlɪç] *a* infinite; **U—keit** *f* infinity.

unent- [ʊn'ɛnt] cpd: **—behrlich** ['-beːrlɪç] *a* indispensable; **—geltlich** [-gɛltlɪç] *a* free (of charge); **—schieden** [-ʃiːdən] *a* undecided; **—schieden enden** *(Sport)* end in a draw; **—schlossen** [-ʃlɔsən] *a* undecided; irresolute; **—wegt** ['-veːkt] *a* unswerving; *(unaufhörlich)* incessant.

uner- [ʊn'eːr] cpd: **—bittlich** bɪtlɪç] *a* unyielding, inexorable; **—fahren** [-faːrən] *a* inexperienced; **—freulich** [-frɔylɪç] *a* unpleasant; **—gründlich** ['-gryntlɪç] *a* unfathomable; —heblich [-he:plɪç] a unimportant; —hört [-hø:rt] a unheard-of; Bitte outrageous; —läßlich [-'lɛslɪç] a indispensable; —laubt [-laupt] a unauthorized; —meßlich ['mɛslɪç] a immeasurable, immense; —müdlich ['my:tlɪç] a indefatigable; —sättlich [-'zɛtlɪç] a insatiable; —schöpflich [-'ʃœpflɪç] a inexhaustible; —schütterlich [-'ʃytərlɪç] a unshakeable; —schwinglich [-'ʃvɪŋlɪç] a Preis exorbitant; too expensive; —träglich [-'trɛːklɪç] a unbearable; Frechheit insufferable; —wartet [-vartət] a unexpected; —wünscht [-vvnʃt] a undesirable, unwelcome; —zogen [-tso:gən] a ill-bred, rude.

unfähig ['unfɛ:ɪç] a incapable (zu of); incompetent; **U—keit** f incapacity; incompetence.

unfair ['unfɛ:r] a unfair.

Unfall ['unfal] m accident; —flucht f hit-and-run (driving); —stelle f scene of the accident; —versicherung f accident insurance.

unfaßbar [un'fasba:r] a inconceivable.

unfehlbar [un'fe:lba:r] a infallible; ad inevitably; **U—keit** f infallibility.

unflätig ['unflɛ:tɪç] a rude.

unfolgsam ['unfɔlkza:m] a disobedient.

unfrankiert ['unfraŋki:rt] a unfranked.

unfrei ['unfraɪ] a not free, unfree; —willig a involuntary, against one's will.

unfreundlich ['unfrɔyntlɪç] a unfriendly; **U—keit** f unfriendliness.

Unfriede(n) ['unfri:də(n)] m dissension, strife.

unfruchtbar ['unfrʊxtba:r] a infertile; Gespräche unfruitful; **U—keit** f infertility; unfruitfulness.

Unfug ['unfu:k] m -s (keine pl) mischief; (Unsinn) nonsense; grober — (Jur) gross misconduct; malicious damage.

ungeachtet ['ungə'axtət] prep +gen notwithstanding.

ungeahnt ['ungə'a:nt] a unsuspected, undreamt-of.

ungebeten ['ungəbe:tən] a uninvited.

ungebildet ['ungəbɪldət] a uneducated; uncultured.

ungebräuchlich ['ungəbrɔyçlɪç] a unusual, uncommon.

ungedeckt ['ungədɛkt] a Scheck uncovered.

Ungeduld ['ungədʊlt] f impatience; **u—ig** [-dɪç] a impatient.

ungeeignet ['ungə'aɪgnət] a unsuitable.

ungefähr ['ungəfɛ:r] a rough, approximate; das kommt nicht von — that's hardly surprising; —lich a not dangerous, harmless.

ungehalten ['ungəhaltən] a indignant.

ungeheuer ['ungəhɔyər] a huge; ad (col) enormously; **U—** nt -s, - monster; —lich [-'hɔyərlɪç] a monstrous.

ungehobelt ['ungəho:bəlt] a (fig) uncouth.

ungehörig ['ungəhø:rɪç] a impertinent, improper; **U—keit** f impertinence.

ungehorsam ['ungəho:rza:m] a disobedient; **U—** m disobedience.

ungeklärt ['ungəklɛ:rt] a not cleared up; Rätsel unsolved; Abwasser untreated.

ungeladen ['ʊngəla:dən] a not loaded; (Elec) uncharged; Gast uninvited.

ungelegen ['ʊngəle:gən] a inconvenient.

ungelernt ['ʊngəlɛrnt] a unskilled.

ungelogen ['ʊngəlo:gən] ad really, honestly.

ungemein ['ʊngəmaɪn] a uncommon.

ungemütlich ['ʊngəmy:tlɪç] a uncomfortable; Person disagreeable.

ungenau ['ʊngənaʊ] a inaccurate; U—igkeit f inaccuracy.

ungeniert ['ʊnʒeni:rt] a free and easy, unceremonious; ad without embarrassment, freely.

ungenießbar ['ʊngəni:sba:r] a inedible; undrinkable; (col) unbearable.

ungenügend ['ʊngəny:gənt] a insufficient, inadequate.

ungepflegt ['ʊngəpfle:kt] a Garten etc untended; Person unkempt; Hände neglected.

ungerade ['ʊngəra:də] a uneven, odd.

ungerecht ['ʊngərɛçt] a unjust; —fertigt a unjustified; U—igkeit f injustice, unfairness.

ungern ['ʊngɛrn] ad unwillingly, reluctantly.

ungeschehen ['ʊngəʃe:ən] a: — machen undo.

Ungeschick- ['ʊngəʃɪk] cpd: —lichkeit f clumsiness; u—t a awkward, clumsy.

ungeschminkt ['ʊngəʃmɪŋkt] a without make-up; (fig) unvarnished.

ungesetzlich ['ʊngəzɛtslɪç] a illegal.

ungestempelt ['ʊngəʃtɛmpəlt] a Briefmarke unfranked, uncancelled.

ungestört ['ʊngəʃtø:rt] a undisturbed.

ungestraft ['ʊngəʃtra:ft] ad with impunity.

ungestüm ['ʊngəʃty:m] a impetuous; tempestuous; U— nt -(e)s impetuosity; passion.

ungesund ['ʊngəzʊnt] a unhealthy.

ungetrübt ['ʊngətry:pt] a clear; (fig) untroubled; Freude unalloyed.

Ungetüm ['ʊngəty:m] nt -(e)s, -e monster.

ungewiß ['ʊngəvɪs] a uncertain; U—heit f uncertainty.

ungewöhnlich ['ʊngəvø:nlɪç] a unusual.

ungewohnt ['ʊngəvo:nt] a unaccustomed.

Ungeziefer ['ʊngətsi:fər] nt -s vermin.

ungezogen ['ʊngətso:gən] a rude, impertinent; U—heit f rudeness, impertinence.

ungezwungen ['ʊngətsvʊŋən] a natural, unconstrained.

ungläubig ['ʊnglɔybɪç] a unbelieving; ein —er Thomas a doubting Thomas; die U—en the infidel(s).

unglaub- cpd: —lich [ʊn'glaʊplɪç] a incredible; —würdig ['ʊnglaʊpvyrdɪç] a untrustworthy, unreliable; Geschichte improbable.

ungleich ['ʊnglaɪç] a dissimilar; unequal; ad incomparably; —artig a different; U—heit f dissimilarity, inequality.

Unglück ['ʊngʏk] nt -(e)s, -e misfortune; (Pech) bad luck; (—sfall) calamity, disaster; (Verkehrs—) accident; u—lich a unhappy; (erfolglos) unlucky; (unerfreulich) unfortunate; u—licherweise ['-'vaɪzə] ad unfortunately; u—selig a calamitous; Person unfortunate; —sfall m accident, calamity.

ungültig ['ongyltɪç] a invalid; U—keit f invalidity.

ungünstig ['ongynstɪç] a unfavourable.

ungut ['ongu:t] a Gefühl uneasy; nichts für — no offence.

unhaltbar ['onhaltbaːr] a untenable.

Unheil ['onhaɪl] nt evil; (Unglück) misfortune; — anrichten cause mischief; u—bar a incurable; u—bringend a fatal, fateful; u—voll a disastrous.

unheimlich ['onhaɪmlɪç] a weird, uncanny; ad (col) tremendously.

unhöflich ['onhøːflɪç] a impolite; U—keit f impoliteness.

unhygienisch ['onhygiˈeːnɪʃ] a unhygienic.

Uni ['oni] f -, -s university; u— [y'niː] a self-coloured.

Uniform [uni'fɔrm] f uniform; u—iert [-'miːrt] a uniformed.

uninteressant ['onɪntɛrɛsant] a uninteresting.

Universität [univɛrziˈtɛːt] f university.

unkenntlich ['onkɛntlɪç] a unrecognizable.

Unkenntnis ['onkɛntnɪs] f ignorance.

unklar ['onklaːr] a unclear; im —en sein über (+acc) be in the dark about; U—heit f unclarity; (Unentschiedenheit) uncertainty.

unklug ['onkluːk] a unwise.

Unkosten ['onkɔstən] pl expense(s).

Unkraut ['onkraʊt] nt weed; weeds pl.

unlängst ['onlɛŋst] ad not long ago.

unlauter ['onlaʊtər] a unfair.

unleserlich ['onleːzɛrlɪç] a illegible.

unlogisch ['onloːgɪʃ] a illogical.

unlösbar ['onløːsbaːr], unlöslich ['onløːslɪç] a insoluble.

Unlust ['onlost] f lack of enthusiasm; u—ig a unenthusiastic.

unmäßig ['onmɛːsɪç] a immoderate.

Unmenge ['onmɛŋə] f tremendous number, hundreds pl.

Unmensch ['onmɛnʃ] m ogre, brute; u—lich a inhuman, brutal; (ungeheuer) awful.

unmerklich ['on'mɛrklɪç] a imperceptible.

unmißverständlich ['onmɪsfɛrʃtɛntlɪç] a unmistakable.

unmittelbar ['onmɪtəlbaːr] a immediate.

unmöbliert ['onmøˈbliːrt] a unfurnished.

unmöglich ['onmøːklɪç] a impossible; U—keit f impossibility.

unmoralisch ['onmoraːlɪʃ] a immoral.

Unmut ['onmuːt] m ill humour.

unnachgiebig ['onnaːxgiːbɪç] a unyielding.

unnahbar ['on'naːbaːr] a unapproachable.

unnötig ['onnøːtɪç] a unnecessary; —erweise ad unnecessarily.

unnütz ['onnyts] a useless.

unordentlich ['on'ɔrdəntlɪç] a untidy.

Unordnung ['on'ɔrdnoŋ] f disorder.

unparteiisch ['onpartaɪʃ] a impartial; U—e(r) m umpire; (Fußball) referee.

unpassend ['onpasənt] a inappropriate; Zeit inopportune.

unpäßlich ['onpɛslɪç] a unwell.

unpersönlich ['unpɛrzøːnlıç] a impersonal.

unpolitisch ['unpoliːtıʃ] a apolitical.

unpraktisch ['unpraktıʃ] a unpractical.

unproduktiv ['unproduktiːf] a unproductive.

unproportioniert ['unproportsionˈiːrt] a out of proportion.

unpünktlich ['unpʏnktlıç] a unpunctual.

unrationell ['unratsionɛl] a inefficient.

unrecht ['unrɛçt] a wrong; **U—** nt wrong; **zu U—** wrongly; **U—haben, im U— sein** be wrong; **—mäßig** a unlawful, illegal.

unregelmäßig ['unreːgəlmɛsıç] a irregular; **U—keit** f irregularity.

unreif ['unraıf] a Obst unripe; (fig) immature.

unrentabel ['unrɛntaːbəl] a unprofitable.

unrichtig ['unrıçtıç] a incorrect, wrong.

Unruh ['unruː] f **-, -en** (von Uhr) balance; **-e** f **-, -n** unrest; **—estifter** m troublemaker; **u—ig** a restless.

uns [uns] pron acc, dat of **wir** us; ourselves.

unsachlich ['unzaxlıç] a not to the point, irrelevant; (persönlich) personal.

unsagbar [un'zaːkbaːr], **unsäglich** [un'zɛːklıç] a indescribable.

unsanft ['unzanft] a rough.

unsauber ['unzaubər] a unclean, dirty; (fig) crooked; (Mus) fuzzy.

unschädlich ['unʃɛːtlıç] a harmless; **jdn/etw — machen** render sb/sth harmless.

unscharf ['unʃarf] a indistinct; Bild etc out of focus, blurred.

unscheinbar ['unʃaınbaːr] a insignificant; Aussehen, Haus etc. unprepossessing.

unschlagbar [un'ʃlaːkbaːr] a invincible.

unschlüssig ['unʃlʏsıç] a undecided.

Unschuld ['unʃult] f innocence; **u—ig** [-dıç] a innocent.

unselbständig ['unzɛlpʃtɛndıç] a dependent, over-reliant on others.

unser ['unzər] pron our; gen of **wir** of us; **—e(r,s)** ours; **—einer, —eins, —esgleichen** pron people like us; **—erseits** ad on our part; **—twegen, —twillen** ad (für uns) for our sake; (wegen uns) on our account; **—ige** pron: **der/die/das —ige** ours.

unsicher ['unzıçər] a uncertain; Mensch insecure; **U—heit** f uncertainty; insecurity.

unsichtbar ['unzıçtbaːr] a invisible; **U—keit** f invisibility.

Unsinn ['unzın] m nonsense; **u—ig** a nonsensical.

Unsitte ['unzıtə] f deplorable habit.

unsittlich ['unzıtlıç] a indecent; **U—keit** f indecency.

unsportlich ['unʃportlıç] a not sporty; unfit; Verhalten unsporting.

unsre ['unzrə] = **unsere**.

unsrige ['unzrıgə] = **unserige**.

unsterblich ['unʃtɛrplıç] a immortal; **U—keit** f immortality.

Unstimmigkeit ['unʃtımıçkaıt] f inconsistency; (Streit) disagreement.

unsympathisch ['unzʏmpaːtıʃ] a unpleasant; **er ist mir —** I don't like him.

untätig ['untɛːtıç] a idle.

untauglich ['untauklıç] a unsuitable; *(Mil)* unfit; **U—keit** f unsuitability; unfitness.

unteilbar [un'taılba:r] a indivisible.

unten ['untən] ad below; *(im Haus)* downstairs; *(an der Treppe etc)* at the bottom; nach — down; — am Berg etc at the bottom of the mountain etc; ich bin bei ihm — durch *(col)* he's through with me.

unter ['untər] prep +acc or dat under, below; *(bei Menschen)* among; *(während)* during; ad under.

Unter- ['untər] cpd: —abteilung f subdivision; —arm m forearm.

unterbe- ['untərbə] cpd: —lichten vt *(Phot)* underexpose; **U—wußtsein** nt subconscious; **—zahlt** a underpaid.

unterbieten [untər'bi:tən] vt insep *(Comm)* undercut; Rekord lower, reduce.

unterbinden [untər'bındən] vt irreg insep stop, call a halt to.

Unterbodenschutz [untər'bo:dənʃuts] m *(Aut)* underseal.

unterbrech- [untər'brɛç] cpd: —en vt irreg insep interrupt; **U—ung** f interruption.

unterbringen ['untərbrıŋən] vt irreg *(in Koffer)* stow away; *(in Hotel etc)* place; Person *(in Hotel etc)* accommodate, put up; *(beruflich)* fix up *(auf, in* with).

unterdessen [untər'dɛsən] ad meanwhile.

Unterdruck ['untərdruk] m low pressure.

unterdrücken [untər'drykən] vt insep suppress; Leute oppress.

untere(r, s) ['untərə(r, z)] a lower.

untereinander [untər'aı'nandər] ad with each other; among themselves etc.

unterentwickelt ['untər'ɛntvıkəlt] a underdeveloped.

unterernährt ['untər'ɛrnɛ:rt] a undernourished, underfed.

Unterernährung f malnutrition.

Unterführung f subway, underpass.

Untergang ['untərgaŋ] m (down)fall, decline; *(Naut)* sinking; *(von Gestirn)* setting.

unter'geben a subordinate.

untergehen ['untərge:ən] vi irreg go down; *(Sonne auch)* set; *(Staat)* fall; *(Volk)* perish; *(Welt)* come to an end; *(im Lärm)* be drowned.

Untergeschoß ['untərgəʃɔs] nt basement.

unter'gliedern vt insep subdivide.

Untergrund ['untərgrunt] m foundation; *(Pol)* underground; **—bahn** f underground, tube, subway *(US)*; **—bewegung** f underground (movement).

unterhalb ['untərhalp] prep +gen, ad below; — von below.

Unterhalt ['untərhalt] m maintenance; **u—en** [untər'haltən] irreg insep vt maintain; *(belustigen)* entertain; vr talk; *(sich belustigen)* enjoy o.s.; **u—end** [untər'haltənt] a entertaining; **—ung** f maintenance; *(Belustigung)* entertainment, amusement; *(Gespräch)* talk.

Unterhändler ['untərhɛntlər] m negotiator.

Unterhemd ['untərhɛmt] nt vest, undershirt *(US)*.

Unterhose ['untərho:zə] f underpants pl.

unterirdisch ['untər'ırdıʃ] a underground.

Unterkiefer ['untərki:fər] m lower jaw.

unterkommen ['untərkɔmən] *vi irreg* find shelter; find work; **das ist mir noch nie untergekommen** I've never met with that.

Unterkunft ['untərkunft] *f* —, **-künfte** accommodation.

Unterlage ['untərla:gə] *f* foundation; *(Beleg)* document; *(Schreibetc)* pad.

unter'lassen *vt irreg insep (versäumen)* fail (to do); *(sich enthalten)* refrain from.

unterlaufen [untər'laufən] *vi irreg insep* happen; **a: mit Blut** — suffused with blood; *(Augen)* bloodshot.

unter'legen ['untərle:gən] *vt* lay or put under; [untər'le:gən] *a* inferior *(dat* to); *(besiegt)* defeated.

Unterleib ['untərlaip] *m* abdomen.

unter'liegen *vi irreg insep* be defeated or overcome *(jdm by sb)*; *(unterworfen sein)* be subject to.

Untermiete ['untərmi:tə] *f:* **zur — wohnen** be a subtenant or lodger; **—r(in** *f) m* subtenant, lodger.

unter'nehmen *vt irreg insep* undertake; **U— ** *nt* **-s, -** undertaking, enterprise *(auch Comm)*; **—d** *a* enterprising, daring.

Unternehmer [untər'ne:mər] *m* **-s, -** entrepreneur, businessman.

Unterprima ['untərpri:ma] *f* —, **-primen** eighth year of secondary school.

Unterredung [untər're:duŋ] *f* discussion, talk.

Unterricht ['untərriçt] *m* **-(e)s, -e** instruction, lessons *pl;* **u—en** [untər'rıçtən] *insep vt* instruct; *(Sch)* teach; *vr* inform o.s. *(über +acc* about).

Unterrock [untərrɔk] *m* petticoat, slip.

unter'sagen *vt insep* forbid *(jdm etw* sb to do sth).

unter'schätzen *vt insep* underestimate.

unter'scheiden *irreg insep* **vt** distinguish; *vr* differ.

Unter'scheidung *f (Unterschied)* distinction; *(Unterscheiden)* differentiation.

Unterschied ['untərʃi:t] *m* **-(e)s, -e** difference, distinction; **im — zu** as distinct from; **u—lich** *a* varying, differing; *(diskriminierend)* discriminatory; **u—slos** *ad* indiscriminately.

unter'schlagen *vt irreg insep* embezzle; *(verheimlichen)* suppress.

Unter'schlagung *f* embezzlement.

Unterschlupf ['untərʃlupf] *m* **-(e)s, -schlüpfe** refuge.

unter'schreiben *vt irreg insep* sign.

Unterschrift ['untərʃrıft] *f* signature.

Unterseeboot ['untərze:bo:t] *nt* submarine.

Untersekunda ['untərzekunda] *f* —, **-sekunden** sixth year of secondary school.

Untersetzer ['untərzɛtsər] *m* tablemat; *(für Gläser)* coaster.

untersetzt [untər'zɛtst] *a* stocky.

unterste(r,s) ['untərstə(r,z)] *a* lowest, bottom.

unterstehen [untər'ʃte:ən] *irreg vi insep* be under *(jdm* sb); *vr* dare; ['untərʃte:ən] *vi* shelter.

unterstellen [untər'ʃtɛlən] *vt insep* subordinate *(dat* to); *(fig)* impute *(jdm etw* sth to sb); ['untərʃtɛlən] *vt Auto* garage, park; *vr* take shelter.

unter'streichen *vt irreg insep (lit, fig)* underline.

Unterstufe ['ʊntərʃtuːfə] f lower grade.

unter'stützen vt insep support.

Unter'stützung f support, assistance.

unter'suchen vt insep (Med) examine; (Polizei) investigate.

Unter'suchung f examination; investigation, inquiry; **—sausschuß** m committee of inquiry; **—shaft** f imprisonment on remand.

Untertan ['ʊntərtaːn] m -s, -en subject.

untertänig ['ʊntərtɛːnɪç] a submissive, humble.

Untertasse ['ʊntərtasə] f saucer.

untertauchen ['ʊntərtauxən] vi dive; (fig) disappear, go underground.

Unterteil ['ʊntərtail] nt or m lower part, bottom; **u—en** [ʊntər'tailən] vt insep divide up.

Untertertia ['ʊntərtɛrtsia] f -, **-tertien** fourth year of secondary school.

Unterwäsche ['ʊntərvɛʃə] f underwear.

unterwegs [ʊntər'veːks] ad on the way.

unter'weisen vt irreg insep instruct.

unter'werfen irreg insep vt subject; Volk subjugate; vr submit (dat to).

unterwürfig [ʊntər'vʏrfɪç] a obsequious, servile.

unter'zeichnen vt insep sign.

unter'ziehen irreg insep vt subject (dat to); vr undergo (etw (dat) sth) / (einer Prüfung) an examination.

untreu ['ʊntrɔy] a unfaithful; **U—e** f unfaithfulness.

untröstlich '' [ʊn'trøːstlɪç] a inconsolable.

Untugend ['ʊntuːgənt] f vice, failing.

unüber- ['ʊn'yːbər] cpd: **—legt** [-leːkt] a ill-considered; ad without thinking; **—sehbar** [-'zeːbaːr] a incalculable.

unum- [ʊn'ʊm] cpd: **—gänglich** [-'gɛnlɪç] a indispensable, vital; absolutely necessary; **—wunden** [-'vʊndən] a candid; ad straight out.

ununterbrochen ['ʊn'ʊntərbrɔxən] a uninterrupted.

unver- [ʊnfɛr] cpd: **—änderlich** [-'ɛndərlɪç] a unchangeable; **—antwortlich** [-'antvɔrtlɪç] a irresponsible; (unentschuldbar) inexcusable; **—äußerlich** [-'ɔysərlɪç] a inalienable; **—besserlich** [-'bɛsərlɪç] a incorrigible; **—bindlich** [-'bɪntlɪç] a not binding; Antwort curt; ad (Comm) without obligation; **—blümt** [-'blyːmt] a,ad plain(ly), blunt(ly); **—daulich** [-'daulɪç] a indigestible; **—dorben** [-'dɔrbən] a unspoilt; **—einbar** [-'ainbaːr] a incompatible; **—fänglich** [-'fɛnlɪç] a harmless; **—froren** [-'froːrən] a impudent; **—hofft** [-'hɔft] a unexpected; **—kennbar** [-'kɛnbaːr] a unmistakable; **—meidlich** [-'maitlɪç] a unavoidable; **—mutet** [-'muːtət] a unexpected; **—nünftig** [-'nʏnftɪç] a foolish; **—schämt** [-'ʃɛːmt] a impudent; **U—schämtheit** f impudence, insolence; **—sehens** [-'zeːəns] ad all of a sudden; **—sehrt** [-'zeːrt] a uninjured; **—söhnlich** [-'zøːnlɪç] a irreconcilable; **—ständlich** [-'ʃtɛntlɪç] a unintelligible; **—träglich** [-'trɛːklɪç] a quarrelsome; Meinungen, (Med) incompatible; **—wüstlich** [-'vyːstlɪç] a indestructible; Mensch

irrespressible; —zeihlich [-'tsaɪlɪç]
a unpardonable; —züglich
[-'tsy:klɪç] a immediate.

unvoll- ['unfɔl] cpd: —kommen a
imperfect; —ständig a incomplete.

unvor- ['unfo:r] cpd: —bereitet a
unprepared; —eingenommen a
unbiased; —hergesehen
[-he:rgəzeːən] a unforeseen;
—sichtig [-zɪçtɪç] a careless, imprudent; —stellbar [-'ʃtɛlba:r] a
inconceivable; —teilhaft [-taɪlhaft]
a disadvantageous.

unwahr ['unva:r] a untrue;
—haftig a untruthful; —scheinlich
a improbable, unlikely; ad (col)
incredibly; U—scheinlichkeit f
improbability, unlikelihood.

unweigerlich [un'vaɪgərlɪç] a
unquestioning; ad without fail.

Unwesen ['unveːzən] nt nuisance;
(Unfug) mischief; sein — treiben
wreak havoc; u—tlich a
inessential, unimportant; u—tlich
besser marginally better.

Unwetter ['unvɛtər] nt thunderstorm.

unwichtig ['unvɪçtɪç] a unimportant.

unwider- [unvi:dər] cpd: —legbar
[-'le:kba:r] a irrefutable; —ruflich
[-'ru:flɪç] a irrevocable; —stehlich
[-'ʃte:lɪç] a irresistible.

unwill- ['unvɪl] cpd: U—e(n) m
indignation; —ig a .indignant;
(widerwillig) reluctant; —kürlich
[-ky:rlɪç] a involuntary; ad
instinctively; lachen involuntarily.

unwirklich ['unvɪrklɪç] a unreal.

unwirsch ['unvɪrʃ] a cross, surly.

unwirtlich ['unvɪrtlɪç] a inhospitable.

unwirtschaftlich ['unvɪrt-ʃaftlɪç]
a uneconomical.

unwissen- ['unvɪsən] cpd: —d a
ignorant; U—heit f ignorance;
—schaftlich a unscientific.

unwohl ['unvo:l] a unwell, ill;
U—sein nt -s indisposition.

unwürdig ['unvyrdɪç] a unworthy
(jds of sb).

unzählig [un'tsɛ:lɪç] a innumerable,
countless.

unzer- [untsɛr] cpd: —brechlich
[-'brɛçlɪç] a unbreakable; —reißbar
[-'raɪsba:r] a untearable; —störbar
[-'ʃtø:rba:r] a indestructible;
—trennlich [-'trɛnlɪç] a inseparable.

Unzucht ['untsuxt] f sexual offence.

unzüchtig ['untsyçtɪç] a immoral;
lewd.

unzu- ['untsu] cpd: —frieden a
dissatisfied; U—friedenheit f
discontent; —länglich ['untsu:lɛn-
lɪç] a inadequate; —lässig
['untsu:lɛsɪç] a inadmissible;
—rechnungsfähig ['untsu:rɛç-
nuŋsfɛ:ɪç] a irresponsible;
—sammenhängend a disconnected;
Äußerung incoherent; —treffend
['untsu:-] a incorrect; —verlässig
['untsu:-] a unreliable.

unzweideutig ['untsvaɪdɔytɪç] adj
unambiguous.

üppig ['ʏpɪç] adj Frau curvaceous;
Busen full, ample; Essen
sumptuous, lavish; Vegetation
luxuriant, lush.

uralt ['u:r'alt] a ancient, very old.

Uran [u'ra:n] nt -s uranium.

Ur- ['u:r] in cpds original; —aufführung f first performance; —einwohner m original inhabitant;
—eltern pl ancestors pl; —enkel(in
f) m great-grandchild; —großmutter f great-grandmother;
—großvater m great-grandfather;
—heber m -s, = originator; (Autor)
author.

Urin [u'ri:n] *m* -s, -e urine.

ur- *cpd:* —**komisch** *a* incredibly funny; **U—kunde** *f* -, -n document, deed; —**kundlich** ['u:rkʊntlɪç] *a* a documentary; —**laub** *m* -(e)s, -e holiday(s *pl*), vacation (US); (Mil etc) leave; —**lauber** *m* -s, - holiday-maker, vacationist (US); —**mensch** *m* primitive man.

Urne ['ʊrnə] *f* -, -n urn.

Ursache ['u:rzaxə] *f* cause.

Ursprung ['u:rʃprʊŋ] *m* origin, source; (von Fluß) source.

ursprünglich [u:rʃprʏŋlɪç] *a, ad* original(ly).

Urteil ['ʊrtaɪl] *nt* -s, -e opinion; (Jur) sentence, judgement; **u—en** *vi* judge; —**spruch** *m* sentence, verdict.

Ur- *cpd:* —**wald** *m* jungle; —**zeit** *f* prehistoric times *pl*.

usw [u:sve:] *abbr of* und so weiter etc.

Utensilien [utɛn'zi:liən] *pl* utensils *pl*.

Utopie [uto'pi:] *f* -, pipedream.

utopisch [u'to:pɪʃ] *a* utopian.

V

V, v [fau] *nt* V, v.

vag(e) [va:k, va:gə] *a* vague.

Vagina [va'gi:na] *f* -, **Vaginen** vagina.

Vakuum ['va:kuʊm] *nt* -s, **Vakua** *or* **Vakuen** vacuum.

Vanille [va'nɪljə] *f* - vanilla.

Variation [variatsi'o:n] *f* variation.

variieren [vari'i:rən] *vti* vary.

Vase ['va:zə] *f* -, -n vase.

Vater ['fa:tər] *m* -s, ⁺ father; —**land** *nt* native country; Fatherland; —**landsliebe** *f* patriotism.

väterlich ['fɛ:tərlɪç] *a* fatherly; —**erseits** *ad* on the father's side.

Vater- *cpd:* —**schaft** *f* paternity; —**unser** *nt* -s, - Lord's prayer.

Vegetarier(in *f*) [vege'ta:riər(ɪn)] *m* -s, - vegetarian.

Veilchen ['faɪlçən] *nt* violet.

Vene ['ve:nə] *f* -, -n vein.

Ventil [vɛn'ti:l] *nt* -s, -e valve; —**ator** [vɛnti'la:tɔr] *m* ventilator.

verab- [fɛr'ap] *cpd:* —**reden** *vt* agree, arrange; *vr* arrange to meet (mit jdm sb); **V—redung** *f* arrange-

ment; (Treffen) appointment; —**scheuen** *vt* detest, abhor; —**schieden** *vt* Gäste say goodbye to; (entlassen) discharge; Gesetz pass; *vr* take one's leave (von of); **V—schiedung** *f* leave-taking; discharge; passing.

ver- [fɛr] *cpd:* —**achten** [-'ʔaxtən] *vt* despise; —**ächtlich** [-'ɛçtlɪç] *a* contemptuous; (verachtenswert) contemptible; **jdn —ächtlich machen** run sb down; **V—achtung** *f* contempt.

verallgemein- [fɛr'algəmaɪn] *cpd:* —**ern** *vt* generalize; **V—erung** *f* generalization.

veralten [fɛr'altən] *vi* become obsolete *or* out-of-date.

Veranda [ve'randa] *f* -, **Veranden** veranda.

veränder- [fɛr'ɛndər] *cpd:* —**lich** *a* changeable; **V—lichkeit** *f* variability, instability; —**n** *vtr* change, alter; **V—ung** *f* change, alteration.

veran- [fɛr''an] *cpd:* —**lagt** a with a ... nature; **V-lagung** *f* disposition, aptitude; —**lassen** *vt* cause; **Maßnahmen** —**lassen** take measures; **sich** —**laßt sehen feel** prompted; **V-lassung** *f* cause; motive; **auf jds V-lassung (hin)** at the instance of sb; —**schaulichen** *vt* illustrate; —**schlagen** *vt* estimate; —**stalten** *vt* organize, arrange; **V-stalter** *m* -s, organizer; **V-staltung** *f* (*Veranstalten*) organizing; (*Veranstaltetes*) event, function.

verantwort- [fɛr''antvort] *cpd:* —**en** *vt* answer for; *vr* justify o.s.; —**lich** a responsible; **V-ung** *f* responsibility; —**ungsbewußt** a responsible; —**ungslos** a irresponsible.

verarbeiten [fɛr''arbaɪtən] *vt* process; (*geistig*) assimilate; **etw zu etw** — make sth into sth.
Verarbeitung *f* processing; assimilation.

verärgern [fɛr''ɛrgərn] *vt* annoy.

verausgaben [fɛr''ausgaːbən] *vr* run out of money; (*fig*) exhaust o.s.

veräußern [fɛr''ɔʏsərn] *vt* dispose of, sell.

Verb [vɛrp] *nt* -s, -en verb.

Verband [fɛr'bant] *m* -(e)s, :e (*Med*) bandage, dressing; (*Bund*) association, society; (*Mil*) unit; —**(s)kasten** *m* medicine chest, first-aid box; —**stoff** *m*, —**zeug** *nt* bandage, dressing material.

verbannen [fɛr'banən] *vt* banish.
Verbannung *f* exile.

verbergen [fɛr'bɛrgən] *vtr irreg* hide (*vor +dat* from).

verbessern [fɛr'bɛsərn] *vtr* improve; (*berichtigen*) correct (o.s.).
Verbesserung *f* improvement; correction.

verbeugen [fɛr'bɔʏgən] *vr* bow.
Verbeugung *f* bow.

ver'biegen *vi irreg* bend.

ver'bieten *vt irreg* forbid (*jdm etw* sb to do sth).

ver'binden *irreg vt* connect; (*kombinieren*) combine; (*Med*) bandage; **jdm die Augen** — blindfold sb; *vr* combine (*auch Chem*), join.

verbindlich [fɛr'bɪntlɪç] a binding; (*freundlich*) friendly; **V-keit** *f* obligation; (*Höflichkeit*) civility.

Ver'bindung *f* connection; (*Zusammensetzung*) combination; (*Chem*) compound; (*Univ*) club.

verbissen [fɛr'bɪsən] a grim, dogged; **V-heit** *f* grimness, doggedness.

ver'bitten *vt irreg:* **sich** (*dat*) **etw** — not tolerate sth, not stand for sth.

verbittern [fɛr'bɪtərn] *vt* embitter; *vi* get bitter.

verblassen [fɛr'blasən] *vi* fade.

Verbleib [fɛr'blaɪp] *m* -(e)s whereabouts; **v-en** [fɛr'blaɪbən] *vi irreg* remain.

Verblendung [fɛr'blɛndʊŋ] *f* (*fig*) delusion.

verblöden [fɛr'bløːdən] *vi* get stupid.

verblüffen [fɛr'blʏfən] *vt* stagger, amaze.
Verblüffung *f* stupefaction.

ver'blühen *vi* wither, fade.

ver'bluten *vi* bleed to death.

verborgen [fɛr'bɔrgən] a hidden.

Verbot [fɛr'boːt] *nt* -(e)s, -e prohibition, ban; **v-en** a forbidden; **Rauchen v—en!** no smoking; **v—enerweise** *ad* though it is forbidden; —**sschild** *nt* prohibitory sign.

Verbrauch [fɛr'braʊx] *m* -(e)s consumption; **v—en** *vt* use up; **—er** *m* -s, - consumer; **v—t** a used up, finished; *Luft* stale; *Mensch* worn-out.

Verbrechen [fɛr'brɛçən] *nt* -s, - crime; **v—** *vt irreg* perpetrate.

Verbrecher [fɛr'brɛçər] *m* -s, - criminal; **v—isch** *a* criminal; **—tum** *nt* -s criminality.

ver'breiten *vtr* spread; **sich über etw** (*acc*) — expound on sth.

verbreitern [fɛr'braɪtərn] *vt* broaden.

Verbreitung *f* spread(ing), propagation.

verbrenn- [fɛr'brɛn] *cpd:* **—bar** *a* combustible; **—en** *vt irreg* burn; *Leiche* cremate; **V—ung** *f* burning; (*in Motor*) combustion; (*von Leiche*) cremation; **V—ungsmotor** *m* internal combustion engine.

ver'bringen *vt irreg* spend.

Verbrüderung [fɛr'bry:dərʊŋ] *f* fraternization.

verbrühen [fɛr'bry:ən] *vt* scald.

verbuchen [fɛr'bu:xən] *vt* (*Fin*) register; *Erfolg* enjoy; *Mißerfolg* suffer.

verbunden [fɛr'bʊndən] *a* connected; **jdm — sein** be obliged *or* indebted to sb; **falsch —** (*Tel*) wrong number; **V—heit** *f* bond, relationship.

verbünden [fɛr'byndən] *vr* ally o.s.

Verbündete(r) [fɛr'byndətə(r)] *mf* ally.

ver'bürgen *vr:* **sich — für** vouch for.

ver'büßen *vt:* **eine Strafe —** serve a sentence.

verchromt [fɛr'kro:mt] *a* chromium-plated.

Verdacht [fɛr'daxt] *m* -(e)s suspicion.

verdächtig [fɛr'dɛçtɪç] *a* suspicious, suspect; **—en** [fɛr'dɛçtɪɡən] *vt* suspect.

verdammen [fɛr'damən] *vt* damn, condemn.

Verdammnis [fɛr'damnɪs] *f* -, -se perdition, damnation.

ver'dampfen *vi* vaporize, evaporate.

ver'danken *vt:* **jdm etw —** owe sb sth.

verdauen [fɛr'daʊən] *vt* (*lit, fig*) digest.

verdaulich [fɛr'daʊlɪç] *a* digestible; **das ist schwer —** that is hard to digest.

Verdauung *f* digestion.

Verdeck [fɛr'dɛk] *nt* -(e)s, -e (*Aut*) hood; (*Naut*) deck; **v—en** *vt* cover (up); (*verbergen*) hide.

ver'denken *vt irreg:* **jdm etw —** blame sb for sth, hold sth against sb.

Verderb- [fɛr'dɛrp] *cpd:* **—en** [fɛr'dɛrbən] *nt* -s ruin; **v—en** *irreg vt* spoil; (*schädigen*) ruin; (*moralisch*) corrupt; **es mit jdm v—en** get into sb's bad books; *vi* (*Essen*) spoil, rot; (*Mensch*) go to the bad; **v—lich** *a* *Einfluß* pernicious; *Lebensmittel* perishable; **v—t** *a* depraved; **—theit** *f* depravity.

verdeutlichen [fɛr'dɔytlɪçən] *vt* make clear.

ver'dichten *vtr* condense.

ver'dienen *vt* earn; (*moralisch*) deserve.

Ver'dienst *m* -(e)s, -e earnings *pl*; *nt* -(e)s, -e merit; (*Leistung*) service (*um* to).

verdient [fɛr'di:nt] a well-earned; *Person* deserving of esteem; **sich um etw — machen** do a lot for sth.

verdoppeln [fɛr'dɔpəln] vt double.

Verdopp(e)lung f doubling.

verdorben [fɛr'dɔrbən] a spoilt; *(geschädigt)* ruined; *(moralisch)* corrupt.

verdrängen [fɛr'drɛŋən] vt oust, displace *(auch Phys)*; *(Psych)* repress.

Verdrängung f displacement; *(Psych)* repression.

ver'drehen vt *(lit, fig)* twist; *Augen* roll; **jdm den Kopf —** *(fig)* turn sb's head.

verdreifachen [fɛr'draifaxən] vt treble.

verdrießlich [fɛr'dri:slɪç] a peevish, annoyed.

verdrossen [fɛr'drɔsən] a cross, sulky.

ver'drücken vt *(col)* put away, eat; vr *(col)* disappear.

Verdruß [fɛr'drʊs] m -sses, -sse annoyance, worry.

ver'duften vi evaporate; **vir** *(col)* disappear.

verdummen [fɛr'dʊmən] vt make stupid; vi grow stupid.

verdunkeln [fɛr'dʊŋkəln] vtr darken; *(fig)* obscure.

Verdunk(e)lung f blackout; *(fig)* obscuring.

verdünnen [fɛr'dʏnən] vt dilute.

verdunsten [fɛr'dʊnstən] vi evaporate.

verdursten [fɛr'dʊrstən] vi die of thirst.

verdutzt [fɛr'dʊtst] a nonplussed, taken aback.

verehr- [fɛr'e:r] cpd: **—en** vt venerate, worship *(auch Rel)*; **jdm etw — en** present sb with sth;

V—er(in f) m -s, - admirer, worshipper *(auch Rel)*; **—t** a esteemed; **V—ung** f respect; *(Rel)* worship.

vereidigen [fɛr'aidɪgən] vt put on oath.

Vereidigung f swearing in.

Verein [fɛr'ain] m -(e)s, -e club, association; **v—bar** a compatible; **v—baren** [-ba:rən] vt agree upon; **—barung** f agreement; **v—fachen** [-faxən] vt simplify; **v—heitlichen** vt standardize; **v—igen** [-ɪgən] vtr unite; **—igung** f union; *(Verein)* association; **v—samen** [-za:mən] vi become lonely; **v—t** a united; **—zelt** a isolated.

vereisen [fɛr'aizən] vi freeze, ice over; vt *(Med)* freeze.

vereiteln [fɛr'aitəln] vt frustrate.

ver'eitern vi suppurate, fester.

verengen [fɛr'ɛŋən] vr narrow.

vererb- [fɛr'ɛrb] cpd: **—en** vt bequeath; *(Biol)* transmit; vr be hereditary; **—lich** [fɛr'ɛrplɪç] a hereditary; **V—ung** f bequeathing; *(Biol)* transmission; *(Lehre)* heredity.

verewigen [fɛr'e:vɪgən] vt immortalize; **vr** *(col)* leave one's name.

ver'fahren *irreg* vi act; **— mit** deal with; vr get lost; a tangled; **V—nt -s,** - procedure; *(Tech)* process; *(Jur)* proceedings pl.

Verfall [fɛr'fal] m -(e)s decline; *(von Haus)* dilapidation; *(Fin)* expiry; **v—en** vi *irreg* decline; *(Haus)* be falling down; *(Fin)* lapse; **v—en in** *(+acc)* lapse into; **v—en auf** *(+acc)* hit upon; **einem Laster v—en sein** be addicted to a vice.

verfänglich [fɛr'fɛŋlɪç] a awkward, tricky.

ver'färben vr change colour.

Verfasser(in f) [fɛr'fasər(ın)] m -s, - author, writer.

Verfassung f constitution (auch Pol); —gericht nt constitutional court; v—smäßig a constitutional; v—swidrig a unconstitutional.

ver'faulen vi rot.

ver'fechten vt irreg advocate; defend.

Verfechter [fɛr'fɛçtər] m -s, - champion; defender.

ver'fehlen vt miss; etw für verfehlt halten regard sth as mistaken.

verfeinern [fɛr'faɪnərn] vt refine.

ver'fliegen vi irreg evaporate; (Zeit) pass, fly.

verflossen [fɛr'flɔsən] a past, former.

ver'fluchen vt curse.

verflüchtigen [fɛr'flʏçtɪɡən] vr vaporize, evaporate; (Geruch) fade.

verflüssigen [fɛr'flʏsɪɡən] vr become liquid.

verfolg- [fɛr'fɔlg] cpd: —en vt pursue; (gerichtlich) prosecute; (grausam, esp Pol) persecute; V—er m -s, - pursuer; V—ung f pursuit; prosecution; persecution; V—ungswahn m persecution mania.

verfremden [fɛr'frɛmdən] vt alienate, distance.

verfrüht [fɛr'fry:t] a premature.

verfüg- [fɛr'fy:g] cpd: —bar a available; —en vt direct, order; vr proceed; vi: —en über (+acc) have at one's disposal; V—ung f direction, order; zur V—ung at one's disposal; jdm zur V—ung stehen be available to sb.

verführ- [fɛr'fy:r] cpd: —en vt tempt; (sexuell) seduce; V—er m tempter; seducer; —erisch a seduc-

tive; V—ung f seduction; (Versuchung) temptation.

ver'gammeln vi (col) go to seed; (Nahrung) go off.

vergangen [fɛr'ɡaŋən] a past; V—heit f past.

vergänglich [fɛr'ɡɛŋlıç] a transitory; V—keit f transitoriness, impermanence.

vergasen [fɛr'ga:zən] vt gasify; (töten) gas.

Vergaser m -s, - (Aut) carburettor.

vergeb- [fɛr'ge:b] cpd: —en vt irreg forgive (jdm etw sb for sth); (weggeben) give away; —en sein be occupied; (col: Mädchen) be spoken—for; —ens ad in vain; —lich [fɛr'ge:plıç] ad in vain; a vain, futile; V—ung f forgiveness.

vergegenwärtigen [fɛr'ge:gənvɛrtıɡən] vr: sich (dat) etw — recall or visualize sth.

ver'gehen irreg vi pass by or away; jdm vergeht etw sb loses sth; vr commit an offence (gegen etw against sth); sich an jdm — (sexually) assault sb; V— nt -s, - offence.

ver'gelten vt irreg pay back (jdm etw sb for sth), repay.

Ver'geltung f retaliation, reprisal; —sschlag m (Mil) reprisal.

vergessen [fɛr'gɛsən] vt irreg forget; V—heit f oblivion.

vergeßlich [fɛr'gɛslıç] a forgetful; V—keit f forgetfulness.

vergeuden [fɛr'ɡɔʏdən] vt squander, waste.

vergewaltigen [fɛrɡə'valtıɡən] vt rape; (fig) violate.

Vergewaltigung f rape.

vergewissern [fɛrɡə'vısərn] vr make sure.

ver'gießen vt irreg shed.

vergiften [fɛr'gɪftən] vt poison.

Vergiftung f poisoning.

Vergißmeinnicht [fɛr'gɪsmaɪnnɪçt] nt -(e)s, -e forget-me-not.

verglasen [fɛr'glɑːzən] vt glaze.

Vergleich [fɛr'glaɪç] m -(e)s, -e comparison; (Jur) settlement; **im — mit** or **zu** compared with or to; **v—bar** a comparable; **v—en** irreg vt compare; vr reach a settlement.

vergnügen [fɛr'gnyːgən] vr enjoy or amuse o.s.; **V— nt -s, -** pleasure; **viel V—!** enjoy yourself

vergnügt [fɛr'gnyːkt] a cheerful.

Vergnügung f pleasure, amusement; **—spark** m amusement park; **v—ssüchtig** a pleasure-loving.

vergolden [fɛr'gɔldən] vt gild.

ver'gönnen vt grant.

vergöttern [fɛr'gœtərn] vt idolize.

ver'graben vt bury.

ver'greifen vr irreg: **sich an jdm — lay hands on sb; sich an etw — misappropriate sth; sich im Ton — say the wrong thing.

vergriffen [fɛr'grɪfən] a Buch out of print; Ware out of stock.

vergrößern [fɛr'grøːsərn] vt enlarge; (mengenmäßig) increase; (Lupe) magnify.

Vergrößerung f enlargement; increase; magnification; **—sglas** nt magnifying glass.

Vergünstigung [fɛr'gynstɪgʊŋ] f concession, privilege.

vergüten [fɛr'gyːtən] vt: **jdm etw — compensate sb for sth.

Vergütung f compensation.

verhaften [fɛr'haftən] vt arrest.

Verhaftete(r) mf prisoner.

Verhaftung f arrest; **—sbefehl** m warrant (for arrest).

ver'hallen vi die away.

ver'halten irreg vr be, stand; (sich benehmen) behave; (Math) be in proportion to; vt hold or keep back; Schritt check; **V— nt -s** behaviour; **V—sforschung** f behavioural science; **V—smaßregel** f rule of conduct.

Verhältnis [fɛr'hɛltnɪs] nt -ses, -se relationship; (Math) proportion, ratio; pl (Umstände) conditions pl; **über seine — se leben** live beyond one's means; **v—mäßig** a, ad relative(ly), comparative(ly).

verhandeln [fɛr'handəln] vi negotiate (über etw (acc) sth); (Jur) hold proceedings; vt discuss; (Jur) hear.

Verhandlung f negotiation; (Jur) proceedings pl.

ver'hängen vt (fig) impose, inflict.

Verhängnis [fɛr'hɛŋnɪs] nt -ses, -se fate, doom; **jdm zum — werden** be sb's undoing; **v—voll** a fatal, disastrous.

verharmlosen [fɛr'harmloːzən] vt make light of, play down.

verharren [fɛr'harən] vi remain; (hartnäckig) persist.

ver'härten [fɛr'hɛrtən] vr harden.

verhaßt [fɛr'hast] a odious, hateful.

verheerend [fɛr'heːrənt] a disastrous, devastating.

verhehlen [fɛr'heːlən] vt conceal.

ver'heilen vi heal.

verheimlichen [fɛr'haɪmlɪçən] vt keep secret (jdm from sb).

verheiratet [fɛr'haraːtət] a married.

ver'heißen vt irreg: **jdm etw — promise sb sth.

ver'helfen vi irreg: **jdm — zu help sb to get.

verherrlichen [fer'hɛrlɪçən] *vt* glorify.

ver'hexen *vt* bewitch; **es ist wie verhext** it's jinxed.

ver'hindern *vt* prevent; **verhindert sein** be unable to make it.

Ver'hinderung *f* prevention.

verhöhnen [fer'hø:nən] *vt* mock, sneer at.

Verhör [fer'hø:r] *nt* -(e)s, -e interrogation; *(gerichtlich)* (cross-)examination; **v—en** *vt* interrogate; (cross-)examine; *vr* misunderstand, mishear.

ver'hungern *vi* starve, die of hunger.

ver'hüten *vt* prevent, avert.

Ver'hütung *f* prevention; **—smittel** *nt* contraceptive.

verirren [fer'ɪrən] *vr* go astray.

ver'jagen *vt* drive away or out.

verjüngen [fer'jyŋən] *vt* rejuvenate; *vr* taper.

verkalken [fer'kalkən] *vi* calcify; *(col)* become senile.

verkalkulieren [fɛrkalku'li:rən] *vr* miscalculate.

verkannt [fer'kant] *a* unappreciated.

Verkauf [fer'kauf] *m* sale; **v—en** *vt* sell.

Verkäufer(in *f)* [fer'kɔyfər(ɪn)] *m* -s, - seller; salesman; *(in Laden)* shop assistant.

verkäuflich [fer'kɔyflɪç] *a* saleable.

Verkehr [fer'ke:r] *m* -s, -e traffic; *(Umgang, esp sexuell)* intercourse; *(Umlauf)* circulation; **v—en** *vi (Fahrzeug)* ply, run; *(besuchen)* visit regularly *(bei jdm sb)*; **v—en mit** associate with; *vtr* turn, transform; **—sampel** *f* traffic lights *pl*; **—sdelikt** *nt* traffic offence; **—sinsel** *f* traffic island;

—sstockung *f* traffic jam, stoppage; **—sunfall** *m* traffic accident; **—swidrig** *a* contrary to traffic regulations; **—szeichen** *nt* traffic sign; **v—t** *a* wrong; *(umgekehrt)* the wrong way round.

ver'kennen *vt irreg* misjudge, not appreciate.

ver'klagen *vt* take to court.

verklären [fer'klɛ:rən] *vt* transfigure; **verklärt lächeln** smile radiantly.

ver'kleben *vt* glue up, stick; *vi* stick together.

verkleiden [fer'klaidən] *vtr* disguise (o.s.), dress up.

Verkleidung *f* disguise; *(Archit)* wainscoting.

verkleinern [fer'klainərn] *vt* make smaller, reduce in size.

verklemmt [fer'klɛmt] *a* *(fig)* inhibited.

ver'klingen *vi irreg* die away.

ver'kneifen *vt (col)* : **sich** *(dat)* **etw — Lachen** stifle; *Schmerz* hide; *(sich versagen)* do without.

verknüpfen [fer'knypfən] *vt* tie (up), knot; *(fig)* connect.

Verknüpfung *f* connection.

verkohlen [fer'ko:lən] *vti* carbonize; *vt (col)* fool.

ver'kommen *vi irreg* deteriorate, decay; *(Mensch)* go downhill, come down in the world; *a (moralisch)* dissolute, depraved; **V—heit** *f* depravity.

verkörpern [fer'kœrpərn] *vt* embody, personify.

verköstigen [fer'kœstɪgən] *vt* feed.

verkraften [fer'kraftən] *vt* cope with.

ver'kriechen *vr irreg* creep away, creep into a corner.

verkrümmt [fɛr'krymt] a crooked.
Verkrümmung f bend, warp; _(Anat)_ curvature.
verkrüppelt [fɛr'krypəlt] a crippled.
verkrustet [fɛr'krʊstət] a encrusted.
ver'kühlen vr get a chill.
ver'kümmern vi waste away.
verkünden [fɛr'kʏndən] vt proclaim; _Urteil_ pronounce.
verkürzen [fɛr'kʏrtsən] vt shorten; _Wort_ abbreviate; **sich** _(dat)_ **die Zeit** — while away the time.
Verkürzung f shortening; abbreviation.
ver'laden vt _irreg_ load.
Verlag [fɛr'la:k] m -(e)s, -e publishing firm.
verlangen [fɛr'laŋən] vt demand; desire; — **Sie Herrn X** ask for Mr X; vi — **nach** ask for, desire; V— nt -s, - desire _(nach for)_; **auf jds V—** (hin) at sb's request.
verlängern [fɛr'lɛŋərn] vt extend; _(länger machen)_ lengthen.
Verlängerung f extension; _(Sport)_ extra time; **—sschnur** f extension cable.
verlangsamen [fɛr'laŋza:mən] vtr decelerate, slow down.
Verlaß [fɛr'las] m: **auf ihn/das ist kein** — he/it cannot be relied upon.
ver'lassen irreg vt leave; vr depend _(auf +acc on)_; **Mensch** abandoned; **V—heit** f loneliness.
verläßlich [fɛr'lɛslɪç] a reliable.
Verlauf [fɛr'laʊf] m course; v—**en** irreg vi _(zeitlich)_ pass; _(Farben)_ **run**; vr get lost; _(Menschenmenge)_ disperse.

ver'lauten vi: **etw — lassen** disclose sth; **wie verlautet** as reported.
ver'leben vt spend.
verlebt [fɛr'le:pt] a dissipated, worn out.
ver'legen vt move; _(verlieren)_ mislay; _(abspielen lassen)_ Handlung set _(nach in)_; _Buch_ publish; vr: **sich auf etw** _(acc)_ — take up or to sth; a embarrassed; **nicht — um** never at a loss for; **V—heit** f embarrassment; _(Situation)_ difficulty, scrape.
Verleger [fɛr'le:gər] m -s, - publisher.
Verleih [fɛr'laɪ] m -(e)s, -e hire service; v—**en** vt irreg lend; _Kraft, Anschein_ confer, bestow; _Preis, Medaille_ award; **—ung** f lending; bestowal; award.
ver'leiten vt lead astray; — **zu** talk into, tempt into.
ver'lernen vt forget, unlearn.
ver'lesen irreg vt read out; _(aussondern)_ sort out; vr make a mistake in reading.
verletz- [fɛr'lɛts] cpd: **—bar** a vulnerable; **—en** vt _(lit, fig)_ injure, hurt; _Gesetz etc_ violate; **—end** a _(fig)_ **Worte** hurtful; **—lich** a vulnerable, sensitive; **V—te(r)** mf injured person; **V—ung** f injury; _(Verstoß)_ violation, infringement.
ver'leugnen vt deny; **Menschen** disown.
Verleugnung f denial.
verleumd- [fɛr'lɔʏmd] cpd: **—en** vt slander; **—erisch** a slanderous; **V—ung** f slander, libel.
ver'lieben vr fall in love _(in jdn with sb)_.
verliebt [fɛr'li:pt] a in love; **V—heit** f being in love.
verlieren [fɛr'li:rən] irreg vti lose;

vr get lost; *(verschwinden)* disappear.

verlob- [fɛr'lo:b] *cpd:* —en vr get engaged *(mit* to); **V—te(r)** [fɛr'lo:ptə(r)] *mf* fiancé(e); **V—ung** *f* engagement.

ver'locken *vt* entice, lure.

Ver'lockung *f* temptation, attraction.

verlogen [fɛr'lo:gən] a untruthful; **V—heit** *f* untruthfulness.

verloren [fɛr'lo:rən] a lost; *Eier* poached; der —e Sohn the prodigal son; etw — geben give sth up for lost; —gehen *vi irreg* get lost.

verlosen [fɛr'lo:zən] *vt* raffle, draw lots for.

Verlosung *f* raffle, lottery.

verlottern [fɛr'lɔtərn], **verludern** [fɛr'lu:dərn] *vi (col)* go to the dogs.

Verlust [fɛr'lʊst] *m* -(e)s, -e loss; *(Mil)* casualty.

ver'machen *vt* bequeath, leave.

Vermächtnis [fɛr'mɛçtnɪs] *nt* -ses, -se legacy.

vermählen [fɛr'mɛːlən] *vr* marry.

Vermählung *f* wedding, marriage.

vermehren [fɛr'me:rən] *vtr* multiply; *(Menge)* increase.

Vermehrung *f* multiplying; increase.

ver'meiden *vt irreg* avoid.

vermeintlich [fɛr'maɪntlɪç] a supposed.

vermengen [fɛr'mɛŋən] *vtr* mix; *(fig)* mix up, confuse.

Vermerk [fɛr'mɛrk] *m* -(e)s, -e note; *(in Ausweis)* endorsement; **v—en** *vt* note.

ver'messen *irreg vt* survey; *vr (falsch messen)* measure incorrectly; a presumptuous, bold; **V—heit** *f* presumptuousness; recklessness.

Ver'messung *f* survey(ing).

ver'mieten *vt* let, rent (out); *Auto* hire out, rent.

Ver'mieter(in *f)* *m* -s, - landlord/landlady.

Ver'mietung *f* letting, renting (out); *(von Autos)* hiring (out).

vermindern [fɛr'mɪndərn] *vtr* lessen, decrease; *Preise* reduce.

Verminderung *f* reduction.

ver'mischen *vtr* mix, blend.

vermissen [fɛr'mɪsən] *vt* miss.

vermißt [fɛr'mɪst] a missing.

vermitteln [fɛr'mɪtəln] *vi* mediate; *vt Gespräch* connect; jdm etw — help sb to obtain sth.

Vermittler [fɛr'mɪtlər] *m* -s, - *(Schlichter)* agent, mediator.

Vermittlung *f* procurement; *(Stellen-)* agency; *(Tel)* exchange; *(Schlichtung)* mediation.

ver'mögen *vt irreg* be capable of; — zu be able to; **V—** *nt* -s, - wealth; *(Fähigkeit)* ability; ein **V—** kosten cost a fortune; **—d** a wealthy.

vermuten [fɛr'mu:tən] *vt* suppose, guess; *(argwöhnen)* suspect.

vermutlich a supposed, presumed; ad probably.

Vermutung *f* supposition; suspicion.

vernachlässigen [fɛr'na:xlɛsɪgən] *vt* neglect.

vernarben [fɛr'narbən] *vi* heal up.

ver'nehmen *vt irreg* perceive, hear; *(erfahren)* learn; *(Jur)* (cross-)examine; dem **V—** nach from what I/we etc hear.

vernehmlich [fɛr'ne:mlɪç] a audible.

Vernehmung *f* (cross-)examination; **v—sfähig** a in a condition to be (cross-)examined.

verneigen [fɛr'naɪgən] vr bow.

verneinen [fɛr'naɪnən] vt Frage answer in the negative; (ablehnen) deny; (Gram) negate; **—d** a negative.

Verneinung f negation.

vernichten [fɛr'nɪçtən] vt annihilate, destroy; **—d** a (fig) crushing; Blick withering; Kritik scathing.

Vernichtung f destruction, annihilation.

verniedlichen [fɛr'niːtlɪçən] vt play down.

Vernunft [fɛr'nʊnft] f - reason, understanding.

vernünftig [fɛr'nʏnftɪç] a sensible, reasonable.

veröden [fɛr'øːdən] vi become desolate; vt (Med) remove.

veröffentlichen [fɛr'œfəntlɪçən] vt publish.

Veröffentlichung f publication.

verordnen [fɛr'ɔrdnən] vt (Med) prescribe.

Verordnung f order, decree; (Med) prescription.

ver'pachten vt lease (out).

ver'packen vt pack.

Ver'packung f, **—smaterial** nt packing, wrapping.

ver'passen vt miss; jdm eine Ohrfeige **—** (col) give sb a clip round the ear.

verpesten [fɛr'pɛstən] vt pollute.

ver'pflanzen vt transplant.

Ver'pflanzung f transplant(ing).

ver'pflegen vt feed, cater for.

Ver'pflegung f feeding, catering; (Kost) food; (in Hotel) board.

verpflichten [fɛr'pflɪçtən] vt oblige, bind; (anstellen) engage; vr undertake; (Mil) sign on; vi carry obligations; jdm zu Dank verpflichtet sein be obliged to sb.

Verpflichtung f obligation, duty.

ver'pfuschen vt (col) bungle, make a mess of.

verplempern [fɛr'plɛmpərn] vt (col) waste.

verpönt [fɛr'pøːnt] a disapproved (of), taboo.

verprassen [fɛr'prasən] vt squander.

ver'prügeln vt (col) beat up, do over.

Verputz [fɛr'pʊts] m plaster, roughcast; **v—en** vt plaster; (col) Essen put away.

verquollen [fɛr'kvɔlən] a swollen; Holz warped.

verrammeln [fɛr'raməln] vt barricade.

Verrat [fɛr'raːt] m -(e)s treachery; (Pol) treason; **v—en** irreg vt betray; Geheimnis divulge; vr give o.s. away.

Verräter [fɛr'rɛːtər] m -s, - traitor; **—in** f traitress; **v—isch** a treacherous.

ver'rechnen vt: **—** mit set off against; vr miscalculate.

Verrechnungsscheck [fɛr'rɛçnʊŋs-ʃɛk] m crossed cheque.

verregnet [fɛr'reːgnət] a spoilt by rain, rainy.

ver'reisen vi go away (on a journey).

ver'reißen vt irreg pull to pieces.

verrenken [fɛr'rɛŋkən] vt contort; (Med) dislocate; sich (dat) den Knöchel **—** sprain one's ankle.

Verrenkung f contortion; (Med) dislocation, sprain.

ver'richten vt do, perform.

verriegeln [fɛr'riːgəln] vt bolt up, lock.

verringern [fɛr'rɪŋərn] vt reduce; vr diminish.

Verringerung f reduction; lessening.

ver'rinnen vi irreg run out or away; (Zeit) elapse.

ver'rosten vi rust.

verrotten [fɛr'rɔtən] vi rot.

ver'rücken vt move, shift.

verrückt [fɛr'rʏkt] a crazy, mad; V—e(r) mf lunatic; V—heit f madness, lunacy.

Verruf [fɛr'ru:f] m: in — geraten/bringen fall/bring into disrepute; v—en a notorious, disreputable.

Vers [fɛrs] m -es, -e verse.

ver'sagen vt: jdm/sich (dat) etw — deny sb/o.s. sth; vi fail; V— nt -s failure.

Versager [fɛr'za:gər] m -s, - failure.

ver'salzen vt irreg put too much salt in; (fig) spoil.

ver'sammeln vtr assemble, gather.

Ver'sammlung f meeting, gathering.

Versand [fɛr'zant] m -(e)s forwarding; dispatch; (—abteilung) dispatch department; (—haus nt mail-order firm.

versäumen [fɛr'zɔymən] vt miss; (unterlassen) neglect, fail.

Versäumnis f -, -se neglect; omission.

ver'schaffen vt: jdm/sich etw — get or procure sth for sb/o.s.

verschämt [fɛr'ʃɛ:mt] a bashful.

verschandeln [fɛr'ʃandəln] vt (col) spoil.

verschanzen [fɛr'ʃantsən] vr: sich hinter etw (dat) — dig in behind sth; (fig) take refuge behind.

verschärfen [fɛr'ʃɛrfən] vtr intensify; Lage aggravate.

ver'schätzen vr be out in one's reckoning.

ver'schenken vt give away.

verscherzen [fɛr'ʃɛrtsən] vt: sich (dat) etw — lose sth, throw away sth.

verscheuchen [fɛr'ʃɔʏçən] vt frighten away.

ver'schicken vt send off; Sträfling transport, deport.

ver'schieben vt irreg shift; (Rail) shunt; Termin postpone; (Comm) push.

Ver'schiebung f shift, displacement; shunting; postponement.

verschieden [fɛr'ʃi:dən] a different; (pl: mehrere) various; ,sie sind — groß they are of different sizes; —e pl various people/things pl; —es pron various things pl; etwas —es something different; —artig a various, of different kinds; zwei so —artige — two such differing —; V—heit f difference; —tlich ad several times.

verschlafen [fɛr'ʃla:fən] irreg vt sleep through; (fig: versäumen) miss; vir oversleep; a sleepy.

Verschlag [fɛr'ʃla:k] m shed; v—en [fɛr'ʃla:gən] vt irreg board up; (Tennis) hit out of play; Buchseite lose; jdm den Atem v—en take sb's breath away; an einen Ort v—en werden wind up in a place; a cunning.

verschlampen [fɛr'ʃlampən] vi fall into neglect; vt lose, mislay.

verschlechtern [fɛr'ʃlɛçtərn] vt make worse; vr deteriorate, get worse.

Verschlechterung f deterioration.

Verschleierung [fɛr'ʃlaɪərʊŋ] f veiling; (fig) concealment; (Mil) screening; —staktik f smoke-screen tactics pl.

Verschleiß [fɛr'ʃlaɪs] *m* -es, -e
wear and tear; *(Aus)* retail trade;
v—en *irreg vt* wear out; retail; *vir*
wear out.

ver'schleppen *vt* carry off,
abduct; *(zeitlich)* drag out, delay.

ver'schleudern *vt* squander;
(Comm) sell dirt-cheap.

verschließ- [fɛr'ʃliːs] *cpd:* —bar a
lockable; —en *irreg vt* close; lock;
vr sich einer Sache — in close one's
mind to sth.

verschlimmern [fɛr'ʃlɪmɐn] *vt*
make worse, aggravate; *vr* get
worse, deteriorate.

Verschlimmerung *f* deterioration.

verschlingen [fɛr'ʃlɪŋən] *vt irreg*
devour, swallow up; *Fäden* twist.

verschlossen [fɛr'ʃlɔsən] *a*
locked; *(fig)* reserved; **V—heit** *f*
reserve.

ver'schlucken *vt* swallow; *vr*
choke.

Verschluß [fɛr'ʃlus] *m* lock; *(von
Kleid etc)* fastener; *(Phot)* shutter;
(Stöpsel) plug; **unter — halten**
keep under lock and key.

verschlüsseln [fɛr'ʃlʏsəln] *vt*
encode.

verschmähen [fɛr'ʃmɛːən] *vt* disdain, scorn.

ver'schmelzen *vti irreg* merge,
blend.

verschmerzen [fɛr'ʃmɛrtsən] *vt*
get over.

verschmutzen [fɛr'ʃmutsən] *vt*
soil; *Umwelt* pollute.

verschneit [fɛr'ʃnaɪt] *a* snowed up,
covered in snow.

verschnüren [fɛr'ʃnyːrən] *vt* tie up.

verschollen [fɛr'ʃɔlən] *a* lost,
missing.

ver'schonen *vt* spare *(jdn mit etw
sb sth)*

verschönern [fɛr'ʃøːnɐn] *vt*
decorate; *(verbessern)* improve.

verschränken [fɛr'ʃrɛŋkən] *vt*
cross, fold.

ver'schreiben *irreg vt Papier* use
up; *(Med)* prescribe; *vr* make a
mistake (in writing); **sich einer
Sache —** devote oneself to sth.

verschrien [fɛr'ʃriːən] *a* notorious.

verschroben [fɛr'ʃroːbən] *a*
eccentric, odd.

verschrotten [fɛr'ʃrɔtən] *vt* scrap.

verschüchtert [fɛr'ʃʏçtɐt] *a* sub-
dued, intimidated.

verschuld- [fɛr'ʃuld] *cpd:* —en *vt*
be guilty of; **V—en** *nt* -s fault,
guilt; —et *a* in debt; **V—ung** *f*
fault; *(Geld)* debts *pl.*

ver'schütten *vt* spill; *(zuschütten)*
fill; *(unter Trümmer)* bury.

ver'schweigen *vt irreg* keep
secret; **jdm etw —** keep sth from
sb.

verschwend- [fɛr'ʃvɛnd] *cpd:* —en
vt squander; **V—er** *m* -s, - spend-
thrift; —erisch *a* wasteful, extravagant; **V—ung** *f* waste; extravagance.

verschwiegen [fɛr'ʃviːgən] *a*
discreet; *Ort* secluded; **V—heit** *f*
discretion; seclusion.

ver'schwimmen *vi irreg* grow
hazy, become blurred.

ver'schwinden *vi irreg* disappear,
vanish; **V— nt** -s disappearance.

ver'schwitzen *vt* stain with
sweat; *(col)* forget.

verschwommen [fɛr'ʃvɔmən] *a*
hazy, vague.

verschwör- [fɛr'ʃvøːr] *cpd:* —en
vr irreg plot, conspire; **V—er** *m* -s,
- conspirator; **V—ung** *f* conspiracy,
plot.

ver'sehen *irreg vt* supply, provide; Pflicht carry out; Amt fill; Haushalt keep; *vr* (fig) make a mistake; ehe er (es) sich — hatte ... before he knew it ...; V— *nt* -s, — oversight; aus V— by mistake; —tlich *ad* by mistake.

Versehrte(r) [fɛrˈzeːrtə(r)] *mf* disabled person.

ver'senden *vt irreg* forward, dispatch.

ver'senken *vt* sink; *vr* become engrossed (*in* +acc in).

ver'sessen *a*: — auf (+acc) mad about.

ver'setzen *vt* transfer; (verpfänden) pawn; (col) stand up; jdm einen Tritt/Schlag — kick/hit sb; etw mit etw — mix sth with sth; jdn in gute Laune — put sb in a good mood; *vr*: sich in jdn or in jds Lage — put o.s. in sb's place.

Ver'setzung *f* transfer.

ver'seuchen [fɛrˈzɔʏçən] *vt* contaminate.

ver'sichern [fɛrˈzɪçərn] *vt* assure; (mit Geld) insure; *vr* sich — (+gen) make sure of.

Versicherung *f* assurance; insurance; —spolice *f* insurance policy.

ver'siegeln [fɛrˈziːɡəln] *vt* seal (up).

ver'siegen *vi* dry up.

ver'sinken *vi irreg* sink.

ver'söhnen [fɛrˈzøːnən] *vt* reconcile; *vr* become reconciled.

Ver'söhnung *f* reconciliation.

ver'sorgen *vt* provide, supply (mit with); Familie etc look after; *vr* look after o.s.

Ver'sorgung *f* provision, (Unterhalt) maintenance; (Alters— etc) benefit, assistance.

ver'späten [fɛrˈʃpɛːtən] *vr* be late.

Ver'spätung *f* delay; — haben be late.

ver'sperren *vt* bar, obstruct.

Ver'sperrung *f* barrier.

ver'spielen *vt* lose.

ver'spielt [fɛrˈʃpiːlt] *a* playful; bei jdm — haben be in sb's bad books.

ver'spotten *vt* ridicule, scoff at.

ver'sprechen *irreg vt* promise; sich (dat) etw von etw — expect sth from sth; V— *nt* -s, — promise.

ver'staatlichen [fɛrˈʃtaːtlɪçən] *vt* nationalize.

Verstand [fɛrˈʃtant] *m* intelligence; mind; den — verlieren go out of one's mind; über jds — gehen go beyond sb; v—esmäßig *a* rational; intellectual.

ver'ständig [fɛrˈʃtɛndɪç] *a* sensible; —en [fɛrˈʃtɛndɪɡən] *vt* inform; *vr* communicate; (sich einigen) come to an understanding; V—keit *f* good sense; V—ung *f* communication; (Benachrichtigung) informing; (Einigung) agreement.

verständ- [fɛrˈʃtɛnt] *cpd*: —lich *a* understandable, comprehensible; V—lichkeit *f* clarity, intelligibility; V—nis *nt* -ses, -se understanding; —nislos *a* uncomprehending; —nisvoll *a* understanding, sympathetic.

verstärk- [fɛrˈʃtɛrk] *cpd*: —en *vt* strengthen; *Ton* amplify; (erhöhen) intensify; *vr* intensify; V—er *m* -s, — amplifier; V—ung *f* strengthening; (Hilfe) reinforcements *pl*; (von Ton) amplification.

ver'stauchen [fɛrˈʃtaʊxən] *vt* sprain.

ver'stauen [fɛrˈʃtaʊən] *vt* stow away.

Versteck [fɛrˈʃtɛk] *nt* -(e)s, -e hiding (place); v—en *vtr* hide;

—spiel *nt* hide-and-seek; **v—t** *a* hidden.

ver'stehen *irreg vt* understand; **vr** get on.

versteifen [fɛr'ʃtaɪfən] *vt* stiffen, brace; *vr (fig)* insist (auf *+acc* on).

versteigern [fɛr'ʃtaɪgərn] *vt* auction.

Versteigerung *f* auction.

verstell- [fɛr'ʃtɛl] *cpd:* **—bar** *a* adjustable, variable; **—en** *vt* move, shift; *Uhr* adjust; `(versperren)` block; *(fig)* disguise; *vr* pretend, put on an act; **V—ung** *f* pretence.

verstiegen [fɛr'ʃtiːgən] *a* exaggerated.

verstimmt [fɛr'ʃtɪmt] *a* out of tune; *(fig)* cross, put out.

verstockt [fɛr'ʃtɔkt] *a* stubborn; **V—heit** *f* stubbornness.

verstohlen [fɛr'ʃtoːlən] *a* stealthy.

verstopfen *vt* block, stop up; *(Med)* constipate.

Ver'stopfung *f* obstruction; *(Med)* constipation.

verstorben [fɛr'ʃtɔrbən] *a* deceased, late.

verstört [fɛr'ʃtøːrt] *a* Mensch distraught.

Verstoß [fɛr'ʃtoːs] *m* infringement, violation (gegen of); **v—en** *irreg vt* disown, reject; *vi:* **v—en gegen** offend against.

ver'streichen *irreg vt* spread; *vi* elapse.

ver'streuen *vt* scatter (about).

ver'stricken *vt (fig)* entangle, ensnare; *vr* get entangled (in *+acc* ·in).

verstümmeln [fɛr'ʃtʏməln] *vt* maim, mutilate *(auch fig)*.

verstummen [fɛr'ʃtʊmən] *vi* go silent; *(Lärm)* die away.

Versuch [fɛr'zuːx] *m* **-(e)s, -e** attempt; *(Sci)* experiment; **v—en** *vt* try; *(verlocken)* tempt; *vr:* sich an etw *(dat)* **v—en** try one's hand at sth; **—skaninchen** *nt* guineapig; **v—sweise** *ad* tentatively; **—ung** *f* temptation.

versunken [fɛr'zʊŋkən] *a* sunken; **— sein** in *(+acc)* be absorbed or engrossed in.

versüßen [fɛr'zyːsən] *vt:* jdm` etw **—** *(fig)* make sth more pleasant for sb.

vertagen [fɛr'taːgən] *vti* adjourn.

Vertagung *f* adjournment.

ver'tauschen *vt* exchange; *(versehentlich)* mix up.

verteidig- [fɛr'taɪdɪg] *cpd:* **—en** *vt* defend; **V—er** *m* **-s, -** defender; *(Jur)* defence counsel; **V—ung** *f* defence.

ver'teilen `vt` distribute; *Rollen* assign; *Salbe* spread.

Verteilung *f* distribution, allotment.

verteufelt [fɛr'tɔʏfəlt] *a,ad (col)* awful(ly), devilish(ly).

vertiefen [fɛr'tiːfən] *vt* deepen; *vr:* sich in etw *(acc)* **—** become engrossed or absorbed in sth.

Vertiefung *f* depression.

vertikal [vɛrti'kaːl] *a* vertical.

vertilgen [fɛr'tɪlgən] *vt* exterminate; *(col)* eat up, consume.

vertippen [fɛr'tɪpən] *vr* make a typing mistake.

vertonen [fɛr'toːnən] *vt* set to music.

Vertrag [fɛr'traːk] *m* **-(e)s, ⁼e** contract, agreement; *(Pol)* treaty; **v—en** [fɛr'taːgən] *irreg vt* tolerate, stand; *vr* get along; *(sich aussöhnen)* become reconciled; **v—lich** *a* contractual.

verträglich [fɛr'trɛːklɪç] a good-natured, sociable; *Speisen* easily digested; *(Med)* easily tolerated; **V—keit** f sociability; good nature; digestibility.

Vertrags— cpd: **—bruch** m breach of contract; **v—brüchig** a in breach of contract; **v—mäßig** a,ad stipulated, according to contract; **—partner** m party to a contract; **—spieler** m *(Sport)* contract professional; **v—widrig** a contrary to contract.

vertrauen [fɛr'trauən] vi trust *(jdm sb)*, **—** auf *(+acc)* rely on; **V—nt** -s confidence; **—erweckend** a inspiring trust; **—sselig** a too trustful; **—svoll** a trustful; **—swürdig** a trustworthy.

vertraulich [fɛr'traulɪç] a familiar; *(geheim)* confidential; **V—keit** f familiarity; confidentiality.

vertraut [fɛr'traut] a familiar; **V—e(r)** mf confidant, close friend; **V—heit** f familiarity.

ver'treiben vt irreg drive away; *(aus Land)* expel; *(Comm)* sell; *Zeit* pass.

Ver'treibung f expulsion.

vertret— [fɛr'treːt] cpd: **—en** vt irreg represent; *Ansicht* hold, advocate; **sich** *(dat)* **die Beine —en** stretch one's legs; **V—er** m -s, **—** representative; *(Verfechter)* advocate; **V—ung** f representation; advocacy.

Vertrieb [fɛr'triːp] m -(e)s, -e marketing.

ver'trocknen vi dry up.

ver'trödeln vt *(col)* fritter away.

ver'trösten vt put off.

vertun [fɛr'tuːn] irreg vt *(col)* waste; vr make a mistake.

vertuschen [fɛr'tuʃən] vt hush or cover up.

verübeln [fɛr'yːbəln] vt: jdm etw **—** be cross or offended with sb on account of sth.

verüben [fɛr'yːbən] vt commit.

verun— [fɛr'un] cpd: **—glimpfen** [-glɪmpfən] vt disparage; **—glücken** [-glʏkən] vi have an accident; **tödlich —glücken** be killed in an accident; **—reinigen** vt soil; *Umwelt* pollute; **—sichern** vt rattle; **—stalten** [-ʃtaltən] vt disfigure; *Gebäude etc* deface; **—treuen** [-trɔyən] vt embezzle.

verur— [fɛr'uːr] cpd: **—sachen** [-zaxən] vt cause; **—teilen** [-tailən] vt condemn; **V—teilung** f condemnation; *(Jur)* sentence.

verviel— [fɛr'fiːl] cpd: **—fachen** [-faxən] vt multiply; **—fältigen** [-fɛltɪgən] vt duplicate, copy; **V—fältigung** f duplication, copying.

vervoll— [fɛr'fɔl] cpd: **—kommnen** [-kɔmnən] vt perfect; **—ständigen** [-ʃtɛndɪgən] vt complete.

ver'wackeln vt *Photo* blur.

ver'wählen vr *(Tel)* dial the wrong number.

verwahr— [fɛr'vaːr] cpd: **—en** vt keep, lock away; vr protest; **—losen** [-loːzən] vi become neglected; *(moralisch)* go to the bad; **—lost** [-loːst] a neglected; wayward.

verwaist [fɛr'vaist] a orphaned.

verwalt— [fɛr'valt] cpd: **—en** vt manage; administer; **V—er** m -s, **—** manager; *(Vermögens—)* trustee; **V—ung** f administration; management; **V—ungsbezirk** m administrative district.

ver'wandeln vtr change, transform.

Ver'wandlung f change, transformation.

verwandt -[fɛr'vant] a related *(mit* to); **V—e(r)** mf relative, relation;

V—**schaft** f relationship;
(Menschen) relations pl.

ver'**warnen** vt caution.

Ver'**warnung** f caution.

ver'**waschen** a faded; *(fig)* vague.

ver**wässern** [fɛr'vɛsərn] vt dilute,
water down. .

ver'**wechseln** vt confuse *(mit*
with); mistake *(mit* for); zum V—
ähnlich as like as two peas.

Ver'**wechslung** f confusion,
mixing up.

ver**wegen** [fɛr've:gən] a daring,
bold; V—**heit** f daring, audacity,
boldness.

Ver**wehung** [fɛr've:ʊŋ] f snow-/
sanddrift.

ver**weichlich**- [fɛr'vaiçlɪç] cpd:
—**en** vt mollycoddle; —**t** a
effeminate, soft.

ver'**weigern** vt refuse *(jdm etw* sb
sth); den Gehorsam/die Aussage
— refuse to obey/testify.

Ver'**weigerung** f refusal.

ver**weilen**-[fɛr'vailən] vi stay; *(fig)*
dwell *(bei* on).

Ver**weis** [fɛr'vais] m -es, -e reprimand, rebuke; *(Hinweis)*
reference; v—**en** [fɛr'vaizən] vt
irreg refer; jdm etw v—**en** *(tadeln)*
scold sb for sth; jdn von der Schule
v—**en** expel sb (from school); jdn
des Landes v—**en** deport or expel
sb; —**ung** f reference; *(Tadel)*
reprimand; *(Landes—)* deportation.

ver'**welken** vi fade.

ver'**wenden** *irreg* vt use; Mühe,
Zeit, Arbeit spend; vr intercede.

Ver'**wendung** f use.

ver'**werfen** vt *irreg* reject.

ver**werflich** [fɛr'vɛrflɪç] a reprehensible.

ver'**werten** vt utilize.

Ver'**wertung** f utilization.

ver**wesen** [fɛr've:zən] vi decay.

Ver**wesung** f decomposition.

ver'**wickeln** vt tangle (up); *(fig)*
involve *(in +acc* in); vr get tangled
(up); **sich — in** *(+acc)* *(fig)* get
involved in.

Ver**wicklung** f complication,
entanglement.

ver**wildern** [fɛr'vɪldərn] vi run wild.

ver'**winden** vt *irreg* get over.

ver**wirklichen** [fɛr'vɪrklɪçən] vt
realize, put into effect.

Ver**wirklichung** f realization.

ver**wirren** [fɛr'vɪrən] vt tangle
(up); *(fig)* confuse.

Ver**wirrung** f confusion.

ver**wittern** [fɛr'vɪtərn] vi weather.

ver**witwet** [fɛr'vɪtvət] a widowed.

ver**wöhnen** [fɛr'vø:nən] vt spoil.

Ver**wöhnung** f spoiling,
pampering.

ver**worfen** [fɛr'vɔrfən] a depraved;
V—**heit** f depravity.

ver**worren** [fɛr'vɔrən] a confused.

ver**wund**- cpd: —**bar** [fɛr'vʊntba:r]
a vulnerable; —**en** [fɛr'vʊndən] vt
wound; —**erlich** [fɛr'vʊndərlɪç] a
surprising; V—**ete(r)** mf injured (person);
[fɛr'vʊndərʊŋ] f astonishment;
V—**ung** f wound, injury.

ver**wünschen** vt curse.

ver**wüsten** [fɛr'vy:stən] vt
devastate.

Ver**wüstung** f devastation.

ver**zagen** [fɛr'tsa:gən] vi despair.

ver'**zahlen** vr miscount.

ver**zehren** [fɛr'tse:rən] vt consume.

ver'**zeichnen** vt list; Niederlage,
Verlust register.

Verzeichnis [fɛr'tsaiçnɪs] nt -ses,
•se list, catalogue; *(in Buch)* index.

verzeih- [fɛrˈtsaɪ] *cpd:* **—en** *vti irreg* forgive (*jdm etw sb* for sth); **—lich** *a* pardonable; **V—ung** *f* forgiveness, pardon; **V—ung!** sorry!, excuse me!

ver'zerren *vt* distort.

Verzicht [fɛrˈtsɪçt] *m* **-(e)s, -e** renunciation (*auf +acc* of); **v—en** *vi* forgo, give up (*auf etw (acc)* sth).

ver'ziehen *irreg vi* move; *vt* put out of shape; *Kind* spoil; *Pflanzen* thin out; **das Gesicht —** pull a face; *vr* go out of shape; *(Gesicht)* contort; *(verschwinden)* disappear.

verzieren [fɛrˈtsiːrən] *vt* decorate, ornament.

verzinsen [fɛrˈtsɪnzən] *vt* pay interest on.

ver'zögern *vt* delay.

Ver'zögerung *f* delay, time-lag; **—staktik** *f* delaying tactics *pl.*

verzollen [fɛrˈtsɔlən] *vt* declare, pay duty on.

verzück- [fɛrˈtsyk] *cpd:* **—en** *vt* send into ecstasies, enrapture; **—t** *a* enraptured; **V—ung** *f* ecstasy.

verzweif- [fɛrˈtsvaɪf] *cpd:* **—eln** *vi* despair; **—elt** *a* desperate; **V—lung** *f* despair.

verzweigen [fɛrˈtsvaɪgən] *vr* branch out.

verzwickt [fɛrˈtsvɪkt] *a* (*col*) awkward, complicated.

Veto [ˈveːto] *nt* **-s, -s** veto.

Vetter [ˈfɛtər] *m* **-s, -n** cousin; **—nwirtschaft** *f* nepotism.

vibrieren [viˈbriːrən] *vi* vibrate.

Vieh [fiː] *nt* **-(e)s** cattle *pl*; **v—isch** *a* bestial.

viel [fiːl] *a* a lot of, much; **—e** *pl* a lot of, many; *a* a lot, much; **— zuwenig** much too little; **—erlei** *a* a great variety of; **—es** *a* a lot; **—fach** *a,ad* many times; **auf**

—fachen Wunsch at the request of many people; **V—falt** *f* **-** variety; **—fältig** *a* varied, many-sided.

vielleicht [fiˈlaɪçt] *ad* perhaps.

viel- *cpd:* **—mal(s)** *ad* many times; **danke —mals** many thanks; **—mehr** *ad* rather, on the contrary; **—sagend** *a* significant; **—seitig** *a* many-sided; **—versprechend** *a* promising.

vier [fiːr] *num* four; **V—eck** *nt* **-(e)s, -e** four-sided figure; *(gleichseitig)* square; **—eckig** *a* four-sided; square; **V—taktmotor** *m* four-stroke engine; **—te(r,s)** [ˈfiːrtə(r,z)] *a* fourth; **—teilen** *vt* quarter; **V—tel** [ˈfɪrtəl] *nt* **-s, -** quarter; **—teljährlich** *a* quarterly; **V—elnote** *f* crotchet; **V—elstunde** [fɪrtəlˈʃtundə] *f* quarter of an hour; **—zehn** [ˈfɪrtseːn] *num* fourteen; **in —zehn Tagen** in a fortnight; **—zehntägig** *a* fortnightly; **—zig** [ˈfɪrtsɪç] *num* forty.

Vikar [viˈkaːr] *m* **-s, -e** curate.

Villa [ˈvɪla] *f* **-,** **Villen** villa.

Villenviertel [ˈvɪlənfɪrtəl] *nt* (prosperous) residential area.

violett [vioˈlɛt] *a* violet.

Violin- [vioˈliːn] *cpd:* **—bogen** *m* violin bow; **—e** *f* **-, -n** violin; **—konzert** *nt* violin concerto; **—schlüssel** *m* treble clef.

Virus [ˈviːrus] *m or nt* **-,** **Viren** virus.

Visier [viˈziːr] *nt* **-s, -e** gunsight; *(am Helm)* visor.

Visite [viˈziːtə] *f* **-, -n** (*Med*) visit; **—nkarte** *f* visiting card.

visuell [vizuˈɛl] *a* visual.

Visum [ˈviːzum] *nt* **-s,** **Visa** *or* **Visen** visa.

vital [viˈtaːl] *a* lively, full of life, vital.

Vitamin [vita'mi:n] *nt* -s, -e vitamin.

Vogel ['fo:gəl] *m* -s, ⁀ bird; einen — haben *(col)* have bats in the belfry; jdm den — zeigen *(col)* tap one's forehead *(to indicate that one thinks sb stupid)*; —bauer *nt* birdcage; —beerbaum *m* rowan tree; —schau *f* bird's-eye view; —scheuche *f* -, -n scarecrow.

Vokab- *cpd:* —el [vo'ka:bəl] *f* -, -n word; —ular [vokabu'la:r] *nt* -s, -e vocabulary.

Vokal [vo'ka:l] *m* -s, -e vowel.

Volk [fɔlk] *nt* -(e)s, ⁀er people; nation.

Völker- ['fœlkər] *cpd:* —bund *m* League of Nations; —recht *nt* international law; v—rechtlich *a* according to international law; —verständigung *f* international understanding; —wanderung *f* migration.

Volks- *cpd:* —abstimmung *f* referendum; —hochschule *f* adult education classes *pl;* —lied *nt* folksong; —republik *f* people's republic; —schule *f* elementary school; —tanz *m* folk dance; v—tümlich ['fɔlksty:mlɪç] *a* popular; —wirtschaft *f* economics.

voll [fɔl] *a* full; — und ganz completely; jdn für — nehmen *(col)* take sb seriously; —auf [fɔl'auf] *ad* amply; —blütig a full-blooded; —'bringen *vt irreg insep* accomplish; —'enden *vt irreg* finish, complete; —ends ['fɔlɛnts] *ad* completely; V—'endung *f* completion; —er *a* fuller (+gen) full of; V—eyball ['vɔlbal] *m* volleyball; V—gas *nt:* mit V—gas at full throttle; V—gas geben step on it.

völlig ['fœlɪç] *a,ad* complete(ly).

voll- *cpd:* —jährig *a* of age; V—kaskoversicherung *f* fully comprehensive insurance; —'kommen *a* perfect; V—'kommenheit *f* perfection; V—kornbrot *nt* wholemeal bread; —machen *vt* fill (up); V—macht *f* -, -en authority, full powers *pl;* V—mond *m* full moon; V—pension *f* full board; —ständig *a* complete; —'strecken *vt insep* execute; —tanken *vti* fill up; —zählig *a* complete; in full number; —'ziehen *vt irreg insep* carry out; *vr* happen; V—'zug *m* execution.

Volt [vɔlt] *nt* - or (e)s, - volt.

Volumen [vo'lu:mən] *nt* -s, - or **Volumina** volume.

vom [fɔm] = von dem.

von [fɔn] *prep +dat* from; *(statt Genitiv, bestehend aus)* of; *(im Passiv)* by; ein Freund — mir a friend of mine; — mir aus *(col)* OK by me; — wegen! no way!; —ei'nander ad from each other; —statten [fɔn'ʃtatən] *ad:* —statten gehen proceed, go.

vor [fo:r] *prep +dat or acc* before; *(räumlich)* in front of; — 2 Tagen 2 days ago; — allem above all; V—abend *m* evening before, eve.

voran [fo'ran] *ad* before, ahead; —gehen *vi irreg* go ahead; einer Sache (dat) —gehen precede sth; —gehend *a* previous; —kommen *vi irreg* come along, make progress.

Vor- [fo:r] *cpd:* —anschlag *m* estimate; —arbeiter *m* foreman.

voraus [fo'raus] *ad* ahead; *(zeitlich)* in advance; jdm — sein be ahead of sb; im — in advance; —bezahlen *vt* pay in advance; —gehen *vi irreg* go (on) ahead;

(fig) precede ; **—haben** vt irreg: jdm etw **—haben** have the edge on sb in sth ; V**—sage** f -, -n prediction ; **—sagen** vt predict ; **—sehen** vt irreg foresee ; **—setzen** vt assume ; **—gesetzt, daß . . .** provided that . . ., V**—setzung** f requirement, prerequisite ; V**—sicht** f foresight ; aller V**—sicht** nach in all probability ; in der V**—sicht, daß . .** anticipating that . . . ; **—sichtlich** ad probably.

vorbauen ['fo:rbauən] vt build up in front ; vi take precautions (dat against).

Vorbehalt ['fo:rbəhalt] m -(e)s, -e reservation, proviso ; **v—en** vt irreg: sich/jdm etw **v—en** reserve sth (to o.s.)/to sb ; **v—los** a,ad unconditional(ly).

vorbei [fɔr'bai] ad by, past ; **—gehen** vi irreg pass by, go past.

vorbe- cpd: **—lastet** ['fo:rbəlastət] a *(fig)* handicapped ; **—reiten** ['fo:rbəraitən] vt prepare ; V**—reitung** f preparation ; **—straft** ['fo:rbəʃtra:ft] a previously convicted, with a record.

vorbeugen ['fo:rbɔygən] vtr lean forward ; vi prevent *(einer Sache* '(dat) sth) ; **—d** a preventive.

Vorbeugung f prevention ; **zur —gegen** for the prevention of.

Vorbild ['fo:rbɪlt] nt model ; **sich** (dat) jdn zum **— nehmen** take sb as one's model, model o.s. on sb ; **v—lich** a model, ideal.

vorbringen ['fo:rbrɪŋən] vt irreg advance, state ; *(col: nach vorne)* bring to the front.

Vorder- ['fɔrdər] cpd: **—achse** f front axle ; **—ansicht** f front view ; **v—e(r,s)** a front ; **—grund** m foreground ; **v—hand** ad for the present ; **—mann** m, pl -**männer** man in front ; jdm auf **—mann**

bringen *(col)* tell sb to pull his socks up ; **—seite** f front (side) ; **v—ste(r,s)** a front.

vordrängen ['fo:rdrɛŋən] vt push to the front.

vorehelich ['fo:r'e:əlɪç] a pre-.marital.

voreilig ['fo:r'ailɪç] a hasty, rash.

voreingenommen ['fo:r'aingənɔmən] a biased ; V**—heit** f bias.

vorenthalten ['fo:r'ɛnthaltən] vt irreg: jdm etw **—** withhold sth from sb.

vorerst ['fo:r'e:rst] ad for the moment or present.

Vorfahr [fo:rfa:r] m -en, -en ancestor ; **v—en** vi irreg drive (on) ahead ; *(vors Haus etc)* drive up ; **—t** f *(Aut)* right of way ; **—t achten!** give way! ; **—tsregel** f right of way ; **—tsschild** nt give way sign.

Vorfall ['fo:rfal] m incident ; **v—en** vi irreg occur.

vorfinden ['fo:rfɪndən] vt irreg find.

vorführen ['fo:rfy:rən] vt show, display ; **dem Gericht —** bring before the court.

Vorgabe ['fo:rga:bə] f *(Sport)* start, handicap.

Vorgang ['fo:rgaŋ] m course of events ; *(esp Sci)* process ; **der —von etw** how sth happens.

Vorgänger(in f) ['fo:rgɛŋər(m)] m -s, - predecessor.

vorgeben ['fo:rge:bən] vt irreg pretend, use as a pretext ; *(Sport)* give an advantage or a start.

vorge- ['fo:rgə] cpd: **—faßt** [-fast] a preconceived ; **—fertigt** [-fɛrtɪçt] a prefabricated ; V**—fühl** [-fyl] nt presentiment, premonition.

vorgehen ['fo:rge:ən] vi irreg *(voraus)* go (on) ahead ; *(nach vorn)* go up front ; *(handeln)* act, proceed; (*Uhr*) be fast; (*Vorrang haben*) take precedence; (*passieren*) go on; **V— nt -s** action.

Vorgeschmack ['foːrgəʃmak] *m* foretaste.

Vorgesetzte(r) ['foːrgəzɛtstə(r)] *mf* superior.

vorgestern ['foːrgɛstərn] *ad* the day before yesterday.

vorgreifen ['foːrgraɪfən] *vi irreg* anticipate, forestall.

vorhaben ['foːrhaːbən] *vt irreg* intend; hast du schon was vor? have you got anything on?; **V— nt -s, -** intention.

Vorhaltung *f* reproach.

vorhalten ['foːrhaltən] *irreg vt* hold or put up; (*fig*) reproach (*jdm etw sb for sth*); *vi* last.

vorhanden [foːr'handən] *a* existing, extant; (*erhältlich*) available; **V—sein nt -s** existence, presence.

Vorhang ['foːrhaŋ] *m* curtain.

Vorhängeschloß ['foːrhɛŋəʃlɔs] *nt* padlock.

Vorhaut ['foːrhaʊt] *f* (*Med*) foreskin.

vorher [foːr'heːr] *ad* before(hand); **—bestimmen** *vt Schicksal* preordain; **—gehen** *vi irreg* precede; **—ig** [foːr'heːrɪç] *a* previous.

Vorherrschaft ['foːrhɛrʃaft] *f* predominance, supremacy.

vorherrschen ['foːrhɛrʃən] *vi* predominate.

vorher- [foːr'heːr] *cpd:* **V—sage** *f* **-, -n** forecast; **—sagen** *vt* forecast, predict; **—sehbar** *a* predictable; **—sehen** *vt irreg* foresee.

vorhin [foːr'hɪn] *ad* not long ago, just now; **—ein** [foːr'hɪnaɪn] *ad:* im **—ein** beforehand.

vorig ['foːrɪç] *a* previous, last.

vorjährig ['foːrjɛːrɪç] *a* of the previous year; last year's.

Vorkehrung ['foːrkeːruŋ] *f* precaution.

vorkommen ['foːrkɔmən] *vi irreg* come forward; (*geschehen*) occur; (*scheinen*) seem (to be); **sich** (*dat*) **dumm etc —** feel stupid etc; **V— nt -s, -** occurrence.

Vorkommnis ['foːrkɔmnɪs] *nt* **-ses, -se** occurrence.

Vorkriegs- ['foːrkriːks] *in cpds* prewar.

Vorladung ['foːrlaːduŋ] *f* summons.

Vorlage ['foːrlaːgə] *f* model, pattern; (*Gesetzes—*) bill; (*Sport*) pass.

vorlassen ['foːrlasən] *vt irreg* admit; (*vorgehen lassen*) allow to go in front.

vorläufig ['foːrlɔyfɪç] *a* temporary, provisional.

vorlaut ['foːrlaʊt] *a* impertinent, cheeky.

Vorleg- ['foːrleːg] *cpd:* **v—en** *vt* put in front of; (*fig*) produce, submit; *jdm* **etw —en** put sth before sb; **—er** *m* **-s, -** mat.

vorlesen ['foːrleːzən] *vt irreg* read (out).

Vorlesung *f* (*Univ*) lecture.

vorletzte(r, s) ['foːrlɛtstə(r,s)] *a* last but one.

Vorliebe ['foːrliːbə] *f* preference, partiality.

vorliebnehmen [foːr'liːpneːmən] *vi irreg:* **— mit** make do with.

vorliegen ['foːrliːgən] *vi irreg* be (here); etw liegt jdm vor sb has sth; **—d** *a* present, at issue.

vormachen ['foːrmaxən] *vt:* *jdm* etw **—** show sb how to do sth; (*fig*) fool sb; have sb on.

Vormachtstellung ['fo:rmaxt-ʃtɛluŋ] f supremacy, hegemony.

Vormarsch ['fo:rmarʃ] m advance.

vormerken ['fo:rmɛrkən] vt book.

Vormittag ['fo:rmita:k] m morning; v–s ad in the morning, before noon.

Vormund ['fo:rmʊnt] m -(e)s, -e or -münder guardian.

vorn(e) ['fɔrn(ə)] ad in front; von — anfangen start at the beginning; nach — to the front.

Vorname ['fo:rna:mə] m first or Christian name.

vornan [fɔrn''an] ad at the front.

vornehm ['fo:rne:m] a distinguished; refined; elegant; v–en vt irreg (fig) carry out; sich (dat) etw —en start on sth; (beschließen) decide to do sth; sich (dat) jdn —en tell sb off; —lich ad chiefly, specially.

vornherein ['fɔrnhɛraɪn] ad: von — from the start.

Vorort ['fo:r'ɔrt] m suburb; —zug m commuter train.

Vorrang ['fo:rraŋ] m precedence, priority; v–ig a of prime importance, primary.

Vorrat ['fo:rra:t] m stock, supply; —skammer f pantry.

vorrätig ['fo:rrɛ:tɪç] a in stock.

Vorrecht ['fo:rrɛçt] nt privilege.

Vorrichtung ['fo:rrɪçtʊŋ] f device, contrivance.

vorrücken ['fo:rrʏkən] vi advance; vt move forward.

vorsagen ['fo:rza:gən] vt recite, say out loud; (Sch: zuflüstern) tell secretly, prompt.

Vorsatz ['fo:rzats] m intention; (Jur) intent; einen — fassen make a resolution.

vorsätzlich ['fo:rzɛtslɪç] a,ad intentional(ly); (Jur) premeditated.

Vorschau ['fo:rʃaʊ] f (Rad, TV) (programme) preview; (Film) trailer.

vorschieben ['fo:rʃi:bən] vt irreg push forward; (vor etw) push across; (fig) put forward as an excuse; jdn — use sb as a front.

Vorschlag ['fo:rʃla:k] m suggestion, proposal; v–en vt irreg suggest, propose.

vorschnell ['fo:rʃnɛl] ad hastily, too quickly.

vorschreiben ['fo:rʃraɪbən] vt irreg prescribe, specify.

Vorschrift ['fo:rʃrɪft] f regulation(s); rule(s); (Anweisungen) instruction(s); Dienst nach — work-to-rule; v–smäßig a as per regulations/instructions.

Vorschuß ['fo:rʃʊs] m advance.

vorschweben ['fo:rʃve:bən] vi: jdm schwebt etw vor sb has sth in mind.

vorsehen ['fo:rze:ən] irreg vt provide for, plan; vr take care, be careful; vi be visible.

Vorsehung f providence.

vorsetzen ['fo:rzɛtsən] vt move forward; (vor etw) put in front; (anbieten) offer.

Vorsicht ['fo:rzɪçt] f caution, care; —! look out!, take care!; (auf Schildern) caution!, danger!; —, Stufe! mind the step!; v–ig a cautious, careful; v–shalber ad just in case.

Vorsilbe ['fo:rzɪlbə] f prefix.

Vorsitz ['fo:rzɪts] m chair(manship); —ende(r) mf chairman/-woman.

Vorsorge ['fo:rzɔrgə] f precaution(s), provision(s); v–n vi; v–en für make provision(s) for.

vorsorglich ['foːrzɔrklɪç] ad as a precaution.

Vorspeise ['foːrʃpaizə] f hors d'oeuvre, appetizer.

Vorspiel ['foːrʃpiːl] nt prelude.

vorsprechen ['foːrʃprɛçən] irreg vt say out loud, recite; vi: bei jdm — call on sb.

Vorsprung ['foːrʃprʊŋ] m projection, ledge; (fig) advantage.

Vorstadt ['foːrʃtat] f suburbs pl.

Vorstand ['foːrʃtant] m executive committee; (Comm) board (of directors); (Person) director, head.

vorstehen ['foːrʃteːən] vi irreg project; etw (dat) — (fig) be the head of sth.

vorstell- ['foːrʃtɛl] cpd: **—bar** a conceivable; **—en** vt put forward; (vor etw) put in front; (bekannt machen) introduce; (darstellen) represent; sich (dat) etw **—en** imagine sth; **V—ung** f (Bekanntmachung) introduction; (Theat etc) performance; (Gedanke) idea, thought.

Vorstoß ['foːrʃtoːs] m advance; **v—en** vti irreg push forward.

Vorstrafe ['foːrʃtraːfə] f previous conviction.

vorstrecken ['foːrʃtrɛkən] vt stretch out; (Geld) advance.

Vorstufe ['foːrʃtuːfə] f first step(s).

Vortag ['foːrtaːk] m day before (einer Sache sth).

vortäuschen ['foːrtɔysən] vt feign, pretend.

Vorteil ['fɔrtail] m **-s, -e** advantage (gegenüber over); im — sein have the advantage; **v—haft** a advantageous.

Vortrag ['foːrtraːk] m **-(e)s**, **Vorträge** talk, lecture; (—sart) delivery, rendering; (Comm)

balance carried forward; **v—en** vt irreg carry forward (auch Comm); (fig) recite; Rede deliver; Lied perform; Meinung etc express.

vortrefflich ['foːrtrɛflɪç] a excellent.

vortreten ['foːrtreːtən] vi irreg step forward; (Augen etc) protrude.

vorüber ['foːrʏbər] ad past, over; **—gehen** vi irreg pass (by); **—gehen an** (+dat) (fig) pass over; **—gehend** a temporary, passing.

Vorurteil ['foːrʔurtail] nt prejudice; **v—sfrei**, **v—slos** a unprejudiced, open-minded.

Vorverkauf ['foːrfɛrkaof] m advance booking.

Vorwahl ['foːrvaːl] f preliminary election; (Tel) dialling code.

Vorwand ['foːrvant] m **-(e)s**, **Vorwände** pretext.

vorwärts ['foːrvɛrts] ad forward; **V—gang** m (Aut etc) forward gear; **—gehen** vi irreg progress; **—kommen** vi irreg get on, make progress.

vorweg ['foːrvɛk] ad in advance; **V—nahme** f **-, -n** anticipation; **—nehmen** vt irreg anticipate.

vorweisen ['foːrvaizən] vt irreg show, produce.

vorwerfen ['foːrvɛrfən] vt irreg: jdm etw — reproach sb for sth, accuse sb of sth; sich (dat) nichts vorzuwerfen haben have nothing to reproach o.s. with.

vorwiegend ['foːrviːgənt] a,ad predominant(ly).

Vorwitz ['foːrvɪts] m cheek; **v—ig** a saucy, cheeky.

Vorwort ['foːrvɔrt] nt **-(e)s**, **-e** preface.

Vorwurf ['foːrvʊrf] m reproach; jdm/sich Vorwürfe machen reproach sb/o.s.; **v—svoll** a reproachful.

vorzeigen ['fo:rtsaɪɡən] *vt* show, produce.

vorzeitig ['fo:rtsaɪtɪç] *a* premature.

vorziehen ['fo:rtsi:ən] *vt irreg* pull forward; *Gardinen* draw; *(lieber haben)* prefer.

Vorzug ['fo:rtsu:k] *m* preference; *(gute Eigenschaft)* merit, good

quality; *(Vorteil)* advantage; *(Rail)* relief train.

vorzüglich [fo:r'tsy:klɪç] *a* excellent, first-rate.

vulgär [vʊl'ɡɛ:r] *a* vulgar.

Vulkan [vʊl'ka:n] *m* -s, -e vol-dano; **v-i'sieren** *vt* vulcanize.

W

W, w [ve:] *nt* W, w.

Waage ['va:ɡə] *f* -, -n scales *pl*; *(Astrol)* Libra; **w-recht** *a* horizontal.

wabb(e)lig ['vab(ə)lɪç] *a* wobbly.

Wabe ['va:bə] *f* -, -n honeycomb.

wach [vax] *a* awake; *(fig)* alert; **W-e** *f* -, -n guard, watch; **W-e halten** keep watch; **W-e stehen** stand guard; **-en** *vi* be awake; *(W-e halten)* guard.

Wacholder [va'xɔldər] *m* -s, - juniper.

Wachs [vaks] *nt* -es, -e wax.

wachsam ['vaxza:m] *a* watchful, vigilant, alert; **W-keit** *f* vigilance.

Wachs- *cpd*: **w-en** *vi irreg* grow; *vt* Skier wax; **-tuch** *nt* oilcloth; **-tum** *nt* -s growth.

Wächter ['vɛçtər] *m* -s, - guard, warder, keeper; *(Parkplatz—)* attendant.

Wacht- [vaxt] *cpd*: **-meister** *m* officer; **-posten** *m* guard, sentry.

wackel- ['vakəl] *cpd*: **-ig** *a* shaky, wobbly; **W-kontakt** *m* loose connection; **-n** *vi* shake; *(fig: Position)* be shaky.

wacker ['vakər] *a* valiant, stout; *ad* well, bravely.

Wade ['va:də] *f* -, -n *(Anat)* calf.

Waffe ['vafə] *f* -, -n weapon; **-l**

f -, -n waffle; wafer; **—nschein** *m* gun licence; **—nstillstand** *m* armistice, truce.

Wagemut ['va:ɡəmu:t] *m* daring.

wagen ['va:ɡən] *vt* venture, dare.

Wagen ['va:ɡən] *m* -s, - vehicle; *(Auto)* car; *(Rail)* carriage; *(Pferde—)* cart; **—führer** *m* driver; **—heber** *m* -s, - jack.

Waggon [va'ɡõ:] *m* -s, -s carriage; *(Güter—)* goods van, freight truck *(US)*.

waghalsig ['va:khalzɪç] *a* foolhardy.

Wagnis ['va:knɪs] *nt* -ses, -se risk.

Wahl ['va:l] *f* -, -en choice; *(Pol)* election; **zweite —** seconds *pl*; **w-berechtigt** *a* entitled to vote.

wähl- ['vɛ:l] *cpd*: **-bar** *a* eligible; **-en** *vti* choose; *(Pol)* elect, vote (for); *(Tel)* dial; **W-er(in** *f)* *m* -s, - voter; **-erisch** *a* fastidious, particular; **W-erschaft** *f* electorate.

Wahl- *cpd*: **-fach** *nt* optional subject; **-gang** *m* ballot; **-kabine** *f* polling booth; **-kampf** *m* election campaign; **-kreis** *m* constituency; **-liste** *f* electoral register; **-lokal** *nt* polling station; **w-los** *ad* at random; **-recht** *nt* franchise; **-spruch** *m* motto; **-urne** *f* ballot box.

Wahn [va:n] *m* -(e)s delusion; folly; —sinn *m* madness; w—sinnig a insane, mad; *ad* (*col*) incredibly.

wahr [va:r] a true; —en *vt* maintain, keep.

währen ['vɛ:rən] *vi* last; —d *prep* +gen during; *cj* while; —ddessen [vɛ:rant'dɛsən] *ad* meanwhile.

wahr- *cpd*: —habage; —haben *vt irreg*: etw nicht —haben wollen refuse to admit sth; —haft *ad* (*tatsächlich*) truly; —haftig [va:r'haftıç] a true, real; *ad* really; —heit *f* truth; —nehmen *vt irreg* perceive, observe; W—nehmung *f* perception; —sagen *vi* prophesy, tell fortunes; W—sager(in *f*) *m* -s, - fortune teller; —scheinlich [va:r'faınlıç] a probable; *ad* probably; W—'scheinlichkeit *f* probability; aller W—scheinlichkeit nach in all probability; W—zeichen *nt* emblem.

Währung ['vɛ:rʊŋ] *f* currency.

Waise ['vaızə] *f* -, -n orphan; —nhaus *nt* orphanage; —nkind *nt* orphan.

Wald [valt] *m* -(e)s, -er wood(s); (*groß*) forest; w—ig ['valdıç] a wooded.

Wäldchen ['vɛltçən] *nt* copse, grove.

Wal(fisch) ['va:l(fıʃ)] *m* -(e)s, -e whale.

Wall [val] *m* -(e)s, -e embankment; (*Bollwerk*) rampart; w—fahren *vi irreg insep* go on a pilgrimage; —fahrer(in *f*) *nt* pilgrim; —fahrt *f* pilgrimage.

Wal- ['val] *cpd*: —nuß *f* walnut; —roß *nt* walrus.

Walze ['valtsə] *f* -, -n (*Gerät*) cylinder; (*Fahrzeug*) roller; w—n *vt* roll (out).

wälzen ['vɛltsən] *vt* roll (over); *Bücher* hunt through; *Probleme* deliberate on; *vr* wallow; (*vor Schmerzen*) roll about; (*im Bett*) toss and turn.

Walzer [valtsar] *m* -s, - waltz.

Wälzer ['vɛltsər] *m* -s, - (*col*) tome.

Wand [vant] *f* -, -e wall; (*Trenn—*) partition; (*Berg—*) precipice.

Wandel ['vandəl] *m* -s change; w—bar a changeable, variable; w—n *vtr* change; *vi* (*gehen*) walk.

Wander- ['vandər] *cpd*: —bühne *f* travelling theatre; —er *m* -s, - hiker, rambler; w—n *vi* hike; (*Blick*) wander; (*Gedanken*) stray; —preis *m* challenge trophy; —schaft *f* travelling; —ung *f* walking tour, hike.

Wand- *cpd*: —lung *f* change, transformation; (*Rel*) transubstantiation; —schirm *m* (folding) screen; —schrank *m* cupboard; —teppich *m* tapestry; —verkleidung *f* wainscoting.

Wange ['vaŋə] *f* -, -n cheek.

wankelmütig [vaŋkəlmy:tıç] a vacillating, inconstant.

wanken ['vaŋkən] *vi* stagger; (*fig*) waver.

wann [van] *ad* when.

Wanne ['vanə] *f* -, -n tub.

Wanze ['vantsə] *f* -, -n bug.

Wappen ['vapən] *nt* -s, - coat of arms, crest; —kunde *f* heraldry.

Ware ['va:rə] *f* -, -n ware; —nhaus *nt* department store; —nlager *nt* stock, store; —nprobe *f* sample; —nzeichen *nt* trademark.

warm [varm] a warm; Essen hot.

Wärm- ['vɛrm] *cpd*: —e *f* -, -n warmth; w—en *vtr* warm, heat; —flasche *f* hot-water bottle.

warm- cpd: —herzig a warm-hearted; —laufen vi irreg (Aut) warm up; W—'wassertank m hot-water tank.

warnen ['varnən] vt warn.

Warnung f warning.

warten ['vartən] vi wait (auf +acc for); auf sich — lassen take a long time.

Wärter(in f) ['vɛrtər(in)] m -s, - attendant.

Warte- cpd: —saal m (Rail), —zimmer nt waiting room.

Wartung f servicing, service.

warum [va'rum] ad why.

Warze [vartsə] f -, -n wart.

was [vas] pron what; (col: etwas) something.

Wasch- ['vaʃ] cpd: **w—bar** a washable; —becken nt washbasin; **w—echt** a colourfast; (fig) genuine.

Wäsche [vɛʃə] f -, -n wash(ing); (Bett—) linen; (Unter—) under-clothing; —klammer f clothes peg, clothespin (US); —leine f washing line.

waschen ['vaʃən] irreg vti wash; vr (have a) wash; sich (dat) die Hände — wash one's hands; — und legen Haare shampoo and set.

Wäsche- cpd: —rei f laundry; —schleuder f spin-drier.

Wasch- cpd: —küche f laundry room; —lappen m face flannel, washcloth (US); (col) sissy; —maschine f washing machine; —mittel nt, —pulver nt detergent, washing powder; —tisch m wash-hand basin.

Wasser ['vasər] nt -s, - water; **w—dicht** a watertight, waterproof; —fall m waterfall; —farbe f water-colour; **w—gekühlt** a (Aut) water-cooled; —hahn m tap, faucet (US).

wässerig ['vɛsərɪç] a watery.

Wasser- cpd: —kraftwerk nt hydroelectric power station; —leitung f water pipe; —mann n (Astrol) Aquarius; **w—n** vi land on the water.

wässern ['vɛsərn] vti water.

Wasser- cpd: **w—scheu** a afraid of the water; —schi nt water-skiing; —stand m water level; —stoff m hydrogen; —stoffbombe f hydrogen bomb; —waage f spirit level; —welle f shampoo and set; —zeichen nt watermark.

waten ['vatən] vi wade.

watscheln ['vatʃəln] vi waddle.

Watt [vat] nt -(e)s, -en mud flats pl; nt -s, - (Elec) watt; —e f -, -n cotton wool, absorbent cotton (US); **w—ieren** [va'tiːrən] vt pad.

Web- ['veːb] cpd: **w—en** vt irreg weave; —er m -s, - weaver; —erei f (Betrieb) weaving mill; —stuhl m loom.

Wechsel ['vɛksəl] m -s, - change; (Comm) bill of exchange; —beziehung f correlation; —geld nt change; **w—haft** a Wetter variable; —jahre pl change of life; —kurs m rate of exchange; **w—n** vt change; Blicke exchange; vi change; vary; (Geld —) have change; —strom m alternating current; —wirkung f interaction.

wecken ['vɛkən] vt wake (up); call.

Wecker ['vɛkər] m -s, - alarm clock.

wedeln ['veːdəln] vi (mit Schwanz) wag; (mit Fächer) fan; (Ski) wedeln.

weder ['veːdər] cj neither; — . . . noch . . . neither . . . nor . . .

weg [vɛk] ad away, off; über etw (acc) — sein be over sth; er war schon — he had already left;

Finger —! hands off!; **W—** ['ve:k] *m* -(e)s, -e way; *(Pfad)* path; *(Route)* route; sich auf den W— machen be on one's way; jdm aus dem W— gehen keep out of sb's way; **W—bereiter** *m* -s, - pioneer; —blasen *vt irreg* blow away; —bleiben *vi irreg* stay away.

wegen ['ve:gən] *prep +gen or (col) dat* because of.

weg- ['vɛk] *cpd:* —fahren *vi irreg* drive away; leave; —fallen *vi irreg* be left out; *(Ferien, Bezahlung)* be cancelled; *(aufhören)* cease; —gehen *vi irreg* go away; leave; —jagen *vt* chase away; —lassen *vt irreg* leave out; —laufen *vi irreg* run away *or* off; —legen *vt* put aside; —machen *vt (col)* get rid of; —müssen *vi irreg (col)* have to go; —nehmen *vt irreg* take away; —räumen *vt* clear away; —schaffen *vt* clear away; —schnappen *vt* snatch away *(jdm etw* sth from sb); —tun *vt irreg* put away; **W—weiser** ['ve:gvaɪzər] *m* -s, - road sign, signpost; —werfen *vt irreg* throw away; —werfend a disparaging; —ziehen *vi irreg* move away.

weh [ve:] *a* sore; — tun hurt, be sore; jdm/sich — tun hurt sb/o.s.; —(e) *interj:* —(e), wenn du ... woe betide you if ...; o —! oh dear! W—e *f* -, -n *(Klage)* pain; —en *vti* blow; *(Fahnen)* flutter; **W—en** *pl (Med)* labour pains *pl*; —klagen *vi insep* wail; —leidig *a* whiny, whining; **W—mut** *f* -melancholy; —mütig *a* melancholy.

Wehr [ve:r] *nt* -(e)s, -e weir; *f*: sich zur — setzen defend o.s.; —dienst *m* military service; **w—en** *vr* defend o.s.; **w—los** *a* defenceless; —macht *f* armed forces *pl*;

—pflicht *f* compulsory military service; **w—pflichtig** *a* liable for military service.

Weib [vaɪp] *nt* -(e)s, -er woman, female; wife; —chen *nt* female; **w—isch** ['vaɪbɪʃ] *a* sissyish; **w—lich** *a* feminine.

weich [vaɪç] *a* soft; **W—e** *f* -, -n *(Rail)* points *pl*; —en *vi irreg* yield, give away; **W—ensteller** *m* -s, - pointsman; **W—heit** *f* softness; —lich *a* soft, namby-pamby; **W—ling** *m* weakling.

Weide ['vaɪdə] *f* -, -n *(Baum)* willow; *(Gras)* pasture; **w—n** *vi* graze; *vr:* sich an etw *(dat)* w—n delight in sth.

weidlich ['vaɪtlɪç] *ad* thoroughly.

weigern ['vaɪgərn] *vr* refuse.

Weigerung ['vaɪgərʊŋ] *f* refusal.

Weih- ['vaɪ] *cpd:* —e *f* -, -n consecration; *(Priester)* ordination; **w—en** *vt* consecrate; ordain; —er *m* -s, - pond; —nacht *f* -, —nachten *nt* - Christmas; **w—nachtlich** a Christmas; —nachtsabend *m* Christmas Eve; —nachtslied *nt* Christmas carol; —nachtsmann *m* Father Christmas, Santa Claus; zweiter —nachtstag *m* Boxing Day; —rauch *m* incense; —wasser *nt* holy water.

weil [vaɪl] *cj* because.

Weile ['vaɪlə] *f* - while, short time.

Wein [vaɪn] *m* -(e)s, -e wine; *(Pflanze)* vine; —bau *m* cultivation of vines; —beere *f* grape; —berg *m* vineyard; —bergschnecke *f* snail; —brand *m* brandy; **w—en** *vti* cry; das ist zum —en it's enough to make you cry or weep; **w—erlich** *a* tearful; —geist *m* spirits of wine; —lese *f* vintage; —rebe *f* vine; —stein *m* tartar; —stock *m* vine; —traube *f* grape.

weise ['vaɪzə] *a* wise; **W—(r)** *mf* wise old man/woman, sage.

Weise ['vaɪzə] *f* -, -n manner, way; (*Lied*) tune; **auf diese —** in this way; **w—n** *vt irreg* show.

Weisheit ['vaɪshaɪt] *f* wisdom; **—szahn** *m* wisdom tooth.

weiß [vaɪs] *a* white; **W—brot** *nt* white bread; **—en** *vt* whitewash; **W—glut** *f* (*Tech*) incandescence; **jdn bis zur W—glut bringen** (*fig*) make sb see red; **W—kohl** *m* (white) cabbage; **W—wein** *m* white wine.

Weisung ['vaɪzʊŋ] *f* instruction.

weit [vaɪt] *a* wide; *Begriff* broad; *Reise, Wurf* long; **wie — ist es . . ?** how far is it . . ?; **in —er Ferne** in the far distance; **das geht zu —** that's going too far; **ad far**; **—aus** *ad* by far; **—blickend** a far-seeing; **W—e** *f* -, -n width; (*Raum*) space; (*von Entfernung*) distance; **—en** *vtr* widen.

weiter ['vaɪtər] *a* wider; broader; farther (away); (*zusätzlich*) further; **ohne —es** without further ado; just like that; *ad* further; **—nichts/niemand** nothing/nobody else; **—arbeiten** *vi* go on working; **—bilden** *vr* continue one's studies; **—empfehlen** *vt irreg* recommend (to others); **W—fahrt** *f* continuation of the journey; **—gehen** *vi irreg* go on; **—hin** *ad*: **etw —hin tun** go on doing sth; **—leiten** *vt* pass on; **—machen** *vti* continue; **—reisen** *vi* continue one's journey.

weit- *cpd*: **—gehend** a considerable; *ad* largely; **—läufig** a *Gebäude* spacious; *Erklärung* lengthy; *Verwandter* distant; **—schweifig** a long-winded; **—sichtig** a (*lit*) long-sighted; (*fig*)

far-sighted; **W—sprung** *m* long jump; **—verbreitet** a widespread; **W—winkelobjektiv** *nt* (*Phot*) wide-angle lens.

Weizen ['vaɪtsən] *m* -s, - wheat.

welch [vɛlç] *pron*: **— ein(e) . . .** what a . . .; **—e** *indef pron* (*col: einige*) some; **—e(r,s)** *rel pron* (*für Personen*) who; (*für Sachen*) which; *interrog pron* (*adjektivisch*) which; (*substantivisch*) which one.

welk [vɛlk] a withered; **—en** *vi* wither.

Well- [vɛl] *cpd*: **—blech** *nt* corrugated iron; **—e** *f* -, -n wave; (*Tech*) shaft; **—enbereich** *m* waveband; **—enbrecher** *m* -s, - breakwater; **—enlänge** *f* (*lit, fig*) wavelength; **—enlinie** *f* wavy line; **—ensittich** *m* budgerigar; **—pappe** *f* corrugated cardboard.

Welt [vɛlt] *f* -, -en world; **—all** *nt* universe; **—anschauung** *f* philosophy of life; **w—berühmt** a world-famous; **—krieg** *m* world war; **w—lich** a worldly; (*nicht kirchlich*) secular; **—macht** *f* world power; **w—männisch** a sophisticated; **—meister** *m* world champion; **—raum** *m* space; **—reise** *f* trip round the world; **—stadt** *f* metropolis; **w—weit** a world-wide; **—wunder** *nt* wonder of the world.

wem [ve:m] *pron* (*dat*) to whom.

wen [ve:n] *pron* (*acc*) whom.

Wende ['vɛndə] *f* -, -n turn; (*Veränderung*) change; **—kreis** *m* (*Geog*) tropic; (*Aut*) turning circle; **—ltreppe** *f* spiral staircase; **w—n** *vtir irreg* turn; **sich an jdn w—n** go/come to sb; **—punkt** *m* turning point.

Wendung *f* turn; (*Rede—*) idiom.

wenig ['ve:nɪç] *a,ad* little; —e ['ve:nɪgə] *pl* few *pl*; W—keit *f* trifle; meine W—keit yours truly, little me; —ste(r,s) *a* least; —stens *ad* at least.

wenn [vɛn] *cj* if; (*zeitlich*) when; — auch … even if …; — ich doch … if only I …; —schon *ad*: na —schon so what?; —schon, dennschon! if a thing's worth doing, it's worth doing properly.

wer [ve:r] *pron* who.

Werbe- ['vɛrbə] *cpd*: —fernsehen *nt* commercial television; —kampagne *f* advertising campaign; w—n *irreg vt* win; (*Mitglied*) recruit; *vi* advertise; sim jdn/etw w—n try to win sb/sth; für jdn/etw w—n promote sb/sth. **Werbung** *f* advertising; (*von Mitgliedern*) recruitment; (*um jdn/etw*) promotion (um of).

Werdegang ['ve:rdəgaŋ] *m* development; (*beruflich*) career.

werden ['ve:rdən] *vi irreg* become; *v aux* (*Futur*) shall, will; (*Passiv*) be; was ist aus ihm/aus der Sache geworden? what became of him/it?; es ist nichts/gut geworden it came to nothing/turned out well; mir wird kalt I'm getting cold; das muß anders — that will have to change; zu Eis — turn to ice.

werfen ['vɛrfən] *vt irreg* throw.

Werft [vɛrft] *f* -, -en shipyard, dockyard.

Werk [vɛrk] *nt* -(e)s, -e work; (*Tätigkeit*) job; (*Fabrik, Mechanismus*) works *pl*; ans — gehen set to work; —statt *f* -, -stätten workshop; (*Aut*) garage; —student *m* self-supporting student; —tag *m* working day; w—tags *ad* on working days; w—tägig *a* working; —zeug *nt*

tool; —zeugschrank *m* tool chest.

Wermut ['ve:rmu:t] *m* -(e)s worm-wood; (*Wein*) vermouth.

Wert [ve:rt] *m* -(e)s, -e worth; (*Fin*) value; — legen auf (+acc) attach importance to; es hat doch keinen — it's useless; w— a worth; (*geschätzt*) dear; worthy; das ist nichts/viel w— it's not worth anything/it's worth a lot; das ist es/er mir w— it's/he's worth that to me; —angabe *f* declaration of value; w—en *vt* rate; —gegenstand *m* article of value; w—los *a* worthless; —losigkeit *f* worthlessness; —papier *nt* security; w—voll *a* valuable; —zuwachs *m* apprecia-tion.

Wesen ['ve:zən] *nt* -s, - (*Geschöpf*) being; (*Natur, Character*) nature; w—tlich *a* significant; (*beträchtlich*) considerable.

weshalb [vɛs'halp] *ad* why.

Wespe ['vɛspə] *f* -, -n wasp.

wessen ['vɛsən] *pron* (*gen*) whose.

West- [vɛst] *cpd*: —e *f* -, -n waist-coat, vest (*US*); (*Woll*—) cardigan; —en *m* -s west; w—lich *a* western; *ad* to the west; w—wärts *ad* westwards.

weswegen [vɛs've:gən] *ad* why.

wett [vɛt] *a* even; W—bewerb *m* competition; W—e *f* -, -n bet, wager; W—eifer *m* rivalry; —en *vti* bet.

Wetter ['vɛtər] *nt* -s, - weather; —bericht *m* weather report; —dienst *m* meteorological service; —lage *f* (weather) situation; —vorhersage *f* weather forecast; —warte *f* -, -n weather station; w—wendisch *a* capricious.

Wett- *cpd*: —kampf *m* contest; —lauf *m* race; w—laufen *vi irreg*

race; w—machen vt make good;
—spiel nt match; —streit m contest.

wetzen ['vɛtsən] vt sharpen.

Wicht [vɪçt] m -(e)s, -e titch; (pej) worthless creature; w—ig a important; —igkeit f importance.

wickeln ['vɪkəln] vt wind; Haare set; Kind change; jdn/etw in etw (acc) — wrap sb/sth in sth.

Widder ['vɪdər] m -s, — ram; (Astrol) Aries.

wider ['vi:dər] prep +acc against; —'fahren vi irreg happen (jdm to sb); —'legen vt refute.

widerlich ['vi:dərlɪç] a disgusting, repulsive: W—keit f repulsiveness.

wider- ['vi:dər] cpd: —rechtlich a unlawful; W—rede f contradiction.

Widerruf ['vi:dərruf] m retraction; countermanding; w—en [vi:dər'ru:fən] vt irreg insep retract; Anordnung revoke; Befehl countermand.

wider'setzen vr insep oppose (jdm/etw sb/sth).

widerspenstig ['vi:dərʃpɛnstɪç] a wilful; W—keit f wilfulness.

widerspiegeln ['vi:dərʃpi:gəln] vt reflect.

wider'sprechen vi irreg insep contradict (jdm sb); —d a contradictory.

Widerspruch ['vi:dərʃprʊx] m contradiction; w—slos ad without. arguing.

Widerstand ['vi:dərʃtant] m resistance; —sbewegung f resistance (movement); w—sfähig a resistant, tough; w—slos a unresisting.

wider'stehen vi irreg insep withstand (jdm/etw sb/sth).

Wider- ['vi:dər] cpd: —streit m conflict; w—wärtig a nasty, horrid;

—wille m aversion (gegen to); w—willig a unwilling, reluctant.

widmen ['vɪtmən] vt dedicate; vtr devote (o.s.).

Widmung f dedication.

widrig ['vi:drɪç] a Umstände adverse; Mensch repulsive.

wie [vi:] ad how; cj — ich schon sagte as I said; (so) schön — . . . as beautiful as . . . ; — du like you; singen — ein . . . sing like a . . .

wieder ['vi:dər] ad again; — da sein be back (again); gehst du schon —? are you off again?; — ein(e) . . . another . . . ; W—aufbau [-'aufbau] m rebuilding [-'aufna:mə] f resumption; —aufnehmen vt irreg resume; —bekommen vt irreg get back; —bringen vt irreg bring back; —erkennen vt irreg recognize; W—erstattung f reimbursement; W—gabe f reproduction; —geben vt irreg (zurückgeben) return; Erzählung etc repeat; Gefühle etc convey; —gutmachen ['-gu:tmaxən] vt make up for; Fehler put right; W—'gutmachung f reparation; —'herstellen vt restore; —'holen vt insep repeat; W—holung f repetition; W—hören nt : auf W—hören (Tel) goodbye; W—kehr f - return; (von Vorfall) repetition, recurrence; W—kunft f -, -e return; —sehen vt irreg see again; auf W—sehen goodbye; —um ad again; (andererseits) on the other hand; —vereinigen vt reunite; W—wahl f re-election.

Wiege ['vi:gə] f -, -n cradle; W—n vt (schaukeln) rock; vti irreg (Gewicht) weigh; —nfest nt birthday.

wiehern ['vi:ərn] *vi* neigh, whinny.

Wiese ['vi:zə] *f* -, -n meadow; —l *nt* -s, - weasel.

wieso [vi:'zo:] *ad* why.

wieviel [vi:'fi:l] *a* how much; — Menschen how many people; —mal *ad* how often; —te(r,s) a: zum —ten Mal? how many times?; den X—ten haben wir? what's the date?; an —ter Stelle? in what place?; der —te Besucher war er? how many visitors were there before him?

wieweit [vi:vait] *ad* to what extent.

wild [vilt] *a* wild; W— *nt* -(e)s game; —ern ['vildərn] *vi* poach; —fremd *a* (col) quite strange or unknown; W—heit *f* wildness; W—leder *nt* suede; W—nis *f* -, -se wilderness; W—schwein *nt* (wild) boar.

Wille ['vilə] *m* -ns, -n will; w—n *prep* +gen: um . . . w—n for the sake of . . .; w—nlos a weakwilled; w—nsstark a strong-willed.

will- *cpd:* —ig *a* willing; —kommen [vil'kɔmən] *a* welcome; jdn —kommen heißen welcome sb; W—kommen *nt* -s, - welcome; —kürlich *a* arbitrary; Bewegung voluntary.

wimmeln ['viməln] *vi* swarm (von with).

wimmern ['vimərn] *vi* whimper.

Wimper ['vimpər] *f* -, -n eyelash.

Wind [vint] *m* -(e)s, -e wind; —beutel *m* cream puff; (fig) windbag; —e ['vində] *f* -, -n (Tech) winch, windlass; (Bot) bindweed; —el ['vindəl] *f* -, -n nappy, diaper (US); w—en ['vindən] *vi* impers be windy; *irreg vt* wind; Kranz weave; (ent—) twist; *vr* wind; (Person) writhe; —hose *f* whirlwind; —hund *m* greyhound;

(Mensch) fly-by-night; w—ig ['vindiç] *a* windy; (fig) dubious; —mühle *f* windmill; —pocken *pl* chickenpox; —schutzscheibe *f* (Aut) windscreen, windshield (US); —stärke *f* wind force; —stille *f* calm; —stoß *m* gust of wind.

Wink [viŋk] *m* -(e)s, -e hint; (mit Kopf) nod; (mit Hand) wave.

Winkel ['viŋkəl] *m* -s, - (Math) angle; (Gerät) set square; (in Raum) corner.

winken ['viŋkən] *vi* wave.

winseln ['vinzəln] *vi* whine.

Winter ['vintər] *m* -s, - winter; w—lich *a* wintry; —sport *m* winter sports *pl*.

Winzer ['vintsər] *m* -s, - vine grower.

winzig ['vintsiç] *a* tiny.

Wipfel ['vipfəl] *m* -s, - treetop.

wir [vi:r] *pron* we; — alle all of us, we all.

Wirbel ['virbəl] *m* -s, - whirl, swirl; (Trubel) hurly-burly (Aufsehen) fuss; (Anat) vertebra; w—n *vi* whirl, swirl; —säule *f* spine; —tier *nt* vertebrate; —wind *m* whirlwind.

wirken ['virkən] *vi* have an effect; (erfolgreich sein) work; (scheinen) seem; *vt* Wunder work.

wirklich ['virkliç] *a* real; W—keit *f* reality.

wirksam ['virkza:m] *a* effective; W—keit *f* effectiveness, efficacy.

Wirkung ['virkuŋ] *f* -, -en effect; w—slos *a* ineffective; w—slos bleiben have no effect; w—svoll *a* effective.

wirr [vir] *a* confused, wild; W—en *pl* disturbances *pl*; W—warr ['var] *m* -s disorder, chaos.

Wirsing(kohl) ['vɪrzɪŋ(ko:l)] m -s savoy cabbage.

Wirt [vɪrt] m -(e)s, -e landlord; —in f landlady; —schaft f (Gaststätte) pub; (Haushalt) housekeeping; (eines Landes) economy; (col: Durcheinander) mess; w—schaftlich a economical; (Pol) economic; —schaftskrise f economic crisis; —schaftsprüfer m chartered accountant; —schaftswunder nt economic miracle; —shaus nt inn.

Wisch [vɪʃ] m -(e)s, -e scrap of paper; w—en vt wipe; —er m -s, - (Aut) wiper.

wispern ['vɪspərn] vti whisper.

Wißbegier(de) ['vɪsbəgi:r(də)] f thirst for knowledge; w—ig a inquisitive, eager for knowledge.

wissen ['vɪsən] vt irreg know; W— nt -s knowledge; W—schaft f science; W—schaftler(in f) m -s, - scientist; w—schaftlich a scientific; —swert a worth knowing; —tlich a knowing.

wittern ['vɪtərn] vt scent; (fig) suspect.

Witterung f weather; (Geruch) scent.

Witwe ['vɪtvə] f -, -n widow; —r m -s, - widower.

Witz [vɪts] m -(e)s, -e joke; —blatt nt comic (paper); —bold m -(e)s, -e joker, wit; w—eln vi joke; w—ig a funny.

wo [vo:] ad where; (col: irgendwo) somewhere; im Augenblick, — . . . the moment (that) . . .; die Zeit, — . . . the time when . . .; cj (wenn) if; —anders [vo:"andərs] ad elsewhere; —bei [vo:'baɪ] ad (rel) by/with which; (interrog) what . . in/by/with.

Woche ['vɔxə] f -, -n week; —nende nt weekend; w—nlang a,ad for weeks; —nschau f newsreel.

wöchentlich ['vœçəntlɪç] a,ad weekly.

wo- cpd: —durch [vo:'dʊrç] ad (rel) through which; (interrog) what . . . through; —für [vo:'fy:r] ad (rel) for which; (interrog) what . . . for.

Woge ['vo:gə] f -, -n wave; w—n vi heave, surge.

wo- cpd: —gegen [vo:'ge:gən] ad (rel) against which; (interrog) what . . . against; —her [vo:'he:r] ad where . . . from; —hin [vo:'hɪn] ad where . . . to.

wohl [vo:l] ad/well; (behaglich) at ease, comfortable; (vermutlich) I suppose, probably; (gewiß) certainly; er weiß das — he knows that perfectly well; W— nt -(e)s welfare; zum W—l cheers!; —auf [vo:l"aʊf] ad well; W—behagen nt comfort; W—behalten ad safe and sound; W—fahrt f welfare; —habend a wealthy; —ig a a contented, comfortable; W—klang m melodious sound; —schmeckend a delicious; —stand m prosperity; W—standsgesellschaft f affluent society; W—tat f relief; act of charity; W—täter(in f) m benefactor; —tätig a charitable; —tun vi irreg do good (jdm sb); —verdient a well-earned, well-deserved; —weislich ad prudently; W—wollen nt -s good will; —wollend a benevolent.

wohn- ['vo:n] cpd: —en vi live; —haft a resident; —lich a comfortable; W—ort m domicile; W—sitz place of residence; W—ung f house; (Etagen-) flat, apartment (US); W—ungsnot f housing shortage; W—wagen m caravan; W—zimmer nt living room.

wölben ['vœlbən] vtr curve.

Wölbung f curve.

Wolf [vɔlf] m -(e)s, ⸚e wolf.

Wölfin ['vœlfɪn] f she-wolf.

Wolke ['vɔlkə] f -, -n cloud; —nkratzer m skyscraper.

wolkig ['vɔlkɪç] a cloudy.

Wolle ['vɔlə] f -, -n wool; w—n a woollen.

wollen ['vɔlən] vti want.

wollüstig ['vɔlʏstɪç] a lusty, sensual.

wo- cpd: —mit [vo:'mɪt] ad (rel) with which; (interrog) what ... with; —möglich [vo:'mø:klɪç] ad probably, I suppose; —nach [vo:'na:x] ad (rel) after/for which; (interrog) what ... for/after.

Wonne ['vɔnə] f -, -n joy, bliss.

wo- cpd: —ran [vo:'ran] ad (rel) on/at which; (interrog) what ... on/at; —rauf [vo:'rauf] ad (rel) on which; (interrog) what ... on; —raus [vo:'raus] ad (rel) from/out of which; (interrog) what ... out of; —rin [vo:'rɪn] ad (rel) in which; (interrog) what ... in.

Wort [vɔrt] nt -(e)s, ⸚e or -er word; jdn beim — nehmen take sb at his word; w—brüchig a not true to one's word.

Wörterbuch ['vœrtərbu:x] nt dictionary.

Wort- cpd: —führer m spokesman; w—getreu a true to one's word; Übersetzung literal; w—karg a taciturn; —laut m wording.

wörtlich ['vœrtlɪç] a literal.

Wort- cpd: w—los a mute; w—reich a wordy, verbose;

—schatz m vocabulary; —spiel nt play on words, pun; —wechsel m dispute.

wo- cpd: —rüber [vo:'ry:bər] ad (rel) over/about which; (interrog) what ... over/about; —rum [vo:'rum] ad (rel) about/round which; (interrog) what ... about/round; —runter [vo:'rʊntər] ad (rel) under which; (interrog) what ... under; —von [vo:'fɔn] ad (rel) from which; (interrog) what ... from; —vor [vo:'fo:r] ad (rel) in front of/before which; (interrog) in front of/before what; of what; —zu [vo:'tsu:] ad (rel) to/for which; (interrog) what ... for/to; (warum) why.

Wrack [vrak] nt -(e)s, -s wreck.

wringen ['vrɪŋən] vt irreg wring.

Wucher ['vu:xər] m -s profiteering; —er m -s, - profiteer; w—isch a profiteering; w—n vi (Pflanzen) grow wild; (Med) growth, tumour.

Wuchs [vu:ks] m -es (Wachstum) growth; (Statur) build.

Wucht [vʊxt] f - force; w—ig a solid, massive.

wühlen ['vy:lən] vi scrabble; (Tier) root; (Maulwurf) burrow; (col: arbeiten) slave away; vt dig.

Wulst [vʊlst] -es, ⸚e bulge; (an Wunde) swelling.

wund [vʊnt] a sore, raw; W—e ['vʊndə] f -, -n wound.

Wunder ['vʊndər] nt -s, - miracle; es ist kein — it's no wonder; w—bar a wonderful, marvellous; —kind nt infant prodigy; w—lich a odd, peculiar; w—n vr be surprised (über +acc at); vt surprise; w—schön a beautiful; w—voll a wonderful.

Wundstarrkrampf ['vʊntʃtar-
krampf] *m* tetanus, lockjaw.
Wunsch [vʊnʃ] *m* -(e)s, ⁼e wish.
wünschen ['vʏnʃən] *vt* wish; sich
(dat) etw — want sth, wish for sth;
—swert *a* desirable.
Würde ['vʏrdə] *f* -, -n dignity;
(Stellung) honour; —nträger *m* dignitary; w—voll *a* dignified.
würdig ['vʏrdɪç] *a* worthy;
(würdevoll) dignified; —en
['vʏrdɪgən] *vt* appreciate; jdn
keines Blickes —en not so much as
look at sb.
Wurf [vʊrf] *m* -s,⁻ ⁼e throw;
(Junge) litter.
Würfel ['vʏrfəl] *m* -s, - dice;
(Math) cube; —becher *m* (dice)
cup; w—n *vi* play dice; *vt* dice;
—spiel *nt* game of dice; —zucker
m lump sugar.
würgen ['vʏrgən] *vti* choke.

Wurm [vʊrm] *m* -(e)s, ⁼er worm;
w—en *vt* *(col)* rile, nettle;
—fortsatz *m* (Med) appendix;
w—ig *a* worm-eaten; —stichig *a*
worm-ridden.
Wurst [vʊrst] *f* -, ⁼e sausage; das
ist mir — *(col)* I don't care, I don't
give a damn.
Würze ['vʏrtsə] *f.* -, -n seasoning,
spice.
Wurzel ['vʊrtsəl] *f* -, -n root.
würz- ['vʏrts] *cpd:* —en *vt* season,
spice; —ig *a* spicy.
wüst [vy:st] *a* untidy, messy; *(ausschweifend)* wild; *(öde)* waste;
(col: heftig) terrible; **W—e** *f* -, -n
desert; **W—ling** *m* rake.
Wut [vu:t] *f* - rage, fury; —anfall
m fit of rage.
wüten ['vy:tən] *vi* rage; —d *a*
furious, mad.

X

X,x [ɪks] *nt* X,x.
X-Beine ['ɪksbaɪnə] *pl* knock-knees
pl.
x-beliebig [ɪksbə'li:bɪç] *a* any
(whatever).
xerokopieren [kseroko'pi:rən] *vt*

xerox, photocopy.
x-mal ['ɪksma:l] *ad* any number of
times, n times.
Xylophon [ksylo'fo:n] *nt* -s, -e
xylophone.

Y

Y,y ['ʏpsilɔn] *nt* Y,y.

Ypsilon *nt* -(s), -s the letter Y.

Z

Z,z [tset] *nt* Z,z.

Zacke ['tsakə] *f* -, -n point; *(Berg—)* jagged peak; *(Gabel—)* prong; *(Kamm—)* tooth.

zackig ['tsakiç] *a* jagged; *(col)* smart; *Tempo* brisk.

zaghaft ['tsa:khaft] *a* timid; Z—igkeit *f* timidity.

zäh [tsɛ:] *a* tough; *Mensch* tenacious; *Flüssigkeit* thick; *(schleppend)* sluggish; Z—igkeit *f* toughness; tenacity.

Zahl [tsa:l] *f*-,-en number; *z—bar a* payable; *z—en vti* pay; *z—en bitte!* the bill please!

zählen ['tsɛ:lən] *vti* count *(auf +acc on)*; — *zu* be numbered among.

Zahl- *cpd:* z—enmäßig *a* numerical; —er *m* -s, - payer.

Zähler ['tsɛ:lər] *m* -s, - *(Tech)* meter; *(Math)* numerator.

Zahl- *cpd:* z—los *a* countless; z—reich *a* numerous; —tag *m* payday; —ung *f* payment; z—ungsfähig *a* solvent; —wort *nt* numeral.

zahm [tsa:m] *a* tame.

zähmen ['tsɛ:mən] *vt* tame; *(fig)* curb.

Zahn [tsa:n] *m* -(e)s, ⁼e tooth; —arzt *m* dentist; —bürste *f* toothbrush; z—en *vi* cut teeth; —fäule *f* - tooth decay, caries; —fleisch *nt* gums *pl*; —pasta, —paste *f* toothpaste; —rad *nt* cog(wheel); —radbahn *f* rack railway; —schmelz *m* (tooth) enamel; —schmerzen *pl* toothache; —stein

m tartar; —stocher *m* -s, - toothpick.

Zange ['tsaŋə] *f* -, -n pliers *pl*; *(Zucker— etc)* tongs *pl*; *(Beiß—, Zool)* pincers *pl*; *(Med)* forceps *pl*; —ngeburt *f* forceps delivery.

Zank- ['tsaŋk] *cpd:* —apfel *m* bone of contention; z—en *vir* quarrel.

zänkisch ['tsɛŋkiʃ] *a* quarrelsome.

Zäpfchen ['tsɛpfçən] *nt* *(Anat)* uvula; *(Med)* suppository.

Zapfen ['tsapfən] *m* -s, - plug; *(Bot)* cone; *(Eis—)* icicle; z— *vt* tap; —streich *m* *(Mil)* tattoo.

zappelig ['tsapəliç] *a* wriggly; *(unruhig)* fidgety.

zappeln ['tsapəln] *vi* wriggle; fidget.

zart [tsart] *a* *(weich, leise)* soft; *Braten etc* tender; *(fein, schwächlich)* delicate; Z—gefühl *nt* tact; Z—heit *f* softness; tenderness; delicacy.

zärtlich ['tsɛ:rtlɪç] *a* tender, affectionate; Z—keit *f* tenderness; *pl* caresses *pl*.

Zauber ['tsaubər] *m* -s, - magic; *(—bann)* spell; —ei [-'rai] *f* magic; —er *m* -s, - magician; conjuror; z—haft *a* magical, enchanting; —künstler *m* conjuror; z—n *vi* conjure, practise magic; —spruch *m* (magic) spell.

zaudern ['tsaudərn] *vi* hesitate.

Zaum [tsaum] *m* -(e)s, Zäume bridle; *etw im* — halten keep sth in check.

Zaun [tsaun] *m* -(e)s, Zäune fence; *vom* —(e) brechen *(fig)* start; —könig *m* wren; —pfahl *m*: ein Wink mit dem — pfahl a broad hint.

Zeche ['tsɛçə] *f* -, -n bill; *(Bergbau)* mine.

Zecke ['tsɛkə] *f* -, -n tick.

Zehe [tse:ə] *f* -, -n toe; *(Knoblauch—)* clove.

zehn [tse:n] *num* ten; —te(r,s) a tenth; **Z—tel** *nt* -s, - tenth (part).

Zeich- ['tsaɪç] *cpd:* —en *nt* -s, - sign; z—nen *vti* draw; *(kenn—)* mark; *(unter—)* sign; —ner *m* -s, - artist; technischer —ner draughtsman; —nung *f* drawing; *(Markierung)* markings *pl*.

Zeig- ['tsaɪg] *cpd:* —efinger *m* index finger; z—en *vt* show; vi point *(auf +acc* to, at); vr show o.s.; es wird sich z—en time will tell; es zeigte sich, daß ... it turned out that ...; —er *m* -s, - pointer; *(Uhr—)* hand.

Zeile ['tsaɪlə] *f* -, -n line; *(Häuser—)* row; —nabstand *m* line spacing.

Zeit [tsaɪt] *f* -, -en time; *(Gram)* tense; **zur** — at the moment; **sich** *(dat)* — lassen take one's time; **von** — **zu** — from time to time; —alter *nt* age; z—gemäß a in keeping with the times; —genosse *m* contemporary; z—ig a early; z—lebens ad all one's life; z—lich a temporal; —lupe *f* slow motion; —raffer *m* -s time-lapse photography; z—raubend a time-consuming; —raum *m* period; —rechnung *f* time, era; nach/vor unserer —rechnung A.D./B.C.; —schrift *f* periodical; —ung *f* newspaper; —verschwendung *f* waste of time; —vertreib *m* pastime, diversion; z—weilig a temporary; z—weise *ad* for a time; —wort *nt*

verb; —zeichen *nt* (Rad) time signal; —zünder *m* time fuse.

Zell- [tsɛl] *cpd:* —e *f* -, -n cell; *(Telefon—)* callbox; —kern *m* cell nucleus; —stoff *m* cellulose; —teilung *f* cell division.

Zelt [tsɛlt] *nt* -(e)s, -e tent; —bahn *f* tarpaulin, groundsheet; z—en *vi* camp.

Zement [tse'mɛnt] *m* -(e)s, -e cement; z—ieren [-'ti:rən] *vt* cement.

zensieren [tsɛn'zi:rən] *vt* censor; *(Sch)* mark.

Zensur [tsɛn'zu:r] *f* censorship; *(Sch)* mark.

Zent- *cpd:* —imeter [tsɛnti'me:tər] *m* or *nt* centimetre; —ner ['tsɛntnər] *m* -s, - hundredweight.

zentral [tsɛn'tra:l] a central; **Z—e** *f* -, -n central office; *(Tel)* exchange; **Z—heizung** *f* central heating; —isieren [tsɛntrali'zi:rən] *vt* centralize.

Zentri- [tsɛntri] *cpd:* —fugalkraft [-fu'ga:lkraft] *f* centrifugal force; —fuge [-'fu:gə] *f* -, -n centrifuge; *(für Wäsche)* spin-dryer.

Zentrum ['tsɛntrʊm] *nt* -s, Zentren centre.

Zepter ['tsɛptər] *nt* -s, - sceptre.

zerbrech- [tsɛr'brɛç] *cpd:* —en *vti irreg* break; —lich a fragile.

zerbröckeln [tsɛr'brœkəln] *vti* crumble (to pieces).

zerdrücken *vt* squash, crush; Kartoffeln mash.

Zeremonie [tseremo'ni:] *f* ceremony.

zerfahren a scatterbrained, distracted.

Zerfall [tsɛr'fal] *m* decay; z—en *vi irreg* disintegrate, decay; *(sich gliedern)* fall (in +acc into).

zerfetzen [tsɛrˈfɛtsən] *vt* tear to pieces.

zer'fließen *vi irreg* dissolve, melt away.

zer'gehen *vi irreg* melt, dissolve.

zerkleinern [tsɛrˈklaɪnərn] *vt* reduce to small pieces.

zerleg- [tsɛrˈleːg] *cpd*: **—bar** *a* able to be dismantled; **—en** *vt* take to pieces; *Fleisch* carve; *Satz* analyse.

zerlumpt [tsɛrˈlʊmpt] *a* ragged.

zermalmen [tsɛrˈmalmən] *vt* crush.

zermürben [tsɛrˈmʏrbən] *vt* wear down.

zer'platzen *vi* burst.

zerquetschen [tsɛrˈkvɛtʃən] *vt* squash.

Zerrbild [ˈtsɛrbɪlt] *nt* caricature, distorted picture.

zer'reden *vt Problem* flog to death.

zer'reiben *vt irreg* grind down.

zer'reißen *irreg vt* tear to pieces; *vi* tear, rip.

zerren [ˈtsɛrən] *vt* drag; *vi* tug (an + *dat* at).

zer'rinnen *vi irreg* melt away.

zerrissen [tsɛrˈrɪsən] *a* torn, tattered; **Z—heit** *f* tattered state; *(Pol)* disunion, discord; *(innere —)* disintegration.

zerrütten [tsɛrˈrʏtən] *vt* wreck, destroy.

zerrüttet *a* wrecked, shattered.

zer'schießen *vt irreg* shoot to pieces.

zer'schlagen *irreg vt* shatter, smash; *vr* fall through.

zerschleißen [tsɛrˈʃlaɪsən] *vti irreg* wear out.

zer'schneiden *vt irreg* cut up.

zer'setzen *vtr* decompose, dissolve.

zersplittern [tsɛrˈʃplɪtərn] *vti* split (into pieces); *(Glas)* shatter.

zer'springen *vi irreg* shatter, burst.

zerstäub- [tsɛrˈʃtɔʏb] *cpd*: **—en** *vt* spray; **Z—er** *m* -s, - atomizer.

zerstör- [tsɛrˈʃtøːr] *cpd*: **—en** *vt* destroy; **Z—ung** *f* destruction.

zer'stoßen *vt irreg* pound, pulverize.

zer'streiten *vr irreg* fall out, break up.

zerstreu- [tsɛrˈʃtrɔʏ] *cpd*: **—en** *vtr* disperse, scatter; *(unterhalten)* divert; *Zweifel etc* dispel; **—t** *a* scattered; *Mensch* absent-minded; **Z—theit** *f* absent-mindedness; **Z—ung** *f* dispersion; *(Ablenkung)* diversion.

zerstückeln [tsɛrˈʃtʏkəln] *vt* cut into pieces.

zer'teilen *vt* divide into parts.

zer'treten *vt irreg* crush underfoot.

zertrümmern [tsɛrˈtrʏmərn] *vt* shatter; *Gebäude etc* demolish.

Zerwürfnis [tsɛrˈvʏrfnɪs] *nt* -ses, -se dissension, quarrel.

zerzausen [tsɛrˈtsaʊzən] *vt Haare* ruffle up, tousle.

zetern [ˈtseːtərn] *vi* shout, shriek.

Zettel [ˈtsɛtəl] *m* -s, - piece of paper, slip; *(Notiz—)* note; *(Formular)* form; **—kasten** *m* card index (box).

Zeug [tsɔʏk] *nt* -(e)s, -e *(col)* stuff; *(Ausrüstung)* gear; **dummes — (stupid)** nonsense; **das — haben zu** have the makings of; **sich ins — legen** put one's shoulder to the wheel.

Zeuge [ˈtsɔʏgə] *m* -n, -n, **Zeugin** [ˈtsɔʏgɪn] *f* witness; **z—n** *vi* bear witness, testify; **es zeugt von . .** . it testifies to . . . ; *vt Kind* father; **—naussage** *f* evidence; **—nstand** *m* witness box.

Zeugnis ['tsɔʏgnɪs] *nt* **-ses, -se**
certificate; *(Sch)* report;
(Referenz) reference; *(Aussage)*
evidence, testimony; — **geben von**
be evidence of, testify to.

Zeugung ['tsɔʏgʊŋ] *f* procreation;
z—**sunfähig** *a* sterile.

Zickzack ['tsɪktsak] *m* **-(e)s, -e**
zigzag.

Ziege ['tsi:gə] *f* **-, -n** goat; —**nleder**
nt kid.

Ziegel ['tsi:gəl] *m* **-s, -** brick;
(Dach—) tile; —**ei** [-'laɪ] *f* brick-
works.

ziehen ['tsi:ən] *irreg vt* draw;
(zerren) pull; *(Schach etc)* move;
(züchten) rear; **etw nach sich** —
lead to sth, entail sth; *vi* draw;
(um—, wandern) move; *(Rauch,
Wolke etc)* drift; *(reißen)* pull; *v
impers*: **es zieht** there is a draught,
it's draughty; *vr (Gummi)* stretch;
(Grenze etc) run; *(Gespräche)* be
drawn out.

Ziehharmonika ['tsi:harmo:nika] *f*
concertina; accordion.

Ziehung ['tsi:ʊŋ] *f (Los—)* drawing.

Ziel [tsi:l] *nt* **-(e)s, -e** *(einer Reise)*
destination; *(Sport)* finish; *(Mil)*
target; *(Absicht)* goal, aim; z—**en**
vi aim *(auf +acc* at); —**fernrohr**
nt telescopic sight; z—**los** *a* aimless; —**scheibe** *f* target; z—**strebig**
a purposeful.

ziemlich ['tsi:mlɪç] *a* quite *a*; fair;
ad rather; quite *a* bit.

zieren ['tsi:rən] *vr* act coy.

Zier- [tsi:r] *cpd*: z—**lich** *a* dainty;
—**lichkeit** *f* daintiness; —**strauch**
m flowering shrub.

Ziffer ['tsɪfər] *f* **-, -n** figure, digit;
—**blatt** *nt* dial, clock-face.

zig [tsɪk] *a (col)* umpteen.

Zigarette [tsiga'rɛtə] *f* cigarette;
—**nautomat** *m* cigarette machine;

—**nschachtel** *f* cigarette packet;
—**nspitze** *f* cigarette holder.

Zigarillo [tsiga'rɪlo] *nt* or *m* **-s, -s**
cigarillo.

Zigarre [tsi'garə] *f* **-, -n** cigar.

Zigeuner(in *f)* [tsi'gɔʏnər(ɪn)] *m*
-s, - gipsy.

Zimmer ['tsɪmər] *nt* **-s, -** room;
—**antenne** *f* indoor aerial; —**decke**
f ceiling; —**herr** *m* lodger;
—**lautstärke** *f* reasonable volume;
—**mädchen** *nt* chambermaid;
—**mann** *m* carpenter; z—**n** *vt*
make, carpenter; —**pflanze** *f*
indoor plant.

zimperlich ['tsɪmpərlɪç] *a*
squeamish; *(pinglig)* fussy, finicky.

Zimt [tsɪmt] *m* **-(e)s, -e** cinnamon;
—**stange** *f* cinnamon stick.

Zink [tsɪŋk] *nt* **-(e)s** zinc; —**e** *f*
-, -n *(Gabel—)* prong; *(Kamm—)*
tooth; z—**en** *vt* **Karten** mark;
—**salbe** *f* zinc ointment.

Zinn [tsɪn] *nt* **-(e)s** *(Element)* tin;
(in —waren) pewter; z—**oberrot**
[tsi'no:bərrot] *a* vermilion; —**soldat**
m tin soldier; —**waren** *pl* pewter.

Zins [tsɪns] *m* **-es, -en** interest;
—**eszins** *m* compound interest;
—**fuß** *m*, —**satz** *m* rate of interest;
z—**los** *a* interest-free.

Zipfel ['tsɪpfəl] *m* **-s, -** corner;
(spitz) tip; *(Hemd—)* tail;
(Wurst—) end; —**mütze** *f* stocking
cap; nightcap.

zirka ['tsɪrka] *ad* (round) about.

Zirkel ['tsɪrkəl] *m* **-s, -** circle;
(Math) pair of compasses;
—**kasten** *m* geometry set.

Zirkus ['tsɪrkus] *m* **-, -se** circus.

Zirrhose [tsɪ'ro:zə] *f* **-, -n** cirrhosis.

zischeln ['tsɪʃəln] *vti* whisper.

zischen ['tsɪʃən] *vi* hiss.

Zitat [tsi'ta:t] nt -(e)s, -e quotation, quote.

zitieren [tsi'ti:rən] vt quote.

Zitronat [tsitro'na:t] nt -(e)s, -e candied lemon peel.

Zitrone [tsi'tro:nə] f -, -n lemon; —nlimonade f lemonade; —nsaft m lemon juice; —nscheibe f lemon slice.

zittern ['tsɪtərn] vi tremble.

Zitze [tsɪtsə] f -, -n teat, dug.

zivil [tsi'vi:l] a civil; Preis moderate; Z— nt -s plain clothes pl; (Mil) civilian clothing; Z—bevölkerung f civilian population; Z—courage f courage of one's convictions; Z—isation [tsivilizatsi'o:n] f civilization; Z—isationserscheinung f phenomenon of civilization; Z—isationskrankheit f disease peculiar to civilization; —isieren vt civilize; Z—ist [tsivi'lɪst] m civilian; Z—recht nt civil law.

Zölibat [tsøli'ba:t] nt or m -(e)s celibacy.

Zoll [tsɔl] m -(e)s, -e customs pl; (Abgabe) duty; —abfertigung f customs clearance; —amt nt customs office; —beamte(r) m customs official; —erklärung f customs declaration; z—frei a duty-free; z—pflichtig a liable to duty, dutiable.

Zone ['tso:nə] f -, -n zone.

Zoo [tso:] m -s, -s zoo; —loge [tsoo'lo:gə] m -n, -n zoologist; —lo'gie f zoology; z—'logisch a zoological.

Zopf [tsɔpf] m -(e)s, -e plait; pigtail; alter — antiquated custom.

Zorn [tsɔrn] m -(e)s anger; z—ig a angry.

Zote [tso:tə] f -, -n smutty joke/remark.

zottig ['tsɔtɪç] a shaggy.

zu [tsu:] (mit Infinitiv) to; prep +dat (bei Richtung, Vorgang) to; (bei Orts-, Zeit-, Preisangabe) at; (Zweck) for; —m Fenster herein through the window; — meiner Zeit in my time; aß too; (in Richtung) towards (sb/sth); a (col) shut.

zualler- [tsu'alər] cpd: —erst first of all; —letzt ad last of all.

Zubehör [tsu:bəhø:r] nt -(e)s, -e accessories pl.

Zuber [tsu:bər] m -s, - tub.

zubereiten ['tsu:bəraɪtən] vt prepare.

zubilligen ['tsu:bɪlɪgən] vt grant.

zubinden ['tsu:bɪndən] vt irreg tie up.

zubleiben ['tsu:blaɪbən] vi irreg (col) stay shut.

zubringen ['tsu:brɪŋən] vt irreg spend; (col) Tür get shut.

Zubringer m -s, - (Tech) feeder, conveyor; —straße f approach or slip road.

Zucht [tsuxt] f -, -en (von Tieren) breed(ing); (von Pflanzen) cultivation; (Rasse) breed; (Erziehung) raising; (Disziplin) discipline.

züchten ['tsʏçtən] vt Tiere breed; Pflanzen cultivate, grow.

Züchter m -s, - breeder; grower.

Zucht- cpd: —haus nt prison, penitentiary (US); —hengst m stallion, stud.

züchtig ['tsʏçtɪç] a modest, demure; —en ['tsʏçtɪgən] vt chastise; Z—ung f chastisement.

zucken ['tsukən] vi jerk, twitch; (Strahl etc) flicker; vt shrug.

zücken ['tsʏkən] vt Schwert draw; Geldbeutel pull out.

Zucker ['tsukər] *m* -s, - sugar;
(*Med*) diabetes; —**dose** *f* sugar
bowl; —**guß** *m* icing; **z**—**krank** a
diabetic; **z**—**n** *vt* sugar; —**rohr** *nt*
sugar cane; —**rübe** *f* sugar beet.

Zuckung ['tsukʊŋ] *f* convulsion,
spasm; (*leicht*) twitch.

zudecken ['tsu:dɛkən] *vt* cover (up).

zudem [tsu'de:m] *ad* in addition (to
this).

zudrehen ['tsu:dre:ən] *vt* turn off.

zudringlich ['tsu:drɪŋlɪç] *a* forward, pushing, obtrusive; **Z**—**keit**
f forwardness, obtrusiveness.

zudrücken ['tsu:drʏkən] *vt* close;
ein Auge — turn a blind eye.

zueinander [tsu'aɪ'nandər] *ad* to
one other; (*in Verbindung*)
together.

zuerkennen ['tsu:'ɛrkɛnən] *vt irreg*
award (*jdm etw sth* to sb, sb sth).

zuerst [tsu'e:rst] *ad* at first; (*zu
Anfang*) at first; — **einmal** first of
all.

Zufahrt ['tsu:fa:rt] *f* approach;
—**straße** *f* approach road; (*von
Autobahn etc*) slip road.

Zufall ['tsu:fal] *m* chance;
(*Ereignis*) coincidence; **durch** — by
accident; **so ein** — what a
coincidence; **z**—**en** *vi irreg* close,
shut itself; (*Anteil, Aufgabe*) fall
(*jdm* to sb).

zufällig ['tsu:fɛlɪç] a chance; *ad* by
chance; (*in Frage*) by any chance.

Zuflucht ['tsu:flʊxt] *f* recourse;
(*Ort*) refuge.

Zufluß ['tsu:flʊs] *m* (*Zufließen*) inflow, influx; (*Geog*) tributary;
(*Comm*) supply.

zufolge [tsu'fɔlgə] *prep* +*dat or
gen* judging by; (*laut*) according to.

zufrieden [tsu'fri:dən] a
content(ed), satisfied; **Z**—**heit** *f*

satisfaction, contentedness;
—**stellen** *vt* satisfy.

zufrieren [tsu'fri:rən] *vi irreg*
freeze up or over.

zufügen ['tsu:fy:gən] *vt* add (*dat*
to); **Leid etc** cause (*jdm etw sth*
to sb).

Zufuhr ['tsu:fu:r] *f* -, -en
(*Herbeibringen*) supplying; (*Met*)
influx; (*Mil*) supplies *pl*.

zuführen ['tsu:fy:rən] *vt* (*leiten*)
bring, conduct; (*transportieren*)
convey to; (*versorgen*) supply; *vi*:
auf etw (*acc*) — lead to sth.

Zug [tsu:k] *m* -(e)s, ⁈e (*Eisenbahn*)
train; (*Luft*—) draught; (*Ziehen*)
pull(ing); (*Gesichts*—) feature;
(*Schach etc*) move; (*Klingel*—)
pull; (*Schrift*—) stroke; (*Atem*—)
breath; (*Charakter*—) trait; (*an
Zigarette*) puff, pull, drag;
(*Schluck*) gulp; (*Menschengruppe*)
procession; (*von Vögeln*) flight;
(*Mil*) platoon; **etw in vollen** —**en
genießen** enjoy sth to the full.

Zu- [tsu:] *cpd*: —**gabe** *f* extra; (*in
Konzert etc*) encore; —**gang** *m*
access, approach; **z**—**gänglich** a
accessible; **Mensch** approachable.

Zug- *cpd*: —**abteil** *nt* train compartment; —**brücke** *f* drawbridge.

zugeben ['tsu:ge:bən] *vt irreg*
(*beifügen*) add, throw in;
(*zugestehen*) admit; (*erlauben*)
permit.

zugehen ['tsu:ge:ən] *vi irreg*
(*schließen*) shut; *vi impers* (*sich
ereignen*) go on, proceed; **auf
jdn/etw** — walk towards sb/sth;
dem Ende — be finishing.

Zugehörigkeit ['tsu:gəhø:rɪçkaɪt] *f*
membership (*zu* of), belonging (*zu*
to); —**gefühl** *nt* feeling of
belonging.

zugeknöpft ['tsu:gəknœpft] a (col) reserved, stand-offish.

Zügel ['tsy:gəl] m -s, - rein(s) ; (fig auch) curb ; z—los a unrestrained, licentious ; —losigkeit f lack of restraint, licentiousness ; z—n vt curb ; Pferd auch rein in.

zuge- ['tsu:gə] cpd: —sellen vr join (jdm up with) ; z—ständnis nt -ses, -se concession ; —stehen vt irreg admit ; Rechte concede (jdm to sb).

Zug- cpd: —führer m (Rail) inspector ; (Mil) platoon commander ; z—ig a draughty.

zügig ['tsy:gıç] a speedy, swift.

Zug- cpd: —luft f draught ; —maschine f traction engine, tractor.

zugreifen ['tsu:graıfən] vi irreg seize or grab it ; (helfen) help ; (beim Essen) help o.s.

zugrunde ['tsu:grundə] ad: —gehen a collapse ; (Mensch) perish ; einer Sache etw — legen base sth on sth ; einer Sache — liegen be based on sth ; — richten ruin, destroy.

zugunsten ['tsu:gunstən] prep +gen or dat in favour of.

zugute ['tsu:gu:tə] ad: jdm etw — halten concede sth ; jdm — kommen be of assistance to sb.

Zug- cpd: —verbindung f train connection ; —vogel m migrating bird.

zuhalten ['tsu:haltən] irreg vt hold shut ; vi: auf jdn/etw — make for sb/sth.

Zuhälter ['tsu:hɛltər] m -s, - pimp.

Zuhause [tsu:hausə] nt - home.

Zuhilfenahme [tsu:hılfəna:mə] f: unter — von with the help of.

zuhören ['tsu:hø:rən] vi listen (dat to).

Zuhörer m -s, - listener ; —schaft f audience.

zujubeln ['tsu:ju:bəln] vi cheer (jdm sb).

zukleben ['tsu:kle:bən] vt paste up.

zuknöpfen ['tsu:knœpfən] vt button up, fasten.

zukommen ['tsu:kəmən] vi irreg come up (auf +acc to) ; (sich gehören) be fitting (jdm for sb) ; (Recht haben auf) be entitled to ; jdm etw — lassen give sb sth ; etw auf sich — lassen wait and see.

Zukunft ['tsu:kunft] f -, Zukünfte future.

zukünftig ['tsu:kynftıç] a future ; mein —er Mann my husband to be ; ad in future.

Zukunfts- cpd: —aussichten pl future prospects pl ; —musik f (col) wishful thinking ; crystal ball gazing ; —roman m science-fiction novel.

Zulage ['tsu:la:gə] f bonus, allowance.

zulassen ['tsu:lasən] vt irreg (hereinlassen) admit ; (erlauben) permit ; Auto license ; (col: nicht öffnen) keep shut.

zulässig ['tsu:lɛsıç] a permissible, permitted.

zulaufen ['tsu:laufən] vi irreg run (auf +acc towards) ; (Tier) adopt (jdm sb) ; spitz — come to a point.

zulegen ['tsu:le:gən] vt add ; Geld put in ; Tempo accelerate, quicken ; (schließen) cover over ; sich (dat) etw — (col) get hold of sth.

zuleide ['tsu:laıdə] a: jdm etw — tun hurt or harm sb.

zuleiten ['tsu:laıtən] vt direct (dat to) ; (schicken) send.

zuletzt [tsu:lɛtst] ad finally, at last.

zuliebe [tsu'li:bə] *ad:* **jdm — to** please sb.

zum [tsum] *= zu dem:* **— dritten Mal** for the third time; **— Scherz as a joke;** **— Trinken** for drinking.

zumachen ['tsu:maxən] *vt·* shut; *Kleidung* do up, fasten; *vi* shut; *(col)* hurry up.

zumal [tsu'ma:l] *cj* especially (as).

zumeist [tsu'maɪst] *ad* mostly.

zumindest [tsu'mɪndəst] *ad* at least.

zumut- *cpd:* **—bar** ['tsu:mu:tba:r] *a* reasonable; **—e wie ist ihm —e?** how does he feel?; **—en** ['tsu:mu:tən] *vt* expect, ask (jdm of sb); **Z—ung** ['tsu:mu:tuŋ] *f* unreasonable expectation or demand, impertinence.

zunächst [tsu'nɛ:çst] *ad* first of all; **— einmal** to start with.

zunähen ['tsu:nɛ:ən] *vt* sew up.

Zunahme ['tsu:na:mə] *f* -, -n increase.

Zuname ['tsu:na:mə] *m* surname.

Zünd- [tsvnd] *cpd:* **z—en** *vi* (Feuer) light, ignite; (Motor) fire; (begeistern) fire (with enthusiasm) (bei jdm sb); **z—end** a fiery; **—er** *m* -s, - fuse; (Mil) detonator; **—holz** ['tsvnt-] *nt* match; **—kerze** *f* (Aut) spark(ing) plug; **—schlüssel** *m* ignition key; **—schnur** *f* fuse wire; **—stoff** *m* fuel; (fig) dynamite; **—ung** *f* ignition.

zunehmen ['tsu:ne:mən] *vi irreg* increase, grow; (Mensch) put on weight.

zuneigen ['tsu:naɪgən] *vi* incline, lean; **sich dem Ende —** draw to a close; **einer Auffassung —** incline towards a view; **jdm zugeneigt sein** be attracted to sb.

Zuneigung *f* affection.

Zunft [tsunft] *f* -, ⁻e guild.

zünftig ['tsynftɪç] *a* proper, real; *Handwerk* decent.

Zunge ['tsuŋə] *f* -, -n tongue; (Fisch) sole; **z—nfertig** a glib.

zunichte [tsu'nɪçtə] *ad:* **— machen** make use of sth. ruin, destroy; **— werden** come to nothing.

zunutze [tsu'nutsə] *ad:* **sich (dat) etw —** machen make use of sth.

zuoberst [tsu'o:bərst] *ad* at the top.

zupfen ['tsupfən] *vt* pull, pick, pluck; *Gitarre* pluck.

zur [tsu:r] *= zu der.*

zurech- ['tsu:rɛç] *cpd:* **—nungsfähig** *a* responsible, accountable; **Z—nungsfähigkeit** *f* responsibility, accountability.

zurecht- ['tsu:rɛçt·] *cpd:* **—finden** *vr irreg* find one's way (about); **—kommen** *vi irreg* (be able to) deal (mit with), manage; **—legen** *vt* get ready; *Ausrede etc* have ready; **—machen** *vt* prepare; *vr* get ready; **—weisen** *vt irreg* reprimand; **Z—weisung** *f* reprimand, rebuff.

zureden ['tsu:re:dən] *vi* persuade, urge (jdm sb).

zurichten ['tsu:rɪçtən] *vt* Essen prepare; (beschädigen) batter, bash up.

zürnen ['tsyrnən] *vi* be angry (jdm with sb).

zurück [tsu'ryk] *ad* back; **—behalten** *vt irreg* keep back; **—bekommen** *vt irreg* get back; **—bezahlen** *vt* repay, pay back; **—bleiben** *vi irreg* (Mensch) remain behind; (nicht nachkommen) fall behind, lag; (Schaden) remain; **—bringen** *vt irreg* bring back; **—drängen** *vt* Gefühle repress; *Feind* push back; **—drehen** *vt* turn back; **—erobern** *vt* reconquer; **—fahren** *irreg vi* travel back; (vor

Schreck) recoil, start; *vt* drive back; **—fallen** *vi irreg* fall back; (*in Laster*) relapse; **—finden** *vi irreg* find one's way back; **—fordern** *vt* demand back; **—führen** *vt* lead back; etw *auf* etw (*acc*) **—führen** trace sth back to sth; **—geben** *vt irreg* give back; (*antworten*) retort with; **—geblieben** a retarded; **—gehen** *vi irreg* go back; (*zeitlich*) date back (*auf +acc* to); (*fallen*) go down, fall; **—gezogen** a retired, withdrawn; **—halten** *irreg vt* hold back; *Mensch* restrain; (*hindern*) prevent; *vr* (*reserviert sein*) be reserved; (*im Essen*) hold back; **—haltend** a reserved; **Z—haltung** f reserve; **—kehren** *vi* return; **—kommen** *vi irreg* come back; *auf* etw (*acc*) **—kommen** return to sth; **—lassen** *vt irreg* leave behind; **—legen** *vt* put back; *Geld* put by; (*reservieren*) keep back; *Strecke* cover; **—nehmen** *vt irreg* take back; **—rufen** *vti irreg* call back; etw ins Gedächtnis **—rufen** recall sth; **—schrecken** *vi* shrink (*vor +dat* from); **—setzen** *vt* put back; (*im Preis*) reduce; (*benachteiligen*) put at a disadvantage; **—stecken** *vt* put back; *vi* (*fig*) moderate (one's wishes); **—stellen** *vt* put back, replace; (*aufschieben*) put off, postpone; (*Mil*) turn down; *Interessen* defer; *Ware* keep; **—stoßen** *vt irreg* repulse; **—treten** *vi irreg* step back; (*vom Amt*) retire; **gegenüber** *or* **hinter** etw **—treten** diminish in importance in view of sth; **—weisen** *vt irreg* turn down; *Mensch* reject; **Z—zahlung** f repayment; **—ziehen** *irreg vt* pull back; *Angebot* withdraw; *vr* retire.

Zuruf ['tsu:ruːf] m shout, cry.

Zusage ['tsuːzaːgə] f -, -n promise; (*Annahme*) consent; **z—n** *vt* promise; *vi* accept; jdm **z—n** (*gefallen*) agree with *or* please sb.

zusammen [tsu'zamən] ad together; **Z—arbeit** f cooperation; **—arbeiten** *vi* cooperate; **—beißen** *vt irreg* Zähne clench; **—bleiben** *vi irreg* stay together; **—brechen** *vi irreg* collapse; (*Mensch auch*) break down; **—bringen** *vt irreg* bring *or* get together; *Geld* get; *Sätze* put together; **Z—bruch** m collapse; **—fahren** *vi irreg* collide; (*erschrecken*) start; **—fassen** *vt* summarize; (*vereinigen*) unite; **—fassend** a summarizing; ad to summarize; **Z—fassung** f summary, résumé; **—finden** *vir irreg* meet (together); **—fließen** *vi irreg* flow together, meet; **Z—fluß** m confluence; **—fügen** *vt* join (together), unite; **—gehören** *vi* belong together; (*Paar*) match; **—gesetzt** a compound, composite; **—halten** *vi irreg* stick together; **Z—hang** m connection; im/aus dem **Z—hang** in/out of context; **—hängen** *vi irreg* be connected *or* linked; **—hang(s)los** a incoherent, disconnected; **—klappbar** a folding, collapsible; **—kommen** *vi irreg* meet, assemble; (*sich ereignen*) occur at once *or* together; **Z—kunft** f meeting; **—laufen** *vi irreg* run *or* come together; (*Straßen, Flüsse etc*) converge, meet; (*Farben*) run into one another; **—legen** *vt* put together; (*stapeln*) pile up; (*falten*) fold; (*verbinden*) combine, unite; *Termine, Fest* amalgamate; *Geld* collect; **—nehmen** *irreg vt* summon up; alles **—genommen** all in all; *vr* pull o.s. together; **—passen** vi go well together, match; **—prallen** vi collide; **—schlagen** vt irreg Mensch beat up; Dinge smash up; (prallen) fold; Hände clap; Hacken click; **—schließen** vtr irreg join (together); **Z—schluß** m amalgamation; **—schreiben** vt irreg write together; Bericht put together; **—schrumpfen** vi shrink, shrivel up; **Z—sein** nt -s gettogether; **—setzen** vt put together; vr be composed of; **Z—setzung** f composition; **—stellen** vt put together; compile; **Z—stellung** f list; (Vorgang) compilation; **Z—stoß** m collision; **—stoßen** vi irreg collide; **—treffen** vi irreg coincide; Menschen meet; **Z—treffen** nt meeting; coincidence; **—wachsen** vi irreg grow together; **—zählen** vt add up; **—ziehen** irreg vt (verengern) draw together; (vereinigen) bring together; (addieren) add up; vr shrink; (sich bilden) form, develop.

Zusatz ['tsu:zats] m addition; **—antrag** m (Pol) amendment.
zusätzlich ['tsu:zɛtslɪç] a additional.
zuschauen ['tsu:ʃauən] vi watch, look on.
Zuschauer m -s, - spectator; pl (Theat) audience.
zuschicken ['tsu:ʃɪkən] vt send, forward (jdm etw sth to sb).
zuschießen ['tsu:ʃi:sən] irreg vt fire (dat at); Geld put in; vi: — auf (+acc) rush towards.
Zuschlag ['tsu:ʃla:k] m extra charge, surcharge; **Z—en** ['tsu:ʃla:gən] irreg vt Tür slam; Ball hit (jdm to sb); (bei Auktion) knock down; Steine etc knock into shape; vi (Fenster, Tür) shut;

(Mensch) hit, punch; **—skarte** f (Rail) surcharge ticket; **z—spflichtig** a subject to surcharge.
zuschließen ['tsu:ʃli:sən] vt irreg lock (up).
zuschmeißen ['tsu:ʃmaɪsən] vt irreg (col) slam, bang shut.
zuschneiden ['tsu:ʃnaɪdən] vt irreg cut out or to size.
zuschnüren ['tsu:ʃny:rən] vt tie up.
zuschrauben ['tsu:ʃraubən] vt screw down or up.
zuschreiben ['tsu:ʃraɪbən] vt irreg (fig) ascribe, attribute; (Comm) credit.
Zuschrift ['tsu:ʃrɪft] f letter, reply.
zuschulden ['tsu:ʃuldən] ad: sich (dat) etw — kommen lassen make o.s. guilty of sth.
Zuschuß ['tsu:ʃus] m subsidy, allowance.
zuschütten ['tsu:ʃʏtən] vt fill up.
zusehen ['tsu:ze:ən] vi irreg watch (jdm/etw sb/sth); (dafür sorgen) take care; **—ds** ad visibly.
zusenden ['tsu:zɛndən] vt irreg forward, send on (jdm etw sth to sb).
zusetzen ['tsu:zɛtsən] vt (beifügen) add; Geld lose; vi: jdm — harass sb; (Krankheit) take a lot out of sb.
zusichern ['tsu:zɪçərn] vt assure (jdm etw sb of sth).
zusperren ['tsu:ʃpɛrən] vt bar.
zuspielen ['tsu:ʃpi:lən] vti pass (jdm to sb).
zuspitzen ['tsu:ʃpɪtsən] vt sharpen; vr (Lage) become critical.
zusprechen ['tsu:ʃpreçən] irreg vt (zuerkennen) award (jdm etw sb sth, sth to sb); jdm Trost — comfort sb; vi speak (jdm to sb); dem Essen/Alkohol — eat/drink a lot.

Zuspruch ['tsu:ʃprʊx] *m* encouragement; appreciation; popularity. *(Anklang)*

Zustand ['tsu:ʃtant] *m* state, condition; z—e ['tsu:ʃtandə] ad: z—e bringen *vt irreg* bring about; z—e kommen *vi irreg* come about.

zuständig ['tsu:ʃtɛndɪç] *a* competent, responsible; Z—keit *f* competence, responsibility.

zustehen ['tsu:ʃte:ən] *vi irreg*: jdm — be sb's right.

zustellen ['tsu:ʃtɛlən] *vt* block; *Post etc* send. *(verstellen)*

zustimmen ['tsu:ʃtɪmən] *vi* agree *(dat* to).

Zustimmung *f* agreement, consent.

zustoßen ['tsu:ʃto:sən] *vi irreg (fig)* happen *(jdm* to sb).

zutage [tsu:ˈta:gə] ad: — bringen bring to light; — treten come to light.

Zutaten ['tsu:ta:tən] *pl* ingredients *pl.*

zuteilen ['tsu:taɪlən] *vt* allocate, assign.

zutiefst [tsu:ˈti:fst] ad deeply.

zutragen ['tsu:tra:gən] *irreg vt* bring *(jdm* etw sth to sb); *Klatsch* tell; *vr* happen.

zuträglich ['tsu:trɛ:klɪç] *a* beneficial.

zutrau- ['tsu:trau] *cpd:* —en *f* credit *(jdm* etw sth with sth); Z—en *nt* -s trust *(zu* in); —lich *a* trusting, friendly; Z—lichkeit *f* trust.

zutreffen ['tsu:trɛfən] *vi irreg* be correct; .apply; Z—des bitte unterstreichen please underline where applicable.

zutrinken ['tsu:trɪŋkən] *vi irreg* drink to *(jdm* sb).

Zutritt ['tsu:trɪt] *m* access, admittance.

Zutun ['tsu:tu:n] *nt* -s assistance; *vt irreg* add; *(schließen)* shut.

zuverlässig ['tsu:fɛrlɛsɪç] **a** reliable; Z—keit *f* reliability.

Zuversicht ['tsu:fɛrzɪçt] *f* - confidence; z—lich a confident; —lichkeit *f* confidence, hopefulness.

zuviel [tsu:ˈfi:l] ad too much.

zuvor [tsu:ˈfo:r] ad before, previously; —kommen *vi irreg* anticipate *(jdm* sb), beat *(jdm* to it); —kommend a obliging, courteous.

Zuwachs ['tsu:vaks] *m* -es increase, growth; *(col)* addition; z—en *vi irreg* become overgrown; *(Wunde)* heal (up).

zuwandern ['tsu:vandərn] *vi* immigrate.

zuwege [tsu:ˈve:gə] ad: etw — bringen accomplish sth; mit etw — kommen manage sth; gut — sein be (doing) well.

zuweilen [tsu:ˈvaɪlən] ad at times, now and then.

zuweisen ['tsu:vaɪzən] *vt irreg* assign, allocate *(jdm* to sb).

zuwenden ['tsu:vɛndən] *irreg vt* turn *(dat* towards); jdm seine Aufmerksamkeit — give sb one's attention; *vr* devote o.s., turn *(dat* to).

zuwenig [tsu:ˈve:nɪç] ad too little.

zuwerfen ['tsu:vɛrfən] *vt irreg* throw *(jdm* to sb).

zuwider [tsu:ˈvi:dər] ad: etw ist jdm — sb loathes sth, sb finds sth repugnant; *prep* +dat contrary to; —handeln *vi* act contrary *(dat* to); einem Gesetz —handeln contravene a law; Z—handlung *f* contravention; —laufen *vi irreg* run counter *(dat* to).

zuziehen ['tsu:tsi:ən] *irreg vt* *(schließen)* Vorhang draw, close; *(herbeirufen)* Experten call in; sich *(dat)* etw — *Krankheit* catch; *Zorn* incur; *vi* move in, come.

zuzüglich ['tsuːtsyːklɪç] *prep* +*gen* plus, with the addition of.

Zwang [tsvaŋ] *m* **-(e)s,** ⁀e compulsion, coercion.

zwängen ['tsvɛŋən] *vtr* squeeze.

Zwang- *cpd:* z—**los** *a* informal; —**losigkeit** *f* informality; —**sarbeit** *f* forced labour; *(Strafe)* hard labour; —**sjacke** *f* straightjacket; —**slage** *f* predicament, tight corner; z—**släufig** *a* necessary, inevitable; —**smaßnahme** *f* sanction, coercive measure; z—**sweise** *ad* compulsorily.

zwanzig ['tsvantsɪç] *num* twenty.

zwar [tsvaːr] *ad* to be sure, indeed; das ist — . . ., aber . . . that may be . . . but . . . ; und — am Sonntag on Sunday to be precise; und — so schnell, daß . . . in fact so quickly that . . .

Zweck [tsvɛk] *m* **-(e)s,** **-e** purpose, aim; z—**dienlich** *a* practical; expedient; —**e** *f* **-,** **-n** hobnail; *(Heft—)* drawing pin, thumbtack *(US)*; —**entfremdung** *f* misuse; z—**los** *a* pointless; z—**mäßig** *a* suitable, appropriate; —**mäßigkeit** *f* suitability; z—**widrig** *a* unsuitable.

zwei [tsvaɪ] *num* two; —**deutig** *a* ambiguous; *(unanständig)* suggestive; —**erlei** *a:* —**erlei** Stoff two different kinds of material; —**erlei** Meinung *a* of differing opinions; —**erlei** zu tun haben have two different things to do; —**fach** *a* double.

Zweifel ['tsvaɪfəl] *m* **-s,** **-** doubt; z—**haft** *a* doubtful, dubious; z—**los** *a* doubtless; z—**n** *vi* doubt (an etw *(dat)* sth); —**sfall** *m:* im —**sfall** in case of doubt.

Zweig [tsvaɪk] *m* **-(e)s,** **-e** branch; —**geschäft** *nt* *(Comm)* branch; —**stelle** *f* branch (office).

zwei- *cpd:* Z—**heit** *f* duality; —**hundert** *num* two hundred; Z—**kampf** *m* duel; —**mal** *ad* twice; —**motorig** *a* twin-engined; —**reihig** *a* *(Anzug)* double-breasted; —**schneidig** *a* *(fig)* two-edged; Z—**sitzer** *m* **-s,** **-** two-seater; —**sprachig** *a* bilingual; —**spurig** *a* *(Aut)* two-lane; —**stimmig** *a* for two voices; Z—**taktmotor** *m* two-stroke engine.

zweit- [tsvaɪt] *cpd:* —**ens** *ad* secondly; —**größte(r,s)** *a* second largest; —**klassig** *a* second-class; —**letzte(r,s)** *a* last but one, penultimate; —**rangig** *a* second-rate; Z—**wagen** *m* second car.

Zwerchfell ['tsvɛrçfɛl] *nt* diaphragm.

Zwerg [tsvɛrk] *m* **-(e)s,** **-e** dwarf.

Zwetsche ['tsvɛtʃə] *f* **-,** **-n** plum.

Zwickel ['tsvɪkəl] *m* **-s,** **-** gusset.

zwicken ['tsvɪkən] *vt* pinch, nip.

Zwieback ['tsviːbak] *m* **-(e)s,** **-e** rusk.

Zwiebel ['tsviːbəl] *f* **-,** **-n** onion; *(Blumen—)* bulb; z—**artig** *a* bulbous.

Zwie- ['tsviː] *cpd:* —**gespräch** *vt* dialogue; —**licht** *nt* twilight; z—**lichtig** *a* shady, dubious; —**spalt** *m* conflict, split; z—**spältig** *a Gefühle* conflicting; *Charakter* contradictory; —**tracht** *f* discord, dissension.

Zwilling ['tsvɪlɪŋ] *m* **-s,** **-e** twin; *pl (Astrol)* Gemini.

zwingen ['tsvɪŋən] *vt* *irreg* force; —**nd** *a* Grund etc compelling.

zwinkern ['tsvɪŋkərn] *vi* blink; *(absichtlich)* wink.

Zwirn [tsvɪrn] *m* **-(e)s, -e** thread.
zwischen ['tsvɪʃən] *prep* +*acc or
dat* between; **Z—bemerkung** *f* (*incidental*) remark; **—blenden** *vt*
(*TV*) insert; **Z—ding** *nt* cross;
—durch [-'durç] *ad* in between;
(*räumlich*) here and there;
Z—ergebnis *nt* intermediate result;
Z—fall *m* incident; **Z—frage** *f*
question; **Z—gas** *nt*: **Z—gas geben**
double-declutch; **Z—handel** *m*
middlemen *pl*; middleman's trade;
Z—händler *m* middleman, agent;
Z—landung *f* stop, intermediate
landing; **—menschlich** *a* inter-
personal; **Z—raum** *m* space;
Z—ruf *m* interjection, interruption;
Z—spiel *nt* interlude; **—staatlich** *a*
interstate; international;
Z—station *f* intermediate station;

Z—stecker *m* (*Elec*) adaptor;
Z—wand *f* partition; **Z—zeit** *f* interval; **in der Z—zeit** in the
interim, meanwhile.
Zwist [tsvɪst] *m* **-es, -e** dispute,
feud.
zwitschern ['tsvɪtʃərn] *vti* twitter,
chirp.
Zwitter ['tsvɪtər] *m* **-s, -**
hermaphrodite.
zwölf [tsvœlf] *num* twelve.
Zyklus ['tsyːklʊs] *m* **-, Zyklen**
cycle.
Zylinder [tsi'lɪndər] *m* **-s, -**
cylinder; (*Hut*) top hat; **z—förmig**
a cylindrical.
Zyniker ['tsyːnikər] *m* **-s, -** cynic.
zynisch ['tsyːnɪʃ] *a* cynical.
Zynismus [tsy'nɪsmʊs] *m* cynicism.
Zyste ['tsystə] *f* **-, -n** cyst.

Länder, Völker und Sprachen

Ich bin Deutscher/Engländer/Albanier I am German/English/Albanian

ein Deutscher/Engländer/Albanier a German/an Englishman/an Albanian; eine Deutsche/Engländerin/Albanierin a German (woman/girl)/an English woman/girl/an Albanian (woman/girl)

sprechen Sie Deutsch/Englisch/Albanisch? do you speak German/ English/Albanian?

Adria (die), Adriatische(s) Meer the Adriatic.
Afrika Africa; Afrikaner(in f) m African; afrikanisch a African.
Ägäis (die), Ägäische(s) Meer the Aegean.
Ägypten Egypt; Ägypter(in f) m; ägyptisch a Egyptian.
Albanien Albania; Albanier(in f) m Albanian; albanisch a Albanian.
Algerien Algeria; Algerier(in f) m Algerian; algerisch a Algerian.
Alpen pl (die) the Alps pl.
Amazonas (der) the Amazon.
Amerika America; Amerikaner(in f) m American; amerikanisch a American.
Anden pl (die) the Andes pl.
Antarktis (die) the Antarctic.
Antillen pl (die) the Antilles pl.
Antwerpen Antwerp.
Arabien Arabia; Araber m Arab, Arabian; arabisch a Arab, Arabic, Arabian.
Argentinien Argentina, the Argentine; Argentinier(in f) m Argentinian; argentinisch a Argentinian.
Ärmelkanal (der) the English Channel.
Armenien Armenia; Armenier(in f) m Armenian; armenisch a Armenian.
Asien Asia; Asiat(in f) m Asian; asiatisch a Asian, Asiatic.
Athen Athens; Athener(in f) m Athenian; athenisch a Athenian.
Äthiopien Ethiopia; Äthiopier(in f) m Ethiopian; äthiopisch a Ethiopian.
Atlantik (der), Atlantische(r) Ozean the Atlantic (Ocean).
Ätna (der) Mount Etna.
Australien Australia; Australier(in f) m Australian; australisch a Australian.
Azoren pl (die) the Azores pl.
Balkan (der) the Balkans pl.
Basel Basle.
Bayern Bavaria; Bayer(in f) m Bavarian; bayerisch a Bavarian.
Belgien Belgium; Belgier(in f) m Belgian; belgisch a Belgian.

Belgrad Belgrade.
Birma Burma; Birmane *m*, Birmanin *f* Burmese; Birmanisch *a* Burmese.
Biskaya (die) the Bay of Biscay.
Bodensee (der) Lake Constance.
Böhmen Bohemia; Böhme *m*, Böhmin *f* Bohemian; böhmisch *a* Bohemian.
Bolivien Bolivia; Bolivianer(in *f*) *m* Bolivian; bolivianisch, bolvisch *a* Bolivian.
Brasilien Brazil; Brasilianer(in *f*) *m* Brazilian; brasilianisch *a* Brazilian.
Braunschweig Brunswick.
Brite *m*, Britin *f* Briton; britisch *a* British.
Brüssel Brussels.
Bulgarien Bulgaria; Bulgare *m*, Bulgarin *f* Bulgarian, Bulgar; bulgarisch *a* Bulgarian.
Burgund Burgundy; burgundisch, Burgunder *a* Burgundian.
Calais: Straße von Calais (die) the Straits of Dover *pl*.
Chile Chile; Chilene *m*, Chilenin *f* Chilean; chilenisch *a* Chilean.
China China; Chinese *m*, Chinesin *f* Chinese; chinesisch *a* Chinese.
Dänemark Denmark; Däne *m*, Dänin *f* Dane; dänisch *a* Danish.
Deutsche Demokratische Republik (die) German Democratic Republic, East Germany.
Deutschland Germany; Deutsche(r) *mf* German; deutsch *a* German.
Dolomiten *pl* (die) the Dolomites *pl*.
Donau (die) the Danube.
Dünkirchen Dunkirk.
Eismeer (das) the Arctic.
Elfenbeinküste (die) the Ivory Coast.
Elsaß (das) Alsace; Elsässer(in *f*) *m* Alsatian; elsässisch *a* Alsatian.
Engadin (das) the Engadine.
England England; Engländer(in *f*) *m* Englishman/-woman; englisch *a* English.
Estland Estonia; Este *m*, Estin *f* Estonian; estnisch *a* Estonian.
Etsch (die) the Adige.
Euphrat (der) the Euphrates.
Eurasien Eurasia.
Europa Europe; Europäer(in *f*) *m* European; europäisch *a* European.
Ferne(r) Osten (der) the Far East.
Finnland Finland; Finne *m*, Finnin *f* Finn; finnisch *a* Finnish.
Flandern Flanders; Flame *m*, Flämin *or* Flamin *f* Fleming; flämisch *a* Flemisn.
Florenz Florence; Florentiner(in *f*) *m* Florentine; florentinisch *a* Florentine.
Frankreich France; Franzose *m*, Französin *f* Frenchman/-woman; französisch *a* French.
Friesland Frisia; Friese *m*, Friesin *f* Frisian; friesisch *a* Frisian.
Genf Geneva.
Genfer See Lake Geneva.
Genua Genoa; Genuese *m*, Genuesin *f* Genoan; genuesisch *a* Genoan.
Griechenland Greece; Grieche *m*, Griechin *f* Greek; griechisch *a* Greek.

Großbritannien Great Britain; **Brite** *m*, **Britin** *f* Briton; **britisch, großbritannisch** *a* British.

Guinea Guinea.

Haag (der), Den Haag the Hague.

Hannover Hanover; **Hannoveraner(in** *f*) *m* Hanoverian; **Hannoveraner, hannoversch** *a* Hanoverian.

Hebriden *pl* (die) the Hebrides *pl*.

Helgoland Heligoland.

Hessen Hesse; **Hesse** *m*, **Hessin** *f* Hessian; **hessisch** *a* Hessian.

Holland Holland; **Holländer(in** *f*) *m* Dutchman/-woman; **holländisch** *a* Dutch.

Iberische Halbinsel (die) the Iberian Peninsula.

Indien India; **Inder(in** *f*) *m*, **Indianer(in** *f*) *m* Indian; **indisch, indianisch** *a* Indian.

Indonesien Indonesia; **Indonesier(in** *f*) *m* Indonesian; **indonesisch** *a* Indonesian.

Irak (*auch* der) Iraq; **Iraker(in** *f*) *m* Iraqi; **irakisch** *a* Iraqi.

Iran (*auch* der) Iran; **Iraner(in** *f*) *m* Iranian; **iranisch** *a* Iranian.

Irland Ireland; **Ire** *m*, **Irin** *f* Irishman/-woman; **irisch** *a* Irish.

Island Iceland; **Isländer(in** *f*) *m* Icelander; **isländisch** *a* Icelandic.

Israel Israel; **Israeli** *mf* Israeli; **israelisch** *a* Israeli.

Italien Italy; **Italiener(in** *f*) *m* Italian; **italienisch** *a* Italian.

Japan Japan; **Japaner(in** *f*) *m* Japanese; **japanisch** *a* Japanese.

Jemen (*auch* der) the Yemen; **Jemenit(in** *f*) *m* Yemeni; **jemenitisch** *a* Yemeni.

Jordanien Jordan; **Jordanier(in** *f*) *m* Jordanian; **jordanisch** *a* Jordanian.

Jugoslawien Yugoslavia; **Jugoslawe** *m*, **Jugoslawin** *f* Yugoslavian; **jugoslawisch** *a* Yugoslavian.

Kanada Canada; **Kanadier(in** *f*) *m* Canadian; **kanadisch** *a* Canadian.

Kanalinseln *pl* (die) the Channel Islands *pl*.

Kanarische Inseln *pl* (die) the Canary Islands *pl*, the Canaries *pl*.

Kap der Guten Hoffnung (das) the Cape of Good Hope.

Kapstadt Cape Town.

Karibische Inseln *pl* (die) the Caribbean Islands *pl*.

Karpaten *pl* (die) the Carpathians *pl*.

Kaspische(s) Meer (das) the Caspian Sea.

Kleinasien Asia Minor.

Köln Cologne.

Konstanz Constance.

Kreml (der) the Kremlin.

Kreta Crete; **Kreter(in** *f*) *m* Cretan; **kretisch** *a* Cretan.

Krim (die) the Crimea.

Kroatien Croatia; **Kroate** *m*, **Kroatin** *f* Croatian; **kroatisch** *a* Croatian.

Lappland Lapland; **Lappe** *m*, **Lappin** *f* Laplander; **lappisch** *a* Lapp.

Lateinamerika Latin America.

Lettland Latvia; **Lette** *m*, **Lettin** *f* Latvian; **lettisch** *a* Latvian.

Libanon the Lebanon; **Libanese** *m*, **Libanesin** *f* Lebanese; **libanesisch** a Lebanese.

Libyen Libya; **Libyer(in** *f*) *m* Libyan; **libyisch** a Libyan.

Lissabon Lisbon.

Litauen Lithuania; **Litauer(in** *f*) *m* Lithuanian; **litauisch** a Lithuanian.

Livland Livonia; **Livländer(in** *f*) *m* Livonian; **livländisch** a Livonian.

London London; **Londoner(in** *f*) *m* Londoner; **Londoner** a London.

Lothringen Lorraine.

Lüneburger Heide (die) the Lüneburg Heath.

Luxemburg Luxembourg.

Maas (die) the Meuse.

Mähren Moravia.

Mailand Milan; **Mailänder(in** *f*) *m* Milanese; **mailändisch** a Milanese..

Mallorca Majorca.

Mandschurei (die) Manchuria; **Mandschure** *m*, **Mandschurin** *f* Manchurian; **mandschurisch** a Manchurian.

Marokko Morocco; **Marokkaner(in** *f*) *m* Moroccan; **marokkanisch** a Moroccan.

Mazedonien Macedonia; **Mazedonier(in** *f*) *m* Macedonian; **mazedonisch** a Macedonian.

Mittelamerika Central America.

Mitteleuropa Central Europe.

Mittelmeer (das) the Mediterranean.

Moldau (die) Moldavia.

Mongolei (die) Mongolia; **Mongole** *m*, **Mongolin** *f* Mongol(ian); **mongolisch** a Mongol(ian).

Moskau Moscow; **Moskauer(in** *f*) *m* Muscovite; **moskauisch** a Muscovite.

München Munich.

Nahe(r) Osten (der) the Near East.

Neapel Naples; **Neapolitaner(in** *f*) *m* Neapolitan; **neapolitanisch** a Neapolitan.

Neufundland Newfoundland; **Neufundländer(in** *f*) *m* Newfoundlander; **neufundländisch** a Newfoundland.

Neuguinea New Guinea.

Neuseeland New Zealand; **Neuseeländer(in** *f*) *m* New. Zealander; **neuseeländisch** a New Zealand.

Niederlande *pl* **(die)** the Netherlands; **Niederländer(in** *f*) *m* Dutchman/-woman; **niederländisch** a Dutch.

Niedersachsen Lower Saxony.

Niederrhein Lower Rhine.

Nil (der) the Nile.

Nordirland Northern Ireland.

Nordsee (die) the North Sea.

Norwegen Norway; **Norweger(in** *f*) *m* Norwegian; **norwegisch** a Norwegian.

Nord-Ostsee-Kanal (der) the Kiel Canal.

Nordrhein-Westfalen North Rhine-Westphalia.

Nürnberg Nuremberg.

Oberbayern Upper Bavaria.

Ostasien Eastern Asia.

Ostende Ostend.

Ostsee (die) the Baltic.

Österreich Austria; **Österreicher(in** f) m Austrian; **österreichisch** a Austrian.

Palästina Palestine; **Palästinenser(in** f) m Palestinian; **palästinensisch a** Palestinian.

Paris Paris; **Pariser(in** f) m Parisian; **Pariser** a Parisian.

Pazifik (der), **Pazifische(r) Ozean** the Pacific.

Peloponnes (der or die) the Peloponnese.

Persien Persia; **Perser(in** f) m Persian; **persisch** a Persian.

Philippinen pl (die) the Philippines pl.

Polen Poland; **Pole** m, **Polin** f Pole; **polnisch** a Polish.

Pommern Pomerania; **Pommer(in** f) m Pomeranian; **pommersch a** Pomeranian.

Portugal Portugal; **Portugiese** m, **Portugiesin** f Portuguese; **portugiesisch a** Portuguese.

Prag Prague.

Preußen Prussia; **Preuße** m, **Preußin** f Prussian; **preußisch** a Prussian.

Pyrenäen pl (die) the Pyrenees pl.

Rhein (der) the Rhine; **rheinisch** a Rhenish.

Rhodesien Rhodesia; **Rhodesier(in** f) m Rhodesian; **rhodesisch** pl Rhodesian.

Rhodos Rhodes.

Rom Rome; **Römer(in** f) m Roman; **römisch** a Roman.

Rote(s) Meer the Red Sea.

Rumänien Ro(u)mania; **Rumäne** m, **Rumänin** f Ro(u)manian; **rumänisch a** Ro(u)manian.

Rußland Russia; **Russe** m, **Russin** f Russian; **russisch** a Russian.

Saarland the Saar.

Sachsen Saxony; **Sachse** m, **Sächsin** f Saxon; **sächsisch** a Saxon.

Sardinien Sardinia; **Sardinier(in** f) m, **Sarde** m, **Sardin** f Sardinian; **sardinisch,** **sardisch** a Sardinian.

Schlesien Silesia; **Schlesier(in** f) m Silesian; **schlesisch** a Silesian.

Schottland Scotland; **Schotte** m, **Schottin** f Scot, Scotsman/-woman; **schottisch** a Scottish, Scots, Scotch.

Schwaben Swabia; **Schwabe** m, **Schwäbin** f Swabian; **schwäbisch** a Swabian.

Schwarzwald (der) the Black Forest.

Schweden Sweden; **Schwede** m, **Schwedin** f Swede; **schwedisch** a Swedish.

Schweiz (die) Switzerland; **Schweizer(in** f) m Swiss; **schweizerisch** a Swiss.

Serbien Serbia; **Serbe** m, **Serbin** f Serbian; **serbisch** a Serbian.

Sibirien Siberia; **sibirisch** a Siberian.

Sizilien Sicily; **Sizilianer(in** f) m, **Sizilier(in** f) m Sicilian; **sizilsch, sizilianisch a** Sicilian.

Skandinavien Scandinavia; Skandinavier(in f) m Scandinavian; skandinavisch a Scandinavian.

Slowakei (die) Slovakia; Slowake m, Slowakin f Slovak; slowakisch a Slovak.

Sowjetunion (die) the Soviet Union; Sowjetbüger(in f) m Soviet; sowjetisch a Soviet.

Spanien Spain; Spanier(in f) m Spaniard; spanisch a Spanish.

Steiermark Styria; Steiermärker(in f) m, Steirer m, Steierin f Styrian; steiermärkisch, steirisch a Styrian.

Stille(r) Ozean the Pacific.

Syrien Syria; Syrer(in f) m Syrian; syrisch a Syrian.

Teneriffa Tenerife.

Themse (die) the Thames.

Thüringen Thuringia; Thüringer(in f) m Thuringian; thüringisch a Thuringian.

Tirol the Tyrol; Tiroler(in f) m Tyrolean; tirolisch a Tyrolean.

Tschechoslowakei (die) Czechoslovakia; Tscheche m, Tschechin f, Tschechoslowake m, Tschechoslowakin f Czech, Czechoslovak(ian); tschechisch, tschechoslowakisch a Czech, Czechoslovak(ian).

Toscana (die) Tuscany.

Trient Trent.

Tunesien Tunisia; Tunesier(in f) m Tunisian; tunesisch a Tunisian.

Türkei (die) Turkey; Türke m, Türkin f Turk; türkisch a Turkish.

Ungarn Hungary; Ungar(in f) m Hungarian; ungarisch a Hungarian.

Venedig Venice; Venetianer(in f) m Venetian; venetianisch a Venetian.

Vereinigte Staaten pl (die) the United States pl.

Vesuv (der) Vesuvius.

Vierwaldstättersee (der) Lake Lucerne.

Vogesen pl (die) the Vosges pl.

Volksrepublik China (die) the Peoples's Republic of China.

Vorderasien the Near East.

Warschau Warsaw.

Weichsel (die) the Vistula.

Westfalen Westphalia; Westfale m, Westfälin f Westphalian; westfälisch a Westphalian.

Westindien the West Indies; westindisch a West Indian.

Wien Vienna; Wiener(in f) m Viennese; Wiener a Viennese.

Zypern Cyprus; Zyprer(in f) m, Zyprier(in f) m, Zypriot(in f) m Cypriot; zyprisch, zypriotisch a Cypriot.

Abf.	Abfahrt *departure, dep*
Abk.	Abkürzung *abbreviation, abbr*
Abs.	Absatz *paragraph;* Absender *sender*
Abt.	Abteilung *department, dept*
AG	Aktiengesellschaft *(Brit) (public) limited company, Ltd, (US) corporation, inc*
Ank.	Ankunft *arrival, arr*
Anm.	Anmerkung *note*
b.a.w.	bis auf weiteres *until further notice*
Best. Nr.	Bestellnummer *order number*
Betr.	Betreff, betrifft *re*
Bhf.	Bahnhof *station*
BRD	Bundesrepublik Deutschland *Federal Republic of Germany*
b.w.	bitte wenden *please turn over, pto*
bzgl.	bezüglich *with reference to, re*
bzw.	beziehungsweise *(see text)*
ca.	circa, ungefähr *approximately, approx*
Cie., Co.	Kompanie *company, co*
DDR	Deutsche Demokratische Republik *German Democratic Republic, GDR*
d.h.	das heißt *that is, i.e.*
d.J.	dieses Jahres *of this year*
d.M.	dieses Monats *instant, inst*
DM	Deutsche Mark *German Mark, Deutschmark*
EDV	elektronische Datenverarbeitung *electronic data processing, EDP*
einschl.	einschließlich *inclusive, including, incl*
Einw.	Einwohner *inhabitant*
empf.	empfohlen(er Preis) *recommended (price)*
ev.	evangelisch *Protestant*
evtl.	eventuell *perhaps, possibly*
EWG	Europäische Wirtschaftsgemeinschaft *European Economic Community, EEC*
e. Wz.	eingetragenes Warenzeichen *registered trademark*
Expl.	Exemplar *sample, copy*
Fa.	Firma *firm;* in Briefen: *Messrs*
ff.	folgende Seiten *pages, pp*
Ffm.	Frankfurt am Main
fl. W.	fließendes Wasser *running water*
Forts.	Fortsetzung *continued, cont'd*

geb.	geboren *born;* geborene *née;* gebunden *bound.*
Gebr.	Gebrüder *Brothers, Bros*
ges. gesch.	gesetzlich geschützt *registered*
GmbH	Gesellschaft mit beschränkter Haftung *(Brit) (private) limited company, Ltd, (US) corporation, inc*
Hbf.	Hauptbahnhof *central station*
hl.	heilig *holy*
Hrsg.	Herausgeber *editor, ed*
i.A.	im Auftrag *for;* in Briefen auch: *pp*
Ing.	Ingenieur *engineer*
Inh.	Inhaber *proprietor, prop;* Inhalt *contents*
i.V.	in Vertretung *by proxy, on behalf of;* im Vorjahre *in the last or previous year;* in Vorbereitung *in preparation*
Jh.	Jahrhundert *century, cent*
jr., jun.	junior, der Jüngere *junior, jun, jr*
kath.	katholisch *Catholic, Cath*
kfm.	kaufmännisch *commercial*
Kfz.	*(see text)*
KG	Kommanditgesellschaft *limited partnership*
led.	ledig *single*
Lkw.	*(see text)*
lt.	laut *according to*
m. E.	meines Erachtens *in my opinion*
Mehrw. St.	Mehrwertsteuer *value-added tax, VAT*
Mrd.	Milliarde *thousand millions, (US) billion*
n. Chr.	nach Christus *AD*
Nr.	Numero, Nummer *number, no*
NS	Nachschrift *postscript, PS;* nationalsozialistisch *National Socialist*
OHG	Offene Handelsgesellschaft *general partnership*
PKW, Pkw.	*(see text)*
Pl.	Platz *square*
Postf.	Postfach *post-office box, PO box*
PS	Pferdestärken *horsepower, HP;* Nachschrift *postscript, PS*
S.	Seite *page, p*
s.	siehe *see*
sen.	senior, der Ältere *senior, sen, sr*
s.o.	siehe oben *see above*
St.	Stück *piece;* Sankt *Saint, St*
Std., Stde.	Stunde *hour, hr*
stdl.	stündlich *every hour*
Str.	Straße *street, St*
s.u.	siehe unten *see below*

tägl.	täglich *daily, per day*
Tsd.	Tausend *thousand*
u.	und *and*
u.a.	und andere(s) *and others;* unter anderem/anderen *among other things, inter alia/among others*
U.A.w.g.	Um Antwort wird gebeten *an answer is requested;* auf Einladung: *RSVP*
UdSSR	Union der Sozialistischen Sowjetrepubliken *Union of Soviet Socialist Republics, USSR*
u.E.	unseres Erachtens *in our opinion*
USA	Vereinigte Staaten (von Amerika) *United States (of America), USA.*
usf.	und so fort *and so forth, etc*
usw.	und so weiter *etcetera, etc*
u.U.	unter Umständen *possibly*
v. Chr.	vor Christus *BC*
Verf., Vf.	Verfasser *author*
verh.	verheiratet *married*
Verl.	Verlag *publishing firm;* Verleger *publisher*
vgl.	vergleiche *compare, cf, cp*
v.H.	vom Hundert *per cent*
Wz.	Warenzeichen *registered trademark*
z.B.	zum Beispiel *for example or instance, eg*
z.H(d)	zu Händen *for the attention of*
z.T.	zum Teil *partly*
zw.	zwischen *between; among*
z.Z(t).	zur Zeit *at the time, at present, for the time being*

German irregular verbs
*with 'sein'

infinitive	present indicative (2nd, 3rd sing.)	preterite	past participle
aufschrecken*	schrickst auf, schrickt auf	schrak *or* schreckte auf	aufgeschreckt
ausbedingen	bedingst aus, bedingt aus	bedang *or* bedingte aus	ausbedungen
backen	bäckst, bäckt	backte *or* buk	gebacken
befehlen	befiehlst, befiehlt	befahl	befohlen
beginnen	beginnst, beginnt	begann	begonnen
beißen	beißt, beißt	biß	gebissen
bergen	birgst, birgt	barg	geborgen
bersten*	birst, birst	barst	geborsten
bescheißen*	bescheißt, bescheißt	beschiß	beschissen
bewegen	bewegst, bewegt	bewog	bewogen
biegen	biegst, biegt	bog	gebogen
bieten	bietest, bietet	bot	geboten
binden	bindest, bindet	band	gebunden
bitten	bittest, bittet	bat	gebeten
blasen	bläst, bläst	blies	geblasen
bleiben*	bleibst, bleibt	blieb	geblieben
braten	brätst, brät	briet	gebraten
brechen*	brichst, bricht	brach	gebrochen
brennen	brennst, brennt	brannte	gebrannt
bringen	bringst, bringt	brachte	gebracht
denken	denkst, denkt	dachte	gedacht
dreschen	drisch(e)st, drischt	drasch	gedroschen
dringen*	dringst, dringt	drang	gedrungen
dürfen	darfst, darf	durfte	gedurft
empfehlen	empfiehlst, empfiehlt	empfahl	empfohlen
erbleichen*	erbleichst, erbleicht	erbleichte	erblichen
erlöschen*	erlischst, erlischt	erlosch	erloschen
erschrecken*	erschrickst, erschrickt	erschrak	erschrocken
essen	ißt, ißt	aß	gegessen
fahren*	fährst, fährt	fuhr	gefahren
fallen*	fällst, fällt	fiel	gefallen
fangen	fängst, fängt	fing	gefangen
fechten	fichtst, ficht	focht	gefochten
finden	findest, findet	fand	gefunden

infinitive	present indicative (2nd, 3rd sing.)	preterite	past participle
flechten	flichst, flicht	flocht	geflochten
fliegen*	fliegst, fliegt	flog	geflogen
fliehen*	fliehst, flieht	floh	geflohen
fließen*	fließt, fließt	floß	geflossen
fressen	frißt, frißt	fraß	gefressen
frieren	frierst, friert	fror	gefroren
gären*	gärst, gärt	gor	gegoren
gebären	gebierst, gebiert	gebar	geboren
geben	gibst, gibt	gab	gegeben
gedeihen*	gedeihst, gedeiht	gedieh	gediehen
gehen*	gehst, geht	ging	gegangen
gelingen*	——, gelingt	gelang	gelungen
gelten	giltst, gilt	galt	gegolten
genesen*	gene(se)st, genest	genas	genesen
genießen	genießt, genießt	genoß	genossen
geraten*	gerätst, gerät	geriet	geraten
geschehen*	——, geschieht	geschah	geschehen
gewinnen	gewinnst, gewinnt	gewann	gewonnen
gießen	gießt, gießt	goß	gegossen
gleichen	gleichst, gleicht	glich	geglichen
gleiten*	gleitest, gleitet	glitt	geglitten
glimmen	glimmst, glimmt	glomm	geglommen
graben	gräbst, gräbt	grub	gegraben
greifen	greifst, greift	griff	gegriffen
haben	hast, hat	hatte	gehabt
halten	hältst, hält	hielt	gehalten
hängen	hängst, hängt	hing	gehangen
hauen	haust, haut	hieb	gehauen
heben	hebst, hebt	hob	gehoben
heißen	heißt, heißt	hieß	geheißen
helfen	hilfst, hilft	half	geholfen
kennen	kennst, kennt	kannte	gekannt
klimmen*	klimmst, klimmt	klomm	geklommen
klingen	klingst, klingt	klang	geklungen
kneifen	kneifst, kneift	kniff	gekniffen
kommen*	kommst, kommt	kam	gekommen
können	kannst, kann	konnte	gekonnt
kriechen*	kriechst, kriecht	kroch	gekrochen
laden	lädst, lädt	lud	geladen
lassen	läßt, läßt	ließ	gelassen
laufen*	läufst, läuft	lief	gelaufen

infinitive	present indicative (2nd, 3rd sing.)	preterite	past participle
leiden	leidest, leidet	litt	gelitten
leihen	leihst, leiht	lieh	geliehen
lesen	liest, liest	las	gelesen
liegen*	liegst, liegt	lag	gelegen
lügen	lügst, lügt	log	gelogen
mahlen	mahlst, mahlt	mahlte	gemahlen
meiden	meidest, meidet	mied	gemieden
melken	milkst, milkt	molk	gemolken
messen	mißt, mißt	maß	gemessen
mißlingen*	——, mißlingt	mißlang	mißlungen
mögen	magst, mag	mochte	gemocht
müssen	mußt, muß	mußte	gemußt
nehmen	nimmst, nimmt	nahm	genommen
nennen	nennst, nennt	nannte	genannt
pfeifen	pfeifst, pfeift	pfiff	gepfiffen
preisen	preist, preist	pries	gepriesen
quellen*	quillst, quillt	quoll	gequollen
raten	rätst, rät	riet	geraten
reiben	reibst, reibt	rieb	gerieben
reißen*	reißt, reißt	riß	gerissen
reiten*	reitest, reitet	ritt	geritten
rennen*	rennst, rennt	rannte	gerannt
riechen	riechst, riecht	roch	gerochen
ringen	ringst, ringt	rang	gerungen
rinnen*	rinnst, rinnt	rann	geronnen
rufen	rufst, ruft	rief	gerufen
salzen	salzt, salzt	salzte	gesalzen
saufen	säufst, säuft	soff	gesoffen
saugen	saugst, saugt	sog	gesogen
schaffen	schaffst, schafft	schuf	geschaffen
schallen	schallst, schallt	scholl	geschollen
scheiden*	scheidest, scheidet	schied	geschieden
scheinen	scheinst, scheint	schien	geschienen
schelten	schiltst, schilt	schalt	gescholten
scheren	scherst, schert	schor	geschoren
schieben	schiebst, schiebt	schob	geschoben
schießen	schießt, schießt	schoß	geschossen
schinden	schindest, schindet	schund	geschunden
schlafen	schläfst, schläft	schlief	geschlafen
schlagen	schlägst, schlägt	schlug	geschlagen
schleichen*	schleichst, schleicht	schlich	geschlichen

Infinitive	present indicative (2nd, 3rd sing.)	preterite	past participle
schleifen	schleifst, schleift	schliff	geschliffen
schließen	schließt, schließt	schloß	geschlossen
schlingen	schlingst, schlingt	schlang	geschlungen
schmeißen	schmeißt, schmeißt	schmiß	geschmissen
schmelzen*	schmilzt, schmilzt	schmolz	geschmolzen
schneiden	schneidest, schneidet	schnitt	geschnitten
schreiben	schreibst, schreibt	schrieb	geschrieben
schreien	schreist, schreit	schrie	geschrie(e)n
schreiten*	schreitest, schreitet	schritt	geschritten
schweigen	schweigst, schweigt	schwieg	geschwiegen
schwellen*	schwillst, schwillt	schwoll	geschwollen
schwimmen*	schwimmst, schwimmt	schwamm	geschwommen
schwinden*	schwindest, schwindet	schwand	geschwunden
schwingen	schwingst, schwingt	schwang	geschwungen
schwören	schwörst, schwört	schwur	geschworen
sehen	siehst, sieht	sah	gesehen
sein*	bist, ist	war	gewesen
senden	sendest, sendet	sandte	gesandt
singen	singst, singt	sang	gesungen
sinken*	sinkst, sinkt	sank	gesunken
sinnen*	sinnst, sinnt	sann	gesonnen
sitzen*	sitzt, sitzt	saß	gesessen
sollen	sollst, soll	sollte	gesollt
speien	speist, speit	spie	gespie(e)n
spinnen	spinnst, spinnt	spann	gesponnen
sprechen	sprichst, spricht	sprach	gesprochen
sprießen*	sprießt, sprießt	sproß	gesprossen
springen*	springst, springt	sprang	gesprungen
stechen	stichst, sticht	stach	gestochen
stecken	steckst, steckt	steckte or stak	gesteckt
stehen	stehst, steht	stand	gestanden
stehlen	stiehlst, stiehlt	stahl	gestohlen
steigen*	steigst, steigt	stieg	gestiegen
sterben*	stirbst, stirbt	starb	gestorben
stinken	stinkst, stinkt	stank	gestunken
stoßen	stößt, stößt	stieß	gestoßen
streichen	streichst, streicht	strich	gestrichen
streiten	streitest, streitet	stritt	gestritten
tragen	trägst, trägt	trug	getragen
treffen	triffst, trifft	traf	getroffen
treiben*	treibst, treibt'	trieb	getrieben

infinitive	present indicative (2nd, 3rd sing.)	preterite	past participle
treten*	trittst, tritt	trat	getreten
trinken	trinkst, trinkt	trank	getrunken
trügen	trügst, trügt	trog	getrogen
tun	tust, tut	tat	getan
verderben	verdirbst, verdirbt	verdarb	verdorben
verdrießen	verdrießt, verdrießt	verdroß	verdrossen
vergessen	vergißt, vergißt	vergaß	vergessen
verlieren	verlierst, verliert	verlor	verloren
verschleißen	verschleißt, verschleißt	verschliß	verschlissen
wachsen*	wächst, wächst	wuchs	gewachsen
wägen	wägst, wägt	wog	gewogen
waschen	wäschst, wäscht	wusch	gewaschen
weben	webst, webt	wob	gewoben
weichen*	weichst, weicht	wich	gewichen
weisen	weist, weist	wies	gewiesen
wenden	wendest, wendet	wandte	gewandt
werben	wirbst, wirbt	warb	geworben
werden*	wirst, wird	wurde	geworden
werfen	wirfst, wirft	warf	geworfen
wiegen	wiegst, wiegt	wog	gewogen
winden	windest, windet	wand	gewunden
wissen	weißt, weiß	wußte	gewußt
wollen	willst, will	wollte	gewollt
wringen	wringst, wringt	wrang	gewrungen
zeihen	zeihst, zeiht	zieh	geziehen
ziehen*	ziehst, zieht	zog	gezogen
zwingen	zwingst, zwingt	zwang	gezwungen

A

A, a [eɪ] *n* A *nt*, a *nt.*

a, an [eɪ, ə; æn, ən] *indef art* ein/eine/ein. **£1 a metre** 1£ pro or das Meter.

aback [ə'bæk] *ad:* **to be taken —** verblüfft sein.

abandon [ə'bændən] *vt (give up)* aufgeben; *(desert)* verlassen; *n* Hingabe *f.*

abashed [ə'bæʃt] *a* verlegen.

abate [ə'beɪt] *vi* nachlassen, sich legen.

abattoir ['æbətwɑ:*] *n* Schlachthaus *nt.*

abbey ['æbɪ] *n* Abtei *f.*

abbot ['æbət] *n* Abt *m.*

abbreviate [ə'bri:vɪeɪt] *vt* abkürzen.

abbreviation [əbri:vɪ'eɪʃən] *n* Abkürzung *f.*

ABC ['eɪbi:'si:] *n (lit, fig)* Abc *nt.*

abdicate ['æbdɪkeɪt] *vt* aufgeben; *vi* abdanken.

abdication [æbdɪ'keɪʃən] *n* Abdankung *f;* (Amts)niederlegung *f.*

abdomen ['æbdəmən] *n* Unterleib *m.*

abdominal [æb'dɒmɪnl] *a* Unterleibs-.

abduct [æb'dʌkt] *vt* entführen; **—ion** [æb'dʌkʃən] Entführung *f.*

aberration [æbə'reɪʃən] *n* (geistige) Verwirrung *f.*

abet [ə'bet] *vt see* **aid** *vt.*

abeyance [ə'beɪəns] *n:* **in —** in der Schwebe; *(disuse)* außer Kraft.

abhor [əb'hɔ:*] *vt* verabscheuen.

abhorrent [əb'hɒrənt] *a* verabscheuungswürdig.

abide [ə'baɪd] *vt* vertragen; leiden; **— by** *vt* sich halten an (+acc).

ability [ə'bɪlɪtɪ] *n (power)* Fähigkeit *f;* *(skill)* Geschicklichkeit *f.*

abject ['æbdʒekt] *a liar* übel; *poverty* größte(r, s); *apology* zerknirscht.

ablaze [ə'bleɪz] *a* in Flammen; *with lights* hell erleuchtet.

able ['eɪbl] *a* geschickt, fähig; **to be — to do sth** etw tun können; **—bodied** *a* kräftig; *seaman* Voll-; *(Mil)* wehrfähig.

ably ['eɪblɪ] *ad* geschickt.

abnormal [æb'nɔ:məl] *a* regelwidrig, abnorm; **—ity** [æbnɔ:'mælɪtɪ] Regelwidrigkeit *f;* *(Med)* krankhafte Erscheinung *f.*

aboard [ə'bɔ:d] *ad, prep* an Bord (+gen).

abode [ə'bəud] *n:* **of no fixed —** ohne festen Wohnsitz.

abolish [ə'bɒlɪʃ] *vt* abschaffen.

abolition [æbə'lɪʃən] *n* Abschaffung *f.*

abominable *a,* **abominably** *ad* [ə'bɒmɪnəbl, -blɪ] scheußlich.

aborigine [æbə'rɪdʒɪni:] *n* Ureinwohner *m.*

abort [ə'bɔ:t] *vt* abtreiben; fehlgebären; **—ion** [ə'bɔ:ʃən] Abtreibung *f;* *(miscarriage)* Fehlgeburt *f;* **—ive** *a* mißlungen.

abound [ə'baʊnd] *vi* im Überfluß vorhanden sein; **to —** in Überfluß haben an (+ *dat*).

about [ə'baʊt] *ad* (*nearby*) in der Nähe; (*roughly*) ungefähr; (*around*) umher, herum; *prep* (*topic*) über (+ *acc*); (*place*) um, um... herum; **to be —** in Begriff sein zu; **I was — to** go out ich wollte gerade weggehen.

above [ə'bʌv] *ad* oben; *prep* über; **a** obig; **— all** vor allem; **—board** **a** offen, ehrlich.

abrasion [ə'breɪʒən] *n* Abschürfung *f*.

abrasive [ə'breɪzɪv] *n* Schleifmittel *nt*; **a** Abschleif-; *personality* zermürbend, aufreibend.

abreast [ə'brest] *ad* nebeneinander; **to keep —** of Schritt halten mit.

abridge [ə'brɪdʒ] *vt* (ab)kürzen.

abroad [ə'brɔːd] *ad* be im Ausland; **go in** Ausland.

abrupt [ə'brʌpt] *a* (*sudden*) abrupt, jäh; (*curt*) schroff.

abscess ['æbsɪs] *n* Geschwür *nt*.

abscond [əb'skɒnd] *vi* flüchten, sich davonmachen.

absence ['æbsəns] *n* Abwesenheit *f*.

absent ['æbsənt] *a* abwesend, nicht da; (*lost in thought*) geistesabwesend; **—ee** [æbsən'tiː] Abwesende(r) *m*; **—eeism** [æbsən'tiːɪzəm] Fehlen *nt* (am Arbeitsplatz/in der Schule); **—minded** *a* zerstreut.

absolute ['æbsəluːt] *a* absolut; *power* unumschränkt; *rubbish* vollkommen, rein; **—ly** ['æbsəluːtlɪ] *ad* absolut, vollkommen; **—!** ganz bestimmt!

absolve [əb'zɒlv] *vt* entbinden; freisprechen.

absorb [əb'zɔːb] *vt* aufsaugen, absorbieren; (*fig*) ganz in Anspruch nehmen, fesseln; **—ent** *a* absorbierend; **—ent cotton** (*US*) Verbandwatte *f*; **—ing** *a* aufsaugend; (*fig*) packend.

abstain [əb'steɪn] *vi* (*in vote*) sich enthalten; **— from** (*keep from*) sich enthalten (+ *gen*).

abstemious [əb'stiːmɪəs] *a* mäßig, enthaltsam.

abstention [əb'stenʃən] *n* (*in vote*) (Stimm)enthaltung *f*.

abstinence ['æbstɪnəns] *n* Enthaltsamkeit *f*.

abstract ['æbstrækt] *a* abstrakt; *n* Abriß *m*; [æb'strækt] *vt* abstrahieren, aussondern.

abstruse [æb'struːs] *a* verworren, abstrus.

absurd [əb'sɜːd] *a* absurd; **—ity** Unsinnigkeit *f*, Absurdität *f*.

abundance [ə'bʌndəns] *n* Überfluß *m* (*of an* + *dat*).

abundant [ə'bʌndənt] *a* reichlich.

abuse [ə'bjuːs] *n* (*rude language*) Beschimpfung *f*; (*ill usage*) Mißbrauch *m*; (*bad practice*) (Amts)mißbrauch *m*; [ə'bjuːz] *vt* (*misuse*) mißbrauchen.

abusive [ə'bjuːsɪv] *a* beleidigend, Schimpf-.

abysmal [ə'bɪzməl] *a* scheußlich; *ignorance* bodenlos.

abyss [ə'bɪs] *n* Abgrund *m*.

academic [ækə'demɪk] *a* akademisch; (*theoretical*) theoretisch.

academy [ə'kædəmɪ] *n* (*school*) Hochschule *f*; (*society*) Akademie *f*.

accede [æk'siːd] *vi*: **— to** *office* antreten; *throne* besteigen; *request* zustimmen (+ *dat*).

accelerate [æk'seləreɪt] *vi* schneller werden; (*Aut*) Gas geben; *vt* beschleunigen.

acceleration [ækselə'reɪʃən] n
Beschleunigung f.

accelerator [ək'seləreɪtə*] n Gas-
(pedal) nt.

accent ['æksent] n Akzent m, Tonfall m; (mark) Akzent m; (stress)
Betonung f; **—uate** [æk'sentjueɪt]
vt betonen.

accept [ək'sept] vt (take) annehmen; (agree to) akzeptieren;
—able a annehmbar; **—ance**
Annahme f.

access ['ækses] n Zugang m; **—ible**
[æk'sesɪbl] a (easy to approach) zugänglich; (within reach) (leicht)
erreichbar; **—ion** [æk'seʃən] f (to
throne) Besteigung f; (to office)
Antritt m.

accessory [æk'sesərɪ] n Zube-
hörteil nt; **accessories** pl Zubehör
nt; **toilet accessories** pl Toilettenartikel pl.

accident ['æksɪdənt] n Unfall m;
(coincidence) Zufall m; **by —**
zufällig; **—al** [æksɪ'dentl] a unbeabsichtigt; (accidental) [æksɪ'dentəli] ad
zufällig; **to be —-prone** zu Unfällen
neigen.

acclaim [ə'kleɪm] vt zujubeln
(+ dat); n Beifall m.

acclimatize [ə'klaɪmətaɪz] vt: **to become —d** sich gewöhnen (to an
+ acc), sich akklimatisieren.

accolade ['ækəleɪd] n Auszeichnung f.

accommodate [ə'kɒmədeɪt] vt
unterbringen; (hold) Platz haben
für; (oblige) (aus)helfen (+ dat).

accommodating [ə'kɒmədeɪtɪŋ] a
entgegenkommend.

accommodation [ə'kɒmə'deɪʃən]
n Unterkunft f.

accompaniment [ə'kʌmpənɪmənt]
n Begleitung f.

accompanist [ə'kʌmpənɪst] n
Begleiter m.

accompany [ə'kʌmpənɪ] vt
begleiten.

accomplice [ə'kʌmplɪs] n Helfers-
helfer m, Komplize m.

accomplish [ə'kʌmplɪʃ] vt (fulfil)
durchführen; (finish) vollenden;
aim erreichen; **—ed** a vollendet,
ausgezeichnet; **—ment** (skill)
Fähigkeit f; (completion) Vollen-
dung f; (feat) Leistung f.

accord [ə'kɔːd] n Übereinstimmung
f; **of one's own —** freiwillig; vt
gewähren; **—ance: in —ance with**
in Übereinstimmung mit; **—ing to**
nach, laut (+ gen); **—ingly** ad
danach, dementsprechend.

accordion [ə'kɔːdɪən] n Ziehharmonika f, Akkordeon nt; **—ist**
Akkordeonspieler m.

accost [ə'kɒst] vt ansprechen.

account [ə'kaʊnt] n (bill) Rechnung
f; (narrative) Bericht m; (report)
Rechenschaftsbericht m; (in bank)
Konto nt; (importance) Geltung f;
on — auf Rechnung; **of no —** ohne
Bedeutung; **on no —** keinesfalls;
on — of wegen; **to take into —**
berücksichtigen; **— for** vt expenditure Rechenschaft ablegen für;
how do you — for that? wie
erklären Sie (sich) das?; **—able** a
verantwortlich; **—ancy** Buchhaltung f; **—ant** Wirtschafts-
prüfer(in f) m.

accoutrements [ə'kuːtrəmənts]
npl Ausrüstung f.

accredited [ə'kredɪtɪd] a
beglaubigt, akkreditiert.

accretion [ə'kriːʃən] n Zunahme f.

accrue [ə'kruː] vi erwachsen, sich
ansammeln.

accumulate [ə'kjuːmjʊleɪt] vt ansammeln; vi sich ansammeln.

accumulation [əkju:mju'leɪʃən] n (act) Aufhäufung f; (result) Ansammlung f.

accuracy ['ækjurəsɪ] n Genauigkeit f.

accurate ['ækjurɪt] a genau; —ly ad genau, richtig.·

accursed, accurst [ə'kɜːst] a verflucht.

accusation [ækju:'zeɪʃən] n Anklage f, Beschuldigung f.

accusative [ə'kju:zətɪv] n Akkusativ m, vierte(r) Fall m.

accuse [ə'kju:z] vt anklagen, beschuldigen; —d Angeklagte(r) mf.

accustom [ə'kʌstəm] vt gewöhnen (to an +acc); —ed a gewohnt.

ace [eɪs] n As nt; (col) As nt, Kanone f.

ache [eɪk] n Schmerz m; vi (be sore) schmerzen, weh tun; I — all over mir tut es überall weh.

achieve [ə'tʃi:v] vt zustande bringen; aim erreichen; —ment Leistung f; (act) Erreichen nt.

acid ['æsɪd] n Säure f; a sauer, scharf; —ity [ə'sɪdɪtɪ] Säuregehalt m; — test (fig) Nagelprobe f.

acknowledge [ək'nɒlɪdʒ] vt receipt bestätigen; (admit) zugeben; —ment Anerkennung f; (letter) Empfangsbestätigung f.

acne ['æknɪ] n Akne f.

acorn ['eɪkɔ:n] n Eichel f.

acoustic [ə'ku:stɪk] a akustisch; —s pl Akustik f.

acquaint [ə'kweɪnt] vt vertraut machen; —ance (person) Bekannte(r) m; (knowledge) Kenntnis f.

acquiesce [ækwɪ'es] vi sich abfinden (in mit).

acquire [ə'kwaɪə*] vt erwerben.

acquisition [ækwɪ'zɪʃən] n Errungenschaft f; (act) Erwerb m.

acquisitive [ə'kwɪzɪtɪv] a gewinnsüchtig.

acquit [ə'kwɪt] vt (free) freisprechen; to — o.s. sich bewähren; —tal Freispruch m.

acre ['eɪkə*] n Morgen m; —age Fläche f.

acrimonious [ækrɪ'məʊnɪəs] a bitter.

acrobat ['ækrəbæt] n Akrobat m.

acrobatics [ækrə'bætɪks] npl akrobatische Kunststücke pl.

across [ə'krɒs] prep über (+acc); he lives — the river er wohnt auf der anderen Seite des Flusses; ad hinüber, herüber; ten metres — zehn Meter weit; he lives — from us er wohnt uns gegenüber; —the-board a pauschal.

act [ækt] n (deed) Tat f; (Jur) Gesetz nt; (Theat) Akt m; (Theat: turn) Nummer f; vi (take action) handeln; (behave) sich verhalten; (pretend) vorgeben; (Theat) spielen; vt (in play) spielen; —ing a stellvertretend; n Schauspielkunst f; (performance) Aufführung f.

action ['ækʃən] n· (deed) Tat f; Handlung f; (motion) Bewegung f; (way of working) Funktionieren nt; (battle) Einsatz m, Gefecht nt; (lawsuit) Klage f, Prozeß m; to take — etwas unternehmen.

activate ['æktɪveɪt]· vt in Betrieb setzen, aktivieren.

active ['æktɪv] a (brisk) rege, tatkräftig; (working) aktiv; (Gram) aktiv, Tätigkeits-; —ly ad aktiv, tätig.

activist ['æktɪvɪst] n Aktivist m.

activity [æk'tɪvɪtɪ] n Aktivität f; (doings) Unternehmungen pl; (occupation) Tätigkeit f.

actor ['æktə*] n Schauspieler m.

actress ['æktrɪs] n Schauspielerin f.

actual ['æktjʊəl] a wirklich; —ly ad tatsächlich; —ly no eigentlich nicht.

acumen ['ækjumen] n Scharfsinn m.

acupuncture ['ækjupʌŋktʃə*] n Akupunktur f.

acute [ə'kju:t] a (severe) heftig, akut; (keen) scharfsinnig; —ly ad akut, scharf.

ad [æd] n abbr of advertisement.

adage ['ædɪdʒ] n Sprichwort m.

Adam ['ædəm] n Adam m; —'s apple Adamsapfel m.

adamant ['ædəmənt] a eisern; hartnäckig.

adapt [ə'dæpt] vt anpassen; vi sich anpassen (to an +acc); —able a anpassungsfähig; —ation [ædæp'teɪʃən] (Theat, etc) Bearbeitung f; (adjustment) Anpassung f; —er (Elec) Zwischenstecker m.

add [æd] vt (join) hinzufügen; numbers addieren; — up vi (make sense) stimmen; — up to vt ausmachen.

addendum [ə'dendəm] n Zusatz m.

adder ['ædə*] n Kreuzotter f, Natter f.

addict ['ædɪkt] n Süchtige(r) mf; —ed a [ə'dɪktɪd] —ed to -süchtig; —ion [ə'dɪkʃən] Sucht f.

adding machine ['ædɪŋməʃi:n] n Addiermaschine f.

addition [ə'dɪʃən] n Anhang m, Addition f; (Math) Addition f, Zusammenzählen nt; in — zusätzlich, außerdem; —al a zusätzlich, weiter.

additive ['ædɪtɪv] n Zusatz m.

addled ['ædld] a faul, schlecht; (fig) verwirrt.

address [ə'dres] n Adresse f; ·(speech) Ansprache f; form of — Anredeform f; vt letter adressieren; (speak to) ansprechen; (make speech to) eine Ansprache halten an (+acc); —ee [ædre'si:] Empfänger(in f) m, Adressat m.

adenoids ['ædənɔɪdz] npl Polypen pl.

adept ['ædept] a geschickt; to be — at gut sein in (+dat).

adequacy ['ædɪkwəsɪ] n Angemessenheit f.

adequate ['ædɪkwɪt] a angemessen; —ly ad hinreichend.

adhere [əd'hɪə*] vi: — to (lit) haften an (+dat); (fig) festhalten an (+dat).

adhesion [əd'hi:ʒən] n Festhaften nt; (Phys) Adhäsion f.

adhesive [əd'hi:zɪv] a klebend; Kleb(e)-; n Klebstoff m.

adieu [ə'dju:] n Adieu nt, Lebewohl nt.

adjacent [ə'dʒeɪsənt] a benachbart.

adjective ['ædʒəktɪv] n Adjektiv nt, Eigenschaftswort nt.

adjoining [ə'dʒɔɪnɪŋ] a benachbart, Neben-.

adjourn [ə'dʒɜ:n] vt vertagen; vi abbrechen.

adjudicate [ə'dʒu:dɪkeɪt] vti entscheiden, ein Urteil fällen.

adjudication [ədʒu:dɪ'keɪʃən] n Entscheidung f.

adjudicator [ə'dʒu:dɪkeɪtə*] n Schiedsrichter m, Preisrichter m.

adjust [ə'dʒʌst] vt (alter) anpassen; (put right) einstellen, richtig stellen; —able a verstellbar; —ment (rearrangement) Anpassung f; (settlement) Schlichtung f.

adjutant ['ædʒətənt] n Adjutant m.

ad-lib [æd'lɪb] vi improvisieren; n Improvisation f; a, ad improvisiert.

administer [əd'mɪnɪstə*] vt (manage) verwalten; (dispense) ausüben; justice sprechen; medicine geben.

administration [ədmɪnɪs'treɪʃən] n Verwaltung f; (Pol) Regierung f.

administrative [əd'mɪnɪstrətɪv] a Verwaltungs-.

administrator [əd'mɪnɪstreɪtə*] n Verwaltungsbeamte(r) m.

admirable ['ædmərəbl] a bewundernswert.

admiral ['ædmərəl] n Admiral m; A—ty Admiralität f.

admiration [ædmɪ'reɪʃən] n Bewunderung f.

admire [əd'maɪə*] vt (respect) bewundern; .(love) verehren; —r Bewunderer m.

admission [əd'mɪʃən] n (entrance) Einlaß m; (fee) Eintritt(spreis) m; (confession) Geständnis nt.

admit [əd'mɪt] vt (let in) einlassen; (confess) gestehen; (accept) anerkennen; —tance Zulassung f; —tedly ad zugegebenermaßen.

ado [ə'du:] n: without more — ohne weitere Umstände.

adolescence [ædə'lesns] n Jugendalter nt.

adolescent [ædə'lesnt] a heranwachsend, jugendlich; n Jugendliche(r) mf.

adopt [ə'dɒpt] vt child adoptieren; idea übernehmen; —ion [ə'dɒpʃən] (of child) Adoption f; (of idea) Übernahme f.

adorable [ə'dɔːrəbl] a anbetungswürdig; (likeable) entzückend.

adoration [ædɒ'reɪʃən] n Anbetung f; Verehrung f.

adore [ə'dɔː*] vt anbeten; verehren.

adoring [ə'dɔːrɪŋ] a verehrend.

adorn [ə'dɔːn] vt schmücken.

adornment [ə'dɔːnmənt] n Schmuck m, Verzierung f.

adrenalin [ə'drenəlɪn] n Adrenalin nt.

adrift [ə'drɪft] ad Wind und Wellen preisgegeben.

adroit [ə'drɔɪt] a gewandt.

adulation [ædjʊ'leɪʃən] n Lobhudelei f.

adult ['ædʌlt] a erwachsen; n Erwachsene(r) mf.

adulterate [ə'dʌltəreɪt] vt verfälschen, mischen.

adultery [ə'dʌltərɪ] n Ehebruch m.

advance [əd'vɑːns] n (progress) Vorrücken nt; (money) Vorschuß m; vt (move forward) vorrücken; money vorschießen; argument vorbringen; vi vorwärtsgehen; in — im voraus; in — of vor (+dat); — booking Vorbestellung f, Vorverkauf m; —d a (ahead) vorgerückt; (modern) fortgeschritten; study für Fortgeschrittene; —ment Förderung f; (promotion) Beförderung f.

advantage [əd'vɑːntɪdʒ] n Vorteil m; —ous [ædvən'teɪdʒəs] a vorteilhaft; to have an — over sb jdm gegenüber im Vorteil sein; to be of — von Nutzen sein; to take — of (misuse) ausnutzen; (profit from) Nutzen ziehen aus.

advent ['ædvent] n Ankunft f; A— Advent m.

adventure [əd'ventʃə*] n Abenteuer nt.

adventurous [əd'ventʃərəs] a abenteuerlich, waghalsig.

aloud [ə'laʊd] ad laut.

alphabet ['ælfəbɛt] n Alphabet nt; —ical [ælfə'bɛtɪkl] a alphabetisch.

alpine ['ælpaɪn] a alpin, Alpen-.

already [ɔːl'rɛdɪ] ad schon, bereits.

also ['ɔːlsəʊ] ad auch, außerdem.

altar ['ɔːltə*] n Altar m.

alter ['ɔːltə*] vti ändern; dress umändern; —ation [ɒltə'reɪʃən] Änderung f; Umänderung f; (of building) Umbau m.

alternate [ɒl'tɜːnɪt] a abwechselnd; [ɒltə:neɪt] vi abwechseln (with mit); —ly ad abwechselnd, wechselweise.

alternative [ɒl'tɜːnətɪv] a andere(r, s); n (Aus)wahl f, Alternative f; what's the —? welche Alternative gibt es?; we have no — uns bleibt keine andere Wahl; —ly ad im anderen Falle.

although [ɔːl'ðəʊ] cj obwohl, wenn auch.

altitude ['æltɪtjuːd] n Höhe f.

alto ['æltəʊ] n Alt m.

altogether [ɔːltə'gɛðə*] ad (on the whole) im ganzen genommen; (entirely) ganz und gar.

altruistic [æltrʊ'ɪstɪk] a uneigennützig, altruistisch.

aluminium [ælju'mɪnɪəm], (US) **aluminum** [ə'luːmɪnəm] n Aluminium nt.

always ['ɔːlweɪz] ad immer; it was — that way es war schon immer so.

amalgam [ə'mælgəm] n Amalgam nt; (fig) Mischung f.

amalgamate [ə'mælgəmeɪt] vi (combine) sich vereinigen; vt (mix) amalgamieren.

amalgamation [əmælgə'meɪʃən] n Verschmelzung f, Zusammenschluß m.

amass [ə'mæs] vt anhäufen.

amateur ['æmətɜ:*] n Amateur m; (pej) Amateur m, Bastler m, Stümper m; a Amateur-, Bastler-; —ish a (pej) dilettantisch, stümperhaft.

amaze [ə'meɪz] vt erstaunen, in Staunen versetzen; —ment höchste(s) (Er)staunen nt.

amazing [ə'meɪzɪŋ] a höchst erstaunlich.

ambassador [æm'bæsədə*] n Botschafter m.

amber ['æmbə*] n Bernstein m.

ambidextrous [æmbɪ'dɛkstrəs] a beidhändig.

ambiguity [æmbɪ'gjuɪtɪ] n Zweideutigkeit f, Unklarheit f.

ambiguous [æm'bɪgjʊəs] a zweideutig; (not clear) unklar.

ambition [æm'bɪʃən] n Ehrgeiz m.

ambitious [æm'bɪʃəs] a ehrgeizig.

ambivalent [æm'bɪvələnt] a attitude zwiespältig.

amble ['æmbl] vi schlendern.

ambulance ['æmbjʊləns] n Krankenwagen m.

ambush ['æmbʊʃ] n Hinterhalt m; vt aus dem Hinterhalt angreifen, überfallen.

ameliorate [ə'miːlɪəreɪt] vt verbessern.

amelioration [əmiːlɪə'reɪʃən] n Verbesserung f.

amen ['ɑː'mɛn] interj amen.

amenable [ə'miːnəbl] a gefügig; (to reason) zugänglich (to dat); (to flattery) empfänglich (to für); (to law) unterworfen (to dat).

amend [ə'mɛnd] vt law etc abändern, ergänzen; to make -s etw wiedergutmachen; —ment Abänderung f.

amenity [ə'mi:nɪtɪ] n (moderne) Einrichtung f.

Americanize [ə'merɪkənaɪz] vt amerikanisieren.

amethyst ['æmɪθɪst] n Amethyst m.

amiable ['eɪmɪəbl] a liebenswürdig, sympathisch.

amicable ['æmɪkəbl] a freundschaftlich; settlement gütlich.

amid(st) [ə'mɪd(st)] prep mitten in or unter (+dat).

amiss [ə'mɪs] a verkehrt, nicht richtig; ad to take sth — etw übelnehmen.

ammeter ['æmɪtə*] n (Aut) Amperemeter m.

ammunition [æmju'nɪʃən] n Munition f.

amnesia [æm'ni:zɪə] n Gedächtnisverlust m.

amnesty ['æmnɪstɪ] n Amnestie f.

amock [ə'mɒk] ad see amuck.

amoeba [ə'mi:bə] n Amöbe f.

among(st) [ə'mʌŋ(st)] prep unter.

amoral [æ'mɒrəl] a unmoralisch.

amorous ['æmərəs] a verliebt.

amorphous [ə'mɔ:fəs] a formlos, gestaltlos.

amount [ə'maʊnt] n (of money) Betrag m; (of time, energy) Aufwand m (of an +dat); (of water, sand) Menge f; no — of ... kein(e) ...; vi: — to (total) sich belaufen auf (+acc); this —s to treachery das kommt Verrat gleich; it —s to the same es läuft aufs gleiche hinaus; he won't — to much aus ihm wird nie was.

amp [æmp] n, ampere ['æmpɛə*] n Ampere nt.

amphibious [æm'fɪbɪəs] a amphibious, Amphibien-.

amphitheatre ['æmfɪθɪətə*] n Amphitheater nt.

ample ['æmpl] a portion reichlich; dress weit, groß; — time genügend Zeit.

amplifier ['æmplɪfaɪə*] n Verstärker m.

amply ['æmplɪ] ad reichlich.

amputate ['æmpjuteɪt] vt amputieren, abnehmen.

amuck [ə'mʌk] ad: to run — Amok laufen.

amuse [ə'mju:z] vt (entertain) unterhalten; (make smile) belustigen; (occupy) unterhalten; I'm not —d das find' ich gar nicht lustig; if that —s you wann es dir Spaß macht; —ment (feeling) Unterhaltung f; (recreation) Zeitvertreib m.

amusing [ə'mju:zɪŋ] a amüsant, unterhaltend.

an [æn, ən] indef art ein(e).

anaemia [ə'ni:mɪə] n Anämie f.

anaemic [ə'ni:mɪk] a blutarm.

anaesthetic [ænɪs'θetɪk] n Betäubungsmittel nt; under — unter Narkose.

anagram ['ænəgræm] n Anagramm nt.

analgesic [ænæl'dʒɪ:sɪk] n schmerzlindernde(s) Mittel nt.

analogous [ə'næləgəs] a analog.

analogy [ə'nælədʒɪ] n Analogie f.

analyse ['ænəlaɪz] vt analysieren.

analysis [ə'næləsɪs] n Analyse f.

analytic [ænə'lɪtɪk] a analytisch.

anarchist ['ænəkɪst] n Anarchist(in f) m.

anarchy ['ænəkɪ] n Anarchie f.

anathema [ə'næθɪmə] n (fig) Greuel m.

anatomical [ænə'tɒmɪkəl] a anatomisch.

anatomy [ə'nætəmɪ] n (structure)

anatomische(r) Aufbau *m*; *(study)* Anatomie *f*.

ancestor ['ænsestə*] *n* Vorfahr *m*.

ancestral [æn'sestrəl] *n* angestammt, Ahnen-.

ancestry ['ænsıstrı] *n* Abstammung *f*; Vorfahren *pl*.

anchor ['æŋkə*] *n* Anker *m*; *vi* ankern, vor Anker liegen; *vt* verankern; —age- Ankerplatz *m*.

anchovy ['æntʃəvı] *n* Sardelle *f*.

ancient ['emʃənt] *a* alt; *car etc* uralt.

and [ænd, ənd, ən] *cj* und.

anecdote ['ænıkdəut] *n* Anekdote *f*.

anemia [ə'ni:mıə] *n* (US) = **anaemia**.

anemone [ə'nemənı] *n* Anemone *f*.

anesthetic [ænıs'θetık] *n* (US) = **anaesthetic**.

anew [ə'nju:] *ad* von neuem.

angel ['eındʒəl] *n* Engel *m*; —ic [æn'dʒelık] *a* engelhaft.

anger ['æŋgə*] *n* Zorn *m*; *vt* ärgern.

angina [æn'dʒamə] *n* Angina *f*, Halsentzündung *f*.

angle ['æŋgl] *n* Winkel *m*; *(point of view)* Standpunkt *m*; at an — nicht gerade; *vt* stellen; **to —** for aussein auf (+*acc*); —r Angler *m*.

Anglican ['æŋglıkən] *a* anglikanisch; *n* Anglikaner(in *f*) *m*.

anglicize ['æŋglısaız] *vt* anglisieren.

angling ['æŋglıŋ] *n* Angeln *nt*.

Anglo- ['æŋgləu] *pref* Anglo-.

angrily ['æŋgrılı] *ad* ärgerlich, böse.

angry ['æŋgrı] *a* ärgerlich, ungehalten, böse; *wound* entzündet.

anguish ['æŋgwıʃ] *n* Qual *f*.

angular ['æŋgjulə*] *a* eckig, winkelförmig; *face* kantig.

animal ['ænıməl] *n* Tier *nt*; *(living creature)* Lebewesen *nt*; *a* tierisch, animalisch.

animate ['ænımeıt] *vt* beleben; ['ænımət] *a* lebhaft; —d *a* lebendig; *film* Zeichentrick-.

animation [ænı'meıʃən] *n* Lebhaftigkeit *f*.

animosity [ænı'mɒsıtı] *n* Feindseligkeit *f*, Abneigung *f*.

aniseed ['ænıs:d] *n* Anis *m*.

ankle ['æŋkl] *n* (Fuß)knöchel *m*.

annex ['æneks] *n* Anbau *m*; [ə'neks] *vt* anfügen; *(Pol)* annektieren, angliedern.

annihilate [ə'naıəleıt] *vt* vernichten.

anniversary [ænı'vɜ:sərı] *n* Jahrestag *m*.

annotate ['ænəteıt] *vt* kommentieren.

announce [ə'nauns] *vt* ankündigen, anzeigen; —ment Ankündigung *f*; *(official)* Bekanntmachung *f*; —r Ansager(in *f*) *m*.

annoy [ə'nɔı] *vt* ärgern; —ance Ärgernis *nt*, Störung *f*; —ing *a* ärgerlich; *person* lästig.

annual ['ænjuəl] *a* jährlich; *salary* Jahres-; *n* *(plant)* einjährige Pflanze *f*; *(book)* Jahrbuch *nt*; —ly *ad* jährlich.

annuity [ə'njuıtı] *n* Jahresrente *f*.

annul [ə'nʌl] *vt* aufheben, annullieren; —ment Aufhebung *f*, Annullierung *f*.

anoint [ə'nɔınt] *vt* salben.

anomalous [ə'nɒmələs] *a* unregelmäßig, anomal.

anomaly [ə'nɒmalı] *n* Abweichung *f* von der Regel.

anon [ə'nɒn] *a* = **anonymous**.

anonymity [ænə'nımıtı] *n* Anonymität *f*.

anonymous [ə'nɒnıməs] *a* anonym.

anorak ['ænəræk] *n* Anorak *m*, Windjacke *f*.

another [ə'nʌðə*] a, pron
(different) ein(e) andere(r, s); (additional) noch eine(r, s).

answer ['ɑ:nsə*] n Antwort f; vi
antworten; (on phone) sich
melden; vt person antworten
(+dat); letter, question beantworten; telephone gehen an
(+acc), abnehmen; door öffnen;
—able a beantwortbar; (responsible) verantwortlich, haftbar; to —
back vi frech sein; to — for sth
für etw verantwortlich sein; to —
to the name of auf den Namen ...
hören.

ant [ænt] n Ameise f.

antagonism [æn'tægənizəm] n
Antagonismus m.

antagonist [æn'tægənist] n Gegner
m, Antagonist m; **—ic**
[æntægə'nistik] a feindselig.

antagonize [æn'tægənaiz] vt reizen.

anteater ['ænti:tə*] n Ameisenbär
m.

antecedent [ænti'si:dənt] n Vorhergehende(s) nt; —s pl Vorleben
nt, Vorgeschichte f.

antelope ['æntiləup] n Antilope f.

antenatal [ænti'neitl] a vor der
Geburt.

antenna [æn'tenə] n (Biol) Fühler
m; (Rad) Antenne f.

anteroom ['æntirum] n Vorzimmer
nt.

anthem ['ænθəm] n Hymne f.

anthology [æn'θɒlədʒi] n Gedichtsammlung f, Anthologie f.

anthropologist [ænθrə'pɒlədʒist]
n Anthropologe m.

anthropology [ænθrə'pɒlədʒi] n
Anthropologie f.

anti- ['ænti] pref Gegen-, Anti-
anti-aircraft ['ænti'eəkrɑ:ft] a
Flugabwehr-.

antibiotic ['æntibai'ɒtik] n Antibiotikum nt.

anticipate [æn'tisipeit] vt (expect)
trouble, question erwarten, rechnen
mit; (look forward to) sich freuen
auf (+acc); (do first) vorwegnehmen; (foresee) ahnen, vorhersehen.

anticipation [æntisi'peiʃən] n
Erwartung f; (foreshadowing)
Vorwegnahme f; that was good —
das war gut vorausgesehen.

anticlimax ['ænti'klaimæks] n
Ernüchterung f.

anticlockwise ['ænti'klɒkwaiz] a
entgegen dem Uhrzeigersinn.

antics ['æntiks] npl Possen pl.

anticyclone ['ænti'saikləun] n
Hoch nt, Hochdruckgebiet nt.

antidote ['æntidəut] n Gegenmittel
nt.

antifreeze ['æntifri:z] n Frostschutzmittel nt.

antipathy [æn'tipəθi] n Abneigung
f, Antipathie f.

antiquarian [ænti'kweəriən] a altertümlich; n Antiquitätensammler m.

antiquated ['æntikweitid] a
antiquiert.

antique [æn'ti:k] n Antiquität f; a
antik; (old-fashioned) altmodisch.

antiquity [æn'tikwiti] n Antike f,
Altertum nt.

antiseptic [ænti'septik] n Antiseptikum nt; a antiseptisch.

antisocial ['ænti'səuʃl] a person ungesellig; law unsozial.

antithesis [æn'tiθisis] n Gegensatz
m, Antithese f.

antlers ['æntləz] npl Geweih nt.

anus ['einəs] n After m.

anvil ['ænvil] n Amboß m.

anxiety [æŋ'zaiəti] n Angst f;
(worry) Sorge f.

anxious ['æŋkʃəs] *a* ängstlich; (*worried*) besorgt; **—ly** *ad* besorgt; **to be — to do sth** etw dringend tun wollen.

any ['enɪ] *a*: **take — one** nimm irgendein(e,n,s)!; **do you want — apples?** willst du Äpfel (haben)?; **do you want —?** willst du welche?; **not — keine**; *ad*: **— faster** schneller; **—body** *pron* irgend jemand; (*everybody*) jedermann; **—how** *ad* sowieso, ohnehin; (*carelessly*) einfach so; **—one** *pron* = **—body**; **—thing** *pron* irgend etwas; **—time** *ad* jederzeit; **—way** *ad* sowieso, ohnehin; **—way, let's stop** na ja *or* sei's drum, hören wir auf; **—where** *ad* irgendwo; (*everywhere*) überall.

apace [ə'peɪs] *ad* rasch.

apart [ə'pɑːt] *ad* (*parted*) auseinander; (*away*) beiseite, abseits; **— from** außer.

apartheid [ə'pɑːteɪt] *n* Apartheid *f*.

apartment [ə'pɑːtmənt] *n* (*US*) Wohnung *f*; **—s** *pl* (möblierte Miet)wohnung *f*.

apathetic [æpə'θetɪk] *a* teilnahmslos, apathisch.

apathy ['æpəθɪ] *n* Teilnahmslosigkeit *f*, Apathie *f*.

ape [eɪp] *n* (Menschen)affe *m*; *vt* nachahmen.

aperitif [ə'perɪtɪv] *n* Aperitif *m*.

aperture ['æpətjʊə*] *n* Öffnung *f*; (*Phot*) Blende *f*.

apex ['eɪpeks] *n* Spitze *f*, Scheitelpunkt *m*.

aphorism ['æfərɪzəm] *n* Aphorismus *m*.

aphrodisiac [æfrəʊ'dɪzɪæk] *n* Aphrodisiakum *nt*.

apiece [ə'piːs] *ad* pro Stück; (*per person*) pro Kopf.

aplomb [ə'plɒm] *n* selbstbewußte(s) Auftreten *nt*.

apocryphal [ə'pɒkrɪfəl] *a* apokryph, unecht.

apologetic [əpɒlə'dʒetɪk] *a* entschuldigend; **to be —** sich sehr entschuldigen.

apologize [ə'pɒlədʒaɪz] *vi* sich entschuldigen.

apology [ə'pɒlədʒɪ] *n* Entschuldigung *f*.

apoplexy ['æpəpleksɪ] *n* Schlaganfall *m*.

apostle [ə'pɒsl] *n* Apostel *m*; (*pioneer*) Vorkämpfer *m*.

apostrophe [ə'pɒstrəfɪ] *n* Apostroph *m*.

appal [ə'pɔːl] *vt* erschrecken; **—ling** *a* schrecklich.

apparatus ['æpərətəs] *n* Apparat *m*, Gerät *nt*.

apparent [ə'pærənt] *a* offenbar; **—ly** *ad* anscheinend.

apparition [æpə'rɪʃən] *n* (*ghost*) Erscheinung *f*, Geist *m*; (*appearance*) Erscheinen *nt*.

appeal [ə'piːl] *vi* dringend ersuchen; dringend bitten (*for* um); sich wenden (*to* an +*acc*); (*to public*) appellieren (*to* an +*acc*); (*Jur*) Berufung einlegen; *n* Aufruf *m*; (*Jur*) Berufung *f*; **—ing** *a* ansprechend.

appear [ə'pɪə*] *vi* (*come into sight*) erscheinen; (*be seen*) auftauchen; (*seem*) scheinen; **—ance** (*coming into sight*) Erscheinen *nt*; (*outward show*) Äußere(s) *nt*; **to put in** *or* **make an —** eine kurze Erscheinung machen.

appease [ə'piːz] *vt* beschwichtigen.

appendage [ə'pendɪdʒ] *n* Anhang *m*, Anhängsel *nt*.

appendicitis [əpendɪ'saɪtɪs] *n* Blinddarmentzündung *f*.

appendix [ə'pendɪks] n (in book) Anhang m; (Med) Blinddarm m.

appetite ['æpɪtaɪt] n Appetit m; (fig) Lust f.

appetizing ['æpɪtaɪzɪŋ] a appetit-anregend.

applaud [ə'plɔːd] vti Beifall klatschen (+dat), applaudieren.

applause [ə'plɔːz] n Beifall m, Applaus m.

apple ['æpl] n Apfel m; — **tree** Apfelbaum m.

appliance [ə'plaɪəns] n Gerät nt.

applicable [ə'plɪkəbl] a anwendbar; (in forms) zutreffend.

applicant ['æplɪkənt] n Bewerber(in f) m.

application [æplɪ'keɪʃən] n (request) Antrag m; (for job) Bewerbung f; (putting into practice) Anwendung f; (hard work) Fleiß m.

applied [ə'plaɪd] a angewandt.

apply [ə'plaɪ] vi (ask) sich wenden (to an +acc), sich melden; (be suitable) zutreffen; vt (place on) auflegen; cream auftragen; (put into practice) anwenden; (devote o.s.) sich widmen (+dat).

appoint [ə'pɔɪnt] vt (to office) ernennen, berufen; (settle) festsetzen; — **ment** (meeting) Verabredung f; (at hairdresser etc) Bestellung f; (in business) Termin m; (choice for a position) Ernennung f; (Univ) Berufung f.

apportion [ə'pɔːʃən] vt zuteilen.

appreciable [ə'priːʃəbl] a (perceptible) merklich; (able to be estimated) abschätzbar.

appreciate [ə'priːʃɪeɪt] vt (value) zu schätzen wissen; (understand) einsehen; vi (increase in value) im Wert steigen.

appreciation [əpriːʃɪ'eɪʃən] n Wertschätzung f; (Comm) Wertzuwachs m.

appreciative [ə'priːʃɪətɪv] a (showing thanks) dankbar; (showing liking) anerkennend.

apprehend [æprɪ'hend] vt (arrest) festnehmen; (understand) erfassen.

apprehension [æprɪ'henʃən] n Angst f.

apprehensive [æprɪ'hensɪv] a furchtsam.

apprentice [ə'prentɪs] n Lehrling m; —**ship** Lehrzeit f.

approach [ə'prəutʃ] vi sich nähern; vt herantreten an (+acc); problem herangehen an (+acc); n Annäherung f; (to problem) Ansatz m; (path) Zugang m, Zufahrt f; —**able** a zugänglich.

approbation [æprə'beɪʃən] n Billigung f.

appropriate [ə'prəuprɪeɪt] vt (take for o.s.) sich aneignen; (set apart) bereitstellen; [ə'prəuprɪət] a angemessen; manner angebracht; —**ly** [ə'prəuprɪətlɪ] ad passend.

approval [ə'pruːvəl] n (show of satisfaction) Beifall m; (permission) Billigung f; (Comm) **on** — bei Gefallen.

approve [ə'pruːv] vti billigen (of acc); I don't — of it/him ich halte nichts davon/von ihm.

approximate [ə'prɒksɪmɪt] a annähernd, ungefähr; [ə'prɒksɪmeɪt] vt nahekommen (+dat); —**ly** ad rund, ungefähr.

approximation [əprɒksɪ'meɪʃən] n Annäherung f.

apricot ['eɪprɪkɒt] n Aprikose f.

April ['eɪprəl] n April m.

apron ['eɪprən] n Schürze f.

apt [æpt] a (*suitable*) passend; (*able*) begabt; (*likely*) geneigt.

aptitude ['æptɪtjuːd] n Begabung f.

aqualung ['ækwəlʌŋ] n Unterwasseratmungsgerät nt.

aquarium [ə'kwɛərɪəm] n Aquarium nt.

Aquarius [ə'kwɛərɪəs] n Wassermann m.

aquatic [ə'kwætɪk] a Wasser-.

aqueduct ['ækwɪdʌkt] n Aquädukt nt.

arable ['ærəbl] a bebaubar, Kultur-.

arbiter ['ɑːbɪtə*] n (Schieds)richter m.

arbitrary ['ɑːbɪtrərɪ] a willkürlich.

arbitrate ['ɑːbɪtreɪt] vti schlichten.

arbitration [ɑːbɪ'treɪʃən] n Schlichtung f; to go to — vor ein Schiedsgericht gehen.

arbitrator ['ɑːbɪtreɪtə*] n Schiedsrichter m, Schlichter m.

arc [ɑːk] n Bogen m.

arcade [ɑː'keɪd] n Säulengang m.

arch [ɑːtʃ] n Bogen m; vt überwölben; back krumm machen; vi sich wölben; a durchtrieben; — enemy Erzfeind m.

archaeologist [ɑːkɪ'ɒlədʒɪst] n Archäologe m.

archaeology [ɑːkɪ'ɒlədʒɪ] n Archäologie f.

archaic [ɑː'keɪɪk] a altertümlich.

archbishop ['ɑːtʃ'bɪʃəp] n Erzbischof m.

archer ['ɑːtʃə*] n Bogenschütze m; —y Bogenschießen nt.

archipelago [ɑːkɪ'pelɪgəʊ] n Archipel m; (sea) Inselmeer nt.

architect ['ɑːkɪtekt] n Architekt(in f) m; —ural [ɑːkɪ'tektʃərəl] a architektonisch; —ure Architektur f.

archives ['ɑːkaɪvz] npl Archiv nt.

archivist ['ɑːkɪvɪst] n Archivar m.

archway ['ɑːtʃweɪ] n Bogen m.

ardent ['ɑːdənt] a glühend.

ardour ['ɑːdə*] n Eifer m.

arduous ['ɑːdjʊəs] a mühsam.

are [ɑː*] see be.

area ['ɛərɪə] n Fläche f; (of land) Gebiet nt; (part of sth) Teil m, Abschnitt m.

arena [ə'riːnə] n Arena f.

aren't [ɑːnt] = are not.

arguable ['ɑːgjʊəbl] a (*doubtful*) diskutabel; (*possible*) it's — that ... man könnte argumentieren daß ...

argue ['ɑːgjuː] vt case vertreten; vi diskutieren; (*angrily*) streiten; don't —! keine Widerrede!; to — with sb sich mit jdm streiten.

argument ['ɑːgjʊmənt] n (*theory*) Argument nt; (*reasoning*) Argumentation f; (*row*) Auseinandersetzung f, Streit m; —ative [ɑːgjʊ'mentətɪv] a streitlustig; to have an — sich streiten.

aria ['ɑːrɪə] n Arie f.

arid ['ærɪd] a trocken; —ity [ə'rɪdɪtɪ] n Dürre f.

Aries ['ɛəriːz] n Widder m.

arise [ə'raɪz] vi irreg aufsteigen; (*get up*) aufstehen; (*difficulties etc*) entstehen; (*case*) vorkommen; to — out of sth herrühren von etw.

aristocracy [ærɪs'tɒkrəsɪ] n Adel m, Aristokratie f.

aristocrat ['ærɪstəkræt] n Adlige(r) mf, Aristokrat(in f) m; —ic [ærɪstə'krætɪk] a adlig, aristokratisch.

arithmetic [ə'rɪθmətɪk] n Rechnen nt, Arithmetik f.

ark [ɑːk] n: Noah's A— die Arche Noah.

arm [ɑːm] n Arm m; (branch of military service) Zweig m; vt bewaffnen; —s pl (weapons) Waffen pl; —chair Lehnstuhl m; —ed a forces Streit-, bewaffnet; robbery bewaffnet; —ful Armvoll m.

armistice ['ɑːmɪstɪs] n Waffenstillstand m.

armour ['ɑːmə*] n (knight's) Rüstung f; (Mil) Panzerplatte f; —y Waffenlager nt; (factory) Waffenfabrik f.

armpit ['ɑːmpɪt] n Achselhöhle f.

army ['ɑːmɪ] n Armee f, Heer nt; (host) Heer nt.

aroma [ə'rəʊmə] n Duft m, Aroma nt; —tic [ærə'mætɪk] a aromatisch, würzig.

around [ə'raʊnd] ad ringsherum; (almost) ungefähr; prep um ... herum; is he —? ist er hier?

arouse [ə'raʊz] vt wecken.

arrange [ə'reɪndʒ] vt time, meeting festsetzen; holidays festlegen; flowers, hair, objects anordnen; I —d to meet him ich habe mit ihm ausgemacht, ihn zu treffen; it's all —d es ist alles arrangiert; —ment (order) Reihenfolge f; (agreement) Übereinkommen nt; (plan) Vereinbarung f.

array [ə'reɪ] n Aufstellung f.

arrears [ə'rɪəz] npl (of debts) Rück-stand m; (of work) Unerledigte(s) nt; in — im Rückstand.

arrest [ə'rest] vt person verhaften; (stop) aufhalten; n Verhaftung f; under — in Haft; you're under — Sie sind verhaftet.

arrival [ə'raɪvl] n Ankunft f.

arrive [ə'raɪv] vi ankommen (at in + dat, bei); to — at a decision zu einer Entscheidung kommen.

arrogance ['ærəgəns] n Überheblichkeit f, Arroganz f.

arrogant ['ærəgənt] a anmaßend, arrogant.

arrow ['ærəʊ] n Pfeil m.

arse [ɑːs] n (col) Arsch m.

arsenal ['ɑːsɪnl] n Waffenlager nt, Zeughaus nt.

arsenic ['ɑːsnɪk] n Arsen nt.

arson ['ɑːsn] n Brandstiftung f.

art [ɑːt] n Kunst f; —s pl Geisteswissenschaften pl; — gallery Kunstgalerie f.

artery ['ɑːtərɪ] n Schlagader f, Arterie f.

artful ['ɑːtfʊl] a verschlagen.

arthritis [ɑː'θraɪtɪs] n Arthritis f.

artichoke ['ɑːtɪtʃəʊk] n Artischocke f.

article ['ɑːtɪkl] n (Press, Gram) Artikel m; (thing) Gegenstand m, Artikel m; (clause) Abschnitt m, Paragraph m.

articulate [ɑː'tɪkjʊlɪt] a (able to express o.s.) redegewandt; (speaking clearly) deutlich, verständlich; to be — sich gut ausdrücken können; [ɑː'tɪkjʊleɪt] vt (connect) zusammenfügen, gliedern; —d vehicle Sattelschlepper m.

artifice ['ɑːtɪfɪs] n (skill) Kunstgriff m; (trick) Kniff m, List f.

artificial [ɑːtɪ'fɪʃl] a künstlich, Kunst-; — respiration künstliche Atmung f.

artillery [ɑː'tɪlərɪ] n Artillerie f.

artisan [ɑː'tɪzæn] n gelernte(r) Handwerker m.

artist ['ɑːtɪst] n Künstler(in f) m; —ic [ɑː'tɪstɪk] a künstlerisch; —ry künstlerische(s) Können nt.

artless ['ɑːtlɪs] a ungekünstelt; character arglos.

arty ['ɑːtɪ] a: to be — auf Kunst machen.

as [æz] *ad, cj* (*since*) da, weil;
(*while*) als; (*like*) wie; (*in role of*)
als; — **soon** — he comes sobald
er kommt; — **big** — so groß wie;
— well auch; — und auch;
— **for him** was ihn anbetrifft; —
if, — **though** als ob; — **it were**
sozusagen; **old** — **he** was so alt
er auch war.

asbestos [æz'bestəs] *n* Asbest *m.*

ascend [ə'send] *vi* aufsteigen; *vt*
besteigen; —**ancy** Oberhand *f.*

ascension [ə'senʃən] *n* (*Eccl*)
Himmelfahrt *f.*

ascent [ə'sent] *n* Aufstieg *m;*
Besteigung *f.*

ascertain [æsə'tein] *vt* feststellen.

ascetic [ə'setik] *a* asketisch.

ascribe [əs'kraib] *vt* zuschreiben
(*to dat*).

ash [æʃ] *n* (*dust*) Asche *f;* (*tree*)
Esche *f.*

ashamed [ə'ʃeimd] *a* beschämt.

ashen [æʃən] *a* (*pale*) aschfahl.

ashore [ə'ʃɔː*] *ad* an Land.

ashtray ['æʃtrei] *n* Aschenbecher
m.

aside [ə'said] *ad* beiseite; — **from**
(*US*) abgesehen von; *n* beiseite
gesprochene Worte *pl.*

ask [uːsk] *vti* fragen; *permission*
bitten um; — **him** his name frage
ihn nach seinem Namen; he —**ed**
to see you er wollte dich sehen;
you —**ed for that!** du bist du selbst
schuld.

askance [əs'kɑːns] *ad:* **to look** —
at s.o. jdn schief ansehen.

askew [əs'kjuː] *ad* schief.

asleep [ə'sliːp] *a, ad:* **to be** —
schlafen; **to fall** — einschlafen.

asp [æsp] *n* Espe *f.*

asparagus [əs'pærəgəs] *n* Spargel
m.

aspect ['æspekt] *n* (*appearance*)
Aussehen *nt;* Aspekt *m.*

asphalt ['æsfælt] *n* Asphalt *m.*

asphyxiate [əs'fiksieit] *vt* ersticken.

asphyxiation [əsfiksi'eiʃən] *n*
Erstickung *f.*

aspirate ['æspərit] *n* Hauchlaut *m.*

aspiration [æspə'reiʃən] *n*
Trachten *nt;* **to have** —**s towards**
sth etw anstreben.

aspire [əs'paiə*] *vi* streben (*to*
nach).

aspirin ['æsprin] *n* Aspirin *nt.*

ass [æs] *n* (*lit, fig*) Esel *m.*

assailant [ə'seilənt] *n* Angreifer *m.*

assassin [ə'sæsin] *n* Attentäter(in
f) *m;* —**ate** *vt* ermorden; —**ation**
[əsæsi'neiʃən] Ermordung *f.*

assault [ə'sɔːlt] *n* Angriff *m;* *vt*
überfallen; *woman* herfallen über
(+*acc*).

assemble [ə'sembl] *vt* versammeln; *parts* zusammensetzen; *vi*
sich versammeln.

assembly [ə'sembli] *n* (*meeting*)
Versammlung *f;* (*construction*)
Zusammensetzung *f,* Montage *f;* —
line Fließband *nt.*

assent [ə'sent] *n* Zustimmung *f;* *vi*
zustimmen (*to dat*).

assert [ə'sɜːt] *vt* erklären; —**ion**
[ə'sɜːʃən] Behauptung *f;* —**ive** *a*
·selbstsicher.

assess [ə'ses] *vt* schätzen; —**ment**
Bewertung *f,* Einschätzung *f;* —**or**
Steuerberater *m.*

asset ['æset] *n* Vorteil *m,* Wert *m;*
—**s** *pl* Vermögen *nt;* (*estate*)
Nachlaß *m.*

assiduous [ə'sidjuəs] *a* fleißig, aufmerksam.

assign [ə'sain] *vt* zuweisen.

assignment [ə'sainmənt] *n* Aufgabe *f,* Auftrag *m.*

assimilate [ə'sɪmɪleɪt] *vt* sich aneignen, aufnehmen.

assimilation [əsɪmɪ'leɪʃən] *n* Assimilierung *f*, Aufnahme *f*.

assist [ə'sɪst] *vt* beistehen (+dat); **—ance** Unterstützung *f*, Hilfe *f*; **—ant** Assistent(in *f*) *m*, Mitarbeiter(in *f*) *m*; (*in shop*) Verkäufer(in *f*) *m*.

assizes [ə'saɪzɪz] *npl* Landgericht *nt*.

associate [ə'səʊʃɪt] *n* (*partner*) Kollege *m*, Teilhaber *m*; (*member*) außerordentliche(s) Mitglied *nt*; [ə'səʊʃɪeɪt] *vt* verbinden (*with* mit); *vi* (*keep company*) verkehren (*with* mit).

association [əsəʊsɪ'eɪʃən] *n* Verband *m*, Verein *m*; (*Psych*) Assoziation *f*; (*link*) Verbindung *f*; **— football** (*Brit*) Fußball *m*.

assorted [ə'sɔːtɪd] *a* gemischt, verschieden.

assortment [ə'sɔːtmənt] *n* Sammlung *f*; (*Comm*) Sortiment *nt* (*of* von), Auswahl *f* (*of an* +dat).

assume [ə'sjuːm] *vt* (*take for granted*) annehmen; (*put on*) annehmen, sich geben; **—d name** Deckname *m*.

assumption [ə'sʌmpʃən] *n* Annahme *f*.

assurance [ə'ʃʊərəns] *n* (*firm statement*) Versicherung *f*; (*confidence*) Selbstsicherheit *f*; (*insurance*) (Lebens)versicherung *f*.

assure [ə'ʃʊə*] *vt* (*make sure*) sicherstellen; (*convince*) versichern (+dat); life versichern.

assuredly [ə'ʃʊərɪdlɪ] *ad* sicherlich.

asterisk ['æstərɪsk] *n* Sternchen *nt*.

astern [əs'tɜːn] *ad* achtern.

asthma ['æsmə] *n* Asthma *nt*; **—tic** [æs'mætɪk] *a* asthmatisch; *n* Asthmatiker(in *f*) *m*.

astir [ə'stɜː*] *ad* in Bewegung.

astonish [əs'tɒnɪʃ] *vt* erstaunen; **—ing** *a* erstaunlich; **—ment** Erstaunen *nt*.

astound [əs'taʊnd] *vt* verblüffen; **—ing** *a* verblüffend.

astray [əs'treɪ] *ad* in die Irre; auf Abwege; *a* irregehend.

astride [əs'traɪd] *ad* rittlings; *prep* rittlings auf.

astringent [əs'trɪndʒənt] *a* (*Med*) zusammenziehend; (*severe*) streng.

astrologer [əs'trɒlədʒə*] *n* Astrologe *m*, Astrologin *f*.

astrology [əs'trɒlədʒɪ] *n* Astrologie *f*.

astronaut ['æstrənɔːt] *n* Astronaut(in *f*) *m*.

astronomer [əs'trɒnəmə*] *n* Astronom *m*.

astronomical [æstrə'nɒmɪkəl] *a* astronomisch; numbers astronomisch; success riesig.

astronomy [əs'trɒnəmɪ] *n* Astronomie *f*.

astute [əs'tjuːt] *a* scharfsinnig; schlau, gerissen.

asunder [ə'sʌndə*] *ad* entzwei.

asylum [ə'saɪləm] *n* (*home*) Heim *nt*; (*refuge*) Asyl *nt*.

at [æt] *prep* **—** home zuhause; **—** John's bei John; **— table** bei Tisch; **— school** in der Schule; **— Easter** an Ostern; **—** 2 o'clock um 2 Uhr; **—** (the age of) 16 mit 16; **— £5** zu 5 Pfund; **— 20 mph** mit 20 Meilen pro Stunde; **— that** darauf; (*also*) dann.

ate [et, eɪt] *pt* of **eat**.

atheism ['eɪθʊɪzəm] *n* Atheismus *m*.

atheist ['eɪθʊɪst] *n* Atheist(in *f*) *m*.

athlete ['æθliːt] *n* Athlet *m*, Sportler *m*.

athletic [æθ'letɪk] a sportlich, athletisch; **—s** pl Leichtathletik f.

atlas ['ætləs] n Atlas m.

atmosphere ['ætməsfɪə*] n Atmosphäre f.

atoll ['ætɒl] n Atoll nt.

atom ['ætəm] n Atom nt; (fig) bißchen nt; **—ic** [ə'tɒmɪk] a atomar, Atom-; **—(ic) bomb** Atombombe f; **—ic power** Atomkraft f; **—izer** Zerstäuber m.

atone [ə'təʊn] vi sühnen (for acc).

atrocious [ə'trəʊʃəs] a gräßlich.

atrocity [ə'trɒsɪtɪ] n Scheußlichkeit f; (deed) Greueltat f.

attach [ə'tætʃ] vt (fasten) befestigen; importance etc legen (to auf +acc), beimessen (to dat); **to be —ed to sb/sth** an jdm/etw hängen; **—é** [ə'tæʃeɪ] n Attaché m.

attack [ə'tæk] vti angreifen; n Angriff m; (Med) Anfall m.

attain [ə'teɪn] vt erreichen; **—ment** Erreichung f; **—ments** pl Kenntnisse pl.

attempt [ə'tempt] n Versuch m; vti versuchen.

attend [ə'tend] vt (go to) teilnehmen (an +dat); besuchen; vi (pay attention) aufmerksam sein; **to —** person sich kümmern um; **—ance** (presence) Anwesenheit f; (people present) Besucherzahl f; **good —ance** gute Teilnahme; **—ant** n (companion) Begleiter(in f) m; Gesellschafter(in f) m; (in car park etc) Wächter(in f) m; (servant) Bediente(r) mf; a begleitend; (fig) verbunden mit.

attention [ə'tenʃən] n Aufmerksamkeit f; (care) Fürsorge f; (for machine etc) Pflege f.

attentive a, **—ly** ad [ə'tentɪv, -lɪ] aufmerksam

attenuate [ə'tenjʊeɪt] vt verdünnen.

attest [ə'test] vt bestätigen; **to —** to sich verbürgen für.

attic ['ætɪk] n Dachstube f, Mansarde f.

attire [ə'taɪə*] n Gewand nt.

attitude ['ætɪtjuːd] n (position) Haltung f; (mental) Einstellung f.

attorney [ə'tɜːnɪ] n (solicitor) Rechtsanwalt; (representative) Bevollmächtigte(r) mf; **A— General** Justizminister m.

attract [ə'trækt] vt anziehen; attention etc erregen; employees anlocken; **—ion** [ə'trækʃən] n Anziehung f; (thing) Attraktion f; **—ive** attraktiv; **the idea —s me** ich finde die Idee attraktiv.

attribute ['ætrɪbjuːt] n Eigenschaft f, Attribut nt; [ə'trɪbjuːt] vt zuschreiben (to dat).

attrition [ə'trɪʃən] n Verschleiß m; **war of —** Zermürbungskrieg m.

aubergine ['əʊbəʒiːn] n Aubergine f.

auburn ['ɔːbən] a kastanienbraun.

auction ['ɔːkʃən] n Versteigerung f, Auktion f; vt versteigern; **—eer** [ɔːkʃə'nɪə*] Versteigerer m.

audacious [ɔː'deɪʃəs] a (daring) verwegen; (shameless) unverfroren.

audacity [ɔː'dæsɪtɪ] n (boldness) Wagemut m; (impudence) Unverfrorenheit f.

audible ['ɔːdɪbl] a hörbar.

audience ['ɔːdɪəns] n Zuhörer pl, Zuschauer pl; (with king etc) Audienz f.

audit ['ɔːdɪt] n Bücherrevision f; vt prüfen.

audition [ɔː'dɪʃən] n Probe f.

auditorium [ɔːdɪ'tɔːrɪəm] n Zuschauerraum m.

augment [ɔːˈgment] vt vermehren; vi zunehmen.

augur [ˈɔːgə*] vti bedeuten, voraussagen; ~s well das ist ein gutes Omen; ~y [-ˈgjʊri] Vorbedeutung f, Omen nt.

August [ˈɔːgəst] n August m.

august [ɔːˈgʌst] a erhaben.

aunt [ɑːnt] n Tante f; ~y, ~ie Tantchen nt.

au pair [ˈəʊ ˈpɛə*] (also ~ girl) Au-pair-Mädchen nt.

aura [ˈɔːrə] n Nimbus m.

auspices [ˈɔːspɪsɪz] npl: ~ of unter der Schirmherrschaft

auspicious [ɔːsˈpɪʃəs] a günstig; verheißungsvoll.

austere [ɒsˈtɪə*] a streng; rein, nüchtern.

austerity [ɒsˈterɪtɪ] n Strenge f; (Pol) wirtschaftliche Einschränkung f.

authentic [ɔːˈθentɪk] a echt, authentisch; ~ate vt beglaubigen; ~ity [ɔːθenˈtɪsɪtɪ] n Echtheit f.

author [ˈɔːθə*] n Autor m, Schriftsteller m; (beginner) Urheber m, Schöpfer m.

authoritarian [ɔːθɒrɪˈtɛərɪən] a autoritär.

authoritative [ɔːˈθɒrɪtətɪv] a account maßgeblich; manner herrisch.

authority [ɔːˈθɒrɪtɪ] n (power) Autorität f; (expert) Autorität f, Fachmann m; the authorities pl die Behörden pl.

authorize [ˈɔːθəraɪz] vt bevollmächtigen; (permit) genehmigen.

auto [ˈɔːtəʊ] n (US) Auto nt, Wagen m.

autobiographical [ɔːtəbaɪə-ˈgræfɪkəl] a autobiographisch.

autobiography [ɔːtəbaɪˈɒgrəfɪ] n Autobiographie f.

autocracy [ɔːˈtɒkrəsɪ] n Autokratie f.

autocratic [ɔːtəˈkrætɪk] a autokratisch.

autograph [ˈɔːtəgrɑːf] n (of celebrity) Autogramm nt; vt mit Autogramm versehen.

automate [ˈɔːtəmeɪt] vt automatisieren, auf Automation umstellen.

automatic [ɔːtəˈmætɪk] a automatisch; n Selbstladepistole f; (car) Automatik m; ~ally ad automatisch.

automation [ɔːtəˈmeɪʃən] n Automation f.

automaton [ɔːˈtɒmətən] n Automat m, Roboter m.

automobile [ˈɔːtəməbiːl] n (US) Auto(mobil) nt.

autonomous [ɔːˈtɒnəməs] a autonom.

autonomy [ɔːˈtɒnəmɪ] n Autonomie f, Selbstbestimmung f.

autopsy [ˈɔːtɒpsɪ] n Autopsie f.

autumn [ˈɔːtəm] n Herbst m.

auxiliary [ɔːgˈzɪljərɪ] a Hilfs-; (Gram) Hilfsverb nt.

avail [əˈveɪl] vt: ~ o.s. of sth sich einer Sache bedienen; n: to no ~ nutzlos; ~ability [əveɪləˈbɪlɪtɪ] Erhältlichkeit f, Vorhandensein nt; ~able a erhältlich; zur Verfügung stehend; person erreichbar, abkömmlich.

avalanche [ˈævəlɑːnʃ] n Lawine f.

avant-garde [ævɑ̃ˈgɑːd] a avantgardistisch; n Avantgarde f.

avarice [ˈævərɪs] n Habsucht f, Geiz m.

avaricious [ævəˈrɪʃəs] a geizig, habsüchtig.

avenge [əˈvendʒ] vt rächen, sühnen.

avenue [ˈævənjuː] n Allee f.

average [ˈævərɪdʒ] n Durchschnitt m; a durchschnittlich, Durchschnitts-; vt figures den Durchschnitt nehmen von; (perform) durchschnittlich leisten; (in car etc) im Schnitt fahren; on — durchschnittlich, im Durchschnitt.

averse [əˈvɜːs] a: to be — to eine Abneigung haben gegen.

aversion [əˈvɜːʃən] n Abneigung f.

avert [əˈvɜːt] vt (turn away) abkehren; (prevent) abwehren.

aviary [ˈeɪvɪərɪ] n Vogelhaus nt.

aviation [eɪvɪˈeɪʃən] n Luftfahrt f, Flugwesen nt.

aviator [ˈeɪvɪeɪtə*] n Flieger m.

avid [ˈævɪd] a gierig (for auf +acc); —ly ad gierig.

avocado [ævəˈkɑːdəʊ] n (also —pear) Avocado(birne) f.

avoid [əˈvɔɪd] vt vermeiden; —able a vermeidbar; —ance Vermeidung f.

avowal [əˈvaʊəl] n Erklärung f.

await [əˈweɪt] vt erwarten, entgegensehen (+dat).

awake [əˈweɪk] a wach irreg vi aufwachen; vt (auf)wecken; —ning Erwachen nt.

award [əˈwɔːd] n (judgment) Urteil nt; (prize) Preis m; vt zuerkennen.

aware [əˈwɛə*] a bewußt; to be — sich bewußt sein (of gen); —ness Bewußtsein nt.

awash [əˈwɒʃ] a überflutet.

away [əˈweɪ] ad weg, fort.

awe [ɔː] n Ehrfurcht f; —-inspiring, —-some a ehrfurchtgebietend; —-struck a von Ehrfurcht ergriffen.

awful [ˈɔːful] a (very bad) furchtbar; —ly ad furchtbar, sehr.

awhile [əˈwaɪl] ad eine kleine Weile, ein bißchen.

awkward [ˈɔːkwəd] a (clumsy) ungeschickt, linkisch; (embarrassing) peinlich; —ness Ungeschicklichkeit f.

awning [ˈɔːnɪŋ] n Markise f.

awry [əˈraɪ] ad, a schief; to go — (person) fehlgehen; (plans) schiefgehen.

ax (US), **axe** [æks] n Axt f, Beil nt; vt (to end suddenly) streichen.

axiom [ˈæksɪəm] n Grundsatz m, Axiom nt; —atic [æksɪəˈmætɪk] a axiomatisch.

axis [ˈæksɪs] n Achse f.

axle [ˈæksl] n Achse f.

ay(e) [aɪ] interj (yes) ja; the —es pl die Jastimmen pl.

azure [ˈeɪʒə*] a himmelblau.

B

B, b [biː] n B nt, b nt.

babble [ˈbæbl] vi schwätzen; (stream) murmeln; n Geschwätz nt.

babe [beɪb] n Rby nt.

baboon [bəˈbuː] n Pavian m.

baby [ˈbeɪbɪ] a Baby nt, Säugling

m; — carriage (US) Kinderwagen m; —ish a kindisch; —-sit vi irreg Kinder hüten, babysitten; —-sitter Babysitter m.

bachelor [ˈbætʃələ*] n Junggeselle m; B— of Arts Bakkalaureus m der philosophischen Fakultät; B— of

Science Bakkalaureus *m* der Natur-wissenschaften.

back [bæk] *n* (of person, horse) Rücken *m*; (of house) Rückseite *f*; (of train) Ende *nt*; (Ftbl) Verteidiger *m*; *vt* (support) unterstützen; (wager) wetten auf (+acc); *car* rückwärts fahren; *vi* (go backwards) rückwärts gehen or fahren; *a* hinter(e, s); *ad* zurück; (to the rear) nach hinten; — **down** *vi* zurückstecken; — **out** *vi* sich zurückziehen; kneifen (col);. —**biting** Verleumdung *f*; —**bone** Rückgrat *nt*; (support) Rückhalt *m*; —**cloth** Hintergrund *m*; — **er** Förderer *m*; —**fire** *vi* (plan) fehlschlagen; (Tech) fehlzünden; —**ground** Hintergrund *m*; (information) Hintergrund *m*, Umstände *pl*; (person's education) Vorbildung *f*; —**hand** (Sport) Rückhand *f*; *a* Rückhand-; —**handed** *a shot* Rückhand-; *compliment* zweifelhaft; —**ing** (support) Unterstützung *f*; —**lash** (Tech) tote(r) Gang *m*; (fig) Gegenschlag *m*; —**log** .(of work) Rückstand *m*; — **number** (Press) alte Nummer *f*; — **pay** (Gehalts-, Lohn)nachzahlung *f*; —**side** (col) Hintern *m*; —**stroke** Rückenschwimmen *nt*; —**ward** *a* (less developed) zurückgebliehen; (primitive) rückständig; —**wardness** (of child) Unterentwicklung *f*; (of country) Rückständigkeit *f*; —**wards** *ad* (in reverse) rückwärts; (towards the past) zurück, rückwärts; —**water** (fig) Kaff *nt*; *cultural* weite tiefste Provinz *f*; —**yard** Hinterhof *m*.

bacon ['beɪkən] *n* Schinkenspeck *m*.
bacteria [bæk'tɪərɪə] *npl* Bakterien *pl*.

bad [bæd] *a* schlecht, schlimm.
badge [bædʒ] *n* Abzeichen *nt*.
badger ['bædʒə*] *n* Dachs *m*; *vt* plagen.
badly ['bædlɪ] *ad* schlecht, schlimm; — **off**: he is — **off** es geht ihm schlecht.
badminton ['bædmɪntən] *n* Federballspiel *nt*.
bad-tempered ['bæd'tempəd] *a* schlecht gelaunt.
baffle ['bæfl] *vt* (puzzle) verblüffen.
bag [bæg] *n* (sack) Beutel *m*; (paper) Tüte *f*; (hand—) Tasche *f*; (suitcase) Koffer *m*; (booty) Jagdbeute *f*; (col: old woman) alte Schachtel *f*; *vi* sich bauschen; *vt* (put in sack) in einen Sack stecken; (hunting) erlegen; —**ful** Sackvoll *m*; —**gage** ['bægɪdʒ] Gepäck *nt*; —**gy** *a* bauschig, sackartig; —**pipes** *pl* Dudelsack *m*.
bail [beɪl] *n* (money) Kaution *f*; *vt prisoner* gegen Kaution freilassen; (also — **out**) *boat* ausschöpfen; *see* bale.
bailiff ['beɪlɪf] *n* Gerichtsvollzieher(in *f*) *m*.
bait [beɪt] *n* Köder *m*; *vt* mit einem Köder versehen; (fig) ködern.
bake [beɪk] *vti* backen; —**r** Bäcker *m*; —**ry** Bäckerei *f*; —**r's dozen** dreizehn.
baking ['beɪkɪŋ] *n* Backen *nt*; — **powder** Backpulver *nt*.
balance ['bæləns] *n* (scales) Waage *f*; (equilibrium) Gleichgewicht *nt*; (Fin: state of account) Saldo *m*; (difference) Bilanz *f*; (amount remaining) Restbetrag *m*; *vt* (weigh) wägen; (make equal) ausgleichen; —**d** *a* ausgeglichen; —**sheet** Bilanz *f*, Rechnungsabschluß *m*.
balcony ['bælkənɪ] *n* Balkon *m*.

bald [bɔːld] a kahl; *statement* knapp.

bale [beɪl] n Ballen m; **to — or bail out** (*from a plane*) abspringen.

baleful ['beɪlful] a (*sad*) unglückselig; (*evil*) böse.

balk [bɔːk] vt (*hinder*) vereiteln; vi scheuen (*at vor* +dat).

ball [bɔːl] n Ball m.

ballad ['bæləd] n Ballade f.

ballast ['bæləst] n Ballast m.

ball bearing ['bɔːl'beərɪŋ] n Kugellager nt.

ballerina [bælə'riːnə] n Ballerina f.

ballet ['bæleɪ] n Ballett nt.

ballistics [bə'lɪstɪks] n Ballistik f.

balloon [bə'luːn] n (Luft)ballon m.

ballot ['bælət] n (*geheime*) Abstimmung f.

ball-point (pen) ['bɔːlpɔɪnt('pen)] n Kugelschreiber m.

ballroom ['bɔːlrum] n Tanzsaal m.

balmy ['bɑːmɪ] a lindernd; mild.

balsa ['bɔːlsə] n (*also* — **wood**) Balsaholz nt.

balustrade [bæləs'treɪd] n Brüstung f.

bamboo [bæm'buː] n Bambus m.

bamboozle [bæm'buːzl] vt übers Ohr hauen.

ban [bæn] n Verbot nt; vt verbieten.

banal [bə'nɑːl] a banal.

banana [bə'nɑːnə] n Banane f.

band [bænd] n Band nt; (*group*) Gruppe f; (*of criminals*) Bande f; (*Mus*) Kapelle f, Band f; vi (+together) sich zusammentun; **—age** Verband m; (*elastic*) Bandage f.

bandit ['bændɪt] n Bandit m.

bandy ['bændɪ] vt wechseln; (**-legged**) a o-beinig.

bang [bæŋ] n (*explosion*) Knall m; (*blow*) Hieb m; vti knallen.

bangle ['bæŋgl] n Armspange f.

banish ['bænɪʃ] vt verbannen.

banister(s) ['bænɪstə*(z)] n(pl) (Treppen)geländer nt.

banjo ['bændʒəʊ] n Banjo nt.

bank [bæŋk] n (*raised ground*) Erdwall m; (*of lake etc*) Ufer nt; (*Fin*) Bank f; vt (*tilt: Aviat*) in die Kurve bringen; *money* einzahlen; **to — on sth** mit etw rechnen; **— account** Bankkonto nt; (*employee*) Bankbeamte(r) m; **— holiday** gesetzliche(r) Feiertag m; **—ing** Bankwesen nt, Bankgeschäft nt; **—note** Banknote f; **—rupt** n Zahlungsunfähige(r) m/f; vt bankrott machen; **to go —rupt** Pleite machen; **—ruptcy** Bankrott m.

banner ['bænə*] n Banner nt.

banns [bænz] npl Aufgebot nt.

banquet ['bæŋkwɪt] n Bankett nt, Festessen nt.

banter ['bæntə*] n Neckerei f.

baptism ['bæptɪzəm] n Taufe f.

baptize [bæp'taɪz] vt taufen.

bar [bɑː*] n (*rod*) Stange f; (*obstacle*) Hindernis nt; (*of chocolate*) Tafel f; (*of soap*) Stück nt; (*for food, drink*) Buffet nt, Bar f; (*pub*) Wirtschaft f; (*Mus*) Takt(strich) m; vt (*fasten*) verriegeln; (*hinder*) versperren; (*exclude*) ausschließen; **the B—:** to be called to the B— als Anwalt zugelassen werden; **— none** ohne Ausnahme.

barbarian [bɑː'beərɪən] n Barbar(in f) m.

barbaric [bɑː'bærɪk] a primitiv, unkultiviert.

barbarity [bɑː'bærɪtɪ] n Grausamkeit f.

barbarous ['bɑːbərəs] a grausam, barbarisch.

barbecue ['bɑːbɪkjuː] n Barbecue nt.

barbed wire ['bɑːbd'waɪə*] n Stacheldraht m.

barber ['bɑːbə*] n Herrenfriseur m.

barbiturate [bɑː'bɪtjʊrɪt] n Barbiturat nt, Schlafmittel nt.

bare [bɛə*] a nackt; trees, country kahl; (mere) bloß; vt entblößen; —back ad ungesattelt; —faced a unverfroren; —foot a barfuß; —headed a mit bloßem Kopf; —ly ad kaum, knapp; —ness Nacktheit f; Kahlheit f.

bargain ['bɑːgɪn] n (sth cheap) günstiger Kauf; (agreement) (written) Kaufvertrag m; (oral) Geschäft nt; into the — obendrein; — for vt rechnen mit.

barge [bɑːdʒ] n Lastkahn m; — in vi hereinplatzen.

baritone ['bærɪtəʊn] n Bariton m.

bark [bɑːk] n (of tree) Rinde f; (of dog) Bellen nt; vi (dog) bellen.

barley ['bɑːlɪ] n Gerste f.

barmaid ['bɑːmeɪd] n Bardame f.

barman ['bɑːmən] n Barkellner m.

barn [bɑːn] n Scheune f.

barnacle ['bɑːnəkl] n Entenmuschel f.

barometer [bə'rɒmɪtə*] n Barometer nt.

baron ['bærən] n Baron m; —ess Baronin f; —ial [bə'rəʊnɪəl] a freiherrlich.

baroque [bə'rɒk] a barock.

barracks ['bærəks] npl Kaserne f.

barrage ['bærɑːʒ] n (gunfire) Sperrfeuer nt; (dam) Staudamm m; Talsperre f.

barrel ['bærəl] n Faß nt; (of gun) Lauf m; — organ Drehorgel f.

barren ['bærən] a unfruchtbar.

barricade [bærɪ'keɪd] n Barrikade f; vt verbarrikadieren.

barrier ['bærɪə*] n (obstruction) Hindernis nt; (fence) Schranke f.

barrister ['bærɪstə*] n (Brit) Rechtsanwalt m.

barrow ['bærəʊ] n (cart) Schubkarren m.

bartender ['bɑːtendə*] n (US) Barmann or -kellner m.

barter ['bɑːtə*] n Tauschhandel m; vi Tauschhandel treiben.

base [beɪs] n (bottom) Boden m, Basis f; (Mil) Stützpunkt m; vt gründen (on auf); to be —d on basieren auf (+dat); a (low) gemein; —ball Baseball m; —less a grundlos; —ment Kellergeschoß nt.

bash [bæʃ] vt (col) (heftig) schlagen.

bashful ['bæʃfʊl] a schüchtern.

basic ['beɪsɪk] a grundlegend; —ally ad im Grunde.

basin ['beɪsn] n (dish) Schüssel f; (for washing, also valley) Becken nt; (dock) (Trocken)becken nt.

basis ['beɪsɪs] n Basis f, Grundlage f.

bask [bɑːsk] vi sich sonnen.

basket ['bɑːskɪt] n Korb m; —ball Basketball m.

bass [beɪs] n (Mus, also instrument) Baß m; (voice) Baßstimme f; — clef Baßschlüssel m.

bassoon [bə'suːn] n Fagott nt.

bastard ['bɑːstəd] n Bastard m; Arschloch nt.

baste [beɪst] vt meat mit Fett begießen.

bastion ['bæstɪən] n (lit, fig) Bollwerk nt.

bat [bæt] n (Sport) Schlagholz nt; Schläger m; (Zool) Fledermaus f; vt: he didn't — an eyelid er hat nicht mit der Wimper gezuckt; off one's own — auf eigene Faust.

batch [bætʃ] *n* (of letters) Stoß *m*; (of samples) Satz *m*.

bated ['beɪtɪd] *a*: with — breath mit verhaltenem Atem.

bath [bɑ:θ] *n* Bad *nt*; (tub) Badewanne *f*; *vt* baden; —**s** [bɑ:ðz] *pl* (Schwimm)bad *nt*; —**chair** Rollstuhl *m*.

bathe [beɪð] *vti* baden; —**r** Badende(r) *mf*.

bathing ['beɪðɪŋ] *n* Baden *nt*; — **cap** Badekappe *f*; — **costume** Badeanzug *m*.

bathmat ['bɑ:θmæt] *n* Badevorleger *m*.

bathroom ['bɑ:θrum] *n* Bad(e-zimmer) *nt*.

baths [bɑ:ðz] *npl* see **bath**.

bath towel ['bɑ:θtaʊəl] *n* Badetuch *nt*.

batman ['bætmən] *n* (Offiziers)-bursche *m*.

baton ['bætən] *n* (of police) Gummiknüppel *m*; (Mus) Taktstock *m*.

battalion [bə'tælɪən] *n* Bataillon *nt*.

batter ['bætə*] *vt* verprügeln; *n* Schlagteig *m*; (for cake) Biskuitteig *m*.

battery ['bætərɪ] *n* (Elec) Batterie *f*; (Mil) Geschützbatterie *f*.

battle ['bætl] *n* Schlacht *f* (small) Gefecht *nt*; *vi* kämpfen; —**axe** (col) Xanthippe *f*; —**field** Schlachtfeld *nt*; —**ments** *pl* Zinnen *pl*; —**ship** Schlachtschiff *nt*.

batty ['bætɪ] *a* (col) plemplem.

bauble ['bɔ:bl] *n* Spielzeug *nt*.

bawdy ['bɔ:dɪ] *a* unflätig.

bawl [bɔ:l] *vi* brüllen; **to** — **sb out** jdn zur Schnecke machen.

bay [beɪ] *n* (of sea) Bucht *f*; **at** — gestellt, in die Enge getrieben; **to keep at** — unter Kontrolle halten.

bayonet ['beɪənet] *n* Bajonett *nt*.

bay window ['beɪ'wɪndəʊ] *n* Erkerfenster *nt*.

bazaar [bə'zɑ:*] *n* Basar *m*.

bazooka [bə'zu:kə] *n* Panzerfaust *f*.

be [bi:] *vi irreg* sein; (become, for passive) werden; (be situated) liegen, sein; **the book is 40p** das Buch kostet 40p; **he wants to** — **a teacher** er will Lehrer werden; **how long have you been here?** wie lange sind Sie schon da?; **have you been to Rome?** warst du schon einmal in Rom?, bist du schon einmal in Rom gewesen?; **his name is on the list** sein Name steht auf der Liste; **there is/are es gibt**.

beach [bi:tʃ] *n* Strand *m*; *vt* ship auf den Strand setzen; —**wear** Strandkleidung *f*.

beacon ['bi:kən] *n* (signal) Leuchtfeuer *nt*; (traffic —)-Bake *f*.

bead [bi:d] *n* Perle *f*; (drop) Tropfen *m*.

beak [bi:k] *n* Schnabel *m*.

beaker ['bi:kə*] *n* Becher *m*.

beam [bi:m] *n* (of wood) Balken *m*; (of light) Strahl *m*; (smile) strahlende(s) Lächeln *nt*; *vi* strahlen.

bean [bi:n] *n* Bohne *f*.

bear [bɛə*] *vt* weight, crops tragen; (tolerate) ertragen; young gebären; *n* Bär *m*; —**able** *a* erträglich; **to** — **on** relevant sein für.

beard [bɪəd] *n* Bart *m*; —**ed** *a* bärtig.

bearer ['bɛərə*] *n* Träger *m*.

bearing ['bɛərɪŋ] *n* (posture) Haltung *f*; (relevance) Relevanz *f*; (relation) Bedeutung *f*; (Tech) Kugellager *nt*; —**s** *pl* (direction)-Orientierung *f*.

bearskin ['bɛəskɪn] *n* Bärenfellmütze *f*.

beast [bi:st] n Tier nt, Vieh nt; (person) Bestie f; (nasty person) Biest nt; **—ly** ad viehisch; (col) scheußlich; **— of burden** Lasttier nt.

beat [bi:t] n (stroke) Schlag m; (pulsation) (Herz)schlag m; (police round) Runde f; Revier nt; (Mus) Takt m; Beat m; vt irreg schlagen; **to — about the bush** wie die Katze um den heißen Brei herumgehen; **to — time** den Takt schlagen; **— off** vt abschlagen; **— up** vt zusammenschlagen; **—en track** gebahnte(r) Weg m; (fig) herkömmliche Art und Weise; **off the —en track** abgelegen; **—er** (for eggs, cream) Schneebesen m.

beautiful ['bju:tiful] a schön; **—ly** ad ausgezeichnet.

beautify ['bju:tifai] vt verschönern.

beauty ['bju:ti] n Schönheit f.

beaver ['bi:və*] n Biber m.

becalm [bi'ka:m] vt: **to be —ed** eine Flaute haben.

because [bi'kɒz] ad, cj weil; prep: **— of** wegen (+gen or (col) dat).

beckon ['bekən] vti ein Zeichen geben (sb jdm).

become [bi'kʌm] vt irreg werden; (clothes) stehen (+dat).

becoming [bi'kʌmiŋ] a (suitable) schicklich; clothes kleidsam.

bed [bed] n Bett nt; (of river) Flußbett nt; (foundation) Schicht f; (in garden) Beet nt; **— and breakfast** Übernachtung f mit Frühstück; **—clothes** pl Bettwäsche f; **—ding** Bettzeug nt.

bedeck [bi'dek] vt schmücken.

bedlam ['bedləm] n (uproar) tolle(s) Durcheinander nt.

bedraggled [bi'drægld] a ramponiert.

bedridden ['bedridn] a bettlägerig.

bedroom ['bedrum] n Schlafzimmer nt.

bedside ['bedsaid] n: **at the —** am Bett.

bed-sitter ['bed'sitə*] n Einzimmerwohnung f, möblierte(s) Zimmer nt.

bedtime ['bedtaim] n Schlafenszeit f.

bee [bi:] n Biene f.

beech [bi:tʃ] n Buche f.

beef [bi:f] n Rindfleisch nt.

beehive ['bi:haiv] n Bienenstock m.

beeline [bi:lain] n: **to make a — for** schnurstracks zugehen auf (+acc).

beer [biə*] n Bier nt.

beetle ['bi:tl] n Käfer m.

beetroot ['bi:tru:t] n rote Bete f.

befall [bi'fɔ:l] irreg vi sich ereignen; vt zustoßen (+dat).

befit [bi'fit] vt sich schicken für.

before [bi'fɔ:*] prep vor; cj bevor; ad (of time) zuvor; früher; **I've done it —** das hab' ich schon mal getan.

befriend [bi'frend] vt sich (jds) annehmen.

beg [beg] vti (implore) dringend bitten; alms betteln; **—gar** Bettler(in) f) m.

begin [bi'gin] vti irreg anfangen, beginnen; (found) gründen; **to — with** zunächst (einmal); **—ner** Anfänger m; **—ning** Anfang m.

begrudge [bi'grʌdʒ] vt (be)neiden; **to — sb sth** jdm etw mißgönnen.

behalf [bi'ha:f] n: **on or in** (US) **—of** im Namen (+gen); **on my —** für mich.

behave [bi'heiv] vi sich benehmen.

behaviour, (US) **behavior** [bi'heivjə*] n Benehmen nt.

behead [bi'hed] vt enthaupten.

behind [bɪ'haɪnd] prep hinter; ad (late) im Rückstand; (in the rear) hinten; n (col) Hinterteil nt.

behold [bɪ'həuld] vt irreg (old) erblicken.

beige [beɪʒ] a beige.

being ['biːɪŋ] n (existence) (Da)sein nt; (person) Wesen nt.

belch [beltʃ] n Rülpsen nt; vi rülpsen; vt smoke ausspeien.

belfry ['belfrɪ] n Glockenturm m.

belie [bɪ'laɪ] vt Lügen strafen (+acc).

belief [bɪ'liːf] n Glaube m (in an +acc); (conviction) Überzeugung f.

believable [bɪ'liːvəbl] a glaubhaft.

believe [bɪ'liːv] vt glauben (+dat); (think) glauben, meinen, denken; vi (have faith) glauben; —r Gläubige(r) mf.

belittle [bɪ'lɪtl] vt herabsetzen.

bell [bel] n Glocke f.

belligerent [bɪ'lɪdʒərənt] a person streitsüchtig; country kriegsführend.

bellow ['beləu] vti brüllen; n Gebrüll nt.

bellows ['beləuz] npl (Tech) Gebläse nt; (for fire) Blasebalg m.

belly ['belɪ] n Bauch m; vi sich ausbauchen.

belong [bɪ'lɒŋ] vi gehören (to sb jdm); (to club) angehören (+dat); it does not — here es gehört nicht hierher; —ings pl Habe f.

beloved [bɪ'lʌvɪd] a innig geliebt; n Geliebte(r) mf.

below [bɪ'ləu] prep unter; ad unten.

belt [belt] n (band) Riemen m; (round waist) Gürtel m; vt (fasten) mit Riemen befestigen; (col: beat) schlagen; vi (col: go fast) rasen.

bench [bentʃ] n (seat) Bank f; (workshop) Werkbank f; (judge's

seat) Richterbank f; (judges) Richterstand m.

bend [bend] vt irreg (curve) biegen; (stoop) beugen; n Biegung f; (in road) Kurve f.

beneath [bɪ'niːθ] prep unter; ad darunter.

benefactor ['benɪfæktə*] n Wohltäter(in f) m.

beneficial [benɪ'fɪʃl] a vorteilhaft; (to health) heilsam.

beneficiary [benɪ'fɪʃərɪ] n Nutznießer(in f) m.

benefit ['benɪfɪt] n (advantage) Nutzen m; vt fördern; vi Nutzen ziehen (from aus).

benevolence [bɪ'nevələns] n Wohlwollen nt.

benevolent [bɪ'nevələnt] a wohlwollend.

benign [bɪ'naɪn] a person gütig; climate mild.

bent [bent] n (inclination) Neigung f; a (col: dishonest) unehrlich; to be — on versessen sein auf (+acc).

bequeath [bɪ'kwiːð] vt vermachen.

bequest [bɪ'kwest] n Vermächtnis nt.

bereaved [bɪ'riːvd] n (person) Hinterbliebene(r) mf.

bereavement [bɪ'riːvmənt] n schmerzliche(r) Verlust m.

beret ['berɪ] n Baskenmütze f.

berry ['berɪ] n Beere f.

berserk [bə'sɜːk] a: to go — wild werden.

berth [bɜːθ] n (for ship) Ankerplatz m; (in ship) Koje f; (in train) Bett nt; vt am Kai festmachen; vi anlegen.

beseech [bɪ'siːtʃ] vt irreg anflehen.

beset [bɪ'set] vt irreg bedrängen.

beside [bɪ'saɪd] prep neben, bei;

(except) außer; to be — o.s. außer sich sein (with our +dat).

besides [bɪ'saɪdz] prep außer, neben; ad zudem, überdies.

besiege [bɪ'siːdʒ] vt (Mil) belagern; (surround) umlagern, bedrängen.

besmirch [bɪ'smɜːtʃ] vt besudeln.

bespectacled [bɪ'spektɪkld] a bebrillt.

bespoke tailor [bɪ'spəʊk 'teɪlə*] n Maßschneider m.

best [best] a beste(r, s); ad am besten; at — höchstens; to make the — of it das Beste daraus machen; for the — zum Besten; — man Trauzeuge m.

bestial ['bestɪəl] a bestialisch.

bestow [bɪ'stəʊ] vt verleihen.

bestseller ['best'selə*] n Bestseller m, meistgekaufte(s) Buch nt.

bet [bet] n Wette f; vti irreg wetten.

betray [bɪ'treɪ] vt verraten; —al Verrat m.

better ['betə*] a, ad besser; vt verbessern; n: to get the — of jdn überwinden; he thought — of it er hat sich eines Besseren besonnen; you had — leave Sie gehen jetzt wohl besser; — off a (richer) wohlhabender.

betting ['betɪŋ] n Wetten nt; — shop Wettbüro nt.

between [bɪ'twiːn] prep zwischen; (among) unter; ad dazwischen.

bevel ['bevəl] n Abschrägung f.

beverage ['bevərɪdʒ] n Getränk nt.

beware [bɪ'weə*] vt sich hüten vor (+dat); '— of the dog' 'Vorsicht, bissiger Hund!'

bewildered [bɪ'wɪldəd] a verwirrt.

bewildering [bɪ'wɪldərɪŋ] a verwirrend.

bewitching [bɪ'wɪtʃɪŋ] a bestrickend.

beyond [bɪ'jɒnd] prep (place) jenseits (+gen); (time) über ... hinaus; (out of reach) außerhalb (+gen); it's — me das geht über meinen Horizont; ad darüber hinaus.

bias ['baɪəs] n (slant) Neigung f; (prejudice) Vorurteil nt; —(s)ed a voreingenommen.

bib [bɪb] n Latz m.

Bible ['baɪbl] n Bibel f.

biblical ['bɪblɪkəl] a biblisch.

bibliography [bɪblɪ'ɒɡrəfɪ] n Bibliographie f.

bicentenary [baɪsen'tiːnərɪ] n Zweihundertjahrfeier f.

biceps ['baɪseps] npl Bizeps m.

bicker ['bɪkə*] vi zanken; —ing Gezänk nt, Gekeife nt.

bicycle ['baɪsɪkl] n Fahrrad nt.

bid [bɪd] n (offer) Gebot nt; (attempt) Versuch m; vt irreg (offer) bieten; to — farewell Lebewohl sagen; —der (person) Steigerer m; —ding (command) Geheiß nt.

bide [baɪd] vt: — one's time abwarten.

big [bɪɡ] a groß.

bigamy ['bɪɡəmɪ] n Bigamie f.

bigheaded ['bɪɡ'hedɪd] a eingebildet.

bigot ['bɪɡət] n Frömmler m; —ed a bigott; —ry Bigotterie f.

bigwig ['bɪɡwɪɡ] n (col) hohe(s) Tier nt.

bike [baɪk] n Rad nt.

bikini [bɪ'kiːnɪ] n Bikini m.

bilateral [baɪ'lætərəl] a bilateral.

bile [baɪl] n (Biol) Galle(nflüssigkeit) f.

bilge [bɪldʒ] n (water) Bilgenwasser nt.

bilingual [baɪˈlɪŋgwəl] a zweisprachig.

bilious [ˈbɪlɪəs] a (sick) gallenkrank; (peevish) verstimmt.

bill [bɪl] n (account) Rechnung f; (Pol) Gesetzentwurf m; (US Fin) Geldschein m; — of exchange Wechsel m.

billet [ˈbɪlɪt] n Quartier nt.

billfold [ˈbɪlfəʊld] n (US) Geldscheintasche f.

billiards [ˈbɪlɪədz] n Billard nt.

billion [ˈbɪlɪən] n Billion f; (US) Milliarde f.

billy goat [ˈbɪlɪgəʊt] n Ziegenbock m.

bin [bɪn] n Kasten m; (dust—) (Abfall)eimer m.

bind [baɪnd] vt irreg (tie) binden; (tie together) zusammenbinden; (oblige) verpflichten; —ing (Buch)einband m; a verbindlich.

binge [bɪndʒ] n (col) Sauferei f.

bingo [ˈbɪŋgəʊ] n Bingo nt.

binoculars [bɪˈnɒkjʊləz] npl Fernglas nt.

biochemistry [ˈbaɪəʊˈkemɪstrɪ] n Biochemie f.

biographer [baɪˈɒgrəfə*] n Biograph m.

biographic(al) [baɪəʊˈgræfɪk(l)] a biographisch.

biography [baɪˈɒgrəfɪ] n Biographie f.

biological [baɪəˈlɒdʒɪkəl] a, biologisch.

biologist [baɪˈɒlədʒɪst] n Biologe m.

biology [baɪˈɒlədʒɪ] n Biologie f.

biped [ˈbaɪped] n Zweifüßler m.

birch [bɜːtʃ] n Birke f.

bird [bɜːd] n Vogel m; (col: girl) Mädchen nt; —'s-eye view Vogelschau f.

birth [bɜːθ] n Geburt f; of good — aus gutem Hause; — certificate Geburtsurkunde f; — control Geburtenkontrolle f; —day Geburtstag m; —place Geburtsort m; — rate Geburtenrate f.

biscuit [ˈbɪskɪt] n Keks m.

bisect [baɪˈsekt] vt halbieren.

bishop [ˈbɪʃəp] n Bischof m.

bit [bɪt] n bißchen, Stückchen nt; (horse's) Gebiß nt; a — tired etwas müde.

bitch [bɪtʃ] n (dog) Hündin f; (unpleasant woman) Weibsstück nt.

bite [baɪt] vti irreg beißen; n Biß m; (mouthful) Bissen m; — to eat Happen m.

biting [ˈbaɪtɪŋ] a beißend.

bitter [ˈbɪtə*] a bitter; memory etc schmerzlich; person verbittert; n (beer) dunkles Bier; to the — end bis zum bitteren Ende; —ness Bitterkeit f; —sweet bittersüß.

bivouac [ˈbɪvʊæk] n Biwak nt.

bizarre [bɪˈzɑː*] a bizarr.

blab [blæb] vi klatschen; vt ausplaudern.

black [blæk] a schwarz; night finster; vt schwärzen; — shoes wichsen; — eye blau schlagen; (industry) boykottieren; — and blue grün und blau; —berry Brombeere f; —bird Amsel f; —board (Wand)tafel f; —currant schwarze Johannisbeere f; —guard [ˈblægɑːd] Schuft m; —leg Streikbrecher(in f) m; —list schwarze Liste f; —mail Erpressung f; vt erpressen; —mailer Erpresser(in f) m; —market Schwarzmarkt m; —ness Schwärze f; —out Verdunkelung f; (Med) to have a — out bewußtlos werden; — sheep schwarze(s) Schaf nt; —smith Schmied m.

bladder ['blædə*] n Blase f.

blade [bleid] n (of weapon) Klinge f; (of grass) Halm m; (of oar) Ruderblatt nt.

blame [bleim] n Tadel m, Schuld f; vt tadeln, Vorwürfe machen (+ dat) he is to — er ist daran schuld; —less a untadelig.

blanch [blɑ:ntʃ] vi bleich werden.

blancmange [blə'mɒnʒ] n Pudding m.

bland [blænd] a mild.

blank [blæŋk] a leer, unbeschrieben; look verdutzt; cheque Blanko-; verse Blank-; n (space) Lücke f; Zwischenraum m; (cartridge) Platzpatrone f.

blanket ['blæŋkɪt] n (Woll)decke f.

blankly ['blæŋklɪ] ad leer; look verdutzt.

blare [blɛə*] vti (radio) plärren; (horn) tuten; (Mus) schmettern; n Geplärr nt; Getute nt; Schmettern nt.

blasé ['blɑ:zeɪ] a blasiert.

blaspheme [blæs'fi:m] vi (God) lästern.

blasphemous ['blæsfɪməs] a lästernd, lästerlich.

blasphemy ['blæsfəmɪ] n (God's) lästerung f, Blasphemie f.

blast [blɑ:st] n Explosion f; (of wind) Windstoß m; vt (blow up) sprengen; —! (col) verflixt!; —furnace Hochofen m; —off (Space) (Raketen)abschuß m.

blatant ['bleitənt] a offenkundig.

blaze [bleiz] n (fire) lodernde(s) Feuer nt; vi lodern; vt: — a trail Bahn brechen.

blazer ['bleizə*] n Klubjacke f, Blazer m.

bleach [bli:tʃ] n Bleichmittel nt; vt bleichen.

bleak [bli:k] a kahl, rauh; future trostlos.

bleary-eyed ['blɪərɪaɪd] a triefäugig; (on waking up) mit verschlafenen Augen.

bleat [bli:t] n (of sheep) Blöken nt; (of goat) Meckern nt; vi blöken; meckern.

bleed [bli:d] irreg vi bluten; vt (draw blood) Blut abnehmen; to — to death verbluten.

bleeding ['bli:dɪŋ] a blutend.

blemish ['blemɪʃ] n Makel m; vt verunstalten.

blench [blentʃ] vi zurückschrecken; see blanch.

blend [blend] n Mischung f; vt mischen; vi sich mischen.

bless [bles] vt segnen; (give thanks) preisen; (make happy) glücklich machen; — you! Gesundheit!; —ing Segen m; (at table) Tischgebet nt; (happiness) Wohltat f; Segen m; (good wish) Glück nt.

blight [blait] n (Bot) Mehltau m; (fig) schädliche(r) Einfluß m; vt zunichte machen.

blimey ['blaimi] interj (Brit col) verflucht.

blind [blaind] a blind; corner unübersichtlich; n (for window) Rouleau nt; vt blenden; — alley Sackgasse f; —fold Augenbinde f; a mit verbundenen Augen; vt die Augen verbinden (sb jdm); —ly ad blind; (fig) blindlings; —ness Blindheit f; — spot (Aut) toter Winkel m; (fig) schwache(r) Punkt m.

blink [blɪŋk] vti blinzeln; —ers pl Scheuklappen pl.

bliss [blis] n (Glück)seligkeit f; —fully ad glückselig.

blister ['blistə*] n Blase f; vt

Blasen werfen auf (+dat); vi Blasen werfen.

blithe [blaɪð] a munter; —ly ad fröhlich.

blitz [blɪts] n Luftkrieg m; vt bombardieren.

blizzard ['blɪzəd] n Schneesturm m.

bloated ['bləʊtɪd] a aufgedunsen; (col: full) nudelsatt.

blob [blɒb] n Klümpchen nt.

bloc [blɒk] n (Pol) Block m.

block [blɒk] n (of wood) Block m, Klotz m; (of houses) Häuserblock m; vt hemmen; —ade [blɒ'keɪd] Blockade f; vt blockieren; —age Verstopfung f.

bloke [bləʊk] n (col) Kerl m, Typ m.

blonde [blɒnd] a blond; n Blondine f.

blood [blʌd] n Blut nt; — donor Blutspender m; — group Blutgruppe f; —less a blutleer; — poisoning Blutvergiftung f; — pressure Blutdruck m; —shed Blutvergießen nt; —shot a blutunterlaufen; —stained a blutbefleckt; —stream Blut n, Blutkreislauf m; —thirsty a blutrünstig; — transfusion Blutübertragung f; —y a (col) verdammt, saumäßig; (lit) blutig; —y-minded a stur.

bloom [blu:m] n Blüte f; (freshness) Glanz m; vi blühen; in — in Blüte.

blossom ['blɒsəm] n Blüte f; vi blühen.

blot [blɒt] n Klecks m; vt beklecksen; ink (ab)löschen; — out auslöschen.

blotchy ['blɒtʃɪ] a fleckig.

blotting paper ['blɒtɪŋpeɪpə*] n Löschpapier nt.

blouse [blaʊz] n Bluse f.

blow [bləʊ] n Schlag m; irreg vt blasen; vi (wind) wehen; to — one's top (vor Wut) explodieren; — over vi vorübergehen; — up vi explodieren; vt sprengen; —lamp Lötlampe f; —out (Aut) geplatzte(r) Reifen m; —up (Phot) Vergrößerung f; —y a windig.

blubber ['blʌbə*] n Walfischspeck m.

bludgeon ['blʌdʒən] vt (fig) zwingen.

blue [blu:] a blau; (col: unhappy) niedergeschlagen; (obscene) pornographisch; joke anzüglich; to have the —s traurig sein; —bell Glockenblume f; —blooded a blaublütig; —bottle · Schmeißfliege f; —print (fig) Entwurf m; —s pl (Mus) Blues m.

bluff [blʌf] vt bluffen, täuschen; n (deception) Bluff m; a gutmütig und derb.

bluish ['blu:ɪʃ] a bläulich.

blunder ['blʌndə*] n grobe(r) Fehler m, Schnitzer m; vi einen groben Fehler machen.

blunt [blʌnt] a knife stumpf; talk unverblümt; vt abstumpfen; —ly ad frei heraus; —ness Stumpfheit f; (fig) Plumpheit f.

blur [blɜ:*] n Fleck m; vi verschwimmen; vt verschwommen machen.

blurb [blɜ:b] n Waschzettel m.

blurt [blɜ:t] vt: — out herausplatzen mit.

blush [blʌʃ] vi erröten; n (Scham)röte f; —ing a errötend.

bluster ['blʌstə*] vi (wind) brausen; (person) darauf lospoltern, schwadronieren; —y a sehr windig.

boa ['bəʊə]. n Boa f.

boar [bɔ:*] n Keiler m, Eber m.

board [bɔ:d] n (of wood) Brett nt; (of card) Pappe f; (committee) Ausschuß m; (of firm) Aufsichtsrat m; (Sch) Direktorium nt; vt train einsteigen in (+acc); ship an Bord gehen (+gen); — and lodging Unterkunft f und Verpflegung; to go by the — flachfallen, über Bord gehen; — up vt mit Brettern vernageln; —er Kostgänger m; (Sch) Internatsschüler(in f) m; —ing house Pension f; —ing school Internat nt; — room Sitzungszimmer nt.

boast [bəʊst] vi prahlen; n Großtuerei f; Prahlerei f; —ful a prahlerisch; —fulness Überheblichkeit f.

boat [bəʊt] n Boot nt; (ship) Schiff nt; —er (hat) Kreissäge f; —ing Bootfahren nt; —swain ['bəʊsn] = bosun; — train Zug m mit Schiffsanschluß.

bob [bɔb] vi sich auf und nieder bewegen.

bobbin ['bɔbɪn] n Spule f.

bobsleigh ['bɔbsleɪ] n Bob m.

bodice ['bɔdɪs] n Mieder nt.

-bodied ['bɔdɪd] a -gebaut.

bodily ['bɔdɪlɪ] a od körperlich.

body ['bɔdɪ] n Körper m; (dead) Leiche f; (group) Mannschaft f; (Aut) Karosserie f; (trunk) Rumpf m; in a — in einer Gruppe; the main — of the work der Hauptanteil der Arbeit; —guard Leibwache f; —work Karosserie f.

bog [bɔg] n Sumpf m; vi: to get —ged down sich festfahren.

bogey ['bəʊgɪ] n Schreckgespenst nt.

boggle ['bɔgl] vi stutzen.

bogus ['bəʊgəs] a unecht, Schein-.

boil [bɔɪl] vti kochen; n (Med) Geschwür nt; to come to the — zu kochen anfangen; —er Boiler m; —ing point Siedepunkt m.

boisterous ['bɔɪstərəs] a ungestüm.

bold [bəʊld] a (fearless) unerschrocken; handwriting fest und klar; —ly ad keck; —ness Kühnheit f; (cheekiness) Dreistigkeit f.

bollard ['bɔləd] n (Naut) Poller m; (on road) Pfosten m.

bolster ['bəʊlstə*] n Polster nt; — up vt unterstützen.

bolt [bəʊlt] n Bolzen m; (lock) Riegel m; vt verriegeln; (swallow) verschlingen; vi (horse) durchgehen.

bomb [bɔm] n Bombe f; vt bombardieren; —ard [bɔm'ba:d] vt bombardieren; —ardment [bɔm'ba:dmənt] Beschießung f; —er Bomber m; —ing Bombenangriff m; —shell (fig) Bombe f.

bombastic [bɔm'bæstɪk] a bombastisch.

bona fide ['bəʊnə'faɪd] a echt.

bond [bɔnd] n (link) Band nt; (Fin) Schuldverschreibung f.

bone [bəʊn] n Knochen m; (of fish) Gräte f; (piece of —) Knochensplitter m; — of contention Zankapfel m; vt die Knochen herausnehmen (+dat); fish entgräten; —dry a knochentrocken; —r (US col) Schnitzer m.

bonfire ['bɔnfaɪə*] n Feuer nt im Freien.

bonnet ['bɔnɪt] n Haube f; (for baby) Häubchen, nt; (Brit Aut) Motorhaube f.

bonny ['bɔnɪ] a (Scot) hübsch.

bonus ['bəʊnəs] n Bonus m; (annual —) Prämie f.

bony ['bəʊnɪ] a knochig, knochendürr.

boo [buː] vt auspfeifen.

book [bʊk] n Buch nt; vt ticket etc vorbestellen; person verwarnen; —able a im Vorverkauf erhältlich; —case Bücherregal nt, Bücherschrank m; —ing office (Rail) Fahrkartenschalter m; (Theat) Vorverkaufsstelle f; —keeping Buchhaltung f; —let Broschüre f; —maker Buchmacher m; —seller Buchhändler m; —shop Buchhandlung f; —stall Bücherstand m; (Rail) Bahnhofsbuchhandlung f; —worm Bücherwurm m.

boom [buːm] n (noise) Dröhnen nt; (busy period) Hochkonjunktur f; vi dröhnen.

boomerang ['buːməræŋ] n Bumerang m.

boon [buːn] n Wohltat f, Segen m.

boorish ['bʊərɪʃ] a grob.

boost [buːst] n Auftrieb m; (fig) Reklame f; vt Auftrieb geben.

boot [buːt] n Stiefel m; (Brit Aut) Kofferraum m; vt (kick) einen Fußtritt geben; to — (in addition) obendrein.

booty ['buːtɪ] n Beute f.

booze [buːz] n (col) Alkohol m, Schnaps m; vi saufen.

border ['bɔːdə*] n Grenze f; (edge) Kante f; (in garden) (Blumen)rabatte f; — on vt grenzen an (+acc); —line Grenze f.

bore [bɔː*] vt bohren, (weary) langweilen; n (person) langweilige(r) Mensch m; (thing) langweilige Sache f; (of gun) Kaliber nt; —dom Langeweile f.

boring ['bɔːrɪŋ] a langweilig.

born [bɔːn] to be — geboren werden.

borough ['bʌrə] n Stadt(gemeinde) f, Stadtbezirk m.

borrow ['bɒrəʊ] vt borgen; —ing (Fin) Anleihe f.

bosom ['bʊzəm] n Busen m.

boss [bɒs] n Chef m, Boß m; vt: — around herumkommandieren; —y a herrisch.

bosun ['bəʊsn] n Bootsmann m.

botanical [bə'tænɪkəl] a botanisch.

botanist ['bɒtənɪst] n Botaniker(in f) m.

botany ['bɒtənɪ] n Botanik f.

botch [bɒtʃ] vt verpfuschen.

both [bəʊθ] a beide(s); — (of) the books beide Bücher; I like them — ich mag sie beide; pron beide(s); ad: — X and Y sowohl X wie or als auch Y.

bother ['bɒðə*] vt (pester) quälen; vi (fuss) sich aufregen; (take trouble) sich Mühe machen; n Mühe f, Umstand m.

bottle ['bɒtl] n Flasche f; vt (in Flaschen) abfüllen; —neck (lit, fig) Engpaß m.

bottom ['bɒtəm] n Boden m; (of person) Hintern m; (riverbed) Flußbett m; at — im Grunde; a unterste(r, s); —less a bodenlos.

bough [baʊ] n Zweig m, Ast m.

boulder ['bəʊldə*] n Felsbrocken m.

bounce [baʊns] vi (ball) hochspringen; (person) herumhüpfen; (cheque) platzen; vt (auf)springen lassen; n (rebound) Aufprall m; —r Rausschmeißer m.

bound [baʊnd] n Grenze f; (leap) Sprung m; vi (spring, leap) (auf)springen; a gebunden, verpflichtet; out of —s Zutritt verboten; to be — to do sth verpflichtet sein, etw zu tun, etw tun müssen; it's — to happen es muß so kommen; to be

— for ... nach ... fahren; **—ary** Grenze *f,* Grenzlinie *f;* **—less** *a* grenzenlos.

bouquet [bʊ'keɪ] *n* Strauß *m;* (*of wine*) Blume *f.*

bourgeois [bʊəʒwɑ:] *a* klein-bürgerlich, bourgeois.

bout [baʊt] *n* (*of illness*) Anfall *m;* (*of contest*) Kampf *m.*

bow¹ [bəʊ] *n* (*ribbon*) Schleife *f;* (*weapon, Mus*) Bogen *m.*

bow² [baʊ] *vi* sich verbeugen; (*submit*) sich beugen (+*dat*); *n* Ver-beugung *f;* (*of ship*) Bug *m.*

bowels ['baʊəlz] *npl* Darm *m;* (*centre*) Innere *nt.*

bowl [bəʊl] *n* (*basin*) Schüssel *f;* (*of pipe*) (Pfeifen)kopf *m;* (*wooden ball*) (Holz)kugel *f; vti* (die Kugel) rollen; **—s** *pl* (*game*) Bowls-Spiel *nt.*

bow-legged ['bəʊlegɪd] *a* o-beinig.

bowler ['bəʊlə*] *n* Werfer *m;* (*hat*) Melone *f.*

bowling ['bəʊlɪŋ] *n* Kegeln *nt;* — **alley** Kegelbahn *f;* — **green** Rasen *m* zum Bowling-Spiel.

bow tie ['bəʊ'taɪ] *n* Fliege *f.*

box [bɒks] *n* Schachtel *f;* (*bigger*) Kasten *m;* (*Theat*) Loge *f; vt* ein-packen; **to** — **sb's ears** jdm eine Ohrfeige geben; *vi* boxen; **—er** Boxer *m;* — **in** *vt* einpferchen; **—ing** (*Sport*) Boxen *nt;* **B—ing Day** zweiter Weihnachtsfeiertag; **—ing ring** Boxring *m;* — **office** (Theater)kasse *f;* — **room** Rumpel-kammer *f.*

boy [bɔɪ] *n* Junge *m;* — **scout** Pfad-finder *m.*

boycott ['bɔɪkɒt] *n* Boykott *m; vt* boykottieren.

boyfriend ['bɔɪfrend] *n* Freund *m.*

boyish ['bɔɪʃ] *a* jungenhaft.

bra [brɑ:] *n* BH *m.*

brace [breɪs] *n* (*Tech*) Stütze *f;* (*Med*) Klammer *f; vt* stützen; **—s** *pl* Hosenträger *pl.*

bracelet ['breɪslɪt] *n* Armband *nt.*

bracing ['breɪsɪŋ] *a* kräftigend.

bracken ['brækən] *n* Farnkraut *nt.*

bracket ['brækɪt] *n* Halter *m,* Klammer *f;* (*in punctuation*) Klammer *f;* (*group*) Gruppe *f; vt* einklammern; (*fig*) in dieselbe Gruppe einordnen.

brag [bræg] *vi* sich rühmen.

braid [breɪd] *n* (*hair*) Flechte *f;* (*trim*) Borte *f.*

Braille [breɪl] *n* Blindenschrift *f.*

brain [breɪn] *n* (*Anat*) Gehirn *nt;* (*intellect*) Intelligenz *f,* Verstand *m;* (*person*) kluge(r) Kopf *m;* **—s** *pl* Verstand *m;* **—less** *a* dumm; **—storm** verrückte(r) Einfall *m;* **—wash** *vt* Gehirnwäsche *f* vor-nehmen bei; **—wave** gute(r) Einfall *m,* Geistesblitz *m;* **—y** gescheit.

braise [breɪz] *vt* schmoren.

brake [breɪk] *n* Bremse *f; vti* bremsen.

branch [brɑ:ntʃ] *n* Ast *m;* (*division*) Zweig *m; vi* (*road*) sich verzweigen.

brand [brænd] *n* (*Comm*) Marke *f,* Sorte *f;* (*on cattle*) Brandmal *nt; vt* brandmarken; (*Comm*) eine Schutzmarke geben (+*dat*).

brandish ['brændɪʃ] *vt* (drohend) schwingen.

brand-new ['brænd'nju:] *a* funkel-nagelneu.

brandy ['brændɪ] *n* Weinbrand *m,* Kognak *m.*

brash [bræʃ] *a* unverschämt.

brass [brɑ:s] *n* Messing *nt;* — **band** Blaskapelle *f.*

brassière [ˈbræsɪə*] n Büstenhalter m.

brat [bræt] n ungezogene(s) Kind nt, Gör nt.

bravado [brəˈvɑːdəʊ] n Tollkühnheit f.

brave [breɪv] a tapfer; n indianische(r) Krieger m; vt die Stirn bieten (+dat); —ly ad tapfer; —ry [ˈbreɪvərɪ] Tapferkeit f.

bravo [ˈbrɑːˈvəʊ] interj bravo!

brawl [brɔːl] n Rauferei f; vi Krawall machen.

brawn [brɔːn] n (Anat) Muskeln pl; (strength) Muskelkraft f; —y a muskulös, stämmig.

bray [breɪ] n Eselsschrei m; vi schreien.

brazen [ˈbreɪzn] a (shameless) unverschämt; vt: — it out sich mit Lügen und Betrügen durchsetzen.

brazier [ˈbreɪzɪə*] n (of workmen) offene(r) Kohlenofen m.

breach [briːtʃ] n (gap) Lücke f; (Mil) Durchbruch m; (of discipline) Verstoß m (gegen die Disziplin); (of faith) Vertrauensbruch m; vt durchbrechen; — of the peace öffentliche Ruhestörung f.

bread [bred] n Brot nt; — and butter Butterbrot nt; —crumbs pl Brotkrumen pl; (Cook) Paniermehl nt; to be on the —line sich gerade so durchschlagen; —winner Ernährer m.

breadth [bretθ] n Breite f.

break [breɪk] irreg vt (destroy) (ab- or zer)brechen; promise brechen, nicht einhalten; vi (fall apart) auseinanderbrechen; (collapse) zusammenbrechen; (of dawn) anbrechen; n (gap) Lücke f; (chance) Chance f, Gelegenheit f; (fracture) Bruch m; (rest) Pause f; — down vi (car) eine Panne haben;

(person) zusammenbrechen; to — free or loose sich losreißen; — in vt animal abrichten; horse zureiten; vi (burglar) einbrechen; — out vi ausbrechen; — up vi zerbrechen; (fig) sich zerstreuen; (Sch) in die Ferien gehen; vt brechen; —able a zerbrechlich; —age Bruch m, Beschädigung f; —down (Tech) Panne f; (of nerves) Zusammenbruch m; —er Brecher m; —fast [ˈbrekfəst] Frühstück nt; —through Durchbruch m; —water Wellenbrecher m.

breast [brest] n Brust f; — stroke Brustschwimmen nt.

breath [breθ] n Atem m; out of — außer Atem; under one's — flüsternd.

breathalize [ˈbreθəlaɪz] vt blasen lassen.

breathe [briːð] vti atmen; —r Verschnaufpause f.

breathless [ˈbreθlɪs] a atemlos.

breath-taking [ˈbreθteɪkɪŋ] a atemberaubend.

breed [briːd] irreg vi sich vermehren; vt züchten; n (race) Rasse f, Zucht f; —er (person) Züchter m; —ing Züchtung f; (up-bringing) Erziehung f; (education) Bildung f.

breeze [briːz] n Brise f.

breezy [ˈbriːzɪ] a windig; manner munter.

brevity [ˈbrevɪtɪ] n Kürze f.

brew [bruː] vt brauen; plot anzetteln; vi (storm) sich zusammenziehen; —ery Brauerei f.

bribe [braɪb] n Bestechungsgeld nt or -geschenk nt; vt bestechen; —ry [ˈbraɪbərɪ] Bestechung f.

bric-à-brac [ˈbrɪkəbræk] n Nippes pl.

brick [brɪk] n Backstein m; —layer Maurer m; —work Mauerwerk nt; —works Ziegelei f.

bridal ['braɪdl] a Braut-, bräutlich.

bride [braɪd] n Braut f; —groom Bräutigam m; —smaid Brautjungfer f.

bridge [brɪdʒ] n Brücke f; (Naut) Kommandobrücke f; (Cards) Bridge nt; (Anat) Nasenrücken m; vt eine Brücke schlagen über (+acc); (fig) überbrücken.

bridle ['braɪdl] n Zaum m; vt (fig) zügeln; horse aufzäumen; — path Saumpfad m.

brief [briːf] a kurz; n (Jur) Akten pl; vt instruieren; —s pl Schlüpfer m, Slip m; —case Aktentasche f; —ing (genaue) Anweisung f; —ly ad kurz; —ness Kürze f.

brigade [brɪ'geɪd] n Brigade f.

brigadier [brɪgə'dɪə*] n Brigadegeneral m.

bright [braɪt] a hell; (cheerful) heiter; idea klug; —en up vt aufhellen; person aufheitern; vi sich aufheitern; —ly ad hell; heiter.

brilliance ['brɪljəns] n Glanz m; (of person) Scharfsinn m.

brilliant a, —ly ad ['brɪljənt, -lɪ] glänzend.

brim [brɪm] n Rand m; vi voll sein; —ful a übervoll.

brine [braɪn] n Salzwasser nt.

bring [brɪŋ] vt irreg bringen; — about vt zustande bringen; — off vt davontragen; success erzielen; — round or to vt wieder zu sich bringen; — up vt aufziehen; question zur Sprache bringen.

brisk [brɪsk] a lebhaft.

bristle ['brɪsl] n Borste f; vi sich sträuben; **bristling with** strotzend vor (+dat).

brittle ['brɪtl] a spröde.

broach [brəʊtʃ] vt subject anschneiden.

broad [brɔːd] a breit; hint deutlich; daylight hellicht; (general) allgemein; accent stark; —cast n Rundfunkübertragung f; vti irreg übertragen, senden; —casting Rundfunk m; —en vt erweitern; vi sich erweitern; —ly ad allgemein gesagt; —-minded a tolerant.

brocade [brə'keɪd] n Brokat m.

broccoli ['brɒkəlɪ] n Spargelkohl m, Brokkoli pl.

brochure ['brəʊʃʊə*] n Broschüre f.

broiler ['brɔɪlə*] n Bratrost m.

broke [brəʊk] a (col) pleite.

broken-hearted ['brəʊkən'hɑːtɪd] a untröstlich.

broker ['brəʊkə*] n Makler m.

bronchitis [brɒŋ'kaɪtɪs] n Bronchitis f.

bronze [brɒnz] n Bronze f; —d a sonnengebräunt.

brooch [brəʊtʃ] n Brosche f.

brood [bruːd] n Brut f; vi brüten; —y a brütend.

brook [brʊk] n Bach m.

broom [bruːm] n Besen m; —stick Besenstiel m.

broth [brɒθ] n Suppe f, Fleischbrühe f.

brothel ['brɒθl] n Bordell nt.

brother ['brʌðə*] n Bruder m; —hood Bruderschaft f; —-in-law Schwager m; —ly a brüderlich.

brow [braʊ] n (eyebrow) (Augen)braue f; (forehead) Stirn f; (of hill) Bergkuppe f; —beat vt irreg einschüchtern.

brown [braʊn] a braun; n Braun nt; vt bräunen; —ie Wichtel m; — paper Packpapier nt.

browse [braʊz] *vi* (*in books*) blättern ; (*in shop*) schmökern, herumschauen.

bruise [bruːz] *n* Bluterguß *m*, blaue(r) Fleck *m*; *vti* einen blauen Fleck geben/bekommen.

brunette [bruː'net] *n* Brünette *f*.

brunt [brʌnt] *n* volle Wucht *f*.

brush [brʌʃ] *n* Bürste *f*; (*for sweeping*) Handbesen *m*; (*for painting*) Pinsel *m*; (*fight*) kurze(r) Kampf *m*; (*Mil*) Scharmützel *nt*; (*fig*) Auseinandersetzung *f*; *vt* (*clean*) bürsten; (*sweep*) fegen; (*touch*) streifen; **give sb the —off** (*col*) jdm eine Abfuhr erteilen; **— aside** *vt* abtun; **—wood** Gestrüpp *nt*.

brusque [bruːsk] *a* schroff.

Brussels sprout [ˈbrʌslz'spraʊt] *n* Rosenkohl *m*.

brutal [ˈbruːtl] *a* brutal; **—ity** [bruːˈtælɪtɪ] *n* Brutalität *f*.

brute [bruːt] *n* (*person*) .Scheusal *nt*; **— force** rohe Kraft; (*violence*) nackte Gewalt *an*.

brutish [ˈbruːtɪʃ] *a* tierisch.

bubble [ˈbʌbl] *n* (Luft)blase *f*; *vi* sprudeln; (*with joy*) übersprudeln.

buck [bʌk] *n* Bock *m*; (*US col*) Dollar *m*; *vi* bocken; **— up** *vi* (*col*) sich zusammenreißen.

bucket [ˈbʌkɪt] *n* Eimer *m*.

buckle [ˈbʌkl] *n* Schnalle *f*; *vt* (an- or zusammen)schnallen; *vi* (*bend*) sich verziehen.

bud [bʌd] *n* Knospe *f*; *vi* knospen, keimen.

Buddhism [ˈbʊdɪzəm] *n* Buddhismus *m*.

Buddhist [ˈbʊdɪst] *n* Buddhist(in *f*) *m*; *a* buddhistisch.

budding [ˈbʌdɪŋ] *a* angehend.

buddy [ˈbʌdɪ] *n* (*col*) Kumpel *m*.

budge [bʌdʒ] *vti* (sich) von der Stelle rühren.

budgerigar [ˈbʌdʒərɪgaː*] *n* Wellensittich *m*.

budget [ˈbʌdʒɪt] *n* Budget *nt*; (*Pol*) Haushalt *m*; *vi* haushalten.

budgie [ˈbʌdʒɪ] *n* = **budgerigar.**

buff [bʌf] *a* colour lederfarben; *n* (*enthusiast*) Fan *m*.

buffalo [ˈbʌfələʊ] *n* Büffel *m*.

buffer [ˈbʌfə*] *n* Puffer *m*.

buffet [ˈbʌfɪt] *n* (*blow*) Schlag *m*; [ˈbʊfeɪ] (*bar*) Imbißraum *m*, Erfrischungsraum *m*; (*food*) (kaltes) Büffet *nt*; *vt* [ˈbʌfɪt] (herum)stoßen.

buffoon [bʌˈfuːn] *n* Hanswurst *m*.

bug [bʌg] *n* (*lit, fig*) Wanze *f*; .*vt* verwanzen; **—bear** Schreckgespenst *nt*.

bugle [ˈbjuːgl] *n* Jagd-, Bügelhorn *nt*.

build [bɪld] *vt irreg* bauen; *n* Körperbau *m*; **—er** *n* Bauunternehmer *m*; **—ing** Gebäude *nt*; **—ing society** Baugenossenschaft *f*; **—up** Aufbau *m*; (*publicity*) Reklame *f*.

built [bɪlt]: **well—** *a person* gut gebaut; **—in** *a cupboard* eingebaut; **—up area** Wohngebiet *nt*.

bulb [bʌlb] *n* (*Bot*) (Blumen)zwiebel *f*; (*Elec*) Glühlampe *f*, Birne *f*; **—ous** *a* knollig.

bulge [bʌldʒ] *n* (Aus)bauchung *f*; *vi* sich aus(bauchen).

bulk [bʌlk] *n* Größe *f*, Masse *f*; (*greater part*) Großteil *m*; **—head** Schott *nt*; **—y** *a* (sehr) umfangreich; *goods* sperrig.

bull [bʊl] *n* (*animal*) Bulle *m*; (*cattle*) Stier· *m*; (*papal*) Bulle *m*; **—dog** Bulldogge *f*.

bulldoze ['buldəuz] vt planieren;
(fig) durchboxen; —r Planierraupe
f, Bulldozer m.

bullet ['bulɪt] n Kugel f.

bulletin ['bulɪtɪn] n Bulletin nt,
Bekanntmachung f.

bullfight ['bulfaɪt] n Stierkampf m.

bullion ['buliən] n Barren m.

bullock ['bulək] n Ochse m.

bull's-eye ['bulzaɪ] n das Schwarze
nt.

bully ['bulɪ] n Raufbold m; vt einschüchtern.

bum [bʌm] n (col: backside)
Hintern m; (tramp) Landstreicher
m; (nasty person) fieser Kerl m;
— around vi herumgammeln.

bumblebee ['bʌmblbi:] n Hummel
f.

bump [bʌmp] n (blow) Stoß m;
(swelling) Beule f; vti stoßen,
prallen; —er n (Brit Aut) Stoßstange
f; a edition dick; harvest Rekord-.

bumptious ['bʌmpʃəs] a
aufgeblasen.

bumpy ['bʌmpɪ] a holprig.

bun [bʌn] n Korinthenbrötchen nt.

bunch [bʌntʃ] n (of flowers) Strauß
m; (of keys) Bund m; (of people)
Haufen m.

bundle ['bʌndl] n Bündel nt; vt
bündeln; — off vt fortschicken.

bung [bʌŋ] n Spund m; vt (col:
throw) schleudern.

bungalow ['bʌŋgələu] n ein-
stöckige(s) Haus nt, Bungalow m.

bungle ['bʌŋgl] vt verpfuschen.

bunion ['bʌniən] n entzündete(r)
Fußballen m.

bunk [bʌŋk] n Schlafkoje m; — bed
Etagenbett nt.

bunker ['bʌŋkə*] n (coal store)
Kohlenbunker m; (golf) Sandloch
nt.

bunny ['bʌnɪ] n Häschen nt.

Bunsen burner ['bʌnsn 'bɜ:nə*] n
Bunsenbrenner m.

bunting ['bʌntɪŋ] n Fahnentuch nt.

buoy [bɔɪ] n Boje f; (lifebuoy)
Rettungsboje f; —ancy Schwimm-
kraft f; —ant a (floating)
schwimmend; (fig) heiter; — up vt
Auftrieb geben (+ dat).

burden ['bɜ:dn] n (weight) Ladung
f, Last f; (fig) Bürde f; vt belasten.

bureau ['bjuərəu] n (desk) Sekretär
m; (for information etc) Büro nt.

bureaucracy [bju'rɒkrəsɪ] n
Bürokratie f.

bureaucrat ['bjuərəkræt] n Büro-
krat(in f) m; —ic [bjuərə'krætɪk] a
bürokratisch.

burglar ['bɜ:glə*] n Einbrecher m;
— alarm Einbruchssicherung f;
—ize vt (US) einbrechen in
(+ acc); —y Einbruch m.

burgle ['bɜ:gl] vt einbrechen in
(+ acc).

burial ['berɪəl] n Beerdigung f; —
ground Friedhof m.

burlesque [bɜ:'lesk] n Burleske f.

burly ['bɜ:lɪ] a stämmig.

burn [bɜ:n] irreg vt verbrennen; vi
brennen; n Brandwunde f; to —
one's fingers sich die Finger verbrennen; —ing question brennende
Frage f.

burnish ['bɜ:nɪʃ] vt polieren.

burrow ['bʌrəu] n (of fox) Bau m;
(of rabbit) Höhle f; vi sich eingraben; vt eingraben.

bursar ['bɜ:sə*] n Kassenverwalter
m, Quästor m.

burst [bɜ:st] irreg vt zerbrechen; vi
platzen; (into tears) ausbrechen; n
Explosion f; (outbreak) Ausbruch
m; (in pipe) Bruch(stelle f) m.

bury ['berɪ] vt vergraben; (in grave) beerdigen; to — the hatchet das Kriegsbeil begraben.

bus [bʌs] n (Auto)bus m, Omnibus m.

bush [bʊʃ] n Busch m.

bushel ['bʊʃl] n Scheffel m.

bushy ['bʊʃɪ] a buschig.

busily ['bɪzɪlɪ] ad geschäftig.

business ['bɪznɪs] n Geschäft f; (concern) Angelegenheit f; it's none of your — es geht dich nichts an; to mean — es ernst meinen; —man Geschäftsmann m.

bus-stop ['bʌsstɒp] n Bushaltestelle f.

bust [bʌst] n Büste f; a (broken) kaputt(gegangen); business pleite; to go — pleite machen.

bustle ['bʌsl] n Getriebe nt; vi hasten.

bustling ['bʌslɪŋ] a geschäftig.

bust-up ['bʌstʌp] n (col) Krach m.

busy ['bɪzɪ] a beschäftigt; road belebt; vt: — o.s. sich beschäftigen; —body Übereifrige(r) mf.

but [bʌt, bət] cj aber; not this — that nicht dies, sondern das; (only) nur; (except) außer.

butane ['bjuːteɪn] n Butan nt.

butcher ['bʊtʃə*] n Metzger m; (murderer) Schlächter m; (kill) schlachten; (kill) abschlachten.

butler ['bʌtlə*] n Butler m.

butt [bʌt] n (cask) große(s) Faß nt;

(target) Zielscheibe f; (thick end) dicke(s) Ende nt; (of gun) Kolben m; (of cigarette) Stummel m; vt (mit dem Kopf) stoßen.

butter ['bʌtə*] n Butter f; vt buttern; —fly Schmetterling m.

buttocks ['bʌtəks] npl Gesäß nt.

button ['bʌtn] n Knopf m; vtf zuknöpfen; —hole Knopfloch nt; Blume f im Knopfloch; vt rankriegen.

buttress ['bʌtrɪs] n Strebepfeiler m; Stützbogen m.

buxom ['bʌksəm] a drall.

buy [baɪ] vt irreg kaufen; — up aufkaufen; —er Käufer(in f) m.

buzz [bʌz] n Summen nt; vi summen.

buzzard ['bʌzəd] n Bussard m.

buzzer ['bʌzə*] n Summer m.

by [baɪ] prep (near) bei; (via) über (+acc); (past) an (+dat) ... vorbei; (before) bis; — day/night tags/nachts; — train/bus mit dem Zug/Bus; done — sb/sth von jdm/durch etw gemacht; — oneself allein; — and large im großen und ganzen; —election Nachwahl f; —gone a vergangen; n: let —gones be —gones laß(t) das Vergangene vergangen sein; —(e)-law Verordnung f; —pass Umgehungsstraße f; —product Nebenprodukt nt; —stander Zuschauer m; —word Inbegriff m.

C

C, c [siː] n C nt, c nt.

cab [kæb] n Taxi nt; (of train)

Führerstand m; (of truck) Führersitz m.

cabaret ['kæbəreɪ] n Kabarett nt.

cabbage ['kæbɪdʒ] n Kohl(kopf) m.

cabin ['kæbɪn] n Hütte f; (Naut) Kajüte f; (Aviat) Kabine f; — cruiser Motorjacht f.

cabinet ['kæbɪnɪt] n Schrank m; (for china) Vitrine f; (Pol) Kabinett nt; —maker Kunsttischler m.

cable ['keɪbl] n Drahtseil nt, Tau nt; (Tel) (Leitungs)kabel nt; (telegram) Kabel nt; vti kabeln, telegraphieren; —car Seilbahn f; —gram (Übersee)telegramm nt; — railway (Draht)seilbahn f.

cache [kæʃ] n Versteck nt; (for ammunition) geheimes Munitionslager nt; (for food) geheimes Proviantlager nt; (supplies of ammunition) Munitionsvorrat m; (supplies of food) Lebensmittelvorrat m.

cackle ['kækl] n Gegacker nt; vi gacken.

cactus ['kæktəs] n Kaktus m, Kaktee f.

caddie ['kædɪ] n Golfjunge m.

caddy ['kædɪ] n Teedose f.

cadence ['keɪdəns] n Tonfall m; (Mus) Kadenz f.

cadet [kə'det] n Kadett m.

cadge [kædʒ] vt schmarotzen, nassauern.

Caesarean [si:'zɛərɪən] a: — (section) Kaiserschnitt m.

café ['kæfɪ] n Café nt, Restaurant nt.

cafeteria [kæfɪ'tɪərɪə] n Selbstbedienungsrestaurant nt.

caffein(e) ['kæfi:n] n Koffein nt.

cage [keɪdʒ] n Käfig m; vt einsperren.

cagey ['keɪdʒɪ] a geheimnistuerisch, zurückhaltend.

cajole [kə'dʒəʊl] vt überreden.

cake [keɪk] n Kuchen m; (of soap) Stück nt; —d a verkrustet.

calamine ['kæləmaɪn] n Galmei m.

calamitous [kə'læmɪtəs] a katastrophal, unglückselig.

calamity [kə'læmɪtɪ] n Unglück nt, (Schicksals)schlag m.

calcium ['kælsɪəm] n Kalzium nt.

calculate ['kælkjʊleɪt] vt berechnen, kalkulieren.

calculating ['kælkjʊleɪtɪŋ] a berechnend.

calculation [kælkjʊ'leɪʃən] n Berechnung f.

calculator ['kælkjʊleɪtə*] n Rechner m.

calculus ['kælkjʊləs] n Rechenart f.

calendar ['kælɪndə*] n Kalender m.

calf [kɑ:f] n Kalb nt; (leather) Kalbsleder nt; (Anat) Wade f.

calibre, (US) caliber ['kælɪbə*] n Kaliber nt.

call [kɔ:l] vt rufen; (summon) herbeirufen; (name) nennen; (meeting) einberufen; (awaken) wecken; (Tel) anrufen; vi (for help) rufen, schreien; (visit) vorbeikommen; n (shout) Schrei m, Ruf m; (visit) Besuch m; (Tel) Anruf m; on — in Bereitschaft; —box Fernsprechzelle f; —er Besucher(in f) m; (Tel) Anrufer m; — girl Call-Girl nt; —ing (vocation) Berufung f; to be —ed heißen; — for vt rufen (nach); (fetch) abholen; (fig: require) erfordern, verlangen; — off vt meeting absagen; — on vt besuchen, aufsuchen; (request) fragen; — up vt (Mil) einziehen, einberufen.

callous a, —ly ad ['kæləs, -lɪ] herzlos; —ness Herzlosigkeit f.

callow ['kæləʊ] a unerfahren, noch nicht flügge.

calm [kɑ:m] n Stille f, Ruhe f; (Naut) Flaute f; vt beruhigen; a

still, ruhig; *person gelassen*; **—ly**
ad ruhig, still; **—ness** Stille *f*, Ruhe
f; (*mental*) Gelassenheit *f*; **—
down** *vi* sich beruhigen; *vt*
beruhigen, besänftigen.

calorie ['kælərɪ] *n* Kalorie *f*,
Wärmeeinheit *f*.

calve [kɑ:v] *vi* kalben.

camber ['kæmbə*] *n* Wölbung *f*.

camel ['kæməl] *n* Kamel *nt*.

cameo ['kæmɪəu] *n* Kamee *f*.

camera ['kæmərə] *n* Fotoapparat
m, Kamera *f*; **in** — unter
Ausschluß der Öffentlichkeit;
—man Kameramann *m*.

camomile ['kæməmaɪl] *n*: **— tea**
Kamillentee *m*.

camouflage ['kæməflɑ:ʒ] *n*
Tarnung *f*; *vt* tarnen; (*fig*) verschleiern, bemänteln.

camp [kæmp] *n* Lager *nt*, Camp *nt*;
(*Mil*) Feldlager *nt*; (*permanent*)
Kaserne *f*; (*camping place*) Zelt-
platz *m*; *vi* zelten, campen.

campaign [kæm'peɪn] *n* Kampagne
f; (*Mil*) Feldzug *m*; *vi* (*Mil*) Krieg
führen; (*participate*) in den Krieg
ziehen; (*fig*) werben, Propaganda
machen; (*Pol*) den Wahlkampf
führen; **electoral** — Wahlkampf *m*.

campbed ['kæmp'bed] *n* Camping-
bett *nt*.

camper ['kæmpə*] *n* Zeltende(r)
mf, Camper *m*.

camping ['kæmpɪŋ] *n*: **to go —**
zelten, Camping machen.

campsite ['kæmpsaɪt] *n* Zeltplatz
m, Campingplatz *m*.

campus ['kæmpəs] *n* (*Sch*)
Schulgelände *nt*; (*Univ*) Univer-
sitätsgelände *nt*, Campus *m*.

can [kæn] *v aux irreg* (*be able*)
können, fähig sein; (*be allowed*)
dürfen, können; *n* Büchse *f*, Dose

f; (*for water*) Kanne *f*; *vt* konservieren, in Büchsen einmachen.

canal [kə'næl] *n* Kanal *m*.

canary [kə'nɛərɪ] *n* Kanarienvogel
m; *a* hellgelb.

cancel ['kænsəl] *vt* (*delete*) durch-
streichen; (*Math*) kürzen; *arrangement* aufheben; *meeting* absagen;
treaty annullieren; *stamp*
entwerten; **—lation** [kænsə'leɪʃən]
Aufhebung *f*; Absage *f*;
Annullierung *f*; Entwertung *f*.

cancer ['kænsə*] *n* (*also Astrol
C—*) Krebs *m*.

candid ['kændɪd] *a* offen, ehrlich;
—ly *ad* ehrlich.

candidate ['kændɪdeɪt] *n*
Bewerber(in *f*) *m*; (*Pol*)
Kandidat(in *f*) *m*.

candle ['kændl] *n* Kerze *f*; **—light**
Kerzenlicht *nt*; **—stick** Kerzen-
leuchter *m*.

candour ['kændə*] *n* Offenheit *f*.

candy ['kændɪ] *n* Kandis(zucker)
m; (*US*) Bonbons *pl*.

cane [keɪn] *n* (*Bot*) Rohr *nt*; (*for
walking*, *Sch*) Stock *m*; *vt* schlagen.

canister ['kænɪstə*] *n* Blechdose *f*.

cannabis ['kænəbɪs] *n* Hanf *m*,
Haschisch *nt*.

canned [kænd] *a* Büchsen-, eingemacht.

cannibal ['kænɪbəl] *n* Menschen-
fresser *m*; **—ism** Kannibalismus *m*.

cannon ['kænən] *n* Kanone *f*.

cannot ['kænɒt] = **can not**.

canny ['kænɪ] *a* (*shrewd*) schlau,
erfahren; (*cautious*) umsichtig, vorsichtig.

canoe [kə'nu:] *n* Paddelboot *nt*,
Kanu *nt*; **—ing** Kanufahren *nt*;
—ist Kanufahrer(in *f*) *m*.

canon ['kænən] *n* Domherr *m*; (*in*

-church law) Kanon m; (standard) Grundsatz m.

canonize ['kænənaız] vt heiligsprechen.

can opener ['kænəupnə*] n Büchsenöffner m.

canopy ['kænəpɪ] n Baldachin m.

can't [kænt] = can not.

cantankerous [kæn'tæŋkərəs] a zänkisch, mürrisch.

canteen [kæn'ti:n] n (in factory) Kantine f; (case of cutlery) Besteckkasten m.

canter ['kæntə*] n Kanter m; kurzer leichter Galopp m; vi in kurzem Galopp reiten.

cantilever ['kæntɪli:və*] n Träger m, Ausleger m.

canvas ['kænvəs] n Segeltuch nt, Zeltstoff m; (sail) Segel nt; (for painting) Leinwand f; (painting) Ölgemälde nt; under — (people) in Zelten; (boat) unter Segel.

canvass ['kænvəs] vt werben; — er Wahlwerber(in f) m.

canyon ['kænjən] n Felsenschlucht f.

cap [kæp] n Kappe f, Mütze f; (lid) (Verschluß)kappe f, Deckel m; vt verschließen; (surpass) übertreffen.

capability [keɪpə'bɪlɪtɪ] n Fähigkeit f.

capable ['keɪpəbl] a fähig; to be — of sth zu etw fähig or imstande sein.

capacity [kə'pæsɪtɪ] n Fassungsvermögen nt; (ability) Fähigkeit f; (position) Eigenschaft f.

cape [keɪp] n· (garment) Cape n, Umhang m; (Geog) Kap nt.

caper ['keɪpə*] n Kaper f.

capital ['kæpɪtl] n (— city) Hauptstadt f; (Fin) Kapital nt; (— letter) Großbuchstabe m; —ism Kapitalismus m; —ist a kapitalistisch; .n

Kapitalist(in f) m; — punishment Todesstrafe f.

capitulate [kə'pɪtjuleɪt] vi kapitulieren.

capitulation [kəpɪtjʊ'leɪʃən] n Kapitulation f.

capricious [kə'prɪʃəs] a launisch.

Capricorn ['kæprɪkɔ:n] n Steinbock m.

capsize [kæp'saɪz] vti kentern.

capstan ['kæpstən] n Ankerwinde f, Poller m.

capsule ['kæpsju:l] n Kapsel f.

captain ['kæptɪn] n Führer m; (Naut) Kapitän m; (Mil) Hauptmann m; (Sport) (Mannschafts)-kapitän m; vt anführen.

caption ['kæpʃən] n Unterschrift f, Text m.

captivate ['kæptɪveɪt] vt· fesseln.

captive ['kæptɪv] n Gefangene(r) mf; a gefangen(gehalten).

captivity [kæp'tɪvɪtɪ] n Gefangenschaft f.

-**capture** ·['kæptʃə*]· vt fassen, gefangennehmen; n Gefangennahme f.

car [ka:*] n Auto nt, Wagen m.

carafe [kə'ræf] n Karaffe f.

caramel ['kærəməl] n Karamelle f.

carat ['kærət] n Karat nt.

caravan ['kærəvæn] n Wohnwagen m; (in desert) Karawane f.

caraway ['kærəweɪ] n: — seed Kümmel m.

carbohydrate [ka:bəʊ'haɪdreɪt] n Kohlenhydrat nt.

carbon ['ka:bən] n Kohlenstoff m; (— paper) Kohlepapier nt; — copy Durchschlag m.

carburettor ['ka:bjuretə*] n Vergaser m.

carcass ['ka:kəs] n Kadaver m.

card [kɑːd] *n* Karte *f*; **—board** Pappe *f*; **—board box** Pappschachtel *f*; **— game** Kartenspiel *nt*.

cardiac ['kɑːdiæk] *a* Herz-.

cardigan ['kɑːdigən] *n* Strickjacke *f*.

cardinal ['kɑːdinl] *a*: **— number** Kardinalzahl *f*.

care [kɛə*] *n* Sorge *f*, Mühe *f*; *(charge)* Obhut *f*, Fürsorge *f*; *vi*: **I don't —** es ist mir egal; **to — about sb/sth** sich kümmern um jdn/etw; **to take —** *(watch)* vorsichtig sein; *(take pains)* darauf achten; **take — of** *vt* sorgen für; **— for** *vt (look after)* sorgen für; *(like)* mögen, gern' haben.

career [kə'riə*] *n* Karriere *f*, Laufbahn *f*; *vi* rasen.

carefree ['kɛəfriː] *a* sorgenfrei.

careful *a*, **—ly** *ad* ['kɛəful, -fəli] sorgfältig.

careless *a*, **—ly** *ad* ['kɛəlis, -li] unvorsichtig; **—ness** Unachtsamkeit *f*; *(neglect)* Nachlässigkeit *f*.

caress [kə'res] *n* Liebkosung *f*; *vt* liebkosen.

caretaker ['kɛəteɪkə*] *n* Hausmeister *m*.

car-ferry ['kɑːferi] *n* Autofähre *f*.

cargo ['kɑːgəu] *n* Kargo *m*, Schiffsladung *f*.

caricature ['kærɪkətjuə*] *n* Karikatur *f*; *vt* karikieren.

carnage ['kɑːnidʒ] *n* Blutbad *nt*.

carnal ['kɑːnl] *a* fleischlich, sinnlich.

carnation [kɑː'neɪʃən] *n* Nelke *f*.

carnival ['kɑːnivəl] *n* Karneval *m*, Fastnacht *f*, Fasching *m*.

carnivorous [kɑː'nivərəs] *a* fleischfressend.

carol ['kærl] *n* (Weihnachts)lied *nt*.

carp [kɑːp] *n (fish)* Karpfen *m*; **— at** *vt* herumnörgeln an (*+dat*).

car park ['kɑːpɑːk] *n* Parkplatz *m*; Parkhaus *nt*.

carpenter ['kɑːpintə*] *n* Zimmermann *m*.

carpentry ['kɑːpintri] *n* Zimmerei *f*.

carpet ['kɑːpit] *n* Teppich *m*; *vt* mit einem Teppich auslegen.

carping ['kɑːpiŋ] *a (critical)* krittelnd, Mecker-.

carriage ['kæridʒ] *n* Wagen *m*; *(of goods)* Beförderung *f*; *(bearing)* Haltung *f*; **—way** *(on road)* Fahrbahn *f*.

carrier ['kæriə*] *n* Träger(in *f*) *m*; *(Comm)* Spediteur *m*; **— bag** Tragetasche *m*; **— pigeon** Brieftaube *f*.

carrion ['kæriən] *n* Aas *nt*.

carrot ['kærət] *n* Möhre *f*, Mohrrübe *f*, Karotte *f*.

carry ['kæri] *vt* tragen; *vi* weit tragen, reichen; **—cot** Babytragetasche *f*; **to be carried away** *(fig)* hingerissen sein; **— on** *vi/t* fortführen, weitermachen; **— out** *vt orders* ausführen.

cart [kɑːt] *n* Wagen *m*, Karren *m*; *vt* schleppen.

cartilage ['kɑːtilidʒ] *n* Knorpel *m*.

cartographer [kɑː'tɒgrəfə*] *n* Kartograph(in *f*) *m*.

carton ['kɑːtən] *n* (Papp)karton *m*; *(of cigarettes)* Stange *f*.

cartoon ' [kɑː'tuːn] *n (Press)* Karikatur *f*; *(Cine)* (Zeichen)trickfilm *m*.

cartridge ['kɑːtridʒ] *n (for gun)* Patrone *f*; *(film)* Rollfilm *m*; *(of record player)* Tonabnehmer *m*.

carve [kɑːv] *vti wood* schnitzen; *stone* meißeln; *meat* (vor)schneiden.

carving ['kɑːviŋ] *n (in wood etc)*

Schnitzerei f; — knife Tranchiermesser nt.

car wash ['kɑːwɒʃ] n Autowäsche f.

cascade [kæs'keɪd] n Wasserfall m; vi kaskadenartig herabfallen.

case [keɪs] n (box) Kasten m, Kiste f; (suit—) Koffer m; (Jur, matter) Fall m; in — falls, im Falle; in any — jedenfalls, auf jeden Fall.

cash [kæʃ] n (Bar)geld nt; vt einlösen; — desk Kasse f; —ier [kæ'ʃɪə*] Kassierer(in f) m; — on delivery per Nachnahme; — register Registrierkasse f.

cashmere ['kæʃmɪə*] n Kaschmirwolle f.

casing ['keɪsɪŋ] n Gehäuse nt.

casino [kə'siːnəʊ] n Kasino nt.

cask [kɑːsk] n Faß nt.

casket ['kɑːskɪt] n Kästchen nt; (US: coffin) Sarg m.

casserole ['kæsərəʊl] n Kasserole f; (food) Auflauf m.

cassock ['kæsək] n Soutane f, Talar m.

cast [kɑːst] irreg vt werfen; horns etc verlieren; metal gießen; (Theat) besetzen; roles verteilen; n (Theat) Besetzung f; — off vi (Naut) losmachen; —off clothing abgelegte Kleidung.

castanets [kæstə'nets] npl Kastagnetten pl.

castaway ['kɑːstəweɪ] n Schiffbrüchige(r) mf.

caste [kɑːst] n Kaste f.

casting ['kɑːstɪŋ] a: — vote entscheidende Stimme f.

castiron [kɑːst'aɪən] n Gußeisen nt; a gußeisern; alibi todsicher.

castle ['kɑːsl] n Burg f; Schloß nt; (country mansion) Landschloß nt; (chess) Turm m.

castor ['kɑːstə*] n (wheel) Laufrolle f; — oil Rizinusöl nt; — sugar Streuzucker m.

castrate [kæs'treɪt] vt kastrieren.

casual ['kæʒjʊl] a arrangement beiläufig; attitude nachlässig; dress leger; meeting zufällig; —ly ad dress zwanglos, leger; remark beiläufig.

casualty ['kæʒjʊltɪ] n Verletzte(r) mf; Tote(r) mf; (department in hospital) Unfallstation f.

cat [kæt] n Katze f.

catalog (US), **catalogue** ['kætəlɒg] n Katalog m; vt katalogisieren.

catalyst ['kætəlɪst] n (lit, fig) Katalysator m.

catapult ['kætəpʌlt] n Katapult nt; Schleuder f.

cataract ['kætərækt] n Wasserfall m; (Med) grauer(r) Star m.

catarrh [kə'tɑː*] n Katarrh m.

catastrophe [kə'tæstrəfɪ] n Katastrophe f.

catastrophic [kætəs'trɒfɪk] a katastrophal.

catch [kætʃ] vt irreg fangen; train etc nehmen; erreichen; (surprise) ertappen; (understand) begreifen; n (of lock) Sperrhaken m; (of fish) Fang m; to — a cold sich erkälten.

catching ['kætʃɪŋ] a (Med, fig) ansteckend.

catch phrase ['kætʃfreɪz] n Schlagwort nt, Slogan m.

catchy ['kætʃɪ] a tune eingängig.

catechism ['kætɪkɪzəm] n Katechismus m.

categorical a, —ly ad [kætə'gɒrɪkl, -kəlɪ] kategorisch.

categorize ['kætɪgəraɪz] vt kategorisieren.

category ['kætɪgərɪ] n Kategorie f.
cater ['keɪtə*] vi versorgen; **—ing** Gastronomie f; Bewirtung f; — for vt (lit) party ausrichten; (fig) eingestellt sein auf (+acc); berücksichtigen.
caterpillar ['kætəpɪlə*] n Raupe f; — track Gleiskette f.
cathedral [kə'θi:drəl] n Kathedrale f, Dom m.
Catholic ['kæθəlɪk] a (Rel) katholisch; n Katholik(in f) m; c— vielseitig.
cattle ['kætl] npl Vieh nt.
catty ['kætɪ] a gehässig.
cauliflower ['kɒlɪflauə*] n Blumenkohl m.
cause [kɔ:z] n Ursache f; Grund m; (purpose) Sache f; in a good — zu einem guten Zweck; vt verursachen.
causeway ['kɔ:zweɪ] n Damm m.
caustic ['kɔ:stɪk] a ätzend; (fig) bissig.
cauterize ['kɔ:təraɪz]·vt ätzen, ausbrennen.
caution ['kɔ:ʃən] n Vorsicht f; (warning) Warnung f; (Jur) Verwarnung f; vt (ver)warnen.
cautious a, **—ly** ad ['kɔ:ʃəs, -lɪ] vorsichtig.
cavalcade [kævəl'keɪd] n Kavalkade f.
cavalier [kævə'lɪə*] a. blasiert.
cavalry ['kævəlrɪ] npl Kavallerie f.
cave [keɪv] n Höhle f; **—man** Höhlenmensch m; — in vi einstürzen.
cavern ['kævən] n Höhle f; **—ous** a cheeks hohl; eyes tiefliegend.
cavil ['kævɪl] vi kritteln (at an + dat).
cavity ['kævɪtɪ] n Höhlung f; (in tooth) Loch nt.

cavort [kə'vɔ:t] vi umherspringen.
cease [si:s] vi aufhören; vt beenden; **—fire** Feuereinstellung f; **—less** a unaufhörlich.
cedar ['si:də*] n Zeder f.
cede [si:d] vt abtreten.
ceiling ['si:lɪŋ] n Decke f; (fig) Höchstgrenze f.
celebrate ['selɪbreɪt] vt feiern; anniversary begehen; vi feiern; **—d** a gefeiert.
celebration [selɪ'breɪʃən] n Feier f.
celebrity [sɪ'lebrɪtɪ] n gefeierte Persönlichkeit f.
celery ['selərɪ] n Sellerie m or f.
celestial [sɪ'lestɪəl] a himmlisch.
celibacy ['selɪbəsɪ] n Zölibat nt or m.
cell [sel] n Zelle f; (Elec) Element nt.
cellar ['selə*] n Keller m.
cellist ['tʃelɪst] n Cellist(in f) m.
cello ['tʃeləu] n Cello nt.
cellophane ® ['seləfeɪn] n Cellophan nt.
cellular ['seljulə*] a zellenförmig, zellular.
cellulose ['seljuləus] n Zellulose f.
cement [sɪ'ment] n Zement m; vt (lit) zementieren; (fig) festigen.
cemetery ['semɪtrɪ] n Friedhof m.
cenotaph ['senətɑ:f] n Ehrenmal nt, Zenotaph f.
censor ['sensə*] n Zensor m; **—ship** Zensur f.
censure ['senʃə*] vt rügen.
census ['sensəs] n Volkszählung f.
centenary [sen'ti:nərɪ] n Jahrhundertfeier f.
center ['sentə*] n (US) = **centre**.
centigrade ['sentɪgreɪd] a: **10** (degrees) — 10 Grad Celsius.
centilitre, (US) **—liter** ['sentɪli:tə*] n Zentiliter nt or m.

centimetre, (US) **—meter** ['sentimi:tə*] n Zentimeter nt.

centipede ['sentipi:d] n Tausendfüßler m.

central ['sentrəl] a **zentral; — heating** Zentralheizung f; **—ize** vt zentralisieren.

centre ['sentə*] n Zentrum nt; **— of gravity** Schwerpunkt m; **to — on** (sich) konzentrieren auf (+acc).

century ['sentjuri] n Jahrhundert nt.

ceramic [si'ræmik] a keramisch.

cereal ['siəriəl] n (any grain) Getreide nt; (at breakfast) Getreideflocken pl.

ceremonial [seri'məuniəl] a zeremoniell.

ceremony ['seriməni] n Feierlichkeiten pl, Zeremonie f.

certain ['sə:tən] a sicher; (particular) gewiß; **for —** ganz bestimmt; **—ly** ad sicher, bestimmt; **—ty** Gewißheit f.

certificate [sə'tifikit] n Bescheinigung f; (Sch etc) Zeugnis nt.

certify ['sə:tifai] vti bescheinigen.

cessation [se'seifən] n Einstellung f, Ende nt.

chafe [tʃeif] vti (wund)reiben, scheuern.

chaffinch ['tʃæfintʃ] n Buchfink m.

chain [tʃein] n Kette f; (also — up) anketten; mit Ketten fesseln; **— reaction** Kettenreaktion f; **— smoker** Kettenraucher(in f) m; **— store** Kettenladen m.

chair [tʃeə*] n Stuhl m; (arm—) Sessel m; (Univ) Lehrstuhl m; vt: **to — a meeting** in einer Versammlung den Vorsitz führen; **—lift** Sessellift m; **—man** Vorsitzende(r) m; (of firm) Präsident m.

chalet ['ʃælei] n Chalet nt.

chalice ['tʃælis] n (Abendmahls)kelch m.

chalk [tʃɔ:k] n Kreide f.

challenge ['tʃælindʒ] n Herausforderung f; vt auffordern; (contest) bestreiten; **—r** Herausforderer m.

challenging ['tʃælindʒiŋ] a statement herausfordernd; work anspruchsvoll.

chamber ['tʃeimbə*] n Kammer f; **— of commerce** Handelskammer f; **—maid** Zimmermädchen nt; **—music** Kammermusik f; **—pot** Nachttopf m.

chameleon [kə'mi:liən] n Chamäleon nt.

chamois ['ʃæmwa:] n Gemse f; **—leather** ['ʃæmi'leðə*] Sämischleder nt.

champagne [ʃæm'pein] n Champagner m, Sekt m.

champion ['tʃæmpiən] n (Sport) Sieger(in f) m, Meister m; (of cause) Verfechter(in f) m; **—ship** Meisterschaft f.

chance [tʃa:ns] n (luck, fate) Zufall m; (possibility) Möglichkeit f; (opportunity) Gelegenheit f, Chance f; (risk) Risiko nt; a zufällig; vt: **to — it** es darauf ankommen lassen; **by —** zufällig; **to take a —** ein Risiko eingehen; **no —** keine Chance.

chancel ['tʃa:nsəl] n Altarraum m, Chor m.

chancellor ['tʃa:nsələ*] n Kanzler m; **C— of the Exchequer** Schatzkanzler m.

chancy ['tʃa:nsi] a (col) riskant.

chandelier [ʃændi'liə*] n Kronleuchter m.

change [tʃeindʒ] vt verändern; money wechseln; vi sich

verändern; (trains) umsteigen; (colour etc) sich verwandeln; (clothes) sich umziehen; n Veränderung f; (money) Wechselgeld nt; (coins) Kleingeld nt; —able a weather wechselhaft; —over Umstellung f, Wechsel m.

changing ['tʃeɪndʒɪŋ] a veränderlich; — room Umkleideraum m.

channel ['tʃænl] n (stream) Bachbett nt; (Naut) Straße f, Meerenge f; (Rad, TV) Kanal m; (fig) Weg m; vt (hindurch)leiten, lenken; through official —s durch die Instanzen; the (English) C— der Ärmelkanal; C— Islands Kanalinseln pl.

chant [tʃɑːnt] n liturgische(r) Gesang m; Sprechgesang m, Sprechchor m; vt intonieren.

chaos ['keɪɔs] n Chaos nt, Durcheinander nt.

chaotic [keɪ'ɒtɪk] a chaotisch.

chap [tʃæp] n (col) Bursche m, Kerl m; vt skin rissig machen; vi (hands etc) aufspringen.

chapel ['tʃæpəl] n Kapelle f.

chaperon ['ʃæpərəʊn] n Anstandsdame f; vt begleiten.

chaplain ['tʃæplɪn] n Geistliche(r) m, Pfarrer m, Kaplan m.

chapter ['tʃæptə*] n Kapitel nt.

char [tʃɑː*] vt (burn) verkohlen; vi (cleaner) putzen gehen.

character ['kærɪktə*] n Charakter m, Wesen nt; (Liter) Figur f, Gestalt f; (Theat) Person f, Rolle f; (peculiar person) Original nt; (in writing) Schriftzeichen nt; —istic [kærɪktə'rɪstɪk] a charakteristisch, bezeichnend (of für); n Kennzeichen nt, Eigenschaft f; —ize vt charakterisieren, kennzeichnen.

charade [ʃə'rɑːd] n Scharade f.

charcoal ['tʃɑːkəʊl] n Holzkohle f.

charge [tʃɑːdʒ] n (cost) Preis m; (Jur) Anklage f; (of gun) Ladung f; (attack) Angriff m; vt gun, battery laden; price verlangen; (Mil) angreifen; vi (rush) angreifen, (an)stürmen; to be in — of verantwortlich sein für; to take — (die Verantwortung) übernehmen.

chariot ['tʃærɪət] n (Streit)wagen m.

charitable ['tʃærɪtəbl] a wohltätig; (lenient) nachsichtig.

charity ['tʃærɪtɪ] n (institution) Wohlfahrtseinrichtung f, Hilfswerk nt; (attitude) Nächstenliebe f, Wohltätigkeit f.

charlady ['tʃɑːleɪdɪ] n Reinemachefrau f, Putzfrau f.

charlatan ['ʃɑːlətən] n Scharlatan m, Schwindler(in f) m.

charm [tʃɑːm] n Charme m, gewinnende(s) Wesen nt; (in superstition) Amulett nt; Talisman m; vt bezaubern; —ing a reizend, liebenswürdig, charmant.

chart [tʃɑːt] n Tabelle f; (Naut) Seekarte f.

charter ['tʃɑːtə*] vt (Naut, Aviat) chartern; n Schutzbrief m; (cost) Schiffsmiete f; — flight Charterflug m; —ed accountant Wirtschaftsprüfer(in f) m.

charwoman ['tʃɑːwʊmən] n Reinemachefrau f, Putzfrau f.

chary ['tʃɛərɪ] a zurückhaltend (of sth mit etw.).

chase [tʃeɪs] vt jagen, verfolgen; n Jagd f.

chasm ['kæzəm] n Kluft f.

chassis ['ʃæsɪ] n Chassis nt, Fahrgestell nt.

chaste [tʃeɪst] a keusch.

chastity ['tʃæstɪtɪ] n Keuschheit f.

chat [tʃæt] vi plaudern, sich (zwanglos) unterhalten; n Plauderei f.

chatter ['tʃætə*] vi schwatzen; (teeth) klappern; n Geschwätz nt; —box Quasselstrippe f.

chatty ['tʃætɪ] a geschwätzig.

chauffeur ['ʃəʊfə*] n Chauffeur m, Fahrer m.

cheap [tʃiːp] a billig; joke schlecht; (of poor quality) minderwertig; to —en o.s. sich herablassen; —ly ad billig.

cheat [tʃiːt] vti betrügen; (Sch) mogeln; n Betrüger(in f) m; —ing Betrug m.

check [tʃek] vt prüfen; (look up, make sure) nachsehen; (control) kontrollieren; (restrain) zügeln; (stop) anhalten; n (examination, restraint) Kontrolle f; (restaurant bill) Rechnung f; (pattern) Karo(muster) nt; (US) = cheque; —ers (US) Damespiel nt; —list Kontrollliste f; —mate Schachmatt nt; —point Kontrollpunkt m; —up (Nach)prüfung f; (Med) (ärztliche) Untersuchung f.

cheek [tʃiːk] n Backe f, Wange f; (fig) Frechheit f, Unverschämtheit f; —bone Backenknochen m; —y a frech, übermütig.

cheep [tʃiːp] n Pieps(er) nt.

cheer [tʃɪə*] n Beifallsruf m, Hochruf m; —s! Prost!; vt zujubeln; (encourage) ermuntern, aufmuntern, vi jauchzen, Hochrufe ausbringen; —ful a fröhlich; —fulness Fröhlichkeit f, Munterkeit f; —ing Applaus m; a aufheiternd; —io interj tschüs!; —less a prospect trostlos; person verdrießlich; — up vt ermuntern; vi: — up! Kopf hoch!

cheese [tʃiːz] n Käse m; —board (gemischte) Käseplatte f; —cake Käsekuchen m.

cheetah ['tʃiːtə] n Gepard m.

chef [ʃef] n Küchenchef m.

chemical ['kemɪkəl] a chemisch.

chemist ['kemɪst] n (Med) Apotheker m, Drogist m; (Chem) Chemiker m; —ry Chemie f; —'s (shop) (Med) Apotheke f, Drogerie f.

cheque [tʃek] n Scheck m; —book Scheckbuch nt; — card Scheckkarte f.

chequered ['tʃekəd] a (fig) bewegt.

cherish ['tʃerɪʃ] vt person lieben; hope hegen; memory bewahren.

cheroot [ʃəˈruːt] n Zigarillo nt or m.

cherry ['tʃerɪ] n Kirsche f.

chervil ['tʃɜːvɪl] n Kerbel m.

chess [tʃes] n Schach nt; —board Schachbrett nt; —man Schachfigur f; —player Schachspieler(in f) m.

chest [tʃest] n Brust f, Brustkasten m; (box) Kiste f, Kasten m; to get sth off one's — seinem Herzen Luft machen; — of drawers Kommode f.

chestnut ['tʃesnʌt] n Kastanie f; (tree) Kastanienbaum m.

chew [tʃuː] vti kauen; —ing gum Kaugummi m.

chic [ʃiːk] a schick, elegant.

chicanery [ʃɪˈkeɪnərɪ] n Schikane f.

chick [tʃɪk] n Küken nt; —en Huhn nt; (food: roast) Hähnchen nt; —enpox Windpocken pl; —pea Kichererbse f.

chicory ['tʃɪkərɪ] n Zichorie f; (plant) Chicorée f.

chief [tʃiːf] n (Ober)haupt nt; Anführer m; (Comm) Chef m; a höchst, Haupt-; —ly ad hauptsächlich.

chieftain ['tʃiːftən] n Häuptling m.

chilblain ['tʃilblein] n Frostbeule f.

child [tʃaild] n Kind nt; —birth Entbindung f; —hood Kindheit f; —ish a kindisch; —like a kindlich; —ren ['tʃildrn] npl of child; —'s play (fig) Kinderspiel nt.

chill [tʃil] n Kühle f; (Med) Erkältung f; —y a kühl, frostig.

chime [tʃaim] n Glockenschlag m, Glockenklang m; vi ertönen, (er)klingen.

chimney ['tʃimni] n Schornstein m, Kamin m.

chimpanzee [tʃimpæn'ziː] n Schimpanse m.

chin [tʃin] n Kinn nt.

china ['tʃainə] n Porzellan nt.

chink [tʃiŋk] n (opening) Ritze f, Spalt m; (noise) Klirren nt.

chintz [tʃints] n Kattun m.

chip [tʃip] n (of wood etc) Splitter m; (potato) —s pl Pommes frites pl; (US: crisp) Chip m; vt absplittern; — vi Zwischenbemerkungen machen.

chiropodist [ki'rɔpədist] n Fußpfleger(in f) m.

chirp [tʃɜːp] n Zwitschern nt; vi zwitschern.

chisel ['tʃizl] n Meißel m.

chit [tʃit] n Notiz f; —chat Plauderei f.

chivalrous ['ʃivələs] a ritterlich.

chivalry ['ʃivəlri] n Ritterlichkeit f; (honour) Ritterschaft f.

chive [tʃaiv] n Schnittlauch m.

chloride ['klɔːraid] n Chlorid nt.

chlorine ['klɔːriːn] n Chlor nt.

chock [tʃɔk] n Keil m; —-a-block a vollgepfropft.

chocolate ['tʃɔklit] n Schokolade f.

choice [tʃɔis] n Wahl f; (of goods) Auswahl f; a auserlesen, Qualitäts-.

choir ['kwaiə*] n Chor m; —boy Chorknabe m.

choke [tʃəuk] vi ersticken; vt erdrosseln; (block) (ab)drosseln; n (Aut) Starterklappe f.

cholera ['kɔlərə] n Cholera f.

choose [tʃuːz] vt irreg wählen; (decide) beschließen.

chop [tʃɔp] vt (zer)hacken; wood spalten; vi to — and change schwanken; n Hieb m; (meat) Kotelett nt; —py a bewegt; —sticks pl (Eß)stäbchen pl.

choral ['kɔːrəl] a Chor-.

chord [kɔːd] n Akkord m; (string) Saite f.

chore [tʃɔː*] n Pflicht f; harte Arbeit f.

choreographer [kɔri'bgrəfə*] n Choreograph(in f) m.

chorister ['kɔristə*] n Chorsänger(in f) m.

chortle ['tʃɔːtl] vi glucksen, tief lachen.

chorus ['kɔːrəs] n Chor m; (in song) Refrain m.

chow [tʃau] n (dog) Chow-Chow m.

Christ [kraist] n Christus m.

christen ['krisn] vt taufen; —ing Taufe f.

Christian ['kristiən] a christlich; —a Christ(in f) m; — name Vorname m; —ity [kristi'æniti] n Christentum nt.

Christmas ['krisməs] n Weihnachten pl; — card Weihnachtskarte f; — tree Weihnachtsbaum m.

chrome [krəum] n = **chromium plating.**

chromium ['krəʊmɪəm] n Chrom nt; — **plating** Verchromung f.

chronic ['krɒnɪk] a (Med) chronisch; (terrible) scheußlich.

chronicle ['krɒnɪkl] n Chronik f.

chronological [krɒnə'lɒdʒɪkəl] a chronologisch.

chrysalis ['krɪsəlɪs] n (Insekten-)puppe f.

chrysanthemum [krɪs'ænθɪməm] n Chrysantheme f.

chubby ['tʃʌbɪ] a child pausbäckig; adult rundlich.

chuck [tʃʌk] vt werfen; n (Tech) Spannvorrichtung f.

chuckle ['tʃʌkl] vi in sich hinein-lachen.

chum [tʃʌm] n (child) Spiel-kamerad m; (adult) Kumpel m.

chunk [tʃʌŋk] n Klumpen m; (of food) Brocken m.

church [tʃɜːtʃ] n Kirche f; (clergy) Geistlichkeit f; —yard Kirchhof m.

churlish ['tʃɜːlɪʃ] a grob.

churn [tʃɜːn] n Butterfaß nt; (for transport) (große) Milchkanne f. — out vt (col) produzieren.

chute [ʃuːt] n Rutsche f.

cicada [sɪ'kɑːdə] n Zikade f.

cider ['saɪdə*] n Apfelwein m.

cigar [sɪ'gɑː*] n Zigarre f; —**ette** [sɪgə'ret] Zigarette f; —**ette case** Zigarettenetui nt; —**ette end** Ziga-rettenstummel m; —**ette holder** Zigarettenspitze f.

cinch [sɪntʃ] n (col) klare(r) Fall m; (easy) Kinderspiel nt.

cinder ['sɪndə*] n Zinder m.

Cinderella [sɪndə'relə] n Aschen-brödel nt.

cine ['sɪnɪ] n: —**camera** Film-kamera f; — **film** Schmalfilm m.

cinema ['sɪnəmə] n Kino nt.

cine-projector [sɪnɪprə'dʒektə*] n Filmvorführapparat m.

cinnamon ['sɪnəmən] n Zimt m.

cipher ['saɪfə*] n (code) Chiffre f; (numeral) Ziffer f.

circle ['sɜːkl] n Kreis m; vi kreisen; vt umkreisen; (attacking) umzingeln.

circuit ['sɜːkɪt] n Umlauf m; (Elec) Stromkreis m; —ous [sɜː'kjuːɪtəs] a weitschweifig.

circular ['sɜːkjʊlə*] a (letter) rund, kreisförmig; n Rundschreiben nt.

circularize ['sɜːkjʊləraɪz] vt (inform) benachrichtigen; letter herumschicken.

circulate ['sɜːkjʊleɪt] vi zirku-lieren; vt in Umlauf setzen.

circulation [sɜːkjʊ'leɪʃən] n (of blood) Kreislauf m; (of newspaper) Auflage f; (of money) Umlauf m.

circumcise ['sɜːkəmsaɪz] vt beschneiden.

circumference [sə'kʌmfərəns] n (Kreis)umfang m.

circumspect ['sɜːkəmspekt] a umsichtig.

circumstances ['sɜːkəmstənsəz] npl (facts connected with sth) Um-stände pl; (financial condition) Ver-hältnisse pl.

circumvent [sɜːkəm'vent] vt umgehen.

circus ['sɜːkəs] n Zirkus m.

cissy ['sɪsɪ] n Weichling m.

cistern ['sɪstən] n Zisterne f; (of W.C.) Spülkasten m.

citation [saɪ'teɪʃən] n Zitat nt.

cite [saɪt] vt zitieren, anführen.

citizen ['sɪtɪzn] n Bürger(in f) m; (of nation) Staatsangehörige(r) mf; —**ship** Staatsangehörigkeit f.

citrus ['sɪtrəs] adj: — **fruit** Zitrus-frucht f.

city ['sɪtɪ] n Großstadt f; (centre) Zentrum nt, City f.

civic ['sɪvɪk] a städtisch, Bürger-.

civil ['sɪvɪl] a (of town) Bürger-; (of state) staatsbürgerlich; (not military) zivil; (polite) höflich; — **engineer** Bauingenieur m; — **engineering** Hoch- und Tiefbau m; —**ian** [sɪ'vɪljən] n Zivilperson f; a zivil, Zivil-; —**ization** [sɪvɪlaɪ'zeɪʃən] n Zivilisation f, Kultur f; —**ized** a zivilisiert; Kultur-; — **law** bürgerliche(s) Recht , Zivilrecht nt; — **rights** pl Bürgerrechte pl; — **servant** Staatsbeamte(r) m; — **service** Staatsdienst m; — **war** Bürgerkrieg m.

clad [klæd] a gekleidet; gehüllt in (+acc).

claim [kleɪm] vt beanspruchen; (have opinion) behaupten; n (demand) Forderung f; (right) Anspruch m; Behauptung f; —**ant** Antragsteller(in f) m.

clairvoyant [klɛə'vɔɪənt] n Hellseher(in f) m; a hellseherisch.

clam [klæm] n Venusmuschel f.

clamber ['klæmbə*] vi kraxeln.

clammy ['klæmɪ] a feucht(kalt); klamm.

clamorous ['klæmərəs] a lärmend, laut.

clamp ['klæmp] n Schraubzwinge f; vt einspannen.

clan [klæn] n Sippe f, Clan m.

clang [klæŋ] n Klang m; Scheppern nt; vi klingen; scheppern.

clap [klæp] vi klatschen; vt Beifall klatschen (+dat); —**ping** (Beifall)klatschen nt.

claret ['klærɪt] n rote(r) Bordeaux(wein) m.

clarification [klærɪfɪ'keɪʃən] n Erklärung f.

clarify ['klærɪfaɪ] vt klären, erklären.

clarinet [klærɪ'net] n Klarinette f.

clarity ['klærɪtɪ] n Klarheit f.

clash [klæʃ] n (fig) Konflikt m, Widerstreit m; (sound) Knall m; vi zusammenprallen; (colours) sich beißen; (argue) sich streiten.

clasp [klɑːsp] n Klammer f, Haken m; (on belt) Schnalle f; vt umklammern.

class [klɑːs] n Klasse f; vt einordnen, einstufen; —**conscious** a klassenbewußt.

classic ['klæsɪk] n Klassiker(in f) m; a (traditional) klassisch; —**al** a klassisch.

classification [klæsɪfɪ'keɪʃən] n Klassifizierung f, Einteilung f.

classify ['klæsɪfaɪ] vt klassifizieren, einteilen.

classroom ['klɑːsrʊm] n Klassenzimmer nt.

classy ['klɑːsɪ] n (col) todschick.

clatter ['klætə*] n Klappern nt, Rasseln nt; (of feet) Getrappel nt; vi klappern, rasseln; (feet) trappeln.

clause [klɔːz] n (Jur) Klausel f; (Gram) Satz(teil) m, Satzglied nt.

claustrophobia [klɔːstrə'fəʊbɪə] n Platzangst f, Klaustrophobie f.

claw [klɔː] n Kralle f; vt (zer)kratzen.

clay [kleɪ] n Lehm m; (for pots) Ton m.

clean [kliːn] a sauber; (fig) schuldlos; shape ebenmäßig; cut glatt; vt saubermachen, reinigen, putzen; —**er** (person) Putzfrau f; (for grease etc) Scheuerpulver nt; —**ers** pl Chemische Reinigung f; —**ing** Reinigen nt, Säubern nt; —**liness** ['klenlɪnɪs] Sauberkeit f.

Reinlichkeit f; —ly ad reinlich; —se [klenz] vt reinigen, säubern; —shaven a glattrasiert; —up Reinigung f; —out vt gründlich putzen; — up vt aufräumen.

clear ['klɪə*] a water klar; glass durchsichtig; sound deutlich, klar, hell; meaning genau, klar; (certain) klar, sicher; road frei; to stand — of sth etw frei halten; vt road etc freimachen; vi (become clear) klarwerden; —ance ['klɪərns] (removal) Räumung f; (free space) Lichtung f; (permission) Freigabe f; —cut a scharf umrissen; case eindeutig; —ing Lichtung f; —ly ad klar, deutlich, zweifellos; —way (Brit) (Straße f mit) Halteverbot nt; — up vi (weather) sich aufklären; vt reinigen, säubern; (solve) aufklären.

clef [klef] n Notenschlüssel m.

clench [klentʃ] vt teeth zusammenbeißen; fist ballen.

clergy ['klɜːdʒɪ] n Geistliche(n) pl; —man Geistliche(r) m.

clerical ['klerɪkəl] a (office)Schreib-, Büro- ; (Eccl) geistlich, Pfarr(er)- ; — error Schreibfehler m.

clerk [klɑːk, US klɜːk] n (in office) Büroangestellte(r) mf; (US: salesman) Verkäufer(in f) m.

clever a, —ly ad ['klevə*, -əlɪ] klug, geschickt, gescheit.

cliché ['kliːʃeɪ] n Klischee nt.

click [klɪk] vi klicken; n Klicken nt; (of door) Zuklinken nt.

client ['klaɪənt] n Klient(in f) m; —ele [kliːˈɒntel] Kundschaft f.

cliff [klɪf] n Klippe f.

climate ['klaɪmɪt] n Klima nt.

climatic [klaɪˈmætɪk] a klimatisch.

climax ['klaɪmæks] n Höhepunkt m.

climb [klaɪm] vt besteigen; vi steigen, klettern; n Aufstieg m; —er Bergsteiger m, Kletterer m; (fig) Streber m; —ing Bergsteigen nt, Klettern nt.

clinch [klɪntʃ] vt (decide) entscheiden; deal festmachen; n (boxing) Clinch m.

cling [klɪŋ] vi irreg anhaften, anhängen.

clinic ['klɪnɪk] n Klinik f; —al a klinisch.

clink [klɪŋk] n (of coins) Klimpern nt; (of glasses) Klirren nt; (col: prison) Knast m; vi klimpern; vt klimpern mit; glasses anstoßen.

clip [klɪp] n Spange f; paper — (Büro-, Heft)klammer f; vt papers heften; hair, hedge stutzen; —pers pl (instrument) (pair of hedge) Heckenschere f; (for hair) Haarschneidemaschine f.

clique [kliːk] n Clique f, Gruppe f.

cloak [kləuk] n lose(r) Mantel m, Umhang m; —room (for coats) Garderobe f; (W.C.) Toilette f.

clobber ['klɒbə*] n (col) Klamotten pl; vt schlagen.

clock [klɒk] n Uhr f; —wise ad im · Uhrzeigersinn; —work Uhrwerk nt; like —work wie am Schnürchen.

clog [klɒg] n Holzschuh m; vt verstopfen.

cloister ['klɔɪstə*] n Kreuzgang m.

close [kləus] a nahe; march geschlossen; thorough genau, gründlich; weather schwül; ad knapp; —ly ad gedrängt, dicht; — to prep in der Nähe (+gen); I had a — shave das war knapp; —up Nahaufnahme f.

close [kləuz] vt schließen, abschließen; vi sich schließen; n (end) Ende nt, Schluß m; to ÷ with sb jdn angreifen; — down vt Geschäft aufgeben; vi eingehen; —d a road gesperrt; shop etc geschlossen; —d shop Gewerkschaftszwang m.

closet ['klɒzɪt] n Abstellraum m, Schrank m.

closure ['kləʊʒə*] n Schließung f.

clot [klɒt] n Klumpen m; (of blood) Blutgerinnsel nt; (fool) Blödmann m; vi gerinnen.

cloth [klɒθ] n (material) Stoff m, Tuch nt; (for washing etc) Lappen m, Tuch nt.

clothe [kləʊð] vt kleiden, bekleiden; —s pl Kleider pl, Kleidung f; see bedclothes; —s brush Kleiderbürste f; —s line Wäscheleine f; —s peg Wäscheklammer f.

clothing ['kləʊðɪŋ] n = clothes.

cloud [klaʊd] n Wolke f; —burst Wolkenbruch m; —y a wolkig, bewölkt.

clout [klaʊt] (col) n Schlag m; vt hauen.

clove [kləʊv] n Gewürznelke f; — of garlic Knoblauchzehe f.

clover ['kləʊvə*] n Klee m; —leaf Kleeblatt nt.

clown [klaʊn] n Clown m, Hanswurst m; vi kaspern, sich albern benehmen.

cloy [klɔɪ] vi: it —s es übersättigt einen.

club [klʌb] n Knüppel m; (society) Klub m; (golf) Golfschläger m; (Cards) Kreuz nt; vt prügeln; — together vi (with money etc) zusammenlegen; —house Klubhaus nt.

cluck [klʌk] vi glucken.

clue [kluː] n Anhaltspunkt m,

Fingerzeig m, Spur f; he hasn't a — er hat keine Ahnung.

clump [klʌmp] n Gebüsch nt.

clumsy ['klʌmzɪ] a person ungelenk, unbeholfen; object, shape unförmig.

cluster ['klʌstə*] n Traube f; (of trees etc) Gruppe f; — round vi sich scharen um; umschwarmen.

clutch [klʌtʃ] n feste(r) Griff m; (Aut) Kupplung f; vt sich festklammern an (+dat); book an sich klammern.

clutter ['klʌtə*] vt vollpropfen; desk etc übersäen; n Unordnung f.

coach [kəʊtʃ] n Omnibus m, (Überland)bus m; (old) Kutsche f; (Rail) (Personen)wagen m; (trainer) Trainer m; vt (Sch) Nachhilfeunterricht geben (+dat); (Sport) trainieren.

coagulate [kəʊˈægjuleɪt] vi gerinnen.

coal [kəʊl] n Kohle f.

coalesce [kəʊəˈles] vi. sich verbinden.

coal face ['kəʊlfeɪs] n (Abbau)sohle f, Streb m; at the — vor Ort.

coalfield ['kəʊlfiːld] n Kohlengebiet nt.

coalition [kəʊəˈlɪʃən] n Zusammenschluß m, (Pol) Koalition f.

coalmine ['kəʊlmaɪn] n Kohlenbergwerk nt; —r Bergarbeiter ·m.

coarse [kɔːs] a (lit) grob; (fig) ordinär.

coast [kəʊst] n Küste f; —al a Küsten-; —er Küstenfahrer m; —guard Küstenwache f; —line Küste(nlinie) f.

coat [kəʊt] n Mantel m; (on animals) Fell nt, Pelz m; (of paint) Schicht f; vt überstreichen; — of arms

Wappen *nt*; —hanger Kleiderbügel *m*; —ing Schicht *f*, Überzug *m*; (*of paint*) Schicht *f*.

coax [kəʊks] *vt* beschwatzen.

cobble(stone)s ['kɒbl(stəʊn)z] *npl* Pflastersteine *pl*.

cobra ['kɒbrə] *n* Kobra *f*.

cobweb ['kɒbweb] *n* Spinnennetz *nt*.

cocaine [kə'keɪn] *n* Kokain *nt*.

cock [kɒk] *n* Hahn *m*; *vt* ears spitzen; *gun* den Hahn spannen; —erel junge(r) Hahn *m*; —eyed *a* (*fig*) verrückt.

cockle ['kɒkl] *n* Herzmuschel *f*.

cockney ['kɒknɪ] *n* echte(r) Londoner *m*.

cockpit ['kɒkpɪt] *n* (*Aviat*) Pilotenkanzel *f*.

cockroach ['kɒkrəʊtʃ] *n* Küchenschabe *f*.

cocktail ['kɒkteɪl] *n* Cocktail *m*; — cabinet Hausbar *f*; — party Cocktailparty *f*; — shaker Mixbecher *m*.

cocoa ['kəʊkəʊ] *n* Kakao *m*.

coconut ['kəʊkənʌt] *n* Kokosnuß *f*.

cocoon [kə'kuːn] *n* Puppe *f*, Kokon *m*.

cod [kɒd] *n* Kabeljau *m*.

code [kəʊd] *n* Kode *m*; (*Jur*) Kodex *m*; in — verschlüsselt, in Kode.

codeine ['kəʊdiːn] *n* Kodein *nt*.

codify ['kəʊdɪfaɪ] *vt message* verschlüsseln; (*Jur*) kodifizieren.

coeducational [kəʊedjʊ'keɪʃənl] *a* koedukativ, gemischt.

coerce [kəʊ'ɜːs] *vt* nötigen, zwingen.

coercion [kəʊ'ɜːʃən] *n* Zwang *m*, Nötigung *f*.

coexistence [kəʊɪg'zɪstəns] *n* Koexistenz *f*.

coffee ['kɒfɪ] *n* Kaffee *m*; — bar Kaffeeausschank *m*, Café *nt*.

coffin ['kɒfɪn] *n* Sarg *m*.

cog [kɒg] *n* (Rad)zahn *m*.

cogent ['kəʊdʒənt] *a* triftig, überzeugend, zwingend.

cognac ['kɒnjæk] *n* Kognak *m*.

coherent [kəʊ'hɪərnt] *a* zusammenhängend, einheitlich.

coil [kɔɪl] *n* Rolle *f*; (*Elec*) Spule *f*; *vt* aufrollen, aufwickeln.

coin [kɔɪn] *n* Münze *f*; *vt* prägen; —age (*word*) Prägung *f*.

coincide [kəʊɪn'saɪd] *vi* (*happen together*) zusammenfallen; (*agree*) übereinstimmen; —nce [kəʊ-'ɪnsɪdəns] Zufall *m*; by a strange —nce merkwürdigerweise; —ntal [kəʊɪnsɪ'dentl] *a* zufällig.

coke [kəʊk] *n* Koks *m*.

colander ['kʌləndə*] *n* Durchschlag *m*.

cold [kəʊld] *a* kalt; I'm — mir ist kalt, ich friere; *n* Kälte *f*; (*illness*) Erkältung *f*; to have — feet (*fig*) kalte Füße haben, Angst haben; to give sb the — shoulder jdm die kalte Schulter zeigen; —ly *ad* kalt; (*fig*) gefühllos; — sore Erkältungsbläschen *nt*.

coleslaw ['kəʊlslɔː] *n* Krautsalat *m*.

colic ['kɒlɪk] *n* Kolik *f*.

collaborate [kə'læbəreɪt] *vi* zusammenarbeiten.

collaboration [kəlæbə'reɪʃən] *n* Zusammenarbeit *f*; (*Pol*) Kollaboration *f*.

collaborator [kə'læbəreɪtə*] *n* Mitarbeiter *m*; (*Pol*) Kollaborateur *m*.

collage [kɒ'lɑːʒ] *n* Collage *f*.

collapse [kə'læps] *vi* (*people*) zusammenbrechen; (*things*) einstürzen; *n* Zusammenbruch *m*, Einsturz *m*.

collapsible [kəˈlæpsəbl] a zusammenklappbar, Klapp-.

collar [ˈkɒlə*] n Kragen m; —bone Schlüsselbein nt.

collate [kɒˈleit] vt zusammenstellen und ordnen.

colleague [ˈkɒliːg] n Kollege m, Kollegin f.

collect [kəˈlekt] vt sammeln; (fetch) abholen; vi sich sammeln; — call (US) R-Gespräch nt; —ed a gefaßt; —ion [kəˈlekʃən] *Sammlung f; (Eccl) Kollekte f; —ive a gemeinsam, (Pol) kollektiv; —or n Sammler m; (tax —or) Steuereinnehmer m.

college [ˈkɒlidʒ] n (Univ) College nt; (Tech) Fach-, Berufsschule f.

collide [kəˈlaid] vi zusammenstoßen; kollidieren, im Widerspruch stehen (with zu).

collie [ˈkɒli] n schottische(r) Schäferhund m, Collie m.

colliery [ˈkɒliəri] n (Kohlen)bergwerk nt, Zeche f.

collision [kəˈliʒən] n Zusammenstoß m, (of opinions) Konflikt m.

colloquial [kəˈləukwiəl] a umgangssprachlich.

collusion [kəˈluːʒən] n geheime(s) Einverständnis nt, Zusammenspiel nt.

colon [ˈkəulɒn] n Doppelpunkt m.

colonel [ˈkɜːnl] n Oberst m.

colonial [kəˈləuniəl] a Kolonial-.

colonize [ˈkɒlənaiz] vt kolonisieren.

colonnade [kɒləˈneid] n Säulengang m.

colony [ˈkɒləni] n Kolonie f.

color [ˈkʌlə*] (US) = colour.

Colorado beetle [kɒləˈraːdəuˈbiːtl] n Kartoffelkäfer m.

colossal [kəˈlɒsl] a kolossal, riesig.

colour [ˈkʌlə*] n Farbe f; off — nicht wohl; vt (lit, fig) färben; vi sich verfärben; —s pl Farbe f; —bar Rassenschranke f; —blind a farbenblind; —ed a farbig; —ed (wo)man Farbige(r) mf; — film Farbfilm m; —ful a bunt; — scheme Farbgebung f; — television Farbfernsehen nt.

colt [kəult] n Fohlen nt.

column [ˈkɒləm] n Säule f; (Mil) Kolonne f; (of print) Spalte f; —ist [ˈkɒləmnist] n Kolumnist m.

coma [ˈkəumə] n Koma nt.

comb [kəum] n Kamm m; vt kämmen; (search) durchkämmen.

combat [ˈkɒmbæt] n Kampf m; vt bekämpfen.

combination [kɒmbiˈneiʃən] n Verbindung f, Kombination f.

combine [kəmˈbain] vt verbinden; vi sich vereinigen; [ˈkɒmbain] n (Comm) Konzern m, Verband m; — harvester Mähdrescher m.

combustible [kəmˈbʌstibl] a brennbar, leicht entzündlich.

combustion [kəmˈbʌstʃən] n Verbrennung f.

come [kʌm] irreg vi kommen, (reach) ankommen, gelangen; — about vi geschehen; — across vt (find) stoßen auf (+acc); — away vi (person) weggehen; (handle etc) abgehen; — by vi vorbeikommen; vt (find) zu etw kommen; — down vi (price) fallen; — forward vi (volunteer) sich melden; — from vt (result) kommen von; where do you — from? wo kommen Sie her? — I — from London ich komme aus London; — in for vt abkriegen; — into vi eintreten in (+acc); (inherit) erben; — of vi: what came of it? was ist daraus geworden?;

— off vi (handle) abgehen; (happen) stattfinden; (succeed) klappen; — off it! laß den Quatsch!; — on vi (progress) vorankommen; how's the book coming on? was macht das Buch?; — on! komm!; (hurry) beeil dich!; (encouraging) los!; — out vi herauskommen; — out with vt herausrücken mit; — round vi (visit) vorbeikommen; (Med) wieder zu sich kommen; — to vi (Med) wieder zu sich kommen; (bill) sich belaufen auf; — up vi hochkommen; (problem) auftauchen — upon vt stoßen auf (+acc); — up to vi (approach) zukommen auf (+acc); (water) reichen bis; (expectation) entsprechen (+dat); to — up with sich etw einfallen lassen; —back Wiederauftreten nt, Comeback nt.

comedian [kə'miːdiən] n Komiker m.

comedown ['kʌmdaʊn] n Abstieg m.

comedy ['kɒmədi] n Komödie f.

comet ['kɒmit] n Komet m.

comfort ['kʌmfət] n Bequemlichkeit f; (of body) Behaglichkeit f; (of mind) Trost m; vt trösten; —s pl Annehmlichkeiten pl; —able a bequem, gemütlich; — station (US) öffentliche Toilette f.

comic ['kɒmik] n Comic(heft) nt; (comedian) Komiker m; a (also —al) komisch, humoristisch.

coming ['kʌmiŋ] n Kommen nt, Ankunft f.

comma ['kɒmə] n Komma nt.

command [kə'mɑːnd] n Befehl m; (control) Führung f; (Mil) Kommando nt, (Ober)befehl m; vt befehlen (+dat); (Mil) komman-

dieren, befehligen; (be able to get) verfügen über (+acc); vi befehlen; —eer [kɒmən'dɪə*] vt (Mil) requirieren; —er Befehlshaber m, Kommandant m; —ing officer Kommandeur m; —ment nt Gebot nt; —o (Mitglied einer) Kommandotruppe f.

commemorate [kə'meməreit] vt gedenken (+gen).

commemoration [kəmemə'reiʃən] n: in — of zum Gedächtnis or Andenken an (+acc).

commemorative [kə'memərətiv] a Gedächtnis-; Gedenk-.

commence [kə'mens] vti beginnen; —ment Beginn m.

commend [kə'mend] vt (recommend) empfehlen; (praise) loben; —able a empfehlenswert, lobenswert; —ation [kɒmen'deiʃən] Empfehlung f; (Sch) Lob nt.

commensurate [kə'menʃurit] a vergleichbar, entsprechend (with dat).

comment ['kɒment] n (remark) Bemerkung f; (note) Anmerkung f; (opinion) Stellungnahme f; vi etw sagen (on zu); sich äußern (on zu); —ary ['kɒməntri] Kommentar m; —ator ['kɒmenteitə*] Kommentator m.

commerce ['kɒmɜːs] n Handel m.

commercial [kə'mɜːʃəl] a kommerziell, geschäftlich; training kaufmännisch; n (TV) Fernsehwerbung f; —ize vt kommerzialisieren; — television Werbefernsehen nt; — vehicle Lieferwagen m.

commiserate [kə'mizəreit] vi Mitleid haben.

commission [kə'miʃən] n Auftrag m; (fee) Provision f; (Mil) Offizierspatent nt; (of offence) Begehen nt; (reporting body) Kommission f; vt bevollmächtigen, beauftragen; out of — außer Betrieb; —aire [kɔmɪʃə'nɛə*] Portier m; —er (Regierungs)bevollmächtigte(r) m.

commit [kə'mɪt] vt *crime* begehen; *(undertake)* sich verpflichten; *(entrust)* übergeben, anvertrauen; I don't want to — myself ich will mich nicht festlegen; —ment Verpflichtung f.

committee [kə'mɪtɪ] n Ausschuß m, Komitee nt.

commodious [kə'məudɪəs] a geräumig.

commodity [kə'mɔdɪtɪ] n Ware f; (Handels-, Gebrauchs)artikel m.

commodore ['kɔmədɔ:*] n Flotilleadmiral m.

common ['kɔmən] a *cause* gemeinsam; *(public)* öffentlich, allgemein; *experience* allgemein, alltäglich; *(pej)* gewöhnlich; *(widespread)* üblich, häufig, gewöhnlich; n gemeinsame öffentliche Anlage f; —ly ad im allgemeinen, gewöhnlich; C— Market Gemeinsame(r) Markt m; —place a alltäglich; n Gemeinplatz m; —room Gemeinschaftsraum m; —sense gesunde(r) Menschenverstand m; the C—wealth das Commonwealth.

commotion [kə'məuʃən] n Aufsehen nt, Unruhe f.

communal ['kɔmju:nl] a Gemeinde-; Gemeinschafts-.

commune ['kɔmju:n] n Kommune f; vi sich mitteilen *(with dat)*, vertraulich verkehren.

communicate [kə'mju:nɪkeɪt] vt *(transmit)* übertragen; vi *(be in touch)* in Verbindung stehen; *(make self understood)* sich verständlich machen.

communication [kəmju:nɪ'keɪʃən] n *(message)* Mitteilung f; *(Rad, TV etc)* Kommunikationsmittel nt; *(making understood)* Kommunikation f; —s pl *(transport etc)* Verkehrswege pl; — cord Notbremse f.

communion [kə'mju:nɪən] n. *(group)* Gemeinschaft f; *(Rel)* Religionsgemeinschaft f; *(Holy)* C— Heilige(s) Abendmahl nt, Kommunion f.

communiqué [kə'mju:nɪkeɪ] n Kommuniqué nt, amtliche Verlautbarung f.

communism ['kɔmjunɪzəm] n Kommunismus m.

communist ['kɔmjunɪst] n Kommunist(in f) m; a kommunistisch.

community [kə'mju:nɪtɪ] n Gemeinschaft f; *(public)* Gemeinwesen nt; — centre Gemeinschaftszentrum nt; — chest *(US)* Wohltätigkeitsfonds m.

commutation ticket [kɔmju'teɪʃən'tɪkɪt] n *(US)* Zeitkarte f.

commute [kə'mju:t] vi pendeln; —r Pendler m.

compact [kəm'pækt] a kompakt, fest, dicht; ['kɔmpækt] n Pakt m, Vertrag m; *(for make-up)* Puderdose f.

companion [kəm'pænɪən] n Begleiter(in f) m; —ship Gesellschaft f.

company ['kʌmpənɪ] n Gesellschaft f; *(Comm also)* Firma f; *(Mil)* Kompanie f; to keep sb — jdm Gesellschaft leisten.

comparable ['kɔmpərəbl] a vergleichbar.

comparative [kəm'pærətɪv] a *(relative)* verhältnismäßig, relativ; *(Gram)* steigernd; —ly ad verhältnismäßig.

compare [kəm'pɛə*] vt vergleichen; vi sich vergleichen lassen.

comparison [kəm'pærɪsn] n Vergleich m; (object) Vergleichsgegenstand m; in — (with) im Vergleich (mit or zu).

compartment [kəm'pɑ:tmənt] n (Rail) Abteil nt; (in drawer etc) Fach nt.

compass ['kʌmpəs] n Kompaß m; —es pl Zirkel m.

compassion [kəm'pæʃən] n Mitleid nt; —ate a mitfühlend.

compatible [kəm'pætɪbl] a vereinbar, im Einklang; we're not — wir vertragen uns nicht.

compel [kəm'pel] vt zwingen; —ling a argument zwingend.

compendium [kəm'pendiəm] n Kompendium nt.

compensate ['kɒmpenseɪt] vt entschädigen; to — for sth Ersatz leisten für, kompensieren.

compensation [kɒmpen'seɪʃən] n Entschädigung f; (money) Schadenersatz m; Entschädigung f; (Jur) Abfindung f; (Psych etc) Kompensation f.

compère ['kɒmpɛə*] n Conférencier m.

compete [kəm'pi:t] vi sich bewerben; konkurrieren, sich messen mit.

competence ['kɒmpɪtəns] n Fähigkeit f; (Jur) Zuständigkeit f.

competent ['kɒmpɪtənt] a kompetent, fähig; (Jur) zuständig.

competition [kɒmpɪ'tɪʃən] n Wettbewerb m; (Comm) Konkurrenz f.

competitive [kəm'petɪtɪv] a Konkurrenz-; (Comm) konkurrenzfähig.

competitor [kəm'petɪtə*] n Mitbewerber(in f) m; (Comm) Kon-

kurrent(in f) m; (Sport) Teilnehmer(in f) m.

compile [kəm'paɪl] vt zusammenstellen.

complacency [kəm'pleɪsnsɪ] n Selbstzufriedenheit f, Gleichgültigkeit f.

complacent [kəm'pleɪsnt] a selbstzufrieden, gleichgültig.

complain [kəm'pleɪn] vi sich beklagen, sich beschweren (about über +acc); —t Beschwerde f; (Med) Leiden nt.

complement ['kɒmplɪmənt] n Ergänzung f; (ship's crew etc) Bemannung f; —ary [kɒmplɪ'mentərɪ] a Komplementär-, (sich) ergänzend.

complete [kəm'pli:t] a vollständig, vollkommen, ganz; vt vervollständigen; (finish) beenden; —ly ad vollständig, ganz.

completion [kəm'pli:ʃən] n Vollständigung f; (of building) Fertigstellung f.

complex ['kɒmpleks] a kompliziert, verwickelt; n Komplex m.

complexion [kəm'plekʃən] n Gesichtsfarbe f, Teint m; (fig) Anstrich m, Aussehen nt.

complexity [kəm'pleksɪtɪ] n Verwicklung f, Kompliziertheit f.

compliance [kəm'plaɪəns] n Fügsamkeit f, Einwilligung f.

complicate ['kɒmplɪkeɪt] vt komplizieren, verwickeln; —d a kompliziert, verwickelt.

complication [kɒmplɪ'keɪʃən] a Komplikation f, Erschwerung f.

compliment ['kɒmplɪmənt] n Kompliment nt; ['kɒmplɪment] vt ein Kompliment machen (sb jdm); —s pl Grüße pl, Empfehlung f; —ary [kɒmplɪ'mentərɪ] a schmeichelhaft; (free) Frei-, Gratis-.

comply [kəm'plaɪ] vi: — with erfüllen (+acc); entsprechen (+dat).

component [kəm'pəʊnənt] a Teil-; n Bestandteil m.

compose [kəm'pəʊz] vt (arrange) zusammensetzen; music komponieren; poetry schreiben; thoughts sammeln; features beherrschen; —d a ruhig, gefaßt; to be —d of bestehen aus; —r Komponist(in f) m.

composite ['kɒmpəzɪt] a zusammengesetzt.

composition [kɒmpə'zɪʃən] n (Mus) Komposition f; (Sch) Aufsatz m; (composing) Zusammensetzung f, Gestaltung f; (structure) Zusammensetzung f, Aufbau m.

compositor [kəm'pɒzɪtə*] n Schriftsetzer m.

compos mentis ['kɒmpɒs'mentɪs] a klar im Kopf.

compost ['kɒmpɒst] n Kompost m; — heap Komposthaufen m.

composure [kəm'pəʊʒə*] n Gelassenheit f, Fassung f.

compound ['kɒmpaʊnd] n (Chem) Verbindung f; (mixture) Gemisch nt; (enclosure) eingezäunte(s) Gelände nt; (Ling) Kompositum nt; a zusammengesetzt; — fracture komplizierte(r) Bruch m; — interest Zinseszinsen pl.

comprehend [kɒmprɪ'hend] vt begreifen; (include) umfassen, einschließen.

comprehension [kɒmprɪ'henʃən] n Fassungskraft f, Verständnis nt.

comprehensive [kɒmprɪ'hensɪv] a umfassend; — school Gesamtschule f.

compress [kəm'pres] vt zusammendrücken, komprimieren; ['kɒmpres] n (Med) Kompresse f, Umschlag m; —ion [kəm'preʃən] Komprimieren nt.

comprise [kəm'praɪz] vt (also be —d of) umfassen, bestehen aus.

compromise ['kɒmprəmaɪz] n Kompromiß m, Verständigung f; vt reputation kompromittieren; vi einen Kompromiß schließen.

compulsion [kəm'pʌlʃən] n Zwang m.

compulsive [kəm'pʌlsɪv] a Gewohnheits-.

compulsory [kəm'pʌlsərɪ] a (obligatory) obligatorisch, Pflicht-.

computer [kəm'pju:tə*] n Computer m, Rechner m.

comrade ['kɒmrɪd] n Kamerad m; (Pol) Genosse m; —ship Kameradschaft f.

concave ['kɒn'keɪv] a konkav, hohlgeschliffen.

conceal [kən'si:l] vt secret verschweigen; to — o.s. sich verbergen.

concede [kən'si:d] vt (grant) gewähren; point zugeben; vi (admit) zugeben.

conceit [kən'si:t] n Eitelkeit f, Einbildung f; —ed a eitel, eingebildet.

conceivable [kən'si:vəbl] a vorstellbar.

conceive [kən'si:v] vt idea ausdenken; imagine sich vorstellen; vti baby empfangen.

concentrate ['kɒnsəntreɪt] vi sich konzentrieren (on auf +acc); vt (gather) konzentrieren.

concentration [kɒnsən'treɪʃən] n Konzentration f; — camp Konzentrationslager nt, KZ nt.

concentric [kən'sentrik] a konzentrisch.

concept ['kɒnsept] n Begriff m; **—ion** [kən'sepʃən] (idea) Vorstellung f; (Physiol) Empfängnis f.

concern [kən'sɜːn] n (affair) Angelegenheit f; (Comm) Unternehmen nt, Konzern m; (worry) Sorge f, Unruhe f; vt (interest) angehen; (be about) handeln von; (have connection with) betreffen; **—ed** a (anxious) besorgt; **—ing** prep betreffend, hinsichtlich (+gen).

concert ['kɒnsət] n Konzert nt; in **—** (with) im Einverständnis (mit); **—ed** [kən'sɜːtɪd] a gemeinsam; (Fin) konzertiert; **—** hall Konzerthalle f.

concertina [kɒnsə'tiːnə] n Handharmonika f.

concerto [kən'tʃɜːtəʊ] n Konzert nt.

concession [kən'seʃən] n (yielding) Zugeständnis nt; (right to do sth) Genehmigung f.

conciliation [kənsɪlɪ'eɪʃən] n Versöhnung f; (official) Schlichtung f.

conciliatory [kən'sɪliətrɪ] a vermittelnd; versöhnlich.

concise [kən'saɪs] a knapp, gedrängt.

conclave ['kɒnkleɪv] n Konklave nt.

conclude [kən'kluːd] vt (end) beenden; treaty (ab)schließen; (decide) schließen, folgern; vi (finish) schließen.

conclusion ['kən'kluːʒən] n (Ab)-schluß m; in **—** zum Schluß, schließlich.

conclusive [kən'kluːsɪv] a überzeugend, schlüssig; **—ly** ad endgültig.

concoct [kən'kɒkt] vt zusammenbrauen.

concord ['kɒŋkɔːd] n Eintracht f.

concourse ['kɒŋkɔːs] n (Bahnhofs)-halle f, Vorplatz m.

concrete ['kɒŋkriːt] n Beton m; a konkret.

concur [kən'kɜː*] vi übereinstimmen.

concurrently [kən'kʌrəntlɪ] ad gleichzeitig.

concussion [kən'kʌʃən] n (Gehirn)-erschütterung f.

condemn [kən'dem] vt verdammen; (Jur) verurteilen; building abbruchreif erklären; **—ation** [kɒndem'neɪʃən] Verurteilung f; (of object) Verwerfung f.

condensation [kɒndən'seɪʃən] n Kondensation f.

condense [kən'dens] vi (Chem) kondensieren; vt (fig) zusammendrängen; **—d milk** Kondensmilch f.

condescend [kɒndɪ'send] vi sich herablassen; **—ing** a herablassend.

condition [kən'dɪʃən] n (state) Zustand m, Verfassung f; (presupposition) Bedingung f; vt hair etc behandeln; (regulate) regeln; on **—** that ... unter der Bedingung, daß ...; **—ed** to gewöhnt an (+acc); **—ed reflex** bedingter Reflex; **—s** pl (circumstances, weather) Verhältnisse pl; **—al** a bedingt; (Gram) Bedingungs-.

condolences [kən'dəʊlənsɪz] npl Beileid nt.

condone [kən'dəʊn] vt gutheißen.

conducive [kən'djuːsɪv] a dienlich (to dat).

conduct ['kɒndʌkt] n (behaviour) Verhalten nt; (management) Führung f; [kən'dʌkt] vt führen, leiten; (Mus) dirigieren; **—or** tour Führung f; **—or** [kən'dʌktə*] (of orchestra) Dirigent m; (in bus)

Schaffner *m*; **—ress** [kən'dʌktrɪs] (*in bus*) Schaffnerin *f*.

conduit ['kɒndɪt] *n* (*water*) Rohrleitung *f*; (*Elec*) Isolierrohr *nt*.

cone [kəʊn] *n* (*Math*) Kegel *m*; (*for ice cream*) (Waffel)tüte *f*; (*fir*) Tannenzapfen *m*.

confectioner [kən'fekʃənə*] *n* Konditor *m*; **—'s** (*shop*) Konditorei *f*; **—y** (*cakes*) Konfekt *nt*, Konditorwaren *pl*; (*sweets*) Süßigkeiten *pl*.

confederation [kənfedə'reɪʃən] *n* Bund *m*.

confer [kən'fɜ:*] *vt* (*degree*) verleihen; *vi* (*discuss*) konferieren, verhandeln; **—ence** ['kɒnfərəns] Konferenz *f*.

confess [kən'fes] *vt* gestehen; (*Eccl*) beichten; **—ion** [kən'feʃən] Geständnis *nt*; (*Eccl*) Beichte *f*; **—ional** [kən'feʃənl] Beichtstuhl *m*; **—or** (*Eccl*) Beichtvater *m*.

confetti [kən'fetɪ] *n* Konfetti *nt*.

confide [kən'faɪd] *vi*: **— in** (sich) anvertrauen (+*dat*); (*trust*) vertrauen (+*dat*); **—nce** ['kɒnfɪdəns] Vertrauen *nt*; (*assurance*) Selbstvertrauen *nt*; (*secret*) vertrauliche Mitteilung *f*, Geheimnis *nt*; **—nce trick** ['kɒnfɪdənstrɪk] Schwindel *m*.

confident ['kɒnfɪdənt] *a* (*sure*) überzeugt; *sicher*; (*self-assured*) selbstsicher; **—ial** [kɒnfɪ'denʃəl] *a* (*secret*) vertraulich, geheim; (*trusted*) Vertrauens-.

confine [kən'faɪn] *vt* (*limit*) begrenzen, einschränken; (*lock up*) einsperren; **—s** ['kɒnfaɪnz] *pl* Grenze *f*; **—d** *a space* eng, begrenzt; **—ment** (*of room*) Beengtheit *f*; (*in prison*) Haft *f*; (*Med*) Wochenbett *nt*.

confirm [kən'fɜ:m] *vt* bestätigen; **—ation** [kɒnfə'meɪʃən] Bestätigung *f*; (*Rel*) Konfirmation *f*; **—ed** *a*

unverbesserlich, hartnäckig; *bachelor* eingefleischt.

confiscate ['kɒnfɪskeɪt] *vt* beschlagnahmen, konfiszieren.

confiscation [kɒnfɪs'keɪʃən] *n* Beschlagnahme *f*.

conflagration [kɒnflə'greɪʃən] *n* Feuersbrunst *f*.

conflict [kən'flɪkt] *n* Kampf *m*; (*of words, opinions*) Konflikt *m*, Streit *m*; [kən'flɪkt] *vi* im Widerspruch stehen; **—ing** [kən'flɪktɪŋ] *a* gegensätzlich; *testimony* sich widersprechend.

conform [kən'fɔ:m] *vt* sich anpassen (*to dat*); (*to rules*) sich fügen (*to dat*); (*to general trends*) sich richten (*to* nach); **—ist** *n* Konformist(in *f*) *m*.

confront [kən'frʌnt] *vt* *enemy* entgegentreten (+*dat*); *sb with sth* konfrontieren; *sb with sb* gegenüberstellen (*with dat*); **—ation** [kɒnfrən'teɪʃən] Gegenüberstellung *f*; (*quarrel*) Konfrontation *f*.

confuse [kən'fju:z] *vt* verwirren; (*sth with sth*) verwechseln.

confusing [kən'fju:zɪŋ] *a* verwirrend.

confusion [kən'fju:ʒən] *n* (*disorder*) Verwirrung *f*; (*tumult*) Aufruhr *m*; (*embarrassment*) Bestürzung *f*.

congeal [kən'dʒi:l] *vi* (*freeze*) gefrieren; (*clot*) gerinnen.

congenial [kən'dʒi:nɪəl] *a* (*agreeable*) angenehm.

congenital [kən'dʒenɪtəl] *a* angeboren.

conger eel ['kɒŋgər'i:l] *n* Meeraal *m*.

congested [kən'dʒestɪd] *a* überfüllt.

congestion [kən'dʒestʃən] *n* Stauung *f*; Stau *m*.

conglomeration [kəngloməˈreɪʃən] n Anhäufung f.

congratulate [kənˈgrætjuleɪt] vt beglückwünschen (on zu).

congratulations [kənˈgrætjuˈleɪʃənz] npl Glückwünsche pl; —! gratuliere!, herzlichen Glückwunsch!

congregate [ˈkɒŋgrɪgeɪt] vi sich versammeln.

congregation [kɒŋgrɪˈgeɪʃən] n Gemeinde f.

congress [ˈkɒŋgres] n Kongreß m; —ional [kɒŋˈgreʃənl] a Kongreß-; —man (US) Mitglied nt des amerikanischen Repräsentantenhauses.

conical [ˈkɒnɪkəl] a kegelförmig, konisch.

conifer [ˈkɒnɪfə*] n Nadelbaum m; —ous [kəˈnɪfərəs] a zapfentragend.

conjecture [kənˈdʒektʃə*] n Vermutung f; vti vermuten.

conjugal [ˈkɒndʒʊgəl] a ehelich.

conjunction [kənˈdʒʌŋkʃən] n Verbindung f; (Gram) Konjunktion f, Verbindungswort nt.

conjunctivitis [kəndʒʌŋktɪˈvaɪtɪs] n Bindehautentzündung f.

conjure [ˈkʌndʒə*] vti zaubern; — up vt heraufbeschwören; —r Zauberer m; (entertainer) Zauberkünstler(in f) m.

conjuring [ˈkʌndʒərɪŋ] n: — trick Zauberkunststück nt.

conk [kɒŋk]: — out vi (col) stehenbleiben, streiken.

connect [kəˈnekt] vt verbinden; train koppeln; —ion [kəˈnekʃən] Verbindung f; (relation) Zusammenhang m; in —ion with in Verbindung mit.

connexion [kəˈnekʃən] n = **connection**.

connoisseur [kɒnɪˈsə:*] n Kenner m.

connotation [kɒnəˈteɪʃən] n Konnotation f.

conquer [ˈkɒŋkə*] vt (overcome) überwinden, besiegen; (Mil) besiegen; vi siegen; —or Eroberer m.

conquest [ˈkɒŋkwest] n Eroberung f.

conscience [ˈkɒnʃəns] n Gewissen nt.

conscientious [kɒnʃɪˈenʃəs] a gewissenhaft; — objector Wehrdienstverweigerer m (aus Gewissensgründen).

conscious [ˈkɒnʃəs] a bewußt; (Med) bei Bewußtsein; —ness Bewußtsein nt.

conscript [ˈkɒnskrɪpt] n Wehrpflichtige(r) m; —ion [kənˈskrɪpʃən] Wehrpflicht f.

consecrate [ˈkɒnsɪkreɪt] vt weihen.

consecutive [kənˈsekjutɪv] a aufeinanderfolgend.

consensus [kənˈsensəs] n allgemeine Übereinstimmung f.

consent [kənˈsent] n Zustimmung f; vi zustimmen (to dat).

consequence [ˈkɒnsɪkwəns] n (importance) Bedeutung f, Konsequenz f; (result, effect) Wirkung f.

consequently [ˈkɒnsɪkwəntlɪ] ad folglich.

conservation [kɒnsəˈveɪʃən] n Erhaltung f, Schutz m.

conservative [kənˈsɜ:vətɪv] a konservativ; (cautious) mäßig, vorsichtig; C— a party konservativ; n Konservative(r) mf.

conservatory [kənˈsɜ:vətrɪ] n (greenhouse) Gewächshaus nt; (room) Wintergarten m.

conserve [kən'sɜːv] vt erhalten.

consider [kən'sɪdə*] vt überlegen; (take into account) in Betracht ziehen; (regard) halten für; —able a beträchtlich; —ate a rücksichtsvoll, aufmerksam; —ation [kənsɪdə'reɪʃən] Rücksicht(nahme) f; (thought) Erwägung f; (reward) Entgelt nt; —ing prep in Anbetracht (+gen); cj da; on no —ation unter keinen Umständen.

consign [kən'saɪn] vt übergeben; —ment (of goods) Sendung f, Lieferung f.

consist [kən'sɪst] vi bestehen (of aus).

consistency [kən'sɪstənsɪ] n (of material) Festigkeit f; (of argument) Folgerichtigkeit f; (of person) Konsequenz f.

consistent [kən'sɪstənt] a gleichbleibend, stetig; argument folgerichtig; she's not — sie ist nicht konsequent.

consolation [kɒnsə'leɪʃən] n Trost m; — prize Trostpreis m.

console [kən'səʊl] vt trösten.

consolidate [kən'sɒlɪdeɪt] vt festigen.

consommé [kən'sɒmeɪ] n Fleischbrühe f.

consonant ['kɒnsənənt] n Konsonant m, Mitlaut m.

consortium [kən'sɔːtɪəm] n Gruppe f, Konsortium nt.

conspicuous [kən'spɪkjʊəs] a (prominent) auffallend; (visible) deutlich, sichtbar.

conspiracy [kən'spɪrəsɪ] n Verschwörung f, Komplott nt.

conspire [kən'spaɪə*] vi sich verschwören.

constable ['kʌnstəbl] n Polizist(in f) m.

constabulary [kən'stæbjʊlərɪ] n Polizei f.

constancy ['kɒnstənsɪ] n Beständigkeit f, Treue f.

constant ['kɒnstənt] a dauernd; —ly ad (continually) andauernd; (faithfully) treu, unwandelbar.

constellation [kɒnstə'leɪʃən] n (temporary) Konstellation f; (permanent) Sternbild nt.

consternation [kɒnstə'neɪʃən] n (dismay) Bestürzung f.

constipated ['kɒnstɪpeɪtəd] a verstopft.

constipation [kɒnstɪ'peɪʃən] n Verstopfung f.

constituency [kən'stɪtjʊənsɪ] n Wahlkreis m.

constituent [kən'stɪtjʊənt] n (person) Wähler m; (part) Bestandteil m.

constitute ['kɒnstɪtjuːt] vt ausmachen.

constitution [kɒnstɪ'tjuːʃən] n Verfassung f; —al a Verfassungs-; monarchy konstitutionell.

constrain [kən'streɪn] vt zwingen; —t Zwang m; (Psych) Befangenheit f.

constrict [kən'strɪkt] vt zusammenziehen; —ion [kən'strɪkʃən] Zusammenziehung f; (of chest) Zusammenschnürung f, Beklemmung f.

construct [kən'strʌkt] vt bauen; —ion [kən'strʌkʃən] (action) (Er)bauen nt, Konstruktion f; (building) Bau m; under —ion im Bau befindlich; —ive a konstruktiv.

construe [kən'struː] vt (interpret) deuten.

consul ['kɒnsl] n Konsul m; —ate ['kɒnsjʊlət] Konsulat nt.

consult [kən'sʌlt] vt um Rat fragen; *doctor* konsultieren; *book* nachschlagen in (+dat); —ant (Med) Facharzt m; (other specialist) Gutachter m; —ation [kɒnsəl'teɪʃən] Beratung f; (Med) Konsultation f; —ing room Sprechzimmer nt.

consume [kən'sjuːm] vt verbrauchen; *food* verzehren, konsumieren; —r Verbraucher m.

consummate ['kɒnsʌmeɪt] vt vollenden; *marriage* vollziehen.

consumption [kən'sʌmpʃən] n Verbrauch m; (of food) Konsum m.

contact ['kɒntækt] n (touch) Berührung f; (connection) Verbindung f; (person) Kontakt m, Beziehung f; vt sich in Verbindung setzen mit; — lenses pl Kontaktlinsen pl.

contagious [kən'teɪdʒəs] a ansteckend.

contain [kən'teɪn] vt enthalten; to — o.s. sich zügeln; —er Behälter m; (transport) Container m.

contaminate [kən'tæmɪneɪt] vt verunreinigen; (germs) infizieren.

contamination [kəntæmɪ'neɪʃən] n Verunreinigung f.

contemplate ['kɒntəmpleɪt] vt (nachdenklich) betrachten; (think about) überdenken; (plan) vorhaben.

contemplation [kɒntəm'pleɪʃən] n Betrachtung f; (Rel) Meditation f.

contemporary [kən'tempərərɪ] a zeitgenössisch; n Zeitgenosse m.

contempt [kən'tempt] n Verachtung f; —ible a verächtlich, nichtswürdig; —uous a voller Verachtung (of für).

contend [kən'tend] vt (fight) kämpfen (um); (argue) behaupten;

—er (for post) Bewerber(in f) m; (Sport) Wettkämpfer(in f) m.

content [kən'tent] a zufrieden; vt befriedigen; ['kɒntent] n (also —s) Inhalt m; —ed a zufrieden.

contention [kən'tenʃən] n (dispute) Streit m; (argument) Behauptung f.

contentment [kən'tentmənt] n Zufriedenheit f.

contest ['kɒntest] n (Wett)kampf m; [kən'test] vt (dispute) bestreiten; (Pol) kandidieren (in dat); —ant [kən'testənt] Bewerber(in f) m.

context ['kɒntekst] n Zusammenhang m.

continent ['kɒntɪnənt] n Kontinent m, Festland nt; the C— das europäische Festland, der Kontinent; —al [kɒntɪ'nentl] a kontinental; n Bewohner(in f) m des Kontinents.

contingency [kən'tɪndʒənsɪ] n Möglichkeit f.

contingent [kən'tɪndʒənt] n (Mil) Kontingent nt; a abhängig (upon von).

continual [kən'tɪnjuəl] a (endless) fortwährend; (repeated) immer wiederkehrend; —ly ad immer wieder.

continuation [kəntɪnju'eɪʃən] n Verlängerung f; Fortsetzung f.

continue [kən'tɪnjuː] vi (go on) anhalten; (last) fortbestehen; shall we —? wollen wir weitermachen?; if this — s wenn das so weitergeht; the rain — d es regnete weiter; vt fortsetzen; to — doing sth fortfahren, etw zu tun.

continuity [kɒntɪ'njuɪtɪ] n Kontinuität nt; (wholeness) Zusammenhang m.

continuous [kən'tɪnjuəs] a ununterbrochen.

contort [kən'tɔ:t] vt verdrehen; **—ion** [kən'tɔ:ʃən] Verzerrung f; **—ionist** [kən'tɔ:ʃənist] Schlangenmensch m.

contour ['kɒntuə*] n Umriß m; (height) Höhenlinie f.

contraband ['kɒntrəbænd] n Schmuggelware f.

contraception [kɒntrə'sepʃən] n Empfängnisverhütung f.

contraceptive [kɒntrə'septɪv] a empfängnisverhütende(s) Mittel nt; a empfängnisverhütend.

contract ['kɒntrækt] n (agreement) Vertrag m, Kontrakt m; [kən'trækt] vi (to do sth) sich vertraglich verpflichten; (muscle) sich zusammenziehen; (become smaller) schrumpfen; **—ion** [kən'trækʃən] (shortening) Verkürzung f; **—or** [kən'træktə*] Unternehmer f; (supplier) Lieferant m.

contradict [kɒntrə'dɪkt] vt widersprechen (+dat); **—ion** [kɒntrə'dɪkʃən] Widerspruch m.

contralto [kən'træltəu] n (tiefe) Altstimme f.

contraption [kən'træpʃən] n (col) komische Konstruktion f, komische(s) Ding nt.

contrary ['kɒntrərɪ] a entgegengesetzt; wind ungünstig, Gegen-; (obstinate) widerspenstig, eigensinnig; n Gegenteil nt; on the **— im** Gegenteil.

contrast ['kɒntrɑ:st] n Kontrast m; [kən'trɑ:st] vt entgegensetzen; **—ing** [kən'trɑ:stɪŋ] a Kontrast-.

contravene [kɒntrə'vi:n] vt verstoßen gegen.

contribute [kən'trɪbju:t] vti beitragen; money spenden.

contribution [kɒntrɪ'bju:ʃən] n Beitrag m.

contributor [kən'trɪbjutə*] n Beitragende(r) m.

contrite ['kɒntraɪt] a zerknirscht.

contrivance [kən'traɪvəns] n Vorrichtung f, Kniff m, Erfindung f.

contrive [kən'traɪv] vt zustande bringen; to **— to do sth** es schaffen, etw zu tun.

control [kən'trəul] vt (direct, test) kontrollieren; n Kontrolle f; (business) Leitung f; **—s** pl (of vehicle) Steuerung f; (of engine) Schalttafel f; **— point** Kontrollstelle f; out of **—** außer Kontrolle; under **—** unter Kontrolle.

controversial [kɒntrə'vɜ:ʃəl] a umstritten, kontrovers.

controversy ['kɒntrəvɜ:sɪ] n Meinungsstreit m, Kontroverse f.

convalesce [kɒnvə'les] vi gesund werden; **—nce** Genesung f; **—nt** auf dem Wege der Besserung; n Genesende(r) mf.

convector [kən'vektə*] n Heizlüfter m.

convene [kən'vi:n] vt zusammenrufen; vi sich versammeln.

convenience [kən'vi:nɪəns] n Annehmlichkeit f; (thing) bequeme Einrichtung f; see public.

convenient [kən'vi:nɪənt] a günstig, bequem.

convent ['kɒnvənt] n Kloster nt.

convention [kən'venʃən] n Versammlung f; (Pol) Übereinkunft f; (custom) Konvention f; **—al** a herkömmlich, konventionell.

converge [kən'vɜ:dʒ] vi zusammenlaufen.

conversant [kən'vɜ:sənt] a

vertraut; (in learning) bewandert (with in +dat).

conversation [kɒnvə'seɪʃən] n Unterhaltung f; **—al** a Unterhaltungs-.

converse [kən'vɜ:s] vi sich unterhalten; ['kɒnvɜ:s] a gegenteilig; **—ly** [kɒn'vɜ:slɪ] ad umgekehrt.

conversion [kən'vɜ:ʃən] n Umwandlung f; (esp Rel) Bekehrung f; **— table** Umrechnungstabelle f.

convert [kən'vɜ:t] vt (change) umwandeln; (Rel) bekehren; ['kɒnvɜ:t] n Bekehrte(r) mf; **Konvertit(in** f) m; **—ible** (Aut) Kabriolett nt; a umwandelbar; (Fin) konvertierbar.

convex ['kɒn'veks] a konvex.

convey [kən'veɪ] vt (carry) befördern; feelings vermitteln; **—or belt** Fließband nt.

convict [kən'vɪkt] vt verurteilen; ['kɒnvɪkt] n Häftling m; **—ion** [kən'vɪkʃən] (verdict) Verurteilung f; (belief) Überzeugung f.

convince [kən'vɪns] vt überzeugen.

convincing [kən'vɪnsɪŋ] a überzeugend.

convivial [kən'vɪvɪəl] a festlich, froh.

convoy ['kɒnvɔɪ] n (of vehicles) Kolonne f; (protected) Konvoi m.

convulse [kən'vʌls] vt zusammenzucken lassen; **to be —d with** laughter sich vor Lachen krümmen.

convulsion [kən'vʌlʃən] n (esp Med) Zuckung f, Krampf m.

coo [ku:] vi (dove) gurren.

cook [kuk] vti kochen; n Koch m, Köchin f; **—book** Kochbuch nt; **—er** Herd m; **—ery** Kochkunst f; **—ery book = —book**; **—ie** (US) Plätzchen nt; **—ing** Kochen nt.

cool [ku:l] a kühl; vti (ab)kühlen; **— down** vti (fig) (sich) beruhigen; **—ing-tower** Kühlturm m; **—ness** Kühle f; (of temperament) kühle(r) Kopf.

coop [ku:p] n Hühnerstall m; vt: **— up** (fig) einpferchen.

co-op ['kəʊɒp] n = cooperative.

cooperate [kəʊ'ɒpəreɪt] vi zusammenarbeiten.

cooperation [kəʊɒpə'reɪʃən] n Zusammenarbeit f.

cooperative [kəʊ'ɒpərətɪv] a hilfsbereit; (Comm) genossenschaftlich; n (of farmers) Genossenschaft f; (— store) Konsumladen m.

coordinate [kəʊ'ɔ:dɪneɪt] vt koordinieren.

coordination [kəʊɔ:dɪ'neɪʃən] n Koordination f.

coot [ku:t] n Wasserhuhn nt.

cop [kɒp] n (col) Polyp m, Bulle m.

cope [kəʊp] vi fertig werden, schaffen (with acc).

co-pilot ['kəʊpaɪlət] n Kopilot m.

copious ['kəʊpɪəs] a reichhaltig.

copper ['kɒpə*] n Kupfer nt; Kupfermünze f; (col: policeman) Polyp m, Bulle m.

coppice ['kɒpɪs], **copse** [kɒps] n Unterholz nt.

copulate ['kɒpjuleɪt] vi sich paaren.

copy ['kɒpɪ] n (imitation) Nachahmung f; (of book etc) Exemplar nt; (of newspaper) Nummer f; vt kopieren, abschreiben; **—cat** Nachäffer m; **—right** Copyright nt; **—right reserved** alle Rechte vorbehalten, Nachdruck verboten.

coral ['kɒrəl] n Koralle f; **— reef** Korallenriff nt.

cord [kɔ:d] n Schnur f, Kordel f; see vocal.

cordial ['kɔ:dɪəl] a herzlich; n Fruchtsaft m; —ly ad herzlich.

cordon ['kɔ:dn] n Absperrkette f.

corduroy ['kɔ:dərɔɪ] n Kord(samt) m.

core [kɔ:*] n Kern m; vt entkernen.

cork [kɔ:k] n (bark) Korkrinde f; (stopper) Korken m; —age Korkengeld nt; —screw Korkenzieher m.

corm [kɔ:m] n Knolle f.

cormorant ['kɔ:mərənt] n Kormoran m.

corn [kɔ:n] n Getreide nt, Korn nt; (US: maize) Mais m; (on foot) Hühnerauge nt.

cornea ['kɔ:nɪə] n Hornhaut f.

corned beef ['kɔ:nd'bi:f] n Corned Beef nt.

corner ['kɔ:nə*] n (road) Ecke f; (nook) Winkel m; (on road) Kurve f; vt in die Enge treiben; vi (Aut) in die Kurve gehen; — flag Eckfahne f; — kick Eckball m; —stone Eckstein m.

cornet ['kɔ:nɪt] n (Mus) Kornett nt; (for ice cream) Eistüte f.

cornflour ['kɔ:nflauə*] n Maizena ® nt, Maismehl nt.

cornice ['kɔ:nɪs] n Gesims nt.

cornstarch ['kɔ:nstɑ:tʃ] n (US) = cornflour.

cornucopia [kɔ:nju'kəupɪə] n Füllhorn nt.

corny ['kɔ:nɪ] a joke blöd(e).

corollary [kə'rɒlərɪ] n Folgesatz m.

coronary ['kɒrənərɪ] a (Med) Koronar-; n Herzinfarkt m; — thrombosis Koronarthrombose f.

coronation [kɒrə'neɪʃən] n Krönung f.

coroner ['kɒrənə*] n Untersuchungsrichter m und Leichenbeschauer m.

coronet ['kɒrənɪt] n Adelskrone f.

corporal ['kɔ:pərəl] n Obergefreite(r) m; a: — punishment Prügelstrafe f.

corporate ['kɔ:pərɪt] a gemeinschaftlich, korporativ.

corporation [kɔ:pə'reɪʃən] n Gemeinde f, Stadt f; (esp business) Körperschaft f, Aktiengesellschaft f.

corps [kɔ:*] n (Armee)korps nt.

corpse [kɔ:ps] n Leiche f.

corpulent ['kɔ:pjulənt] a korpulent.

Corpus Christi ['kɔ:pəs'krɪstɪ] n Fronleichnamsfest nt.

corpuscle ['kɔ:pʌsl] n Blutkörperchen nt.

corral [kə'rɑ:l] n Pferch m, Korral m.

correct [kə'rekt] a (accurate) richtig; (proper) korrekt; vt mistake berichtigen; pupil tadeln; —ion [kə'rekʃən] Berichtigung f; —ly ad richtig; korrekt.

correlate ['kɒrɪleɪt] vt aufeinander beziehen; vi korrelieren.

correlation [kɒrɪ'leɪʃən] n Wechselbeziehung f.

correspond [kɒrɪs'pɒnd] vi übereinstimmen; (exchange letters) korrespondieren; —ence (similarity) Entsprechung f; Briefwechsel m, Korrespondenz f; —ence course Fernkurs m; —ent (Press) Berichterstatter m; —ing a entsprechend, gemäß (to dat).

corridor ['kɒrɪdɔ:*] n Gang m.

corroborate [kə'rɒbəreɪt] vt bestätigen, erhärten.

corroboration [kərɒbə'reɪʃən] n Bekräftigung f.

corrode [kə'rəud] vt zerfressen; vi rosten.

corrosion [kəˈrəʊʒən] n Rost m, Korrosion f.

corrugated [ˈkɒrəgeɪtɪd] a gewellt; — **cardboard** Wellpappe f; — **iron** Wellblech nt.

corrupt [kəˈrʌpt] a korrupt; vt verderben; (bribe) bestechen; —**ion** [kəˈrʌpʃən] (of society) Verdorbenheit f; (bribery) Bestechung f.

corset [ˈkɔːsɪt] n Korsett nt.

cortège [kɔːˈteːʒ] n Zug m; (of funeral) Leichenzug m.

cortisone [ˈkɔːtɪzəʊn] n Kortison nt.

cosh [kɒʃ] n Totschläger m; vt über den Schädel hauen.

cosignatory [ˈkəʊˈsɪgnətərɪ] n Mitunterzeichner(in f) m.

cosine [ˈkəʊsaɪn] n Kosinus m.

cosiness [ˈkəʊzɪnɪs] n Gemütlichkeit f.

cosmetic [kɒzˈmetɪk] n Schönheitsmittel nt, kosmetische(s) Mittel nt; a kosmetisch.

cosmic [ˈkɒzmɪk] a kosmisch.

cosmonaut [ˈkɒzmənɔːt] n Kosmonaut(in f) m.

cosmopolitan [kɒzməˈpɒlɪtən] a international; city Welt-.

cosmos [ˈkɒzmɒs] n Weltall nt, Kosmos m.

cost [kɒst] n Kosten pl, Preis m; vt irreg kosten; it — him his life/job es kostete ihm sein Leben/seine Stelle; at all —s um jeden Preis; — of living Lebenshaltungskosten pl.

co-star [ˈkəʊstɑː*] n zweite(r) or weitere(r) Hauptdarsteller(in f) m.

costing [ˈkɒstɪŋ] n Kostenberechnung f.

costly [ˈkɒstlɪ] a kostspielig.

cost price [ˈkɒstˈpraɪs] n Selbstkostenpreis m.

costume [ˈkɒstjuːm] n Kostüm nt; (fancy dress) Maskenkostüm nt; (for bathing) Badeanzug m; — **jewellery** Modeschmuck m.

cosy [ˈkəʊzɪ] a behaglich, gemütlich.

cot [kɒt] n Kinderbett(chen) nt.

cottage [ˈkɒtɪdʒ] n kleine(s) Haus nt (auf dem Land); — **cheese** Hüttenkäse m.

cotton [ˈkɒtn] n (material) Baumwollstoff m; (thread) etc Baumwoll-, Kattun-; a dress etc Baumwoll-, Kattun-; — **wool** Watte f.

couch [kautʃ] n Couch f; vt (in Worte) fassen, formulieren.

cougar [ˈkuːgə*] n Puma m.

cough [kɒf] vi husten; n Husten m; — **drop** Hustenbonbon nt.

could [kʊd] pt of **can**; —**n't** = could not.

council [ˈkaʊnsl] n (of town) Stadtrat m; — **estate/house** Siedlung f/Haus nt des sozialen Wohnungsbaus; —**lor** [ˈkaʊnsɪlə*] Stadtrat m.

counsel [ˈkaʊnsl] n (barrister) Anwalt m, Rechtsbeistand m; (advice) Rat(schlag) m; —**lor** Berater m.

count [kaʊnt] vti zählen; vi (be important) zählen, gelten; n (reckoning) Abrechnung f; (nobleman) Graf m; —**down** Countdown m; — **on** vt zählen auf (+acc); — **up** vt zusammenzählen.

counter [ˈkaʊntə*] n (in shop) Ladentisch m; (in café) Tresen m, Theke f; (in bank, post office) Schalter m; vt entgegnen; ad entgegen; —**act** [ˈkaʊntəˈrækt] vt entgegenwirken (+dat); —**attack** Gegenangriff m; —**balance** vt aufwiegen; —**clockwise** ad entgegen dem Uhrzeigersinn; —**espionage** Spionageabwehr f; —**feit** Fälschung f; vt fälschen; a gefälscht, unecht; **—foil** (Kontroll)-abschnitt m; **—part** (object) Gegenstück nt; (person) Gegenüber nt.

countess ['kauntɪs] n Gräfin f.

countless ['kauntlɪs] a zahllos, unzählig.

countrified ['kʌntrɪfaɪd] a ländlich.

country ['kʌntrɪ] n Land nt; in the — auf dem Land(e); **— dancing** Volkstanztanzen nt; **— house** Landhaus nt; **—man** (national) Landsmann m; (rural) Bauer m; **—side** Landschaft f.

county ['kauntɪ] n Landkreis m; (Brit) Grafschaft f; **— town** Kreisstadt f.

coup [ku:] n Coup m; **— d'état** Staatsstreich m, Putsch m.

coupé [ku:'peɪ] n (Aut) Coupé nt.

couple ['kʌpl] n Paar nt; **a — of** ein paar; vt koppeln.

couplet ['kʌplɪt] n Reimpaar nt.

coupling ['kʌplɪŋ] n Kupplung f.

coupon ['ku:pɒn] n Gutschein m.

courage ['kʌrɪdʒ] n Mut m; **—ous** [kə'reɪdʒəs] a mutig.

courier ['kurɪə*] n (for holiday) Reiseleiter m; (messenger) Kurier m, Eilbote m.

course [kɔ:s] n (race) Strecke f, Bahn f; (of stream) Lauf m; (of action) Richtung f; (of lectures) Vortragsreihe f; (of study) Studiengang m; summer — Sommerkurs m; (Naut) Kurs m; (in meal) Gang m; of — natürlich; in the — of im Laufe (+gen); in due — zu gegebener Zeit; see golf.

court [kɔ:t] n (royal) Hof m; (Jur) Gericht nt; vt gehen mit; see tennis.

courteous ['kɜ:tɪəs] a höflich, zuvorkommend.

courtesan [kɔ:tɪ'zæn] n Kurtisane f.

courtesy ['kɜ:təsɪ] n Höflichkeit f.

courthouse ['kɔ:thaus] n (US) Gerichtsgebäude nt.

courtier ['kɔ:tɪə*] n Höfling m.

court-martial ['kɔ:t'mɑ:ʃəl] n Kriegsgericht nt; vt vor ein Kriegsgericht stellen.

courtroom ['kɔ:trum] n Gerichtssaal m.

courtyard ['kɔ:tjɑ:d] n Hof m.

cousin ['kʌzn] n Cousin m, Vetter m; Kusine f.

cove [kəuv] n kleine Bucht f.

covenant ['kʌvənənt] n feierliche(s) Abkommen nt.

cover ['kʌvə*] vt (spread over) bedecken; (shield) abschirmen; (include) sich erstrecken über (+acc); (protect) decken; n (lid) Deckel m; (for bed) Decke f; (Mil) Bedeckung f; **—age** ['kʌvərɪdʒ] (Press) (reports) Berichterstattung f; (distribution) Verbreitung f; **—charge** Bedienungsgeld m; **—ing** Bedeckung f; **—ing letter** Begleitbrief m.

covet ['kʌvɪt] vt begehren.

covetous ['kʌvɪtəs] a begehrlich.

cow [kau] n Kuh f.

coward ['kauəd] n Feigling m; **—ice** ['kauədɪs] Feigheit f; **—ly** a feige.

cowboy ['kaubɔɪ] n Cowboy m.

cower ['kauə*] vi kauern; (movement) sich kauern.

co-worker ['kəu'wɜ:kə*] n Mitarbeiter(in f) m.

cowshed ['kauʃed] n Kuhstall m.

coxswain ['kɒksn] n (abbr cox) Steuermann m.

coy [kɔɪ] a schüchtern; **girl** spröde.

coyote [kɔɪˈəʊti] n Präriewolf m.

crab [kræb] n Krebs m; —**apple** Holzapfel m.

crack [kræk] n Riß m, Sprung m; (noise) Knall m; vt (break) springen lassen; joke reißen; vi (noise) krachen, knallen; a erstklassig; troops Elite-; —er n (firework) Knallkörper m, Kracher m; (biscuit) Keks m; (Christmas —) Knallbonbon m; — up vi (fig) zusammenbrechen.

crackle ['krækl] vi knistern; (fire) prasseln.

crackling ['kræklɪŋ] n Knistern n; (rind) Kruste f (des Schweinebratens).

cradle ['kreɪdl] n Wiege f.

craft [krɑːft] n (skill) (Hand- or Kunst)fertigkeit f; (trade) Handwerk nt; (cunning) Verschlagenheit f; (Naut) Fahrzeug nt, Schiff nt; —**sman** gelernte(r) Handwerker m; —**smanship** (quality) handwerkliche Ausführung f; (ability) handwerkliche(s) Können nt; —**y** a schlau, gerieben.

crag [kræg] n Klippe f; —**gy** a schroff, felsig.

cram [kræm] vt vollstopfen; (col) (teach) einpauken; vi (learn) pauken.

cramp [kræmp] n Krampf m; vt (hinder) einengen, hemmen.

crampon ['kræmpən] n Steigeisen nt.

cranberry ['krænbərɪ] n Preiselbeere f.

crane [kreɪn] n (machine) Kran m; (bird) Kranich m.

cranium ['kreɪnɪəm] n Schädel m.

crank [kræŋk] n (lever) Kurbel f; (person) Spinner m; vt ankurbeln; —**shaft** Kurbelwelle f.

cranky ['kræŋkɪ] a verschroben.

cranny ['krænɪ] n Ritze f.

crap [kræp] n (col) Mist m, Scheiße f.

craps [kræps] n (US) Würfelspiel nt.

crash [kræʃ] n (noise) Krachen nt; (with cars) Zusammenstoß m; (with plane) Absturz m; vi stürzen; (cars) zusammenstoßen; (plane) abstürzen; (economy) zusammenbrechen; (noise) knallen; a course Schnell-; — helmet Sturzhelm m; — **landing** Bruchlandung f.

crass [kræs] a kraß.

crate [kreɪt] n (lit, fig) Kiste f.

crater ['kreɪtə*] n Krater m.

cravat(e) [krəˈvæt] n Krawatte f.

crave [kreɪv] vi verlangen (for nach).

craving ['kreɪvɪŋ] n Verlangen nt.

crawl [krɔːl] vi kriechen; (baby) krabbeln; n Kriechen nt; (swim) Kraul m.

crayon ['kreɪən] n Buntstift m.

craze [kreɪz] n Fimmel m.

crazy ['kreɪzɪ] a (foolish) verrückt; (insane) wahnsinnig; (eager for) versessen (auf +acc); — **paving** Mosaikpflaster nt.

creak [kriːk] n Knarren nt; vi quietschen, knarren.

cream [kriːm] n (from milk) Rahm m, Sahne f; (polish, cosmetic) Creme f; (colour) Cremefarbe f; (fig: people) Elite f; — **cake** (small) Sahnetörtchen nt; (big) Sahnekuchen m; — **cheese** Rahmquark m; —**ery** Molkerei f; —**y** a sahnig.

crease [kriːs] n Falte f; vt falten; (untidy) zerknittern.

create [krɪ'eɪt] *vt* erschaffen; (cause) verursachen.

creation [krɪ'eɪʃən] *n* Schöpfung *f*.

creative [krɪ'eɪtɪv] *a* schöpferisch, kreativ.

creator [krɪ'eɪtə*] *n* Schöpfer *m*.

creature ['kriːtʃə*] *n* Geschöpf *nt*.

credence [kriːdəns] *n* Glauben *m*.

credentials [krɪ'denʃəlz] *npl* Beglaubigungsschreiben *nt*.

credibility [kredɪ'bɪlɪtɪ] *n* Glaubwürdigkeit *f*.

credible ['kredɪbl] *a person* glaubwürdig; *story* glaubhaft.

credit ['kredɪt] *n* (Comm) Kredit *m*; Guthaben *nt*; *vt* Glauben schenken (+ dat); to sb's — zu jds Ehre; —s *pl* (of film) die Mitwirkenden; —able *a* rühmlich; —card Kreditkarte *f*; —or Gläubiger *m*.

credulity [krɪ'djuːlɪtɪ] *n* Leichtgläubigkeit *f*.

creed [kriːd] *n* Glaubensbekenntnis *nt*.

creek [kriːk] *n* (inlet) kleine Bucht *f*; (US: river) kleine(r) Wasserlauf *m*.

creep [kriːp] *vi irreg* kriechen; —**er** Kletterpflanze *f*; —**y** *a* (frightening) gruselig.

cremate [krɪ'meɪt] *vt* einäschern.

cremation [krɪ'meɪʃən] *n* Einäscherung *f*.

crematorium [kremə'tɔːrɪəm] *n* Krematorium *nt*.

creosote ['krɪəsəʊt] *n* Kreosot *nt*.

crepe [kreɪp] *n* Krepp *m*; — bandage Elastikbinde *f*.

crescent ['kresnt] *n* (of moon) Halbmond *m*.

cress [kres] *n* Kresse *f*.

crest [krest] *n* (of cock) Kamm *m*; (of wave) Wellenkamm *m*; (coat of arms) Wappen *nt*; —**fallen** *a* niedergeschlagen.

cretin ['kretɪn] *n* Idiot *m*.

crevasse [krɪ'væs] *n* Gletscherspalte *f*.

crevice ['krevɪs] *n* Riß *m*; (in rock) Felsspalte *f*.

crew [kruː] *n* Besatzung *f*, Mannschaft *f*; —**cut** Bürstenschnitt *m*; —**neck** runde(r) Ausschnitt *m*.

crib [krɪb] *n* (bed) Krippe *f*; (translation) wortwörtliche Übersetzung *f*, Klatsche *f*.

crick [krɪk] *n* Muskelkrampf *m*.

cricket ['krɪkɪt] *n* (insect) Grille *f*; (game) Kricket *nt*; —**er** Kricketspieler *m*.

crime [kraɪm] *n* Verbrechen *nt*.

criminal ['krɪmɪnl] *n* Verbrecher *m*; *a* kriminell, strafbar.

crimp [krɪmp] *vt* hair drehen.

crimson ['krɪmzn] *n* Karmesin *nt*; *a* leuchtend rot.

cringe [krɪndʒ] *vi* sich ducken.

crinkle ['krɪŋkl] *vt* zerknittern; *vi* knittern.

crinkly ['krɪŋklɪ] *a* hair kraus.

cripple ['krɪpl] *n* Krüppel *m*; *vt* lahmlegen; (Med) lähmen, verkrüppeln.

crisis ['kraɪsɪs] *n* Krise *f*.

crisp [krɪsp] *a* knusprig; *n* Chip *m*.

criss-cross ['krɪskrɒs] *a* gekreuzt, Kreuz-.

criterion [kraɪ'tɪərɪən] *n* Kriterium *nt*.

critic ['krɪtɪk] *n* Kritiker(in *f*) *m*; —**al** *a* kritisch; —**ally** *ad* kritisch; ill gefährlich; —**ism** ['krɪtɪsɪzəm] Kritik *f*; —**ize** ['krɪtɪsaɪz] *vt* kritisieren; (comment) beurteilen.

croak [krəʊk] *vi* krächzen; (frog) quaken; *n* Krächzen *nt*; Quaken *nt*.

crochet ['krəʊʃeɪ] n Häkelei f.

crockery ['krɒkərɪ] n Geschirr nt.

crocodile ['krɒkədaɪl] n Krokodil nt.

crocus ['krəʊkəs] n Krokus m.

croft [krɒft] n kleine(s) Pachtgut nt; —er Kleinbauer m.

crony ['krəʊnɪ] n (col) Kumpel m.

crook [krʊk] n (criminal) Gauner m, Schwindler m; (stick) Hirtenstab m; —ed ['krʊkɪd] a krumm.

crop [krɒp] n (harvest) Ernte f; (col: series) Haufen m; — up vi auftauchen; (thing) passieren.

croquet ['krəʊkeɪ] n Krocket nt.

croquette [krə'ket] n Krokette f.

cross [krɒs] n Kreuz nt; (Biol) Kreuzung f; vt road überqueren; legs übereinander legen; (write) einen Querstrich ziehen; (Biol) kreuzen; cheque als Verrechnungsscheck kennzeichnen; a (annoyed) ärgerlich, böse; —bar Querstange f; —breed Kreuzung f; —country (race) Geländelauf m; —examination Kreuzverhör nt; —examine vt ins Kreuzverhör nehmen; —eyed a: to be —eyed schielen; —ing (crossroads) Kreuzung f; (of ship) Überfahrt f; (for pedestrians) Fußgängerübergang m; — out vt streichen; to be at — purposes von verschiedenen Dingen reden; —reference Querverweis m; —roads Straßenkreuzung f; (fig) Scheideweg m; — section Querschnitt m; —wind Seitenwind m; —word (puzzle) Kreuzworträtsel nt.

crotch [krɒtʃ] n Zwickel m; (Anat) Unterleib m.

crotchet ['krɒtʃɪt] n Viertelnote f.

crotchety ['krɒtʃɪtɪ] a person launenhaft.

crouch [kraʊtʃ] vi hocken.

crouton ['kru:tɔn] n geröstete(r) Brotwürfel m.

crow [krəʊ] n Krähen nt; vi krähen.

crowbar ['krəʊbɑ:*] n Stemmeisen nt.

crowd [kraʊd] n Menge f, Gedränge nt; vt (fill) überfüllen; vi drängen; —ed a überfüllt.

crown [kraʊn] n Krone f; (of head, hat) Kopf m; vt krönen; — jewels pl Kronjuwelen pl; — prince Kronprinz m.

crow's-nest ['krəʊznest] n Krähennest nt, Ausguck m.

crucial ['kru:ʃəl] a entscheidend.

crucifix ['kru:sɪfɪks] n Kruzifix nt; —ion [kru:sɪ'fɪkʃən] Kreuzigung f.

crucify ['kru:sɪfaɪ] vt kreuzigen.

crude [kru:d] a (raw) roh; humour, behaviour grob, unfein; —ly ad grob; —ness Roheit f.

crudity ['kru:dɪtɪ] n = **crudeness**.

cruel [krʊəl] a grausam; (distressing) schwer; (hard-hearted) hart, gefühllos; —ty Grausamkeit f.

cruet ['kru:ɪt] n Gewürzständer m, Menage f.

cruise [kru:z] n Kreuzfahrt f; vi kreuzen; —r (Mil) Kreuzer m.

cruising-speed ['kru:zɪŋspi:d] n Reisegeschwindigkeit f.

crumb [krʌm] n Krume f; (fig) Bröckchen nt.

crumble ['krʌmbl] vti zerbröckeln.

crumbly ['krʌmblɪ] a krümelig.

crumpet ['krʌmpɪt] n Tee(pfann)-kuchen m.

crumple ['krʌmpl] vt zerknittern.

crunch [krʌntʃ] n Knirschen nt; (fig) der entscheidende Punkt m; vt knirschen; —y a knusprig.

crusade [kru:'seɪd] n Kreuzzug m; —r Kreuzfahrer m.

crush [krʌʃ] n Gedränge nt; vt zerdrücken; (rebellion) unterdrücken, niederwerfen; vi (material) knittern; —ing a überwältigend.

crust [krʌst] n (of bread) Rinde f, Kruste f; (Med) Schorf m.

crutch [krʌtʃ] n Krücke f; see also crotch.

crux [krʌks] n (crucial point) der springende Punkt, Haken m (col).

cry [krai] vi (call) ausrufen; (shout) schreien; (weep) weinen; n (call) Schrei m; —ing a (fig) himmelschreiend; — off vi (plötzlich) absagen.

crypt [krɪpt] n Krypta f.

cryptic ['krɪptɪk] a (secret) geheim; (mysterious) rätselhaft.

crystal ['krɪstl] n Kristall m; (glass) Kristallglas nt; (mineral) Bergkristall m; —clear a kristallklar; —lize vti (lit) kristallisieren; (fig) klären.

cub [kʌb] n Junge(s) nt; (young Boy Scout) Wölfling m.

cubbyhole ['kʌbihəul] n Eckchen nt.

cube [kju:b] n Würfel m; (Math) Kubikzahl f.

cubic ['kju:bik] a würfelförmig; centimetre etc Kubik-.

cubicle ['kju:bikl] n Kabine f.

cubism ['kju:bizəm] n Kubismus m.

cuckoo ['kuku:] n Kuckuck m; —clock Kuckucksuhr f.

cucumber ['kju:kʌmbə*] n Gurke f.

cuddle ['kʌdl] vt herzen, drücken (col); n enge Umarmung f.

cuddly ['kʌdli] a anschmiegsam; teddy zum Drücken.

cudgel ['kʌdʒəl] n Knüppel m.

cue [kju:] n Wink m; (Theat) Stichwort nt; Billardstock m.

cuff [kʌf] n (of shirt, coat etc) Manschette f; Aufschlag m; (US = turn-up) Umschlag m; —link Manschettenknopf m.

cuisine [kwi'zi:n] n Kochkunst f, Küche f.

cul-de-sac ['kʌldəsæk] n Sackgasse f.

culinary ['kʌlinəri] a Koch-.

culminate ['kʌlmineit] vi gipfeln.

culmination [kʌlmi'neiʃən] n Höhepunkt m.

culpable ['kʌlpəbl] a strafbar, schuldhaft.

culprit ['kʌlprɪt] n Täter m.

cult [kʌlt] n Kult m.

cultivate ['kʌltiveit] vt (Agr) bebauen; mind bilden; —d a (Agr) bebaut; (cultured) kultiviert.

cultivation [kʌlti'veiʃən] n (Agr) Bebauung f; (of person) Bildung f.

cultural ['kʌltʃərəl] a kulturell, Kultur-.

culture ['kʌltʃə*] n (refinement) Kultur f, Bildung f; (of community) Kultur f; —d a gebildet, kultiviert.

cumbersome ['kʌmbəsəm] a task beschwerlich; object schwer zu handhaben.

cummerbund ['kʌmbʌnd] n Kummerbund m.

cumulative ['kju:mjulətɪv] a gehäuft; to be — sich häufen.

cunning ['kʌnɪŋ] n Verschlagenheit f; a schlau.

cup [kʌp] n Tasse f; (prize) Pokal m; —board ['kʌbəd] Schrank m; — final Meisterschaftsspiel nt; —ful Tasse(voll) f.

cupola ['kju:pələ] n Kuppel f.

curable ['kjurəbəl] a heilbar.

curator [kju'reitə*] n Kustos m.

curb [kз:b] vt zügeln; n Zaum m; (on spending etc) Einschränkung f.

cure [kjʊə*] *n* Heilmittel *nt*; (*process*) Heilverfahren *nt*; there's no — for ... es gibt kein Mittel gegen ...; *vt* heilen.

curfew ['kɜ:fju:] *n* Ausgangssperre *f*; Sperrstunde *f*.

curiosity [kjʊərɪ'ɒsɪtɪ] *n* Neugier *f*; (*for knowledge*) Wißbegierde *f*; (*object*) Merkwürdigkeit *f*.

curious ['kjʊərɪəs] *a* neugierig; (*strange*) seltsam; —ly *ad* besonders.

curl [kɜ:l] *n* Locke *f*; *vti* locken; —er Lockenwickler *m*.

curlew ['kɜ:lju:] *n* Brachvogel *m*.

curly ['kɜ:lɪ] *a* lockig.

currant ['kʌrənt] *n* Korinthe *f*; Johannisbeere *f*.

currency ['kʌrənsɪ] *n* Währung *f*; (*of ideas*) Geläufigkeit *f*.

current ['kʌrənt] *n* Strömung *f*; *a* expression gängig, üblich; *issue* neueste; — **account** Girokonto *nt*; — **affairs** *pl* Zeitgeschehen *nt*; —ly *ad* zur Zeit.

curriculum [kə'rɪkjʊləm] *n* Lehrplan *m*; — **vitae** Lebenslauf *m*.

curry ['kʌrɪ] *n* Currygericht *nt*; — **powder** Currypulver) *nt*.

curse [kɜ:s] *vi* (*swear*) fluchen (*at* auf +*acc*); *vt* (*insult*) verwünschen; *n* Fluch *m*.

cursory ['kɜ:sərɪ] *a* flüchtig.

curt [kɜ:t] *a* schroff.

curtail [kɜ:'teɪl] *vt* abkürzen; *rights* einschränken.

curtain ['kɜ:tn] *n* Vorhang *m*, Gardine *f*; (*Theat*) Vorhang *m*.

curtsy ['kɜ:tsɪ] *n* Knicks *m*; *vi* knicksen.

cushion ['kʊʃən] *n* Kissen *nt*; *vt* polstern.

custard ['kʌstəd] *n* Vanillesoße *f*.

custodian [kʌs'təʊdɪən] *n* Kustos *m*, Verwalter(in *f*) *m*.

custody ['kʌstədɪ] *n* Aufsicht *f*; (*police*) Polizeigewahrsam *m*.

custom ['kʌstəm] *n* (*tradition*) Brauch *m*; (*business dealing*) Kundschaft *f*; —**s** (*taxes*) Einfuhrzoll *m*; C—**s** Zollamt *nt*; —**ary** *a* üblich; —**er** Kunde *m*, Kundin *f*; —**-made** *a* speziell angefertigt; C—**s officer** Zollbeamte(r) *mf*.

cut [kʌt] *vt* irreg schneiden; *wages* kürzen; *prices* heruntersetzen; I — my hand ich habe mir in die Hand geschnitten; *n* Schnitt *m*; (*wound*) Schnittwunde *f*; (*in book, income etc*) Kürzung *f*; (*share*) Anteil *m*.

cute [kju:t] *a* reizend, niedlich.

cuticle ['kju:tɪkl] *n* (*on nail*) Nagelhaut *f*.

cutlery ['kʌtlərɪ] *n* Besteck *nt*.

cutlet ['kʌtlɪt] *n* (*pork*) Kotelett *nt*; (*veal*) Schnitzel *nt*.

cutout ['kʌtaʊt] *n* (*Elec*) Sicherung *f*.

cut-price ['kʌtpraɪs] *a* verbilligt.

cutting ['kʌtɪŋ] *a* schneidend; *n* (*from paper*) Ausschnitt *m*.

cyanide ['saɪənaɪd] *n* Zyankali *nt*.

cybernetics [saɪbə'netɪks] *n* Kybernetik *f*.

cyclamen ['sɪkləmən] *n* Alpenveilchen *nt*.

cycle ['saɪkl] *n* Fahrrad *nt*; (*series*) Reihe *f*; (*of songs*) Zyklus *m*; *vi* radfahren.

cycling ['saɪklɪŋ] *n* Radfahren *nt*; (*Sport*) Radsport *m*.

cyclist ['saɪklɪst] *n* Radfahrer(in *f*) *m*.

cyclone ['saɪkləʊn] *n* Zyklon *m*.

cygnet ['sɪgnɪt] *n* junge(r) Schwan *m*.

cylinder ['sılındə*] n Zylinder m; (Tech) Walze f; — **block** Zylinderblock m; — **capacity** Zylindervolumen nt, Zylinderinhalt m; — **head** Zylinderkopf m.

cymbals ['sımbəlz] npl Becken nt.

cynic ['sınık] n Zyniker(in f) m; —**al** a zynisch; —**ism** Zynismus m.

cypress ['saıprıs] n Zypresse f.

cyst [sıst] n Zyste f.

czar [za:*] n Zar m; —**ina** [za'ri:nə] Zarin f.

D

D, d [di:] n D nt, d nt.

dab [dæb] vt wound, paint betupfen; n (little bit) bißchen nt; (of paint) Tupfer m; (smear) Klecks m.

dabble ['dæbl] vi (splash) plätschern; (fig) to — in sth in etw (dat) machen.

dachshund ['dækshʊnd] n Dackel m.

dad(dy) ['dæd, -ı] n Papa m, Vati m; **daddy-long-legs** Weberknecht m.

daffodil ['dæfədıl] n Osterglocke f.

daft [da:ft] a (col) blöd(e), doof.

dagger ['dægə*] n Dolch m.

dahlia ['deılıə] n Dahlie f.

daily ['deılı] a täglich; n (Press) Tageszeitung f; (woman) Haushaltshilfe f.

dainty ['deıntı] a zierlich; (attractive) reizend.

dairy ['dεərı] n (shop) Milchgeschäft nt; (on farm) Molkerei f; a Milch-.

daisy ['deızı] n Gänseblümchen nt.

dally ['dælı] vi tändeln.

dam [dæm] n (Stau)damm m; vt stauen.

damage ['dæmıdʒ] n Schaden m; vt beschädigen; —**s** (Jur) Schaden(s)ersatz m.

dame [deım] n Dame f; (col) Weibsbild nt.

damn [dæm] vt verdammen, verwünschen; a (col) verdammt; — it! verflucht!; —**ing** a vernichtend.

damp [dæmp] n Feuchtigkeit f; vt (also —**en**) befeuchten; (discourage) dämpfen; —**ness** Feuchtigkeit f.

damson ['dæmzən] n Damaszenerpflaume f.

dance [da:ns] n Tanz m; (party) Tanz(abend) m; vi tanzen; — **hall** Tanzlokal nt; —**r** Tänzer m.

dancing ['da:nsıŋ] n Tanzen nt.

dandelion ['dændılaıən] n Löwenzahn m.

dandruff ['dændrəf] n (Kopf)schuppen pl.

dandy ['dændı] n Dandy m.

danger ['deındʒə*] n Gefahr f; —**!** (sign) Achtung!; **in** — in Gefahr; **on the** —**list** in Lebensgefahr; —**ous** a, —**ously** ad gefährlich.

dangle ['dæŋgl] vi baumeln; vt herabhängen lassen.

dapper ['dæpə*] a elegant.

dare [dεə*] vt herausfordern; vi: — (to) do sth es wagen, etw zu tun; **I** — **say** ich würde sagen.

daring ['dεərıŋ] a (audacious) verwegen; (bold) wagemutig; **dress** gewagt; n Mut m.

dark [dɑːk] a dunkel; (fig) düster, trübe; (deep colour) dunkel-; n Dunkelheit f; after — nach Anbruch der Dunkelheit; D— Ages (finsteres) Mittelalter nt; —en vti verdunkeln; —ness Finsternis nt; — room Dunkelkammer f.

darling ['dɑːlɪŋ] n Liebling m; a lieb.

darn [dɑːn] n Gestopfte(s) nt; vt stopfen.

dart [dɑːt] n (leap) Satz m; (weapon) Pfeil m; vi sausen; —s (game) Pfeilwerfen nt; —board Zielscheibe f.

dash [dæʃ] n Sprung m; (mark) (Gedanken)strich m; vt (lit) schmeißen; vi stürzen; —board Armaturenbrett nt; —ing a schneidig.

data ['deɪtə] npl Einzelheiten pl, Daten pl; — processing Datenverarbeitung f.

date [deɪt] n Datum nt; (for meeting etc) Termin m; (with person) Verabredung f; (fruit) Dattel f; vt letter etc datieren; person gehen mit; —d a altmodisch; —line Datumsgrenze f.

dative ['deɪtɪv] n Dativ m; a Dativ-.

daub [dɔːb] vt beschmieren; paint schmieren.

daughter ['dɔːtə*] n Tochter f; —in-law Schwiegertochter f.

daunt [dɔːnt] vt entmutigen.

davenport ['dævnpɔːt] n Sekretär m; (US: sofa) Sofa nt.

dawdle ['dɔːdl] vi trödeln.

dawn [dɔːn] n Morgendämmerung f; vi dämmern; (fig) dämmern (on dat).

day [deɪ] n Tag m; (daylight) Tageslicht nt; — by — Tag für Tag, täglich; one — eines Tages; —break Tagesanbruch m; —dream n Wachtraum m, Träumerei f; vi

irreg (mit offenen Augen) träumen; —light Tageslicht nt; —time Tageszeit f.

daze [deɪz] vt betäuben; n Betäubung f; —d a benommen.

dazzle ['dæzl] vt blenden; n Blenden nt.

deacon ['diːkən] n Diakon m; Kirchenvorsteher m.

dead [ded] a tot, gestorben; (without feeling) gefühllos; (without movement) leer, verlassen; — centre genau in der Mitte; ad völlig; the — pl die Toten pl; —en vt pain abtöten; sound ersticken; — end Sackgasse f; — heat tote(s) Rennen nt; —line Frist(ablauf) m, Stichtag m; —lock Stillstand m; —ly a tödlich; —pan a undurchdringlich.

deaf [def] a taub; —aid Hörgerät nt; —en vt taub machen; —ening a ohrenbetäubend; —ness Taubheit f; —mute Taubstumme(r) m.

deal [diːl] n Geschäft nt; vti irreg austeilen; a great — of sehr viel; to — with person behandeln; —er (Comm) Händler m; (Cards) Kartengeber m; —ings pl (Fin) Geschäfte pl; (relations) Beziehungen pl, Geschäftsverkehr m.

dean [diːn] n (Protestant) Superintendent m; (Catholic) Dechant m; (Univ) Dekan m.

dear [dɪə*] a lieb; (expensive) teuer; n Liebling m; — me! du liebe Zeit!; D— Sir Sehr geehrter Herr!; D— John Lieber John!; —ly ad love herzlich; pay teuer.

dearth [dɜːθ] n Mangel m (of an + dat).

death [deθ] n Tod m; (end) Ende nt; (statistic) Sterbefall m; —bed

Sterbebett *nt*; — certificate Totenschein *m*; — duties (Brit) Erbschaftssteuer *f*; —ly *a* totenähnlich, Toten-; — penalty Todesstrafe *f*; — rate Sterblichkeitsziffer *f*.

debar [dɪ'bɑ:*] *vt* ausschließen.

debase [dɪ'beɪs] *vt* entwerten.

debatable [dɪ'beɪtəbl] *a* anfechtbar.

debate [dɪ'beɪt] *n* Debatte *f*, Diskussion *f*; *vt* debattieren, diskutieren; *(consider)* überlegen.

debauched [dɪ'bɔ:tʃt] *a* ausschweifend.

debauchery [dɪ'bɔ:tʃərɪ] *n* Ausschweifungen *pl*.

debit [debɪt] *n* Schuldposten *m*; *vt* belasten.

debris ['debri:] *n* Trümmer *pl*.

debt [det] *n* Schuld *f*; to be in — verschuldet sein; —or Schuldner *m*.

début [deɪbu:] *n* Debüt *nt*.

decade [dekeɪd] *n* Jahrzehnt *nt*.

decadence ['dekədəns] *n* Verfall *m*, Dekadenz *f*.

decadent ['dekədənt] *a* dekadent.

decanter [dɪ'kæntə*] *n* Karaffe *f*.

decarbonize [di:'kɑ:bənaɪz] *vt* entkohlen.

decay [dɪ'keɪ] *n* Verfall *m*; *vi* verfallen; *teeth*, *meat etc* faulen; *leaves etc* verrotten.

decease [dɪ'si:s] *n* Hinscheiden *nt*; —d *v* verstorben.

deceit [dɪ'si:t] *n* Betrug *m*; —ful *a* falsch.

deceive [dɪ'si:v] *vt* täuschen.

decelerate [di:'seləreɪt] *vti* (sich) verlangsamen, die Geschwindigkeit verringern.

December [dɪ'sembə*] *n* Dezember *m*.

decency ['di:sənsɪ] *n* Anstand *m*.

decent [di:sənt] *a* (*respectable*) anständig; (*pleasant*) annehmbar.

decentralization [di:sentralaɪ'zeɪʃən] *n* Dezentralisierung *f*.

deception [dɪ'sepʃən] *n* Betrug *m*.

deceptive [dɪ'septɪv] *a* täuschend, irreführend.

decibel ['desɪbel] *n* Dezibel *nt*.

decide [dɪ'saɪd] *vt* entscheiden; *vi* sich entscheiden; to — on sth etw beschließen; —d *a* bestimmt, entschieden; —dly *ad* entschieden.

deciduous [dɪ'sɪdjʊəs] *a* jedes Jahr abfallend, Laub-.

decimal ['desɪml] *a* dezimal; *n* Dezimalzahl *f*; — point Komma *nt* (eines Dezimalbruches); — system Dezimalsystem *nt*.

decimate ['desɪmeɪt] *vt* dezimieren.

decipher [dɪ'saɪfə*] *vt* entziffern.

decision [dɪ'sɪʒən] *n* Entscheidung *f*, Entschluß *m*.

decisive [dɪ'saɪsɪv] *a* entscheidend, ausschlaggebend.

deck [dek] *n* (Naut) Deck *nt*; (of cards) Pack *m*; —chair Liegestuhl *m*; —hand Matrose *m*.

declaration [deklə'reɪʃən] *n* Erklärung *f*.

declare [dɪ'kleə*] *vt* (*state*) behaupten; *war* erklären; (*Customs*) verzollen.

decline [dɪ'klaɪn] *n* (*decay*) Verfall *m*; (*lessening*) Rückgang *m*, Niedergang *m*; *vt invitation* ausschlagen, ablehnen; *vi* (*of strength*) nachlassen; (*say no*) ablehnen.

declutch ['di:'klʌtʃ] *vi* auskuppeln.

decode [di:'kəʊd] *vt* entschlüsseln.

decompose [di:kəm'pəʊz] *vi* (sich) zersetzen.

decomposition [di:kɒmpə'zɪʃən] *n* Zersetzung *f*.

decontaminate [di:kən'tæmɪneɪt] *vt* entgiften.

décor ['deɪkɔ:*] n Ausstattung f.

decorate ['dekəreɪt] vt room tapezieren; streichen; (adorn) (aus)schmücken; cake verzieren; (honour) auszeichnen.

decoration [dekə'reɪʃən] n (of house) (Wand)dekoration f; (medal) Orden m.

decorative [dekərətɪv] a dekorativ, Schmuck-.

decorator ['dekəreɪtə*] n Maler m, Anstreicher m.

decorum [dɪ'kɔ:rəm] n Anstand m.

decoy ['di:kɔɪ] n (lit, fig) Lockvogel m.

decrease [dɪ'kri:s] n Abnahme f; vt vermindern; vi abnehmen.

decree [dɪ'kri:] n Verfügung f, Erlaß m.

decrepit [dɪ'krepɪt] a hinfällig.

dedicate ['dedɪkeɪt] vt (to God) weihen; book widmen.

dedication [dedɪ'keɪʃən] n (devotion) Ergebenheit f.

deduce [dɪ'dju:s] vt ableiten, schließen (from aus).

deduct [dɪ'dʌkt] vt abziehen; —ion [dɪ'dʌkʃən] (of money) Abzug m; (conclusion) Schluß(folgerung f.

deed [di:d] n Tat f; (document) Urkunde f.

deep [di:p] a tief; —en vt vertiefen; —freeze Tiefkühlung f; —seated a tiefsitzend; —set a tiefliegend.

deer [dɪə*] n Reh nt; (with antlers) Hirsch m.

deface [dɪ'feɪs] vt entstellen.

defamation [defə'meɪʃən] n Verleumdung f.

default [dɪ'fɔ:lt] n Versäumnis nt; vi versäumen; by — durch Nichterscheinen nt; —er Schuldner m, Zahlungsunfähige(r) m.

defeat [dɪ'fi:t] n (overthrow) Vernichtung f; (battle) Niederlage f; vt schlagen, zu Fall bringen; —ist a defätistisch.

defect ['di:fekt] n Defekt m, Fehler m; [dɪ'fekt] vi überlaufen; —ive [dɪ'fektɪv] a fehlerhaft, schadhaft.

defence [dɪ'fens] n (Mil, Sport) Verteidigung f; (excuse) Rechtfertigung f; —less a wehrlos.

defend [dɪ'fend] vt verteidigen; —ant Angeklagte(r) m; —er Verteidiger m.

defensive [dɪ'fensɪv] a defensiv, Schutz-.

defer [dɪ'fɜ:*] vt verschieben; —ence ['defərəns] Hochachtung f, Rücksichtnahme f; —ential [defə'renʃəl] a ehrerbietig.

defiance [dɪ'faɪəns] n Trotz m, Unnachgiebigkeit f; in — of the order dem Befehl zum Trotz.

defiant [dɪ'faɪənt] a trotzig, unnachgiebig.

deficiency [dɪ'fɪʃənsɪ] n Unzulänglichkeit f, Mangel m.

deficient [dɪ'fɪʃənt] a unzureichend.

deficit ['defɪsɪt] n Defizit nt, Fehlbetrag m.

defile [dɪ'faɪl] vt beschmutzen; n ['di:faɪl] Schlucht f.

define [dɪ'faɪn] vt bestimmen; (explain) definieren.

definite ['defɪnɪt] a bestimmt; (clear) klar, eindeutig; —ly ad bestimmt.

definition [defɪ'nɪʃən] n Definition f; (Phot) Schärfe f.

definitive [dɪ'fɪnɪtɪv] a definitiv, endgültig.

deflate [di:'fleɪt] vt die Luft ablassen aus.

deflation [di:'fleɪʃən] n (Fin) Deflation f.

deflect [dɪ'flekt] *vt* ablenken.

deform [dɪ'fɔːm] *vt* deformieren, entstellen; **—ed** *a* deformiert; **—ity** Verunstaltung *f*, Mißbildung *f*.

defraud [dɪ'frɔːd] *vt* betrügen.

defray [dɪ'freɪ] *vt* bestreiten.

defrost [diː'frɒst] *vt* *fridge* abtauen; *food* auftauen.

deft [deft] *a* geschickt.

defunct [dɪ'fʌŋkt] *a* verstorben.

defy [dɪ'faɪ] *vt* (*challenge*) sich widersetzen (+ *dat*); (*resist*) trotzen (+ *dat*), sich stellen gegen.

degenerate [dɪ'dʒenəreɪt] *vi* degenerieren; [dɪ'dʒenərɪt] *a* degeneriert.

degradation [degrə'deɪʃən] *n* Erniedrigung *f*.

degrading [dɪ'greɪdɪŋ] *a* erniedrigend.

degree [dɪ'griː] *n* Grad *m*; (*Univ*) akademische(r) Grad *m*; **by —s** allmählich; **to take one's —** sein Examen machen.

dehydrated [diːhaɪ'dreɪtɪd] *a* getrocknet, Trocken-.

de-ice [diː'aɪs] *vt* enteisen, auftauen.

deign [deɪn] *vi* sich herablassen.

deity ['diːɪtɪ] *n* Gottheit *f*.

dejected [dɪ'dʒektɪd] *a* niedergeschlagen.

dejection [dɪ'dʒekʃən] *n* Niedergeschlagenheit *f*.

delay [dɪ'leɪ] *vt* (*hold back*) aufschieben; **the flight was —ed** die Maschine hatte Verspätung; *vi* (*linger*) sich aufhalten, zögern; *n* Aufschub *m*, Verzögerung *f*; **without —** unverzüglich; **—ed** *a* *action* verzögert.

delegate ['delɪgɪt] *n* Delegierte(r) *mf*, Abgeordnete(r) *mf*; ['delɪgeɪt] *vt* delegieren.

delegation [delɪ'geɪʃən] *n* Abordnung *f*; (*foreign*) Delegation *f*.

delete [dɪ'liːt] *vt* (aus)streichen.

deliberate *a* (*intentional*) bewußt, überlegt; (*slow*) bedächtig; [dɪ'lɪbəreɪt] *vi* (*consider*) überlegen; (*debate*) sich beraten; **—ly** *ad* vorsätzlich.

deliberation [dɪlɪbə'reɪʃən] *n* Überlegung *f*, Beratung *f*.

delicacy ['delɪkəsɪ] *n* Zartheit *f*; (*weakness*) Anfälligkeit *f*; (*tact*) Zartgefühl *nt*; (*food*) Delikatesse *f*.

delicate ['delɪkɪt] *a* (*fine*) fein; (*fragile*) zart; (*situation*) heikel; (*Med*) empfindlich; **—ly** *ad* bedenklich.

delicatessen [delɪkə'tesn] *n* Feinkostgeschäft *nt*.

delicious [dɪ'lɪʃəs] *a* köstlich, lecker, delikat.

delight [dɪ'laɪt] *n* Wonne *f*; *vt* entzücken; **—ful** *a* entzückend, herrlich.

delinquency [dɪ'lɪŋkwənsɪ] *n* Straffälligkeit *f*, Delinquenz *f*.

delinquent [dɪ'lɪŋkwənt] *n* Straffällige(r) *mf*; *a* straffällig.

delirious [dɪ'lɪrɪəs] *a* irre, im Fieberwahn.

delirium [dɪ'lɪrɪəm] *n* Fieberwahn *m*, Delirium *nt*.

deliver [dɪ'lɪvə*] *vt* *goods* (ab)liefern; *letter* bringen, zustellen; *verdict* aussprechen; *speech* halten; **—y** (Ab)lieferung *f*; (*of letter*) Zustellung *f*; (*of speech*) Vortragsweise *f*; **—y van** Lieferwagen *m*.

delouse [diː'laʊs] *vt* entlausen.

delta ['deltə] *n* Delta *nt*.

delude [dɪ'luːd] *vt* täuschen.

deluge ['delju:dʒ] *n* Überschwemmung *f*; (*fig*) Flut *f*; *vt* (*fig*) überfluten.

delusion [dɪ'lu:ʒən] *n* (Selbst)täuschung *f*.

de luxe [dɪ'lʌks] *a* Luxus-.

demand [dɪ'mɑːnd] *vt* verlangen; *n* (*request*) Verlangen *nt*; (*Comm*) Nachfrage *f*; **in** — begehrt, gesucht; **on** — auf Verlangen; **—ing** *a* anspruchsvoll.

demarcation [diːmɑː'keɪʃən] *n* Abgrenzung *f*.

demeanour [dɪ'miːnə*] *n* Benehmen *nt*.

demented [dɪ'mentɪd] *a* wahnsinnig.

demi- ['demɪ] *pref* halb-.

demise [dɪ'maɪz] *n* Ableben *nt*.

demobilization [ˌdiːməubɪlaɪ'zeɪʃən] *n* Demobilisierung *f*.

democracy [dɪ'mɒkrəsɪ] *n* Demokratie *f*.

democrat ['deməkræt] *n* Demokrat *m*; **—ic** *a*, **—ically** *ad* [demə'krætɪk, -lɪ] demokratisch.

demolish [dɪ'mɒlɪʃ] *vt* (*lit*) abreißen; (*destroy*) zerstören; (*fig*) vernichten.

demolition [demə'lɪʃən] *n* Abbruch *m*.

demon ['diːmən] *n* Dämon *m*.

demonstrate ['demənstreɪt] *vti* demonstrieren.

demonstration [demən'streɪʃən] *n* Demonstration *f*; (*proof*) Beweisführung *f*.

demonstrative [dɪ'mɒnstrətɪv] *a* demonstrativ.

demonstrator ['demənstreɪtə*] *n* (*Pol*) Demonstrant(in *f*) *m*.

demoralize [dɪ'mɒrəlaɪz] *vt* demoralisieren.

demote [dɪ'məut] *vt* degradieren.

demure [dɪ'mjuə*] *a* ernst.

den [den] *n* (*of animal*) Höhle *f*, Bau *m*; Bude *f*; — **of vice** Lasterhöhle *f*.

denationalize [diː'næʃnəlaɪz] *vt* reprivatisieren.

denial [dɪ'naɪəl] *n* Leugnung *f*; **official** — Dementi *nt*.

denigrate ['denɪgreɪt] *vt* verunglimpfen.

denim ['denɪm] *n* Denim-; **—s** *pl* Denim-Jeans.

denomination [dɪnɒmɪ'neɪʃən] *n* (*Eccl*) Bekenntnis *nt*; (*type*) Klasse *f*; (*Fin*) Wert *m*.

denominator [dɪ'nɒmɪneɪtə*] *n* Nenner; **common** — gemeinsame(r) Nenner *m*.

denote [dɪ'nəut] *vt* bedeuten.

denounce [dɪ'nauns] *vt* brandmarken.

dense [dens] *a* dicht, dick; (*stupid*) schwer von Begriff; **—ly** *ad* dicht.

density ['densɪtɪ] *n* Dichte *f*.

dent [dent] *n* Delle *f*; *vt* einbeulen.

dental ['dentl] *a* Zahn-; — **surgeon** = dentist.

dentifrice ['dentɪfrɪs] *n* Zahnputzmittel *nt*.

dentist ['dentɪst] *n* Zahnarzt *m*/-ärztin *f*; **—ry** Zahnmedizin *f*.

denture ['dentʃə*] *n* künstliche(s) Gebiß *nt*.

denude [dɪ'nju:d] *vt* entblößen.

deny [dɪ'naɪ] *vt* leugnen; *rumour* widersprechen (+ *dat*); *knowledge* verleugnen; *help* abschlagen; **to — o.s. sth** sich etw versagen.

deodorant [diː'əudərənt] *n* Desodorans *nt*.

depart [dɪ'pɑːt] *vi* abfahren.

department [dɪ'pɑːtmənt] *n* (*Comm*) Abteilung *f*, Sparte *f*;

(*Univ, Sch*) Fachbereich *m*; (*Pol*) Ministerium *nt*, Ressort *nt*; **—al** [di:pa:'t'mǝntl] *a* Fach-; **—** store Warenhaus *nt*.

departure [di'pa:tʃǝ*] *n* (*of person*) Weggang *m*; (*on journey*) Abreise *f*; (*of train*) Abfahrt *f*; (*of plane*) Abflug *m*; new — Neuerung *f*.

depend [di'pend] *vi*: it —s es kommt darauf an; — on vt abhängen von; *parents etc* angewiesen sein auf (+*acc*); —able *a* zuverlässig; **—ence** *n* Abhängigkeit *f*; **—ent** *n* (*person*) Familienangehörige(r) *mf*; *a* bedingt (*on* durch).

depict [di'pikt] *vt* schildern.

depleted [di'pli:tid] *a* aufgebraucht.

deplorable [di'plɔ:rǝbl] *a* bedauerlich.

deplore [di'plɔ:*] *vt* mißbilligen.

deploy [di'plɔi] *vt* einsetzen.

depopulation ['di:pɒpju'leiʃǝn] *n* Entvölkerung *f*.

ᵈeport [di'pɔ:t] *vt* deportieren; **—ation** [di:pɔ:'teiʃǝn] Abschiebung *f*; **—ation order** Ausweisung *f*; **—ment** Betragen *nt*.

depose [di'pǝuz] *vt* absetzen.

deposit [di'pɒzit] *n* (*in bank*) Guthaben *nt*; (*down payment*) Anzahlung *f*; (*security*) Kaution *f*; (*Chem*) Niederschlag *m*; *vt* (*in bank*) deponieren; (*put down*) niederlegen; — account Sparkonto *nt*; **—or** Kontoinhaber *m*.

depot ['depǝu] *n* Depot *nt*.

deprave [di'preiv] *vt* (*moralisch*) verderben; **—d** *a* verworfen.

depravity [di'præviti] *n* Verworfenheit *f*.

deprecate ['deprikeit] *vt* mißbilligen.

depreciate [di'pri:ʃieit] *vi* im Wert sinken.

depreciation [dipri:ʃi'eiʃǝn] *n* Wertminderung *f*.

depress [di'pres] *vt* (*press down*) niederdrücken; (*in mood*) deprimieren; **—ed** *a person* niedergeschlagen, deprimiert; **—ed** area Notstandsgebiet *nt*; **—ing** *a* deprimierend; **—ion** [di'preʃǝn] (*mood*) Depression *f*; (*in trade*) Wirtschaftskrise *f*; (*hollow*) Vertiefung *f*; (*Met*) Tief(druckgebiet) *nt*.

deprivation [depri'veiʃǝn] *n* Entbehrung *f*, Not *f*.

deprive [di'praiv] *vt* berauben (*of* +*gen*); **—d** *a child* sozial benachteiligt; *area* unterentwickelt.

depth [depθ] *n* Tiefe *f*; in the **—s** of despair in tiefster Verzweiflung; to be out of one's — den Boden unter den Füßen verloren haben; — charge Wasserbombe *f*.

deputation [depju'teiʃǝn] *n* Abordnung *f*.

deputize ['depjutaiz] *vi* vertreten (*for* +*acc*).

deputy ['depjuti] *a* stellvertretend; *n* (*Stell*)vertreter *m*.

derail [di'reil] *vt* entgleisen lassen; to be **—ed** entgleisen; **—ment** Entgleisung *f*.

deranged [di'reindʒd] *a* irr, verrückt.

derby ['da:bi] *n* (*US*) Melone *f*.

derelict ['derilikt] *a* verlassen; *building* baufällig.

deride [di'raid] *vt* auslachen.

derision [di'riʒǝn] *n* Hohn *m*, Spott *m*.

derisory [di'raisǝri] *a* spöttisch.

derivation [deri'veiʃǝn] *n* Ableitung *f*.

derivative [dɪ'rɪvətɪv] *n* Abgeleitete(s) *nt*; *a* abgeleitet.

derive [dɪ'raɪv] *vt* (*get*) gewinnen; (*deduce*) ableiten; *vi* (*come from*) abstammen.

dermatitis [dɜ:mə'taɪtɪs] *n* Hautentzündung *f*.

derogatory [dɪ'rɒgətərɪ] *a* geringschätzig.

derrick ['derɪk] *n* Drehkran *m*.

desalination [di:sælɪ'neɪʃən] *n* Entsalzung *f*.

descend [dɪ'send] *vti* hinuntersteigen; to — from abstammen von; —ant Nachkomme *m*.

descent [dɪ'sent] *n* (*coming down*) Abstieg *m*; (*origin*) Abstammung *f*.

describe [dɪs'kraɪb] *vt* beschreiben.

description [dɪs'krɪpʃən] *n* Beschreibung *f*; (*sort*) Art *f*.

descriptive [dɪs'krɪptɪv] *a* beschreibend; *word* anschaulich.

desecrate ['desɪkreɪt] *vt* schänden.

desegregation [di:segrə'geɪʃən] *n* Aufhebung *f* der Rassentrennung.

desert¹ ['dezət] *n* Wüste *f*.

desert² [dɪ'zɜ:t] *vt* verlassen; (*temporarily*) im Stich lassen; *vi* (*Mil*) desertieren; —er Deserteur *m*; —ion [dɪ'zɜ:ʃən] (*of wife*) böswillige(s) Verlassen *nt*; (*Mil*) Fahnenflucht *f*.

deserve [dɪ'zɜ:v] *vt* verdienen.

deserving [dɪ'zɜ:vɪŋ] *a* person würdig; *action* verdienstvoll.

design [dɪ'zaɪn] *n* (*plan*) Entwurf; (*drawing*) Zeichnung *f*; (*planning*) Gestaltung *f*, Design *nt*; *vt* entwerfen; (*intend*) bezwecken; to have —s on sb/sth es auf jdn/etw abgesehen haben.

designate ['dezɪgneɪt] *vt* bestimmen; ['dezɪgnɪt] *a* designiert.

designation [dezɪg'neɪʃən] *n* Bezeichnung *f*.

designer [dɪ'zaɪnə*] *n* Designer *m*; (*Theat*) Bühnenbildner(in *f*) *m*.

desirability [dɪzaɪərə'bɪlɪtɪ] *n* Erwünschtheit *f*.

desirable [dɪ'zaɪərəbl] *n* wünschenswert; *woman* begehrenswert.

desire [dɪ'zaɪə*] *n* Wunsch *m*, Verlangen *nt*; *vt* (*lust*) begehren, wünschen; (*ask for*) verlangen, wollen.

desirous [dɪ'zaɪərəs] *a* begierig (*of* auf +*acc*).

desist [dɪ'zɪst] *vi* Abstand nehmen, aufhören.

desk [desk] *n* Schreibtisch *m*.

desolate ['desəlɪt] *a* öde; (*sad*) trostlos.

desolation [desə'leɪʃən] *n* Trostlosigkeit *f*.

despair [dɪs'peə*] *n* Verzweiflung *f*; *vi* verzweifeln (*of an* +*dat*).

despatch [dɪs'pætʃ] = **dispatch**.

desperate ['despərɪt] *a* verzweifelt; *situation* hoffnungslos; to be — for sth etw unbedingt brauchen; —ly *ad* verzweifelt.

desperation [despə'reɪʃən] *n* Verzweiflung *f*.

despicable [dɪs'pɪkəbl] *a* abscheulich.

despise [dɪs'paɪz] *vt* verachten.

despite [dɪs'paɪt] *prep* trotz (+*gen*).

despondent [dɪs'pɒndənt] *a* mutlos.

dessert [dɪ'zɜ:t] *n* Nachtisch *m*; —spoon Dessertlöffel *m*.

destination [destɪ'neɪʃən] *n* (*of person*) (Reise)ziel *nt*; (*of goods*) Bestimmungsort *m*.

destine ['destɪn] *vt* (*set apart*) bestimmen.

destiny ['destɪnɪ] n Schicksal nt.

destitute ['destɪtjuːt] a notleidend.

destitution [destɪtjuːʃən] n Elend f.

destroy [dɪs'trɔɪ] vt zerstören; —er (Naut) Zerstörer m.

destruction [dɪs'trʌkʃən] n Zerstörung f.

destructive [dɪs'trʌktɪv] a zerstörend.

detach [dɪ'tætʃ] vt loslösen; —able a abtrennbar; —ed a attitude distanziert, objektiv; house Einzel-; —ment (Mil) Abteilung f, Sonderkommando nt; (fig) Abstand m, Unvoreingenommenheit f.

detail ['diːteɪl] n Einzelheit f, Detail nt; (minor part) unwichtige Einzelheit f; vt (relate) ausführlich berichten; (appoint) abkommandieren; in — ausführlichst, bis ins kleinste.

detain [dɪ'teɪn] vt aufhalten; (imprison) in Haft halten.

detect [dɪ'tekt] vt entdecken; —ion [dɪ'tekʃən] Aufdeckung f; —ive Detektiv m; —ive story Kriminalgeschichte f) m; —or Detektor m.

détente [deɪtɑːnt] n Entspannung f.

detention [dɪ'tenʃən] n Haft f; (Sch) Nachsitzen nt.

deter [dɪ'tɜː*] vt abschrecken.

detergent [dɪ'tɜːdʒənt] n Waschmittel nt; Reinigungsmittel nt.

deteriorate [dɪ'tɪərɪəreɪt] vi sich verschlechtern.

deterioration [dɪtɪərɪə'reɪʃən] n Verschlechterung f.

determination [dɪtɜːmɪ'neɪʃən] n Entschlossenheit f.

determine [dɪ'tɜːmɪn] vt bestimmen; —d a entschlossen.

deterrent [dɪ'terənt] n Ab-

schreckungsmittel nt; a abschreckend.

detest [dɪ'test] vt verabscheuen; —able a abscheulich.

dethrone [diː'θrəʊn] vt entthronen.

detonate ['detəneɪt] vt detonieren.

detonator ['detəneɪtə*] n Sprengkapsel f.

detour ['deɪtuə*] n Umweg m; (on road sign) Umleitung f.

detract [dɪ'trækt] vi schmälern (from acc).

detriment ['detrɪmənt] n: to the — of zum Schaden (+gen); —al [detrɪ'mentl] a schädlich.

deuce [djuːs] n (tennis) Einstand m.

devaluation [dɪvæljʊ'eɪʃən] n Abwertung f.

devalue ['diː'væljuː] vt abwerten.

devastate ['devəsteɪt] vt verwüsten.

devastating ['devəsteɪtɪŋ] a verheerend.

develop [dɪ'veləp] vt entwickeln; resources erschließen; vi sich entwickeln; —er (Phot) Entwickler m; (of land) Bauunternehmer m; —ing a country Entwicklungs-; —ment Entwicklung f.

deviant ['diːvɪənt] a abweichend; Abweichler m.

deviate ['diːvɪeɪt] vi abweichen.

deviation [diːvɪ'eɪʃən] n Abweichung f.

device [dɪ'vaɪs] n Vorrichtung f, Gerät nt.

devil ['devl] n Teufel m; --ish a teuflisch.

devious ['diːvɪəs] a route gewunden; means krumm; person verschlagen.

devise [dɪ'vaɪz] vt entwickeln.

devoid [dɪ'vɔɪd] a: — of ohne, bar (+gen).

devolution [di:vəˈluːʃən] *n* Dezentralisierung *f.*

devote [dɪˈvəut] *vt* widmen (*to dat*); **—d** ergeben zu; **—e** [devəuˈtiː] Anhänger(in *f*) *m*, Verehrer(in *f*) *m.*

devotion [dɪˈvəuʃən] *n* (*piety*) Andacht *f*; (*loyalty*) Ergebenheit *f*, Hingabe *f.*

devour [dɪˈvauə*] *vt* verschlingen.

devout [dɪˈvaut] *a* andächtig.

dew [djuː] *n* Tau *m.*

dexterity [deksˈterɪtɪ] *n* Geschicklichkeit *f.*

diabetes [daɪəˈbiːtiːz] *n* Zuckerkrankheit *f.*

diabetic [daɪəˈbetɪk] *a* zuckerkrank; *n* Diabetiker *m.*

diagnose ['daɪəgnəuz] *vt* (*Med*) diagnostizieren; feststellen.

diagnosis [daɪəgˈnəusɪs] *n* Diagnose *f.*

diagonal [daɪˈægənl] *a* diagonal, schräg; *n* Diagonale *f.*

diagram ['daɪəgræm] *n* Diagramm *nt*, Schaubild *nt.*

dial ['daɪəl] *n* (*Tel*) Wählscheibe *f*; (*of clock*) Zifferblatt *nt*; *vt* wählen; **—ling tone** Amtszeichen *nt.*

dialect ['daɪəlekt] *n* Dialekt *m.*

dialogue ['daɪəlɒg] *n* Gespräch *nt*; (*Liter*) Dialog *m.*

diameter [daɪˈæmɪtə*] *n* Durchmesser *m.*

diametrically [daɪəˈmetrɪkəlɪ] *ad*: **— opposed to** genau entgegengesetzt (+*dat*).

diamond ['daɪəmənd] *n* Diamant *m*; (*Cards*) Karo *nt.*

diaper ['daɪəpə*] *n* (*US*) Windel *f.*

diaphragm ['daɪəfræm] *n* Zwerchfell *nt.*

diarrhoea [daɪəˈriːə] *n* Durchfall *m.*

diary ['daɪərɪ] *n* Taschenkalender *m*; (*account*) Tagebuch *nt.*

dice [daɪs] *n* Würfel *pl*; *vt* (*Cook*) in Würfel schneiden.

dicey ['daɪsɪ] *a* (*col*) riskant.

dichotomy [dɪˈkɒtəmɪ] *n* Kluft *f.*

dictate [dɪkˈteɪt] *vt* diktieren; (*of circumstances*) gebieten; ['dɪkteɪt] *n* Mahnung *f*, Gebot *nt.*

dictation [dɪkˈteɪʃən] *n* Diktat *nt.*

dictator [dɪkˈteɪtə*] *n* Diktator *m.*

dictatorship [dɪkˈteɪtəʃɪp] *n* Diktatur *f.*

diction ['dɪkʃən] *n* Ausdrucksweise *f.*

dictionary ['dɪkʃənrɪ] *n* Wörterbuch *nt.*

didn't ['dɪdənt] = **did not**.

diddle ['dɪdl] *vt* (*col*) übers Ohr hauen.

die [daɪ] *vi* sterben; (*end*) aufhören; **— away** *vi* schwächer werden; **— down** *vi* nachlassen; **— out** *vi* aussterben; (*fig*) nachlassen.

diesel ['diːzəl] *n*: **— engine** Dieselmotor *m.*

diet ['daɪət] *n* Nahrung *f*, Kost *f*; (*special food*) Diät *f*; (*slimming*) Abmagerungskur *f*; *vi* eine Abmagerungskur machen.

differ ['dɪfə*] *vi* sich unterscheiden; (*disagree*) anderer Meinung sein; **we —** wir sind unterschiedlicher Meinung; **—ence** Unterschied *m*; (*disagreement*) (Meinungs)unterschied *m*; **—ent** *a* verschieden; **that's —ent** das ist anders; **—ently** *ad* verschieden, anders; **—ential** [dɪfəˈrenʃəl] (*Aut*) Differentialgetriebe *nt*; (*in wages*) Lohnstufe *f*; **—entiate** [dɪfəˈrenʃɪeɪt] *vti* unterscheiden.

difficult ['dɪfɪkəlt] *a* schwierig; **—y**

Schwierigkeit *f*; with —y nur schwer.

diffidence ['dɪfɪdəns] *n* mangelnde(s) Selbstvertrauen *nt.*

diffident ['dɪfɪdənt] *a* schüchtern.

diffuse [dɪ'fjuːs] *a* langatmig; [dɪ'fjuːz] *vt* verbreiten.

dig [dɪg] *vti irreg hole* graben; *garden* (um)graben; *claws* senken; *n* (*prod*) Stoß *m*; — in *vi* (*Mil*) sich eingraben; (*to food*) sich hermachen über (+*acc*); — in! greif zu!; — up *vt* ausgraben; (*fig*) aufgabeln.

digest [daɪ'dʒest] *vt* (*lit, fig*) verdauen; ['daɪdʒest] *n* Auslese *f*; —ible *a* verdaulich; —ion Verdauung *f.*

digit ['dɪdʒɪt] *n* einstellige Zahl *f*; (*Anat*) Finger *m*; Zehe *f*; —al computer Einzahlencomputer *m.*

dignified ['dɪgnɪfaɪd] *a* würdevoll.

dignify ['dɪgnɪfaɪ] *vt* Würde verleihen (+*dat*).

dignitary ['dɪgnɪtərɪ] *n* Würdenträger *m.*

dignity ['dɪgnɪtɪ] *n* Würde *f.*

digress [daɪ'gres] *vi* abschweifen; —ion [daɪ'greʃən] Abschweifung *f.*

digs [dɪgz] *npl* (*Brit col*) Bude *f.*

dilapidated [dɪ'læpɪdeɪtɪd] *a* baufällig.

dilate [daɪ'leɪt] *vti* (sich) weiten.

dilatory ['dɪlətərɪ] *a* hinhaltend.

dilemma [daɪ'lemə] *n* Dilemma *nt.*

dilettante [dɪlɪ'tæntɪ] *n* Dilettant *m.*

diligence ['dɪlɪdʒəns] *n* Fleiß *m.*

diligent ['dɪlɪdʒənt] *a* fleißig.

dill [dɪl] *n* Dill *m.*

dilly-dally ['dɪlɪdælɪ] *vi* (*col*) herumtrödeln.

dilute [daɪ'luːt] *vt* verdünnen; *a* verdünnt.

dim [dɪm] *a* trübe, matt; (*stupid*) schwer von Begriff; to take a — view of sth etw mißbilligen; *vt* verdunkeln.

dime [daɪm] (*US*) Zehncentstück *nt.*

dimension [dɪ'menʃən] *n* Dimension *f*; —s *pl* Maße *pl.*

diminish [dɪ'mɪnɪʃ] *vti* verringern.

diminutive [dɪ'mɪnjʊtɪv] *a* winzig; *n* Verkleinerungsform *f.*

dimly ['dɪmlɪ] *ad* trübe.

dimple ['dɪmpl] *n* Grübchen *nt.*

dim-witted ['dɪm'wɪtɪd] *a* (*col*) dämlich.

din [dɪn] *n* Getöse *nt.*

dine [daɪn] *vi* speisen; —r Tischgast *m*; (*Rail*) Speisewagen *m.*

dinghy ['dɪŋgɪ] *n* kleine(s) Ruderboot *nt*; Dinghy *nt.*

dingy ['dɪndʒɪ] *a* armselig.

dining car ['daɪnɪŋkɑː*] *n* Speisewagen *m.*

dining room ['daɪnɪŋrʊm] *n* Eßzimmer *nt*; (*in hotel*) Speisezimmer *nt.*

dinner ['dɪnə*] *n* Mittagessen *nt*, Abendessen *nt*; (*public*) Festessen *nt*; — jacket Smoking *m*; — party Tischgesellschaft *f*; — time Tischzeit *f.*

dinosaur ['daɪnəsɔː*] *n* Dinosaurier *m.*

diocese ['daɪəsɪs] *n* Diözese *f*, Sprengel *m.*

dip [dɪp] *n* (*hollow*) Senkung *f*; (*bathe*) kurze(s) Bad(en) *nt*; *vt* eintauchen; (*Aut*) abblenden; *vi* (*slope*) sich senken, abfallen.

diphtheria [dɪf'θɪərɪə] *n* Diphtherie *f.*

diphthong ['dɪfθɒŋ] *n* Diphthong *m.*

diploma [dɪ'pləʊmə] *n* Urkunde *f*, Diplom *nt.*

diplomat ['dɪpləmæt] *n* Diplomat(in *f*) *m*; —ic [dɪplə'mætɪk] *a* diplomatisch; —ic corps diplomatische(s) Korps *nt*.

dipstick ['dɪpstɪk] *n* Ölmeßstab *m*.

dire [daɪə*] *a* schrecklich.

direct [daɪ'rekt] *a* direkt; *vt* leiten; *film* die Regie führen (+*gen*); *jury* anweisen; *(aim)* richten, lenken; *(tell way)* den Weg erklären (+*dat*); *(order)* anweisen; — **current** Gleichstrom *m*; — **hit** Volltreffer *m*; —**ion** [dɪ'rekʃən] Führung *f*, Leitung *f*; *(course)* Richtung *f*; *(Cine)* Regie *f*; —**ions** *pl (for use)* Gebrauchsanleitung *f*; *(orders)* Anweisungen *pl*; —**ional** [dɪ'rekʃənl] *a* Richt-; —**ive** Direktive *f*; —**ly** *ad (in straight line)* gerade, direkt; *(at once)* unmittelbar, sofort; —**or** Direktor *m*, Leiter *m*; *(of film)* Regisseur *m*; —**ory** Adreßbuch *nt*; *(Tel)* Telefonbuch *nt*.

dirt [dɜːt] *n* Schmutz *m*, Dreck *m*; — **road** unbefestigte Straße; —**y** *a* schmutzig, dreckig; gemein; *vt* beschmutzen; — **cheap** *a* spottbillig.

disability [dɪsə'bɪlɪtɪ] *n* Körperbehinderung *f*.

disabled [dɪs'eɪbld] *a* körperbehindert.

disabuse [dɪsə'bjuːz] *vt* befreien.

disadvantage [dɪsəd'vɑːntɪdʒ] *n* Nachteil *m*; —**ous** [dɪsædvɑːn-'teɪdʒəs] *a* ungünstig.

disagree [dɪsə'griː] *vi* nicht übereinstimmen; *(quarrel)* (sich) streiten; *(food)* nicht bekommen *(with dat)*; —**able** *a person* widerlich; *task* unangenehm; —**ment** *(between persons)* Streit *m*; *(between things)* Widerspruch *m*.

disallow [dɪsə'lau] *vt* nicht zulassen.

disappear [dɪsə'pɪə*] *vi* verschwinden; —**ance** Verschwinden *nt*.

disappoint [dɪsə'pɔɪnt] *vt* enttäuschen; —**ing** *a* enttäuschend; —**ment** Enttäuschung *f*.

disapproval [dɪsə'pruːvəl] *n* Mißbilligung *f*.

disapprove [dɪsə'pruːv] *vi* mißbilligen *(of acc)*; **she —s** sie mißbilligt es.

disarm [dɪs'ɑːm] *vt* entwaffnen; *(Pol)* abrüsten; —**ament** Abrüstung *f*.

disaster [dɪ'zɑːstə*] *n* Unglück *nt*; Katastrophe *f*.

disastrous [dɪ'zɑːstrəs] *a* verhängnisvoll.

disband [dɪs'bænd] *vt* auflösen.

disbelief [dɪsbə'liːf] *n* Ungläubigkeit *f*.

disc [dɪsk] *n* Scheibe *f*; *(record)* (Schall)platte *f*.

discard [dɪskɑːd] *vt* ablegen.

disc brake ['dɪsk breɪk] *n* Scheibenbremse *f*.

discern [dɪ'sɜːn] *vt* unterscheiden (können), erkennen; —**ing** *a* scharfsinnig.

discharge [dɪs'tʃɑːdʒ] *vt ship* entladen; *duties* nachkommen (+*dat*); *(dismiss)* entlassen; *gun* abschießen; *n (of ship)* Entladung *f*; ['dɪstʃɑːdʒ] *(Med)* Ausfluß *m*.

disciple [dɪ'saɪpl] *n* Jünger *m*.

disciplinary ['dɪsɪplɪnərɪ] *a* disziplinarisch.

discipline ['dɪsɪplɪn] *n* Disziplin *f*; *vt (train)* schulen; *(punish)* bestrafen.

disc jockey ['dɪskdʒɒkɪ] *n* Diskjockey *m*.

disclaim [dɪs'kleɪm] *vt* nicht anerkennen; *(Pol)* dementieren.

disclose [dɪs'kləʊz] vt enthüllen.
disclosure [dɪs'kləʊʒə*] n Enthüllung f.
disco ['dɪskəʊ] n abbr of **discotheque**.
discoloured [dɪs'kʌləd] a verfärbt, verschossen.
discomfort [dɪs'kʌmfət] n Unbehagen nt; (embarrassment) Verlegenheit ·f.
disconcert [dɪskən'sɜ:t] vt aus der Fassung bringen; (puzzle) verstimmen.
disconnect ['dɪskə'nekt] vt abtrennen.
discontent [dɪskən'tent] n Unzufriedenheit f; **—ed** a unzufrieden.
discontinue ['dɪskən'tɪnju:] vt einstellen; vi aufhören.
discord ['dɪskɔ:d] n Zwietracht f; (noise) Dissonanz f; **—ant** [dɪs'kɔ:dənt] a uneinig; noise mißtönend.
discotheque ['dɪskəʊtek] n Diskothek f.
discount ['dɪskaʊnt] n Rabatt m; [dɪs'kaʊnt] vt außer acht lassen.
discourage [dɪs'kʌrɪdʒ] vt entmutigen; (prevent) abraten, abhalten.
discouraging [dɪs'kʌrɪdʒɪŋ] a entmutigend.
discourteous [dɪs'kɜ:tɪəs] a unhöflich.
discover [dɪs'kʌvə*] vt entdecken; **—y** Entdeckung f.
discredit [dɪs'kredɪt] vt in Verruf bringen.
discreet a, **—ly** ad [dɪskri:t, -lɪ] taktvoll, diskret.
discrepancy [dɪs'krepənsɪ] n Unstimmigkeit f, Diskrepanz f.

discretion [dɪs'kreʃən] n Takt m, Diskretion f; (decision) Gutdünken nt; to leave sth to sb's **—** etw jds Gutdünken überlassen.
discriminate [dɪs'krɪmɪneɪt] vi unterscheiden; to **—** against diskriminieren.
discriminating [dɪs'krɪmɪneɪtɪŋ] a klug; taste anspruchsvoll.
discrimination [dɪskrɪmɪ'neɪʃən] n Urteilsvermögen nt; (pej) Diskriminierung f.
discus ['dɪskəs] n Diskus m.
discuss [dɪs'kʌs] vt diskutieren, besprechen; **—ion** [dɪs'kʌʃən] Diskussion f, Besprechung f.
disdain [dɪs'deɪn] vt verachten, für unter seiner Würde halten; n Verachtung· f; **—ful** a geringschätzig.
disease [dɪ'zi:z] n Krankheit f; **—d** a erkrankt.
disembark [dɪsɪm'ba:k] vt aussteigen lassen; vi von ·Bord gehen.
disenchanted ['dɪsɪn'tʃɑ:ntɪd] a desillusioniert.
disengage [dɪsɪn'geɪdʒ] vt (Aut) auskuppeln.
disentangle ['dɪsɪn'tæŋgl] vt entwirren.
disfavour [dɪs'feɪvə*] n Ungunst f.
disfigure [dɪs'fɪgə*] vt entstellen.
disgrace [dɪs'greɪs] n Schande f; (thing) Schandfleck m; vt Schande bringen über (+acc); (less strong) blamieren; **—ful** a schändlich, unerhört; it's **—ful** es ist eine Schande.
disgruntled [dɪs'grʌntld] a verärgert.
disguise [dɪs'gaɪz] vt verkleiden; feelings verhehlen; voice ver-

stellen; n Verkleidung f; in — verkleidet, maskiert.

disgust [dɪs'gʌst] n Abscheu f; vt anwidern; —ing a abscheulich; (terrible) gemein.

dish [dɪʃ] n Schüssel f; (food) Gericht nt; — up vt auftischen; —cloth Spüllappen m.

dishearten [dɪs'hɑ:tn] vt entmutigen.

dishevelled [dɪ'ʃevəld] a hair zerzaust; clothing ungepflegt.

dishonest [dɪs'ɒnɪst] a unehrlich; —y Unehrlichkeit f.

dishonour [dɪs'ɒnə*] n Unehre f; vt cheque nicht einlösen; —able a unehrenhaft.

dishwasher ['dɪʃwɒʃə*] n Geschirrspülmaschine f.

disillusion [dɪsɪ'lu:ʒən] vt enttäuschen, desillusionieren.

disinfect [dɪsɪn'fekt] vt desinfizieren; —ant Desinfektionsmittel nt.

disingenuous [dɪsɪn'dʒenjuəs] a unehrlich.

disinherit ['dɪsɪn'herɪt] vt enterben.

disintegrate [dɪs'ɪntɪgreɪt] vi sich auflösen.

disinterested [dɪs'ɪntrɪstɪd] a uneigennützig; (col) uninteressiert.

disjointed [dɪs'dʒɔɪntɪd] a unzusammenhängend.

disk [dɪsk] n = disc.

dislike [dɪs'laɪk] n Abneigung f; vt nicht leiden können.

dislocate ['dɪsləʊkeɪt] vt auskugeln; (upset) in Verwirrung bringen.

dislodge [dɪs'lɒdʒ] vt verschieben; (Mil) aus der Stellung werfen.

disloyal ['dɪs'lɔɪəl] a treulos.

dismal ['dɪzməl] a trostlos, trübe.

dismantle [dɪs'mæntl] vt demontieren.

dismay [dɪs'meɪ] n Bestürzung f; vt bestürzen.

dismiss [dɪs'mɪs] vt employee entlassen; idea von sich weisen; (send away) wegschicken; (Jur) complaint abweisen; —al Entlassung f.

disobedience [dɪsə'bi:dɪəns] n Ungehorsam m.

disobedient [dɪsə'bi:dɪənt] a ungehorsam.

disobey ['dɪsə'beɪ] vt nicht gehorchen (+dat).

disorder [dɪs'ɔ:də*] n (confusion) Verwirrung f; (commotion) Aufruhr m; (Med) Erkrankung f.

disorderly [dɪs'ɔ:dəlɪ] a (untidy) unordentlich; (unruly) ordnungswidrig.

disorganized [dɪs'ɔ:gənaɪzd] a unordentlich.

disown [dɪs'əʊn] vt son verstoßen; I — you ich will nichts mehr mit dir zu tun haben.

disparaging [dɪs'pærɪdʒɪŋ] a geringschätzig.

disparity [dɪs'pærɪtɪ] n Verschiedenheit f.

dispassionate [dɪs'pæʃnɪt] a gelassen, unparteiisch.

dispatch [dɪs'pætʃ] vt goods abschicken, abfertigen; n Absendung f; (esp Mil) Meldung f.

dispel [dɪs'pel] vt zerstreuen.

dispensable [dɪs'pensəbl] a entbehrlich.

dispensary [dɪs'pensərɪ] n Apotheke f.

dispensation [dɪspen'seɪʃən] n (Eccl) Befreiung f.

dispense [dɪs'pens]: — with vt verzichten auf (+acc); —r (container) Spender m.

dispensing [dɪs'pensɪŋ] a: — chemist Apotheker m.

dispersal [dɪs'pɜ:səl] n Zerstreuung f.

disperse [dɪs'pɜ:s] vt zerstreuen; vi sich verteilen.

dispirited [dɪs'pɪrɪtɪd] a niedergeschlagen.

displace [dɪs'pleɪs] vt verschieben; —d a: — person Verschleppte(r) mf.

display [dɪs'pleɪ] n (of goods) Auslage f; (of feeling) Zurschaustellung f; (Mil) Entfaltung f; vt zeigen, entfalten.

displease [dɪs'pli:z] vt mißfallen (+dat).

displeasure [dɪs'pleʒə*] n Mißfallen nt.

disposable [dɪs'pəʊzəbl] a container etc Wegwerf-.

disposal [dɪs'pəʊzəl] n (of property) Verkauf m; (throwing away) Beseitigung f; to be at one's — einem zur Verfügung stehen.

dispose [dɪs'pəʊz]: — of vt los-werden.

disposed [dɪs'pəʊzd] a geneigt.

disposition [dɪspə'zɪʃən] n Wesen nt, Natur f.

disproportionate [dɪsprə'pɔ:ʃnɪt] a unverhältnismäßig.

disprove [dɪs'pru:v] vt widerlegen.

dispute [dɪs'pju:t] n Streit m; vt bestreiten.

disqualification [dɪskwɒlɪfɪ'keɪʃən] n Disqualifizierung f.

disqualify [dɪs'kwɒlɪfaɪ] vt disqualifizieren.

disquiet [dɪs'kwaɪət] n Unruhe f.

disregard [dɪsrɪ'gɑ:d] vt nicht (be)achten.

disreputable [dɪs'repjʊtəbl] a verrufen.

disrepute ['dɪsrɪ'pju:t] n Verruf m.

disrespectful [dɪsrɪs'pektfʊl] a respektlos.

disrupt [dɪs'rʌpt] vt stören; programme unterbrechen; —ion [dɪs'rʌpʃən] n Störung f, Unterbrechung f.

dissatisfaction ['dɪssætɪs'fækʃən] n Unzufriedenheit f.

dissatisfied ['dɪs'sætɪsfaɪd] a unzufrieden.

dissect [dɪ'sekt] vt zerlegen, sezieren.

disseminate [dɪ'semɪneɪt] vt verbreiten.

dissent [dɪ'sent] n abweichende Meinung f; vi nicht übereinstimmen.

dissident ['dɪsɪdənt] a andersdenkend; n Dissident m.

dissimilar ['dɪ'sɪmɪlə*] a unähnlich (to dat.).

dissipate ['dɪsɪpeɪt] vt (waste) verschwenden; (scatter) zerstreuen; —d a ausschweifend.

dissipation [dɪsɪ'peɪʃən] n Ausschweifung f.

dissociate [dɪ'səʊʃɪeɪt] vt trennen.

dissolute ['dɪsəlu:t] a liederlich.

dissolve [dɪ'zɒlv] vt auflösen; vi sich auflösen.

dissuade [dɪ'sweɪd] vt abraten (+dat.).

distance ['dɪstəns] n Entfernung f; in the — in der Ferne.

distant ['dɪstənt] a entfernt, fern; (with time) fern; (formal) distanziert.

distaste [dɪs'teɪst] n Abneigung f; —ful a widerlich.

distemper [dɪs'tempə*] n (paint) Temperafarbe f; (Med) Staupe f.

distend [dɪs'tend] vti (sich) ausdehnen.

distil [dɪs'tɪl] vt destillieren ; —lery Brennerei f.

distinct [dɪs'tɪŋkt] a (separate) getrennt ; (clear) klar, deutlich ; —ion [dɪs'tɪŋkʃən] Unterscheidung f; (eminence) Berühmtheit f; (in exam) Auszeichnung f; —ive a bezeichnend ; —ly ad deutlich.

distinguish [dɪs'tɪŋgwɪʃ] vt unterscheiden ; —ed a (eminent) berühmt ; —ing a unterscheidend, bezeichnend.

distort [dɪs'tɔːt] vt verdrehen ; (misrepresent) entstellen ; —ion [dɪs'tɔːʃən] Verzerrung f.

distract [dɪs'trækt] vt ablenken ; (bewilder) verwirren ; —ing a verwirrend ; —ion [dɪs'trækʃən] Zerstreutheit f; (distress) Raserei f; (diversion) Zerstreuung f.

distraught [dɪs'trɔːt] a bestürzt.

distress [dɪs'tres] n Not f; (suffering) Qual f; vt quälen ; —ing a erschütternd ; — signal Notsignal nt.

distribute [dɪs'trɪbjuːt] vt verteilen.

distribution [dɪstrɪ'bjuːʃən] n Verteilung f.

distributor [dɪs'trɪbjʊtə*] n Verteiler m.

district [dɪstrɪkt] n (of country) Kreis m; (of town) Bezirk m; — attorney (US) Oberstaatsanwalt m; — nurse (Brit) Kreiskrankenschwester f.

distrust [dɪs'trʌst] n Mißtrauen nt; vt mißtrauen (+ dat).

disturb [dɪs'tɜːb] vt stören ; (agitate) erregen ; —ance Störung f; —ing a beunruhigend.

disuse ['dɪs'juːs] n Nichtgebrauch m; to fall into — außer Gebrauch kommen.

disused ['dɪs'juːzd] a aufgegeben, außer Gebrauch.

ditch [dɪtʃ] n Graben m; vt im Stich lassen.

dither ['dɪðə*] vi verdattert sein.

ditto ['dɪtəu] n dito, ebenfalls.

divan [dɪ'væn] n Liegesofa nt.

dive [daɪv] n (into water) Kopfsprung m; (Aviat) Sturzflug m; vi tauchen ; —r Taucher m.

diverge [daɪ'vɜːdʒ] vi auseinandergehen.

diverse [daɪ'vɜːs] a verschieden.

diversification [daɪvɜːsɪfɪ'keɪʃən] n Verzweigung f.

diversify [daɪ'vɜːsɪfaɪ] vt (ver)ändern ; vi variieren.

diversion [daɪ'vɜːʃən] n Ablenkung f; (traffic) Umleitung f.

diversity [daɪ'vɜːsɪtɪ] n Verschiedenheit f; (variety) Mannigfaltigkeit f.

divert [daɪ'vɜːt] vt ablenken ; traffic umleiten.

divide [dɪ'vaɪd] vt teilen ; vi sich teilen.

dividend ['dɪvɪdend] n Dividende f; (fig) Gewinn m.

divine [dɪ'vaɪn] a göttlich ; vt erraten.

diving board ['daɪvɪŋbɔːd] n Sprungbrett nt.

divinity [dɪ'vɪnɪtɪ] n Gottheit f, Gott m; (subject) Religion f.

divisible [dɪ'vɪzəbl] a teilbar.

division [dɪ'vɪʒən] n Teilung f; (Math) Division f, Teilung f; (Mil) Division f; (part) Teil m, Abteilung f; (in opinion) Uneinigkeit f.

divorce [dɪ'vɔːs] n (Ehe)scheidung f; vt scheiden ; —d a geschieden ; —e [dɪvɔː'siː] Geschiedene(r) mf.

divulge [daɪ'vʌldʒ] vt preisgeben.

dizziness ['dɪzɪnəs] n Schwindelgefühl nt.

dizzy ['dızı] a schwindlig.

do [du:] irreg vt tun, machen; vi (proceed) vorangehen; (be suitable) passen; (be enough) genügen; n (party) Party f; how — you —? guten Tag! etc.

docile ['dəusaıl] a gefügig; dog gutmütig.

dock [dɒk] n Dock nt; (Jur) Anklagebank f; vi ins Dock gehen; —er Hafenarbeiter m.

docket ['dɒkıt] n Inhaltsvermerk m.

dockyard ['dɒkja:d] n Werft f.

doctor ['dɒktə*] n Arzt m, Ärztin f; (Univ) Doktor m.

doctrinaire [dɒktrı'nɛə*] a doktrinär.

doctrine ['dɒktrın] n Doktrin f.

document ['dɒkjumənt] n Dokument nt; —ary [dɒkju'mentərı] Dokumentarbericht m; (film) Dokumentarfilm m; a dokumentarisch; —ation [dɒkjumen'teıʃən] dokumentarische(r) Nachweis m.

doddering ['dɒdərıŋ], **doddery** ['dɒdərı] a zittrig.

dodge [dɒdʒ] n Kniff m; vt umgehen; ausweichen (+dat); —m Boxauto nt.

dodo ['dəudəu] n Dronte f: as dead as the — von Anno dazumal.

dog [dɒg] n Hund m; — biscuit Hundekuchen m; — collar Hundehalsband nt; (Eccl) Kragen m des Geistlichen; —eared a mit Eselsohren; —fish Hundsfisch m; — food Hundefutter nt.

dogged ['dɒgıd] a hartnäckig.

dogma ['dɒgmə] n Dogma nt; —tic [dɒg'mætık] a dogmatisch.

doings ['du:ıŋz] npl (activities) Treiben nt.

do-it-yourself ['du:ıtjə'self] n Do-it-yourself nt; a zum Selbermachen.

doldrums ['dɒldrəmz] npl: to be in the — Flaute haben; (person) deprimiert sein.

dole [dəul] n (Brit) Stempelgeld nt; to be on the — stempeln gehen; — out vt ausgeben, austeilen.

doleful ['dəulful] a traurig.

doll [dɒl] n Puppe f; vt: — o.s. up sich aufdonnern.

dollar ['dɒlə*] n Dollar m.

dollop ['dɒləp] n Brocken m.

dolphin ['dɒlfın] n Delphin m, Tümmler m.

domain [dəu'meın] n Sphäre f, Bereich m.

dome [dəum] n Kuppel f.

domestic [də'mestık] a häuslich; (within country) Innen-, Binnen-; animal Haus-; —ated a person häuslich; animal zahm.

domicile ['dɒmısaıl] n (ständiger) Wohnsitz m.

dominant ['dɒmınənt] a vorherrschend.

dominate ['dɒmıneıt] vt beherrschen.

domination [dɒmı'neıʃən] n (Vor)herrschaft f.

domineering [dɒmı'nıərıŋ] a herrisch, überheblich.

dominion [də'mınıən] n (rule) Regierungsgewalt f; (land) Staatsgebiet nt mit Selbstverwaltung.

dominoes ['dɒmınəuz] n Domino(spiel) nt.

don [dɒn] n akademische(r) Lehrer m.

donate [dəu'neıt] vt (blood, little money) spenden; (lot of money) stiften.

donation [dəu'neıʃən] n Spende f.

donkey ['dɒŋkı] n Esel m.

donor ['dəunə*] n Spender m.

don't [dəunt] = do not.

doom [du:m] n böse(s) Geschick nt; (downfall) Verderben nt; vt: to be —ed zum Untergang verurteilt sein.

door [dɔ:*] n Tür f; —bell Türklingel f; —handle Türklinke f; —man Türsteher m; —mat Fußmatte f; —step Türstufe f; —way Türöffnung f.

dope [dəup] n (drug) Aufputschmittel nt.

dopey ['dəupi] a (col) bekloppt.

dormant ['dɔ:mənt] a schlafend, latent.

dormitory ['dɔ:mitri] n Schlafsaal m.

dormouse ['dɔ:maus] n Haselmaus f.

dosage ['dəusidʒ] n Dosierung f.

dose [dəus] n Dosis f; vt dosieren.

dossier ['dɔsiei] n Dossier m, Aktenbündel nt.

dot [dɔt] n Punkt m; on the — pünktlich.

dote [dəut]: — on vt vernarrt sein in (+acc).

double ['dʌbl] a, ad doppelt; n Doppelgänger m; vt verdoppeln; (fold) zusammenfalten; vi (in amount) sich verdoppeln; at the — im Laufschritt; —s (tennis) Doppel nt; — bass Kontrabaß m; — bed Doppelbett nt; —breasted a zweireihig; —cross n Betrug m; vt hintergehen; —decker Doppeldecker m; — room Doppelzimmer nt.

doubly ['dʌbli] ad doppelt.

doubt [daut] n Zweifel m; vi zweifeln; vt bezweifeln; without — zweifellos; —ful a zweifelhaft, fraglich; —less ad ohne Zweifel, sicherlich.

dough [dəu] n Teig m; —nut Krapfen m, Pfannkuchen m.

dove [dʌv] n Taube f; —tail n Schwalbenschwanz m, Zinke f; vt verzahnen, verzinken.

dowdy ['daudi] a unmodern, schlampig.

down [daun] n (fluff) Flaum m; (hill) Hügel m; ad unten; (motion) herunter; hinunter; prep he came — the street er kam die Straße herunter; to go — the street die Straße hinuntergehen; he lives — the street er wohnt unten an der Straße; vt niederschlagen; — with X! nieder mit X!; —and-out a abgerissen; n Tramp m; —at-heel a schäbig; —cast a niedergeschlagen; —fall n Sturz m; —hearted a niedergeschlagen, mutlos; —hill ad bergab; —pour Platzregen m; —right a völlig, ausgesprochen; —stairs ad unten; (motion) nach unten; a untere(r, s); —stream ad flußabwärts —town ad in die/der Innenstadt; a (US) im Geschäftsviertel, City- —ward a sinkend, Abwärts- —wards ad abwärts, nach unten.

dowry ['dauri] n Mitgift f.

doze [dəuz] vi dösen; n Schläfchen nt, Nickerchen nt.

dozen ['dʌzn] n Dutzend nt.

drab [dræb] a düster, eintönig.

draft [dru:ft] n Skizze f, Entwurf m; (Fin) Wechsel m; (US Mil) Einberufung f; vt skizzieren.

drag [dræg] vt schleifen, schleppen; river mit einem Schleppnetz absuchen; vi sich (dahin)schleppen; n (bore) etwas Blödes; (Theat) Klotz m am Bein; in — als Tunte; — on vi sich in die Länge ziehen.

dragon ['drægən] n Drache m;
—fly Libelle f.

drain [dreɪn] n (lit) Abfluß m;
(ditch) Abflußgraben m; (fig:
burden) Belastung f; vt
(exhaust) erschöpfen; vi (of water)
abfließen; —age Kanalisation f;
—pipe Abflußrohr nt.

drama ['drɑːmə] n (lit, fig) Drama
nt; —tic [drə'mætɪk] a dramatisch;
—tist Dramatiker m.

drape [dreɪp] vt drapieren; npl: —s
(US) Vorhänge pl; —r Tuch-
händler m.

drastic ['dræstɪk] a drastisch.

draught [drɑːft] n Zug m; (Naut)
Tiefgang m; —s Damespiel nt;
(beer) on — vom Faß; —board
Zeichenbrett nt; —sman tech-
nische(r) Zeichner m; —y a zugig.

draw [drɔː] irreg vt ziehen; crowd
anlocken; picture zeichnen; money
abheben; water schöpfen; vi
(Sport) unentschieden spielen; n
(Sport) Unentschieden nt; (lottery)
Ziehung f; to — to a close (speech)
zu Ende kommen; (year) zu Ende
gehen; — out vi (train) ausfahren;
(lengthen) sich hinziehen; vt
money abheben; — up vi (stop)
halten; vt document aufsetzen; —
back (disadvantage) Nachteil m;
(obstacle) Haken m; —bridge Zug-
brücke f; —er Schublade f; —ing
Zeichnung f; Zeichnen nt; —ing
pin Reißzwecke f; —ing room
Salon·m.

drawl [drɔːl] n schleppende Sprechweise f; vi gedehnt sprechen.

drawn [drɔːn] a game unentschieden; face besorgt.

dread [dred] n Furcht f, Grauen nt;
vt fürchten; sich grauen vor
(+dat); —ful a furchtbar.

dream [driːm] n Traum m; (fancy)
Wunschtraum m; vti irreg träumen
(about von); a house etc Traum-;
—er Träumer m; — world Traum-
welt f; —y a verträumt.

dreary ['drɪərɪ] a trostlos, öde.

dredge [dredʒ] vt ausbaggern;
(with flour etc) mit Mehl etc
bestreuen; —r Baggerschiff nt;
(for flour etc) (Mehl etc)streuer m.

dregs [dregz] npl Bodensatz m;
(fig) Abschaum m.

drench [drentʃ] vt durchnässen.

dress [dres] n Kleidung f; (garment) Kleid nt; vt anziehen; (Med)
verbinden; (Agr) düngen; food
anrichten; to get — ed sich
anziehen; — up vi sich fein
machen; — circle erste(r) Rang m;
—er (furniture) Anrichte f,
Geschirrschrank m; she's a smart
—er sie zieht sich elegant an; —ing
(Med) Verband m; (Cook) Soße f;
—ing gown Morgenrock m; —ing
room (Theat) Garderobe f; (Sport)
Umkleideraum m; —ing table
Toilettentisch m; —maker Schnei-
derin f; —making Schneidern nt;
— rehearsal Generalprobe f; —
shirt Frackhemd nt.

dribble ['drɪbl] vi tröpfeln; vt
sabbern.

drift [drɪft] n Trift f, Strömung f;
(snow—) Schneewehe f; (fig)
Richtung f; vi getrieben werden;
(aimlessly) sich treiben lassen;
—wood Treibholz nt.

drill [drɪl] n Bohrer m; (Mil) Drill
m; vt bohren; (Mil) ausbilden; vi
(Mil) exerzieren; bohren (for
nach); —ing Bohren nt; (hole)
Bohrloch nt; (Mil) Exerzieren nt.

drink [drɪŋk] n Getränk nt; (spirits)
Drink m; vti irreg trinken; —able

a trinkbar; —er Trinker *m*; —ing water Trinkwasser *nt*.

drip [drɪp] *n* Tropfen *m*; (*dripping*) Tröpfeln *nt*; *vi* tropfen; —dry *a* bügelfrei; —ping Bratenfett *nt*; —ping wet *a* triefend.

drive [draɪv] *n* Fahrt *f*; (*road*) Einfahrt *f*; (*campaign*) Aktion *f*; (*energy*) Schwung *m*, Tatkraft *f*; (*Sport*) Schlag *m*; *irreg vt car* fahren; *animals* treiben; *nail* einschlagen; *ball* schlagen; (*power*) antreiben; (*force*) treiben; *vi* fahren; to — sb mad jdn verrückt machen; what are you driving at? worauf willst du hinaus?; —in *a* Drive-in-.

drivel [ˈdrɪvl] *n* Faselei *f*.

driver [ˈdraɪvə*] *n* Fahrer *m*; —'s license (*US*) Führerschein *m*.

driving [ˈdraɪvɪŋ] *a* rain stürmisch; — instructor Fahrlehrer *m*; — lesson Fahrstunde *f*; — license (*Brit*) Führerschein *m*; — school Fahrschule *f*; — test Fahrprüfung *f*.

drizzle [ˈdrɪzl] *n* Nieselregen *m*; *vi* nieseln.

droll [drəʊl] *a* drollig.

dromedary [ˈdrɒmɪdərɪ] *n* Dromedar *nt*.

drone [drəʊn] *n* (*sound*) Brummen *nt*; (*bee*) Drohne *f*.

drool [druːl] *vi* sabbern.

droop [druːp] *vi* (*schlaff*) herabhängen.

drop [drɒp] *n* (*of liquid*) Tropfen *m*; (*fall*) Fall *m*; *vt* fallen lassen; (*lower*) senken; (*abandon*) fallenlassen; *vi* (*fall*) herunterfallen; — off *vi* (*sleep*) einschlafen; — out *vi* (*withdraw*) ausscheiden; —out Ausgeflippte(r) *mf*, Drop-out *mf*.

dross [drɒs] *n* Unrat *m*.

drought [draʊt] *n* Dürre *f*.

drove [drəʊv] *n* (*crowd*) Herde *f*.

drown [draʊn] *vt* ertränken; *sound* übertönen; *vi* ertrinken.

drowsy [ˈdraʊzɪ] *a* schläfrig.

drudge [drʌdʒ] *n* Kuli *m*; —ry [ˈdrʌdʒərɪ] Plackerei *f*.

drug [drʌg] *n* (*Med*) Arznei *f*; (*narcotic*) Rauschgift *nt*; *vt* betäuben; — addict Rauschgiftsüchtige(r) *mf*; —gist (*US*) Drogist *m*; —store (*US*) Drogerie *f*.

drum [drʌm] *n* Trommel *f*; —mer Trommler *m*.

drunk [drʌŋk] *a* betrunken; *n* Betrunkene(r) *m*; Trinker(in *f*) *m*; —ard Trunkenbold *m*; —en *a* betrunken; —enness Betrunkenheit *f*.

dry [draɪ] *a* trocken; *vt* (ab)trocknen; *vi* trocknen, trocken werden; — up *vi* austrocknen; (*dishes*) abtrocknen; —clean *vt* chemisch reinigen; —cleaning chemische Reinigung *f*; — Trockner *m*; —ness Trockenheit *f*; — rot Hausschwamm *m*.

dual [ˈdjʊəl] *a* doppelt; — carriageway zweispurige Fahrbahn *f*; — nationality doppelte Staatsangehörigkeit *f*; —purpose *a* Mehrzweck-.

dubbed [dʌbd] *a* film synchronisiert.

dubious [ˈdjuːbɪəs] *a* zweifelhaft.

duchess [ˈdʌtʃɪs] *n* Herzogin *f*.

duck [dʌk] *n* Ente *f*; *vt* (ein)tauchen; *vi* sich ducken; —ling Entchen *nt*.

duct [dʌkt] *n* Röhre *f*.

dud [dʌd] *n* Niete *f*; *a* wertlos, miserabel; *cheque* ungedeckt.

due [djuː] *a* fällig; (*fitting*) angemessen; the train is — der

Zug soll ankommen; n Gebühr f; (right) Recht nt; ad south very genau, gerade; — to infolge (+gen), wegen (+gen).

duel ['djʊəl] n Duell nt.

duet [djuː'et] n Duett nt.

duke [djuːk] n Herzog m.

dull [dʌl] a colour, weather trübe; (stupid) schwer von Begriff; (boring) langweilig; vt (soften, weaken) abstumpfen.

duly ['djuːlɪ] ad ordnungsgemäß, richtig; (on time) pünktlich.

dumb [dʌm] a (lit) stumm; (col: stupid) doof, blöde.

dummy ['dʌmɪ] n Schneiderpuppe f; (substitute) Attrappe f; (teat) Schnuller m; a Schein-.

dump [dʌmp] n Abfallhaufen m; (Mil) Stapelplatz m; (col: place) Nest nt; vt abladen, auskippen; —ing (Comm) Schleuderexport m; (of rubbish) Schuttabladen nt.

dumpling ['dʌmplɪŋ] n Kloß m, Knödel m.

dunce [dʌns] n Dummkopf m.

dune [djuːn] n Düne f.

dung [dʌŋ] n Mist m; (Agr) Dünger m.

dungarees [dʌŋgə'riːz] npl Arbeitsanzug m, Arbeitskleidung pl.

dungeon ['dʌndʒən] n Kerker m.

dupe [djuːp] n Gefoppte(r) mf; vt hintergehen, anführen.

duplicate ['djuːplɪkɪt] a doppelt; n Duplikat nt; ['djuːplɪkeɪt] vt verdoppeln; (make copies) kopieren; **in** — in doppelter Ausführung.

duplicator ['djuːplɪkeɪtə*] n Vervielfältigungsapparat m.

durability [djʊərə'bɪlɪtɪ] n Haltbarkeit f.

durable ['djʊərəbl] a haltbar.

duration [djʊə'reɪʃən] n Dauer f.

during ['djʊərɪŋ] prep während (+gen).

dusk [dʌsk] n Abenddämmerung f.

dust [dʌst] n Staub m; vt abstauben; (sprinkle) bestäuben; **—bin** (Brit) Mülleimer m; **—er** Staubtuch nt; **—man** (Brit) Müllmann m; **—storm** Staubsturm m; **—y** a staubig.

dutiable ['djuːtɪəbl] a zollpflichtig.

duty ['djuːtɪ] n Pflicht f; (job) Aufgabe f; (tax) Einfuhrzoll m; on — im Dienst, diensthabend; **—free** a zollfrei; **—free articles** zollfreie Waren pl.

dwarf [dwɔːf] n Zwerg m.

dwell [dwel] vi irreg wohnen; — on vt verweilen bei; **—ing** Wohnung f.

dwindle ['dwɪndl] vi schwinden.

dye [daɪ] n Farbstoff m; vt färben.

dying ['daɪŋ] a person sterbend; moments letzt.

dynamic [daɪ'næmɪk] a dynamisch; **—s** Dynamik f.

dynamite ['daɪnəmaɪt] n Dynamit nt.

dynamo ['daɪnəməʊ] n Dynamo m.

dynasty ['dɪnəstɪ] n Dynastie f.

dysentery ['dɪsntrɪ] n Ruhr f.

dyspepsia [dɪs'pepsɪə] n Verdauungsstörung f.

E

E, e [i:] *n* E *nt*, e *nt*.

each [i:tʃ] *a* jeder/jede/jedes; *pron* (ein) jeder/(eine) jede/(ein) jedes; — *other* einander, sich.

eager *a*, **—ly** *ad* ['i:ga*, -lɪ] eifrig; **—ness** Eifer *m*; Ungeduld *f*.

eagle ['i:gl] *n* Adler *m*.

ear [ɪə*] *n* Ohr *nt*; (*of corn*) Ähre *f*; **—ache** Ohrenschmerzen *pl*; **—drum** Trommelfell *nt*.

earl [ɜ:l] *n* Graf *m*.

early ['ɜ:lɪ] *a, ad* früh; you're — du bist früh dran.

earmark ['ɪəmɑ:k] *vt* vorsehen.

earn [ɜ:n] *vt* verdienen.

earnest ['ɜ:nɪst] *a* ernst; **in** — im Ernst.

earnings ['ɜ:nɪŋz] *npl* Verdienst *m*.

earphones ['ɪəfəʊnz] *npl* Kopfhörer *pl*.

earplug ['ɪəplʌg] *n* Ohropax ® *nt*.

earring ['ɪərɪŋ] *n* Ohrring *m*.

earshot ['ɪəʃɒt] *n* Hörweite *f*.

earth [ɜ:θ] *n* Erde *f*; (*Elec*) Erdung *f*; *vt* erden; **—enware** Steingut *nt*; **—quake** Erdbeben *nt*.

earthy ['ɜ:θɪ] *a* roh; (*sensual*) sinnlich.

earwig ['ɪəwɪg] *n* Ohrwurm *m*.

ease [i:z] *n* (*simplicity*) Leichtigkeit *f*; (*social*) Ungezwungenheit *f*; *vt pain* lindern; *burden* erleichtern; **at** — ungezwungen; (*Mil*) rührt euch!; **to feel at** — sich wohl fühlen; — *off or up vi* nachlassen.

easel ['i:zl] *n* Staffelei *f*.

easily ['i:zɪlɪ] *ad* leicht.

east [i:st] *n* Osten *m*; *a* östlich; *ad* nach Osten.

Easter ['i:stə*] *n* Ostern *nt*.

eastern ['i:stən] *a* östlich; orientalisch.

eastward(s) ['i:stwəd(z)] *ad* ostwärts.

easy ['i:zɪ] *a task* einfach; *life* bequem; *manner* ungezwungen, natürlich; *ad* leicht.

eat [i:t] *vt irreg* essen; (*animals*) fressen; (*destroy*) (zer)fressen; — *away vt* (*corrode*) zerfressen; **—able** *a* genießbar.

eaves [i:vz] *npl* (überstehender) Dachrand *m*.

eavesdrop ['i:vzdrɒp] *vi* horchen, lauschen; **to** — **on sb** jdn belauschen.

ebb [eb] *n* Ebbe *f*; *vi* ebben.

ebony ['ebənɪ] *n* Ebenholz *nt*.

ebullient [ɪ'bʌlɪənt] *a* sprudelnd, temperamentvoll.

eccentric [ɪk'sentrɪk] *a* exzentrisch, überspannt; *n* exzentrische(r) Mensch *m*.

ecclesiastical [ɪkli:zɪ'æstɪkəl] *a* kirchlich, geistlich.

echo ['ekəʊ] *n* Echo *nt*; *vt* zurückwerfen; (*fig*) nachbeten; *vi* widerhallen.

eclipse [ɪ'klɪps] *n* Verfinsterung *f*, Finsternis *f*; *vt* verfinstern.

ecology [ɪ'kɒlədʒɪ] *n* Ökologie *f*.

economic [i:kə'nɒmɪk] *a* (volks)wirtschaftlich, ökonomisch; **—al** *a* wirtschaftlich; *person* sparsam; **—s** Volkswirtschaft *f*.

economist [ɪ'kɒnəmɪst] *n* Volkswirt(schaftler) *m*.

economize [ɪ'kɒnəmaɪz] vi sparen
(on an + dat.)

economy [ɪ'kɒnəmɪ] n (thrift)
Sparsamkeit f; (of country) Wirtschaft f.

ecstasy ['ekstəsɪ] n Ekstase f.

ecstatic [eks'tætɪk] a hingerissen.

ecumenical [iːkjʊ'menɪkəl] a
ökumenisch.

eczema ['eksɪmə] n Ekzem nt.

Eden ['iːdn] n (Garten m) Eden nt.

edge [edʒ] n Rand m; (of knife)
Schneide f; on — nervös; (nerves)
überreizt.

edging ['edʒɪŋ] n Einfassung f.

edgy ['edʒɪ] a nervös.

edible ['edɪbl] a eßbar.

edict ['iːdɪkt] n Erlaß m.

edifice ['edɪfɪs] n Gebäude nt.

edit ['edɪt] vt edieren, redigieren;
—ion [ɪ'dɪʃən] Ausgabe f; —or (of
newspaper) Redakteur m; (of
book) Lektor m; —orial [edɪ'tɔːrɪəl]
a Redaktions-; n Leitartikel m.

educate ['edjukeɪt] vt erziehen,
(aus)bilden.

education [edju'keɪʃən] n (teaching) Unterricht m; (system) Schulwesen nt; (schooling) Erziehung f;
Bildung f; —al a pädagogisch.

eel [iːl] n Aal m.

eerie ['ɪərɪ] a unheimlich.

efface [ɪ'feɪs] vt auslöschen.

effect [ɪ'fekt] n Wirkung f; vt
bewirken; in — in der Tat; —s pl
(sound, visual) Effekte pl; —ive a
wirksam, effektiv.

effeminate [ɪ'femɪnɪt] a weibisch.

effervescent [efə'vesnt] a (lit, fig)
sprudelnd.

efficiency [ɪ'fɪʃənsɪ] n Leistungsfähigkeit f.

efficient a, —ly ad [ɪ'fɪʃənt, -lɪ]

tüchtig; (Tech) leistungsfähig;
method wirksam.

effigy ['efɪdʒɪ] n Abbild nt.

effort ['efət] n Anstrengung f; to
make an — sich anstrengen; —less
a mühelos.

effrontery [ɪ'frʌntərɪ] n Unverfrorenheit f.

egalitarian [ɪgælɪ'tɛərɪən] a Gleichheits-, egalitär.

egg [eg] n Ei nt; — on vt
anstacheln; —cup Eierbecher m;
—plant Aubergine f; —shell
Eierschale f.

ego ['iːgəu] n Ich nt, Selbst nt.

egotism ['egəutɪzəm] n Ichbezogenheit f.

egotist ['egəutɪst] n Egozentriker m.

eiderdown ['aɪdədaun] n Daunendecke f.

eight [eɪt] num acht; —een num
achtzehn; —h [eɪtθ] a achte(r,s);
n Achtel nt; —y num achtzig.

either ['aɪðə*] cj — ... oder; pron
— of the two eine(r,s)
von beiden; I don't want — ich will
keins von beiden; a on — side auf
beiden Seiten; ad I don't — ich
auch nicht.

eject [ɪ'dʒekt] vt ausstoßen, vertreiben; —or seat Schleudersitz m.

elaborate [ɪ'læbərɪt] a sorgfältig
ausgearbeitet, ausführlich;
[ɪ'læbəreɪt] vt sorgfältig ausarbeiten; —ly ad genau, ausführlich.

elaboration [ɪlæbə'reɪʃən] n Ausarbeitung f.

elapse [ɪ'læps] vi vergehen.

elastic [ɪ'læstɪk] n Gummiband nt;
a elastisch; — band Gummiband nt.

elated [ɪ'leɪtɪd] a froh, in gehobener
Stimmung.

elation [ɪ'leɪʃən] n gehobene Stimmung f.

elbow ['elbəʊ] n Ellbogen m.

elder ['eldə*] a älter; n Ältere(r) mf; —ly a ältere(r,s).

elect [ɪ'lekt] vt wählen; a zukünftig; —ion Wahl f; —ioneering [ɪlekʃə'nɪərɪŋ] Wahlpropaganda f; —or Wähler m; —oral a Wahl-; —orate Wähler pl, Wählerschaft f.

electric [ɪ'lektrɪk] a elektrisch, Elektro-; —al a elektrisch; — blanket Heizdecke f; — chair elektrische(r) Stuhl m; — cooker Elektroherd m; — current elektrische(r) Strom m; — fire elektrische(r) Heizofen m; —ian [ɪlek'trɪʃən] Elektriker m; —ity [ɪlek'trɪsɪtɪ] Elektrizität f.

electrification [ɪlektrɪfɪ'keɪʃən] n Elektrifizierung f.

electrify [ɪ'lektrɪfaɪ] vt elektrifizieren; (fig) elektrisieren.

electro- [ɪ'lektrəʊ] pref Elektro-.

electrocute [ɪ'lektrəʊkjuːt] vt elektrisieren; durch elektrischen Strom töten.

electrode [ɪ'lektrəʊd] n Elektrode f.

electron [ɪ'lektrɒn] n Elektron nt.

electronic [ɪlek'trɒnɪk] a elektronisch, Elektronen-; —s Elektronik f.

elegance ['elɪgəns] n Eleganz f.

elegant ['elɪgənt] a elegant.

elegy ['elɪdʒɪ] n Elegie f.

element ['elɪmənt] n Element nt; (fig) Körnchen nt; —ary [elɪ'mentərɪ] a einfach; (primary) grundlegend, Anfangs-.

elephant ['elɪfənt] n Elefant m.

elevate ['elɪveɪt] vt emporheben.

elevation [elɪ'veɪʃən] n (height) Erhebung f; (of style) Niveau nt; (Archit) (Quer)schnitt m.

elevator ['elɪveɪtə*] n (US) Fahrstuhl m, Aufzug m.

eleven [ɪ'levn] num elf; n (team) Elf f.

elf [elf] n Elfe f.

elicit [ɪ'lɪsɪt] vt herausbekommen.

eligible ['elɪdʒəbl] a wählbar; he's not — er kommt nicht in Frage; to be — for a pension/competition pensions-/teilnahmeberechtigt sein; — bachelor gute Partie f.

eliminate [ɪ'lɪmɪneɪt] vt ausschalten; beseitigen.

elimination [ɪlɪmɪ'neɪʃən] n Ausschaltung f; Beseitigung f.

elite [eɪ'liːt] n Elite f.

elm [elm] n Ulme f.

elocution [elə'kjuːʃən] n Sprecherziehung f; (clarity) Artikulation f.

elongated ['iːlɒŋgeɪtɪd] a verlängert.

elope [ɪ'ləʊp] vi entlaufen; —ment Entlaufen nt.

eloquence ['eləkwəns] n Beredsamkeit f.

eloquent a, —ly ad ['eləkwənt, -lɪ] redegewandt.

else [els] ad sonst; —where ad anderswo, woanders; who —? wer sonst?; sb — jd anders; or — sonst.

elucidate [ɪ'luːsɪdeɪt] vt erläutern.

elude [ɪ'luːd] vt entgehen (+dat).

elusive [ɪ'luːsɪv] a schwer faßbar.

emaciated [ɪ'meɪsɪeɪtɪd] a abgezehrt.

emanate ['eməneɪt] vi ausströmen (from aus).

emancipate [ɪ'mænsɪpeɪt] vt emanzipieren; slave freilassen.

emancipation [ɪmænsɪ'peɪʃən] n Emanzipation f; Freilassung f.

embalm [ɪm'bɑːm] vt einbalsamieren.

embankment [ɪmˈbæŋkmənt] n (of river) Uferböschung f; (of road) Straßendamm m.

embargo [ɪmˈbɑ:gəʊ] n Embargo nt.

embark [ɪmˈbɑ:k] vi sich einschiffen; — **on** vt unternehmen; —**ation** [embɑ:ˈkeɪʃən] Einschiffung f.

embarrass [ɪmˈbærəs] vt in Verlegenheit bringen; —**ed** a verlegen; —**ing** a peinlich; —**ment** Verlegenheit f.

embassy [ˈembəsɪ] n Botschaft f.

embed [ɪmˈbed] vt einbetten.

embellish [ɪmˈbelɪʃ] vt verschönern.

embers [ˈembəz] npl Glut(asche) f.

embezzle [ɪmˈbezl] vt unterschlagen; —**ment** Unterschlagung f.

embitter [ɪmˈbɪtə*] vt verbittern.

emblem [ˈembləm] n Emblem nt, Abzeichen nt.

embodiment [ɪmˈbɒdɪmənt] n Verkörperung f.

embody [ɪmˈbɒdɪ] vt ideas verkörpern; new features (in sich) vereinigen.

emboss [ɪmˈbɒs] vt prägen.

embrace [ɪmˈbreɪs] vt umarmen; (include) einschließen; n Umarmung f.

embroider [ɪmˈbrɔɪdə*] vt (be)sticken; story ausschmücken; —**y** Stickerei f.

embryo [ˈembrɪəʊ] n (lit) Embryo m; (fig) Keim m.

emerald [ˈemərəld] n Smaragd m; a smaragdgrün.

emerge [ɪˈmɜ:dʒ] vi auftauchen; (truth) herauskommen; —**nce** Erscheinen nt; —**ncy** n Notfall m; a action Not-; —**ncy exit** Notausgang m.

emery [ˈemərɪ] n: — **paper** Schmirgelpapier nt.

emetic [ɪˈmetɪk] n Brechmittel nt.

emigrant [ˈemɪgrənt] n Auswanderer m, Emigrant m; a Auswanderungs-.

emigrate [ˈemɪgreɪt] vi auswandern, emigrieren.

emigration [emɪˈgreɪʃən] n Auswanderung f, Emigration f.

eminence [ˈemɪnəns] n hohe(r) Rang m; E— Eminenz f.

eminent [ˈemɪnənt] a bedeutend.

emission [ɪˈmɪʃən] n (of gases) Ausströmen nt.

emit [ɪˈmɪt] vt von sich (dat) geben.

emotion [ɪˈməʊʃən] n Emotion f, Gefühl nt; —**al** a person emotional; scene ergreifend; —**ally** ad gefühlsmäßig; behave emotional; sing ergreifend.

emotive [ɪˈməʊtɪv] a gefühlsbetont.

emperor [ˈempərə*] n Kaiser m.

emphasis [ˈemfəsɪs] n (Ling) Betonung f; (fig) Nachdruck m.

emphasize [ˈemfəsaɪz] vt betonen.

emphatic [emˈfætɪk, -əlɪ] nachdrücklich; **to be** — **about sth** etw nachdrücklich betonen.

empire [ˈempaɪə*] n Reich nt.

empirical [emˈpɪrɪkəl] a empirisch.

employ [ɪmˈplɔɪ] vt (hire) anstellen; (use) verwenden; —**ee** [emplɔɪˈi:] Angestellte(r) mf; —**er** Arbeitgeber(in f) m; —**ment** Beschäftigung f; **in** —**ment** beschäftigt.

empress [ˈemprɪs] n Kaiserin f.

emptiness [ˈemptɪnɪs] n Leere f.

empty [ˈemptɪ] a leer; vt contents leeren; container ausleeren; — **handed** a mit leeren Händen.

emu [ˈi:mju:] n Emu m.

emulate [ˈemjʊleɪt] vt nacheifern (+ dat).

enable [ɪ'neɪbl] vt ermöglichen; it —s us to ... das ermöglicht es uns, zu ...

enamel [ɪ'næməl] n Email nt; (of teeth) (Zahn)schmelz m.

enamoured [ɪ'næməd] a verliebt sein (of in +dat).

encase [ɪn'keɪs] vt einschließen; (Tech) verschalen.

enchant [ɪn'tʃɑːnt] vt bezaubern; —ing a entzückend.

encircle [ɪn'sɜːkl] vt umringen.

enclose [ɪn'kləʊz] vt einschließen; (in letter) beilegen (in, with dat); —d (in letter) beiliegend, anbei.

enclosure [ɪn'kləʊʒə*] n Einfriedung f; (in letter) Anlage f.

encore ['ɒŋkɔː*] n Zugabe f; —! da capo!

encounter [ɪn'kaʊntə*] n Begegnung f; (Mil) Zusammenstoß m; vt treffen; resistance stoßen auf (+acc).

encourage [ɪn'kʌrɪdʒ] vt ermutigen; —ment Ermutigung f, Förderung f.

encouraging [ɪn'kʌrɪdʒɪŋ] a ermutigend, vielversprechend.

encroach [ɪn'krəʊtʃ] vi eindringen ((up)on in +acc), überschreiten ((up)on acc).

encyclop(a)edia [ensaɪkləʊ'piːdɪə] n Konversationslexikon nt.

end [end] n Ende nt, Schluß m; (purpose) Zweck m; a End-; vt beenden; vi zu Ende gehen; — up vi landen.

endanger [ɪn'deɪndʒə*] vt gefährden.

endeavour [ɪn'devə*] n Bestrebung f; vi sich bemühen.

ending ['endɪŋ] n Ende nt.

endless ['endlɪs] a endlos; plain unendlich.

endorse [ɪn'dɔːs] vt unterzeichnen; (approve) unterstützen; —ment Bestätigung f; (of document) Unterzeichnung f; (on licence) Eintrag m.

endow [ɪn'daʊ] vt: — sb with sth jdm etw verleihen; (with money) jdm etw stiften.

end product ['endprɒdʌkt] n Endprodukt nt.

endurable [ɪn'djʊərəbl] a erträglich.

endurance [ɪn'djʊərəns] n Ausdauer f; (suffering) Ertragen nt.

endure [ɪn'djʊə*] vt ertragen; vi (last) (fort)dauern.

enemy ['enɪmɪ] n Feind m; a feindlich.

energetic [enə'dʒetɪk] a tatkräftig.

energy ['enədʒɪ] n (of person) Energie f, Tatkraft f; (Phys) Energie f.

enervating ['enɜːveɪtɪŋ] a nervenaufreibend.

enforce [ɪn'fɔːs] vt durchsetzen; obedience erzwingen.

engage [ɪn'geɪdʒ] vt (employ) einstellen; (in conversation) verwickeln; (Mil) angreifen; (Tech) einrasten lassen, einschalten; —d a verlobt; (Tel, toilet) besetzt; (busy) beschäftigt, unabkömmlich; to get —d sich verloben; —ment (appointment) Verabredung f; (to marry) Verlobung f; (Mil) Gefecht nt; —ment ring Verlobungsring m.

engaging [ɪn'geɪdʒɪŋ] a gewinnend.

engender [ɪn'dʒendə*] vt hervorrufen.

engine ['endʒɪn] n (Aut) Motor m; (Rail) Lokomotive f; —er [endʒɪ'nɪə*] n Ingenieur m; (US Rail) Lokomotivführer m; —ering [endʒɪ'nɪərɪŋ] n Technik f; Maschinenbau m; — failure, — trouble Maschinenschaden m; (Aut) Motorschaden m.

engrave [in'greiv] vt (carve) einschneiden; (fig) tief einprägen; (print) gravieren.

engraving [in'greiviŋ] n Stich m.

engrossed [in'graust] a vertieft.

engulf [in'gʌlf] vt verschlingen.

enhance [in'hɑːns] vt steigern, heben.

enigma [i'nigmə] n Rätsel nt; **—tic** [enig'mætik] a rätselhaft.

enjoy [in'dʒɔi] vt genießen; privilege besitzen; **—able** a erfreulich; **—ment** Genuß m, Freude f.

enlarge [in'lɑːdʒ] vt erweitern; (Phot) vergrößern; **to —** on sth etw weiter ausführen; **—ment** Vergrößerung f.

enlighten [in'laitn] vt aufklären; **—ment** Aufklärung f.

enlist [in'list] vt gewinnen; vi (Mil) sich melden.

enmity ['enmiti] n Feindschaft f.

enormity [i'nɔːmiti] n Ungeheuerlichkeit f.

enormous a, **—ly** ad [i'nɔːməs, -li] ungeheuer.

enough [i'nʌf] a genug; ad genug, genügend; **—!** genug!; that's **—!** das reicht!

enquire [in'kwaiə*] = **inquire.**

enrich [in'ritʃ] vt bereichern.

enrol [in'rəul] vt (Mil) anwerben; vi (register) sich anmelden; **—ment** (for course) Anmeldung f; (Univ) Einschreibung f.

en route [ɑːn'ruːt] ad unterwegs.

ensign ['ensain] n (Naut) Flagge f; (Mil) Fähnrich m.

enslave [in'sleiv] vt versklaven.

ensue [in'sjuː] vi folgen, sich ergeben.

ensuing [in'sjuːiŋ] a (nach)folgend.

ensure [in'ʃuə*] vt garantieren.

entail [in'teil] vt mit sich bringen.

enter ['entə*] vt eintreten in (+ dat), betreten; club beitreten (+ dat); (in book) eintragen; vi hereinkommen, hineingehen; **—** for vt sich beteiligen an (+ dat); **— into** vt agreement eingehen; argument sich einlassen auf (+ acc); **— upon** vt beginnen.

enterprise ['entəpraiz] n (in person) Initiative f, Unternehmungsgeist m; (Comm) Unternehmen nt, Betrieb m.

enterprising ['entəpraiziŋ] a unternehmungslustig.

entertain [entə'tein] vt guest bewirten; (amuse) unterhalten; **—er** Unterhaltungskünstler(in f) m; **—ing** a unterhaltend, amüsant; **—ment** (amusement) Unterhaltung f; (show) Veranstaltung f.

enthralled [in'θrɔːld] a gefesselt.

enthusiasm [in'θjuːziæzəm] n Begeisterung f.

enthusiast [in'θjuːziæst] n Enthusiast m, Schwärmer(in f) m; **—ic** [inθjuːzi'æstik] a begeistert.

entice [in'tais] vt verleiten, locken.

entire [in'taiə*] a ganz; **—ly** ad ganz, völlig; **—ty** [in'taiərəti] in **—ty** in seiner Gesamtheit.

entitle [in'taitl] vt (allow) berechtigen; (name) betiteln.

entity ['entiti] n Ding nt, Wesen nt.

entrance ['entrəns] n Eingang m; (entering) Eintritt m; [in'trɑːns] vt hinreißen; **— examination** Aufnahmeprüfung f; **— fee** Eintrittsgeld nt.

entrancing [in'trɑːnsiŋ] a bezaubernd.

entrant ['entrənt] n (for exam) Kandidat m; (into job) Anfänger m; (Mil) Rekrut m; (in race) Teilnehmer m.

entreat [ɪn'triːt] *vt* anflehen, beschwören; **—y** flehende Bitte *f*, Beschwörung *f*.

entrée ['ɒntreɪ] *n* Zwischengang *m*.

entrenched [ɪn'trentʃt] *a* (*fig*) verwurzelt.

entrust [ɪn'trʌst] *vt* anvertrauen (*sb with sth* jdm etw).

entry ['entrɪ] *n* Eingang *m*; (*Theat*) Auftritt *m*; (*in account*) Eintragung *f*; (*in dictionary*) Eintrag *m*; 'no —' 'Eintritt verboten'; (*for cars*) 'Einfahrt verboten'; **— form** Anmeldeformular *nt*.

enunciate [ɪ'nʌnsɪeɪt] *vt* (deutlich) aussprechen.

envelop [ɪn'veləp] *vt* einhüllen; **—e** ['envələʊp] *n* Umschlag *m*.

enviable ['envɪəbl] *a* beneidenswert.

envious ['envɪəs] *a* neidisch.

environment [ɪn'vaɪərənmənt] *n* Umgebung *f*, (*ecology*) Umwelt *f*; **—al** [ɪnvaɪərən'mentl] *a* Umwelt-.

envisage [ɪn'vɪzɪdʒ] *vt* sich (*dat*) vorstellen; (*plan*) ins Auge fassen.

envoy ['envɔɪ] *n* Gesandte(r) *mf*.

envy ['envɪ] *n* Neid *m*; (*object*) Gegenstand *m* des Neides; *vt* beneiden (*sb sth* jdn um etw).

enzyme ['enzaɪm] *n* Enzym *nt*.

ephemeral [ɪ'femərəl] *a* kurzlebig, vorübergehend.

epic ['epɪk] *n* Epos *nt*; (*film*) Großfilm *m*; *a* episch; (*fig*) heldenhaft.

epidemic [epɪ'demɪk] *n* Epidemie *f*.

epigram ['epɪɡræm] *n* Epigramm *nt*.

epilepsy ['epɪlepsɪ] *n* Epilepsie *f*.

epileptic [epɪ'leptɪk] *a* epileptisch; *n* Epileptiker(in *f*) *m*.

epilogue ['epɪlɒɡ] *n* (*of drama*) Epilog *m*; (*of book*) Nachwort *nt*.

episode ['epɪsəʊd] *n* (*incident*) Vorfall *m*; (*story*) Episode *f*.

epistle [ɪ'pɪsl] *n* Brief *m*.

epitaph ['epɪtɑːf] *n* Grab(in)schrift *f*.

epitome [ɪ'pɪtəmɪ] *n* Inbegriff *m*.

epitomize [ɪ'pɪtəmaɪz] *vt* verkörpern.

epoch ['iːpɒk] *n* Epoche *f*.

equable ['ekwəbl] *a* ausgeglichen.

equal ['iːkwl] *a* gleich; **— to** the task der Aufgabe gewachsen; *n* Gleichgestellte(r) *mf*; *vt* gleichkommen (+*dat*); **two times two —s** four zwei mal zwei ist (gleich) vier; **without —** ohne seinesgleichen; **—ity** [ɪ'kwɒlɪtɪ] Gleichheit *f*; (*equal rights*) Gleichberechtigung *f*; **—ize** *vt* gleichmachen; *vi* (*Sport*) ausgleichen; **—izer** (*Sport*) Ausgleich(streffer) *m*; **—ly** *ad* gleich; **—s sign** Gleichheitszeichen *nt*.

equanimity [ekwə'nɪmɪtɪ] *n* Gleichmut *m*.

equate [ɪ'kweɪt] *vt* gleichsetzen.

equation [ɪ'kweɪʒən] *n* Gleichung *f*.

equator [ɪ'kweɪtə*] *n* Äquator *m*; **—ial** [ekwə'tɔːrɪəl] *a* Äquator-.

equilibrium [iːkwɪ'lɪbrɪəm] *n* Gleichgewicht *nt*.

equinox ['iːkwɪnɒks] *n* Tag- und Nachtgleiche *f*.

equip [ɪ'kwɪp] *vt* ausrüsten; **—ment** Ausrüstung *f*; (*Tech*) Gerät *nt*.

equitable ['ekwɪtəbl] *a* gerecht, billig.

equity ['ekwɪtɪ] *n* Billigkeit *f*, Gerechtigkeit *f*.

equivalent [ɪ'kwɪvələnt] *a* gleichwertig (*to dat*), entsprechend (*to dat*); *n* (*amount*) gleiche Menge *f*; (*in money*) Gegenwert *m*; Äquivalent *nt*.

equivocal [ɪ'kwɪvəkəl] *a* zweideutig; (*suspect*) fragwürdig.

era [ˈɪərə] n Epoche f, Ära f.

eradicate [ɪˈrædɪkeɪt] vt ausrotten.

erase [ɪˈreɪz] vt ausradieren; tape löschen; **—r** Radiergummi m.

erect [ɪˈrekt] a aufrecht; vt errichten; **—ion** Errichtung f; (Physiol) Erektion f.

ermine [ˈɜːmɪn] n Hermelin(pelz) m.

erode [ɪˈrəʊd] vt zerfressen; land auswaschen.

erosion [ɪˈrəʊʒən] n Auswaschen nt, Erosion f.

erotic [ɪˈrɒtɪk] a erotisch; **—ism** [ɪˈrɒtɪsɪzəm] Erotik f.

err [ɜː*] vi sich irren.

errand [ˈerənd] n Besorgung f; **—boy** Laufbursche m.

erratic [ɪˈrætɪk] a sprunghaft; driving unausgeglichen.

erroneous [ɪˈrəʊnɪəs] a irrig, irrtümlich.

error [ˈerə*] n Fehler m.

erudite [ˈerʊdaɪt] a gelehrt.

erudition [erʊˈdɪʃən] n Gelehrsamkeit f.

erupt [ɪˈrʌpt] vi ausbrechen; **—ion** Ausbruch m.

escalate [ˈeskəleɪt] vt steigern; vi sich steigern.

escalator [ˈeskəleɪtə*] n Rolltreppe f.

escapade [ˈeskəpeɪd] n Eskapade f, Streich m.

escape [ɪsˈkeɪp] n Flucht f; (of gas) Entweichen nt; vti entkommen (+ dat); (prisoners) fliehen; (leak) entweichen; **to — notice** unbemerkt bleiben; **the word —s me** das Wort ist mir entfallen.

escapism [ɪsˈkeɪpɪzəm] n Flucht f (vor der Wirklichkeit).

escort [ˈeskɔːt] n (person accompanying) Begleiter m; (guard) Eskorte f; [ɪsˈkɔːt] vt lady begleiten; (Mil) eskortieren.

especially [ɪsˈpeʃəlɪ] ad besonders.

espionage [ˈespɪənɑːʒ] n Spionage f.

esplanade [ˈespləneɪd] n Esplanade f, Promenade f.

Esquire [ɪsˈkwaɪə*] n (in address) J. Brown, Esq Herrn J. Brown.

essay [ˈeseɪ] n Aufsatz m; (Liter) Essay m.

essence [ˈesəns] n (quality) Wesen nt; (extract) Essenz f, Extrakt m.

essential [ɪˈsenʃəl] a (necessary) unentbehrlich; (basic) wesentlich; n Hauptbestandteil m, Allernötigste(s) nt; **—ly** ad in der Hauptsache, eigentlich.

establish [ɪsˈtæblɪʃ] vt (set up) gründen, einrichten; (prove) nachweisen; **—ment** (setting up) Einrichtung f; (business) Unternehmen nt; **the E—ment** das Establishment.

estate [ɪsˈteɪt] n Gut nt; (housing —) Siedlung f; (will) Nachlaß m; **— agent** Grundstücksmakler m; **— car** (Brit) Kombiwagen m.

esteem [ɪsˈtiːm] n Wertschätzung f.

estimate [ˈestɪmət] n (opinion) Meinung f; (of price) (Kosten)voranschlag m; [ˈestɪmeɪt] vt schätzen.

estimation [estɪˈmeɪʃən] n Einschätzung f; (esteem) Achtung f.

estuary [ˈestjʊərɪ] n Mündung f.

etching [ˈetʃɪŋ] n Kupferstich m.

eternal a, **—ly** ad [ɪˈtɜːnl, -nəlɪ] ewig.

eternity [ɪˈtɜːnɪtɪ] n Ewigkeit f.

ether [ˈiːθə*] n (Med) Äther m.

ethical [ˈeθɪkəl] a ethisch.

ethics [ˈeθɪks] npl Ethik f.

ethnic ['eθnɪk] a Volks-, ethnisch.

etiquette ['etɪket] n Etikette f.

Eucharist ['juːkərɪst] n heilige(s) Abendmahl nt.

eulogy ['juːlədʒɪ] n Lobrede f.

eunuch ['juːnək] n Eunuch m.

euphemism ['juːfɪmɪzəm] n Euphemismus m.

euphoria [juːˈfɔːrɪə] n Taumel m, Euphorie f.

euthanasia [juːθəˈneɪzɪə] n Euthanasie f.

evacuate [ɪˈvækjʊeɪt] vt place räumen; people evakuieren; (Med) entleeren.

evacuation [ɪvækjuˈeɪʃən] n Evakuierung f; Räumung f; Entleerung f.

evade [ɪˈveɪd] vt (escape) entkommen (+dat); (avoid) meiden; duty sich entziehen (+dat).

evaluate [ɪˈvæljʊeɪt] vt bewerten; information auswerten.

evangelical [iːvænˈdʒelɪkəl] a evangelisch.

evangelist [ɪˈvændʒəlɪst] n Evangelist m.

evaporate [ɪˈvæpəreɪt] vi verdampfen; vt verdampfen lassen; —d milk Kondensmilch f.

evaporation [ɪvæpəˈreɪʃən] n Verdunstung f.

evasion [ɪˈveɪʒən] n Umgehung f; (excuse) Ausflucht f.

evasive [ɪˈveɪzɪv] a ausweichend.

even ['iːvən] a eben; gleichmäßig; score etc unentschieden; number gerade; (ein)ebnen, glätten; ad — you selbst or sogar du; he — said ... er hat sogar gesagt...; — as he spoke (gerade) da er sprach; — if sogar or selbst wenn, wenn auch; — so dennoch; — out or up vi sich ausgleichen; vt ausgleichen; get — sich revanchieren.

evening ['iːvnɪŋ] n Abend m; in the — abends, am Abend; in the — class Abendschule f; — dress (man's) Gesellschaftsanzug m; (woman's) Abendkleid nt.

evenly ['iːvənlɪ] ad gleichmäßig.

evensong ['iːvənsɒŋ] n (Rel) Abendandacht f.

event [ɪˈvent] n (happening) Ereignis nt; (Sport) Disziplin f; (horses) Rennen nt; the next — der nächste Wettkampf; in the — of im Falle (+gen); —ful a ereignisreich.

eventual [ɪˈventʃʊəl] a (final) schließlich; —ity [ɪventʃʊˈælɪtɪ] Möglichkeit f; —ly ad (at last) am Ende; (given time) schließlich.

ever ['evə*] ad (always) immer; (at any time) je(mals); — so big sehr groß; — so many sehr viele; —green a immergrün; n Immergrün nt; —lasting a immerwährend.

every ['evrɪ] a jeder/jede/jedes; —day jeden Tag; — other day jeden zweiten Tag; —body pron jeder, alle pl; —day a (daily) täglich; (commonplace) alltäglich, Alltags-; —one = —body; — so often hin und wieder; —thing pron alles; —where ad überall.

evict [ɪˈvɪkt] vt ausweisen; —ion Ausweisung f.

evidence ['evɪdəns] n (sign) Spur f; (proof) Beweis m; (testimony) Aussage f; in — (obvious) zu sehen.

evident ['evɪdənt] a augenscheinlich; —ly ad offensichtlich.

evil ['iːvl] a böse, übel; n Übel nt; Unheil nt; (sin) Böse(s) nt.

evocative [ɪˈvɒkətɪv] a to be — of sth an etw (acc) erinnern.

evoke [ɪ'vəʊk] vt hervorrufen.

evolution [iːvə'luːʃən] n Entwicklung f; (of life) Evolution f.

evolve [ɪ'vɒlv] vt entwickeln; vi sich entwickeln.

ewe [juː] n Mutterschaf nt.

ex- [eks] a Ex-, Alt-, ehemalig.

exact a, **—ly** ad [ɪg'zækt, -lɪ] genau; vt (demand) verlangen; (compel) erzwingen; money, fine einziehen; punishment vollziehen; **—ing** a anspruchsvoll; **—itude** Genauigkeit f; **—ness** Genauigkeit f, Richtigkeit f.

exaggerate [ɪg'zædʒəreɪt] vti übertreiben; **—d** a übertrieben.

exaggeration [ɪgzædʒə'reɪʃən] n Übertreibung f.

exalt [ɪg'zɔːlt] vt (praise) verherrlichen.

exam [ɪg'zæm] n Prüfung f.

examination [ɪgzæmɪ'neɪʃən] n Untersuchung f; (Sch, Univ) Prüfung f, Examen nt; (customs) Kontrolle f.

examine [ɪg'zæmɪn] vt untersuchen; (Sch) prüfen; (consider) erwägen; **—r** Prüfer m.

example [ɪg'zɑːmpl] n Beispiel nt; for — zum Beispiel.

exasperate [ɪg'zɑːspəreɪt] vt zum Verzweifeln bringen.

exasperating [ɪg'zɑːspəreɪtɪŋ] a ärgerlich, zum Verzweifeln bringend.

exasperation [ɪgzɑːspə'reɪʃən] n Verzweiflung f.

excavate ['ekskəveɪt] vt (hollow out) aushöhlen; (unearth) ausgraben.

excavation [ekskə'veɪʃən] n Ausgrabung f.

excavator ['ekskəveɪtə*] n Bagger m.

exceed [ɪk'siːd] vt überschreiten; hopes übertreffen; **—ingly** ad in höchstem Maße.

excel [ɪk'sel] vi sich auszeichnen; vt übertreffen; **—lence** ['eksələns] Vortrefflichkeit f; His E—llency ['eksələnsɪ] Seine Exzellenz f; **—lent** ['eksələnt] a ausgezeichnet.

except [ɪk'sept] prep (also — for) außer (+dat); vt ausnehmen; **—ing** prep = except; **—ion** [ɪk'sepʃən] Ausnahme f; to take **—ion** to Anstoß nehmen an (+dat); **—ional** a, **—ionally** ad [ɪk'sepʃənl, -nəlɪ] außergewöhnlich.

excerpt ['eksɜːpt] n Auszug m.

excess [ek'ses] n Übermaß nt (of an +dat); Exzeß m; a money Nach-; baggage Mehr-; **—es** pl Ausschweifungen pl, Exzesse pl; (violent) Ausschreitungen pl; **—weight** (of thing) Mehrgewicht nt; (of person) Übergewicht nt; **—ive**, **—ively** ad übermäßig.

exchange [ɪks'tʃeɪndʒ] n Austausch m; (Fin) Wechselstube f; (Tel) Vermittlung f, Zentrale f; (Post Office) (Fernsprech)amt nt; vt goods tauschen; greetings austauschen; money, blows wechseln; see rate.

exchequer [ɪks'tʃekə*] n Schatzamt nt.

excisable [ek'saɪzbl] a (ver-brauchs)steuerpflichtig.

excise ['eksaɪz] n Verbrauchssteuer f; [ek'saɪz] vt (Med) herausschneiden.

excitable [ɪk'saɪtəbl] a erregbar, nervös.

excite [ɪk'saɪt] vt erregen; **—d** a aufgeregt; to get **—d** sich aufregen; **—ment** Aufgeregtheit f; (of interest) Erregung f.

exciting [ɪk'saɪtɪŋ] a aufregend; book, film spannend.

exclaim [ɪks'kleɪm] vt ausrufen.

exclamation [eksklə'meɪʃən] n Ausruf m; — mark Ausrufezeichen nt.

exclude [ɪks'klu:d] vt ausschließen.

exclusion [ɪks'klu:ʒən] n Ausschluß m.

exclusive [ɪks'klu:sɪv] a (select) exklusiv; (sole) ausschließlich, Allein-; — of ausschließlich (+gen); —ly ad nur, ausschließlich.

excommunicate [ekskə'mju:nɪkeɪt] vt exkommunizieren.

excrement ['ekskrɪmənt] n Kot m.

excruciating [ɪks'kru:ʃɪeɪtɪŋ] a qualvoll.

excursion [ɪks'kɜ:ʃən] n Ausflug m.

excusable [ɪks'kju:zəbl] a entschuldbar.

excuse [ɪks'kju:s] n Entschuldigung f; [ɪks'kju:z] vt entschuldigen; — me! entschuldigen Sie!

execute ['eksɪkju:t] vt (carry out) ausführen; (kill) hinrichten.

execution [eksɪ'kju:ʃən] n Ausführung f; (killing) Hinrichtung f; —er Scharfrichter m.

executive [ɪg'zekjutɪv] n (Comm) leitende(r) Angestellte(r) m, Geschäftsführer m; (Pol) Exekutive f; a Exekutiv-, ausführend.

executor [ɪg'zekjutə*] n Testamentsvollstrecker m.

exemplary [ɪg'zempləri] a musterhaft.

exemplify [ɪg'zemplɪfaɪ] vt veranschaulichen.

exempt [ɪg'zempt] a befreit; vt befreien; —ion [ɪg'zempʃən] Befreiung f.

exercise ['eksəsaɪz] n Übung f; vt power ausüben; muscle, patience üben; dog ausführen; — book (Schul)heft nt.

exert [ɪg'zɜ:t] vt influence ausüben; — o.s. sich anstrengen; —ion Anstrengung f.

exhaust [ɪg'zɔ:st] n (fumes) Abgase pl; (pipe) Auspuffrohr nt; vt (weary) ermüden; (use up) erschöpfen; —ed a erschöpft; —ing a anstrengend; —ion Erschöpfung f; —ive a erschöpfend.

exhibit [ɪg'zɪbɪt] n (Art) Ausstellungsstück nt; (Jur) Beweisstück nt; vt ausstellen; —ion [eksɪ'bɪʃən] (Art) Ausstellung f; (of temper etc) Zurschaustellung f; —ionist [eksɪ'bɪʃənɪst] Exhibitionist m; —or Aussteller m.

exhilarating [ɪg'zɪləreɪtɪŋ] a erhebend.

exhilaration [ɪgzɪlə'reɪʃən] n erhebende(s) Gefühl nt.

exhort [ɪg'zɔ:t] vt ermahnen; beschwören.

exile ['eksaɪl] n Exil nt; (person) im Exil Lebende(r) mf; vt verbannen; in — im Exil.

exist [ɪg'zɪst] vi existieren; (live) leben; —ence Existenz f; (way of life) Leben nt, Existenz f; —ing a vorhanden, bestehend.

exit ['eksɪt] n Ausgang m; (Theat) Abgang m.

exonerate [ɪg'zɒnəreɪt] vt entlasten.

exorbitant [ɪg'zɔ:bɪtənt] a übermäßig; price Phantasie-.

exotic [ɪg'zɒtɪk] a exotisch.

expand [ɪks'pænd] vt (spread) ausspannen; operations ausdehnen; vi sich ausdehnen.

expanse [ɪks'pæns] n weite Fläche f, Weite f.

expansion [ɪks'pænʃən] n Erweiterung f.

expatriate [eks'pætrɪeɪt] a Exil-; n im Exil Lebende(r) mf; vt ausbürgern.

expect [ɪks'pekt] vt erwarten; (suppose) annehmen; vi: to be —ing ein Kind erwarten; —ant a (hopeful) erwartungsvoll; mother werdend; —ation [ekspek'teɪʃən] (hope) Hoffnung f; —ations pl Erwartungen pl; (prospects) Aussicht f.

expedience [ɪks'piːdɪəns], **expediency** [ɪks'piːdɪənsɪ] n Zweckdienlichkeit f.

expedient [ɪks'piːdɪənt] a zweckdienlich; n (Hilfs)mittel nt.

expedite ['ekspɪdaɪt] vt beschleunigen.

expedition [ekspɪ'dɪʃən] n Expedition f.

expel [ɪks'pel] vt ausweisen; student (ver)weisen.

expend [ɪks'pend] vt money ausgeben; effort aufwenden; —able a (entbehrlich; —iture Kosten pl, Ausgaben pl.

expense [ɪks'pens] n (cost) Auslage f, Ausgabe f; (high cost) Aufwand m; —s pl Spesen pl; at the — of auf Kosten von; — account Spesenkonto nt.

expensive [ɪks'pensɪv] a teuer.

experience [ɪks'pɪərɪəns] n (incident) Erlebnis nt; (practice) Erfahrung f; vt erfahren, erleben; hardship durchmachen; —d a erfahren.

experiment [ɪks'perɪmənt] n Versuch m, Experiment nt; [ɪks'perɪment] vi experimentieren; —al [eksperɪ'mentl] a versuchsweise, experimentell.

expert [eksp3ːt] n Fachmann m; (official) Sachverständige(r) m; a erfahren; (practised) gewandt;

—ise [ekspə'tiːz] Sachkenntnis f.

expiration [ekspaɪə'reɪʃən] n (breathing) Ausatmen nt; (fig) Ablauf m.

expire [ɪks'paɪə*] vi (end) ablaufen; (die) sterben; (ticket) verfallen.

expiry [ɪks'paɪərɪ] n Ablauf m.

explain [ɪks'pleɪn] vt (make clear) erklären; (account for) begründen; — away vt wegerklären.

explanation [eksplə'neɪʃən] n Erklärung f.

explanatory [ɪks'plænətərɪ] a erklärend.

explicable [eks'plɪkəbl] a erklärlich.

explicit [ɪks'plɪsɪt] a (clear) ausdrücklich; (outspoken) deutlich; —ly ad deutlich.

explode [ɪks'pləʊd] vi explodieren; vt bomb zur Explosion bringen; theory platzen lassen.

exploit [eksplɔɪt] n (Helden)tat f; [ɪks'plɔɪt] vt ausbeuten; —ation [eksplɔɪ'teɪʃən] Ausbeutung f.

exploration [eksplɔː'reɪʃən] n Erforschung f.

exploratory [eks'plɔrətərɪ] a sondierend, Probe-.

explore [ɪks'plɔː*] vt (travel) erforschen; (search) untersuchen; —r Forschungsreisende(r) mf, Erforscher(in f) m.

explosion [ɪks'pləʊʒən] n (lit) Explosion f; (fig) Ausbruch m.

explosive [ɪks'pləʊzɪv] a explosiv, Spreng-; n Sprengstoff m.

exponent [eks'pəʊnənt] n Exponent m.

export [ɪks'pɔːt] vt exportieren; ['ekspɔːt] n Export m; a trade Export-; —ation [ekspɔː'teɪʃən] Ausfuhr f; —er Exporteur m.

expose [ɪks'pəʊz] vt (to danger etc) aussetzen (to dat); imposter entlarven; lie aufdecken.

exposé [eks'pəʊzeɪ] n (of scandal) Enthüllung f.

exposed [ɪks'pəʊzd] a position exponiert.

exposure [ɪks'pəʊʒə*] m (Med) Unterkühlung f; (Phot) Belichtung f; —meter Belichtungsmesser m.

expound [ɪks'paʊnd] vt entwickeln.

express [ɪks'pres] a ausdrücklich; (speedy) Expreß-, Eil-; n (Rail) Zug m; vt ausdrücken; to — o.s. sich ausdrücken; —ion [ɪks'preʃən] (phrase) Ausdruck m; (look) (Gesichts)ausdruck m; —ive a ausdrucksvoll; —ly ad ausdrücklich, extra.

expropriate [eks'prəʊprɪeɪt] vt enteignen.

expulsion [ɪks'pʌlʃən] n Ausweisung f.

exquisite [ɪks'kwɪzɪt] a erlesen; —ly ad ausgezeichnet.

extend [ɪks'tend] vt visit etc verlängern; building vergrößern, ausbauen; hand ausstrecken; welcome bieten.

extension [ɪks'tenʃən] n Erweiterung f; (of building) Anbau m; (Tel) Nebenanschluß m, Apparat m.

extensive [ɪks'tensɪv] a knowledge umfassend; use weitgehend.

extent [ɪks'tent] n Ausdehnung f; (fig) Ausmaß m.

extenuating [eks'tenjʊeɪtɪŋ] a mildernd.

exterior [eks'tɪərɪə*] a äußere(r,s), Außen-; n Äußere(s) nt.

exterminate [eks'tɜːmɪneɪt] vt ausrotten.

extermination [ekstɜːmɪ'neɪʃən] n Ausrottung f.

external [eks'tɜːnl] a äußere(r,s), Außen-; —ly ad äußerlich.

extinct [ɪks'tɪŋkt] a ausgestorben; —ion [ɪks'tɪŋkʃən] Aussterben nt.

extinguish [ɪks'tɪŋgwɪʃ] vt (aus)löschen; —er Löschgerät nt.

extort [ɪks'tɔːt] vt erpressen (sth from sb jdn um etw); —ion [ɪks'tɔːʃən] Erpressung f; —ionate [ɪks'tɔːʃənɪt] a überhöht, erpresserisch.

extra [ekstrə] a zusätzlich; ad besonders; n (work) Sonderarbeit f; (benefit) Sonderleistung f; (charge) Zuschlag m; (Theat) Statist m.

extract [ɪks'trækt] vt (heraus)ziehen; (select) auswählen; ['ekstrækt] n (from book etc) Auszug m; (Cook) Extrakt m; —ion (Heraus)ziehen nt; (origin) Abstammung f.

extradite ['ekstrədaɪt] vt ausliefern.

extradition [ekstrə'dɪʃən] n Auslieferung f.

extraneous [eks'treɪnɪəs] a unwesentlich; influence äußere(r,s).

extraordinary [ɪks'trɔːdnrɪ] a außerordentlich; (amazing) erstaunlich.

extravagance [ɪks'trævəgəns] n Verschwendung f; (lack of restraint) Zügellosigkeit f; (an —) Extravaganz f.

extravagant [ɪks'trævəgənt] a extravagant.

extreme [eks'triːm] a edge äußerste(r,s), hinterste(r,s); cold äußerste(r,s); behaviour außergewöhnlich, übertrieben; n Extrem nt, das Äußerste; —s pl (excesses) Ausschreitungen pl; (opposites)

Extreme *pl*; —ly *ad* äußerst, höchst.

extremist [iks'tri:mist] *a* extremistisch; *n* Extremist(in *f*) *m*.

extremity [iks'tremiti] *n* (*end*) Spitze *f*, äußerste(s) Ende *nt*; (*hardship*) bitterste Not *f*; (*Anat*) Hand *f*; Fuß *m*.

extricate ['ekstrikeit] *vt* losmachen, befreien.

extrovert ['ekstrəuvə:t] *n* Extravertierte(r) *mf*; *a* extravertiert.

exuberance [ig'zu:bərəns] *n* Überschwang *m*.

exuberant [ig'zu:bərənt] *a* ausgelassen.

exude [ig'zju:d] *vt* absondern; *vi* sich absondern.

exult [ig'zʌlt] *vi* frohlocken; —ation [egzʌl'teiʃən] Jubel *m*.

eye [ai] *n* Auge *nt*; (*of needle*) Öhr *nt*; *vt* betrachten; (*up and down*) mustern; to keep an — on *im* Auge behalten; (*watch*) aufpassen auf (+*acc*); in the —s of in den Augen (+*gen*); up to the —s in bis zum Hals in; —ball Augapfel *m*; —bath Augenbad *nt*; —brow Augenbraue *f*; —lash Augenwimper *f*; —lid Augenlid *nt*; that was an —opener das hat mir die Augen geöffnet; —shadow Lidschatten *m*; —sight Sehkraft *f*; —sore Schandfleck *m*; —wash (*lit*) Augenwasser *nt*; (*fig*) Schwindel *m*; Quatsch *m*; — witness Augenzeuge *m*.

F

F,f [ef] *n* F *nt*, f *nt*.

fable ['feibl] *n* Fabel *f*.

fabric ['fæbrik] *n* Stoff *m*, Gewebe *nt*; (*fig*) Gefüge *nt*.

fabricate ['fæbrikeit] *vt* fabrizieren.

fabulous ['fæbjuləs] *a* (*imaginary*) legendär, sagenhaft; (*unbelievable*) unglaublich; (*wonderful*) fabelhaft, unglaublich.

façade [fə'sa:d] *n* (*lit, fig*) Fassade *f*.

face [feis] *n* Gesicht *nt*; (*grimace*) Grimasse *f*; (*surface*) Oberfläche *f*; (*of clock*) Zifferblatt *nt*; *vt* (*point towards*) liegen nach; (*situation*) sich gegenübersehen (+*dat*); (*difficulty*) mutig entgegentreten (+*dat*); in the — of angesichts (+*gen*); to — up to sth einer Sache ins Auge sehen; — cream Gesichtscreme *f*;

— powder (Gesichts)puder *m*.

facet ['fæsit] *n* Seite *f*, Aspekt *m*; (*of gem*) Kristallfläche *f*, Schliff *m*.

facetious [fə'si:ʃəs] *a* schalkhaft; (*humorous*) witzig; —ly *ad* spaßhaft, witzig.

face to face [feistə'feis] *ad* Auge in Auge, direkt.

face value ['feis 'vælju:] *n* Nennwert *m*; (*fig*) to take sth at its — etw für bare Münze nehmen.

facial ['feiʃəl] *a* Gesichts-.

facile ['fæsail] *a* oberflächlich; (*US*: *easy*) leicht.

facilitate [fə'siliteit] *vt* erleichtern.

facility [fə'siliti] *n* (*ease*) Leichtigkeit *f*; (*skill*) Gewandtheit *f*; facilities *pl* Einrichtungen *pl*.

facing ['feisiŋ] *a* zugekehrt; *prep* gegenüber.

facsimile ['fæk'sımılı] n Faksimile nt.

fact [fækt] n Tatsache f; in — in der Tat. ·

faction ['fækʃən] n Splittergruppe f.

factor ['fæktə*] n Faktor m.

factory ['fæktərı] n Fabrik f.

factual ['fæktjʊəl] a Tatsachen-, sachlich.

faculty ['fækltı] n Fähigkeit f; (Univ) Fakultät f; (US: teaching staff) Lehrpersonal nt.

fade [feɪd] vi (lose colour) verschießen, verblassen; (grow dim) nachlassen, schwinden; (sound, memory) schwächer werden; (wither) verwelken; vt material verblassen lassen; —d a verwelkt; colour verblichen; to — in/out (Cine) ein-/ausblenden.

fag [fæg] n Plackerei f; (col: cigarette) Kippe f; —ged a (exhausted) erschöpft.

Fahrenheit ['færənhaɪt] a Fahrenheit.

fail [feɪl] vt exam nicht bestehen; student durchfallen lassen; (courage) verlassen; (memory) im Stich lassen; vi (supplies) zu Ende gehen; (student) durchfallen; (eyesight) nachlassen; (light) schwächer werden; (crop) fehlschlagen; (remedy) nicht wirken; — to do sth (neglect) es unterlassen, etw zu tun; (be unable) es nicht schaffen, etw zu tun; without — ganz bestimmt, unbedingt; —ing n Fehler m, Schwäche f; prep' in Ermangelung (+gen); —ing this falls nicht, sonst; —ure ['feɪljə*] n (person) Versager m; (act) Versagen nt; (Tech) Defekt m.

faint [feɪnt] a schwach, matt; n Ohnmacht f; vi ohnmächtig wer-

den; —hearted a mutlos, kleinmütig; —ly ad schwach; —ness Schwäche f; (Med) Schwächegefühl nt.

fair [fɛə*] a schön; hair blond; skin hell; weather schön, trocken; (just) gerecht, fair; (not very good) leidlich, mittelmäßig; conditions günstig, gut; (sizeable) ansehnlich; ad play ehrlich, fair; n (Comm) Messe f; (fun —) Jahrmarkt m; —ly ad (honestly) gerecht, fair; (rather) ziemlich; —ness Schönheit f; (of hair) Blondheit f; (of game) Ehrlichkeit f, Fairneß f; —way n Fahrrinne f.

fairy ['fɛərı] n Fee f; —land Märchenland nt; — tale Märchen nt.

faith [feɪθ] n Glaube m; (trust) Vertrauen nt; (sect) Bekenntnis n, Religion f; —ful a treu; —fully ad treu; yours —fully hochachtungsvoll.

fake [feɪk] n (thing) Fälschung f; (person) Schwindler m; a vorgetäuscht; vt fälschen.

falcon ['fɔːlkən] n Falke m.

fall [fɔːl] n Fall m, Sturz m; (decrease) Fallen nt; (of snow) (Schnee)fall m; (US: autumn) Herbst m; vi irreg (lit, fig) fallen; (night) hereinbrechen; —s pl (waterfall) Fälle pl; — back on vt in Reserve haben; — down vi (person) hinfallen; (building) einstürzen; — flat vi (lit) platt hinfallen; (joke) nicht ankommen; the plan fell flat aus dem Plan wurde nichts; — for vt trick hereinfallen auf (+acc); person sich verknallen in (+acc); — off vi herunterfallen (von); (diminish) sich vermindern; — out vi sich streiten; — through vi (plan) ins Wasser fallen.

fallacy ['fæləsɪ] n Trugschluß m.

fallible ['fæləbl] a fehlbar.

fallout ['fɔ:laʊt] n radioaktive(r) Niederschlag m.

fallow ['fæləʊ] a brach(liegend).

false [fɔ:ls] a falsch; (artificial) gefälscht, künstlich; under — pretences unter Vorspiegelung falscher Tatsachen; — alarm Fehlalarm m; —ly ad fälschlicherweise; — teeth pl Gebiß nt.

falter ['fɔ:ltə*] vi schwanken; (in speech) stocken.

fame [feɪm] n Ruhm m.

familiar [fə'mɪlɪə*] a vertraut, bekannt; (intimate) familiär; to be — with vertraut sein mit, gut kennen; —ity [fə'mɪlɪ'ærɪtɪ] Vertrautheit f; —ize vt vertraut machen.

family ['fæmɪlɪ] n Familie f; (relations) Verwandtschaft f; — allowance Kindergeld nt; — business Familienunternehmen nt; — doctor Hausarzt m; — life Familienleben nt; — planning Geburtenkontrolle f.

famine ['fæmɪn] n Hungersnot f.

famished ['fæmɪʃt] a ausgehungert.

famous ['feɪməs] a berühmt.

fan [fæn] n (folding) Fächer m; (Elec) Ventilator m; (admirer) begeisterte(r) Anhänger m; Fan m; vt fächeln; — out vi sich (fächerförmig) ausbreiten.

fanatic [fə'nætɪk] n Fanatiker(in f) m; —al a fanatisch.

fan belt ['fænbelt] n Keilriemen m.

fancied ['fænsɪd] a beliebt, populär.

fanciful ['fænsɪfʊl] a (odd) seltsam; (imaginative) phantasievoll.

fancy ['fænsɪ] n (liking) Neigung f; (imagination) Phantasie f, Ein-

bildung f; a schick, ausgefallen; vt (like) gern haben; wollen; (imagine) sich einbilden; (just) — (that)! stellen Sie sich (das nur) vor!; — dress Verkleidung f, Maskenkostüm nt; —-dress ball Maskenball m.

fanfare ['fænfeə*] n Fanfare f.

fang [fæŋ] n Fangzahn m; (snake's) Giftzahn m.

fanlight ['fænlaɪt] n Oberlicht nt.

fantastic [fæn'tæstɪk] a phantastisch.

fantasy ['fæntəzɪ] n Phantasie f.

far [fɑ:*] a weit; ad weit entfernt; (very much) weitaus, (sehr) viel; — away, — off weit weg; by — bei weitem; so — soweit; bis jetzt; —away a weit entfernt; the F— East der Ferne Osten.

farce [fɑ:s] n Schwank m, Posse f; (fig) Farce f.

farcical ['fɑ:sɪkəl] a possenhaft; (fig) lächerlich.

fare [feə*] n Fahrpreis m; Fahrgeld nt; (food) Kost f; vi: he is faring well es ergeht ihm gut; —well Abschied(sgruß) m; interj lebe wohl!; a Abschieds-.

far-fetched ['fɑ:'fetʃt] a weit hergeholt.

farm [fɑ:m] n Bauernhof m, Farm f; vt bewirtschaften; vi Landwirt m sein; —er Bauer m, Landwirt m; —hand Landarbeiter m; —house Bauernhaus nt; —ing Landwirtschaft f; —land Ackerland nt; —yard Hof m.

far-reaching ['fɑ:'ri:tʃɪŋ] a weitgehend.

far-sighted ['fɑ:'saɪtɪd] a weitblickend.

fart [fɑ:t] n (col) Furz m; vi (col) furzen.

farther ['fɑːðə*] a, ad weiter.

farthest ['fɑːðist] a weiteste(r,s), fernste(r,s); ad am weitesten.

fascinate ['fæsineit] vt faszinieren, bezaubern.

fascinating ['fæsineitiŋ] a faszinierend, spannend.

fascination [fæsi'neiʃən] n Faszination f, Zauber m.

fascism ['fæʃizəm] n Faschismus m.

fascist ['fæʃist] n Faschist m; a faschistisch.

fashion ['fæʃən] n (of clothes) Mode f; (manner) Art f (und Weise f); vt machen, gestalten; in — in Mode; out of — unmodisch; —able a clothes modern, modisch; place elegant; — show Mode(n)-schau f.

fast [fɑːst] a schnell; (firm) fest; dye waschecht; to be — (clock) vorgehen; ad schnell; (firmly) fest; n Fasten nt; vi fasten.

fasten ['fɑːsn] vt (attach) befestigen; seat belt festmachen; (with rope) zuschnüren; vi sich schließen lassen; —er, —ing Verschluß m.

fastidious [fæs'tidiəs] a wählerisch.

fat [fæt] a dick, fett; n (on person) Fett m, Speck m (col); (on meat) Fett nt; (for cooking) (Braten)fett nt.

fatal ['feitl] a tödlich; (disastrous) verhängnisvoll; —ism n Fatalismus m, Schicksalsglaube m; —ity [fə'tæliti] (road death etc) Todesopfer nt; —ly ad tödlich.

fate [feit] n Schicksal nt; a (prophetic) schicksalsschwer; (important) schicksalhaft.

father ['fɑːðə*] n Vater m; (Rel) Pater m; —-in-law Schwiegervater m; —ly a väterlich.

fathom ['fæðəm] n Klafter m; vt ausloten; (fig) ergründen.

fatigue [fə'tiːg] n Ermüdung f; vt ermüden.

fatness ['fætnis] n Dicke f.

fatten ['fætn] vt dick machen; animals mästen; vi dick werden.

fatty ['fæti] a food fettig.

fatuous ['fætjuəs] a albern, affig.

faucet ['fɔːsit] n (US) Wasserhahn m.

fault [fɔːlt] n (defect) Defekt m; (Elec) Störung f; (blame) Fehler m, Schuld f; (Geog) Verwerfung f; it's your — du bist daran schuld; at — schuldig, im Unrecht; vt: — sth etwas an etw (dat) auszusetzen haben; —less a fehlerfrei, tadellos; —y a fehlerhaft, defekt.

fauna ['fɔːnə] n Fauna f.

favour, (US) favor ['feivə*] n (approval) Wohlwollen nt; (kindness) Gefallen m; vt (prefer) vorziehen; in — of für; zugunsten (+gen); —able a, —ably ad günstig; —ite ['feivərit] a Lieblings-; n Günstling m; (child) Liebling m; (Sport) Favorit m; —itism (Sch) Bevorzugung f; (Pol) Günstlingswirtschaft f.

fawn [fɔːn] n rehbraun; n (colour) Rehbraun nt; (animal) (Reh)kitz nt.

fawning ['fɔːniŋ] a kriecherisch.

fear [fiə*] n Furcht f; vt fürchten; no —! keine Angst!; —ful a (timid) furchtsam; (terrible) fürchterlich; —less a, —lessly ad furchtlos; —lessness Furchtlosigkeit f.

feasibility [fiːzə'biliti] n Durchführbarkeit f.

feasible ['fiːzəbl] a durchführbar, machbar.

feast [fiːst] n Festmahl m; (Rel) Kirchenfest nt; vi sich gütlich tun (on an +dat); — day kirchliche(r) Feiertag m.

feat [fi:t] n Leistung f.

feather ['feðə*] n Feder f.

feature ['fi:tʃə*] n (Gesichts)zug m; (important part) Grundzug m; (Cine, Press) Feature nt; vt darstellen; (advertising etc) groß herausbringen; **featuring X** mit X; vi vorkommen; — **film** Spielfilm m; **—less** a nichtssagend.

February ['februəri] n Februar m.

federal ['fedərəl] a Bundes-.

federation [fedə'reiʃən] n (society) Verband m; (of states) Staatenbund m.

fed-up [fed'ʌp] a: **to be — with sth** etw satt haben; **I'm —** ich habe die Nase voll.

fee [fi:] n Gebühr f.

feeble ['fi:bl] a (person) schwach; (excuse) lahm; **—-minded** a geistesschwach.

feed [fi:d] n (for baby) Essen nt; (for animals) Futter nt; vt (baby) füttern; (support) ernähren; **to —on** leben von, fressen; **—back** (Tech) Rückkopplung f; (information) Feedback nt.

feel [fi:l] n: **it has a soft —** es fühlt sich weich an; **to get the —** of sth sich an etw (acc) gewöhnen; irreg vt (sense) fühlen; (touch) anfassen; (think) meinen; vi (person) sich fühlen; (thing) sich anfühlen; **I — cold** mir ist kalt; **I — like a cup of tea** ich habe Lust auf eine Tasse Tee; **—er** n Fühler m; **—ing** Gefühl nt; (opinion) Meinung f.

feet [fi:t] npl of **foot**.

feign [fein] vt vortäuschen; **—ed** a vorgetäuscht, Schein-.

feint [feint] n Täuschungsmanöver nt.

feline ['fi:lain] a Katzen-, katzenartig.

fell [fel] vt tree fällen; n (hill) kahle(r) Berg m; a: **with one —** swoop mit einem Schlag; auf einen Streich.

fellow ['feləu] n (companion) Gefährte m, Kamerad m; (man) Kerl m; — **citizen** Mitbürger(in f) m; — **countryman** Landsmann m; — **feeling** Mitgefühl nt; — **men** pl Mitmenschen pl; **—ship** (group) Körperschaft f; (friendliness) Gemeinschaft f, Kameradschaft f; (scholarship) Forschungsstipendium nt; — **worker** Mitarbeiter(in f) m.

felony ['feləni] n schwere(s) Verbrechen nt.

felt [felt] n Filz m.

female ['fi:meil] n (of animals) Weibchen nt; a weiblich.

feminine ['feminin] a (Gram) weiblich; qualities fraulich.

femininity [femi'niniti] n Weiblichkeit f; (quality) Fraulichkeit f.

feminist ['feminist] n Feminist(in f) m.

fence [fens] n Zaun m; (crook) Hehler m; vi fechten; — **in** vt einzäunen; — **off** vt absperren.

fencing ['fensiŋ] n Zaun m; (Sport) Fechten nt.

fend [fend] vi: — **for o.s.** sich (allein) durchschlagen.

fender ['fendə*] n Kaminvorsetzer m; (US Aut) Kotflügel m.

ferment [fə'ment] vi (Chem) gären; ['fɜ:ment] n (excitement) Unruhe f; **—ation** [fɜ:men'teiʃən] n Gärung f.

fern [fɜ:n] n Farn m.

ferocious [fə'rəuʃəs] a wild, grausam; **—ly** ad wild.

ferocity [fəˈrɒsɪtɪ] n Wildheit f, Grimmigkeit f.

ferry [ˈferɪ] n Fähre f; vt übersetzen.

fertile [ˈfɜːtaɪl] a fruchtbar.

fertility [fəˈtɪlɪtɪ] n Fruchtbarkeit f.

fertilization [fɜːtɪlaɪˈzeɪʃən] n Befruchtung f.

fertilize [ˈfɜːtɪlaɪz] vt (Agr) düngen; (Biol) befruchten; —r (Kunst)dünger m.

fervent [ˈfɜːvənt] a admirer glühend; hope innig.

festival [ˈfestɪvəl] n (Rel etc) Fest nt; (Art, Mus) Festspiele pl; Festival nt.

festive [ˈfestɪv] a festlich; the — season (Christmas) die Festzeit f.

festivity [fesˈtɪvɪtɪ] n Festlichkeit f.

fetch [fetʃ] vt holen; (in sale) einbringen, erzielen.

fetching [ˈfetʃɪŋ] a einnehmend, reizend.

fête [feɪt] n Fest nt.

fetish [ˈfiːtɪʃ] n Fetisch m.

fetters [ˈfetəz] npl (lit, fig) Fesseln pl.

fetus [ˈfiːtəs] n (US) = foetus.

feud [fjuːd] n Fehde f; vi sich befehden; —al a lehnsherrlich, Feudal-; —alism Lehnswesen nt, Feudalismus m.

fever [ˈfiːvə*] n Fieber nt; —ish a (Med) fiebrig, Fieber-; (fig) fieberhaft; —ishly ad (fig) fieberhaft.

few [fjuː] a wenig; pron wenige; a — a, pron einige; —er weniger; —est wenigste(r,s); a good — ziemlich viele.

fiancé [fɪˈɑːnseɪ] n Verlobte(r) m; —e Verlobte f.

fiasco [fɪˈæskəʊ] n Fiasko nt, Reinfall m.

fib [fɪb] n Flunkerei f; vi flunkern.

fibre, (US) **fiber** [ˈfaɪbə*] n Faser f, Fiber f; (material) Faserstoff m; —glass Glaswolle f.

fickle [ˈfɪkl] a unbeständig, wankelmütig; —ness Unbeständigkeit f, Wankelmut m.

fiction [ˈfɪkʃən] n (novels) Romanliteratur f; (story) Erdichtung f; —al a erfunden.

fictitious [fɪkˈtɪʃəs] a erfunden, fingiert.

fiddle [ˈfɪdl] n Geige f, Fiedel f; (trick) Schwindelei f; vt accounts frisieren; — with vi herumfummeln an (+dat); —r Geiger m.

fidelity [fɪˈdelɪtɪ] n Treue f.

fidget [ˈfɪdʒɪt] vi zappeln; n Zappelphilipp m; —y a nervös, zappelig.

field [fiːld] n Feld nt; (range) Gebiet nt; — day (gala) Paradetag m; — marshal Feldmarschall m; —work (Mil) Schanze f; (Univ) Feldforschung f.

fiend [fiːnd] n Teufel m; (beast) Unhold m; Fanatiker(in f) m; —ish a teuflisch.

fierce [fɪəs] —ly ad [fɪəs, -lɪ] wild; —ness Wildheit f.

fiery [ˈfaɪərɪ] a glühend; (blazing) brennend; (hot-tempered) hitzig, heftig.

fifteen [fɪfˈtiːn] num fünfzehn.

fifth [fɪfθ] a fünfte(r,s); n Fünftel nt.

fifty [ˈfɪftɪ] num fünfzig; ——— halbe halbe, fifty fifty (col).

fig [fɪg] n Feige f.

fight [faɪt] n Kampf m; (brawl) Schlägerei f; (argument) Streit m; irreg vt kämpfen gegen; sich schlagen mit; (fig) bekämpfen; vi kämpfen; sich schlagen; streiten; —er Kämpfer(in f) m; (plane)

Jagdflugzeug *nt*; —**ing** Kämpfen *nt*; (*war*) Kampfhandlungen *pl*.

figment ['fɪgmənt] *n* — of imagination reine Einbildung *f*.

figurative *a* bildlich.

figure ['fɪgə*] *n* Form *f*; (*of person*) Figur *f*; (*person*) Gestalt *f*; (*illustration*) Zeichnung *f*; (*number*) Ziffer *f*; *vt* (*US: imagine*) glauben; *vi* (*appear*) eine Rolle spielen, erscheinen; (*US: make sense*) stimmen; — **out** *vt* verstehen, herausbekommen; —**head** (*Naut*, *fig*) Galionsfigur *f*; — **skating** Eiskunstlauf *m*.

filament ['fɪləmənt] *n* Faden *m*; (*Elec*) Glühfaden *m*.

file [faɪl] *n* (*tool*) Feile *f*; (*dossier*) Akte *f*; (*folder*) Aktenordner *m*; (*row*) Reihe *f*; *vt metal, nails* feilen; *papers* abheften; *claim* einreichen; *vi*: — **in/out** hintereinander hereinkommen/hinausgehen; **in single** — einer hinter dem anderen.

filing ['faɪlɪŋ] *n* Feilen *nt*; —**s** *pl* Feilspäne *pl*; — **cabinet** Aktenschrank *m*.

fill [fɪl] *vt* füllen; (*occupy*) ausfüllen; (*satisfy*) sättigen; *n*: **to eat one's** — sich richtig satt essen; **to have had one's** — genug haben; **to** — **the bill** (*fig*) allen Anforderungen genügen; — **in** *vt hole* (auf)füllen; *form* ausfüllen; — **up** *vt container* auffüllen; *form* ausfüllen.

fillet ['fɪlɪt] *n* Filet *nt*; *vt* als Filet herrichten.

filling ['fɪlɪŋ] *n* (*Cook*) Füllung *f*; (*for tooth*) (Zahn)plombe *f*; — **station** Tankstelle *f*.

fillip ['fɪlɪp] *n* Anstoß *m*, Auftrieb *m*.

film [fɪlm] *n* Film *m*; (*layer*) Häutchen *nt*, Film *m*; *vt scene*

filmen; — **star** Filmstar *m*; —**strip** Filmstreifen *m*.

filter ['fɪltə*] · *n* Filter *m*; (*for traffic*) Verkehrsfilter *m*; *vt* filtern; *vi* durchsickern; — **tip** Filter *m*, Filtermundstück *nt*; —**tipped cigarette** Filterzigarette *f*.

filth [fɪlθ] *n* (*lit*) Dreck *m*; (*fig*) Unflat *m*; —**y** *a* dreckig; (*behaviour*) gemein; **weather** scheußlich.

fin [fɪn] *n* Flosse *f*.

final [faɪnl] *a* letzte(r,s) End-; (*conclusive*) endgültig; *n* (*Ftbl etc*) Endspiel *nt*; —**s** *pl* (*Univ*) Abschlußexamen *nt*; (*Sport*) Schlußrunde *f*; —**e** [fɪ'nɑːlɪ] (*Theat*) Schlußszene *f*; (*Mus*) Finale *nt*; —**ist** (*Sport*) Schlußrundenteilnehmer *m*; —**ize** *vt* endgültige Form geben (+*dat*); abschließen; —**ly** *ad* (*lastly*) zuletzt; (*eventually*) endlich; (*irrevocably*) endgültig.

finance [faɪ'næns] *n* Finanzwesen *nt*; —**s** *pl* Finanzen *pl*; (*income*) Einkünfte *pl*; *vt* finanzieren.

financial [faɪ'nænʃəl] *a* Finanz-; finanziell; —**ly** *ad* finanziell.

financier [faɪ'nænsɪə*] *n* Finanzier *m*.

find [faɪnd] *irreg vt* finden; *vi* (*realize*) erkennen; *n* Fund *m*; **to** — **sb guilty** jdn für schuldig erklären; **to** — **out** herausfinden; —**ings** *pl* (*Jur*) Ermittlungsergebnis *nt*; (*of report*) Feststellung *f*, Befund *m*.

fine [faɪn] *a* fein; (*thin*) dünn, fein; (*good*) gut; *clothes* elegant; *weather* schön; *ad* (*well*) gut; (*small*) klein; *n* (*Jur*) Geldstrafe *f*; *vt* (*Jur*) mit einer Geldstrafe belegen; **to cut it** — (*fig*) knapp rechnen; — **arts** *pl* die schönen

Künste pl; **—ness** n Feinheit f;
—ry ['faɪnərɪ] Putz m; **—sse**
[fɪ'nɛs] Finesse f.

finger ['fɪŋgə*] n Finger m; vt
befühlen; **—nail** Fingernagel m;
—print Fingerabdruck m; **—stall**
Fingerling m; **—tip** Fingerspitze f;
to have sth at one's —tips etw
parat haben.

finicky ['fɪnɪkɪ] a pingelig.

finish ['fɪnɪʃ] n Ende nt; (Sport)
Ziel nt; (of object) Verarbeitung f;
(of paint) Oberflächenwirkung f; vt
beenden; book zu Ende lesen; **to
be —ed** with sth fertig sein mit
etw; vi aufhören; (Sport) ans Ziel
kommen; **—ing line** Ziellinie f;
—ing school Mädchenpensionat nt.

finite ['faɪnaɪt] a endlich, begrenzt;
(Gram) finit.

fiord [fjɔːd] n Fjord m.

fir [fɜː*] n Tanne f, Fichte f.

fire [faɪə*] n (lit, fig) Feuer nt;
(damaging) Brand m, Feuer nt; **to
set — to sth** in Brand stecken;
to be on — brennen; vt (Aut)
zünden; gun abfeuern; (fig)
imagination entzünden; (dismiss)
hinauswerfen; vi (Aut) zünden; **to
— at sb** auf jdn schießen; **— away!**
schieß los!; **— alarm** Feueralarm
m; **—arm** Schußwaffe f; **—
brigade** Feuerwehr f; **— engine**
Feuerwehrauto nt; **— escape** Feuer-
leiter f; **— extinguisher** Löschgerät
nt; **—man** Feuerwehrmann m;
—place offene(r) Kamin m;
—proof a feuerfest; **—side** Kamin
m; **—station** Feuerwehrwache f;
—wood Brennholz nt; **—works** pl
Feuerwerk nt.

firing ['faɪərɪŋ] n Schießen nt; **—
squad** Exekutionskommando nt.

firm a, **—ly** ad [fɜːm,-lɪ] fest;
(determined) entschlossen; n

Firma f; **—ness** Festigkeit f; Entschlossenheit f.

first [fɜːst] a erste(r,s); ad zuerst;
arrive als erste(r); happen zum
erstenmal; n (person: in race)
Erste(r) mf; (Univ) Eins f; (Aut)
erste(r) Gang m; at — zuerst,
anfangs; **— of all** zu allererst; **—
aid** Erste Hilfe f; **—aid kit**
Verbandskasten m; **—class** a
erstklassig; (travel) erste(r)
Klasse; **—hand** a aus erster Hand; **—
lady** (US) First Lady f; **—ly** ad
erstens; **— name** Vorname m; **—
night** Premiere f; Erstaufführung f;
—rate a erstklassig.

fiscal ['fɪskəl] a fiskalisch, Finanz-.

fish [fɪʃ] n Fisch m; vt river angeln
in (+ dat); sea fischen in (+ dat);
vi fischen; angeln; **— out**
herausfischen; **to go —ing** angeln
gehen; (in sea) fischen gehen; **—
erman** Fischer m; **—ery** Fisch-
grund m; **— finger** Fischstäbchen
nt; **— hook** Angelhaken m; **—ing
boat** Fischerboot nt; **—ing line**
Angelschnur f; **—ing rod** Angel-
(rute) f; **—ing tackle** Angelzeug nt;
— market Fischmarkt m; **—
monger** Fischhändler m; **— slice**
Fischvorlegemesser nt; **—y** a (col:
suspicious) faul.

fission ['fɪʃən] n Spaltung f.

fissure ['fɪʃə*] n Riß m.

fist [fɪst] n Faust f.

fit [fɪt] a (Med) gesund; (Sport) in
Form, fit; (suitable) geeignet; vt
passen (+ dat); (insert, attach)
einsetzen; vi (correspond) passen
(zu); (clothes) passen; (in space,
gap) hineinpassen; n (of clothes)
Sitz m; (Med, of anger) Anfall m;
(of laughter) Krampf m; **— in** vi
sich einfügen; vt einpassen; **— out**
vt, **— up** vt ausstatten; **—fully, by**

—s and starts *move* ruckweise; *work* unregelmäßig; **—ment** Einrichtungsgegenstand *m*; **—ness** (*suitability*) Eignung *f*; (*Med*) Gesundheit *f*; (*Sport*) Fitneß *f*; **—ter** (*Tech*) Monteur *m*; **—ting** *a* passend; *n* (*of dress*) Anprobe *f*; (*piece of equipment*) (Ersatz)teil *nt*; **—tings** *pl* Zubehör *nt*.

five [faɪv] *num* fünf; **—r** (*Brit*) Fünf-Pfund-Note *f*.

fix [fɪks] *vt* befestigen; (*settle*) festsetzen; (*repair*) richten, reparieren; *drink* zurechtmachen; *n*: in a — in der Klemme; **—ed** *a* repariert; *. time* abgemacht; it was **—ed** (*dishonest*) das war Schiebung; **—ture** ['fɪkstʃə*] Installationsteil *m*; (*Sport*) Spiel *nt*.

fizz [fɪz] *n* Sprudeln *nt*; *vi* sprudeln.

fizzle ['fɪzl] *vi* zischen; **— out** *vi* verpuffen.

fizzy ['fɪzɪ] *a* Sprudel-, sprudelnd.

fjord [fjɔːd] *n* = fiord.

flabbergasted ['flæbəgɑːstɪd] *a* (*col*) platt.

flabby ['flæbɪ] *a* wabbelig.

flag [flæg] *n* Fahne *f*; *vi* (*strength*) nachlassen; (*spirit*) erlahmen; **— down** *vt* stoppen, abwinken.

flagon ['flægən] *n* bauchige (Wein)-flasche *f*, Krug *m*.

flagpole ['flægpəʊl] *n* Fahnenstange *f*.

flagrant ['fleɪgrənt] *a* offenkundig; *offence* schamlos; *violation* flagrant.

flagstone ['flægstəʊn] *n* Steinplatte *f*.

flair [fleə*] *n* (*talent*) Talent *nt*; (*of style*) Schick *m*.

flake [fleɪk] *n* (*of snow*) Flocke *f*; (*of rust*) Schuppe *f*; *vi* (*also* **— off**) abblättern.

flamboyant [flæm'bɔɪənt] *a* extravagant; *colours* brillant; *gesture* großartig.

flame [fleɪm] *n* Flamme *f*.

flaming ['fleɪmɪŋ] *a* (*col*) verdammt; *row* irre.

flamingo [flə'mɪŋgəʊ] *n* Flamingo *m*.

flan [flæn] *n* Obsttorte *f*.

flank [flæŋk] *n* Flanke *f*; *vt* flankieren.

flannel ['flænl] *n* Flanell *m*; (*face* —) Waschlappen *m*; (*col*) Geschwafel *nt*; **—s** *pl* Flanellhose *f*.

flap [flæp] *n* Klappe *f*; (*col: crisis*) (helle) Aufregung *f*; *vt wings* schlagen mit; *vi* lose herabhängen; flattern; (*col: panic*) sich aufregen.

flare [fleə*] *n* (*signal*) Leuchtsignal *nt*; (*in skirt etc*) Weite *f*; **— up** *vi* aufflammen; (*fig*) aufbrausen; (*revolt*) (plötzlich) ausbrechen.

flared [fleəd] *a trousers* ausgestellt.

flash [flæʃ] *n* Blitz *m*; (*news* —) Kurzmeldung *f*; (*Phot*) Blitzlicht *nt*; *vt* aufleuchten lassen; *message* durchgeben; *vi* aufleuchten; in a — im Nu; to — by *or* past vorbeirasen; **—back** Rückblende *f*; **—bulb** Blitzlichtbirne *f*; **—er** (*Aut*) Blinker *m*.

flashy ['flæʃɪ] *a* (*pej*) knallig.

flask [flɑːsk] *n* Reiseflasche *f*; (*Chem*) Kolben *m*; (*vacuum* —) Thermosflasche *f*.

flat [flæt] *a* flach; (*dull*) matt; (*Mus*) erniedrigt; *beer* schal; *tyre* platt; A — as; *ad* (*Mus*) zu tief; *n* (*rooms*) Wohnung *f*; (*Mus*) b *nt*; (*Aut*) Reifenpanne *f*, Platte(r) *m*; **— broke** *a* (*col*) völlig pleite; **—footed** *a* plattfüßig; **—ly** *ad* glatt; **—ness** Flachheit *f*; **—ten** (*also*

(*also* **—ten out**) platt machen, (ein)-
ebnen.

flatter ['flætə*] *vt* schmeicheln
(+*dat*); **—er** Schmeichler(in *f*) *m*;
—ing a schmeichelhaft; **—y**
Schmeichelei *f*.

flatulence ['flætjuləns] *n*
Blähungen *pl*.

flaunt [flɔ:nt] *vt* prunken mit.

flavour, (*US*) **flavor** ['fleɪvə*] *n*
Geschmack *m*; *vt* würzen; **—ing**
Würze *f*.

flaw [flɔ:] *n* Fehler *m*; (*in argument*) schwache(r) Punkt *m*;
—less a einwandfrei.

flax [flæks] *n* Flachs *m*; **—en** a
flachsfarben.

flea [fli:] *n* Floh *m*.

flee [fli:] *irreg vi* fliehen
vor (+*dat*); *country* fliehen aus.

fleece [fli:s] *n* Schaffell *nt*, Vlies *nt*;
vt (*col*) schröpfen.

fleet [fli:t] *n* Flotte *f*.

fleeting ['fli:tɪŋ] a flüchtig.

flesh [fleʃ] *n* Fleisch *nt*; (*of fruit*)
Fruchtfleisch *nt*; **— wound** Fleisch-
wunde *f*.

flex [fleks] *n* (Leitungs)kabel *nt*; *vt*
beugen, biegen; **—ibility**
[fleksɪ'bɪlɪtɪ] Biegsamkeit *f*; (*fig*)
Flexibilität *f*; **—ible** a biegsam;
plans flexibel.

flick [flɪk] *n* Schnippen *nt*; (*blow*)
leichte(r) Schlag *m*; *vt* leicht
schlagen; **— through** *vt* durchblättern; **to — sth off** etw weg-
schnippen.

flicker ['flɪkə*] *n* Flackern *nt*; (*of
emotion*) Funken *m*; *vi* flackern.

flier ['flaɪə*] *n* Flieger *m*.

flight [flaɪt] *n* Fliegen *nt*; (*journey*)
Flug *m*; (*fleeing*) Flucht *f*; **— of
stairs** Treppe *f*; **to take —** die
Flucht ergreifen; **to put to —** in

die Flucht schlagen; **— deck** Flug-
deck *nt*; **—y** a flatterhaft.

flimsy ['flɪmzɪ] a nicht stabil,
windig; (*thin*) hauchdünn; *excuse*
fadenscheinig.

flinch [flɪntʃ] *vi* zurückschrecken
(*away from* vor +*dat*).

fling [flɪŋ] *vt irreg* schleudern.

flint [flɪnt] *n* (*in lighter*) Feuerstein
m.

flip [flɪp] *vt* werfen; **he —ped the
lid off** er klappte den Deckel auf.

flippancy ['flɪpənsɪ] *n* Leichtfertigkeit *f*.

flippant ['flɪpənt] a schnippisch; **to
be — about sth** etw nicht ernst
nehmen.

flirt [flɜ:t] *vi* flirten; *n* kokette(s)
Mädchen *nt*; **he/she is a —** er/sie
flirtet gern; **—ation** [flɜ:'teɪʃən]
Flirt *m*.

flit [flɪt] *vi* flitzen.

float [fləʊt] *n* (*Fishing*) Schwimmer
m; (*esp in procession*) Plattform-
wagen *m*; *vi* schwimmen; (*in air*)
schweben; *vt* schwimmen lassen;
(*Comm*) gründen; *currency*
floaten; **—ing** a (*lit*) schwimmend;
fig) *votes* unentschieden.

flock [flɒk] *n* (*of sheep, Rel*) Herde
f; (*of birds*) Schwarm *m*; (*of
people*) Schar *f*.

flog [flɒg] *vt* prügeln; peitschen;
(*col: sell*) verkaufen.

flood [flʌd] *n* Überschwemmung *f*;
(*fig*) Flut *f*; **the F—** die Sintflut *f*;
to be in — Hochwasser haben; *vt*
(*lit, fig*) überschwemmen; **—ing**
Überschwemmung *f*; **—light** *n* Flut-
licht *nt*; *vt* anstrahlen; **—lighting**
Beleuchtung *f*.

floor [flɔ:*] *n* (Fuß)boden *m*;
(*storey*) Stock *m*; **— person** zu
Boden schlagen; **ground —** (*Brit*),
first — (*US*) Erdgeschoß *nt*; **first**

— (Brit), second — (US) erste(r)
Stock m; —board Diele f; — show
Kabarettvorstellung f; —walker
(Comm) Abteilungsaufseher m.

flop [flɒp] n Plumps m; (failure)
Reinfall m; vi (fail) durchfallen;
the project —ped aus dem Plan
wurde nichts.

floppy ['flɒpɪ] a hängend; — hat
Schlapphut m.

flora ['flɔːrə] n Flora f; —l a
Blumen-.

florid ['flɒrɪd] a style blumig.

florist ['flɒrɪst] n Blumenhändler(in
f) m; —'s (shop) Blumengeschäft
nt.

flotsam ['flɒtsəm] n Strandgut nt.

flounce [flaʊns] n (on dress) Besatz
m; vi: — in/out hinein-/hinaus-
stürmen.

flounder ['flaʊndə*] vi herum-
strampeln; (fig) ins Schleudern
kommen.

flour ['flaʊə*] n Mehl nt.

flourish ['flʌrɪʃ] vi blühen;
gedeihen; vt (wave) schwingen; n
(waving) Schwingen nt; (of
trumpets) Tusch m, Fanfare f;
—ing a blühend.

flout [flaʊt] vt mißachten, sich hin-
wegsetzen über (+acc).

flow [fləʊ] n Fließen nt; (of sea)
Flut f; vi fließen.

flower ['flaʊə*] n Blume f; vi
blühen; — bed Blumenbeet nt;
—pot Blumentopf m; —y a style
blumenreich.

flowing ['fləʊɪŋ] a fließend; hair
wallend; style flüssig.

flu [fluː] n Grippe f.

fluctuate ['flʌktjʊeɪt] vi schwanken.

fluctuation [flʌktjʊ'eɪʃən] n
Schwankung f.

fluency ['fluːənsɪ] n Flüssigkeit f;
his — in English seine Fähigkeit,
fließend Englisch zu sprechen.

fluent a —ly ad ['fluːənt,-lɪ] speech
flüssig; to be — in German fließend
Deutsch sprechen.

fluff [flʌf] n Fussel f; —y a
flaumig; pastry flockig.

fluid ['fluːɪd] n Flüssigkeit f; a (lit)
flüssig; (fig) plans veränderbar.

fluke [fluːk] n (col) Dusel m.

fluorescent [fluə'resnt] a fluores-
zierend, Leucht-.

fluoride ['fluəraɪd] n Fluorid nt.

flurry ['flʌrɪ] n (of activity)
Aufregung f; (of snow) Gestöber nt.

flush [flʌʃ] n Erröten nt; (of excitement) Glühen nt; (Cards) Sequenz
f; vt (aus)spülen; vi erröten; a
glatt; —ed a rot.

fluster ['flʌstə*] n Verwirrung f;
—ed a verwirrt.

flute [fluːt] n Querflöte f.

fluted ['fluːtɪd] a gerillt.

flutter ['flʌtə*] n (of wings)
Flattern nt; (of excitement) Beben
nt; vi flattern; (person) rotieren.

flux [flʌks] n: in a state of — im
Fluß.

fly [flaɪ] n (insect) Fliege f; (on
trousers, also flies) (Hosen)schlitz
m; irreg vt fliegen; vi fliegen;
(flee) fliehen; (flag) wehen; —
open vi auffliegen; let — vti
(shoot) losschießen; (verbally) los-
wettern; insults loslassen; —ing n
Fliegen nt; with —ing colours mit
fliegenden Fahnen; —ing saucer
fliegende Untertasse f; —ing start
gute(r) Start m; —ing visit Stipp-
visite f; —over (Brit) Überführung
f; —paper Fliegenfänger m; —past
Luftparade f; —sheet (for tent)
Regendach nt; —swatter Fliegen-
wedel m; —wheel Schwungrad nt.

foal [fəul] n Fohlen nt.

foam [fəum] n Schaum m; (plastic etc) Schaumgummi m; vi schäumen.

fob [fɔb] a : — **off** vt andrehen (sb with sth jdm etw); (with promise) abspeisen.

focal ['fəukəl] a im Brennpunkt (stehend), Brennpunkt-.

focus ['fəukəs] n Brennpunkt m; (fig) Mittelpunkt m; vt attention konzentrieren; camera scharf einstellen; vi sich konzentrieren (on auf +acc); **in** — scharf eingestellt; **out of** — unscharf eingestellt.

fodder ['fɔdə*] n Futter nt.

foe [fəu] n (liter) Feind m, Gegner m.

foetus ['fi:təs] n Fötus m.

fog [fɔg] n Nebel m; vt issue verunklären, verwirren; —**gy** a neblig, trüb.

foible ['fɔibl] n Schwäche f, Faible nt.

foil [fɔil] vt vereiteln; n (metal, also fig) Folie f; (fencing) Florett nt.

fold [fəuld] n (bend, crease) Falte f; (Agr) Pferch m; (for sheep) Pferch m; vt falten; —**up** vt map etc zusammenfalten; vi (business) eingehen; —**er** (pamphlet) Broschüre f; (portfolio) Schnellhefter m; —**ing** a chair etc zusammenklappbar, Klapp-.

foliage ['fəulidʒ] n Laubwerk nt.

folio ['fəuliəu] n Foliant m.

folk [fəuk] n Volk nt; a Volks-; — s pl Leute pl; —**lore** (study) Volkskunde f; (tradition) Folklore f; —**song** Volkslied nt; (modern) Folksong m.

follow ['fɔləu] vt folgen (+dat); (obey) befolgen; fashion mitmachen; profession nachgehen (+dat); (understand) folgen können (+dat); vi folgen; (result) sich ergeben; — **as** wie im folgenden; — **up** vt (weiter) verfolgen; —**er** Anhänger(in f) m; —**ing** a folgend; n Folgende(s) nt; (people) Gefolgschaft f.

folly ['fɔli] n Torheit f.

fond [fɔnd] a: to be — of haben; —**ly** ad (with love) liebevoll; (foolishly) törichterweise; —**ness** Vorliebe f; (for people) Liebe f.

font [fɔnt] n Taufbecken nt.

food [fu:d] n Essen nt, Nahrung f; (for animals) Futter nt; — **mixer** Küchenmixer m; —**poisoning** Lebensmittelvergiftung f; —**stuffs** pl Lebensmittel pl.

fool [fu:l] n Narr m, Närrin f; (jester) (Hof)narr m, Hanswurst m; (food) Mus nt; vt (deceive) hereinlegen; vi (behave like a —) (herum)albern; —**hardy** a tollkühn; —**ish** a, —**ishly** ad dumm; albern; —**ishness** Dummheit f; —**proof** a idiotensicher.

foot [fut] n Fuß m; (of animal) Pfote f; **to put one's** — **in it** ins Fettnäpfchen treten; **on** — zu Fuß; vt bill bezahlen; —**ball** Fußball m; —**baller** Fußballer m; —**brake** Fußbremse f; —**bridge** Fußgängerbrücke f; —**hills** pl Ausläufer pl; —**hold** Halt m; Stütze f; —**ing** (lit) Halt m; (fig) Verhältnis nt; **to get a** —**ing in society** in der Gesellschaft Fuß fassen; **to be on a good** —**ing with sb** mit jdm auf gutem Fuß stehen; —**light** Rampenlicht nt; —**man** Bediente(r) m; —**and-mouth (disease)** Maul- und Klauenseuche f; —**note** Fußnote f; —**path** Fußweg m; —**rest** Fußstütze f; —**sore** a fußkrank; —**step** Schritt m; **in his father's**

—steps in den Fußstapfen seines Vaters; —wear Schuhzeug *nt.*

fop [fɒp] *n* Geck *m.*

for [fɔ:*] *prep* für; *cj* denn; what —? wozu?

forage ['fɒrɪdʒ] *n* (Vieh)futter *nt*; *vi* nach Nahrung suchen.

foray ['fɒreɪ] *n* Raubzug *m.*

forbearing [fɔ:'bɛərɪŋ] *a* geduldig.

forbid [fə'bɪd] *vt irreg* verbieten; —den *a* verboten; —ding *a* einschüchternd, abschreckend.

force [fɔ:s] *n* Kraft *f,* Stärke *f*; (compulsion) Zwang *m*; (Mil) Truppen *pl*; *vt* zwingen; lock aufbrechen; plant hochzüchten; in — rule gültig; group in großer Stärke; the F—s *pl* die Armee; —d *a* smile gezwungen; landing Not-; —ful *a* speech kraftvoll; personality resolut.

forceps ['fɔ:seps] *npl* Zange *f.*

forcible ['fɔ:səbl] *a* (convincing) wirksam, überzeugend; (violent) gewaltsam.

forcibly ['fɔ:səblɪ] *ad* unter Zwang, zwangsweise.

ford [fɔ:d] *n* Furt *f*; *vt* durchwaten.

fore [fɔ:*] *a* vorder, Vorder-; *n*: to the — in den Vordergrund.

forearm ['fɔ:rɑ:m] *n* Unterarm *m.*

foreboding [fɔ:'bəʊdɪŋ] *n* Vorahnung *f.*

forecast ['fɔ:kɑ:st] *n* Vorhersage *f*; *vt irreg* voraussagen.

forecourt ['fɔ:kɔ:t] *n* (of garage) Vorplatz *m.*

forefathers ['fɔ:fɑ:ðəz] *npl* Vorfahren *pl.*

forefinger ['fɔ:fɪŋgə*] *n* Zeigefinger *m.*

forefront ['fɔ:frʌnt] *n* Spitze *f.*

forego [fɔ:'gəʊ] *vt irreg* verzichten auf (+*acc*); —ing *a* vorangehend;

—ne conclusion ausgemachte Sache.

foreground ['fɔ:graʊnd] *n* Vordergrund *m.*

forehead ['fɒrɪd] *n* Stirn *f.*

foreign ['fɒrɪn] *a* Auslands-; country, accent ausländisch; trade Außen-; body Fremd-; —er Ausländer(in *f*) *m*; — exchange Devisen *pl*; — minister Außenminister *m.*

foreman ['fɔ:mən] *n* Vorarbeiter *m.*

foremost ['fɔ:məʊst] *a* erste(r,s).

forensic [fə'rensɪk] *a* gerichtsmedizinisch.

forerunner ['fɔ:rʌnə*] *n* Vorläufer *m.*

foresee [fɔ:'si:] *vt irreg* vorhersehen; —able *a* absehbar.

foreshore ['fɔ:ʃɔ:*] *n* Küste *f,* Küstenland *nt.*

foresight ['fɔ:saɪt] *n* Voraussicht *f.*

forest ['fɒrɪst] *n* Wald *m.*

forestall [fɔ:'stɔ:l] *vt* zuvorkommen (+*dat*).

forestry ['fɒrɪstrɪ] *n* Forstwirtschaft *f.*

foretaste ['fɔ:teɪst] *n* Vorgeschmack *m.*

foretell [fɔ:'tel] *vt irreg* vorhersagen.

forever [fə'revə*] *ad* für immer.

forewarn [fɔ:'wɔ:n] *vt* vorherwarnen.

foreword ['fɔ:wɜ:d] *n* Vorwort *nt.*

forfeit ['fɔ:fɪt] *n* Einbuße *f*; *vt* verwirken.

forge [fɔ:dʒ] *n* Schmiede *f*; *vt* fälschen; iron schmieden; — ahead *vi* Fortschritte machen; —r Fälscher *m*; —ry Fälschung *f.*

forget [fə'get] *vti irreg* vergessen; —ful *a* vergeßlich; —fulness Vergeßlichkeit *f.*

forgive [fə'gɪv] *vt irreg* verzeihen (*sb for sth* jdm etw).

forgiveness [fə'gɪvnəs] *n* Verzeihung *f*.

forgo [fɔː'gəʊ] *see* **forego.**

fork [fɔːk] *n* Gabel *f*; (*in road*) Gabelung *f*; *vi* (*road*) sich gabeln; — out *vti* (*col: pay*) blechen; —ed a gegabelt; *lightning* zickzackförmig.

forlorn [fə'lɔːn] *a person* verlassen; *hope* vergeblich.

form [fɔːm] *n* Form *f*; (*type*) Art *f*; (*figure*) Gestalt *f*; (*Sch*) Klasse *f*; (*bench*) (Schul)bank *f*; (*document*) Formular *nt*; *vt* formen; (*be part of*) bilden.

formal ['fɔːməl] *a* förmlich, formell; *occasion* offiziell; —ity [fɔː'mælɪtɪ] Förmlichkeit *f*; (*of occasion*) offizielle(r) Charakter *m*; —ities *pl* Formalitäten *pl*; —ly *ad* (*ceremoniously*) formell; (*officially*) offiziell.

format ['fɔːmæt] *n* Format *nt.*

formation [fɔː'meɪʃən] *n* Bildung *f*; Gestaltung *f*; (*Aviat*) Formation *f.*

formative ['fɔːmətɪv] *a years* formend.

former ['fɔːmə*] *a* früher; (*opposite of latter*) erstere(r,s); —ly *ad* früher.

Formica ® [fɔː'maɪkə] *n* Resopal ® *nt.*

formidable ['fɔːmɪdəbl] *a* furchtbar; gewaltig.

formula ['fɔːmjʊlə] *n* Formel *f*; —te [fɔːmjʊlert] *vt* formulieren.

forsake [fə'seɪk] *vt irreg* im Stich lassen, verlassen; *habit* aufgeben.

fort [fɔːt] *n* Feste *f*, Fort *nt.*

forte ['fɔːtɪ] *n* Stärke *f*, starke Seite *f.*

forth [fɔːθ] *ad:* and so — und so weiter; —coming *a* kommend; *character* entgegenkommend; —right *a* offen, gerade heraus.

fortification [fɔːtɪfɪ'keɪʃən] *n* Befestigung *f.*

fortify ['fɔːtɪfaɪ] *vt* (ver)stärken; (*protect*) befestigen.

fortitude ['fɔːtɪtjuːd] *n* Seelenstärke *f*, Mut *m.*

fortnight ['fɔːtnaɪt] *n* zwei Wochen *pl*, vierzehn Tage *pl*; —ly *a* zweiwöchentlich; *ad* alle vierzehn Tage.

fortress ['fɔːtrɪs] *n* Festung *f.*

fortuitous [fɔː'tjuːɪtəs] *a* zufällig.

fortunate ['fɔːtʃənɪt] *a* glücklich; —ly *ad* glücklicherweise, zum Glück.

fortune ['fɔːtʃən] *n* Glück *nt*; (*money*) Vermögen *nt*; —teller Wahrsager(in *f*) *m.*

forty ['fɔːtɪ] *num* vierzig.

forum ['fɔːrəm] *n* Forum *nt.*

forward ['fɔːwəd] *a* vordere(r,s); *movement* vorwärts; *person* vorlaut; *planning* Voraus-; *ad* vorwärts; *n* (*Sport*) Stürmer *m*; *vt* (*send*) schicken; (*help*) fördern; —s *ad* vorwärts.

fossil ['fɒsl] *n* Fossil *nt*, Versteinerung *f.*

foster ['fɒstə*] *vt talent* fördern; — *child* Pflegekind *nt*; — *mother* Pflegemutter *f.*

foul [faʊl] *a* schmutzig; *language* gemein; *weather* schlecht; *n* (*Sport*) Foul *nt*; *vt mechanism* blockieren; (*Sport*) foulen.

found [faʊnd] *vt* (*establish*) gründen; —ation [faʊn'deɪʃən] (*act*) Gründung *f*; (*fig*) Fundament *nt*; —ations *pl* Fundament *nt.*

founder ['faʊndə*] *n* Gründer(in *f*) *m*; *vi* sinken.

foundry ['faʊndrɪ] *n* Gießerei *f*, Eisenhütte *f*.

fount [faʊnt] *n* (*liter*) Quell *m*; **—ain** (Spring)brunnen *m*; **—ain pen** Füllfederhalter *m*.

four [fɔ:*] *num* vier; **—on all —s** auf allen vieren; **—some** Quartett *nt*; **—teen** *num* vierzehn; **—th** *a* vierte(r,s).

fowl [faʊl] *n* Huhn *nt*; (*food*) Geflügel *nt*.

fox [fɒks] *n* Fuchs *m*; **—ed** *a* verblüfft; **—hunting** Fuchsjagd *f*; **—trot** Foxtrott *m*.

foyer ['fɔɪeɪ] *n* Foyer *nt*, Vorhalle *f*.

fracas ['fræka:] *n* Radau *m*.

fraction ['frækʃən] *n* (*Math*) Bruch *m*; (*part*) Bruchteil *m*.

fracture ['fræktʃə*] *n* (*Med*) Bruch *m*; *vt* brechen.

fragile ['frædʒaɪl] *a* zerbrechlich.

fragment ['frægmənt] *n* Bruchstück *m*, Fragment *nt*; (*small part*) Stück *nt*, Splitter *m*; **—ary** ['frægˈmentərɪ] *a* bruchstückhaft, fragmentarisch.

fragrance ['freɪgrəns] *n* Duft *m*.

fragrant ['freɪgrənt] *a* duftend.

frail [freɪl] *a* schwach, gebrechlich.

frame [freɪm] *n* Rahmen *m*; (*body*) Gestalt *f*; *vt* einrahmen; (*make*) gestalten, machen; (*col: incriminate*) to **—** sb jdm etw anhängen; **— of mind** Verfassung *f*; **—work** Rahmen *m*; (*of society*) Gefüge *nt*.

franchise ['fræntʃaɪz] *n* (aktives) Wahlrecht *nt*.

frank [fræŋk] *a* offen; **—furter** Saitenwürstchen *nt*; **—ly** *ad* offen gesagt; **—ness** Offenheit *f*.

frankincense ['fræŋkɪnsens] *n* Weihrauch *m*.

frantic ['fræntɪk] *a* effort verzweifelt; **— with worry** außer sich vor Sorge; **—ally** *ad* außer sich; verzweifelt.

fraternal [frə'tɜ:nl] *a* brüderlich.

fraternity [frə'tɜ:nɪtɪ] *n* (*club*) Vereinigung *f*; (*spirit*) Brüderlichkeit *f*; (*US Sch*) Studentenverbindung *f*.

fraternization [frætənaɪ'zeɪʃən] *n* Verbrüderung *f*.

fraternize ['frætənaɪz] *vi* fraternisieren.

fraud [frɔ:d] *n* (*trickery*) Betrug *m*; (*trick*) Schwindel *m*, Trick *m*; (*person*) Schwindler(in *f*) *m*.

fraudulent ['frɔ:djʊlənt] *a* betrügerisch.

fraught [frɔ:t] *a* voller (*with gen*).

fray [freɪ] *n* Rauferei *f*; *vti* ausfransen.

freak [fri:k] *n* Monstrosität *f*; (*crazy person*) Irre(r) *mf*; (*storm etc*) Ausnahmeerscheinung *f*; *a storm, conditions* anormal; *animal* monströs; **— out** *vi* (*col*) durchdrehen.

freckle ['frekl] *n* Sommersprosse *f*; **—d** *a* sommersprossig.

free [fri:] *a* frei; (*loose*) lose; (*liberal*) freigebig; **to get sth —** etw umsonst bekommen; **you're — to ...** es steht dir frei zu ...; *vt* (*set free*) befreien; (*unblock*) freimachen; **—dom** Freiheit *f*; **—for-all** allgemeine(r) Wettbewerb *m*; (*fight*) allgemeine(s) Handgemenge *nt*; **— kick** Freistoß *m*; **—lance** *a* frei; *artist* freischaffend; **—ly** *ad* frei; lose; (*generously*) reichlich; **admit** offen; **—mason** Freimaurer *m*; **—masonry** Freimaurerei *f*; **—trade** Freihandel *m*; **—way** (*US*) Autobahn *f*; **—wheel** *vi* im Freilauf fahren.

freesia ['friːʒə] n Freesie f.

freeze [friːz] irreg vi gefrieren; (feel cold) frieren; vt (lit, fig) einfrieren; n (fig, Fin) Stopp m; —r Tiefkühltruhe f; (in fridge) Gefrierfach nt.

freezing ['friːzɪŋ] a eisig; (— cold) eiskalt; — point Gefrierpunkt m.

freight [freɪt] n (goods) Fracht f; (money charged) Fracht(gebühr) f; — car (US) Güterwagen m; —er (Naut) Frachtschiff nt.

French [frentʃ] a: — fried potatoes pl Pommes frites pl; — window Verandatür f; see appendix.

frenzy ['frenzɪ] n Raserei f, wilde Aufregung f.

frequency ['friːkwənsɪ] n Häufigkeit f; (Phys) Frequenz f.

frequent a, —ly ad ['friːkwənt,-lɪ] häufig; [frɪ'kwent] vt (regelmäßig) besuchen.

fresco ['freskəʊ] n Fresko nt.

fresh [freʃ] a frisch; (new) neu; (cheeky) frech; —en (also —en up) vi (sich) auffrischen; (person) sich frisch machen; vt auffrischen; —ly ad gerade; —ness Frische f; —water a fish Süßwasser-.

fret [fret] vi sich (dat) Sorgen machen (about über +acc).

friar ['fraɪə*] n Klosterbruder m.

friction ['frɪkʃən] n (lit, fig) Reibung f.

Friday ['fraɪdeɪ] n Freitag m; see good.

fridge [frɪdʒ] n Kühlschrank m.

fried [fraɪd] a gebraten.

friend [frend] n Bekannte(r) mf; (more intimate) Freund(in f) m; —liness Freundlichkeit f; —ly a freundlich; relations freundschaftlich; —ship Freundschaft f.

frieze [friːz] n Fries m.

frigate ['frɪgɪt] n Fregatte f.

fright [fraɪt] n Schrecken m; you look a — (col) du siehst unmöglich aus!; —en vt erschrecken; to be —ened Angst haben; —ening a schrecklich; ängstigend; —ful a, —fully ad (col) schrecklich, furchtbar.

frigid ['frɪdʒɪd] a kalt, eisig; woman frigid; —ity [frɪ'dʒɪdɪtɪ] Kälte f; Frigidität f.

frill [frɪl] n Rüsche f.

fringe [frɪndʒ] n Besatz m; (hair) Pony m; (fig) äußere(r) Rand m, Peripherie f.

frisky ['frɪskɪ] a lebendig, ausgelassen.

fritter ['frɪtə*] : — away vt vertun, verplempern.

frivolity [frɪ'vɒlɪtɪ] n Leichtfertigkeit f, Frivolität f.

frivolous ['frɪvələs] a frivol, leichtsinnig.

frizzy ['frɪzɪ] a kraus.

fro [frəʊ] see **to**.

frock [frɒk] n Kleid nt.

frog [frɒg] n Frosch m; —man Froschmann m.

frolic ['frɒlɪk] n lustige(r) Streich m; vi ausgelassen sein.

from [frɒm] prep von; (place) aus; (judging by) nach; (because of) wegen (+gen).

front [frʌnt] n Vorderseite f; (of house) Fassade f; (promenade) Strandpromenade f; (Mil, Pol, Met) Front f; (fig: appearances) Fassade f; a (forward) vordere(r,s), Vorder-; (first) vorderste(r,s); page erste(r,s); door Eingangs-, Haus-; in — ad vorne; in — of prep vor; —age Vorderfront f; —al a frontal, Vorder-; —ier ['frʌntɪə*] Grenze f;

— **room** (Brit) Vorderzimmer nt, Wohnzimmer nt; —**-wheel drive** Vorderradantrieb m.

frost [frɒst] n Frost m; —**bite** Erfrierung f; —**ed** a glass Milch-; —**y** a frostig.

froth [frɒθ] n Schaum m; —**y** a schaumig.

frown [fraun] n Stirnrunzeln nt; (vi) die Stirn runzeln.

frozen [frəuzn] a food gefroren; (Fin) assets festgelegt.

frugal ['fru:gəl] a sparsam, bescheiden.

fruit [fru:t] n (particular) Frucht f; I like — ich esse gern Obst; —**erer** Obsthändler m; —**ful** a fruchtbar; —**ion** fru:'ıʃən Verwirklichung f; to come to —**ion** in Erfüllung gehen; — **machine** Spielautomat m; — **salad** Obstsalat m.

frustrate [frʌs'treıt] vt vereiteln; —**d** a gehemmt; (Psych) frustriert.

frustration [frʌs'treıʃən] n Behinderung f; Frustration f.

fry [fraı] vt braten; small — pl kleine Leute pl; (children) Kleine(n) pl; —**ing pan** Bratpfanne f.

fuchsia ['fju:ʃə] n Fuchsie f.

fuddy-duddy ['fʌdıdʌdı] n altmodische(r) Kauz m.

fudge [fʌdʒ] n Karamellen pl.

fuel [fjuəl] n Treibstoff m; (for heating) Brennstoff m; (for cigarette lighter) Benzin nt; — **oil** (diesel fuel) Heizöl nt; — **tank** Tank m.

fugitive ['fju:dʒıtıv] n Flüchtling m; (from prison) Flüchtige(r) m.

fulfil [ful'fıl] vt duty erfüllen; promise einhalten; —**ment** Erfüllung f; Einhaltung f.

full [ful] a box, bottle, price voll; person (satisfied) satt, member,

power, employment, moon Voll-; (complete) vollständig, Voll-; —**speed** höchste(r, s); skirt weit; **in** — vollständig, ungekürzt; —**back** Verteidiger m; —**ness** Fülle f; — **stop** Punkt m; —**-time** a job Ganztags-; ad work hauptberuflich; —**y** ad völlig; —**y-fledged** a (lit, fig) flügge; a —**y-fledged** teacher ein vollausgebildeter Lehrer.

fumble ['fʌmbl] vi herumfummeln (with, at an+dat).

fume [fju:m] vi rauchen, qualmen; (fig) wütend sein, kochen (col); —**s** pl Abgase pl; Qualm m.

fumigate ['fju:mıgeıt] vt ausräuchern.

fun [fʌn] n Spaß m; to make — of sich lustig machen über (+acc).

function ['fʌŋkʃən] n Funktion f; (occasion) Veranstaltung f, Feier f; vi funktionieren; —**al** a funktionell, praktisch.

fund [fʌnd] n (money) Geldmittel pl, Fonds m; (store) Schatz m, Vorrat m.

fundamental [fʌndə'mentl] a fundamental, grundlegend; —**s** pl Grundbegriffe pl; —**ly** ad im Grunde.

funeral ['fju:nərəl] n Beerdigung f; a Beerdigungs-.

fungus ['fʌŋgəs] n, pl fungi or funguses Pilz m.

funicular [fju:'nıkjulə*] n (Draht-) seilbahn f.

funnel ['fʌnl] n Trichter m; (Naut) Schornstein m.

funnily ['fʌnılı] ad komisch; — **enough** merkwürdigerweise.

funny ['fʌnı] a komisch; — **bone** Musikantenknochen m.

fur [fɜ:*] n Pelz m; — **coat** Pelzmantel m.

furious *a*, **—ly** *ad* ['fjʊəriəs, -li] wütend; *attempt* heftig.

furlong ['fɜːlɒŋ] *n* = 220 yards.

furlough ['fɜːləʊ] *n* (US) Urlaub *m*.

furnace ['fɜːnis] *n* (Brenn)ofen *m*.

furnish ['fɜːniʃ] *vt* einrichten, möblieren; (*supply*) versehen; **—ings** *pl* Einrichtung *f*.

furniture ['fɜːnitʃə*] *n* Möbel *pl*.

furrow ['fʌrəʊ] *n* Furche *f*.

furry ['fɜːri] *a* pelzartig; *tongue* pelzig; *animal* Pelz-.

further ['fɜːðə*] *comp of* **far**; *a* weitere(r,s); *ad* weiter; *vt* fördern; **— education** Weiterbildung *f*; **—more** *ad* Erwachsenenbildung *f*; ferner.

furthest ['fɜːðist] *superl of* **far**.

furtive *a*, **—ly** *ad* ['fɜːtiv, -li] verstohlen.

fury ['fjʊəri] *n* Wut *f*, Zorn *m*.

fuse [fjuːz] *n* (Elec) Sicherung *f*;

(of bomb) Zünder *m*; *vt* verschmelzen; *vi* (Elec) durchbrennen; **— box** Sicherungskasten *m*.

fuselage ['fjuːzəlɑːʒ] *n* Flugzeugrumpf *m*.

fusion ['fjuːʒən] *n* Verschmelzung *f*.

fuss [fʌs] *n* Theater *nt*; **—y** *a* (*difficult*) heikel; (*attentive to detail*) kleinlich.

futile ['fjuːtail] *a* zwecklos, sinnlos.

futility [fjuːˈtiliti] *n* Zwecklosigkeit *f*.

future ['fjuːtʃə*] *a* zukünftig; *n* Zukunft *f*; **in (the) —** in Zukunft, zukünftig.

futuristic [fjuːtʃəˈristik] *a* futuristisch.

fuze [fjuːz] (US) = **fuse**.

fuzzy ['fʌzi] *a* (*indistinct*) verschwommen; *hair* kraus.

G

G, g [dʒiː] *n* G *nt*, g *nt*.

gabble ['gæbl] *vi* plappern.

gable ['geibl] *n* Giebel *m*.

gadget ['gædʒit] *n* Vorrichtung *f*; **—ry** Kinkerlitzchen *pl*.

gaffe [gæf] *n* Fauxpas *m*.

gag [gæg] *n* Knebel *m*; (*Theat*) Gag *m*; *vt* knebeln; (*Pol*) mundtot machen.

gaiety ['geiti] *n* Fröhlichkeit *f*.

gaily ['geili] *ad* lustig, fröhlich.

gain [gein] *vt* (*obtain*) erhalten; (*win*) gewinnen; *vi* (*improve*) gewinnen (*in an + dat*); (*make progress*) Vorsprung gewinnen; (*clock*) vorgehen; *n* Gewinn *m*; **—ful employment** Erwerbstätigkeit

f.

gala ['gɑːlə] *n* Fest *nt*.

galaxy ['gæləksi] *n* Sternsystem *nt*.

gale [geil] *n* Sturm *m*.

gallant ['gælənt] *a* tapfer, ritterlich; (*polite*) galant; **—ry** Tapferkeit *f*, Ritterlichkeit *f*; Galanterie *f*.

gall-bladder ['gɔːlblædə*] *n* Gallenblase *f*.

gallery ['gæləri] *n* Galerie *f*.

galley ['gæli] *n* (*ship's kitchen*) Kombüse *f*; (*ship*) Galeere *f*.

gallon ['gælən] *n* Gallone *f*.

gallop ['gæləp] *n* Galopp *m*; *vi* galoppieren.

gallows ['gæləʊz] *npl* Galgen *m*.

gallstone ['gɔːlstəʊn] *n* Gallenstein *m*.

gamble ['gæmbl] *vi* (um Geld) spielen; *vt* (*risk*) aufs Spiel setzen; *n* Risiko *nt*; **—r** Spieler(in *f*) *m*.

gambling ['gæmblɪŋ] *n* Glücksspiel *nt*.

game [geɪm] *n* Spiel *nt*; (*hunting*) Wild *nt*; *a* bereit (*for* zu); (*brave*) mutig; **—keeper** Wildhüter *m*.

gammon ['gæmən] *n* geräucherte(r) Schinken *m*.

gander ['gændə*] *n* Gänserich *m*.

gang [gæŋ] *n* (*of criminals, youths*) Bande *f*; (*of workmen*) Kolonne *f*.

gangrene ['gæŋgriːn] *n* Brand *m*.

gangster ['gæŋstə*] *n* Gangster *m*.

gangway ['gæŋweɪ] *n* (Naut) Laufplanke *f*.

gaol [dʒeɪl] *n* = jail.

gap [gæp] *n* (*hole*) Lücke *f*; (*space*) Zwischenraum *m*.

gape [geɪp] *vi* glotzen.

gaping ['geɪpɪŋ] *a wound* klaffend; *hole* gähnend.

garage ['gærɑːʒ] *n* Garage *f*; (*for repair*) (Auto)reparaturwerkstatt *f*; (*for petrol*) Tankstelle *f*; *vt* einstellen.

garbage ['gɑːbɪdʒ] *n* Abfall *m*; **—can** (*US*) Mülltonne *f*.

garbled ['gɑːbld] *a story* verdreht.

garden ['gɑːdn] *n* Garten *m*; *vi* gärtnern; **—er** Gärtner(in *f*) *m*; **—ing** Gärtnern *nt*; **— party** Gartenfest *nt*.

gargle ['gɑːgl] *vi* gurgeln; *n* Gurgelmittel *nt*.

gargoyle ['gɑːgɔɪl] *n* Wasserspeier *m*.

garish ['gɛərɪʃ] *a* grell.

garland ['gɑːlənd] *n* Girlande *f*.

garlic ['gɑːlɪk] *n* Knoblauch *m*.

garment ['gɑːmənt] *n* Kleidungsstück *nt*.

garnish ['gɑːnɪʃ] *vt food* garnieren; *n* Garnierung *f*.

garret ['gærɪt] *n* Dachkammer *f*, Mansarde *f*.

garrison ['gærɪsən] *n* Garnison *f*; *vt* besetzen.

garrulous ['gærʊləs] *a* geschwätzig.

garter ['gɑːtə*] *n* Strumpfband *nt*.

gas [gæs] *n* Gas *nt*; (*Med*) Betäubungsmittel *nt*; (*esp US: petrol*) Benzin *nt*; **to step on the — Gas geben; *vt* vergasen; **—cooker** Gasherd *m*; **— cylinder** Gasflasche *f*; **— fire** Gasofen *m*, Gasheizung *f*.

gash [gæʃ] *n* klaffende Wunde *f*; *vt* tief verwunden.

gasket ['gæskɪt] *n* Dichtungsring *m*.

gasmask ['gæsmɑːsk] *n* Gasmaske *f*.

gas meter ['gæsmiːtə*] *n* Gaszähler *m*.

gasoline ['gæsəliːn] *n* (*US*) Benzin *nt*.

gasp [gɑːsp] *vi* keuchen; (*in astonishment*) tief Luft holen; *n* Keuchen *nt*.

gas ring ['gæsrɪŋ] *n* Gasring *m*.

gas station ['gæssteɪʃən] *n* (*US*) Tankstelle *f*.

gas stove ['gæsstəʊv] *n* Gaskocher *m*.

gassy ['gæsɪ] *a drink* sprudelnd.

gastric ['gæstrɪk] *a* Magen-; **—ulcer** Magengeschwür *nt*.

gastronomy [gæs'trɒnəmɪ] *n* Kochkunst *f*.

gate [geɪt] *n* Tor *nt*; (*barrier*) Schranke *f*; **—crash** *vt party* platzen in (+*acc*); **—way** Toreingang *m*.

gather ['gæðə*] *vt people* versammeln; *things* sammeln; *vi* (*understand*) annehmen; (*deduce*) schließen (*from* aus); (*assemble*) sich versammeln; **—ing** Versammlung *f.*

gauche [gəʊʃ] *a* linkisch.

gaudy ['gɔːdɪ] *a* schreiend.

gauge [geɪdʒ] *n* Normalmaß *nt;* (*Rail*) Spurweite *f;* (*dial*) Anzeiger *m;* (*measure*) Maß *nt;* *vt* (*lit*) (ab)messen; (*fig*) abschätzen.

gaunt [gɔːnt] *a* hager.

gauntlet ['gɔːntlɪt] *n* (*knight's*) Fehdehandschuh *m;* Handschuh *m.*

gauze [gɔːz] *n* Mull *m,* Gaze *f.*

gawk [gɔːk] *vi* dumm (an)glotzen (*at* acc).

gay [geɪ] *a* lustig; (*coloured*) bunt; (*col*) schwul.

gaze [geɪz] *n* Blick *m;* *vi* (an)blicken (*at* acc).

gazelle [gə'zel] *n* Gazelle *f.*

gazetteer [gæzɪ'tɪə*] *n* geographische(s) Lexikon *nt.*

gear [gɪə*] *n* Getriebe *nt;* (*equipment*) Ausrüstung *f;* (*Aut*) Gang *m;* **to be out of/in** — aus-/eingekuppelt sein; **—box** Getriebe(gehäuse) *nt;* **—lever,** **—shift** (US) Schalthebel *m.*

geese [giːs] *pl of* **goose.**

gelatin(e) ['dʒelətiːn] *n* Gelatine *f.*

gem [dʒem] *n* Edelstein *m;* ˜(*fig*) Juwel *nt.*

Gemini ['dʒemɪniː] *n* Zwillinge *pl.*

gen [dʒen] *n* (*col: information*) Infos *pl* (*on* über +acc).

gender ['dʒendə*] *n* (*Gram*) Geschlecht *nt.*

gene [dʒiːn] *n* Gen *nt.*

general ['dʒenərəl] *n* General *m;* *a* allgemein; **— election** allgemeine Wahlen .*pl;* **—ization** Verall-

gemeinerung *f;* **—ize** *vi* verallgemeinern; **—ly** *ad* allgemein, im allgemeinen.

generate ['dʒenəreɪt] *vt* erzeugen.

generation [dʒenə'reɪʃən] *n* Generation *f;* (*act*) Erzeugung *f.*

generator ['dʒenəreɪtə*] *n* Generator *m.*

generosity [dʒenə'rɒsɪtɪ] *n* Großzügigkeit *f.*

generous *a,* **—ly** *ad* ['dʒenərəs, -lɪ] (*noble-minded*) hochherzig; (*giving freely*) großzügig.

genetics [dʒɪ'netɪks] *n* Genetik *f,* Vererbungslehre *f.*

genial ['dʒiːnɪəl] *a* freundlich, jovial.

genitals ['dʒenɪtlz] *npl* Geschlechtsteile *pl,* Genitalien *pl.*

genitive ['dʒenɪtɪv] *n* Genitiv- *m,* Wesfall *m.*

genius ['dʒiːnɪəs] *n* Genie *nt.*

genocide ['dʒenəʊsaɪd] *n* Völkermord *m.*

genteel [dʒen'tiːl] *a* (*polite*) wohlanständig; (*affected*) affektiert.

gentile ['dʒentaɪl] *n* Nichtjude *m.*

gentle ['dʒentl] *a* sanft, zart; **—man** Herr *m;* (*polite*) Gentleman *m;* **—ness** Zartheit *f,* Milde *f.*

gently ['dʒentlɪ] *ad* zart, sanft.

gentry ['dʒentrɪ] *n* Landadel *m.*

gents [dʒents] *n:* **'G—'** (*lavatory*) 'Herren'.

genuine ['dʒenjʊɪn] *a* echt, wahr; **—ly** *ad* wirklich, echt.

geographer [dʒɪ'ɒgrəfə*] *n* Geograph(in *f*) *m.*

geographical [dʒɪə'græfɪkəl] *a* geographisch.

geography [dʒɪ'ɒgrəfɪ] *n* Geographie *f,* Erdkunde *f.*

geological [dʒɪəʊ'lɒdʒɪkəl] *a* geologisch.

geologist [dʒɪ'ɒlədʒɪst] n Geologe m, Geologin f.

geology [dʒɪ'ɒlədʒɪ] n Geologie f.

geometric(al) [dʒɪə'metrɪk(əl)] a geometrisch.

geometry [dʒɪ'ɒmɪtrɪ] n Geometrie f.

geranium [dʒɪ'reɪnɪəm] n Geranie f.

germ [dʒɜːm] n Keim m; (Med) Bazillus m.

germination [dʒɜːmɪ'neɪʃən] n Keimen nt.

gesticulate [dʒes'tɪkjʊleɪt] vi gestikulieren.

gesticulation [dʒestɪkjʊ'leɪʃən] n Gesten pl, Gestikulieren nt.

gesture [dʒestʃə*] n Geste f.

get [get] vt irreg (receive) bekommen, kriegen; (become) werden; (go, travel) kommen; (arrive) ankommen; to — sb to do sth jdn dazu bringen, etw zu tun, jdn etw machen lassen; — along vi (people) (gut) zurechtkommen; (depart) sich (acc) auf den Weg machen; — at sb facts herausbekommen; to — at sb (nag) an jdm herumnörgeln; — away vi (leave) sich (acc) davonmachen; (escape) entkommen (from dat); — away with you! laß den Quatsch!; — down vi (her)untergehen; vt (depress) fertigmachen; — in vi (train) ankommen; (arrive home) heimkommen; — off vi (from train etc) aussteigen (aus); (from horse) absteigen (von); — on vi (progress) vorankommen; (be friends) auskommen; (age) alt werden; vt train etc einsteigen (in + acc); horse aufsteigen (auf + acc); — out vi (of house) herauskommen; (of vehicle) aussteigen; vt (take out) herausholen; — over vt illness sich (acc) erholen von;

surprise verkraften; news fassen; loss sich abfinden mit; I couldn't — over her ich konnte sie nicht vergessen; — up vi aufstehen; —away Flucht f.

geyser ['giːzə*] n Geiser m; (heater) Durchlauferhitzer m.

ghastly ['gɑːstlɪ] a (horrible) gräßlich; (pale) totenbleich.

gherkin ['gɜːkɪn] n Gewürzgurke f.

ghetto ['getəʊ] n G(h)etto nt.

ghost [gəʊst] n Gespenst nt, Geist m; —ly gespenstisch; — story Gespenstergeschichte f.

giant ['dʒaɪənt] n Riese m; a riesig, Riesen-.

gibberish ['dʒɪbərɪʃ] n dumme(s) Geschwätz f.

.**gibe** [dʒaɪb] n spöttische Bemerkung f.

giblets ['dʒɪblɪts] npl Geflügelinnereien pl.

giddiness ['gɪdɪnəs] n Schwindelgefühl nt.

giddy ['gɪdɪ] a schwindlig; (frivolous) leichtsinnig.

gift [gɪft] n Geschenk nt; (ability) Begabung f; —ed a begabt.

gigantic [dʒaɪ'gæntɪk] a riesenhaft, ungeheuer groß.

giggle ['gɪgl] vi kichern; n Gekicher nt.

gild [gɪld] vt vergolden.

gill¹ [dʒɪl] n (1/4 pint) Viertelpinte f.

gill² [gɪl] n (of fish) Kieme f.

gilt [gɪlt] n Vergoldung f; a vergoldet.

gimlet ['gɪmlɪt] n Handbohrer m.

gimmick ['gɪmɪk] n (for sales, publicity) Gag m; it's so —y es ist alles nur ein Gag.

gin [dʒɪn] n Gin m.

ginger ['dʒɪndʒə*] n Ingwer m; — **ale**, — **beer** Ingwerbier nt; —**bread** Pfefferkuchen m; —**haired** a rothaarig.

gingerly ['dʒɪndʒəlɪ] ad behutsam.

gipsy ['dʒɪpsɪ] n Zigeuner(in f) m.

giraffe [dʒɪ'rɑːf] n Giraffe f.

girder ['gɜːdə*] n (steel) Eisenträger m; (wood) Tragebalken m.

girdle ['gɜːdl] n (woman's) Hüftgürtel m; vt umgürten.

girl [gɜːl] n Mädchen nt; —**friend** Freundin f; —**ish** a mädchenhaft.

girth [gɜːθ] n (measure) Umfang m; (strap) Sattelgurt m.

gist [dʒɪst] n Wesentliche(s) nt, Quintessenz f.

give [gɪv] irreg vt geben; vi (break) nachgeben; — **away** vt (give free) verschenken; (betray) verraten; — **back** vt zurückgeben; — **in** vi (yield) aufgeben; (agree) nachgeben; vt (hand in) abgeben; — **up** vti aufgeben; — **way** vi (traffic) Vorfahrt lassen; (to feelings) nachgeben (+dat).

glacier ['glæsɪə*] n Gletscher m.

glad [glæd] a froh; **I was — to hear...** ich habe mich gefreut, zu hören...; —**den** vt erfreuen.

gladiator ['glædɪeɪtə*] n Gladiator m.

gladioli [glædɪ'əʊlaɪ] npl Gladiolen pl.

gladly ['glædlɪ] ad gern(e).

glamorous ['glæmərəs] a bezaubernd; **life** reizvoll.

glamour ['glæmə*] n Zauber m, Reiz m.

glance [glɑːns] n flüchtige(r) Blick m; vi schnell (hin)blicken (at auf +acc); — **off** vi (fly off) abprallen von.

glancing ['glɑːnsɪŋ] a blow abprallend, Streif-.

gland [glænd] n Drüse f; —**ular fever** Drüsenentzündung f.

glare [gleə*] n (light) grelle(s) Licht nt; (stare) wilde(r) Blick m; vi grell scheinen; (angrily) böse ansehen (at acc).

glaring ['gleərɪŋ] a injustice schreiend; mistake kraß.

glass [glɑːs] n Glas nt; (mirror) Spiegel m; —**es** pl Brille f; —**house** Gewächshaus nt; —**ware** Glaswaren pl; —**y** a glasig.

glaze [gleɪz] vt verglasen; (finish with a —) glasieren; n Glasur f.

glazier ['gleɪzɪə*] n Glaser m.

gleam [gliːm] n Schimmer m; vi schimmern; —**ing** a schimmernd.

glee [gliː] n Frohsinn m; —**ful** a fröhlich.

glen [glen] n Bergtal nt.

glib [glɪb] a (re)gewandt; (superficial) oberflächlich; —**ly** ad glatt.

glide [glaɪd] vi gleiten; n Gleiten nt; (Aviat) Segelflug m; —**r** (Aviat) Segelflugzeug nt.

gliding ['glaɪdɪŋ] n Segelfliegen nt.

glimmer ['glɪmə*] n Schimmer m; — **of hope** Hoffnungsschimmer m.

glimpse [glɪmps] n flüchtige(r) Blick m; vt flüchtig erblicken.

glint [glɪnt] n Glitzern nt; vi glitzern.

glisten ['glɪsn] vi glänzen.

glitter ['glɪtə*] vi funkeln; n Funkeln nt; —**ing** a glitzernd.

gloat over ['gləʊtəʊvə*] vt sich weiden an (+dat).

global ['gləʊbl] a global.

globe [gləʊb] n Erdball m; (sphere) Globus m; —**trotter** Weltenbummler(in f) m, Globetrotter(in f) m.

gloom [gluːm] n (also —**iness**) (darkness) Dunkel nt, Dunkelheit f; (depression) düstere Stimmung f; —**ily** ad, —**y** a düster.

glorification [glɔːrɪfɪˈkeɪʃən] n Verherrlichung f.

glorify [ˈglɔːrɪfaɪ] vt verherrlichen; just a glorified cafe nur ein besseres Café.

glorious [ˈglɔːrɪəs] a glorreich; (splendid) prächtig.

glory [ˈglɔːrɪ] n Herrlichkeit f; (praise) Ruhm m; to — in sich sonnen in (+dat).

gloss [glɒs] n (shine) Glanz m; — **paint** Ölfarbe f; — **over** vt übertünchen.

glossary [ˈglɒsərɪ] n Glossar nt.

glossy [ˈglɒsɪ] a surface glänzend.

glove [glʌv] n Handschuh m.

glow [gləu] vi glühen, leuchten; n (heat) Glühen nt; (colour) Röte f; (feeling) Wärme f.

glower [ˈglauə*] vi: — at finster anblicken.

glucose [ˈgluːkəus] n Traubenzucker m.

glue [gluː] n Klebstoff m, Leim m; vt leimen, kleben.

glum [glʌm] a bedrückt.

glut [glʌt] n Überfluß m; vt überladen.

glutton [ˈglʌtn] n Vielfraß m; (fig) Unersättliche(r) mf; —**ous** a gierig; —**y** Völlerei f; Unersättlichkeit f.

glycerin(e) [ˈglɪsəriːn] n Glyzerin nt.

gnarled [nɑːld] a knorrig.

gnat [næt] n Stechmücke f.

gnaw [nɔː] vt nagen an (+dat).

gnome [nəum] n Gnom m.

go [gəu] vi irreg gehen; (travel) reisen, fahren; (depart: train) (ab)fahren; (money) ausgehen; (vision) verschwinden; (smell) verfliegen; (disappear) (fort)gehen; (be sold) kosten; (at auction) weggehen; (work) gehen, funktionieren; (fit, suit) passen (with zu); (become) werden; (break etc) nachgeben; n (energy) Schwung m; (attempt) Versuch m; can I have another —? darf ich noch mal?; — **ahead** vi (proceed) weitergehen; — **along with** vt (agree to support) zustimmen (+dat), unterstützen; — **away** vi (depart) weggehen; — **back** vi (return) zurückgehen; — **back on** vt promise nicht halten; — **by** vi (years, time) vergehen; — **down** vi (sun) untergehen; — **for** vt (fetch) holen (gehen); (like) mögen; (attack) sich stürzen auf (+acc); — **in** vi hineingehen; — **into** vt (enter) hineingehen in (+acc); (study) sich befassen mit; — **off** vi (depart) weggehen; (lights) ausgehen; (milk etc) sauer werden; (explode) losgehen; (lights) nicht mehr mögen; — **on** vi (continue) weitergehen; (col: complain) meckern; (lights) angehen; to — **on with** sth mit etw weitermachen; — **out** vi (fire, light) ausgehen; (of house) hinausgehen; — **over** vt (examine, check) durchgehen; — **up** vi (price) steigen; — **without** vt sich behelfen ohne; food untbehren.

goad [gəud] vt anstacheln; n Treibstock m.

go-ahead [ˈgəuəhed] a zielstrebig; (progressive) fortschrittlich; n grünes Licht nt.

goal [gəul] n Ziel nt; (Sport) Tor nt; —**keeper** Torwart m; —**post** Torpfosten m.

goat [gəʊt] n Ziege f.

gobble ['gɒbl] vt hinunterschlingen.

go-between ['gəʊbɪtwi:n] n Mittelsmann m.

goblet ['gɒblɪt] n Kelch(glas nt) m.

goblin ['gɒblɪn] n Kobold m.

god [gɒd] n Gott m; —child Patenkind nt; —dess Göttin f; —father Pate m; —forsaken a gottverlassen; —mother Patin f; —send Geschenk nt des Himmels.

goggle ['gɒgl] vi (stare) glotzen; to — at anglotzen; —s pl Schutzbrille f.

going ['gəʊɪŋ] n (condition of ground) Straßenzustand m; (horse-racing) Bahn f; it's hard — es ist schwierig; a rate gängig; concern gutgehend; —s-on pl Vorgänge m.

gold [gəʊld] n Gold nt; —en a golden, Gold-; —fish Goldfisch m; — mine Goldgrube f.

golf [gɒlf] n Golf nt; — club (society) Golfklub m; (stick) Golfschläger m; — course Golfplatz m; —er Golfspieler(in f) m.

gondola ['gɒndələ] n Gondel f.

gong [gɒŋ] n Gong m.

good [gʊd] n (benefit) Wohl m; (moral excellence) Güte f; a gut; (suitable) passend; —s pl Ware(n pl) f, Güter pl; a — deal of ziemlich viel; a — many ziemlich viele; —bye! auf Wiedersehen!; G— Friday Karfreitag m; —looking a gutaussehend; — morning! guten Morgen!; —ness Güte f, (virtue) Tugend f; —will (favour) Wohlwollen nt; (Comm) Firmenansehen nt.

goose [gu:s] n Gans f; —berry [ˈgʊzbərɪ] Stachelbeere f; —flesh, — pimples pl Gänsehaut f.

gore [gɔ:*] vt durchbohren; aufspießen; n Blut nt.

gorge [gɔ:dʒ] n Schlucht f; vti (sich voll)fressen.

gorgeous ['gɔ:dʒəs] a prächtig; person bildhübsch.

gorilla [gəˈrɪlə] n Gorilla m.

gorse [gɔ:s] n Stechginster m.

gory ['gɔ:rɪ] a blutig.

go-slow ['gəʊ'sləʊ] n Bummelstreik m.

gospel ['gɒspəl] n Evangelium nt.

gossamer ['gɒsəmə*] n Spinnfäden pl.

gossip ['gɒsɪp] n Klatsch m; (person) Klatschbase f; vi klatschen.

goulash ['gu:læʃ] n Gulasch nt or m.

gout [gaʊt] n Gicht f.

govern ['gʌvən] vt regieren; verwalten; (Gram) bestimmen; —ess Gouvernante f; —ing a leitend; (fig) bestimmend; —ment Regierung f; a Regierungs-; —or Gouverneur m.

gown [gaʊn] n Gewand nt; (Univ) Robe f.

grab [græb] vt packen; an sich reißen; n plötzliche(r) Griff m; (crane) Greifer m.

grace [greɪs] n Anmut f; (favour) Güte f, Gefälligkeit f; (blessing) Gnade f; (prayer) Tischgebet nt; (Comm) Zahlungsfrist f; vt (adorn) zieren; (honour) auszeichnen; 5 days' — 5 Tage Aufschub m; —ful a —fully ad anmutig, graziös.

gracious ['greɪʃəs] a gnädig; (kind, courteous) wohlwollend, freundlich.

gradation [grəˈdeɪʃən] n (Ab-)stufung f.

grade [greɪd] n Grad m; (slope) Gefälle m; to make the — es schaffen; vt (classify) einstufen; — crossing (US) Bahnübergang m.

gradient ['greɪdɪənt] n Steigung f; Gefälle nt.

gradual a, —ly ad ['grædjʊəl,-lɪ] allmählich.

graduate ['grædjʊɪt] n: to be a — das Staatsexamen haben; ['grædjʊeɪt] vi das Staatsexamen machen or bestehen.

graduation [grædjʊ'eɪʃən] n Erlangung f eines akademischen Grades.

graft [grɑːft] n (on plant) Pfropfreis nt; (hard work) Schufterei f; (Med) Verpflanzung f; (unfair self-advancement) Schiebung f; vt propfen; (fig) aufpfropfen; (Med) verpflanzen.

grain [greɪn] n Korn nt, Getreide nt; (particle) Körnchen nt, Korn nt; (in wood) Maserung f.

grammar ['græmə*] n Grammatik f.

grammatical [grə'mætɪkəl] a grammatisch.

gram(me) [græm] n Gramm nt.

gramophone ['græməfəʊn] n Grammophon nt.

granary ['grænərɪ] n Kornspeicher m.

grand [grænd] a großartig; —daughter Enkelin f; —eur ['grændjə*] Erhabenheit f; —father Großvater m; —iose (imposing) großartig; (pompous) schwülstig; —mother Großmutter f; —piano Flügel m; —son Enkel m; —stand Haupttribüne f; — total Gesamtsumme f.

granite ['grænɪt] n Granit m.

granny ['grænɪ] n Oma f.

grant [grɑːnt] vt gewähren; (allow) zugeben; n Unterstützung f; (Univ) Stipendium nt; to take sb/sth for —ed jdn/etw als selbstverständlich (an)nehmen.

granulated ['grænjʊleɪtɪd] a sugar raffiniert.

granule ['grænjuːl] n Körnchen nt.

grape [greɪp] n (Wein)traube f; —fruit Pampelmuse f, Grapefruit f; — juice Traubensaft m.

graph [grɑːf] n Schaubild nt; —ic a (descriptive) anschaulich, lebendig; drawing graphisch.

grapple ['græpl] vi sich raufen; — with (lit, fig) kämpfen mit.

grasp [grɑːsp] vt ergreifen; (understand) begreifen; n Griff m; (possession) Gewalt f; (of subject) Beherrschung f; —ing a habgierig.

grass [grɑːs] n Gras nt; —hopper Heuschrecke f; —land Weideland nt; — roots pl (fig) Basis f; —snake Ringelnatter f; —y a grasig, Gras-.

grate [greɪt] n Feuerrost m, Kamin m; vi kratzen; (sound) knirschen; (on nerves) zerren (on an +dat); vt reiben.

grateful a, —ly ad ['greɪtfʊl, -fəlɪ] dankbar.

grater ['greɪtə*] n (in kitchen) Reibe f.

gratification [grætɪfɪ'keɪʃən] n Befriedigung f.

gratify ['grætɪfaɪ] vt befriedigen; —ing a erfreulich.

grating ['greɪtɪŋ] n (iron bars) Gitter nt; a noise knirschend.

gratitude ['grætɪtjuːd] n Dankbarkeit f.

gratuitous [grə'tjuːɪtəs] a (uncalled-for) grundlos, überflüssig; (given free) unentgeltlich, gratis.

gratuity [grə'tjuːɪtɪ] n (Geld)geschenk nt; (Comm) Gratifikation f.

grave [greɪv] n Grab nt; a (serious) ernst, schwerwiegend; (solemn) ernst, feierlich; **—digger** Totengräber m.

gravel ['grævəl] n Kies m.

gravely ['greivli] ad schwer, ernstlich.

gravestone ['greivstəun] n Grabstein m.

graveyard ['greivjɑːd] n Friedhof m.

gravitate ['græviteit] vi streben; (fig) tendieren.

gravity ['græviti] n Schwerkraft f; (seriousness) Schwere f, Ernst m.

gravy ['greivi] n (Braten)soße f.

gray [grei] a = **grey**.

graze [greiz] vi grasen; vt (touch) streifen; (Med) abschürfen; n (Med) Abschürfung f.

grease [griːs] n (fat) Fett nt; (lubricant) Schmiere f; vt (ab)schmieren; einfetten; — **gun** Schmierspritze f; **—proof** a paper Butterbrot-.

greasy ['griːsi] a fettig.

great [greit] a groß; (important) groß, bedeutend; (distinguished) groß, hochstehend; (col: good) prima; **—grandfather** Urgroßvater m; **—grandmother** Urgroßmutter f; **—ly** ad sehr; **—ness** Größe f.

greed [griːd] n (also **—iness**) Gier f (for nach); (meanness) Geiz m; **—ily** ad gierig; **—y** a gefräßig, gierig; **—y for money** geldgierig.

green [griːn] a grün; n (village —) Dorfwiese f; **—grocer** Obst- und Gemüsehändler m; **—house** Gewächshaus nt; **—ish** a grünlich; **— light** (lit, fig) grüne(s) Licht nt.

greet [griːt] vt grüßen; **—ing** Gruß m, Begrüßung f.

gregarious [gri'gɛəriəs] a gesellig.

grenade [gri'neid] n Granate f.

grey [grei] a grau; **—-haired** a grauhaarig; **—hound** Windhund m; **—ish** a gräulich.

grid [grid] n Gitter nt; (Elec) Leitungsnetz nt; (on map) Gitternetz nt; **—iron** Bratrost m.

grief [griːf] n Gram m, Kummer m.

grievance ['griːvəns] n Beschwerde f.

grieve [griːv] vi sich grämen; vt betrüben.

grill [gril] n (on cooker) Grill m; vt grillen; (question) in die Mangel nehmen.

grille [gril] n (on car etc) (Kühler)gitter nt.

grim [grim] a grimmig; situation düster.

grimace [gri'meis] n Grimasse f; vi Grimassen schneiden.

grime [graim] n Schmutz m.

grimly ['grimli] ad grimmig, finster.

grimy ['graimi] a schmutzig.

grin [grin] n Grinsen nt; vi grinsen.

grind [graind] vt irreg mahlen; (sharpen) schleifen; teeth knirschen mit; n (bore) Plackerei f.

grip [grip] n Griff m; (mastery) Griff m, Gewalt f; (suitcase) kleine(r) Handkoffer m; vt packen.

gripes [graips] npl (bowel pains) Bauchschmerzen pl, Bauchweh nt.

gripping ['gripiŋ] a (exciting) spannend.

grisly ['grizli] a gräßlich.

gristle ['grisl] n Knorpel m.

grit [grit] n Splitt m; (courage) Mut m, Mumm m; vt teeth knirschen mit; road (mit Splitt be)streuen.

groan [grəun] n Stöhnen nt; vi stöhnen.

grocer ['grəusə*] n Lebensmittelhändler m; **—ies** pl Lebensmittel pl.

grog [grɒg] n Grog m.

groggy ['grɒgi] a benommen; (boxing) angeschlagen.

groin [grɔin] n Leistengegend f.

groom [gru:m] n Bräutigam m; (for horses) Pferdeknecht m; — o.s. (of man) sich zurechtmachen, sich pflegen; (well) -ed gepflegt; to — sb for a career jdn auf eine Laufbahn vorbereiten.

groove [gru:v] n Rille f, Furche f.

grope [grəup] vi tasten.

gross [grəus] a (coarse) dick, plump; (bad) grob, schwer; (Comm) brutto; Gesamt-; n Gros nt; —ly ad höchst, ungeheuerlich.

grotesque [grəu'tesk] a grotesk.

grotto ['grɒtəu] n Grotte f.

ground [graund] n Boden m, Erde f; (land) Grundbesitz m; (reason) Grund m; —s pl (dregs) Bodensatz m; (around house) (Garten)anlagen pl; vt (run ashore) auf Strand setzen; aircraft stillegen; (instruct) die Anfangsgründe beibringen (+ dat); vi (run ashore) stranden, auflaufen; — floor (Brit) Erdgeschoß nt, Parterre nt; —ing (instruction) Anfangsunterricht m; —sheet Zeltboden m; —work Grundlage f.

group [gru:p] n Gruppe f; vti (sich) gruppieren.

grouse [graus] n (bird) schottische(s) Moorhuhn nt; (complaint) Nörgelei f; vi (complain) meckern.

grove [grəuv] n Gehölz nt, Hain m.

grovel ['grɒvl] vi auf dem Bauch kriechen; (fig) kriechen.

grow [grəu] irreg vi wachsen, größer werden; (grass) wachsen; (become) werden; it — s on you man gewöhnt sich daran; vt (raise) anbauen, ziehen; — up vi auf-

wachsen; (mature) erwachsen werden; —er Züchter m; —ing a wachsend; (fig) zunehmend.

growl [graul] vi knurren; n Knurren nt.

grown-up ['grəun'ʌp] a erwachsen; n Erwachsene(r) mf.

growth [grəuθ] n Wachstum nt, Wachsen nt; (increase) Anwachsen nt, Zunahme f; (of beard etc) Wuchs m.

grub [grʌb] n Made f, Larve f; (col: food) Futter nt; —by a schmutzig, schmuddelig.

grudge [grʌdʒ] n Groll m; vt missgönnen (sb sth jdm etw); to bear sb a — einen Groll gegen jdn hegen.

grudging ['grʌdʒiŋ] a neidisch; (unwilling) widerwillig.

gruelling ['grəuliŋ] a climb, race mörderisch.

gruesome ['gru:səm] a grauenhaft.

gruff [grʌf] a barsch.

grumble ['grʌmbl] vi murren, schimpfen; n Brummen nt, Murren nt.

grumpy ['grʌmpi] a verdrießlich.

grunt [grʌnt] vi grunzen; n Grunzen nt.

guarantee [gærən'ti:] n (promise to pay) Gewähr f; (promise to replace) Garantie f; vt gewährleisten; garantieren.

guarantor [gærən'tɔ:*] n Gewährsmann m, Bürge m.

guard [gɑ:d] n (defence) Bewachung f; (sentry) Wache f; (Rail) Zugbegleiter m; to be on — Wache stehen; to be on one's — aufpassen; vt bewachen, beschützen; —ed a vorsichtig, zurückhaltend; —ian Vormund m; (keeper) Hüter m; —'s van (Brit Rail) Dienstwagen m.

guerrilla [gə'rɪlə] *n* Guerilla-(kämpfer) *m*; **—** warfare Guerillakrieg *m*.

guess [ges] *vti* (er)raten, schätzen; *n* Vermutung *f*; **—work** Raterei *f*; good **—** gut geraten.

guest [gest] *n* Gast *m*; **—-house** Pension *f*; **— room** Gastzimmer *nt*.

guffaw [gʌ'fɔ:] *n* schallende(s) Gelächter *nt*; *vi* schallend lachen.

guidance ['gaɪdəns] *n* (control) Leitung *f*; (advice) Rat *m*, Beratung *f*.

guide [gaɪd] *n* Führer *m*; *vt* führen; girl — Pfadfinderin *f*; **—book** Reiseführer *m*; **—d missile** Fernlenkgeschoß *nt*; **— lines** *pl* Richtlinien *pl*.

guild [gɪld] *n* (Hist) Gilde *f*; (society) Vereinigung *f*; **—hall** (Brit) Stadthalle *f*.

guile [gaɪl] *n* Arglist *f*; **—less** a arglos.

guillotine [gɪlə'ti:n] *n* Guillotine *f*.

guilt [gɪlt] *n* Schuld *-f*; **—y** a schuldig.

guise [gaɪz] *n* (appearance) Verkleidung *f*; in the **—** of (things) in der Form *f* (+gen); (people) gekleidet als.

guitar [gɪ'tɑ:*] *n* Gitarre *f*; **—ist** Gitarrist(in *f*) *m*.

gulf [gʌlf] *n* Golf *m*; (fig) Abgrund *m*.

gull [gʌl] *n* Möwe *f*.

gullet ['gʌlɪt] *n* Schlund *m*.

gullible ['gʌlɪbl] a leichtgläubig.

gully ['gʌlɪ] *n* (Wasser)rinne *f*; (gorge) Schlucht *f*.

gulp [gʌlp] *vi* hinunterschlucken; (gasp) schlucken; *n* große(r) Schluck *m*.

gum [gʌm] *n* (around teeth) Zahnfleisch *nt*; (glue) Klebstoff *m*;

(chewing **—**) Kaugummi *m*; *vt* gummieren, kleben; **—boots** *pl* Gummistiefel *pl*.

gumption ['gʌmpʃən] *n* (col) Mumm *m*.

gum tree ['gʌmtri:] *n* Gummibaum *m*; up a **—** (col) in der Klemme.

gun [gʌn] *n* Schußwaffe *f*; **—fire** Geschützfeuer *nt*; **—man** bewaffnete(r) Verbrecher *m*; **—ner** Kanonier *m*, Artillerist *m*; **—powder** Schießpulver *nt*; **—shot** Schuß *m*; **— down** *vt* niederknallen.

gurgle ['gɜ:gl] *n* Gluckern *nt*; *vi* gluckern.

gush [gʌʃ] *n* Strom *m*, Erguß *m*; *vi* (rush out) hervorströmen; (fig) schwärmen.

gusset ['gʌsɪt] *n* Keil *m*, Zwickel *m*.

gust [gʌst] *n* Windstoß *m*, Bö *f*.

gusto ['gʌstəu] *n* Genuß *m*, Lust *f*.

gut [gʌt] *n* (Anat) Gedärme *pl*; (string) Darm *m*; **—s** *pl* (fig) Schneid *m*.

gutter ['gʌtə*] *n* Dachrinne *f*; (in street) Gosse *f*.

guttural ['gʌtərəl] a guttural, Kehl-.

guy [gaɪ] *n* (rope) Halteseil *nt*; (man) Typ *m*, Kerl *m*.

guzzle ['gʌzl] *vti* (drink) saufen; (eat) fressen.

gym(nasium) [dʒɪm'neɪzɪəm] *n* Turnhalle *f*.

gymnast ['dʒɪmnæst] *n* Turner(in *f*) *m*; **—ics** [dʒɪm'næstɪks] Turnen *nt*, Gymnastik *f*.

gyn(a)ecologist [gaɪnɪ'kɒlədʒɪst] *n* Frauenarzt *m*/-ärztin *f*, Gynäkologe *m*, Gynäkologin *f*.

gyn(a)ecology [gaɪnɪ'kɒlədʒɪ] *n* Gynäkologie *f*, Frauenheilkunde *f*.

gypsy ['dʒɪpsɪ] *n* = gipsy.

gyrate [dʒaɪ'reɪt] *vi* kreisen.

H

H, h [eitʃ] *n* H *nt*, h *nt*.
haberdashery [hæbə'dæʃərɪ] *n* Kurzwaren *pl*.
habit ['hæbɪt] *n* (An)gewohnheit *f*; (monk's) Habit *m* or *m*.
habitable ['hæbɪtəbl] *a* bewohnbar.
habitat ['hæbɪtæt] *n* Lebensraum *m*.
habitation [hæbɪ'teɪʃən] *n* Bewohnen *nt*; (place) Wohnung *f*.
habitual [hə'bɪtjʊəl] *a* üblich, gewohnheitsmäßig; **—ly** *ad* gewöhnlich.
hack [hæk] *vt* hacken; *n* Hieb *m*; (writer) Schreiberling *m*.
hackney cab ['hæknɪ'kæb] *n* Taxi *nt*.
hackneyed ['hæknɪd] *a* abgedroschen.
haddock ['hædək] *n* Schellfisch *m*.
hadn't ['hædnt] = **had not**.
haemorrhage, (US) **hemo-** ['hemərɪdʒ] *n* Blutung *f*.
haemorrhoids, (US) **hemo-** ['hemərɔɪdz] Hämorrhoiden *pl*.
haggard ['hægəd] *a* abgekämpft.
haggle ['hægl] *vi* feilschen.
haggling ['hæglɪŋ] *n* Feilschen *nt*.
hail [heɪl] *n* Hagel *m*; *vt* zujubeln; to — sb as emperor jdn zum Kaiser ausrufen; *vi* hageln; **—storm** *n* Hagelschauer *m*.
hair [heə*] *n* Haar *nt*, Haare *pl*; (one —) Haar *nt*; **—brush** Haarbürste *f*; **—cut** Haarschnitt *m*; to get a **—cut** sich (dat) die Haare schneiden lassen; **—do** Frisur *f*; **—dresser** Friseur *m*, Friseuse *f*; **—drier** Trockenhaube *f*; (hand) Fön *m*; **—net** Haarnetz *nt*; **— oil**

Haaröl *nt*; **—piece** (lady's) Haarteil *nt*; (man's) Toupet *nt*; **—pin** (lit) Haarnadel *f*; (bend) Haarnadelkurve *f*; **—raising** *a* haarsträubend; **—'s breadth** Haaresbreite *f*; **— style** Frisur *f*; **—y** *a* haarig.
hake [heɪk] *n* Seehecht *m*.
half [hɑːf] *n* Hälfte *f*; *a* halb; *ad* halb, zur Hälfte; **—back** Läufer *m*; **—breed**, **—caste** Mischling *m*; **—hearted** *a* lustlos, unlustig; **—hour** halbe Stunde *f*; **—penny** ['heɪpnɪ] halbe(r) Penny *m*; **—price** halbe(r) Preis *m*; **—time** Halbzeit *f*; **—way** *ad* halbwegs, auf halbem Wege.
halibut ['hælɪbət] *n* Heilbutt *m*.
hall [hɔːl] *n* Saal *m*; (entrance —) Hausflur *m*; (building) Halle *f*.
hallmark ['hɔːlmɑːk] *n* (lit, fig) Stempel *m*.
hallo [hʌ'ləʊ] see **hello**.
hallucination [həluːsɪ'neɪʃən] *n* Halluzination *f*.
halo ['heɪləʊ] *n* (of saint) Heiligenschein *m*; (of moon) Hof *m*.
halt [hɔːlt] *n* Halt *m*; *vti* anhalten.
halve [hɑːv] *vt* halbieren.
ham [hæm] *n* Schinken *m*; **— sandwich** Schinkenbrötchen *nt*; **—burger** Frikadelle *f*.
hamlet ['hæmlɪt] *n* Weiler *m*.
hammer ['hæmə*] *n* Hammer *m*; *vt* hämmern.
hammock ['hæmək] *n* Hängematte *f*.
hamper ['hæmpə*] *vt* (be)hindern; *n* Picknickkorb *m*; Geschenkkorb *m*.

hand [hænd] n Hand f; (of clock) (Uhr)zeiger m; (worker) Arbeiter m; vt (pass) geben; **to give sb a —** jdm helfen; **at first —** aus erster Hand; **to —** zur Hand; **in —** (under control) in fester Hand, unter Kontrolle; (being done) im Gange; (extra) übrig; **—bag** Handtasche f; **—ball** Handball m; **—book** Handbuch nt; **—brake** Handbremse f; **— cream** Handcreme f; **—cuffs** pl Handschellen pl; **—ful** Handvoll f; (col: person) Plage f.

handicap ['hændikæp] n Handikap nt; vt benachteiligen.

handicraft ['hændikrɑːft] n Kunsthandwerk nt.

handkerchief ['hæŋkətʃif] n Taschentuch nt.

handle ['hændl] n (of door etc) Klinke f; (of cup etc) Henkel m; (for winding) Kurbel f; vt (touch) anfassen; (deal with) things sich befassen mit; people umgehen mit; **—bars** pl Lenkstange f.

hand-luggage ['hændlʌgidʒ] Handgepäck nt.

handmade ['hændmeɪd] a handgefertigt.

handshake ['hændʃeɪk] n Händedruck f.

handsome ['hænsəm] a gutaussehend; (generous) großzügig.

handwriting ['hændraɪtɪŋ] n Handschrift f.

handy ['hændɪ] a praktisch; shops leicht erreichbar.

handyman ['hændɪmən] n Mädchen nt für alles; (do-it-yourself) Bastler m; (general —) Gelegenheitsarbeiter m.

hang [hæŋ] irreg vt aufhängen; (execute) hängen; **to — sth on sth** etw an etw (acc) hängen; vi

(droop) hängen; **— about** vi sich herumtreiben.

hangar ['hæŋə*] n Hangar m, Flugzeughalle f.

hanger ['hæŋə*] n Kleiderbügel m.

hanger-on ['hæŋər'ɒn] n Anhänger (-in f) m.

hangover ['hæŋəʊvə*] n Kater m.

hank [hæŋk] n Strang m.

hanker ['hæŋkə*] vi sich sehnen (for, after nach).

haphazard ['hæp'hæzəd] a wahllos, zufällig.

happen ['hæpən] vi sich ereignen, passieren; **—ing** n Ereignis nt; (Art) Happening nt.

happily ['hæpɪlɪ] ad glücklich; (fortunately) glücklicherweise.

happiness ['hæpɪnɪs] n Glück nt.

happy ['hæpɪ] a glücklich; **—-lucky** a sorglos.

harass ['hærəs] vt bedrängen, plagen.

harbour, (US) harbor ['hɑːbə*] n Hafen m.

hard [hɑːd] a (firm) hart, fest; (difficult) schwer, schwierig; (physically) schwer; (harsh) hart(herzig), gefühllos; ad work hart; try sehr; push, hit fest; **— by** (close) dicht or nahe an(+dat); he **took it —** er hat es schwer genommen; **—back** n kartonierte Ausgabe; **—boiled** a hartgekocht; **—en** vt erhärten; (fig) verhärten; vi hart werden; (fig) sich verhärten; **—-hearted** a hartherzig; **—ly** ad kaum; **—ship** Not f; (injustice) Unrecht nt; **—-up** a knapp bei Kasse; **—ware** Eisenwaren pl.

hardy ['hɑːdɪ] a (strong) widerstandsfähig; (brave) verwegen.

hare [hɛə*] n Hase m.

harem [hɑː'riːm] n Harem m.

harm [hɑːm] n Schaden m; Leid nt; vt schaden (+dat); it won't do any — es kann nicht schaden; —ful a schädlich; —less a harmlos, unschädlich.

harmonica [hɑː'mɒnɪkə] n Mundharmonika f.

harmonious [hɑː'məʊnɪəs] a harmonisch.

harmonize ['hɑːmənaɪz] vt abstimmen; vi harmonieren.

harmony ['hɑːmənɪ] n Harmonie f; (fig also) Einklang m.

harness ['hɑːnɪs] n Geschirr nt; vt horse anschirren; (fig) nutzbar machen.

harp [hɑːp] n Harfe f; to — on about sth auf etw (dat) herumreiten; —ist n Harfenspieler(in f) m.

harpoon [hɑː'puːn] n Harpune f.

harrow ['hærəʊ] n Egge f; vt eggen.

harrowing ['hærəʊɪŋ] a nervenaufreibend.

harsh [hɑːʃ] a (rough) rauh, grob; (severe) schroff, streng; —ly ad rauh, barsch; —ness Härte f.

harvest ['hɑːvɪst] n Ernte f; (time) Erntezeit f; vt ernten.

harvester ['hɑːvɪstə*] n Mähbinder m.

hash [hæʃ] vt kleinhacken; n (mess) Kuddelmuddel m; (meat cooked) Haschee nt; (raw) Gehackte(s) nt.

hashish ['hæʃɪʃ] n Haschisch nt.

haste [heɪst] n (speed) Eile f; (hurry) Hast f; —n ['heɪsn] vt beschleunigen; vi eilen, sich beeilen.

hasty a, **hastily** ad [heɪstɪ, -lɪ] hastig; (rash) vorschnell.

hat [hæt] n Hut m.

hatbox ['hætbɒks] n Hutschachtel f.

hatch [hætʃ] n (Naut) Luke f; (in house) Durchreiche f; vi brüten; (young) ausschlüpfen; vt brood ausbrüten; plot aushecken.

hatchet ['hætʃɪt] n Beil nt.

hate [heɪt] vt hassen; I — queuing ich stehe nicht gern Schlange; n Haß m; —ful a verhaßt.

hatred ['heɪtrɪd] n Haß m; (dislike) Abneigung f.

hat trick ['hættrɪk] n Hattrick m.

haughty a, haughtily ad [hɔːtɪ, -lɪ] hochnäsig, überheblich.

haul [hɔːl] vt ziehen, schleppen; n (pull) Zug m; (catch) Fang m; —age Transport m; (Comm) Spedition f; —ier n Transportunternehmer m, Spediteur m.

haunch [hɔːntʃ] n Lende f; to sit on one's —es hocken.

haunt [hɔːnt] vt (ghost) spuken in (+dat), umgehen in (+dat); (memory) verfolgen; pub häufig besuchen; the castle is —ed in dem Schloß spukt es; n Lieblingsplatz m.

have [hæv] vt irreg haben; (at meal) essen; trinken; (col: trick) hereinlegen; to — sth done etw machen lassen; to — to do sth etw tun müssen; to — sb on jdn auf den Arm nehmen.

haven ['heɪvn] n Hafen m; (fig) Zufluchtsort m.

haversack ['hævəsæk] n Rucksack m.

havoc ['hævək] n Verwüstung f.

hawk [hɔːk] n Habicht m.

hay [heɪ] n Heu nt; — fever Heuschnupfen m; —stack Heuschober m.

haywire ['heɪwaɪə*] *a* (col) durcheinander.

hazard ['hæzəd] *n* (chance) Zufall *m*; (danger) Wagnis *nt*, Risiko *nt*; *vt* aufs Spiel setzen; **—ous** *a* gefährlich, riskant.

haze [heɪz] *n* Dunst *m*; (fig) Unklarheit *f*.

hazelnut ['heɪzlnʌt] *n* Haselnuß *f*.

hazy ['heɪzɪ] *a* (misty) dunstig, diesig; (vague) verschwommen.

he [hi:] *pron er*.

head [hed] *n* Kopf *m*; (top) Spitze *f*; (leader) Leiter *m*; *a* Kopf-; (leading) Ober-; *vt* (an)führen, leiten; **—** for Richtung nehmen auf (+acc), zugehen auf (+acc); **—ache** Kopfschmerzen *pl*, Kopfweh *nt*; **—ing** Überschrift *f*; **—lamp** Scheinwerfer *m*; **—land** Landspitze *f*; **—light** = **—lamp**; **—line** Schlagzeile *f*; **—long** *ad* kopfüber; **—master** (of primary school) Rektor *m*; (of secondary school) Direktor *m*; **—mistress** (of primary school) Rektorin *f*; Direktorin *f*; **—on** *a* Frontal-; **—quarters** *pl* Zentrale *f*; (Mil) Hauptquartier *nt*; **—rest** Kopfstütze *f*; **—room** (of bridges etc) lichte Höhe *f*; Platz *m* für den Kopf; **—s** (on coin) Kopf *m*, Wappen *nt*; **—strong** *a* eigenwillig; **—waiter** Oberkellner *m*; **—way** Fahrt *f* (voraus); (fig) Fortschritte *pl*; **—wind** Gegenwind *m*; **—y** *a* (rash) hitzig; (intoxicating) stark, berauschend.

heal [hi:l] *vt* heilen; *vi* verheilen.

health [helθ] *n* Gesundheit *f*; your **—!** *int* prost; **—y** *a* gesund.

heap [hi:p] *n* Haufen *m*; *vt* häufen.

hear [hɪə*] *irreg vt* hören; (listen to) anhören; *vi* hören; **—ing** Gehör *nt*; (Jur) Verhandlung *f*; (of witnesses) Vernehmung *f*; to give sb a **—ing** jdn anhören; **—ing aid** Hörapparat *m*; **—say** Hörensagen *nt*.

hearse [hɜ:s] *n* Leichenwagen *m*.

heart [hɑ:t] *n* Herz *nt*; (centre also) Zentrum *nt*; (courage) Mut *m*; by **—** auswendig; the **—** of the matter der Kern des Problems; **—** attack Herzanfall *m*; **—beat** Herzschlag *m*; **—breaking** *a* herzzerbrechend; **—broken** *a* (ganz)gebrochen; **—burn** Sodbrennen *nt*; **—failure** Herzschlag *m*; **—felt** *a* aufrichtig.

hearth [hɑ:θ] *n* Herd *m*.

heartily ['hɑ:tɪlɪ] *ad* herzlich; *eat* herzhaft.

heartless ['hɑ:tlɪs] *a* herzlos.

hearty ['hɑ:tɪ] *a* kräftig; (friendly) freundlich.

heat [hi:t] *n* Hitze *f*; (of food, water etc) Wärme *f*; (Sport) Ausscheidungsrunde *f*; (excitement) Feuer *nt*; in the **—** of the moment in der Hitze des Gefechts; *vt house* heizen; *substance* heiß machen, erhitzen; **—** up *vi* warm werden; *vt aufwärmen*; **—** *a* erhitzt; (fig) hitzig; **—er** (Heiz)ofen *m*.

heath [hi:θ] *n* (Brit) Heide *f*.

heathen ['hi:ðən] *n* Heide *m*; *a* heidnisch, Heiden-.

heather ['heðə*] *n* Heidekraut *nt*, Erika *f*.

heating ['hi:tɪŋ] *n* Heizung *f*.

heatstroke ['hi:tstrəʊk] *n* Hitzschlag *m*.

heatwave ['hi:tweɪv] *n* Hitzewelle *f*.

heave [hi:v] *vt* hochheben; *sigh* ausstoßen; *vi* wogen; (breast) sich heben; *n* Heben *nt*.

heaven ['hevn] *n* Himmel *m*; (bliss) (der siebte) Himmel *m*; **—ly**

a himmlisch; **—ly body** Himmels-
körper *m.*

heavy *a*, **heavily** *ad* ['hevɪ, -lɪ]
schwer.

heckle ['hekl] *vt* unterbrechen; *vi*
dazwischenrufen, störende Fragen
stellen.

hectic ['hektɪk] *a* hektisch.

he'd [hi:d] = **he had; he would.**

hedge [hedʒ] *n* Hecke *f*; *vt*
einzäunen; **to — one's bets** sich
absichern; *vi* (*fig*) ausweichen.

hedgehog ['hedʒhɒg] *n* Igel *m.*

heed [hi:d] *vt* beachten; *n* Beachtung *f*; **—ful** *a* achtsam; **—less** *a*
achtlos.

heel [hi:l] *n* Ferse *f*; (*of shoe*)
Absatz *m*; *vt* shoes mit Absätzen
versehen.

hefty ['heftɪ] *a person* stämmig;
portion reichlich; *bite* kräftig;
weight schwer.

heifer ['hefə*] *n* Färse *f.*

height [haɪt] *n* (*of person*) Größe
f; (*of object*) Höhe *f*; (*high place*)
Gipfel *m*; **—en** *vt* erhöhen.

heir [ɛə*] *n* Erbe *m*; **—ess** ['ɛərɪs]
Erbin *f*; **—loom** Erbstück *nt.*

helicopter ['helɪkɒptə*] *n* Hubschrauber *m.*

hell [hel] *n* Hölle *f*; *interj* verdammt!

he'll [hi:l] = **he will, he shall.**

hellish ['helɪʃ] *a* höllisch, verteufelt.

hello [hʌ'ləu] *interj* (*greeting*)
Hallo; (*surprise*) nanu, hallo, he.

helm [helm] *n* Ruder *nt*, Steuer *nt.*

helmet ['helmɪt] *n* Helm *m.*

helmsman ['helmzmən] *n* Steuermann *m.*

help [help] *n* Hilfe *f*; *vt* helfen
(+*dat*); **I can't —** ich kann
nichts dafür; **I couldn't —** laughing ich mußte einfach lachen; **—
yourself** bedienen Sie sich; **—er**

Helfer *m*; **—ful** *a* hilfreich; **—ing**
Portion *f*; **—less** *a* hilflos.

hem [hem] *n* Saum *m*; **— in** *vt* einschließen; (*fig*) einengen.

hemisphere ['hemɪsfɪə*] *n* Halb-
kugel *f*; Hemisphäre *f.*

hemline ['hemlaɪn] *n* Rocklänge *f.*

hemp [hemp] *n* Hanf *m.*

hen [hen] *n* Henne *f.*

hence [hens] *ad* von jetzt an;
(*therefore*) daher.

henchman ['hentʃmən] *n*
Anhänger *m*, Gefolgsmann *m.*

henpecked ['henpekt] *a*: **to be —
**under dem Pantoffel stehen; **— hus-
band** Pantoffelheld *m.*

her [h3:*] *pron* (*acc*) sie; (*dat*) ihr;
a ihr.

herald ['herəld] *n* Herold *m*; (*fig*)
(Vor)bote *m*; *vt* verkünden,
anzeigen.

heraldry ['herəldrɪ] *n* Wappen-
kunde *f.*

herb [h3:b] *n* Kraut *nt.*

herd [h3:d] *n* Herde *f.*

here [hɪə*] *ad* hier; (*to this place*)
hierher; **—after** *ad* hernach,
künftig; *n* Jenseits *nt*; **—by** *ad*
hiermit.

hereditary [hɪ'redɪtərɪ] *a* erblich.

heredity [hɪ'redɪtɪ] *n* Vererbung *f.*

heresy ['herəsɪ] *n* Ketzerei *f.*

heretic ['herətɪk] *n* Ketzer *m*; **—al**
[hɪ'retɪkəl] *a* ketzerisch.

herewith ['hɪə'wɪð] *ad* hiermit;
(*Comm*) anbei.

heritage ['herɪtɪdʒ] *n* Erbe *nt.*

hermetically [h3:'metɪkəlɪ] *ad* luft-
dicht, hermetisch.

hermit ['h3:mɪt] *n* Einsiedler *m.*

hernia ['h3:nɪə] *n* Bruch *m.* •

hero ['hɪərəu] *n* Held *m*; **—ic**
[hɪ'rəuɪk] *a* heroisch.

heroin ['herəʊɪn] n Heroin nt.

heroine ['herəʊɪn] n Heldin f.

heroism ['herəʊɪzəm] n Heldentum nt.

heron ['herən] n Reiher m.

herring ['herɪŋ] n Hering m.

hers [hɜ:z] pron ihre(r,s).

herself [hɜ:'self] pron sich (selbst); (emphatic) selbst; she's not — mit ihr ist etwas los or nicht in Ordnung.

he's [hi:z] = he is, he has.

hesitant ['hezɪtənt] a zögernd; speech stockend.

hesitate ['hezɪteɪt] vi zögern; (feel doubtful) unschlüssig sein.

hesitation [hezɪ'teɪʃən] n Zögern nt, Schwanken nt.

het up [het'ʌp] a (col) aufgeregt.

hew [hju:] vt irreg hauen, hacken.

hexagon ['heksəgən] n Sechseck nt; **—al** [hek'sægənəl] a sechseckig.

heyday ['heɪdeɪ] n Blüte f, Höhepunkt m.

hi [haɪ] interj he, hallo.

hibernate ['haɪbəneɪt] vi Winterschlaf halten.

hibernation [haɪbə'neɪʃən] n Winterschlaf m.

hiccough, hiccup ['hɪkʌp] vi den Schluckauf haben; **—s** pl Schluckauf m.

hide [haɪd] n (skin) Haut f, Fell nt; irreg vt verbergen; (keep secret) verbergen; vi sich verstecken; **—and-seek** Versteckspiel nt.

hideous ['hɪdɪəs] a abscheulich; **—ly** ad scheußlich.

hiding ['haɪdɪŋ] n (beating) Tracht f Prügel; **to be in —** sich versteckt halten; **— place** Versteck nt.

hierarchy ['haɪərɑ:kɪ] n Hierarchie f.

high [haɪ] a hoch; importance groß; spirits Hoch-; wind stark; living extravagant, üppig; ad hoch; **—brow** n Intellektuelle(r) mf; a (betont) intellektuell; (pej) hochgestochen; **—chair** Hochstuhl m, Sitzer m; **—handed** a eigenmächtig; **—heeled** a hochhackig; **—jack** = hijack; **—level** a meeting wichtig, Spitzen-; **—light** (fig) Höhepunkt m; **—ly** ad in hohem Maße, höchst; praise in hohen Tönen; **—ly strung** a überempfindlich, reizbar; H— Mass Hochamt nt; **—ness** Höhe f; H—ness Hoheit f; **—pitched** a voice hoch, schrill, hell; **—school** Oberschule f; **—speed** a Schnell-; **—tide** Flut f; **—way** Landstraße f.

hijack ['haɪdʒæk] vt hijacken, entführen.

hike [haɪk] vi wandern; n Wanderung f; **—r** Wanderer m.

hiking ['haɪkɪŋ] n Wandern nt.

hilarious [hɪ'lɛərɪəs] a lustig; zum Schreien komisch.

hilarity [hɪ'lærɪtɪ] n Lustigkeit f.

hill [hɪl] n Berg m; **—side** (Berg)hang m; **—top** Bergspitze f; **—y** a hügelig.

hilt [hɪlt] n Heft nt; up to the — ganz und gar.

him [hɪm] pron (acc) ihn; (dat) ihm.

himself [hɪm'self] pron sich (selbst); (emphatic) selbst; he's not — mit ihm ist etwas los or nicht in Ordnung.

hind [haɪnd] a hinter, Hinter-; n Hirschkuh f.

hinder ['hɪndə*] vt (stop) hindern; (delay) behindern.

hindrance ['hɪndrəns] n (delay) Behinderung f; (obstacle) Hindernis nt.

hinge [hɪndʒ] *n* Scharnier *nt*; (on door) Türangel *f*; *vt* mit Scharnieren versehen; *vi* (fig) abhängen (on von).

hint [hɪnt] *n* Tip *m*, Andeutung *f*; (trace) Anflug *m*; *vi* andeuten (at acc), anspielen (at auf +acc).

hip [hɪp] *n* Hüfte *f*.

hippopotamus [hɪpə'pɒtəməs] *n* Nilpferd *nt*.

hire ['haɪə*] *vt* worker anstellen; car mieten; *n* Miete *f*; for — taxi frei; **to have for** — verleihen; — **purchase** Teilzahlungskauf *m*.

his [hɪz] *poss a* sein; *poss pron* seine(r,s).

hiss [hɪs] *vi* zischen; *n* Zischen *nt*.

historian [hɪs'tɔ:rɪən] *n* Geschichtsschreiber *m*; Historiker *m*.

historic [hɪs'tɒrɪk] *a* historisch.

historical [hɪs'tɒrɪkl] *a* historisch, geschichtlich.

history ['hɪstərɪ] *n* Geschichte *f*; (personal) Entwicklung *f*, Werdegang *m*.

hit [hɪt] *vt* irreg schlagen; (injure) treffen, verletzen; *n* (blow) Schlag *m*, Stoß *m*; (success) Erfolg *m*, Treffer *m*; (Mus) Hit *m*.

hitch [hɪtʃ] *vt* festbinden; (pull up) hochziehen; *n* (loop) Knoten *m*; (difficulty) Schwierigkeit *f*, Haken *m*.

hitch-hike ['hɪtʃhaɪk] *vi* trampen, per Anhalter fahren; —**r** Tramper *m*.

hitherto ['hɪðə'tu:] *ad* bislang.

hive [haɪv] *n* Bienenkorb *m*.

hoard [hɔ:d] *n* Schatz *m*; *vt* horten, hamstern.

hoarding ['hɔ:dɪŋ] *n* Bretterzaun *m*; (for advertising) Reklamewand *f*.

hoarfrost ['hɔ:'frɒst] *n* (Rauh)reif *m*.

hoarse [hɔ:s] *a* heiser, rauh.

hoax [həʊks] *n* Streich *m*.

hobble ['hɒbl] *vi* humpeln.

hobby ['hɒbɪ] *n* Steckenpferd *nt*, Hobby *nt*.

hobo ['həʊbəʊ] *n* (US) Tippelbruder *m*.

hock [hɒk] *n* (wine) weiße(r) Rheinwein *m*.

hockey ['hɒkɪ] *n* Hockey *nt*.

hoe [həʊ] *n* Hacke *f*; *vt* hacken.

hog [hɒg] *n* Schlachtschwein *nt*; *vt* mit Beschlag belegen.

hoist [hɔɪst] *n* Winde *f*; *vt* hochziehen.

hold [həʊld] irreg *vt* halten; (keep) behalten; (contain) enthalten; (be able to contain) fassen; (keep back) zurück(be)halten; breath anhalten; meeting abhalten; *vi* (withstand pressure) standhalten, aushalten; *n* (grasp) Halt *m*; (claim) Anspruch *m*; (Naut) Schiffsraum *m*; — **back** *vt* zurückhalten; — **down** *vt* niederhalten; — **out** *vt* hinhalten; bieten; *vi* aushalten; — **up** *vt* (delay) aufhalten; (rob) überfallen; —**all** Reisetasche *f*; —**er** Behälter *m*; —**ing** (share) (Aktien)-anteil *m*; —**up** (in traffic) Stockung *f*; (robbery) Überfall *m*.

hole [həʊl] *n* Loch *nt*; *vt* durchlöchern.

holiday ['hɒlədɪ] *n* (day) Feiertag *m*; freie(r) Tag *m*; (vacation) Urlaub *m*, (Sch) Ferien *pl*; —**maker** Feriengast *m*, Urlauber(in *f*) *m*.

holiness ['həʊlɪnɪs] *n* Heiligkeit *f*.

hollow ['hɒləʊ] *a* hohl; (fig) leer; *n* Vertiefung *f*; (in rock) Höhle *f*; — **out** *vt* aushöhlen.

holly ['hɒlɪ] *n* Stechpalme *f*.

holster ['həʊlstə*] *n* Pistolenhalfter *m*.

holy ['həʊlɪ] *a* heilig; (*religious*) fromm.

homage ['hɒmɪdʒ] *n* Huldigung *f*; to pay — to huldigen (+*dat*).

home [həʊm] *n* Heim *nt*, Zuhause *nt*; (*institution*) Heim *nt*, Anstalt *f*; *a* einheimisch; (*Pol*) _inner_; *ad* heim, nach Hause; at — zu Hause; —coming Heimkehr *f*; —less *a* obdachlos; —ly *a* häuslich; (*US*: *ugly*) unscheinbar; —made *a* selbstgemacht; —sick *a*: to be —sick Heimweh haben; —ward(s) *a* heimwärts; —work Hausaufgaben *pl*.

homicide ['hɒmɪsaɪd] *n* (*US*) Totschlag *m*, Mord *m*.

homoeopathy [həʊmɪ'ɒpəθɪ] *n* Homöopathie *f*.

homogeneous [hɒmə'dʒiːnɪəs] *a* homogen, gleichartig.

homosexual [hɒməʊ'seksjʊəl] *a* homosexuell; *n* Homosexuelle(r) *m*.

hone [həʊn] *n* Schleifstein *m*; *vt* feinschleifen.

honest ['ɒnɪst] *a* ehrlich; (*upright*) aufrichtig; —ly *ad* ehrlich; —y *n* Ehrlichkeit *f*.

honey ['hʌnɪ] *n* Honig *m*; —comb Honigwabe *f*; —moon Flitterwochen *pl*, Hochzeitsreise *f*.

honk [hɒŋk] *n* (*Aut*) Hupensignal *nt*; *vi* hupen.

honorary ['ɒnərərɪ] *a* Ehren-.

honour, (*US*) **honor** ['ɒnə*] *vt* ehren; *cheque* einlösen; *debts* begleichen; *contract* einhalten; *n* (*respect*) Ehre *f*; (*reputation*) Ansehen *nt*, gute(r) Ruf *m*; (*sense of right*) Ehrgefühl *nt*; —s *pl* (*titles*) Auszeichnungen *pl*; —able

a ehrenwert, rechtschaffen; *intention* ehrenhaft.

hood [hʊd] *n* Kapuze *f*; (*Aut*) Verdeck *nt*; (*US Aut*) Kühlerhaube *f*; —wink *vt* reinlegen.

hoof [huːf] *n* Huf *m*.

hook [hʊk] *n* Haken *m*; *vt* einhaken; —up Gemeinschaftssendung *f*.

hooligan ['huːlɪgən] *n* Rowdy *m*.

hoop [huːp] *n* Reifen *m*.

hoot [huːt] *vi* (*Aut*) hupen; to — with laughter schallend lachen; *n* (*shout*) Johlen *nt*; (*Aut*) Hupen *nt*; —er *n* (*Naut*) Dampfpfeife *f*; (*Aut*) Hupe *f*.

hop[1] [hɒp] *vi* hüpfen, hopsen; *n* (*jump*) Hopser *m*.

hop[2] [hɒp] *n* (*Bot*) Hopfen *m*.

hope [həʊp] *vi* hoffen; I — that... hoffentlich...; *n* Hoffnung *f*; —ful *a* hoffnungsvoll; (*promising*) vielversprechend; —less *a* hoffnungslos; (*useless*) unmöglich.

horde [hɔːd] *n* Horde *f*.

horizon [hə'raɪzn] *n* Horizont *m*; —tal [hɒrɪ'zɒntl] *a* horizontal.

hormone ['hɔːməʊn] *n* Hormon *nt*.

horn [hɔːn] *n* Horn *nt*; (*Aut*) Hupe *f*; —ed *a* gehörnt, Horn-.

hornet ['hɔːnɪt] *n* Hornisse *f*.

horny ['hɔːnɪ] *a* schwielig; (*US*) scharf.

horoscope ['hɒrəskəʊp] *n* Horoskop *nt*.

horrible, a, horribly *ad* ['hɒrɪbl, -blɪ] fürchterlich.

horrid *a,* —ly *ad* ['hɒrɪd, -lɪ] abscheulich, scheußlich.

horrify ['hɒrɪfaɪ] *vt* entsetzen.

horror ['hɒrə*] *n* Schrecken *m*; (*great dislike*) Abscheu *m* (*of* vor +*dat*).

hors d'oeuvre [ɔːˈdɜːvr] *n* Vorspeise *f*.

horse [hɔːs] *n* Pferd *nt*; on —back beritten; — chestnut Roßkastanie *f*; —-drawn *a* von Pferden gezogen, Pferde-; —power Pferdestärke *f*, PS *nt*; —-racing Pferderennen *nt*; —shoe Hufeisen *nt*.

horsy [ˈhɔːsɪ] *a* pferdenärrisch.

horticulture [ˈhɔːtɪkʌltʃə*] *n* Gartenbau *m*.

hose(pipe) [ˈhəʊzpaɪp] *n* Schlauch *m*.

hosiery [ˈhəʊzɪərɪ] *n* Strumpfwaren *pl*.

hospitable [hɒsˈpɪtəbl] *a* gastfreundlich.

hospital [ˈhɒspɪtl] *n* Krankenhaus *nt*.

hospitality [hɒspɪˈtælɪtɪ] *n* Gastlichkeit *f*, Gastfreundschaft *f*.

host [həʊst] *n* Gastgeber *m*; (innkeeper) (Gast)wirt *m*; (large number) Heerschar *f*; (Eccl) Hostie *f*.

hostage [ˈhɒstɪdʒ] *n* Geisel *f*.

hostel [ˈhɒstəl] *n* Herberge *f*.

hostess [ˈhəʊstes] *n* Gastgeberin *f*.

hostile [ˈhɒstaɪl] *a* feindlich.

hostility [hɒsˈtɪlɪtɪ] *n* Feindschaft *f*; hostilities *pl* Feindseligkeiten *pl*.

hot [hɒt] *a* heiß; *drink, food, water* warm; (*spiced*) scharf; (*angry*) hitzig; — air (*col*) Gewäsch *nt*; —bed (*lit*) Mistbeet *nt*; (*fig*) Nährboden *m*; —-blooded *a* heißblütig; — dog heiße(s) Würstchen *m*.

hotel [həʊˈtel] *n* Hotel *nt*; —ier Hotelier *m*.

hotheaded [ˈhɒtˈhedɪd] *a* hitzig, aufbrausend.

hothouse [ˈhɒthaʊs] *n* (*lit, fig*) Treibhaus *nt*.

hot line [ˈhɒtlaɪn] *n* (*Pol*) heiße(r) Draht *m*.

hotly [ˈhɒtlɪ] *ad* argue hitzig; pursue dicht.

hot news [ˈhɒtˈnjuːz] *n* das Neueste vom Neuen.

hotplate [ˈhɒtpleɪt] *n* Kochplatte *f*.

hot-water bottle [hɒtˈwɔːtəbɒtl] *n* Wärmflasche *f*.

hound [haʊnd] *n* Jagdhund *m*; *vt* jagen, hetzen.

hour [aʊə*] *n* Stunde *f*; (*time of day*) (Tages)zeit *f*; —ly *a* stündlich.

house [haʊs] *n* Haus *nt*; [haʊz] *vt* (*accommodate*) unterbringen; (*shelter*) aufnehmen; —boat Hausboot *nt*; —breaking Einbruch *m*; —hold Haushalt *m*; —keeper Haushälterin *f*; —keeping Haushaltung *f*; —wife Hausfrau *f*; —work Hausarbeit *f*.

housing [ˈhaʊzɪŋ] *n* (*act*) Unterbringung *f*; (*houses*) Wohnungen *pl*; (*Pol*) Wohnungsbau *m*; (*covering*) Gehäuse *nt*; — estate (Wohn)-siedlung *f*.

hovel [ˈhɒvəl] *n* elende Hütte *f*; Loch *nt*.

hover [ˈhɒvə*] *vi* (*bird*) schweben; (*person*) wartend herumstehen; —craft Luftkissenfahrzeug *nt*.

how [haʊ] *ad* wie; — many wie viele; — much wieviel; —ever *ad* (*but*) (je)doch, aber; —ever you phrase it wie Sie es auch ausdrücken.

howl [haʊl] *n* Heulen *nt*; *vi* heulen.

howler [ˈhaʊlə*] *n* grobe(r) Schnitzer *m*.

hub [hʌb] *n* Radnabe *f*; (*of the world*) Mittelpunkt *m*; (*of commerce*) Zentrum *nt*.

hubbub [ˈhʌbʌb] *n* Tumult *m*.

hub cap ['hʌbkæp] *n* Radkappe *f.*

huddle ['hʌdl] *vi* sich zusammendrängen; *n* Grüppchen *nt.*

hue [hju:] *n* Färbung *f*, Farbton *m*; — **and cry** Zetergeschrei *nt.*

huff [hʌf] *n* Eingeschnapptsein *nt*; **to go into a** — einschnappen.

hug [hʌg] *vt* umarmen; (*fig*) sich dicht halten **an** (+*acc*); *n* Umarmung *f.*

huge [hju:dʒ] *a* groß, riesig.

hulk [hʌlk] *n* (*ship*) abgetakelte(s) Schiff *nt*; (*person*) Koloß *m*; —**ing** *a* ungeschlacht.

hull [hʌl] *n* Schiffsrumpf *m.*

hullo [hʌ'ləu] *see* **hello.**

hum [hʌm] *vi* summen; (*bumble-bee*) brummen; *vt* summen; *n* Summen *nt.*

human ['hju:mən] *a* menschlich; *n* (*also* — **being**) Mensch *m.*

humane [hju:'mein] *a* human.

humanity [hju:'mæniti] *n* Menschheit *f*; (*kindliness*) Menschlichkeit *f.*

humble ['hʌmbl] *a* demütig; (*modest*) bescheiden; *vt* demütigen.

humbly ['hʌmbli] *ad* demütig.

humdrum ['hʌmdrʌm] *a* eintönig, langweilig.

humid ['hju:mid] *a* feucht; —**ity** [hju:'miditi] Feuchtigkeit *f.*

humiliate [hju:'milieit] *vt* demütigen.

humiliation [hju:mili'eiʃən] *n* Demütigung *f.*

humility [hju:'militi] *n* Demut *f.*

humorist ['hju:mərist] *n* Humorist *m.*

humorous ['hju:mərəs] *a* humorvoll, komisch.

humour, (*US*) **humor** ['hju:mə*] *n* (*fun*) Humor *m*; (*mood*) Stimmung *f*; *vt* nachgeben (+*dat*); **bei** Stimmung halten.

hump [hʌmp] *n* Buckel *m.*

hunch [hʌntʃ] *n* (*presentiment*) (Vor)ahnung *f*; *vt* **shoulders** hochziehen; —**back** Bucklige(r) *m.*

hundred ['hʌndrid] *num*, **a**, **n** hundert; —**weight** Zentner *m.*

hunger ['hʌŋgə*] *n* Hunger *m*; (*fig*) Verlangen *nt* (*for* nach); *vi* hungern.

hungry *a*, **hungrily** *ad* ['hʌŋgri, -li] hungrig; **to be** — Hunger haben.

hunt [hʌnt] *vt* jagen; (*search*) suchen (*for acc*); *vi* jagen; *n* Jagd *f*; —**er** Jäger *m*; —**ing** Jagen *nt*, Jagd *f.*

hurdle ['hɜ:dl] *n* (*lit, fig*) Hürde *f.*

hurl [hɜ:l] *vt* schleudern.

hurrah [hu'rɑ:], **hurray** [hu'rei] *n* Hurra *nt.*

hurricane ['hʌrikən] *n* Orkan *m.*

hurried ['hʌrid] *a* eilig; (*hasty*) übereilt; —**ly** *ad* übereilt, hastig.

hurry ['hʌri] *n* Eile *f*; **to be in a** — es eilig haben; *vi* sich beeilen; —**!** mach schnell! *vt* (an)treiben; **job** übereilen.

hurt [hɜ:t] *irreg vt* weh tun (+*dat*); (*injure, fig*) verletzen; *vi* weh tun; —**ful** *a* schädlich; **remark** verletzend.

hurtle ['hɜ:tl] *vt* schleudern; *vi* sausen.

husband ['hʌzbənd] *n* (Ehe)mann *m*, Gatte *m.*

hush [hʌʃ] *n* Stille *f*; *vt* zur Ruhe bringen; *vi* still sein; — *interj* pst, still.

husk [hʌsk] *n* Spelze *f.*

husky ['hʌski] *a* **voice** rauh; **figure** stämmig; *n* Eskimohund *m.*

hustle ['hʌsl] *vt* (*push*) stoßen; (*hurry*) antreiben, drängen;

(Hoch)betrieb *m*; — **and bustle**
Geschäftigkeit *f.*

hut [hʌt] *n* Hütte *f.*

hutch [hʌtʃ] *n* (Kaninchen)stall *m.*

hyacinth ['haɪəsɪnθ] *n* Hyazinthe *f.*

hybrid ['haɪbrɪd] *n* Kreuzung *f*; *a*
Misch-

hydrant ['haɪdrənt] *n* Hydrant *m.*

hydraulic [haɪ'drɒlɪk] *a*
hydraulisch.

hydroelectric ['haɪdrəʊɪ'lektrɪk] *a*
hydroelektrisch.

hydrofoil ['haɪdrəʊfɔɪl] *n* Tragflügel
m; Tragflügelboot *nt.*

hydrogen ['haɪdrɪdʒən] *n* Wasser-
stoff *m.*

hyena [haɪ'iːnə] *n* Hyäne *f.*

hygiene ['haɪdʒiːn] *n* Hygiene *f.*

hygienic [haɪ'dʒiːnɪk] *a* hygienisch.

hymn [hɪm] *n* Kirchenlied *nt.*

hyphen ['haɪfən] *n* Bindestrich *m*;
Trennungszeichen *nt.*

hypnosis [hɪp'nəʊsɪs] *n* Hypnose *f.*

hypnotism ['hɪpnətɪzəm] *n*
Hypnotismus *m.*

hypnotist ['hɪpnətɪst] *n*
Hypnotiseur *m.*

hypnotize ['hɪpnətaɪz] *vt*
hypnotisieren.

hypochondriac [haɪpəʊ'kɒndrɪæk]
n eingebildete(r) Kranke(r) *mf.*

hypocrisy [hɪ'pɒkrɪsɪ] *n* Heuchelei
f, Scheinheiligkeit *f.*

hypocrite ['hɪpəkrɪt] *n* Heuchler *m,*
Scheinheilige(r) *m.*

hypocritical [hɪpə'krɪtɪkəl] *a*
scheinheilig, heuchlerisch.

hypothesis [haɪ'pɒθɪsɪs] *n*
Hypothese *f.*

hypothetic(al) [haɪpəʊ'θetɪk(əl)] *a*
hypothetisch.

hysteria [hɪs'tɪərɪə] *n* Hysterie *f.*

hysterical [hɪs'terɪkəl] *a* hysterisch.

hysterics [hɪs'terɪks] *npl*
hysterische(r) Anfall *m.*

I

I, i [aɪ] *n* I *nt*, i *nt*; **I** *pron* ich.

ice [aɪs] *n* Eis *nt*; *vt* (*Cook*) mit
Zuckerguß überziehen; *vi* (*also* —
up) vereisen; —**axe** Eispickel *m.*;
—**berg** Eisberg *m*; —**box** (*US*)
Kühlschrank *m*; —**cream** Eis *nt*;
—**cold** *a* eiskalt; —**cube**
Eiswürfel *m*; — **hockey** Eishockey
nt; — **rink** (Kunst)eisbahn *f.*

icicle ['aɪsɪkl] *n* Eiszapfen *m.*

icing ['aɪsɪŋ] *n* (*on cake*) Zuckerguß
m; (*on window*) Vereisung *f.*

icon ['aɪkɒn] *n* Ikone *f.*

icy ['aɪsɪ] *a* (*slippery*) vereist; (*cold*)
eisig.

I'd [aɪd] = **I would**; **I had.**

idea [aɪ'dɪə] *n* Idee *f*; no' — **keine**
Ahnung; **my** — **of a holiday we**
ich mir einen Urlaub vorstelle.

ideal [aɪ'dɪəl] *n* Ideal *nt*; *a* ideal;
—**ism** Idealismus *m*; —**ist** Idealist
m; —**ly** *ad* ideal(erweise).

identical [aɪ'dentɪkəl] *a* identisch;
twins eineiig.

identification [aɪdentɪfɪ'keɪʃən] *n*
Identifizierung *f.*

identify [aɪ'dentɪfaɪ] *vt*
identifizieren; (*regard as the same*)
gleichsetzen.

identity [aɪ'dentɪtɪ] *n* Identität *f*; —
card Personalausweis *m*; — **papers**
pl (Ausweis)papiere *pl.*

ideology [aɪdɪ'ɒlədʒɪ] n Ideologie f.

idiocy ['ɪdɪəsɪ] n Idiotie f.

idiom ['ɪdɪəm] n (expression) Redewendung f; (dialect) Idiom nt.

idiosyncrasy [ɪdɪə'sɪŋkrəsɪ] n Eigenart f.

idiot ['ɪdɪət] n Idiot(in f) m; **-ic** [ɪdɪ'ɒtɪk] a idiotisch.

idle ['aɪdl] a (doing nothing) untätig, müßig; (lazy) faul; (useless) vergeblich, nutzlos; machine still-(stehend); threat, talk leer; **-ness** Müßiggang m; Faulheit f; **-r** Faulenzer m.

idol ['aɪdl] n Idol nt; **-ize** vt vergöttern.

idyllic ['ɪdɪlɪk] a idyllisch.

if [ɪf] cj wenn, falls; (whether) ob; **- only …** wenn … doch nur; **-not** falls nicht.

igloo ['ɪgluː] n Iglu m or nt.

ignite [ɪg'naɪt] vt (an)zünden.

ignition [ɪg'nɪʃən] n Zündung f; **-key** (Aut) Zündschlüssel m.

ignoramus [ɪgnə'reɪməs] n Ignorant m.

ignorance ['ɪgnərəns] n Unwissenheit f, Ignoranz f.

ignorant ['ɪgnərənt] a unwissend.

ignore [ɪg'nɔː*] vt ignorieren.

ikon ['aɪkɒn] n = icon.

I'll [aɪl] = I will, I shall.

ill [ɪl] a krank; (evil) schlecht, böse; n Übel nt; **-advised** a schlecht beraten, unklug; **-at-ease** unbehaglich.

illegal a, **-ly** ad [ɪ'liːgəl, -ɪ] illegal.

illegible [ɪ'ledʒəbl] a unleserlich.

illegitimate [ɪlɪ'dʒɪtɪmət] a unzulässig; child unehelich.

ill-fated ['ɪl'feɪtɪd] a unselig.

ill-feeling ['ɪl'fiːlɪŋ] n Verstimmung f.

illicit [ɪ'lɪsɪt] a verboten.

illiterate [ɪ'lɪtərət] a ungebildet.

ill-mannered ['ɪl'mænəd] a ungehobelt.

illness ['ɪlnəs] n Krankheit f.

illogical [ɪ'lɒdʒɪkl] a unlogisch.

ill-treat ['ɪl'triːt] vt mißhandeln.

illuminate [ɪ'luːmɪneɪt] vt beleuchten.

illumination [ɪluːmɪ'neɪʃən] n Beleuchtung f.

illusion [ɪ'luːʒən] n Illusion f.

illusive [ɪ'luːsɪv], **illusory** [ɪ'luːsərɪ] a illusorisch, trügerisch.

illustrate ['ɪləstreɪt] vt illustrieren; (explain) veranschaulichen.

illustration [ɪləs'treɪʃən] n Illustration f; (explanation) Veranschaulichung f.

illustrious [ɪ'lʌstrɪəs] a berühmt.

ill will ['ɪl'wɪl] n Groll m.

I'm [aɪm] = I am.

image ['ɪmɪdʒ] n Bild nt; (likeness) Abbild nt; (public -) Image nt; **-ry** Symbolik f.

imaginable ['ɪmædʒɪnəbl] a vorstellbar.

imaginary ['ɪmædʒɪnərɪ] a eingebildet; world Phantasie-.

imagination [ɪmædʒɪ'neɪʃən] n Einbildung f; (creative) Phantasie f.

imaginative ['ɪmædʒɪnətɪv] a phantasiereich, einfallsreich.

imagine ['ɪmædʒɪn] vt 'sich vorstellen; (wrongly) sich einbilden.

imbalance [ɪm'bæləns] n Unausgeglichenheit f.

imbecile ['ɪmbəsiːl] n Schwachsinnige(r) mf.

imbue [ɪm'bjuː] vt durchdringen.

imitate ['ɪmɪteɪt] vt nachmachen, imitieren.

imitation [ımı'teıʃən] n Nachahmung f, Imitation f.

imitator ['ımıteıtə*] n Nachahmer m.

immaculate [ı'mækjʊlıt] a makellos; dress tadellos; (Eccl) unbefleckt.

immaterial [ımə'tıərıəl] a unwesentlich.

immature [ımə'tjʊə*] a unreif.

immaturity [ımə'tjʊərıtı] n Unreife f.

immediate [ı'mi:dıət] a (instant) sofortig; (near) unmittelbar; relatives nächste(r, s); needs dringlich; —ly ad sofort; (in position) unmittelbar.

immense [ı'mens] a unermeßlich; —ly ad ungeheuerlich; grateful unheimlich.

immerse [ı'mɜ:s] vt eintauchen.

immersion heater [ı'mɜ:ʃənhi:tə*] n Heißwassergerät nt.

immigrant ['ımıgrənt] n Einwanderer m.

immigration [ımı'greıʃən] n Einwanderung f.

imminent ['ımınənt] a bevorstehend; danger drohend.

immobilize [ı'məʊbılaız] vt lähmen.

immoderate [ı'mɒdərət] a maßlos, übertrieben.

immoral [ı'mɒrəl] a unmoralisch; (sexually) unsittlich; —ity [ımə'rælıtı] Verderbtheit f.

immortal [ı'mɔ:tl] a unsterblich; n Unsterbliche(r) mf; —ity [ımɔ:'tælıtı] Unsterblichkeit f; (of book etc) Unvergänglichkeit f; —ize vt unsterblich machen.

immune [ı'mju:n] a (secure) geschützt (from gegen), sicher (from vor + dat); (Med) immun.

immunity [ı'mju:nıtı] n (Med, Jur) Immunität f; (fig) Freiheit f.

immunization [ımjʊnaı'zeıʃən] n Immunisierung f.

immunize ['ımjʊnaız] vt immunisieren.

impact ['ımpækt] n (lit) Aufprall m; (force) Wucht f; (fig) Wirkung f.

impair [ım'pεə*] vt beeinträchtigen.

impale [ım'peıl] vt aufspießen.

impartial [ım'pα:ʃəl] a unparteiisch; —ity [ımpα:ʃı'ælıtı] Unparteilichkeit f.

impassable [ım'pα:səbl] a unpassierbar.

impassioned [ım'pæʃnd] a leidenschaftlich.

impatience [ım'peıʃəns] n Ungeduld f.

impatient a, —ly ad [ım'peıʃənt, -lı] ungeduldig; to be — to do sth es nicht erwarten können, etw zu tun.

impeccable [ım'pekəbl] a tadellos.

impede [ım'pi:d] vt (be)hindern.

impediment [ım'pedımənt] n Hindernis nt; (in speech) Sprachfehler m.

impending [ım'pendıŋ] a bevorstehend.

impenetrable [ım'penıtrəbl] a (lit, fig) undurchdringlich; forest unwegsam; theory undurchsichtig; mystery unerforschlich.

imperative [ım'perətıv] a (necessary) unbedingt erforderlich; n (Gram) Imperativ m, Befehlsform f.

imperceptible [ımpə'septəbl] a nicht wahrnehmbar.

imperfect [ım'pɜ:fıkt] a (faulty) fehlerhaft; (incomplete) unvollständig; —ion [ımpə'fekʃən]

Unvollkommenheit f; (fault) Fehler m; (faultiness) Fehlerhaftigkeit f.

imperial [ɪmˈpɪərɪəl] a kaiserlich; —ism Imperialismus m.

imperil [ɪmˈperɪl] vt gefährden.

impersonal [ɪmˈpɜːsnl] a unpersönlich.

impersonate [ɪmˈpɜːsəneɪt] vt sich ausgeben als; (for amusement) imitieren.

impersonation [ɪmpɜːsəˈneɪʃən] n Verkörperung f; (Theat) Imitation f.

impertinence [ɪmˈpɜːtɪnəns] n Unverschämtheit f.

impertinent [ɪmˈpɜːtɪnənt] a unverschämt, frech.

imperturbable [ɪmpəˈtɜːbəbl] a unerschütterlich, gelassen.

impervious [ɪmˈpɜːvɪəs] a undurchlässig; (fig) unempfänglich (to für).

impetuous [ɪmˈpetjʊəs] a heftig, ungestüm.

impetus [ˈɪmpɪtəs] n Triebkraft f; (fig) Auftrieb m.

impinge [ɪmˈpɪndʒ]: — on vt beeinträchtigen; (light) fallen auf (+acc).

implausible [ɪmˈplɔːzəbl] a unglaubwürdig, nicht überzeugend.

implement [ˈɪmplɪmənt] n Werkzeug nt, Gerät nt; [ˈɪmplɪment] vt ausführen.

implicate [ˈɪmplɪkeɪt] vt verwickeln, hineinziehen.

implication [ɪmplɪˈkeɪʃən] n (meaning) Bedeutung f; (effect) Auswirkung f; (hint) Andeutung f; (in crime) Verwicklung f; by — folglich.

implicit [ɪmˈplɪsɪt] a (suggested) unausgesprochen; (utter) vorbehaltlos.

implore [ɪmˈplɔː*] vt anflehen.

imply [ɪmˈplaɪ] vt (hint) andeuten; (be evidence for) schließen lassen auf (+acc); what does that —? was bedeutet das?

impolite [ɪmpəˈlaɪt] a unhöflich.

impolitic [ɪmˈpɒlɪtɪk] a undiplomatisch.

imponderable [ɪmˈpɒndərəbl] a unwägbar.

import [ɪmˈpɔːt] vt einführen, importieren; [ˈɪmpɔːt] n Einfuhr f, Import m; (meaning) Bedeutung f, Tragweite f.

importance [ɪmˈpɔːtəns] n Bedeutung f; (influence) Einfluß m.

important [ɪmˈpɔːtənt] a wichtig; (influential) bedeutend, einflußreich.

import duty [ˈɪmpɔːtdjuːtɪ] n Einfuhrzoll m.

imported [ɪmˈpɔːtɪd] a eingeführt, importiert.

importer [ɪmˈpɔːtə*] n Importeur m.

import licence [ˈɪmpɔːtlaɪsəns] n Einfuhrgenehmigung f.

impose [ɪmˈpəʊz] vti auferlegen (on dat); penalty, sanctions verhängen (on gegen); to — (o.s.) on sb sich jdm aufdrängen; to — on sb's kindness jds Liebenswürdigkeit ausnützen.

imposing [ɪmˈpəʊzɪŋ] a eindrucksvoll.

imposition [ɪmpəˈzɪʃən] n (of burden, fine) Auferlegung f; (Sch) Strafarbeit f.

impossibility [ɪmpɒsəˈbɪlɪtɪ] n Unmöglichkeit f.

impossible a, **impossibly** ad [ɪmˈpɒsəbl, -blɪ] unmöglich.

impostor [ɪmˈpɒstə*] n Betrüger m; Hochstapler m.

impotence ['ɪmpətəns] Impotenz f.

impotent ['ɪmpətənt] a machtlos; (sexually) impotent.

impound [ɪm'paʊnd] vt beschlagnahmen.

impoverished [ɪm'pɒvərɪʃt] a verarmt.

impracticable [ɪm'præktɪkəbl] a undurchführbar.

impractical [ɪm'præktɪkəl] a unpraktisch.

imprecise [ɪmprə'saɪs] a ungenau.

impregnable [ɪm'pregnəbl] a (castle) uneinnehmbar.

impregnate ['ɪmpregneɪt] vt (saturate) sättigen; (fertilize) befruchten; (fig) durchdringen.

impresario [ɪmpre'saːrɪəʊ] n Impresario m.

impress [ɪm'pres] vt (influence) beeindrucken; (imprint) (auf)-drücken; to — sth on sb jdm etw einschärfen; —ion Eindruck m; (on wax, footprint) Abdruck m; (of stamp) Aufdruck m; (of book) Auflage f; (take-off) Nachahmung f; I was under the —ion ich hatte den Eindruck; —ionable a leicht zu beeindrucken(d); —ionist Impressionist m; —ive a eindrucksvoll.

imprison [ɪm'prɪzn] vt ins Gefängnis schicken; —ment Inhaftierung f; Gefangenschaft f; 3 years' —ment eine Gefängnisstrafe von 3 Jahren.

improbable [ɪm'prɒbəbl] a unwahrscheinlich.

impromptu [ɪm'prɒmptjuː] a, ad aus dem Stegreif, improvisiert.

improper [ɪm'prɒpə*] a (indecent) unanständig; (wrong) unrichtig, falsch; (unsuitable) unpassend.

impropriety [ɪmprə'praɪətɪ] n Ungehörigkeit f.

improve [ɪm'pruːv] vt verbessern; vi besser werden; —ment (Ver)-besserung f; (of appearance) Verschönerung f.

improvisation [ɪmprəvaɪ'zeɪʃən] n Improvisation f.

improvise ['ɪmprəvaɪz] vti improvisieren.

imprudence [ɪm'pruːdəns] n Unklugheit f.

imprudent [ɪm'pruːdənt] a unklug.

impudent ['ɪmpjʊdənt] a unverschämt.

impulse ['ɪmpʌls] n (desire) Drang m; (driving force) Antrieb m, Impuls m; my first — was to... ich wollte zuerst...

impulsive [ɪm'pʌlsɪv] a impulsiv.

impunity [ɪm'pjuːnɪtɪ] n Straflosigkeit f.

impure [ɪm'pjʊə*] a (dirty) unrein; (mixed) gemischt; (bad) schmutzig, unanständig.

impurity [ɪm'pjʊərɪtɪ] n Unreinheit f; (Tech) Verunreinigung f.

in [ɪn] prep in; (made of) aus; — Dickens/a child bei Dickens/einem Kind; — him you'll have... an ihm hast du...; — doing this he has ... dadurch, daß er das tat, hat er ...; — saying that I mean ... wenn ich das sage, meine ich ...; I haven't seen him — years ich habe ihn seit Jahren nicht mehr gesehen; 15 pence — the £ 15 Pence per Pfund; blind — the left eye auf dem linken Auge or links blind; — itself an sich; — that, — so or as far as insofern als; ad hinein; to be — zuhause sein; (train) da sein; (in fashion) in (Mode) sein; to have it — for sb es auf jdn abgesehen haben; —s and outs pl Einzelheiten pl; to

know the —s and outs sich auskennen.

inability [ɪnə'bɪlɪtɪ] n Unfähigkeit f.

inaccessible [ɪnæk'sesəbl] a
.unzugänglich.

inaccuracy [ɪn'ækjʊrəsɪ] n
Ungenauigkeit f.

inaccurate [ɪn'ækjʊrɪt] a ungenau;
(wrong) unrichtig.

inaction [ɪn'ækʃən] n Untätigkeit f.

inactive [ɪn'æktɪv] a untätig.

inactivity [ɪnæk'tɪvɪtɪ] n Untätigkeit f.

inadequacy [ɪn'ædɪkwəsɪ] n
Unzulänglichkeit f; (of punishment) Unangemessenheit f.

inadequate [ɪn'ædɪkwət] a
unzulänglich; punishment
unangemessen.

inadvertently [ɪnəd'vɜːtəntlɪ] ad
unabsichtlich.

inadvisable [ɪnəd'vaɪzəbl] a nicht
ratsam.

inane [ɪ'neɪn] a dumm, albern.

inanimate [ɪn'ænɪmət] a leblos.

inapplicable [ɪnə'plɪkəbl] a
unzutreffend.

inappropriate [ɪnə'prəʊprɪət] a
clothing ungeeignet; remark
unangebracht.

inapt [ɪn'æpt] a unpassend;
(clumsy) ungeschickt; —itude
Untauglichkeit f.

inarticulate [ɪnɑː'tɪkjʊlət] a
unklar; to be — sich nicht ausdrücken können.

inartistic [ɪnɑː'tɪstɪk] a unkünst-
lerisch.

inasmuch as [ɪnəz'mʌtʃəz] ad da,
weil; (in so far as) soweit.

inattention [ɪnə'tenʃən] n Unauf-
merksamkeit f.

inattentive [ɪnə'tentɪv] a unauf-
merksam.

inaudible [ɪn'ɔːdəbl] a unhörbar.

inaugural [ɪ'nɔːgjʊrəl] a Eröff-
nungs-; (Univ) Antritts-.

inaugurate [ɪ'nɔːgjʊreɪt] vt (open)
einweihen; (admit to office) (feierlich) einführen.

inauguration [ɪnɔːgjʊ'reɪʃən] n
Eröffnung f; (feierliche) Amtsein-
führung f.

inborn [ɪn'bɔːn] a angeboren.

inbred [ɪn'bred] a quality
angeboren; they are — bei ihnen
herrscht Inzucht.

inbreeding [ɪn'briːdɪŋ] n Inzucht f.

incalculable [ɪn'kælkjʊləbl] a
person unberechenbar; consequences unabsehbar.

incapability [ɪnkeɪpə'bɪlɪtɪ] n
Unfähigkeit f.

incapable [ɪn'keɪpəbl] a unfähig (of
doing sth etw zu tun); (not able)
nicht einsatzfähig.

incapacitate [ɪnkə'pæsɪteɪt] vt
untauglich machen; —d behindert;
machine nicht gebrauchsfähig.

incapacity [ɪnkə'pæsɪtɪ] n Unfähigkeit f.

incarcerate [ɪn'kɑːsəreɪt] vt
einkerkern.

incarnate [ɪn'kɑːnɪt] a menschge-
worden; (fig) leibhaftig.

incarnation [ɪnkɑː'neɪʃən] n (Eccl)
Menschwerdung f; (fig) Inbegriff
m.

incendiary [ɪn'sendɪərɪ] a brand-
stifterisch, Brand-; (fig) aufrührerisch; n Brandstifter m;
(bomb) Brandbombe f.

incense ['ɪnsens] n Weihrauch m;
[ɪn'sens] vt erzürnen.

incentive [ɪn'sentɪv] n Anreiz m.

incessant a, —ly ad [ɪn'sesnt, -lɪ]
unaufhörlich.

incest ['ɪnsest] n Inzest m.

inch [ɪntʃ] n Zoll m.

incidence ['ɪnsɪdəns] n Auftreten nt; (of crime) Quote f.

incident ['ɪnsɪdənt] n Vorfall m; (disturbance) Zwischenfall m; **—al** [ɪnsɪ'dentl] a music Begleit-; expenses Neben-; (unplanned) zufällig; (unimportant) nebensächlich; remark beiläufig; **—al to sth** mit etw verbunden; **—ally** [ɪnsɪ'dentlɪ] ad (by chance) nebenbei; (by the way) nebenbei bemerkt, übrigens.

incinerator [ɪn'sɪnəreɪtə*] n Verbrennungsofen m.

incision [ɪn'sɪʒən] n Einschnitt m.

incisive [ɪn'saɪsɪv] a style treffend; person scharfsinnig.

incite [ɪn'saɪt] vt anstacheln.

inclement [ɪn'klemənt] a weather rauh.

inclination [ɪnklɪ'neɪʃən] n Neigung f.

incline ['ɪnklaɪn] n Abhang m; [ɪn'klaɪn] vt neigen; (fig) veranlassen; **to be —d to do sth** Lust haben, etw zu tun; (have tendency) dazu neigen, etw zu tun; vi sich neigen.

include [ɪn'kluːd] vt einschließen; (on list, in group) aufnehmen.

including [ɪn'kluːdɪŋ] prep: **— X X** inbegriffen.

inclusion [ɪn'kluːʒən] n Aufnahme f, Einbeziehung f.

inclusive [ɪn'kluːsɪv] a einschließlich; (Comm) inklusive.

incognito [ɪnkɒg'niːtəʊ] ad inkognito.

incoherent [ɪnkəʊ'hɪərənt] a zusammenhanglos.

income ['ɪnkʌm] n Einkommen nt; (from business) Einkünfte pl; **—**

tax Lohnsteuer f; (of self-employed) Einkommensteuer f.

incoming ['ɪnkʌmɪŋ] a ankommend; (succeeding) folgend; mail eingehend; tide steigend.

incomparable [ɪn'kɒmpərəbl] a unvergleichlich.

incompatible [ɪnkəm'pætəbl] a unvereinbar; people unverträglich.

incompetence [ɪn'kɒmpɪtəns] n Unfähigkeit f.

incompetent [ɪn'kɒmpɪtənt] a unfähig; (not qualified) nicht berechtigt.

incomplete [ɪnkəm'pliːt] a unvollständig.

incomprehensible [ɪnkɒmprɪ'hensəbl] a unverständlich.

inconceivable [ɪnkən'siːvəbl] a unvorstellbar.

inconclusive [ɪnkən'kluːsɪv] a nicht schlüssig.

incongruity [ɪnkɒn'gruːɪtɪ] n Seltsamkeit f; (of remark etc) Unangebrachtsein nt.

incongruous [ɪn'kɒŋgruəs] a seltsam; remark unangebracht.

inconsequential [ɪnkɒnsɪ'kwenʃəl] a belanglos.

inconsiderable [ɪnkən'sɪdərəbl] a unerheblich.

inconsiderate [ɪnkən'sɪdərət] a rücksichtslos; (hasty) unüberlegt.

inconsistency [ɪnkən'sɪstənsɪ] n innere(r) Widerspruch m; (state) Unbeständigkeit f.

inconsistent [ɪnkən'sɪstənt] a unvereinbar; behaviour inkonsequent; action, speech widersprüchlich; person, work unbeständig.

inconspicuous [ɪnkən'spɪkjuəs] a unauffällig.

inconstancy [ɪn'kɒnstənsɪ] *n* Unbeständigkeit *f.*

inconstant [ɪn'kɒnstənt] *a* unbeständig.

incontinence [ɪn'kɒntɪnəns] *n* (Med) Unfähigkeit *f*, Stuhl und Harn zurückzuhalten; (fig) Zügellosigkeit *f.*

incontinent [ɪn'kɒntɪnənt] *a* (Med) nicht fähig, Stuhl und Harn zurückzuhalten; (fig) zügellos.

inconvenience [ɪnkən'vi:nɪəns] *n* Unbequemlichkeit *f*; (trouble to others) Unannehmlichkeiten *pl.*

inconvenient [ɪnkən'vi:nɪənt] *a* ungelegen; journey unbequem.

incorporate [ɪn'kɔ:rpəreɪt] *vt* (include) aufnehmen; (unite) vereinigen.

incorporated [ɪn'kɔ:rpəreɪtɪd] *a* eingetragen; (US) GmbH.

incorrect [ɪnkə'rekt] *a* unrichtig; behaviour inkorrekt.

incorrigible [ɪn'kɒrɪdʒəbl] *a* unverbesserlich.

incorruptible [ɪnkə'rʌptəbl] *a* unzerstörbar; person unbestechlich.

increase ['ɪnkri:s] *n* Zunahme *f*, Erhöhung *f*; (pay —) Gehaltserhöhung *f*; (in size) Vergrößerung *f*; [ɪn'kri:s] *vt* erhöhen; wealth, rage vermehren; business erweitern; *vi* zunehmen; (prices) steigen; (in size) größer werden; (in number) sich vermehren.

increasingly [ɪn'kri:sɪŋlɪ] *ad* zunehmend.

incredible *a*, **incredibly** *ad* [ɪn'kredəbl, -blɪ] unglaublich.

incredulity [ɪnkrɪ'dju:lɪtɪ] *n* Ungläubigkeit *f.*

incredulous [ɪn'kredjʊləs] *a* ungläubig.

increment ['ɪnkrɪmənt] *n* Zulage *f.*

incriminate [ɪn'krɪmɪneɪt] *vt* belasten.

incubation [ɪnkjʊ'beɪʃən] *n* Ausbrüten *nt*; — period Inkubationszeit *f.*

incubator ['ɪnkjʊbeɪtə*] *n* Brutkasten *m.*

incur [ɪn'kɜ:*] *vt* sich zuziehen; debts machen.

incurable [ɪn'kjʊərəbl] *a* unheilbar; (fig) unverbesserlich.

incursion [ɪn'kɜ:ʃən] *n* (feindlicher) Einfall *m.*

indebted [ɪn'detɪd] *a* (obliged) verpflichtet (to sb jdm); (owing) verschuldet.

indecency [ɪn'di:snsɪ] *n* Unanständigkeit *f.*

indecent [ɪn'di:snt] *a* unanständig.

indecision [ɪndɪ'sɪʒən] *n* Unschlüssigkeit *f.*

indecisive [ɪndɪ'saɪsɪv] *a* battle nicht entscheidend; result unentschieden; person unentschlossen.

indeed [ɪn'di:d] *ad* tatsächlich, in der Tat.

indefinable [ɪndɪ'faɪnəbl] *a* undefinierbar; (vague) unbestimmt.

indefinite [ɪn'defɪnɪt] *a* unbestimmt; —ly *ad* auf unbestimmte Zeit; wait unbegrenzt lange.

indelible [ɪn'deləbl] *a* unauslöschlich; — pencil Tintenstift *m.*

indemnify [ɪn'demnɪfaɪ] *vt* entschädigen; (safeguard) versichern.

indentation [ɪnden'teɪʃən] *n* Einbuchtung *f*; (Print) Einrückung *f.*

independence [ɪndɪ'pendəns] *n* Unabhängigkeit *f.*

independent [ɪndɪ'pendənt] *a* (free) unabhängig; (unconnected) unabhängig von.

indescribable [ɪndɪs'kraɪbəbl] a unbeschreiblich.

index ['ɪndeks] n Index m (also 'Eccl'), Verzeichnis nt; — finger Zeigefinger m.

indicate ['ɪndɪkeɪt] vt anzeigen; (hint) andeuten.

indication [ɪndɪ'keɪʃən] n Anzeichen nt; (information) Angabe f.

indicative [ɪn'dɪkətɪv] n (Gram) Indikativ m.

indicator ['ɪndɪkeɪtə*] n (sign) (An)-zeichen nt; (Aut) Richtungsanzeiger m.

indict [ɪn'daɪt] vt anklagen; —able a person strafrechtlich verfolgbar; offence strafbar; —ment Anklage f.

indifference [ɪn'dɪfrəns] n (lack of interest) Gleichgültigkeit f; (unimportance) Unwichtigkeit f.

indifferent [ɪn'dɪfrənt] a (not caring) gleichgültig; (unimportant) unwichtig; (mediocre) mäßig.

indigenous [ɪn'dɪdʒɪnəs] a einheimisch; a plant — to X eine in X vorkommende Pflanze.

indigestible [ɪndɪ'dʒestəbl] a unverdaulich.

indigestion [ɪndɪ'dʒestʃən] n Verdauungsstörung f; verdorbene(r) Magen m.

indignant [ɪn'dɪgnənt] a ungehalten, entrüstet.

indignation [ɪndɪg'neɪʃən] n Entrüstung f.

indignity [ɪn'dɪgnɪtɪ] n Demütigung f.

indigo ['ɪndɪgəʊ] n Indigo m or nt; a indigoblau.

indirect a, —ly ad [ɪndɪ'rekt, -lɪ] indirekt; answer nicht direkt; by — means auf Umwegen.

indiscernible [ɪndɪ'sɜːnəbl] a nicht wahrnehmbar.

indiscreet [ɪndɪs'kriːt] a (insensitive) unbedacht; (improper) taktlos; (telling secrets) indiskret.

indiscretion [ɪndɪs'kreʃən] n Taktlosigkeit f; Indiskretion f.

indiscriminate [ɪndɪs'krɪmɪnət] a wahllos; kritiklos.

indispensable [ɪndɪs'pensəbl] a unentbehrlich.

indisposed [ɪndɪs'pəʊzd] a unpäßlich.

indisposition [ɪndɪspə'zɪʃən] n Unpäßlichkeit f.

indisputable [ɪndɪs'pjuːtəbl] a unbestreitbar; evidence unanfechtbar.

indistinct [ɪndɪs'tɪŋkt] a undeutlich.

indistinguishable [ɪndɪs'tɪŋgwɪʃəbl] a nicht unterscheidbar; difference unmerklich.

individual [ɪndɪ'vɪdjʊəl] n Einzelne(r) mf, Individuum nt; a individuell; case Einzel-; (of, for one person) eigen, individuell; (characteristic) eigentümlich; —ist Individualist m; —ity [ɪndɪvɪdjʊ'ælɪtɪ] Individualität f; —ly ad einzeln, individuell.

indoctrinate [ɪn'dɒktrɪneɪt] vt indoktrinieren.

indoctrination [ɪndɒktrɪ'neɪʃən] n Indoktrination f.

indolence ['ɪndələns] n Trägheit f.

indolent ['ɪndələnt] a träge.

indoor ['ɪndɔː*] a Haus-; Zimmer-; Innen-; (Sport) Hallen-; —s ad drinnen, im Haus; to go —s hinein or ins Haus gehen.

indubitable [ɪn'djuːbɪtəbl] a unzweifelhaft.

indubitably [ɪn'djuːbɪtəblɪ] ad zweifellos.

induce [in'dju:s] *vt* dazu bewegen, veranlassen; *reaction* herbeiführen; **—ment** Veranlassung *f*; (*incentive*) Anreiz *m*.

induct [in'dʌkt] *vt* in sein Amt einführen.

indulge [in'dʌldʒ] *vt* (*give way*) nachgeben (+*dat*); (*gratify*) frönen (+*dat*); to — o.s. in sth sich (*dat*) etw gönnen; *vi* frönen (*in dat*), sich gönnen (*in acc*); **—nce** Nachsicht *f*; (*enjoyment*) (übermäßiger) Genuß *m*; **—nt** *a* nachsichtig, (*pej*) nachgiebig.

industrial [in'dʌstriəl] *a* Industrie-, industriell; *dispute, injury* Arbeits-; **—ist** Industrielle(r) *mf*; **—ize** *vt* industrialisieren.

industrious [in'dʌstriəs] *a* fleißig.

industry [indəstri] *n* Industrie *f*; (*diligence*) Fleiß *m*; *hotel* — Hotelgewerbe *nt*.

inebriated [i'ni:brieitid] *a* betrunken, berauscht.

inedible [in'edibl] *a* ungenießbar.

ineffective [ini'fektiv], **ineffectual** [ini'fektjuəl] *a* unwirksam, wirkungslos; *person* untauglich.

inefficiency [ini'fiʃənsi] *n* Ineffizienz *f*.

inefficient [ini'fiʃənt] *a* ineffizient; (*ineffective*) unwirksam.

inelegant [in'eligənt] *a* unelegant.

ineligible [in'elidʒəbl] *a* nicht berechtigt; *candidate* nicht wählbar.

ineluctable [ini'lʌktəbl] *a* unausweichlich.

inept [i'nept] *a* *remark* unpassend; *person* ungeeignet.

inequality [ini'kwɒliti] *n* Ungleichheit *f*.

ineradicable [ini'rædikəbl] *a* unausrottbar; *mistake* unabänderlich; *guilt* tiefsitzend.

inert [i'nɜ:t] *a* träge; (*Chem*) inaktiv; (*motionless*) unbeweglich.

inertia [i'nɜ:ʃə] *n* Trägheit *f*.

inescapable [inis'keipəbl] *a* unvermeidbar.

inessential [ini'senʃəl] *a* unwesentlich.

inestimable [in'estiməbl] *a* unschätzbar.

inevitability [inevitə'biliti] *n* Unvermeidlichkeit *f*.

inevitable [in'evitəbl] *a* unvermeidlich.

inexact [inig'zækt] *a* ungenau.

inexcusable [iniks'kju:zəbl] *a* unverzeihlich.

inexhaustible [inig'zɔ:stəbl] *a* *wealth* unerschöpflich; *talker* unermüdlich; *curiosity* unstillbar.

inexorable [in'eksərəbl] *a* unerbittlich.

inexpensive [iniks'pensiv] *a* preiswert.

inexperience [iniks'piəriəns] *n* Unerfahrenheit *f*; **—d** *a* unerfahren.

inexplicable [iniks'plikəbl] *a* unerklärlich.

inexpressible [iniks'presəbl] *a* *pain, joy* unbeschreiblich; *thoughts* nicht ausdrückbar.

inextricable [iniks'trikəbl] *a* un(auf)lösbar.

infallibility [infælə'biliti] *n* Unfehlbarkeit *f*.

infallible [in'fæləbl] *a* unfehlbar.

infamous ['infəməs] *a* *place* verrufen; *deed* schändlich; *person* niederträchtig.

infamy ['infəmi] *n* Verrufenheit *f*; Niedertracht *f*; (*disgrace*) Schande *f*.

infancy ['ɪnfənsɪ] n frühe Kindheit f; (fig) Anfangsstadium nt.

infant ['ɪnfənt] n kleine(s) Kind nt, Säugling m; —ile a kindisch, infantil; — **school** Vorschule f.

infantry ['ɪnfəntrɪ] n Infanterie f; —man Infanterist m.

infatuated [ɪn'fætjʊeɪtɪd] a vernarrt; to become — with sich vernarren in (+acc).

infatuation [ɪnfætjʊ'eɪʃən] n Vernarrtheit f (with in +acc).

infect [ɪn'fekt] vt anstecken (also fig), infizieren; —ion Ansteckung f, Infektion f; —ious [ɪn'fekʃəs] a ansteckend.

infer [ɪn'fɜ:*] vt schließen; —ence ['ɪnfərəns] a Schlußfolgerung f.

inferior [ɪn'fɪərɪə*] a minder geordnet, niedriger; quality minderwertig; n Untergebene(r) mf; —ity [ɪnfɪərɪ'ɒrɪtɪ] Minderwertigkeit f; (in rank) untergeordnete Stellung f; —ity complex Minderwertigkeitskomplex m.

infernal [ɪn'fɜ:nl] a höllisch.

inferno [ɪn'fɜ:nəʊ] n Hölle f, Inferno nt.

infertile [ɪn'fɜ:taɪl] a unfruchtbar.

infertility [ɪnfɜ:'tɪlɪtɪ] n Unfruchtbarkeit f.

infest [ɪn'fest] vt plagen, heimsuchen; to be —ed with wimmeln von.

infidel ['ɪnfɪdəl] n Ungläubige(r) mf.

infidelity [ɪnfɪ'delɪtɪ] n Untreue f.

in-fighting ['ɪnfaɪtɪŋ] n Nahkampf m.

infiltrate ['ɪnfɪltreɪt] vt infiltrieren; spies einschleusen; (liquid) durchdringen; vi (Mil, liquid) einsickern; (Pol) unterwandern (into acc).

infinite ['ɪnfɪnɪt] a unendlich.

infinitive [ɪn'fɪnɪtɪv] n Infinitiv m, Nennform f.

infinity [ɪn'fɪnɪtɪ] n Unendlichkeit f.

infirm [ɪn'fɜ:m] a schwach, gebrechlich; (irresolute) willensschwach.

infirmary [ɪn'fɜ:mərɪ] n Krankenhaus nt.

infirmity [ɪn'fɜ:mɪtɪ] n Schwäche f, Gebrechlichkeit f.

inflame [ɪn'fleɪm] vt (Med) entzünden; person reizen; anger erregen.

inflammable [ɪn'flæməbl] a feuergefährlich.

inflammation [ɪnflə'meɪʃən] n Entzündung f.

inflate [ɪn'fleɪt] vt aufblasen; tyre aufpumpen; prices hochtreiben.

inflation [ɪn'fleɪʃən] n Inflation f; —ary a increase inflationistisch; situation inflationär.

inflexible [ɪn'fleksəbl] a person nicht flexibel; opinion starr; thing unbiegsam.

inflict [ɪn'flɪkt] vt zufügen (sth on sb jdm etw); punishment auferlegen (on dat); wound beibringen (on dat); —ion Zufügung f; Auferlegung f; (suffering) Heimsuchung f.

inflow ['ɪnfləʊ] n Einfließen nt, Zustrom m.

influence ['ɪnfluəns] n Einfluß m; vt beeinflussen.

influential [ɪnflʊ'enʃəl] a einflußreich.

influenza [ɪnflʊ'enzə] n Grippe f.

influx ['ɪnflʌks] n (of water) Einfluß m; (of people) Zustrom m; (of ideas) Eindringen nt.

inform [ɪn'fɔ:m] vt informieren; to keep sb —ed jdn auf dem laufenden halten.

informal [ɪn'fɔ:məl] a zwanglos; **—ity** [ɪnfɔ:'mælɪtɪ] Ungezwungenheit f.

information [ɪnfə'meɪʃən] n Auskunft f, Information f.

informative [ɪn'fɔ:mətɪv] a informativ; *person* mitteilsam.

informer [ɪn'fɔ:mə*] n Denunziant(in f) m.

infra-red ['ɪnfrə'red] a infrarot.

infrequent [ɪn'fri:kwənt] a selten.

infringe [ɪn'frɪndʒ] vt *law* verstoßen gegen; — upon vt verletzen; **—ment** Verstoß m, Verletzung f.

infuriate [ɪn'fjʊərɪeɪt] vt wütend machen.

infuriating [ɪn'fjʊərɪeɪtɪŋ] a ärgerlich.

ingenious [ɪn'dʒi:nɪəs] a genial; *thing* raffiniert.

ingenuity [ɪndʒɪ'nju:ɪtɪ] n Findigkeit f, Genialität f; Raffiniertheit f.

ingot ['ɪŋgət] n Barren m.

ingratiate [ɪn'greɪʃɪeɪt] vt einschmeicheln (o.s. with sb sich bei jdm).

ingratitude [ɪn'grætɪtju:d] n Undankbarkeit f.

ingredient [ɪn'gri:dɪənt] n Bestandteil m; (*Cook*) Zutat f.

inhabit [ɪn'hæbɪt] vt bewohnen; **—ant** Bewohner(in f) m; (*of island, town*) Einwohner(in f) m.

inhale [ɪn'heɪl] vt einatmen; (*Med, cigarettes*) inhalieren.

inherent [ɪn'hɪərənt] a innewohnend (in dat).

inherit [ɪn'herɪt] vt erben; **—ance** Erbe nt, Erbschaft f.

inhibit [ɪn'hɪbɪt] vt hemmen; (*restrain*) hindern; **—ion** [ɪnhɪ'bɪʃən] Hemmung f.

inhospitable [ɪnhɒs'pɪtəbl] a *person* ungastlich; *country* unwirtlich.

inhuman [ɪn'hju:mən] a unmenschlich.

inimitable [ɪ'nɪmɪtəbl] a unnachahmlich.

iniquity [ɪ'nɪkwɪtɪ] n Ungerechtigkeit f.

initial [ɪ'nɪʃəl] a anfänglich, Anfangs-; n Anfangsbuchstabe m, Initiale f; vt abzeichnen; (*Pol*) paraphieren; **—ly** ad anfangs.

initiate [ɪ'nɪʃɪeɪt] vt einführen; *negotiations* einleiten; (*instruct*) einweihen.

initiation [ɪnɪʃɪ'eɪʃən] n Einführung f; Einleitung f.

initiative [ɪ'nɪʃɪətɪv] n Initiative f.

inject [ɪn'dʒekt] vt einspritzen; (*fig*) einflößen; **—ion** Spritze f, Injektion f.

injure ['ɪndʒə*] vt verletzen; (*fig*) schaden (+dat).

injury ['ɪndʒərɪ] n Verletzung f.

injustice [ɪn'dʒʌstɪs] n Ungerechtigkeit f.

ink [ɪŋk] n Tinte f.

inkling ['ɪŋklɪŋ] n (dunkle) Ahnung f.

inlaid ['ɪn'leɪd] a eingelegt, Einlege-.

inland ['ɪnlænd] a Binnen-; (*domestic*) Inlands-; ad landeinwärts; — revenue (*Brit*) Fiskus m.

in-law ['ɪnlɔ:] n angeheiratete(r) Verwandte(r) mf.

inlet ['ɪnlet] n Öffnung f, Einlaß m; (*bay*) kleine Bucht f.

inmate ['ɪnmeɪt] n Insasse m.

inn [ɪn] n Gasthaus nt, Wirtshaus nt.

innate [ɪ'neɪt] a angeboren, eigen (+dat).

inner ['ɪnə*] a inner, Innen-; (fig) verborgen, innerste(r,s).

innocence ['ɪnəsns] n Unschuld f; (ignorance) Unkenntnis f.

innocent ['ɪnəsnt] a unschuldig.

innocuous [ɪ'nɒkjuəs] a harmlos.

innovation [ɪnəʊ'veɪʃən] n Neuerung f.

innuendo [ɪnju'endəʊ] n (versteckte) Anspielung f.

innumerable [ɪ'njuːmərəbl] a unzählig.

inoculation [ɪnɒkju'leɪʃən] n Impfung f.

inopportune [ɪn'ɒpətjuːn] a remark unangebracht; visit ungelegen.

inordinately [ɪ'nɔːdɪntlɪ] ad unmäßig.

inorganic [ɪnɔː'gænɪk] a unorganisch; (Chem) anorganisch.

in-patient ['ɪnpeɪʃənt] n stationäre(r) Patient(in f) m.

input ['ɪnpʊt] n (Elec) (Auf)ladung f; (Tech) zugeführte Menge f; (labour) zugeführte Arbeitsleistung f; (money) Investitionssumme f.

inquest ['ɪnkwest] n gerichtliche Untersuchung f.

inquire [ɪn'kwaɪə*] vi sich erkundigen; vt price sich erkundigen nach; — into vt untersuchen.

inquiring [ɪn'kwaɪərɪŋ] a mind wissensdurstig.

inquiry [ɪn'kwaɪərɪ] n (question) Erkundigung f, Nachfrage f; (investigation) Untersuchung f; — office Auskunft(sbüro nt) f.

inquisitive [ɪn'kwɪzɪtɪv] a neugierig; look forschend.

inroad ['ɪnrəʊd] n (Mil) Einfall m; (fig) Eingriff m.

insane [ɪn'seɪn] a wahnsinnig; (Med) geisteskrank.

insanitary [ɪn'sænɪtərɪ] a unhygienisch, gesundheitsschädlich.

insanity [ɪn'sænɪtɪ] n Wahnsinn m.

insatiable [ɪn'seɪʃəbl] a unersättlich.

inscription [ɪn'skrɪpʃən] n (on stone) Inschrift f; (in book) Widmung f.

inscrutable [ɪn'skruːtəbl] a unergründlich.

insect ['ɪnsekt] n Insekt nt; **—icide** [ɪn'sektɪsaɪd] Insektenvertilgungsmittel nt.

insecure [ɪnsɪ'kjʊə*] a person unsicher; thing nicht fest or sicher.

insecurity [ɪnsɪ'kjʊərɪtɪ] n Unsicherheit f.

insensible [ɪn'sensɪbl] a gefühllos; (unconscious) bewußtlos; (imperceptible) unmerklich; — of or to sth unempfänglich für etw.

insensitive [ɪn'sensɪtɪv] a (to pain) unempfindlich; (without feelings) gefühllos.

inseparable [ɪn'sepərəbl] a people unzertrennlich; word untrennbar.

insert [ɪn'sɜːt] vt einfügen; coin einwerfen; (stick into) hineinstecken; advert aufgeben; ['ɪnsɜːt] n Beifügung f; (in book) Einlage f; (in magazine) Beilage f; **—ion** Einfügung f; (Press) Inserat nt.

inshore ['ɪnʃɔː*] a Küsten-; ['ɪn'ʃɔː*] ad an der Küste.

inside ['ɪn'saɪd] n Innenseite f, Innere(s) nt; a innere(r,s), Innen-; ad (place) innen; (direction) nach innen, hinein; prep (place) in (+dat); (direction) in (+acc) ... hinein; (time) innerhalb (+gen); — forward (Sport) Halbstürmer m; — out ad linksherum; know in-

und auswendig; —r Eingeweihte(r) mf; (member) Mitglied nt.

insidious [ɪn'sɪdɪəs] a heimtückisch.

insight ['ɪnsaɪt] n Einsicht f; Einblick m (into in +acc).

insignificant [ɪnsɪg'nɪfɪkənt] a unbedeutend.

insincere [ɪnsɪn'sɪə*] a unaufrichtig, falsch.

insincerity [ɪnsɪn'serɪtɪ] n Unaufrichtigkeit f.

insinuate [ɪn'sɪnjʊeɪt] vt (hint) andeuten; (— o.s. into sth) sich in etw (acc) einschleichen.

insinuation [ɪnsɪnjʊ'eɪʃən] n Anspielung f.

insipid [ɪn'sɪpɪd] a fad(e).

insist [ɪn'sɪst] vi bestehen (on auf +acc); —ence Bestehen nt; —ent a hartnäckig; (urgent) dringend.

insolence ['ɪnsələns] n Frechheit f.

insolent ['ɪnsələnt] a frech.

insoluble [ɪn'sɒljʊbl] a unlösbar; (Chem) unlöslich.

insolvent [ɪn'sɒlvənt] a zahlungsunfähig.

insomnia [ɪn'sɒmnɪə] n Schlaflosigkeit f.

inspect [ɪn'spekt] vt besichtigen, prüfen; (officially) inspizieren; —ion Besichtigung f, Inspektion f; —or (official) Aufsichtsbeamte(r) m, Inspektor m; (police) Polizeikommissar m; (Rail) Kontrolleur m.

inspiration [ɪnspɪ'reɪʃən] n Inspiration f.

inspire [ɪn'spaɪə*] vt respect einflößen (in dat); hope wecken (in in +dat); person inspirieren; to — sb to do sth jdn dazu anregen, etw zu tun; —d a begabt, einfallsreich.

inspiring [ɪn'spaɪərɪŋ] a begeisternd.

instability [ɪnstə'bɪlɪtɪ] n Unbeständigkeit f, Labilität f.

install [ɪn'stɔ:l] vt (put in) einbauen, installieren; telephone anschließen; (establish) einsetzen; —ation [ɪnstə'leɪʃən] (of person) (Amts)einsetzung f; (of machinery) Einbau m, Installierung f; (machines etc) Anlage f.

instalment, (US) installment [ɪn'stɔ:lmənt] n Rate f; (of story) Fortsetzung f; to pay in —s auf Raten zahlen.

instance ['ɪnstəns] n Fall m; (example) Beispiel nt; for — zum Beispiel.

instant ['ɪnstənt] n Augenblick m; a augenblicklich, sofortig; — coffee Pulverkaffee m; —ly ad sofort.

instead [ɪn'sted] ad stattdessen; — of prep anstatt (+gen).

instigation [ɪnstɪ'geɪʃən] n Veranlassung f; (of crime etc) Anstiftung f.

instil [ɪn'stɪl] vt (fig) beibringen (in sb jdm).

instinct ['ɪnstɪŋkt] n Instinkt m; —ive a, —ively ad [ɪn'stɪŋktɪv, -lɪ] instinktiv.

institute ['ɪnstɪtju:t] n Institut nt; (society also) Gesellschaft f; vt einführen; search einleiten.

institution [ɪnstɪ'tju:ʃən] n (custom) Einrichtung f, Brauch m; (society) Institution f; (home) Anstalt f; (beginning) Einführung f, Einleitung f.

instruct [ɪn'strʌkt] vt anweisen; (officially) instruieren; —ion [ɪn'strʌkʃən] Unterricht m; —ions pl Anweisungen pl; (for use) Gebrauchsanweisung f; —ive a lehrreich; —or Lehrer m; (Mil) Ausbilder m.

instrument ['ɪnstrəmənt] n (tool) Instrument nt, Werkzeug nt; (Mus) (Musik)instrument nt; — al [ɪnstru'mentl] a (Mus) Instrumental-; (helpful) behilflich (in bei); —alist [ɪnstru'mentəlɪst] Instrumentalist m; — panel Armaturenbrett nt.

insubordinate [ɪnsə'bɔːdɪnət] a aufsässig, widersetzlich.

insubordination ['ɪnsəbɔːdɪ'neɪʃən] n Gehorsamsverweigerung f.

insufferable [ɪn'sʌfərəbl] a unerträglich.

insufficient a, —ly ad [ɪn'səfɪʃənt, -lɪ] ungenügend.

insular ['ɪnsjələ*] a (fig) engstirnig; —ity [ɪnsju'lærɪtɪ] (fig) Engstirnigkeit f.

insulate ['ɪnsjuleɪt] vt (Elec) isolieren; (fig) abschirmen (from vor +dat).

insulating tape ['ɪnsjuleɪtɪŋteɪp] n Isolierband nt.

insulation [ɪnsju'leɪʃən] n Isolierung f.

insulator ['ɪnsjuleɪtə*] n Isolator m.

insulin ['ɪnsjulɪn] n Insulin nt.

insult ['ɪnsʌlt] n Beleidigung f; [ɪn'sʌlt] vt beleidigen; —ing [ɪn'sʌltɪŋ] a beleidigend.

insuperable [ɪn'suːpərəbl] a unüberwindlich.

insurance [ɪn'ʃuərəns] n Versicherung f; — agent Versicherungsvertreter m; — policy Versicherungspolice f.

insure [ɪn'ʃuə*] vt versichern.

insurmountable [ɪnsə'mauntəbl] a unüberwindlich.

insurrection [ɪnsə'rekʃən] n Aufstand m.

intact [ɪn'tækt] a intakt, unangetastet, ganz.

intake ['ɪnteɪk] n (place) Einlaßöffnung f; (act) Aufnahme f; (amount) aufgenommene Menge f; (Sch) Neuaufnahme f.

intangible [ɪn'tændʒəbl] a unfaßbar; thing nicht greifbar.

integer ['ɪntɪdʒə*] n ganze Zahl f.

integral ['ɪntɪgrəl] a (essential) wesentlich; (complete) vollständig; (Math) Integral-.

integrate ['ɪntɪgreɪt] vt vereinigen; people eingliedern, integrieren.

integration [ɪntɪ'greɪʃən] n Eingliederung f, Integration f.

integrity [ɪn'tegrɪtɪ] n (honesty) Redlichkeit f, Integrität f.

intellect ['ɪntɪlekt] n Intellekt m; —ual [ɪntɪ'lektjuəl] a geistig, intellektuell; n Intellektuelle(r) mf.

intelligence [ɪn'telɪdʒəns] n (understanding) Intelligenz f; (news) Information f; (Mil) Geheimdienst m.

intelligent [ɪn'telɪdʒənt] a intelligent; beings vernunftbegabt; —ly ad klug; write, speak verständlich.

intelligible [ɪn'telɪdʒəbl] a verständlich.

intemperate [ɪn'tempərət] a unmäßig.

intend [ɪn'tend] vt beabsichtigen; that was —ed for you das war für dich gedacht.

intense [ɪn'tens] a stark, intensiv; person ernsthaft; —ly ad äußerst; study intensiv.

intensify [ɪn'tensɪfaɪ] vt verstärken, intensivieren.

intensity [ɪn'tensɪtɪ] n Intensität f, Stärke f.

intensive *a*, **—ly** *ad* [ɪn'tensɪv, -lɪ] intensiv.

intent [ɪn'tent] *n* Absicht *f*; **to all —s and purposes** praktisch; **—ly** *ad* aufmerksam; *look* forschend; **to be — on** doing sth fest entschlossen sein, etw zu tun.

intention [ɪn'tenʃən] *n* Absicht *f*; **with good —s** mit guten Vorsätzen; **—al** *a*, **—ally** *ad* absichtlich.

inter [ɪn'tɜ:*] *vt* beerdigen.

inter- ['ɪntə*] *pref* zwischen-, Zwischen-.

interact [ɪntər'ækt] *vi* aufeinander einwirken; **—ion** Wechselwirkung *f*.

intercede [ɪntə'si:d] *vi* sich verwenden; (*in argument*) vermitteln.

intercept [ɪntə'sept] *vt* abfangen; **—ion** Abfangen *nt*.

interchange ['ɪntə'tʃeɪndʒ] *n* (*exchange*) Austausch *m*; (*on roads*) Verkehrskreuz *nt*; [ɪntə'tʃeɪndʒ] *vt* austauschen; **—able** [ɪntə'tʃeɪndʒəbl] *a* austauschbar.

intercom ['ɪntəkɒm] *n* (Gegen-) sprechanlage *f*.

interconnect [ɪntəkə'nekt] *vt* miteinander verbinden; *vi* miteinander verbunden sein; (*roads*) zusammenführen.

intercontinental ['ɪntəkɒntɪ'nentl] *a* interkontinental.

intercourse ['ɪntəkɔ:s] *n* (*exchange*) Verkehr *m*, Beziehungen *pl*; (*sexual*) Geschlechtsverkehr *m*.

interdependence [ɪntədɪ'pendəns] *n* gegenseitige Abhängigkeit *f*.

interest ['ɪntrest] *n* Interesse *nt*; (*Fin*) Zinsen *pl*; (*Comm*: share) Anteil *m*; (*group*) Interessengruppe *f*; **to be of —** von Interesse

sein; *vt* interessieren; **—ed** *a* (*having claims*) beteiligt; (*attentive*) interessiert; **to be —ed in** sich interessieren für; **—ing** *a* interessant.

interfere [ɪntə'fɪə*] *vi* (*meddle*) sich einmischen (*with* in + acc) stören (*with* acc); (*with an object*) sich zu schaffen machen (*with* an + *dat*); **—nce** Einmischung *f*; (*TV*) Störung *f*.

interim ['ɪntərɪm] *a* vorläufig; *n*: **in the —** inzwischen.

interior [ɪn'tɪərɪə*] *n* Innere(s) *nt*; *a* innere(r,s), Innen-.

interjection [ɪntə'dʒekʃən] *n* Ausruf *m*; (*Gram*) Interjektion *f*.

interlock [ɪntə'lɒk] *vi* ineinandergreifen; *vt* zusammenschließen, verzahnen.

interloper ['ɪntələupə*] *n* Eindringling *m*.

interlude ['ɪntəlu:d] *n* Pause *f*; (*in entertainment*) Zwischenspiel *nt*.

intermarriage [ɪntə'mærɪdʒ] *n* Mischehe *f*.

intermarry [ɪntə'mærɪ] *vi* untereinander heiraten.

intermediary [ɪntə'mi:dɪərɪ] *n* Vermittler *m*.

intermediate [ɪntə'mi:dɪət] *a* Zwischen-, Mittel-.

interminable [ɪn'tɜ:mɪnəbl] *a* endlos.

intermission [ɪntə'mɪʃən] *n* Pause *f*.

intermittent [ɪntə'mɪtənt] *a* periodisch, stoßweise; **—ly** *ad* mit Unterbrechungen.

intern [ɪn'tɜ:n] *vt* internieren; ['ɪntɜ:n] *n* (*US*) Assistenzarzt *m*/-ärztin *f*.

internal [ɪn'tɜ:nl] *a* (*inside*) innere(r,s); (*domestic*) Inlands-.

—ly *ad* innen; (*Med*) innerlich; intern; — **revenue** (*US*) Sozialprodukt *nt*.

international [intə'næʃnəl] *a* international; *n* (*Sport*) Nationalspieler *m*; (*match*) internationale(s) Spiel *nt*.

internment [in'tɜ:nmənt] *n* Internierung *f*.

interplanetary [intə'plænitəri] *a* interplanetar.

interplay ['intəplei] *n* Wechselspiel *nt*.

Interpol ['intəpɒl] *n* Interpol *f*.

interpret [in'tɜ:prit] *vt* (*explain*) auslegen, interpretieren; (*translate*) verdolmetschen; (*represent*) darstellen; —**ation** Deutung *f*, Interpretation *f*; (*translation*) Dolmetschen *nt*; —**er** Dolmetscher(in *f*) *m*.

interrelated [intəri'leitid] *a* untereinander zusammenhängend.

interrogate [in'terəgeit] *vt* befragen; (*Jur*) verhören.

interrogation [intərə'geiʃən] *n* Verhör *nt*.

interrogative [intə'rɒgətiv] *a* fragend, Frage-.

interrogator [in'terəgeitə*] *n* Vernehmungsbeamte(r) *m*.

interrupt [intə'rʌpt] *vt* unterbrechen; —**ion** Unterbrechung *f*.

intersect [intə'sekt] *vt* (durch)schneiden; *vi* sich schneiden; —**ion** (*of roads*) Kreuzung *f*; (*of lines*) Schnittpunkt *m*.

intersperse [intə'spɜ:s] *vt* (*scatter*) verstreuen; **to** — **sth with sth** etw mit etw durchsetzen.

intertwine [intə'twain] *vti* (sich) verflechten.

interval ['intəvəl] *n* Abstand *m*; (*break*) Pause *f*; (*Mus*) Intervall

nt; **at** —**s** hier und da; (*time*) dann und wann.

intervene [intə'vi:n] *vi* dazwischenliegen; (*act*) einschreiten (*in* gegen), eingreifen (*in* in +*acc*).

intervening [intə'vi:niŋ] *a* dazwischenliegend.

intervention [intə'venʃən] *n* Eingreifen *nt*, Intervention *f*.

interview ['intəvju:] *n* (*Press etc*) Interview *nt*; (*for job*) Vorstellungsgespräch *nt*; *vt* interviewen; —**er** Interviewer *m*.

intestate [in'testeit] *a* ohne Hinterlassung eines Testaments.

intestinal [in'testinl] *a* Darm-.

intestine [in'testin] *n* Darm *m*; —**s** *pl* Eingeweide *nt*.

intimacy ['intiməsi] *n* vertraute(r) Umgang *m*, Intimität *f*.

intimate ['intimət] *a* (*inmost*) innerste(r,s); *knowledge* eingehend; (*familiar*) vertraut; *friends* eng; ['intimeit] *vt* andeuten; —**ly** *ad* vertraut, eng.

intimidate [in'timideit] *vt* einschüchtern.

intimidation [intimi'deiʃən] *n* Einschüchterung *f*.

into ['intu] *prep* (*motion*) in (+*acc*) ... hinein; **5** — **25** 25 durch 5.

intolerable [in'tɒlərəbl] *a* unerträglich.

intolerance [in'tɒlərəns] *n* Intoleranz *f*.

intolerant [in'tɒlərənt] *a* intolerant.

intonation [intə'neiʃən] *n* Intonation *f*.

intoxicate [in'tɒksikeit] *vt* betrunken machen; (*fig*) berauschen; —**d** *a* betrunken; (*fig*) trunken.

intoxication [intɒksi'keiʃən] *n* Rausch *m*.

intractable [ɪn'træktəbl] a schwer zu handhaben(d); **problem** schwer lösbar.

intransigent [ɪn'trænsɪdʒənt] a unnachgiebig.

intransitive [ɪn'trænsɪtɪv] a intransitiv.

intravenous [ɪntrə'vi:nəs] a intravenös.

intrepid [ɪn'trepɪd] a unerschrocken.

intricacy ['ɪntrɪkəsɪ] a Kompliziertheit f.

intricate ['ɪntrɪkət] a kompliziert.

intrigue [ɪn'tri:g] n Intrige f; vt faszinieren.

intriguing [ɪn'tri:gɪŋ] a faszinierend.

intrinsic [ɪn'trɪnsɪk] a innere(r,s); **difference** wesentlich.

introduce [ɪntrə'dju:s] vt person vorstellen (to sb jdm); sth new einführen; subject anschneiden; to — sb to sth jdn in etw (acc) einführen.

introduction [ɪntrə'dʌkʃən] n Einführung f; (to book) Einleitung f.

introductory [ɪntrə'dʌktərɪ] a Einführungs-, Vor-.

introspective [ɪntrəʊ'spektɪv] a nach innen gekehrt.

introvert ['ɪntrəʊvɜːt] n Introvertierte(r) mf; a introvertiert.

intrude [ɪn'tru:d] vi stören (on acc); —r Eindringling m.

intrusion [ɪn'tru:ʒən] n Störung f; (coming into) Eindringen nt.

intrusive [ɪn'tru:sɪv] a aufdringlich.

intuition [ɪn'tju:ɪʃən] n Intuition f.

intuitive a, —ly ad [ɪn'tju:ɪtɪv, -lɪ] intuitiv.

inundate ['ɪnʌndeɪt] vt (lit, fig) überschwemmen.

invade [ɪn'veɪd] vt einfallen in (+ acc); —r Eindringling m.

invalid ['ɪnvəlɪd] n (disabled) Kranke(r) mf; Invalide m; a (ill) krank; (disabled) invalide; [ɪn'vælɪd] (not valid) ungültig; —ate [ɪn'vælɪdeɪt] vt passport (für) ungültig erklären; (fig) entkräften.

invaluable [ɪn'væljʊəbl] a unschätzbar.

invariable [ɪn'veərɪəbl] a unveränderlich.

invariably [ɪn'veərɪəblɪ] ad ausnahmslos.

invasion [ɪn'veɪʒən] n Invasion f, Einfall m.

invective [ɪn'vektɪv] n Beschimpfung f.

invent [ɪn'vent] vt erfinden; —ion [ɪn'venʃən] Erfindung f; —ive a erfinderisch; —iveness Erfindungsgabe f; —or Erfinder m.

inventory ['ɪnvəntrɪ] n (Bestands)verzeichnis nt, Inventar nt.

inverse ['ɪn'vɜːs] n Umkehrung f; a, —ly [ɪn'vɜːs, -lɪ] ad umgekehrt.

invert [ɪn'vɜːt] vt umdrehen; —ed commas pl Anführungsstriche pl.

invertebrate [ɪn'vɜːtɪbrət] n wirbellose(s) Tier nt.

invest [ɪn'vest] vt (Fin) anlegen, investieren; (endue) ausstatten.

investigate [ɪn'vestɪgeɪt] vt untersuchen.

investigation [ɪnvestɪ'geɪʃən] n Untersuchung f.

investigator [ɪn'vestɪgeɪtə*] n Untersuchungsbeamte(r) m.

investiture [ɪn'vestɪtʃə*] n Amtseinsetzung f.

investment [ɪn'vestmənt] n Investition f.

investor [ɪn'vestə*] n (Geld)anleger m.

inveterate [ɪn'vetərət] a unverbesserlich.

invigorating [ɪn'vɪgəreɪtɪŋ] a stärkend.

invincible [ɪn'vɪnsəbl] a unbesiegbar.

inviolate [ɪn'vaɪələt] a unverletzt.

invisible [ɪn'vɪzəbl] a unsichtbar; *ink* Geheim-.

invitation [ɪnvɪ'teɪʃən] n Einladung f.

invite [ɪn'vaɪt] vt einladen; *criticism, discussion* herausfordern.

inviting [ɪn'vaɪtɪŋ] a einladend.

invoice ['ɪnvɔɪs] n Rechnung f, Lieferschein m; vt *goods in* Rechnung stellen (*sth for sb* jdm etw acc).

invoke [ɪn'vəʊk] vt anrufen.

involuntary a, **involuntarily** ad [ɪn'vɒləntərɪ, -lɪ] (*unwilling*) unfreiwillig; (*unintentional*) unabsichtlich.

involve [ɪn'vɒlv] vt (*entangle*) verwickeln; (*entail*) mit sich bringen; —d a verwickelt; the person —d die betreffende Person; —ment Verwicklung f.

invulnerable [ɪn'vʌlnərəbl] a unverwundbar, (*fig*) unangreifbar.

inward ['ɪnwəd] a innere(r,s); *curve* Innen-; —(s) ad nach innen; —ly ad im Inneren.

iodine ['aɪədi:n] n Jod nt.

iota [aɪ'əʊtə] n (*fig*) bißchen nt.

irascible [ɪ'ræsɪbl] a reizbar.

irate [aɪ'reɪt] a zornig.

iris ['aɪərɪs] n Iris f.

irk [ɜːk] vt verdrießen.

irksome ['ɜːksəm] a lästig.

iron ['aɪən] n Eisen nt; (*for ironing*) Bügeleisen nt; (*golf club*) Golfschläger m, Metallschläger m; a eisern; vt bügeln; —s pl (*chains*) Hand-/Fußschellen pl; — out vt (*lit, fig*) ausbügeln; *differences aus-*

gleichen; I— Curtain Eiserne(r) Vorhang m.

ironic(al) [aɪ'rɒnɪk(əl)] a ironisch; *coincidence etc* witzig; —ally ad ironisch; witzigerweise.

ironing ['aɪənɪŋ] n Bügeln nt; (*laundry*) Bügelwäsche f; — board Bügelbrett nt.

ironmonger ['aɪənmʌŋgə*] n Eisenwarenhändler m; —'s (shop) Eisenwarenhandlung f.

iron ore ['aɪənɔ:*] n Eisenerz nt.

ironworks ['aɪənwɜ:ks] n Eisenhütte f.

irony ['aɪərənɪ] n Ironie f; the — of it was ... das Witzige daran war

irrational [ɪ'ræʃənl] a unvernünftig, irrational.

irreconcilable [ɪrekən'saɪləbl] a unvereinbar.

irredeemable [ɪrɪ'di:məbl] a (*Comm*) *money* nicht einlösbar; *loan* unkündbar; (*fig*) rettungslos.

irrefutable [ɪrɪ'fju:təbl] a unwiderlegbar.

irregular [ɪ'regjʊlə*] a unregelmäßig; *shape* ungleich(mäßig); (*fig*) unüblich; *behaviour* ungehörig; —ity [ɪregjʊ'lærɪtɪ] Unregelmäßigkeit f; Ungleichmäßigkeit f; (*fig*) Vergehen nt.

irrelevance [ɪ'reləvəns] n Belanglosigkeit f.

irrelevant [ɪ'reləvənt] a belanglos, irrelevant.

irreligious [ɪrɪ'lɪdʒəs] a ungläubig.

irreparable [ɪ'repərəbl] a nicht gutzumachen(d).

irreplaceable [ɪrɪ'pleɪsəbl] a unersetzlich.

irrepressible [ɪrɪ'presəbl] a nicht zu unterdrücken(d); *joy* unbändig.

irreproachable [ɪrɪˈprəʊtʃəbl] a untadelig.

irresistible [ɪrɪˈzɪstəbl] a unwiderstehlich.

irresolute [ɪˈrezəluːt] a unentschlossen.

irrespective [ɪrɪˈspektɪv] : — **of** *prep* ungeachtet (+*gen*).

irresponsibility [ɪrɪspɒnsəˈbɪlɪtɪ] n Verantwortungslosigkeit f.

irresponsible [ɪrɪsˈpɒnsəbl] a verantwortungslos.

irretrievably [ɪrɪˈtriːvəblɪ] ad unwiederbringlich; *lost* unrettbar.

irreverence [ɪˈrevərəns] n Mißachtung f.

irreverent [ɪˈrevərənt] a respektlos.

irrevocable [ɪˈrevəkəbl] a unwiderrufbar.

irrigate [ˈɪrɪgeɪt] vt bewässern.

irrigation [ɪrɪˈgeɪʃən] n Bewässerung f.

irritability [ɪrɪtəˈbɪlɪtɪ] n Reizbarkeit f.

irritable [ˈɪrɪtəbl] a reizbar.

irritant [ˈɪrɪtənt] n Reizmittel nt.

irritate [ˈɪrɪteɪt] vt irritieren, reizen (*also Med*).

irritating [ˈɪrɪteɪtɪŋ] a irritierend, aufreizend.

irritation [ɪrɪˈteɪʃən] n (*anger*) Ärger m; (*Med*) Reizung f.

is [ɪz] see **be**.

Islam [ˈɪzlɑːm] n Islam m.

island [ˈaɪlənd] n Insel f; **—er** Inselbewohner(in f) m.

isle [aɪl] n (kleine) Insel f.

isn't [ˈɪznt] = **is not**.

isobar [ˈaɪsəʊbɑːʳ] n Isobare f.

isolate [ˈaɪsəʊleɪt] vt isolieren; **—d** a isoliert; *case* Einzel-.

isolation [aɪsəʊˈleɪʃən] n Isolierung f; **to treat sth in —** etw vereinzelt *or* isoliert behandeln.

isolationism [aɪsəʊˈleɪʃənɪzəm] n Isolationismus m.

isotope [ˈaɪsətəʊp] n Isotop nt.

issue [ˈɪʃuː] n (*matter*) Problem nt, Frage f; (*outcome*) Resultat nt, Ausgang m; (*of newspaper, shares*) Ausgabe f; (*offspring*) Nachkommenschaft f; (*of river*) Mündung f; **that's not at —** das steht nicht zur Debatte; **to make an — out of sth** ein Theater machen wegen etw (dat); vt ausgeben; *warrant* erlassen; *documents* ausstellen; *orders* erteilen; *books* herausgeben; *verdict* aussprechen; **to — sb with sth** etw (acc) an jdn ausgeben.

isthmus [ˈɪsməs] n Landenge f.

it [ɪt] pron (nom, acc) es; (dat) ihm.

italic [ɪˈtælɪk] a kursiv; **—s** pl Kursivschrift f; **in —s** kursiv gedruckt.

itch [ɪtʃ] n Jucken nt; (fig) brennende(s) Verlangen nt; vi jucken; **to be —ing to do sth** darauf brennen, etw zu tun; **—ing** Jucken nt; **—y** a juckend.

it'd [ˈɪtd] = **it would**; **it had**.

item [ˈaɪtəm] n Gegenstand m; (on list) Posten m; (in programme) Nummer f; (in agenda) (Programm)punkt m; (in newspaper) (Zeitungs)notiz f; **—ize** vt verzeichnen.

itinerant [ɪˈtɪnərənt] a person umherreisend.

itinerary [aɪˈtɪnərərɪ] n Reiseroute f; (*records*) Reisebericht m.

it'll [ˈɪtl] = **it will**, **it shall**.

its [ɪts] poss a (masculine, neuter) sein; (feminine) ihr; poss pron seine(r,s); ihre(r,s).

it's [ɪts] = **it is**; **it has**.

itself [ɪtˈself] pron sich (selbst); (emphatic) selbst.

I've [aɪv] = **I have.**

ivory ['aɪvərɪ] n Elfenbein nt; — **ivy** ['aɪvɪ] n Efeu nt.

J

J, j [dʒeɪ] n J nt, j nt.

jab [dʒæb] vti (hinein)stechen; n Stich m, Stoß m; (col) Spritze f.

jabber ['dʒæbə*] vi plappern.

jack [dʒæk] n (Wagen)heber m; (Cards) Bube m; — **up** vt aufbocken.

jackdaw ['dʒækdɔ:] n Dohle f.

jacket ['dʒækɪt] n Jacke f, Jackett nt; (of book) Schutzumschlag m; (Tech) Ummantelung f.

jack-knife ['dʒæknaɪf] n Klappmesser nt; vi (truck) sich zusammenschieben.

jackpot ['dʒækpɒt] n Haupttreffer m.

jade [dʒeɪd] n (stone) Jade m.

jaded ['dʒeɪdɪd] a ermattet.

jagged ['dʒægɪd] a zackig; blade schartig.

jail [dʒeɪl] n Gefängnis nt; vt einsperren; —**break** Gefängnisausbruch m; —**er** Gefängniswärter m.

jam [dʒæm] n Marmelade f; (crowd) Gedränge nt; (col: trouble) Klemme f; see **traffic**; vt people zusammendrängen; (wedge) einklemmen; (cram) hineinzwängen; (obstruct) blockieren; to — **on the brakes** auf die Bremse treten.

jamboree [dʒæmbə'ri:] n (Pfadfinder)treffen nt.

jangle ['dʒæŋgl] vti klimpern; (bells) bimmeln.

janitor ['dʒænɪtə*] n Hausmeister m.

January ['dʒænjʊərɪ] n Januar m.

jar [dʒɑ:*] n Glas nt; vi kreischen; (colours etc) nicht harmonieren.

jargon ['dʒɑ:gən] n Fachsprache f, Jargon m.

jarring ['dʒɑ:rɪŋ] a sound kreischend; colour unharmonisch.

jasmin(e) ['dʒæzmɪn] n Jasmin m.

jaundice ['dʒɔ:ndɪs] n Gelbsucht f; —**d** a (fig) mißgünstig.

jaunt [dʒɔ:nt] n Spritztour f; —**y** a (lively) munter; (brisk) flott; attitude unbekümmert.

javelin ['dʒævlɪn] n Speer m.

jaw [dʒɔ:] n Kiefer m; —**s** pl (fig) Rachen m.

jaywalker ['dʒeɪwɔ:kə*] n unvorsichtige(r) Fußgänger m, Verkehrssünder m.

jazz [dʒæz] n Jazz m; — **up** vt (Mus) verjazzen; (enliven) aufpolieren; —**band** Jazzkapelle f; —**y** a colour schreiend, auffallend.

jealous ['dʒeləs] a (envious) mißgünstig; husband eifersüchtig; (watchful) bedacht (of auf +acc); —**ly** ad mißgünstig; eifersüchtig; sorgsam; —**y** Mißgunst f; Eifersucht f.

jeans [dʒi:nz] npl Jeans pl.

jeep [dʒi:p] n Jeep m.

jeer [dʒɪə*] vi höhnisch lachen (at über +acc), verspotten (at sb jdn); n Hohn m; (remark) höhnische Bemerkung f; —**ing** a höhnisch.

jelly ['dʒelɪ] n Gelee nt; (on meat)

Gallert *nt*; (*dessert*) Grütze *f*.
—fish Qualle *f*.

jemmy ['dʒemɪ] *n* Brecheisen *nt*.

jeopardize ['dʒepədaɪz] *vt* gefährden.

jeopardy ['dʒepədɪ] *n* Gefahr *f*.

jerk [dʒɜːk] *n* Ruck *m*; (col: *idiot*) Trottel *m*; *vt* ruckartig bewegen; *vi* sich ruckartig bewegen; (*muscles*) zucken.

jerkin ['dʒɜːkɪn] *n* Wams ·*nt*.

jerky ['dʒɜːkɪ] *a* movement ruckartig; *writing* zitterig; *ride* rüttelnd.

jersey ['dʒɜːzɪ] *n* Pullover *m*.

jest [dʒest] *n* Scherz *m*; in — im Spaß; *vi* spaßen.

jet [dʒet] *n* (*stream: of water etc*) Strahl *m*; (*spout*) Düse *f*; (*Aviat*) Düsenflugzeug *nt*; —black *a* rabenschwarz; — engine Düsenmotor *m*.

jetsam ['dʒetsəm] *n* Strandgut *nt*.

jettison ['dʒetɪsn] *vt* über Bord werfen.

jetty ['dʒetɪ] *n* Landesteg *m*, Mole *f*.

Jew [dʒuː] *n* Jude *m*.

jewel ['dʒuːəl] *n* (*lit, fig*) Juwel *nt*; (*stone*) Edelstein *m*; —(l)er Juwelier *m*; —(l)er's (*shop*) Schmuckwarengeschäft *nt*, Juwelier *m*; —(le)ry Schmuck *m*, Juwelen *pl*.

Jewess ['dʒuːɪs] *n* Jüdin *f*.

Jewish ['dʒuːɪʃ] *a* jüdisch.

jib [dʒɪb] *n* (*Naut*) Klüver *m*; *vi* sich scheuen (*at* vor +*dat*).

jibe [dʒaɪb] *n* spöttische Bemerkung *f*.

jiffy ['dʒɪfɪ] *n* (*col*) in a — sofort.

jigsaw (puzzle) ['dʒɪgsɔː(pʌzl)] *n* Puzzle(spiel) *nt*.

jilt [dʒɪlt] *vt* den Laufpaß geben (+*dat*).

jingle ['dʒɪŋgl] *n* (*advertisement*) Werbesong *m*; (*verse*) Reim *m*; *vti* klimpern; (*bells*) bimmeln.

jinx [dʒɪŋks] *n* Fluch *m*; to put a — on sth etw verhexen.

jitters ['dʒɪtəz] *npl* (*col*) to get the — einen Bammel kriegen.

jittery ['dʒɪtərɪ] *a* (*col*) nervös.

jiujitsu [dʒuː·dʒɪtsuː] *n* Jiu-Jitsu *nt*.

job [dʒɒb] *n* (*piece of work*) Arbeit *f*; (*occupation*) Stellung *f*, Arbeit *f*; (*duty*) Aufgabe *f*; (*difficulty*) Mühe *f*; what's your — ? was machen Sie von Beruf?; it's a good — he... es ist ein Glück, daß er...; just the — genau das Richtige; —bing *a* (*in factory*) Akkord-; (*freelance*) Gelegenheits-; —less *a* arbeitslos.

jockey ['dʒɒkɪ] *n* Jockei *m*; *vi*: to — for position sich in einer gute Position drängeln.

jocular ['dʒɒkjulə*] *a* scherzhaft, witzig.

jodhpurs ['dʒɒdpɜːz] *npl* Reithose *f*.

jog [dʒɒg] *vt* (an)stoßen; *vi* (*run*) einen Dauerlauf machen.

john [dʒɒn] *n* (*US col*) Klo *nt*.

join [dʒɔɪn] *vt* (*put together*) verbinden (*to* mit); *club* beitreten (+*dat*); *person* sich anschließen (+*dat*); *vi* (*unite*) sich vereinigen; (*bones*) zusammenwachsen; *n* Verbindungsstelle *f*, Naht *f*; — in mitmachen; — up *vi* (*Mil*) zur Armee gehen; —er Schreiner *m*; —ery Schreinerei *f*; —t *n* (*Tech*) Fuge *f*; (*of bones*) Gelenk *nt*; (*of meat*) Braten *m*; (*col: place*) Lokal *nt*; *a*, —tly *ad* gemeinsam.

joist [dʒɔɪst] *n* Träger *m*.

joke [dʒəʊk] *n* Witz *m*; it's no — es ist nicht zum Lachen; *vi* spaßen,

Witze machen; you must be joking das ist doch wohl nicht dein Ernst; —er Witzbold m; (Cards) Joker m.

joking ['dʒəʊkɪŋ] a scherzhaft; —ly ad zum Spaß; talk im Spaß, scherzhaft.

jollity ['dʒɒlɪtɪ] n Fröhlichkeit f.

jolly ['dʒɒlɪ] a lustig, vergnügt; ad (col) ganz schön; — good! prima!; to — sb along jdn ermuntern.

jolt [dʒəʊlt] n (shock) Schock m; (jerk) Stoß m, Rütteln nt; vt (push) stoßen; (shake) durchschütteln; (fig) aufrütteln; vi holpern.

jostle ['dʒɒsl] vt anrempeln.

jot [dʒɒt] n: not one — kein Jota nt; — down vt schnell aufschreiben, notieren; —ter Notizbuch nt; (Sch) Schulheft nt.

journal ['dʒɜːnl] n (diary) Tagebuch nt; (magazine) Zeitschrift f; —ese [dʒɜːnə'liːz] Zeitungsstil m; —ism Journalismus m; —ist Journalist(in f) m.

journey ['dʒɜːnɪ] n Reise f.

jovial ['dʒəʊvɪəl] a jovial.

joy [dʒɔɪ] n Freude f; —ful ä freudig; (gladdening) erfreulich; —fully ad freudig; —ous a freudig; — ride Schwarzfahrt f; —stick Steuerknüppel m.

jubilant ['dʒuːbɪlənt] a triumphierend.

jubilation [dʒuːbɪ'leɪʃən] n Jubel m.

jubilee ['dʒuːbɪliː] n Jubiläum nt.

judge [dʒʌdʒ] n Richter m; (fig) Kenner m; vt (Jur) person de Verhandlung führen über (+ acc); case verhandeln; (assess) beurteilen; (criticize) verurteilen; vi ein Urteil abgeben; as far as I can — soweit ich das beurteilen kann; judging by sth nach etw zu urteilen; —ment (Jur) Urteil nt; (Eccl) Gericht nt;

(opinion) Ansicht f; (ability) Urteilsvermögen nt.

judicial [dʒuː'dɪʃəl] a gerichtlich, Justiz-.

judicious [dʒuː'dɪʃəs] a weis(e).

judo ['dʒuːdəʊ] n Judo nt.

jug [dʒʌg] n Krug m.

juggernaut ['dʒʌgənɔːt] n (truck) Fernlastwagen m.

juggle ['dʒʌgl] vi jonglieren; vt facts verdrehen; figures frisieren; —r Jongleur m.

jugular ['dʒʌgjʊlə*] a vein Hals-.

juice [dʒuːs] n Saft m.

juiciness ['dʒuːsɪnɪs] n Saftigkeit f.

juicy ['dʒuːsɪ] a (lit, fig) saftig; story schlüpfrig.

jukebox ['dʒuːkbɒks] n Musikautomat m.

July [dʒuː'laɪ] n Juli m.

jumble ['dʒʌmbl] n Durcheinander nt; (also — up) durcheinanderwerfen; facts durcheinanderbringen; — sale (Brit) Basar m, Flohmarkt m.

jumbo (jet) ['dʒʌmbəʊ(dʒet)] n Jumbo(-Jet) m.

jump [dʒʌmp] vi springen; (nervously) zusammenzucken; to — to conclusions voreilige Schlüsse ziehen; vt überspringen; to — the gun (fig) voreilig handeln; to — the queue sich vordrängeln; n Sprung m; to give sb a — jdn erschrecken; —ed-up a (col) eingebildet; —er Pullover m; —y a nervös.

junction ['dʒʌŋkʃən] n (of roads) (Straßen)kreuzung f; (Rail) Knotenpunkt m.

juncture ['dʒʌŋktʃə*] n: at this — in diesem Augenblick.

June [dʒuːn] n Juni m.

jungle ['dʒʌŋgl] n Dschungel m, Urwald m.

junior ['dʒuːnɪə*] a (*younger*) jünger; (*after name*) junior; (*Sport*) Junioren-; (*lower position*) untergeordnet; (*for young people*) Junioren-; n Jüngere(r) m.

junk [dʒʌŋk] n (*rubbish*) Plunder m; (*ship*) Dschunke f; **—shop** Ramschladen m.

junta ['dʒʌntə] n Junta f.

jurisdiction [dʒuərɪs'dɪkʃən] n Gerichtsbärkeit f; (*range of authority*) Zuständigkeit(sbereich m) f.

jurisprudence [dʒuərɪs'pruːdəns] n Rechtswissenschaft f, Jura no art.

juror ['dʒuərə*] n Geschworene(r) mf; Schöffe m, Schöffin f; (*in competition*) Preisrichter m.

jury ['dʒuərɪ] n (*court*) Geschworene pl; (*in competition*) Jury f, Preisgericht nt; **—man** = juror.

just [dʒʌst] a gerecht; ad (*recently, now*) gerade, eben; (*barely*) gerade noch; (*exactly*) genau, gerade; (*only*) nur, bloß; (*a small distance*) gleich; (*absolutely*) einfach; — as I arrived gerade als ich ankam; — as nice genauso nett; — as well um so besser; — about so etwa; — now soeben, gerade; not — now

nicht im Moment; — try versuch es bloß or mal.

justice ['dʒʌstɪs] n (*fairness*) Gerechtigkeit f; (*magistrate*) Richter m; — of the peace Friedensrichter m.

justifiable ['dʒʌstɪfaɪəbl] a berechtigt.

justifiably ['dʒʌstɪfaɪəblɪ] ad berechtigterweise, zu Recht.

justification [dʒʌstɪfɪ'keɪʃən] n Rechtfertigung f.

justify ['dʒʌstɪfaɪ] vt rechtfertigen.

justly ['dʒʌstlɪ] ad say mit Recht; condemn gerecht.

justness ['dʒʌstnəs] n Gerechtigkeit f.

jut [dʒʌt] vi (*also* — out) herausragen, vorstehen.

juvenile ['dʒuːvənaɪl] a (*young*) jugendlich; (*for the young*) Jugend-; n Jugendliche(r) mf; — delinquency Jugendkriminalität f; — delinquent jugendliche(r) Straftäter(in f) m.

juxtapose ['dʒʌkstəpəuz] vt nebeneinanderstellen.

juxtaposition [dʒʌkstəpə'zɪʃən] n Nebeneinanderstellung f.

K

K, k [keɪ] n K nt, k nt.

kaleidoscope [kə'laɪdəskəup] n Kaleidoskop nt.

kangaroo [kæŋgə'ruː] n Känguruh nt.

kayak ['kaɪæk] n Kajak m or nt.

keel [kiːl] n Kiel m; on an even — (fig) im Lot.

keen [kiːn] a eifrig, begeistert; intelligence, wind, blade scharf;

sight, hearing gut; price günstig; **—ly** ad leidenschaftlich; (*sharply*) scharf; **—ness** Schärfe f; (*eagerness*) Begeisterung f.

keep [kiːp] irreg vt (*retain*) behalten; (*have*) haben; animals, one's word halten; (*support*) versorgen; (*maintain in state*) halten; (*preserve*) aufbewahren; (*restrain*) abhalten; vi (*continue in* *direction*) sich halten; (*food*) sich halten; (*remain: quiet etc*) sein, bleiben; it —s happening es passiert immer wieder; *n* Unterhalt *m*; (*tower*) Burgfried *m*; — back *vt* fernhalten; secret verschweigen; — on *vi*: — on doing sth etw immer weiter tun; *vt* anbehalten; *hat* aufbehalten; — out *vt* draußen lassen, nicht hereinlassen; '— out!' 'Eintritt verboten!'; — up *vi* Schritt halten; *vt* aufrechterhalten; (*continue*) weitermachen; —ing (*care*) Obhut *f*; in —ing (with) in Übereinstimmung (mit).

keg [keg] *n* Faß *nt*.

kennel ['kenl] *n* Hundehütte *f*.

kerb(stone) ['kɜːbstəʊn] *n* Bordstein *m*.

kernel ['kɜːnl] *n* Kern *m*.

kerosene ['kerəsiːn] *n* Kerosin *nt*.

kestrel ['kestrəl] *n* Turmfalke *m*.

ketchup ['ketʃəp] *n* Ketchup *nt* or *m*.

kettle ['ketl] *n* Kessel *m*; —drum Pauke *f*.

key [kiː] *n* Schlüssel *m*; (*solution, answers*) Schlüssel *m*, Lösung *f*; (*of piano, typewriter*) Taste *f*; (*Mus*) Tonart *f*; (*explanatory note*) Zeichenerklärung *f*; a position etc Schlüssel-; —board (*of piano, typewriter*) Tastatur *f*; —hole Schlüsselloch *nt*; —note Grundton *m*; — ring Schlüsselring *m*.

khaki ['kɑːkɪ] *n* K(h)aki *nt*; a k(h)aki(farben).

kick [kɪk] *vt* einen Fußtritt geben (+*dat*), treten; *vi* treten; (*baby*) strampeln; (*horse*) ausschlagen; *n* (Fuß)tritt *m*; (*thrill*) Spaß *m*; — around *vt* person herumstoßen; — off *vi* (*Sport*) anstoßen; — up *vt*

(*col*) schlagen; —off (*Sport*) Anstoß *m*.

kid [kɪd] *n* (*child*) Kind *nt*; (*goat*) Zicklein *nt*; (*leather*) Glacéleder *nt*; *vt* auf den Arm nehmen; *vi* Witze machen.

kidnap ['kɪdnæp] *vt* entführen, kidnappen; —per Kidnapper *m*, Entführer *m*; —ping Entführung *f*, Kidnapping *nt*.

kidney ['kɪdnɪ] *n* Niere *f*.

kill [kɪl] *vt* töten, umbringen; chances ruinieren; *vi* töten; *n* Tötung *f*; (*hunting*) (Jagd)beute *f*; —er Mörder *m*.

kiln [kɪln] *n* Brennofen *m*.

kilo ['kiːləʊ] *n* Kilo *nt*; —gram(me) Kilogramm *nt*; —metre, (*US*) —meter Kilometer *m*; —watt Kilowatt *nt*.

kilt [kɪlt] *n* Schottenrock *m*.

kimono [kɪ'məʊnəʊ] *n* Kimono *m*.

kin [kɪn] *n* Verwandtschaft *f*, Verwandte(n) *pl*.

kind [kaɪnd] *a* freundlich, gütig; *n* Art *f*; a — of eine Art von; (*two*) of a — (zwei) von der gleichen Art; in — auf dieselbe Art; (*in goods*) in Naturalien.

kindergarten ['kɪndəgɑːtn] *n* Kindergarten *m*.

kind-hearted ['kaɪnd'hɑːtɪd] *a* gutherzig.

kindle ['kɪndl] *vt* (*set on fire*) anzünden; (*rouse*) reizen, (er)wecken.

kindliness ['kaɪndlɪnəs] *n* Freundlichkeit *f*, Güte *f*.

kindly ['kaɪndlɪ] *a* freundlich; *ad* liebenswürdig(erweise); would you — ...? wären Sie so freundlich und ...?

kindness ['kaɪndnəs] *n* Freundlichkeit *f*.

kindred ['kɪndrɪd] a verwandt; — **spirit** Gleichgesinnte(r) mf.

kinetic [kɪ'netɪk] a kinetisch.

king [kɪŋ] n König m; —**fisher** Eisvogel m; —**pin** (Tech) Bolzen m; (Aut) Achsschenkelbolzen m; (fig) Stütze f; —**size** a cigarette King-size.

kink [kɪŋk] n Knick m; —**y** a (fig) exzentrisch.

kiosk ['kiːɒsk] n (Tel) Telefonhäuschen nt.

kipper ['kɪpə*] n Räucherhering m.

kiss [kɪs] n Kuß m; vt küssen; vi: **they —ed** sie küßten sich.

kit [kɪt] n Ausrüstung f; (tools) Werkzeug nt; —**bag** Seesack m.

kitchen ['kɪtʃɪn] n Küche f; —**garden** Gemüsegarten m; — **sink** Spülbecken nt; —**ware** Küchengeschirr nt.

kite [kaɪt] n Drachen m.

kith [kɪθ] n: — **and kin** Blutsverwandte pl; **with — and kin** mit Kind und Kegel.

kitten ['kɪtn] n Kätzchen nt.

kitty ['kɪtɪ] n (money) (gemeinsame) Kasse f.

kleptomaniac [kleptəʊ'meɪnɪæk] n Kleptomane m, Kleptomanin f.

knack [næk] n Dreh m, Trick m.

knapsack ['næpsæk] n Rucksack m; (Mil) Tornister m.

knave [neɪv] n (old) Schurke m.

knead [niːd] vt kneten.

knee [niː] n Knie nt; —**cap** Kniescheibe f; —**deep** a knietief.

kneel [niːl] vi irreg knien.

knell [nel] n Grabgeläute nt.

knickers ['nɪkəz] npl Schlüpfer m.

knife [naɪf] n Messer nt; vt erstechen.

knight [naɪt] n Ritter m; (chess) Springer m, Pferd nt; —**hood** Ritterwürde f.

knit [nɪt] vti stricken; vi (bones) zusammenwachsen; (people) harmonieren; —**ting** (occupation) Stricken nt; (work) Strickzeug nt; —**ting machine** Strickmaschine f; —**ting needle** Stricknadel f; —**wear** Strickwaren pl.

knob [nɒb] n Knauf m; (on instrument) Knopf m; (of butter etc) kleine(s) Stück nt.

knock [nɒk] vt schlagen; (criticise) heruntermachen; vi klopfen; (knees) zittern; n Schlag m; (on door) Klopfen nt; — **off** vt (do quickly) hinhauen; (col: steal) klauen; vi (finish) Feierabend machen; — **out** vt ausschlagen; (boxing) k.o. schlagen; —**er** (on door) Türklopfer m; — **kneed** a x-beinig; —**out** (lit) k.o.-Schlag m; (fig) Sensation f.

knot [nɒt] n Knoten m; (in wood) Astloch nt; (group) Knäuel nt or m; vt (ver)knoten; —**ted** a verknotet.

knotty ['nɒtɪ] a knorrig; problem kompliziert.

know [nəʊ] vti irreg wissen; (be able to) können; (be acquainted with) kennen; (recognize) erkennen; **to — how to do sth** wissen, wie man etw macht, etw tun können; **you —** nicht (wahr); **to be well —n** bekannt sein; —**how** Kenntnis f, Know-how nt; —**ing** a schlau; look, smile wissend; —**ingly** ad wissend; (intentionally) wissentlich; —**all** Alleswisser m.

knowledge ['nɒlɪdʒ] n Wissen nt, Kenntnis f; —**able** a informiert.

knuckle ['nʌkl] n Fingerknöchel m. **kudos** ['kjuːdɒs] n Ehre f.

L

L, 1 [el] n L nt, 1 nt.

lab [læb] n (col) Labor nt.

label ['leɪbl] n Etikett nt, Schild nt; vt mit einer Aufschrift versehen, etikettieren.

laboratory [lə'bɒrətəri] n Laboratorium nt.

laborious a, **—ly** ad [lə'bɔːrɪəs, -lɪ] mühsam.

labour, (US) **labor** ['leɪbə*] n Arbeit f; (workmen) Arbeitskräfte pl; (Med) Wehen pl; (a Pol) Labour-; **hard —** Zwangsarbeit f; n Mangel **—er** Arbeiter m; **—saving** a arbeitssparend.

laburnum [lə'bɜːnəm] n Goldregen m.

labyrinth ['læbərɪnθ] n (lit, fig) Labyrinth nt.

lace [leɪs] n (fabric) Spitze f; (of shoe) Schnürsenkel m; (braid) Litze f; vt (also **— up**) (zu)schnüren.

lacerate ['læsəreɪt] vt zerschneiden, tief verwunden.

lack [læk] vt nicht haben; **sb —s sth** jdm fehlt etw (nom); vi: **to be —ing** fehlen; **sb is —ing in sth** es fehlt jdm an etw (dat); n Mangel m; **for — of** aus Mangel an (+dat).

lackadaisical [lækə'deɪzɪkəl] a lasch.

lackey ['lækɪ] n Lakei m.

lacklustre, (US) **lackluster** ['læklʌstə*] a glanzlos, matt.

laconic [lə'kɒnɪk] a lakonisch.

lacquer ['lækə*] n Lack m.

lacrosse [lə'krɒs] n Lacrosse nt.

lacy ['leɪsɪ] a spitzenartig, Spitzen-.

lad [læd] n (boy) Junge m; (young man) Bursche m.

ladder ['lædə*] n (lit) Leiter f; (fig) Stufenleiter f; (Brit: in stocking) Laufmasche f; vt Laufmaschen bekommen in (+dat).

laden ['leɪdn] a beladen, voll.

ladle ['leɪdl] n Schöpfkelle f.

lady ['leɪdɪ] n Dame f; (title) Lady f; 'Ladies' (lavatory) 'Damen'; **—bird,** (US) **—bug** Marienkäfer m; **—in-waiting** Hofdame f; **—like** a damenhaft, vornehm.

lag [læg] n (delay) Verzug m; (time —) Zeitabstand m; vi (also — behind) zurückbleiben; vt pipes verkleiden.

lager ['lɑːgə*] n Lagerbier nt, helles Bier nt.

lagging ['lægɪŋ] n Isolierung f.

lagoon [lə'guːn] n Lagune f.

laid [leɪd] n: **to be — up** ans Bett gefesselt sein.

lair [lɛə*] n Lager nt.

laissez-faire ['leɪsɪ'fɛə*] n Laisser-faire nt.

laity ['leɪtɪ] n Laien pl.

lake [leɪk] n See m.

lamb [læm] n Lamm nt; (meat) Lammfleisch nt; **— chop** Lammkotelett nt; **—'s wool** Lammwolle f.

lame [leɪm] a lahm; person also gelähmt; excuse faul.

lament [lə'ment] n Klage f; vt beklagen; **—able** ['læməntəbl] a bedauerlich; *(bad)* erbärmlich; —ation [læmən'teɪʃən] Wehklage *f.*

laminated ['læmɪneɪtɪd] *a* beschichtet.

lamp [læmp] *n* Lampe *f*; *(in street)* Straßenlaterne *f*; —**post** Laternenpfahl *m*; —**shade** Lampenschirm *m.*

lance [lɑːns] *n* Lanze *f*; *vt (Med)* aufschneiden; — **corporal** Obergefreite(r) *m.*

lancet ['lɑːnsɪt] *n* Lanzette *f.*

land [lænd] *n* Land *nt*; *vi (from ship)* an Land gehen; *(Aviat, end up)* landen; *vt (obtain)* gewinnen, kriegen; *passengers* absetzen; *goods* abladen; *troops, space probe* landen; —**ed** *a* Land-; —**ing** Landung *f*; *(on stairs)* (Treppen)absatz *m*; —**ing craft** Landungsboot *nt*; —**ing stage** Landesteg *m*; —**ing strip** Landebahn *f*; —**lady** (Haus)wirtin *f*; —**locked** *a* landumschlossen, Binnen-; —**lord** *(of house)* Hauswirt *m*, Besitzer *m*; *(of pub)* Gastwirt *m*; *(of land)* Grundbesitzer *m*; —**lubber** Landratte *f*; —**mark** Wahrzeichen *nt*; *(fig)* Meilenstein *m*; —**owner** Grundbesitzer *m*; —**scape** Landschaft *f*; —**slide** *(Geog)* Erdrutsch *m*; *(Pol)* überwältigende(r) Sieg *m.*

lane [leɪn] *n (in town)* Gasse *f*; *(in country)* Weg *m*; Sträßchen *nt*; *(of motorway)* Fahrbahn *f*, Spur *f*; *(Sport)* Bahn *f.*

language ['læŋgwɪdʒ] *n* Sprache *f*; *(style)* Ausdrucksweise *f.*

languid ['læŋgwɪd] *a* schlaff, matt.

languish ['læŋgwɪʃ] *vi* schmachten; *(pine)* sich sehnen *(for* nach).

languor ['læŋgə*] *n* Mattigkeit *f.*

languorous ['læŋgərəs] *a* schlaff, träge.

lank [læŋk] *a* dürr; —**y** *a* schlaksig.

lantern ['læntən] *n* Laterne *f.*

lanyard ['lænjəd] *n (Naut)* Taljereep *nt*; *(Mil)* Kordel *f.*

lap [læp] *n* Schoß *m*; *(Sport)* Runde *f*; *vt* auflecken; *vi (water)* plätschern; —**dog** Schoßhund *m.*

lapel [lə'pel] *n* Rockaufschlag *m*, Revers *nt* or *m.*

lapse [læps] *n (mistake)* Irrtum *m*; *(moral)* Fehltritt *m*; *(time)* Zeitspanne *f.*

larceny ['lɑːsənɪ] *n* Diebstahl *m.*

lard [lɑːd] *n* Schweineschmalz *nt.*

larder ['lɑːdə*] *n* Speisekammer *f.*

large [lɑːdʒ] *a* groß; **at** — auf freiem Fuß; **by and** — im großen und ganzen; —**ly** *ad* zum größten Teil; —**scale** *a* groß angelegt, Groß-; —**sse** [lɑː'ʒes] Freigebigkeit *f.*

lark [lɑːk] *n (bird)* Lerche *f*; *(joke)* Jux *m*; — **about** *vi (col)* herumalbern.

larva ['lɑːvə] *n* Larve *f.*

laryngitis [lærɪn'dʒaɪtɪs] *n* Kehlkopfentzündung *f.*

larynx ['lærɪŋks] *n* Kehlkopf *m.*

lascivious *a*, —**ly** [lə'sɪvɪəs, -lɪ] wollüstig.

lash [læʃ] *n* Peitschenhieb *m*; *vt (beat against)* schlagen an *(+acc)*; *(rain)* schlagen gegen; *(whip)* peitschen; *(bind)* festbinden; — **out** *vi (with fists)* um sich schlagen; *(spend money)* sich in Unkosten stürzen; *vt money etc* springen lassen; —**ing** *(beating)* Tracht *f* Prügel; *(tie)* Schleife *f*; —**ings of** *(col)* massenhaft.

lass [læs] *n* Mädchen *nt.*

lassitude ['læsɪtjuːd] *n* Abgespanntheit *f.*

lasso [læˈsuː] *n* Lasso *nt*; *vt* mit einem Lasso fangen.

last [lɑːst] *a* letzte(r, s); *ad* zuletzt; *(last time)* das letztemal; *n (person)* Letzte(r) *mf*; *(thing)* Letzte(s) *nt*; *(for shoe)* (Schuh)leisten *m*; *vi (continue)* dauern; *(remain good)* sich halten; *(money)* ausreichen; at — endlich; — **night** gestern abend; —**ing** *a* dauerhaft, haltbar; *shame etc* andauernd; —**minute** *a* in letzter Minute.

latch [lætʃ] *n* Riegel *m*; —**key** Hausschlüssel *m*.

late [leɪt] *a* spät; zu spät; *(recent)* jüngste(r, s); *(former)* frühere(r,s); *(dead)* verstorben; *ad* spät; *(after proper time)* zu spät; **to be** — zu spät kommen; *of* — in letzter Zeit; — **in the day** *(lit)* spät; *(fig)* reichlich spät; —**comer** Nachzügler *m*; —**ly** *ad* in letzter Zeit.

lateness [ˈleɪtnəs] *n (of person)* Zuspätkommen *nt*; *(of train)* Verspätung *f*; — **of the hour** die vorgerückte Stunde.

latent [ˈleɪtənt] *a* latent.

lateral [ˈlætərəl] *a* seitlich.

latest [ˈleɪtɪst] *n (news)* Neu(e)ste(s) *nt*; **at the** — spätestens.

latex [ˈleɪteks] *n* Milchsaft *m*.

lath [læθ] *n* Latte *f*, Leiste *f*.

lathe [leɪð] *n* Drehbank *f*.

lather [ˈlɑːðə*] *n* (Seifen)schaum *m*; *vt* einschäumen; *vi* schäumen.

latitude [ˈlætɪtjuːd] *n (Geog)* Breite *f*; *(freedom)* Spielraum *m*.

latrine [ləˈtriːn] *n* Latrine *f*.

latter [ˈlætə*] *a (second of two)* letztere; *(coming at end)* letzte(r, s), später; —**ly** *ad* in letzter Zeit; —**day** *a* modern.

lattice work [ˈlætɪswɜːk] *n* Lattenwerk *nt*, Gitterwerk *nt*.

laudable [ˈlɔːdəbl] *a* löblich.

laugh [lɑːf] *n* Lachen *nt*; *vi* lachen; — **at** *vt* lachen über *(+acc)*; — **off** *vt* lachend abtun; —**able** *a* lachhaft; —**ing** *a* lachend; —**ing stock** Zielscheibe *f* des Spottes; —**ter** Lachen *nt*, Gelächter *nt*.

launch [lɔːntʃ] *n (of ship)* Stapellauf *m*; *(of rocket)* Raketenabschuß *m*; *(boat)* Barkasse *f*; *(pleasure boat)* Vergnügungsboot *nt*; *vt (set afloat)* vom Stapel laufen lassen; *rocket* abschießen; *(set going)* in Gang setzen, starten; —**ing** Stapellauf *m*; —**(ing) pad** Abschußrampe *f*.

launder [ˈlɔːndə*] *vt* waschen und bügeln; —**ette** [lɔːndəˈret] Waschsalon *m*.

laundry [ˈlɔːndrɪ] *n (place)* Wäscherei *f*; *(clothes)* Wäsche *f*.

laureate [ˈlɔːrɪət] *a* see **poet.**

laurel [ˈlɔːrəl] *n* Lorbeer *m*.

lava [ˈlɑːvə] *n* Lava *f*.

lavatory [ˈlævətrɪ] *n* Toilette *f*.

lavender [ˈlævɪndə*] *n* Lavendel *m*.

lavish [ˈlævɪʃ] *a (extravagant)* verschwenderisch; *(generous)* großzügig; *vt money* verschwenden *(on auf +acc)*; *attentions, gifts* überschütten mit *(on sb jdn)*; —**ly** *ad* verschwenderisch.

law [lɔː] *n* Gesetz *nt*; *(system)* Recht *nt*; *(of game etc)* Regel *f*; *(as studies)* Jura *no art*; —**abiding** *a* gesetzestreu; —**breaker** Gesetzesübertreter *m*; —**court** Gerichtshof *m*; —**ful** *a* gesetzlich, rechtmäßig; —**fully** *ad* rechtmäßig; —**less** *a* gesetzlos.

lawn [lɔːn] *n* Rasen *m*; —**mower** Rasenmäher *m*; — **tennis** Rasentennis *m*.

law school [ˈlɔːskuːl] *n* Rechtsakademie *f*.

law student ['lɔ:stju:dənt] *n* Jura-student *m*.

lawsuit ['lɔ:su:t] *n* Prozeß *m*.

lawyer ['lɔ:jə*] *n* Rechtsanwalt *m* Rechtsanwältin *f*.

lax [læks] *a* lax.

laxative ['læksətɪv] *n* Abführmittel *nt*.

laxity ['læksɪtɪ] *n* Laxheit *f*.

lay [leɪ] *a* Laien—; *vt irreg (place)* legen; — *table* decken; *fire* anrichten; *egg* legen; *trap* stellen; *money* wetten; — **aside** vt zurücklegen; — **by** vt *(set aside)* beiseite legen; — **down** vt hinlegen; *rules* vorschreiben; *arms* strecken; — **off** vt *workers* (vorübergehend) entlassen; — **on** vt auftragen; *concert etc* veranstalten; — **out** vt (her)auslegen; *money* ausgeben; *corpse* aufbahren; — **up** vt *(store)* aufspeichern; *supplies* anlegen; *(save)* zurücklegen; —**about** Faulenzer *m*; —**by** Parkbucht *f*; *(bigger)* Rastplatz *m*; —**er** Schicht *f*; —**ette** [leɪ'et] Babyausstattung *f*; —**man** Laie *m*; —**out** Anlage *f*; *(Art)* Layout *nt*.

laze [leɪz] *vi* faulenzen.

lazily ['leɪzɪlɪ] *ad* träge, faul.

laziness ['leɪzɪnəs] *n* Faulheit *f*.

lazy ['leɪzɪ] *a* faul; *(slow-moving)* träge.

lead¹ [led] *n* Blei *nt*; *(of pencil)* (Bleistift)mine *f*; *a* bleiern, Blei-.

lead² [li:d] *n (front position)* Führung *f*; *(distance, time ahead)* Vorsprung *f*; *(example)* Vorbild *nt*; *(clue)* Tip *m*; *(of police)* Spur *f*; *(Theat)* Hauptrolle *f*; *(dog's)* Leine *f*; *irreg vt (guide)* führen; *group etc* leiten; *vi (be first)* führen; — **astray** vt irreführen; — **away** vt wegführen; *prisoner* abführen; — **back** vi zurückführen; — **on** vt

anführen; — **to** vt *(street)* (hin)führen nach; *(result in)* führen zu; — **up to** vt *(drive)* führen zu; *(speaker etc)* hinführen auf (+acc); —**er** Führer *m*, Leiter *m*; *(of party)* Vorsitzende(r) *m*; *(Press)* Leitartikel *m*; —**ership** *(office)* Leitung *f*; *(quality)* Führerschaft *f*; —**ing** *a* führend; —**ing lady** *(Theat)* Hauptdarstellerin *f*; —**ing light** *(person)* führende(r) Geist *m*; —**ing man** *(Theat)* Hauptdarsteller *m*.

leaf [li:f] *n* Blatt *nt*; *(of table)* Ausziehplatte; —**let** Blättchen *nt*; *(advertisement)* Prospekt *m*; *(pamphlet)* Flugblatt *nt*; *(for information)* Merkblatt *nt*; —**y** *a* belaubt.

league [li:g] *n (union)* Bund *m*, Liga *f*; *(Sport)* Liga *f*, Tabelle *f*; *(measure)* 3 englische Meilen.

leak [li:k] *n* undichte Stelle *f*; *(in ship)* Leck *nt*; *vt liquid etc* durchlassen; *vi (pipe etc)* undicht sein; *(liquid etc)* auslaufen; — **out** vi *(liquid etc)* auslaufen; *(information)* durchsickern.

leaky ['li:kɪ] *a* undicht.

lean [li:n] *a* mager; *n* Magere(s) *nt*; *irreg vi* sich neigen; — **against** *sth* an etw *(dat)* angelehnt sein; *sich an etw (acc)* anlehnen; vt *(an)lehnen; — **back** vi sich zurücklehnen; — **forward** vi sich vorbeugen; — **on** vi sich stützen auf (+acc); — **over** vi sich hinüberbeugen; — **towards** vt neigen zu; —**ing** Neigung *f*; —**to** Anbau *m*.

leap [li:p] *n* Sprung *m*; *vi irreg* springen; **by** —**s and bounds** schnell; —**frog** Bockspringen *nt*; — **year** Schaltjahr *nt*.

learn [lɜ:n] *vti irreg* lernen; *(find out)* erfahren, hören; —**ed** ['lɜ:nɪd] *a* gelehrt; **—er** Anfänger(in *f*) *m*; (*Aut*) Fahrschüler(in *f*) *m*; **—ing** Gelehrsamkeit *f*.

lease [li:s] *n* (*of property*) Mietvertrag *m*; (*of land*) Pachtvertrag *m*; *vt* mieten; pachten.

leash [li:ʃ] *n* Leine *f*.

least [li:st] *a* kleinste(r, s); (*slightest*) geringste(r, s); *n* Mindeste(s) *nt*; *at* — zumindest; not in the —! durchaus nicht!

leather [ˈleðə*] *n* Leder *nt*; *a* ledern, Leder-; **—y** *a* zäh, ledern.

leave [li:v] *irreg vt* verlassen; (— *behind*) zurücklassen; (*forget*) vergessen; (*allow to remain*) lassen; (*after death*) hinterlassen; (*entrust*) überlassen (*to sb* jdm); **to be left** (*remain*) übrigbleiben; *vi* weggehen, wegfahren; (*for journey*) abreisen; (*bus, train*) abfahren; *n* Erlaubnis *f*; (*Mil*) Urlaub *m*; *on* — auf Urlaub; **to take one's** — Abschied nehmen von; **— off** *vi* aufhören; **— out** *vt* auslassen.

lecherous [ˈletʃərəs] *a* lüstern.

lectern [ˈlekts:n] *n* Lesepult *nt*.

lecture [ˈlektʃə*] *n* Vortrag *m*; (*Univ*) Vorlesung *f*; *vi* einen Vortrag halten; (*Univ*) lesen; **—r** Vortragende(r) *mf*; (*Univ*) Dozent(in *f*) *m*.

ledge [ledʒ] *n* Leiste *f*; (*window* —) Sims *m or nt*; (*of mountain*) (Fels)vorsprung *m*.

ledger [ˈledʒə*] *n* Hauptbuch *nt*.

lee [li:] *n* Windschatten *m*; (*Naut*) Lee *f*.

leech [li:tʃ] *n* Blutegel *m*.

leek [li:k] *n* Lauch *m*.

leer [lɪə*] *n* schiefe(r) Blick *m*; *vi* schielen (*at* nach).

leeway [ˈli:wei] *n* (*fig*) Rückstand *m*; (*freedom*) Spielraum *m*.

left [left] *a* linke(r, s); *ad* links; nach links; *n* (*side*) linke Seite *f*; **the L—** (*Pol*) die Linke *f*; **—hand drive** Linkssteuerung *f*; **—handed** *a* linkshändig; **—hand side** linke Seite *f*; **—luggage (office)** Gepäckaufbewahrung *f*; **—overs** *pl* Reste *pl*, Überbleibsel *pl*; **— wing** linke(r) Flügel *m*; **—wing** *a* linke(r, s).

leg [leg] *n* Bein *nt*; (*of meat*) Keule *f*; (*stage*) Etappe *f*.

legacy [ˈlegəsi] *n* Erbe *nt*, Erbschaft *f*.

legal [ˈli:gəl] *a* gesetzlich, rechtlich; (*allowed*) legal, rechtsgültig; **to take — action** prozessieren; **—ize** *vt* legalisieren; **—ly** *ad* gesetzlich, legal; **— tender** gesetzliche(s) Zahlungsmittel *nt*.

legation [liˈgeɪʃən] *n* Gesandtschaft *f*.

legend [ˈledʒənd] *n* Legende *f*; **—ary** *a* legendär.

-legged [legid] *a* suf -beinig.

leggings [ˈlegɪnz] *npl* (hohe) Gamaschen *pl*; (*for baby*) Gamaschenhose *f*.

legibility [ledʒɪˈbɪlɪtɪ] *n* Leserlichkeit *f*.

legible *a*, **legibly** *ad* [ˈledʒəbl, -blɪ] leserlich.

legion [ˈli:dʒən] *n* Legion *f*.

legislate [ˈledʒɪsleɪt] *vi* Gesetze geben.

legislation [ledʒɪsˈleɪʃən] *n* Gesetzgebung *f*.

legislative [ˈledʒɪslətɪv] *a* gesetzgebend.

legislator [ˈledʒɪsleɪtə*] *n* Gesetzgeber *m*.

legislature [ˈledʒɪslətʃə*] *n* Legislative *f*.

legitimacy [lɪˈdʒɪtɪməsɪ] *n* Rechtmäßigkeit f; (of birth) Ehelichkeit f.

legitimate [lɪ'dʒɪtɪmət] a rechtmäßig, legitim; child ehelich.

legroom ['legrum] n Platz m für die Beine.

leisure ['leʒə*] n 'Freizeit f; a Freizeit-; to be at — Zeit haben; —ly ad gemächlich.

lemming ['lemɪŋ] n Lemming m.

lemon ['lemən] n Zitrone f; (colour) Zitronengelb nt; —ade [lemə'neɪd] Limonade f.

lend [lend] vt irreg leihen; to — sb sth jdm etw leihen; it —s itself to es eignet sich zu; —er Verleiher m; —ing library Leihbibliothek f.

length [leŋθ] n Länge f; (section of road, pipe etc) Strecke f; (of material) Stück nt; — of time Zeitdauer f; at — (lengthy) ausführlich; (at last) schließlich; —en vt verlängern; vi länger werden; —ways ad längs; —y a sehr lang; langatmig.

leniency ['liːnɪənsɪ] n Nachsicht f.

lenient ['liːnɪənt] a nachsichtig; —ly ad milde.

lens [lenz] n Linse f; (Phot) Objektiv nt.

Lent [lent] n Fastenzeit f.

lentil ['lentl] n Linse f.

Leo ['liːəu] n Löwe m.

leopard ['lepəd] n Leopard m.

leotard ['liːətɑːd] n Trikot nt, Gymnastikanzug m.

leper ['lepə*] n Leprakranke(r) mf.

leprosy ['leprəsɪ] n Lepra f.

lesbian ['lezbɪən] a lesbisch; n Lesbierin f.

less [les] a, ad, n weniger.

lessen ['lesn] vi abnehmen; vt verringern, verkleinern.

lesser ['lesə*] a kleiner, geringer.

lesson ['lesn] n (Sch) Stunde f; (unit of study) Lektion f; (fig) Lehre f; (Eccl) Lesung f; —s start at 9 der Unterricht beginnt um 9.

lest [lest] cj damit ... nicht.

let [let] n: without — or hindrance völlig unbehindert; vt irreg lassen; (lease) vermieten; —'s go! gehen wir!; — down vt hinunterlassen; (disappoint) enttäuschen; — go vi loslassen; vt things loslassen; person gehen lassen; — off vt gun abfeuern; steam ablassen; (forgive) laufen lassen; — out vt herauslassen; scream fahren lassen; — up vi nachlassen; (stop) aufhören; —down Enttäuschung f.

lethal ['liːθəl] a tödlich.

lethargic [le'θɑːdʒɪk] a lethargisch, träge.

lethargy ['leθədʒɪ] n Lethargie f, Teilnahmslosigkeit f.

letter ['letə*] n (of alphabet) Buchstabe m; (message) Brief m; —s pl (literature) (schöne) Literatur f; —box Briefkasten m; —ing n Beschriftung f.

lettuce ['letɪs] n (Kopf)salat m.

let-up ['letʌp] n (col) Nachlassen nt.

leukaemia, (US) **leukemia** [luː'kiːmɪə] n Leukämie f.

level ['levl] a ground eben; (at same height) auf gleicher Höhe; (equal) gleich gut; head kühl; to do one's — best sein möglichstes tun; ad auf gleicher Höhe; to draw — with gleichziehen mit; a (instrument) Wasserwaage f; (altitude) Höhe f; (flat place) ebene Fläche f; (position on scale) Niveau nt; (amount, degree) Grad m; talks on a high — Gespräche auf hoher Ebene; profits keep on the same — Gewinne halten sich auf dem gleichen Stand; **on the moral —** aus moralischer Sicht; **on the —** (lit) auf gleicher Höhe; (fig: honest) ehrlich; vt ground einebnen; building abreißen; town dem Erdboden gleichmachen; blow versetzen (at sb jdm); remark richten (at gegen); — off or out vi flach or eben werden; (fig) (sich) ausgleichen; (plane) horizontal fliegen; vt ground planieren; differences ausgleichen; — **crossing** Bahnübergang m; —**headed** a vernünftig.

lever ['li:və*, (US) 'levə*] n Hebel m; (fig) Druckmittel nt; vt (hoch)stemmen; —**age** Hebelkraft f; (fig) Einfluß m.

levity ['levɪtɪ] n Leichtfertigkeit f.

levy ['levɪ] n (of taxes) Erhebung f; (tax) Abgabe pl; (Mil) Aushebung f; vt erheben; (Mil) ausheben.

lewd [lu:d] a unzüchtig, unanständig.

liability [laɪə'bɪlɪtɪ] n (burden) Belastung f; (duty) Pflicht f; (debt) Verpflichtung \ f; (proneness) Anfälligkeit f; (responsibility) Haftung f.

liable ['laɪəbl] a (responsible) haftbar; (prone) anfällig; **to be —** for etw (dat) unterliegen; **it's — to happen** es kann leicht vorkommen.

liaison [li:'eɪzɒn] n Verbindung f.

liar ['laɪə*] n Lügner m.

libel ['laɪbəl] n Verleumdung f; vt verleumden; —**(l)ous** a verleumderisch.

liberal ['lɪbərəl] a (generous) großzügig; (open-minded) aufgeschlossen; (Pol) liberal; n liberal denkende(r) Mensch m; **L—** (Pol) Liberale(r) mf; —**ly** ad (abundantly) reichlich.

liberate ['lɪbəreɪt] vt befreien.

liberation [lɪbə'reɪʃən] n Befreiung f.

liberty ['lɪbətɪ] n Freiheit f; (permission) Erlaubnis f; **to be at —** to do sth etw tun dürfen; **to take liberties with** sich (dat) Freiheiten herausnehmen gegenüber.

Libra ['li:brə] n Waage f.

librarian [laɪ'breərɪən] n Bibliothekar(in f) m.

library ['laɪbrərɪ] n Bibliothek f; (lending —) Bücherei f.

libretto [lɪ'bretəʊ] n Libretto nt.

lice [laɪs] npl of louse.

licence, (US) license ['laɪsəns] n (permit) Erlaubnis f, amtliche Zulassung f; (driving —) Führerschein m; (excess) Zügellosigkeit f; — **plate** (US Aut) Nummernschild nt.

license ['laɪsəns] vt genehmigen, konzessionieren; —**e** [laɪsən'si:] n Konzessionsinhaber m.

licentious [laɪ'senʃəs] a ausschweifend.

lichen ['laɪkən] n Flechte f.

lick [lɪk] vt lecken; vi (flames) züngeln; n Lecken nt; (small amount) Spur f.

licorice ['lɪkərɪs] n Lakritze f.

lid [lɪd] n Deckel m; (eye—) Lid nt.

lido ['li:dəʊ] n Freibad nt.

lie [laɪ] n Lüge f; vi lügen; irreg (rest, be situated) liegen; (put o.s. in position) sich legen; **to — idle** stillstehen; — **detector** Lügendetektor m.

lieu [lu:] n: **in —** of anstatt (+gen).

lieutenant [lef'tenənt], (US) [lu:'tenənt] n Leutnant m.

life [laɪf] n Leben nt; (story) Lebensgeschichte f; (energy) Lebendigkeit f; — **assurance** Lebensversicherung *f;* **—belt** Rettungsring *m;* **—boat** Rettungsboot *nt;* **-guard** Badewärter *m;* Rettungsschwimmer *m;* **—jacket** Schwimmweste *f;* **—less** *a* (dead) leblos, tot; (dull) langweilig; **—like** *a* lebenswahr, naturgetreu; **—line** (lit) Rettungsleine *f;* (fig) Rettungsanker *m;* **—long** *a* lebenslang; **—preserver** Totschläger *m;* **—raft** Rettungsfloß *nt;* **—sized** *a* in Lebensgröße; **—span** Lebensspanne *f;* **—time** Lebenszeit *f.*

lift [lɪft] *vt* hochheben; *vi* sich heben; *n* (raising) (Hoch)heben *nt;* (elevator) Aufzug *m,* Lift *m;* **to give sb a —** jdn mitnehmen; **—off** Abheben *nt* (vom Boden).

ligament ['lɪgəmənt] *n* Sehne *f,* Band *nt.*

light [laɪt] *n* Licht *nt;* (lamp) Lampe *f;* (flame) Feuer *nt;* **—s** *pl* (Aut) Beleuchtung *f;* **in the —** *of* angesichts (+gen); *vt irreg* beleuchten; *lamp* anmachen; *fire, cigarette* anzünden; (brighten) erleuchten, erhellen; *a* (bright) hell, licht; (pale) hell-; (not heavy, easy) leicht; *punishment* milde; *taxes* niedrig; *touch* leicht; **— up** *vi* (lamp) angehen; (face) aufleuchten; *vt* (illuminate) beleuchten; *lights* anmachen; **—bulb** Glühbirne *f;* **—en** *vi* (brighten) hell werden; (lightning) blitzen; *vt* (give light to) erhellen; *hair* aufhellen; (gloom) aufheitern; (make less heavy) leichter machen; (fig) erleichtern; **—er** (cigarette —) Feuerzeug *nt;* (boat) Leichter *m;* **—headed** *a* (thoughtless) leichtsinnig; (giddy) schwindlig; **—hearted** *a* fröhlich; **—house** Leuchtturm *m;* **—ing** Beleuchtung *f;* **—ing-up time** Zeit *f* des Ein-

schaltens der Straßen-/Autobeleuchtung; **—ly** *ad* leicht; (irresponsibly) leichtfertig; **— meter** (Phot) Belichtungsmesser *m;* **—ness** (of weight) Leichtigkeit *f;* (of colour) Helle *f;* (light) Helligkeit *f;* **—ning** Blitz *m;* **—ning conductor** Blitzableiter *m;* **—weight** *a suit* leicht; **—weight boxer** Leichtgewicht *nt;* **—year** Lichtjahr *nt.*

lignite ['lɪgnaɪt] *n* Lignit *m.*

like [laɪk] *vt* mögen, gernhaben; **would you — ...?** hätten Sie gern ...?; **would you — to ...?** möchten Sie gern...?; *prep wie;* **what's it/he —?** wie ist es/er?; **that's just —** him das sieht ihm ähnlich; **— that/this** so; *a* (similar) ähnlich; (equal) gleich; *n* Gleiche(s) *nt;* **—able** *a* sympathisch; **—lihood** Wahrscheinlichkeit *f;* **—ly** *a* (probable) wahrscheinlich; (suitable) geeignet; *ad* wahrscheinlich; **—minded** *a* gleichgesinnt; **—n** *vt* vergleichen (to mit); **—wise** *ad* ebenfalls.

liking ['laɪkɪŋ] *n* Zuneigung *f;* (taste for) Vorliebe *f.*

lilac ['laɪlək] *n* Flieder *m.*

lilting ['lɪltɪŋ] *a accent* singend; *tune* munter.

lily ['lɪlɪ] *n* Lilie *f;* **— of the valley** Maiglöckchen *nt.*

limb [lɪm] *n* Glied *nt.*

limber ['lɪmbə*]:* **— up** *vi* sich auflockern; (fig) sich vorbereiten.

limbo ['lɪmbəʊ] *n:* **to be in —** (fig) in der Schwebe sein.

lime [laɪm] *n* (tree) Linde *f;* (fruit) Limone *f;* (substance) Kalk *m;* **—juice** Limonensaft *m;* **—light** (fig) Rampenlicht *nt.*

limerick ['lɪmərɪk] *n* Limerick *m.*

limestone ['laɪmstəʊn] *n* Kalkstein *m.*

limit ['lɪmɪt] n Grenze f; (col) Höhe f; vt begrenzen, einschränken; **—ation** Grenzen pl, Einschränkung f; **—ed** a beschränkt; **—ed company** Gesellschaft f mit beschränkter Haftung, GmbH f.

limousine ['lɪməziːn] n Limousine f.

limp [lɪmp] n Hinken nt; vi hinken; a (without firmness) schlaff.

limpet ['lɪmpɪt] n (lit) Napfschnecke f; (fig) Klette f.

limpid ['lɪmpɪd] a klar.

limply ['lɪmplɪ] ad schlaff.

line [laɪn] n Linie f; (rope) Leine f, Schnur f; (on face) Falte f; (row) Reihe f; (of hills) Kette f; (US: queue) Schlange f; (company) Linie f, Gesellschaft f; (Rail) Strecke f; (pl) Geleise pl; (Tel) Leitung f; (written) Zeile f; (direction) Richtung f; (fig: business) Branche f, Beruf m; (range of items) Kollektion f; **it's a bad —** (Tel) die Verbindung ist schlecht; **hold the —** bleiben Sie am Apparat; **in —** with in Übereinstimmung mit; vt coat füttern; (border) säumen; **— up** vi sich aufstellen; vt aufstellen; (prepare) sorgen für; support mobilisieren; surprise planen.

linear ['lɪnɪə*] a gerade; (measure) Längen-.

linen ['lɪnɪn] n Leinen nt; (sheets etc) Wäsche f.

liner ['laɪnə*] n Überseedampfer m.

linesman ['laɪnzmən] n (Sport) Linienrichter m.

line-up ['laɪnʌp] n Aufstellung f.

linger ['lɪŋgə*] vi (remain long) verweilen; (taste) (zurück)bleiben; (delay) zögern, verharren.

lingerie ['lænʒəriː] n Damenunterwäsche f.

lingering ['lɪŋgərɪŋ] a lang; doubt zurückbleibend; disease langwierig; taste nachhaltend; look lang.

lingo ['lɪŋgəʊ] n (col) Sprache f.

linguist ['lɪŋgwɪst] n Sprachkundige(r) mf; (Univ) Sprachwissenschaftler(in f) m.

linguistic [lɪŋ'gwɪstɪk] a sprachlich; sprachwissenschaftlich; **—s** Sprachwissenschaft f, Linguistik f.

liniment ['lɪnɪmənt] n Einreibemittel nt.

lining ['laɪnɪŋ] n (of clothes) Futter nt.

link [lɪŋk] n Glied nt; (connection) Verbindung f; vt verbinden; **—s** Golfplatz m; **—-up** (Tel) Verbindung f; (of spaceships) Kopplung f.

lino ['laɪnəʊ] n, **linoleum** [lɪ'nəʊlɪəm] n Linoleum nt.

linseed oil ['lɪnsiːd'ɔɪl] n Leinöl nt.

lint [lɪnt] n Verbandstoff m.

lintel ['lɪntl] n (Archit) Sturz m.

lion ['laɪən] n Löwe m; **—ess** Löwin f.

lip [lɪp] n Lippe f; (of jug) Tülle f, Schnabel m; **—-read** vi irreg von den Lippen ablesen; **to pay — service (to)** ein Lippenbekenntnis ablegen (zu); **—stick** Lippenstift m.

liquefy ['lɪkwɪfaɪ] vt verflüssigen.

liqueur [lɪ'kjʊə*] n Likör m.

liquid ['lɪkwɪd] n Flüssigkeit f; a flüssig; **—ate** vt liquidieren; **—ation** Liquidation f.

liquor ['lɪkə*] n Alkohol m, Spirituosen pl.

lisp [lɪsp] n Lispeln nt; vti lispeln.

list [lɪst] n Liste f, Verzeichnis nt; (of ship) Schlagseite f; vt (write down) eine Liste machen von;

(verbally) aufzählen; *vi (ship)* Schlagseite haben.

listen ['lɪsn] *vi* hören, horchen; — to *vt* zuhören (+ *dat*); —**er** (Zu)hörer(in *f*) *m*.

listless *a*, —**ly** *ad* ['lɪstləs, -lɪ] lustlos, teilnahmslos; —**ness** Lustlosigkeit *f*, Teilnahmslosigkeit *f*.

litany ['lɪtənɪ] *n* Litanei *f*.

literacy ['lɪtərəsɪ] *n* Fähigkeit *f* zu lesen und zu schreiben.

literal ['lɪtərəl] *a* eigentlich, buchstäblich; *translation* wortwörtlich; —**ly** *ad* wörtlich; buchstäblich.

literary ['lɪtərərɪ] *a* literarisch, Literatur-.

literate ['lɪtərət] *a* des Lesens und Schreibens kundig.

literature ['lɪtrətʃə*] *n* Literatur *f*.

lithograph ['lɪθəugrɑ:f] *n* Lithographie *f*.

litigate ['lɪtɪgeɪt] *vi* prozessieren.

litmus ['lɪtməs] *n*: — **paper** Lackmuspapier *nt*.

litre, *(US)* **liter** ['li:tə*] *n* Liter *m*.

litter ['lɪtə*] *n (rubbish)* Abfall *m*; *(of animals)* Wurf *m*; *vt* in Unordnung bringen; **to be** —**ed with** übersät sein mit.

little ['lɪtl] *a* klein; *(unimportant)* unbedeutend; *ad*, *n* wenig; **a** — ein bißchen; **the** — das wenige.

liturgy ['lɪtədʒɪ] *n* Liturgie *f*.

live[1] ['lɪv] *vi* leben; *(last)* fortleben; *(dwell)* wohnen; *vt life* führen; — **down** *vt* Gras wachsen lassen über (+*acc*); **I'll never** — **it down** das wird man mir nie vergessen; — **on** *vi* weiterleben; — **on sth** von etw leben; — **up to** *vt standards* gerecht werden (+*dat*); *principles* anstreben; *hopes* entsprechen (+*dat*).

live[2] [laɪv] *a* lebendig; *(burning)* glühend; *(Mil)* scharf; *(Elec)* geladen; *broadcast* live.

livelihood ['laɪvlɪhud] *n* Lebensunterhalt *m*.

liveliness ['laɪvlɪnəs] *n* Lebendigkeit *f*.

lively ['laɪvlɪ] *a* lebhaft, lebendig.

liver ['lɪvə*] *n (Anat)* Leber *f*; —**ish** *a (bad-tempered)* gallig.

livery ['lɪvərɪ] *n* Livree *f*.

livestock ['laɪvstɔk] *n* Vieh *nt*, Viehbestand *m*.

livid ['lɪvɪd] *a (lit)* bläulich; *(furious)* fuchsteufelswild.

living ['lɪvɪŋ] *n (Lebens)unterhalt *m*; *a* lebendig; *language etc* lebend; *wage* ausreichend; — **room** Wohnzimmer· *nt*.

lizard ['lɪzəd] *n* Eidechse *f*.

llama ['lɑ:mə] *n* Lama *nt*.

load [ləud] *n (burden)* Last *f*; *(amount)* Ladung *f*, Fuhre *f*; —**s of** *(col)* massenhaft; *vt* (be)laden; *(fig)* überhäufen; *camera* Film einlegen in (+*acc*); *gun* laden.

loaf [ləuf] *n* Brot *nt*, Laib *m*; *vi* herumlungern, faulenzen.

loam [ləum] *n* Lehmboden *m*.

loan [ləun] *n* Leihgabe *f*, *(Fin)* Darlehen *nt*; *vt* leihen; **on** — geliehen.

loathe [ləuð] *vt* verabscheuen.

loathing ['ləuðɪŋ] *n* Abscheu *f*.

lobby ['lɔbɪ] *n* Vorhalle *f*, *(Pol)* Lobby *f*; *vt* politisch beeinflussen (wollen).

lobe [ləub] *n* Ohrläppchen *nt*.

lobster ['lɔbstə*] *n* Hummer *m*.

local ['ləukəl] *a* ortsansässig, hiesig, Orts-; *anaesthetic* örtlich; *a (pub)* Stammwirtschaft *f*; **the** —**s** *pl* die Ortsansässigen *pl*; — **colour** Lokalkolorit nt; —ity [ləʊˈkælɪtɪ] Ort m; —ly ad örtlich, am Ort.

locate [ləʊˈkeɪt] vt ausfindig machen; *(establish)* errichten.

location [ləʊˈkeɪʃən] n Platz m, Lage f; on — *(Cine)* auf Außenaufnahme.

loch [lɒx] n *(Scot)* See m.

lock [lɒk] n Schloß nt; *(Naut)* Schleuse f; *(of hair)* Locke f; vt *(fasten)* (ver)schließen; vi *(door etc)* sich schließen (lassen); *(wheels)* blockieren.

locker [ˈlɒkə*] n Spind m.

locket [ˈlɒkɪt] n Medaillon nt.

locomotive [ləʊkəˈməʊtɪv] n Lokomotive f.

locust [ˈləʊkəst] n Heuschrecke f.

lodge [lɒdʒ] n *(gatehouse)* Pförtnerhaus nt; *(freemasons')* Loge f; vi *(in Untermiete)* wohnen *(with* bei); *(get stuck)* stecken(bleiben); vt *protest* einreichen; —r *(Unter)mieter m.

lodgings [ˈlɒdʒɪŋz] n *(Miet)*wohnung f; Zimmer nt.

loft [lɒft] n *(Dach)boden m.

lofty [ˈlɒftɪ] a hoch(ragend); *(proud)* hochmütig.

log [lɒg] n Klotz m; *(Naut)* Log nt.

logarithm [ˈlɒgərɪθəm] n Logarithmus m.

logbook [ˈlɒgbʊk] n Bordbuch nt, Logbuch nt; *(for lorry)* Fahrtenschreiber m; *(Aut)* Kraftfahrzeugbrief m.

loggerheads [ˈlɒgəhedz] n: to be at — sich in den Haaren liegen.

logic [ˈlɒdʒɪk] n Logik f; —al a logisch; —ally ad logisch(erweise).

logistics [lɒˈdʒɪstɪks] npl Logistik f.

loin [lɔɪn] n Lende f.

loiter [ˈlɔɪtə*] vi herumstehen, sich herumtreiben.

loll [lɒl] vi sich rekeln.

lollipop [ˈlɒlɪpɒp] n *(Dauer)*lutscher m.

lone [ləʊn] a einsam.

loneliness [ˈləʊnlɪnəs] n Einsamkeit f.

lonely [ˈləʊnlɪ] a einsam.

long [lɒŋ] a lang; *distance* weit; ad lange; **two-day—** zwei Tage lang; vi sich sehnen *(for* nach); — **ago** vor langer Zeit; **before** — bald; **as — as** solange; **in the — run** auf die Dauer; **—distance** a Fern-; **—haired** a langhaarig; **—hand** Langschrift f; **—ing** Verlangen nt, Sehnsucht f; a sehnsüchtig; **—ish** a ziemlich lang; **—itude** Längengrad m; — **jump** Weitsprung m; **—lost** a längst verloren geglaubt; **—playing record** Langspielplatte f; **—range** a Langstrecken-, Fern-; **—sighted** a weitsichtig; **—standing** a alt, seit langer Zeit bestehend; **—suffering** a schwer geprüft; **—term** a langfristig; — **wave** Langwelle f; **—winded** a langatmig.

loo [luː] n *(col)* Klo nt.

loofah [ˈluːfɑ*] n *(plant)* Luffa f; *(sponge)* Luffa(schwamm) m.

look [lʊk] vi schauen, blicken; *(seem)* aussehen; *(face)* liegen nach, gerichtet sein nach; n Blick m; —s pl Aussehen nt; — **after** vt *(care for)* sorgen für; *(watch)* aufpassen auf *(+acc)*; — **down on** vt *(fig)* herabsehen auf *(+acc)*; — **for** vt *(seek)* suchen (nach); *(expect)* erwarten; — **forward to** vt sich freuen auf *(+acc)*; — **out** **for** vt Ausschau halten nach; *(be careful)* achtgeben auf *(+acc)*; — **to** vt *(take care of)* achtgeben auf

(+acc); (rely on) sich verlassen auf (+acc); — **up** vi aufblicken; (improve) sich bessern; vt word nachschlagen; person besuchen; — **up to** vt aufsehen zu; —**out** (watch) Ausschau f; (person) Wachposten m; (place) Ausguck m; (prospect) Aussichten pl.

loom [lu:m] n Webstuhl m; vi sich abzeichnen.

loop [lu:p] n Schlaufe f, Schleife f; vt schlingen; —**hole** (fig) Hintertürchen nt.

loose [lu:s] a lose, locker; (free) frei; (inexact) unpräzise; vt lösen, losbinden; **to be at a —** end nicht wissen, was man tun soll; —**ly** ad locker, lose; —**ly speaking** grob gesagt; —**n** vt lockern, losmachen; —**ness** Lockerheit f.

loot [lu:t] n Beute f; vt plündern; —**ing** Plünderung f.

lop [lɒp]: — **off** vt abhacken.

lop-sided ['lɒp'saɪdd] a schief.

lord [lɔ:d] n (ruler) Herr m, Gebieter m; (Brit, title) Lord m; **the L—** (Gott) der Herr m; —**ly** a vornehm; (proud) stolz.

lore [lɔ:*] n Überlieferung f.

lorry ['lɒrɪ] n Lastwagen m.

lose [lu:z] irreg vt verlieren; chance verpassen; — **out** on zu kurz kommen bei; vi verlieren; —**r** Verlierer m.

losing ['lu:zɪŋ] a Verlierer-; (Comm) verlustbringend.

loss [lɒs] n Verlust m; **at a —** (Comm) mit Verlust; (unable) außerstande; **I am at a — for words** mir fehlen die Worte.

lost [lɒst] a verloren; — **cause** aussichtslose Sache f; — **property** Fundsachen pl.

lot [lɒt] n (quantity) Menge f; (fate, at auction) Los nt; (col: people,

things) Haufen m; **the —** alles; (people) alle; **a —** of viel; pl viele; —**s of** massenhaft, viel(e).

lotion ['ləʊʃən] n Lotion f.

lottery ['lɒtərɪ] n Lotterie f.

loud [laʊd] a laut; (showy) schreiend; ad laut; —**ly** ad laut; —**ness** Lautheit f; —**speaker** Lautsprecher m.

lounge [laʊndʒ] n (in hotel) Gesellschaftsraum m; (in house) Wohnzimmer m; (on ship) Salon m; vi sich herumlümmeln; — **suit** Straßenanzug m.

louse [laʊs] n Laus f.

lousy ['laʊzɪ] a (lit) verlaust; (fig) lausig, miserabel.

lout [laʊt] n Lümmel m.

lovable ['lʌvəbl] a liebenswert.

love [lʌv] n Liebe f; (person) Liebling m, Schatz m; (Sport) null; vt person lieben; (activity etc) gerne mögen; — **to do sth** etw (sehr) gerne tun; **to make** sich lieben; **to make — to/with sb** jdn lieben; — **affair** Liebesverhältnis nt; — **letter** Liebesbrief m; — **life** Liebesleben nt; —**ly** a schön; person, object also entzückend, reizend; —**making** Liebe f; —**r** Liebhaber m; Geliebte f; (of books etc) Liebhaber m; **the —rs** die Liebenden, das Liebespaar; —**song** Liebeslied nt.

loving ['lʌvɪŋ] a liebend, liebevoll; —**ly** ad liebevoll.

low [ləʊ] a niedrig; rank niedere(r, s); level, note, neckline tief; (vulgar) ordinär; (not loud) leise; (depressed) gedrückt; ad (not high) niedrig; (not loudly) leise; n (low point) Tiefstand m; (Met) Tief nt; —**cut** a dress tiefausgeschnitten.

lower ['ləʊə*] vt herunterlassen;

eyes, gun senken; *(reduce)* herabsetzen, senken.

lowly ['ləʊlɪ] a bescheiden.

loyal ['lɔɪəl] a *(true)* treu; *(to king)* loyal, treu; **—ly** ad treu; loyal; **—ty** Treue f; Loyalität f.

lozenge ['lɒzɪndʒ] n Pastille f.

lubricant ['lu:brɪkənt] n Schmiermittel nt.

lubricate ['lu:brɪkeɪt] vt (ab)schmieren, ölen.

lubrication [lu:brɪ'keɪʃən] n (Einor Ab)schmierung f.

lucid ['lu:sɪd] a klar; *(sane)* bei klarem Verstand; *moment* licht; **—ity** [lu:'sɪdɪtɪ] Klarheit f; **—ly** ad klar.

luck [lʌk] n Glück nt; bad **—** Pech nt; **—ily** ad glücklicherweise, zum Glück; **—y** a glücklich, Glücks-; to be **—** Glück haben.

lucrative ['lu:krətɪv] a einträglich.

ludicrous ['lu:dɪkrəs] a grotesk.

ludo ['lu:dəʊ] n Mensch ärgere dich nicht nt.

lug [lʌg] vt schleppen.

luggage ['lʌgɪdʒ] n Gepäck nt; **— rack** Gepäcknetz nt.

lugubrious [lu:'gu:brɪəs] a traurig.

lukewarm ['lu:kwɔ:m] a lauwarm; *(indifferent)* lau.

lull [lʌl] n Flaute f; vt einlullen; *(calm)* beruhigen; **—aby** ['lʌləbaɪ] Schlaflied nt.

lumbago [lʌm'beɪgəʊ] n Hexenschuß m.

lumber ['lʌmbə*] n Plunder m; *(wood)* Holz nt; **—jack** Holzfäller m.

luminous ['lu:mɪnəs] a leuchtend, Leucht-.

lump [lʌmp] n Klumpen m; *(Med)* Schwellung f; *(in breast)* Knoten m; *(of sugar)* Stück nt; vt

zusammentun; *(judge together)* in einen Topf werfen; **— sum** Pauschalsumme f; **—y** klumpig; to go **—y** klumpen.

lunacy ['lu:nəsɪ] n Irrsinn m.

lunar ['lu:nə*] a Mond-.

lunatic ['lu:nətɪk] n Wahnsinnige(r) mf; a wahnsinnig, irr.

lunch [lʌntʃ] n *(also* **—eon** [-ən] *)* Mittagessen nt; **— hour** Mittagspause f; **—time** Mittagszeit f; **—eon meat** Frühstücksfleisch nt.

lung [lʌŋ] n Lunge f; **— cancer** Lungenkrebs m.

lunge [lʌndʒ] vi (los)stürzen.

lupin ['lu:pɪn] n Lupine f.

lurch [lɜ:tʃ] vi taumeln; *(Naut)* schlingern; n Taumeln nt; *(Naut)* plötzliche(s) Schlingern nt.

lure [ljʊə*] n Köder m; *(fig)* Lockung f; vt (ver)locken.

lurid ['ljʊərɪd] a *(shocking)* grausig, widerlich; *colour* grell.

lurk [lɜ:k] vi lauern.

luscious ['lʌʃəs] a köstlich; *colour* satt.

lush [lʌʃ] a satt; *vegetation* üppig.

lust [lʌst] n sinnliche Begierde f *(for* nach)*; *(sensation)* Wollust f; *(greed)* Gier f; vi gieren *(after* nach)*; **—ful** a wollüstig, lüstern.

lustre, *(US)* **luster** ['lʌstə*] n Glanz m.

lusty ['lʌstɪ] a gesund und munter; *old person* rüstig.

lute [lu:t] n Laute f.

luxuriant [lʌg'zjʊərɪənt] a üppig.

luxurious [lʌg'zjʊərɪəs] a luxuriös, Luxus-.

luxury ['lʌkʃərɪ] n Luxus m; the little luxuries die kleinen Genüsse.

lying ['laɪɪŋ] n Lügen nt; a verlogen.

lynch [lɪntʃ] vt lynchen.

lynx [lɪŋks] n Luchs m.
lyre ['laɪə*] n Leier f.
lyric ['lɪrɪk] n Lyrik f; (pl: words

for song) (Lied)text m; a lyrisch;
—al a lyrisch, gefühlvoll.

M

M, m [em] n M nt, m nt.
mac [mæk] n (Brit col) Regenmantel m.
macabre [mə'kɑ:br] a makaber.
macaroni [mækə'rəʊnɪ] n Makkaroni pl.
mace [meɪs] n Amtsstab m; (spice) Muskat m.
machine [mə'ʃi:n] n Maschine f; vt dress etc mit der Maschine nähen; maschinell herstellen/bearbeiten; —gun Maschinengewehr nt; —ry [mə'ʃi:nərɪ] Maschinerie f, Maschinen pl; — tool Werkzeugmaschine f.
machinist [mə'ʃi:nɪst] n Maschinist m.
mackerel ['mækrəl] n Makrele f.
mackintosh ['mækɪntɒʃ] n Regenmantel m.
macro- ['mækrəʊ] pref Makro-, makro-.
mad [mæd] a verrückt; dog tollwütig; (angry) wütend; — about (fond of) verrückt nach, versessen auf (+acc).
madam ['mædəm] n gnädige Frau f.
madden ['mædn] vt verrückt machen; (make angry) ärgern; —ing a ärgerlich.
made-to-measure ['meɪdtə'meʒə*] a Maß-.
made-up ['meɪd'ʌp] a story erfunden.
madly ['mædlɪ] ad wahnsinnig.

madman ['mædmən] n Verrückte(r) m, Irre(r) m.
madness ['mædnəs] n Wahnsinn m.
Madonna [mə'dɒnə] n Madonna f.
madrigal ['mædrɪgəl] n Madrigal nt.
magazine ['mægəzi:n] n Zeitschrift f; (in gun) Magazin nt.
maggot ['mægət] n Made f.
magic ['mædʒɪk] n Zauberei f, Magie f; (fig) Zauber m; —al a magisch, Zauber-; —ian [mə'dʒɪʃən] Zauberer m.
magistrate ['mædʒɪstreɪt] n (Friedens)richter m.
magnanimity [mægnə'nɪmɪtɪ] n Großmut f.
magnanimous [mæg'nænɪməs] a großmütig.
magnate ['mægneɪt] n Magnat m.
magnet ['mægnɪt] n Magnet m; —ic [mæg'netɪk] a magnetisch; (fig) anziehend, unwiderstehlich; —ism Magnetismus m; (fig) Ausstrahlungskraft f.
magnification [mægnɪfɪ'keɪʃən] n Vergrößerung f.
magnificence [mæg'nɪfɪsəns] n Großartigkeit f.
magnificent a, —ly ad [mæg'nɪfɪsənt, -lɪ] großartig.
magnify ['mægnɪfaɪ] vt vergrößern; —ing glass Vergrößerungsglas nt, Lupe f.
magnitude ['mægnɪtju:d] n (size) Größe f; (importance) Ausmaß nt.

magnolia [mæg'nəʊlɪə] n Magnolie f.

magpie ['mægpaɪ] n Elster f.

maharajah [mɑːhə'rɑːdʒə] n Maharadscha m.

mahogany [mə'hɒgənɪ] n Mahagoni nt; a Mahagoni-.

maid [meɪd] n Dienstmädchen nt; old — alte Jungfer f; —en (liter) Maid f; a flight, speech Jungfern-; —en name Mädchenname m.

mail [meɪl] n Post f; vt aufgeben; — box (US) Briefkasten m; —ing list Anschreibeliste f; — order Bestellung f durch die Post; — order firm Versandhaus nt.

maim [meɪm] vt verstümmeln.

main [meɪn] a hauptsächlich, Haupt-; n (pipe) Hauptleitung f; in the — im großen und ganzen; —land Festland nt; — road Hauptstraße f; —stay (fig) Hauptstütze f.

maintain [meɪn'teɪn] vt machine, roads instand halten; (support) unterhalten; (keep up) aufrechterhalten; (claim) behaupten; innocence beteuern.

maintenance ['meɪntənəns] n (Tech) Wartung f; (of family) Unterhalt m.

maisonette [meɪzə'net] n kleine(s) Eigenheim nt; Wohnung f.

maize [meɪz] n Mais m.

majestic · [mə'dʒestɪk] a majestätisch.

majesty ['mædʒɪstɪ] n Majestät f.

major ['meɪdʒə*] n Major m; a (Mus) Dur-; (more important) Haupt-; (bigger) größer.

majority [mə'dʒɒrɪtɪ] n Mehrheit f; (Jur) Volljährigkeit f.

make [meɪk] vt irreg machen; (appoint) ernennen (zu); (cause to

do sth) veranlassen; (reach) erreichen; (in time) schaffen; (earn) verdienen; to — sth happen etw geschehen lassen; n Marke f, Fabrikat nt; — for vi gehen/fahren nach; — out vi zurechtkommen; vt (write out) ausstellen; (understand) verstehen; (pretend) (so) tun (als ob); — up vi (make) machen, herstellen; face schminken; quarrel beilegen; story etc erfinden; vi sich versöhnen; — up for vi wiedergutmachen; (Comm) vergüten; ——believe n it's ——believe es ist nicht wirklich; a Phantasie-, ersonnen; —r (Comm) Hersteller m; ——shift a behelfsmäßig, Not-; ——up Schminke f, Make-up nt.

making ['meɪkɪŋ] n: in the — im Entstehen; to have the —s of das Zeug haben zu.

maladjusted ['mælə'dʒʌstɪd] a fehlangepaßt, umweltgestört.

malaise [mæ'leɪz] n Unbehagen nt.

malaria [mə'lɛərɪə] n Malaria f.

male [meɪl] n Mann m; (animal) Männchen nt; a männlich.

malevolence [mə'levələns] n Böswilligkeit f.

malevolent [mə'levələnt] a übelwollend.

malfunction [mæl'fʌŋkʃən] vi versagen, nicht funktionieren.

malice ['mælɪs] n Bosheit f.

malicious [mə'lɪʃəs] —ly ad [mə'lɪʃəs, -lɪ] böswillig, gehässig.

malign [mə'laɪn] vt verleumden.

malignant [mə'lɪgnənt] a bösartig.

malinger [mə'lɪŋgə*] vi simulieren; ——er Drückeberger m, Simulant m.

malleable ['mælɪəbl] a formbar.

mallet ['mælɪt] n Holzhammer m.

malnutrition ['mælnju:'trıʃən] *n* Unterernährung *f.*

malpractice [mæl'præktıs] *n* Amtsvergehen *nt.*

malt [mɔ:lt] *n* Malz *nt.*

maltreat [mæl'tri:t] *vt* mißhandeln.

mammal ['mæml] *n* Säugetier *nt.*

mammoth ['mæməθ] *a* Mammut-, Riesen-.

man [mæn] *n, pl* **men** Mann *m*; *(human race)* der Mensch, die Menschen *pl*; *vt* bemannen.

manage ['mænıdʒ] *vi* zurechtkommen; *vt (control)* führen, leiten; *(cope with)* fertigwerden mit; **to — to** do sth etw schaffen; **—able** *a person, animal* lenksam, fügsam; *object* handlich; **—ment** *(control)* Führung *f,* Leitung *f*; *(directors)* Management *nt*; **—r** Geschäftsführer *m,* (Betriebs)leiter *m*; **—ress** ['mænıdʒə'res] Geschäftsführerin *f*; **—rial** [mænə'dʒıərıəl] *a* leitend; *problem etc* Management-.

managing ['mænıdʒıŋ] *a*: **— director** Betriebsleiter *m.*

mandarin ['mændərın] *n (fruit)* Mandarine *f*; *(Chinese official)* Mandarin *m.*

mandate ['mændeıt] *n* Mandat *nt.*

mandatory ['mændətərı] *a* obligatorisch.

mandolin(e) ['mændəlın] *n* Mandoline *f.*

mane [meın] *n* Mähne *f.*

maneuver [mə'nu:və*] *(US)* =**manoeuvre**.

manful *a,* **—ly** *ad* ['mænful, -fəlı] beherzt; mannhaft.

mangle ['mæŋgl] *vt* verstümmeln.

mango ['mæŋgəu] *n* Mango(pflaume) *f.*

mangrove ['mæŋgrəuv] *n* Mangrove *f.*

mangy ['meındʒı] *a dog* räudig.

manhandle ['mænhændl] *vt* grob behandeln.

manhole ['mænhəul] *n* (Straßen)schacht *m.*

manhood ['mænhud] *n* Mannesalter *nt*; *(manliness)* Männlichkeit *f.*

man-hour ['mæn'auə*] *n* Arbeitsstunde *f.*

manhunt ['mænhʌnt] *n* Fahndung *f.*

mania ['meınıə] *n* *(craze)* Sucht *f,* Manie *f*; *(madness)* Wahn(sinn) *m*; **—c** ['meınıæk] Wahnsinnige(r) *mf,* Verrückte(r) *mf.*

manicure ['mænıkjuə*] *n* Maniküre *f*; *vt* maniküren; **— set** Necessaire *nt.*

manifest ['mænıfest] *vt* offenbaren; *a* offenkundig; **—ation** *(showing)* Ausdruck *m,* Bekundung *f*; *(sign)* Anzeichen *nt*; **—ly** *ad* offenkundig; **—o** [mænı'festəu] Manifest *nt.*

manipulate [mə'nıpjuleıt] *vt* handhaben; *(fig)* manipulieren.

manipulation [mənıpju'leıʃən] *n* Manipulation *f.*

mankind [mæn'kaınd] *n* Menschheit *f.*

manliness ['mænlınəs] *n* Männlichkeit *f.*

manly ['mænlı] *a* männlich; mannhaft.

man-made ['mæn'meıd] *a fibre* künstlich.

manner ['mænə*] *n* Art *f,* Weise *f*; *(style)* Stil *m*; **in such a —** so; **in a — of** speaking sozusagen; **—s** *pl* Manieren *pl*; **—ism** *(of person)*

Angewohnheit f; (of style) Manieriertheit f.

manoeuvrable [məˈnuːvrəbl] a manövrierfähig.

manoeuvre [məˈnuːvə*] vti manövrieren; n (Mil) Feldzug m; (general) Manöver nt, Schachzug m; —s pl Truppenübungen pl, Manöver nt.

manor [ˈmænə*] n Landgut nt; — house Herrenhaus nt.

manpower [ˈmænpauə*] n Arbeitskräfte pl.

manservant [ˈmænsɜːvənt] n Diener m.

mansion [ˈmænʃən] n Herrenhaus nt, Landhaus nt.

manslaughter [ˈmænslɔːtə*] n Totschlag m.

mantelpiece [ˈmæntlpiːs] n Kaminsims m.

mantle [ˈmæntl] n (cloak) lange(r) Umhang m.

manual [ˈmænjuəl] a manuell, Hand-; n Handbuch nt.

manufacture [mænjuˈfæktʃə*] vt herstellen; n Herstellung f; —r Hersteller m.

manure [məˈnjuə*] n Dünger m.

manuscript [ˈmænjuskrɪpt] n Manuskript nt.

many [ˈmenɪ] a viele; as — as 20 sage und schreibe 20; — a good soldier so mancher gute Soldat; —'s the time oft.

map [mæp] n (Land)karte f; (of town) Stadtplan m; vt eine Karte machen von; — out vt (fig) ausarbeiten.

maple [ˈmeɪpl] n Ahorn m.

mar [maː*] vt verderben, beeinträchtigen.

marathon [ˈmærəθən] n (Sport) Marathonlauf m; (fig) Marathon m.

marauder [məˈrɔːdə*] n Plünderer m.

marble [ˈmaːbl] n Marmor m; (for game) Murmel f.

March [maːtʃ] n März m.

march [maːtʃ] vi marschieren; n Marsch m; —-past Vorbeimarsch m.

mare [meə*] n Stute f; —'s nest Windei nt.

margarine [maːdʒəˈriːn] n Margarine f.

margin [ˈmaːdʒɪn] n Rand m; (extra amount) Spielraum m; (Comm) Spanne f; —al a note Rand-; difference etc geringfügig; —ally ad nur wenig.

marigold [ˈmærɪgould] n Ringelblume f.

marijuana [mærɪˈhwaːnə] n Marihuana nt.

marina [məˈriːnə] n Yachthafen m.

marine [məˈriːn] a Meeres-, See-; n (Mil) Marineinfanterist m; (fleet) Marine f; —r [ˈmærɪnə*] n Seemann m.

marionette [mærɪəˈnet] n Marionette f.

marital [ˈmærɪtl] a ehelich, Ehe-.

maritime [ˈmærɪtaɪm] a See-.

marjoram [ˈmaːdʒərəm] n Majoran m.

mark [maːk] n (coin) Mark f; (spot) Fleck m; (scar) Kratzer m; (sign) Zeichen nt; (target) Ziel nt; (Sch) Note f; quick off the — blitzschnell; on your —s auf die Plätze; vt (make mark) Kratzer machen auf (+acc); (indicate) markieren, bezeichnen; (note) sich (dat) merken; exam korrigieren; to — time (lit, fig) auf der Stelle treten; — out vt bestimmen; area abstecken; —ed a deutlich; —edly [ˈmaːkɪdlɪ] ad merklich; —er (in

book) (Lese)zeichen nt; (on road)
Schild nt.

market ['ma:kɪt] n Markt m; (stock
—) Börse f; vt (Comm: new product) auf den Markt bringen; (sell)
vertreiben; —day Markttag m; —
garden (Brit) Handelsgärtnerei f;
—ing Marketing nt; —place
Marktplatz m.

marksman ['ma:ksmən] n Scharf-
schütze m; —ship Treffsicherheit f.

marmalade ['ma:məleɪd] n
Orangenmarmelade f.

maroon [mə'ru:n] vt aussetzen; a
(colour) kastanienbraun.

marquee [ma:'ki:] n große(s) Zelt
nt.

marquess, marquis ['ma:kwɪs] n
Marquis m.

marriage ['mærɪdʒ] n Ehe f;
(wedding) Heirat f; (fig) Verbindung f.

married ['mærɪd] a person verheiratet; couple, life Ehe-.

marrow ['mærəʊ] n (Knochen)-
mark nt; (vegetable) Kürbis m.

marry ['mærɪ] vt (join) trauen;
(take as husband, wife) heiraten;
vi (also get married) heiraten.

marsh [ma:ʃ] n Marsch f,
Sumpfland nt.

marshal ['ma:ʃəl] n (US) Bezirks-
polizeichef m; vt (an)ordnen,
arrangieren.

marshy ['ma:ʃɪ] a sumpfig.

martial ['ma:ʃəl] a kriegerisch; —
law Kriegsrecht nt.

martyr ['ma:tə*] n (lit, fig)
Märtyrer(in f) m; vt zum Märtyrer
machen; —dom Martyrium nt.

marvel ['ma:vəl] n Wunder nt; vi
sich wundern (at über +acc);
—lous, (US) —ous a, —lously, (US)
—ously ad wunderbar.

Marxism ['ma:ksɪzəm] n
Marxismus m.

Marxist ['ma:ksɪst] n Marxist(in f)
m.

marzipan [ma:zɪ'pæn] n Marzipan
nt.

mascara [mæs'ka:rə] n
Wimperntusche f.

mascot ['mæskət] n Maskottchen
nt.

masculine ['mæskjʊlɪn] a männlich; n Maskulinum nt.

masculinity [mæskjʊ'lɪnɪtɪ] n
Männlichkeit f.

mashed [mæʃt] a: — potatoes pl
Kartoffelbrei m or -püree nt.

mask [ma:sk] n (lit, fig) Maske f;
vt maskieren, verdecken.

masochist ['mæzəʊkɪst] n
Masochist(in f) m.

mason ['meɪsn] n (stone—) Steinmetz m; (free—) Freimaurer m;
—ic [mə'sɒnɪk] a Freimaurer-;
—ry Mauerwerk nt.

masquerade [mæskə'reɪd] n
Maskerade f; vi sich maskieren,
sich verkleiden; to — as sich ausgeben als.

mass [mæs] n Masse f; (greater
part) Mehrheit f; (Rel) Messe f;
—es of massenhaft; vt sammeln,
anhäufen; vi sich sammeln.

massacre ['mæsəkə*] n Blutbad
nt; vt niedermetzeln, massakrieren.

massage ['mæsa:ʒ] n Massage f;
vt massieren.

masseur [mæ'sɜ:*] n Masseur m.

masseuse [mæ'sɜ:z] n Masseuse f.

massive ['mæsɪv] a gewaltig,
massiv.

mass media ['mæs'mi:dɪə] npl
Massenmedien pl.

mass-produce ['mæsprə'dju:s] vt
serienmäßig herstellen.

mass production ['mæsprə'dʌk-ʃən] *n* Serienproduktion *f*, Massenproduktion *f*.

mast [maːst] *n* Mast *m*.

master ['maːstə*] *n* Herr *m*; (Naut) Kapitän *m*; (teacher) Lehrer *m*; (artist) Meister *m*; *vt* meistern; language etc beherrschen; —ly a meisterhaft; —mind *n* Kapazität *f*; *vt* geschickt lenken; M— of Arts Magister Artium *m*; —piece Meisterstück *nt*; (Art) Meisterwerk *nt*; — stroke Glanzstück *nt*; —y Können *nt*; to gain — y over sb die Oberhand gewinnen über jdn.

masturbate ['mæstəbeɪt] *vi* masturbieren, onanieren.

masturbation [mæstə'beɪʃən] *n* Masturbation *f*, Onanie *f*.

mat [mæt] *n* Matte *f*; (for table) Untersetzer *m*; *vi* sich verfilzen; *vt* verfilzen.

match [mætʃ] *n* Streichholz *nt*; (sth corresponding) Pendant *nt*; (Sport) Wettkampf *m*; (ball games) Spiel *nt*; it's a good — es paßt gut (for zu); to be a — for sb sich mit jdm messen können; jdm gewachsen sein; he's a good — er ist eine gute Partie (*vt* be alike, suit) passen zu; (equal) gleichkommen (+dat); (Sport) antreten lassen; *vi* zusammenpassen; —box Streichholzschachtel *f*; —ing a passend; —less a unvergleichlich; —maker Kuppler(in *f*) *m*.

mate [meɪt] *n* (companion) Kamerad *m*; (spouse) Lebensgefährte *m*; (of animal) Weibchen *nt*/Männchen *nt*; (Naut) Schiffsoffizier *m*; *vi* (chess) (schach)matt sein; (animals) sich paaren; *vt* (chess) matt setzen.

material [mə'tɪərɪəl] *n* Material *nt*; (for book, cloth) Material *nt*, Stoff *m*; a (important) wesentlich; damage Sach-; comforts etc materiell; —s *pl* Materialien *pl*; —istic a materialistisch; —ize *vi* sich verwirklichen, zustande kommen; —ly ad grundlegend.

maternal [mə'tɜːnl] a mütterlich, Mutter-; — grandmother Großmutter mütterlicherseits.

maternity [mə'tɜːnɪti] a Schwangeren-; — dress Umstandskleid *nt*; — benefit Wochen-.

matey ['meɪtɪ] a (Brit col) kameradschaftlich.

mathematical a, —ly ad [mæθə'mætɪkəl, -ɪ] mathematisch.

mathematician [mæθəmə'tɪʃən] *n* Mathematiker *m*.

mathematics [mæθə'mætɪks] *n* Mathematik *f*.

maths [mæθs] *n* Mathe *f*.

matinée ['mætɪneɪ] *n* Matinee *f*.

mating ['meɪtɪŋ] *n* Paarung *f*; — call Lockruf *m*.

matins ['mætɪnz] *n* (Früh)mette *f*.

matriarchal [meɪtrɪ'ɑːkl] a matriarchalisch.

matrimonial [mætrɪ'məʊnɪəl] a ehelich, Ehe-.

matrimony ['mætrɪmənɪ] *n* Ehestand *m*.

matron ['meɪtrən] *n* (Med) Oberin *f*; (Sch) Hausmutter *f*; —ly a matronenhaft.

matt [mæt] a paint matt.

matter ['mætə*] *n* (substance) Materie *f*; (affair) Sache *f*; Angelegenheit *f*; (content) Inhalt *m*; (Med) Eiter *m*; *vi* darauf ankommen; it doesn't — es macht nichts; no — how/what egal wie/was; what is the —? was ist los?; **as a — of fact** eigentlich; **—-of-fact** a sachlich, nüchtern.

mattress ['mætrəs] n Matratze f.

mature [mə'tjuə*] a reif; vi reif werden.

maturity [mə'tjuərɪtɪ] n Reife f.

maudlin ['mɔːdlɪn] a weinerlich; gefühlsduselig.

maul [mɔːl] vt übel zurichten.

mausoleum [mɔːsə'liːəm] n Mausoleum nt.

mauve [məʊv] a mauve.

mawkish ['mɔːkɪʃ] a kitschig; taste süßlich.

maxi ['mæksɪ] pref Maxi-.

maxim ['mæksɪm] n Maxime f.

maximize ['mæksɪmaɪz] vt maximieren.

maximum ['mæksɪməm] a höchste(r, s), Höchst-, Maximal-; n Höchstgrenze f, Maximum nt.

May [meɪ] n Mai m.

may [meɪ] v aux (be possible) können; (have permission) dürfen; **I — come** ich komme vielleicht, es kann sein, daß ich komme; **we — as well go** wir können ruhig gehen; **— you be very happy** ich hoffe, ihr seid glücklich; **—be** ad vielleicht.

Mayday ['meɪdeɪ] n (message) SOS nt.

mayonnaise [meɪə'neɪz] n Mayonnaise f.

mayor [mɛə*] n Bürgermeister m; **—ess** (wife) (die) Frau f Bürgermeister; (lady —) Bürgermeisterin f.

maypole ['meɪpəʊl] n Maibaum m.

maze [meɪz] n (lit) Irrgarten m; (fig) Wirrwarr m; **to be in a —** (fig) durcheinander sein.

me [miː] pron (acc) mich; (dat) mir; **it's —** ich bin's.

meadow ['medəʊ] n Wiese f.

meagre, (US) **meager** ['miːgə*] a dürftig, spärlich.

meal [miːl] n Essen nt, Mahlzeit f; (grain) Schrotmehl nt; **to have a — essen** (gehen); **—time** Essenszeit f; **—y-mouthed** a: **to be —y-mouthed** wie d(a)rum herumreden.

mean [miːn] a (stingy) geizig; (spiteful) gemein; (shabby) armselig, schäbig; (average) durchschnittlich, Durchschnitts-; irreg vt (signify) bedeuten; vi (intend) vorhaben, beabsichtigen; (be resolved) entschlossen sein; **he —s well** er meint es gut; **I — it!** ich meine das ernst!; **do you — me?** meinen Sie mich?; **it —s nothing to me** es sagt mir nichts; n (average) Durchschnitt m; **—s** pl Mittel pl; (wealth) Vermögen nt; **by —s of** durch; **by all —s** selbstverständlich; **by no —s** keineswegs.

meander [mɪ'ændə*] vi sich schlängeln.

meaning ['miːnɪŋ] n Bedeutung f; (of life) Sinn m; **—ful** a bedeutungsvoll; life sinnvoll; **—less** a sinnlos.

meanness ['miːnnəs] n (stinginess) Geiz m; (spitefulness) Gemeinheit f; (shabbiness) Schäbigkeit f.

meantime ['miːntaɪm] ad, **meanwhile** ['miːnwaɪl] ad inzwischen, mittlerweile; **for the —** vorerst.

measles ['miːzlz] n Masern pl; **German —** Röteln pl.

measly ['miːzlɪ] a (col) poplig.

measurable ['meʒərəbl] a meßbar.

measure ['meʒə*] vti messen; n Maß nt; (step) Maßnahme f; **to be a — of sth** etw erkennen lassen; **—d** a (slow) gemessen; **—ment** (way of measuring) Messung f; (amount measured) Maß nt.

meat [mi:t] *n* Fleisch *nt*; **-y** *a (lit)* fleischig; *(fig)* gehaltvoll.

mechanic [mɪ'kænɪk] *n* Mechaniker *m*; **-s** Mechanik *f*; **-al** *a* mechanisch.

mechanism ['mekənɪzəm] *n* Mechanismus *m*.

mechanization [mekənaɪ'zeɪʃən] *n* Mechanisierung *f*.

mechanize ['mekənaɪz] *vt* mechanisieren.

medal ['medl] *n* Medaille *f*; *(decoration)* Orden *m*; **-lion** [mɪ'dælɪən] Medaillon *nt*; **-list**, *(US)* **-ist** Medaillengewinner(in *f*) *m*.

meddle ['medl] *vi* sich einmischen *(in* in *+acc)*; *(tamper)* hantieren *(with* an *+dat)*; **- with sb** sich mit jdm einlassen.

media ['mi:dɪə] *npl* Medien *pl*.

mediate ['mi:dɪeɪt] *vi* vermitteln.

mediation [mi:dɪ'eɪʃən] *n* Vermittlung *f*.

mediator ['mi:dɪeɪtə*] *n* Vermittler *m*.

medical ['medɪkəl] *a* medizinisch; Medizin-; ärztlich; *n* (ärztliche) Untersuchung *f*.

medicated ['medɪkeɪtɪd] *a* medizinisch.

medicinal [me'dɪsɪnl] *a* medizinisch, Heil-.

medicine ['medsɪn] *n* Medizin *f*; *(drugs)* Arznei *f*; **- chest** Hausapotheke *f*.

medieval [medɪ'i:vəl] *a* mittelalterlich.

mediocre [mi:dɪ'əʊkə*] *a* mittelmäßig.

mediocrity [mi:dɪ'ɒkrɪtɪ] *n* Mittelmäßigkeit *f*; *(person also)* kleine(r) Geist *m*.

meditate ['medɪteɪt] *vi* nachdenken

(on über *+acc)*; meditieren *(on* über *+acc)*.

meditation [medɪ'teɪʃən] *n* Nachsinnen *nt*; Meditation *f*.

medium ['mi:dɪəm] *a* mittlere(r, s), Mittel-, mittel-; *n* Mitte *f*; *(means)* Mittel *nt*; *(person)* Medium *nt*.

medley ['medlɪ] *n* Gemisch *nt*.

meek *a*, **-ly** *ad* [mi:k, -lɪ] sanft(mütig); *(pej)* duckmäuserisch.

meet [mi:t] *irreg vt (encounter)* treffen, begegnen *(+dat)*; *(by arrangement)* sich treffen mit; *(difficulties* stoßen auf *(+acc)*; *(become acquainted with)* kennenlernen; *(fetch)* abholen; *(join)* zusammentreffen mit; *(river)* fließen in *(+acc)*; *(satisfy)* entsprechen *(+dat)*; *debt* bezahlen; **pleased to - you!** angenehm!; *vi* sich treffen; *(become acquainted)* sich kennenlernen; *(join)* sich treffen; *(rivers)* ineinanderfließen; *(roads)* zusammenlaufen; **- with** *vt problems* stoßen auf *(+acc)*; *(US: people)* zusammentreffen mit; **-ing** Treffen *nt*; *(business -)* Besprechung *f*, Konferenz *f*; *(discussion)* Sitzung *f*; *(assembly)* Versammlung *f*; **-ing place** Treffpunkt *m*.

megaphone ['megəfəʊn] *n* Megaphon *nt*.

melancholy ['melənkəlɪ] *n* Melancholie *f*; *a person* melancholisch, schwermütig; *sight, event* traurig.

mellow ['meləʊ] *a* mild, weich; *fruit* reif, weich; *(fig)* gesetzt; *vi* reif werden.

melodious [mɪ'ləʊdɪəs] *a* wohlklingend.

melodrama ['meləʊdrɑ:mə] *n* Melodrama *nt*; **-tic** [meləʊdrə'mætɪk] *a* melodramatisch.

melody ['melədɪ] n Melodie f.

melon ['melən] n Melone f.

melt [melt] vi schmelzen; (anger) verfliegen; vt schmelzen; — away vi dahinschmelzen; — down vt einschmelzen; —ing point Schmelzpunkt m; —ing pot (fig) Schmelztiegel m; to be in the —ing pot in der Schwebe sein.

member ['membə*] n Mitglied nt; (of tribe, species) Angehörige(r) m; (Anat) Glied nt; —ship Mitgliedschaft f.

membrane ['membreɪn] n Membrane f.

memento [mə'mentəʊ] n Andenken nt.

memo ['meməʊ] n Notiz f; Mitteilung f.

memoirs ['memwɑ:*z] npl Memoiren pl.

memorable ['memərəbl] a denkwürdig.

memorandum [memə'rændəm] n Notiz f; Mitteilung f; (Pol) Memorandum nt.

memorial [mɪ'mɔ:rɪəl] n Denkmal nt; a Gedenk-.

memorize ['memərɑɪz] vt sich einprägen.

memory ['memərɪ] n Gedächtnis nt; (of computer) Speicher m; (sth recalled) Erinnerung f; in — of zur Erinnerung an (+acc); from — aus dem Kopf.

men [men] npl of **man.**

menace ['menɪs] n Drohung f; Gefahr f; vt bedrohen.

menacing a, —ly ad ['menɪsɪŋ, -lɪ] drohend.

ménage [me'nɑ:ʒ] n Haushalt m.

menagerie [mɪ'nædʒərɪ] n Tierschau f.

mend [mend] vt reparieren, flicken; n ausgebesserte Stelle f; on the — auf dem Wege der Besserung.

menial ['mi:nɪəl] a niedrig, untergeordnet.

meningitis [menɪn'dʒɑɪtɪs] n Hirnhautentzündung f, Meningitis f.

menopause ['menəʊpɔ:z] n Wechseljahre pl, Menopause f.

menstrual ['menstruəl] a Menstruations-.

menstruate ['menstrʊeɪt] vi menstruieren.

menstruation [menstrʊ'eɪʃən] n Menstruation f.

mental ['mentl] a geistig, Geistes-; arithmetic Kopf-; hospital Nerven-; cruelty seelisch; (col: abnormal) verrückt; —ity [men'tælɪtɪ] Mentalität f; —ly ad geistig; —ly ill geisteskrank.

mentholated ['menθəletɪd] a Menthol-.

mention ['menʃən] n Erwähnung f; vt erwähnen; names nennen; don't — it! bitte (sehr), gern geschehen.

menu ['menju:] n Speisekarte f; (food) Speisen pl.

mercantile ['mɜ:kəntaɪl] a Handels-.

mercenary ['mɜ:sɪnərɪ] a person geldgierig; (Mil) Söldner-; n Söldner m.

merchandise ['mɜ:tʃəndaɪz] n (Handels)ware f.

merchant ['mɜ:tʃənt] n Kaufmann m; a Handels-; — navy Handelsmarine f.

merciful ['mɜ:sɪful] a gnädig, barmherzig; —ly ['mɜ:sɪfəlɪ] ad gnädig; (fortunately) glücklicherweise.

merciless a, —ly ['mɜ:sɪləs, -lɪ] erbarmungslos.

mercurial [mɜːˈkjuərɪəl] a quecksilbrig, Quecksilber-.

mercury [ˈmɜːkjurɪ] n Quecksilber nt.

mercy [ˈmɜːsɪ] n Erbarmen nt; Gnade f; (blessing) Segen m; at the — of ausgeliefert (+dat).

mere a, —ly ad [mɪə*, ˈmɪəlɪ] bloß.

merge [mɜːdʒ] vt verbinden; (Comm) fusionieren; vi verschmelzen; (roads) zusammenlaufen; (Comm) fusionieren; to — into übergehen in (+acc); —r (Comm) Fusion f.

meridian [məˈrɪdɪən] n Meridian m.

meringue [məˈræŋ] n Baiser nt, Schaumgebäck nt.

merit [ˈmerɪt] n Verdienst nt; (advantage) Vorzug m; to judge on — nach Leistung beurteilen; vt verdienen.

mermaid [ˈmɜːmeɪd] n Wassernixe f, Meerjungfrau f.

merrily [ˈmerɪlɪ] ad lustig.

merriment [ˈmerɪmənt] n Fröhlichkeit f; (laughter) Gelächter nt.

merry [ˈmerɪ] a fröhlich; (col) angeheitert; **—-go-round** Karussell nt.

mesh [meʃ] n Masche f; vi (gears) ineinandergreifen.

mesmerize [ˈmezməraɪz] vt hypnotisieren; (fig) faszinieren.

mess [mes] n Unordnung f; (dirt) Schmutz m; (trouble) Schwierigkeiten pl; (Mil) Messe f; to look a — fürchterlich aussehen; to make a — of sth etw verpfuschen; — about vi (tinker with) herummurksen (with an +dat); (play fool) herumalbern; (do nothing in particular) herumgammeln; — up vt verpfuschen; (make untidy) in Unordnung bringen.

message [ˈmesɪdʒ] n Mitteilung f, Nachricht f; to get the — kapieren.

messenger [ˈmesɪndʒə*] n Bote m.

messy [ˈmesɪ] a schmutzig; (untidy) unordentlich.

metabolism [meˈtæbəlɪzəm] n Stoffwechsel m.

metal [ˈmetl] n Metall nt; **—lic** [mɪˈtælɪk] a metallisch; **—lurgy** [meˈtælədʒɪ] Metallurgie f.

metamorphosis [metəˈmɔːfəsɪs] n Metamorphose f.

metaphor [ˈmetəfɔː*] n Metapher f; **—ical** [metəˈfɒrɪkəl] a bildlich, metaphorisch.

metaphysics [metəˈfɪzɪks] n Metaphysik f.

meteor [ˈmiːtɪə*] n Meteor m; **—ic** [miːtɪˈɒrɪk] a meteorisch, Meteor-; **—ite** Meteorit m; **—ological** [miːtɪərəˈlɒdʒɪkəl] a meteorologisch; **—ology** [miːtɪəˈrɒlədʒɪ] Meteorologie f.

meter [ˈmiːtə*] n Zähler m; (US) = **metre**.

method [ˈmeθəd] n Methode f; **—ical** [mɪˈθɒdɪkəl] a methodisch; **—ology** [meθəˈdɒlədʒɪ] Methodik f.

methylated spirit [ˈmeθɪleɪtɪdˈspɪrɪt] n (also **meths**) (Brenn)spiritus m.

meticulous [mɪˈtɪkjuləs] a (über)genau.

metre [ˈmiːtə*] n Meter m or nt; (verse) Metrum nt.

metric [ˈmetrɪk] a (also **—al**) metrisch; **—ation** Umstellung f auf das Dezimalsystem; **— system** Dezimalsystem nt.

metronome [ˈmetrənəum] n Metronom nt.

metropolis [meˈtrɒpəlɪs] n Metropole f.

mettle ['metl] n Mut m.

mezzanine ['mezəni:n] n Hochparterre nt.

miaow [mi:'au] vi miauen.

mice [mais] npl of mouse.

mickey ['mɪkɪ] n: to take the — out of sb (col) jdn auf den Arm nehmen.

microbe ['maikrəub] n Mikrobe f.

microfilm ['maikrəufilm] n Mikrofilm m; vt auf Mikrofilm aufnehmen.

microphone ['maikrəfəun] n Mikrophon nt.

microscope ['maikrəskəup] n Mikroskop nt.

microscopic [maikrə'skɒpik] a mikroskopisch.

mid [mid] a mitten in (+dat); in the — eighties Mitte der achtziger Jahre; in — course mittendrin.

midday ['mɪdeɪ] n Mittag m.

middle ['mɪdl] n Mitte f; (waist) Taille f; in the — of mitten in (+dat); a mittlere(r, s), Mittel-; —aged a mittleren Alters; the M-Ages pl das Mittelalter; —class Mittelstand m or -klasse f; a Mittelstands-, Mittelklassen-; the M-East der Nahe Osten; —man (Comm) Zwischenhändler m; —name zweiter Vorname m; —of-the-road a gemäßigt.

middling ['mɪdlɪŋ] a mittelmäßig.

midge [mɪdʒ] n Mücke f.

midget ['mɪdʒɪt] n Liliputaner(in f) m; a Kleinst-.

midnight ['mɪdnaɪt] n Mitternacht f.

midriff ['mɪdrɪf] n Taille f.

midst [mɪdst] n in the — of persons mitten unter (+dat); things mitten in (+dat); in our — unter uns.

midsummer ['mɪd'sʌmə*] n Hoch-

sommer m; M—'s Day Sommersonnenwende f.

midway ['mɪd'weɪ] ad auf halbem Wege; a Mittel-.

midweek ['mɪd'wi:k] a, ad in der Mitte der Woche.

midwife ['mɪdwaɪf] n Hebamme f; —ry ['mɪdwɪfərɪ] Geburtshilfe f.

midwinter ['mɪd'wɪntə*] n tiefste(r) Winter m.

might [maɪt] n Macht f, Kraft f; pt of may; I — come ich komme vielleicht; —ily ad mächtig; —n't = might not; —y, a mächtig.

migraine ['mi:greɪn] n Migräne f.

migrant ['maɪgrənt] n (bird) Zugvogel m; (worker) Saison- or Wanderarbeiter m; a Wander-; bird Zug-.

migrate [maɪ'greɪt] vi (ab)wandern; (birds) (fort)ziehen.

migration [maɪ'greɪʃən] n Wanderung f, Zug m.

mike [maɪk] n = microphone.

mild [maɪld] a mild; medicine, interest leicht; person sanft.

mildew ['mɪldju:] n (on plants) Mehltau m; (on food) Schimmel m.

mildly ['maɪldlɪ] ad leicht; to put it — gelinde gesagt.

mildness ['maɪldnəs] n Milde f.

mile [maɪl] n Meile f; —age Meilenzahl f; —stone (lit, fig) Meilenstein m.

milieu ['mi:ljɜ:] n Milieu nt.

militant ['mɪlɪtənt] n Militante(r) mf; a militant.

militarism ['mɪlɪtərɪzəm] n Militarismus m.

military ['mɪlɪtərɪ] a militärisch, Militär-, Wehr-; n Militär nt.

militate ['mɪlɪteɪt] vi sprechen; entgegenwirken (against dat).

militia [mɪˈlɪʃə] n Miliz f, Bürgerwehr f.

milk [mɪlk] n Milch f; vt (lit, fig) melken; — chocolate Milchschokolade f; —ing Melken nt; —man Milchmann m; — shake Milchmixgetränk nt; M—y Way Milchstraße f.

mill [mɪl] n Mühle f; (factory) Fabrik f; vt mahlen; vi (move around) umherlaufen; —ed a gemahlen.

millennium [mɪˈlenɪəm] n Jahrtausend nt.

miller [ˈmɪlə*] n Müller m.

millet [ˈmɪlɪt] n Hirse f.

milligram(me) [ˈmɪlɪgræm] n Milligramm nt.

millilitre, (US) **—liter** [ˈmɪlɪliːtə*] n Milliliter m.

millimetre, (US) **—meter** [ˈmɪlɪmiːtə*] n Millimeter m.

milliner [ˈmɪlɪnə*] n Hutmacher(in f) m; —y (hats) Hüte pl, Modewaren pl; (business) Hutgeschäft nt.

million [ˈmɪljən] n Million f; —aire [mɪljəˈneə*] n Millionär(in f) m.

millwheel [ˈmɪlwiːl] n Mühlrad nt.

milometer [maɪˈlɒmɪtə*] n Kilometerzähler m.

mime [maɪm] n Pantomime f; (actor) Mime m, Mimin f; vti mimen.

mimic [ˈmɪmɪk] n Mimiker m; vt nachahmen; —ry [ˈmɪmɪkrɪ] Nachahmung f; (Biol) Mimikry f.

mince [mɪns] vt (zer)hacken; vi (walk) trippeln; n (meat) Hackfleisch nt; —meat süße Pastetenfüllung f; — pie gefüllte (süße) Pastete f.

mincing [ˈmɪnsɪŋ] a manner affektiert.

mind [maɪnd] n Verstand m, Geist m; (opinion) Meinung f; on my — auf dem Herzen; to my — meiner Meinung nach; to be out of one's — wahnsinnig sein; to bear or keep in — bedenken, nicht vergessen; to change one's — es sich (dat) anders überlegen; to make up one's — sich entschließen; to have sth in — an etw (acc) denken; etw beabsichtigen; to have a good — to do sth große Lust haben, etw zu tun; vt aufpassen auf (+acc); (object to) etwas haben gegen; vi etwas dagegen haben; I don't —! the rain der Regen macht mir nichts aus; do you — if I ... macht es Ihnen etwas aus, wenn ich ...; do you —! na hören Sie mal!; never —! macht nichts!; '— the step' 'Vorsicht Stufe'; — your own business kümmern Sie sich um Ihre eigenen Angelegenheiten; —ful a achtsam (of auf +acc); —less a achtlos, dumm.

mine [maɪn] poss pron meine(r, s); n (coal—) Bergwerk nt; (Mil) Mine f; (source) Fundgrube f; vt abbauen; (Mil) verminen; vi Bergbau betreiben; — for sth etw gewinnen; — detector Minensuchgerät nt; —field Minenfeld nt; —r Bergarbeiter m.

mineral [ˈmɪnərəl] a mineralisch, Mineral-; n Mineral nt; — water Mineralwasser nt.

minesweeper [ˈmaɪnswiːpə*] n Minensuchboot nt.

mingle [ˈmɪŋgl] vt vermischen; vi sich mischen (with unter +acc).

mingy [ˈmɪndʒɪ] a (col) knickerig.

mini [ˈmɪnɪ] pref Mini-, Klein-.

miniature [ˈmɪnɪtʃə*] a Miniatur-, Klein-; n Miniatur f; in — en miniature.

minibus ['mɪnɪbʌs] n Kleinbus m, Minibus m.

minicab ['mɪnɪkæb] n Kleintaxi nt.

minim ['mɪnɪm] n halbe Note f.

minimal ['mɪnɪml] a kleinste(r, s), minimal, Mindest-.

minimize ['mɪnɪmaɪz] vt auf das Mindestmaß beschränken; (belittle) herabsetzen.

minimum ['mɪnɪməm] n Minimum nt; a Mindest-.

mining ['maɪnɪŋ] n Bergbau m; a Bergbau-, Berg-.

minion ['mɪnjən] n (pej) Trabant m.

miniskirt ['mɪnɪskɜ:t] n Minirock m.

minister ['mɪnɪstə*] n (Pol) Minister m; (Eccl) Geistliche(r) m, Pfarrer m; --ial [mɪnɪs'tɪərɪəl] a ministeriell, Minister-.

ministry ['mɪnɪstrɪ] n (government body) Ministerium nt; (Eccl) (office) geistliche(s) Amt nt; (all ministers) Geistlichkeit f.

mink [mɪŋk] n Nerz m.

minnow ['mɪnəʊ] n Eiritze f.

minor ['maɪnə*] a kleiner; operation leicht; problem, poet unbedeutend; (Mus) Moll; Smith — Smith der Jüngere; n (Brit: under 18) Minderjährige(r) mf; --ity [maɪ'nɒrɪtɪ] Minderheit f.

minster ['mɪnstə*] n Münster nt, Kathedrale f.

minstrel ['mɪnstrəl] n (Hist) Spielmann m, Minnesänger m.

mint [mɪnt] n Minze f; (sweet) Pfefferminzbonbon nt; (place) Münzstätte f; a condition (wie) neu; stamp ungestempelt; — sauce Minzsoße f.

minuet [mɪnjʊ'et] n Menuett nt.

minus ['maɪnəs] n Minuszeichen nt; (amount) Minusbetrag m; prep minus, weniger.

minute [maɪ'nju:t] a winzig, sehr klein; (detailed) minuziös; ['mɪnɪt] n Minute f; (moment) Augenblick m; —s pl Protokoll nt; —ly [maɪ'nju:tlɪ] ad (in detail) genau.

miracle ['mɪrəkl] n Wunder nt; — play geistliche(s) Drama nt.

miraculous [mɪ'rækjʊləs] a wunderbar; —ly ad auf wunderbare Weise.

mirage ['mɪrɑ:ʒ] n Luftspiegelung f, Fata Morgana f.

mirror ['mɪrə*] n Spiegel m; vt (wider)spiegeln.

mirth [mɜ:θ] n Freude f; Heiterheit f.

misadventure [mɪsəd'ventʃə*] n Mißgeschick nt, Unfall m.

misanthropist [mɪ'zænθrəpɪst] n Menschenfeind m.

misapprehension ['mɪsæprɪ'henʃən] n Mißverständnis nt; to be under the — that . . . irrtümlicherweise annehmen, daß. . .

misappropriate ['mɪsə'prəʊprɪeɪt] vt funds veruntreuen.

misappropriation ['mɪsəprəʊprɪ'eɪʃən] n Veruntreuung f.

misbehave ['mɪsbɪ'heɪv] vi sich schlecht benehmen.

miscalculate ['mɪs'kælkjʊleɪt] vt falsch berechnen.

miscalculation ['mɪskælkjʊ'leɪʃən] n Rechenfehler m.

miscarriage ['mɪskærɪdʒ] n (Med) Fehlgeburt f; — of justice Fehlurteil nt.

miscellaneous [mɪsɪ'leɪnɪəs] a verschieden.

miscellany [mɪ'selənɪ] n (bunte) Sammlung f.

mischance [mɪs'tʃɑ:ns] n Mißgeschick nt.

25

mischief ['mɪstʃɪf] *n* Unfug *m*; *(harm)* Schaden *m*.

mischievous *a*, **-ly** *ad* ['mɪstʃɪvəs, -lɪ] *person* durchtrieben; *glance* verschmitzt; *rumour* bösartig.

misconception ['mɪskən'sepʃən] *n* fälschliche Annahme *f*.

misconduct [mɪs'kɒndʌkt] *n* Vergehen *nt*.

misconstrue ['mɪskən'stru:] *vt* mißverstehen.

miscount ['mɪs'kaʊnt] *vt* falsch (be)rechnen.

misdemeanour, *(US)* **misdemeanor** [mɪsdɪ'mi:nə*] *n* Vergehen *nt*.

misdirect ['mɪsdɪ'rekt] *vt* *person* irreleiten; *letter* fehlleiten.

miser ['maɪzə*] *n* Geizhals *m*.

miserable ['mɪzərəbl] *a* *(unhappy)* unglücklich; *headache, weather* fürchterlich; *(poor)* elend; *(contemptible)* erbärmlich.

miserably ['mɪzərəblɪ] *ad* unglücklich; *fail* kläglich.

miserly ['maɪzəlɪ] *a* geizig.

misery ['mɪzərɪ] *n* Elend *nt*, Qual *f*.

misfire ['mɪs'faɪə*] *vi* *(gun)* versagen; *(engine)* fehlzünden; *(plan)* fehlgehen.

misfit ['mɪsfɪt] *n* Außenseiter *m*.

misfortune [mɪs'fɔ:tʃən] *n* Unglück *nt*.

misgiving [mɪs'gɪvɪŋ] *n (often pl)* Befürchtung *f*, Bedenken *pl*.

misguided [mɪs'gaɪdɪd] *a* fehlgeleitet; *opinions* irrig.

mishandle [mɪs'hændl] *vt* falsch handhaben.

mishap ['mɪshæp] *n* Unglück *nt*; *(slight)* Panne *f*.

mishear ['mɪs'hɪə*] *vt irreg* mißverstehen.

misinform [mɪsɪn'fɔ:m] *vt* falsch unterrichten.

misinterpret ['mɪsɪn'tɜ:prɪt] *vt* falsch auffassen; **—ation** ['mɪsɪntɜ:prɪ'teɪʃən] falsche Auslegung *f*.

misjudge [mɪs'dʒʌdʒ] *vt* falsch beurteilen.

mislay [mɪs'leɪ] *vt irreg* verlegen.

mislead [mɪs'li:d] *vt irreg (deceive)* irreführen; **—ing** *a* irreführend.

mismanage ['mɪs'mænɪdʒ] *vt* schlecht verwalten; **—ment** Mißwirtschaft *f*.

misnomer [mɪs'nəʊmə*] *n* falsche Bezeichnung *f*.

misogynist [mɪ'sɒdʒɪnɪst] *n* Weiberfeind *m*.

misplace ['mɪs'pleɪs] *vt* verlegen.

misprint ['mɪsprɪnt] *n* Druckfehler *m*.

mispronounce ['mɪsprə'naʊns] *vt* falsch aussprechen.

misread ['mɪs'ri:d] *vt irreg* falsch lesen.

misrepresent ['mɪsreprɪ'zent] *vt* falsch darstellen.

miss [mɪs] *vt (fail to hit, catch)* verfehlen; *(not notice)* verpassen; *(be too late)* versäumen, verpassen; *(omit)* auslassen; *(regret the absence of)* vermissen; **I — you** du fehlst mir; *vi* fehlen; *n (shot)* Fehlschuß *m*; *(failure)* Fehlschlag *m*; *(title)* Fräulein *nt*.

missal ['mɪsəl] *n* Meßbuch *nt*.

misshapen ['mɪs'ʃeɪpən] *a* mißgestaltet.

missile ['mɪsaɪl] *n* Geschoß *nt*, Rakete *f*.

missing ['mɪsɪŋ] *a person* vermißt; *thing* fehlend; **to be —** fehlen.

mission ['mɪʃən] *n* (work) Auftrag *m*, Mission *f*; (people) Delegation *f*; (Rel) Mission *f*; —**ary** Missionar(in *f*) *m*.

misspent ['mɪs'spent] *a youth* vergeudet.

mist [mɪst] *n* Dunst *m*, Nebel *m*; *vi* (also — over, — up) sich beschlagen.

mistake [mɪs'teɪk] *n* Fehler *m*; *vt irreg* (misunderstand) mißverstehen; (mix up) verwechseln (for mit); —**n** idea falsch; —**n** identity Verwechslung *f*; to be —**n** sich irren.

mister ['mɪstə*] *n* (abbr Mr) Herr *m*.

mistletoe ['mɪsltəʊ] *n* Mistel *f*.

mistranslation ['mɪstræns'leɪʃən] *n* falsche Übersetzung *f*.

mistreat [mɪs'triːt] *vt* schlecht behandeln.

mistress ['mɪstrɪs] *n* (teacher) Lehrerin *f*; (in house) Herrin *f*; (lover) Geliebte *f*; (abbr Mrs) Frau *f*.

mistrust [mɪs'trʌst] *vt* mißtrauen (+ dat).

misty ['mɪstɪ] *a* neblig.

misunderstand ['mɪsʌndə'stænd] *vti irreg* mißverstehen, falsch verstehen; —**ing** Mißverständnis *nt*; (disagreement) Meinungsverschiedenheit *f*.

misunderstood ['mɪsʌndə'stʊd] *a person* unverstanden.

misuse ['mɪs'juːs] *n* falsche(r) Gebrauch *m*; ['mɪs'juːz] *vt* falsch gebrauchen.

mite [maɪt] *n* Milbe *f*; (fig) bißchen *nt*.

mitigate ['mɪtɪgeɪt] *vt pain* lindern; *punishment* mildern.

mitre, (US) **miter** ['maɪtə*] *n* (Eccl) Mitra *f*.

mitt(en) ['mɪt(n)] *n* Fausthandschuh *m*.

mix [mɪks] *vt* (blend) (ver)mischen; *vi* (liquids) sich (ver)mischen lassen; (people) (get on) sich vertragen; (associate) Kontakt haben; he —**es** well er ist kontaktfreudig; *n* (mixture) Mischung *f*; —**ed** *a* gemischt; —**er** (for food) Mixer *m*; —**ture** (assortment) Mischung *f*; (Med) Saft *m*; —**up** Durcheinander *nt*, Verwechslung *f*; — up *vt* (mix) zusammenmischen; (confuse) verwechseln; to be —**ed** up in sth in etw (dat) verwickelt sein; —**ed-up** *a papers, person* durcheinander.

moan [məʊn] *n* Stöhnen *nt*; (complaint) Klage *f*; *vi* stöhnen; (complain) maulen; —**ing** Stöhnen *nt*; Gemaule *nt*.

moat [məʊt] *n* (Burg)graben·*m*.

mob [mɒb] *n* Mob *m*; (the masses) Pöbel *m*; *vt star* herfallen über (+ acc).

mobile ['məʊbaɪl] *a* beweglich; *library etc* fahrbar; *n* (decoration) Mobile *nt*; — home Wohnwagen *m*.

mobility [məʊ'bɪlɪtɪ] *n* Beweglichkeit *f*.

moccasin ['mɒkəsɪn] *n* Mokassin *m*.

mock [mɒk] *vt* verspotten; (defy) trotzen (+ dat); *a* Schein-; —**ery** Spott *m*; (person) Gespött *nt*; —**ing** *a tone* spöttisch; —**ing bird** Spottdrossel *f*; —**up** Modell *nt*.

mode [məʊd] *n* (Art *f* und) Weise *f*.

model ['mɒdl] *n* Modell *nt*; (example) Vorbild *nt*; (in fashion) Mannequin *nt*; *vt* (make) formen, modellieren, bilden; (clothes) vorführen; a *railway* Modell-; *(perfect)* Muster-; vorbildlich; **—ling**, (US) **—ing** ['mɒdlɪŋ] (— *making*) Basteln *nt*.

moderate ['mɒdərət] a gemäßigt; *(fairly good)* mittelmäßig; *n (Pol)* Gemäßigte(r) *mf*; ['mɒdəreɪt] *vi* sich mäßigen; *vt* mäßigen; **—ly** ['mɒdərətlɪ] *ad* mäßig.

moderation [mɒdə'reɪʃən] *n* Mäßigung *f*; **in —** mit Maßen.

modern ['mɒdən] a modern; *history, languages* neuere(r, s); *Greek etc* Neu-; **—ity** [mɒ'dɜːnɪtɪ] Modernität *f*; **—ization** [mɒdənaɪ'zeɪʃən] Modernisierung *f*; **—ize** *vt* modernisieren.

modest a, **—ly** ad ['mɒdɪst, -lɪ] *attitude* bescheiden; *meal, home* einfach; *(chaste)* schamhaft; **—y** Bescheidenheit *f*; *(chastity)* Schamgefühl *nt*.

modicum ['mɒdɪkəm] *n* bißchen *nt*.

modification [mɒdɪfɪ'keɪʃən] *n* (Ab)änderung *f*.

modify ['mɒdɪfaɪ] *vt* abändern; *(Gram)* modifizieren.

modulation [mɒdjʊ'leɪʃən] *n* Modulation *f*.

module ['mɒdjʊl] *n* (Raum)kapsel *f*.

mohair ['məʊhɛə*] *n* Mohair *m*; a Mohair-.

moist [mɔɪst] a feucht; **—en** ['mɔɪsn] *vt* befeuchten; **—ure** Feuchtigkeit *f*; **—urizer** Feuchtigkeitscreme *f*.

molar ['məʊlə*] *n* Backenzahn *m*.

molasses [mə'læsɪz] *npl* Melasse *f*.

mold [məʊld] (US) = **mould**.

mole [məʊl] *n (spot)* Leberfleck *m*; *(animal)* Maulwurf *m*; *(pier)* Mole *f*.

molecular [mə'lekjʊlə*] a molekular, Molekular-.

molecule [mɒlɪkjuːl] *n* Molekül *nt*.

molest [məʊ'lest] *vt* belästigen.

mollusc ['mɒləsk] *n* Molluske *f*, Weichtier *nt*.

mollycoddle ['mɒlɪkɒdl] *vt* verhätscheln.

molt [məʊlt] (US) = **moult**.

molten ['məʊltən] a geschmolzen.

moment ['məʊmənt] *n* Moment *m*, Augenblick *m*; *(importance)* Tragweite *f*; **— of truth** Stunde *f* der Wahrheit; **any —** jeden Augenblick; **—arily** [məʊmən'tærəlɪ] *ad* momentan; **—ary** a kurz; **—ous** [məʊ'mentəs] a folgenschwer; **—um** [məʊ'mentəm] Schwung *m*.

monarch ['mɒnək] *n* Herrscher(in *f*) *m*; **—ist** Monarchist(in *f*) *m*; **—y** Monarchie *f*.

monastery ['mɒnəstrɪ] *n* Kloster *nt*.

monastic [mə'næstɪk] a klösterlich, Kloster-.

Monday ['mʌndeɪ] *n* Montag *m*.

monetary ['mʌnɪtərɪ] a geldlich, Geld-; *(of currency)* Währungs-, monetär.

money ['mʌnɪ] *n* Geld *nt*; **—ed** vermögend; **—lender** Geldverleiher *m*; **—making** a einträglich, lukrativ; *n* Gelderwerb *m*; **— order** Postanweisung *f*.

mongol ['mɒŋgəl] *n (Med)* mongoloide(s) Kind *nt*; a mongolisch; *(Med)* mongoloid.

mongoose ['mɒŋguːs] *n* Mungo *m*.

mongrel ['mʌŋgrəl] *n* Promenadenmischung *f*; a Misch-.

monitor ['mɒnɪtə*] *n (Sch)* Klassenordner *m*; *(television —)* Monitor *m*; *vt broadcasts* abhören; *(control)* überwachen.

monk [mʌŋk] *n* Mönch *m*.

monkey ['mʌŋki] *n* Affe *m*; — nut Erdnuß *f*; — wrench (Tech) Engländer *m*, Franzose *m*.

mono- ['mɒnəu] *pref* Mono-.

monochrome ['mɒnəkrəum] *a* schwarz-weiß.

monocle ['mɒnəkl] *n* Monokel *nt*.

monogram ['mɒnəgræm] *n* Monogramm *nt*.

monolithic [mɒnəu'lɪθɪk] *a* monolithisch.

monologue ['mɒnəlɒg] *n* Monolog *m*.

monopolize [mə'nɒpəlaɪz] *vt* beherrschen.

monopoly [mə'nɒpəlɪ] *n* Monopol *nt*.

monorail ['mɒnəureɪl] *n* Einschienenbahn *f*.

monosyllabic ['mɒnəusɪ'læbɪk] *a* einsilbig.

monotone ['mɒnətəun] *n* gleichbleibende(r) Ton(fall) *m*.

monotonous [mə'nɒtənəs] *a* eintönig, monoton.

monotony [mə'nɒtənɪ] *n* Eintönigkeit *f*, Monotonie *f*.

monseigneur [mɒnsen'jɜ:*] *n*
monsignor [mɒn'si:njə*] *n* Monsignore *m*.

monsoon [mɒn'su:n] *n* Monsun *m*.

monster ['mɒnstə*] *n* Ungeheuer *nt*; (person) Scheusal *nt*; *a* (col) Riesen-.

monstrosity [mɒns'trɒsɪtɪ] *n* Ungeheuerlichkeit *f*; (thing) Monstrosität *f*.

monstrous ['mɒnstrəs] *a* (shocking) gräßlich, ungeheuerlich; (huge) riesig.

montage [mɒn'tɑːʒ] *n* Montage *f*.

month [mʌnθ] *n* Monat *m*; —ly *a* monatlich, Monats-; *ad* einmal im Monat; *n* (magazine) Monatsschrift *f*.

monument ['mɒnjumənt] *n* Denkmal *nt*; —al [mɒnju'mentl] *a* (huge) gewaltig; *ignorance* ungeheuer.

moo [mu:] *vi* muhen.

mood [mu:d] *n* Stimmung *f*, Laune *f*; to be in the — for aufgelegt sein zu; I am not in the — for laughing mir ist nicht zum Lachen zumute; —ily *ad* launisch; —iness Launenhaftigkeit *f*; —y *a* launisch.

moon [mu:n] *n* Mond *m*; —beam Mondstrahl *m*; —less *a* mondlos; —light Mondlicht *nt*; —lit *a* mondhell; —shot Mondflug *m*.

moor [muə*] *n* Heide *f*, Hochmoor *nt*; *vt* ship festmachen, verankern; *vi* anlegen; —ings *pl* Liegeplatz *m*; —land Heidemoor *nt*.

moose [mu:s] *n* Elch *m*.

moot [mu:t] *vt* aufwerfen; *a*: — point strittige(r) Punkt *m*.

mop [mɒp] *n* Mop *m*; *vt* (auf)wischen; — of hair Mähne *f*.

mope [məup] *vi* Trübsal blasen.

moped ['məuped] *n* (Brit) Moped *nt*.

moping ['məupɪŋ] *a* trübselig.

moquette [mə'ket] *n* Plüschgewebe *nt*.

moral ['mɒrəl] *a* moralisch; *values* sittlich; (virtuous) tugendhaft; *n* Moral *f*; —s *pl* Moral *f*; —e [mɒ'rɑːl] Moral *f*, Stimmung *f*; —ity [mə'rælɪtɪ] Sittlichkeit *f*; —ly *ad* moralisch.

morass [mə'ræs] *n* Sumpf *m*.

morbid ['mɔːbɪd] *a* morbid, krankhaft; *jokes* makaber.

more [mɔː*] *a, n, pron, ad* mehr; — or less mehr oder weniger; — than ever mehr denn je; a few —

noch ein paar; — beautiful schöner; —over ad überdies.

morgue [mɔːg] n Leichenschauhaus nt.

moribund ['mɒrɪbʌnd] a aussterbend.

morning ['mɔːnɪŋ] n Morgen m; a morgendlich, Morgen-, Früh-; in the — am Morgen; — sickness (Schwangerschafts)erbrechen nt.

moron ['mɔːrɒn] n Schwachsinnige(r) m; —ic [məˈrɒnɪk] a schwachsinnig.

morose [məˈrəʊs] a mürrisch.

morphine ['mɔːfiːn] n Morphium nt.

Morse [mɔːs] n (also — code) Morsealphabet nt.

morsel ['mɔːsl] n Stückchen nt, bißchen nt.

mortal ['mɔːtl] a sterblich; (deadly) tödlich; (very great) Todes-; n (human being) Sterbliche(r) mf; —ity [mɔːˈtælɪtɪ] n Sterblichkeit f; (death rate) Sterblichkeitsziffer f; —ly ad tödlich.

mortar ['mɔːtə*] n (for building) Mörtel m; (bowl) Mörser m; (Mil) Granatwerfer m.

mortgage ['mɔːgɪdʒ] n Hypothek f; vt eine Hypothek aufnehmen (+acc).

mortification [mɔːtɪfɪˈkeɪʃən] n Beschämung f.

mortified ['mɔːtɪfaɪd] a: I was — es war mir schrecklich peinlich.

mortuary ['mɔːtjʊərɪ] n Leichenhalle f.

mosaic [məʊˈzeɪɪk] n Mosaik nt.

mosque [mɒsk] n Moschee f.

mosquito [mɒsˈkiːtəʊ] n Moskito m.

moss [mɒs] n Moos nt; —y a bemoost.

most [məʊst] a a meiste(r, s); — men die meisten Männer; ad am meisten; (very) höchst; the — das meiste, der größte Teil; (people) die meisten; — of the time meistens, die meiste Zeit; — of the winter fast den ganzen Winter über; the — beautiful die/der/das Schönste; at the (very) — allerhöchstens; to make the — of das Beste machen aus; —ly ad größtenteils.

motel [məʊˈtel] n Motel nt.

moth [mɒθ] n Nachtfalter m; (wooleating) Motte f; —ball Mottenkugel f; —eaten a mottenzerfressen.

mother ['mʌðə*] n Mutter f; vt bemuttern; a tongue Mutter-; country Heimat-; —hood Mutterschaft f; —in-law Schwiegermutter f; —ly a mütterlich; —to-be werdende Mutter f.

mothproof ['mɒθpruːf] a mottenfest.

motif [məʊˈtiːf] n Motiv nt.

motion ['məʊʃən] n Bewegung f; (in meeting) Antrag m; vti winken (+dat), zu verstehen geben (+dat); —less a regungslos; — picture Film m.

motivated ['məʊtɪveɪtɪd] a motiviert.

motivation [məʊtɪˈveɪʃən] n Motivierung f.

motive ['məʊtɪv] n Motiv nt, Beweggrund m; a treibend.

motley ['mɒtlɪ] a bunt.

motor ['məʊtə*] n Motor m; (car) Auto nt; vi (im Auto) fahren; a Motor-; —bike Motorrad nt; —boat Motorboot nt; —car Auto nt; —cycle Motorrad nt; —cyclist Motorradfahrer(in f) m; —ing n Autofahren nt; a Auto-; —ist ['məʊtərɪst] Autofahrer(in f) m; —

oil Motorenöl *nt;* — **racing** Autorennen *nt;* — **scooter** Motorroller *m;* — **vehicle** Kraftfahrzeug *nt;* —**way** (Brit) Autobahn *f.*

mottled ['mɒtld] *a* gesprenkelt.

motto ['mɒtəʊ] *n* Motto *nt,* Wahlspruch *m.*

mould [məʊld] *n* Form *f;* (mildew) Schimmel *m;* *vt* (lit, fig) formen; —**er** *vi* (decay) vermodern; —**ing** Formen *nt;* —**y** *a* schimmelig.

moult [məʊlt] *vi* sich mausern.

mound [maʊnd] *n* (Erd)hügel *m.*

mount [maʊnt] *n* (liter: hill) Berg *m;* (horse) Pferd *nt;* (for jewel etc) Fassung *f; vt* horse steigen auf (+acc); (put in setting) fassen; exhibition veranstalten; attack unternehmen; *vi* (also — up) sich häufen; (on horse) aufsitzen; —**ain** ['maʊntɪn] *n* Berg *m;* —**aineer** [maʊntɪ'nɪə*] Bergsteiger(in *f*) *m;* —**aineering** Bergsteigen *nt;* to go —**aineering** klettern gehen; —**ainous** *a* bergig; —**ainside** Berg(ab)hang *m.*

mourn [mɔːn] *vt* betrauern, beklagen; *vi* trauern (for um); —**er** Trauernde(r) *mf;* —**ful** *a* traurig; —**ing** (grief) Trauer *f;* in —**ing** (period etc) in Trauer; (dress) in Trauerkleidung *f.*

mouse [maʊs] *n, pl* **mice** Maus *f;* —**trap** Mausefalle *f.*

moustache [məs'taː∫] *n* Schnurrbart *m.*

mousy ['maʊsɪ] *a colour* mausgrau; *person* schüchtern.

mouth [maʊθ] *n* Mund *m;* (general) Öffnung *f;* (of river) Mündung *f;* (of harbour) Einfahrt *f;* [maʊð] *vt* words affektiert sprechen; **down in the** — niedergeschlagen; —**ful** Mundvoll *m;* —**organ** Mundharmonika *f;* —**piece** (lit) Mund-

stück *nt;* (fig) Sprachrohr *nt;* —**wash** Mundwasser *nt;* —**watering** *a* lecker, appetitlich.

movable ['muːvəbl] *a* beweglich.

move [muːv] *n* (movement) Bewegung *f;* (in game) Zug *m;* (step) Schritt *m;* (of house) Umzug *m;* *vt* bewegen; object rücken; people transportieren; (in job) versetzen; (emotionally) bewegen, ergreifen; **to** — **sb to do sth** jdn veranlassen, etw zu tun; *vi* sich bewegen; (change place) gehen; (vehicle, ship) fahren; (take action) etwas unternehmen; (go to another house) umziehen; **to get a** — **on** sich beeilen; **on the** — in Bewegung; **to** — **house** umziehen; **to** — **closer to** or **towards sth** sich etw (dat) nähern; — **about** *vi* sich hin- und herbewegen; (travel) unterwegs sein; — **away** *vi* weggehen; — **back** *vi* zurückgehen; (to the rear) zurückweichen; — **forward** *vi* vorwärtsgehen, sich vorwärtsbewegen; *vt* vorschieben; time vorverlegen; — **in** *vi* (to house) einziehen; (troops) einrücken; — **on** *vi* weitergehen; *vt* weitergehen lassen; — **out** *vi* (of house) ausziehen; (troops) abziehen; — **up** *vi* aufsteigen; (in job) befördert werden; *vt* nach oben bewegen; (in job) befördern; (Sch) versetzen; —**ment** Bewegung *f;* (Mus) Satz *m;* (of clock) Uhrwerk *nt.*

movie ['muːvɪ] *n* Film *m;* **the —s** (the cinema) das Kino; — **camera** Filmkamera *f.*

moving ['muːvɪŋ] *a* beweglich; *force* treibend; (touching) ergreifend.

mow [məʊ] *vt* irreg mähen; — **down** *vt* (fig) niedermähen; —**er**

(machine) Mähmaschine *f;* *(lawn—)* Rasenmäher *m.*

Mr [mɪstə*] Herr *m.*

Mrs ['mɪsɪz] Frau *f.*

Ms [mɪz] n Frau *f.*

much [mʌtʃ] *a* viel; *ad* sehr; viel; *n* viel, eine Menge *f;* — better viel besser; — the same size so ziemlich gleich groß; how —? wieviel?; too — zuviel; — to my surprise zu meiner großen Überraschung; — as I should like to so gern ich möchte.

muck [mʌk] n *(lit)* Mist *m;* *(fig)* Schmutz *m;* — about *(col)* vi herumlungern; *(meddle)* herumalbern *(with an +dat);* vt — sb about mit jdm treiben, was man will; — up vt *(col: ruin)* vermasseln; *(dirty)* dreckig machen; —y *a (dirty)* dreckig.

mucus ['mju:kəs] n Schleim *m.*

mud [mʌd] n Schlamm *m;* *(fig)* Schmutz *m.*

muddle ['mʌdl] n Durcheinander *nt;* vt *(also — up)* durcheinanderbringen; — through vi sich durchwursteln.

muddy ['mʌdɪ] a schlammig.

mudguard ['mʌdgɑ:d] n Schutzblech *nt.*

mudpack ['mʌdpæk] n Moorpackung *f.*

mud-slinging ['mʌdslɪŋɪŋ] n *(col)* Verleumdung *f.*

muff [mʌf] n Muff *m.*

muffin ['mʌfɪn] n süße(s) Teilchen *nt.*

muffle ['mʌfl] vt *sound* dämpfen; *(wrap up)* einhüllen.

mufti ['mʌftɪ] n: in — in Zivil.

mug [mʌg] n *(cup)* Becher *m;* *(col: face)* Visage *f;* *(col: fool)* Trottel

m; vt überfallen und ausrauben; —ging Überfall *m.*

muggy ['mʌgɪ] a *weather* schwül.

mulatto [mju:'lætəʊ] n Mulatte *m,* Mulattin *f.*

mule [mju:l] n Maulesel *m.*

mull [mʌl]: — over vt nachdenken über *(+acc).*

mulled [mʌld] a *wine* Glüh-.

multi- ['mʌltɪ] pref Multi-, multi-.

multicoloured, *(US)* **multicolored** ['mʌltɪˈkʌləd] a mehrfarbig.

multifarious [mʌltɪˈfɛərɪəs] a mannigfaltig.

multilateral [mʌltɪˈlætərəl] a multilateral.

multiple ['mʌltɪpl] n Vielfache(s) *nt;* a mehrfach; *(many)* mehrere; — sclerosis multiple Sklerose *f;* — store Kaufhauskette *f.*

multiplication [mʌltɪplɪˈkeɪʃən] n Multiplikation *f.*

multiply ['mʌltɪplaɪ] vt multiplizieren *(by* mit*);* vi *(Biol)* sich vermehren.

multiracial ['mʌltɪˈreɪʃəl] a gemischtrassig; — policy Rassenintegration *f.*

multitude ['mʌltɪtjuːd] n Menge *f.*

mum[1] [mʌm] a: to keep — den Mund halten *(about* über *+acc).*

mum[2] [mʌm] n *(col)* Mutti *f.*

mumble ['mʌmbl] vti murmeln; n Gemurmel *nt.*

mummy ['mʌmɪ] n *(dead body)* Mumie *f;* *(col)* Mami *f.*

mumps [mʌmps] n Mumps *m.*

munch [mʌntʃ] vti mampfen.

mundane ['mʌn'deɪn] a weltlich; *(fig)* profan.

municipal [mju:'nɪsɪpəl] a städtisch, Stadt-; —ity

[mju:nɪsɪ'pælɪtɪ] Stadt f mit Selbstverwaltung.

munificence [mju:'nɪfɪsns] n Freigebigkeit f.

munitions [mju:'nɪʃənz] npl Munition f.

mural ['mjuərəl] n Wandgemälde nt.

murder ['mɜ:də*] n Mord m; it was — (fig) es war möderisch; to get away with — (fig) sich alles erlauben können; vt ermorden; —er Mörder m; —ess Mörderin f; —ous a Mord-; (fig) mörderisch.

murk [mɜ:k] n Dunkelheit f —y a finster.

murmur ['mɜ:mə*] n Murmeln nt; (of water, wind) Rauschen nt; without a — ohne zu murren; vti murmeln.

muscle ['mʌsl] n Muskel m.

muscular ['mʌskjulə*] a Muskel-; (strong) muskulös.

muse [mju:z] vi (nach)sinnen; M— Muse f.

museum [mju:'zɪəm] n Museum nt.

mushroom ['mʌʃrum] n Champignon m; Pilz m; vi (fig) emporschießen.

mushy [mʌʃɪ] a breiig; (sentimental) gefühlsduselig.

music ['mju:zɪk] n Musik f; (printed) Noten pl; —al a sound melodisch; person musikalisch; n (show) Musical nt; —al box Spieldose f; —al instrument Musikinstrument nt; —ally ad musikalisch; sing melodisch; —hall (Brit) Varieté nt; —ian [mju:'zɪʃən] n Musiker(in f) m.

muslin ['mʌzlɪn] n Musselin m.

mussel [mʌsl] n Miesmuschel f.

must [mʌst] v aux müssen; (in negation) dürfen; n Muß nt; the

film is a — den Film muß man einfach gesehen haben.

mustache ['mʌstæʃ] (US) = moustache.

mustard ['mʌstəd] n Senf m.

muster ['mʌstə*] vt (Mil) antreten lassen; courage zusammennehmen.

mustiness ['mʌstɪnəs] n Muffigkeit f.

mustn't ['mʌsnt] = must not.

musty ['mʌstɪ] a. muffig.

mute [mju:t] a stumm; n (person) Stumme(r) mf; (Mus) Dämpfer m.

mutilate ['mju:tɪleɪt] vt verstümmeln.

mutilation [mju:tɪ'leɪʃən] n Verstümmelung f.

mutinous ['mju:tɪnəs] a meuterisch.

mutiny ['mju:tɪnɪ] n Meuterei f; vi meutern.

mutter ['mʌtə*] vti murmeln.

mutton ['mʌtn] n Hammelfleisch nt.

mutual ['mju:tjuəl] a gegenseitig; beiderseitig; —ly ad gegenseitig; auf beiden Seiten; für beide Seiten.

muzzle ['mʌzl] n (of animal) Schnauze f; (for animal) Maulkorb m; (of gun) Mündung f; vt einen Maulkorb anlegen (+dat).

my [maɪ] poss a mein.

myopic [maɪ'ɒpɪk] a kurzsichtig.

myrrh [mɜ:*] n Myrrhe f.

myself [maɪ'self] pron mich (acc); mir (dat); (emphatic) selbst; I'm not — mit mir ist etwas nicht in Ordnung.

mysterious [mɪs'tɪərɪəs] a geheimnisvoll, mysteriös; —ly ad auf unerklärliche Weise.

mystery ['mɪstərɪ] n (secret) Geheimnis nt; (sth difficult) Rätsel nt; — play Mysterienspiel nt.

mystic ['mɪstɪk] n Mystiker m; a einmystisch; —al a mystisch; —ism ['mɪstɪsɪzəm] Mystizismus m.

mystification [mɪstɪfɪ'keɪʃən] n Verblüffung f.

mystify ['mɪstɪfaɪ] vt ein Rätsel sein (+dat); verblüffen.

mystique [mɪs'tiːk] n geheimnisvolle Natur f.

myth [mɪθ] n Mythos m; (fig) Erfindung f; —ical a mythisch, Sagen-; —ological [mɪθə'lɒdʒɪkəl] a mythologisch; —ology [mɪ'θɒlədʒɪ] Mythologie f.

N

N, n [en] n N nt, n nt.

nab [næb] vt (col) schnappen.

nadir ['neɪdɪə*] n Tiefpunkt m.

nag [næg] n (horse) Gaul m; (person) Nörgler(in f) m; vti herumnörgeln (sb an jdm); —ging a doubt nagend; n Nörgelei f.

nail [neɪl] n Nagel m; vt nageln; — down vt (lit, fig) festnageln; —brush Nagelbürste f; —file Nagelfeile f; — polish Nagellack m; — scissors pl Nagelschere f.

naive a, —ly ad [naɪ'iːv, -lɪ] naiv.

naked ['neɪkɪd] a nackt; —ness Nacktheit f.

name [neɪm] n Name m; (reputation) Ruf m; vt nennen; sth new benennen; (appoint) ernennen; what's your —? wie heißen Sie?; in the — of im Namen (+gen); (for the sake of) um willen (+gen); he's always — dropping er wirft immer mit großen Namen um sich; —less a namenlos; —ly ad nämlich; —sake Namensvetter m.

nanny ['nænɪ] n Kindermädchen nt.

nap [næp] n (sleep) Nickerchen nt; (on cloth) Strich m; to have a — ein Nickerchen machen.

napalm ['neɪpɑːm] n Napalm nt.

nape [neɪp] n Nacken m.

napkin ['næpkɪn] n (at table) Serviette f; (Brit: for baby) Windel f.

nappy ['næpɪ] n (Brit: for baby) Windel f.

narcissism [nɑːˈsɪsɪzəm] n Narzißmus m.

narcotic [nɑːˈkɒtɪk] n Betäubungsmittel nt.

narrate [nə'reɪt] vt erzählen.

narration [nə'reɪʃən] n Erzählung f.

narrative ['nærətɪv] n Erzählung f; a erzählend.

narrator [nə'reɪtə*] n Erzähler(in f) m.

narrow ['nærəʊ] a eng, schmal; (limited) beschränkt; vi sich verengen; to — sth down to sth etw auf etw (acc) einschränken; —ly ad miss knapp; escape mit knapper Not; —-minded a engstirnig; —-mindedness Engstirnigkeit f.

nasal ['neɪzəl] a Nasal-.

nastily ['nɑːstɪlɪ] ad böse, schlimm.

nastiness ['nɑːstɪnəs] n Ekligkeit f.

nasty ['nɑːstɪ] a ekelhaft, fies; business, wound schlimm; to turn — gemein werden.

nation ['neɪʃən] n Nation f, Volk nt; —al ['næʃənl] a national, National-, Landes-; n Staatsangehörige(r) mf; —al anthem

Nationalhymne f; —alism
['næɲəlɪzəm] Nationalismus m;
—alist ['næʃnəlɪst] n Nationalist(in
f) m; a nationalistisch; —ality
[næʃə'nælɪtɪ] Staatsangehörigkeit f,
Nationalität f; —alization
[næʃnəlar'zeɪʃən] Verstaatlichung
f; —alize ['næʃnəlaɪz] vt verstaat-
lichen; —ally ['næʃnəlɪ] ad
national, auf Staatsebene; —wide
a, ad allgemein, landesweit.

native ['neɪtɪv] n (born in) Ein-
heimische(r) mf; (original inhabit-
tant) Eingeborene(r) mf; a (coming
from a certain place) einheimisch;
(of the original inhabitants) Ein-
geborenen-; (belonging by birth)
heimatlich, Heimat-; (inborn) angeboren, natürlich; a — of Germany
ein gebürtiger Deutscher; — language Muttersprache f.

natter ['nætə*] vi (col: chat)
quatschen; n Gequatsche nt.

natural ['nætʃrəl] a natürlich;
Natur-; (inborn) (an)geboren; —ist
Naturkundler(in f) m; —ize vt
foreigner einbürgern, naturali-
sieren; plant etc einführen; —ly ad
natürlich; —ness Natürlichkeit f.

nature ['neɪtʃə*] n Natur f; by —
von Natur (aus).

naught [nɔːt] n Null f.

naughtily ['nɔːtɪlɪ] ad unartig.

naughtiness ['nɔːtɪnəs] n Unartig-
keit f.

naughty ['nɔːtɪ] a child unartig, ungezogen; action ungehörig.

nausea ['nɔːsɪə] n (sickness) Übelkeit f; (disgust) Ekel m; —te
['nɔːsɪeɪt] vt anekeln.

nauseating ['nɔːsɪeɪtɪŋ] a ekeler-
regend; job widerlich.

nautical ['nɔːtɪkəl] a nautisch,
See-; expression seemännisch.

naval ['neɪvəl] a Marine-, Flotten-.
nt.

nave [neɪv] n Kirchen(haupt)schiff
nt.

navel ['neɪvəl] n Nabel m.

navigable ['nævɪgəbl] a schiffbar.

navigate ['nævɪgeɪt] vt ship etc
steuern; vi (sail) (zu Schiff) fahren.

navigation [nævɪ'geɪʃən] n
Navigation f.

navigator ['nævɪgeɪtə*] n Steuermann m; (explorer) Seefahrer m;
(Aviat) Navigator m; (Aut) Bei-
fahrer(in f) m.

navvy ['nævɪ] n Straßenarbeiter m;
(on railway) Streckenarbeiter m.

navy ['neɪvɪ] n Marine f, Flotte f;
(warships etc) (Kriegs)flotte f; a —
blue Marineblau nt; a marineblau.

nay [neɪ] ad (old) (no) nein; (even)
ja sogar.

neap [niːp] a: — tide Nippflut f.

near [nɪə*] a nah; the holidays are
— es sind bald Ferien; ad in der
Nähe; to come —er näher
kommen; (time) näher rücken;
prep (also — to) (space) in der
Nähe (+gen); (time) um (+acc) …
herum; vt sich nähern (+dat); —
at hand weit weg; —by a
nahe (gelegen); ad in der Nähe;
—ly ad fast; a — miss knapp
daneben; —ness Nähe f; —side
(Aut) Beifahrerseite f; a auf der Beifahrerseite; a — thing knapp.

neat a, —ly ad ['niːt, -lɪ] (tidy)
ordentlich; (clever) treffend; solution sauber; (pure) unverdünnt,
rein; —ness Ordentlichkeit f,
Sauberkeit f.

nebulous ['nebjuləs] a nebelhaft,
verschwommen.

necessarily ['nesɪsərɪlɪ] ad
unbedingt; notwendigerweise.

necessary ['nesɪsərɪ] a notwendig,
nötig.

necessitate [ni'sesiteit] vt erforderlich machen.

necessity [ni'sesiti] n (need) Not f; (compulsion) Notwendigkeit f; in case of — im Notfall; necessities of life Bedürfnisse pl des Lebens.

neck [nek] n Hals m; — and — Kopf an Kopf; —lace Halskette f; —line Ausschnitt m; —tie (US) Krawatte f.

nectar [nektə*] n Nektar m.

née [nei] a geborene.

need [ni:d] n Bedarf m no pl (for an +dat); Bedürfnis nt (for für); (want) Mangel m; (necessity) Notwendigkeit f; (poverty) Not f; to brauchen; to — to do tun müssen; if — be wenn nötig; to be in — of brauchen; there is no — for you to come du brauchst nicht zu kommen; there's no — es ist nicht nötig.

needle [ni:dl] n Nadel f.

needless a, —ly ad ['ni:dlis, -li] unnötig.

needlework ['ni:dlwɜ:k] n Handarbeit f.

needy ['ni:di] a bedürftig.

negation [ni'geiʃən] n Verneinung f.

negative ['negətiv] n (Phot) Negativ nt; a negativ; answer abschlägig.

neglect [ni'glekt] vt (leave undone) versäumen; (take no care of) vernachlässigen; n Vernachlässigung f.

negligée ['negliʒei] n Negligé nt.

negligence ['neglidʒəns] n Nachlässigkeit f.

negligent a, —ly ad ['neglidʒənt, -li] nachlässig, unachtsam.

negligible ['neglidʒəbl] a unbedeutend, geringfügig.

negotiable [ni'gəuʃəbl] a cheque übertragbar, einlösbar.

negotiate [ni'gəuʃieit] vi verhandeln; vt treaty abschließen, aushandeln; difficulty überwinden; corner nehmen.

negotiation [nigəuʃi'eiʃən] n Verhandlung f.

negotiator [ni'gəuʃieitə*] n Unterhändler m.

Negress ['ni:gres] n Negerin f.

Negro ['ni:grəu] n Neger m; a Neger-.

neighbour, (US) **neighbor** ['neibə*] n Nachbar(in f) m; —hood Nachbarschaft f; Umgebung f; —ing a benachbart, angrenzend; —ly a freundlich.

neither ['naiðə*] a, pron keine(r, s) (von beiden); cj weder; he can't do it, and — can I er kann es nicht und ich auch nicht.

neo- ['ni:əu] pref neo-.

neon ['ni:ɒn] n Neon nt; — light Neonlicht nt.

nephew ['nefju:] n Neffe m.

nerve [nɜ:v] n Nerv m; (courage) Mut m; (impudence) Frechheit f; —racking a nervenaufreibend.

nervous ['nɜ:vəs] a (of the nerves) Nerven-; (timid) nervös, ängstlich; — breakdown Nervenzusammenbruch m; —ly ad nervös; —ness Nervosität f.

nest [nest] n Nest nt.

nestle ['nesl] vi sich kuscheln; (village) sich schmiegen.

net [net] n Netz nt; a: —(t) netto, Netto-, Rein-; —ball Netzball m.

netting ['netiŋ] n Netz(werk) nt, Drahtgeflecht nt.

network ['netwɜ:k] n Netz nt.

neurosis [njuə'rəusis] n Neurose f.

neurotic [njuə'rɒtɪk] a neurotisch; n Neurotiker(in f) m.

neuter ['nju:tə*] a (Biol) geschlechtslos; (Gram) sächlich; n (Biol) kastrierte(s) Tier nt; (Gram) Neutrum nt.

neutral ['nju:trəl] a neutral; —ity [nju:'trælɪtɪ] Neutralität f.

never ['nevə*] ad nie(mals); well I — na so was!; —ending a endlos; —theless [nevəðə'les] ad trotzdem, dennoch.

new [nju:] a neu; they are still — to the work die Arbeit ist ihnen noch neu; — from frisch aus or von; —born a neugeboren; —comer Neuankömmling m; —ly ad frisch, neu; — moon Neumond m; —ness Neuheit f.

news [nju:z] n Nachricht f; (Rad, TV) Nachrichten pl; —agent Zeitungshändler m; — flash Kurzmeldung f; —letter Rundschreiben nt; —paper Zeitung f; —reel Wochenschau f.

New Year ['nju:'jɪə*] n Neujahr nt; —'s Day Neujahrstag m; —'s Eve Silvester(abend m) nt.

next [nekst] a nächste(r, s); ad (after) dann, darauf; (next time) das nächstemal; prep: — to (gleich) neben (+dat); — nothing so gut wie nichts; to do sth — etw als nächstes tun; what —! was denn noch (alles)?; the — day am nächsten or folgenden Tag; — door ad nebenan; — year nächstes Jahr; — of kin Familienangehörige(r) mf.

nib [nɪb] n Spitze f.

nibble ['nɪbl] vt knabbern an (+dat).

nice [naɪs] a hübsch, nett, schön; (subtle) fein; —-looking a hübsch, gutaussehend; —ly ad gut, fein, nett.

nick [nɪk] n Einkerbung f; in the — of time gerade rechtzeitig.

nickel ['nɪkl] n Nickel nt; (US) Nickel m (5 cents).

nickname ['nɪkneɪm] n Spitzname m.

nicotine ['nɪkəti:n] n Nikotin nt.

niece [ni:s] n Nichte f.

niggardly ['nɪgədlɪ] a schäbig; person geizig.

niggling ['nɪglɪŋ] a pedantisch; doubt, worry quälend; detail kleinlich.

night [naɪt] n Nacht f; (evening) Abend m; good —! gute Nacht!; at or by — nachts; abends; —cap (drink) Schlummertrunk m; —club Nachtlokal nt; —dress Nachthemd nt; —fall Einbruch m der Nacht; —ie (col) Nachthemd nt; —ingale Nachtigall f; —life Nachtleben nt; —ly a, ad jeden Abend; jede Nacht; —mare Alptraum m; —school `Abendschule f; —time Nacht f; at — time nachts; —watchman Nachtwächter m.

nil [nɪl] n Nichts nt, Null f (also Sport).

nimble ['nɪmbl] a behend(e), flink; mind beweglich.

nimbly ['nɪmblɪ] ad flink.

nine [naɪn] n Neun f; a neun; —teen Neunzehn f; a neunzehn; —ty Neunzig f; a neunzig.

ninth [naɪnθ] a neunte(r, s); n Neuntel nt.

nip [nɪp] vt kneifen; n Kneifen nt.

nipple ['nɪpl] n Brustwarze f.

nippy ['nɪpɪ] a (col) person flink; car flott; (cold) frisch.

nit [nɪt] n Nisse f.

nitrogen ['naɪtrədʒən] n Stickstoff m.

no [nəu] *a* kein ; *ad* nein ; *n* Nein
nt ; — further nicht weiter ; —
more time keine Zeit mehr ; in —
time schnell.

nobility [nəu'bılıtı] *n* Adel *m* ; the
— of this deed diese edle Tat.

noble ['nəubl] *a* rank adlig ;
(splendid) nobel, edel ; *n* Adlige(r)
mf ; —man Edelmann *m*, Adlige(r)
m.

nobly ['nəublı] *ad* edel, großmütig.

nobody ['nəubədı] *pron* niemand,
keiner ; *n* Niemand *m*.

nod [nɒd] *vi* nicken ; — off einnicken ; *n* Nicken *nt*.

noise [nɔız] *n* (sound) Geräusch *nt* ;
(unpleasant, loud) Lärm *m*.

noisily ['nɔızılı] *ad* lärmend, laut.

noisy ['nɔızı] *a* laut ; crowd lärmend.

nomad ['nəumæd] *n* Nomade *m* ;
—ic [nəu'mædık] *a* nomadisch.

no-man's land ['nəumænzlænd] *n*
(lit, fig) Niemandsland *nt*.

nominal ['nɒmınl] *a* nominell ;
(Gram) Nominal-.

nominate ['nɒmıneıt] *vt* (suggest)
vorschlagen ; (in election) aufstellen ; (appoint) ernennen.

nomination [nɒmı'neıʃən] *n*
(election) Nominierung *f* ; (appointment) Ernennung *f*.

nominee [nɒmı'ni:] *n* Kandidat(in
f) *m*.

non- [nɒn] *pref* Nicht-, un- ; —alcoholic *a* alkoholfrei.

nonchalant ['nɒnʃələnt] *a* lässig.

nondescript ['nɒndıskrıpt] *a*
mittelmäßig.

none [nʌn] *a, pron* kein(e, r, s) ; *ad*
— the wiser keineswegs klüger ; —
of your cheek! sei nicht so frech!

nonentity [nɒ'nentıtı] *n* Null *f* (col).

nonetheless [nʌnðə'les] *ad* nichts-
destoweniger.

non-fiction [nɒn'fıkʃən] *n* Sach-
bücher *pl*.

nonplussed [nɒn'plʌst] *a* verdutzt.

nonsense ['nɒnsəns] *n* Unsinn *m*.

non-stop [nɒn'stɒp] *a* pausenlos,
Nonstop-.

noodles ['nu:dlz] *npl* Nudeln *pl*.

nook [nuk] *n* Winkel *m*, Eckchen
nt.

noon [nu:n] *n* (12 Uhr) Mittag *m*.

no one ['nəuwʌn] *pron* = **nobody**.

noose [nu:s] *n* Schlinge *f*.

norm [nɔ:m] *n* Norm *f*, Regel *f*.

normal ['nɔ:məl] *a* normal ; —ly *ad*
normal ; (usually) normalerweise.

north [nɔ:θ] *n* Norden *m* ; *a* nördlich, Nord- ; *ad* nördlich, nach or
im Norden ; —east Nordosten *m* ;
—ern ['nɔ:ðən] *a* nördlich, Nord-
—ward(s) *ad* nach Norden ; —
west Nordwesten *m*.

nose [nəuz] *n* Nase *f* ; —bleed
Nasenbluten *nt* ; —dive Sturzflug
m ; —y *a* neugierig.

nostalgia [nɒs'tældʒıə] *n* Sehnsucht *f*, Nostalgie *f*.

nostalgic [nɒs'tældʒık] *a* weh-
mütig, nostalgisch.

nostril ['nɒstrıl] *n* Nasenloch *nt* ;
(of animal) Nüster *f*.

not [nɒt] *ad* nicht ; he is — an
expert er ist kein Experte ; — at
all keineswegs ; (don't mention it)
gern geschehen.

notable ['nəutəbl] *a* bemerkenswert.

notably ['nəutəblı] *ad* (especially)
besonders ; (noticeably) bemerkenswert.

notch [nɒtʃ] *n* Kerbe *f*, Einschnitt
m.

note [nəut] *n* (Mus) Note *f*, Ton *m* ;
(short letter) Nachricht *f* ; (Pol)
Note *f* ; (comment, attention) Notiz
f ; (of lecture etc) Aufzeichnung *f* ;

(bank—) Schein *m; (fame)* Ruf *m,*
Ansehen *nt;* vt *(observe)*
bemerken; *(write down)* notieren;
to take —s of sich Notizen machen
über *(+acc);* —book Notizbuch
nt; —case Brieftasche *f;* —d a
bekannt; —paper Briefpapier *nt.*

nothing ['nʌθɪŋ] *n* nichts; for —
umsonst; it is — to me es bedeutet
mir nichts.

notice ['nəʊtɪs] *n (announcement)*
Anzeige *f,* Bekanntmachung *f;*
(attention) Beachtung *f; (warning)*
Ankündigung *f; (dismissal)*
Kündigung *f;* vt bemerken; to take
— of beachten; to bring sth to sb's
— jdn auf etw *(acc)* aufmerksam
machen; take no —! kümmere dich
nicht darum!; —able a merklich;
— board Anschlagtafel *f.*

notification [nəʊtɪfɪ'keɪʃən] *n*
Benachrichtigung *f.*

notify ['nəʊtɪfaɪ] vt benachrichtigen.

notion ['nəʊʃən] *n (idea)* Vorstellung *f,* Idee *f; (fancy)* Lust *f.*

notorious [nəʊ'tɔːrɪəs] a berüchtigt.

notwithstanding [nɒtwɪð'
stændɪŋ] ad trotzdem; prep trotz.

nougat ['nuːgɑː] *n* weiße(r) Nougat
m.

nought [nɔːt] *n* Null *f.*

noun [naʊn] *n* Hauptwort *nt,* Substantiv *nt.*

nourish ['nʌrɪʃ] vt nähren; —ing a
nahrhaft; —ment Nahrung *f.*

novel ['nɒvəl] *n* Roman *m;* a
neu(artig); —ist Schriftsteller(in *f)*
m; —ty Neuheit *f.*

November [nəʊ'vembə*] *n*
November *m.*

novice ['nɒvɪs] *n* Neuling *m; (Eccl)*
Novize *m.*

now [naʊ] ad jetzt; right — jetzt,
gerade; do it right — tun Sie es
sofort; — and then, — and again

ab und zu, manchmal; —, — na,
na; — ... — or then bald ... bald,
mal ... mal; —adays ad heutzutage.

nowhere ['nəʊwɛə*] ad nirgends.

nozzle ['nɒzl] *n* Düse *f.*

nuance ['njuːɑːns] *n* Nuance *f.*

nuclear ['njuːklɪə*] a energy etc
Atom-, Kern-.

nucleus ['njuːklɪəs] *n* Kern *m.*

nude [njuːd] a nackt; *n (person)*
Nackte(r) *mf; (Art)* Akt *m;* in the
— nackt.

nudge [nʌdʒ] vt leicht anstoßen.

nudist ['njuːdɪst] *n* Nudist(in *f) m.*

nudity ['njuːdɪtɪ] *n* Nacktheit *f.*

nuisance ['njuːsns] *n* Ärgernis *nt;*
that's a — das ist ärgerlich; he's
a — er geht einem auf die Nerven.

null [nʌl] a: — and void null und
nichtig; —ify vt für null und
nichtig erklären.

numb [nʌm] a taub, gefühllos; vt
betäuben.

number ['nʌmbə*] *n* Nummer *f;*
(numeral also) Zahl *f; (quantity)*
(An)zahl *f; (Gram)* Numerus *m;*
(of magazine also) Ausgabe *f;* vt
(give a number to) numerieren;
(amount to) sein; his days are —ed
seine Tage sind gezählt; — plate
(Brit Aut) Nummernschild *nt.*

numbness ['nʌmnəs] *n* Gefühllosig-
keit *f.*

numbskull ['nʌmskʌl] *n* Idiot *m.*

numeral ['njuːmərəl] *n* Ziffer *f.*

numerical [njuː'merɪkl] a order
zahlenmäßig.

numerous ['njuːmərəs] a zahlreich.

nun [nʌn] *n* Nonne *f.*

nurse [nɜːs] *n* Krankenschwester *f;*
(for children) Kindermädchen *nt;*
vt patient pflegen; doubt etc
hegen; —ry *(for children)* Kinder-
zimmer *nt; (for plants)* Gärtner-

f; (for trees) Baumschule *f;* **—ry rhyme** Kinderreim *m;* **—ry school** Kindergarten *m.*

nursing ['nɜ:sɪŋ] *n (profession)* Krankenpflege *f;* **—home** Privatklinik *f.*

nut [nʌt] *n* Nuß *f; (screw)* Schraubenmutter *f; (col)* Verrückte(r) *mf;* **—s a** *(col: crazy)* verrückt.

nutcase ['nʌtkeɪs] *n (col)* Verrückte(r) *mf.*

nutcrackers ['nʌtkrækəz] *npl* Nußknacker *m.*

nutmeg ['nʌtmeg] *n* Muskat(nuß *f)*
m.

nutrient ['nju:trɪənt] *n* Nährstoff *m.*

nutrition [nju:'trɪʃən] *n* Nahrung *f.*

nutritious [nju:'trɪʃəs] *a* nahrhaft.

nutshell ['nʌtʃel] *n:* **in a —** in aller Kürze.

nylon ['naɪlɒn] *n* Nylon *nt;* **a** Nylon-.

O

O, o [əʊ] *n* O *nt, o nt; (Tel)* Null *f; see* oh.

oaf [əʊf] *n* Trottel *m.*

oak [əʊk] *n* Eiche *f; a* Eichen(holz)-.

oar [ɔ:*] *n* Ruder *nt.*

oasis [əʊ'eɪsɪs] *n* Oase *f.*

oath [əʊθ] *n (statement)* Eid *m,* Schwur *m; (swearword)* Fluch *m.*

oatmeal ['əʊtmi:l] *n* Haferschrot *m.*

oats [əʊts] *n pl* Hafer *m; (Cook)* Haferflocken *pl.*

obedience [ə'bi:dɪəns] *n* Gehorsam *m.*

obedient [ə'bi:dɪənt] *a* gehorsam, folgsam.

obelisk ['ɒbɪlɪsk] *n* Obelisk *m.*

obesity [əʊ'bi:sɪtɪ] *n* Korpulenz *f,* Fettleibigkeit *f.*

obey [ə'beɪ] *vti* gehorchen (+*dat),* folgen (+*dat).*

obituary [ə'bɪtjʊərɪ] *n* Nachruf *m.*

object ['ɒbdʒɪkt] *n (thing)* Gegenstand *m,* Objekt *nt; (of feeling etc)* Gegenstand *m; (purpose)* Ziel *nt; (Gram)* Objekt *nt;* [əb'dʒekt] *vi* dagegen sein, Einwände haben *(to* gegen);

(morally) Anstoß nehmen *(to an* +*acc);* **—ion** [əb'dʒekʃən] *(reason against)* Einwand *m,* Einspruch *m; (dislike)* Abneigung *f;* **—ionable** [əb'dʒekʃnəbl] *a* nicht einwandfrei; *language* anstößig; **—ive** [əb'dʒektɪv] *n* Ziel *nt; a* objektiv; **—ively** [əb'dʒektɪvlɪ] *ad* objektiv; **—ivity** [ɒbdʒɪk'tɪvɪtɪ] Objektivität *f;* **—or** [əb'dʒektə*] Gegner(in *f) m.*

obligation [ɒblɪ'geɪʃən] *n (duty)* Pflicht *f; (promise)* Verpflichtung *f;* **no —** unverbindlich; **be under an —** verpflichtet sein.

obligatory [ɒ'blɪgətərɪ] *a* bindend, obligatorisch; **it is — to . . .** es ist Pflicht, zu . . .

oblige [ə'blaɪdʒ] *vt (compel)* zwingen; *(do a favour)* einen Gefallen tun (+*dat);* **you are not —d to do it** Sie sind nicht verpflichtet, es zu tun; **much —d** herzlichen Dank.

obliging [ə'blaɪdʒɪŋ] *a* entgegenkommend.

oblique [ə'bli:k] *a* schräg, schief; **n** Schrägstrich *m.*

obliterate [ə'blɪtəreɪt] vt auslöschen.

oblivion [ə'blɪvɪən] n Vergessenheit f.

oblivious [ə'blɪvɪəs] a nicht bewußt (of gen); he was — of it er hatte es nicht bemerkt.

oblong ['ɒblɒŋ] n Rechteck nt; a länglich.

obnoxious [əb'nɒkʃəs] a abscheulich, widerlich.

oboe ['əʊbəʊ] n Oboe f.

obscene [əb'si:n] a obszön, unanständig.

obscenity [əb'senɪtɪ] n Obszönität f; **obscenities** Zoten pl.

obscure [əb'skjʊə*] a unklar; (indistinct) undeutlich; (unknown) unbekannt, obskur; (dark) düster; vt verdunkeln; view verbergen; (confuse) verwirren.

obscurity [əb'skjʊərɪtɪ] n Unklarheit f; (being unknown) Verborgenheit f; (darkness) Dunkelheit f.

obsequious [əb'si:kwɪəs] a servil.

observable [əb'zɜ:vəbl] a wahrnehmbar, sichtlich.

observance [əb'zɜ:vəns] n Befolgung f.

observant [əb'zɜ:vənt] a aufmerksam.

observation [ɒbzə'veɪʃən] n (noticing) Beobachtung f; (surveillance) Überwachung f; (remark) Bemerkung f.

observatory [əb'zɜ:vətrɪ] n Sternwarte f, Observatorium nt.

observe [əb'zɜ:v] vt (notice) bemerken; (watch) beobachten; customs einhalten; **—er** Beobachter(in f) m.

obsess [əb'ses] vt verfolgen, quälen; to be **—ed** with an idea von einem Gedanken besessen sein;

—ion [əb'seʃən] Besessenheit f, Wahn m; **—ive** a krankhaft.

obsolescence [ɒbsə'lesns] n Veralten nt.

obsolescent [ɒbsə'lesnt] a veraltend.

obsolete ['ɒbsəli:t] a überholt, veraltet.

obstacle ['ɒbstəkl] n Hindernis nt; **— race** Hindernisrennen nt.

obstetrics [ɒb'stetrɪks] n Geburtshilfe f.

obstinacy ['ɒbstɪnəsɪ] n Hartnäckigkeit f, Sturheit f.

obstinate a, **—ly** ad ['ɒbstɪnət, -lɪ] hartnäckig, stur.

obstreperous [əb'strepərəs] a aufmüpfig.

obstruct [əb'strʌkt] vt versperren; pipe verstopfen; (hinder) hemmen; **—ion** [əb'strʌkʃən] Versperrung f; Verstopfung f; (obstacle) Hindernis nt; **—ive** a hemmend.

obtain [əb'teɪn] vt erhalten, bekommen; result erzielen; **—able** a erhältlich.

obtrusive [əb'tru:sɪv] a aufdringlich.

obtuse [əb'tju:s] a begriffsstutzig; angle stumpf.

obviate ['ɒbvɪeɪt] vt beseitigen; danger abwenden.

obvious ['ɒbvɪəs] a offenbar, offensichtlich; **—ly** ad offensichtlich.

occasion [ə'keɪʒən] n Gelegenheit f; (special event) große(s) Ereignis nt; (reason) Grund m, Anlaß m; **on —** gelegentlich; vt veranlassen; **—al** a, **—ally** ad gelegentlich; very **—ally** sehr selten.

occult [ɒ'kʌlt] n the **—** der Okkultismus; a okkult.

occupant ['ɔkjupənt] n Inhaber(in f) m; (of house etc) Bewohner(in f) m.

occupation [ɔkju'peɪʃən] n (employment) Tätigkeit f, Beruf m; (pastime) Beschäftigung f; (of country) Besetzung f, Okkupation f; —al a hazard Berufs-; therapy Beschäftigungs-.

occupier ['ɔkjupaɪə*] n Bewohner(in f) m.

occupy ['ɔkjupaɪ] vt (take possession of) besetzen; seat belegen; (live in) bewohnen; position, office bekleiden; position in sb's life einnehmen; time beanspruchen; mind beschäftigen.

occur [ə'kɜ:*] vi (happen) vorkommen, geschehen; (appear) vorkommen; (come to mind) einfallen (to dat); —rence [ə'kʌrəns] n Ereignis nt; (appearing) Auftreten nt.

ocean ['əuʃən] n Ozean m, Meer nt; —going a Hochsee-.

ochre ['əukə*] n Ocker m or nt.

o'clock [ə'klɔk] ad: it is 5 — es ist 5 Uhr.

octagonal [ɔk'tægənl] a achteckig.

octane ['ɔkteɪn] n Oktan nt.

octave ['ɔktɪv] n Oktave f.

October [ɔk'təubə*] n Oktober m.

octopus ['ɔktəpəs] n Krake f; (small) Tintenfisch m.

oculist ['ɔkjulɪst] n Augenarzt m/-ärztin f.

odd [ɔd] a (strange) sonderbar; (not even) ungerade; (the other part missing) einzeln; (about) ungefähr; (surplus) übrig; (casual) Gelegenheits-, zeitweilig; —ity (strangeness) Merkwürdigkeit f; (queer person) seltsame(r) Kauz m; (thing) Kuriosität f; —ly ad seltsam; —ly enough merkwürdigerweise; —ment Rest m,

Einzelstück nt; —s pl Chancen pl; (betting) Gewinnchancen pl; it makes no —s es spielt keine Rolle; at —s uneinig; —s and ends pl Reste pl; Krimskrams m.

ode [əud] n Ode f.

odious ['əudɪəs] a verhaßt; action abscheulich.

odour, (US) **odor** ['əudə*] n Geruch m; —less a geruchlos.

of [ɔv, əv] prep von; (indicating material) aus; the first — May der erste Mai; within a month — his death einen Monat nach seinem Tod; a girl — ten ein zehnjähriges Mädchen; fear — God Gottesfurcht f; love — money Liebe f zum Geld; the six — us wir sechs.

off [ɔf] ad (absent) weg, fort; (switch) aus(geschaltet), ab(geschaltet); (milk) sauer; I'm — ich gehe jetzt; the button's — der Knopf ist ab; to be well-/badly — reich/arm sein; prep von; (distant from) ab(gelegen) von; 3% — 3% Nachlaß gewähren; just — Piccadilly gleich bei Piccadilly; I'm — smoking ich rauche nicht mehr.

offal ['ɔfəl] n Innereien pl.

off-colour ['ɔf'kʌlə*] a nicht wohl.

offence, (US) **offense** ['əfens] n (crime) Vergehen nt, Straftat f; (insult) Beleidigung f.

offend [ə'fend] vt beleidigen; —er Gesetzesübertreter m; —ing a verletzend.

offensive [ə'fensɪv] a (unpleasant) übel, abstoßend; weapon Kampf-; remark verletzend; n Angriff m, Offensive f.

offer ['ɔfə*] n Angebot f; on — zum Verkauf angeboten; vt anbieten; reward aussetzen; opinion äußern; resistance leisten;

—ing Gabe f; (collection) Kollekte f.

offhand ['ɒf'hænd] a lässig; ad ohne weiteres.

office ['ɒfɪs] n Büro nt; (position) Amt nt; (duty) Aufgabe f; (Eccl) Gottesdienst m; — **block** Büro(hoch)haus nt; — **boy** Laufjunge m; —**r** (Mil) Offizier m; (public —) Beamte(r) m im öffentlichen Dienst; — **work** Büroarbeit f; — **worker** Büroangestellte(r) mf.

official [ə'fɪʃəl] a offiziell, amtlich; n Beamte(r) m; (Pol) amtliche(r) Sprecher m (of club etc) Funktionär m, Offizielle(r) m; —**ly** ad offiziell.

officious [ə'fɪʃəs] a aufdringlich.

offing ['ɒfɪŋ] n: in the — in (Aus)sicht.

off-licence ['ɒflaɪsəns] n Wein- und Spirituosenhandlung f.

off-peak ['ɒfpiːk] a heating Speicher-; charges verbilligt.

off-season ['ɒfsiːzn] a außer Saison.

offset [ɒfset] vt irreg ausgleichen.

offshore ['ɒf'ʃɔ:*] ad in einiger Entfernung von der Küste; a küstennah, Küsten-.

offside ['ɒf'saɪd] a (Sport) im Abseits (stehend); ad abseits; n (Aut) Fahrerseite f.

offspring ['ɒfsprɪŋ] n Nachkommenschaft f; (one) Sprößling m.

offstage ['ɒf'steɪdʒ] ad hinter den Kulissen.

off-the-cuff ['ɒfðəkʌf] a unvorbereitet, aus dem Stegreif.

often ['ɒfən] ad oft.

ogle ['əʊgl] vt liebäugeln mit.

oh [əʊ] interj oh, ach.

oil [ɔɪl] n Öl nt; vt ölen; —**can** Ölkännchen nt; —**field** Ölfeld nt; —**fired** a Öl-; — **level** Ölstand m; — **painting** Ölgemälde nt; — **refinery** Ölraffinerie f; —**rig** Ölplattform f; —**skins** pl Ölzeug nt; — **tanker** (Öl)tanker m; — **well** Ölquelle f; —**y** a ölig; (dirty) ölbeschmiert; manners schleimig.

ointment ['ɔɪntmənt] n Salbe f.

O.K., okay ['əʊ'keɪ] interj in Ordnung, O.K.; a in Ordnung; that's — with or by me ich bin damit .einverstanden; n Zustimmung f; vt genehmigen.

old [əʊld] a alt; (former also) ehemalig; in the — days früher; any — thing irgend etwas; — **age** Alter nt; —**en** a (liter) alt, vergangen; —**fashioned** a altmodisch; — **maid** alte Jungfer f.

olive ['ɒlɪv] n (fruit) Olive f; (colour) Olive nt; a Oliven-; (coloured) olivenfarbig; — **branch** Ölzweig m; — **oil** Olivenöl nt.

Olympic [əʊ'lɪmpɪk] a olympisch; — Games, —**s** pl Olympische Spiele pl.

omelet(te) ['ɒmlət] n Omelett nt.

omen ['əʊmən] n Zeichen nt, Omen nt.

ominous ['ɒmɪnəs] a bedrohlich.

omission [əʊ'mɪʃən] n Auslassung f; (neglect) Versäumnis nt.

omit [əʊ'mɪt] vt auslassen; (fail to do) versäumen.

on [ɒn] prep auf; — TV im Fernsehen; I have it — me ich habe es bei mir; a ring — his finger ein Ring am Finger; — the main road/the bank of the river an der Hauptstraße/dem Flußufer; — foot zu Fuß; a lecture — Dante eine Vorlesung über Dante; — the left links; — the right rechts; — Sunday am Sonntag; — Sundays sonntags; — hearing this, he left als er das hörte, ging er; ad (dar)auf; she had nothing — se hatte nichts an; (no plans) sie hatte nichts vor; what's — at the cinema? was läuft im Kino?; move — weitergehen; go — mach weiter; the light is — das Licht ist an; you're — (col) akzeptiert; it's not — (col) das ist nicht drin; — and off hin und wieder.

once [wʌns] ad einmal; cj wenn ... einmal; — you've seen him wenn du ihn erst einmal gesehen hast; — she had seen him sobald sie ihn gesehen hatte; at — sofort; (at the same time) gleichzeitig; all at — plötzlich; — more noch einmal; more than — mehr als einmal; in a while and dann und zu; — and for all ein für allemal; — upon a time es war einmal.

oncoming ['ɒnkʌmɪŋ] a traffic Gegen-, entgegenkommend.

one [wʌn] a ein; (only) einzig; n Eins f; pron eine(r, s); (people, you) man; this —, that — das; dieser/diese/dieses; — day eines Tages; the blue — der/die/das blaue; which — welche(r, s); he is — of us er ist einer von uns; — by — einzeln; — another einander; —man a Einmann-; —self pron sich (selber); —way a street Einbahn-.

ongoing ['ɒngəʊɪŋ] a stattfindend, momentan; (progressing) sich entwickelnd.

onion ['ʌnjən] n Zwiebel f.

onlooker ['ɒnlʊkə*] n Zuschauer(in f) m.

only ['əʊnlɪ] ad nur, bloß; a einzige(r, s); — yesterday erst

gestern; — just arrived gerade erst angekommen.

onset ['ɒnset] n (beginning) Beginn m.

onshore ['ɒnʃɔ:*] ad an Land; a Küsten-.

onslaught ['ɒnslɔ:t] n Angriff m.

onto ['ɒntʊ] prep = on to.

onus ['əʊnəs] n Last f, Pflicht f.

onwards ['ɒnwədz] ad (place) voran, vorwärts; from that day —, von dem Tag an; from today — ab heute.

onyx ['ɒnɪks] n Onyx m.

ooze [u:z] vi sickern.

opacity [əʊ'pæsɪtɪ] n Undurchsichtigkeit f.

opal ['əʊpəl] n Opal m.

opaque [əʊ'peɪk] a undurchsichtig.

open ['əʊpən] a offen; (public) öffentlich; mind aufgeschlossen; sandwich belegt; in the — (air) im Freien; to keep a day — einen Tag freihalten; vt öffnen, aufmachen; trial, motorway, account eröffnen; vi (begin) anfangen; (shop) aufmachen; (door, flower) aufgehen; (play) Premiere haben; — out vt ausbreiten; hole, business erweitern; vi (person) aus sich herausgehen; — up vt route erschließen; shop, prospects eröffnen; —-air a Frei(luft)-; —er Öffner m; —ing (hole) Öffnung f, Loch nt; (beginning) Eröffnung f, Anfang m; (good chance) Gelegenheit f; —ly ad offen; (publicly) öffentlich; —-minded a aufgeschlossen; —necked a offen.

opera ['ɒpərə] n Oper f; — glasses pl Opernglas nt; — house Opernhaus nt.

operate ['ɒpəreɪt] vt machine bedienen; brakes, light betätigen; vi (machine) laufen, in Betrieb sein; *(person)* arbeiten; *(Med)* to — on operieren.

operatic [ɒpə'rætik] *a* Opern-.

operation [ɒpə'reiʃən] *n (working)* Betrieb *m*, Tätigkeit *f*; *(Med)* Operation *f*; *(undertaking)* Unternehmen *nt*; *(Mil)* Einsatz *m*; in full — in vollem Gang; to be in — *(Jur)* in Kraft sein; *(machine)* in Betrieb sein; —al *a* einsatzbereit.

operative ['ɒprətiv] *a* wirksam; *law* rechtsgültig; *(Med)* operativ; *n* Mechaniker *m*; Agent *m*.

operator ['ɒprəreitə*] *n (of machine)* Arbeiter *m*; *(Tel)* Telefonist(in *f*) *m*; phone the — rufen Sie die Vermittlung *or* das Fernamt an.

operetta [ɒpə'retə] *n* Operette *f*.

opinion [ə'pinjən] *n* Meinung *f*; in my — meiner Meinung nach; a matter of — Ansichtssache *f*; —ated *a* starrsinnig.

opium ['əupiəm] *n* Opium *nt*.

opponent [ə'pəunənt] *n* Gegner *m*.

opportune ['ɒpətju:n] *a* günstig; *remark* passend.

opportunist [ɒpə'tju:nist] *n* Opportunist *m*.

opportunity [ɒpə'tju:niti] *n* Gelegenheit *f*, Möglichkeit *f*.

oppose [ə'pəuz] *vt* entgegentreten (+*dat*); *argument, plea* ablehnen; *plan* bekämpfen; —d *a*: to be —d to sth gegen etw sein; as —d to im Gegensatz zu.

opposing [ə'pəuziŋ] *a* gegnerisch; *points of view* entgegengesetzt.

opposite ['ɒpəzit] *a house* gegenüberliegend; *direction* entgegengesetzt; *ad* gegenüber; *prep* gegenüber; — me mir gegenüber; *n* Gegenteil *nt*; — number *(person)* Pendant *nt*; *(Sport)* Gegenspieler *m*.

opposition [ɒpə'ziʃən] *n (resistance)* Widerstand *m*; *(Pol)* Opposition *f*; *(contrast)* Gegensatz *m*.

oppress [ə'pres] *vt* unterdrücken; *(heat etc)* bedrücken; —ion [ə'preʃən] Unterdrückung *f*; —ive *a authority, law* ungerecht; *burden, thought* bedrückend; *heat* drückend.

opt [ɒpt] *vi*: — for sth sich entscheiden für etw; to — to do sth sich entscheiden, etw zu tun; — out of *vi* sich drücken vor (+*dat*); *(of society)* ausflippen aus (+*dat*).

optical ['ɒptikl] *a* optisch.

optician [ɒp'tiʃən] *n* Optiker *m*.

optimism ['ɒptimizəm] *n* Optimismus *m*.

optimist ['ɒptimist] *n* Optimist *m*; —ic ['ɒpti'mistik] *a* optimistisch.

optimum ['ɒptiməm] *a* optimal.

option ['ɒpʃən] *n* Wahl *f*; *(Comm)* Vorkaufsrecht *m*, Option *f*; —al *a* freiwillig; *subject* wahlfrei; —al extras Extras auf Wunsch.

opulence ['ɒpjuləns] *n* Reichtum *m*.

opulent ['ɒpjulənt] *a* sehr reich.

opus ['əupəs] *n* Werk *nt*, Opus *nt*.

or [ɔ:*] *cj* oder; he could not read — write er konnte weder lesen noch schreiben.

oracle ['ɒrəkl] *n* Orakel *nt*.

oral [ɔ:'rəl] *a* mündlich; *n (exam)* mündliche Prüfung *f*, Mündliche(s) *nt*.

orange ['ɒrindʒ] *n (fruit)* Apfelsine *f*, Orange *f*; *(colour)* Orange *nt*; *a* orange.

orang-outang, orang-utan [ɔ:'ræŋu:'tæn] *n* Orang-Utan *m*.

oration [ɔ:'reiʃən] *n* feierliche Rede *f*.

orator ['ɔrətə*] n Redner(in f) m.

oratorio [ɔrə'tɔ:rɪəʊ] n Oratorium nt.

orbit ['ɔ:bɪt] n Umlaufbahn f; 2 —s 2 Umkreisungen; **to be in** — (die Erde/den Mond etc) umkreisen; vt umkreisen.

orchard ['ɔ:tʃəd] n Obstgarten m.

orchestra ['ɔ:kɪstrə] n Orchester nt; —l [ɔ:'kestrəl] a Orchester-, orchestral; —te ['ɔ:kɪstreɪt] vt orchestrieren.

orchid ['ɔ:kɪd] n Orchidee f.

ordain [ɔ:'deɪn] vt (Eccl) weihen; (decide) verfügen.

ordeal [ɔ:'di:l] n schwere Prüfung f, Qual f.

order ['ɔ:də*] n (sequence) Reihenfolge f; (good arrangement) Ordnung f; (command) Befehl m; (Jur) Anordnung f; (peace) Ordnung f, Ruhe f; (condition) Zustand m; (rank) Klasse f; (Comm) Bestellung f; (Eccl, honour) Orden m; **out of** — außer Betrieb; **in** — **to do sth um etw zu tun**; **in** — **that damit**; **holy** —**s** Priesterweihe f; vt (arrange) ordnen; (command) befehlen (sth etw acc, sb jdm); (Comm) bestellen; — **form** Bestellschein m; —**ly** n (Mil) Offiziersbursche m; (Mil Med) Sanitäter m; (Med) Pfleger m; a (tidy) ordentlich; (well-behaved) ruhig; —**ly officer** diensthabender Offizier.

ordinal ['ɔ:dɪnl] a Ordnungs-, Ordinal-.

ordinarily ['ɔ:dnrɪlɪ] ad gewöhnlich.

ordinary ['ɔ:ndrɪ] a (usual) gewöhnlich, normal; (commonplace) gewöhnlich, alltäglich.

ordination [ɔ:dɪ'neɪʃən] n Priesterweihe f; (Protestant) Ordination f.

ordnance ['ɔ:dnəns] n Artillerie f; Munition f; — **factory** Munitionsfabrik f.

ore [ɔ:*] n Erz nt.

organ ['ɔ:gən] n (Mus) Orgel f; (Biol, fig) Organ nt; —**ic** [ɔ:'gænɪk] a organisch; —**ism** ['ɔ:gənɪzm] Organismus m; —**ist** Organist(in f) m.

organization [ɔ:gənaɪ'zeɪʃən] n Organisation f; (make-up) Struktur f.

organize ['ɔ:gənaɪz] vt organisieren; —**r** Organisator m, Veranstalter m.

orgasm ['ɔ:gæzəm] n Orgasmus m.

orgy ['ɔ:dʒɪ] n Orgie f.

Orient ['ɔ:rɪənt] n Orient m.

oriental [ɔ:rɪ'entəl] a orientalisch; n Orientale m, Orientalin f.

orientate ['ɔ:rɪentet] vt orientieren.

orifice ['ɒrɪfɪs] n Öffnung f.

origin ['ɒrɪdʒɪn] n Ursprung m; (of the world) Anfang m, Entstehung f.

original [ə'rɪdʒɪnl] a (first) ursprünglich; painting original; idea originell; n Original nt —**ity** [ərɪdʒɪ'nælɪtɪ] Originalität f —**ly** ad ursprünglich; originell.

originate [ə'rɪdʒɪnet] vi entstehen; **to** — **from** stammen aus; vt ins Leben rufen.

originator [ə'rɪdʒɪneɪtə*] n (of movement) Begründer m; (of invention) Erfinder m.

ornament ['ɔ:nəmənt] n Schmuck m; (on mantelpiece) Nippesfigur f; (fig) Zierde f; —**al** [ɔ:nə'mentl] a schmückend, Zier-; —**ation** Verzierung f.

ornate [ɔ:'neɪt] a reich verziert; style überladen.

ornithologist [ɔ:nɪˈθɒlədʒɪst] n Ornithologe m, Ornithologin f.

ornithology [ɔ:nɪˈθɒlədʒɪ] n Vogelkunde f, Ornithologie f.

orphan [ˈɔ:fən] n Waise f, Waisenkind nt; vt zur Waise machen; **—age** Waisenhaus nt.

orthodox [ˈɔ:θədɒks] a orthodox.

orthopaedic, (US) **orthopedic** [ɔ:θəuˈpi:dɪk] a orthopädisch.

oscillation [ɔsɪˈleɪʃən] n Schwingung f, Oszillation f.

ostensible a, **ostensibly** ad [ɒsˈtensəbl, -blɪ] vorgeblich, angeblich.

ostentation [ɒstenˈteɪʃən] n Zurschaustellen nt.

ostentatious [ɒstenˈteɪʃəs] a großtuerisch, protzig.

ostracize [ˈɒstrəsaɪz] vt ausstoßen.

ostrich [ˈɒstrɪtʃ] n Strauß m.

other [ˈʌðə*] a ander(e, s); the — day neulich; every — day jeden .zweiten Tag; any person — than him alle außer ihm; there are 6 —s da sind noch 6; pron andere(r, s); ad: — than anders als; —wise ad (in a different way) anders; (in other ways) sonst, im übrigen; (or else) sonst.

otter [ˈɒtə*] n Otter m.

ought [ɔ:t] v aux sollen; he behaves as he — er benimmt sich, wie es .sich gehört; you — to do that Sie sollten das tun; he — to win er müßte gewinnen; that — to do das müßte or dürfte reichen.

ounce [auns] n Unze f.

our [auə*] poss a unser; **—s** poss pron unsere(r, s); **—selves** pron uns (selbst); (emphatic) (wir) selbst.

oust [aust] vt verdrängen.

out [aut] ad hinaus/heraus; (not indoors) draußen; (not alight) aus; (unconscious) bewußtlos; (results) bekanntgegeben; to eat/go — auswärts essen/ausgehen; that fashion's — das ist nicht mehr Mode; the ball was — der Ball war aus; the flowers are — die Blumen blühen; he was — in his calculations seine Berechnungen waren nicht richtig; to be — for sth auf. etw (acc) aus sein; — loud ad laut; — of prep aus; (away from) außerhalb (+gen); to be — of milk etc keine Milch etc mehr haben; made — of wood aus Holz gemacht; — of danger außer Gefahr; — of place fehl am Platz; — of curiosity aus Neugier; nine — of ten neun von zehn; — and — durch und durch; —of-bounds a verboten; —of-date a veraltet; —of-doors ad im Freien; —of-the-way a (off the general route) abgelegen; (un- usual) ungewöhnlich.

outback [ˈautbæk] n Hinterland nt.

outboard (motor) [ˈautbɔ:d (ˈməutə*)] n Außenbordmotor m.

outbreak [ˈautbreɪk] n Ausbruch m.

outbuilding [ˈautbɪldɪŋ] n Nebengebäude nt.

outburst [ˈautbɜ:st] n Ausbruch m.

outcast [ˈautka:st] n Ausgestoßene(r) mf.

outclass [autˈkla:s] vt übertreffen.

outcome [ˈautkʌm] n Ergebnis nt.

outcry [ˈautkraɪ] n Protest m.

outdated [autˈdeɪtɪd] a veraltet, überholt.

outdo [autˈdu:] vt irreg übertrumpfen.

outdoor [ˈautdɔ:*] a Außen-; (Sport) im Freien.

outdoors [ˈautˈdɔ:z] ad draußen, im

Freien; **to go** — ins Freie or nach draußen gehen.

outer ['autə*] a äußere(r, s); — **space** Weltraum m.

outfit ['autfit] n Ausrüstung f; (set of clothes) Kleidung f; —**ters** (for men's clothes) Herrenausstatter m.

outgoings ['autgəʊɪŋz] npl Ausgaben pl.

outgrow [aut'grəʊ] vt irreg clothes herauswachsen aus; habit ablegen.

outing ['autɪŋ] n Ausflug m.

outlandish [aut'lændɪʃ] a eigenartig.

outlaw ['autlɔ:] n Geächtete(r) m; vt ächten; (thing) verbieten.

outlay ['autleɪ] n Auslage f.

outlet ['autlet] n Auslaß m, Abfluß m; (Comm) Absatzmarkt m; (for emotions) Ventil nt.

outline ['autlaɪn] n Umriß m.

outlive [aut'lɪv] vt überleben.

outlook ['autlʊk] n (lit, fig) Aussicht f; (attitude) Einstellung f.

outlying ['autlaɪŋ] a entlegen; district Außen-.

outmoded [aut'məʊdɪd] a veraltet.

outnumber [aut'nʌmbə*] vt zahlenmäßig überlegen sein (+dat).

outpatient ['autpeɪʃənt] n ambulante(r) Patient(in f) m.

outpost ['autpəʊst] n (Mil, fig) Vorposten m.

output ['autput] n Leistung f, Produktion f.

outrage ['autreɪdʒ] n (cruel deed) Ausschreitung f, Verbrechen nt; (indecency) Skandal m; vt morals verstoßen gegen; person empören; —**ous** [aut'reɪdʒəs] a unerhört, empörend.

outright ['autraɪt] ad (at once) sofort; (openly) ohne Umschweife; **to refuse** — rundweg ablehnen; a

denial völlig; sale Total-; winner unbestritten.

outset ['autset] n Beginn m.

outside ['aut'saɪd] n Außenseite f; on the — außen; at the very — höchstens; a äußere(r, s), Außen-; price Höchst-; chance gering; ad außen; **to go** — nach draußen or hinaus gehen; prep außerhalb (+gen); —**r** Außenseiter(in f) m.

outsize ['autsaɪz] a übergroß.

outskirts ['autskɜ:ts] npl Stadtrand m.

outspoken [aut'spəʊkən] a offen, freimütig.

outstanding [aut'stændɪŋ] a hervorragend; debts etc ausstehend.

outstay [aut'steɪ] vt: — one's welcome länger bleiben als erwünscht.

outstretched ['autstretʃt] a ausgestreckt.

outward [aut'wəd] a äußere(r, s); journey Hin-; freight ausgehend; ad nach außen; —**ly** ad äußerlich.

outweigh [aut'weɪ] vt (fig) überwiegen.

outwit [aut'wɪt] vt überlisten.

outworn [aut'wɔ:n] a expression abgedroschen.

oval ['əʊvəl] a oval; n Oval nt.

ovary ['əʊvərɪ] n Eierstock m.

ovation [əʊ'veɪʃən] n Beifallssturm m.

oven ['ʌvn] n Backofen m.

over ['əʊvə*] ad (across) hinüber/herüber; (finished) vorbei; (left) übrig; (again) wieder, noch einmal; prep über; (in every part of) in; pref (excessively) übermäßig; **famous the world** — in der ganzen Welt berühmt; **five times** — fünfmal; — **the weekend** übers Wochenende; — **coffee bei**

einer Tasse Kaffee; **—** the phone am Telephon; **all** — *(everywhere)* überall; *(finished)* vorbei; — **and** — immer wieder; — **and above** darüber hinaus.

over- ['əʊvə*] pref über-.

overact [əʊvər'ækt] vi übertreiben.

overall ['əʊvərɔ:l] n *(Brit)* *(for woman)* Kittelschürze f; a situation allgemein; length Gesamt-; ad insgesamt; **~s** pl *(for man)* Overall m.

overawe [əʊvər'ɔ:] vt *(frighten)* einschüchtern; *(make impression)* überwältigen.

overbalance [əʊvə'bæləns] vi Übergewicht bekommen.

overbearing [əʊvə'bɛərɪŋ] a aufdringlich.

overboard ['əʊvəbɔ:d] ad über Bord.

overcast ['əʊvəka:st] a bedeckt.

overcharge [əʊvə'tʃɑ:dʒ] vt zuviel verlangen von.

overcoat ['əʊvəkəʊt] n Mantel m.

overcome [əʊvə'kʌm] vt irreg überwinden; *(sleep, emotion)* übermannen; **—** **by the song** vom Lied gerührt.

overcrowded [əʊvə'kraʊdɪd] a überfüllt.

overcrowding [əʊvə'kraʊdɪŋ] n Überfüllung f.

overdo [əʊvə'du:] vt irreg *(cook too much)* verkochen; *(exaggerate)* übertreiben.

overdose ['əʊvədəʊs] n Überdosis f.

overdraft ['əʊvədrɑ:ft] n *(Konto)*überziehung f; **to have an —** sein Konto überzogen haben.

overdrawn ['əʊvə'drɔ:n] a account überzogen.

overdrive ['əʊvədraɪv] n *(Aut)* Schnellgang m.

overdue ['əʊvə'dju:] a überfällig.

overenthusiastic ['əʊvərɪn-θju:zi'æstɪk] a zu begeistert.

overestimate [əʊvər'estɪmeɪt] vt überschätzen.

overexcited [əʊvərɪk'saɪtɪd] a überreizt; children aufgeregt.

overexertion [əʊvərɪg'zɜ:ʃən] n Überanstrengung f.

overexpose [əʊvərɪks'pəʊz] vt *(Phot)* überbelichten.

overflow [əʊvə'fləʊ] vi überfließen; ['əʊvəfləʊ] n *(excess)* Überschuß m; *(outlet)* Überlauf m.

overgrown [əʊvə'grəʊn] a garden verwildert.

overhaul [əʊvə'hɔ:l] vt car überholen; plans überprüfen; ['əʊvəhɔ:l] n Überholung f.

overhead [əʊvə'hed] ad Hoch-; wire oberirdisch; lighting Decken-; ['əʊvəhed] ad oben; **—s** pl allgemeine Unkosten pl.

overhear [əʊvə'hɪə*] vt irreg *(mit an)*hören.

overjoyed [əʊvə'dʒɔɪd] a überglücklich.

overland ['əʊvəlænd] a Überland-; [əʊvə'lænd] ad travel über Land.

overlap [əʊvə'læp] vi sich überschneiden; *(objects)* sich teilweise decken; ['əʊvəlæp] n Überschneidung f.

overload [əʊvə'ləʊd] vt überladen.

overlook [əʊvə'lʊk] vt *(view from above)* überblicken; *(not to notice)* übersehen; *(pardon)* hinwegsehen über *(+acc)*.

overlord ['əʊvəlɔ:d] n Lehnsherr m.

overnight ['əʊvə'naɪt] a journey Nacht-; ad über Nacht; **— bag**

Reisetasche f; — stay Übernachtung f.

overpass ['əʊvəpɑ:s] n Überführung f.

overpower [əʊvə'paʊə*] vt überwältigen; —ing a überwältigend.

overrate ['əʊvə'reɪt] vt überschätzen.

override [əʊvə'raɪd] vt irreg order, decision aufheben; objection übergehen.

overriding [əʊvə'raɪdɪŋ] a Haupt-, vorherrschend.

overrule [əʊvə'ru:l] vt verwerfen; we were —d unser Vorschlag wurde verworfen.

overseas ['əʊvə'si:z] ad nach/in Übersee; a überseeisch, Übersee-.

overseer ['əʊvəsɪə*] n Aufseher m.

overshadow [əʊvə'ʃædəʊ] vt überschatten.

overshoot ['əʊvə'ʃu:t] vt irreg runway hinausschießen über (+acc).

oversight ['əʊvəsaɪt] n (mistake) Versehen nt.

oversimplify ['əʊvə'sɪmplɪfaɪ] vt zu sehr vereinfachen.

oversleep ['əʊvə'sli:p] vi irreg verschlafen.

overspill ['əʊvəspɪl] n (Bevölkerungs)überschuß m.

overstate ['əʊvə'steɪt] vt übertreiben; —ment Übertreibung f.

overt [əʊ'vɜ:t] a offen(kundig).

overtake [əʊvə'teɪk] vti irreg überholen.

overthrow [əʊvə'θrəʊ] vt irreg (Pol) stürzen.

overtime ['əʊvətaɪm] n Überstunden pl.

overtone ['əʊvətəʊn] n (fig) Note f.

overture ['əʊvətjʊə*] n Ouvertüre f; —s pl (fig) Angebot nt.

overturn [əʊvə'tɜ:n] vti umkippen.

overweight ['əʊvə'weɪt] a zu dick, zu schwer.

overwhelm [əʊvə'welm] vt überwältigen; —ing a überwältigend.

overwork ['əʊvə'wɜ:k] n Überarbeitung f; vt überlasten; vi sich überarbeiten.

overwrought ['əʊvə'rɔ:t] a überreizt.

owe [əʊ] vt schulden; to — sth to sb money jdm etw schulden; favour etc jdm etw verdanken.

owing ['əʊɪŋ'tu:] prep wegen (+gen).

owl [aʊl] n Eule f.

own [əʊn] vt besitzen; (admit) zugeben; who —s that? wem gehört das?; a eigen; **I have money of my** — ich habe selbst Geld; all my — mein Eigentum nt; all my — mein Eigentum; on one's — allein; — up vi zugeben (to sth etw acc); —er Besitzer(in f) m, Eigentümer(in f) m; . —ership Besitz m.

ox [ɒks] n Ochse m.

oxide ['ɒksaɪd] n Oxyd nt.

oxtail ['ɒksteɪl] n: — soup Ochsenschwanzsuppe f.

oxyacetylene ['ɒksɪ'setɪli:n] a Azetylensauerstoff-.

oxygen ['ɒksɪdʒən] n Sauerstoff m; — mask Sauerstoffmaske f; — tent Sauerstoffzelt nt.

oyster ['ɔɪstə*] n Auster f.

ozone ['əʊzəʊn] n Ozon nt.

P

P, p [pi:] n P nt, p nt.

pa [pɑ:] n (col) Papa m.

pace [peɪs] n Schritt m; (speed) Geschwindigkeit f, Tempo nt; vi schreiten; **to keep — with** Schritt halten mit; **—maker** Schrittmacher m.

pacification [pæsɪfɪ'keɪʃən] n Befriedung f.

pacifism ['pæsɪfɪzəm] n Pazifismus m.

pacifist ['pæsɪfɪst] n Pazifist m.

pacify ['pæsɪfaɪ] vt befrieden; (calm) beruhigen.

pack [pæk] n Packen m; (of wolves) Rudel nt; (of hounds) Meute f; (of cards) Spiel nt; (gang) Bande f; vti case packen; clothes einpacken; —age Paket nt; —age **tour** Pauschalreise; f; —et Päckchen nt; — **horse** Packpferd nt; — **ice** Packeis nt; —ing (action) Packen nt; (material) Verpackung f; —ing case (Pack)kiste f.

pact [pækt] n Pakt m, Vertrag m.

pad [pæd] n (of paper) (Schreib)block m; (for inking) Stempelkissen nt; (padding) Polster nt; vt polstern.

paddle ['pædl] n Paddel nt; vt boat paddeln; vi (in sea) plantschen.

paddling pool ['pædlɪŋ pu:l] n Plantschbecken nt.

paddock ['pædək] n Koppel f.

paddy ['pædɪ] n — **field** Reisfeld nt.

padlock ['pædlɒk] n Vorhängeschloß nt.

padre ['pɑ:drɪ] n Militärgeistliche(r) m.

paediatrics [pi:dɪ'ætrɪks] n Kinderheilkunde f.

pagan ['peɪgən] a heidnisch.

page [peɪdʒ] n Seite f; (person) Page m; vt (in hotel etc) ausrufen lassen.

pageant ['pædʒənt] n Festzug m; —ry Gepränge nt.

pagoda [pə'gəʊdə] n Pagode f.

pail [peɪl] n Eimer m.

pain [peɪn] n Schmerz m, Schmerzen pl; —s pl (efforts) große Mühe f, große Anstrengungen pl; **to be at —s to** do sth sich (dat) Mühe geben, etw zu tun; —ed a expression gequält; —ful a (physically) schmerzhaft; (embarrassing) peinlich; (difficult) mühsam; —**killing drug** schmerzstillende(s) Mittel nt; —less a schmerzlos; —**staking** a gewissenhaft.

paint [peɪnt] n Farbe f; vt anstreichen; picture malen; —**brush** Pinsel m; (decorator) Maler m; (decorator) Maler m, Anstreicher m; —ing (act) Malen nt; (Art) Malerei f; (picture) Bild nt, Gemälde nt.

pair [peə*] n Paar nt; — **of scissors** Schere f; — **of trousers** Hose f.

pajamas (US) [pə'dʒɑ:məz] npl Schlafanzug m.

pal [pæl] n (col) Kumpel m; (woman) (gute) Freundin f.

palace ['pæləs] n Palast m, Schloß nt.

palatable ['pælətəbl] a schmackhaft.

palate ['pælɪt] n Gaumen m; (taste) Geschmack m.

palaver [pə'lɑ:və*] n (col) Theater nt.

pale [peɪl] a face blaß, bleich; colour hell, blaß; —ness Blässe f.

palette ['pælɪt] n Palette f.

palisade [pælɪ'seɪd] n Palisade f.

pall [pɔ:l] n Bahr- or Leichentuch nt; (of smoke) (Rauch)wolke f; vi jeden Reiz verlieren, verblassen; —bearer Sargträger m.

pallid ['pælɪd] a blaß, bleich.

pally ['pælɪ] a (col) befreundet.

palm [pɑ:m] n (of hand) Handfläche f; (also — tree) Palme f; —ist Handleserin f; P— Sunday Palmsonntag m.

palpable ['pælpəbl] a (lit, fig) greifbar.

palpably ['pælpəblɪ] ad offensichtlich.

palpitation [pælpɪ'teɪʃən] n Herzklopfen nt.

paltry ['pɔ:ltrɪ] a armselig.

pamper ['pæmpə*] vt verhätscheln.

pamphlet ['pæmflət] n Broschüre f.

pan [pæn] n Pfanne f; vi (Cine) schwenken.

pan- [pæn] pref Pan-, All-.

panacea [pænə'sɪə] n (fig) Allheilmittel nt.

panache [pə'næʃ] n Schwung m.

pancake ['pænkeɪk] n Pfannkuchen m.

panda ['pændə] n Panda m.

pandemonium [pændɪ'məunɪəm] n Hölle f; (noise) Höllenlärm m.

pander ['pændə*] vi sich richten (to nach).

pane [peɪn] n (Fenster)scheibe f.

panel ['pænl] n (of wood) Tafel f; (TV) Diskussionsteilnehmer pl; —ing (US), —ling Täfelung f.

pang [pæŋ] n Stich m, Qual f; —s of conscience Gewissensbisse pl.

panic ['pænɪk] n Panik f; a panisch; vi von panischem Schrecken erfaßt werden, durchdrehen; don't — (nur) keine Panik; —ky a person überängstlich.

pannier ['pænɪə*] n (Trage)korb m; (on bike) Satteltasche f.

panorama [pænə'rɑ:mə] n Rundblick m, Panorama nt.

panoramic [pænə'ræmɪk] a Panorama-.

pansy ['pænzɪ] n (flower) Stiefmütterchen nt; (col) Schwule(r) m.

pant [pænt] vi keuchen; (dog) hecheln.

pantechnicon [pæn'teknɪkən] n Möbelwagen m.

panther ['pænθə*] n Panther m.

panties ['pæntɪz] npl (Damen)slip m.

pantomime ['pæntəmaɪm] n Märchenkomödie f um Weihnachten.

pantry ['pæntrɪ] n Vorratskammer f.

pants [pænts] npl Unterhose f; (trousers) Hose f.

papal ['peɪpəl] a päpstlich.

paper ['peɪpə*] n Papier nt; (newspaper) Zeitung f; (essay) Vortrag m, Referat nt; a Papier-, aus Papier; vt wall tapezieren; —s pl (identity) Ausweis(papiere pl) m; —back Taschenbuch nt; — bag Tüte f; — clip Büroklammer f; —weight Briefbeschwerer m; —work Schreibarbeit f.

papier-mâché ['pæpɪeɪ'mæʃeɪ] n Papiermaché nt.

paprika ['pæprɪkə] n Paprika m.

papyrus [pə'paɪərəs] n Papyrus m.

par [pɑ:*] n (Comm) Nennwert m; (Golf) Par nt; on a — with ebenbürtig (+dat); to be on a — with sb sich mit jdm messen können; below — unter (jds) Niveau.

parable ['pærəbl] n Parabel f; (Rel) Gleichnis nt.

parachute ['pærəʃu:t] n Fallschirm m; vi (mit dem · Fallschirm) abspringen.

parachutist ['pærəʃu:tɪst] n Fallschirmspringer m.

parade [pə'reɪd] n Parade f; vt aufmarschieren lassen; vi paradieren, vorbeimarschieren.

paradise ['pærədaɪs] n Paradies nt.

paradox ['pærədɒks] n Paradox nt; —ical [pærə'dɒksɪkəl] a paradox, widersinnig; —ically [pærə'dɒksɪkəlɪ] ad paradoxerweise.

paraffin ['pærəfɪn] n Paraffin nt.

paragraph ['pærəgrɑ:f] n Absatz m, Paragraph m.

parallel ['pærəlel] a parallel; n Parallele f.

paralysis [pə'rælɪsɪs] n Lähmung f.

paralyze ['pærəlaɪz] vt lähmen.

paramount ['pærəmaʊnt] a höchste(r, s), oberste(r, s).

paranoia [pærə'nɔɪə] n Paranoia f.

parapet ['pærəpɪt] n Brüstung f.

paraphernalia ['pærəfə'neɪlɪə] n Zubehör nt, Utensilien pl.

paraphrase ['pærəfreɪz] vt umschreiben.

paraplegic [pærə'pli:dʒɪk] n Querschnittsgelähmte(r) mf.

parasite ['pærəsaɪt] n (lit, fig) Schmarotzer m, Parasit m.

parasol ['pærəsɒl] n Sonnenschirm m.

paratrooper ['pærətru:pə*] n Fallschirmjäger m.

parcel ['pɑ:sl] n Paket nt; vt (also — up) einpacken.

parch [pɑ:tʃ] vt (aus)dörren; I'm —ed ich bin am Verdursten.

parchment ['pɑ:tʃmənt] n Pergament nt.

pardon ['pɑ:dn] n Verzeihung f; vt (Jur) begnadigen; — me!, I beg your —! verzeihen Sie bitte!; (objection) aber ich bitte Sie! ; — me? (US), (I beg your) —? wie bitte?

parent ['pɛərənt] n Elternteil m; —al [pə'rentl] a elterlich, Eltern-; —hood Elternschaft f; —s pl Eltern pl; — ship Mutterschiff nt.

parenthesis [pə'renθɪsɪs] n Klammer f; (sentence) Parenthese f.

parish ['pærɪʃ] n Gemeinde · f; —ioner [pə'rɪʃənə*] Gemeindemitglied nt.

parity ['pærɪtɪ] n (Fin) Umrechnungskurs m, Parität f.

park [pɑ:k] n Park m; vti parken; —ing Parken nt; 'no —ing' Parken verboten; —ing lot (US) Parkplatz m; —ing meter Parkuhr f; —ing place Parkplatz m.

parliament ['pɑ:ləmənt] n Parlament nt; —ary [pɑ:lə'mentərɪ] a parlamentarisch, Parlaments-.

parlour, (US) **parlor** ['pɑ:lə*] n Salon m, Wohnzimmer nt.

parlous ['pɑ:ləs] a äußerst schlimm.

parochial [pə'rəʊkɪəl] a Gemeinde-, gemeindlich; (narrow-minded) eng(stirnig), Provinz-.

parody ['pærədɪ] n Parodie f; · vt parodieren.

parole [pə'rəʊl] n: on — (prisoner) auf Bewährung.

parquet ['pɑːkeɪ] n Parkett(fußboden m) nt.

parrot ['pærət] n Papagei m; — fashion ad wie ein Papagei.

parry ['pærɪ] vt parieren, abwehren.

parsimonious a, —ly ad [pɑːsɪˈməʊnɪəs, -lɪ] knauserig.

parsley ['pɑːslɪ] n Petersilie m.

parsnip ['pɑːsnɪp] n Pastinake f, Petersilienwurzel f.

parson ['pɑːsn] n Pfarrer m.

part [pɑːt] n (piece) Teil m, Stück nt; (Theat) Rolle f; (of machine) Teil nt; a Teil-; ad = partly; vt trennen; hair scheiteln, vi (people) sich trennen, Abschied nehmen; for my — ich für meinen Teil; for the most — meistens, größtenteils; — with vt hergeben; (renounce) aufgeben; in — exchange in Zahlung; —ial ['pɑːʃəl] a (incomplete) teilweise, Teil-; (biased) eingenommen, parteiisch; eclipse partiell; to be —ial to eine (besondere) Vorliebe haben für; —ially ['pɑːʃəlɪ] ad teilweise, zum Teil.

participate [pɑːˈtɪspeɪt] vi teilnehmen (in an +dat).

participation [pɑːtɪsɪˈpeɪʃən] n Teilnahme f; (sharing) Beteiligung f.

participle ['pɑːtɪsɪpl] n Partizip nt, Mittelwort nt.

particular [pəˈtɪkjʊlə*] a bestimmt, speziell; (exact) genau; (fussy) eigen; n Einzelheit f; —s pl (details) Einzelheiten pl; Personalien pl; —ly ad besonders.

parting ['pɑːtɪŋ] n (separation) Abschied m, Trennung f; (of hair) Scheitel m; a Abschieds-.

partisan [pɑːtɪˈzæn] n Parteigänger m; (guerrilla) Partisan m; a Partei-; Partisanen-.

partition [pɑːˈtɪʃən] n (wall) Trennwand f; (division) Teilung f.

partly ['pɑːtlɪ] ad zum Teil, teilweise.

partner ['pɑːtnə*] n Partner m; (Comm also) Gesellschafter m, Teilhaber m; vt der Partner sein von; —ship Partnerschaft f, Gemeinschaft f; (Comm) Teilhaberschaft f.

partridge ['pɑːtrɪdʒ] n Rebhuhn m.

part-time ['pɑːt'taɪm] a (half-day only) halbtägig, Halbtags-; (part of the week only) nebenberuflich; ad halbtags; nebenberuflich.

party ['pɑːtɪ] n (Pol, Jur) Partei f; (group) Gesellschaft f; (celebration) Party f; a dress Gesellschafts-, Party-; politics Partei-.

pass [pɑːs] vt vorbeikommen an (+dat); (on foot) vorbeigehen an (+dat); vorbeifahren an (+dat); (surpass) übersteigen; (hand on) weitergeben; (approve) gelten lassen, genehmigen; time verbringen; exam bestehen; vi (go by) vorbeigehen; vorbeifahren; (years) vergehen; (be successful) bestehen; n (in mountains) Paß m; (permission) Durchgangs- or Passierschein m; (Sport) Paß m, Abgabe f; (in exam) Bestehen nt; to get a — bestehen; — away vi (euph) verscheiden; —by vi vorbeigehen; vorbeifahren; (years) vergehen; — for vt gelten or gehalten werden für; — out vi (faint) ohnmächtig werden; —able a road passierbar, befahrbar; (fairly good) passabel, leidlich; also ad leidlich, ziemlich; —age ['pæsɪdʒ] n (corridor) Gang m, Korridor m; (in book) (Text)stelle f; (voyage) Überfahrt f; —ageway Passage f, Durchgang m.

passenger ['pæsɪndʒə*] n Passagier m; (on bus) Fahrgast m; (in aeroplane also) Fluggast m.

passer-by ['pɑːsə'baɪ] n Passant(in f) m.

passing ['pɑːsɪŋ] n (death) Ableben nt; a car vorbeifahrend; thought, affair momentan; in — en passant.

passion ['pæʃən] n Leidenschaft f; —ate a, —ately ad leidenschaftlich.

passive ['pæsɪv] n Passiv nt; a Passiv-, passiv.

Passover ['pɑːsəʊvə*] n Passahfest nt.

passport ['pɑːspɔːt] n (Reise)paß m.

password ['pɑːswɜːd] n Parole f, Kennwort nt, Losung f.

past [pɑːst] n Vergangenheit f; ad vorbei; prep to go — sth an etw (dat) vorbeigehen; to be — 10 (with age) über 10 sein; (with time) nach 10 sein; a years vergangen; president etc ehemalig.

paste [peɪst] n (for pastry) Teig m; (fish — etc) Paste f; (glue) Kleister m; vt kleben; (put — on) mit Kleister bestreichen.

pastel ['pæstəl] a colour Pastell-.

pasteurized ['pæstəraɪzd] a pasteurisiert.

pastille ['pæstɪl] n Pastille f.

pastime ['pɑːstaɪm] n Hobby nt, Zeitvertreib m.

pastor ['pɑːstə*] n Pastor m, Pfarrer m.

pastoral ['pɑːstərəl] a literature Schäfer-, Pastoral-.

pastry ['peɪstrɪ] n Blätterteig m; (tarts etc) Stückchen pl; Tortengebäck nt.

pasture ['pɑːstʃə*] n Weide f.

pasty ['pæstɪ] n (Fleisch)pastete f; ['peɪstɪ] a bläßlich, käsig.

pat [pæt] n leichte(r) Schlag m, Klaps m; vt tätscheln.

patch [pætʃ] n Fleck m; vt flicken; — of fog Nebelfeld nt; a bad — eine Pechsträhne; —work Patchwork nt; —y a (irregular) ungleichmäßig.

pate [peɪt] n Schädel m.

patent ['peɪtənt] n Patent nt; vt patentieren lassen; (by authorities) patentieren; a offenkundig; — leather Lackleder nt; —ly ad offensichtlich; — medicine pharmazeutische(s) Präparat nt.

paternal [pə'tɜːnl] a väterlich; his — grandmother seine Großmutter väterlicherseits; —istic [pətɜːnə'lɪstɪk] a väterlich, onkelhaft.

paternity [pə'tɜːnɪtɪ] n Vaterschaft f.

path [pɑːθ] n Pfad m; Weg m; (of the sun) Bahn f.

pathetic [pə'θetɪk], —ally ad [pə'θetɪk, -lɪ] (very bad) kläglich; it's — es ist zum Weinen.

pathological [pæθə'lɒdʒɪkəl] a krankhaft, pathologisch.

pathologist [pə'θɒlədʒɪst] n Pathologe m.

pathology [pə'θɒlədʒɪ] n Pathologie f.

pathos ['peɪθɒs] n Rührseligkeit f.

pathway ['pɑːθweɪ] n Pfad m, Weg m.

patience ['peɪʃəns] n Geduld f; (Cards) Patience f.

patient ['peɪʃənt] n Patient(in f) m, Kranke(r) mf; a, —ly a geduldig.

patio ['pætɪəʊ] n Innenhof m; (outside) Terrasse f.

patriotic [pætrɪ'ɒtɪk] a patriotisch.

patriotism ['pætrɪɒtɪzəm] n Patriotismus m.

patrol [pə'trəʊl] n Patrouille f; (police) Streife f; vt patrouillieren in (+dat); vi (police) die Runde machen; (Mil) patrouillieren; on — (police) auf Streife; — car Streifenwagen m; —man (US) (Streifen)polizist m.

patron ['peitrən] n (in shop) (Stamm)kunde m; (in hotel) (Stamm)gast m; (supporter) Förderer m; —age ['pætrənidʒ] Förderung f; Schirmherrschaft f; (Comm) Kundschaft f; —ize also ['pætrənaiz] vt (support) unterstützen; shop besuchen; ['pætrənaiz] (treat condescendingly) von oben herab behandeln; —izing a attitude herablassend; — saint Schutzheilige(r) mf, Schutzpatron(in f) m.

patter ['pætə*] n (sound) (of feet) Trappeln n; (of rain) Prasseln nt; (sales talk) Art f zu reden, Gerede nt; vi (feet) trappeln; (rain) prasseln.

pattern ['pætən] n Muster nt; (sewing) Schnittmuster nt; (knitting) Strickanleitung f; vt — sth on sth etw nach etw bilden.

paunch [pɔ:ntʃ] n dicke(r) Bauch m, Wanst m.

pauper ['pɔ:pə*] n Arme(r) mf.

pause [pɔ:z] n Pause f; vi innehalten.

pave [peiv] vt pflastern; to — the way for den Weg bahnen für; —ment (Brit) Bürgersteig m.

pavilion [pə'viliən] n Pavillon m; (Sport) Klubhaus nt.

paving ['peiviŋ] n Straßenpflaster nt.

paw [pɔ:] n Pfote f; (of big cats) Tatze f, Pranke f; vt (scrape) scharren; (handle) betatschen.

pawn [pɔ:n] n Pfand nt; (chess) Bauer m; vt versetzen, verpfänden; —broker Pfandleiher m; —shop Pfandhaus nt.

pay [pei] n Bezahlung f, Lohn m; to be in sb's — von jdm bezahlt werden; irreg vt bezahlen; it would — you to … es würde sich für dich lohnen, zu …; to — attention achtgeben (to auf +acc); vi zahlen; (be profitable) sich bezahlt machen; it doesn't — es lohnt sich nicht; — for vt bezahlen für; — up vi bezahlen, seine Schulden begleichen; —able a zahlbar, fällig; —day Zahltag m; —ee [per'i:] Zahlungsempfänger m; —ing a einträglich, rentabel; —load Nutzlast f; —ment Bezahlung f; —packet Lohntüte f; —roll Lohnliste f.

pea [pi:] n Erbse f; — souper (col) Suppe f, Waschküche f.

peace [pi:s] n Friede(n) m; —able a, —ably ad friedlich; —ful a friedlich, ruhig; —keeping a Friedens-; —keeping role Vermittlerrolle f; — offering Friedensangebot nt; —time Friede(n) m.

peach [pi:tʃ] n Pfirsich m.

peacock ['pi:kɒk] n Pfau m.

peak [pi:k] n Spitze f; (of mountain) Gipfel m; (fig) Höhepunkt m; (of cap) (Mützen)schirm m; — period Stoßzeit f, Hauptzeit f.

peal [pi:l] n (Glocken)läuten nt.

peanut ['pi:nʌt] n Erdnuß f; — butter Erdnußbutter f.

pear [peə*] n Birne f.

pearl [pɜ:l] n Perle f.

peasant ['pezənt] n Bauer m.

peat [pi:t] n Torf m.

pebble ['pebl] n Kiesel m.

peck [pek] vti picken; n (with beak) Schnabelhieb m; (kiss) flüchtige(r) Kuß m; —ish a (col) ein bißchen hungrig.

peculiar [pɪ'kju:lɪə*] a (odd) seltsam; — to charakteristisch für; —ity [pɪkjuli'erɪtɪ] (singular quality) Besonderheit f; (strangeness) Eigenartigkeit f; —ly ad seltsam; (especially) besonders.

pecuniary [pɪ'kju:nɪərɪ] a Geld-, finanziell, pekuniär.

pedal ['pedl] n Pedal nt; vti (cycle) fahren, radfahren.

pedant ['pedənt] n Pedant m.

pedantic [pɪ'dæntɪk] a pedantisch.

pedantry ['pedəntrɪ] n Pedanterie f.

peddle ['pedl] vt hausieren gehen mit.

pedestal ['pedɪstl] n Sockel m.

pedestrian [pɪ'destrɪən] n Fußgänger m; a Fußgänger-; (humdrum) langweilig; — crossing Fußgängerübergweg m; — precinct Fußgängerzone f.

pediatrics [pi:dɪ'ætrɪks] n (US) = **paediatrics**.

pedigree ['pedɪgri:] n Stammbaum m; a animal reinrassig, Zucht-.

pee [pi:] vi (col) pissen, pinkeln.

peek [pi:k] n flüchtige(r) Blick m; vi gucken.

peel [pi:l] n Schale f; vt schälen; vi (paint etc) abblättern; (skin) sich schälen; —ings pl Schalen pl.

peep [pi:p] n (look) neugierige(r) Blick m; (sound) Piepsen nt; vi (look) neugierig gucken; —hole Guckloch m.

peer [pɪə*] vi spähen; angestrengt schauen (at auf +acc); (peep) gucken; n (nobleman) Peer m; (equal) Ebenbürtige(r) m; his —s

seinesgleichen; —age Peerswürde f; —less a unvergleichlich.

peeve [pi:v] vt (col) verärgern; —d a ärgerlich; person sauer.

peevish ['pi:vɪʃ] a verdrießlich, brummig; —ness Verdrießlichkeit f.

peg [peg] n Stift m; (hook) Haken m; (stake) Pflock m; (clothes —) Wäscheklammer f; off the — von der Stange.

pejorative [pɪ'dʒɒrɪtɪv] a pejorativ, herabsetzend.

pekinese [pi:kɪ'ni:z] n Pekinese m.

pelican ['pelɪkən] n Pelikan m.

pellet ['pelɪt] n Kügelchen nt.

pelmet ['pelmɪt] n Blende f, Schabracke f.

pelt [pelt] vt bewerfen; n Pelz m, Fell nt; — down vi niederprasseln.

pelvis ['pelvɪs] n Becken nt.

pen [pen] n (fountain —) Federhalter m; (ball-point) Kuli m; (for sheep) Pferch m; have you got a —? haben Sie etwas zum Schreiben?

penal ['pi:nl] a Straf-; —ize vt (make punishable) unter Strafe stellen; (punish) bestrafen; (disadvantage) benachteiligen; —ty ['penltɪ] Strafe f; (Ftbl) Elfmeter m; —ty area Strafraum m; —ty kick Elfmeter m.

penance ['penəns] n Buße f.

pence [pens] npl (pl of penny) Pence pl.

penchant [pã:ŋʃã:ŋ] n Vorliebe f, Schwäche f.

pencil ['pensl] n Bleistift m; — sharpener Bleistiftspitzer m.

pendant ['pendənt] n Anhänger m.

pending ['pendɪŋ] prep bis (zu); a unentschieden, noch offen.

pendulum ['pendjʊləm] n Pendel nt.

penetrate ['penɪtreɪt] vt durchdringen; (enter into) eindringen in (+acc).

penetrating ['penɪtreɪtɪŋ] a durchdringend; analysis scharfsinnig.

penetration [penɪ'treɪʃən] n Durchdringen nt; Eindringen nt.

penfriend ['penfrend] n Brieffreund(in f) m.

penguin ['peŋgwɪn] n Pinguin m.

penicillin [penɪ'sɪlɪn] n Penizillin nt.

peninsula [pɪ'nɪnsjulə] n Halbinsel f.

penis ['piːnɪs] n Penis m, männliche(s) Glied nt.

penitence ['penɪtəns] n Reue f.

penitent ['penɪtənt] a reuig; **—iary** [penɪ'tenʃərɪ] (US) Zuchthaus nt.

penknife ['pennaɪf] n Federmesser nt.

pen name ['pen'neɪm] n Pseudonym nt.

pennant ['penənt] n Wimpel m; (official —) Stander m.

penniless ['penɪlɪs] a mittellos, ohne einen Pfennig.

penny ['penɪ] n Penny m.

pension ['penʃən] n Rente f; (for civil servants, executives etc) Ruhegehalt nt, Pension f; **—able** a person pensionsberechtigt; job mit Renten- or Pensionsanspruch; **—er** Rentner(in f) m; (civil servant, executive) Pensionär m; **— fund** Rentenfonds m.

pensive ['pensɪv] a nachdenklich.

pentagon ['pentəgən] n Fünfeck nt.

Pentecost ['pentɪkɒst] n Pfingsten pl or nt.

penthouse ['penthaʊs] n Dachterrassenwohnung f.

pent-up ['pentʌp] a feelings angestaut.

penultimate [pɪ'nʌltɪmət] a vorletzte(r, s).

people ['piːpl] n (nation) Volk nt; (inhabitants) Bevölkerung f; (persons) Leute pl; **— think** man glaubt; vt besiedeln.

pep [pep] n (col) Schwung m, Schmiß m; **— up** vt aufmöbeln.

pepper ['pepə*] n Pfeffer m; (vegetable) Paprika m; vt (pelt) bombardieren; **—mint** (plant) Pfefferminze f; (sweet) Pfefferminz f.

peptalk ['peptɔːk] n (col) Anstachelung f.

per [pɜː*] prep pro; **— annum** pro Jahr; **— cent** Prozent nt.

perceive [pə'siːv] vt (realize) wahrnehmen, spüren; (understand) verstehen.

percentage [pə'sentɪdʒ] n Prozentsatz m.

perceptible [pə'septəbl] a merklich, wahrnehmbar.

perception [pə'sepʃən] n Wahrnehmung f; (insight) Einsicht f.

perceptive [pə'septɪv] a person aufmerksam; analysis tiefgehend.

perch [pɜːtʃ] n Stange f; (fish) Flußbarsch m; vi sitzen, hocken.

percolator ['pɜːkəleɪtə*] n Kaffeemaschine f.

percussion [pɜː'kʌʃən] n (Mus) Schlagzeug nt.

peremptory [pə'remptərɪ] a schroff.

perennial [pə'renɪəl] a wiederkehrend; (everlasting) unvergänglich; n perennierende Pflanze f.

perfect ['pɜːfɪkt] a vollkommen; crime, solution perfekt; (Gram) vollendet; n (Gram) Perfekt nt; [pə'fekt] vt vervollkommnen; **—ion**

[pə'fekʃən] Vollkommenheit f;
Perfektion f; —ionist [pə'fekʃənɪst]
Perfektionist m; —ly ad vollkommen, perfekt; (quite) ganz,
einfach.

perforate ['pɜ:fəreɪt] vt durchlöchern; —d a durchlöchert,
perforiert.

perforation [pɜ:fə'reɪʃən] n
Perforation f.

perform [pə'fɔ:m] vt (carry out)
durch- or ausführen; task ver-
richten; (Theat) spielen, geben; vi
(Theat) auftreten; —ance Durchführung f; (efficiency) Leistung f;
(show) Vorstellung f; —er
Künstler(in f) m; —ing a animal
dressiert.

perfume ['pɜ:fju:m] n Duft m;
(lady's) Parfüm nt.

perfunctory [pə'fʌŋktərɪ] a oberflächlich, mechanisch.

perhaps [pə'hæps] ad vielleicht.

peril ['perɪl] n Gefahr f; —ous a,
—ously ad gefährlich.

perimeter [pə'rɪmɪtə*] n Peripherie
f; (of circle etc) Umfang m.

period ['pɪərɪəd] n Periode f, Zeit
f; (Gram) Punkt m; (Med) Periode
f; a costume historisch; —ic(al)
[pɪərɪ'ɒdɪk(əl)] a periodisch; —ical
n Zeitschrift f; —ically
[pɪərɪ'ɒdɪkəlɪ] ad periodisch.

peripheral [pə'rɪfərəl] a Rand-,
peripher.

periphery [pə'rɪfərɪ] n Peripherie f,
Rand m.

periscope ['perɪskəup] n Periskop
nt, Sehrohr nt.

perish ['perɪʃ] vi umkommen;
(material) unbrauchbar werden;
(fruit) verderben; — the thought!
daran wollen wir nicht denken;
—able a fruit leicht verderblich;
—ing a (col: cold) eisig.

perjure ['pɜ:dʒə*] vr: — o.s. einen
Meineid leisten.

perjury ['pɜ:dʒərɪ] n Meineid m.

perk [pɜ:k] n (col: fringe benefit)
Vorteil m, Vergünstigung f; — up
vi munter werden; vt ears spitzen;
—y a (cheerful) keck.

perm [pɜ:m] n Dauerwelle f.

permanence ['pɜ:mənəns] n
Dauer(haftigkeit) f, Beständigkeit f.

permanent a, —ly ad ['pɜ:mənənt,
—lɪ] dauernd, ständig.

permissible [pə'mɪsəbl] a zulässig.

permission [pə'mɪʃən] n Erlaubnis
f, Genehmigung f.

permissive [pə'mɪsɪv] a nachgiebig; society etc permissiv.

permit [pə'mɪt] n Zulassung f,
Erlaubnis(schein) m f; ['pɜ:mɪt] vt
erlauben, zulassen.

permutation [pɜ:mju'teɪʃən] n Veränderung f; (Math) Permutation f.

pernicious [pɜ:'nɪʃəs] a schädlich.

perpendicular [pɜ:pən'dɪkjulə*] a
senkrecht.

perpetrate ['pɜ:pɪtreɪt] vt begehen,
verüben.

perpetual a, —ly ad [pə'petjuəl, -ɪ]
dauernd, ständig.

perpetuate [pə'petjueɪt] vt
verewigen, bewahren.

perpetuity [pɜ:pɪ'tjuːɪtɪ] n Ewigkeit
f.

perplex [pə'pleks] vt verblüffen;
—ed a verblüfft, perplex; —ing a
verblüffend; —ity Verblüffung f.

persecute ['pɜ:sɪkjuːt] vt verfolgen.

persecution [pɜ:sɪ'kjuːʃən] n Verfolgung f.

perseverance [pɜ:sɪ'vɪərəns] n Ausdauer f.

persevere [pɜ:sɪ'vɪə*] vi beharren,
durchhalten.

persist [pə'sɪst] vi (in belief etc) bleiben (in bei); (rain, smell) andauern; (continue) nicht aufhören; —ence Beharrlichkeit f; —ent a, —ently ad beharrlich; (unending) ständig.

person ['pɜːsn] n Person f, Mensch m; (Gram) Person f; on one's — bei sich; in — persönlich; —able a gut aussehend; —al a persönlich; (private) privat; (of body) körperlich, Körper-; —ality [pɜːsə'nælɪtɪ] Persönlichkeit f; —ally ad persönlich; —ification [pɜːsɒnɪfɪ'keɪʃən] Verkörperung f; —ify ['pɜːsɒnɪfaɪ] vt verkörpern, personifizieren.

personnel [pɜːsə'nel] n Personal nt; (in factory) Belegschaft f; — manager Personalchef m.

perspective [pə'spektɪv] n Perspektive f.

Perspex ® ['pɜːspeks] n Plexiglas ® nt.

perspicacity [pɜːspɪ'kæsɪtɪ] n Scharfsinn m.

perspiration [pɜːspə'reɪʃən] n Transpiration f.

perspire [pəs'paɪə*] vi transpirieren.

persuade [pə'sweɪd] vt überreden; (convince) überzeugen.

persuasion [pə'sweɪʒən] n Überredung f; Überzeugung f.

persuasive a, —ly ad [pə'sweɪsɪv, -lɪ] überzeugend.

pert [pɜːt] a keck.

pertain [pɜː'teɪn] vt gehören (to zu).

pertaining [pɜː'teɪnɪŋ]: — to betreffend (+acc).

pertinent [pɜː'tɪnənt] a relevant.

perturb [pə'tɜːb] vt beunruhigen.

perusal [pə'ruːzəl] n Durchsicht f.

peruse [pə'ruːz] vt lesen.

pervade [pɜː'veɪd] vt erfüllen, durchziehen.

pervasive [pɜː'veɪsɪv] a durchdringend; influence etc allgegenwärtig.

perverse a, —ly ad [pə'vɜːs, -lɪ] pervers; (obstinate) eigensinnig; —ness Perversität f; Eigensinn m.

perversion [pə'vɜːʃən] n Perversion f; (of justice) Verdrehung f.

perversity [pə'vɜːsɪtɪ] n Perversität f.

pervert [pɜː'vɜːt] n perverse(r) Mensch m; [pə'vɜːt] vt verdrehen; (morally) verderben.

pessimism ['pesɪmɪzəm] n Pessimismus m.

pessimist ['pesɪmɪst] n Pessimist m; —ic [pesɪ'mɪstɪk] a pessimistisch.

pest [pest] n Plage f; (insect) Schädling m; (fig) (person) Nervensäge f; (thing) Plage f.

pester ['pestə*] vt plagen.

pesticide ['pestɪsaɪd] n Insektenvertilgungsmittel nt.

pestle ['pesl] n Stößel m.

pet [pet] n (animal) Haustier nt; (person) Liebling m; vt liebkosen, streicheln.

petal ['petl] n Blütenblatt nt.

peter out ['piːtə aʊt] vi allmählich zu Ende gehen.

petite [pə'tiːt] a zierlich.

petition [pə'tɪʃən] n Bittschrift f.

petrel ['petrəl] n Sturmvogel m.

petrified ['petrɪfaɪd] a versteinert; person starr (vor Schreck).

petrify ['petrɪfaɪ] vt versteinern; person erstarren lassen.

petrol ['petrəl] n (Brit) Benzin nt, Kraftstoff m; —engine Benzin-

motor *m*; **—eum** [pɪˈtrəʊliəm]
Petroleum *nt*; **—** **pump** (*in car*)
Benzinpumpe *f*; (*at garage*) Zapf-
säule *f*, Tanksäule *f*; **—** **station**
Tankstelle *f*; **—** **tank** Benzintank *m*.

petticoat [ˈpetɪkəʊt] *n* Petticoat *m*.

pettifogging [ˈpetɪfɒgɪŋ] *a*
kleinlich.

pettiness [ˈpetɪnəs] *n* Gering-
fügigkeit *f*; (*meanness*) Klein-
lichkeit *f*.

petty [ˈpetɪ] *a* (*unimportant*) geringfügig, unbedeutend; (*mean*)
kleinlich; **—** **cash** Portokasse *f*; **—**
officer Maat *m*.

petulant [ˈpetjʊlənt] *a* leicht
reizbar.

pew [pjuː] *n* Kirchenbank *f*.

pewter [ˈpjuːtə*] *n* Zinn *nt*.

phallic [ˈfælɪk] *a* phallisch, Phallus-.

phantom [ˈfæntəm] *n* Phantom *nt*,
Geist *m*.

pharmacist [ˈfɑːməsɪst] *n* Pharma-
zeut *m*; (*druggist*) Apotheker *m*.

pharmacy [ˈfɑːməsɪ] *n* Pharmazie
f; (*shop*) Apotheke *f*.

phase [feɪz] *n* Phase *f*; **—** **out** *vt*
langsam abbauen; *model* auslaufen
lassen; *person* absetzen.

pheasant [ˈfeznt] *n* Fasan *m*.

phenomenal *a*, **—ly** *ad* [fɪˈnɒmɪnl,
-nəlɪ] phänomenal.

phenomenon [fɪˈnɒmɪnən] *n*
Phänomen *nt*; **common** **—** häufige
Erscheinung *f*.

phial [ˈfaɪəl] *n* Fläschchen *nt*,
Ampulle *f*.

philanderer [fɪˈlændərə*] *n*
Schwerenöter *m*.

philanthropic [fɪlənˈθrɒpɪk] *a*
philanthropisch.

philanthropist [fɪˈlænθrəpɪst] *n*
Philanthrop *m*, Menschenfreund *m*.

philatelist [fɪˈlætəlɪst] *n* Brief-
markensammler *m*, Philatelist *m*.

philately [fɪˈlætəlɪ] *n* Briefmarkensammeln *nt*, Philatelie *f*.

philosopher [fɪˈlɒsəfə*] *n*
Philosoph *m*.

philosophical [fɪləˈsɒfɪkəl] *a*
philosophisch.

philosophize [fɪlɒsəfaɪz] *vi*
philosophieren.

philosophy [fɪˈlɒsəfɪ] *n* Philosophie
f; Weltanschauung *f*.

phlegm [flem] *n* (*Med*) Schleim *m*;
(*calmness*) Gelassenheit *f*; **—atic**
[flegˈmætɪk] *a* gelassen.

phobia [ˈfəʊbɪə] *n* krankhafte
Furcht *f*, Phobie *f*.

phoenix [ˈfiːnɪks] *n* Phönix *m*.

phone [fəʊn] (*abbr of telephone*) *n*
Telefon *nt*; *vti* telefonieren,
anrufen.

phonetics [fəʊˈnetɪks] *n* Phonetik *f*,
Laut(bildungs)lehre *f*; *pl* Laut-
schrift *f*.

phon(e)y [ˈfəʊnɪ] *a* (*col*) unecht;
excuse faul; *money* gefälscht; *n*
(*person*) Schwindler *m*; (*thing*)
Fälschung *f*; (*pound note*) Blüte *f*.

phonograph [ˈfəʊnəgrɑːf] *n* (*US*)
Grammophon *nt*.

phonology [fəʊˈnɒlədʒɪ] *n*
Phonologie *f*, Lautlehre *f*.

phosphate [ˈfɒsfeɪt] *n* Phosphat *nt*.

phosphorus [ˈfɒsfərəs] *n* Phosphor
m.

photo [ˈfəʊtəʊ] *n* (*abbr of photograph*) Foto *nt*.

photocopier [ˈfəʊtəʊˈkɒpɪə*] *n*
Kopiergerät *nt*.

photocopy [ˈfəʊtəʊkɒpɪ] *n*
Fotokopie *f*; *vt* fotokopieren.

photoelectric [ˈfəʊtəʊɪˈlektrɪk] *a*
fotoelektrisch.

photo finish ['fəʊtəʊ'fɪnɪʃ] *n* Zielfotografie *f*.

photogenic [fəʊtəʊ'dʒenɪk] *a* fotogen.

photograph ['fəʊtəgrɑ:f] *n* Fotografie *f*, Aufnahme *f*; *vt* fotografieren, aufnehmen; **—er** [fə'tɒgrəfə] Fotograf *m*; **—ic** ['fəʊtə'græfɪk] *a* fotografisch; **—y** [fə'tɒgrəfɪ] Fotografie *f*, Fotografieren *nt*; *(of film, book)* Aufnahmen *pl*.

photostat ['fəʊtəʊstæt] *n* Fotokopie *f*.

phrase [freɪz] *n* (kurzer) Satz *m*; *(Gram)* Phrase *f*; *(expression)* Redewendung *f*, Ausdruck *m*; *vt* ausdrücken, formulieren; **— book** Sprachführer *m*.

physical *a*, **—ly** *ad* ['fɪzɪkəl, -ɪ] physikalisch; *(bodily)* körperlich, physisch; **— training** Turnen *nt*.

physician [fɪ'zɪʃən] *n* Arzt *m*.

physicist ['fɪzɪsɪst] *n* Physiker(in *f*) *m*.

physics ['fɪzɪks] *n* Physik *f*.

physiology [fɪzɪ'ɒlədʒɪ] *n* Physiologie *f*.

physiotherapist [fɪzɪə'θerəpɪst] *n* Heilgymnast(in *f*) *m*.

physiotherapy [fɪzɪə'θerəpɪ] *n* Heilgymnastik *f*, Physiotherapie *f*.

physique [fɪ'zi:k] *n* Körperbau *m*; *(in health)* Konstitution *f*.

pianist ['pɪənɪst] *n* Pianist(in *f*) *m*.

piano ['pjɑ:nəʊ] *n* Klavier *nt*, Piano *nt*; **—accordion** Akkordeon *nt*.

piccolo ['pɪkələʊ] *n* Pikkoloflöte *f*.

pick [pɪk] *n* *(tool)* Pickel *m*; *(choice)* Auswahl *f*; **the —** of das Beste *m*; *vt* *(gather)* sammeln, *fruit* pflücken; *(choose)* aussuchen; *(Mus)* zupfen; **to — one's nose** in der Nase bohren; **to**

— sb's pocket jdm bestehlen; **to — at one's food** im Essen herumstochern; **— on** *vt* person herumhacken auf *(+dat)*; **why — on me?** warum ich?; **— out** *vt* auswählen; **— up** *vi* *(improve)* sich erholen; *vt* *(lift up)* aufheben; *(learn)* (schnell) mitbekommen; *word* aufschnappen; *(collect)* abholen; *girl* (sich *dat*) anlachen; *speed* gewinnen an *(+dat)*; **— axe** Pickel *m*.

picket ['pɪkɪt] *n* *(stake)* Pfahl *m*, Pflock *m*; *(guard)* Posten *m*; *(striker)* Streikposten *m*; *vt factory* (Streik)posten aufstellen vor *(+dat)*; *vi* (Streik)posten stehen; **—ing** Streikwache *f*; **— line** Streikpostenlinie *f*.

pickle ['pɪkl] *n* *(salty mixture)* Pökel *m*; *(col)* Klemme *f*; *vt* (in Essig) einlegen; einpökeln.

pick-me-up ['pɪkmi:ʌp] *a* Schnäpschen *nt*.

pickpocket ['pɪkpɒkɪt] *n* Taschendieb *m*.

pickup ['pɪkʌp] *n* *(on record player)* Tonabnehmer *m*; *(small truck)* Lieferwagen *m*.

picnic ['pɪknɪk] *n* Picknick *nt*; *vi* picknicken.

pictorial [pɪk'tɔ:rɪəl] *a* in Bildern; *n* Illustrierte *f*.

picture ['pɪktʃə*] *n* Bild *nt*; *(likeness also)* Abbild *nt*; *(in words also)* Darstellung *f*; **in the —** *(fig)* im Bild; *vt* darstellen; *(fig: paint)* malen; *(visualize)* sich *(dat)* vorstellen; **the —s** *(Brit)* Kino *nt*; **— book** Bilderbuch *nt*; **—sque** [pɪktʃə'resk] *a* malerisch.

piddling ['pɪdlɪŋ] *a* *(col)* lumpig; *task* pingelig.

pidgin ['pɪdʒɪn] *a*: **— English** Pidgin-Englisch *nt*.

pie [paɪ] n (meat) Pastete f; (fruit) Torte f.

piebald ['paɪbɔːld] a gescheckt.

piece [piːs] n Stück nt; to go to —s (work, standard) wertlos werden; he's gone to —s er ist vollkommen fertig; in —s entzwei, kaputt; (taken apart) auseinandergenommen; a — of cake (col) ein Kinderspiel nt; — meal ad stückweise, Stück für Stück; —work Akkordarbeit f; — together vt zusammensetzen.

pier [pɪə*] n Pier m, Mole f.

pierce [pɪəs] vt durchstechen, durchbohren (also look); durchdringen (also fig).

piercing ['pɪəsɪŋ] a durchdringend; cry also gellend; look also durchbohrend.

piety ['paɪətɪ] n Frömmigkeit f.

pig [pɪg] n Schwein nt.

pigeon ['pɪdʒən] n Taube f; —hole (compartment) Ablegefach nt; vt ablegen; idea zu den Akten legen.

piggy bank ['pɪgɪbæŋk] n Sparschwein nt.

pigheaded ['pɪg'hedɪd] a dickköpfig.

piglet ['pɪglət] n Ferkel nt, Schweinchen nt.

pigment ['pɪgmənt] n Farbstoff m, Pigment nt (also Biol); —ation [pɪgmən'teɪʃən] Färbung f, Pigmentation f.

pigmy ['pɪgmɪ] n = **pygmy**.

pigskin ['pɪgskɪn] n Schweinsleder nt; a schweinsledern.

pigsty ['pɪgstaɪ] n (lit, fig) Schweinestall m.

pigtail ['pɪgteɪl] n Zopf m.

pike [paɪk] n Pike f; (fish) Hecht m.

pilchard ['pɪltʃəd] n Sardine f.

pile [paɪl] n Haufen m; (of books, wood) Stapel m, Stoß m; (in ground) Pfahl m; (of bridge) Pfeiler m; (on carpet) Flausch m; vti (also — up) sich anhäufen.

piles [paɪlz] n Hämorrhoiden pl.

pile-up ['paɪlʌp] n (Aut) Massenzusammenstoß m.

pilfer ['pɪlfə*] vt stehlen, klauen; —ing Diebstahl m.

pilgrim ['pɪlgrɪm] n Wallfahrer(in f) m, Pilger(in f) m; —age Wallfahrt f, Pilgerfahrt f.

pill [pɪl] n Tablette f, Pille f; the P— die (Antibaby)pille.

pillage ['pɪlɪdʒ] vt plündern.

pillar ['pɪlə*] n Pfeiler m, Säule f (also fig); — box (Brit) Briefkasten m.

pillion ['pɪljən] n Soziussitz m; — passenger Soziusfahrer m.

pillory ['pɪlərɪ] n Pranger m; vt an den Pranger stellen; (fig) anprangern.

pillow ['pɪləʊ] n Kissen nt; —case Kissenbezug m.

pilot ['paɪlət] n Pilot m; (Naut) Lotse m; a scheme etc Versuchs-; vt führen; ship lotsen; — light Zündflamme f.

pimp [pɪmp] n Zuhälter m.

pimple ['pɪmpl] n Pickel m.

pimply ['pɪmplɪ] a pick(e)lig.

pin [pɪn] n Nadel f; (sewing) Stecknadel f; (Tech) Stift m, Bolzen m; vt stecken, heften (to an +acc); (keep in one position) pressen, drücken; —s and needles Kribbeln nt; I have —s and needles in my leg mein Bein ist (mir) eingeschlafen; — down vt (fig) person festnageln (to auf +acc).

pinafore ['pɪnəfɔː*] n Schürze f; — dress Kleiderrock m.

pincers ['pɪnsəz] npl Kneif- or Beißzange f; (Med) Pinzette f.

pinch [pɪntʃ] n Zwicken, Kneifen nt; (of salt) Prise f; vti zwicken, kneifen; (shoe) drücken; vt (col) (steal) klauen; (arrest) schnappen; at a — notfalls, zur Not; to feel the — die Not or es zu spüren bekommen.

pincushion ['pɪnkuʃən] n Nadelkissen nt.

pine [paɪn] n (also — tree) Kiefer f, Föhre f, Pinie f; vi: — for sich sehnen or verzehren nach; to — away sich zu Tode sehnen.

pineapple ['paɪnæpl] n Ananas f.

ping [pɪŋ] n Peng nt; Kling nt; —pong Pingpong nt.

pink [pɪŋk] n (plant) Nelke f; (colour) Rosa nt; a rosa inv.

pinnacle ['pɪnəkl] n Spitze f.

pinpoint ['pɪnpɔɪnt] vt festlegen.

pinstripe ['pɪnstraɪp] n Nadelstreifen m.

pint [paɪnt] n Pint nt.

pinup ['pɪnʌp] n Pin-up-girl nt.

pioneer [paɪə'nɪə*] n Pionier m; (fig also) Bahnbrecher m.

pious ['paɪəs] a fromm; literature geistlich.

pip [pɪp] n Kern m; (sound) Piepen nt; (on uniform) Stern m; to give sb the — (col) jdn verrückt machen.

pipe [paɪp] n (smoking) Pfeife f; (Mus) Flöte f; (tube) Rohr nt; (in house) (Rohr)leitung f; vti (durch Rohre) leiten; (Mus) blasen; — down vi (be quiet) die Luft anhalten; —dream Luftschloß nt; —line (for oil) Pipeline f; — r n Pfeifer m; (bagpipes) Dudelsackbläser m; — tobacco Pfeifentabak m.

piping ['paɪpɪŋ] n Leitungsnetz nt; (on cake) Dekoration f; (on uniform) Tresse f; ad: — hot siedend heiß.

piquant ['pi:kənt] a pikant.

pique [pi:k] n gekränkte(r) Stolz m; —d a pikiert.

piracy ['paɪərəsɪ] n Piraterie f, Seeräuberei f; (plagiarism) Plagiat nt.

pirate ['paɪərɪt] n Pirat m, Seeräuber m; (plagiarist) Plagiator m; — radio Schwarzsender m; (extraterritorial) Piratensender m.

pirouette [pɪru'et] n Pirouette f; vi pirouettieren, eine Pirouette drehen.

Pisces ['paɪsi:z] n Fische pl.

pissed [pɪst] a (col) blau, besoffen.

pistol ['pɪstl] n Pistole f.

piston ['pɪstən] n Kolben m.

pit [pɪt] n Grube f; (Theat) Parterre nt; (orchestra —) Orchestergraben m; vt (mark with scars) zerfressen; (compare) o.s. messen (against mit); sb/sth messen (against an +dat); the —s pl (motor racing) die Boxen.

pitch [pɪtʃ] n Wurf m; (of trader) Stand m; (Sport) (Spiel)feld nt; (slope) Neigung f; (degree) Stufe f; (Mus) Tonlage f; (substance) Pech nt; perfect — absolute(r) Gehör nt; to queer sb's — (col) jdm alles verderben; vt werfen, schleudern; (set up) aufschlagen; song anstimmen; vi fall (längelang) hinschlagen; (Naut) rollen; —black a pechschwarz; —ed battle offene Schlacht f.

pitcher ['pɪtʃə*] n Krug m.

pitchfork ['pɪtʃfɔ:k] n Heugabel f.

piteous ['pɪtɪəs] a kläglich, erbärmlich.

pitfall ['pɪtfɔ:l] n (fig) Falle f.

pith [pɪθ] n Mark nt; (of speech) Kern m.

pithead ['pɪthed] n Schachtkopf m.

pithy ['pɪθɪ] a prägnant.

pitiable ['pɪtɪəbl] a bedauernswert; (contemptible) jämmerlich.

pitiful a, —ly ad ['pɪtɪful, -fəlɪ] mitleidig; (deserving pity) bedauernswert; (contemptible) jämmerlich.

pitiless a, —ly ad ['pɪtɪləs, -lɪ] erbarmungslos.

pittance ['pɪtəns] n Hungerlohn m.

pity ['pɪtɪ] n (sympathy) Mitleid nt; (shame) Jammer. m; **to** have or take — on sb Mitleid mit jdm haben; for —'s sake um Himmels willen; what a —! wie schade!; it's a — es ist schade; vt Mitleid haben mit; I — you du tust· mir leid; —ing a mitleidig. ·

pivot ['pɪvət] n Drehpunkt m; (pin) (Dreh)zapfen m; (fig) Angelpunkt m; vi sich drehen (on um).

pixie ['pɪksɪ] n Elf(e f) m.

placard ['plækɑːd] n Plakat nt, Anschlag m; vt anschlagen.

placate [plə'keɪt] vt beschwichtigen, besänftigen..

place [pleɪs] n Platz m; (spot) Stelle f; (town etc) Ort m; vt setzen, stellen, legen; order aufgeben; (Sport) plazieren; (identify) unterbringen; **in** — am rechten Platz; **out of** — nicht am rechten Platz; (fig) remark unangebracht; **in** — **of** anstelle von; **in the first/second etc** — erstens/zweitens etc; **to give** — **to** Platz machen (+dat); **to invite sb to one's** — jdn zu sich (nach Hause) einladen; **to keep sb in his** — jdn in seinen Schranken halten; **to put sb in his** — jdn in seine Schranken (ver)weisen; — **of wor**-

ship Stätte f des Gebets; — **mat** Platzdeckchen nt.

placid ['plæsɪd] a gelassen, ruhig; —ity [plə'sɪdɪtɪ] Gelassenheit f, Ruhe f.

plagiarism ['pleɪdʒɪərɪzəm] n Plagiat nt.

plagiarist ['pleɪdʒɪərɪst] n Plagiator m.

plagiarize ['pleɪdʒɪəraɪz] vt abschreiben, plagiieren.

plague [pleɪg] n Pest f; (fig) Plage f; vt plagen.

plaice [pleɪs] n Scholle f.

plaid [plæd] n Plaid nt.

plain a, —ly ad [pleɪn, '—lɪ] (clear) klar, deutlich; (simple) einfach, schlicht; (not beautiful) einfach, nicht attraktiv; (honest) offen; n Ebene f; **in** — **clothes** (police) in Zivil(kleidung); **it is** — **sailing** das ist ganz einfach; —**ness** Einfachheit f.

plaintiff ['pleɪntɪf] n Kläger m.

plait [plæt] n Zopf m; vt flechten.

plan [plæn] n Plan m; vti planen; (intend also) vorhaben; — **out** vt vorbereiten; **according to** — planmäßig.

plane [pleɪn] n Ebene f; (Aviat) Flugzeug nt; (tool) Hobel m; (tree) Platane f; a eben, flach; vt hobeln.

planet ['plænɪt] n Planet m.

planetarium [plænɪ'tɛərɪəm] n Planetarium nt.

planetary ['plænɪtərɪ] a planetarisch.

plank [plæŋk] n Planke f, Brett nt; (Pol) Programmpunkt m.

plankton ['plæŋktən] n Plankton nt.

planner ['plænə*] n Planer m.

planning ['plænɪŋ] n Planen nt, Planung f.

plant [plɑ:nt] n Pflanze f; (Tech) (Maschinen)anlage f; (factory) Fabrik f, Werk nt; vt pflanzen; (set firmly) stellen.

plantain ['plæntɪn] n (Mehl)banane f.

plantation [plæn'teɪʃən] n Pflanzung f, Plantage f.

planter ['plɑ:ntə*] n Pflanzer nt.

plaque [plæk] n Gedenktafel f.

plasma ['plæzmə] n Plasma nt.

plaster ['plɑ:stə*] n Gips m; (whole surface) Verputz m; (Med) Pflaster nt; (for fracture: also — of Paris) Gipsverband m; in — (leg etc) in Gips; vt gipsen; hole zugipsen; ceiling verputzen; (fig: with pictures etc) be- or verkleben; —ed a (col) besoffen; —er Gipser m.

plastic ['plæstɪk] n Kunststoff m; a (made of plastic) Kunststoff-, Plastik-; (soft) formbar, plastisch; (Art) plastisch, bildend; p—ine ['plæstɪsi:n] Plastilin nt; — surgery plastische Chirurgie f; Schönheitsoperation f.

plate [pleɪt] n Teller m; (gold/silver) vergoldete(s)/versilberte(s) Tafelgeschirr nt; (flat 'sheet') Platte f; (in book) (Bild)tafel f; vt überziehen, plattieren; to silver-/gold— versilbern/vergolden.

plateau ['plætəʊ] n, pl —x Hochebene f, Plateau nt.

plateful ['pleɪtful] n Teller(voll) m.

plate glass ['pleɪt'glɑ:s] n Tafelglas nt.

platform ['plætfɔ:m] n (at meeting) Plattform f; Podium nt; (stage) Bühne f; (Rail) Bahnsteig m; (Pol) Parteiprogramm nt; — ticket Bahnsteigkarte f.

platinum ['plætɪnəm] n Platin nt.

platitude ['plætɪtju:d] n Gemeinplatz m, Platitüde f.

platoon [plə'tu:n] n (Mil) Zug m.

platter ['plætə*] n Platte f.

plausibility [plɔ:zə'bɪlɪtɪ] n Plausibilität f.

plausible a, **plausibly** ad ['plɔ:zəbl, -blɪ] plausibel, einleuchtend; liar überzeugend.

play [pleɪ] n Spiel nt (also Tech); (Theat) (Theater)stück nt, Schauspiel nt; vi spielen; another team spielen gegen; (put sb in a team) einsetzen, spielen lassen; to — a joke on sb jdm einen Streich spielen; to — sb off against sb else jdn gegen jdn anders ausspielen; to — a part in (fig) eine Rolle spielen bei; — down vt bagatellisieren; — up vi (cause trouble) frech werden; (bad leg etc) weh tun; vt person plagen; to — up to sb jdm flattieren; —acting n Schauspielerei f; —boy Playboy m; —er Spieler(in f) m; —ful a spielerisch, verspielt; —goer Theaterfreund m; —ground Spielplatz m; —group Kindergarten m; —ing card Spielkarte f; —ing field Sportplatz m; —mate Spielkamerad m; —off (Sport) Entscheidungsspiel nt; —pen Laufstall m; —thing Spielzeug nt; —wright Theaterschriftsteller m.

plea [pli:] n (dringende) Bitte f, Gesuch nt; (Jur) Antwort f des Angeklagten; (excuse) Ausrede f, Vorwand m; (objection) Einrede f; — of guilty Geständnis nt.

plead [pli:d] vt poverty zur Entschuldigung anführen; (Jur) sb's case vertreten; vi (beg) dringend bitten (with sb jdn); (Jur) plädieren; to — guilty schuldig plädieren.

pleasant a, **—ly** ad ['pleznt, .lɪ] angenehm; freundlich; . **—ness** Angenehme(s) nt; (of person) angenehme(s) Wesen nt, Freundlichkeit f; **—ry** Scherz m.

please [pli:z] vt (be agreeable to) gefallen (+dat); —I bitte! ; — yourself! wie du willst!; do what you — mach' was du willst; **—d** a zufrieden; (glad) erfreut (with über +acc).

pleasing ['pli:zɪŋ] a erfreulich.

pleasurable a, **pleasurably** ad ['pleʒərəbl, -blɪ] angenehm, erfreulich.

pleasure ['pleʒə*] n Vergnügen nt, Freude f; (old: will) Wünsche pl; it's a — gern geschehen; they take (no/great) — in doing . . . es macht ihnen (keinen/großen) Spaß zu...; — ground Vergnügungspark m; — seeking a vergnügungshungrig; — steamer Vergnügungsdampfer m.

pleat [pli:t] n Falte f.

plebeian [plɪ'bi:ən] n Plebejer(in f) m; a plebejisch.

plebiscite ['plebɪsɪt] n Volksentscheid m, Plebiszit nt.

plebs [plebz] npl Plebs m, Pöbel m.

plectrum ['plektrəm] n Plektron nt.

pledge [pledʒ] n Pfand nt; (promise) Versprechen nt; vt verpfänden; (promise) geloben, versprechen; to take the — dem Alkohol abschwören.

plenipotentiary [plenɪpə'tenʃərɪ] m Bevollmächtiger m; a bevollmächtigt; — power Vollmacht f.

plentiful ['plentɪful] a reichlich.

plenty ['plentɪ] n Fülle f, Überfluß m; ad (col) ganz schön; — of eine Menge, viel; in — reichlich, massenhaft; to be — genug sein, reichen.

plethora ['pleθərə] n Überfülle f.

pleurisy ['pluərɪsɪ] n Rippenfellentzündung f.

pliability [plaɪə'bɪlɪtɪ] n Biegsamkeit f; (of person) Beeinflußbarkeit f.

pliable ['plaɪəbl] a biegsam; person beeinflußbar. : ·

pliers ['plaɪəz] npl (Kneif)zange f.

plight [plaɪt] n (Not)lage f; (schrecklicher) Zustand m.

plimsolls ['plɪmsəlz] npl Turnschuhe pl.

plinth [plɪnθ] n Säulenplatte f, Plinthe f.

plod [plɒd] vi (work) sich abplagen; (walk) trotten; **—der** Arbeitstier nt; **—ding** a schwerfällig.

plonk [plɒŋk] n (col: wine) billige(r) Wein m; vt: — sth down etw hinknallen.

plot [plɒt] n Komplott nt, Verschwörung f; (story) Handlung f; (of land) Stück nt Land, Grundstück nt; vt markieren; curve zeichnen; movements. nachzeichnen; vi (plan secretly) sich verschwören, ein Komplott schmieden; **—ter** Verschwörer m; **—ting** Intrigen pl.

plough, (US) plow [plau] n Pflug m; vt pflügen; (col) exam candidate durchfallen lassen; — back vt (Comm) wieder in das Geschäft stecken; — through vt water durchpflügen; book sich kämpfen durch; **—ing** Pflügen nt.

ploy [plɔɪ] n Masche f.

pluck [plʌk] vt fruit pflücken; guitar zupfen; goose rupfen; n Mut m; to — up courage all seinen Mut zusammennehmen; **—y** a beherzt.

plug [plʌg] n Stöpsel m; (Elec) Stecker m; (of tobacco) Priem m;

(col: publicity) Schleichwerbung f; *(Aut)* Zündkerze f; vt (zu)stopfen; *(col: advertise)* Reklame machen für; **to — in** a lamp den Stecker einer Lampe einstecken.

plum [plʌm] n Pflaume f, Zwetschge f; a **job etc** Bomben-.

plumage ['pluːmɪdʒ] n Gefieder nt.

plumb [plʌm] n Lot nt; **out of —** nicht im Lot; a senkrecht; ad *(exactly)* genau; vt ausloten; *(fig)* .sondieren; **mystery** ergründen.

plumber ['plʌmə*] n Klempner m, Installateur m.

plumbing ['plʌmɪŋ] n *(craft)* Installieren nt; *(fittings)* Leitungen pl, Installationen pl.

plumbline ['plʌmlaɪn] n Senkblei nt.

plume [pluːm] n Feder f; *(of smoke etc)* Fahne f; *(bird)* putzen.

plummet ['plʌmɪt] n Senkblei nt; vi (ab)stürzen.

plump [plʌmp] a rundlich, füllig; vi plumpsen, sich fallen lassen; vt plumpsen lassen; **to — for** *(col: choose)* wählen, sich entscheiden für; **—ness** Rundlichkeit f.

plunder ['plʌndə*] n Plünderung f; *(loot)* Beute f; vt plündern; **things** rauben.

plunge [plʌndʒ] n Sprung m, Stürzen nt; vt stoßen; vi (sich) stürzen; *(ship)* tollen; a **room — into darkness** ein in Dunkelheit getauchtes Zimmer.

plunging ['plʌndʒɪŋ] a **neckline** offenherzig.

pluperfect ['pluː'pɜːfɪkt] n Plusquamperfekt nt, Vorvergangenheit f.

plural ['pluərəl] a Plural-, Mehrzahl-; n Plural m, Mehrzahl f; **—istic** [pluərə'lɪstɪk] a pluralistische.

plus [plʌs] prep plus, und; a Plus-.

plush [plʌʃ] a *(also* **—y:** *col: luxurious)* feudal; n Plüsch m.

ply [plaɪ] n as in: **three-—** wool dreischichtig; **wool** Dreifach-; vt **trade** (be)treiben; *(with questions)* zusetzen *(+dat)*; *(ship, taxi)* befahren; vi *(ship, taxi)* verkehren; **—wood** Sperrholz nt.

pneumatic [njuː'mætɪk] a pneumatisch; *(Tech)* Luft-; **— drill** Preßlufthammer m; **— tyre** Luftreifen m.

pneumonia [njuː'məʊnɪə] n Lungenentzündung f.

poach [pəʊtʃ] vt *(Cook)* pochieren; **game** stehlen; vi *(steal)* wildern *(for nach)*; **—ed** a **egg** pochiert, verloren; **—er** Wilddieb m; **—ing** Wildern nt.

pocket ['pɒkɪt] n Tasche f; *(of ore)* Ader f; *(of resistance)* (Widerstands)nest nt; **air —** Luftloch nt; vt einstecken, in die Tasche stecken; **to be out of —** kein Geld haben; **—book** Taschenbuch nt; **—ful** Tasche(voll) f; **— knife** Taschenmesser nt; **— money** Taschengeld nt.

pockmarked ['pɒkmɑːkt] a **face** pockennarbig.

pod [pɒd] n Hülse f; *(of peas also)* Schote f.

podgy ['pɒdʒɪ] a pummelig.

poem ['pəʊəm] n Gedicht nt.

poet ['pəʊɪt] n Dichter m, Poet m; **—ic** [pəʊ'etɪk] a poetisch, dichterisch; **beauty** malerisch, stimmungsvoll; **— laureate** Hofdichter m; **—ry** Poesie f; *(poems)* Gedichte pl.

poignant a, **—ly** ad ['pɔɪnjənt, -lɪ] scharf, stechend; *(touching)* ergreifend, quälend.

point [pɔɪnt] n Punkt m *(also in discussion, scoring)*; *(spot also)*

Stelle f; (sharpened tip) Spitze f; (moment) (Zeit)punkt m, Moment m; (purpose) Zweck m; (idea) Argument nt; (decimal) Dezimalstelle f; (personal characteristic) Seite f; vt zeigen mit; gun richten; vi zeigen; —s pl (Rail) Weichen pl; — of view Stand- or Gesichtspunkt m; what's the —? was soll das?; you have a — there da hast du recht; three — two drei Komma zwei; — out vt hinweisen auf (+acc); — to vt zeigen auf (+acc); —-blank ad (at close range) aus nächster Entfernung; (bluntly) unverblümt; — duty Verkehrsregelungsdienst m; —ed a, —edly ad spitz, scharf; (fig) gezielt; —er Zeigestock m; (on dial) Zeiger m; —less a, —lessly ad zwecklos, sinnlos; —lessness Zwecklosigkeit f, Sinnlosigkeit f.

poise [pɔɪz] n Haltung f, (fig also) Gelassenheit f; vti balancieren; knife, pen bereithalten; o.s. sich bereitmachen; —d a beherrscht.

poison ['pɔɪzn] n (lit, fig) Gift nt; vt vergiften; —ing Vergiftung f; —ous a giftig, Gift-.

poke [pəʊk] vt stoßen; (put) stecken; fire schüren; hole bohren; n Stoß m; —'s one's nose into seine Nase stecken in (+acc); to — fun at sb sich über jdn lustig machen; — about vi herumstochern; herumwühlen; —r Schürhaken m; (Cards) Poker nt; —r-faced a undurchdringlich.

poky ['pəʊkɪ] a eng.

polar ['pəʊlə*] a Polar-, polar; — bear Eisbär m; —ization [pəʊləraɪ'zeɪʃən] n Polarisation f; —ize vt polarisieren; vi sich polarisieren.

pole [pəʊl] n Stange f, Pfosten m; (flag—, telegraph — also) Mast m; (Elec, Geog) Pol m; (Sport) (vaulting —) Stab m; (ski —) Stock m; —s apart durch Welten getrennt; —cat (US) Skunk m; — star Polarstern m; — vault Stabhochsprung m.

polemic [pɒ'lemɪk] n Polemik f.

police [pə'liːs] n Polizei f; vt polizeilich überwachen; kontrollieren; — car Polizeiwagen m; —man Polizist m; — state Polizeistaat m; — station (Polizei)revier nt, Wache f; —woman Polizistin f.

policy ['pɒlɪsɪ] n Politik f; (of business also) Usus m; (insurance) (Versicherungs)police f; (prudence) Klugheit f; (principle) Grundsatz m; — decision/statement Grundsatzentscheidung f/-erklärung f.

polio ['pəʊlɪəʊ] n (spinale) Kinderlähmung f, Polio f.

polish ['pɒlɪʃ] n Politur f; (for floor) Wachs nt; (for shoes) Creme f; (nail —) Lack m; (shine) Glanz m; (of furniture) Politur f; (fig) Schliff m; vt polieren; shoes putzen; (fig) den letzten Schliff geben (+dat), aufpolieren; — off vt (col: work) erledigen; food wegputzen; drink hinunterschütten; — up vt essay aufpolieren; knowledge auffrischen; —ed a glänzend (also fig); manners verfeinert.

polite a, —ly ad [pə'laɪt, -lɪ] höflich; society fein; —ness Höflichkeit f; Feinheit f.

politic ['pɒlɪtɪk] a (prudent) diplomatisch; —al a [pə'lɪtɪkəl, -l] politisch; —ally ad [pə'lɪtɪkəl, -l] politisch; —al science Politologie f; —ian [pɒlɪ'tɪʃən] n Politiker m, Staatsmann m; —s pl Politik f.

polka ['pɒlkə] n Polka f; — **dot** Tupfen m.

poll [pəʊl] n Abstimmung f; (in election) Wahl f; (votes cast) Wahlbeteiligung f; (opinion —) Umfrage f; vt votes erhalten, auf sich vereinigen.

pollen ['pɒlən] n Blütenstaub m, Pollen m; — **count** Pollenkonzentration f.

pollination [pɒlɪ'neɪʃən] n Befruchtung f.

polling booth ['pəʊlɪŋbu:ð] n Wahlkabine f.

polling day ['pəʊlɪŋ deɪ] n Wahltag m.

polling station ['pəʊlɪŋ steɪʃən] n Wahllokal nt.

pollute [pə'lu:t] vt verschmutzen, verunreinigen.

pollution [pə'lu:ʃən] n Verschmutzung f.

polo ['pəʊləʊ] n Polo nt.

poly- [pɒlɪ] pref Poly-.

polygamy [pɒ'lɪgəmɪ] n Polygamie f.

polytechnic [pɒlɪ'teknɪk] n technische Hochschule f.

polythene ['pɒlɪθi:n] n Plastik nt; — **bag** Plastiktüte f.

pomegranate ['pɒməgrænɪt] n Granatapfel m.

pommel ['pʌml] vt mit den Fäusten bearbeiten; n Sattelknopf m.

pomp [pɒmp] n Pomp m, Prunk m.

pompous a, —**ly** ad ['pɒmpəs, -lɪ] aufgeblasen; language geschwollen.

ponce [pɒns] n (col) (pimp) Louis m; (queer) Schwule m.

pond [pɒnd] n Teich m, Weiher m.

ponder ['pɒndə*] vt nachdenken or nachgrübeln über (+acc); —**ous** a schwerfällig.

pontiff ['pɒntɪf] n Pontifex m.

pontificate [pɒn'tɪfɪkeɪt] vi (fig) geschwollen reden.

pontoon [pɒn'tu:n] n Ponton m; (Cards) 17-und-4 nt.

pony ['pəʊnɪ] n Pony nt; —**tail** Pferdeschwanz m.

poodle ['pu:dl] n Pudel m.

pooh-pooh [pu:'pu:] vt die Nase rümpfen über (+acc).

pool [pu:l] n (swimming —) Schwimmbad nt; (private) Swimming-pool m; (of spilt liquid, blood) Lache f; (fund) (gemeinsame) Kasse f; (billiards) Poolspiel nt; vt money etc zusammenlegen.

poor [pʊə*] a arm; (not good) schlecht, schwach; **the** — pl die Armen pl; —**ly** ad schlecht, schwach; dressed ärmlich; a schlecht, elend.

pop [pɒp] n Knall m; (music) Popmusik f; (drink) Limo(nade) f; (US col) Pa m; vt (put) stecken; balloon platzen lassen; vi knallen; — **in/out** (person) vorbeikommen/hinausgehen; hinein-/hinausspringen; —**concert** Popkonzert nt; —**corn** Puffmais m.

Pope [pəʊp] n Papst m.

poplar ['pɒplə*] n Pappel f.

poplin ['pɒplɪn] n Popelin m.

poppy ['pɒpɪ] n Mohn m; —**cock** (col) Quatsch m.

populace ['pɒpjʊləs] n Volk nt.

popular ['pɒpjʊlə*] a beliebt, populär; (of the people) volkstümlich, Populär-; (widespread) allgemein; —**ity** [pɒpjʊ'lærɪtɪ] Beliebtheit f, Popularität f; —**ize** vt popularisieren; —**ly** ad allgemein, überall.

populate ['pɒpjʊleɪt] vt bevölkern; town bewohnen.

population [pɒpjʊ'leɪʃən] n Bevölkerung f; (of town) Einwohner pl.

populous ['pɒpjuləs] a dicht besiedelt.

porcelain ['pɔ:slɪn] n Porzellan nt.

porch [pɔ:tʃ] n Vorbau m, Veranda f; (in church) Vorhalle f.

porcupine ['pɔ:kjupaɪn] n Stachelschwein nt.

pore [pɔ:*] n Pore f; — over vt brüten or hocken über (+dat).

pork [pɔ:k] n Schweinefleisch nt.

pornographic a, —ally ad [pɔ:nə'græfik, -əli] pornographisch.

pornography [pɔ:'nɒgrəfɪ] n Pornographie f.

porous ['pɔ:rəs] a porös; skin porig.

porpoise ['pɔ:pəs] n Tümmler m.

porridge ['pɒrɪdʒ] n Porridge m, Haferbrei m.

port [pɔ:t] n Hafen m; (town) Hafenstadt f; (Naut: left side) Backbord nt; (opening for loads) Luke f; (wine) Portwein m.

portable ['pɔ:təbl] a tragbar; radio Koffer-; typewriter Reise-.

portal ['pɔ:tl] n Portal nt.

portcullis [pɔ:t'kʌlɪs] n Fallgitter nt.

portend [pɔ:'tend] vt anzeigen, hindeuten auf (+acc).

portent ['pɔ:tent] n schlimme(s) Vorzeichen nt; —ous [pɔ:'tentəs] a schlimm, ominös; (amazing) ungeheuer.

porter ['pɔ:tə*] n Pförtner(in f) m; (for luggage) (Gepäck)träger m.

porthole ['pɔ:thəul] n Bullauge nt.

portico ['pɔ:tɪkəu] n Säulengang m.

portion ['pɔ:ʃən] n Teil m, Stück nt; (of food) Portion f.

portly ['pɔ:tlɪ] a korpulent, beleibt.

portrait ['pɔ:trɪt] n Porträt nt, Bild(nis) nt.

portray [pɔ:'treɪ] vt darstellen; (describe) schildern; —al Darstellung f; Schilderung f.

pose [pəuz] n Stellung f, Pose f (also affectation); vi posieren, sich in Positur setzen; vt stellen; to — as sich ausgeben als; —r knifflige Frage f.

posh [pɒʃ] a (col) (piek)fein.

position [pə'zɪʃən] n Stellung f; (place) Position f, Lage f; (job) Stelle f; (attitude) Standpunkt m, Haltung f; to be in a — to do sth in der Lage sein, etw zu tun; vt aufstellen.

positive a, —ly ad ['pɒzɪtɪv, -lɪ] positiv; (convinced) sicher; (definite) eindeutig.

posse ['pɒsɪ] n (US) Aufgebot nt.

possess [pə'zes] vt besitzen; what —ed you to . . .? was ist in dich gefahren, daß...?; —ed a besessen; —ion [pə'zeʃən] n Besitz m; —ive a besitzergreifend, eigensüchtig; (Gram) Possessiv-, besitzanzeigend; —ively ad besitzergreifend, eigensüchtig; —or Besitzer m.

possibility [pɒsə'bɪlɪtɪ] n Möglichkeit f.

possible ['pɒsəbl] a möglich; if — wenn möglich, möglichst; as big as — so groß wie möglich, möglichst groß.

possibly ['pɒsəblɪ] ad möglicherweise, vielleicht; as soon as I — can sobald ich irgendwie kann.

post [pəust] n Post f; (pole) Pfosten m, Pfahl m; (place of duty) Posten m; (job) Stelle f; vt notice anschlagen; letters aufgeben; soldiers aufstellen; —age Postgebühr f, Porto nt; —al a Post-; —al order Postanweisung f; —card Postkarte f; —date vt cheque nach-

datieren; —er Plakat nt, Poster m;
—e restante Aufbewahrungsstelle f
für postlagernde Sendungen; to
send sth —e restante etw post-
lagernd schicken.

posterior [pɒsˈtɪərɪə*] n (col)
Hintern m.

posterity [pɒsˈterɪtɪ] n Nachwelt f;
(descendants) Nachkommenschaft
f.

postgraduate [ˈpəʊstˈgrædjuət] n
Weiterstudierender(in f) m.

posthumous a, —ly ad
[ˈpɒstjuməs, -lɪ] post(h)um.

postman [ˈpəʊstmən] n Briefträger
m, Postbote m.

postmark [ˈpəʊstmɑːk] n Post-
stempel m.

postmaster [ˈpəʊstmɑːstə*] n Post-
meister m; P— General Post-
minister m.

post-mortem [ˈpəʊstˈmɔːtəm] n
Autopsie f.

post office [ˈpəʊstɒfɪs] n Postamt
nt, Post f (also organization).

postpone [pəˈspəʊn] vt verschieben, aufschieben; —ment Verschiebung f, Aufschub m.

postscript [ˈpəʊsskrɪpt] n Nach-
schrift f, Postskript nt; (in book)
Nachwort nt.

postulate [ˈpɒstjulət] vt voraussetzen; (maintain) behaupten.

postulation [pɒstjuˈleɪʃən] n
Voraussetzung f; Behauptung f.

posture [ˈpɒstʃə*] n Haltung f; vi
posieren.

postwar [ˈpəʊstˈwɔː*] a Nach-
kriegs-.

posy [ˈpəʊzɪ] n Blumenstrauß m.

pot [pɒt] n Topf m; (tea—) Kanne
f; (col: marijuana) Hasch nt; vt
plant eintopfen.

potash [ˈpɒtæʃ] n Pottasche f.

potato [pəˈteɪtəʊ] n, pl -es Kartoffel
f.

potency [ˈpəʊtənsɪ] n Stärke f,
Potenz f.

potent [ˈpəʊtənt] a stark; argument
zwingend.

potentate [ˈpəʊtənteɪt] n Macht-
haber m.

potential [pəʊˈtenʃəl] a potentiell;
he is a — virtuoso or hat das Zeug
zum Virtuosen; n Potential nt;
—ly ad potentiell.

pothole [ˈpɒthəʊl] n Höhle f; (in
road) Schlagloch nt; —r Höhlen-
forscher m.

potholing [ˈpɒthəʊlɪŋ] n: to go —
Höhlen erforschen.

potion [ˈpəʊʃən] n Trank m.

potluck [ˈpɒtˈlʌk] n: to take — with
sth etw auf gut Glück nehmen.

potpourri [pəʊˈpʊrɪ] n Potpourri nt.

potshot [ˈpɒtʃɒt] n: to take a —
at sth auf etw (acc) ballern.

potted [ˈpɒtɪd] a food eingelegt,
eingemacht; plant Topf-; (fig:
book, version) konzentriert.

potter [ˈpɒtə*] n Töpfer m; vi
herumhantieren, herumwursteln;
—y Töpferwaren pl, Steingut nt;.
(place) Töpferei f.

potty [ˈpɒtɪ] a (col) verrückt; n
Töpfchen nt.

pouch [paʊtʃ] n Beutel m; (under
eyes) Tränensack m; (for tobacco)
Tabaksbeutel m.

pouffe [puːf] n Sitzkissen nt.

poultice [ˈpəʊltɪs] n Packung f.

poultry [ˈpəʊltrɪ] n Geflügel nt; —
farm Geflügelfarm f.

pounce [paʊns] vi sich stürzen (on
auf +acc); n Sprung m, Satz m.

pound [paʊnd] n (Fin, weight)
Pfund nt; (for cars, animals)

Auslösestelle f; (for stray animals) (Tier)asyl nt; vi klopfen, hämmern; vt (zer)stampfen; —ing starke(s) Klopfen nt, Hämmern nt; (Zer)stampfen nt.

pour [pɔ:*] vt gießen, schütten; vi gießen; (crowds etc) strömen; — away vt, — off vt abgießen; —ing rain strömende(r) Regen m.

pout [paut] n Schnute f, Schmollmund m; vi eine Schnute ziehen, schmollen.

poverty ['pɒvəti] n Armut f; —stricken a verarmt, sehr arm.

powder ['paudə*] n Pulver nt; (cosmetic) Puder m; vt pulverisieren; (sprinkle) bestreuen; to — one's nose sich (dat) die Nase pudern; — room Damentoilette f; —y a pulverig, Pulver-.

power [pauə*] n Macht f (also Pol); (ability) Fähigkeit f; (strength) Stärke f; (authority) Macht f, Befugnis f; (Math) Potenz f; (Elec) Strom m; vt betreiben, antreiben; — cut Stromausfall m; —ful a person mächtig; engine, government stark; —less a machtlos; — line (Haupt)stromleitung f; — point elektrische(r) Anschluß m; — station Elektrizitätswerk nt.

powwow ['pauwau] n Besprechung f; vi eine Besprechung abhalten.

practicability [præktikə'bɪlti] n Durchführbarkeit f.

practicable ['præktikəbl] a durchführbar.

practical a, —ly ad ['præktikəl, -i] praktisch; — joke Streich m.

practice ['præktis] n Übung f; (reality) Praxis f; (custom) Brauch m; (in business) Usus m; (doctor's, lawyer's) Praxis f; in — (in reality)

in der Praxis; out of — außer Übung.

practise, (US) **practice** ['præktis] vt üben; profession ausüben; to — law/medicine als Rechtsanwalt/Arzt arbeiten; vi (sich) üben; (doctor, lawyer) praktizieren; —d a erfahren.

practising, (US) **practicing** ['præktisiŋ] a praktizierend; Christian etc aktiv.

practitioner [præk'tiʃənə*] n. praktische(r) Arzt m.

pragmatic [præg'mætik] a pragmatisch.

pragmatism ['prægmətizəm] n Pragmatismus m.

pragmatist ['prægmətist] n Pragmatiker m.

prairie ['preəri] n Prärie f, Steppe f.

praise [preiz] n Lob nt, Preis m; vt loben; (worship) (lob)preisen, loben; —worthy a lobenswert.

pram [præm] n Kinderwagen m.

prance [prɑ:ns] vi (horse) tänzeln; (person) stolzieren; (gaily) herumhüpfen.

prank [præŋk] n Streich m.

prattle ['prætl] vi schwatzen, plappern.

prawn [prɔ:n] n Garnele f; Krabbe f.

pray [prei] vi beten; —er [preə*] n Gebet nt; —er book Gebetbuch nt.

pre- [pri:] pref prä-, vor(her)-.

preach [pri:tʃ] vi predigen; —er n Prediger m.

preamble [pri:'æmbl] n Einleitung f.

prearrange ['pri:ə'reindʒ] vt vereinbaren, absprechen; —d a vereinbart; —ment Vereinbarung f, vorherige Absprache f.

precarious a, —ly ad [prɪˈkɛərɪəs, -lɪ] prekär, unsicher.

precaution [prɪˈkɔːʃən] n (Vorsichts)maßnahme f, Vorbeugung f; —ary a measure vorbeugend, Vorsichts-.

precede [prɪˈsiːd] vti vorausgehen (+dat); (be more important) an Bedeutung übertreffen; —nce ['presɪdəns] Priorität f, Vorrang m; to take —nce over den Vorrang haben vor (+dat); —nt ['presɪdənt] Präzedenzfall m.

preceding [prɪˈsiːdɪŋ] a vorhergehend.

precept ['priːsept] n Gebot nt, Regel f.

precinct ['priːsɪŋkt] n Gelände nt; (district) Bezirk m; (shopping —) Einkaufszone f.

precious ['preʃəs] a kostbar, wertvoll; (affected) preziös, geziert.

precipice ['presɪpɪs] n Abgrund m.

precipitate a, —ly ad [prɪˈsɪpɪtɪt, -lɪ] überstürzt, übereilt; [prɪˈsɪpɪteɪt] vt hinunterstürzen; events heraufbeschwören.

precipitation [prɪsɪpɪˈteɪʃən] n Niederschlag m.

precipitous a, —ly ad [prɪˈsɪpɪtəs, -lɪ] abschüssig; action überstürzt.

précis ['preɪsiː] n (kurze) Übersicht f, Zusammenfassung f; (Sch) Inhaltsangabe f.

precise a, —ly ad [prɪˈsaɪs, -lɪ] genau, präzis.

preclude [prɪˈkluːd] vt ausschließen; person abhalten.

precocious [prɪˈkəʊʃəs] a frühreif.

preconceived [priːkənˈsiːvd] a idea vorgefaßt.

precondition ['priːkənˈdɪʃən] n Vorbedingung f, Voraussetzung f.

precursor [priːˈkɜːsə*] n Vorläufer m.

predator ['predətə*] n Raubtier nt; —y a Raub-; räuberisch.

predecessor ['priːdɪsesə*] n Vorgänger m.

predestination [priːdestɪˈneɪʃən] n Vorherbestimmung f, Prädestination f.

predestine [priːˈdestɪn] vt vorherbestimmen.

predetermine ['priːdɪˈtɜːmɪn] vt vorherentscheiden, vorherbestimmen.

predicament [prɪˈdɪkəmənt] n mißliche Lage f; to be in a — in der Klemme sitzen.

predicate ['predɪkət] n Prädikat n, Satzaussage f.

predict [prɪˈdɪkt] vt voraussagen; —ion [prɪˈdɪkʃən] Voraussage f.

predominance [prɪˈdɒmɪnəns] n (in power) Vorherrschaft f; (fig) Vorherrschen nt, Überwiegen nt.

predominant [prɪˈdɒmɪnənt] a vorherrschend; (fig also) überwiegend; —ly ad überwiegend, hauptsächlich.

predominate [prɪˈdɒmɪneɪt] vi vorherrschen; (fig also) überwiegen.

pre-eminent [priːˈemɪnənt] a hervorragend, herausragend.

pre-empt [priːˈempt] vt action, decision vorwegnehmen.

preen [priːn] vt putzen; to — o.s. on sth sich (dat) etwas auf etw (acc) einbilden.

prefab ['priːfæb] n Fertighaus nt.

prefabricated ['priːˈfæbrɪkeɪtɪd] a vorgefertigt, Fertig-.

preface ['prefɪs] n Vorwort nt, Einleitung f.

prefect ['priːfekt] n Präfekt m; (Sch) Aufsichtsschüler(in f) m.

prefer [pri'f3:*] vt vorziehen, lieber mögen; to — to do sth etw lieber tun; —able ['prefərəbl] a vorzuziehen(d) (to dat); —ably ['prefərəbli] ad vorzugsweise, am liebsten; —ence ['prefərəns] Präferenz f, Vorzug m; —ential [prefə'renʃəl] a bevorzugt, Vorzugs-.

prefix ['pri:fiks] n Vorsilbe f, Präfix nt.

pregnancy ['pregnənsɪ] n Schwangerschaft f.

pregnant ['pregnənt] a schwanger; — with meaning (fig) bedeutungsschwer or -voll.

prehistoric ['pri:his'tɒrɪk] a prähistorisch, vorgeschichtlich.

prehistory ['pri:'hɪstərɪ] n Urgeschichte f.

prejudge ['pri:dʒʌdʒ] vt vorschnell beurteilen.

prejudice ['predʒudɪs] n Vorurteil nt; Voreingenommenheit f; (harm) Schaden m; vt beeinträchtigen; —d a person voreingenommen.

prelate ['prelət] n Prälat m.

preliminary [prɪ'lɪmɪnərɪ] a einleitend, Vor-; the preliminaries pl die vorbereitenden Maßnahmen pl.

prelude ['prelju:d] n Vorspiel nt; (Mus) Präludium nt; (fig also) Auftakt m.

premarital ['pri:'mærɪtl] a vorehelich.

premature ['premətʃʊə*] a vorzeitig, verfrüht; birth Früh-; decision voreilig; —ly ad vorzeitig; verfrüht; voreilig.

premeditate [pri:'medɪteɪt] vt im voraus planen; —d a geplant; murder vorsätzlich.

premeditation [pri:medɪ'teɪʃən] n Planung f.

premier ['premɪə*] a erste(r, s), oberste(r, s), höchste(r, s); n Premier m.

premiere [premɪ'eə*] n Premiere f; Uraufführung f.

premise ['premɪs] n Voraussetzung f; Prämisse f; —s pl Räumlichkeiten pl; (grounds) Grundstück m.

premium ['pri:mɪəm] n Prämie f; to sell at a — mit Gewinn verkaufen.

premonition [premə'nɪʃən] n Vorahnung f.

preoccupation [pri:ɒkjʊ'peɪʃən] n Sorge f.

preoccupied [pri:'ɒkjʊpaɪd] a look geistesabwesend; to be — with sth mit dem Gedanken an etw (acc) beschäftigt sein.

prep [prep] n (Sch: study) Hausaufgabe f.

prepaid ['pri:'peɪd] a vorausbezahlt; letter frankiert.

preparation [prepə'reɪʃən] n Vorbereitung f.

preparatory [prɪ'pærətərɪ] a Vor(bereitungs)-.

prepare [prɪ'peə*] vt vorbereiten (for auf +acc); vi sich vorbereiten; to be —d to . . . bereit sein zu . . .

preponderance [prɪ'pɒndərəns] n Übergewicht nt.

preposition [prepə'zɪʃən] n Präposition f, Verhältniswort nt.

preposterous [prɪ'pɒstərəs] a absurd, widersinnig.

prerequisite ['pri:'rekwɪzɪt] n (unerläßliche) Voraussetzung f.

prerogative [prɪ'rɒgətɪv] n Vorrecht nt, Privileg nt.

presbytery ['prezbɪtərɪ] n (house)

Presbyterium *nt*; *(Catholic)* Pfarrhaus *nt*.

prescribe [prɪs'kraɪb] *vt* vorschreiben, anordnen; *(Med)* verschreiben.

prescription [prɪs'krɪpʃən] *n* Vorschrift *f*; *(Med)* Rezept *nt*.

prescriptive [prɪs'krɪptɪv] *a* normativ.

presence ['prezns] *n* Gegenwart *f*, Anwesenheit *f*; — of mind Geistesgegenwart *f*.

present ['preznt] *a* anwesend; *(existing)* gegenwärtig, augenblicklich; *n* Gegenwart *f*; at — im Augenblick; Präsens *nt* *(Gram)*; *(gift)* Geschenk *nt*; [prɪ'zent] *vt* vorlegen; *(introduce)* vorstellen; *(show)* zeigen; *(give)* überreichen; to — sb with sth jdm etw überreichen; —able [prɪ'zentəbl] *a* präsentabel; —ation Überreichung *f*; —day a heutig, gegenwärtig, modern; —ly *ad* bald; *(at present)* im Augenblick; —participle Partizip *nt* des Präsens, Mittelwort *nt* der Gegenwart; — tense Präsens *nt*, Gegenwart *f*.

preservation [prezə'veɪʃən] *n* Erhaltung *f*.

preservative [prɪ'zɜ:vətɪv] *n* Konservierungsmittel *nt*.

preserve [prɪ'zɜ:v] *vt* erhalten, schützen; *food* einmachen, konservieren; *n (jam)* Eingemachte(s) *nt*; *(hunting)* Schutzgebiet *nt*.

preside [prɪ'zaɪd] *vi* den Vorsitz haben.

presidency ['prezɪdənsɪ] *n (Pol)* Präsidentschaft *f*.

president ['prezɪdənt] *n* Präsident *m*; —ial [prezɪ'denʃəl] *a* Präsidenten-; election Präsidentschafts-; system Präsidial-.

press [pres] *n* Presse *f*; *(printing house)* Druckerei *f*; to give the clothes a — die Kleider bügeln; *vt* drücken, pressen; *(iron)* bügeln; *(urge)* (be)drängen; *vi (push)* drücken, pressen; to be —ed for time unter Zeitdruck stehen; to be —ed for money/space wenig Geld/Platz haben; to — for sth drängen auf etw *(acc)*; — on *vi* vorwärtsdrängen; — agency Presseagentur *f*; — conference Pressekonferenz *f*; — cutting Zeitungsausschnitt *m*; —ing *a* dringend; —stud Druckknopf *m*.

pressure ['preʃə*] *n* Druck *m*; — cooker Schnellkochtopf *m*; — gauge Druckmesser *m*; — group Interessenverband *m*, Pressure Group *f*.

pressurized ['preʃəraɪzd] *a* Druck-.

prestige [pres'ti:ʒ] *n* Ansehen *nt*, Prestige *nt*.

prestigious [pres'tɪdʒəs] *a* Prestige-.

presumably [prɪ'zju:məblɪ] *ad* vermutlich.

presume [prɪ'zju:m] *vti* annehmen; *(dare)* sich erlauben.

presumption [prɪ'zʌmpʃən] *n* Annahme *f*; *(impudent behaviour)* Anmaßung *f*.

presumptuous [prɪ'zʌmptjʊəs] *a* anmaßend.

presuppose [prɪ:sə'pəʊz] *vt* voraussetzen.

presupposition [prɪ:sʌpə'zɪʃən] *n* Voraussetzung *f*.

pretence [prɪ'tens] *n* Vorgabe *f*, Vortäuschung *f*; *(false claim)* Vorwand *m*.

pretend [prɪ'tend] *vt* vorgeben, so tun als ob ...; *vi* so tun; to — to sth Anspruch erheben auf etw *(acc)*.

pretense [prɪ'tens] n (US) = **pretence.**

pretension [prɪ'tenʃən] n Anspruch m; (impudent claim) Anmaßung f.

pretentious [prɪ'tenʃəs] a angeberisch.

pretext ['pri:tekst] n Vorwand m.

prettily ['prɪtɪlɪ] ad hübsch, nett.

pretty ['prɪtɪ] a hübsch, nett; ad (col) ganz schön.

prevail [prɪ'veɪl] vi siegen (against, over über +acc); (custom) vorherrschen; to — upon sb to do sth jdn dazu bewegen, etw zu tun; —ing a vorherrschend.

prevalent ['prevələnt] a vorherrschend.

prevarication [prɪværɪ'keɪʃən] n Ausflucht f.

prevent [prɪ'vent] vt (stop) verhindern, verhüten; to — sb from doing sth jdn (daran) hindern, etw zu tun; —able a verhütbar; —ative Vorbeugungsmittel nt; —ion [prɪ'venʃən] Verhütung f, Schutz m (of gegen); —ive a vorbeugend, Schutz-.

preview ['pri:vju:] n private Voraufführung f; (trailer) Vorschau f; vt film privat vorführen.

previous ['pri:vɪəs] a früher, vorherig; —ly ad früher.

prewar ['pri:'wɔ:] a Vorkriegs-.

prey [preɪ] n Beute f; — on vt Jagd machen auf (+acc); mind nagen an (+dat); bird/beast of — Raubvogel m/Raubtier nt.

price [praɪs] n Preis m; (value) Wert m; vt schätzen; (label) auszeichnen; —less a (lit, fig) unbezahlbar; — list Preisliste f; —y a (col) teuer.

prick [prɪk] n Stich m, vt stechen; to — up one's ears die Ohren spitzen.

prickle ['prɪkl] n Stachel m, Dorn m; vi brennen.

prickly ['prɪklɪ] a stachelig; (fig) person reizbar; — heat Hitzebläschen pl; — pear Feigenkaktus m; (fruit) Kaktusfeige f.

pride [praɪd] n Stolz m; (arrogance) Hochmut m; to — o.s. on sth auf etw (acc) stolz sein.

priest [pri:st] n Priester m; —ess Priesterin f; —hood Priesteramt nt.

prig [prɪg] n Selbstgefällige(r) mf.

prim a, —ly ad [prɪm, -lɪ] prüde.

prima donna ['pri:mə 'dɒnə] n Primadonna f.

primarily ['praɪmərɪlɪ] ad vorwiegend, hauptsächlich.

primary ['praɪmərɪ] a Haupt-, Grund-, primär; — colour Grundfarbe f; — education Grundschul(aus)bildung f; — election Vorwahl f; — school Grundschule f, Volksschule f.

primate ['praɪmɪt] n (Eccl) Primas m; (Biol) Primat m.

prime [praɪm] a oberste(r, s), erste(r, s), wichtigste(r, s); (excellent) erstklassig, prima inv; vt vorbereiten; gun laden; n (of life) beste(s) Alter nt; — minister Premierminister m, Ministerpräsident m; —r Elementarlehrbuch nt, Fibel f.

primeval [praɪ'mi:vəl] a vorzeitlich; forests Ur-.

primitive ['prɪmɪtɪv] a primitiv.

primrose ['prɪmrəuz] n (gelbe) Primel f.

primula ['prɪmjulə] n Primel f.

primus (stove) ® ['praɪməs (stəuv)] n Primuskocher m.

prince [prɪns] n Prinz m; (ruler) Fürst m; —ss [prɪn'ses] Prinzessin f; Fürstin f.

principal ['prɪnsɪpəl] a Haupt-; wichtigste(r, s); n (Sch) (Schul)direktor m, Rektor m; (money) (Grund)kapital nt; —ity [prɪnsɪ'pælɪtɪ] Fürstentum nt; —ly a hauptsächlich.

principle ['prɪnsɪpl] n Grundsatz m, Prinzip nt; in/on — im/aus Prinzip, prinzipiell.

print [prɪnt] n Druck m; (made by feet, fingers) Abdruck m; (Phot) Abzug m; (cotton) Kattun m; vt drucken; name in Druckbuchstaben schreiben; Photo abziehen; —ed matter Drucksache f; —er Drucker m; —ing Drucken nt; (of photos) Abziehen nt; —ing press Druckerpresse f; is the book still in —? wird das Buch noch gedruckt?; out of — vergriffen.

prior [praɪə*] a früher; — to sth vor etw (dat); — to going abroad, she had . . . bevor sie ins Ausland ging, hatte sie . . .; n Prior m; —ess Priorin f; —ity [praɪ'ɒrɪtɪ] Vorrang m; Priorität f; —y Kloster nt.

prise [praɪz] vt: — open aufbrechen.

prism ['prɪzəm] n Prisma nt.

prison ['prɪzn] n Gefängnis nt; —er Gefangene(r) mf; —er of war Kriegsgefangene(r) m; to be taken —er in Gefangenschaft geraten.

prissy ['prɪsɪ] a (col) etepetete.

pristine ['prɪstiːn] a makellos.

privacy ['prɪvəsɪ] n Ungestörtheit f, Ruhe f; Privatleben nt.

private [praɪvɪt] a privat, Privat-; (secret) vertraulich, geheim; soldier einfach; n einfache(r) Soldat m; in — privat, unter vier Augen; — eye Privatdetektiv m; —ly privat; vertraulich, geheim.

privet ['prɪvɪt] n Liguster m.

privilege ['prɪvɪlɪdʒ] n Vorrecht nt,

Vergünstigung f, Privileg nt; —d a bevorzugt, privilegiert.

privy ['prɪvɪ] a geheim, privat; — council Geheime(r) Staatsrat m.

prize [praɪz] n Preis m; a example erstklassig; idiot Voll-; vt (hoch)schätzen; — fighting Preisboxen nt; — giving Preisverteilung f; — money Geldpreis m; —winner Preisträger(in f) m; (of money) Gewinner(in f) m.

pro- [prəʊ] pref pro-; n: the —s and cons pl das Für und Wider.

pro [prəʊ] n (professional) Profi m.

probability [prɒbə'bɪlɪtɪ] n Wahrscheinlichkeit f; in all — aller Wahrscheinlichkeit nach.

probable a, **probably** ad ['prɒbəbl, -blɪ] wahrscheinlich.

probation [prə'beɪʃən] n Probe(zeit) f; (Jur) Bewährung f; on — auf Probe; auf Bewährung; — officer Bewährungshelfer m; —ary a Probe-; —er (nurse) Lernschwester f; Pfleger m in der Ausbildung; (Jur) auf Bewährung freigelassene(r) Gefangene(r) m.

probe [prəʊb] n Sonde f; (enquiry) Untersuchung f; vti untersuchen, erforschen, sondieren.

probity ['prəʊbɪtɪ] n Rechtschaffenheit f.

problem ['prɒbləm] n Problem nt; —atic [prɒblɪ'mætɪk] a problematisch.

procedural [prə'siːdjʊrəl] a verfahrensmäßig, Verfahrens-.

procedure [prə'siːdʒə*] n Verfahren nt, Vorgehen nt.

proceed [prə'siːd] vi (advance) vorrücken; (start) anfangen; (carry on) fortfahren; (set about) vorgehen; (come from) vorgehen (from aus); (Jur) gerichtlich vorgehen; —ings pl Verfahren nt;

(record of things) Sitzungsbericht *m*; —s ['prəʊsiːds] *pl* Erlös *m*, Gewinn *m*.

process ['prəʊses] *n* Vorgang *m*, Prozeß *m*; *(method also)* Verfahren *nt*; *vt* bearbeiten; *food* verarbeiten; *film* entwickeln; —ing *(Phot)* Entwickeln *nt*.

procession [prə'seʃən] *n* Prozession *f*, Umzug *m*.

proclaim [prə'kleɪm] *vt* verkünden, proklamieren; **to — sb king** jdn zum König ausrufen.

proclamation [prɒklə'meɪʃən] *n* Verkündung *f*, Proklamation *f*; Ausrufung *f*.

procrastination [prəʊkræstɪ-\'neɪʃən] *n* Hinausschieben *nt*.

procreation [prəʊkrɪ'eɪʃən] *n* (Er)zeugung *f*.

procure [prə'kjʊə*] *vt* beschaffen.

prod [prɒd] *vt* stoßen; **to — sb** *(fig)* bohren; *n* Stoß *m*.

prodigal ['prɒdɪgəl] *a* verschwenderisch (of mit); **the — son** der verlorene Sohn.

prodigious [prə'dɪdʒəs] *a* gewaltig, erstaunlich; *(wonderful)* wunderbar.

prodigy ['prɒdɪdʒɪ] *n* Wunder *nt*; **a child —** ein Wunderkind.

produce ['prɒdjuːs] *n (Agr)* (Boden)produkte *pl*, (Natur-) erzeugnis *nt*; [prə'djuːs] *vt* herstellen, produzieren; *(cause)* hervorrufen; *(farmer)* erzeugen; *(yield)* liefern, bringen; *play* inszenieren; —r Erzeuger *m*, Hersteller *m*, Produzent *m (also Cine)*.

product ['prɒdʌkt] *n* Produkt *nt*, Erzeugnis *nt*; —ion [prə'dʌkʃən] Produktion *f*, Herstellung *f*; *(thing)* Erzeugnis *nt*, Produkt *nt*; *(Theat)* Inszenierung *f*; —ion line Fließband *nt*; —ive *a* produktiv;

(fertile) ertragreich, fruchtbar; **to be —ive of** führen zu, erzeugen.

productivity [prɒdʌk'tɪvɪtɪ] *n* Produktivität *f*; *(Comm)* Leistungsfähigkeit *f*; *(fig)* Fruchtbarkeit *f*.

prof [prɒf] *n (col)* Professor *m*.

profane [prə'feɪn] *a* weltlich, profan, Profan-.

profess [prə'fes] *vt* bekennen; *(show)* zeigen; *(claim to be)* vorgeben; —ion [prə'feʃən] Beruf *m*; *(declaration)* Bekenntnis *nt*; —ional [prə'feʃənl] Fachmann *m*; *(Sport)* Berufsspieler(in *f*) *m*; *a* Berufs-; *(expert)* fachlich; *player* professionell; —ionalism [prə'feʃnəlɪzəm] (fachliches) Können *nt*; Berufssportlertum *nt*; —or Professor *m*.

proficiency [prə'fɪʃənsɪ] *n* Fertigkeit *f*, Können *nt*.

proficient [prə'fɪʃənt] *a* fähig.

profile ['prəʊfaɪl] *n* Profil *nt*; *(fig: report)* Kurzbiographie *f*.

profit ['prɒfɪt] *n* Gewinn *m*, Profit *m*; *vi* profitieren *(by, from* von), Nutzen *or* Gewinn ziehen *(by, from* aus); · —ability ['prɒfɪtə'bɪlɪtɪ] Rentabilität *f*; —able *a* einträglich, rentabel; —ably *ad* nützlich; —eering [prɒfɪ'tɪərɪŋ] Profitmacherei *f*.

profound [prə'faʊnd] *a* tief; *knowledge* profund; *bole, thinker* tiefschürfend; —ly *ad* zutiefst.

profuse [prə'fjuːs] *a* überreich; **to be — in** überschwenglich sein bei; —ly *ad* überschwenglich; *sweat* reichlich.

profusion [prə'fjuːʒən] *n* Überfülle *f*, Überfluß *m (of an* +dat).

progeny ['prɒdʒɪnɪ] *n* Nachkommenschaft *f*.

programme, *(US)* **program** ['prəʊgræm] *n* Programm *nt*; *vt*

planen; *computer* programmieren.
programming, *(US)* **programing**
['prəʊgræmɪŋ] *n* Programmieren *nt*,
Programmierung *f*.
progress ['prəʊgres] *n* Fortschritt
m; **to be in** — im Gang sein; **to
make** — Fortschritte machen;
[prə'gres] *vi* fortschreiten, weitergehen; —**ion** [prə'grefən] Fortschritt *m*, Progression *f*; *(walking
etc)* Fortbewegung *f*; —**ive**
[prə'gresɪv] *a* fortschrittlich,
progressiv; —**ively** [prə'gresɪvlɪ] *ad*
zunehmend.
prohibit [prə'hɪbɪt] *vt* verbieten;
—**ion** [prəʊɪ'bɪʃən] Verbot *nt*; *(US)*
Alkoholverbot *nt*, Prohibition *f*;
—**ive** *a price etc* unerschwinglich.
project ['prɒdʒekt] *n* Projekt *nt*;
[prə'dʒekt] *vt* vorausplanen,
(Psych) hineinprojizieren; *film etc*
projizieren; *personality, voice* zum
Tragen bringen; *vi* *(stick out)*
hervorragen, (her)vorstehen; —**ile**
[prə'dʒektaɪl] Geschoß *nt*, Projektil
nt; —**ion** [prə'dʒekʃən] Projektion
f; *(sth prominent)* Vorsprung *m*;
—**or** [prə'dʒektə*] Projektor *m*,
Vorführgerät *nt*.
proletarian [prəʊlə'teərɪən] *a*
proletarisch, Proletarier-; *n*
Proletarier(in *f*) *m*.
proletariat [prəʊlə'teərɪət] *n*
Proletariat *nt*.
proliferate [prə'lɪfəreɪt] *vi* sich
vermehren.
proliferation [prəlɪfə'reɪʃən] *n*
Vermehrung *f*.
prolific [prə'lɪfɪk] *a* fruchtbar;
author etc produktiv.
prologue ['prəʊlɒg] *n* Prolog *m*;
(event) Vorspiel *nt*.
prolong [prə'lɒŋ] *vt* verlängern;
—**ed** *a* lang.

prom [prɒm] *n abbr of* promenade
and promenade concert; *(US:
college ball)* Studentenball *m*.
promenade [prɒmɪ'nɑ:d] *n*
Promenade *f*; — **concert**
Promenadenkonzert *nt*,
Stehkonzert *nt*; — **deck**
Promenadendeck *nt*.
prominence ['prɒmɪnəns] *n*
(große) Bedeutung *f*, Wichtigkeit *f*;
(sth standing out) vorspringende(r)
Teil *m*.
prominent ['prɒmɪnənt] *a*
bedeutend; *politician* prominent;
(easily seen) herausragend,
auffallend.
promiscuity [prɒmɪs'kju:ɪtɪ] *n*
Promiskuität *f*.
promiscuous [prə'mɪskjʊəs] *a*
lose, *(mixed up)* wild.
promise ['prɒmɪs] *n* Versprechen
nt; *(hope)* Aussicht *f* (*of* auf +
acc); **to show** — vielversprechend
sein; **a writer of** — ein vielver-
sprechender Schriftsteller; *vti* versprechen; **the** —**d land** das Gelobte
Land.
promising ['prɒmɪsɪŋ] *a* vielversprechend.
promontory ['prɒməntrɪ] *n*
Vorsprung *m*.
promote [prə'məʊt] *vt* befördern;
(help on) fördern, unterstützen;
—**r** *(in sport, entertainment)*
Veranstalter *m*; *(for charity etc)*
Organisator *m*.
promotion [prə'məʊʃən] *n* *(in
rank)* Beförderung *f*; *(furtherance)*
Förderung *f*; *(Comm)* Werbung *f*
(of für).
prompt [prɒmpt] *a* prompt,
schnell; **to be** — to do sth etw
sofort tun; *ad (punctually)* genau;
at two o'clock — punkt zwei Uhr;
vt veranlassen; *(Theat)* einsagen

(+dat), soufflieren (+dat); **—er**
(Theat) Souffleur m, Souffleuse f;
—ly ad sofort; **—ness** Schnelligkeit
f, Promptheit f.

promulgate ['prɒməlgeɪt] vt
(öffentlich) bekanntmachen,
verkünden; beliefs verbreiten.

prone [prəʊn] a hingestreckt; **to be**
— to sth zu etw neigen.

prong [prɒŋ] n Zinke f.

pronoun ['prəʊnaʊn] n Pronomen
nt, Fürwort nt.

pronounce [prə'naʊns] vt aussprechen; (Jur) verkünden; vi
(give an opinion) sich äußern (on
zu); **—d** a ausgesprochen; **—ment**
n Erklärung f.

pronto ['prɒntəʊ] ad (col) fix,
pronto.

pronunciation [prənʌnsɪ'eɪʃən] n
Aussprache f.

proof [pru:f] n Beweis m; (Print)
Korrekturfahne f; (of alcohol)
Alkoholgehalt m; **to put to the —**
unter Beweis stellen; a sicher;
alcohol prozentig; **rain—**
regendicht.

prop [prɒp] n Stütze f (also fig);
(Min) Stempel m; (Theat) Requisit
nt; vt (also **— up**) (ab)stützen.

propaganda [prɒpə'gændə] n
Propaganda f.

propagate ['prɒpəgeɪt] vt fort-
pflanzen; news propagieren,
verbreiten.

propagation [prɒpə'geɪʃən] n Fortpflanzung f; (of knowledge also)
Verbreitung f.

propel [prə'pel] vt (an)treiben;
—ler Propeller m; **—ling pencil**
Drehbleistift m.

propensity [prə'pensɪtɪ] n Tendenz
f.

proper ['prɒpə*] a richtig;
(seemly) schicklich; **—ly** ad

richtig; **—ly speaking** genau
genommen; **it is not — to . . . es**
schickt sich nicht, zu . . .; **— noun**
Eigenname m.

property ['prɒpətɪ] n Eigentum nt,
Besitz m, Gut nt; (quality) Eigenschaft f; (land) Grundbesitz m;
(Theat) properties pl Requisiten pl;
— owner Grundbesitzer m.

prophecy ['prɒfɪsɪ] n Prophezeiung
f.

prophesy ['prɒfɪsaɪ] vt
prophezeien, vorhersagen.

prophet ['prɒfɪt] n Prophet m; **—ic**
[prə'fetɪk] a prophetisch.

proportion [prə'pɔ:ʃən] n
Verhältnis nt, Proportion f; (share)
Teil m; vt abstimmen (to auf
+acc); **—al** a, **—ally** ad
proportional, verhältnismäßig; **to**
be —al to entsprechen (+dat);
—ate a, **—ately** ad verhältnismäßig; **—ed** a proportioniert.

proposal [prə'pəʊzl] n Vorschlag
m, Antrag m; (of marriage)
Heiratsantrag m.

propose [prə'pəʊz] vt vorschlagen;
toast ausbringen; vi (offer marriage) einen Heiratsantrag machen;
—r n Antragsteller m.

proposition [prɒpə'zɪʃən] n
Angebot nt; (Math) Lehrsatz m;
(statement) Satz m.

propound [prə'paʊnd] vt theory
vorlegen.

proprietary [prə'praɪətərɪ] a
Eigentums-; medicine gesetzlich
geschützt.

proprietor [prə'praɪətə*] n Besitzer
m, Eigentümer m.

props [prɒps] npl Requisiten pl.

propulsion [prə'pʌlʃən] n Antrieb
m.

pro-rata [prəʊ'rɑ:tə] ad anteilmäßig.

prosaic [prə'zeɪɪk] *a* prosaisch, alltäglich.

prose [prəuz] *n* Prosa *f.*

prosecute ['prɒsɪkju:t] *vt* (strafrechtlich) verfolgen.

prosecution [prɒsɪ'kju:ʃən] *n* Durchführung *f;* (Jur) strafrechtliche Verfolgung *f;* (party) Anklage *f;* Staatsanwaltschaft *f.*

prosecutor ['prɒsɪkju:tə*] *n* Vertreter *m* der Anklage; Public P— Staatsanwalt *m.*

prospect ['prɒspekt] *n* Aussicht *f;* [prəs'pekt] *vi* suchen (for nach); —ing [prəs'pektɪŋ] (for minerals) Suche *f;* —ive [prəs'pektɪv] *a* möglich; —or [prəs'pektə*] (Gold)sucher *m;* —us [prəs'pektəs] (Werbe)prospekt *m.*

prosper ['prɒspə*] *vi* blühen, gedeihen; (person) erfolgreich sein; —ity [prɒs'perɪtɪ] Wohlstand *m;* —ous [prɒs'perəs] *a* wohlhabend, reich; business gutgehend, blühend.

prostitute ['prɒstɪtju:t] *n* Prostituierte *f.*

prostrate ['prɒstreɪt] *a* ausgestreckt (liegend); — with grief/exhaustion von Schmerz/Erschöpfung übermannt.

protagonist [prəu'tægənɪst] *n* Hauptperson *f,* Held *m.*

protect [prə'tekt] *vt* (be)schützen; —ion [prə'tekʃən] Schutz *m;* —ive *a* Schutz-, (be)schützend; —or (Be)schützer *m.*

protégé ['prɒteʒeɪ] *n* Schützling *m.*

protein ['prəuti:n] *n* Protein *nt,* Eiweiß *nt.*

protest ['prəutest] *n* Protest *m;* [prə'test] *vi* protestieren (against gegen); to — that . . . beteuern . . .; P—ant *a* protestantisch; *n* Protestant(in *f) m.*

protocol ['prəutəkɒl] *n* Protokoll *nt.*

prototype ['prəutəutaɪp] *n* Prototyp *m.*

protracted [prə'træktɪd] *a* sich hinziehend.

protractor [prə'træktə*] *n* Winkelmesser *m.*

protrude [prə'tru:d] *vi* (her)vorstehen.

protuberance [prə'tju:bərəns] *n* Auswuchs *m.*

protuberant [prə'tju:bərənt] *a* (her)vorstehend.

proud *a,* —ly *ad* [praud, -lɪ] stolz (of auf +acc).

prove [pru:v] *vt* beweisen; *vi* sich herausstellen, sich zeigen.

proverb ['prɒvɜ:b] *n* Sprichwort *nt;* —ial *a,* —ially *ad* [prə'vɜ:bɪəl, -ɪ] sprichwörtlich.

provide [prə'vaɪd] *vt* versehen; (supply) besorgen; person versorgen; — for *vt* sorgen für, sich kümmern um; emergency Vorkehrungen treffen für; blankets will be —d Decken werden gestellt; —d (that) *cj* vorausgesetzt (daß); P—nce ['prɒvɪdəns] die Vorsehung.

providing [prə'vaɪdɪŋ] *cj* = **provided (that).**

province ['prɒvɪns] *n* Provinz *f;* (division of work) Bereich *m;* the —s die Provinz.

provincial [prə'vɪnʃəl] *a* provinziell, Provinz-; *n* Provinzler(in *f) m.*

provision · [prə'vɪʒən] *n* Vorkehrung *f,* Maßnahme *f;* (condition) Bestimmung *f;* —s *pl* (food) Vorräte *pl,* Proviant *m;* —al *a,* —ally *ad* vorläufig, provisorisch.

proviso [prə'vaɪzəu] *n* Vorbehalt *m,* Bedingung *f.*

provocation' [prɒvə'keɪʃən] *n*
Provokation *f*, Herausforderung *f*.
provocative [prə'vɒkətɪv] *a*
provokativ, herausfordernd.
provoke [prə'vəʊk] *vt* provozieren;
(cause) hervorrufen.
prow [praʊ] *n* Bug *m*; —**ess** überragende(s) Können *nt*; *(valour)*
Tapferkeit *f*.
prowl [praʊl] *vt* streets durchstreifen; *vi* herumstreichen;
(animal) schleichen; *n*: on the —
umherstreifend; *(police)* auf der
Streife; —er Eindringling *m*.
proximity [prɒk'smɪtɪ] *n* Nähe *f*.
proxy ['prɒksɪ] *n* (Stell)vertreter *m*,
Bevollmächtigte(r) *m*; *(document)*
Vollmacht *f*; **to vote by** —
Briefwahl machen.
prudence ['pru:dəns] *n* Klugheit *f*,
Umsicht *f*.
prudent *a*, —**ly** *ad* ['pru:dənt, -lɪ]
klug, umsichtig.
prudish ['pru:dɪʃ] *a* prüde; —**ness**
Prüderie *f*.
prune [pru:n] *n* Backpflaume *f*; *vt*
ausputzen; *(fig)* zurechtstutzen.
pry [praɪ] *vi* seine Nase stecken
(into in +*acc).*
psalm [sɑ:m] *n* Psalm *m*.
pseudo ['sju:dəʊ] *a* Pseudo-; *(false)*
falsch, unecht; —**nym** ['sju:dənɪm]
Pseudonym *nt*, Deckname *m*.
psyche ['saɪkɪ] *n* Psyche *f*.
psychiatric [saɪkɪ'ætrɪk] *a*
psychiatrisch.
psychiatrist [saɪ'kaɪətrɪst] *n*
Psychiater *m*.
psychiatry [saɪ'kaɪətrɪ] *n*
Psychiatrie *f*.
psychic(al) ['saɪkɪk(əl)] *a*
übersinnlich; *person* paranormal
begabt; **you must be** — **du** kannst
wohl hellsehen.

psychoanalyse, *(US)* **psychoanalyze** [saɪkəʊ'ænəlaɪz] *vt*
psychoanalytisch behandeln.
psychoanalysis [saɪkəʊə'nælɪsɪs]
n Psychoanalyse *f*.
psychoanalyst [saɪkəʊ'ænəlɪst] *n*
Psychoanalytiker(in *f*) *m*.
psychological *a*, —**ly** *ad*
[saɪkə'lɒdʒɪkəl, -ɪ]. psychologisch.
psychologist [saɪ'kɒlədʒɪst] *n*
Psychologe *m*, Psychologin *f*.
psychology [saɪ'kɒlədʒɪ] *n*
Psychologie *f*.
psychopath ['saɪkəʊpæθ] *n*
Psychopath(in *f*) *m*.
psychosomatic
['saɪkəʊsəʊ'mætɪk] *a* psychosomatisch.
psychotherapy [saɪkəʊ'θerəpɪ] *n*
Psychotherapie *f*.
psychotic [saɪ'kɒtɪk] *a*
psychotisch; *n* Psychotiker(in *f*) *m*.
pub [pʌb] *n* Wirtschaft *f*, Kneipe *f*.
puberty ['pju:bətɪ] *n* Pubertät *f*.
pubic ['pju:bɪk] *a* Scham-.
public *a*, —**ly** *ad* ['pʌblɪk, -lɪ]
öffentlich; *n* *(also* general —*)*
Öffentlichkeit *f*; —**an** Wirt *m*;
—**ation** [pʌblɪ'keɪʃən] Publikation *f*,
Veröffentlichung *f*; — **company**
Aktiengesellschaft *f*; — **convenience** öffentliche Toiletten *pl*;
— **house** Lokal *nt*, Kneipe *f*; —**ity**
[pʌb'lɪsɪtɪ] Publicity *f*, Werbung *f*;
— **opinion** öffentliche Meinung *f*;
— **relations** *pl* Public Relations *pl*;
— **school** *(Brit)* Privatschule *f*,
Internatsschule *f*; —**-spirited** a mit
Gemeinschaftssinn; **to be**
—**-spirited** Gemeinschaftssinn
haben..
publish ['pʌblɪʃ] *vt* veröffentlichen,
publizieren; *event* bekanntgeben;
—**er** Verleger *m*; —**ing** Herausgabe

f, Verlegen nt; (business) Verlagswesen nt.

puce [pjuːs] a violettbraun.

puck [pʌk] n Puck m, Scheibe f.

pucker ['pʌkə*] vt face verziehen; lips kräuseln.

pudding ['pudɪŋ] n (course) Nachtisch m; Pudding m.

puddle ['pʌdl] n Pfütze f.

puerile ['pjuəraɪl] a kindisch.

puff [pʌf] n (of wind etc) Stoß m; (cosmetic) Puderquaste f; vt blasen, pusten; pipe paffen; vi keuchen, schnaufen; (smoke) paffen; —ed a (col: out of breath) außer Puste.

puffin ['pʌfɪn] n Papageitaucher m.

puff pastry, (US) **puff paste** ['pʌfˌpeɪstrɪ, 'pʌfˌpeɪst] n Blätterteig m.

puffy ['pʌfɪ] a aufgedunsen.

pull [pul] n Ruck m; Zug m; (influence) Beziehung f; vt ziehen; trigger abdrücken; vi ziehen; to — a face ein Gesicht schneiden; to — sb's leg jdn auf den Arm nehmen; to — to pieces (lit) in Stücke reißen; (fig) verreißen; to — one's weight sich in die Riemen legen; to — o.s. together sich zusammenreißen; — apart vt (break) zerreißen; (dismantle) auseinandernehmen; fighters trennen; — down vt house abreißen; — in vi hineinfahren; (stop) anhalten; (Rail) einfahren; — off vt deal etc abschließen; — out vi (of lane) ausfahren; (fig: partner) aussteigen; vt herausziehen; — round, — through vi durchkommen; — up vi anhalten.

pulley ['pulɪ] n Rolle f, Flaschenzug m.

pullover ['puləuvə*] n Pullover m.

pulp [pʌlp] n Brei m; (of fruit) Fruchtfleisch nt.

pulpit ['pulpɪt] n Kanzel f.

pulsate [pʌl'seɪt] vi pulsieren.

pulse [pʌls] n Puls m.

pulverize ['pʌlvəraɪz] vt pulverisieren, in kleine Stücke zerlegen (also fig).

puma ['pjuːmə] n Puma m.

pummel ['pʌml] vt mit den Fäusten bearbeiten.

pump [pʌmp] n Pumpe f; (shoe) leichter (Tanz)schuh m; vt pumpen; — up vt tyre aufpumpen.

pumpkin ['pʌmpkɪn] n Kürbis m.

pun [pʌn] n Wortspiel nt.

punch [pʌntʃ] n (tool) Stanze f; Locher m; (blow) (Faust)schlag m; (drink) Punsch m, Bowle f; vt stanzen; lochen; (strike) schlagen, boxen; —drunk a benommen; —up (col) Keilerei f.

punctual ['pʌŋktjuəl] a pünktlich; —ity [pʌŋktjuˈælɪt] Pünktlichkeit f.

punctuate ['pʌŋktjueɪt] vt mit Satzzeichen versehen, interpunktieren; (fig) unterbrechen.

punctuation [pʌŋktjuˈeɪʃən] n Zeichensetzung f, Interpunktion f.

puncture ['pʌŋktʃə*] n Loch nt; (Aut) Reifenpanne f; vt durchbohren.

pundit ['pʌndɪt] n Gelehrte(r) m.

pungent ['pʌndʒənt] a scharf.

punish ['pʌnɪʃ] vt bestrafen; (in boxing etc) übel zurichten; —able a strafbar; —ment Strafe f; (action) Bestrafung f.

punitive ['pjuːnɪtɪv] a strafend.

punt [pʌnt] n Stechkahn m.

punter ['pʌntə*] n (better) Wetter m.

puny ['pjuːnɪ] a kümmerlich.

pup [pʌp] n = **puppy**.

pupil ['pju:pl] n Schüler(in f) m; (in eye) Pupille f.

puppet ['pʌpɪt] n Puppe f; Marionette f.

puppy ['pʌpɪ] n junge(r) Hund m.

purchase ['pɜːtʃɪs] n Kauf m, Anschaffung f; (grip) Halt m; vt kaufen, erwerben; —r Käufer(in f) m.

pure [pjuə*] a pur; rein (also fig); —ly ['pju:əlɪ] ad rein; (only) nur; (with a also) rein.

purée ['pjuəreɪ] n Püree nt.

purgatory ['pɜːgətərɪ] n Fegefeuer nt.

purge [pɜːdʒ] n Säuberung f (also Pol); (medicine) Abführmittel nt; vt reinigen; body entschlacken.

purification [pjuərɪfɪ'keɪʃən] n Reinigung f.

purify ['pjuərɪfaɪ] vt reinigen.

purist ['pjuərɪst] n Purist m.

puritan ['pjuərɪtən] n Puritaner m; —ical [pjuərɪ'tænɪkəl] a puritanisch.

purity ['pjuərɪtɪ] n Reinheit f.

purl [pɜːl] n linke Masche f; vt links stricken.

purple ['pɜːpl] a violett; face dunkelrot; n Violett nt.

purpose ['pɜːpəs] n Zweck m, Ziel nt; (of person) Absicht f; on — absichtlich; —ful a zielbewußt, entschlossen; —ly ad absichtlich.

purr [pɜː*] n Schnurren nt; vi schnurren.

purse [pɜːs] n Portemonnaie nt, Geldbeutel m; vt lips zusammenpressen, schürzen.

purser ['pɜːsə*] n Zahlmeister m.

pursue [pə'sju:] vt verfolgen, nachjagen (+dat); study nachgehen (+dat); —r Verfolger m.

pursuit [pə'sju:t] n Jagd f (of nach), Verfolgung f; (occupation) Beschäftigung f.

purveyor [pɜː'veɪə*] n Lieferant m.

pus [pʌs] n Eiter m.

push [pʊʃ] n Stoß m, Schub m; (energy) Schwung m; (Mil) Vorstoß m; vt stoßen, schieben; button drücken; idea durchsetzen; vi stoßen, schieben; at a — zur Not; — aside vt beiseiteschieben; — off (col) abschieben; — on vi weitermachen; — through vt durchdrücken; policy durchsetzen; — up vt total erhöhen; prices hochtreiben; —chair (Kinder)sportwagen m; —ing a aufdringlich; —over (col) Kinderspiel nt; —y a (col) aufdringlich.

puss [pʊs] n Mieze(katze) f.

put [pʊt] vt irreg setzen, stellen, legen; (express) ausdrücken, sagen; (write) schreiben; — about vi (turn back) wenden; vt (spread) verbreiten; — across vt (explain) erklären; — away vt weglegen; (store) beiseitelegen; — back vt zurückstellen or -legen; — by vt zurücklegen, sparen; — down vt hinstellen or -legen; (stop) niederschlagen; animal einschläfern; (in writing) niederschreiben; — forward vt idea vorbringen; clock vorstellen; — off vt verlegen, verschieben; (discourage) abbringen von; it — me off smoking das hat mir die Lust am Rauchen verdorben; — on vt clothes etc anziehen; light etc anschalten, anmachen; play etc aufführen; brake anziehen; — out vt hand etc (her)ausstrecken; news, rumour verbreiten; light etc ausschalten, ausmachen; — up vt tent aufstellen; building errichten; price erhöhen; *person* unterbringen; **to — up with** sich abfinden mit; **I won't — up with it** das laß ich mir nicht gefallen.

putrid ['pju:trɪd] *a* faul.

putsch [putʃ] *n* Putsch *m*.

putt [pʌt] *vt* (*golf*) putten, einlochen; *n* (*golf*) Putten *nt*, leichte(r) Schlag *m*; **—er** Putter *m*.

putty ['pʌtɪ] *n* Kitt *m*; (*fig*) Wachs *nt*.

put-up ['putʌp] *a*: **— job** abgekartete(s) Spiel *nt*.

puzzle ['pʌzl] *n* Rätsel *nt*; (*toy*) Geduldspiel *nt*; *vt* verwirren; *vi* sich den Kopf zerbrechen.

puzzling ['pʌzlɪŋ] *a* rätselhaft, verwirrend.

pygmy ['pɪgmɪ] *n* Pygmäe *m*; (*fig*) Zwerg *m*.

pyjamas [pɪ'dʒɑ:məz] *npl* Schlafanzug *m*, Pyjama *m*.

pylon ['paɪlən] *n* Mast *m*.

pyramid ['pɪrəmɪd] *n* Pyramide *f*.

python ['paɪθən] *n* Pythonschlange *f*.

Q

Q, q [kju:] *n* Q *nt*, q *nt*.

quack [kwæk] *n* Quacken *nt*; (*doctor*) Quacksalber *m*.

quad [kwɒd] *abbr of* **quadrangle, quadruple, quadruplet.**

quadrangle ['kwɒdræŋgl] *n* (*court*) Hof *m*; (*Math*) Viereck *nt*.

quadruped ['kwɒdruped] *n* Vierfüßler *m*.

quadruple ['kwɒ'dru:pl] *a* vierfach; *vi* sich vervierfachen; *vt* vervierfachen.

quadruplet [kwɒ'dru:plət] *n* Vierling *m*.

quagmire ['kwægmaɪə*] *n* Morast *m*.

quaint [kweɪnt] *a* kurios; malerisch; **—ly** *ad* kurios; **—ness** malerischer Anblick *m*; Kuriosität *f*.

quake [kweɪk] *vi* beben, zittern; **Q—r** Quäker *m*.

qualification [kwɒlɪfɪ'keɪʃən] *n* Qualifikation *f*; (*sth which limits*) Einschränkung *f*.

qualified ['kwɒlɪfaɪd] *a* (*compe*tent) qualifiziert; (*limited*) bedingt.

qualify ['kwɒlɪfaɪ] *vt* (*prepare*) befähigen; (*limit*) einschränken; *vi* sich qualifizieren.

qualitative ['kwɒlɪtətɪv] *a* qualitativ.

quality ['kwɒlɪtɪ] *n* Qualität *f*; (*characteristic*) Eigenschaft *f*; *a* Qualitäts-.

qualm [kwɑ:m] *n* Bedenken *nt*, Zweifel *m*.

quandary ['kwɒndərɪ] *n* Verlegenheit *f*; **to be in a — in** Verlegenheit sein.

quantitative ['kwɒntɪtətɪv] *a* quantitativ.

quantity ['kwɒntɪtɪ] *n* Menge *f*, Quantität *f*.

quarantine ['kwɒrəntiːn] *n* Quarantäne *f*.

quarrel ['kwɒrəl] *n* Streit *m*; *vi* sich streiten; **—some** a streitsüchtig.

quarry ['kwɒrɪ] *n* Steinbruch *m*; (*animal*) Wild *nt*; (*fig*) Opfer *nt*.

quart [kwɔ:t] n Quart nt.

quarter ['kwɔ:tə*] n Viertel nt; (of year) Quartal nt, Vierteljahr nt; vt (divide) vierteln, in Viertel teilen; (Mil) einquartieren; —s pl (esp Mil) Quartier nt; — of an hour Viertelstunde f; — past three viertel nach drei; — to three dreiviertel drei, viertel vor drei; —deck Achterdeck nt; — final Viertelfinale nt; —ly a vierteljährlich; —master Quartiermeister m.

quartet(te) [kwɔ:'tet] n Quartett nt.

quartz ['kwɔ:ts] n Quarz m.

quash ['kwɔʃ] vt verdict aufheben.

quasi ['kwɑ:zi] ad quasi.

quaver ['kweivə*] n (Mus) Achtelnote f; vi (tremble) zittern.

quay [ki:] n Kai m.

queasiness ['kwi:zməs] n Übelkeit f.

queasy ['kwi:zi] a übel; he feels — ihm ist übel.

queen [kwi:n] n Königin f; — mother Königinmutter f.

queer [kwiə*] a seltsam, sonderbar, kurios; — fellow komische(r) Kauz m; n (col: homosexual) Schwule(r) m.

quell [kwel] vt unterdrücken.

quench [kwentʃ] vt thirst löschen, stillen; (extinguish) löschen.

query ['kwiəri] n (question) (An)frage f; (question mark) Fragezeichen nt; vt in Zweifel ziehen, in Frage stellen.

quest [kwest] n Suche f.

question ['kwestʃən] n Frage f; vt (ask) (be)fragen; suspect verhören; (doubt) in Frage stellen, bezweifeln; beyond — ohne Frage; out of the — ausgeschlossen; —able a zweifelhaft; —er Frage

steller m; —ing a fragend; — mark Fragezeichen nt; —naire Fragebogen m; (enquiry) Umfrage f.

queue [kju:] n Schlange f; vi (also — up) Schlange stehen.

quibble ['kwibl] n Spitzfindigkeit f; vi kleinlich sein.

quick a, —ly ad [kwik, -li] a schnell, n (of nail) Nagelhaut f; (old: the living) die Lebenden; to the — (fig) bis ins Innerste; — en vt (hasten) beschleunigen; (stir) anregen; vi sich beschleunigen; — fire a questions etc Schnellfeuer-; —ness Schnelligkeit f; (mental) Scharfsinn m; —sand Treibsand m; —step Quickstep m; —witted a schlagfertig, hell.

quid [kwid] n (Brit col: £1) Pfund nt.

quiet ['kwaiət] a (without noise) leise; (peaceful, calm) still, ruhig; n Stille f, Ruhe f; —en (also —en down) vi ruhig werden; vt beruhigen; —ly ad leise, ruhig; —ness Ruhe f, Stille f.

quill [kwil] n (of porcupine) Stachel m; (pen) Feder f.

quilt [kwilt] n Steppdecke f; —ing Füllung f, Wattierung f.

quin [kwin] abbr of quintuplet.

quince [kwins] n Quitte f.

quinine [kwi'ni:n] n Chinin nt.

quinsy ['kwinzi] n Mandelentzündung f.

quintet(te) [kwin'tet] n Quintett nt.

quintuplet [kwin'tju:plət] n Fünfling m.

quip [kwip] n witzige Bemerkung f; vi witzeln.

quirk [kwə:k] n (oddity) Eigenart f.

quit [kwit] irreg vt verlassen; vi aufhören.

quite [kwaɪt] ad *(completely)* ganz, völlig; *(fairly)* ziemlich; — *(so!)* richtig!

quits [kwɪts] a quitt.

quiver ['kwɪvə*] vi zittern; n *(for arrows)* Köcher m.

quiz [kwɪz] n *(competition)* Quiz nt; *(series of questions)* Befragung f; vt prüfen; —zical a fragend, verdutzt.

quoit [kwɔɪt] n Wurfring m.

quorum ['kwɔ:rəm] n beschlußfähige Anzahl f.

quota ['kwəʊtə] n Anteil m; *(Comm)* Quote f.

quotation [kwəʊ'teɪʃən] n Zitat nt; *(price)* Kostenvoranschlag m; — marks pl Anführungszeichen pl.

quote [kwəʊt] n see quotation; vi *(from book)* zitieren; vt *(from book)* zitieren; price angeben.

quotient ['kwəʊʃənt] n Quotient m.

R

R, r [ɑ:*] n R nt, r nt.

rabbi ['ræbaɪ] n Rabbiner m; *(title)* Rabbi m.

rabbit ['ræbɪt] n Kaninchen nt; — hutch Kaninchenstall m.

rabble ['ræbl] n Pöbel m.

rabies ['reɪbi:z] n Tollwut f.

raccoon [rə'ku:n] n Waschbär m.

race [reɪs] n *(species)* Rasse f; *(competition)* Rennen nt; *(on foot also)* Wettlauf m; *(rush)* Hetze f; vt um die Wette laufen mit; horses laufen lassen; vi *(run)* rennen; *(in contest)* am Rennen teilnehmen; —course *(for horses)* Rennbahn f; —horse Rennpferd nt; — meeting *(for horses)* (Pferde)rennen nt; — relations pl Beziehungen f zwischen den Rassen; —track *(for cars etc)* Rennstrecke f.

racial ['reɪʃəl] a Rassen-; — discrimination Rassendiskriminierung f; —ism Rassismus m; —ist a rassistisch; n Rassist m.

racing ['reɪsɪŋ] n Rennen nt; — car Rennwagen m; — driver Rennfahrer m.

racism ['reɪsɪzm] n Rassismus m.

racist ['reɪsɪst] · n Rassist m; a rassistisch.

rack [ræk] n Ständer m, Gestell nt; vt (zer)martern; to go to — and ruin verfallen.

racket ['rækɪt] n *(din)* Krach m; *(scheme)* (Schwindel)geschäft nt; *(tennis)* (Tennis)schläger m.

racquet ['rækɪt] n = racket *(tennis)*.

racy ['reɪsɪ] a gewagt; style spritzig.

radar ['reɪdɑ:*] n Radar nt or m.

radiance ['reɪdɪəns] n strahlende(r) Glanz m.

radiant ['reɪdɪənt] a *(bright)* strahlend; *(giving out rays)* Strahlungs-.

radiate ['reɪdɪeɪt] vti ausstrahlen; *(roads, lines)* strahlenförmig wegführen.

radiation [reɪdɪ'eɪʃən] n (Aus)strahlung f.

radiator ['reɪdɪeɪtə*] n *(for heating)* Heizkörper m; *(Aut)* Kühler m; — cap Kühlerdeckel m.

radical a, —ly ad ['rædɪkəl, -ɪ] radikal.

radio ['reɪdɪəʊ] n Rundfunk m, Radio nt; (set) Radio nt, Radioapparat m; —active a radioaktiv; —activity Radioaktivität f; —grapher [reɪdɪ'ɒgrəfə*] Röntgenassistent(in f) m; —graphy [reɪdɪ'ɒgrəfɪ] Radiographie f, Röntgenphotographie f; —logy [reɪdɪ'ɒlədʒɪ] Strahlenkunde f; — station Rundfunkstation f; — telephone Funksprechanlage f; — telescope Radioteleskop nt; —therapist Radiologieassistent(in f) m.

radish ['rædɪʃ] n (big) Rettich m; (small) Radieschen nt.

radium ['reɪdɪəm] n Radium nt.

radius ['reɪdɪəs] n Radius m, Halbkreis m; (area) Umkreis m.

raffia ['ræfɪə] n (Raffia)bast m.

raffish ['ræfɪʃ] a liederlich; clothes gewagt.

raffle ['ræfl] n Verlosung f, Tombola f.

raft [rɑːft] n Floß nt.

rafter ['rɑːftə*] n Dachsparren m.

rag [ræg] n (cloth) Lumpen m, Lappen m; (col: newspaper) Käseblatt nt; (Univ: for charity) studentische Sammelaktion f; vt auf den Arm nehmen; —bag (fig) Sammelsurium nt.

rage [reɪdʒ] n Wut f; (desire) Sucht f; (fashion) große Mode f; to be in a — wütend sein; vi wüten, toben.

ragged ['rægɪd] a edge gezackt; clothes zerlumpt.

raging ['reɪdʒɪŋ] a tobend; thirst Heiden-.

raid [reɪd] n Überfall m; (Mil) Angriff m; (by police) Razzia f; vt überfallen; —er m; (Bank)räuber m; (Naut) Kaperschiff nt.

rail [reɪl] n Schiene f, Querstange f; (on stair) Geländer nt; (of ship) Reling f; (Rail) Schiene f; by — per Bahn; —ing(s) Geländer nt; —road (US), —way (Brit) Eisenbahn f; —road or —way station Bahnhof m.

rain [reɪn] n Regen m; vti regnen; the —s pl die Regenzeit; —bow Regenbogen m; —coat Regenmantel m; —drop Regentropfen m; —fall Niederschlag m; —storm heftige(r) Regenguß m; —y a region, season Regen-; day regnerisch, verregnet.

raise [reɪz] n (esp US: increase) (Lohn- or Gehalts- or Preis)erhöhung f; vt (lift) (hoch)heben; (increase) erhöhen; question aufwerfen; doubts äußern; funds beschaffen; family großziehen; livestock züchten; (build) errichten.

raisin ['reɪzən] n Rosine f.

rajah ['rɑːdʒə] n Radscha m.

rake [reɪk] n Rechen m, Harke f; (person) Wüstling m; vt rechen, harken; (with gun) (mit Feuer) bestreichen; (search) (durch)suchen; to — in or together zusammenscharren.

rakish ['reɪkɪʃ] a verwegen.

rally ['rælɪ] n (Pol etc) Kundgebung f; (Aut) Sternfahrt f, Rallye f; (improvement) Erholung f; vt (Mil) sammeln; vi Kräfte sammeln; — round vti (sich) scharen um; (help) zu Hilfe kommen (+dat).

ram [ræm] n Widder m; (instrument) Ramme f; vt (strike) rammen; (stuff) (hinein)stopfen.

ramble ['ræmbl] n Wanderung f, Ausflug m; vi (wander) umherstreifen; (talk) schwafeln; —r Wanderer m; (plant) Kletterrose f.

rambling ['ræmbliŋ] *a plant* Kletter-; *speech* weitschweifig; *town* ausgedehnt.

ramification [ræmɪfɪ'keɪʃən] *n* Verästelung *f*; —s *pl* Tragweite *f*.

ramp [ræmp] *n* Rampe *f*.

rampage [ræm'peɪdʒ] *n*: to be on the — (*also* — *vi*) rahdalieren.

rampant ['ræmpənt] *a (heraldry)* aufgerichtet; to be — überhandnehmen.

rampart ['ræmpɑːt] *n* (Schutz)wall *m*.

ramshackle ['ræmʃækl] *a* baufällig.

ranch [rɑːntʃ] *n* Ranch *f*; —er Rancher *m*.

rancid ['rænsɪd] *a* ranzig.

rancour, (US) **rancor** ['ræŋkə*] *n* Verbitterung *f*, Groll *m*.

random ['rændəm] *a* ziellos, wahllos; *n*: at — aufs Geratewohl.

randy ['rændɪ] *a (Brit)* geil, scharf.

range [reɪndʒ] *n* Reihe *f*; *(of mountains)* Kette *f*; *(Comm)* Sortiment *nt*; *(selection)* (große) Auswahl *f* (*of an +dat*); *(reach)* (Reich)weite *f*; *(of gun)* Schußweite *f*; *(for shooting practice)* Schießplatz *m*; *(stove)* (großer) Herd *m*; *vt* (set in row) anordnen, aufstellen; *(roam)* durchstreifen; *vi* *(extend)* sich erstrecken; prices ranging from £5 to £10 Preise, die sich zwischen 5£ und 10£ bewegen; —r Förster *m*.

rank [ræŋk] *n* (row) Reihe *f*; *(for taxis)* Stand *m*; *(Mil)* Dienstgrad *m*, Rang *m*; *(social position)* Stand *m*; *vt* einschätzen; *vi* *(have* —) gehören *(among* zu); *a* *(strongsmelling)* stinkend; *(extreme)* krass; the —s *pl (Mil)* die Mannschaften *pl*; the — and file *(fig)* die breite Masse.

rankle ['ræŋkl] *vi* nagen.

ransack ['rænsæk] *vt (plunder)* plündern; *(search)* durchwühlen.

ransom ['rænsəm] *n* Lösegeld *nt*; to hold sb to — jdn gegen Lösegeld festhalten.

rant [rænt] *vi* hochtrabend reden; —ing Wortschwall *m*.

rap [ræp] *n* Schlag *m*; *vt* klopfen.

rape [reɪp] *n* Vergewaltigung *f*; *vt* vergewaltigen.

rapid ['ræpɪd] *a* rasch, schnell; —s *pl* Stromschnellen *pl*; —ity [rə'pɪdɪtɪ] Schnelligkeit *f*; —ly *ad* schnell.

rapier ['reɪpɪə*] *n* Florett *nt*.

rapist ['reɪpɪst] *n* Vergewaltiger *m*.

rapport [ræ'pɔː*] *n* gute(s) Verhältnis *nt*.

rapprochement [ræ'prɒʃmɑ̃:ŋ] *n* (Wieder)annäherung *f*.

rapt [ræpt] *a* hingerissen.

rapture ['ræptʃə*] *n* Entzücken *nt*.

rapturous ['ræptʃərəs] *a applause* stürmisch; *expression* verzückt.

rare [rɛə*] *a* selten, rar; *(especially good)* vortrefflich; *(underdone)* nicht durchgebraten; —fied ['rɛərɪfaɪd] *a air, atmosphere* dünn; —ly *ad* selten.

rarity ['rɛərɪtɪ] *n* Seltenheit *f*.

rascal ['rɑːskəl] *n* Schuft *m*; *(child)* Strick *m*.

rash [ræʃ] *a* übereilt; *(reckless)* unbesonnen; *n* (Haut)ausschlag *m*.

rasher ['ræʃə*] *n* Speckscheibe *f*.

rashly ['ræʃlɪ] *ad* vorschnell, unbesonnen.

rashness ['ræʃnəs] *n* Voreiligkeit *f*; *(recklessness)* Unbesonnenheit *f*.

rasp [rɑːsp] *n* Raspel *f*.

raspberry ['rɑːzbərɪ] *n* Himbeere *f*.

rasping ['rɑːspɪŋ] *a noise* kratzend.

rat [ræt] *n (animal)* Ratte *f*; *(person)* Halunke *m*.

ratable ['reɪtəbl] *a*: — value Grundsteuer *f.*

ratchet ['rætʃɪt] *n* Sperrad *nt.*

rate [reɪt] *n* (proportion) Ziffer *f*, Rate *f*; (price) Tarif *m*, Gebühr *f*; (speed) Geschwindigkeit *f*; *vt* (ein)schätzen; —s *pl* (Brit) Grundsteuer *f*, Gemeindeabgaben *pl*; at any — jedenfalls; (at least) wenigstens; at this — wenn es so weitergeht; — of exchange (Wechsel)kurs *m*; —payer Steuerzahler(in *f*) *m*; see first.

rather ['rɑːðə*] *ad* (in preference) lieber, eher; (to some extent) ziemlich; —! und ob!

ratification [rætɪfɪ'keɪʃən] *n* Ratifikation *f.*

ratify ['rætɪfaɪ] *vt* bestätigen; (Pol) ratifizieren.

rating ['reɪtɪŋ] *n* Klasse *f*; (sailor) Matrose *m.*

ratio ['reɪʃɪəʊ] *n* Verhältnis *nt.*

ration ['ræʃən] *n* (usually pl) Ration *f*; *vt* rationieren.

rational *a*, —**ly** *ad* ['ræʃənl, -nəlɪ] rational, vernünftig; —**e** [ræʃə'nɑːl] Grundprinzip *nt*; —**ization** [ræʃnəlaɪ'zeɪʃən] Rationalisierung *f*; —**ize** ['ræʃnəlaɪz] *vt* rationalisieren.

rationing ['ræʃnɪŋ] *n* Rationierung *f.*

rat race ['rætreɪs] *n* Konkurrenzkampf *m.*

rattle ['rætl] *n* (sound) Rattern *nt*, Rasseln *nt*; (toy) Rassel *f*; *vi* ratteln, klappern; —**snake** Klapperschlange *f.*

raucous *a*, —**ly** *ad* ['rɔːkəs, -lɪ] heiser, rauh.

ravage ['rævɪdʒ] *vt* verheeren; —**s** *pl* verheerende Wirkungen *pl*; the —**s** of time der Zahn der Zeit.

rave [reɪv] *vi* (talk wildly) phantasieren; (rage) toben.

raven ['reɪvn] *n* Rabe *m.*

ravenous ['rævənəs] *a* heißhungrig; appetite unersättlich.

ravine [rə'viːn] *n* Schlucht *f*, Klamm *f.*

raving ['reɪvɪŋ] *a* tobend; — **mad** total verrückt.

ravioli [rævɪ'əʊlɪ] *n* Ravioli *pl.*

ravish ['rævɪʃ] *vt* (delight) entzücken; (Jur) woman vergewaltigen; —**ing** *a* hinreißend.

raw [rɔː] *a* roh; (tender) wund(gerieben); wound offen; (inexperienced) unerfahren; — material Rohmaterial *nt.*

ray [reɪ] *n* (of light) (Licht)strahl *m*; (gleam) Schimmer *m.*

rayon ['reɪɒn] *n* Kunstseide *f*, Reyon *m* or *nt.*

raze [reɪz] *vt* dem Erdboden gleichmachen.

razor ['reɪzə*] *n* Rasierapparat *m*; — **blade** Rasierklinge *f.*

re- [riː] *pref* wieder-.

re [riː] *prep* (Comm) betreffs (+ gen).

reach [riːtʃ] *n* Reichweite *f*; (of river) Flußstrecke *f*; within — (shops etc) in erreichbarer Weite or Entfernung; *vt* erreichen; (pass on) reichen, geben; *vi* (try to get) langen (for nach); (stretch) sich erstrecken; — **out** *vi* die Hand ausstrecken.

react [riː'ækt] *vi* reagieren; —**ion** [riː'ækʃən] Reaktion *f*; —**ionary** [riː'ækʃənrɪ] *a* reaktionär; —**or** Reaktor *m.*

read [riːd] *vti* irreg lesen; (aloud) vorlesen; the — **s** as follows es lautet folgendermaßen; —**able** *a* leserlich; (worth —**ing**) lesenswert; —er (person) Leser(in f) m; (book) Lesebuch nt; —ership Leserschaft f.

readily ['redɪlɪ] ad (willingly) bereitwillig; (easily) prompt.

readiness ['redɪnəs] n (willingness) Bereitwilligkeit f; (being ready) Bereitschaft f.

reading ['riːdɪŋ] n Lesen nt; (interpretation) Deutung f, Auffassung f; — lamp Leselampe f; — matter Lesestoff m, Lektüre f; — room Lesezimmer nt, Lesesaal m.

readjust ['riːə'dʒʌst] vt wieder in Ordnung bringen; neu einstellen; to — (o.s.) to sth sich wieder anpassen an etw (acc); —ment Wiederanpassung f.

ready ['redɪ] a (prepared) bereit, fertig; (willing) bereit, willens; (in condition to) reif; (quick) schlagfertig; money verfügbar, bar; ad bereit; n: at the — bereit; —made a gebrauchsfertig, Fertig-; clothes Konfektions-; —reckoner Rechentabelle f.

real [rɪəl] a wirklich; (actual) eigentlich; (true) wahr; (not fake) echt; — estate Grundbesitz m; —ism Realismus m; —ist Realist m; —istic a, —istically ad realistisch; —ity [riː'ælɪtɪ] (real existence) Wirklichkeit f, Realität f; (facts) Tatsachen pl; —ization (understanding) Erkenntnis f; (fulfilment) Verwirklichung f; —ize vt (understand) begreifen; (make real) verwirklichen; money einbringen; I didn't —ize . . . ich wußte nicht, . . . ; ad wirklich.

realm [relm] n Reich nt.

ream [riːm] n Ries nt.

reap [riːp] vt ernten; —er Mähmaschine f.

reappear ['riːə'pɪə*], vi wieder erscheinen; —ance Wiedererscheinen nt.

reapply ['riːə'plaɪ] vi wiederholt beantragen (for acc); (for job) sich erneut bewerben (for acc).

reappoint ['riːə'pɔɪnt] vt wieder anstellen; wiederernennen.

reappraisal ['riːə'preɪzəl] n Neubeurteilung f.

rear [rɪə*] a hintere(r, s), Rück-; n Rückseite f, (last part) Schluß m; vt (bring up) aufziehen; vi (horse) sich aufbäumen; —engined a mit Heckmotor; —guard Nachhut f.

rearm ['riː'ɑːm] vt wiederbewaffnen; vi wiederaufrüsten; —ament Wiederaufrüstung f.

rearrange ['riːə'reɪndʒ] vt umordnen; plans ändern.

rear-view ['rɪəvjuː] a: — mirror Rückspiegel m.

reason ['riːzn] n (cause) Grund m; (ability to think) Verstand m; (sensible thoughts) Vernunft f; vi (think) denken; (use arguments) argumentieren; to — with sb mit jdm diskutieren; —able a vernünftig; —ably ad vernünftig; (fairly reasonable) ziemlich; one could —ably suppose man könnte doch (mit gutem Grund) annehmen; —ed a argument durchdacht; .—ing Urteilen nt; (argumentation) Beweisführung f.

reassemble ['riːə'sembl] vt wieder versammeln; (Tech) wieder zusammensetzen, wieder zusammenbauen; vi sich wieder versammeln.

reassert ['riːə'sɜːt] vt wieder geltend machen.

reassurance ['riːə'ʃuərəns] n Beruhigung f; (confirmation) nochmalige Versicherung f.

reassure [ri:ə'ʃuə*] vt beruhigen; (confirm) versichern (sb jdm).

reassuring [ri:ə'ʃuərɪŋ] a beruhigend.

reawakening [ri:ə'weɪknɪŋ] n Wiedererwachen nt.

rebate ['ri:beɪt] n Rabatt m; (money back) Rückzahlung f.

rebel ['rebl] n Rebell m; a Rebellen-; —lion [rɪ'beljən] rebellion f, Aufstand m; —lious [rɪ'beljəs] a rebellisch; (fig) widerspenstig.

rebirth ['ri:'bɜ:θ] n Wiedergeburt f.

rebound [rɪ'baund] vi zurückprallen; ['ri:baund] n Rückprall m; on the — (fig) als Reaktion.

rebuff [rɪ'bʌf] n Abfuhr f; vt abblitzen lassen.

rebuild ['ri:'bɪld] vt irreg wiederaufbauen; (fig) wiederherstellen; —ing Wiederaufbau m.

rebuke [rɪ'bju:k] n Tadel m; vt tadeln, rügen.

rebut [rɪ'bʌt] vt widerlegen.

recalcitrant [rɪ'kælsɪtrənt] a widerspenstig.

recall [rɪ'kɔ:l] vt (call back) zurückrufen; (remember) sich erinnern an (+acc).

recant [rɪ'kænt] vi (öffentlich) widerrufen.

recap ['ri:kæp] n kurze Zusammenfassung f; vti information wiederholen.

recapture ['ri:'kæptʃə*] vt wieder (ein)fangen.

recede [rɪ'si:d] vi zurückweichen.

receding [rɪ'si:dɪŋ] a: — hair Stirnglatze f.

receipt [rɪ'si:t] n (document) Quittung f; (receiving) Empfang m; —s pl Einnahmen pl.

receive [rɪ'si:v] vt erhalten; visitors etc empfangen; —r (Tel) Hörer m.

recent ['ri:snt] a vor kurzem (geschehen), neuerlich; (modern) neu; —ly ad kürzlich, neulich.

receptacle [rɪ'septəkl] n Behälter m.

reception [rɪ'sepʃən] n Empfang m; (welcome) Aufnahme f; (in hotel) Rezeption f; —ist (in hotel) Empfangschef m/-dame f; (Med) Sprechstundenhilfe f.

receptive [rɪ'septɪv] a aufnahmebereit.

recess [rɪ'ses] n (break) Ferien pl; (hollow) Nische f; —es pl Winkel m; —ion [rɪ'seʃən] Rezession f.

recharge [rɪ:'tʃɑ:dʒ] vt battery aufladen.

recipe ['resɪpɪ] n Rezept nt.

recipient [rɪ'sɪpɪənt] n Empfänger m.

reciprocal [rɪ'sɪprəkəl] a gegenseitig; (mutual) wechselseitig.

reciprocate [rɪ'sɪprəkeɪt] vt erwidern.

recital [rɪ'saɪtl] n (Mus) Konzert nt, Vortrag m.

recitation [resɪ'teɪʃən] n Rezitation f.

recite [rɪ'saɪt] vt vortragen, aufsagen; (give list of also) aufzählen.

reckless a, —ly ad [rekləs, -lɪ] leichtsinnig; driving fahrlässig; —ness Rücksichtslosigkeit f.

reckon ['rekən] vt (count) (be- or er)rechnen; (consider) halten für; vi (suppose) annehmen; — on vt rechnen mit; —ing (calculation) Rechnen nt.

reclaim [rɪ'kleɪm] vt land abgewinnen (from dat); expenses zurückverlangen.

reclamation [reklə'meɪʃən] n (of land) Gewinnung f.

recline [rɪ'klaɪn] vi sich zurücklehnen.

reclining [rɪ'klaɪnɪŋ] a verstellbar, Liege-.

recluse [rɪ'kluːs] n Einsiedler m.

recognition [rekəg'nɪʃən] n (recognizing) Erkennen nt; (acknowledgement) Anerkennung f.

recognizable [rekəgnaɪzəbl] a erkennbar.

recognize ['rekəgnaɪz] vt erkennen; (Pol, approve) anerkennen.

recoil [rɪ'kɔɪl] n Rückstoß m; vi (in horror) zurückschrecken; (rebound) zurückprallen.

recollect [rekə'lekt] vt sich erinnern an (+acc); —ion [rekə'lekʃən] Erinnerung f.

recommend [rekə'mend] vt empfehlen; —ation Empfehlung f.

recompense ['rekəmpens] n (compensation) Entschädigung f; (reward) Belohnung f; vt entschädigen; belohnen.

reconcilable ['rekənsaɪləbl] a vereinbar.

reconcile ['rekənsaɪl] vt facts vereinbaren, in Einklang bringen; people versöhnen.

reconciliation [rekənsɪlɪ'eɪʃən] n Versöhnung f.

reconditioned ['riːkən'dɪʃənd] a überholt, erneuert.

reconnaissance [rɪ'kɒnɪsəns] n Aufklärung f.

reconnoitre, (US) reconnoiter [rekə'nɔɪtə*] vt erkunden; vi aufklären.

reconsider ['riːkən'sɪdə*] vti von neuem erwägen, (es) überdenken.

reconstitute ['riː'kɒnstɪtjuːt] vt neu bilden.

reconstruct ['riːkən'strʌkt] vt wiederaufbauen; crime rekonstruieren; —ion ['riːkən'strʌkʃən] Rekonstruktion f.

record ['rekɔːd] n (of) Aufzeichnung f; (Mus) Schallplatte f; (best performance) Rekord m; a time Rekord-; [rɪ'kɔːd] vt aufzeichnen; (Mus etc) aufnehmen; — card (in file) Karteikarte f; —ed music Musikaufnahmen pl; —er [rɪ'kɔːdə*] (officer) Protokollführer m; (Mus) Blockflöte f; — holder (Sport) Rekordinhaber m; —ing [rɪ'kɔːdɪŋ] (Mus) Aufnahme f; — library Schallplattenarchiv nt; — player Plattenspieler m.

recount [rɪ'kaʊnt] n Nachzählung f; vt (count again) nachzählen; [rɪ'kaʊnt] (tell) berichten.

recoup [rɪ'kuːp] vt wettmachen.

recourse [rɪ'kɔːs] n Zuflucht f.

recover [rɪ'kʌvə*] vt (get back) zurückerhalten; [riː'kʌvə*] quilt etc neu überziehen; vi sich erholen; —y Wiedererlangung f; (of health) Genesung f.

recreate ['riːkrɪ'eɪt] vt wiederherstellen.

recreation [rekrɪ'eɪʃən] n Erholung f; Freizeitbeschäftigung f; —al a Erholungs-.

recrimination [rɪkrɪmɪ'neɪʃən] n Gegenbeschuldigung f.

recruit [rɪ'kruːt] n Rekrut m; vt rekrutieren; —ing office Wehrmeldeamt nt; —ment Rekrutierung f.

rectangle ['rektæŋgl] n Rechteck nt.

rectangular [rek'tæŋgjələ*] a rechteckig, rechtwinklig.

rectify ['rektɪfaɪ] vt berichtigen.

rectory ['rektərɪ] n Pfarrhaus nt.

recuperate [rɪ'ku:pəreɪt] vi sich erholen.

recur [rɪ'kɜ:*]* vi sich wiederholen; —rence Wiederholung f; —rent a wiederkehrend.

red [red] n Rot nt; (Pol) Rote(r) m; a rot; **in the** — in den roten Zahlen; R— Cross Rote(s) Kreuz nt; —den vti (sich) röten; (blush) erröten; —dish a rötlich.

redecorate ['ri:'dekəreɪt] vt renovieren.

redecoration [ri:dekə'reɪʃən] n Renovierung f.

redeem [rɪ'di:m] vt (Comm) einlösen; (set free) freikaufen; (compensate) retten; **to** — sb from sin jdn von seinen Sünden erlösen; —ing ['ri:dɪ:mɪŋ] a virtue, feature rettend.

redeploy ['ri:dɪ'plɔɪ] vt resources umverteilen.

red-haired ['red'heəd] a rothaarig.

red-handed ['red'hændɪd] ad auf frischer Tat.

redhead ['redhed] n Rothaarige(r) mf.

red herring ['red'herɪŋ] n Ablenkungsmanöver nt.

red-hot ['red'hɒt] a rotglühend; (excited) hitzig; tip heiß.

redirect [ri:daɪ'rekt] vt umleiten.

rediscovery ['ri:dɪs'kʌvərɪ] n Wiederentdeckung f.

redistribute ['ri:dɪs'trɪbju:t] vt neu verteilen.

red-letter day ['red'letədeɪ] n (lit, fig) Festtag m.

redness ['rednəs] n Röte f.

redo ['ri:'du:] vt irreg nochmals tun or machen.

redolent ['redəʊlənt] a: — of riechend nach; (fig) erinnernd an (+acc).

redouble [ri:'dʌbl] vt verdoppeln.

red tape ['red'teɪp] n Bürokratismus m.

reduce [rɪ'dju:s] vt price herabsetzen (to auf +acc); speed, temperature vermindern; photo verkleinern; **to** — sb **to tears/silence** jdn zum Weinen/Schweigen bringen.

reduction [rɪ'dʌkʃən] n Herabsetzung f; Verminderung f; Verkleinerung f; (amount of money) Nachlaß m.

redundancy [rɪ'dʌndənsɪ] n Überflüssigkeit f; (of workers) Entlassung f.

redundant [rɪ'dʌndənt] a überflüssig; workers ohne Arbeitsplatz; **to be made** — arbeitslos werden.

reed [ri:d] n Schilf nt; (Mus) Rohrblatt nt.

reef [ri:f] n Riff nt.

reek [ri:k] vi stinken (of nach).

reel [ri:l] n Spule f, Rolle f; vt (wind) wickeln, spulen; (stagger) taumeln.

re-election ['ri:ɪ'lekʃən] n Wiederwahl f.

re-engage ['ri:ɪn'geɪdʒ] vt wieder einstellen.

re-enter ['ri:'entə*] vti wieder eintreten (in +acc).

re-entry ['ri:'entrɪ] n Wiedereintritt m.

re-examine ['ri:ɪg'zæmɪn] vt neu überprüfen.

ref [ref] n (col) Schiri m.

refectory [rɪ'fektərɪ] n (Univ) Mensa f; (Sch) Speisesaal m; (Eccl) Refektorium nt.

refer [rɪ'fɜ:*] vt: — sb to sb/sth jdn an jdn/etw verweisen; vi: — to hinweisen auf (+acc); (to book) nachschlagen in (+dat); (mention) sich beziehen auf (+acc).

referee [refə'ri:] n Schiedsrichter m; (for job) Referenz f; vt schiedsrichtern.

reference ['refrəns] n (mentioning) Hinweis m; (allusion) Anspielung f; (for job) Referenz f; (in book) Verweis m; (number, code) Aktenzeichen nt; Katalognummer f; with — to in bezug auf (+acc) — book Nachschlagewerk nt.

referendum [refə'rendəm] n Volksabstimmung f.

refill ['ri:'fɪl] vt nachfüllen; ['ri:fɪl] n Nachfüllung f; (for pen) Ersatzpatrone f; Ersatzmine f.

refine [rɪ'faɪn] vt (purify) raffinieren, läutern; (fig) bilden, kultivieren; —d a gebildet, kultiviert; —ment Bildung f, Kultiviertheit f; —ry Raffinerie f.

reflect [rɪ'flekt] vt light reflektieren; (fig) (wider)spiegeln, zeigen; vi (meditate) nachdenken (on über +acc); —ion Reflexion f; (image) Spiegelbild nt; (thought) Überlegung f, Gedanke m; —or Reflektor m.

reflex ['ri:fleks] n Reflex m; —ive [rɪ'fleksɪv] a (Gram) Reflexiv-, rückbezüglich, reflexiv.

reform [rɪ'fɔ:m] n Reform f; vt person bessern; the R—ation [refə'meɪʃən] die Reformation; —er Reformer m; (Eccl) Reformator m.

refrain [rɪ'freɪn] vi unterlassen (from acc).

refresh [rɪ'freʃ] vt erfrischen; —er course Wiederholungskurs m; —ing a erfrischend; —ments pl Erfrischungen pl.

refrigeration [rɪfrɪdʒə'reɪʃən] n Kühlung f.

refrigerator [rɪ'frɪdʒəreɪtə*] n Kühlschrank m.

refuel ['ri:'fjuəl] vti auftanken; —ling Auftanken nt.

refuge ['refju:dʒ] n Zuflucht f; —e [refjʊ'dʒi:] Flüchtling m.

refund [rɪ'fʌnd] n Rückvergütung f; [rɪ'fʌnd] vt zurückerstatten, rückvergüten.

refurbish ['ri:'fɜ:bɪʃ] vt aufpolieren.

refurnish ['ri:'fɜ:nɪʃ] vt neu möblieren.

refusal [rɪ'fju:zəl] n (Ver)weigerung f; (official) abschlägige Antwort f.

refuse [rɪ'fju:z] n Abfall m, Müll m; [rɪ'fju:z] vt abschlagen; vi sich weigern.

refute [rɪ'fju:t] vt widerlegen.

regain [rɪ'geɪn] vt wiedergewinnen; consciousness wiedererlangen.

regal ['ri:gəl] a königlich; —ia [rɪ'geɪlɪə] pl Insignien pl; (of mayor etc) Amtsornat nt.

regard [rɪ'gɑ:d] n Achtung f; vt ansehen; —s pl Grüße pl; —ing, as —s, with — to bezüglich (+gen), in bezug auf (+acc); —less a ohne Rücksicht (of auf +acc); ad unbekümmert, ohne Rücksicht auf die Folgen.

regatta [rɪ'gætə] n Regatta f.

regency ['ri:dʒənsɪ] n Regentschaft f.

regent ['ri:dʒənt] n Regent m.

régime [reɪ'ʒi:m] n Regime nt.

regiment ['redʒɪmənt] n Regiment nt; —al [redʒɪ'mentl] a Regiments-; —ation Reglementierung f.

region ['ri:dʒən] n Gegend f, Bereich m; —al a örtlich, regional.

register ['redʒɪstə*] n Register nt, Verzeichnis nt, Liste f; vt (list) registrieren, eintragen; emotion zeigen; (write down) eintragen; vi (at hotel) sich eintragen; (with police) sich melden (with bei); (make impression) wirken, ankommen; **—ed** a design eingetragen; letter Einschreibe-, eingeschrieben.

registrar [redʒɪs'trɑ:*] n Standesbeamte(r) m.

registration [redʒɪs'treɪʃən] n (act) Erfassung f, Registrierung f; (number) Autonummer f, polizeiliche(s) Kennzeichen nt.

registry office ['redʒɪstrɪɒfɪs] n Standesamt nt.

regret [rɪ'gret] n Bedauern nt; to have no **—s** nichts bedauern; to bedauern; **—ful** a traurig; to be **—ful** about sth etw bedauern; **—fully** ad mit Bedauern, ungern; **—table** a bedauerlich.

regroup ['ri:'gru:p] vt umgruppieren; vi sich umgruppieren.

regular ['regjulə*] a regelmäßig; (usual) üblich; (fixed by rule) geregelt; (col) regelrecht; n (client etc) Stammkunde m; (Mil) Berufssoldat m; **—ity** [regju'lærɪtɪ] Regelmäßigkeit f; **—ly** ad regelmäßig.

regulate ['regjulet] vt regeln, regulieren.

regulation [regju'leɪʃən] n (rule) Vorschrift f; (control) Regulierung f; (order) Anordnung f, Regelung f.

rehabilitation ['ri:həbɪlɪ'teɪʃən] n (of criminal) Resozialisierung f.

rehash ['ri:'hæʃ] vt (col) aufwärmen.

rehearsal [rɪ'hɜ:səl] n Probe f.

rehearse [rɪ'hɜ:s] vt proben.

reign [reɪn] n Herrschaft f; vi herrschen; **—ing** a monarch herrschend; champion gegenwärtig.

reimburse [ri:ɪm'bɜ:s] vt entschädigen, zurückzahlen (sb for sth jdm etw).

rein [reɪn] n Zügel m.

reincarnation ['ri:ɪnkɑ:'neɪʃən] n Wiedergeburt f.

reindeer ['reɪndɪə*] n Ren nt.

reinforce [ri:ɪn'fɔ:s] vt verstärken; **—d** a verstärkt; concrete Eisen-; **—ment** Verstärkung f; **—ments** pl (Mil) Verstärkungstruppen pl.

reinstate ['ri:ɪn'steɪt] vt wiedereinsetzen.

reissue ['ri:'ɪʃu:] vt neu herausgeben.

reiterate [ri:'ɪtəreɪt] vt wiederholen.

reject ['ri:dʒekt] n (Comm) Ausschuß(artikel) m; [rɪ'dʒekt] vt ablehnen; (throw away) ausrangieren; **—ion** [rɪ'dʒekʃən] Zurückweisung f.

rejoice [rɪ'dʒɔɪs] vi sich freuen.

rejuvenate [rɪ'dʒu:vɪneɪt] vt verjüngen.

rekindle ['ri:'kɪndl] vt wieder anfachen.

relapse [rɪ'læps] n Rückfall m.

relate [rɪ'leɪt] vt (tell) berichten, erzählen; (connect) verbinden; **—d** a verwandt (to mit).

relating [rɪ'leɪtɪŋ] prep: **— to** bezüglich (+gen).

relation [rɪ'leɪʃən] n Verwandte(r) mf; (connection) Beziehung f; **—ship** Verhältnis nt, Beziehung f.

relative ['relətɪv] n Verwandte(r) mf; a relativ, bedingt; **—ly** ad verhältnismäßig; **— pronoun** Verhältniswort nt, Relativpronomen nt.

relax [rɪ'læks] vi (slacken) sich lockern; (muscles, person) sich entspannen; (be less strict) freundlicher werden; vt (ease) lockern, entspannen; —! reg' dich nicht auf!; **—ation** [riːlæk'seɪʃən] Entspannung f; —ed a entspannt, locker; —ing a entspannend.

relay ['riːleɪ] n (Sport) Staffel f; vt message weiterleiten; (Rad, TV) übertragen.

release [rɪ'liːs] n (freedom) Entlassung f; (Tech) Auslöser m; vt befreien; prisoner entlassen; report, news verlautbaren, bekanntgeben.

relent [rɪ'lent] vi nachgeben; —less a, —lessly ad unnachgiebig.

relevance ['relәvәns] n Bedeutung f, Relevanz f.

relevant ['relәvәnt] a wichtig, relevant.

reliability [rɪlaɪә'bɪlɪtɪ] n Zuverlässigkeit f.

reliable, reliably ad [rɪ'laɪәbl, -blɪ] zuverlässig.

reliance [rɪ'laɪәns] n Abhängigkeit f (on von).

relic ['relɪk] n (from past) Überbleibsel nt; (Rel) Reliquie f.

relief [rɪ'liːf] n Erleichterung f; (help) Hilfe f, Unterstützung f; (person) Ablösung f; (Art) Relief nt; (distinctness) Hervorhebung f.

relieve [rɪ'liːv] vt (ease) erleichtern; (bring help) entlasten; person ablösen; to — sb of sth jdm etw abnehmen.

religion [rɪ'lɪdʒәn] n Religion f.

religious [rɪ'lɪdʒәs] a religiös; —ly ad religiös; (conscientiously) gewissenhaft.

reline ['riː'laɪn] vt brakes neu beschuhen.

relinquish [rɪ'lɪŋkwɪʃ] vt aufgeben.

relish ['relɪʃ] n Würze f, pikante Beigabe f; vt genießen.

relive [riː'lɪv] vt noch einmal durchleben.

reluctance [rɪ'lʌktәns] n Widerstreben nt, Abneigung f.

reluctant [rɪ'lʌktәnt] a widerwillig; —ly ad ungern.

rely [rɪ'laɪ]: — on vt sich verlassen auf (+acc).

remain [rɪ'meɪn] vi (be left) übrigbleiben; (stay) bleiben; —der Rest m; —ing a übrig(geblieben); —s pl Überreste pl; (dead body) sterbliche Überreste pl.

remand [rɪ'mɑːnd]: — on — in Untersuchungshaft; vt: — in custody in Untersuchungshaft schicken.

remark [rɪ'mɑːk] n Bemerkung f; vt bemerken; —able a, —ably ad bemerkenswert.

remarry ['riː'mærɪ] vi sich wieder verheiraten.

remedial [rɪ'miːdɪәl] a Heil-; teaching Hilfsschul-.

remedy ['remәdɪ] n Mittel nt; vt pain abhelfen (+dat); trouble in Ordnung bringen.

remember [rɪ'membә*] vt sich erinnern an (+acc); — me to them grüße sie von mir.

remembrance [rɪ'membrәns] n Erinnerung f; (official) Gedenken nt.

remind [rɪ'maɪnd] vt erinnern; —er Mahnung f.

reminisce [remɪ'nɪs] vi in Erinnerungen schwelgen; —nces [remɪ'nɪsәnsɪz] pl Erinnerungen pl; —nt a erinnernd (of an +acc), Erinnerungen nachrufend (of an +acc).

remit [rɪ'mɪt] vt money überweisen (to an +acc); **—tance** Geldanweisung f.

remnant ['remnənt] n Rest m.

remorse [rɪ'mɔ:s] n Gewissensbisse pl; **—ful** a reumütig; **—less** a, **—lessly** ad unbarmherzig.

remote [rɪ'məut] a abgelegen, entfernt; (slight) gering; **— control** Fernsteuerung f; **—ly** ad entfernt; **—ness** Entlegenheit f.

removable [rɪ'mu:vəbl] a entfernbar.

removal [rɪ'mu:vəl] n Beseitigung f; (of furniture) Umzug m; (from office) Entlassung f; **— van** Möbelwagen m.

remove [rɪ'mu:v] vt beseitigen, entfernen; (dismiss) entlassen; **—r** (for paint etc) Fleckenentferner m; **—rs** pl Möbelspedition f.

remuneration [rɪmju:nə'reɪʃən] n Vergütung f, Honorar n.

Renaissance [rə'neɪsɑ̃:ns]: the **—** die Renaissance.

rename ['ri:'neɪm] vt umbenennen.

rend [rend] vt irreg zerreißen.

render ['rendə*] vt machen; (translate) übersetzen; **—ing** (Mus) Wiedergabe f.

rendezvous ['rɒndɪvu:] n Verabredung f, Rendezvous n.

renegade ['renɪgeɪd] n Überläufer m.

renew [rɪ'nju:] vt erneuern; contract, licence verlängern; (replace) ersetzen; **—al** Erneuerung f; Verlängerung f.

renounce [rɪ'naʊns] vt (give up) verzichten auf (+acc); (disown) verstoßen.

renovate ['renəʊveɪt] vt renovieren; building restaurieren.

renovation [renəʊ'veɪʃən] n Renovierung f; Restauration f.

renown [rɪ'naʊn] n Ruf m; **—ed** a namhaft.

rent [rent] n (for land) Pacht f; vt (hold as tenant) mieten; pachten; (let) vermieten; car etc mieten; (firm) vermieten; **—al** Miete f; Pacht f, Pachtgeld n.

renunciation [rɪnʌnsɪ'eɪʃən] n Verzicht m (of auf +acc).

reopen ['ri:'əʊpən] vt wiedereröffnen.

reorder ['ri:'ɔ:də*] vt wieder bestellen.

reorganization ['ri:ɔ:gənaɪ'zeɪʃən] n Neugestaltung f; (Comm etc) Umbildung f.

reorganize ['ri:'ɔ:gənaɪz] vt umgestalten, reorganisieren.

rep [rep] n (Comm) Vertreter m; (Theat) Repertoire m.

repair [rɪ'pɛə*] n Reparatur f; in good **—** in gutem Zustand; vt reparieren; damage wiedergutmachen; **— kit** Werkzeugkasten m; **— man** Mechaniker m; **— shop** Reparaturwerkstatt f.

repartee [repɑ:'ti:] n Witzeleien pl.

repay [ri:'peɪ] vt irreg zurückzahlen; (reward) vergelten; **—ment** Rückzahlung f; (fig) Vergelten n.

repeal [rɪ'pi:l] n Aufhebung f; vt aufheben.

repeat [rɪ'pi:t] n (Rad, TV) Wiederholung(ssendung) f; vt wiederholen; **—edly** ad wiederholt.

repel [rɪ'pel] vt (drive back) zurückschlagen; (disgust) abstoßen; **—lent** a abstoßend; n: insect **—lent** Insektenmittel m.

repent [rɪ'pent] vti bereuen; **—ance** Reue f.

repercussion [ri:pə'kʌʃən] n Auswirkung f; (of rifle) Rückstoß m.

repertoire ['repətwa:*] n Repertoire nt.

repertory ['repətəri] n Repertoire nt.

repetition [repə'tiʃən] n Wiederholung f.

repetitive [ri'petitiv] a sich wiederholend.

rephrase [ri:'freiz] vt anders formulieren.

replace [ri'pleis] vt ersetzen; (put back) zurückstellen; —ment Ersatz m.

replenish [ri'pleniʃ] vt (wieder) auffüllen.

replete [ri'pli:t] a (zum Platzen) voll.

replica ['replikə] n Kopie f.

reply [ri'plai] n Antwort f, Erwiderung f; vi antworten, erwidern.

report [ri'pɔ:t] n Bericht m; (Sch) Zeugnis nt; (of gun) Knall m; vt (tell) berichten; (give information against) melden; (to police) anzeigen; vi (make report) Bericht erstatten; (present o.s.) sich melden; —er Reporter m.

reprehensible [repri'hensibl] a tadelnswert.

represent [repri'zent] vt darstellen, zeigen; (act) darstellen; (speak for) vertreten; —ation Darstellung f; (being represented) Vertretung f; —ative n (person) Vertreter m; a räpresentativ.

repress [ri'pres] vt unterdrücken; —ion [ri'preʃən] Unterdrückung f; —ive a Unterdrückungs-; (Psych) Hemmungs-.

reprieve [ri'pri:v] n Aufschub m; (cancellation) Begnadigung f; (fig) Atempause f; vt Gnadenfrist gewähren (+dat); begnadigen.

reprimand ['reprima:nd] n Verweis m; vt einen Verweis erteilen (+dat).

reprint ['ri:print] n Neudruck m; [ri:'print] vt wieder abdrucken.

reprisal [ri'praizəl] n Vergeltung f.

reproach [ri'prəutʃ] n (blame) Vorwurf m, Tadel m; (disgrace) Schande f; beyond — über jeden Vorwurf erhaben; vt Vorwürfe machen (+dat), tadeln; —ful a vorwurfsvoll.

reproduce [ri:prə'dju:s] vt reproduzieren; vi (have offspring) sich vermehren.

reproduction [ri:prə'dʌkʃən] n Wiedergabe f; (Art, Phot) Reproduktion f; (breeding) Fortpflanzung f.

reproductive [ri:prə'dʌktiv] a reproduktiv; (breeding) Fortpflanzungs-.

reprove [ri'pru:v] vt tadeln.

reptile ['reptail] n Reptil nt.

republic [ri'pʌblik] n Republik f; —an a republikanisch; n Republikaner m.

repudiate [ri'pju:dieit] vt zurückweisen, nicht anerkennen.

repugnance [ri'pʌgnəns] n Widerwille m.

repugnant [ri'pʌgnənt] a widerlich.

repulse [ri'pʌls] vt (drive back) zurückschlagen; (reject) abweisen.

repulsion [ri'pʌlʃən] n Abscheu m.

repulsive [ri'pʌlsiv] a abstoßend.

repurchase ['ri:'pə:tʃəs] vt zurückkaufen.

reputable ['repjutəbl] a angesehen.

reputation [repju'teiʃən] n Ruf m.

repute [ri'pju:t] n hohe(s) Ansehen nt; —d a, —dly ad angeblich.

request [rɪ'kwest] n (asking) Ansuchen nt; (demand) Wunsch m; at sb's — auf jds Wunsch; vt thing erbitten; person ersuchen.

requiem ['rekwiem] n Requiem nt.

require [rɪ'kwaɪə*] vt (need) brauchen; (wish) wünschen; to be —d to do sth etw tun müssen; —ment (condition) Anforderung f; (need) Bedarf m.

requisite ['rekwɪzɪt] n Erfordernis nt; a erforderlich.

requisition [rekwɪ'zɪʃən] n Anforderung f; vt beschlagnahmen; (order) anfordern.

reroute ['ri:'ru:t] vt umleiten.

rescind [rɪ'sɪnd] vt aufheben.

rescue ['reskju:] n Rettung f; vt retten; — party Rettungsmannschaft f; —r Retter m.

research [rɪ'sɜ:tʃ] n Forschung f; vi Forschungen anstellen (into über + acc); vt erforschen; —er Forscher m; — work Forschungsarbeit f; — worker wissenschaftliche(r) Mitarbeiter(in f) m.

resemblance [rɪ'zemblans] n Ähnlichkeit f.

resemble [rɪ'zembl] vt ähneln (+dat).

resent [rɪ'zent] vt übelnehmen; —ful a nachtragend, empfindlich; —ment Verstimmung f, Unwille m.

reservation [rezə'veɪʃən] n (of seat) Reservierung f; (Theat) Vorbestellung f; (doubt) Vorbehalt m; (land) Reservat nt.

reserve [rɪ'zɜ:v] n (store) Vorrat m, Reserve f; (manner) Zurückhaltung f; (game) Naturschutzgebiet nt; (native —) Reservat nt; (Sport) Ersatzspieler(in f) m; vt reservieren; judgement sich (dat) vorbehalten; —s pl (Mil) Reserve f; in — in Reserve; —d a

reserviert; all rights —d alle Rechte vorbehalten.

reservist [rɪ'zɜ:vɪst] n Reservist m.

reservoir ['rezəvwɑ:*] n Reservoir nt.

reshape ['ri:'ʃeɪp] vt umformen.

reshuffle ['ri:'ʃʌfl] vt (Pol) umbilden.

reside [rɪ'zaɪd] vi wohnen, ansässig sein; —nce ['rezɪdəns] (house) Wohnung f, Wohnsitz m; (living) Wohnen nt, Aufenthalt m; —nt ['rezɪdənt] (in house) Bewohner m; (in area) Einwohner m; a wohnhaft, ansässig; —ntial [rezɪ'denʃəl] a Wohn-.

residue ['rezɪdju:] n Rest m; (Chem) Rückstand m; (fig) Bodensatz m.

resign [rɪ'zaɪn] vt office aufgeben, zurücktreten von; to be —ed to sth, to — o.s. to sth sich mit etw abfinden; vi (from office) zurücktreten; —ation [rezɪg'neɪʃən] (resigning) Aufgabe f; (Pol) Rücktritt m; (submission) Resignation f; —ed a resigniert.

resilience [rɪ'zɪlɪəns] n Spannkraft f, Elastizität f; (of person) Unverwüstlichkeit f.

resilient [rɪ'zɪlɪənt] a unverwüstlich.

resin ['rezɪn] n Harz nt.

resist [rɪ'zɪst] vt widerstehen (+dat); —ance Widerstand m; —ant a widerstandsfähig (to gegen); (to stains etc) abstoßend.

resolute ['rezəlu:t] a, —ly ad ['rezəlu:t, -lɪ] entschlossen, resolut.

resolution [rezə'lu:ʃən] n (firmness) Entschlossenheit f; (intention) Vorsatz m; (decision) Beschluß m; (personal) Entschluß m.

resolve [rɪ'zɒlv] n Vorsatz m, Entschluß m; vt (decide) beschließen;

it —d itself es löste sich; —d a (fest) entschlossen.

resonant ['rezənənt] a widerhallend; *voice* volltönend.

resort [ri'zo:t] n *(holiday place)* Erholungsort m; *(help)* Zuflucht f; vi Zuflucht nehmen (to zu); as a last — als letzter Ausweg.

resound [ri'zaund] vi widerhallen; —ing a nachhallend; *success* groß.

resource [ri'so:s] n Findigkeit f; —s pl *(of energy)* Energiequellen pl; *(of money)* Quellen pl; *(of a country etc)* Bodenschätze pl; —ful a findig; —fulness Findigkeit f.

respect [ris'pekt] n Respekt m; *(esteem)* (Hoch)achtung f; vt achten,\respektieren; —s pl Grüße pl; with — to in bezug auf (+acc), hinsichtlich (+gen); in — of in bezug auf (+acc); in this — in dieser Hinsicht; —ability [rispektə'biliti] n Anständigkeit f, Achtbarkeit f; —able a *(decent)* angesehen, achtbar; *(fairly good)* leidlich; —ed a angesehen; —ful a höflich; —fully ad ehrerbietig; *(in letter)* mit vorzüglicher Hochachtung; —ing prep betreffend; —ive a jeweilig; —ively ad beziehungsweise.

respiration [respi'reiʃən] n Atmung f, Atmen pl.

respiratory [ris'pirətəri] a Atmungs-.

respite ['respait] n Ruhepause f; without — ohne Unterlaß.

resplendent [ris'plendənt] a strahlend.

respond [ris'pɒnd] vi antworten; *(react)* reagieren (to auf +acc).

response [ris'pɒns] n Antwort f; Reaktion f; *(to advert etc)* Resonanz f.

responsibility [rispɒnsə'biliti] n Verantwortung f.

responsible [ris'pɒnsəbl] a verantwortlich; *(reliable)* verantwortungsvoll.

responsibly [ris'pɒnsəbli] ad verantwortungsvoll.

responsive [ris'pɒnsiv] a empfänglich.

rest [rest] n Ruhe f; *(break)* Pause f; *(remainder)* Rest m; the — of them die übrigen; vi sich ausruhen; *(be supported)* (auf)liegen; *(remain)* liegen (with bei).

restaurant ['restərɒ:n] n Restaurant nt, Gaststätte f; — car Speisewagen m.

rest cure ['restkjuə*] n Erholung f.

restful ['restful] a erholsam, ruhig.

rest home ['resthəum] n Erholungsheim nt.

restitution [resti'tju:ʃən] n Rückgabe f, Entschädigung f.

restive ['restiv] a unruhig; *(disobedient)* störrisch.

restless ['restləs] a unruhig; —ly ad ruhelos; —ness Ruhelosigkeit f.

restock ['ri:'stɒk] vt auffüllen.

restoration [restə'reiʃən] n Wiederherstellung f; Neueinführung f; Wiedereinsetzung f; Rückgabe f; Restauration f; the R— die Restauration.

restore [ris'to:*] vt *order* wiederherstellen; *customs* wieder einführen; *person to position* wiedereinsetzen; *(give back)* zurückgeben; *paintings* restaurieren.

restrain [ris'trein] vt zurückhalten; *curiosity etc* beherrschen; —ed a *style etc* gedämpft, verhalten; —t *(restraining)* Einschränkung f; *(being restrained)* Beschränkung f; *(self-control)* Zurückhaltung f.

restrict [rɪsˈtrɪkt] vt einschränken; **—ed** a beschränkt; **—ion** [rɪsˈtrɪkʃən] Einschränkung f; **—ive** a einschränkend.

rest room [ˈrestrʊm] n (US) Toilette f.

result [rɪˈzʌlt] n Resultat nt, Folge f; (of exam, game) Ergebnis nt; vi zur Folge haben (in acc); **—ant** a (daraus) entstehend or resultierend.

resume [rɪˈzjuːm] vt fortsetzen; (occupy again) wieder einnehmen.

résumé [ˈreɪzjuːmeɪ] n Zusammenfassung f.

resumption [rɪˈzʌmpʃən] n Wiederaufnahme f.

resurgence [rɪˈsɜːdʒəns] n Wiedererwachen nt.

resurrection [rezəˈrekʃən] n Auferstehung f.

resuscitate [rɪˈsʌsɪteɪt] vt wiederbeleben.

resuscitation [rɪsʌsɪˈteɪʃən] n Wiederbelebung f.

retail [ˈriːteɪl] n Einzelhandel m; a Einzelhandels-, Laden-; [ˈriːteɪl] vt im kleinen verkaufen; vi im Einzelhandel kosten; **—er** [ˈriːteɪlə*] Einzelhändler m, Kleinhändler m; **— price** Ladenpreis m.

retain [rɪˈteɪn] vt (keep) (zurück)behalten; (pay) unterhalten; **—er** (servant) Gefolgsmann m; (fee) Honorar(vorschuß m.

retaliate [rɪˈtælɪeɪt] vi zum Vergeltungsschlag ausholen.

retaliation [rɪtælɪˈeɪʃən] n Vergeltung f.

retarded [rɪˈtɑːdɪd] a zurückgeblieben.

retention [rɪˈtenʃən] n Behalten nt.

retentive [rɪˈtentɪv] a memory gut.

rethink [ˈriːˈθɪŋk] vt irreg nochmals durchdenken.

reticence [ˈretɪsəns] n Schweigsamkeit f.

reticent [ˈretɪsənt] a schweigsam.

retina [ˈretɪnə] n Netzhaut f.

retinue [ˈretɪnjuː] n Gefolge nt.

retire [rɪˈtaɪə*] vi (from work) in den Ruhestand treten; (withdraw) sich zurückziehen; (go to bed) schlafen gehen; **—d** a person pensioniert, im Ruhestand; **—ment** Ruhestand m.

retiring [rɪˈtaɪərɪŋ] a zurückhaltend, schüchtern.

retort [rɪˈtɔːt] n (reply) Erwiderung f; (Sci) Retorte f; vi (sharp) erwidern.

retrace [rɪˈtreɪs] vt zurückverfolgen.

retract [rɪˈtrækt] vt statement zurücknehmen; claws einziehen; **—able** a aerial ausziehbar.

retrain [ˈriːˈtreɪn] vt umschulen; **—ing** n Umschulung f.

retreat [rɪˈtriːt] n Rückzug m; (place) Zufluchtsort m; vi sich zurückziehen.

retrial [ˈriːˈtraɪəl] n Wiederaufnahmeverfahren nt.

retribution [retrɪˈbjuːʃən] n Strafe f.

retrieval [rɪˈtriːvəl] n Wiedergewinnung f.

retrieve [rɪˈtriːv] vt wiederbekommen; (rescue) retten; **—r** Apportierhund m.

retroactive [retrəʊˈæktɪv] a rückwirkend.

retrograde [ˈretrəʊɡreɪd] a step Rück-; policy rückschrittlich.

retrospect [ˈretrəʊspekt] n: in — im Rückblick, rückblickend; **—ive** [retrəʊˈspektɪv] a rückwirkend; rückblickend.

return [rɪˈtɜːn] n Rückkehr f; (profits) Ertrag m, Gewinn m;

(report) amtliche(r) Bericht *m; (rail ticket etc)* Rückfahrkarte *f; (plane)* Rückflugkarte *f; (bus)* Rückfahrschein *m;* a by .— of post postwendend; *journey, match* Rück-; *vi* zurückkehren or -kommen; *vt* zurückgeben, zurücksenden; *(pay back)* zurückzahlen; *(elect)* wählen; *verdict* aussprechen; —able *a bottle etc* mit Pfand.

reunion [ri:'ju:njən] *n* Wiedervereinigung *f; (Sch etc)* Treffen *nt.*

reunite ['ri:ju:'naɪt] *vt* wiedervereinigen.

rev [rev] *n* Drehzahl *f; vti (also—up)* (den Motor) auf Touren bringen.

revamp ['ri:'væmp] *vt* aufpolieren.

reveal [rɪ'vi:l] *vt* enthüllen; —ing *a* aufschlußreich.

reveille [rɪ'vælɪ] *n* Wecken *nt.*

revel ['revl] *vi* genießen *(in acc).*

revelation [revə'leɪʃən] *n* Offenbarung *f.*

reveller ['revələ*] *n* Schwelger *m.*

revelry [revlrɪ] *n* Rummel *m.*

revenge [rɪ'vendʒ] *n* Rache *f; vt* rächen; —ful *a* rachsüchtig.

revenue ['revənju:] *n* Einnahmen *pl,* Staatseinkünfte *pl.*

reverberate [rɪ'vɜ:bəreɪt] *vi* widerhallen.

reverberation [rɪvɜ:bə'reɪʃən] *n* Widerhall *m.*

revere [rɪ'vɪə*] *vt* (ver)ehren; —nce ['revərəns] *n* Ehrfurcht *f;* ['revərənd] R—nd . . . Hochwürden . . .; —nt ['revərənt] *a* ehrfurchtsvoll.

reverie [revərɪ] *n* Träumerei *f.*

reversal [rɪ'vɜ:səl] *n* Umkehrung *f.*

reverse [rɪ'vɜ:s] *n* Gegenteil *nt; (Aut: gear)* Rückwärtsgang *m; a order, direction* entgegengesetzt;

vt umkehren; *vi (Aut)* rückwärts fahren.

reversion [rɪ'vɜ:ʃən] *n* Umkehrung *f.*

revert [rɪ'vɜ:t] *vi* zurückkehren.

review [rɪ'vju:] *n (Mil)* Truppenschau *f; (of book)* Besprechung *f,* Rezension *f; (magazine)* Zeitschrift *f;* to be under — untersucht werden; *vt* Rückschau halten auf (+acc); *(Mil)* mustern; *book* besprechen, rezensieren; *(re-examine)* von neuem untersuchen; —er *(critic)* Rezensent *m.*

revise [rɪ'vaɪz] *vt* durchsehen, verbessern; *book* überarbeiten; *(reconsider)* ändern, revidieren.

revision [rɪvɪʒən] *n* Durchsicht *f,* Prüfung *f; (Comm)* Revision *f; (of book)* verbesserte Ausgabe *f; (Sch)* Wiederholung *f.*

revisit ['ri:'vɪzɪt] *vt* wieder besuchen.

revitalize ['ri:'vaɪtəlaɪz] *vt* neu beleben.

revival [rɪ'vaɪvəl] *n* Wiederbelebung *f; (Rel)* Erweckung *f; (Theat)* Wiederaufnahme *f.*

revive [rɪ'vaɪv] *vt* wiederbeleben; *(fig)* wieder auffrischen; *vi* wiedererwachen; *(fig)* wieder aufleben.

revoke [rɪ'vəuk] *vt* aufheben.

revolt [rɪ'vəult] *n* Aufstand *m,* Revolte *f; vi* sich auflehnen; *vt* entsetzen; —ing *a* widerlich.

revolution [revə'lu:ʃən] *n (turn)* Umdrehung *f; (change)* Umwälzung *f; (Pol)* Revolution *f;* —ary *a* revolutionär; *n* Revolutionär *m;* —ize *vt* revolutionieren.

revolve [rɪ'vɒlv] *vi* kreisen; *(on own axis)* sich drehen; —*r* Revolver *m.*

revue [rɪ'vjuː] *n* Revue *f.*

revulsion [rɪ'vʌlʃən] *n* (*disgust*) Ekel *m.*

reward [rɪ'wɔːd] *n* Belohnung *f; vt* belohnen; **—ing** *a* lohnend.

reword · [riː'wɜːd] *vt* anders formulieren·

rewrite [riː'raɪt] *vt irreg* umarbeiten, neu schreiben.

rhapsody ['ræpsədɪ] *n* Rhapsodie *f; (fig)* Schwärmerei *f.*

rhetoric [rɛtərɪk] *n* Rhetorik *f*, Redekunst *f;* **—al** [rɪ'tɒrɪkəl] *a* rhetorisch.

rheumatic [ruː'mætɪk] *a* rheumatisch.

rheumatism ['ruːmətɪzəm] *n* Rheumatismus *m*, Rheuma *nt.*

rhinoceros [raɪ'nɒsərəs] *n* Nashorn *nt*, Rhinozeros *nt.*

rhododendron [rəʊdə'dendrən] *n* Rhododendron *m.*

rhubarb ['ruːbɑːb] *n* Rhabarber *m.*

rhyme [raɪm] *n* Reim *m.*

rhythm ['rɪðəm] *n* Rhythmus *m;* **—ic(al)** *a*, **—ically** *ad* ['rɪðmɪk(l), -l] rhythmisch.

rib [rɪb] *n* Rippe *f; vt* (*mock*) hänseln, aufziehen.

ribald ['rɪbəld] *a* saftig.

ribbon ['rɪbən] *n* Band *nt.*

rice [raɪs] *n* Reis *m;* **— pudding** Milchreis *m.*

rich [rɪtʃ] *a* reich, wohlhabend; (*fertile*) fruchtbar; (*splendid*) kostbar; *food* reichhaltig; **—es** *pl* Reichtum *m*, Reichtümer *pl;* **—ly** *ad* reich; *deserve* völlig; **—ness** Reichtum *m;* (*of food*) Reichhaltigkeit *f;* (*of colours*) Sattheit *f.*

rick [rɪk] *n* Schober *m.*

rickets ['rɪkɪts] *n* Rachitis *f.*

rickety ['rɪkɪtɪ] *a* wack(e)lig.

rickshaw ['rɪkʃɔː] *n* Riksha *f.*

ricochet ['rɪkəʃeɪ] *n* Abprallen *nt;* (*shot*) Querschläger *m; vi* abprallen.

rid [rɪd] *vt irreg* befreien (*of* von); **to get —** *of* loswerden; *good* **—dance!** den/die/das wären wir los!

riddle ['rɪdl] *n* Rätsel *nt; vt* (*esp passive*) durchlöchern.

ride [raɪd] *n* (*in vehicle*) Fahrt *f;* (*on horse*) Ritt *m; irreg vt horse* reiten; *bicycle* fahren; *vi* fahren; reiten; (*ship*) vor Anker liegen; **—r** Reiter *m;* (*addition*) Zusatz *m.*

ridge [rɪdʒ] *n* (*of hills*) Bergkette *f;* (*top*) Grat *m*, Kamm *m;* (*of roof*) Dachfirst *m.*

ridicule ['rɪdɪkjuːl] *n* Spott *m; vt* lächerlich machen.

ridiculous *a*, **—ly** *ad* [rɪ'dɪkjʊləs, -lɪ] lächerlich.

riding ['raɪdɪŋ] *n* Reiten *nt;* **to go —** reiten gehen; **— habit** Reitkleid *nt;* **— school** Reitschule *f.*

rife [raɪf] *a* weit verbreitet.

riffraff ['rɪfræf] *n* Gesindel *nt*, Pöbel *m.*

rifle ['raɪfl] *n* Gewehr *nt; vt* berauben; **— range** Schießstand *m.*

rift [rɪft] *n* Ritze *f*, Spalte *f; (fig)* Bruch *m.*

rig [rɪg] *n* (*outfit*) Takelung *f; (fig)* Aufmachung *f;* (*oil —*) Bohrinsel *f; vt election* etc manipulieren; **—ging** Takelage *f;* **— out** *vt* ausstatten; **— up** *vt* zusammenbasteln, konstruieren.

right [raɪt] *a* (*correct, just*) richtig, recht; (*right side*) rechte(r, s); *n* Recht *nt;* (*not left, Pol*) Rechte *f; ad* (*on the right*) rechts; (*to the right*) nach rechts; *look, work* richtig, recht; (*directly*) gerade; (*exactly*) genau; *vt* in Ordnung bringen, korrigieren; *interj* gut; — away sofort; to be — recht haben; all —! gut!, in Ordnung!, schön!; — now in diesem Augenblick; eben; by —s von Rechts wegen; — to the end bis ans Ende; on the — rechts; — angle Rechteck *nt*; —eous ['raɪtʃəs] *a* rechtschaffen; —eousness Rechtschaffenheit *f*; —ful *a* rechtmäßig; —fully auf rechtmäßig; (*justifiably*) zu Recht; —hand drive: to have —hand drive das Steuer rechts haben; —handed *a* rechtshändig; —hand man rechte Hand *f*; —hand side rechte Seite *f*; —ly *ad* mit Recht; —minded *a* rechtschaffen; — of way Vorfahrt *f*; —wing rechte(r) Flügel *m*.

rigid ['rɪdʒɪd] *a* (*stiff*) starr, steif; (*strict*) streng; —ity [rɪ'dʒɪdɪtɪ] Starrheit *f*, Steifheit *f*; Strenge *f*; —ly starr, steif; (*fig*) hart, unbeugsam.

rigmarole ['rɪɡmərəʊl] *n* Gewäsch *nt*.

rigor mortis ['rɪɡə'mɔ:tɪs] *n* Totenstarre *f*.

rigorous *a*, —ly *ad* ['rɪɡərəs, -lɪ] streng.

rigour, (*US*) **rigor** ['rɪɡə*] *n* Strenge *f*, Härte *f*.

rig-out ['rɪɡaʊt] *n* (*col*) Aufzug *m*.

rile [raɪl] *vt* ärgern.

rim [rɪm] *n* (*edge*) Rand *m*; (*of wheel*) Felge *f*; —less *a* randlos; —med *a* gerändert.

·rind [raɪnd] *n* Rinde *f*.

ring [rɪŋ] *n* Ring *m*; (*of people*) Kreis *m*; (*arena*) Ring *m*, Manege *f*; (*of telephone*) Klingeln *nt*, Läuten *nt*; to give sb a — jdn anrufen; that has a familiar — es klingt bekannt; *vti irreg bell* läuten; (*also* — up) anrufen; — off

vi aufhängen; — binder Ringbuch *nt*; —leader Anführer *m*, Rädelsführer *m*; —lets *pl* Ringellocken *pl*; — road Umgehungsstraße *f*.

rink [rɪŋk] *n* (*ice* —) Eisbahn *f*.

rinse [rɪns] *n* Spülen *nt*; *vt* spülen.

riot ['raɪət] *n* Aufruhr *m*; *vi* randalieren; —er Aufrührer *m*; —ous *a*, —ously *ad* aufrührerisch; (*noisy*) lärmend.

rip [rɪp] *n* Schlitz *m*, Riß *m*; *vti* (zer)reißen.

ripcord ['rɪpkɔ:d] *n* Reißleine *f*.

ripe [raɪp] *a* (*fruit*) reif; (*cheese*) ausgereift; —n *vi* reifen, reif werden (lassen); —ness Reife *f*.

riposte [rɪ'pɒst] *n* Nachstoß *m*; (*fig*) schlagfertige Antwort *f*.

ripple ['rɪpl] *n* kleine Welle *f*; *vt* kräuseln; *vi* sich kräuseln.

rise [raɪz] *n* (*slope*) Steigung *f*; (*esp in wages*) Erhöhung *f*; (*growth*) Aufstieg *m*; *vi irreg* aufstehen; (*sun*) aufgehen; (*smoke*) aufsteigen; (*mountain*) sich erheben; (*ground*) ansteigen; (*prices*) steigen; (*in revolt*) sich erheben; to give — to Anlaß geben zu; to — to the occasion sich der Lage gewachsen zeigen.

risk [rɪsk] *n* Gefahr *f*, Risiko *nt*; *vt* (*venture*) wagen; (*chance loss of*) riskieren, aufs Spiel setzen; —y *a* gewagt, gefährlich, riskant.

risqué ['rɪ:skeɪ] *a* gewagt.

rissole ['rɪsəʊl] *n* Fleischklößchen *nt*.

rite [raɪt] *n* Ritus *m*; last —s *pl* Letzte Ölung *f*.

ritual ['rɪtjʊəl] *n* Ritual *nt*; *a* rituell, Ritual-; (*fig*) rituell.

rival ['raɪvəl] *n* Rivale *m*, Konkurrent *m*; *a* rivalisierend; *vt* rivalisieren mit; (*Comm*) kon-

kurrieren mit; —ry Rivalität f;
Konkurrenz f.

river ['rɪvə*] n Fluß m, Strom m;
—bank Flußufer nt; —bed Flußbett
nt; —side n Flußufer nt; a am Ufer
gelegen, Ufer-.

rivet ['rɪvɪt] n Niete f; vt (fasten)
(ver)nieten.

road [rəʊd] n Straße f; —block
Straßensperre f; —hog Verkehrs-
rowdy m; —map Straßenkarte f;
— side n Straßenrand m; a an der
Landstraße (gelegen); — sign
Straßenschild nt; — user
Verkehrsteilnehmer m; —way
Fahrbahn f; —worthy a verkehrs-
sicher.

roam [rəʊm] vi (umher)streifen; vt
durchstreifen.

roar [rɔ:*] n Brüllen nt, Gebrüll nt;
vi brüllen; —ing a fire Bomben-,
prasselnd; trade schwunghaft,
Bomben-.

roast [rəʊst] n Braten m; vt braten,
rösten, schmoren.

rob [rɒb] vt bestehlen, berauben;
bank ausrauben; —ber Räuber m;
—bery Raub m.

robe [rəʊb] n (dress) Gewand nt;
(US) Hauskleid nt; (judge's) Robe
f; vt feierlich ankleiden.

robin ['rɒbɪn] n Rotkehlchen nt.

robot ['rəʊbɒt] n Roboter m.

robust [rəʊ'bʌst] a stark, robust.

rock [rɒk] n Felsen m; (piece)
Stein m; (bigger) Fels(brocken) m;
(sweet) Zuckerstange f; vt wiegen,
schaukeln; on the —s drink mit
Eis(würfeln); marriage
gescheitert; ship aufgelaufen; —
bottom (fig) Tiefpunkt m; —
climber (Steil)kletterer m; to go —
climbing (steil)klettern gehen;
—ery Steingarten m.

rocket ['rɒkɪt] n Rakete f.

rock face ['rɒkfeɪs] n Felswand f.

rocking chair ['rɒkɪŋtʃeə*] n
Schaukelstuhl m.

rocking horse ['rɒkɪŋhɔ:s] n
Schaukelpferd nt.

rocky ['rɒkɪ] a felsig.

rococo [rəʊ'kəʊkəʊ] a Rokoko-; n
Rokoko nt.

rod [rɒd] n (bar) Stange f; (stick)
Rute f.

rodent ['rəʊdənt] n Nagetier nt.

rodeo ['rəʊdɪəʊ] n Rodeo m or nt.

roe [rəʊ] n (deer) Reh nt; (of fish)
Rogen m.

rogue [rəʊg] n Schurke m; (hum)
Spitzbube m.

roguish ['rəʊgɪʃ] a schurkisch;
hum schelmisch.

role [rəʊl] n Rolle f.

roll [rəʊl] n Rolle f; (bread)
Brötchen nt, Semmel f; (list)
(Namens)liste f, Verzeichnis nt; (of
drum) Wirbel m; vt (turn) rollen,
(herum)wälzen; grass etc walzen;
vi (swing) schlingern; (sound)
(g)rollen; — by vi (time)
verfliegen; — in vi (mail)
hereinkommen; — over vi sich
(herum)drehen; — up vi (arrive)
kommen, auftauchen; vt carpet aufrollen; — call Namensaufruf m;
—ed a umbrella zusammengerollt;
—er Rolle f, Walze f; (road —er)
Straßenwalze f; —er skates pl Roll-
schuhe pl.

rollicking ['rɒlɪkɪŋ] a ausgelassen.

rolling ['rəʊlɪŋ] a landscape wellig;
— pin Nudel- or Wellholz nt; —
stock Wagenmaterial nt.

Roman ['rəʊmən] a römisch; n
Römer(in f) m; — Catholic — a
römisch-katholisch; n Katholik(in
f) m.

romance [rəʊˈmæns] n Romanze f; (story) (Liebes)roman m; vi aufschneiden, erfinden; **—r** (storyteller) Aufschneider m.

romantic [rəʊˈmæntɪk] a romantisch; **R—ism** [rəʊˈmæntɪsɪzəm] Romantik f.

romp [rɒmp] n Tollen nt; vi (also — about) herumtollen; **—ers** pl Spielanzug m.

rondo [ˈrɒndəʊ] n (Mus) Rondo nt.

roof [ruːf] n Dach nt; (of mouth) Gaumen nt; vt überdachen, überdecken; **—ing** Deckmaterial nt.

rook [rʊk] n (bird) Saatkrähe f; (chess) Turm m; vt (cheat) betrügen.

room [rʊm] n Zimmer nt, Raum m; (space) Platz m; (fig) Spielraum m; **—s** pl Wohnung f. **—iness** Geräumigkeit f; **—mate** Mitbewohner(in f) m; **— service** Zimmerbedienung f; **—y** a geräumig.

roost [ruːst] n Hühnerstange f; vi auf der Stange hocken.

root [ruːt] n (lit, fig) Wurzel f; vt einwurzeln; **—ed** a (fig) verwurzelt; **— about** vi (fig) herumwühlen; **— for** vt Stimmung machen für; **— out** vt ausjäten; (fig) ausrotten.

rope [rəʊp] n Seil nt, Strick m; vt (tie) festschnüren; **to — sb in** jdn gewinnen; **— off** vt absperren; **to know the —s** sich auskennen; **—ladder** Strickleiter f.

rosary [ˈrəʊzərɪ] n Rosenkranz m.

rose [rəʊz] n Rose f; a Rosen-, rosenrot.

rosé [ˈrəʊzeɪ] n Rosé m.

rosebed [ˈrəʊzbed] n Rosenbeet nt.

rosebud [ˈrəʊzbʌd] n Rosenknospe f.

rosebush [ˈrəʊzbʊʃ] n Rosenstock m, Rosenstrauch m.

rosemary [ˈrəʊzmərɪ] n Rosmarin m.

rosette [rəʊˈzet] n Rosette f.

roster [ˈrɒstə*] n Dienstplan m.

rostrum [ˈrɒstrəm] n Rednerbühne f.

rosy [ˈrəʊzɪ] a rosig.

rot [rɒt] n Fäulnis f; (nonsense) Quatsch m, Blödsinn m; vti verfaulen (lassen).

rota [ˈrəʊtə] n Dienstliste f.

rotary [ˈrəʊtərɪ] a rotierend, sich drehend.

rotate [rəʊˈteɪt] vt rotieren lassen; (two or more things in order) turnusmäßig wechseln; vi rotieren.

rotating [rəʊˈteɪtɪŋ] a rotierend.

rotation [rəʊˈteɪʃən] n Umdrehung f, Rotation f; **in —** der Reihe nach, abwechselnd.

rotor [ˈrəʊtə*] n Rotor m.

rotten [ˈrɒtn] n faul, verfault; (fig) schlecht, gemein.

rotund [rəʊˈtʌnd] a rund; person rundlich.

rouge [ruːʒ] n Rouge nt.

rough [rʌf] a (not smooth) rauh; path uneben; (violent) roh, grob; crossing stürmisch; wind rauh; (without comforts) hart, unbequem; (unfinished, makeshift) grob; (approximate) ungefähr; n (grass) unebene(r) Boden m; (person) Rowdy m, Rohling m; **to — it** primitiv leben; **to play —** (Sport) hart spielen; **to sleep —** im Freien schlafen; **— out** vt entwerfen, flüchtig skizzieren; **— up** vt aufrauhen; **—ly** ad grob; (about) ungefähr; **—ness** Rauheit f; (of manner) Ungeschliffenheit f.

roulette [ru:'let] n Roulette nt.

round [raund] a rund; figures abgerundet, aufgerundet; ad (in a circle) rundherum; prep um . . . herum; — Runde f; (of ammunition) Magazin nt; (song) Kanon m; theatre in the — Rundtheater nt; vt corner biegen um; — off vt abrunden; — up vt (end) abschließen; figures aufrunden; — of applause Beifall m; —about n (traffic) Kreisverkehr m; (merry-go-round) Karussell nt; a auf Umwegen; —ed a gerundet; —ly ad (fig) gründlich; —shouldered a mit abfallenden Schultern; —sman (general) Austräger m; (milk —) Milchmann m; —up Zusammentreiben nt, Sammeln nt.

rouse [rauz] vt (waken) (auf)wecken; (stir up) erregen.

rousing ['rauzıŋ] a welcome stürmisch; speech zündend.

rout [raut] n wilde Flucht f; Überwältigung f; vt in die Flucht schlagen.

route [ru:t] n Weg m, Route f.

routine [ru:'ti:n] n Routine f; a Routine-.

rover ['rəuvə*] n Wanderer m.

roving ['rəuvıŋ] a reporter im Außendienst.

row [rəu] n (line) Reihe f; vti boat rudern.

row [rau] n (noise) Lärm m, Krach m, Radau m; (dispute) Streit m; (scolding) Krach m; vi sich streiten.

rowboat ['rəubəut] n (US) Ruderboot nt.

rowdy ['raudı] a rüpelhaft; n (person) Rowdy m.

rowing ['rauıŋ] n Rudern nt; (Sport) Rudersport m; — boat Ruderboot nt.

rowlock ['rɔlək] n Rudergabel f.

royal ['rɔıəl] a königlich, Königs-; —ist n Royalist m; a königstreu; —ty (family) königliche Familie f; (for invention) Patentgebühr f; (for book) Tantieme f.

rub [rʌb] n (problem) Haken m; to give sth a — etw (ab)reiben; vt reiben; — off vi (lit, fig) abfärben (on auf +acc); to — it in darauf herumreiten.

rubber ['rʌbə*] n Gummi m; (Brit) Radiergummi m; — band Gummiband nt; — plant Gummibaum m; —y a gummiartig, wie Gummi.

rubbish ['rʌbıʃ] n (waste) Abfall m; (nonsense) Blödsinn m, Quatsch m; — dump Müllabladeplatz m.

rubble ['rʌbl] n (Stein)schutt m.

ruby ['ru:bı] n Rubin m; a rubinrot.

rucksack ['rʌksæk] n Rucksack m.

rudder ['rʌdə*] n Steuerruder nt.

ruddy ['rʌdı] a (colour) rötlich; (col: bloody) verdammt.

rude, a, —ly ad [ru:d, -lı] unhöflich, unverschämt; shock hart; awakening unsanft; (unrefined, rough) grob; —ness n Unhöflichkeit f, Unverschämtheit f; Grobheit f.

rudiment ['ru:dımənt] n Grundlage f; —ary [ru:dı'mentərı] a rudimentär.

ruff [rʌf] n Halskrause f.

ruffian ['rʌfıən] n Rohling m.

ruffle ['rʌfl] vt kräuseln; durcheinanderbringen.

rug [rʌg] n Brücke f; (in bedroom) Bettvorleger m; (for knees) (Reise)decke f.

rugged ['rʌgıd] a coastline zerklüftet; features markig.

ruin ['ru:ın] n Ruine f; (downfall) Ruin m; vt ruinieren; —s pl

Trümmer pl; —ation Zerstörung f, Ruinierung f; —ous a ruinierend.

rule [ru:l] n Regel f; (government) Herrschaft f, Regierung f; (for measuring) Lineal nt; vti (govern) herrschen über (+acc), regieren; (decide) anordnen, entscheiden; (make lines) linieren; as a — in der Regel; —d a paper liniert; —r Lineal nt; Herrscher m.

ruling ['ru:lɪŋ] a party Regierungs-; class herrschend.

rum [rʌm] n Rum m; a (col) komisch.

rumble ['rʌmbl] n Rumpeln nt; (of thunder) Rollen nt; vi rumpeln; grollen.

ruminate ['ru:mɪneɪt] vi grübeln; (cows) wiederkäuen.

rummage ['rʌmɪdʒ] n Durch-suchung f; vi durchstöbern.

rumour, (US) **rumor** ['ru:mə*] n Gerücht nt; vt: it is —ed that man sagt or man munkelt, daß.

rump [rʌmp] n Hinterteil nt; (of fowl) Bürzel m; — steak Rumpsteak m.

rumpus ['rʌmpəs] n Spektakel m, Krach m.

run [rʌn] n Lauf m; (in car) (Spazier)fahrt f; (series) Serie f, Reihe f; (of play) Spielzeit f; (sudden demand) Ansturm m, starke Nachfrage f; (of animals) Auslauf m; (ski —) (Ski)abfahrt f; (in stocking) Laufmasche f; irreg vt (cause to run) laufen lassen; car, train, bus fahren; (pay for) unter-halten; race, distance laufen, rennen; (manage) leiten, ver-walten; knife stoßen; (pass) hand, eye gleiten lassen; vi laufen; (move quickly also) rennen; (bus, train) fahren; (flow) fließen, laufen; (colours)

(ab)färben; on the — auf der Flucht; in the long — auf die Dauer; to — riot Amok laufen; to — a risk ein Risiko eingehen; — about vi (children) umherspringen (+acc); — across vt (find) stoßen auf (+acc); — away vi weglaufen; — down vi (clock) ablaufen; vt (with car) überfahren; (talk against) her-untermachen; to be — down erschöpft or abgespannt sein; to — for president für die Präsident-schaft kandidieren; — off vi fort-laufen; — out vi (person) hinaus-rennen; (liquid) auslaufen; (lease) ablaufen; (money) ausgehen; he ran out of money/petrol ihm ging das Geld/Benzin aus; — over vt (in accident) überfahren; (read quickly) überfliegen; — through vt instructions durchgehen; — up vt debt, bill machen; — up against vt difficulties stoßen auf (+acc); —about (small car) kleine(r) Flitzer m; —away a horse ausgebrochen; vi flüchtig.

rung [rʌŋ] n Sprosse f.

runner ['rʌnə*] n Läufer(in f) m; (messenger) Bote m; (for sleigh) Kufe f; —up Zweite(r) mf.

running ['rʌnɪŋ] n (of business) Leitung f; (of machine) Laufen nt, Betrieb m; a water fließend; commentary laufend; 3 days — 3 Tage lang or hintereinander.

run-of-the-mill ['rʌnəvðə'mɪl] a gewöhnlich, alltäglich.

runny ['rʌnɪ] a dünn.

runway ['rʌnweɪ] n Startbahn f, Landebahn f, Rollbahn f.

rupture ['rʌptʃə*] n (Med) Bruch m; vt: —o.s. sich (dat) einen Bruch zuziehen.

rural ['ruərəl] a ländlich, Land-.

ruse [ru:z] *n* Kniff *m*, List *f*.

rush [rʌʃ] *n* Eile *f*, Hetze *f*; (Fin) starke Nachfrage *f*; *vt* (carry along) auf dem schnellsten Weg schaffen or transportieren; (attack) losstürmen auf (+acc); don't — me dräng mich nicht; *vi* (hurry) eilen, stürzen; to — into sth etw überstürzen; —es *pl* Schilf(rohr) *nt*; — hour Hauptverkehrszeit *f*.

rusk [rʌsk] *n* Zwieback *m*.

rust [rʌst] *n* Rost *m*; *vi* rosten.

rustic ['rʌstɪk] *a* bäuerlich, ländlich, Bauern-.

rustle ['rʌsl] *n* Rauschen *nt*, Rascheln *nt*; *vi* rauschen, rascheln; *vt* rascheln lassen; cattle stehlen.

rustproof ['rʌstpru:f] *a* nichtrostend, rostfrei.

rusty ['rʌstɪ] *a* rostig.

rut [rʌt] *n* (in track) Radspur *f*; (of deer) Brunst *f*; (fig) Trott *m*.

ruthless *a*, —ly *ad* ['ru:θləs, -lɪ] erbarmungslos, rücksichtslos; —ness Unbarmherzigkeit *f*; Rücksichtslosigkeit *f*.

rye [raɪ] *n* Roggen *m*; — bread Roggenbrot *nt*.

S

S, s [es] *n* S *nt*, s *nt*.

sabbath ['sæbəθ] *n* Sabbat *m*.

sabbatical [sə'bætɪkəl] *a*: — year Beurlaubungs- or Forschungsjahr *nt*.

sabotage ['sæbətɑ:ʒ] *n* Sabotage *f*; *vt* sabotieren.

sabre, (US) **saber** ['seɪbə*] *n* Säbel *m*.

saccharin(e) ['sækərɪn] *n* Saccharin *nt*.

sachet ['sæʃeɪ] *n* (of shampoo) Briefchen *nt*, Kissen *nt*.

sack [sæk] *n* Sack *m*; to give sb the — (col) jdn hinauswerfen; *vt* (col) hinauswerfen; (pillage) plündern; —ful Sack(voll) *m*; —ing (material) Sackleinen *nt*; (col) Rausschmiß *m*.

sacrament ['sækrəmənt] *n* Sakrament *nt*.

sacred ['seɪkrɪd] *a* building, music etc geistlich, Kirchen-; altar, oath heilig.

sacrifice ['sækrɪfaɪs] *n* Opfer *nt*; *vt* (lit, fig) opfern.

sacrilege ['sækrɪlɪdʒ] *n* Schändung *f*.

sacrosanct ['sækrəʊsæŋkt] *a* sakrosankt.

sad [sæd] *a* traurig; —den *vt* traurig machen, betrüben.

saddle ['sædl] *n* Sattel *m*; *vt* (burden) aufhalsen (sb with sth jdm etw); — bag Satteltasche *f*.

sadism ['seɪdɪzəm] *n* Sadismus *m*.

sadist ['seɪdɪst] *n* Sadist *m*; —ic [sə'dɪstɪk] *a* sadistisch.

sadly ['sædlɪ] *ad* betrübt, beklagenswert; (very) arg.

sadness ['sædnəs] *n* Traurigkeit *f*.

safari [sə'fɑ:rɪ] *n* Safari *f*.

safe [seɪf] *a* (free from danger) sicher; (careful) vorsichtig; it's — to say man kann ruhig behaupten; *n* Safe *m*, Tressor *m*, Geldschrank *m*; —guard *n* Sicherung *f*; *vt* sichern, schützen; —keeping sichere Verwahrung *f*; **—ly** *ad* sicher; *arrive* wohlbehalten; **—ness** Zuverlässigkeit *f*; **—ty** Sicherheit *f*; **—ty belt** Sicherheitsgurt *m*; **—ty current** eiserne(r) Vorhang *m*; **—ty first** (slogan) Sicherheit geht vor; **—ty pin** Sicherheitsnadel *f*.

sag [sæg] *vi* (durch)sacken, sich senken.

saga ['sɑːgə] *n* Sage *f*.

sage [seidʒ] *n* (herb) Salbei *m*; (man) Weise(r) *m*.

Sagittarius [sædʒɪˈtɛərɪəs] *n* Schütze *m*.

sago ['seigəu] *n* Sago *m*.

said [sed] *n* besagt.

sail [seil] *n* Segel *nt*; (trip) Fahrt *f*; *vt* segeln; *vi* segeln; mit dem Schiff fahren; (begin voyage) abfahren; (ship) auslaufen; (fig: cloud etc) dahinsegeln; **—boat** (US) Segelboot *nt*; **—ing** Segeln *nt*; **to go —ing** segeln gehen; **—ing ship** Segelschiff *nt*; **—or** Matrose *m*, Seemann *m*.

saint [seint] *n* Heilige(r) *mf*; **—liness** Heiligkeit *f*; **—ly** *a* heilig, fromm.

sake [seik] *n*: **for the — of** um (+gen) willen; **for your —** um deinetwillen, deinetwegen, wegen dir.

salad ['sæləd] *n* Salat *m*; **— cream** gewürzte Mayonnaise *f*; **— dressing** Salatsoße *f*; **— oil** Speiseöl *nt*, Salatöl *nt*.

salami [səˈlɑːmi] *n* Salami *f*.

salaried ['sælərid] *a*: **— staff** Gehaltsempfänger *pl*.

salary ['sæləri] *n* Gehalt *nt*.

sale [seil] *n* Verkauf *m*; (reduced prices) Schlußverkauf *m*; **—room** Verkaufsraum *m*; **—sman** Verkäufer *m*; (representative) Vertreter *m*; **—smanship** Geschäftstüchtigkeit *f*; **—swoman** Verkäuferin *f*.

salient ['seiliənt] *a* hervorspringend, bemerkenswert.

saliva [səˈlaivə] *n* Speichel *m*.

sallow ['sæləu] *a* fahl; *face* bleich.

salmon ['sæmən] *n* Lachs *m*.

salon ['sælɔːŋ] *n* Salon *m*.

saloon [səˈluːn] *n* (Aut) Limousine *f*; (ship's lounge) Salon *m*.

salt [sɔːlt] *n* Salz *nt*; *vt* (cure) einsalzen; (flavour) salzen; **—cellar** Salzfaß *nt*; **— mine** Salzbergwerk *nt*; **—y** *a* salzig.

salubrious [səˈluːbriəs] *a* gesund; *district etc* -ersprießlich.

salutary ['sæljutəri] *a* gesund, heilsam.

salute [səˈluːt] *n* (Mil) Gruß *m*, Salut *m*; (with guns) Salutschüsse *pl*; *vt* (Mil) salutieren.

salvage ['sælvidʒ] *n* (from ship) Bergung *f*; (property) Rettung *f*; *vt* bergen; retten.

salvation [sælˈveiʃən] *n* Rettung *f*; **S— Army** Heilsarmee *f*.

salver ['sælvə*] *n* Tablett *nt*.

salvo ['sælvəu] *n* Salve *f*.

same [seim] *a* (similar) gleiche(r,s); (identical) derselbe/dieselbe/ dasselbe; **all or just the —** trotzdem; **it's all the —** to me das ist mir egal; **they all look the —** to me für mich lehnen sie alle gleich aus; **the — to you** gleichfalls; **at the — time** zur gleichen Zeit, gleichzeitig; **(however)** zugleich, andererseits.

sampan ['sæmpæn] *n* Sampan *m*.

sample ['sɑːmpl] *n* (specimen) Probe *f*; (example of sth) Muster *nt*, Probe *f*; *vt* probieren.

sanatorium [sænəˈtɔːrɪəm] n Sanatorium nt.

sanctify [ˈsæŋktɪfaɪ] vt weihen.

sanctimonious [sæŋktɪˈməʊnɪəs] a scheinheilig.

sanction [ˈsæŋkʃən] n Sanktion f. vt strength schwächen; health untergraben.

sanctity [ˈsæŋktɪtɪ] n Heiligkeit f; (fig) Unverletzlichkeit f.

sanctuary [ˈsæŋktjʊərɪ] n Heiligtum nt; (for fugitive) Asyl nt; (refuge) Zufluchtsort m; (for animals) Naturpark m, Schutzgebiet nt.

sand [sænd] n Sand m; vt mit Sand bestreuen; furniture schmirgeln; —s pl Sand m.

sandal [ˈsændl] n Sandale f.

sandbag [ˈsændbæg] n Sandsack m.

sand dune [ˈsænddjuːn] n (Sand)düne f.

sandpaper [ˈsændpeɪpə*] n Sandpapier nt.

sandpit [ˈsændpɪt] n Sandkasten m.

sandstone [ˈsændstəʊn] n Sandstein m.

sandwich [ˈsænwɪdʒ] n Sandwich m or nt; vt einklemmen.

sandy [ˈsændɪ] a sandig, Sand-; (colour) sandfarben; hair rotblond.

sane [seɪn] a geistig gesund or normal; (sensible) vernünftig, gescheit.

sanguine [ˈsæŋgwɪn] a (hopeful) zuversichtlich.

sanitarium [sænɪˈtɛərɪəm] n (US) = sanatorium.

sanitary [ˈsænɪtərɪ] a hygienisch (einwandfrei); (against dirt) hygienisch, Gesundheits-; — napkin (US), — towel (Monats)binde f.

sanitation [sænɪˈteɪʃən] n sanitäre Einrichtungen pl; Gesundheitswesen nt.

sanity [ˈsænɪtɪ] n geistige Gesundheit f; (good sense) gesunde(r) Verstand m, Vernunft f.

Santa Claus [sæntəˈklɔːz] n Nikolaus m, Weihnachtsmann m.

sap [sæp] n (of plants) Saft m; vt strength schwächen; health untergraben.

sapling [ˈsæplɪŋ] n junge(r) Baum m.

sapphire [ˈsæfaɪə*] n Saphir m.

sarcasm [ˈsɑːkæzəm] n Sarkasmus m.

sarcastic [sɑːˈkæstɪk] a sarkastisch.

sarcophagus [sɑːˈkɒfəgəs] n Sarkophag m.

sardine [sɑːˈdiːn] n Sardine f.

sardonic [sɑːˈdɒnɪk] a zynisch.

sari [ˈsɑːrɪ] n Sari m.

sash [sæʃ] n Schärpe f.

Satan [ˈseɪtn] n Satan m, Teufel m; s—ic [səˈtænɪk] a satanisch, teuflisch.

satchel [ˈsætʃəl] n (Sch) Schulranzen m, Schulmappe f.

satellite [ˈsætəlaɪt] n Satellit m; (fig) Trabant m; a Satelliten-.

satin [ˈsætɪn] n Satin m; a Satin-.

satire [ˈsætaɪə*] n Satire f.

satirical [səˈtɪrɪkəl] a satirisch.

satirize [ˈsætəraɪz] vt (durch Satire) verspotten.

satisfaction [sætɪsˈfækʃən] n Befriedigung f, Genugtuung f.

satisfactorily [sætɪsˈfæktərɪlɪ] ad zufriedenstellend.

satisfactory [sætɪsˈfæktərɪ] a zufriedenstellend, befriedigend.

satisfy [ˈsætɪsfaɪ] vt befriedigen, zufriedenstellen; (convince) überzeugen; conditions erfüllen; —ing a befriedigend; meal sättigend.

saturate [ˈsætʃəreɪt] vt (durch)tränken.

saturation [sætʃə'reɪʃən] n Durchtränkung f; (Chem, fig) Sättigung f.

Saturday ['sætədeɪ] n Samstag m, Sonnabend m.

sauce [sɔːs] n Soße f, Sauce f; —pan Kasserolle f; —r Untertasse f.

saucily ['sɔːsɪlɪ] ad frech.

sauciness ['sɔːsɪnəs] n Frechheit f.

saucy ['sɔːsɪ] a frech, keck.

sauna ['sɔːnə] n Sauna f.

saunter ['sɔːntə*] vi schlendern; n Schlendern nt.

sausage ['sɒsɪdʒ] n Wurst f; — roll Wurst f im Schlafrock, Wurstpastete f.

savage ['sævɪdʒ] a (fierce) wild, brutal, grausam; (uncivilized) wild, primitiv; n Wilde(r) mf; (animals) zerfleischen; —ly ad grausam; —ry Roheit f, Grausamkeit f.

save [seɪv] vt retten; money, electricity etc sparen; strength etc aufsparen; to — you the trouble um dir Mühe zu ersparen; n (Sport) (Ball)abwehr f; prep, cj außer, ausgenommen.

saving ['seɪvɪŋ] a rettend; n Sparen nt, Ersparnis f; —s pl Ersparnisse pl; —s bank Sparkasse f.

saviour ['seɪvjə*] n Retter m; (Eccl) Heiland m, Erlöser m.

savoir-faire ['sævwɑː'feə*] n Gewandtheit f.

savour, (US) **savor** ['seɪvə*] n Wohlgeschmack m; vt (taste) schmecken; (fig) genießen; vi schmecken (of nach), riechen (of nach); —y a schmackhaft f; food pikant, würzig.

savvy ['sævɪ] n (col) Grips m.

saw [sɔː] n (tool) Säge f; vti irreg sägen; —dust Sägemehl nt; —mill Sägewerk nt.

saxophone ['sæksəfəʊn] n Saxophon nt.

say [seɪ] n Meinung f; (right) Mitspracherecht nt; to have no — in sth (kein) Mitspracherecht bei etw haben; let him have his — laß ihn doch reden; vti irreg sagen; **I** couldn't — schwer zu sagen; how old would you — he is? wie alt schätzt du ihn?; you don't —! was du nicht sagst! don't — you forgot sag bloß nicht, daß du es vergessen hast; there are, —, 50 es sind, sagen wir mal, 50...; that is to — das heißt; (more precisely) beziehungsweise, mit anderen Worten; to — nothing of ... ganz zu schweigen von...; —ing Sprichwort nt; —so (col) Ja nt, Zustimmung f.

scab [skæb] n Schorf m; (of sheep) Räude f; (pej) Streikbrecher m.

scabby ['skæbɪ] a sheep räudig; skin schorfig.

scaffold ['skæfəʊld] n (for execution) Schafott nt; —ing (Bau)gerüst nt.

scald [skɔːld] n Verbrühung f; vt (burn) verbrühen; (clean) (ab)brühen; —ing a brühheiß.

scale [skeɪl] n (of fish) Schuppe f; (Mus) Tonleiter f; (dish for measuring) Waagschale f; (on map, size) Maßstab m; (gradation) Skala f; vt (climb) erklimmen; —s pl (balance) Waage f; on a large — (fig) im großen, in großem Umfang; — drawing maßstabgerechte Zeichnung f.

scallop ['skɒləp] n Kammuschel f.

scalp [skælp] n Kopfhaut f; vt skalpieren.

scalpel ['skælpəl] n Skalpell nt.

scamp [skæmp] vt schlud(e)rig machen, hinschlampen.

scamper ['skæmpə*] vi huschen.

scan [skæn] vt (examine) genau prüfen; (quickly) überfliegen; horizon absuchen; poetry skandieren.

scandal ['skændl] n (disgrace) Skandal m; (gossip) böswillige(r) Klatsch m; **—ize** vt schockieren; **—ous** a skandalös, schockierend.

scant [skænt] a knapp; **—ily** ad knapp, dürftig; **—iness** Knappheit f; **—y** knapp, unzureichend.

scapegoat ['skeɪpgəʊt] n Sündenbock m.

scar [skɑ:*] n Narbe f; vt durch Narben entstellen.

scarce ['skɛəs] a selten, rar; goods knapp; **—ly** ad kaum; **—ness** Seltenheit f.

scarcity ['skɛəsɪtɪ] n Mangel m, Knappheit f.

scare ['skɛə*] n Schrecken m, Panik f; vt erschrecken; ängstigen; to be **—d** Angst haben; **—crow** Vogelscheuche f; **—monger** Bangemacher m.

scarf [skɑ:f] n Schal m; (on head) Kopftuch nt.

scarlet ['skɑ:lət] a scharlachrot; n Scharlachrot nt; **— fever** Scharlach m.

scarred [skɑ:d] a narbig.

scary ['skɛərɪ] a (col) schaurig.

scathing ['skeɪðɪŋ] a scharf, vernichtend.

scatter ['skætə*] n Streuung f; vt (sprinkle) (ver)streuen; (disperse) zerstreuen; vi sich zerstreuen; **—brained** a flatterhaft, schusselig; **—ing (of)** ein paar.

scavenger ['skævɪndʒə*] n (animal) Aasfresser m.

scene [si:n] n (of happening) Ort m; (of play, incident) Szene f; (canvas etc) Bühnenbild nt; (view) Anblick m; (argument) Szene f, Auftritt m; on the — am Ort, dabei; behind the —s hinter den Kulissen; **—ry** ['si:nərɪ] (Theat) Bühnenbild nt; (landscape) Landschaft f.

scenic ['si:nɪk] a landschaftlich, Landschafts-.

scent [sent] n Parfüm nt; (smell) Duft m; (sense) Geruchsinn m; vt parfümieren.

sceptic ['skeptɪk] n Skeptiker m; **—al** a skeptisch; **—ism** ['skeptɪsɪzəm] Skepsis f.

sceptre, (US) **scepter** ['septə*] n Szepter nt.

schedule ['fedju:l] n (list) Liste f, Tabelle f; (plan) Programm nt; vt: it is —d for 2 es soll um 2 abfahren/stattfinden etc; on — pünktlich, fahrplanmäßig; behind — mit Verspätung.

scheme [ski:m] n Schema nt; (dishonest) Intrige f; (plan of action) Plan m, Programm nt; vi sich verschwören, intrigieren; vt planen.

scheming ['ski:mɪŋ] a intrigierend, ränkevoll.

schism ['skɪzəm] n Spaltung f; (Eccl) Schisma nt, Kirchenspaltung f.

schizophrenic [skɪtsəʊ'frenɪk] a schizophren.

scholar ['skɒlə*] n Gelehrte(r) m; (holding scholarship) Stipendiat m; **—ly** a gelehrt; **—ship** Gelehrsamkeit f, Belesenheit f; (grant) Stipendium nt.

school [sku:l] n Schule f; (Univ) Fakultät f; vt schulen; dog

trainieren; —book Schulbuch nt;
—boy Schüler m, Schuljunge m;
—days pl (alte) Schulzeit f; —girl
Schülerin f, Schulmädchen nt;
—ing Schulung f, Ausbildung f;
—master Lehrer m; —mistress
Lehrerin f; —room Klassenzimmer
nt; —teacher Lehrer(in f) m.

schooner ['sku:nə*] n Schoner m;
(glass) große(s) Sherryglas nt.

sciatica [saɪ'ætɪkə] n Ischias m or
nt.

science ['saɪəns] n Wissenschaft f;
(natural —) Naturwissenschaft f;
— fiction Science-fiction f.

scientific [saɪən'tɪfɪk] a wissenschaftlich; (natural sciences) natur-
wissenschaftlich.

scientist ['saɪəntɪst] n Wissen-
schaftler(in f) m.

scintillating ['sɪntɪleɪtɪŋ] a
sprühend.

scissors ['sɪzəz] npl Schere f; a
pair of — eine Schere.

scoff [skɒf] vt (eat) fressen; vi
(mock) spotten (at über +acc).

scold [skəʊld] vt schimpfen.

scone [skɒn] n weiche(s) Teege-
bäck nt.

scoop [sku:p] n Schaufel f; (news)
sensationelle Erstmeldung f; vt
(also — out or up) schaufeln.

scooter ['sku:tə*] n Motorroller m;
(child's) Roller m.

scope [skəʊp] n Ausmaß nt; (opportunity) Spielraum m, Bewegungs-
freiheit f.

scorch [skɔ:tʃ] n Brandstelle f; vt
versengen, verbrennen; —er (col)
heiße(r) Tag m; —ing a brennend,
glühend.

score [skɔ:*] n (in game) Punktzahl
f; (Spiel)ergebnis nt; (Mus)
Partitur f; (line) Kratzer m;
(twenty) 20, 20 Stück; on that —

in dieser Hinsicht; what's the —?
wie steht's?; vt goal schießen;
points machen; (mark) einkerben,
zerkratzen, einritzen; vi (keep
record) Punkte zählen; —board
Anschreibetafel f; —card (Sport)
Punktliste f; —r Torschütze m;
(recorder) (Auf)schreiber m.

scorn [skɔ:n] n Verachtung f; vt
verhöhnen; —ful a, —fully ad
höhnisch, verächtlich.

Scorpio ['skɔ:pɪəʊ] n Skorpion m.

scorpion ['skɔ:pɪən] n Skorpion m.

scotch [skɒtʃ] vt (end) unterbinden.

scoundrel ['skaʊndrəl] n Schurke
m, Schuft m.

scour ['skaʊə*] vt (search)
absuchen; (clean) schrubben; —er
Topfkratzer m.

scourge [skɜ:dʒ] n (whip) Geißel f;
(plague) Qual f.

scout [skaʊt] n (Mil) Späher m,
Aufklärer m; vi (reconnoitre) auskundschaften; see boy.

scowl [skaʊl] n finstere(r) Blick m;
vi finster blicken.

scraggy ['skrægɪ] a dürr, hager.

scram [skræm] vi (col)
verschwinden, abhauen.

scramble ['skræmbl] n (climb)
Kletterei f; (struggle) Kampf m; vi
klettern; (fight) sich schlagen; —d
eggs pl Rührei nt.

scrap [skræp] n (bit) Stückchen nt;
(fight) Keilerei f; a Abfall- vt verwerfen; vi (fight) streiten, sich
prügeln; —book Einklebealbum
nt; —s pl (waste) Abfall m.

scrape [skreɪp] n Kratzen nt;
(trouble) Klemme f; vt kratzen;
car zerkratzen; (clean) abkratzen;
vi (make harsh noise) kratzen; —r
Kratzer m.

scrap heap ['skræphi:p] n Abfallhaufen m; (for metal) Schrotthaufen m.

scrap iron ['skræp'aɪən] n Schrott m.

scrappy ['skræpɪ] a zusammengestoppelt.

scratch ['skrætʃ] n (wound) Kratzer m, Schramme f; to start from — ganz von vorne anfangen; a (improvised) zusammengewürfelt; vt kratzen; car zerkratzen; vi (sich) kratzen.

scrawl [skrɔ:l] n Gekritzel nt; vti kritzeln.

scream [skri:m] n Schrei m; vi schreien.

scree ['skri:] n Geröll(halde f) nt.

screech [skri:tʃ] n Schrei m; vi kreischen.

screen [skri:n] n (protective) Schutzschirm m; (film) Leinwand f; (TV) Bildschirm m; (against insects) Fliegengitter nt; (Eccl) Lettner m; vt (shelter) (be)schirmen; film zeigen, vorführen.

screw [skru:] n Schraube f; (Naut) Schiffsschraube f; vt (fasten) schrauben; (vulgar) bumsen; to — money out of sb (col) jdm das Geld aus der Tasche ziehen; **—driver** Schraubenzieher m; **—y** a (col) verrückt.

scribble ['skrɪbl] n Gekritzel nt; vti kritzeln.

scribe [skraɪb] n Schreiber m; (Jewish) Schriftgelehrte(r) m.

script [skrɪpt] n (handwriting) Handschrift f; (for film) Drehbuch nt; (Theat) Manuskript nt, Text m.

Scripture ['skrɪptʃə*] n Heilige Schrift f.

scriptwriter ['skrɪptraɪtə*] n Textverfasser m.

scroll [skrəʊl] n Schriftrolle f.

scrounge [skraʊndʒ] vt schnorren; n: on the — beim Schnorren.

scrub [skrʌb] n (clean) Schrubben nt; (in countryside) Gestrüpp nt; vt (clean) schrubben; (reject) fallenlassen.

scruff [skrʌf] n Genick nt, Kragen m; **—y** a unordentlich, vergammelt.

scrum(mage) ['skrʌm(ɪdʒ)] n Getümmel nt.

scruple ['skru:pl] n Skrupel m; Bedenken nt.

scrupulous a, **—ly** ad ['skru:pjʊləs, -lɪ] peinlich genau, gewissenhaft.

scrutinize ['skru:tɪnaɪz] vt genau prüfen or untersuchen.

scrutiny ['skru:tɪnɪ] n genaue Untersuchung f.

scuff [skʌf] vt shoes abstoßen.

scuffle ['skʌfl] n Handgemenge nt.

scullery ['skʌlərɪ] n Spülküche f; Abstellraum m.

sculptor ['skʌlptə*] n Bildhauer m.

sculpture ['skʌlptʃə*] n (art) Bildhauerei f; (statue) Skulptur f.

scum [skʌm] n (lit, fig) Abschaum m.

scurrilous ['skʌrɪləs] a unflätig.

scurry ['skʌrɪ] vi huschen.

scurvy ['skɜ:vɪ] n Skorbut m.

scuttle ['skʌtl] n Kohleneimer m; vt ship versenken; vi (scamper) (+ away, off) sich davonmachen.

scythe [saɪð] n Sense f.

sea [si:] n Meer nt (also fig), See f; a Meeres-, See-; **—** bird Meervogel m; **—board** Küste f; **—** breeze Seewind m; **—dog** Seebär m; **—farer** Seefahrer m; **—faring** a seefahrend; **—food** Meeresfrüchte pl; **—** front Strandpromenade f;

—going a seetüchtig, Hochsee-;
—gull Möwe f.

seal [si:l] n (animal) Robbe f, See-
hund m; (stamp, impression)
Siegel nt; vt versiegeln.

sea level ['si:levl] n Meeresspiegel
m.

sealing wax ['si:lɪŋwæks] n
Siegellack m.

sea lion ['si:laɪən] n Seelöwe m.

seam [si:m] n Saum m; (edges
joining) Naht f; (layer) Schicht f;
(of coal) Flöz nt.

seaman ['si:mən] n Seemann m.

seamless ['si:mlɪs] a nahtlos.

seamy ['si:mɪ] a people, café
zwielichtig; life anrüchig; — **side
of life** dunkle Seite f des Lebens.

seaport ['si:pɔ:t] n Seehafen m,
Hafenstadt f.

search [sɜ:tʃ] n Suche f (for nach);
vi suchen; vt (examine) durch-
suchen; —**ing** a look forschend,
durchdringend; —**light** Scheinwerfer m; — **party** Suchmann-
schaft f.

seashore ['si:ʃɔ:*] n Meeresküste f.

seasick ['si:sɪk] a seekrank; —**ness**
Seekrankheit f.

seaside ['si:saɪd] n Küste f; at the
— an der See; to go to the — an
die See fahren.

season ['si:zn] n Jahreszeit f; (eg
Christmas) Zeit f, Saison f; vt
(flavour) würzen; —**al** a Saison-;
—**ing** Gewürz nt, Würze f; —
ticket (Rail) Zeitkarte f; (Theat)
Abonnement nt.

seat [si:t] n Sitz m, Platz m; (in
Parliament) Sitz m; (part of body)
Gesäß nt; (part of garment) Sitz-
fläche f, Hosenboden m; vt (place)
setzen; (have space for) Sitzplätze
bieten für; — **belt** Sicherheitsgurt

m; —**ing** Anweisen nt von Sitz-
plätzen.

sea water ['si:wɔ:tə*] n Meer-
wasser nt, Seewasser nt.

seaweed ['si:wi:d] n (See)tang m,
Alge f.

seaworthy ['si:wɜ:ðɪ] a seetüchtig.

secede [sɪ'si:d] vi sich trennen.

secluded [sɪ'klu:dɪd] a abgelegen,
ruhig.

seclusion [sɪ'klu:ʒən] n Zurück-
gezogenheit f.

second ['sekənd] n zweite(r,s); ad
(in — position) an zweiter Stelle;
(Rail) zweite(r) Klasse; n Sekunde
f; (person) Zweite(r) m; (Comm:
imperfect) zweite Wahl f; (Sport)
Sekundant m; vt (support) unterstützen; —**ary** a zweitrangig;
—**ary education** Sekundarstufe f;
—**ary school** höhere Schule f,
Mittelschule f; —**er** Unterstützer
m; —**hand** a aus zweiter Hand; car
etc gebraucht; —**ly** ad zweitens;
it is — **nature** to him es ist ihm
zur zweiten Natur geworden; —
rate a mittelmäßig; to have —
thoughts es sich (dat) anders überlegen.

secrecy ['si:krəsɪ] n Geheimhaltung
f.

secret ['si:krət] n Geheimnis nt; a
geheim, heimlich, Geheim-; in —
geheim, heimlich.

secretarial [sekrə'tɛərɪəl] a
Sekretärs-.

secretariat [sekrə'tɛərɪət] n Sekretariat nt.

secretary ['sekrətrɪ] n Sekretär(in
f) m; (government) Staats-
sekretär(in f) m; Minister m.

secretive ['si:krətɪv] a geheim-
tuerisch.

secretly ['si:krətlɪ] ad heimlich.

sect [sekt] n Sekte f; —arian [sek'tɛərɪən] a (belonging to a sect) Sekten-.

section ['sekʃən] n Teil m, Ausschnitt m; (department) Abteilung f; (of document) Abschnitt m, Paragraph m; —al a (regional) partikularistisch.

sector ['sektə*] n Sektor m.

secular ['sekjulə*] a weltlich, profan.

secure [sɪ'kjuə*] a (safe) sicher; (firmly fixed) fest; vt (make firm) befestigen, sichern; (obtain) sichern; —ly ad sicher,·fest.

security [sɪ'kjuərɪtɪ] n Sicherheit f; (pledge) Pfand nt; (document) Sicherheiten pl; (national —) Staatssicherheit f; —guard Sicherheitsbeamte(r) m; see social.

sedate [sɪ'deɪt] a (calm) gelassen; (serious) gesetzt; vt (Med) ein Beruhigungsmittel geben (+dat).

sedation [sɪ'deɪʃən] n (Med) Einfluß m von Beruhigungsmitteln.

sedative ['sedətɪv] n Beruhigungsmittel nt; a beruhigend, einschläfernd.

sedentary ['sedntrɪ] a job sitzend.

sediment ['sedɪmənt] n (Boden)satz m; —ary [sedɪ'mentərɪ] a (Geol) Sediment-.

seduce [sɪ'djuːs] vt verführen.

seduction [sɪ'dʌkʃən] n Verführung f.

seductive [sɪ'dʌktɪv] a verführerisch.

see [siː] irreg vt sehen; (understand) (ein)sehen, erkennen; (find out) sehen, herausfinden; (make sure) dafür sorgen (daß); (accompany) begleiten, bringen; (visit) besuchen; to — a doctor zum Arzt gehen; vi (be aware) sehen; (find out) nachsehen; I —

ach so, ich verstehe; let me — warte mal; we'll — werden (mal) sehen; in (Eccl) Bistum nt; (Protestant) Kirchenkreis m; to — sth through etw durchfechten; to — through sb/sth jdn/etw durchschauen; to — to it dafür sorgen; to — sb off jdn zum Zug etc begleiten.

seed [siːd] n Samen m, (Samen)korn nt; vt (Tennis) plazieren; —ling Setzling m; —y a (ill) flau, angeschlagen; clothes schäbig; person zweifelhaft.

seeing ['siːɪŋ] cj da.

seek [siːk] vt irreg suchen.

seem [siːm] vi scheinen; —ingly ad anscheinend; —ly a geziemend,.

seep [siːp] vi sickern.

seer [sɪə*] n Seher m.

seesaw ['siːsɔː] n Wippe f.

seethe [siːð] vi kochen; (with crowds) wimmeln von.

see-through ['siːθruː] a dress durchsichtig.

segment ['segmənt] n Teil m; (of circle) Ausschnitt m.

segregate ['segrɪgeɪt] vt trennen, absondern.

segregation [segrɪ'geɪʃən] n Rassentrennung f.

seismic ['saɪzmɪk] a seismisch, Erdbeben-.

seize [siːz] vt (grasp) (er)greifen, packen; power ergreifen; (take legally) beschlagnahmen; point erfassen, begreifen; — up vi (Tech) sich festfressen.

seizure ['siːʒə*] n (illness) Anfall m.

seldom ['seldəm] ad selten.

select [sɪ'lekt] a ausgewählt; vt auswählen; —ion [sɪ'lekʃən] Auswahl f; —ive a person wählerisch.

self [self] n Selbst nt, Ich nt; ---
adhesive a selbstklebend; ---
appointed a selbsternannt; ---
assurance Selbstsicherheit f; ---
assured a selbstbewußt; ---
coloured, (US) ---colored a einfarbig; ---**confidence** Selbstvertrauen nt, Selbstbewußtsein nt; ---
confident a selbstsicher; ---
conscious a gehemmt, befangen;
---**contained** a (complete) (in sich)
geschlossen; person verschlossen;
---**defeating** a: to be ---defeating
ein Widerspruch in sich sein; ---
defence Selbstverteidigung f; (Jur)
Notwehr f; ---**employed** a frei-
(schaffend) ---**evident** a offensichtlich; ---**explanatory** a für sich
(selbst) sprechend; ---**indulgent** a
zügellos; ---**interest** Eigennutz m;
---**ish** a, ---**ishly** ad egoistisch, selbst-
süchtig; ---**ishness** Egoismus m,
Selbstsucht f; ---**lessly** ad
selbstlos; ---**made** a selbstgemacht; ---**pity** Selbstmitleid nt;
---**portrait** Selbstbildnis nt; ---
propelled a mit Eigenantrieb; ---
reliant a unabhängig; ---**respect**
Selbstachtung f; ---**respecting** a
mit Selbstachtung; ---**righteous** a
selbstgerecht; ---**satisfied** a selbstzufrieden; ---**service** a Selbst-
bedienungs-; ---**sufficient** a selbst-
genügsam; ---**supporting** a (Fin)
Eigenfinanzierungs-; person eigen-
ständig.

sell [sel] irreg vt verkaufen; vi
verkaufen; (goods) sich verkaufen
(lassen); ---**er** Verkäufer m; ---**ing**
price Verkaufspreis m.

semantic [sɪ'mæntɪk] a seman-
tisch; ---**s** Semantik f.

semaphore ['seməfɔ:*] n Wink-
zeichen pl.

semi ['semɪ] n = ---**detached**
house; ---**circle.** Halbkreis m; ---
colon Semikolon nt; ---**conscious**
a halbbewußt; ---**detached house**
Zweifamilienhaus nt, Doppelhaus
nt; ---**final** Halbfinale nt.

seminar ['semɪnɑ:*] n Seminar nt.

semiquaver ['semɪkweɪvə*] n
Sechzehntel nt.

semiskilled ['sem'skɪld] a
angelernt.

semitone ['semɪtəun] n Halbton m.

semolina [seməˈliːnə] n Grieß m.

senate ['senət] n Senat m.

senator ['senətə*] n Senator m.

send [send] vt irreg senden,
schicken; (col: inspire) hinreißen;
--- **away** vt wegschicken; --- **away**
for vt holen lassen; --- **back** vt
zurückschicken; --- **for** vt holen
lassen; --- **off** vt goods abschicken;
player vom Feld schicken; --- **out**
vt invitation aussenden; --- **up** vt
hinaufsenden; (col) verulken; ---**er**
Absender m; ---**off** Verab-
schiedung f; ---**up** (col) Verulkung
f.

senile ['si:naɪl] a senil, Alters-.

senility [sɪ'nɪlɪtɪ] n Altersschwäch-
heit f.

senior ['si:nɪə*] a (older) älter;
(higher rank) Ober-; n (older
person) Ältere(r) mf; (higher rank-
ing) Rangälteste(r) m; ---**ity**
[si:nɪ'brɪtɪ] (of age) höhere(s) Alter
nt; (in rank) höhere(r) Dienstgrad
m.

sensation [sen'seɪʃən] n
Empfindung f, Gefühl nt; (excitement) Sensation f, Aufsehen nt;
---**al** a sensationell, Sensations-.

sense [sens] n Sinn m; (understanding) Verstand m, Vernunft f;
(meaning) Sinn m, Bedeutung f;
(feeling) Gefühl nt; to make ---

Sinn ergeben; *vt* fühlen, spüren; **—less** *a* sinnlos; (*unconscious*) besinnungslos; **—lessly** *ad* (*stupidly*) sinnlos.

sensibility [sensɪ'bɪlɪtɪ] *n* Empfindsamkeit *f*; (*feeling hurt*) Empfindlichkeit *f*.

sensible *a*, **sensibly** *ad* ['sensəbl, -blɪ] vernünftig.

sensitive ['sensɪtɪv] *a* empfindlich (*to gegen*); (*easily hurt*) sensibel, feinfühlig; *film* lichtempfindlich.

sensitivity [sensɪ'tɪvɪtɪ] *n* Empfindlichkeit *f*; (*artistic*) Feingefühl *nt*; (*tact*) Feinfühligkeit *f*.

sensual ['sensjʊəl] *a* sinnlich.

sensuous ['sensjʊəs] *a* sinnlich, sinnenfreudig.

sentence ['sentəns] *n* Satz *m*; (*Jur*) Strafe *f*; Urteil *nt*; *vt* verurteilen.

sentiment ['sentɪmənt] *n* Gefühl *nt*; (*thought*) Gedanke *m*, Gesinnung *f*; **—al** [sentɪ'mentl] *a* sentimental; (*of feelings rather than reason*) gefühlsmäßig; **—ality** [sentɪmen'tælɪtɪ] Sentimentalität *f*.

sentinel ['sentɪnl] *n* Wachtposten *m*.

sentry ['sentrɪ] *n* (Schild)wache *f*.

separable ['separəbl] *a* (ab)trennbar.

separate ['seprət] *a* getrennt, separat; ['sepəreɪt] *vt* trennen; *vi* sich trennen; **—ly** *ad* getrennt.

separation [sepə'reɪʃən] *n* Trennung *f*.

sepia ['siːpɪə] *a* Sepia-.

September [sep'tembə*] *n* September *m*.

septic ['septɪk] *a* vereitert, septisch.

sequel ['siːkwəl] *n* Folge *f*.

sequence ['siːkwəns] *n* (Reihen)folge *f*.

sequin ['siːkwɪn] *n* Paillette *f*.

serenade [serə'neɪd] *n* Ständchen *nt*, Serenade *f*; *vt* ein Ständchen bringen (+*dat*).

serene *a*, **—ly** *ad* [sə'riːn, -lɪ] heiter, gelassen, ruhig.

serenity [sɪ'renɪtɪ] *n* Heiterkeit *f*, Gelassenheit *f*, Ruhe *f*.

serf [sɜːf] *n* Leibeigene(r) *mf*.

serge [sɜːdʒ] *n* Serge *f*.

sergeant ['sɑːdʒənt] *n* Feldwebel *m*; (*police*) (Polizei)wachtmeister *m*.

serial ['sɪərɪəl] *n* Fortsetzungsroman *m*; (*TV*) Fernsehserie *f*; **—** *number* (fort)laufend; **—ize** *vt* in Fortsetzungen veröffentlichen/senden.

series ['sɪərɪz] *n* Serie *f*, Reihe *f*.

serious ['sɪərɪəs] *a* ernst; *injury* schwer; *development* ernstzunehmend; **i'm —** das meine ich ernst; **—ly** *ad* ernst(haft); *hurt* schwer; **—ness** Ernst *m*, Ernsthaftigkeit *f*.

sermon ['sɜːmən] *n* Predigt *f*.

serpent ['sɜːpənt] *n* Schlange *f*.

serrated [se'reɪtɪd] *a* gezackt; **—** *knife* Sägemesser *nt*.

serum ['sɪərəm] *n* Serum *nt*.

servant ['sɜːvənt] *n* Bedienstete(r) *mf*, Diener(in *f*) *m*; see *civil*.

serve [sɜːv] *vt* dienen (+*dat*); *guest, customer* bedienen; *food* servieren; *writ* zustellen (*on sb* jdm); *vi* dienen, nützen; (*at table*) servieren; (*tennis*) geben, aufschlagen; **it —s him right** das geschieht ihm recht; **that'll — the purpose** das reicht; **that'll — as a** table das geht aus Tisch; **— out** *or* up *vt* food auftragen, servieren.

service ['sɜːvɪs] *n* (*help*) Dienst *m*; (*trains etc*) Verkehrsverbindungen, *pl*; (*hotel*) Service *m*, Bedienung *f*; (*set of dishes*) Service *nt*; (*Rel*) Gottesdienst *m*; (*Mil*) Waffengattung f; (car) Inspektion f; (for TVs etc) Kundendienst m; (tennis) Aufschlag m; to be of — to sb jdm einen großen Dienst erweisen; can I be of —? kann ich Ihnen behilflich sein?; vt (Aut, Tech) warten, überholen; the S—s pl (armed forces) Streitkräfte pl; (car) brauchbar; — area (on motorway) Raststätte f; — charge Bedienung f; —man (soldier etc) Soldat m; — station (Groß)tankstelle f.

servicing ['sɜːvɪsɪŋ] n Wartung f.

serviette [sɜːvɪ'et] n Serviette f.

servile ['sɜːvaɪl] a sklavisch, unterwürfig.

session ['seʃən] n Sitzung f; (Pol) Sitzungsperiode f.

set [set] n (collection of things) Satz m, Set nt; (Rad, TV) Apparat m; (tennis) Satz m; (group of people) Kreis m; (Cine) Szene f; (Theat) Bühnenbild nt; a festgelegt; (ready) bereit; — phrase feststehende(r) Ausdruck m; — square Zeichendreieck nt; Irreg vt (place) setzen, stellen, legen; (arrange) (an)ordnen; table decken; time, price festsetzen; alarm, watch stellen; jewels (ein)-fassen; task stellen; exam ausarbeiten; to — one's hair die Haare eindrehen; vi (sun) untergehen; (become hard) fest werden; (bone) zusammenwachsen; to — on fire anstecken; to — free freilassen; to — sth going etw in Gang bringen; to — sail losfahren; — about vt task anpacken; — aside vt beiseitelegen; — back vt zurückwerfen; — down vt absetzen; — off vi ausbrechen; vt (explode) zur Explosion bringen; alarm losgehen lassen; (show up well) hervorheben; — out vi aufbrechen; vt

(arrange) anlegen, arrangieren; (state) darlegen; — up vt organization aufziehen; record aufstellen; monument erstellen; —back Rückschlag m.

settee [se'tiː] n Sofa nt.

setting ['setɪŋ] n (Mus) Vertonung f; (scenery) Hintergrund m.

settle ['setl] vt beruhigen; (pay) begleichen, bezahlen; (agree) regeln; vi (also — down) sich einleben; (come to rest) sich niederlassen; (sink) sich setzen; (calm down) sich beruhigen; —ment (payment) Begleichung f; (colony) Siedlung f, Niederlassung f; —r Siedler m.

setup ['setʌp] n (arrangement) Aufbau m, Gliederung f; (situation) Situation f, Lage f.

seven ['sevn] num sieben; —teen num siebzehn; —th a siebte(r,s) f; n Siebtel nt; —ty num siebzig.

sever ['sevə*] vt abtrennen.

several ['sevrəl] a mehrere, verschiedene; pron mehrere.

severance ['sevərəns] n Abtrennung f; (fig) Abbruch m.

severe [sɪ'vɪə*] a (strict) streng; (serious) schwer; climate rauh; (plain) streng, schmucklos; —ly ad (strictly) streng, strikt; (seriously) schwer, ernstlich.

severity [sɪ'verɪtɪ] n Strenge f; Schwere f; Ernst m.

sew [səʊ] vti irreg nähen; — up vt zunähen.

sewage ['sjuːɪdʒ] n Abwässer pl.

sewer ['sjuə*] n (Abwasser)kanal m.

sewing ['səʊɪŋ] n Näharbeit f; — machine Nähmaschine f.

sex [seks] n Sex m; (gender) Geschlecht nt; — act Geschlechtsakt m.

sextant ['sekstənt] *n* Sextant *m*.

sextet [seks'tet] *n* Sextett *nt*.

sexual ['seksjʊəl] *a* sexuell, geschlechtlich, Geschlechts-; —**ly** *ad* geschlechtlich, sexuell.

sexy ['seksɪ] *a* sexy.

shabbily ['ʃæbɪlɪ] *ad* schäbig.

shabbiness ['ʃæbɪnəs] *n* Schäbigkeit *f*.

shabby ['ʃæbɪ] *a* (*lit, fig*) schäbig.

shack [ʃæk] *n* Hütte *f*.

shackle ['ʃækl] *vt* fesseln; —**s** *pl* (*lit, fig*) Fesseln *pl*, Ketten *pl*.

shade [ʃeɪd] *n* Schatten *m*; (*for lamp*) Lampenschirm *m*; (*colour*) Farbton *m*; (*small quantity*) Spur *f*, Idee *f*; *vt* abschirmen.

shadow ['ʃædəʊ] *n* Schatten *m*; *vt* (*follow*) beschatten; a: — **cabinet** (*Pol*) Schattenkabinett *nt*; —**y** *a* schattig.

shady ['ʃeɪdɪ] *a* schattig; (*fig*) zwielichtig.

shaft [ʃɑːft] *n* (*of spear etc*) Schaft *m*; (*in mine*) Schacht *m*; (*Tech*) Welle *f*; (*of light*) Strahl *m*.

shaggy ['ʃægɪ] *a* struppig.

shake [ʃeɪk] *irreg vt* schütteln, rütteln; (*shock*) erschüttern; to — hands die Hand geben (*with dat*); they shook hands sie gaben sich die Hand; to — one's head den Kopf schütteln; *vi* (*move*) schwanken; (*tremble*) zittern, beben; a (*jerk*) Schütteln *nt*, Rütteln *nt*; — off *vt* abschütteln; — up *vt* (*lit*) aufschütteln; (*fig*) aufrütteln; —**up** Aufrüttelung *f*; (*Pol*) Umgruppierung *f*.

shakily ['ʃeɪkɪlɪ] *ad* zitternd, unsicher.

shakiness ['ʃeɪkɪnəs] *n* Wackeligkeit *f*.

shaky ['ʃeɪkɪ] *a* zittrig; (*weak*) unsicher.

shale [ʃeɪl] *n* Schiefer(ton) *m*.

shall [ʃæl] *v aux irreg* werden; (*must*) sollen.

shallow ['ʃæləʊ] *a* flach, seicht (*also fig*); —**s** *pl* flache Stellen *pl*.

sham [ʃæm] *n* Täuschung *f*, Trug *m*, Schein *m*; *a* unecht, falsch.

shambles ['ʃæmblz] *n sing* Durcheinander *nt*.

shame [ʃeɪm] *n* Scham *f*; (*disgrace, pity*) Schande *f*; *vt* beschämen; what a —! wie schade! — on you! schäm dich!; —faced *a* beschämt; —ful *a*, —fully *ad* schändlich; —less *a* schamlos; (*immodest*) unverschämt.

shampoo [ʃæm'puː] *n* Schampoon *nt*; *vt* schampunieren; — and set Waschen und Legen.

shamrock ['ʃæmrɒk] *n* Kleeblatt *nt*.

shandy ['ʃændɪ] *n* Radlermaß *nt*.

shan't [ʃɑːnt] = **shall not**.

shanty ['ʃæntɪ] *n* (*cabin*) Hütte *f*, Baracke *f*; — **town** Elendsviertel *nt*.

shape [ʃeɪp] *n* Form *f*, Gestalt *f*; *vt* formen, gestalten; to take — Gestalt annehmen; —less *a* formlos; —**ly** *a* wohlgeformt, wohlproportioniert.

share [ʃεə*] *n* (An)teil *m*; (*Fin*) Aktie *f*; *vt* teilen; —**holder** Aktionär *m*.

shark [ʃɑːk] *n* Hai(fisch) *m*; (*swindler*) Gauner *m*.

sharp [ʃɑːp] *a* scharf; *pin* spitz; *person* clever; *child* aufgeweckt; (*unscrupulous*) gerissen, raffiniert; (*Mus*) erhöht; — **practices** *pl* Machenschaften *pl*; *n* (*Mus*) Kreuz *nt*; *ad* (*Mus*) zu hoch; **nine o'clock** — Punkt neun; **look** —! mach schnell!; —**en** *vt* schärfen; *pencil* spitzen; —ener Spitzer m; —-eyed a scharfsichtig; —ness Schärfe f; —-witted a scharfsinnig, aufgeweckt.

shatter ['ʃætə*] vt zerschmettern; (fig) zerstören; vi zerspringen; —ed a (lit, fig) kaputt; —ing a experience unfaßbar.

shave [ʃeɪv] n Rasur f, Rasieren nt; to have a — sich rasieren (lassen); vt rasieren; vi sich rasieren; —n a head geschoren; —r (Elec) Rasierapparat m, Rasierer m.

shaving ['ʃeɪvɪŋ] n (action) Rasieren nt; —s pl (of wood etc) Späne pl; — brush Rasierpinsel m; — cream Rasierkrem f; — point Rasiersteckdose f; — soap Rasierseife f.

shawl [ʃɔːl] n Schal m, Umhang m.

she [ʃiː] pron sie; a weiblich; — bear Bärenweibchen nt.

sheaf [ʃiːf] n Garbe f.

shear [ʃɪə*] vt irreg scheren; — off vt abscheren; —s pl Heckenschere f.

sheath [ʃiːθ] n Scheide f; —e [ʃiːð] vt einstecken; (Tech) verkleiden.

shed [ʃed] n Schuppen m; (for animals) Stall m; vt irreg leaves etc abwerfen, verlieren; tears vergießen.

she'd [ʃiːd] = she had; she would.

sheep [ʃiːp] n Schaf nt; —dog Schäferhund m; —ish a verschämt, betreten; —skin Schaffell nt.

sheer [ʃɪə*] a bloß, rein; (steep) steil, jäh; (transparent) (hauch-) dünn, durchsichtig; ad (directly) direkt.

sheet [ʃiːt] n Bettuch nt, Bettlaken nt; (of paper) Blatt nt; (of metal etc) Platte f; (of ice) Fläche f; — lightning Wetterleuchten nt.

sheik(h) [ʃeɪk] n Scheich m.

shelf [ʃelf] n Bord nt, Regal nt.

she'll [ʃiːl] = she will; she shall.

shell [ʃel] n Schale f; (sea-) Muschel f; (explosive) Granate f; (of building) Mauern pl; vt peas schälen; (fire on) beschießen; —fish Schalentier nt; (as food) Meeresfrüchte pl.

shelter ['ʃeltə*] n Schutz m; Bunker m; vt schützen, bedecken; refugees aufnehmen; vi sich unterstellen; —ed a life behütet; spot geschützt.

shelve [ʃelv] vt aufschieben; vi abfallen.

shelving ['ʃelvɪŋ] n Regale pl.

shepherd ['ʃepəd] n Schäfer m; vt treiben, führen; —ess Schäferin f.

sheriff ['ʃerɪf] n Sheriff m.

sherry ['ʃerɪ] n Sherry m.

she's [ʃiːz] = she is; she has.

shield [ʃiːld] n Schild m; (fig) Schirm m, Schutz m; vt (be)schirmen; (Tech) abschirmen.

shift [ʃɪft] n Veränderung f, Verschiebung f; (work) Schicht f; vt (ver)rücken, verschieben; office verlegen; arm wegnehmen; vi sich verschieben; (col) schnell fahren; — work Schichtarbeit f; —y a verschlagen.

shilling ['ʃɪlɪŋ] n (old) Shilling m.

shilly-shally ['ʃɪlɪʃælɪ] vi zögern.

shimmer ['ʃɪmə*] n Schimmer m; vi schimmern.

shin [ʃɪn] n Schienbein nt.

shine [ʃaɪn] n Glanz m, Schein m; irreg vt polieren; to — a torch on sb jdn (mit einer Lampe) anleuchten; vi scheinen; (fig) glänzen.

shingle ['ʃɪŋgl] n Schindel f; (on

beach) Strandkies *m*; **—s** *pl (Med)*
Gürtelrose *f*.

shining ['ʃaɪnɪŋ] *a light* strahlend.

shiny ['ʃaɪnɪ] *a* glänzend.

ship [ʃɪp] *n* Schiff *nt*; *vt* an Bord
bringen, verladen; *(transport as
cargo)* verschiffen; **—building**
Schiffbau *m*; **—** canal Seekanal *m*;
—ment Verladung *f*; *(goods
shipped)* Schiffsladung *f*; **—per**
Verschiffer *m*; **—ping** *(act)* Ver-
schiffung *f*; *(ships)* Schiffahrt *f*;
—shape a in Ordnung; **—wreck**
Schiffbruch *m*; *(destroyed ship)*
Wrack *nt*; **—yard** Werft *f*.

shirk [ʃɜːk] *vt* ausweichen (+ *dat.*).

shirt [ʃɜːt] *n* (Ober)hemd *nt*; in
—sleeves in Hemdsärmeln; **—y** *a
(col)* mürrisch.

shiver ['ʃɪvə*] *n* Schauer *m*; *vi*
frösteln, zittern.

shoal [ʃəʊl] *n* (Fisch)schwarm *m*.

shock [ʃɒk] *n* Stoß *m*,
Erschütterung *f*; *(mental)* Schock
m; *(Elec)* Schlag *m*; *vt*
erschüttern; *(offend)* schockieren;
— absorber Stoßdämpfer *m*; **—ing**
a unerhört, schockierend; **—proof**
a watch stoßsicher.

shoddiness ['ʃɒdɪnəs] *n* Schäbigkeit *f*.

shoddy ['ʃɒdɪ] *a* schäbig.

shoe [ʃuː] *n* Schuh *m*; *(of horse)*
Hufeisen *nt*; *vt irreg horse*
beschlagen; **—brush** Schuhbürste
f; **—horn** Schuhlöffel *m*; **—lace**
Schnürsenkel *m*.

shoot [ʃuːt] *n (branch)* Schößling
m; *irreg vt gun* abfeuern; *goal,
arrow* schießen; *(kill)* erschießen;
film drehen, filmen; **shot in the leg**
ins Bein getroffen; *vi (gun, move
quickly)* schießen; **don't —!** nicht
schießen!; **— down** *vt* abschießen;

—ing Schießerei *f*; **—ing star** Stern-
schnuppe *f*.

shop [ʃɒp] *n* Geschäft *nt*, Laden *m*;
(workshop) Werkstatt *f*; *vi (also* **go
—ping)** einkaufen gehen; **—**
assistant Verkäufer(in *f*) *m*; **—**
keeper Geschäftsinhaber *m*; **—**
lifter Ladendieb *m*; **—lifting**
Ladendiebstahl *m*; **—per** Käufer(in
f) *m*; **—ping** Einkaufen *nt*, Einkauf
m; **—ping bag** Einkaufstasche *f*;
—ping centre, *(US)* **—ping center**
Einkaufszentrum *nt*; **—soiled** *a*
angeschmutzt; **— steward**
Betriebsrat *m*; **— window**
Schaufenster *nt*; *see* **talk**.

shore [ʃɔː*] *n* Ufer *nt*; *(of sea)*
Strand *m*, Küste *f*; *vt:* **— up**
abstützen.

short [ʃɔːt] *a* kurz; *person* klein;
(curt) kurz angebunden; *(measure)*
zu knapp; **to be —** of zu wenig
... haben; **two —** zwei zu wenig;
n (Elec—circuit) Kurzschluß *m*;
ad (suddenly) plötzlich; *vi (Elec)*
einen Kurzschluß haben; **to cut —**
abkürzen; **to fall —** nicht
erreichen; **for —** kurz; **—age**
Knappheit *f*, Mangel *m*; **—bread**
Mürbegebäck *nt*, Heidesand *m*; **—**
circuit Kurzschluß *m*; *vi* einen
Kurzschluß haben; **—coming**
Fehler *m*, Mangel *m*; **— cut**
Abkürzung *f*; **—en** *vt* (ab)kürzen;
clothes kürzer machen; **—hand**
Stenographie *f*, Kurzschrift *f*;
—hand typist Stenotypistin *f*;
—list engere Wahl *f*; **—lived** *a*
kurzlebig; **—ly** *ad* bald; **—ness**
Kürze *f*; **—s** *pl* Shorts *pl*; **—**
sighted *a (lit, fig)* kurzsichtig; **—**
sightedness Kurzsichtigkeit *f*; **—**
story Kurzgeschichte *f*; **—**
tempered *a* leicht aufbrausend; **—**

term *a effect* kurzfristig; — **wave** (Rad) Kurzwelle *f.*

shot [ʃɒt] *n (from gun)* Schuß *m;* *(person)* Schütze *m; (try)* Versuch *m; (injection)* Spritze *f; (Phot)* Aufnahme *f,* Schnappschuß *m;* like **a** — wie der Blitz; —**gun** Schrotflinte *f.*

should [ʃʊd] *v aux:* I — go now ich sollte jetzt gehen; I — say ich würde sagen; I — like to ich möchte gerne, ich würde gerne.

shoulder [ˈʃəʊldə*] *n* Schulter *f; vt* **rifle** schultern; *(fig)* auf sich nehmen; —**blade** Schulterblatt *nt.*

shouldn't [ˈʃʊdnt] = **should not.**

shout [ʃaʊt] *n* Schrei *m; (call)* Ruf *m; vt* rufen; *vi* schreien, laut rufen; **to** — **at** anbrüllen; —**ing** Geschrei *nt.*

shove [ʃʌv] *n* Schubs *m,* Stoß *m; vt* schieben, stoßen, schubsen; — **off** *vi (Naut)* abstoßen; *(fig col)* abhauen.

shovel [ˈʃʌvl] *n* Schaufel *f; vt* schaufeln.

show [ʃəʊ] *n (display)* Schau *f; (exhibition)* Ausstellung *f; (Cine, Theat)* Vorstellung *f,* Show *f; irreg vt zeigen; kindness* erweisen; *vi zu* sehen sein; **to** — **sb** in jdn hereinführen; **to** — **sb out** jdn hinausbegleiten; — **off** *vi (pej)* angeben, protzen; *vt (display)* ausstellen; — **up** *vi (stand out)* sich abheben; *(arrive)* erscheinen; *vt* aufzeigen; *(unmask)* bloßstellen; — **business** Showbusineß *nt;* —**down** Kraftprobe *f,* endgültige Auseinandersetzung *f.*

shower [ˈʃaʊə*] *n* Schauer *m; (of stones)* (Stein)hagel *m; (of sparks)* (Funken)regen *m;* (— *bath)* Dusche *f;* **to have a** — duschen; *vt (fig)* überschütten; —**proof a**

wasserabstoßend; —**y** *a weather* regnerisch.

showground [ˈʃəʊgraʊnd] *n* Ausstellungsgelände *nt.*

showing [ˈʃəʊɪŋ] *n (of film)* Vorführung *f.*

show jumping [ˈʃəʊdʒʌmpɪŋ] *n* Turnierreiten *nt.*

showmanship [ˈʃəʊmənʃɪp] *n* Talent *nt* als Showman.

show-off [ˈʃəʊɒf] *n* Angeber *m.*

showpiece [ˈʃəʊpiːs] *n* Paradestück *nt.*

showroom [ˈʃəʊrʊm] *n* Ausstellungsraum *m.*

shrapnel [ˈʃræpnl] *n* Schrapnell *nt.*

shred [ʃred] *n* Fetzen *m; vt* zerfetzen; *(Cook)* raspeln; **in** —**s** in Fetzen.

shrewd *a,* —**ly** *ad* [ʃruːd, -lɪ] scharfsinnig, clever; —**ness** Scharfsinn *m.*

shriek [ʃriːk] *n* Schrei *m; vti* kreischen, schreien.

shrill [ʃrɪl] *a* schrill, gellend.

shrimp [ʃrɪmp] *n* Krabbe *f,* Garnele *f.*

shrine [ʃraɪn] *n* Schrein *m.*

shrink [ʃrɪŋk] *irreg vi* schrumpfen, eingehen; *vt* einschrumpfen lassen; —**age** Schrumpfung *f;* — **away** *vi* zurückschrecken *(from* vor *+ dat).*

shrivel [ˈʃrɪvl] *vti (also* — **up)** schrumpfen, schrumpeln.

shroud [ʃraʊd] *n* Leichentuch *nt; vt* umhüllen, (ein)hüllen.

Shrove Tuesday [ˈʃrəʊvˈtjuːzdeɪ] *n* Fastnachtsdienstag *m.*

shrub [ʃrʌb] *n* Busch *m,* Strauch *m;* —**bery** Gebüsch *nt.*

shrug [ʃrʌg] *n* Achselzucken *nt; vi* die Achseln zucken; — **off** *vt* auf die leichte Schulter nehmen.

shrunken ['ʃrʌŋkən] a eingelaufen..
shudder ['ʃʌdə*] n Schauder m; vi schaudern.
shuffle ['ʃʌfl] n (Cards) (Karten)mischen nt; vt cards mischen; vi (walk) schlurfen.
shun [ʃʌn] vt scheuen, (ver)meiden.
shunt [ʃʌnt] vt rangieren.
shut [ʃʌt] irreg vt schließen, zumachen; vi sich schließen (lassen); — **down** vti schließen; — **off** vt supply abdrehen; — **up** vi (keep quiet) den Mund halten; vt (close) zuschließen; (silence) zum Schweigen bringen; — up! halt den Mund!; —**ter** Fensterladen m, Rolladen m; (Phot) Verschluß m.
shuttlecock ['ʃʌtlkɒk] n Federball m; Federballspiel nt.
shuttle service ['ʃʌtls3:vɪs] n Pendelverkehr m.
shy a, —**ly** ad [ʃaɪ, -lɪ] schüchtern, scheu; —**ness** Schüchternheit f, Zurückhaltung f.
Siamese [saɪəˈmiːz] a: — cat Siamkatze f; — **twins** pl siamesische Zwillinge pl.
sick [sɪk] a krank; humour schwarz; joke makaber; I feel — mir ist schlecht; I was — ich habe gebrochen; to be — of sb/sth jdn/etw satt haben; — **bay** (Schiffs)lazarett nt; —**bed** Krankenbett nt; —**en** vt (disgust) krankmachen; vi krank werden; —**ening** a (sight ekelig; (annoying) zum Weinen.
sickle ['sɪkl] n Sichel f.
sick leave ['sɪkliːv] n: to be on — krank geschrieben sein.
sick list ['sɪklɪst] n Krankenliste f.
sickly ['sɪklɪ] a kränklich, blaß; (causing nausea) widerlich.
sickness ['sɪknəs] n Krankheit f; (vomiting) Übelkeit f, Erbrechen nt.

sick pay ['sɪkpeɪ] n Krankengeld nt.
side [saɪd] n Seite f; a door, entrance Seiten-, Neben-; by the — of neben; on all —s von allen Seiten; to take —s (with) Partei nehmen (für); vi: — with sb es halten mit jdm; —**board** Anrichte f, Sideboard nt; —**boards**, —**burns** pl Koteletten pl; — **effect** Nebenwirkung f; —**light** (Aut) Parkleuchte f, Standlicht nt; — **line** (Sport) Seitenlinie f; (fig: hobby) Nebenbeschäftigung' f; — **road** Nebenstraße f; — **show** Nebenausstellung f; —**track** vt (fig) ablenken; —**walk** (US) Bürgersteig m; —**ways** ad seitwärts.
siding ['saɪdɪŋ] n. Nebengleis nt.
sidle ['saɪdl] vi: — up sich heranmachen (to an + acc).
siege [siːdʒ] n Belagerung f.
siesta [sɪˈestə] n Siesta f.
sieve [sɪv] n Sieb nt; vt sieben.
sift [sɪft] vt sieben; (fig) sichten.
sigh [saɪ] n Seufzer m; vi seufzen.
sight [saɪt] n (power of seeing) Sehvermögen nt, Augenlicht nt; (view) (An)blick m; (scene) Aussicht f, Blick m; (of gun) Zielvorrichtung f, Korn nt; —s pl (of city etc) Sehenswürdigkeiten pl; in — in Sicht; out of — außer Sicht; vt sichten; —**seeing** Besuch m von Sehenswürdigkeiten; to go —**seeing** Sehenswürdigkeiten besichtigen; —**seer** Tourist m.
sign [saɪn] n Zeichen nt; (notice, road — etc) Schild nt; vt unterschreiben; — **out** vi sich austragen; — **up** vi (Mil) sich verpflichten; vt verpflichten.
signal ['sɪgnl] n Signal nt; vi ein Zeichen geben (+ dat).
signatory ['sɪgnətrɪ] n Signatar m.

signature ['sɪgnətʃə*] n Unterschrift f; — **tune** Erkennungsmelodie f.

signet ring ['sɪgnətrɪŋ] n Siegelring m.

significance [sɪg'nɪfɪkəns] n Bedeutung f.

significant [sɪg'nɪfɪkənt] a (meaning sth) bedeutsam; (important) bedeutend, wichtig; —**ly** ad bezeichnenderweise.

signify ['sɪgnɪfaɪ] vt bedeuten; (show) andeuten, zu verstehen geben.

sign language ['saɪnlæŋgwɪdʒ] n Zeichensprache f, Fingersprache f.

signpost ['saɪnpəʊst] n Wegweiser m, Schild nt.

silence ['saɪləns] n Stille f, Ruhe f; (of person) Schweigen nt; vt zum Schweigen bringen; —**r** (on gun) Schalldämpfer m; (Aut) Auspufftopf m.

silent ['saɪlənt] a still; person schweigsam; —**ly** ad schweigend, still.

silhouette [sɪlu:'et] n Silhouette f, Umriß m; (picture) Schattenbild nt; vt: to be —d against sth sich als Silhouette abheben gegen etw.

silk [sɪlk] n Seide f; a seiden, Seiden-; —**y** a seidig.

silliness ['sɪlɪnəs] n Albernheit f, Dummheit f.

silly ['sɪlɪ] a dumm, albern.

silo ['saɪləʊ] n Silo m.

silt [sɪlt] n Schlamm m, Schlick m.

silver ['sɪlvə*] n Silber nt; a silbern, Silber-; — **paper** Silberpapier nt; —**plate** Silber(geschirr) nt; —**plated** a versilbert; —**smith** Silberschmied m; —**ware** Silber nt; —**y** a silbern.

similar ['sɪmɪlə*] a ähnlich (to dat); —**ity** [sɪmɪ'lærɪtɪ] n Ähnlichkeit f; —**ly** ad in ähnlicher Weise.

simile ['sɪmɪlɪ] n Vergleich m.

simmer ['sɪmə*] vti sieden (lassen).

simple ['sɪmpl] a einfach; dress also schlicht; —(-minded) a naiv, einfältig.

simplicity [sɪm'plɪsɪtɪ] n Einfachheit f; (of person) Einfältigkeit f.

simplification [sɪmplɪfɪ'keɪʃən] n Vereinfachung f.

simplify ['sɪmplɪfaɪ] vt vereinfachen.

simply ['sɪmplɪ] ad einfach; (only) bloß, nur.

simulate ['sɪmjʊleɪt] vt simulieren.

simulation [sɪmjʊ'leɪʃən] n Simulieren nt.

simultaneous a, —**ly** ad [sɪml'teɪnɪəs, -lɪ] gleichzeitig.

sin [sɪn] n Sünde f; vi sündigen.

since [sɪns] ad seither; prep seit, seitdem; cj (time) seit; (because) da, weil.

sincere [sɪn'sɪə*] a aufrichtig, ehrlich, offen; —**ly** ad aufrichtig; yours —**ly** mit freundlichen Grüßen.

sincerity [sɪn'serɪtɪ] n Aufrichtigkeit f.

sinecure ['saɪnɪkjʊə*] n einträgliche(r) Ruheposten m.

sinew ['sɪnju:] n Sehne f; (of animal) Flechse f.

sinful ['sɪnfʊl] a sündig, sündhaft.

sing [sɪŋ] vti irreg singen.

singe [sɪndʒ] vt versengen.

singer ['sɪŋə*] n Sänger(in f) m.

singing ['sɪŋɪŋ] n Singen nt, Gesang m.

single ['sɪŋgl] a (one only) einzig; bed, room Einzel-, einzeln; (unmarried) ledig; ticket einfach; (having one part only) einzeln; n

.(ticket) einfache Fahrkarte f; —s (tennis) Einzel nt; — out vt aussuchen, auswählen; —-breasted a einreihig in — file hintereinander; —-handed a allein; —-minded a zielstrebig.

singlet ['sɪŋglət] n Unterhemd nt.

single ['sɪŋglɪ] ad einzeln, allein.

singular ['sɪŋgjʊlə*] a (Gram) Singular-; (odd) merkwürdig, seltsam; n (Gram) Einzahl f, Singular m; —ly ad besonders, höchst.

sinister ['sɪnɪstə*] a (evil) böse; (ghostly) unheimlich.

sink [sɪŋk] n Spülbecken nt, Ausguß m; irreg vt ship versenken; (dig) einsenken; vi sinken; — in vi (news etc) eingehen (+dat); —ing a feeling flau.

sinner ['sɪnə*] n Sünder(in f) m.

sinuous ['sɪnjʊəs] a gewunden, sich schlängelnd.

sinus ['saɪnəs] n (Anat) Nasenhöhle f, Sinus m.

sip [sɪp] n Schlückchen nt; vt nippen an (+dat).

siphon ['saɪfən] n Siphon(flasche f) m; — off vt absaugen; (fig) abschöpfen.

sir [sɜ:*] n (respect) Herr m; (knight) Sir m; yes S— ja(wohl, mein Herr).

siren ['saɪərən] n Sirene f.

sirloin ['sɜ:lɔɪn] n Lendenstück nt.

sirocco [sɪ'rɒkəʊ] n Schirokko m.

sissy ['sɪsɪ] n = cissy.

sister ['sɪstə*] n Schwester f; (nurse) Oberschwester f; (nun) Ordensschwester f; —-in-law Schwägerin f.

sit [sɪt] irreg vi sitzen; (hold session) tagen, Sitzung halten; vt exam machen; to — tight

abwarten; — down vi sich hinsetzen; — up vi (after lying) sich aufsetzen; (straight) sich gerade setzen; (at night) aufbleiben.

site [saɪt] n Platz m; vt plazieren, legen.

sit-in ['sɪtɪn] n Sit-in nt.

siting ['saɪtɪŋ] n (location) Platz m, Lage f.

sitting ['sɪtɪŋ] n (meeting) Sitzung f, Tagung f; — room Wohnzimmer nt.

situated ['sɪtjʊeɪtɪd] a: to be — liegen.

situation [sɪtjʊ'eɪʃən] n Situation f, Lage f; (place) Lage f; (employment) Stelle f.

six [sɪks] num sechs; —teen num sechzehn; —th a sechste(r,s); n Sechstel nt; —ty num sechzig.

size [saɪz] n Größe f; (of project) Umfang m; (glue) Kleister m; — up vt (assess) abschätzen, einschätzen; —able a ziemlich groß, ansehnlich.

sizzle ['sɪzl] n Zischen nt; vi zischen; (Cook) brutzeln.

skate [skeɪt] n Schlittschuh m; vi Schlittschuh laufen; —r Schlittschuhläufer(in f) m.

skating ['skeɪtɪŋ] n Eislauf m; to go — Eislaufen gehen; — rink Eisbahn f.

skeleton ['skelɪtn] n Skelett nt; (fig) Gerüst nt; — key Dietrich m.

skeptic ['skeptɪk] n (US) = sceptic.

sketch [sketʃ] n Skizze f; (Theat) Sketch m; vt skizzieren, eine Skizze machen von; —book Skizzenbuch nt; —ing Skizzieren nt; — pad Skizzenblock m; —y a skizzenhaft.

skewer ['skjuə*] *n* Fleischspieß *m*.

ski [ski:] *n* Ski *m*, Schi *m*; *vi* Ski or Schi laufen; — **boot** Skistiefel *m*.

skid [skɪd] *n* (*Aut*) Schleudern *nt*; *vi* rutschen; (*Aut*) schleudern.

skidmark ['skɪdmɑ:k] *n* Rutschspur *f*.

skier ['ski:ə*] *n* Skiläufer(in *f*) *m*.

skiing ['ski:ɪŋ] *n:* to go — Skilaufen gehen.

ski-jump ['ski:dʒʌmp] . *n* Sprungschanze *f*; *vi* Ski springen.

ski-lift ['ski:lɪft] *n* Skilift *m*.

skilful *a*, **—ly** *ad* ['skɪlful, -fəlɪ] geschickt.

skill [skɪl] *n* Können *nt*, Geschicklichkeit *f*; **—ed** *a* geschickt; **worker** Fach-, gelernt.

skim [skɪm] *vt liquid* abschöpfen; *milk* entrahmen; (*read*) überfliegen; (*glide over*) gleiten über (+*acc*).

skimp [skɪmp] *vt* (*do carelessly*) oberflächlich tun; **—y** *a work* schlecht gemacht; *dress* knapp.

skin [skɪn] *n* Haut *f*; (*peel*) Schale *f*; *vt* abhäuten; schälen; **—deep** *a* oberflächlich; **—diving** Schwimmtauchen *nt*; **—ny** *a* dünn; **—tight** *a dress etc* hauteng.

skip [skɪp] *n* Sprung *m*, Hopser *m*; *vi* hüpfen, springen; (*with rope*) Seil springen; *vt* (*pass over*) übergehen.

ski pants ['ski:'pænts] *npl* Skihosen *pl*.

skipper ['skɪpə*] *n* (*Naut*) Schiffer *m*, Kapitän *m*; (*Sport*) Mannschaftskapitän *m*; *vt* führen.

skipping rope ['skɪpɪŋrəup] *n* Hüpfseil *nt*.

skirmish ['skɜ:mɪʃ] *n* Scharmützel *nt*.

skirt [skɜ:t] *n* Rock *m*; *vt* herumgehen um; (*fig*) umgehen.

ski run ['ski:rʌn] *n* Skiabfahrt *f*.

skit [skɪt] *n* Parodie *f*.

ski tow ['ski:təu] *n* Schlepplift *m*.

skittle ['skɪtl] *n* Kegel *m*; **—s** (*game*) Kegeln *nt*.

skive [skarv] *vi* (*Brit col*) schwänzen.

skulk [skʌlk] *vi* sich herumdrücken.

skull [skʌl] *n* Schädel *m*; — **and crossbones** Totenkopf *m*.

skunk [skʌŋk] *n* Stinktier *nt*.

sky [skaɪ] *n* Himmel *m*; **—blue** *a* himmelblau; *n* Himmelblau *nt*; **—light** Dachfenster *nt*, Oberlicht *nt*; **—scraper** Wolkenkratzer *m*.

slab [slæb] *n* (*of stone*) Platte *f*; (*of chocolate*) Tafel *f*.

slack [slæk] *a* (*loose*) lose, schlaff, locker; *business* flau; (*careless*) nachlässig, lasch; *vi* nachlässig sein; *n* (*in rope etc*) durchhängende(r) Teil *nt*; to take up the — straffziehen; **—s** *pl* Hose(n *pl*) *f*; **—en** (*also* — **en off**) *vi* schlaff/locker werden; (*become slower*) nachlassen, stocken; *vt* (*loosen*) lockern; **—ness** Schlaffheit *f*.

slag [slæg] *n* Schlacke *f*; **—heap** Halde *f*.

slalom ['slɑ:ləm] *n* Slalom *m*.

slam [slæm] *n* Knall *m*; *vt door* zuschlagen, zuknallen; (*throw down*) knallen; *vi* zuschlagen.

slander ['slɑ:ndə*] *n* Verleumdung *f*; *vt* verleumden; **—ous** *a* verleumderisch.

slang [slæŋ] *n* Slang *m*; Jargon *m*.

slant [slɑ:nt] *n* (*lit*) Schräge *f*; (*fig*) Tendenz *f*, Einstellung *f*; *vt* schräg legen; *vi* schräg liegen; **—ing** *a* schräg.

slap [slæp] n Schlag m, Klaps m; vt schlagen, einen Klaps geben (+dat); ad (directly) geradewegs; —dash a salopp; —stick (comedy) Klamauk m; —up a meal erstklassig, prima.

slash [slæʃ] n Hieb m, Schnittwunde f; vt (auf)schlitzen; expenditure radikal kürzen.

slate [sleit] n (stone) Schiefer m; (roofing) Dachziegel m; vt (criticize) verreißen.

slaughter ['slɔːtə*] n (of animals) Schlachten nt; (of people) Gemetzel nt; vt schlachten; people niedermetzeln.

slave [sleiv] n Sklave m Sklavin f; vi schuften, sich schinden; —ry Sklaverei f; (work) Schinderei f.

slavish a, —ly ad ['sleiviʃ, -li] sklavisch.

slay [slei] vt irreg ermorden.

sleazy ['sliːzi] a place schmierig.

sledge ['sledʒ] n Schlitten m; —hammer Schmiedehammer m.

sleek [sliːk] a glatt, glänzend; shape rassig.

sleep [sliːp] n Schlaf m; vi irreg schlafen; to go to — einschlafen; — in vi ausschlafen; (oversleep) verschlafen; —er (person) Schläfer m; (Rail) Schlafwagen m; (beam) Schwelle f; —ily ad schläfrig; —iness Schläfrigkeit f; —ing bag Schlafsack m; —ing car Schlafwagen m; —ing pill Schlaftablette f; —less a night schlaflos; —lessness Schlaflosigkeit f; —walker Schlafwandler m; —y schläfrig.

sleet [sliːt] n Schneeregen m.

sleeve [sliːv] n Ärmel m; (of record) Umschlag m; —less a garment ärmellos.

sleigh [slei] n Pferdeschlitten m.

sleight [slait] n: — of hand Fingerfertigkeit f.

slender ['slendə*] a schlank; (fig) gering.

slice [slais] n Scheibe f; vt in Scheiben schneiden.

slick [slik] a (clever) raffiniert, aalglatt; n Ölteppich m.

slide [slaid] n Rutschbahn f; (Phot) Dia(positiv) nt; (for hair) (Haar)spange f; (fall in prices) (Preis)rutsch m; irreg vt schieben; vi (slip) gleiten, rutschen; to let things — die Dinge schleifen lassen; — rule Rechenschieber m.

sliding ['slaidiŋ] a door Schiebe-.

slight [slait] a zierlich; (trivial) geringfügig; (small) leicht, gering; n Kränkung f; vt (offend) kränken; —ly ad etwas, ein bißchen.

slim [slim] a schlank; book dünn; chance gering; vi eine Schlankheitskur machen.

slime [slaim] n Schlamm m; Schleim m.

slimming ['slimiŋ] n Schlankheitskur f.

slimness ['slimnəs] n Schlankheit f.

slimy ['slaimi] a glitschig; (dirty) schlammig; person schmierig.

sling [sliŋ] n Schlinge f; (weapon) Schleuder f; vt irreg werfen; (hurl) schleudern.

slip [slip] n (slipping) Ausgleiten nt, Rutschen nt; (mistake) Flüchtigkeitsfehler m; (petticoat) Unterrock m; (of paper) Zettel m; to give sb the — jdn entwischen; — of the tongue Versprecher m; vt (put) stecken, schieben; it —ped my mind das ist mir entfallen, ich habe es vergessen; vi (lose balance) ausrutschen; (move) gleiten, rutschen; (make mistake) einen Fehler machen; (*decline*) nachlassen; **to let things** — die Dinge schleifen lassen; — **away** *vi* sich wegstehlen; — **by** *vi* (*time*) verstreichen; — **in** *vt* hineingleiten lassen; *vi* (*errors*) sich einschleichen; — **out** *vi* hinausschlüpfen; —**per** Hausschuh *m*; —**pery** *a* glatt; (*tricky*) aalglatt, gerissen; —**road** Auffahrt *f*/Auffahrt *f*; —**shod** *a* schlampig; —**stream** Windschatten *m*; —**up** Panne *f*; —**way** Auslaufbahn *f*.

slit [slɪt] *n* Schlitz *m*; *vt irreg* aufschlitzen.

slither ['slɪðə*] *vi* schlittern; (*snake*) sich schlängeln.

slob [slɒb] *n* (*col*) Klotz *m*.

slog [slɒg] *n* (*great effort*) Plackerei *f*; *vi* (*work hard*) schuften.

slogan ['sləʊgən] *n* Schlagwort *nt*; (*Comm*) Werbespruch *m*.

slop [slɒp] *vi* überschwappen; *vt* verschütten.

slope [sləʊp] *n* Neigung *f*, Schräge *f*; (*of mountains*) (Ab)hang *m*; *vi*: — **down** sich senken; — **up** ansteigen.

sloping ['sləʊpɪŋ] *a* schräg; *shoulders* abfallend; *ground* abschüssig.

sloppily ['slɒpɪlɪ] *ad* schlampig.

sloppiness ['slɒpɪnəs] *n* Matschigkeit *f*; (*of work*) Nachlässigkeit *f*.

sloppy ['slɒpɪ] *a* (*wet*) matschig; (*careless*) schlampig; (*silly*) rührselig.

slot [slɒt] *n* Schlitz *m*; *vt*: — **sth in** etw einlegen; — **machine** Automat *m*.

slouch [slaʊtʃ] *vi* krumm dasitzen or dastehen.

slovenly ['slʌvnlɪ] *a* schlampig; *speech* salopp.

slow [sləʊ] *a* langsam; **to be** — (*clock*) nachgehen; · (*stupid*) begriffsstutzig sein; — **down** *vi* langsamer werden; — **down!** mach langsam!; *vt* aufhalten, langsamer machen, verlangsamen; — **up** *vi* sich verlangsamen, sich verzögern; *vt* aufhalten, langsamer machen; —**ly** *ad* langsam; allmählich; **in** — **motion** in Zeitlupe.

sludge [slʌdʒ] *n* Schlamm *m*, Matsch *m*.

slug [slʌg] *n* Nacktschnecke *f*; (*col: bullet*) Kugel *f*; —**gish** *a* träge; (*Comm*) schleppend; —**gishly** *ad* träge; —**gishness** *n* Langsamkeit *f*, Trägheit *f*.

sluice [sluːs] *n* Schleuse *f*.

slum [slʌm] *n* Elendsviertel *nt*, Slum *m*.

slumber ['slʌmbə*] *n* Schlummer *m*.

slump [slʌmp] *n* Rückgang *m*; *vi* fallen, stürzen.

slur [slɜː*] *n* Undeutlichkeit *f*; (*insult*) Verleumdung *f*; *vt* (*also* — *over*) hinweggehen über (+*acc*); —**red** [slɜːd] *a* *pronunciation* undeutlich.

slush [slʌʃ] *n* (*snow*) Schneematsch *m*; (*mud*) Schlamm *m*; —**y** *a* (*lit*) matschig; (*fig: sentimental*) schmalzig.

slut [slʌt] *n* Schlampe *f*.

sly *a*, —**ly** [slaɪ, -lɪ] *ad* schlau, verschlagen; —**ness** *n* Schlauheit *f*.

smack [smæk] *n* Klaps *m*; *vt* einen Klaps geben (+*dat*); **to** — **one's lips** schmatzen, sich (*dat*) die Lippen lecken; *vi* — **of** riechen nach.

small [smɔːl] *a* klein; — **change** Kleingeld *nt*; —**holding** Kleinlandbesitz *m*; —**hours** *pl* frühe Morgenstunden *pl*; —**ish** *a* ziemlich klein; —**ness** Kleinheit *f*; —**pox** Pocken pl; **—-scale** a klein, in kleinem Maßstab; — **talk** Konversation f, Geplauder nt.

smarmy ['smɑ:mi] a (col) schmierig.

smart a, **—ly** ad [smɑ:t, -li] (fashionable) elegant, schick; (neat) adrett; (clever) clever; (quick) scharf; vi brennen, schmerzen; **—en up** vi sich in Schale werfen; vt herausputzen; **—ness** Gescheitheit f; Eleganz f.

smash [smæʃ] n Zusammenstoß m; (tennis) Schmetterball m; vt (break) zerschmettern; (destroy) vernichten; vi (break) zersplittern, zerspringen; **—ing** a (col) toll, großartig.

smattering ['smætərɪŋ] n oberflächliche Kenntnis f.

smear [smɪə*] n Fleck m; vt beschmieren.

smell [smɛl] n Geruch m; (sense) Geruchssinn m; vti irreg riechen (of nach); **—y** a übelriechend.

smile [smaɪl] n Lächeln nt; vi lächeln.

smirk [smɜ:k] n blöde(s) Grinsen nt; vi blöde grinsen.

smith [smɪθ] n Schmied m; **—y** ['smɪðɪ] n Schmiede f.

smock [smɒk] n Kittel m.

smog [smɒg] n Smog m.

smoke [sməuk] n Rauch m; vt rauchen; food räuchern; vi rauchen; **—r** Raucher m; (Rail) Raucherabteil nt; **— screen** Rauchwand f.

smoking ['sməukɪŋ] n Rauchen nt; 'no —' Rauchen verboten'.

smoky ['sməukɪ] a rauchig; room verraucht; taste geräuchert.

smolder ['sməuldə*] vi US) = **smoulder.**

smooth [smu:ð] a glatt; movement geschmeidig; person glatt, gewandt; vt (also — out) glätten, glattstreichen; **—ly** ad glatt, eben; (fig) reibungslos; **—ness** Glätte f.

smother ['smʌðə*] vt ersticken.

smoulder ['sməuldə*] vi glimmen, schwelen.

smudge [smʌdʒ] n Schmutzfleck m; vt beschmieren.

smug [smʌg] a selbstgefällig.

smuggle ['smʌgl] vt schmuggeln; **—r** Schmuggler m.

smuggling ['smʌglɪŋ] n Schmuggel m.

smugly ['smʌglɪ] ad selbstgefällig.

smugness ['smʌgnəs] n Selbstgefälligkeit f.

smutty ['smʌtɪ] a (fig: obscene) obszön, schmutzig.

snack [snæk] n Imbiß m; **— bar** Imbißstube f.

snag [snæg] n Haken m; (in stocking) gezogene(r) Faden m.

snail [sneɪl] n Schnecke f.

snake [sneɪk] n Schlange f.

snap [snæp] n Schnappen nt; (photograph) Schnappschuß m; a decision schnell; vt (break) zerbrechen; (Phot) knipsen; to — one's fingers mit den Fingern schnipsen; vi (break) brechen; (bite) schnappen; (speak) anfauchen; **— out of it!** raff dich auf!; **— off** vt (break) abbrechen; **— up** vt aufschnappen; **—py** a flott; **— shot** Schnappschuß m.

snare [snɛə*] n Schlinge f; vt mit einer Schlinge fangen.

snarl [snɑ:l] n Zähnefletschen nt; vi (dog) knurren; (engine) brummen, dröhnen.

snatch [snætʃ] n (grab) Schnappen

nt; (small amount) Bruchteil m; vt
schnappen, packen.

sneak [sni:k] vi schleichen.

sneakers ['sni:kəz] npl (US)
Freizeitschuhe pl.

sneer [snɪə*] n Hohnlächeln nt; vi
höhnisch grinsen; spötteln.

sneeze [sni:z] n Niesen nt; .vi
niesen.

snide [snaɪd] a (col: sarcastic)
schneidend.

sniff [snɪf] n Schnüffeln nt; vi
schnieben; (smell) schnüffeln; vt
schnuppern.

snigger ['snɪgə*] n Kichern nt; vi
hämisch kichern.

snip [snɪp] n Schnippel m,
Schnipsel m; vt schnippeln.

sniper ['snaɪpə*] n Heckenschütze
m.

snippet ['snɪpɪt] n Schnipsel m; (of
conversation) Fetzen m.

snivelling ['snɪvlɪŋ] a weinerlich.

snob [snɒb] n Snob m; —bery
Snobismus m; —ish a versnobt; —
bishness Versnobtheit f,
Snobismus m.

snooker ['snu:kə*] n Snooker nt.

snoop [snu:p] vi: — about herum-
schnüffeln.

snooty ['snu:tɪ] a (col) hochnäsig;
restaurant stinkfein.

snooze [snu:z] n Nickerchen nt; vi
ein Nickerchen machen, dösen.

snore [snɔ:*] vi schnarchen.

snoring ['snɔ:rɪŋ] n Schnarchen nt.

snorkel ['snɔ:kl] n Schnorchel m.

snort [snɔ:t] n Schnauben nt; vi
schnauben.

snotty ['snɒtɪ] a (col) rotzig.

snout [snaʊt] n Schnauze f; (of
pig) Rüssel m.

snow [snəʊ] n Schnee m; vi
schneien; —ball Schneeball m; —

blind a schneeblind; —bound a
eingeschneit; —drift Schneewehe
f; —drop Schneeglöckchen nt;
—fall Schneefall m; —flake
Schneeflocke f; —line Schnee-
grenze f; —man Schneemann m;
—plough, —plow Schneepflug
m; —storm Schneesturm m.

snub [snʌb] vt schroff abfertigen;
n Verweis m, schroffe Abfertigung
f; a —nosed stupsnasig.

snuff [snʌf] n Schnupftabak m;
—box Schnupftabakdose f.

snug [snʌg] a gemütlich, behaglich.

so [səʊ] ad so; cj daher, folglich,
also; — as to um zu; or — so
etwa; — long! (goodbye) tschüs!;
— many so viele; — much soviel;
— that damit.

soak [səʊk] vt durchnässen; (leave
in liquid) einweichen; n vi einsickern in (+acc); —ing Einweichen nt; —ing wet a klatschnaß.

soap [səʊp] n Seife f; —flakes pl
Seifenflocken pl; —powder Wasch-
pulver nt; —y a seifig, Seifen-.

soar [sɔ:*] vi aufsteigen; (prices) in
die Höhe schnellen.

sob [sɒb] n Schluchzen nt; vi
schluchzen.

sober ['səʊbə*] a (lit, fig) nüchtern;
— up vi nüchtern werden; —ly ad
nüchtern.

so-called ['səʊ'kɔ:ld] a sogenannt.

soccer ['sɒkə*] n Fußball m.

sociability [səʊʃə'bɪlɪtɪ] n
Umgänglichkeit f.

sociable ['səʊʃəbl] a umgänglich,
gesellig.

social ['səʊʃəl] a sozial; (friendly,
living with others) gesellig; —ism
Sozialismus m; —ist Sozialist(in f)
m; a sozialistisch; —ly ad gesell-
schaftlich, privat; — science Sozial-
wissenschaft f; — security Sozial-

versicherung f; — welfare Fürsorge f; — work Sozialarbeit f; — worker Sozialarbeiter(in f) m.

society [sə'saɪətɪ] n Gesellschaft f; (fashionable world) die große Welt.

sociological [səʊsɪə'lɒdʒɪkəl] a soziologisch.

sociologist [səʊsɪ'ɒlədʒɪst] n Soziologe m, Soziologin f.

sociology [səʊsɪ'ɒlədʒɪ] n Soziologie f.

sock [sɒk] n Socke f; vt (col) schlagen.

socket ['sɒkɪt] n (Elec) Steckdose f; (of eye) Augenhöhle f; (Tech) Rohransatz m.

sod [sɒd] n Rasenstück nt; (col) Saukerl m.

soda ['səʊdə] n Soda f; — water Mineralwasser nt, Soda(wasser) nt.

sodden ['sɒdn] a durchweicht.

sofa ['səʊfə] n Sofa nt.

soft [sɒft] a weich; (not loud) leise, gedämpft; (kind) weichherzig, gutmütig; (weak) weich, nachgiebig; — drink alkoholfreie(s) Getränk nt; — en ['sɒfn] vt weich machen; blow. abschwächen, mildern; vi weich werden; — hearted a weichherzig; —ly ad sanft; leise; —ness Weichheit f; (fig) Sanftheit f.

soggy ['sɒgɪ] a ground sumpfig; bread aufgeweicht.

soil [sɔɪl] n Erde f, Boden m; vt beschmutzen; —ed a beschmutzt, schmutzig.

solace ['sɒlɪs] n Trost m.

solar ['səʊlə*] a Sonnen-; — system Sonnensystem nt.

solder ['səʊldə*] vt löten; n Lötmetall nt.

soldier ['səʊldʒə*] n Soldat m.

sole [səʊl] n Sohle f; (fish) Seezunge f; vt besohlen; a alleinig, Allein-; —ly ad ausschließlich, nur.

solemn ['sɒləm] a feierlich; (serious) feierlich, ernst.

solicitor [sə'lɪsɪtə*] n Rechtsanwalt m.

solid ['sɒlɪd] a (hard) fest; (of same material) rein, massiv; (not hollow) massiv, stabil; (without break) voll, ganz; (reliable) solide, zuverlässig; (sensible) solide, gut; (united) eins, einig; meal kräftig; n Feste(s) nt; —arity [sɒlɪ'dærɪtɪ] Solidarität f, Zusammenhalt m; —figure (Math) Körper m; —ify [sə'lɪdɪfaɪ] vi fest werden, sich verdichten, erstarren; vt fest machen, verdichten; —ity [sə'lɪdɪtɪ] Festigkeit f; —ly ad (fig) behind einmütig; work ununterbrochen.

soliloquy [sə'lɪləkwɪ] n Monolog m.

solitaire [sɒlɪ'teə*] n (Cards) Patience f; (gem) Solitär m.

solitary ['sɒlɪtərɪ] a einsam, einzeln, solitude ['sɒlɪtjuːd] n Einsamkeit f.

solo ['səʊləʊ] n Solo nt; —ist Soloist(in f) m.

solstice ['sɒlstɪs] n Sonnenwende f.

soluble ['sɒljʊbl] a substance löslich; problem (auf)lösbar.

solution [sə'luːʃən] n (lit, fig) Lösung f; (of mystery) Erklärung f.

solve [sɒlv] vt (auf)lösen.

solvent ['sɒlvənt] a (Fin) zahlungsfähig.

sombre, (US) **somber** a, —ly ad ['sɒmbə*, -əlɪ] düster.

some [sʌm] a people etc einige; water etc etwas; (unspecified) (irgend)ein; (remarkable) toll, enorm; that's — house das ist vielleicht ein Haus; pron (amount) etwas; (number) einige; —body *pron* (irgend) jemand ; he is —body er ist jemand *or* wer ; —day *ad* irgendwann ; —how *ad* (*in a certain way*) irgendwie ; (*for a certain reason*) aus irgendeinem Grunde ; —one *pron* = somebody ; —place *ad* (*US*) = somewhere.

somersault ['sʌməsɔːlt] *n* Purzelbaum *m* ; Salto *m* ; *vi* Purzelbäume schlagen ; einen Salto machen.

something ['sʌmθɪŋ] *pron* (irgend) etwas.

sometime ['sʌmtaɪm] *ad* (irgend) einmal ; —s *ad* manchmal, gelegentlich.

somewhat ['sʌmwɒt] *ad* etwas, ein wenig, ein bißchen.

somewhere ['sʌmwɛə*] *ad* irgendwo ; (*to a place*) irgendwohin.

son [sʌn] *n* Sohn *m*.

sonata [sə'nɑːtə] *n* Sonate *f*.

song [sɒŋ] *n* Lied *nt*; —writer Texter *m*.

sonic ['sɒnɪk] *a* Schall- ; — boom Überschallknall *m*.

son-in-law ['sʌnɪnlɔː] *n* Schwiegersohn *m*.

sonnet ['sɒnɪt] *n* Sonett *nt*.

sonny ['sʌnɪ] *n* (col) Kleine(r) *m*.

soon [suːn] *ad* bald ; too — zu früh ; as — as possible so bald wie möglich ; —er *ad* (*time*) eher, früher ; (*for preference*) lieber ; no —er kaum.

soot [sut] *n* Ruß *m*.

soothe [suːð] *vt person* beruhigen ; *pain* lindern.

soothing ['suːðɪŋ] *a* (*for person*) beruhigend ; (*for pain*) lindernd.

sop [sɒp] *n* (*bribe*) Schmiergeld *nt*.

sophisticated [sə'fɪstɪkeɪtɪd] *a person* kultiviert, weltgewandt ; *machinery* differenziert, hochentwickelt ; *plan* ausgeklügelt.

sophistication [səfɪstɪ'keɪʃən] *n* Weltgewandtheit *f*, Kultiviertheit *f* ; (*Tech*) technische Verfeinerung *f*.

sophomore ['sɒfəmɔː*] *n* (*US*) College-Student *m im* 2. Jahr.

soporific [sɒpə'rɪfɪk] *a* einschläfernd, Schlaf-.

sopping ['sɒpɪŋ] *a* (*very wet*) patschnaß, triefend.

soppy ['sɒpɪ] *a* (col) schmalzig.

soprano [sə'prɑːnəʊ] *n* Sopran *m*.

sordid ['sɔːdɪd] *a* (*dirty*) schmutzig ; (*mean*) niederträchtig.

sore [sɔː*] *a* schmerzend ; *point* wund ; to be — weh tun ; (*angry*) böse sein ; *n* Wunde *f* ; —ly *ad* tempted stark, sehr ; —ness Schmerzhaftigkeit *f*, Empfindlichkeit *f*.

sorrow ['sɒrəʊ] *n* Kummer *m*, Leid *nt* ; —ful *a* sorgenvoll ; —fully *ad* traurig, betrübt, kummervoll.

sorry ['sɒrɪ] *a* traurig, erbärmlich ; (I'm) — es tut mir leid ; I feel — for him er tut mir leid.

sort [sɔːt] *n* Art *f*, Sorte *f* ; *vt* (*also* — out) papers sortieren, sichten ; *problems* in Ordnung bringen.

so-so ['səʊ'səʊ] *ad* so(-so) la-la, mäßig.

soufflé ['suːfleɪ] *n* Auflauf *m*, Soufflé *nt*.

soul [səʊl] *n* Seele *f* ; (*music*) Soul *m* ; —destroying a trostlos ; —ful *a* seelenvoll ; —less *a* seelenlos, gefühllos.

sound [saʊnd] *a* (*healthy*) gesund ; (*safe*) sicher, solide ; (*sensible*) vernünftig ; *theory* stichhaltig ; (*thorough*) tüchtig, gehörig ; (*noise*) Geräusch *nt*, Laut *m* ; (*Geog*) Meerenge *f*, Sund *m* ; *vt* erschallen lassen ; *alarm* (Alarm) schlagen ; (*Med*) abhorchen ; to — one's horn hupen ; *vi* (*make a* *sound*) schallen, tönen; (*seem*) klingen; — out *vt* *opinion* erforschen; *person* auf den Zahn fühlen (+*dat*); — barrier Schallmauer *f*; —ing (*Naut etc*) Lotung *f*; —ly *ad* sleep fest, tief; *beat* tüchtig; —proof a room schalldicht; *vt* schalldicht machen; —track Tonstreifen *m*; Filmmusik *f*.

soup [su:p] *n* Suppe *f*; in the — (*col*) in der Tinte; —spoon Suppenlöffel *m*.

sour [sauə*] *a* (*lit*, *fig*) sauer.

source [sɔ:s] *n* (*lit*, *fig*) Quelle *f*.

sourness [ˈsauənəs] *n* Säure *f*; (*fig*) Bitterkeit *f*.

south [sauθ] *n* Süden *m*; a Süd-, südlich; *ad* nach Süden, südwärts; —east Südosten *m*; · —erly [ˈsʌðəlɪ] a südlich; —ern [ˈsʌðən] a südlich, Süd-; —ward(s) *ad* südwärts, nach Süden; —west Südwesten *m*.

souvenir [su:vəˈnɪə*] *n* Andenken *nt*, Souvenir *nt*.

sovereign [ˈsɒvrɪn] *n* (*ruler*) Herrscher *m*; a (*independent*) souverän; —ty Oberhoheit *f*, Souveränität *f*.

sow [sau] *n* Sau *f*; [səu] *vt irreg* (*lit*, *fig*) säen.

soya bean [ˈsɔɪəˈbi:n] *n* Sojabohne *f*.

spa [spa:] *n* (*spring*) Mineralquelle *f*; (*place*) Kurort *m*, Bad *nt*.

space [speɪs] *n* Platz *m*, Raum *m*; (*universe*) Weltraum *m*, All *nt*; (*length of time*) Abstand *m*; — out *vt* Platz lassen zwischen; (*typing*) gesperrt schreiben; —craft Raumschiff *nt*; —man Raumfahrer *m*.

spacious [ˈspeɪʃəs] *a* geräumig, weit.

spade [speɪd] *n* Spaten *m*; —s

(*Cards*) Pik *nt*, Schippe *f*; —work (*fig*) Vorarbeit *f*.

spaghetti [spəˈgetɪ] *n* Spaghetti *pl*.

span [spæn] *n* Spanne *f*; Spannweite *f*; *vt* überspannen.

spaniel [ˈspænjəl] *n* Spaniel *m*.

spank [spæŋk] *vt* verhauen, versohlen.

spanner [ˈspænə*] *n* Schraubenschlüssel *m*.

spar [spa:*] *n* (*Naut*) Sparren *m*; *vi* (*boxing*) einen Sparring machen.

spare [speə*] *a* Ersatz-; *n* — part; *vt* *lives*, *feelings* verschonen; *trouble* ersparen; 4 to — 4 übrig; — part Ersatzteil *nt*; — time Freizeit *f*.

spark [spa:k] *n* Funken *m*; —(ing) plug Zündkerze *f*.

sparkle [ˈspa:kl] *n* Funkeln *nt*, Glitzern *nt*; (*gaiety*) Lebhaftigkeit *f*, Schwung *m*; *vi* funkeln, glitzern.

sparkling [ˈspa:klɪŋ] *a* funkelnd, sprühend; *wine* Schaum-; *conversation* spritzig, geistreich.

sparrow [ˈspærəu] *n* Spatz *m*.

sparse a, —ly *ad* [spa:s, -lɪ] spärlich, dünn.

spasm [ˈspæzəm] *n* (*Med*) Krampf *m*; (*fig*) Anfall *m*; —odic [spæzˈmɒdɪk] a krampfartig, spasmodisch; (*fig*) sprunghaft.

spastic [ˈspæstɪk] *a* spastisch.

spate [speɪt] *n* (*fig*) Flut *f*, Schwall *m*; in — *river* angeschwollen.

spatter [ˈspætə*] *n* Spritzer *m*; *vt* bespritzen, verspritzen; *vi* spritzen.

spatula [ˈspætjulə] *n* Spatel *m*; (*for building*) Spachtel *f*.

spawn [spɔ:n] *vt* laichen.

speak [spi:k] *irreg vt* sprechen, reden; *truth* sagen; *vi* sprechen (*to* mit *or* zu); — for *vt* sprechen *or* eintreten für; — up *vi* lauter sprechen; —er Sprecher *m*, Redner *m*; loud— Lautsprecher *m*; not to be on —ing terms nicht miteinander sprechen.

spear [spiə*] *n* Speer *m*, Lanze *f*, Spieß *m*; *vt* aufspießen, durchbohren.

spec [spek] *n* (*col*) on — auf gut Glück.

special ['speʃəl] *a* besondere(r,s); speziell; *n* (*Rail*) Sonderzug *m*; —ist Spezialist *m*; (*Tech*) Fachmann *m*; (*Med*) Facharzt *m*; —ity [speʃi'ælɪtɪ] Spezialität *f*; (*study*) Spezialgebiet *nt*; —ize *vi* sich spezialisieren (*in* auf +*acc*); —ly *ad* besonders; (*explicitly*) extra, *ausdrücklich.

species ['spi:ʃi:z] *n* Art *f*.

specific [spə'sɪfɪk] *a* spezifisch, eigentümlich, besondere(r,s); —ally *ad* genau, spezifisch; —ations *pl* [spesɪfɪ'keɪʃənz] genaue Angaben *pl*; (*Tech*) technische Daten *pl*.

specify ['spesɪfaɪ] *vt* genau angeben.

specimen ['spesɪmɪn] *n* Probe *f*, Muster *nt*.

speck [spek] *n* Fleckchen *nt*; —led *a* gesprenkelt.

specs [speks] *npl* (*col*) Brille *f*.

spectacle ['spektəkl] *n* Schauspiel *nt*; —s *pl* Brille *f*.

spectacular [spek'tækjulə*] *a* aufsehenerregend, spektakulär.

spectator [spek'teɪtə*] *n* Zuschauer *m*.

spectre, (*US*) **specter** ['spektə*] *n* Geist *m*, Gespenst *nt*.

spectrum ['spektrəm] *n* Spektrum *nt*.

speculate ['spekjulət] *vi* vermuten, spekulieren (*also* Fin).

speculation [spekju'leɪʃən] *n* Vermutung *f*, Spekulation *f* (*also* Fin).

speculative ['spekjulətɪv] *a* spekulativ.

speech [spi:tʃ] *n* Sprache *f*; (*address*) Rede *f*, Ansprache *f*; (*manner of speaking*) Sprechweise *f*; — day (*Sch*) (Jahres)schlußfeier *f*; —less *a* sprachlos; — therapy Sprachheilpflege *f*.

speed [spi:d] *n* Geschwindigkeit *f*; (*gear*) Gang *m*; *vi irreg* rasen; (*Jur*) (zu) schnell fahren; — up *vt* beschleunigen; *vi* schneller werden/ fahren; —boat Schnellboot *nt*; —ily *ad* schnell, schleunigst; —ing zu schnelles Fahren; — limit Geschwindigkeitsbegrenzung *f*; —ometer [spɪ'dɒmɪtə*] Tachometer *m*; —way (*bike racing*) Motorradrennstrecke *f*; —y *a* schnell, zügig.

spell [spel] *n* (*magic*) Bann *m*, Zauber *m*; (*period of time*) Zeit *f*, Zeitlang *f*, Weile *f*; sunny —s *pl* Aufheiterungen *pl*; rainy —s *pl* vereinzelte Schauer *pl*; *vt irreg* buchstabieren; (*imply*) bedeuten; how do you — ...? wie schreibt man ...?; —bound *a* (wie) gebannt; —ing Buchstabieren *nt*; English —ing die englische Rechtschreibung.

spend [spend] *vt irreg* money ausgeben; *time* verbringen; —ing money Taschengeld *nt*.

spent [spent] *a* patience erschöpft.

sperm [spɜ:m] *n* (*Biol*) Samenflüssigkeit *f*.

spew [spju:] *vt* (er)brechen.

sphere [sfɪə*] *n* (*globe*) Kugel *f*; (*fig*) Sphäre *f*, Gebiet *nt*.

spherical ['sferɪkəl] *a* kugelförmig.

sphinx [sfıŋks] *n* Sphinx *f*.

spice [spaıs] *n* Gewürz *nt*; *vt* würzen.

spiciness ['spaısmıs] *n* Würze *f*.

spick-and-span ['spıkən'spæn] *a* blitzblank.

spicy ['spaısı] *a* würzig, pikant (*also fig*).

spider ['spaıdə*] *n* Spinne *f*; **—y** *a writing* krakelig.

spike [spaık] *n* Dorn *m*, Spitze *f*; **—s** *pl* Spikes *pl*.

spill [spıl] *irreg vt* verschütten; *vi* sich ergießen.

spin [spın] *n* Umdrehung *f*; (*trip in car*) Spazierfahrt *f*; (*Aviat*) (Ab)trudeln *nt*; (*on ball*) Drall *m*; *irreg vt thread* spinnen; (*like top*) schnell drehen, (herum)wirbeln; *vi* sich drehen; **— out** *vt* in die Länge ziehen; *story* ausmalen.

spinach ['spınıtʃ] *n* Spinat *m*.

spinal ['spaınl] *a* spinal, Rückgrat-, Rückenmark-; **— cord** Rückenmark *nt*.

spindly ['spındlı] *a* spindeldürr.

spin-drier ['spın'draıə*] *n* Wäscheschleuder *f*.

spin-dry ['spın'draı] *vt* schleudern.

spine [spaın] *n* Rückgrat *nt*; (*thorn*) Stachel *m*; **—less** *a* (*lit, fig*) rückgratlos.

spinet [spı'nɛt] *n* Spinett *nt*.

spinner ['spınə*] *n* (*of thread*) Spinner *m*.

spinning ['spınıŋ] *n* (*of thread*) (Faden)spinnen *nt*; **— wheel** Spinnrad *nt*.

spinster ['spınstə*] *n* unverheiratete Frau *f*; (*pej*) alte Jungfer *f*.

spiral ['spaıərəl] *n* Spirale *f*; *a* gewunden, spiralförmig, Spiral-; *vi*

sich ringeln; **— staircase** Wendeltreppe *f*.

spire ['spaıə*] *n* Turm *m*.

spirit ['spırıt] *n* Geist *m*; (*humour, mood*) Stimmung *f*; (*courage*) Mut *m*; (*verve*) Elan *m*; (*alcohol*) Alkohol *m*; **—s** *pl* Spirituosen *pl*; **in good —s** gut aufgelegt; **—ed** *a* beherzt; **— level** Wasserwaage *f*; **—ual** *a* geistig, seelisch; (*Rel*) geistlich; *n* Spiritual *nt*; **—ualism** Spiritismus *m*.

spit [spıt] *n* (*for roasting*) (Brat)spieß *m*; (*saliva*) Spucke *f*; *vi irreg* spucken; (*rain*) sprühen; (*make a sound*) zischen; (*cat*) fauchen.

spite [spaıt] *n* Gehässigkeit *f*; *vt* ärgern, kränken; **in — of** trotz (+*gen or dat*); **—ful** *a* gehässig.

splash [splæʃ] *n* Spritzer *m*; (*of colour*) (Farb)fleck *m*; *vt* bespritzen; *vi* spritzen; **—down** Wasserlandung *f*.

spleen [spli:n] *n* (*Anat*) Milz *f*.

splendid *a*, **—ly** *ad* ['splɛndıd, -lı] glänzend, großartig.

splendour, (*US*) **splendor** ['splɛndə*] *n* Pracht *f*.

splice [splaıs] *vt* spleißen.

splint [splınt] *n* Schiene *f*.

splinter ['splıntə*] *n* Splitter *m*; *vi* (zer)splittern.

split [splıt] *n* Spalte *f*; (*fig*) Spaltung *f*; (*division*) Trennung *f*; *irreg vt* spalten; *vi* (*divide*) reißen; **sich spalten**; (*col: depart*) abhauen; **— up** *vi* sich trennen; *vt* aufteilen, teilen; **—ting** *a headache* rasend, wahnsinnig.

splutter ['splʌtə*] *vi* spritzen; (*person, engine*) stottern.

spoil [spɔıl] *irreg vt* (*ruin*) verderben; (*child* verwöhnen, verziehen; *vi* (*food*) verderben; **—s** *pl* Beute *f*; **—sport** Spielverderber *m*.

spoke [spəʊk] n Speiche f; —sman Sprecher m, Vertreter m.

sponge [spʌndʒ] n Schwamm m; vt mit dem Schwamm abwaschen; vi auf Kosten leben (on gen); —bag Kulturbeutel m; —cake Rührkuchen m; —r (col) Schmarotzer m.

spongy ['spʌndʒɪ] a schwammig.

sponsor ['spɒnsə*] n Bürge m; (in advertising) Sponsor m; vt bürgen für; fördern; —ship Bürgschaft f; (public) Schirmherrschaft f.

spontaneity [spɒntə'neɪtɪ] n Spontanität f.

spontaneous a, —ly ad [spɒn'teɪnɪəs, -lɪ] spontan.

spooky ['spuːkɪ] a (col) gespenstisch.

spool [spuːl] n Spule f, Rolle f.

spoon [spuːn] n Löffel m; —feed vt irreg (lit) mit dem Löffel füttern; (fig) hochpäppeln; —ful Löffel(voll) m.

sporadic [spə'rædɪk] a vereinzelt, sporadisch.

sport [spɔːt] n Sport m; (fun) Spaß m; (person) feine(r) Kerl m; —ing a (fair) sportlich, fair; —s car Sportwagen m; —(s) coat, —(s) jacket Sportjackett nt; —sman Sportler m; (fig) anständige(r) Kerl m; —smanship Sportlichkeit f; (fig) Anständigkeit f; —s page Sportseite f; —swear Sportkleidung f; —swoman Sportlerin f; —y a sportlich.

spot [spɒt] n Punkt m; (dirty) Fleck(en) m; (place) Stelle f, Platz m; (Med) Pickel m, Pustel f; (small amount) Schluck m, Tropfen m; vt erspähen; mistake bemerken; —check Stichprobe f; —less a, —ly ad fleckenlos; —light Scheinwerferlicht nt; (lamp) Scheinwerfer m;

—ted a gefleckt; dress gepunktet; —ty a face pickelig.

spouse [spauz] n Gatte m/Gattin f.

spout [spaut] n (of pot) Tülle f; (jet) Wasserstrahl m; vi speien, spritzen.

sprain [spreɪn] n Verrenkung f; vt verrenken.

sprawl [sprɔːl] n (of city) Ausbreitung f; vi sich strecken.

spray [spreɪ] n Spray nt; (of sea) Gischt f; (instrument) Zerstäuber m; Spraydose f; (of flowers) Zweig m; vt besprühen, sprayen.

spread [spred] n (extent) Verbreitung f; (of wings) Spannweite f; (col: meal) Schmaus m; (for bread) Aufstrich m; vt irreg ausbreiten; (scatter) verbreiten; butter streichen.

spree [spriː] n lustige(r) Abend m; (shopping) Einkaufsbummel m; to go out on a — einen draufmachen.

sprig [sprɪg] n kleine(r) Zweig m.

sprightly ['spraɪtlɪ] a munter, lebhaft.

spring [sprɪŋ] n (leap) Sprung m; (metal) Feder f; (season) Frühling m; (water) Quelle f; vi irreg (leap) springen; — up vi (problem) entstehen, auftauchen; —board Sprungbrett nt; —clean vt Frühjahrsputz machen in (+dat); —cleaning Frühjahrsputz m; —iness Elastizität f; —time Frühling m; —y a federnd, elastisch.

sprinkle ['sprɪŋkl] n Prise f; vt salt streuen; liquid spritzen.

sprinkling ['sprɪŋklɪŋ] n Spur f, ein bißchen.

sprint [sprɪnt] n Kurzstreckenlauf m; Sprint m; vi sprinten; —er Sprinter m, Kurzstreckenläufer m.

sprite [spraɪt] n Elfe f; Kobold m.

sprout [spraʊt] vi sprießen; n see Brussels —.

spruce [spru:s] n Fichte f; a schmuck, adrett.

spry [spraɪ] a flink, rege.

spud [spʌd] n (col) Kartoffel f.

spur [spɜ:*] n Sporn m; (fig) Ansporn m; vt (also — on) (fig) anspornen; **on the — of the moment** spontan.

spurious ['spjʊərɪəs] a falsch, unecht, Pseudo-.

spurn [spɜ:n] vt verschmähen.

spurt [spɜ:t] n (jet) Strahl m; (acceleration) Spurt m; vt spritzen; vi (jet) steigen; (liquid) schießen; (run) spurten.

spy [spaɪ] n Spion m; vt spionieren; vt erspähen; **to — on sb** jdm nachspionieren; —ing Spionage f.

squabble ['skwɒbl] n Zank m; vi sich zanken.

squabbling ['skwɒblɪŋ] n Zankerei f.

squad [skwɒd] n (Mil) Abteilung f; (police) Kommando nt.

squadron ['skwɒdrən] n (cavalry) Schwadron f; (Naut) Geschwader nt; (air force) Staffel f.

squalid ['skwɒlɪd] a schmutzig, verkommen.

squall [skwɔ:l] n Bö f, Windstoß m; —y a, **weather** stürmisch; **wind** böig.

squalor ['skwɒlə*] n Verwahrlosung f, Schmutz m.

squander ['skwɒndə*] vt verschwenden.

square [skwɛə*] n (Math) Quadrat nt; (open space) Platz m; (instrument) Winkel m; (col: person) Spießer m; a viereckig, quad-

ratisch; (fair) ehrlich, reell; (meal) reichlich; (col) ideas, tastes spießig; ad (exactly) direkt, gerade; vt (arrange) ausmachen, aushandeln; (Math) ins Quadrat erheben; (bribe) schmieren; vi (agree) übereinstimmen; all — quitt; **2 metres — 2 Meter im** Quadrat; **2 — metres** 2 Quadratmeter; —ly ad fest, gerade.

squash [skwɒʃ] n (drink) Saft m; vt zerquetschen.

squat [skwɒt] a untersetzt, gedrungen; vi hocken; —ter Squatter m, Siedler m ohne Rechtstitel; Hausbesetzer m.

squaw [skwɔ:] n Squaw f.

squawk [skwɔ:k] n Kreischen nt; vi kreischen.

squeak [skwi:k] n Gequiek(s)e nt; vi quiek(s)en; (spring, door etc) quietschen; —y a quiek(s)end; quietschend.

squeal [skwi:l] n schrille(r) Schrei m; (of brakes etc) Quietschen nt; vi schrill schreien.

squeamish ['skwi:mɪʃ] a empfindlich; **that made me —** davon wurde mir übel; —ness f Überempfindlichkeit f.

squeeze [skwi:z] n (lit) Pressen nt; (Pol) Geldknappheit f, wirtschaftl. liche(r) Engpaß m; vt pressen, drücken; orange auspressen; — **out** vt ausquetschen.

squid [skwɪd] n Tintenfisch m.

squint [skwɪnt] n Schielen nt; vi schielen.

squire ['skwaɪə*] n Gutsherr m.

squirm [skwɜ:m] vi sich winden.

squirrel ['skwɪrəl] n Eichhörnchen nt.

squirt [skwɜ:t] n Spritzer m, Strahl m; vti spritzen.

stab [stæb] n (blow) Stoß m, Stich m; (col: try) Versuch m; vt erstechen; —bing Messerstecherei f.

stability [stə'bɪlɪtɪ] n Festigkeit f, Stabilität f.

stabilization [steɪbəlaɪ'zeɪʃən] n Festigung f, Stabilisierung f.

stabilize ['steɪbəlaɪz] vt festigen, stabilisieren; —r Stabilisator m.

stable ['steɪbl] n Stall m; vt im Stall unterbringen; a fest, stabil; person gefestigt.

staccato [stə'kɑːtəʊ] a stakkato.

stack [stæk] n Stoß m, Stapel m; vt (auf)stapeln.

stadium ['steɪdɪəm] n Stadion nt.

staff [stɑːf] n (stick, Mil) Stab m; (personnel) Personal nt; (Sch) Lehrkräfte pl; vt (with people) besetzen.

stag [stæg] n Hirsch m.

stage [steɪdʒ] n Bühne f; (of journey) Etappe f; (degree) Stufe f; (point) Stadium nt; vt (put on) aufführen; play inszenieren; demonstration veranstalten; in —s etappenweise; —coach Postkutsche f; — door Bühneneingang m; — manager Spielleiter m, Intendant m.

stagger ['stægə*] vi wanken, taumeln; vt (amaze) verblüffen; hours staffeln; —ing a unglaublich.

stagnant ['stægnənt] a stagnierend; water stehend.

stagnate [stæg'neɪt] vi stagnieren.

stagnation [stæg'neɪʃən] n Stillstand m, Stagnation f.

staid [steɪd] a gesetzt.

stain [steɪn] n Fleck m; (colouring for wood) Beize f; vt beflecken, Flecken machen auf (+acc); beizen; —ed glass window buntes

Glasfenster nt; —less a steel rostfrei, nichtrostend; — remover Fleckentferner m.

stair [steə*] n (Treppen)stufe f; —case Treppenhaus nt, Treppe f; —s pl Treppe f; —way Treppenaufgang m.

stake [steɪk] n (post) Pfahl m, Pfosten m; (money) Einsatz m; vt (bet money) setzen; to be at — auf dem Spiel stehen.

stalactite ['stæləktaɪt] n Stalaktit m.

stalagmite ['stæləgmaɪt] n Stalagmit m.

stale [steɪl] a alt; beer schal; bread altbacken; —mate (chess) Patt nt; (fig) Stillstand m.

stalk [stɔːk] n Stengel m, Stiel m; vt game sich anpirschen an (+acc), jagen; vi (walk) stolzieren.

stall [stɔːl] n (in stable) Stand m, Box f; (in market) (Verkaufs)stand m; (Aut) (den Motor) abwürgen; vi (Aut) stehenbleiben; (avoid) Ausflüchte machen, ausweichen; —s pl (Theat) Parkett nt.

stallion ['stælɪən] n Zuchthengst m.

stalwart ['stɔːlwət] a standhaft; n treue(r) Anhänger m.

stamina ['stæmɪnə] n Durchhaltevermögen nt, Zähigkeit f.

stammer ['stæmə*] n Stottern nt; vti stottern, stammeln.

stamp [stæmp] n Briefmarke f; (with foot) Stampfen nt; (for document) Stempel m; vt stampfen; vt (mark) stempeln; mail frankieren; foot stampfen mit; — album Briefmarkenalbum nt; — collecting Briefmarkensammeln nt.

stampede [stæm'piːd] n panische Flucht f.

stance [stæns] n (posture) Haltung

f, Stellung f; (opinion) Einstellung
f.

stand [stænd] n Standort m, Platz
m; (for objects) Gestell nt; (seats)
Tribüne f; to make a — Widerstand
leisten; irreg vi stehen; (rise) aufstehen; (decision) feststehen; to —
still still stehen; vt setzen, stellen;
(endure) aushalten; person ausstehen, leiden können; nonsense
dulden; it —s to reason es ist einleuchtend; — by vi (be ready)
bereitstehen; vt obligation treu
bleiben (+dat); — for vt (signify)
stehen für; (permit, tolerate)
hinnehmen; — in for vt einspringen für; — out vi (be
prominent) hervorstehen; — up vi
(rise) aufstehen; — up for vt sich
einsetzen für.

standard ['stændəd] n (measure)
Standard m, Norm f; (flag)
Standarte f, Fahne f; a size etc
Normal-, Durchschnitts-; —ization
Vereinheitlichung f; —ize vt verein-
heitlichen, normen; — lamp
Stehlampe f; — of living Lebens-
standard m; — time Ortszeit f.

stand-by ['stændbai] n Reserve f;
— flight Standby-Flug m.

stand-in ['stændin] n Ersatz(mann)
m, Hilfskraft f.

standing ['stændiŋ] a (erect)
stehend; (permanent) ständig,
dauernd; invitation offen; n
(duration) Dauer f; (reputation)
Ansehen nt; — jump Sprung m aus
dem Stand; — order (at bank)
Dauerauftrag m; — orders pl (Mil)
Vorschrift; — room only nur
Stehplatz.

stand-offish ['stænd'ɒfiʃ] a
zurückhaltend, sehr reserviert.

standpoint ['stændpɔint] n Standpunkt m.

standstill ['stændstil] n: to be at
a — stillstehen; to come to a —
zum Stillstand kommen.

stanza ['stænzə] n (verse) Strophe
f; (poem) Stanze f.

staple ['steipl] n (clip) Krampe f;
(in paper) Heftklammer f; (article)
Haupterzeugnis nt; a Grund-;
Haupt-; vt (fest)klammern; —r
Heftmaschine f.

star [stɑ:*] n Stern m; (person)
Star m; vi die Hauptrolle spielen;
vt actor in der Hauptrolle zeigen.

starboard ['stɑ:bəd] n Steuerbord
nt; a Steuerbord-.

starch [stɑ:tʃ] n Stärke f; vt
stärken; —y a stärkehaltig;
(formal) steif.

stardom ['stɑ:dəm] n Berühmtheit
f.

stare [stɛə*] n starre(r) Blick m;
vi starren (at auf +acc); — at vt
anstarren.

starfish ['stɑ:fiʃ] n Seestern m.

staring ['stɛəriŋ] a eyes starrend.

stark [stɑ:k] a öde; ad: — naked
splitternackt.

starless ['stɑ:ləs] a sternlos.

starlight ['stɑ:lait] n Sternenlicht nt.

starling ['stɑ:liŋ] n Star m.

starlit ['stɑ:lit] a sternklar.

starring ['stɑ:riŋ] a mit ... in der
Hauptrolle.

star-studded ['stɑ:stʌdid] a mit
Spitzenstars.

starry ['stɑ:ri] a Sternen-; —eyed
a (innocent) blauäugig.

start [stɑ:t] n Beginn m, Anfang m,
Start m; (Sport) Start m; (lead)
Vorsprung m; to give a —
zusammenfahren; to give sb a —
jdn zusammenfahren lassen; vt in
Gang setzen, anfangen; car
anlassen; vi anfangen; (car)

anspringen; (on journey) aufbrechen; (Sport) starten; — over vi (US) wieder anfangen; — up vi anfangen; (startled) auffahren; vt beginnen; car anlassen; engine starten; —er (Aut) Anlasser m; (for race) Starter m; —ing handle Anlaßkurbel f; —ing point Ausgangspunkt m.

startle ['stɑːtl] vt erschrecken.
startling ['stɑːtlɪŋ] a erschreckend.
starvation [stɑːˈveɪʃən] n Verhungern nt; to die of — verhungern.
starve [stɑːv] vi verhungern; vt verhungern lassen; to be —d of affection unter Mangel an Liebe leiden; — out vt aushungern.
starving ['stɑːvɪŋ] a (ver)hungernd.
state [steɪt] n (condition) Zustand m; (Pol) Staat m; (col: anxiety) (schreckliche) Verfassung f; vt erklären; facts angeben; — control staatliche Kontrolle f; —d a festgesetzt; —liness Pracht f, Würde f; —ly a würdevoll, erhaben; —ment Aussage f; (Pol) Erklärung f; — secret Staatsgeheimnis nt; —sman Staatsmann m.
static ['stætɪk] n Statik f; a statisch.
station ['steɪʃən] n (Rail etc) Bahnhof m; (police etc) Station f, Wache f; (in society) gesellschaftliche Stellung f; vt aufstellen; to be —ed stationiert sein.
stationary ['steɪʃənrɪ] a stillstehend; car parkend.
stationer ['steɪʃənə*] n Schreibwarenhändler m; —'s (shop) Schreibwarengeschäft nt; —y Schreibwaren pl.
station master ['steɪʃənmɑːstə*] n Bahnhofsvorsteher m.
station wagon ['steɪʃənwægən] n Kombiwagen m.

statistic [stəˈtɪstɪk] n Statistik f; —al a statistisch; —s pl Statistik f.
statue ['stætjuː] n Statue f.
statuesque [stætjuˈesk] a statuenhaft.
stature ['stætʃə*] n Wuchs m, Statur f; (fig) Größe f.
status ['steɪtəs] n Stellung f, Status m; the — quo der Status quo; — symbol Statussymbol nt.
statute ['stætjuːt] n Gesetz nt.
statutory ['stætjʊtərɪ] a gesetzlich.
staunch a, —ly ad [stɔːntʃ, -lɪ] treu, zuverlässig; Catholic standhaft, erz-.
stave [steɪv]: — off vt attack abwehren; threat abwenden.
stay [steɪ] n Aufenthalt m; (support) Stütze f; (for tent) Schnur f; vi bleiben; (reside) wohnen; to — put an Ort und Stelle bleiben; to — with friends bei Freunden untergebracht sein; to — the night übernachten; to — behind vi zurückbleiben; — in vi (at home) zu Hause bleiben; — on vi (continue) länger bleiben; — up vi (at night) aufbleiben.
steadfast ['stedfəst] a standhaft, treu.
steadily ['stedɪlɪ] ad stetig, regelmäßig.
steadiness ['stedɪnəs] n Festigkeit f; (fig) Beständigkeit f.
steady ['stedɪ] a (firm) fest, stabil; (regular) gleichmäßig; (reliable) zuverlässig, beständig; hand ruhig; job, boyfriend fest; vt festigen; to — o.s. sich stützen.
steak [steɪk] n Steak nt; (fish) Filet nt.
steal [stiːl] irreg vti stehlen; vi sich stehlen; —th [stelθ] Heimlichkeit

f; **—thy** ['stelθɪ] a verstohlen, heimlich.

steam [sti:m] n Dampf m; vt (Cook) im Dampfbad erhitzen; vi dampfen; (ship) dampfen, fahren; **— engine** Dampfmaschine f; **—er** Dampfer m; **—roller** Dampfwalze f; **—y** a dampfig.

steel [sti:l] n Stahl m; a Stahl-; (fig) stählern; **—works** Stahlwerke pl.

steep [sti:p] a steil; price gepfeffert; vt einweichen.

steeple ['sti:pl] n Kirchturm m; **—chase** Hindernisrennen nt; **—jack** Turmarbeiter m.

steeply ['sti:plɪ] ad steil.

steepness ['sti:pnəs] n Steilheit f.

steer [stɪə*] n Mastochse m; vt steuern; car etc lenken; **—ing** (Aut) Steuerung f; **—ing column** Lenksäule f; **—ing wheel** Steuer- or Lenkrad nt.

stellar ['stelə*] a Stern(en)-.

stem [stem] n (Biol) Stengel m, Stiel m; (of glass) Stiel m; vt aufhalten; **— from** vi abstammen von.

stench [stentʃ] n Gestank m.

stencil ['stensl] n Schablone f; (paper) Matrize f; vt (auf)drucken.

stenographer [ste'nɒɡrəfə*] n Stenograph(in f) m.

step [step] n Schritt m; (stair) Stufe f; **to take —s** Schritte unternehmen; vi treten, schreiten; **—s = —ladder**; **— down** vi (fig) abtreten; **— up** vt steigern; **—brother** Stiefbruder m; **—child** Stiefkind nt; **—father** Stiefvater m; **—ladder** Trittleiter f; **—mother** Stiefmutter f.

steppe [step] n Steppe f.

stepping stone ['stepɪŋstəun] Stein m; (fig) Sprungbrett nt.·

stereo ['steriəu] n Stereoanlage f; **—phonic** a stereophonisch; **—type** n Prototyp m; vt stereotypieren; (fig) stereotyp machen.

sterile ['sterail] a steril, keimfrei; person unfruchtbar; (after operation) steril.

sterility [ste'rɪlɪtɪ] n Unfruchtbarkeit f, Sterilität f.

sterilization [sterilai'zeɪʃən] n Sterilisation f.

sterilize ['sterilaiz] vt (make unproductive) unfruchtbar machen; (make germfree) sterilisieren, keimfrei machen.

sterling ['stɜ:lɪŋ] a (Fin) Sterling-; silver von Standardwert; character bewährt, gediegen; **£ —** Pfund Sterling; **— area** Sterlingblock m.

stern a, **—ly** ad [stɜ:n, -lɪ] streng; n Heck nt, Achterschiff nt; **—ness** Strenge f.

stethoscope ['steθəskəup] n Stethoskop nt, Hörrohr nt.

stevedore ['sti:vədɔ:*] n Schauermann m.

stew [stju:] n Eintopf m; vti schmoren.

steward ['stju:əd] n Steward m; (in club) Kellner m; (organizer) Verwalter m; **—ess** Stewardess f.

stick [stik] n Stock m, Stecken m; (of chalk etc) Stück nt; irreg vt (stab) stechen; (fix) stecken; (put) stellen; (gum) (an)kleben; (col: tolerate) vertragen; vi (stop) steckenbleiben; (get stuck) klemmen; (hold fast) kleben, haften; **— out** vi (project) hervorstehen aus; **— up** vi (project) in die Höhe stehen; **— up for** vt (defend) eintreten für; **—er** Klebezettel m, Aufkleber m.

stickleback ['stiklbæk] n Stichling m.

stickler ['stɪklə*] n Pedant m (for in + acc).

stick-up ['stɪkʌp] n (col) (Raub)- überfall m.

sticky ['stɪkɪ] a klebrig; atmosphere stickig.

stiff [stɪf] a steif; (difficult) schwierig, hart; paste dick, zäh; drink stark; —en vt versteifen, (ver)stärken; vi sich versteifen; —ness Steifheit f.

stifle ['staɪfl] vt yawn etc unter- drücken.

stifling ['staɪflɪŋ] a atmosphere drückend.

stigma ['stɪgmə] n (disgrace) Stigma nt.

stile [staɪl] n Steige f.

still [stɪl] a steif; ad (immer) noch; (anyhow) immerhin; —born a totgeboren; — life Stilleben nt; —ness Stille f.

stilt [stɪlt] n Stelze f.

stilted ['stɪltɪd] a gestelzt.

stimulant ['stɪmjʊlənt] n Anregungsmittel nt, Stimulans m.

stimulate ['stɪmjʊleɪt] vt anregen, stimulieren.

stimulating ['stɪmjʊleɪtɪŋ] a anregend, stimulierend.

stimulation [stɪmjʊ'leɪʃən] n Anregung f, Stimulation f.

stimulus ['stɪmjʊləs] n Anregung f, Reiz m.

sting [stɪŋ] n Stich m; (organ) Stachel m; vti irreg stechen; (on skin) brennen.

stingily ['stɪndʒɪlɪ] ad knickerig, geizig.

stinginess ['stɪndʒɪməs] n Geiz m.

stinging nettle ['stɪŋɪŋnetl] n Brennessel f.

stingy ['stɪndʒɪ] a geizig, knauserig.

stink [stɪŋk] n Gestank m; vi irreg stinken; —er (col) (person) gemeine(r) Hund m; (problem) böse Sache f; —ing a (fig) wider- lich; —ing rich stinkreich.

stint [stɪnt] n Pensum nt; (period) Betätigung f; vt einschränken, knapphalten.

stipend ['staɪpend] n Gehalt nt.

stipulate ['stɪpjʊleɪt] vt festsetzen.

stipulation [stɪpjʊ'leɪʃən] n Bedingung f.

stir [stɜ:*] n Bewegung f; (Cook) Rühren nt; (sensation) Aufsehen nt; vt (um)rühren; vi sich rühren; — up vt mob aufhetzen; fire ent- fachen; mixture umrühren; dust aufwirbeln; to — things up Ärger machen; —ring a ergreifend.

stirrup ['stɪrəp] n Steigbügel m.

stitch [stɪtʃ] n (with needle) Stich m; (Med) Faden m; (of knitting) Masche f; (pain) Stich m, Stechen nt; vt nähen.

stoat [stəʊt] n Wiesel nt.

stock [stɒk] n Vorrat m; (Comm) (Waren)lager nt; (live—) Vieh nt; (Cook) Brühe f; (Fin) Grundkapital nt; a stets vorrätig; (standard) Normal-; vt versehen, versorgen; (in shop) führen; in — auf Vorrat; to take — Inventur machen; (fig) Bilanz ziehen; to — up with Reserven anlegen von; —ade [stɒ'keɪd] f; Palisade f; —broker Börsenmakler m; — exchange Börse f.

stocking ['stɒkɪŋ] n Strumpf m.

stockist ['stɒkɪst] n Händler m.

stock market ['stɒkmɑ:kɪt] n Börse f, Effektenmarkt m.

stockpile ['stɒkpaɪl] n Vorrat m; nuclear — Kernwaffenvorräte pl; vt aufstapeln.

stocktaking ['stɒkteɪkɪŋ] n Inventur f, Bestandsaufnahme f.

stocky ['stɒkɪ] a untersetzt.

stodgy ['stɒdʒɪ] a füllend, stopfend; (fig) langweilig, trocken.

stoic ['stəʊɪk] n Stoiker m; —al a stoisch; —ism ['stəʊɪsɪzəm] Stoizismus m; (fig) Gelassenheit f.

stoke [stəʊk] vt schüren; —r Heizer m.

stole [stəʊl] n Stola f; —n a gestohlen.

stolid ['stɒlɪd] a schwerfällig; silence stur.

stomach ['stʌmək] n Bauch m, Magen m; I have no — for it das ist nichts für mich; vt vertragen; —ache Magen- or Bauchschmerzen pl.

stone [stəʊn] n Stein m; (seed) Stein m, Kern m; (weight) Gewichtseinheit f = 6.35 kg; a steinern, Stein-; vt entkernen; (kill) steinigen; —cold a eiskalt; — deaf a stocktaub; —mason Steinmetz m; —work Mauerwerk nt.

stony ['stəʊnɪ] a steinig.

stool [stuːl] n Hocker m.

stoop [stuːp] vi sich bücken.

stop [stɒp] n Halt m; (bus—) Haltestelle f; (punctuation) Punkt m; vt anhalten, anhalten; (bring to end) aufhören (mit), sein lassen; vi aufhören; (clock) stehenbleiben; (remain) bleiben; to — doing stn aufhören, etw zu tun; — it! hör auf (damit)!; — dead vi plötzlich aufhören, innehalten; — in vi (at home) zu Hause bleiben; — off vi kurz haltmachen; — out vi (of house) ausbleiben; — over vi übernachten, über Nacht bleiben; — up vi (at night) aufbleiben; vt hole zustopfen, verstopfen; — lights pl (Aut) Bremslichter pl;

—over (on journey) Zwischenaufenthalt m; —page ['stɒpɪdʒ] (An)halten m; (traffic) Verkehrsstockung f; (strike) Arbeitseinstellung f; —per Propfen m, Stöpsel m; —press letzte Meldung f; —watch Stoppuhr f.

storage ['stɔːrɪdʒ] n Lagerung f.

store [stɔː*] n Vorrat m; (place) Lager nt, Warenhaus nt; (large shop) Kaufhaus nt; vt lagern; — up vt sich eindecken mit; —room Lagerraum m, Vorratsraum m.

storey ['stɔːrɪ] n (Brit) Stock m, Stockwerk nt.

stork [stɔːk] n Storch m.

storm [stɔːm] n (lit, fig) Sturm m; vti stürmen; to take by — im Sturm nehmen; —cloud Gewitterwolke f; —y a stürmisch.

story ['stɔːrɪ] n Geschichte f, Erzählung f; (lie) Märchen nt; (US: storey) Stock m, Stockwerk nt; —book Geschichtenbuch nt; —teller Geschichtenerzähler m.

stout [staʊt] a (bold) mannhaft, tapfer; (too fat) beleibt, korpulent; —ness Festigkeit f; (of body) Korpulenz f.

stove [staʊv] n (Koch)herd m; (for heating) Ofen m.

stow [stəʊ] vt verstauen; —away blinde(r) Passagier m.

straddle ['strædl] vt horse, fence rittlings sitzen auf (+dat); (fig) überbrücken.

strafe [straːf] vt beschießen, bombardieren.

straggle ['strægl] vi (branches etc) wuchern; (people) nachhinken; —r Nachzügler m.

straight [streɪt] a gerade; (honest) offen, ehrlich; (in order) in Ordnung; drink pur, unverdünnt; n ad (direct) direkt, geradewegs; n

(Sport) Gerade f; —away ad sofort, unverzüglich; — off ad sofort; direkt nacheinander; — on ad geradeaus; —en vt (also — out) (lit) gerade machen; (fig) in Ordnung bringen, klarstellen; —forward a einfach, unkompliziert.

strain [strein] n Belastung f; (streak, trace) Zug m; (of music) Fetzen m; vt überanstrengen; (stretch) anspannen; muscle zerren; (filter) (durch)seihen; don't — yourself überanstrenge dich nicht; vi (make effort) sich anstrengen; —ed a laugh gezwungen; relations gespannt; —er Sieb nt.

strait [streit] n Straße f, Meerenge f; —ened a circumstances beschränkt; —jacket Zwangsjacke f; —laced a engherzig, streng.

strand [strænd] n (lit, fig) Faden m; (of hair) Strähne f; to be —ed (lit, fig) gestrandet sein.

strange [streindʒ] a fremd; (unusual) merkwürdig, seltsam; —ly ad merkwürdig, fremd; —ly enough merkwürdigerweise; —ness Fremdheit f; —r Fremde(r) mf; I'm a —r here ich bin hier fremd.

strangle ['stræŋgl] vt erdrosseln, erwürgen; —hold (fig) Unklammerung f.

strangulation [stræŋgju'leiʃən] n Erdrosseln nt.

strap [stræp] n Riemen m; (on clothes) Träger m; vt (fasten) festschnallen; —less a dress trägerlos a stramm.

stratagem ['strætədʒəm] n (Kriegs)list f.

strategic a, —ally ad [strə'ti:dʒik, -əli] strategisch.

strategist ['strætədʒist] n Stratege m.

strategy ['strætədʒi] n Kriegskunst f; (fig) Strategie f.

stratosphere ['strætəusfiə*] n Stratosphäre f.

stratum ['stra:təm] n Schicht f.

straw [stro:] n Stroh nt; (single stalk, drinking —) Strohhalm m; a Stroh-; —berry Erdbeere f.

stray [strei] n verirrte(s) Tier nt; vi herumstreunen; a animal verirrt; thought zufällig.

streak ['stri:k] n Streifen m; (in character) Einschlag m; (in hair) Strähne f; — of bad luck Pechsträhne f; vt streifen; —y a gestreift; bacon durchwachsen.

stream [stri:m] n (brook) Bach m; (fig) Strom m; (flow of liquid) Strom m, Flut f; vi strömen, fluten; —er (pennon) Wimpel m; (of paper) Luftschlange f; —lined a stromlinienförmig; (effective) rationell.

street [stri:t] n Straße f; —car (US) Straßenbahn f; — lamp Straßenlaterne f.

strength [streŋθ] n Stärke f (also fig); Kraft f; —en vt (ver)stärken.

strenuous ['strenjuəs] a anstrengend; —ly ad angestrengt.

stress [stres] n Druck m; (mental) Streß m; (Gram) Betonung f; vt betonen.

stretch [stretʃ] n Stück nt, Strecke f; vt ausdehnen, strecken; vi sich erstrecken; (person) sich strecken; at a — (continuously) ununterbrochen; — out vi sich ausstrecken; vt ausstrecken; —er Tragbahre f.

stricken ['strikən] a person befallen, ergriffen; city, country heimgesucht.

strict [strɪkt] *a (exact)* genau; *(severe)* streng; **—ly** *ad* streng, genau; **—ly speaking** streng or genau genommen; **—ness** Strenge f.

stride [straɪd] *n* lange(r) Schritt *m*; *vi irreg* schreiten.

strident ['straɪdənt] *a* schneidend, durchdringend.

strife [straɪf] *n* Streit *m*.

strike [straɪk] *n* Streik *m*, Ausstand *m*; *(discovery)* Fund *m*; *(attack)* Schlag *m*; *vi irreg vt (hit)* schlagen; treffen; *(collide)* stoßen gegen; *(come to mind)* einfallen (+ *dat*); *(stand out)* auffallen; *(find)* stoßen auf (+ *acc*), finden; *vi (stop work)* streiken; *(attack)* zuschlagen; *(clock)* schlagen; **— down** *vt (lay low)* niederschlagen; **— out** *vt (cross out)* ausstreichen; **— up** *vt music* anstimmen; *friendship* schließen; **— pay** Streikgeld *nt*; **—r** Streikende(r) *mf*.

striking *a*, **—ly** *ad* ['straɪkɪŋ, -lɪ] auffallend, bemerkenswert.

string [strɪŋ] *n* Schnur *f*, Kordel *f*, Bindfaden *m*; *(row)* Reihe *f*; *(Mus)* Saite *f*; **— bean** grüne Bohne *f*.

stringency ['strɪndʒənsɪ] *n* Schärfe *f*.

stringent ['strɪndʒənt] *a* streng, scharf.

strip [strɪp] *n* Streifen *m*; *vt (uncover)* abstreifen, abziehen; *clothes* ausziehen; *(Tech)* auseinandernehmen; *vi (undress)* sich ausziehen; **— cartoon** Bildserie *f*.

stripe [straɪp] *n* Streifen *m*; **—d** *a* gestreift.

strip light ['strɪplaɪt] *n* Leuchtröhre *f*.

stripper ['strɪpə*] *n* Striptease-tänzerin *f*.

striptease ['strɪptiːz] *n* Striptease *nt*.

strive [straɪv] *vi irreg* streben (*for* nach).

stroke [strəʊk] *n* Schlag *m*, Hieb *m*; *(swim, row)* Stoß *m*; *(Tech)* Hub *m*; *(Med)* Schlaganfall *m*; *(caress)* Streicheln *nt*; *vt* streicheln; **at a —** mit einem Schlag; **on the —** of 5 Schlag 5.

stroll [strəʊl] *n* Spaziergang *m*; *vi* spazierengehen, schlendern.

strong [strɒŋ] *a* stark; *(firm)* fest; **they are 50 —** sie sind 50 Mann stark; **—hold** Hochburg *f*; **—ly** *ad* stark; **—room** Tresor *m*.

structural ['strʌktʃərəl] *a* strukturell.

structure ['strʌktʃə*] *n* Struktur *f*, Aufbau *m*; *(building)* Gebäude *nt*, Bau *m*.

struggle ['strʌgl] *n* Kampf *m*, Anstrengung *f*; *vi (fight)* kämpfen; **to — to do sth** sich (ab)mühen etw zu tun.

strum [strʌm] *vt guitar* klimpern auf (+ *dat*).

strung [strʌŋ] *see* **highly**.

strut [strʌt] *n* Strebe *f*, Stütze *f*; *vi* stolzieren.

strychnine ['strɪkniːn] *n* Strychnin *nt*.

stub [stʌb] *n* Stummel *m*; *(of cigarette)* Kippe *f*.

stubble ['stʌbl] *n* Stoppel *f*.

stubbly ['stʌblɪ] *a* stoppelig, Stoppel-.

stubborn *a*, **—ly** *ad* ['stʌbən, -lɪ] stur, hartnäckig; **—ness** Sturheit *f*, Hartnäckigkeit *f*.

stubby ['stʌbɪ] *a* untersetzt.

stucco ['stʌkəʊ] *n* Stuck *m*.

stuck-up ['stʌk'ʌp] *a* hochnäsig.

stud [stʌd] n (nail) Beschlagnagel m; (button) Kragenknopf m; (number of horses) Stall m; (place) Gestüt nt; —ded with übersät mit.

student ['stju:dənt] n Student(in f) m; (US also) Schüler(in f) m; —fellow — Kommilitone m; Kommilitonin f.

studied ['stʌdɪd] a absichtlich.

studio ['stju:dɪəʊ] n Studio nt; (for artist) Atelier nt.

studious [—ly ad ['stju:dɪəs, -lɪ] lernbegierig.

study ['stʌdɪ] n Studium nt; (investigation also) Untersuchung f; (room) Arbeitszimmer nt; (essay etc) Studie f; vt studieren; face erforschen; evidence prüfen; vi studieren; — group Arbeitsgruppe f.

stuff [stʌf] n Stoff m; (col) Zeug nt; that's hot —! das ist Klasse!; vt stopfen, füllen; animal ausstopfen; to — o.s. sich vollstopfen; —ed full vollgepfropft; —iness Schwüle f; Spießigkeit f; —ing Füllung f; —y a room schwül; person spießig.

stumble ['stʌmbl] vi stolpern; to — on zufällig stoßen auf (+acc).

stumbling block ['stʌmblɪŋblɒk] n Hindernis nt, Stein m des Anstoßes.

stump [stʌmp] n Stumpf m; vt umwerfen.

stun [stʌn] vt betäuben; (shock) niederschmettern.

stunning ['stʌnɪŋ] a betäubend; news überwältigend, umwerfend; —ly beautiful traumhaft schön.

stunt [stʌnt] n Kunststück nt, Trick m; vt verkümmern lassen; —ed a verkümmert.

stupefy ['stju:pɪfaɪ] vt betäuben; (by news) bestürzen; —ing a betäubend; bestürzend.

stupendous [stju'pendəs] a erstaunlich, enorm.

stupid a, —ly ad ['stju:pɪd, -lɪ] dumm; —ity [stju:'pɪdɪtɪ] Dummheit f.

stupor ['stju:pə*] n Betäubung f.

sturdily ['stɜ:dɪlɪ] ad kräftig, stabil.

sturdiness [ʃtɜ:dɪnəs] n Robustheit f.

sturdy ['stɜ:dɪ] a kräftig, robust.

stutter ['stʌtə*] n Stottern nt; vi stottern.

sty [staɪ] n Schweinestall m.

stye [staɪ] n Gerstenkorn nt.

style [staɪl] n (fashion) Mode f; hair — Frisur f; in — mit Stil; vt hair frisieren.

styling ['staɪlɪŋ] n (of car etc) Formgebung f.

stylish a, —ly ad ['staɪlɪʃ, -lɪ] modisch, schick, flott.

stylized ['staɪlaɪzd] a stilisiert.

stylus ['staɪləs] n (Grammophon-)nadel f.

styptic ['stɪptɪk] a: — pencil blutstillende(r) Stift m.

suave [swɑ:v] a zuvorkommend.

sub- pref Unter-.

subconscious ['sʌb'kɒnʃəs] a unterbewußt; n: the — das Unterbewußte.

subdivide ['sʌbdɪ'vaɪd] vt unterteilen.

subdivision ['sʌbdɪvɪʒən] n Unterteilung f; (department) Unterabteilung f.

subdue [səb'dju:] vt unterwerfen; —d a lighting gedämpft; person still.

subject ['sʌbdʒɪkt] n (of kingdom) Untertan m; (citizen) Staatsangehörige(r) mf; (topic) Thema m; (Sch) Fach nt; (Gram) Subjekt nt, Satzgegenstand m;

[səb'dʒekt] vt (subdue) unterwerfen, abhängig machen; (expose) aussetzen; to be — to unterworfen sein (+dat); (exposed) ausgesetzt sein (+dat); —ion [səb'dʒekʃən] Unterwerfung f; (being controlled) Abhängigkeit f; —ive a, —ively ad [səb'dʒektɪv, -lɪ] subjektiv; — matter Thema nt.

sub judice [sʌb'dju:dɪsɪ] a in gerichtliche(r) Untersuchung.

subjunctive [səb'dʒʌŋktɪv] n Konjunktiv m, Möglichkeitsform f; a Konjunktiv-, konjunktivisch.

sublet ['sʌb'let] vt irreg untervermieten.

sublime [sə'blaɪm] a erhaben.

submarine [sʌbmə'ri:n] n Unterseeboot nt, U-Boot nt.

submerge [səb'mɜ:dʒ] vt untertauchen; (flood) überschwemmen; vi untertauchen.

submission [səb'mɪʃən] n (obedience) Ergebenheit f, Gehorsam m; (claim) Behauptung f; (of plan) Unterbreitung f.

submit [səb'mɪt] vt behaupten; plan unterbreiten; vi (give in) sich ergeben.

subnormal ['sʌb'nɔ:məl] a minderbegabt.

subordinate [sə'bɔ:dɪnət] a untergeordnet; n Untergebene(r) mf.

subpoena [sə'pi:nə] n Vorladung f; vt vorladen.

subscribe [səb'skraɪb] vi spenden, Geld geben; (to view etc) unterstützen, beipflichten (+dat); (to newspaper) abonnieren (to acc); —r (to periodical) Abonnent m; (Tel) Telefonteilnehmer m.

subscription [səb'skrɪpʃən] n Abonnement nt; (Mitglieds)beitrag m.

subsequent ['sʌbsɪkwənt] a folgend, später; —ly ad später.

subside [səb'saɪd] vi sich senken; —nce [sʌb'saɪdəns] Senkung f.

subsidiary [səb'sɪdɪərɪ] n Neben-; n (company) Zweig m, Tochtergesellschaft f.

subsidize ['sʌbsɪdaɪz] vt subventionieren.

subsidy ['sʌbsɪdɪ] n Subvention f.

subsistence [səb'sɪstəns] n Unterhalt m; — level Existenzminimum nt.

substance ['sʌbstəns] n Substanz f, Stoff m; (most important part) Hauptbestandteil m.

substandard [sʌb'stændəd] a unterdurchschnittlich.

substantial [səb'stænʃəl] a (strong) fest, kräftig; (important) wesentlich; —ly ad erheblich.

substantiate [səb'stænʃɪeɪt] vt begründen, belegen.

substation ['sʌbsteɪʃən] n (Elec) Nebenwerk nt.

substitute ['sʌbstɪtju:t] n Ersatz m; vt ersetzen.

substitution [sʌbstɪ'tju:ʃən] n Ersetzung f.

subterfuge ['sʌbtəfju:dʒ] n Vorwand m; Tricks pl.

subterranean [sʌbtə'reɪnɪən] a unterirdisch.

subtitle ['sʌbtaɪtl] n Untertitel m.

subtle ['sʌtl] a fein; (sly) raffiniert; —ty subtile Art f, Raffinesse f.

subtly ['sʌtlɪ] ad fein, raffiniert.

subtract [səb'trækt] vt abziehen, subtrahieren; —ion [səb'trækʃən] Abziehen nt, Subtraktion f.

subtropical ['sʌb'trɒpɪkəl] a subtropisch.

suburb ['sʌbɜ:b] n Vorort m; —an [sə'bɜ:bən] a Vorort(s)-,

Stadtrand-; **—ia** [sə'bɜ:biə]
Vorstadt f.

subvention [səb'venʃən] n (US)
Unterstützung f, Subvention f.

subversive [səb'vɜ:ʃɪv] a subversiv.

subway ['sʌbweɪ] n (US) U-Bahn
f, Untergrundbahn f; (Brit)
Unterführung f.

sub-zero ['sʌb'zɪərəʊ] a unter Null,
unter dem Gefrierpunkt.

succeed [sək'si:d] vi gelingen
(+dat), Erfolg haben; he —ed es
gelang ihm; vt (nach)folgen
(+dat); —ing a (nach)folgend.

success [sək'ses] n Erfolg m; —ful
a, —fully ad erfolgreich; —ion
[sək'seʃən] (Aufeinander)folge f;
(to throne) Nachfolge f; —ive a
[sək'sesɪv] aufeinanderfolgend; —
or Nachfolger(in f) m.

succinct [sək'sɪŋkt] a kurz und
bündig, knapp.

succulent ['sʌkjulənt] a saftig.

succumb [sə'kʌm] vi zusammenbrechen (to unter +dat); (yield)
nachgeben (die) unterliegen.

such [sʌtʃ] a solche(r, s); — a so
ein; — a lot so viel; — is life so
ist das Leben; — is my wish das
ist mein Wunsch; — as wie; pron
solch; — as I have die, die ich
habe; —like a derartig; pron
dergleichen.

suck [sʌk] vt saugen; ice cream etc
lecken; toffee etc lutschen; vi
saugen; —er (col) Idiot m,
Dummkopf m.

suckle ['sʌkl] vt säugen; child
stillen; vi saugen.

suction ['sʌkʃən] n Saugen nt,
Saugkraft f.

sudden ['sʌdn] a, —ly ad ['sʌdn,
plötzlich; all of a — ganz plötzlich,
auf einmal; —ness Plötzlichkeit f.

sue [su:] vt verklagen.

suède [sweɪd] n Wildleder nt; a
Wildleder-.

suet ['su:ɪt] n Nierenfett nt.

suffer ['sʌfə*] vt (er)leiden; (old:
allow) zulassen, dulden; vi leiden;
—er Leidende(r) mf; —ering
Leiden nt.

suffice [sə'faɪs] vi genügen.

sufficient a, —ly ad [sə'fiʃənt, -lɪ]
ausreichend.

suffix ['sʌfɪks] n Nachsilbe f.

suffocate ['sʌfəkeɪt] vti ersticken.

suffocation [sʌfə'keɪʃən] n
Ersticken nt.

suffragette [sʌfrə'dʒet] n
Suffragette f.

sugar ['ʃʊgə*] n Zucker m; vt
zuckern; — beet Zuckerrübe f; —
cane Zuckerrohr nt; —y a süß.

suggest [sə'dʒest] vt vorschlagen;
(show) schließen lassen auf
(+acc); what does this painting —
to you? was drückt das Bild für dich
aus?; —ion [sə'dʒestʃən]
Vorschlag m; —ive a anregend;
(indecent) zweideutig; to be —ive
of sth an etw (acc) erinnern.

suicidal [suɪ'saɪdl] a
selbstmörderisch; that's — das ist
Selbstmord.

suicide ['suɪsaɪd] n Selbstmord m;
to commit — Selbstmord begehen.

suit [su:t] n Anzug m; (Cards)
Farbe f; vt passen (+dat); clothes
stehen (+dat); (adapt) anpassen;
— yourself mach doch, was du
willst; —ability [su:tə'bɪlɪtɪ]
Eignung f; —able a geeignet,
passend; —ably ad passend,
angemessen; —case (Hand)koffer
m.

suite [swi:t] n (of rooms) Zimmer-
flucht f; (of furniture) Einrichtung

f; (*Mus*) Suite f; **three-piece —** Couchgarnitur f.

sulfur ['sʌlfə*] n (*US*) = **sulphur.**

sulk [sʌlk] *vi* schmollen; **—y** *a* schmollend.

sullen ['sʌlən] *a* (*gloomy*) düster; (*bad-tempered*) mürrisch, verdrossen.

sulphur ['sʌlfə*] n Schwefel m.

sulphuric [sʌl'fjuərɪk] *a:* **— acid** Schwefelsäure f.

sultan ['sʌltən] n Sultan m; **—a** [sʌl'tɑːnə] (*woman*) Sultanin f; (*raisin*) Sultanine f.

sultry ['sʌltrɪ] *a* schwül.

sum [sʌm] n Summe f; (*money also*) Betrag m; (*arithmetic*) Rechenaufgabe f; **—s** *pl* Rechnen nt; **— up** *vti* zusammenfassen; **—marize** *vt* kurz zusammenfassen; **—mary** Zusammenfassung f; (*of book etc*) Inhaltsangabe f.

summer ['sʌmə*] n Sommer m; *a* Sommer-; **—house** (*in garden*) Gartenhaus nt; **—time** Sommerzeit f.

summing-up ['sʌmɪŋ'ʌp] n Zusammenfassung f.

summit ['sʌmɪt] n Gipfel m; **— conference** Gipfelkonferenz f.

summon ['sʌmən] *vt* bestellen, kommen lassen; (*Jur*) vorladen; (*gather up*) aufbieten, aufbringen; **—s** (*Jur*) Vorladung f.

sump [sʌmp] n Ölwanne f.

sumptuous ['sʌmptjuəs] *a* prächtig; **—ness** Pracht f.

sun [sʌn] n Sonne f; **—bathe** *vi* sich sonnen; **—bathing** Sonnenbaden nt; **—burn** Sonnenbrand m; **to be —burnt** einen Sonnenbrand haben.

Sunday ['sʌndeɪ] n Sonntag m.

sundial ['sʌndaɪəl] n Sonnenuhr f.

sundown ['sʌndaun] n Sonnenuntergang m.

sundry ['sʌndrɪ] *a* verschieden; n: **sundries** *pl* Verschiedene(s) nt; **all and — alle.**

sunflower ['sʌnflauə*] n Sonnenblume f.

sunglasses ['sʌnglɑːsɪz] *npl* Sonnenbrille f.

sunken ['sʌŋkən] *a* versunken; *eyes* eingesunken.

sunlight ['sʌnlaɪt] n Sonnenlicht nt.

sunlit ['sʌnlɪt] *a* sonnenbeschienen.

sunny ['sʌnɪ] *a* sonnig.

sunrise ['sʌnraɪz] n Sonnenaufgang m.

sunset ['sʌnset] n Sonnenuntergang m.

sunshade ['sʌnʃeɪd] n Sonnenschirm m.

sunshine ['sʌnʃaɪn] n Sonnenschein m.

sunspot ['sʌnspɒt] n Sonnenfleck m.

sunstroke ['sʌnstrəuk] n Hitzschlag m.

sun tan ['sʌntæn] n (Sonnen)-bräune f; **to get a —** braun werden.

suntrap ['sʌntræp] n sonnige(r) Platz m.

sunup ['sʌnʌp] n (col) Sonnenaufgang m.

super ['su:pə*] *a* (col) prima, klasse; Super-, Über-.

superannuation [su:pər-ænjueɪʃən] n Pension f.

superb *a*, **—ly** *ad* [su:'pɜːb, -lɪ] ausgezeichnet, hervorragend.

supercilious [su:pə'sɪlɪəs] *a* herablassend.

superficial *a*, **—ly** *ad* [su:pə'fɪʃəl, -ɪ] oberflächlich.

superfluous [su:'pɜːfluəs] *a* überflüssig.

superhuman [su:pə'hju:mən] *a* effort übermenschlich.

superimpose ['su:pərɪm'pəʊz] *vt* übereinanderlegen.

superintendent [su:pərɪn'tendənt] *n* Polizeichef *m*.

superior [su'pɪərɪə*] *a* (*higher*) höher(stehend); (*better*) besser; (*proud*) überlegen; *n* Vorgesetzte(r) *mf*; **—ity** [supɪərɪ'brɪtɪ] Überlegenheit *f*.

superlative [su'pɜ:lətɪv] *a* höchste(r,s); *n* (*Gram*) Superlativ *m*.

superman ['su:pəmæn] *n* Übermensch *m*.

supermarket ['su:pəma:kɪt] *n* Supermarkt *m*.

supernatural [su:pə'nætʃərəl] *a* übernatürlich.

superpower ['su:pəpaʊə*] *n* Weltmacht *f*.

supersede [su:pə'si:d] *vt* ersetzen.

supersonic ['su:pə'sɒnɪk] *n* Überschall-.

superstition [su:pə'stɪʃən] *n* Aberglaube *m*.

superstitious [su:pə'stɪʃəs] *a* abergläubisch.

supervise ['su:pəvaɪz] *vt* beaufsichtigen, kontrollieren.

supervision [su:pə'vɪʒən] *n* Aufsicht *f*.

supervisor ['su:pəvaɪzə*] *n* Aufsichtsperson *f*; **—y** *a* Aufsichts-.

supper ['sʌpə*] *n* Abendessen *nt*.

supple ['sʌpl] *a* gelenkig, geschmeidig; *wire* biegsam.

supplement ['sʌplɪmənt] *n* Ergänzung *f*; (*in book*) Nachtrag *m*; [sʌplɪ'ment] *vt* ergänzen; **—ary** [sʌplɪ'mentərɪ] *a* ergänzend, Ergänzungs-, Zusatz-.

supplier [sə'plaɪə*] *n* Lieferant *m*.

supply [sə'plaɪ] *vt* liefern; *n* Vorrat *m*; (*supplying*) Lieferung *f*; **supplies** *pl* (*food*) Vorräte *pl*; (*Mil*) Nachschub *m*; **— and demand** Angebot *nt* und Nachfrage.

support [sə'pɔ:t] *n* Unterstützung *f*; (*Tech*) Stütze *f*; *vt* (*hold up*) stützen, tragen; (*provide for*) ernähren; (*speak in favour of*) befürworten, unterstützen; **—er** Anhänger *m*; **—ing** *a* programme Bei-; *role* Neben-.

suppose [sə'pəʊz] *vti* annehmen, denken, glauben; **I —** so ich glaube schon; **— he comes ...** angenommen, er kommt ...; **—dly** [sə'pəʊzɪdlɪ] *ad* angeblich.

supposing [sə'pəʊzɪŋ] *cj* angenommen.

supposition [sʌpə'zɪʃən] *n* Voraussetzung *f*.

suppress [sə'pres] *vt* unterdrücken; **—ion** [sə'preʃən] Unterdrückung *f*; **—or** (*Elec*) Entstörungselement *nt*.

supra- ['su:prə] *pref* Über-.

supremacy [su'preməsɪ] *n* Vorherrschaft *f*, Oberhoheit *f*.

supreme *a*, **—ly** *ad* [su'pri:m, -lɪ] oberste(r,s), höchste(r,s).

surcharge ['sɜ:tʃa:dʒ] *n* Zuschlag *m*.

sure [ʃʊə*] *a* sicher, gewiß; **to be — sicher sein**; **to be — about sth** sich (*dat*) einer Sache sicher sein; **we are — to win** wir werden ganz sicher gewinnen; *ad* sicher; **—!** (*of course*) ganz bestimmt!, natürlich!, klar!; **to make —** of sich vergewissern (*+gen*); **—footed** *a* sicher (auf den Füßen); **—ly** *ad* (*certainly*) sicherlich, gewiß; **—ly** it's wrong das ist doch wohl falsch; **—ly not!** das ist doch wohl nicht wahrl; **—ty** Sicherheit *f*; (*person*) Bürge *m*.

surf [sɜːf] *n* Brandung *f*.

surface ['sɜːfɪs] *n* Oberfläche *f*; *vt* roadway teeren; *vi* auftauchen; **—mail** gewöhnliche Post *f*, Post per Bahn *f*.

surfboard ['sɜːfbɔːd] *n* Wellenreiterbrett *nt*.

surfeit ['sɜːfɪt] *n* Übermaß *nt*.

surfing ['sɜːfɪŋ] *n* Wellenreiten *nt*, Surfing *nt*.

surge [sɜːdʒ] *n* Woge *f*; *vi* wogen.

surgeon ['sɜːdʒən] *n* Chirurg(in *f*) *m*.

surgery ['sɜːdʒərɪ] *n* Praxis *f*; (*room*) Sprechzimmer *nt*; (*time*) Sprechstunde *f*; (*treatment*) operative(r) Eingriff *m*, Operation *f*; **he needs —** er muß operiert werden.

surgical ['sɜːdʒɪkəl] *a* chirurgisch.

surly ['sɜːlɪ] *a* verdrießlich, grob.

surmise [sɜːˈmaɪz] *vt* vermuten.

surmount [sɜːˈmaunt] *vt* überwinden.

surname ['sɜːneɪm] *n* Zuname *m*.

surpass [sɜːˈpɑːs] *vt* übertreffen.

surplus ['sɜːpləs] *n* Überschuß *m*; *a* überschüssig, Über(schuß)-.

surprise [səˈpraɪz] *n* Überraschung *f*; *vt* überraschen.

surprising [səˈpraɪzɪŋ] *a* überraschend; **—ly** *ad* überraschend(erweise).

surrealism [səˈrɪəlɪzəm] *n* Surrealismus *m*.

surrealist [səˈrɪəlɪst] *a* surrealistisch; *n* Surrealist *m*.

surrender [səˈrendə*] *n* Übergabe *f*; Kapitulation *f*; *vi* sich ergeben, kapitulieren; *vt* aufgeben.

surreptitious *a*, **—ly** *ad*. [sʌrəpˈtɪʃəs, -lɪ] verstohlen.

surround [səˈraund] *vt* umgeben; (*come all round*) umringen; **—ed by** umgeben von; **—ing** *a* country-side umliegend; *n*: **—ings** *pl* Umgebung *f*; (*environment*) Umwelt *f*.

surveillance [sɜːˈveɪləns] *n* Überwachung *f*.

survey ['sɜːveɪ] *n* Übersicht *f*; [sɜːˈveɪ] *vt* überblicken; land vermessen; **—ing** [səˈveɪŋ] (*of land*) (Land)vermessung *f*; **—or** [səˈveɪə*] Land(ver)messer *m*.

survival [səˈvaɪvl] *n* Überleben *nt*; (*sth from earlier times*) Überbleibsel *nt*.

survive [səˈvaɪv] *vti* überleben.

survivor [səˈvaɪvə*] *n* Überlebende(r) *mf*.

susceptible [səˈseptəbl] *a* empfindlich (*to* gegen); empfänglich (*to* für).

suspect ['sʌspekt] *n* Verdächtige(r) *mf*; *a* verdächtig; [səsˈpekt] *vt* verdächtigen; (*think*) vermuten.

suspend [səsˈpend] *vt* verschieben; (*from work*) suspendieren; (*hang up*) aufhängen; (*Sport*) sperren; *n*: **—ers** *pl* Strumpfhalter *m*; (*men's*) Sockenhalter *m*; (*US*) Hosenträger *m*.

suspense [səsˈpens] *n* Spannung *f*.

suspension [səsˈpenʃən] *n* (*hanging*) (Auf)hängen *nt*, Aufhängung *f*; (*postponing*) Aufschub *m*; (*from work*) Suspendierung *f*; (*Sport*) Sperrung *f*; (*Aut*) Federung *f*; **— bridge** Hängebrücke *f*.

suspicion [səsˈpɪʃən] *n* Mißtrauen *nt*; Verdacht *m*.

suspicious *a*, **—ly** *ad* [səsˈpɪʃəs, -lɪ] mißtrauisch; (*causing suspicion*) verdächtig; **—ness** Mißtrauen *nt*.

sustain [səs'teɪn] vt (*hold up*) stützen, tragen; (*maintain*) aufrechterhalten; (*confirm*) bestätigen; (*Jur*) anerkennen; *injury* davontragen; **—ed** a effort anhaltend.

sustenance ['sʌstɪnəns] n Nahrung f.

swab [swɒb] n (*Med*) Tupfer m; vt *decks* schrubben; *wound* abtupfen.

swagger ['swægə*] vi stolzieren; (*behave*) prahlen, angeben.

swallow ['swɒləʊ] n (*bird*) Schwalbe f; (*of food etc*) Schluck m; vt (ver)schlucken; **— up** vt verschlingen.

swamp [swɒmp] n Sumpf m; vt überschwemmen; **—y** a sumpfig.

swan [swɒn] n Schwan m; **— song** Schwanengesang m.

swap [swɒp] n Tausch m; vt (ein)tauschen (*for* gegen); vi tauschen.

swarm [swɔːm] n Schwarm m; vi wimmeln (*with* von).

swarthy ['swɔːðɪ] a dunkel, braun.

swastika ['swɒstɪkə] n Hakenkreuz nt.

swat [swɒt] vt totschlagen.

sway [sweɪ] vi schwanken; (*branches*) schaukeln, sich wiegen; vt schwenken; (*influence*) beeinflussen, umstimmen.

swear [swɛə*] vi irreg (*promise*) schwören; (*curse*) fluchen; to — to sth schwören auf etw (acc); **—word** Fluch m.

sweat [swet] n Schweiß m; vi schwitzen; **—er** Pullover m; **—y** a verschwitzt.

swede [swiːd] n Steckrübe f.

sweep [swiːp] n (*cleaning*) Kehren nt; (*wide curve*) Bogen m; (*with arm*) schwungvolle Bewegung f;

(*chimney* —) Schornsteinfeger m; irreg vt fegen, kehren; vi (*road*) sich dahinziehen; (*go quickly*) rauschen; **— away** vt wegfegen; (*river*) wegspülen; **— past** vi vorbeisausen; **— up** vt zusammenkehren; **—ing** a gesture schwungvoll; statement verallgemeinernd; **—stake** Toto nt.

sweet [swiːt] n (*course*) Nachtisch m; (*candy*) Bonbon nt; a, **—ly** ad süß; **—corn** Zuckermais m; **—en** vt süßen; (*fig*) versüßen; **—heart** Liebste(r) mf; **—ness** Süße f; **—pea** Gartenwicke f; **to have a — tooth** ein Leckermaul sein.

swell [swel] n Seegang m; a (*col*) todschick; irreg vt numbers vermehren; vi (*also* **— up**) (an)schwellen; **—ing** Schwellung f.

sweltering ['sweltərɪŋ] a drückend.

swerve [swɜːv] n Ausschwenken nt; vti ausscheren, zur Seite schwenken.

swift [swɪft] n Mauersegler m; a, **—ly** ad geschwind, schnell, rasch; **—ness** Schnelligkeit f.

swig [swɪg] n Zug m.

swill [swɪl] n (*for pigs*) Schweinefutter nt; vt spülen.

swim [swɪm] n: to go for a — schwimmen gehen; irreg vi schwimmen; my head is **—ming** mir dreht sich der Kopf; vt (*cross*) (durch)schwimmen; **—mer** Schwimmer(in f) m; **—ming** Schwimmen nt; to go **—ming** schwimmen gehen; **—ming baths** pl Schwimmbad nt; **—ming cap** Badehaube f, Badekappe f; **—ming costume** Badeanzug m; **—ming pool** Schwimmbecken nt; (*private*) Swimming-Pool m; **—suit** Badeanzug m.

swindle ['swɪndl] *n* Schwindel *m*, Betrug *m*; *vt* betrügen; **—r** Schwindler *m*.

swine [swaɪn] *n* (*lit, fig*) Schwein *nt*.

swing [swɪŋ] *n* (*child's*) Schaukel *f*; (*swinging*) Schwingen *nt*, Schwung *m*; (*Mus*) Swing *m*; *irreg vt* schwingen, (herum)schwenken; *vi* schwingen, pendeln, schaukeln; (*turn quickly*) schwenken; **in full —** in vollem Gange; **—bridge** Drehbrücke *f*; **—door** Schwingtür *f*.

swipe [swaɪp] *n* Hieb *m*; *vt* (*col*) (*hit*) hart schlagen; (*steal*) klauen.

swirl [swɜːl] *n* Wirbel *m*; *vi* wirbeln.

switch [swɪtʃ] *n* (*Elec*) Schalter *m*; (*change*) Wechsel *m*; *vti* (*Elec*) schalten; (*change*) wechseln; **— off** *vt* ab- or ausschalten; **— on** *vt* an- or einschalten; **—back** Achterbahn *f*; **—board** Vermittlung *f*, Zentrale *f*; (*board*) Schaltbrett *nt*.

swivel ['swɪvl] *vti* (*also* **— round**) (sich) drehen.

swollen ['swəʊlən] *a* geschwollen.

swoon [swuːn] *vi* (*old*) in Ohnmacht fallen.

swoop [swuːp] *n* Sturzflug *m*; (*esp by police*) Razzia *f*; *vi* (*also* **— down**) stürzen.

swop [swɒp] = **swap**.

sword [sɔːd] *n* Schwert *nt*; **—fish** Schwertfisch *m*; **—sman** Fechter *m*.

sworn [swɔːn] *a*: **— enemies** *pl* Todfeinde *pl*.

sycamore ['sɪkəmɔː*] *n* (*US*) Platane *f*; (*Brit*) Bergahorn *m*.

sycophantic [sɪkə'fæntɪk] *a* schmeichlerisch, kriecherisch.

syllable ['sɪləbl] *n* Silbe *f*.

syllabus ['sɪləbəs] *n* Lehrplan *m*.

symbol ['sɪmbəl] *n* Symbol *nt*; **—ic(al)** [sɪm'bɒlɪk(əl)] *a*

symbolisch; **—ism** symbolische Bedeutung *f*; (*Art*) Symbolismus *m*; **—ize** *vt* versinnbildlichen, symbolisieren.

symmetrical *a*, **—ly** *ad* [sɪ'metrɪkəl, -ɪ] symmetrisch, gleichmäßig.

symmetry ['sɪmɪtrɪ] *n* Symmetrie *f*.

sympathetic *a*, **—ally** *ad* [sɪmpə'θetɪk, -əlɪ] mitfühlend.

sympathize ['sɪmpəθaɪz] *vi* sympathisieren; mitfühlen; **—r** Mitfühlende(r) *mf*; (*Pol*) Sympathisant *m*.

sympathy ['sɪmpəθɪ] *n* Mitleid *nt*, Mitgefühl *nt*; (*condolence*) Beileid *nt*.

symphonic [sɪm'fɒnɪk] *a* sinfonisch.

symphony ['sɪmfənɪ] *n* Sinfonie *f*; **— orchestra** Sinfonieorchester *nt*.

symposium [sɪm'pəʊzɪəm] *n* Tagung *f*.

symptom ['sɪmptəm] *n* Symptom *nt*, Anzeichen *nt*; **—atic** [sɪmptə'mætɪk] *a* (*fig*) bezeichnend (*of* für).

synagogue ['sɪnəgɒg] *n* Synagoge *f*.

synchromesh ['sɪŋkrəʊ'meʃ] *n* Synchronschaltung *f*.

synchronize ['sɪŋkrənaɪz] *vt* synchronisieren; *vi* gleichzeitig sein or ablaufen.

syndicate ['sɪndɪkət] *n* Konsortium *nt*, Verband *m*, Ring *m*.

syndrome ['sɪndrəʊm] *n* Syndrom *nt*.

synonym ['sɪnənɪm] *n* Synonym *nt*; **—ous** [sɪ'nɒnɪməs] *a* gleichbedeutend.

synopsis [sɪ'nɒpsɪs] *n* Abriß *m*, Zusammenfassung *f*.

syntactic [sɪn'tæktɪk] a syntaktisch.
syntax ['sɪntæks] n Syntax f.
synthesis ['sɪnθəsɪs] n Synthese f.
synthetic a, **—ally** ad [sɪn'θetɪk, -əlɪ] synthetisch, künstlich.
syphilis ['sɪfɪlɪs] n Syphilis f.
syphon ['saɪfən] = **siphon**.

syringe [sɪ'rɪndʒ] n Spritze f.
syrup ['sɪrəp] n Sirup m; (of sugar) Melasse f.
system ['sɪstəm] n System nt; **—atic** a, **—atically** ad [sɪstə'mætɪk, -əlɪ] systematisch, planmäßig.

T

T, t [tiː] n T nt, t nt; **to a —** genau.
ta [taː] interj (Brit col) danke.
tab [tæb] n Schlaufe f, Aufhänger m; (name —) Schild nt.
tabby ['tæbɪ] n (female cat) (weibliche) Katze f; a (black-striped) getigert.
tabernacle ['tæbənækl] n Tabernakel nt or m.
table ['teɪbl] n Tisch m; (list) Tabelle f, Tafel f; **to lay sth on the —** (fig) etw zur Diskussion stellen; vt (Parl: propose) vorlegen, einbringen.
tableau ['tæbləʊ] n lebende(s) Bild nt.
tablecloth ['teɪblklɒθ] n Tischtuch nt, Tischdecke f.
table- d'hôte ['taːbl'dəʊt] n Tagesmenu nt.
tablemat ['teɪblmæt] n Untersatz m.
tablespoon ['teɪblspuːn] n Eßlöffel m; **—ful** Eßlöffel(voll) m.
tablet ['tæblət] n (Med) Tablette f; (for writing) Täfelchen nt; (of paper) Schreibblock m; (of soap) Riegel m.
table talk ['teɪbltɔːk] n Tischgespräch nt.
table tennis ['teɪbltenɪs] n Tischtennis nt.
table wine ['teɪblwaɪn] n Tafelwein

m.
taboo [tə'buː] n Tabu nt; a tabu.
tabulate ['tæbjʊleɪt] vt tabellarisch ordnen.
tacit a, **—ly** ad ['tæsɪt, -lɪ] stillschweigend; **—urn** a schweigsam, wortkarg.
tack [tæk] n (small nail) Stift m; (US: thumb—) Reißzwecke f; (stitch) Heftstich m; (Naut) Lavieren nt; (course) Kurs m.
tackle ['tækl] n (for lifting) Flaschenzug m; (Naut) Takelage f; (Sport) Tackling nt; vt (deal with) anpacken, in Angriff nehmen; person festhalten; player angehen; **he couldn't —** it er hat es nicht bewältigt.
tacky ['tækɪ] a klebrig.
tact [tækt] n Takt m; **—ful** a, **—fully** ad taktvoll.
tactical ['tæktɪkəl] a taktisch.
tactics ['tæktɪks] npl Taktik f.
tactless a, **—ly** ad ['tæktləs, -lɪ] taktlos.
tadpole ['tædpəʊl] n Kaulquappe f.
taffeta ['tæfɪtə] n Taft m.
taffy ['tæfɪ] n (US) Sahnebonbon nt.
tag [tæg] n (label) Schild nt, Anhänger m; (maker's name) Etikett nt; (phrase) Floskel f, Spruch m; **— along** vi mit-

kommen; — question Bestätigungsfrage f.

tail [teil] n Schwanz m; (of list) Schluß m; (of comet) Schweif m; —s (of coin) Zahl(seite) f; vt folgen (+ dat); — off vi abfallen, schwinden; — end Schluß m, Ende nt.

tailor ['teilə*] n Schneider m; —ing Schneidern nt, Schneiderarbeit f; —made a (lit) maßgeschneidert; (fig) wie auf den Leib geschnitten (for sb jdm).

tailwind ['teilwind] n Rückenwind m.

tainted ['teintid] a verdorben.

take [teik] vt irreg nehmen; prize entgegennehmen; trip, exam machen; (capture) person fassen; town einnehmen; disease bekommen; (carry to a place) bringen; (Math: subtract) abziehen (from von); (extract) quotation entnehmen (from dat); (get for o.s.) sich (dat) nehmen; (gain, obtain) bekommen; (Fin, Comm) einnehmen; (record) aufnehmen; (consume) zu sich nehmen; (Phot) aufnehmen, machen; (put up with) hinnehmen; (respond to) aufnehmen; (understand, interpret) auffassen; (assume) annehmen; (contain) fassen, Platz haben für; (Gram) stehen mit; it —s 4 hours man braucht 4 Stunden; it —s him 4 hours er braucht 4 Stunden; to — sth from sb jdm etw wegnehmen; to — part in teilnehmen an (+ dat); to — place stattfinden; — after vt ähnlich sein (+ dat); — back vt (return) zurückbringen; (retract) zurücknehmen; (remind) zurückversetzen (to in + acc); — down vt (pull down) abreißen; (write down) auf-

schreiben; — in vt (deceive) hereinlegen; (understand) begreifen; (include) einschließen; — off vi (plane) starten; vt (remove) wegnehmen, abmachen; clothing ausziehen; (imitate) nachmachen; — on vt (undertake) übernehmen; (engage) einstellen; (opponent) antreten gegen; — out vt (girl, dog) ausführen; (extract) herausnehmen; insurance abschließen; licence sich (dat) geben lassen; book ausleihen; (remove) entfernen; to — sth out on sb etw an jdm auslassen; — over vt übernehmen; vi ablösen (from acc); — to vt (like) mögen; (adopt as practice) sich (dat) angewöhnen; — up vt (raise) aufnehmen; hem kürzer machen; (occupy) in Anspruch nehmen; (absorb) aufsaugen; (engage in) sich befassen mit; to — sb up on sth jdn beim Wort nehmen; to be —n with begeistert sein von; —off (Aviat) Abflug m, Start m; (imitation) Nachahmung f; —over (Comm) Übernahme f; —over bid Übernahmeangebot nt.

takings ['teikinz] npl, (Comm) Einnahmen pl.

talc [tælk] n (also —um powder) Talkumpuder m.

tale [teil] n Geschichte f, Erzählung f.

talent ['tælənt] n Talent nt, Begabung f; —ed a talentiert, begabt.

talk [tɔːk] n (conversation) Gespräch nt; (rumour) Gerede nt; (speech) Vortrag m; vi sprechen, reden; (gossip) klatschen, reden; —ing of ... da wir gerade von ... sprechen; — about impertinence! so eine Frechheit! to — sb into doing sth jdn überreden, etw zu tun; to — shop fachsimpeln; — over vt besprechen; —ative a redselig, gesprächig; —er Schwätzer m.

tall [tɔ:l] a groß; building hoch; —boy Kommode f; —ness Größe f; Höhe f; — story übertriebene Geschichte f.

tally ['tælɪ] n Abrechnung f; vi übereinstimmen.

talon ['tælən] n Kralle f.

tambourine [tæmbə'ri:n] n Tamburin nt.

tame [teɪm] a zahm; (fig) fade, langweilig; vt zähmen; —ness Zahmheit f; (fig) Langweiligkeit f.

tamper ['tæmpə*]: — with vt herumpfuschen an (+dat); documents fälschen.

tampon ['tæmpən] n Tampon m.

tan [tæn] n (on skin) (Sonnen)bräune f; (colour) Gelbbraun nt; a (colour) (gelb)braun.

tandem ['tændəm] n Tandem nt.

tang [tæŋ] n Schärfe f, scharfe(r) Geschmack m or Geruch m.

tangent ['tændʒənt] n Tangente f.

tangerine [tændʒə'ri:n] n Mandarine f.

tangible ['tændʒəbl] a (lit) greifbar; (real) wirklich.

tangle ['tæŋgl] n Durcheinander nt; (trouble) Schwierigkeiten pl; vt verwirren.

tango ['tæŋgəʊ] n Tango m.

tank [tæŋk] n (container) Tank m, Behälter m; (Mil) Panzer m.

tankard ['tæŋkəd] n Seidel nt, Deckelkrug m.

tanker ['tæŋkə*] n (ship) Tanker m; (vehicle) Tankwagen m.

tankful ['tæŋkful] n volle(r) Tank m.

tanned [tænd] a skin gebräunt, sonnenverbrannt.

tantalizing ['tæntəlaɪzɪŋ] a verlockend; (annoying) quälend.

tantamount ['tæntəmaʊnt] a gleichbedeutend (to mit).

tantrum ['tæntrəm] n Wutanfall m.

tap [tæp] n Hahn m; (gentle blow) leichte(r) Schlag m, Klopfen nt; vt (strike) klopfen; supply anzapfen.

tap-dance ['tæpdɑ:ns] vi steppen.

tape [teɪp] n Band nt; (magnetic) (Ton)band nt; (adhesive) Klebstreifen m; vt (record) (auf Band) aufnehmen; — measure Maßband nt.

taper ['teɪpə*] n (dünne) Wachskerze f; vi spitz zulaufen.

tape recorder ['teɪprɪkɔ:də*] n Tonbandgerät nt.

tapered ['teɪpəd], **tapering** ['teɪpərɪŋ] a spitz zulaufend.

tapestry ['tæpɪstrɪ] n Wandteppich m, Gobelin m.

tapioca [tæpɪ'əʊkə] n Tapioka f.

tappet ['tæpɪt] n (Aut) Nocke f.

tar [tɑ:*] n Teer m.

tarantula [tə'ræntjʊlə] n Tarantel f.

tardy ['tɑ:dɪ] a langsam, spät.

target ['tɑ:gɪt] n Ziel nt; (board) Zielscheibe f.

tariff ['tærɪf] n (duty paid) Zoll m; (list) Tarif m.

tarmac ['tɑ:mæk] n (Aviat) Rollfeld nt.

tarn [tɑ:n] n Gebirgssee m.

tarnish ['tɑ:nɪʃ] vt (lit) matt machen; (fig) beflecken.

tarpaulin [tɑ:'pɔ:lɪn] n Plane f, Persenning f.

tarry ['tærɪ] vi (liter) bleiben; (delay) säumen.

tart [tɑ:t] n (Obst)torte f; (col)

Nutte f; a scharf, sauer; **remark** scharf, spitz.

tartan ['tɑːtən] n schottisch-karierte(r) Stoff m; Schottenkaro nt.

tartar ['tɑːtə*] n Zahnstein m; —(e) sauce Remouladensoße f.

tartly ['tɑːtlɪ] ad spitz.

task [tɑːsk] n Aufgabe f; (duty) Pflicht f; — force Sondertrupp m.

tassel ['tæsəl] n Quaste f.

taste [teɪst] n Geschmack m; (sense) Geschmackssinn m; (small quantity) Kostprobe f; (liking) Vorliebe f; vt schmecken; (try) versuchen; vi schmecken (of nach); —ful a, —fully ad geschmackvoll; —less a (insipid) ohne Geschmack, fade; (in bade taste) geschmacklos; —lessly ad geschmacklos.

tastily ['teɪstɪlɪ] ad schmackhaft.

tastiness ['teɪstɪnəs] n Schmackhaftigkeit f.

tasty ['teɪstɪ] a schmackhaft.

tata ['tæ'tɑː] interj (Brit col) tschüß.

tattered ['tætəd] a zerrissen, zerlumpt.

tatters ['tætəz] npl: in — in Fetzen.

tattoo [tə'tuː] n (Mil) Zapfenstreich m; (on skin) Tätowierung f; vt tätowieren.

tatty ['tætɪ] a (col) schäbig.

taunt [tɔːnt] n höhnische Bemerkung f; vt verhöhnen.

Taurus ['tɔːrəs] n Stier m.

taut [tɔːt] a straff.

tavern ['tævən] n Taverne f.

tawdry ['tɔːdrɪ] a (bunt und) billig.

tawny ['tɔːnɪ] a gelbbraun.

tax [tæks] n Steuer f; vt besteuern; (strain) strapazieren; **strength** angreifen; —ation [tæk'seɪʃən] n Besteuerung f; — **collector**

Steuereinnehmer m; —free a steuerfrei.

taxi ['tæksɪ] n Taxi nt; vi (plane) rollen.

taxidermist ['tæksɪdɜːmɪst] n Tierausstopfer m.

taxi driver ['tæksɪ draɪvə*] n Taxifahrer m.

taxi rank ['tæksɪræŋk] n Taxistand m.

taxpayer ['tækspeɪə*] n Steuerzahler m.

tax return ['tæksrɪ'tɜːn] n Steuererklärung f.

tea [tiː] n Tee m; (meal) (frühes) Abendessen nt; — **bag** Tee(aufguß)beutel m; — **break** Teepause f; — **cake** Rosinenbrötchen nt.

teach [tiːtʃ] vti irreg lehren; (Sch also) unterrichten; (show) zeigen, beibringen (sb sth jdm etw); that'll — him! das hat er nun davon!; —er Lehrer(in f) m; —in Teach-in nt; —ing (teacher's work) Unterricht m, Lehren nt; (doctrine) Lehre f.

tea cosy ['tiːkəʊzɪ] n Teewärmer m.

teacup ['tiːkʌp] n Teetasse f.

teak [tiːk] n Teakbaum m; a Teak(holz)-.

tea leaves ['tiːliːvz] npl Teeblätter pl.

team [tiːm] n (workers) Team nt; (Sport) Mannschaft f; (animals) Gespann nt; — **spirit** Gemeinschaftsgeist m; (Sport) Mannschaftsgeist m; —**work** Zusammenarbeit f, Teamwork nt.

tea party ['tiːpɑːtɪ] n Kaffeeklatsch m.

teapot ['tiːpɒt] n Teekanne f.

tear [teə*] n Riß m; irreg vt zerreißen; muscle zerren; I am torn between ... ich schwanke zwischen ...; *vi* (zer)reißen; (*rush*) rasen, sausen.

tear [tɪə*] *n* Träne *f*; in —s in Tränen (aufgelöst); —ful *a* weinend; *voice* weinerlich; — gas Tränengas *nt*.

tearing [ˈtɛərɪŋ] *a*: to be in a — hurry es schrecklich eilig haben.

tearoom [ˈtiːrʊm] *n* Teestube *f*.

tease [tiːz] *n* Hänsler *m*; *vt* necken, aufziehen; *animal* quälen; I was only teasing ich habe nur Spaß gemacht.

tea set [ˈtiːset] *n* Teeservice *nt*.

teashop [ˈtiːʃɒp] *n* Café *nt*.

teaspoon [ˈtiːspuːn] *n* Teelöffel *m*; —ful Teelöffel(voll) *m*.

tea strainer [ˈtiːstreɪnə*] *n* Teesieb *nt*.

teat [tiːt] *n* (*of woman*) Brustwarze *f*; (*of animal*) Zitze *f*; (*of bottle*) Sauger *m*.

tea towel [ˈtiːtaʊəl] *n* Küchenhandtuch *nt*.

tea urn [ˈtiːзːn] *n* Teemaschine *f*.

technical [ˈteknɪkəl] *a* technisch; *knowledge, terms* Fach-; —ity [teknɪˈkælɪtɪ] technische Einzelheit *f*; (*Jur*) Formsache *f*; —ly *ad* technisch; *speak* spezialisiert; (*fig*) genau genommen.

technician [tekˈnɪʃən] *n* Techniker *m*.

technique [tekˈniːk] *n* Technik *f*.

technological [teknəˈlɒdʒɪkəl] *a* technologisch.

technologist [tekˈnɒlədʒɪst] *n* Technologe *m*.

technology [tekˈnɒlədʒɪ] *n* Technologie *f*.

teddy (bear) [ˈtedɪ(bɛə*)] *n* Teddybär *m*.

tedious *a*, —ly *ad* [ˈtiːdɪəs, -lɪ] langweilig, ermüdend.

tedium [ˈtiːdɪəm] *n* Langweiligkeit *f*.

tee [tiː] *n* (*golf*) Abschlagstelle *f*; (*object*) Tee *nt*.

teem [tiːm] *vi* (*swarm*) wimmeln (*with* von); (*pour*) gießen.

teenage [ˈtiːneɪdʒ] *a fashions etc* Teenager-, jugendlich; —r Teenager *m*, Jugendliche(r) *mf*.

teens [tiːnz] *npl* Teenagerjahre *pl*, Jugendjahre *pl*.

teeter [ˈtiːtə*] *vi* schwanken.

teeth [tiːθ] *npl of* **tooth**.

teethe [tiːð] *vi* zahnen.

teething ring [ˈtiːðɪŋrɪŋ] *n* Beißring *m*.

teetotal [ˈtiːtəʊtl] *a* abstinent; —ler, (*US*) —er Antialkoholiker *m*, Abstinenzler *m*.

telecommunications [ˈtelɪkəmjuːnɪˈkeɪʃənz] *npl* Fernmeldewesen *nt*.

telegram [ˈtelɪgræm] *n* Telegramm *nt*.

telegraph [ˈtelɪgrɑːf] *n* Telegraph *m*; —ic [telɪˈgræfɪk] *a address* Telegramm-; — pole Telegraphenmast *m*.

telepathic [telɪˈpæθɪk] *a* telepathisch.

telepathy [təˈlepəθɪ] *n* Telepathie *f*, Gedankenübertragung *f*.

telephone [ˈtelɪfəʊn] *n* Telefon *nt*, Fernsprecher *m*; *vi* telefonieren; *vt* anrufen; *message* telefonisch mitteilen; — booth, — box Telefonhäuschen *nt*, Telefonzelle *f*; — call Telefongespräch *nt*, Anruf *m*; — directory Telefonbuch *nt*; — exchange Telefonvermittlung *f*, Telefonzentrale *f*; — number Telefonnummer *f*.

telephonist [təˈlefənɪst] *n* Telefonist(in *f*) *m*.

telephoto lens ['telɪ'fəʊtəʊ'lenz] n
Teleobjektiv nt.

teleprinter ['telɪprɪntə*] n
Fernschreiber m.

telescope ['telɪskəʊp] n Teleskop
nt, Fernrohr nt; vt ineinander-
schieben.

telescopic [telɪs'kɒpɪk] a tele-
skopisch; aerial etc ausziehbar.

televiewer ['telɪvjuːə*] n Fernseh-
teilnehmer(in f) m.

televise ['telɪvaɪz] vt durch das
Fernsehen übertragen.

television ['telɪvɪʒən] n Fernsehen
nt; to watch — fernsehen; — (set)
Fernsehapparat m, Fernseher m;
on — im Fernsehen.

telex ['teleks] n Telex nt.

tell [tel] irreg vt story erzählen;
secret ausplaudern; (say, make
known) sagen (sth to sb jdm etw);
(distinguish) erkennen (sb by sth
jdn an etw dat); (be sure) wissen;
(order) sagen, befehlen (sb jdm);
to — a lie lügen; to — sb about
sth jdm von etw erzählen; vi (be
sure) wissen; (divulge) es
verraten; (have effect) sich aus-
wirken; — off vt schimpfen; — on
vt verraten, verpetzen; **—er**
Kassenbeamte(r) mf; **—ing**
verräterisch; blow hart; moment
der Wahrheit; **—tale** a verräterisch.

telly ['telɪ] n (col) Fernseher m.

temerity [tɪ'merɪtɪ] n (Toll)-
kühnheit f.

temper ['tempə*] n (disposition)
Temperament nt, Gemütsart f;
(anger) Gereiztheit f, Zorn m; to
be in a (bad) — wütend or gereizt
sein; vt (tone down) mildern;
metal härten; **quick** **—ed** jähzornig,
aufbrausend; **—ament** Temperament nt, Veranlagung f; **—amental**
[tempərə'mentl] a (moody) launisch.

temperance ['tempərəns] n
Mäßigung f; (abstinence) Enthalt-
samkeit f; — hotel alkoholfreie(s)
Hotel nt.

temperate ['tempərət] a gemäßigt.

temperature ['temprɪtʃə*] n
Temperatur f; (Med: high —)
Fieber nt.

tempered ['tempəd] a steel
gehärtet.

tempest ['tempɪst] n (wilder)
Sturm m; **—uous** [tem'pestjʊəs] a
stürmisch; (fig) ungestüm.

template ['templət] n Schablone f.

temple ['templ] n Tempel m;
(Anat) Schläfe f.

tempo ['tempəʊ] n Tempo nt.

temporal ['tempərəl] a (of time)
zeitlich; (worldly) irdisch, weltlich.

temporarily ['tempərərɪlɪ] ad
zeitweilig, vorübergehend.

temporary ['tempərərɪ] a
vorläufig; road, building
provisorisch.

tempt [tempt] vt (persuade)
verleiten, in Versuchung führen;
(attract) reizen, (ver)locken;
—ation [temp'teɪʃən] Versuchung
f; **—ing** a person verführerisch;
object, situation verlockend.

ten [ten] num zehn.

tenable ['tenəbl] a haltbar; to be
— (post) vergeben werden.

tenacious [tə'neɪʃəs], **—ly** ad [tə'neɪʃəs, -lɪ]
zäh, hartnäckig.

tenacity [tə'næsɪtɪ] n Zähigkeit f,
Hartnäckigkeit f.

tenancy ['tenənsɪ] n Mietverhältnis
nt; Pachtverhältnis nt.

tenant ['tenənt] n Mieter m; (of
larger property) Pächter m.

tend [tend] vt (look after) sich
kümmern um; vi neigen, tendieren
(to zu); to — to do sth (things)

etw gewöhnlich tun; **—ency**
Tendenz f; (of person also)
Neigung f.

tender ['tendə*] a (soft) weich,
zart; (delicate) zart; (loving) liebevoll, zärtlich; n (Comm: offer)
Kostenanschlag m; **—ize** vt weich
machen; **—ly** ad liebevoll; touch
also zart; **—ness** Zartheit f; (being
loving) Zärtlichkeit f.

tendon ['tendən] n Sehne f.

tenement ['tenəmənt] n Mietshaus
nt.

tenet ['tenət] n Lehre f.

tennis ['tenɪs] n Tennis nt; **— ball**
Tennisball m; **— court** Tennisplatz
m; **— racket** Tennisschläger m.

tenor ['tenə*] n (voice) Tenor-
(stimme f) m; (singer) Tenor m;
(meaning) Sinn m, wesentliche(r)
Inhalt m.

tense [tens] a angespannt,
(stretched tight) gespannt, straff; n
Zeitform f; **—ly** ad (an)gespannt;
—ness Spannung f, (strain)
Angespanntheit f.

tension ['tenʃən] n Spannung f;
(strain) (An)gespanntheit f.

tent [tent] n Zelt nt.

tentacle ['tentəkl] n Fühler m; (of
sea animals) Fangarm m.

tentative ['tentətɪv] a movement
unsicher; offer Probe-; arrangement vorläufig; suggestion unverbindlich; **—ly** ad versuchsweise;
try, move vorsichtig.

tenterhooks ['tentəhuks] npl: to be
on **—** auf die Folter gespannt sein.

tenth [tenθ] a zehnte(r,s); n
Zehntel nt.

tent peg ['tentpeg] n Hering m.

tent pole ['tentpəʊl] n Zeltstange
f.

tenuous ['tenjʊəs] a fein; air dünn;
connection, argument schwach.

tenure ['tenjʊə*] n (of land) Besitz
m; (of office) Amtszeit f.

tepid ['tepɪd] a lauwarm.

term [tɜːm] n (period of time)
Zeit(raum m) f; (limit) Frist f;
(Sch) Quartal nt; (Univ) Trimester
nt; (expression) Ausdruck m; vt
(be)nennen; **—s** pl (conditions)
Bedingungen pl; (relationship)
Beziehungen pl; to be on good **—s**
with sb mit jdm gut auskommen;
—inal (Rail, bus **—inal**; also
—inus) Endstation f; (Aviat) Ter-
minal m; a Schluß-; (Med)
unheilbar; **—inal** cancer Krebs m
im Endstadium; **—inate** vt
beenden; vi enden, aufhören (in auf
+ dat); **—ination** [tɜːmɪˈneɪʃən]
Ende nt; (act) Beendigung f;
—inology [tɜːmɪˈnɒlədʒɪ]
Terminologie f.

termite ['tɜːmaɪt] n Termite f.

terrace ['terəs] n (of houses)
Häuserreihe f; (in garden etc)
Terrasse f; **—d** a garden terrassen-
förmig angelegt; house Reihen-.

terracotta ['terəˈkɒtə] n Terrakotta
f.

terrain [te'reɪn] n Gelände nt,
Terrain nt.

terrible ['terəbl] a schrecklich,
entsetzlich, fürchterlich.

terribly ['terəblɪ] ad fürchterlich.

terrier ['terɪə*] n Terrier m.

terrific a, **—ally** ad [təˈrɪfɪk, -lɪ]
unwahrscheinlich; **—!** klasse!

terrify ['terɪfaɪ] vt erschrecken;
—ing a erschreckend, grauenvoll.

territorial [terɪˈtɔːrɪəl] a Gebiets-,
territorial; **— waters** pl Hoheitsge-
wässer pl.

territory ['terɪtərɪ] n Gebiet nt.

terror ['terə*] n Schrecken m; (Pol) Terror m; **—ism** Terrorismus m; **—ist** Terrorist(in f) m; **—ize** vt terrorisieren.

terse [tɜ:s] a knapp, kurz, bündig.

Terylene ® ['terəli:n] n Terylen(e) nt.

test [test] n Probe f; (examination) Prüfung f; (Psych,' Tech) Test m; vt prüfen; (Psych) testen.

testament ['testəmənt] n Testament nt.

test card ['testkɑ:d] n (TV) Testbild nt.

test case ['testkeɪs] n (Jur) Präzedenzfall m; (fig) Musterbeispiel nt.

test flight ['testflaɪt] n Probeflug m.

testicle ['testɪkl] n Hoden m.

testify ['testɪfaɪ] vi aussagen; bezeugen (to acc).

testimonial [testɪ'məʊnɪəl] n (of character) Referenz f.

testimony ['testɪmənɪ] n (Jur) Zeugenaussage f; (fig) Zeugnis nt.

test match ['testmætʃ] n (Sport) Länderkampf m.

test paper ['testpeɪpə*] n schriftliche (Klassen)arbeit f.

test pilot ['testpaɪlət] n Testpilot m.

test tube ['testtju:b] n Reagenzglas nt.

testy ['testɪ] a gereizt; reizbar.

tetanus ['tetənəs] n Wundstarrkrampf m, Tetanus m.

tether ['teðə*] vt anbinden; to be at the end of one's — völlig am Ende sein.

text [tekst] n Text m; (of document) Wortlaut m; **—book** Lehrbuch nt.

textile ['tekstaɪl] n Gewebe nt; **—s** pl Textilien pl.

texture ['tekstʃə*] n Beschaffenheit f, Struktur f.

than [ðæn] prep, cj als.

thank [θæŋk] vt danken (+dat); you've him to — for your success Sie haben Ihren Erfolg ihm zu verdanken; **—ful** a dankbar; **—fully** ad (luckily) zum Glück; **—less** a undankbar; **—s** pl Dank m; **—s** to dank (+gen); — you, **—s** interj danke, dankeschön; T—sgiving (US) (Ernte)dankfest nt.

that [ðæt] a der/die/das, jene(r,s); pron das; cj daß; and **—'s** — und damit Schluß; **—** is das heißt; **after —** danach; **at —** dazu noch; **—** big so groß.

thatched [θætʃt] a strohgedeckt.

thaw [θɔ:] n Tauwetter nt; vi tauen; (frozen foods, fig: people) auftauen; vt auftauen lassen.

the [ði, ðə] def art der/die/das; to play — piano Klavier spielen; — sooner — better je eher desto besser.

theatre, (US) theater ['θɪətə*] n Theater nt; (for lectures etc) Saal m; (Med) Operationssaal m; **—goer** Theaterbesucher(in f) m.

theatrical [θɪ'ætrɪkl] a Theater-; career Schauspieler-; (showy) theatralisch.

theft [θeft] n Diebstahl m.

their [ðɛə*] poss a ihr; **—s** poss pron ihre(r,s).

them [ðem, ðəm] pron (acc) sie; (dat) ihnen.

theme [θi:m] n Thema nt; (Mus) Motiv nt; — song Titelmusik f.

themselves [ðəm'selvz] pl pron (reflexive) sich (selbst); (emphatic) selbst.

then [ðen] ad (at that time) damals; (next) dann; cj also, folglich; (furthermore) ferner; **a**

daniàlig; from — on von da an;
before — davor; by — bis dahin;
not till — erst dann.

theologian [θɪəˈlɒudʒən] *n*
Theologe *m*, Theologin *f*.

theological [θɪəˈlɒdʒɪkəl] *a*
theologisch.

theology [θɪˈɒlədʒɪ] *n* Theologie *f*.

theorem [ˈθɪərəm] *n* Grundsatz *m*,
Theorem *n*.

theoretical *a*, **—ly** *ad* [θɪəˈretɪkəl,
-ɪ] theoretisch.

theorize [ˈθɪəraɪz] *vi* theoretisieren.

theory [ˈθɪərɪ] *n* Theorie *f*.

therapeutic(al) [θerəˈpjuːtɪk(əl)] *a*
(Med) therapeutisch; erholsam.

therapist [ˈθerəpɪst] *n* Therapeut(in
f) *m*.

therapy [ˈθerəpɪ] *n* Therapie *f*,
Behandlung *f*.

there [ðɛə*] *ad* dort; (to a place)
dorthin; *interj* (see) na also; (to
child) (sei) ruhig, na na; — is es
gibt; — are es sind, es gibt; —
abouts *ad* so ungefähr; —after
[ðɛərˈɑːftə*] *ad* danach, später;
—by *ad* dadurch; —fore *ad* daher,
deshalb; —'s = there is.

thermal [ˈθɜːməl] *a* *springs*
Thermal-; (Phys) thermisch.

thermodynamics [ˈθɜːməʊdaɪ-
ˈnæmɪks] *n* Thermodynamik *f*.

thermometer [θəˈmɒmɪtə*] *n*
Thermometer *m*.

thermonuclear' [ˈθɜːməʊˈnjuːklɪə*]
a thermonuklear.

Thermos ® [ˈθɜːməs] *n* Thermosflasche *f*.

thermostat [ˈθɜːməstæt] *n* Thermostat *m*.

thesaurus [θɪˈsɔːrəs] *n* Synonym-
wörterbuch *n*.

these [ðiːz] *pl pron*, a diese.

thesis [ˈθiːsɪs] *n* (for discussion)
These *f*; (Univ) Dissertation *f*,
Doktorarbeit *f*.

they [ðeɪ] *pl pron* sie; (people in
general) man; —'d = they had;
they would; —'ll = they shall, they
will; —'re = they are; —'ve =
they have.

thick [θɪk] *a* dick; forest dicht;
liquid dickflüssig; (slow, stupid)
dumm, schwer von Begriff; *n:* in
the — of mitten in (+dat); —en
vi (fog) dichter werden; *vt* sauce
etc verdicken; —ness (of object)
Dicke *f*; Dichte *f*; Dickflüssigkeit
f; (of person) Dummheit *f*; —set
a untersetzt; —skinned *a* dick-
häutig.

thief [θiːf] *n* Dieb(in *f*) *m*.

thieving [ˈθiːvɪŋ] *n* Stehlen *nt*; *a*
diebisch.

thigh [θaɪ] *n* Oberschenkel *m*;
—bone Oberschenkelknochen *m*.

thimble [ˈθɪmbl] *n* Fingerhut *m*.

thin [θɪn] *a* dünn; person also
mager; (not abundant) spärlich;
fog, rain leicht; excuse schwach.

thing [θɪŋ] *n* Ding *nt*; (affair) Sache
f; my —s *pl* meine Sachen *pl*.

think [θɪŋk] *vti* irreg denken;
(believe) meinen, denken; to — of
doing sth vorhaben or beabsichtigen, etw zu tun; — over *vt*
überdenken; — up *vt* sich (dat)
ausdenken; —ing *a* denkend.

thinly [ˈθɪnlɪ] *ad* dünn; disguised
kaum.

thinness [ˈθɪnnəs] *n* Dünnheit *f*;
Magerkeit *f*; Spärlichkeit *f*.

third [θɜːd] *a* dritte(r,s); *n* (person)
Dritte(r) *mf*; (part) Drittel *nt*; —ly
ad drittens; — party insurance
Haftpflichtversicherung *f*; —rate
a minderwertig.

thirst [θɜːst] n (lit, fig) Durst m; (fig) Verlangen nt; **—y** a person durstig; work durstig machend; **to be —y** Durst haben.

thirteen [ˈθɜːˈtiːn] num dreizehn.

thirty [ˈθɜːtɪ] num dreißig.

this [ðɪs] a diese(r,s); pron dies/das; **it was — long** es war so lang.

thistle [ˈθɪsl] n Distel f.

thong [θɒŋ] n (Leder)riemen m.

thorn [θɔːn] n Dorn m, Stachel m; (plant) Dornbusch m; **—y** a dornig; problem schwierig.

thorough [ˈθʌrə] a gründlich; contempt tief; **—bred** Vollblut nt; a reinrassig, Vollblut-; **—fare** Straße f; **—ly** ad gründlich; (extremely) vollkommen, äußerst; **—ness** Gründlichkeit f.

those [ðəʊz] pl pron die (da), jene; a die, jene; **— who** diejenigen, die.

though [ðəʊ] cj obwohl; ad trotzdem; **as — als** ob.

thought [θɔːt] n (idea) Gedanke m; (opinion) Auffassung f; (thinking) Denken nt, Denkvermögen nt; **—ful** a (thinking) gedankenvoll, nachdenklich; (kind) rücksichtsvoll, aufmerksam; **—less** a gedankenlos, unbesonnen; (unkind) rücksichtslos.

thousand [ˈθaʊzənd] num tausend.

thrash [θræʃ] vt (lit) verdreschen; (fig) (vernichtend) schlagen.

thread [θred] n Faden m, Garn nt; (on screw) Gewinde nt; (in story) Faden m, Zusammenhang m; vt needle einfädeln; **— one's way** sich hindurchschlängeln; **—bare** a (lit, fig) fadenscheinig.

threat [θret] n Drohung f; (danger) Bedrohung f, Gefahr f; **—en vt** bedrohen; vi drohen; **to —en sb with sth** jdm etw androhen;

—ening a drohend; letter Droh-.

three [θriː] num drei; **—-dimensional** a dreidimensional; **—-fold** a dreifach; **—-piece suit** dreiteilige(r) Anzug m; **—-piece suite** dreiteilige Polstergarnitur f; **—-ply** a wool dreifach; wood dreischichtig; **—-quarter** [ˈθriːˈkwɔːtə*] a dreiviertel; **—-wheeler** Dreiradwagen m.

thresh [θreʃ] vti dreschen; **—ing machine** Dreschmaschine f.

threshold [ˈθreʃhəʊld] n Schwelle f.

thrift [θrɪft] n Sparsamkeit f; **—y** a sparsam.

thrill [θrɪl] n Reiz m, Erregung f; **it gave me quite a — to ...** es war ein Erlebnis für mich,·zu ...; vt begeistern, packen; vi beben, zittern; **—er** Krimi m; **—ing** a spannend, packend; news aufregend.

thrive [θraɪv] vi gedeihen (on bei), **thriving** [ˈθraɪvɪŋ] a blühend, gut gedeihend.

throat [θrəʊt] n Hals m, Kehle f.

throb [θrɒb] n Pochen nt, Schlagen nt; (Puls)schlag m; vi klopfen, pochen.

throes [θrəʊz] npl: **in the — of** mitten in (+ dat).

thrombosis [θrɒmˈbəʊsɪs] n Thrombose f.

throne [θrəʊn] n Thron m; (Eccl) Stuhl m.

throttle [ˈθrɒtl] n Gashebel m; **to open the — Gas** geben; vt erdrosseln.

through [θruː] prep durch; (time) während (+ gen); (because of) aus, durch; ad durch; **to put sb —** (Tel) jdn verbinden (to mit); a ticket, train durchgehend; (finished) fertig; **—out** [θruːˈaʊt] prep (place) überall in (+ dat); (time) während (+ gen); ad überall; die ganze Zeit; we're — es ist aus zwischen uns.

throw [θrəʊ] n Wurf m; vt irreg werfen; — **out** vt hinauswerfen; rubbish wegwerfen; plan verwerfen; — **up** vti (vomit) speien; —**away** a (disposable) Wegwerf-; bottle Einweg-; —**in** Einwurf m.

thru [θruː] (US) = **through**.

thrush [θrʌʃ] n Drossel f.

thrust [θrʌst] n (Tech) Schubkraft f; vti irreg (push) stoßen; (fig) sich drängen; **to** — oneself on sb sich jdm aufdrängen; —**ing** a person aufdringlich, unverfroren.

thud [θʌd] n dumpfe(r) (Auf)schlag m.

thug [θʌg] n Schlägertyp m.

thumb [θʌm] n Daumen m; vt book durchblättern; a well-—ed book ein abgegriffenes Buch; **to** — a lift per Anhalter fahren (wollen); — **index** Daumenregister nt; —**nail** Daumennagel m; —**tack** (US) Reißzwecke f.

thump [θʌmp] n (blow) Schlag m; (noise) Bums m; vi hämmern, pochen; vt schlagen auf (+ acc).

thunder [θʌndə*] n Donner m; vi donnern; vt brüllen; —**ous** a stürmisch; —**storm** Gewitter nt, Unwetter nt; —**struck** a wie vom Donner gerührt; —**y** a gewitterschwül.

Thursday [θɜːzdeɪ] n Donnerstag m.

thus [ðʌs] ad (in this way) so; (therefore) somit, also, folglich.

thwart [θwɔːt] vt vereiteln, durchkreuzen; person hindern.

thyme [taɪm] n Thymian m.

thyroid [θaɪrɔɪd] n Schilddrüse f.

tiara [tɪˈɑːrə] n Diadem nt; (pope's) Tiara f.

tic [tɪk] n Tick m.

tick [tɪk] n (sound) Ticken nt; (mark) Häkchen nt; **in a** — (col) sofort; vi ticken; vt abhaken.

ticket [ˈtɪkɪt] n (for travel) Fahrkarte f; (for entrance) (Eintritts)karte f; (price —) Preisschild nt; (luggage —) (Gepäck)schein m; (raffle —) Los nt; (parking —) Strafzettel m; (permission) Parkschein m; — **collector** Fahrkartenkontrolleur m; — **holder** Karteninhaber m; — **office** (Rail etc) Fahrkartenschalter m; (Theat etc) Kasse f.

ticking-off [ˈtɪkɪŋˈɒf] n (col) Anschnauzer m.

tickle [ˈtɪkl] n Kitzeln nt; vt kitzeln; (amuse) amüsieren; that —d her fancy das gefiel ihr.

ticklish [ˈtɪklɪʃ] a (lit, fig) kitzlig.

tidal [ˈtaɪdl] a Flut-, Tide-.

tidbit [ˈtɪdbɪt] n (US) Leckerbissen m.

tiddlywinks [ˈtɪdlɪwɪŋks] n Floh(hüpf)spiel nt.

tide [taɪd] n Gezeiten pl, Ebbe f und Flut; **the** — **is in/out** es ist Flut/Ebbe.

tidily [ˈtaɪdɪlɪ] ad sauber, ordentlich.

tidiness [ˈtaɪdɪnəs] n Ordnung f.

tidy [ˈtaɪdɪ] a ordentlich; vt aufräumen, in Ordnung bringen.

tie [taɪ] n (necktie) Kravatte f; Schlips m; (sth connecting) Band nt; (Sport) Unentschieden nt; vt (fasten, restrict) binden; knot schnüren, festbinden; vi (Sport) unentschieden spielen; (in competition) punktgleich sein; — **down** vt (lit) festbinden; (fig) binden; — **up** vt dog anbinden;

parcel verschnüren; *boat* festmachen; *person* fesseln; **I am —d up** right now ich bin im Moment beschäftigt.

tier [tɪə*] *n* Reihe *f*, Rang *m*; (*of cake*) Etage *f*.

tiff [tɪf] *n* kleine Meinungsverschiedenheit *f*.

tiger ['taɪgə*] *n* Tiger *m*.

tight [taɪt] *a* (*close*) eng, knapp; *schedule* gedrängt; (*firm*) fest, dicht; *screw* festsitzend; *control* streng; (*stretched*) stramm, (an)gespannt; (*col*) blau, stramm; **—s** *pl* Strumpfhose *f*; **—en** *vt* anziehen, anspannen; *restrictions* verschärfen; *vi* sich spannen; **—fisted** *a* knauserig; **—ly** *ad* eng; fest, dicht; *stretched* straff; **—ness** Enge *f*; Festigkeit *f*; Straffheit *f*; (*of money*) Knappheit *f*; **—rope** Seil *nt*.

tile [taɪl] *n* (*in roof*) Dachziegel *m*; (*on wall or floor*) Fliese *f*; **—d** *a roof* gedeckt, Ziegel-; *floor, wall* mit Fliesen belegt.

till [tɪl] *n* Kasse *f*; *vt* bestellen; *prep,cj* bis; **not —** (*in future*) nicht vor; (*in past*) erst.

tiller ['tɪlə*] *n* Ruderpinne *f*.

tilt [tɪlt] *vt* kippen, neigen; *vi* sich neigen.

timber ['tɪmbə*] *n* Holz *nt*; (*trees*) Baumbestand *m*.

time [taɪm] *n* Zeit *f*; (*occasion*) Mal *nt*; (*rhythm*) Takt *m*; *vt* zur rechten Zeit tun, zeitlich einrichten; (*Sport*) stoppen; **I have no — for** people like him für Leute wie ihn habe ich nichts übrig; **in 2 weeks' —** in 2 Wochen; **for the —** being vorläufig; **at all —s** immer; **at one —** früher; **at no —** nie; **at —s** manchmal; **by the —** bis; **this —** diesmal, dieses Mal; **to have a**

good — viel Spaß haben, sich amüsieren; **in —** (*soon enough*) rechtzeitig; (*after some time*) mit der Zeit; (*Mus*) im Takt; **on —** pünktlich, rechtzeitig; **five —s** fünfmal; **just imagine! what — is it?** wieviel Uhr ist es?, wie spät ist es?; **—keeper** Zeitnehmer *m*; **—lag** (*in travel*) Verzögerung *f*; (*difference*) Zeitunterschied *m*; **—less** *a beauty* zeitlos; **— limit** Frist *f*; **—ly** *a* rechtzeitig; *günstig; **—saving** *a* zeitsparend; **— switch** Zeitschalter *m*; **—table** Fahrplan *m*; (*Sch*) Stundenplan *m*; **— zone** Zeitzone *f*.

timid ['tɪmɪd] *a* ängstlich, schüchtern; **—ity** [tɪ'mɪdtɪ] Ängstlichkeit *f*; **—ly** *ad* ängstlich.

timing ['taɪmɪŋ] *n* Wahl *f* des richtigen Zeitpunkts, Timing *nt*; (*Aut*) Einstellung *f*.

timpani ['tɪmpənɪ] *npl* Kesselpauken *pl*.

tin [tɪn] *n* (*metal*) Blech *nt*; (*container*) Büchse *f*, Dose *f*; **—foil** Staniolpapier *nt*.

tinge [tɪndʒ] *n* (*colour*) Färbung *f*; (*fig*) Anflug *m*; *vt* färben, einen Anstrich geben (+*dat*).

tingle ['tɪŋgl] *n* Prickeln *nt*; *vi* prickeln.

tinker ['tɪŋkə*] *n* Kesselflicker *m*; **— with** *vt* herumpfuschen an (+*dat*).

tinkle ['tɪŋkl] *n* Klingeln *nt*; *vi* klingeln.

tinned [tɪnd] *a food* Dosen-, Büchsen-.

tinny ['tɪnɪ] *a* Blech-, blechern.

tin opener ['tɪnəʊpnə*] *n* Dosen- *or* Büchsenöffner *m*.

tinsel ['tɪnsəl] *n* Rauschgold *nt*; Lametta *nt*.

tint [tɪnt] n Farbton m; (slight colour) Anflug m; (hair) Tönung f.

tiny ['taɪnɪ] a winzig.

tip [tɪp] n (pointed end) Spitze f; (money) Trinkgeld nt; (hint) Wink m, Tip m; it's on the — of my tongue es liegt mir auf der Zunge; vt (slant) kippen; hat antippen; (— over) umkippen; waiter ein Trinkgeld geben (+dat); —off Hinweis m, Tip m; —ped a cigarette Filter-.

tipple ['tɪpl] n (drink) Schnäpschen nt.

tipsy ['tɪpsɪ] a beschwipst.

tiptoe ['tɪptəʊ] n: on — auf Zehenspitzen.

tiptop ['tɪp'tɒp] a: in — condition tipptopp, erstklassig.

tire ['taɪə*] n (US) = tyre; vti ermüden, müde machen/werden; —d a müde; to be —d of sth etw satt haben; —dness Müdigkeit f; —less a, —lessly ad unermüdlich; —some a lästig.

tiring ['taɪərɪŋ] a ermüdend.

tissue ['tɪʃuː] n Gewebe nt; (paper handkerchief) Papiertaschentuch nt; — paper Seidenpapier nt.

tit [tɪt] n (bird) Meise f; (col: breast) Titte f; — for tat wie du mir, so ich dir.

titbit ['tɪtbɪt] n Leckerbissen m.

titillate ['tɪtɪleɪt] vt kitzeln.

titillation [tɪtɪ'leɪʃən] n Kitzeln nt.

titivate ['tɪtɪveɪt] vt schniegeln.

title ['taɪtl] n Titel m; (in law) Rechtstitel m, Eigentumsrecht nt; — deed Eigentumsurkunde f; — role Hauptrolle f.

tittle-tattle ['tɪtltætl] n Klatsch m.

titter ['tɪtə*] vi kichern.

titular ['tɪtjʊlə*] a Titular-, nominell; possessions Titel-.

to [tuː, tə] prep (towards) zu; (with countries, towns) nach; (indir obj) dat; (as far as) bis; (next to, attached to) an (+dat); (per) pro; cj (in order to) um... zu; ad — and fro hin und her; to go — school/the theatre/bed in die Schule/ins Theater/ins Bett gehen; I have never been — Germany ich war noch nie in Deutschland; to give sth — sb jdm etw geben; — this day bis auf den heutigen Tag; 20 (minutes) — 4 20 (Minuten) vor 4; superior — sth besser als etw; they tied him — a tree sie banden ihn an einen Baum.

toad [təʊd] n Kröte f; —stool Giftpilz m; —y Speichellecker m, Kriecher m; vi kriechen (to vor +dat).

toast [təʊst] n (bread) Toast m; (drinking) Trinkspruch m; vt trinken auf (+acc); bread toasten; (warm) wärmen; —er Toaster m; —master Zeremonienmeister m; —rack Toastständer m.

tobacco [tə'bækəʊ] n Tabak m; —nist [tə'bækənɪst] Tabakhändler m; —nist's (shop) Tabakladen m.

toboggan [tə'bɒgən] n (Rodel)-schlitten m.

today [tə'deɪ] ad heute; (at the present time) heutzutage; n (day) heutige(r) Tag m; (time) Heute nt, heutige Zeit f.

toddle ['tɒdl] vi watscheln.

toddler ['tɒdlə*] n Kleinkind nt.

toddy ['tɒdɪ] n (Whisky)grog m.

to-do [tə'duː] n Aufheben nt, Theater nt.

toe [təʊ] n Zehe f; (of sock, shoe) Spitze f; vt: — the line (fig) sich einfügen; — hold Halt m für die Fußspitzen; —nail Zehennagel m.

toffee ['tɒfi] n Sahnebonbon nt; **—apple** kandierte(r) Apfel m.

toga ['təʊgə] n Toga f.

together [tə'geðə*] ad zusammen; (at the same time) gleichzeitig; **—ness** (company) Beisammensein nt; (feeling) Zusammengehörigkeitsgefühl nt.

toil [tɔɪl] n harte Arbeit f, Plackerei f; vi sich abmühen, sich plagen.

toilet ['tɔɪlət] n Toilette f; a Toiletten-; **— bag** Waschbeutel m; **— paper** Toilettenpapier nt; **—ries** ['tɔɪlətrɪz] pl Toilettenartikel pl; **—roll** Rolle f Toilettenpapier; **— soap** Toilettenseife f; **— water** Toilettenwasser nt.

token ['təʊkən] n Zeichen nt; (gift —) Gutschein m.

tolerable ['tɒlərəbl] a (bearable) erträglich; (fairly good) leidlich.

tolerably ['tɒlərəblɪ] ad ziemlich, leidlich.

tolerance ['tɒlərəns] n Toleranz f.

tolerant a, **—ly** ad ['tɒlərənt, -lɪ] tolerant; (patient) geduldig.

tolerate ['tɒləreɪt] vt dulden; noise ertragen.

toleration [tɒlə'reɪʃən] n Toleranz f.

toll [təʊl] n Gebühr f; it took a heavy — of human life es forderte or kostete viele Menschenleben; vi (bell) läuten; **—bridge** gebührenpflichtige Brücke f; **—road** gebührenpflichtige Autostraße f.

tomato [tə'mɑːtəʊ] n, pl **-es** Tomate f.

tomb [tuːm] n Grab(mal) nt.

tombola [tɒm'bəʊlə] n Tombola f.

tomboy ['tɒmbɔɪ] n Wildfang m; she's a — sie ist sehr burschikos.

tombstone ['tuːmstəʊn] n Grabstein m.

tomcat ['tɒmkæt] n Kater m.

tome [təʊm] n (volume) Band m; (big book) Wälzer m.

tomorrow [tə'mɒrəʊ] n Morgen nt; ad morgen.

ton [tʌn] n Tonne f; **-s of** (col) eine Unmenge von.

tonal ['təʊnl] a tonal; Klang-.

tone [təʊn] n Ton m; vi (harmonize) passen (zu), harmonisieren (mit); vt eine Färbung geben (+ dat); **— down** vt criticism, demands mäßigen; colours abtonen; **—deaf** a ohne musikalisches Gehör.

tongs [tɒŋz] npl Zange f; (curling —) Lockenstab m.

tongue [tʌŋ] n Zunge f; (language) Sprache f; with — in cheek ironisch, scherzhaft; **—tied** a stumm, sprachlos; **—twister** Zungenbrecher m.

tonic ['tɒnɪk] n (Med) Stärkungsmittel nt; (Mus) Grundton m, Tonika f; **— water** Tonic(water) m.

tonight [tə'naɪt] n heutige(r) Abend m; diese Nacht f; ad heute abend; heute nacht.

tonnage ['tʌnɪdʒ] n Tonnage f.

tonsil ['tɒnsl] n Mandel f; **—itis** [tɒnsɪ'laɪtɪs] Mandelentzündung f.

too [tuː] ad zu; (also) auch.

tool [tuːl] n (lit, fig) Werkzeug nt; **—box** Werkzeugkasten m; **—kit** Werkzeug nt.

toot [tuːt] n Hupen nt; vi tuten; (Aut) hupen.

tooth [tuːθ] n, pl **teeth** Zahn m; **—ache** Zahnschmerzen pl, Zahnweh nt; **—brush** Zahnbürste f; **—paste** Zahnpasta f; **—pick**

Zahnstocher *m;* — powder Zahnpulver *nt.*

top [tɔp] *n* Spitze *f;* (of mountain) Gipfel *m;* (of tree) Wipfel *m;* (toy) Kreisel *m;* (— gear) vierte(r) Gang *m;* a oberste(r,s); *vt* list an erster Stelle stehen auf (+*dat*); **to — it all,** he said ... und er setzte dem noch die Krone auf, indem er sagte ...; **from —,** to toe von oben bis Fuß; **—coat** Mantel *m;* **—flight** a erstklassig, prima; **— hat** Zylinder *m;* **—heavy** a oben schwerer als unten, kopflastig.

topic [tɔpɪk] *n* Thema *nt,* Gesprächsgegenstand *m;* **—al** a aktuell.

topless [tɔpləs] *a dress* oben ohne.

top-level [tɔp'levl] a auf höchster Ebene.

topmost [tɔpməust] a oberste(r,s), höchste(r,s).

topple [tɔpl] *vti* stürzen, kippen.

top-secret [tɔp'si:krət] a streng geheim.

topsy-turvy [tɔpsɪ'tɜ:vɪ] ad durcheinander; a auf den Kopf gestellt.

torch [tɔ:tʃ] *n* (Elec) Taschenlampe *f;* (with flame) Fackel *f.*

torment [tɔ:ment] *n* Qual *f;* [tɔ:'ment] *vt* (annoy) plagen; (distress) quälen.

torn [tɔ:n] a hin- und hergerissen.

tornado [tɔ:'neɪdəu] *n* Tornado *m,* Wirbelsturm *m.*

torpedo [tɔ:'pi:dəu] *n* Torpedo *m.*

torpor [tɔ:pə*] *n* Erstarrung *f.*

torrent [tɔrənt] *n* Sturzbach *m;* **—ial** [tɔ'renʃəl] a wolkenbruchartig.

torso [tɔ:səu] *n* Torso *m.*

tortoise [tɔ:təs] *n* Schildkröte *f.*

tortuous [tɔ:tjuəs] a (winding) gewunden; (deceitful) krumm, unehrlich.

torture [tɔ:tʃə*] *n* Folter *f;* *vt* foltern.

Tory [tɔ:rɪ] *n* Tory *m;* a Tory-, konservativ.

toss [tɔs] *vt* werfen, schleudern; *n* (of coin) Hochwerfen *nt;* **to — a coin, to — up for sth** etw mit einer Münze entscheiden.

tot [tɔt] *n* (small quantity) bißchen *nt;* (small child) Knirps *m.*

total [təutl] *n* Gesamtheit *f,* Ganze(s) *nt;* a ganz, gesamt, total; *vt* (add . up) zusammenzählen; (amount to) sich belaufen auf; **—itarian** [təutælɪ'teərɪən] a totalitär; **—ity** [təu'tælɪtɪ] Gesamtheit *f;* **—ly** ad gänzlich, total.

totem pole [təutəmpəul] *n* Totempfahl *m.*

totter [tɔtə*] *vi* wanken, schwanken, wackeln.

touch [tʌtʃ] *n* Berührung *f;* (sense of feeling) Tastsinn *m;* (small amount) Spur *f;* (style) Stil *m;* *vt* (feel) berühren; (come against) leicht anstoßen; (emotionally) bewegen, rühren; **in — with** in Verbindung mit; **— on** *vt topic* berühren, erwähnen; **— up** *vt paint* auffrischen; **—-and-go** a riskant, knapp; **—down** Landen *nt,* Niedergehen *nt;* **—iness** Empfindlichkeit *f;* **—ing** a rührend, ergreifend; **—line** Seitenlinie *f;* **—y** a empfindlich, reizbar.

tough [tʌf] a (strong) zäh, widerstandsfähig; (difficult) schwierig, hart; meat zäh; **— luck** Pech *nt;* n Schläger(typ) *m;* **—en** *vt* zäh machen; (make strong) abhärten; *vi* zäh werden; **—ness** Zähigkeit *f;* Härte *f.*

toupée [tu:peɪ] *n* Toupet *nt.*

tour ['tʊə*] n Reise f, Tour f, Fahrt f; vi umherreisen; (Theat) auf Tour sein/gehen; —ing Umherreisen nt; (Theat) Tournee f; —ism Fremdenverkehr m, Tourismus m; —ist Tourist(in f); a (class) Touristen-; ad Touristenklasse; —ist office Verkehrsamt nt.

tournament ['tʊənəmənt] n Turnier nt.

tousled ['taʊzld] a zerzaust.

tow [təʊ] n Schleppen nt; vt (ab)schleppen.

toward(s) [tə'wɔ:d(z)] prep (with time) gegen; (in direction of) nach; he walked — me/the town er kam auf mich zu/er ging auf die Stadt zu; my feelings — him meine Gefühle ihm gegenüber.

towel ['taʊəl] n Handtuch nt.

tower ['taʊə*] n Turm m; — over vi (lit, fig) überragen; —ing a hochragend; rage rasend.

town [taʊn] n Stadt f; — clerk Stadtdirektor m; — hall Rathaus nt; — planner Stadtplaner m; — planning Stadtplanung f.

towpath ['təʊpɑ:θ] n Leinpfad m.

towrope ['təʊrəʊp] n Abschlepptau nt.

toxic ['tɒksɪk] a giftig, Gift-.

toy [tɔɪ] n Spielzeug nt; — with vt spielen mit; —shop Spielwarengeschäft nt.

trace [treɪs] n Spur f; vt (follow a course) nachspüren (+dat); (find out) aufspüren; (copy) zeichnen, durchpausen.

track [træk] n (mark) Spur f; (path) Weg m, Pfad m; (race—) Rennbahn f; (Rail) Gleis nt; vt verfolgen; to keep — of sb jdn im Auge behalten; to keep — of an argument einer Argumentation folgen können; to keep — of the situation die Lage verfolgen; to

make —s (for) gehen (nach); — down vt aufspüren; —er dog Spürhund m; —less a pfadlos.

tract [trækt] n (of land) Gebiet nt; (booklet) Abhandlung f, Traktat nt.

tractor ['træktə*] n Traktor m.

trade [treɪd] n (commerce) Handel m; (business) Geschäft nt; (people) Geschäftsleute pl; (skilled manual work) Handwerk nt; vi handeln (in mit); vt tauschen; — in vt in Zahlung geben; —mark Warenzeichen nt; — name Handelsbezeichnung f; —r Händler m; —sman (shopkeeper) Geschäftsmann m; (workman) Handwerker m; (delivery man) Lieferant m; — union Gewerkschaft f; — unionist Gewerkschaftler(in f) m.

trading ['treɪdɪŋ] n Handel m; —estate Industriegelände nt; —stamp Rabattmarke f.

tradition [trə'dɪʃən] n Tradition f; —al a traditionell, herkömmlich; —ally ad üblicherweise, schon immer.

traffic ['træfɪk] n Verkehr m; (esp in drugs) Handel m (in mit); vt esp drugs handeln; — circle (US) Kreisverkehr m; — jam Verkehrsstauung f; — lights pl Verkehrsampeln pl.

tragedy ['trædʒədɪ] n (lit, fig) Tragödie f.

tragic ['trædʒɪk] a tragisch; —ally ad tragisch, auf tragische Weise.

trail [treɪl] n (track) Spur f, Fährte f; (of meteor) Schweif m; (of smoke) Rauchfahne f; (of dust) Staubwolke f; (road) Pfad m, Weg m; vt animal verfolgen; person folgen (+dat); (drag) schleppen; vi (hang loosely) schleifen; (plants) sich ranken; (be behind) hinter-

herhinken; (Sport) weit zurück-
liegen; (walk) zuckeln; on the —
auf der Spur; — behind vi zurückbleiben; —er Anhänger m; (US:
caravan) Wohnwagen m; (for film)
Vorschau f.

train [trein] n Zug m; (of dress)
Schleppe f; (series) Folge f, Kette
f; vt (teach) person ausbilden;
animal abrichten; mind schulen;
(Sport) trainieren; (aim) richten
(on auf +acc); plant wachsen
lassen, ziehen; vi (exercise)
trainieren; (study) ausgebildet
werden; —ed a eye geschult;
person, voice ausgebildet; —ee
Anlernling m; Lehrling m;
Praktikant(in f) m; —er (Sport)
Trainer m; Ausbilder m; —ing (for
occupation) Ausbildung f; (Sport)
Training nt; in —ing im Training;
—ing college Pädagogische Hochschule f, Lehrerseminar nt; (for
priests) Priesterseminar nt.

traipse [treips] vi latschen.

trait [trei(t)] n Zug m, Merkmal nt.

traitor ['treitə*] n Verräter m.

trajectory [trə'dʒektəri] n
Flugbahn f.

tram(car) ['træm(ka:*)] n
Straßenbahn f; —line Straßenbahn-
schiene f; (route) Straßenbahnlinie
f.

tramp [træmp] n Landstreicher m;
vi (walk heavily) stampfen,
stapfen; (travel on foot) wandern;
—le ['træmpl] vt (nieder)trampeln;
vi (herum)trampeln; —oline
Trampolin nt.

trance [tra:ns] n Trance f.

tranquil ['træŋkwil] a ruhig, friedlich; —ity [træŋ'kwliti] Ruhe f;
—izer Beruhigungsmittel nt.

trans- [trænz] pref Trans-.

transact [træn'zækt]' vt (durch)-
führen, abwickeln; —ion Durchführung f, Abwicklung f; (piece of
business) Geschäft nt; Transaktion
f.

transatlantic ['trænzət'læntik] a
transatlantisch.

transcend [træn'send] vt
übersteigen.

transcendent [træn'sendənt] a
transzendent.

transcript ['trænskript] n Abschrift
f, Kopie f; (Jur) Protokoll nt; —ion
[træn'skripʃən] Transkription f;
(product) Abschrift f.

transept ['trænsept] n Querschiff
nt.

transfer ['trænsfə*] n (trans-
ferring) Übertragung f; (of
business) Umzug m; (being trans-
ferred) Versetzung f; (design)
Abziehbild nt; (Sport) Transfer m;
(player) Transferspieler m;
[træns'fə:*] vt business verlegen;
person versetzen; prisoner über-
führen; drawing übertragen;
money überweisen; —able
[træns'fə:rəbl] a übertragbar.

transform [træns'fɔ:m] vt
umwandeln, verändern; —ation
[trænsfə'meiʃən] Umwandlung f,
Veränderung f, Verwandlung f;
—er (Elec) Transformator m.

transfusion [træns'fju:ʒən] n
Blutübertragung f, Transfusion f.

transient ['trænziənt] a kurz(lebig).

transistor [træn'zistə*] n (Elec)
Transistor m; (radio) Transistor-
radio nt.

transit ['trænzit] n: in —
unterwegs, auf dem Transport.

transition [træn'ziʃən] n Übergang
m; —al a Übergangs-.

transitive a, —ly ad ['trænzitiv,
-li] transitiv.

transitory ['trænzɪtərɪ] a vorübergehend.

translate [trænz'leɪt] vti übersetzen.

translation [trænz'leɪʃən] n Übersetzung f.

translator [trænz'leɪtə*] n Übersetzer(in f) m.

transmission [trænz'mɪʃən] n (of information) Übermittlung f; (Elec, Med, TV) Übertragung f; (Aut) Getriebe nt; (process) Übersetzung f.

transmit [trænz'mɪt] vt message übermitteln; (Elec, Med, TV) übertragen; **—ter** Sender m.

transparency [træns'pærənsɪ] n Durchsichtigkeit f, Transparenz f; (Phot also [-'pærənsɪ] Dia(positiv) nt.

transparent [træns'pærənt] a (lit) durchsichtig; (fig) offenkundig.

transplant [træns'plɑ:nt] vt umpflanzen; (Med) verpflanzen; (fig) person verpflanzen; ['træns'plɑ:nt] n (Med) Transplantation f; (organ) Transplantat nt.

transport ['trænspɔ:t] n Transport m, Beförderung f; (vehicle) fahrbare(r) Untersatz m; means of — Transportmittel nt; [træns'pɔ:t] vt befördern; transportieren; **—able** [træns'pɔ:təbl] a transportfähig; **—ation** [trænspɔ:'teɪʃən] n Transport m, Beförderung f; (means) Beförderungsmittel nt; (cost) Transportkosten pl.

transverse ['trænzvɜ:s] a Quer-; position horizontal; engine querliegend.

transvestite [trænz'vestaɪt] n Transvestit m.

trap [træp] n Falle f; (carriage) zweirädrige(r) Einspänner m; (col: mouth) Klappe f; vt fangen;

person in eine Falle locken; the miners were **—ed** die Bergleute waren eingeschlossen; **—door** Falltür f.

trapeze [trə'pi:z] n Trapez nt.

trapper ['træpə*] n Fallensteller m, Trapper m.

trappings ['træpɪŋz] npl Aufmachung f.

trash [træʃ] n (rubbish) wertlose(s) Zeug nt, Plunder m; (nonsense) Mist m, Blech nt; — **can** (US) Mülleimer m; **—y** a wertlos; novel etc Schund-.

trauma ['trɔ:mə] n Trauma nt; **—tic** [trɔ:'mætɪk] a traumatisch.

travel ['trævl] n Reisen nt; vi reisen, eine Reise machen; vt distance zurücklegen; country bereisen; **—ler**, (US) **—er** Reisende(r) mf; (salesman) Handlungsreisende(r) m; **—ler's cheque**, (US) **—er's check** Reisescheck m; **—ling**, (US) **—ing** Reisen nt; **—ling bag** Reisetasche f; — **sickness** Reisekrankheit f.

traverse [trə'vɜ:s] vt (cross) durchqueren; (lie across) überspannen.

travesty ['trævəstɪ] n Zerrbild nt, Travestie f; a — of justice ein Hohn m auf die Gerechtigkeit.

trawler ['trɔ:lə*] n Fischdampfer m, Trawler m.

tray [treɪ] n (tea —) Tablett nt; (receptacle) Schale f; (for mail) Ablage f.

treacherous ['tretʃərəs] a verräterisch; memory unzuverlässig; road tückisch.

treachery ['tretʃərɪ] n Verrat m; (of road) tückische(r) Zustand m.

treacle ['tri:kl] n Sirup m, Melasse f.

tread [tred] n Schritt m, Tritt m; (of stair) Stufe f; (on tyre) Profil

nt; vi irreg treten; (walk) gehen;
— on vt treten.auf (+acc).
treason ['tri:zn] n Verrat m (to an
+dat).
treasure ['treʒə*] n Schatz m; vt
schätzen; — hunt Schatzsuche f;
—r Kassenverwalter m,
Schatzmeister m.
treasury ['treʒəri] n (Pol) Finanz-
ministerium nt.
treat [tri:t] n besondere Freude f;
(school — etc) Fest nt; (outing)
Ausflug m; vt (deal with)
behandeln; (entertain) bewirten;
to — sb to sth jdn zu etw einladen,
jdm etw spendieren.
treatise ['tri:tiz] n Abhandlung f.
treatment ['tri:tmənt] n
Behandlung f.
treaty ['tri:ti] n Vertrag m.
treble ['trebl] a dreifach; vt verdreifachen; n (voice) Sopran m;
(music) Diskant m; — clef Violin-
schlüssel m.
tree [tri:] n Baum m; —-lined a
baumbestanden; — trunk Baum-
stamm m.
trek [trek] n Treck m, Zug m; vi
trecken.
trellis ['trelis] n Gitter nt; (for
gardening) Spalier m.
tremble ['trembl] vi zittern;
(ground) beben.
trembling ['tremblin] n Zittern nt;
a zitternd.
tremendous [trə'mendəs] a
gewaltig, kolossal; (col: very good)
prima; —ly ad ungeheuer, enorm;
(col) unheimlich.
tremor ['tremə*] n Zittern nt; (of
earth) Beben nt.
trench [trentʃ] n Graben m; (Mil)
Schützengraben m.

trend [trend] n Richtung f, Tendenz
f; vi sich neigen, tendieren; —y a
(col) modisch.
trepidation [trepɪ'deɪʃən] n
Beklommenheit f.
trespass ['trespas] vi widerrecht-
lich betreten (on acc); '—ers will
be prosecuted' 'Betreten verboten.'
tress [tres] n Locke f.
trestle ['tresl] n Bock m; — table
Klapptisch m.
tri- [traɪ] pref Drei-, drei-.
trial ['traɪəl] n (Jur) Prozeß m, Verfahren nt; (test) Versuch m, Probe
f; (hardship) Prüfung f; by — and
error durch Ausprobieren.
triangle ['traɪæŋgl] n Dreieck nt;
(Mus) Triangel f.
triangular [traɪ'æŋgjulə*] a
dreieckig.
tribal ['traɪbəl] a Stammes-.
tribe [traɪb] n Stamm m; —sman
Stammesangehörige(r) m.
tribulation [trɪbju'leɪʃən] n Not f,
Mühsal f.
tribunal [traɪ'bju:nl] n Gericht nt;
(inquiry) Untersuchungsausschuß
m.
tributary ['trɪbjutəri] n Nebenfluß
m.
tribute [trɪbju:t] n (admiration)
Zeichen nt der Hochachtung.
trice [traɪs] n: in a — im Nu.
trick [trɪk] n Trick m; (mischief)
Streich m; (habit) Angewohnheit
f; (Cards) Stich m; vt überlisten,
beschwindeln; —ery Betrügerei f,
Tricks pl.
trickle ['trɪkl] n Tröpfeln nt; (small
river) Rinnsal nt; vi tröpfeln;
(seep) sickern.
tricky ['trɪkɪ] a problem schwierig;
situation kitzlig.

tricycle ['traɪsɪkl] *n* Dreirad *nt*.

tried [traɪd] *a* erprobt, bewährt.

trier ['traɪə*] *n*: **to be a —** sich·(*dat*) ernsthaft Mühe geben.

trifle ['traɪfl] *n* Kleinigkeit *f*; (*Cook*) Trifle *m*; *ad*: **a —** ein bißchen.

trifling ['traɪflɪŋ] *a* geringfügig.

trigger ['trɪgə*] *n* Drücker *m*; **—off** *vt* auslösen.

trigonometry [trɪgə'nɒmɪtrɪ] *n* Trigonometrie *f*.

trilby ['trɪlbɪ] *n* weiche(r) Filzhut *m*.

trill [trɪl] *n* (*Mus*) Triller *m*.

trilogy ['trɪlədʒɪ] *n* Trilogie *f*.

trim [trɪm] *a* ordentlich, gepflegt; *figure* schlank; *n* (gute) Verfassung *f*; (*embellishment*) Verzierung *f*; **to give sb's hair a —** jdm die Haare etwas schneiden; *vt* (*clip*) schneiden; *trees* stutzen; (*decorate*) besetzen; *sails* trimmen; **—mings** *pl* (*decorations*) Verzierung(en *pl*) *f*; (*extras*) Zubehör *nt*.

Trinity ['trɪnɪtɪ] *n*: **the —** die Dreieinigkeit.

trinket ['trɪŋkɪt] *n* kleine(s) Schmuckstück *nt*.

trio ['triːəʊ] *n* Trio *nt*.

trip [trɪp] *n* (kurze) Reise *f*; (*outing*) Ausflug *m*; (*stumble*) Stolpern *nt*; *vi* (*walk quickly*) trippeln; (*stumble*) stolpern; **— over** *vt* stolpern über (*+acc*); **— up** *vi* stolpern; (*fig also*) einen Fehler machen; *vt* zu Fall bringen; (*fig*) hereinlegen.

tripe [traɪp] *n* (*food*) Kutteln *pl*; (*rubbish*) Mist *m*.

triple ['trɪpl] *n* dreifach; **—ts** ['trɪplɪts] *pl* Drillinge *pl*.

triplicate ['trɪplɪkət] *n*: **in — in** dreifacher Ausfertigung.

tripod ['traɪpɒd] *n* Dreifuß *m*; (*Phot*) Stativ *nt*.

tripper ['trɪpə*] *n* Ausflügler(in *f*) *m*.

trite [traɪt] *a* banal.

triumph ['traɪʌmf] *n* Triumph *m*; *vi* triumphieren; **—al** [traɪˈʌmfəl] *a* triumphal, Sieges-; **—ant** [traɪˈʌmfənt] *a* triumphierend; (*victorious*) siegreich; **—antly** *ad* triumphierend; siegreich.

trivial ['trɪvɪəl] *a* gering(fügig), trivial; **—lity** [trɪvɪˈælɪtɪ] *n* Trivialität *f*, Nebensächlichkeit *f*.

trolley ['trɒlɪ] *n* Handwagen *m*; (*in shop*) Einkaufswagen; (*for luggage*) Kofferkuli *m*; (*table*) Teewagen *m*; **— bus** O(berleitungs)bus *m*.

trollop ['trɒləp] *n* Hure *f*; (*slut*) Schlampe *f*.

trombone [trɒmˈbəʊn] *n* Posaune *f*.

troop [truːp] *n* Schar *f*; (*Mil*) Trupp *m*; **—s** *pl* Truppe *pl*; **— in/out** *vi* hinein-/hinausströmen; **—er** Kavallerist *m*; **—ship** Truppentransporter *m*.

trophy ['trəʊfɪ] *n* Trophäe *f*.

tropic ['trɒpɪk] *n* Wendekreis *m*; **the —s** *pl* die Tropen *pl*; **—al** *a* tropisch.

trot [trɒt] *n* Trott *m*; *vi* trotten.

trouble ['trʌbl] *n* (*worry*) Sorge *f*, Kummer *m*; (*in country, industry*) Unruhen *pl*; (*effort*) Umstand *m*, Mühe *f*; *vt* (*disturb*) beunruhigen, stören, belästigen; **to —** sich·(*dat*) etw tun; **to make —** Schwierigkeiten oder Unannehmlichkeiten machen; **to have — with** Ärger haben mit; **to be in —** Probleme oder Ärger haben; **—d** *a person* beunruhigt; *country* geplagt; **—free** *a* sorglos;

—**maker** Unruhestifter m;
—**shooter** Vermittler m; —**some** a
lästig, unangenehm; child
schwierig.

trough [trɒf] n (vessel) Trog m;
(channel) Rinne f, Kanal m; (Met)
Tief nt.

trounce [trauns] vt (esp Sport)
vernichtend schlagen.

troupe [tru:p] n Truppe f.

trousers ['trauzəz] npl (lange)
Hose f, Hosen pl.

trousseau ['tru:səu] n Aussteuer f.

trout [traut] n Forelle f.

trowel ['trauəl] n Kelle f.

truant ['truənt] n: to play — (die
Schule) schwänzen.

truce [tru:s] n Waffenstillstand m.

truck [trʌk] n Lastwagen m,
Lastauto nt; (Rail) offene(r) Güterwagen m; (barrow) Gepäckkarren
m; to have no — with sb nichts
zu tun haben wollen mit jdm; —
driver Lastwagenfahrer m; —**farm**
(US) Gemüsegärtnerei f.

truculent ['trʌkjulənt] a trotzig.

trudge [trʌdʒ] vi sich (mühselig)
dahinschleppen.

true [tru:] ·a (exact) wahr;
(genuine) echt; friend treu.

truffle ['trʌfl] n Trüffel f.

truly ['tru:li] ad (really) wirklich;
(exactly) genau; (faithfully) treu;
yours — Ihr sehr ergebener.

trump [trʌmp] n (Cards) Trumpf
m; —**ed-up** a erfunden.

trumpet ['trʌmpit] n Trompete f;
vt ausposaunen; vi trompeten.

truncated [trʌŋ'keitid] a
verstümmelt.

truncheon ['trʌntʃən] n
Gummiknüppel m.

trundle ['trʌndl] vt schieben; vi: —

along (person) dahinschlendern;
(vehicle) entlangrollen.

trunk [trʌŋk] n (of tree) (Baum)-
stamm m; (Anat) Rumpf m; (box)
Truhe f, Überseekoffer m; (of
elephant) Rüssel m; —**s** pl
Badehose f; — **call** Ferngespräch
nt.

truss [trʌs] n (Med) Bruchband nt.

trust [trʌst] n (confidence)
Vertrauen nt; (for property etc)
Treuhandvermögen nt; vt (rely on)
vertrauen (+dat), sich verlassen
auf (+acc); (hope) hoffen; — him
to break it! er muß es natürlich
kaputt machen, typisch!; to — sth
to sb jdm etw anvertrauen; —**ed**
a treu; —**ee** [trʌs'ti:] Vermögens-
verwalter m; —**ful**, a, —**ing** a vertrauensvoll; —**worthy** a vertrauens-
würdig; account glaubwürdig; —**y**
a treu, zuverlässig.

truth [tru:θ] n Wahrheit f; —**ful** a
ehrlich; —**fully** ad
wahrheitsgemäß; —**fulness** Ehrlichkeit f; (of statement) Wahrheit f.

try [trai] n Versuch m; to have a
— es versuchen; vt (attempt)
versuchen; (test) (aus)probieren;
(Jur) person unter Anklage stellen;
case verhandeln; (strain)
anstrengen; courage, patience auf
die Probe stellen; vi (make effort)
versuchen, sich bemühen; — on vt
dress anprobieren; hat auf-
probieren; — out vt ausprobieren;
—**ing** a schwierig; —**ing** for
anstrengend für.

tsar [zɑː*] n Zar m.

T-shirt ['ti:ʃɜ:t] n T-shirt nt.

T-square ['ti:skwɛə*] n
Reißschiene f.

tub [tʌb] n Wanne f, Kübel m; (for
margarine etc) Becher m.

tuba ['tju:bə] n Tuba f.

tubby ['tʌbɪ] a rundlich, klein und dick.

tube [tju:b] n (pipe) Röhre f, Rohr nt; (for toothpaste etc) Tube f; (in London) U-Bahn f; (Aut: for tyre) Schlauch m; **—less** a (Aut) schlauchlos.

tuber ['tju:bə*] n Knolle f.

tuberculosis [tjubɜ:kju'ləʊsɪs] n Tuberkulose f.

tube station ['tju:bsteɪʃən] n U-Bahnstation f.

tubular ['tju:bjʊlə*] a röhrenförmig.

tuck [tʌk] n (fold) Falte f, Einschlag m; vt (put) stecken; (gather) fälteln, einschlagen; **— away** vt wegstecken; **— in** vt hineinstecken; blanket etc feststecken; person zudecken; vi (eat) hineinhauen, zulangen; **— up** vt child warm zudecken; **— shop** Süßwarenladen m.

Tuesday ['tju:zdeɪ] n Dienstag m.

tuft [tʌft] n Büschel m.

tug [tʌg] n (jerk) Zerren nt, Ruck m; (Naut) Schleppdampfer m; vti zerren, ziehen; boat schleppen; **—of-war** Tauziehen nt.

tuition [tju:'ɪʃən] n Unterricht m.

tulip ['tju:lɪp] n Tulpe f.

tumble ['tʌmbl] n. (fall) Sturz m; vi (fall) fallen, stürzen; **— to** vt kapieren; **—down** a baufällig; **—r** (glass) Trinkglas nt, Wasserglas nt; (for drying) Trockenautomat m.

tummy ['tʌmɪ] n (col) Bauch m.

tumour ['tju:mə*] n Tumor m, Geschwulst f.

tumult ['tju:mʌlt] n Tumult m; **—uous** [tju:'multjʊəs] a lärmend, turbulent.

tumulus ['tju:mjʊləs] n Grabhügel m.

tuna ['tju:nə] n Thunfisch m.

tundra ['tʌndrə] n Tundra f.

tune [tju:n] n Melodie f; vt (put in tune) stimmen; (Aut) richtig einstellen; to sing in **—/out of —** richtig/falsch singen; to be out of **—** with nicht harmonieren mit; **— in** vi einstellen (to acc); **— up** vi (Mus) stimmen; **—er** (person) (Instrumenten)stimmer m; (radio set) Empfangsgerät nt, Steuergerät nt; (part) Tuner m, Kanalwähler m; **—ful** a melodisch.

tungsten ['tʌŋstən] n Wolfram nt.

tunic ['tju:nɪk] n Waffenrock m; (loose garment) lange Bluse f.

tuning ['tju:nɪŋ] n (Rad, Aut) Einstellen nt; (Mus) Stimmen nt.

tunnel ['tʌnl] n Tunnel m, Unterführung f; vi einen Tunnel anlegen.

tunny ['tʌnɪ] n Thunfisch m.

turban ['tɜ:bən] n Turban m.

turbid ['tɜ:bɪd] a trübe; (fig) verworren.

turbine ['tɜ:baɪn] n Turbine f.

turbot ['tɜ:bət] n Steinbutt m.

turbulence ['tɜ:bjʊləns] n (Aviat) Turbulenz f.

turbulent ['tɜ:bjʊlənt] a stürmisch.

tureen [tjʊri:n] n Terrine f.

turf [tɜ:f] n Rasen m; (piece) Sode f.

turgid ['tɜ:dʒɪd] a geschwollen.

turkey ['tɜ:kɪ] n Puter m, Truthahn m.

turmoil ['tɜ:mɔɪl] n Aufruhr m, Tumult m.

turn [tɜ:n] n (rotation) (Um)drehung f; (performance) (Programm)nummer f; (Med) Schock m; vt (rotate) umdrehen; (change position of) umdrehen, wenden; page umblättern; (transform) verwandeln; (direct) zuwenden; *vi* (*rotate*) sich drehen; (*change direction*) (*in car*) abbiegen; (*wind*) drehen; (*round*) umdrehen, wenden; (*become*) werden; (*leaves*) sich verfärben; (*milk*) sauer werden; (*weather*) umschlagen; (*become*) werden; **to make a —** to the left nach links abbiegen; **the —** of the tide der Gezeitenwechsel; **the —** of the century die Jahrhundertwende; **to take a —** for the worse sich zum Schlechten wenden; it's your **—** du bist dran or an der Reihe; **in —**, **by —s** abwechselnd; **to take —s** sich abwechseln; **to do sb a good/bad —** jdm einen guten/schlechten Dienst erweisen; it gave me quite a **—** das hat mich schön erschreckt; **to — sb loose** jdn los- or freilassen; **— back** *vt* umdrehen; *person* zurückschicken; *clock* zurückstellen; *vi* umkehren; **— down** *vt* (*refuse*) ablehnen; (*fold down*) umschlagen; **— in** *vi* (*go to bed*) ins Bett gehen; *vt* (*fold inwards*) einwärts biegen; **— into** *vi* sich verwandeln in (*+acc*); **— off** *vi* abbiegen; *vt* ausschalten; *tap* zudrehen; *machine, electricity* abstellen; **— on** *vt* (*light*) anschalten, einschalten; *tap* aufdrehen; *machine* anstellen; **— out** *vi* (*prove to be*) sich herausstellen, sich erweisen; (*people*) sich entwickeln; **how did the cake — out?** wie ist der Kuchen geworden?; *vt light* ausschalten; *gas* abstellen; (*produce*) produzieren; **— to** *vt* sich zuwenden (*+dat*); **— up** *vi* auftauchen; (*happen*) passieren, sich ereignen; *vt collar* hochklappen, hochstellen; *nose*

rümpfen; (*increase*) *radio* lauter stellen; *heat* höher drehen; **—about** Kehrtwendung *f*; **—ed-up** a nose Stups-; **—ing** (*in road*) Abzweigung *f*; **—ing point** Wendepunkt *m*.

turnip ['tə:nɪp] *n* Steckrübe *f*.

turnout ['tə:naut] *n* (*Besucher*)zahl *f*; (*Comm*) Produktion *f*.

turnover ['tə:nəuvə*] *n* Umsatz *m*; (*of staff*) Wechsel *m*; (*Cook*) Tasche *f*.

turnpike ['tə:npaɪk] *n* (*US*) gebührenpflichtige Straße *f*.

turnstile ['tə:nstaɪl] *n* Drehkreuz *nt*.

turntable ['tə:nteɪbl] *n* (*of record-player*) Plattenteller · *m*; (*Rail*) Drehscheibe *f*.

turn-up ['tə:nʌp] *n* (*on trousers*) Aufschlag *m*.

turpentine ['tə:pəntaɪn] *n* Terpentin *nt*.

turquoise ['tə:kwɔɪz] *n* (*gem*) Türkis *m*; (*colour*) Türkis *nt*; a türkisfarben.

turret ['tʌrɪt] *n* Turm *m*.

turtle ['tə:tl] *n* Schildkröte *f*.

tusk [tʌsk] *n* Stoßzahn *m*.

tussle ['tʌsl] *n* Balgerei *f*.

tutor ['tju:tə*] *n* (*teacher*) Privatlehrer *m*; (*college instructor*) Tutor *m*; **—ial** [tju:'tɔ:rɪəl] (*Univ*) Kolloquium *nt*, Seminarübung *f*.

tuxedo [tʌk'si:dəu] *n* (*US*) Smoking *m*.

TV ['ti:'vi:] *n* Fernseher *m*; a Fernseh-.

twaddle ['twɒdl] *n* (*col*) Gewäsch *nt*.

twang [twæŋ] *n* scharfe(r) Ton *m*; (*of voice*) Näseln *nt*; *vt* zupfen; *vi* klingen; (*talk*) näseln.

tweed [twi:d] *n* Tweed *m*.

tweezers ['twi:zəz] *npl* Pinzette *f.*

twelfth [twelfθ] *a* zwölfte(r,s); **T— Night** Dreikönigsabend *m.*

twelve [twelv] *num a* zwölf.

twenty ['twentɪ] *num a* zwanzig.

twerp [twɜ:p] *n (col)* Knülch *m.*

twice [twaɪs] *ad* zweimal; — **as much** doppelt soviel; — **my age** doppelt so alt wie ich.

twig [twɪg] *n* dünne(r) Zweig *m*; *vt (col)* kapieren, merken.

twilight ['twaɪlaɪt] *n* Dämmerung *f*, Zwielicht *nt.*

twill [twɪl] *n* Köper *m.*

twin [twɪn] *n* Zwilling *m*; **a** Zwillings-; *(very similar)* Doppel-.

twine [twaɪn] *n* Bindfaden *m*; *vi* binden.

twinge [twɪndʒ] *n* stechende(r) Schmerz *m*, Stechen *nt.*

twinkle ['twɪŋkl] *n* Funkeln *nt*, Blitzen *nt*; *vi* funkeln.

twin town ['twɪntaʊn] *n* Partnerstadt *f.*

twirl [twɜ:l] *n* Wirbel *m*; *vti* (herum)wirbeln.

twist [twɪst] *n (twisting)* Biegen *nt*, Drehung *f*; *(bend)* Kurve *f*; *vt (turn)* drehen; *(make crooked)* verbiegen; *(distort)* verdrehen; *vi (wind)* sich drehen; *(curve)* sich winden.

twit [twɪt] *n (col)* Idiot *m.*

twitch [twɪtʃ] *n* Zucken *nt*; *vi* zucken.

two [tu:] *num a* zwei; **to break in —** in zwei Teile brechen; **— by —** zu zweit; **to be in — minds** nicht genau wissen; **to put — and — together** seine Schlüsse ziehen; **—-door a** zweitürig; **—-faced a** falsch; **—-fold a, ad** zweifach, doppelt; **—-piece a** zweiteilig; **—-seater** *(plane, car)* Zweisitzer *m*; **—-some** Paar *nt*; **—-way a** *traffic* Gegen-.

tycoon [taɪ'ku:n] *n* (Industrie)magnat *m.*

type [taɪp] *n* Typ *m*, Art *f*; *(Print)* Type *f*; *vti* maschineschreiben, tippen; **—-cast a** *(Theat, TV)* auf eine Rolle festgelegt; **—-script** maschinegeschriebene(r) Text *m*; **—-writer** Schreibmaschine *f*; **—-written a** maschinegeschrieben.

typhoid ['taɪfɔɪd] *n* Typhus *m.*

typhoon [taɪ'fu:n] *n* Taifun *m.*

typhus ['taɪfəs] *n* Flecktyphus *m.*

typical *a*, **—-ly** *ad* ['tɪpɪkəl, -klɪ] typisch *(of* für).

typify ['tɪpɪfaɪ] *vt* typisch sein für.

typing ['taɪpɪŋ] *n* Maschineschreiben *nt.*

typist ['taɪpɪst] *n* Maschinenschreiber(in *f*) *m*, Tippse *f (col).*

tyranny ['tɪrənɪ] *n* Tyrannei *f*, Gewaltherrschaft *f.*

tyrant ['taɪərnt] *n* Tyrann *m.*

tyre [taɪə*] *n* Reifen *m.*

U

U, u [ju:] *n* U *nt*, u *nt.*

ubiquitous [ju:'bɪkwɪtəs] *adj* überall zu finden(d); allgegenwärtig.

udder ['ʌdə*] *n* Euter *nt.*

ugh [ɜ:h] *Interj* hu.

ugliness ['ʌglɪnəs] *n* Häßlichkeit *f.*

ugly ['ʌglɪ] *a* häßlich; *(bad)* böse, schlimm.

ukulele [juːkəˈleɪlɪ] n Ukulele f.

ulcer [ˈʌlsə*] n Geschwür nt.

ulterior [ʌlˈtɪərɪə*] a: — motive Hintergedanke m.

ultimate [ˈʌltɪmət] a äußerste(r,s), allerletzte(r,s); —ly ad schließlich, letzten Endes.

ultimatum [ʌltɪˈmeɪtəm] n Ultimatum nt.

ultra- [ˈʌltrə] pref ultra-.

ultraviolet [ʌltrəˈvaɪələt] a ultraviolett.

umbilical cord [ʌmˈbɪlɪkl kɔːd] n Nabelschnur f.

umbrage [ˈʌmbrɪdʒ] n: to take — Anstoß nehmen (at an +dat).

umbrella [ʌmˈbrelə] n Schirm m.

umpire [ˈʌmpaɪə*] n Schiedsrichter m; vti schiedsrichtern.

umpteen [ˈʌmptiːn] num (col) zig.

un- [ʌn] pref un-.

unabashed [ʌnəˈbæʃt] a unerschrocken.

unabated [ʌnəˈbeɪtɪd] a unvermindert.

unable [ʌnˈeɪbl] a außerstande; to be — to do sth etw nicht tun können.

unaccompanied [ʌnəˈkʌmpənɪd] a ohne Begleitung.

unaccountably [ʌnəˈkaʊntəblɪ] ad unerklärlich.

unaccustomed [ʌnəˈkʌstəmd] a nicht gewöhnt (to an +acc); (unusual) ungewohnt.

unadulterated [ʌnˈdʌltəreɪtɪd] a rein, unverfälscht.

unaided [ʌnˈeɪdɪd] a selbständig, ohne Hilfe.

unanimity [juːnəˈnɪmɪtɪ] n Einstimmigkeit f.

unanimous a, —ly ad [juːˈnænɪməs, -lɪ] einmütig; vote einstimmig.

unattached [ʌnəˈtætʃt] a ungebunden.

unattended [ʌnəˈtendɪd] a person unbeaufsichtigt; thing unbewacht.

unattractive [ʌnəˈtræktɪv] a unattraktiv.

unauthorized [ʌnˈɔːθəraɪzd] a unbefugt.

unavoidable a, **unavoidably** ad [ʌnəˈvɔɪdəbl, -blɪ] unvermeidlich.

unaware [ʌnəˈweə*] a: to be — of sth sich (dat) einer Sache nicht bewußt sein; —s ad unversehens.

unbalanced [ʌnˈbælənst] a unausgeglichen; (mentally) gestört.

unbearable [ʌnˈbeərəbl] a unerträglich.

unbeatable [ʌnˈbiːtəbl] a unschlagbar.

unbeaten [ʌnˈbiːtn] a ungeschlagen.

unbecoming [ʌnbɪˈkʌmɪŋ] a dress unkleidsam; behaviour unpassend, unschicklich.

unbeknown [ʌnbɪˈnəʊn] ad ohne jedes Wissen (to gen).

unbelief [ʌnbɪˈliːf] n Unglaube m.

unbelievable [ʌnbɪˈliːvəbl] a unglaublich.

unbend [ʌnˈbend] irreg vt geradebiegen, gerademachen; vi aus sich herausgehen.

unbounded [ʌnˈbaʊndɪd] a unbegrenzt.

unbreakable [ʌnˈbreɪkəbl] a unzerbrechlich.

unbridled [ʌnˈbraɪdld] a ungezügelt.

unbroken [ʌnˈbrəʊkən] a period ununterbrochen; spirit ungebrochen; record unübertroffen.

unburden [ʌnˈbɜːdn] vt: — o.s. (jdm) sein Herz ausschütten.

unbutton [ʌnˈbʌtn] vt aufknöpfen.

uncalled-for [ʌn'kɔ:ldfɔ:*] a unnötig.

uncanny [ʌn'kæni] a unheimlich.

unceasing [ʌn'si:sɪŋ] a unaufhörlich.

uncertain [ʌn'sɜ:tn] a unsicher; (doubtful) ungewiß a; (unreliable) unbeständig; (vague) undeutlich, vage; —ty Ungewißheit f.

unchanged [ʌn'tʃeɪndʒd] a unverändert.

uncharitable [ʌn'tʃærɪtəbl] a hartherzig; remark unfreundlich.

uncharted [ʌn'tʃɑ:tɪd] a nicht verzeichnet.

unchecked [ʌn'tʃekt] a ungeprüft; (not stopped) advance ungehindert.

uncivil [ʌn'sɪvɪl] a unhöflich, grob.

uncle [ʌŋkl] n Onkel m.

uncomfortable [ʌn'kʌmfətəbl] a unbequem, ungemütlich.

uncompromising [ʌn'kɒm-prəmaɪzɪŋ] a kompromißlos, unnachgiebig.

unconditional [ʌnkən'dɪʃənl] a bedingungslos.

uncongenial [ʌnkən'dʒi:nɪəl] a unangenehm.

unconscious [ʌn'kɒnʃəs] a (Med) bewußtlos; (not aware) nicht bewußt; (not meant) unbeabsichtigt; the — das Unbewußte; —ly ad unwissentlich, unbewußt; —ness Bewußtlosigkeit f.

uncontrollable [ʌnkən'trəʊləbl] a unkontrollierbar, unbändig.

uncork [ʌn'kɔ:k] vt entkorken.

uncouth [ʌn'ku:θ] a grob, ungehobelt.

uncover [ʌn'kʌvə*] vt aufdecken.

unctuous [ʌŋktjʊəs] a salbungs-voll.

undaunted [ʌn'dɔ:ntɪd] a unerschrocken.

undecided [ʌndɪ'saɪdɪd] a unschlüssig.

undeniable [ʌndɪ'naɪəbl] a unleugbar.

undeniably [ʌndɪ'naɪəblɪ] ad unbestreitbar.

under ['ʌndə*] prep unter; ad darunter; — repair in Reparatur; —age a minderjährig.

undercarriage ['ʌndəkærɪdʒ] n Fahrgestell nt.

underclothes ['ʌndəkləʊðz] npl Unterwäsche f.

undercoat ['ʌndəkəʊt] n (paint) Grundierung f.

undercover ['ʌndəkʌvə*] a Geheim-.

undercurrent ['ʌndəkʌrənt] n Unterströmung f.

undercut ['ʌndəkʌt] vt irreg unter-bieten.

underdeveloped ['ʌndədɪ'veləpt] a Entwicklungs-, unterentwickelt.

underdog ['ʌndədɒg] n Unter-legene(r) mf.

underdone ['ʌndə'dʌn] a (Cook) nicht gar, nicht durchgebraten.

underestimate ['ʌndər'estɪmeɪt] vt unterschätzen.

underexposed ['ʌndərɪks'pəʊzd] a unterbelichtet.

underfed ['ʌndə'fed] a unterernährt.

underfoot ['ʌndə'fʊt] ad unter den Füßen.

undergo ['ʌndə'gəʊ] vt irreg experience durchmachen; operation, test sich unterziehen (+dat).

undergraduate ['ʌndə'grædjʊət] n Student(in f) m.

underground ['ʌndəgraʊnd] n

Untergrundbahn f, U-Bahn f; a press etc Untergrund-.

undergrowth ['ʌndəgrəʊθ] n Gestrüpp nt, Unterholz nt.

underhand ['ʌndəhænd] a hinterhältig.

underlie [ʌndə'laɪ] vt irreg (form the basis of) zugrundeliegen (+dat).

underline [ʌndə'laɪn] vt unterstreichen; (emphasize) betonen.

underling ['ʌndəlɪŋ] n Handlanger m.

undermine [ʌndə'maɪn] vt unterhöhlen; (fig) unterminieren, untergraben.

underneath [ʌndə'niːθ] ad darunter; prep unter.

underpaid ['ʌndə'peɪd] a unterbezahlt.

underpants ['ʌndəpænts] npl Unterhose f.

underpass ['ʌndəpɑːs] n Unterführung f.

underplay ['ʌndə'pleɪ] vt herunterspielen.

underprice [ʌndə'praɪs] vt zu niedrig ansetzen.

underprivileged [ʌndə'prɪvɪlɪdʒd] a benachteiligt, unterprivilegiert.

underrate [ʌndə'reɪt] vt unterschätzen.

undershirt ['ʌndəʃɜːt] n (US) Unterhemd nt.

undershorts ['ʌndəʃɔːts] npl (US) Unterhose f.

underside ['ʌndəsaɪd] n Unterseite f.

underskirt ['ʌndəskɜːt] n Unterrock m.

understand [ʌndə'stænd] vt irreg verstehen; I — that ... ich habe gehört, daß ...; am I to — that ...? soll das (etwa) heißen, daß

...?; what do you — by that? was verstehen Sie darunter?; it is understood that ... es wurde vereinbart, daß ...; to make o.s. understood sich verständlich machen; is that understood? is das klar?; —able a verständlich; —ing Verständnis nt; a verständnisvoll.

understatement ['ʌndəsteɪtmənt] n Untertreibung f, Understatement nt.

understudy ['ʌndəstʌdɪ] n Ersatz(schau)spieler(in) f m.

undertake [ʌndə'teɪk] irreg vt unternehmen; vi (promise) sich verpflichten; —r Leichenbestatter m; —r's Beerdigungsinstitut nt.

undertaking [ʌndə'teɪkɪŋ] n (enterprise) Unternehmen nt; (promise) Verpflichtung f.

underwater [ʌndə'wɔːtə*] ad unter Wasser; a Unterwasser-.

underwear ['ʌndəwɛə*] n Unterwäsche f.

underweight [ʌndə'weɪt] a: to be — Untergewicht haben.

underworld ['ʌndəwɜːld] n (of crime) Unterwelt f.

underwriter ['ʌndəraɪtə*] n Assekurant m.

undesirable [ʌndɪ'zaɪərəbl] a unerwünscht.

undies ['ʌndɪz] npl (col) (Damen)unterwäsche f.

undiscovered ['ʌndɪs'kʌvəd] a unentdeckt.

undisputed ['ʌndɪs'pjuːtɪd] a unbestritten.

undistinguished ['ʌndɪs'tɪŋgwɪʃt] a unbekannt, nicht ausgezeichnet.

undo ['ʌn'duː] vt irreg (unfasten) öffnen, aufmachen; work zunichte machen; —ing Verderben nt.

undoubted [ʌn'dautɪd] *a*
unbezweifelt; —ly *ad* zweifellos,
ohne Zweifel.

undress [ʌn'dres] *vti* (sich)
ausziehen.

undue ['ʌndju:] *a* übermäßig.

undulating ['ʌndjuleɪtɪŋ] *a* wellenförmig; *country* wellig.

unduly [ʌn'dju:lɪ] *ad* übermäßig.

unearth [ʌn'ɜ:θ] *vt* (*dig up*) ausgraben; (*discover*) ans Licht
bringen; **—ly** *a* schauerlich.

unease [ʌn'i:z] *n* Unbehagen *nt*;
(*public*) Unruhe *f*.

uneasy [ʌn'i:zɪ] *a* (*worried*)
unruhig; *feeling* ungut;
(*embarrassed*) unbequem; **I feel —
about it** mir ist nicht wohl dabei.

uneconomic(al) ['ʌni:kə'-
nɒmɪk(əl)] *a* unwirtschaftlich.

uneducated [ʌn'edjukeɪtɪd] *a*
ungebildet.

unemployed [ʌnɪm'plɔɪd] *a*
arbeitslos; **the — die Arbeitslosen**
pl.

unemployment [ʌnɪm'plɔɪmənt] *n*
Arbeitslosigkeit *f*.

unending [ʌn'endɪŋ] *a* endlos.

unenviable ['ʌn'envɪəbl] *a* wenig
beneidenswert.

unerring ['ʌn'ɜ:rɪŋ] *a* unfehlbar.

uneven [ʌn'i:vən] *a* *surface*
uneben; *quality* ungleichmäßig.

unexploded ['ʌnɪks'pləudɪd] *a*
nicht explodiert.

unfailing [ʌn'feɪlɪŋ] *a* nie versagend.

unfair *a*, **—ly** *ad* ['ʌn'feə*, -əlɪ]
ungerecht, unfair.

unfaithful [ʌn'feɪθful] *a* untreu.

unfasten ['ʌn'fɑ:sn] *vt* öffnen,
aufmachen.

unfavourable, (*US*) **unfavorable**
['ʌn'feɪvərəbl] *a* ungünstig.

unfeeling [ʌn'fi:lɪŋ] *a* gefühllos,
kalt.

unfinished ['ʌn'fɪnɪʃt] *a*
unvollendet.

unfit ['ʌn'fɪt] *a* ungeeignet (*for* zu,
für); (*in bad health*) nicht fit.

unflagging [ʌn'flægɪŋ] *a*
unermüdlich.

unflappable [ʌn'flæpəbl] *a*
unerschütterlich.

unflinching [ʌn'flɪntʃɪŋ] *a*
unerschrocken.

unfold [ʌn'fəuld] *vt* entfalten;
paper auseinanderfalten; *vi*
(*develop*) sich entfalten.

unforeseen ['ʌnfɔ:'si:n] *a* unvorhergesehen.

unforgivable ['ʌnfə'gɪvəbl] *a* unverzeihlich.

unfortunate [ʌn'fɔ:tʃnət] *a*
unglücklich, bedauerlich; **—ly** *ad*
leider.

unfounded ['ʌn'faundɪd] *a*
unbegründet.

unfriendly ['ʌn'frendlɪ] *a*
unfreundlich.

unfurnished ['ʌn'fɜ:nɪʃt] *a*
unmöbliert.

ungainly [ʌn'geɪnlɪ] *a* linkisch.

ungodly [ʌn'gɒdlɪ] *a* *hour*
nachtschlafend; *row* heillos.

unguarded ['ʌn'gɑ:dɪd] *a* *moment*
unbewacht.

unhappiness [ʌn'hæpɪnəs] *n*
Unglück *nt*, Unglückseligkeit *f*.

unhappy [ʌn'hæpɪ] *a* unglücklich.

unharmed [ʌn'hɑ:md] *a*
wohlbehalten, unversehrt.

unhealthy [ʌn'helθɪ] *a* ungesund.

unheard-of [ʌn'hɜ:dɒv] *a* unerhört.

unhurt [ʌn'hɜ:t] *a* unverletzt.

unicorn ['ju:nɪkɔ:n] *n* Einhorn *nt*.

unidentified ['ʌnaɪ'dentɪfaɪd] *a*
unbekannt, nicht identifiziert.

unification [ju:nıfı'keıʃən] n
Vereinigung f.

uniform ['ju:nıfɔ:m] n Uniform f;
a einheitlich; **-ity** [ju:nı'fɔ:mıtı]
Einheitlichkeit f.

unify ['ju:nıfaı] vt vereinigen.

unilateral ['ju:nı'lætərəl] a einseitig.

unimaginable [ʌnı'mædʒınəbl] a
unvorstellbar.

uninjured ['ʌn'ındʒəd] a unverletzt.

unintentional ['ʌnın'tenʃənl] a
unabsichtlich.

union ['ju:njən] n (uniting)
Vereinigung f; (alliance) Bund m,
Union f; (trade —) Gewerkschaft
f; U— Jack Union Jack m.

unique [ju:'ni:k] a einzig(artig).

unison ['ju:nızn] n Einstimmigkeit
f; in — einstimmig.

unit ['ju:nıt] n Einheit f.

unite [ju:'naıt] vt vereinigen; vi
sich vereinigen; **—d** a vereinigt;
(together) vereint; U—d Nations
Vereinte Nationen pl.

unit trust ['ju:nıt'trʌst] n (Brit)
Treuhandgesellschaft f.

unity ['ju:nıtı] n Einheit f; (agreement) Einigkeit f.

universal a, **—ly** ad [ju:nı'vɜ:səl,
-ı] allgemein.

universe ['ju:nıvɜ:s] n (Welt)all nt,
Universum nt.

university [ju:nı'vɜ:sıtı] n
Universität f.

unjust ['ʌn'dʒʌst] a ungerecht.

unjustifiable [ʌn'dʒʌstıfaıəbl] a
ungerechtfertigt.

unkempt ['ʌn'kempt] a ungepflegt,
verwahrlost.

unkind [ʌn'kaınd] a unfreundlich.

unknown ['ʌn'nəun] a unbekannt
(to dat).

unladen ['ʌn'leıdn] a weight Leer-,
unbeladen.

unleash ['ʌn'li:ʃ] vt entfesseln.

unleavened ['ʌn'levnd] a
ungesäuert.

unless [ən'les] cj wenn nicht, es sei
denn ...

unlicensed ['ʌn'laısənst] a (to sell
alcohol) unkonzessioniert.

unlike ['ʌn'laık] a unähnlich; prep
im Gegensatz zu.

unlimited [ʌn'lımıtıd] a unbegrenzt.

unload ['ʌn'ləud] vt entladen.

unlock ['ʌn'lɒk] vt aufschließen.

unmannerly [ʌn'mænəlı] a
unmanierlich.

unmarried ['ʌn'mærıd] a
unverheiratet, ledig.

unmask ['ʌn'mɑ:sk] vt
demaskieren; (fig) entlarven.

unmistakable ['ʌnmıs'teıkəbl] a
unverkennbar.

unmistakably ['ʌnmıs'teıkəblı] ad
unverwechselbar, unverkennbar.

unmitigated [ʌn'mıtıgeıtıd] a
ungemildert, ganz.

unnecessary ['ʌn'nesəsərı] a
unnötig.

unobtainable ['ʌnəb'teınəbl] a: this
number is — kein Anschluß unter
dieser Nummer.

unoccupied ['ʌn'ɒkjupaıd] a seat
frei.

unopened ['ʌn'əupənd] a
ungeöffnet.

unorthodox ['ʌn'ɔ:θədɒks] a
unorthodox.

unpack ['ʌn'pæk] vti auspacken.

unpalatable [ʌn'pælətəbl] a truth
bitter.

unparalleled [ʌn'pærəleld] a
beispiellos.

unpleasant [ʌn'pleznt] a
unangenehm.

unplug ['ʌn'plʌg] vt den Stecker
herausziehen von.

unpopular [ʌn'pɒpjʊlə*] *a* unbeliebt, unpopulär.

unprecedented [ʌn'presɪdəntɪd] *a* noch nie dagewesen; beispiellos.

unqualified ['ʌn'kwɒlɪfaɪd] *a success* uneingeschränkt, voll; *person* unqualifiziert.

unravel [ʌn'rævəl] *vt (disentangle)* auffasern, entwirren; *(solve)* lösen.

unreal ['ʌn'rɪəl] *a* unwirklich.

unreasonable [ʌn'riːznəbl] *a* unvernünftig; *demand* übertrieben; *that's —* das ist zuviel verlangt.

unrelenting ['ʌnrɪ'lentɪŋ] *a* unerbittlich.

unrelieved ['ʌnrɪ'liːvd] *a monotony* ungemildert.

unrepeatable ['ʌnrɪ'piːtəbl] *a* nicht zu wiederholen(d).

unrest [ʌn'rest] *n (discontent)* Unruhe *f*; *(fighting)* Unruhen *pl*.

unroll ['ʌn'rəʊl] *vt* aufrollen.

unruly [ʌn'ruːlɪ] *a child* undiszipliniert; schwer lenkbar.

unsafe ['ʌn'seɪf] *a* nicht sicher.

unsaid ['ʌn'sed] *a*: to leave sth — etw ungesagt sein lassen.

unsatisfactory ['ʌnsætɪs'fæktərɪ] *a* unbefriedigend; unzulänglich.

unsavoury, *(US)* **unsavory** ['ʌn'seɪvərɪ] *a (fig)* widerwärtig.

unscrew ['ʌn'skruː] *vt* aufschrauben.

unscrupulous [ʌn'skruːpjʊləs] *a* skrupellos.

unselfish ['ʌn'selfɪʃ] *a* selbstlos, uneigennützig.

unsettled ['ʌn'setld] *a* unstet; *person* rastlos; *weather* wechselhaft; *dispute* nicht beigelegt.

unshaven ['ʌn'ʃeɪvn] *a* unrasiert.

unsightly [ʌn'saɪtlɪ] *a* unansehnlich.

unskilled ['ʌn'skɪld] *a* ungelernt.

unsophisticated ['ʌnsə'fɪstɪkeɪtɪd] *a* einfach, natürlich.

unsound ['ʌn'saʊnd] *a ideas* anfechtbar.

unspeakable [ʌn'spiːkəbl] *a joy* unsagbar; *crime* scheußlich.

unstuck [ʌn'stʌk] *a*: to come — *(lit)* sich lösen; *(fig)* ins Wasser fallen.

unsuccessful ['ʌnsək'sesfʊl] *a* erfolglos.

unsuitable ['ʌn'suːtəbl] *a* unpassend.

unsuspecting ['ʌnsəs'pektɪŋ] *a* nichtsahnend.

unswerving [ʌn'swɜːvɪŋ] *a loyalty* unerschütterlich.

untangle ['ʌn'tæŋgl] *vt* entwirren.

untapped ['ʌn'tæpt] *a resources* ungenützt.

unthinkable [ʌn'θɪŋkəbl] *a* unvorstellbar.

untidy ['ʌn'taɪdɪ] *a* unordentlich.

untie ['ʌn'taɪ] *vt* aufmachen, aufschnüren.

until [ən'tɪl] *prep*, *cj* bis.

untimely [ʌn'taɪmlɪ] *a death* vorzeitig.

untold ['ʌn'təʊld] *a* unermeßlich.

untoward [ʌntə'wɔːd] *a* widrig, ungünstig.

untranslatable ['ʌntræns'leɪtəbl] *a* unübersetzbar.

untried ['ʌn'traɪd] *a plan* noch nicht ausprobiert.

unused ['ʌn'juːzd] *a* unbenutzt.

unusual *a*, **—ly** *ad* [ʌn'juːʒʊəl, -ɪ] ungewöhnlich.

unveil [ʌn'veɪl] *vt* enthüllen.

unwary [ʌn'wɛərɪ] *a* unbedacht(sam).

unwavering [ʌn'weɪvərɪŋ] *a* standhaft, unerschütterlich.

unwell ['ʌn'wel] *a* unpäßlich.

unwieldy [ʌn'wi:ldɪ] *a* unhandlich, sperrig.

unwilling ['ʌn'wɪlɪŋ] *a* unwillig.

unwind ['ʌn'waɪnd] *Irreg vt - (lit)* abwickeln; *vi (relax)* sich entspannen.

unwitting [ʌn'wɪtɪŋ] *a* unwissentlich.

unwrap ['ʌn'ræp] *vt* aufwickeln, auspacken.

unwritten ['ʌn'rɪtn] *a* ungeschrieben.

up [ʌp] *prep* auf; *ad* nach oben, hinauf; *(out of bed)* auf; it is — to you es liegt bei Ihnen; what is he — to? was hat er vor?; he is not — to it er kann es nicht (tun); what's —? was ist los?; — to *(temporally)* bis; —-and-coming *a* im Aufstieg; the —s and downs das Auf und Ab.

upbringing ['ʌpbrɪŋɪŋ] *n* Erziehung *f.*

update [ʌp'deɪt] *vt* auf den neuesten Stand bringen.

upend [ʌp'end] *vt* auf Kante stellen.

upgrade [ʌp'greɪd] *vt* höher einstufen.

upheaval [ʌp'hi:vəl] *n* Umbruch *m.*

uphill ['ʌp'hɪl] *a* (steep), *(fig)* mühsam; *ad* bergauf.

uphold [ʌp'həʊld] *vt irreg* unterstützen.

upholstery [ʌp'həʊlstərɪ] *n* Polster *nt;* Polsterung *f.*

upkeep ['ʌpki:p] *n* Instandhaltung *f.*

upon [ə'pɒn] *prep* auf.

upper ['ʌpə*] *n (on shoe)* Oberleder *nt; a* obere(r,s), höhere(r,s); the — class die Oberschicht; —-class *a* vornehm; —most *a* oberste(r,s), höchste(r,s).

upright ['ʌpraɪt] *a (erect)* aufrecht; *(honest)* aufrecht, rechtschaffen; *n* Pfosten *m.*

uprising [ʌp'raɪzɪŋ] *n* Aufstand *m.*

uproar ['ʌprɔ:*] *n* Aufruhr *m.*

uproot [ʌp'ru:t] *vt* ausreißen; *tree* entwurzeln.

upset ['ʌpset] *n* Aufregung *f.* [ʌp'set] *vt irreg (overturn)* umwerfen; *(disturb)* aufregen, bestürzen; *plans* durcheinanderbringen; —ting *a* bestürzend.

upshot ['ʌpʃɒt] *n* (End)ergebnis *nt,* Ausgang *m.*

upside-down ['ʌpsaɪd'daʊn] *ad* verkehrt herum; *(fig)* drunter und drüber.

upstairs ['ʌp'stɛəz] *ad* oben, im oberen Stockwerk; *go* nach oben; *a room* obere(r,s), Ober-; *n* obere(s) Stockwerk *nt.*

upstart ['ʌpstɑ:t] *n* Emporkömmling *m.*

upstream ['ʌp'stri:m] *ad* stromaufwärts.

uptake ['ʌpteɪk] *n:* to be quick on the — schnell begreifen; to be slow on the — schwer von Begriff sein.

uptight ['ʌp'taɪt] *a (col) (nervous)* nervös; *(inhibited)* verklemmt.

up-to-date ['ʌptə'deɪt] *a clothes* modisch, modern; *information* neueste(r,s); to bring sth up to date etw auf den neuesten Stand bringen.

upturn ['ʌptɜ:n] *n (in luck)* Aufschwung *m.*

upward ['ʌpwəd] *a* nach oben gerichtet; —(s) *ad* aufwärts.

uranium [jʊə'reɪnɪəm] *n* Uran *nt.*

urban ['ɜ:bən] *a* städtisch, Stadt-.

urbane [ɜ:'beɪn] *a* höflich, weltgewandt.

urchin ['ɜ:tʃɪn] *n (boy)* Schlingel *m;* (sea —) Seeigel *m.*

urge [ɜ:dʒ] n Drang m; vt drängen,
dringen in (+acc); **— on** vt
antreiben.

urgency [ˈɜ:dʒənsɪ] n Dringlichkeit
f.

urgent a, **-ly** ad [ˈɜ:dʒənt, -lɪ]
dringend.

urinal [ˈjʊərɪnl] n (Med) Urinflasche
f; (public) Pissoir nt.

urinate [ˈjʊərɪneɪt] vi urinieren,
Wasser lassen.

urine [ˈjʊərɪn] n Urin m, Harn m.

urn [ɜ:n] n Urne f; (tea —) Teemaschine f.

us [ʌs] pron uns.

usage [ˈju:zɪdʒ] n Gebrauch m;
(esp Ling) Sprachgebrauch m.

use [ju:s] n Verwendung f;
(custom) Brauch m, Gewohnheit f;
(employment) Gebrauch m; (point)
Zweck m; **in —** in Gebrauch; **out
of —** außer Gebrauch; **it's no —
es** hat keinen Zweck; **what's the
—?** was soll's?; [ju:z] vt
gebrauchen; **—d to** [ju:st] gewöhnt
an (+acc); she **—d** to live here sie
hat früher mal hier gewohnt; **— up**
[ju:z] vt aufbrauchen, verbrauchen; **—d** [ju:zd] a car
Gebraucht-; **—ful** a nützlich;
—fulness Nützlichkeit f; **—less** a
nutzlos, unnütz; **—lessly** ad

nutzlos; **—lessness** Nutzlosigkeit
f; **—r** [ˈju:zə*] Benutzer m.

usher [ˈʌʃə*] n Platzanweiser m;
—ette [ʌʃəˈret] Platzanweiserin f.

usual [ˈju:ʒʊəl] a gewöhnlich,
üblich; **—ly** ad gewöhnlich.

usurp [ju:ˈzɜ:p] vt an sich reißen;
—er Usurpator m.

usury [ˈju:ʒʊrɪ] n Wucher m.

utensil [ju:ˈtensl] n Gerät nt,
Utensil n.

uterus [ˈju:tərəs] n Gebärmutter f,
Uterus m.

utilitarian [ju:tɪlɪˈtɛərɪən] a
Nützlichkeits-.

utility [ju:ˈtɪlɪtɪ] n (usefulness)
Nützlichkeit f; (also public —)
öffentliche(r) Versorgungsbetrieb
m.

utilization [ju:tɪlaɪˈzeɪʃən] n
Nutzbarmachung f; Benutzung f.

utilize [ˈju:tɪlaɪz] vt nutzbar
machen; benützen.

utmost [ˈʌtməʊst] a äußerste(r,s);
n: to do one's **—** sein möglichstes
tun.

utter [ˈʌtə*] a äußerste(r,s)
höchste(r,s), völlig; vt äußern, aussprechen; **—ance** Äußerung f; **—ly**
ad äußerst, absolut, völlig.

U-turn [ˈju:tɜ:n] n (Aut)
Kehrtwendung f.

V

V, v [vi:] n V nt, v nt.

vacancy [ˈveɪkənsɪ] n (job) offene
Stelle f; (room) freies Zimmer nt.

vacant [ˈveɪkənt] a leer; (unoccupied) frei; house leerstehend,
unbewohnt; (stupid) (gedanken)-

leer; **'—'** (on door) 'frei'.

vacate [vəˈkeɪt] vt seat frei
machen; room räumen.

vacation [vəˈkeɪʃən] n Ferien pl,
Urlaub m; **—ist** (US) Ferien-
reisende(r) mf.

vaccinate ['væksɪneɪt] vt impfen.

vaccination [væksɪ'neɪʃən] n Impfung f.

vaccine ['væksi:n] n Impfstoff m.

vacuum ['vækjʊm] n luftleere(r) Raum m, Vakuum nt; — bottle (US), — flask (Brit) Thermosflasche f; — cleaner Staubsauger m.

vagary ['veɪgərɪ] n Laune f.

vagina [və'dʒaɪnə] n Scheide f, Vagina f.

vagrant ['veɪgrənt] n Landstreicher m.

vague [veɪg] a unbestimmt, vage; outline verschwommen; (absentminded) geistesabwesend; —ly ad unbestimmt, vage; understand, correct ungefähr; —ness Unbestimmtheit f; Verschwommenheit f.

vain [veɪn] a (worthless) eitel, nichtig; attempt vergeblich; (conceited) eitel, eingebildet; in — vergebens, umsonst; —ly ad vergebens, vergeblich; eitel, eingebildet.

valentine ['væləntaɪn] n Valentinsgruß m.

valiant a, —ly ad ['vælɪənt, -lɪ] tapfer.

valid ['vælɪd] a gültig; argument stichhaltig; objection berechtigt; —ity [və'lɪdɪtɪ] Gültigkeit f; Stichhaltigkeit f.

valise [və'li:z] n Reisetasche f.

valley ['vælɪ] n Tal nt.

valuable ['væljʊəbl] a wertvoll; time kostbar; —s pl Wertsachen pl.

valuation [væljʊ'eɪʃən] n (Fin) Schätzung f; Beurteilung f.

value ['vælju:] n Wert m; (usefulness) Nutzen m; vt (prize) (hoch)-schätzen, werthalten; (estimate)

schätzen; —d a (hoch)geschätzt; —less a wertlos; —r Schätzer m.

valve [vælv] n Ventil nt; (Biol) Klappe f; (Rad) Röhre f.

vampire ['væmpaɪə*] n Vampir m.

van [væn] n Lieferwagen m; Kombiwagen m.

vandal ['vændəl] n Vandale m; —ism mutwillige Beschädigung f, Vandalismus m.

vanilla [və'nɪlə] n Vanille f.

vanish ['vænɪʃ] vi verschwinden.

vanity ['vænɪtɪ] n Eitelkeit f, Einbildung f; — case Schminkkoffer m.

vantage ['vɑ:ntɪdʒ] n: — point gute(r) Aussichtspunkt m.

vapour, (US) **vapor** ['veɪpə*] n (mist) Dunst m; (gas) Dampf m.

variable ['vɛərɪəbl] a wechselhaft, veränderlich; speed, height regulierbar.

variance ['vɛərɪəns] n: to be at — uneinig sein.

variant ['vɛərɪənt] n Variante f.

variation [vɛərɪ'eɪʃən] n Variation f, Veränderung f; (of temperature, prices) Schwankung f.

varicose ['værɪkəʊs] a: — veins Krampfadern pl.

varied ['vɛərɪd] a verschieden, unterschiedlich; life abwechslungsreich.

variety [və'raɪətɪ] n (difference) Abwechslung f; (varied collection) Vielfalt f; (Comm) Auswahl f; (sorte) Sorte f, Art f; — show Varieté nt.

various ['vɛərɪəs] a verschieden; (several) mehrere.

varnish ['vɑ:nɪʃ] n Lack m; (on pottery) Glasur f; vt lackieren; truth beschönigen.

vary ['vɛərɪ] vt (alter) verändern; (give variety to) abwechslungsreicher gestalten; vi sich (ver)ändern; (prices) schwanken; (weather) unterschiedlich sein; **to — from** sth sich von etw unterscheiden; **—ing** a unterschiedlich; veränderlich.

vase [vɑːz] n Vase f.

vast [vɑːst] a weit, groß, riesig; **—ly** ad wesentlich; grateful, amused äußerst; **—ness** Unermeßlichkeit f, Weite f.

vat [væt] n große(s) Faß nt.

Vatican ['vætɪkən] n: the — der Vatikan.

vaudeville ['vəudəvɪl] n (US) Varieté nt.

vault [vɔːlt] n (of roof) Gewölbe nt; (tomb) Gruft f; (in bank) Tresorraum m; (leap) Sprung m; vt überspringen.

vaunted ['vɔːntɪd] a gerühmt, gepriesen.

veal [viːl] n Kalbfleisch nt.

veer [vɪə*] vi sich drehen; (of car) ausscheren.

vegetable ['vedʒətəbl] n Gemüse nt; (plant) Pflanze f.

vegetarian [vedʒɪ'tɛərɪən] n Vegetarier(in f) m; a vegetarisch.

vegetate ['vedʒɪteɪt] vi (dahin)vegetieren.

vegetation [vedʒɪ'teɪʃən] n Vegetation f.

vehemence ['viːɪməns] n Heftigkeit f.

vehement ['viːɪmənt] a heftig; feelings leidenschaftlich.

vehicle ['viːɪkl] n Fahrzeug nt; (fig) Mittel nt.

vehicular [vɪ'hɪkjulə*] a Fahrzeug-; traffic Kraft-.

veil [veɪl] n (lit, fig) Schleier m; vt verschleiern.

vein [veɪn] n Ader f; (Anat) Vene f; (mood) Stimmung f.

velocity [vɪ'lɒsɪtɪ] n Geschwindigkeit f.

velvet ['velvɪt] n Samt m.

vendetta [ven'detə] n Fehde f; (in family) Blutrache f.

vending machine ['vendɪŋməʃiːn] n Automat m.

vendor ['vendɔ:*] n Verkäufer m.

veneer [və'nɪə*] n (lit) Furnier(holz) nt; (fig) äußere(r) Anstrich m.

venerable ['venərəbl] a ehrwürdig.

venereal [vɪ'nɪərɪəl] a disease Geschlechts-.

venetian [vɪ'niːʃən] a: — blind Jalousie f.

vengeance ['vendʒəns] n Rache f; **with a —** gewaltig.

venison ['venɪsn] n Reh(fleisch) nt.

venom ['venəm] n Gift nt; **—ous** a, **—ously** ad giftig, gehässig.

vent [vent] n Öffnung f; (in coat) Schlitz m; (fig) Ventil nt; vt emotion abreagieren.

ventilate ['ventɪleɪt] vt belüften; question erörtern.

ventilation [ventɪ'leɪʃən] n (Be)lüftung f, Ventilation f.

ventilator ['ventɪleɪtə*] n Ventilator m.

ventriloquist [ven'trɪləkwɪst] n Bauchredner m.

venture ['ventʃə*] n Unternehmung f, Projekt nt; vt wagen; life aufs Spiel setzen; vi sich wagen.

venue ['venjuː] n Schauplatz m, Treffpunkt m.

veranda(h) [və'rændə] a Veranda f.

verb [vɜːb] n Zeitwort nt, Verb nt; **—al** a (spoken) mündlich; trans-

lation wörtlich; (*of a verb*) verbal, Verbal-; **—ally** *ad* mündlich; (*as a verb*) verbal; **—atim** [vɜː'beɪtɪm] *ad* Wort für Wort; a wortwörtlich.

verbose [vɜː'bəʊs] *a* wortreich.

verdict ['vɜːdɪkt] *n* Urteil *nt*.

verge [vɜːdʒ] *n* Rand *m*; on the — of doing sth im Begriff, etw zu tun; *vi*: — on grenzen an (+*acc*).

verger ['vɜːdʒə*] *n* Kirchendiener *m*, Küster *m*.

verification [verɪfɪ'keɪʃən] *n* Bestätigung *f*; (*checking*) Überprüfung *f*; (*proof*) Beleg *m*.

verify ['verɪfaɪ] *vt* (über)prüfen; (*confirm*) bestätigen; *theory* beweisen.

vermin ['vɜːmɪn] *npl* Ungeziefer *nt*.

vermouth ['vɜːməθ] *n* Wermut *m*.

vernacular [və'nækjʊlə*] *n* Landessprache *f*; (*dialect*) Dialekt *m*, Mundart *f*; (*jargon*) Fachsprache *f*.

versatile ['vɜːsətaɪl] *a* vielseitig.

versatility [vɜːsə'tɪlɪtɪ] *n* Vielseitigkeit *f*.

verse [vɜːs] *n* (*poetry*) Poesie *f*; (*stanza*) Strophe *f*; (*of Bible*) Vers *m*; in — in Versform; **—d** *a*: —d in bewandert in (+*dat*), beschlagen in (+*dat*).

version ['vɜːʃən] *n* Version *f*; (*of car*) Modell *nt*.

versus ['vɜːsəs] *prep* gegen.

vertebra ['vɜːtɪbrə] *n* (Rücken)-wirbel *m*.

vertebrate ['vɜːtɪbrət] *a animal* Wirbel-.

vertical ['vɜːtɪkəl] *a* senkrecht, vertikal; **—ly** *ad* senkrecht, vertikal.

vertigo ['vɜːtɪgəʊ] *n* Schwindel *m*, Schwindelgefühl *nt*.

verve [vɜːv] *n* Schwung *m*.

very ['verɪ] *ad* sehr; a (*extreme*) äußerste(r,s); the — book genau das Buch; at that — moment gerade *or* genau in dem Augenblick; · at the — latest allerspätestens; the — same day noch am selben Tag; the — thought der Gedanke allein, der bloße Gedanke.

vespers ['vespəz] *npl* Vesper *f*.

vessel ['vesl] *n* (*ship*) Schiff *nt*; (*container*) Gefäß *nt*.

vest [vest] *n* Unterhemd *nt*; (*US: waistcoat*) Weste *f*; *vt*: — sb with sth *or* sth in sb jdm etw verleihen; **—ed** a: —ed interests *pl* finanzielle Beteiligung *f*; (*people*) · finanziell Interessierte *pl*; (*fig*) persönliche(s) Interesse *nt*.

vestibule ['vestɪbjuːl] *n* Vorhalle *f*.

vestige ['vestɪdʒ] *n* Spur *f*.

vestry ['vestrɪ] *n* Sakristei *f*.

vet [vet] *n* Tierarzt *m/*-ärztin *f*; *vt* genau prüfen.

veteran ['vetərən] *n* Veteran *m*; a altgedient.·

veterinary ['vetmərɪ] *a* Veterinär-; **— surgeon** Tierarzt *m/*-ärztin *f*.

veto ['viːtəʊ] *n* Veto *nt*; power of — Vetorecht *nt*; *vt* sein Veto einlegen gegen.

vex [veks] *vt* ärgern; **—ed** a verärgert; **—ed question** umstrittene Frage *f*; **—ing** a ärgerlich.

via [vaɪə] *prep* über (+*acc*).

viability [vaɪə'bɪlɪtɪ] *n* (*of plan, scheme*) Durchführbarkeit *f*; (*of company*) Rentabilität *f*; (*of life forms*) Lebensfähigkeit *f*.

viable ['vaɪəbl] *a plan* durchführbar; *company* rentabel; *plant, economy* lebensfähig.

viaduct ['vaɪədʌkt] *n* Viadukt *m*.

vibrate [vaɪˈbreɪt] *vi* zittern, beben; (*machine, string*) vibrieren; (*notes*) schwingen.

vibration [vaɪˈbreɪʃən] *n* Schwingung *f*; (*of machine*) Vibrieren *·nt*; (*of voice, ground*) Beben *nt*.

vicar [ˈvɪkə*] *n* Pfarrer *m*; —age Pfarrhaus *nt*.

vice [vaɪs] *n* (*evil*) Laster *nt*; (*Tech*) Schraubstock *m*; *pref:* —chairman stellvertretende(r) Vorsitzende(r) *m*; —president Vizepräsident *m*; — versa *ad* umgekehrt.

vicinity [vɪˈsɪnɪtɪ] *n* Umgebung *f*; (*closeness*) Nähe *f*.

vicious [ˈvɪʃəs] *a* gemein, böse; — circle Teufelskreis *m*; —ness Bösartigkeit *f*, Gemeinheit *f*.

vicissitudes [vɪˈsɪsɪtjuːdz] *npl* Wechselfälle *pl*.

victim [ˈvɪktɪm] *n* Opfer *nt*; —ization [vɪktɪmaɪˈzeɪʃən] Benachteiligung *f*; —ize *vt* benachteiligen.

victor [ˈvɪktə*] *n* Sieger *m*.

Victorian [vɪkˈtɔːrɪən] *a* viktorianisch; (*fig*) (sitten)streng.

victorious [vɪkˈtɔːrɪəs] *a* siegreich.

victory [ˈvɪktərɪ] *n* Sieg *m*.

video [ˈvɪdɪəʊ] *a* Fernseh-, Bild-.

vie [vaɪ] *vi* wetteifern.

view [vjuː] *n* (*sight*) Sicht *f*, Blick *m*; (*scene*) Aussicht *f*; (*opinion*) Ansicht *f*, Meinung *f*; (*intention*) Absicht *f*; **to have sth in** — etw beabsichtigen; **in** — **of** wegen (+gen), angesichts (+gen); *vt* situation betrachten; house besichtigen; —**er** (*viewfinder*) Sucher *m*; (Phot: small projector) Gucki *m*; (*TV*) Fernsehteilnehmer(in *f*) *m*; —**finder** Sucher *m*; —**point** Standpunkt *m*.

vigil [ˈvɪdʒɪl] *n* (Nacht)wache *f*; —ance Wachsamkeit *f*; —ant *a* wachsam; —antly *ad* aufmerksam.

vigorous *a*, —ly *ad* [ˈvɪgərəs, -lɪ] kräftig; protest energisch, heftig.

vigour, (US) **vigor** [ˈvɪgə*] *n* Kraft *f*, Vitalität *f*; (*of protest*) Heftigkeit *f*.

vile [vaɪl] *a* (*mean*) gemein; (*foul*) abscheulich.

vilify [ˈvɪlɪfaɪ] *vt* verleumden.

villa [ˈvɪlə] *n* Villa *f*.

village [ˈvɪlɪdʒ] *n* Dorf *nt*; —**r** Dorfbewohner(in *f*) *m*.

villain [ˈvɪlən] *n* Schurke *m*, Bösewicht *m*. ·

vindicate [ˈvɪndɪkeɪt] *vt* rechtfertigen; (*clear*) rehabilitieren.

vindication [vɪndɪˈkeɪʃən] *n* Rechtfertigung *f*; Rehabilitation *f*.

vindictive [vɪnˈdɪktɪv] *a* nachtragend, rachsüchtig.

vine [vaɪn] *n* Rebstock *m*, Rebe *f*.

vinegar [ˈvɪnɪgə*] *n* Essig *m*.

vineyard [ˈvɪnjəd] *n* Weinberg *m*.

vintage [ˈvɪntɪdʒ] *n* (*of wine*) Jahrgang *m*; — **car** Vorkriegsmodell *nt*; — **wine** edle(r) Wein *m*; — **year** besondere(s) Jahr *nt*.

viola [vɪˈəʊlə] *n* Bratsche *f*.

violate [ˈvaɪəleɪt] *vt* promise brechen; law übertreten; rights, rule, neutrality verletzen; sanctity, woman schänden.

violation [vaɪəˈleɪʃən] *n* Verletzung *f*; Übertretung *f*.

violence [ˈvaɪələns] *n* (*force*) Heftigkeit *f*; (*brutality*) Gewalttätigkeit *f*.

violent *a*, —ly *ad* [ˈvaɪələnt, -lɪ] (*strong*) heftig; (*brutal*) gewalttätig, brutal; contrast kraß; death gewaltsam.

violet [ˈvaɪələt] *n* Veilchen *nt*; *a* veilchenblau, violett.

violin [vaɪə'lɪn] n Geige f, Violine f.

viper ['vaɪpə*] n Viper· f; (fig) Schlange f.

virgin ['vɜːdʒɪn] n Jungfrau f; a jungfräulich, unberührt; —ity [vɜːˈdʒɪnɪtɪ] Unschuld f.

Virgo ['vɜːgəʊ] n Jungfrau f.

virile ['vɪraɪl] a männlich; (fig) kraftvoll.

virility [vɪ'rɪlɪtɪ] n Männlichkeit f.

virtual ['vɜːtjʊəl] a eigentlich; it was a — disaster es war geradezu eine Katastrophe; —ly ad praktisch, fast.

virtue ['vɜːtjuː] n (moral goodness) Tugend f; (good quality) Vorteil m, Vorzug m; by — of aufgrund (+gen).

virtuoso [vɜːtjʊ'əʊzəʊ] n Virtuose m.

virtuous ['vɜːtjʊəs] a tugendhaft.

virulence ['vɪrjʊləns] n Bösartigkeit f.

virulent ['vɪrjʊlənt] a (poisonous) scharf, (bitter) scharf, geharnischt.

virus ['vaɪərəs] n Virus m.

visa ['viːzə] n Visum nt, Sichtvermerk m.

vis-à-vis ['viːzævɪː] prep gegenüber.

visibility [vɪzɪ'bɪlɪtɪ] n Sichtbarkeit f; (Met) Sicht(weite) f.

visible ['vɪzəbl] a sichtbar.

visibly ['vɪzəblɪ] ad sichtlich.

vision ['vɪʒən] n (ability) Sehvermögen nt; (foresight) Weitblick m; (in dream, image) Vision f; —ary Hellseher m; (dreamer) Phantast m; a phantastisch.

visit ['vɪzɪt] n Besuch m; vt besuchen; town,. country fahren nach; —ing a professor Gast-; —ing card Visitenkarte f; —or (in house) Besucher(in f) m; (in hotel) Gast m; —or's book Gästebuch nt.

visor ['vaɪzə*] n Visier nt; (on cap) Schirm m; (Aut) Blende f.

vista ['vɪstə] n Aussicht f.

visual ['vɪzjʊəl] a Seh-, visuell; — aid Anschauungsmaterial nt; —ize vt (imagine) sich (dat) vorstellen; (expect) erwarten; —ly ad visuell.

vital ['vaɪtl] a (important) unerläßlich; (necessary for life) Lebens-, lebenswichtig; (lively) vital; —ity [vaɪ'tælɪtɪ] Vitalität f, Lebendigkeit f; —ly ad äußerst, ungeheuer.

vitamin ['vɪtəmɪn] n Vitamin nt.

vitiate ['vɪʃɪeɪt] vt verunreinigen; theory etc ungültig machen.

vivacious [vɪ'veɪʃəs] a lebhaft.

vivacity [vɪ'væsɪt] n Lebhaftigkeit f, Lebendigkeit f.

vivid a, —ly ad ['vɪvɪd, -lɪ] (graphic) lebendig, deutlich; memory lebhaft; (bright) leuchtend.

vivisection [vɪvɪ'sekʃən] n Vivisektion f.

vocabulary [vəʊ'kæbjʊlərɪ] n Wortschatz m, Vokabular nt.

vocal ['vəʊkəl] a Vokal-, Gesang-; (fig) lautstark; — cord Stimmband nt; —ist Sänger(in f) m.

vocation [vəʊ'keɪʃən] n (calling) Berufung f; —al a Berufs-.

vociferous a, —ly ad [vəʊ'sɪfərəs, -lɪ] lautstark.

vodka ['vɒdkə] n Wodka m.

vogue [vəʊg] n Mode f.

voice [vɔɪs] n (lit) Stimme f; (fig) Mitspracherecht nt; (Gram) Aktionsart f; active/passive — Aktiv nt/Passiv nt; with one — einstimmig; vt äußern; —d consonant stimmhafte(r) Konsonant m.

void [vɔɪd] n Leere f; a (empty) leer; (lacking) ohne (of acc), bar (of gen); (Jur) ungültig; see null.

volatile ['vɒlətaɪl] a gas flüchtig; person impulsiv; situation brisant.

volcanic [vɒl'kænɪk] a vulkanisch, Vulkan-.

volcano [vɒl'keɪnəʊ] n Vulkan m.

volition [vəʊ'lɪʃən] n Wille m; **of** one's own — aus freiem Willen.

volley ['vɒlɪ] n (of guns) Salve f; (of stones) Hagel m; (of words) Schwall m; (tennis) Flugball m; —ball Volleyball m.

volt [vəʊlt] n Volt nt; —age (Volt)-spannung f.

volte-face [vɒlt'fɑ:s] n (Kehrt)-wendung f.

voluble ['vɒljʊbl] a redselig.

volume ['vɒlju:m] n (book) Band m; (size) Umfang m; (space) Rauminhalt m, Volumen nt; (of sound) Lautstärke f.

voluntary, a, voluntarily ad ['vɒləntəri, -lɪ] freiwillig.

volunteer [vɒlən'tɪə*] n Freiwillige(r) mf; vi sich freiwillig melden; vt anbieten.

voluptuous [və'lʌptjʊəs] a sinnlich, wollüstig.

vomit ['vɒmɪt] n Erbrochene(s) nt; (act) Erbrechen nt; vt speien; vi sich übergeben.

vote [vəʊt] n Stimme f; (ballot) Wahl f, ·Abstimmung f; (result) Wahl- or Abstimmungsergebnis nt; (right to vote) Wahlrecht nt; vti wählen; —r Wähler(in f) m.

voting ['vəʊtɪŋ] n Wahl f; low — geringe Wahlbeteiligung f.

vouch [vautʃ]: — for vi bürgen für.

voucher ['vautʃə*] n Gutschein m.

vow [vaʊ] n Versprechen nt; (Rel) Gelübde nt; vt geloben; vengeance schwören.

vowel ['vaʊəl] n Vokal m, Selbstlaut m.

voyage ['vɔɪdʒ] n Reise f.

vulgar ['vʌlgə*] a (rude) vulgär; (of common people) allgemein, Volks-; —ity [vʌl'gærɪtɪ] Gewöhnlichkeit f, Vulgarität f.

vulnerability [vʌlnərə'bɪlɪtɪ] n Verletzlichkeit f.

vulnerable ['vʌlnərəbl] a (easily injured) verwundbar; (sensitive) verletzlich.

vulture ['vʌltʃə*] n Geier m.

W

W, w ['dʌblju:] n W nt, w nt.

wad [wɒd] n (bundle) Bündel nt; (of paper) Stoß m; (of money) Packen m.

wade [weɪd] vi waten.

wafer ['weɪfə*] n Waffel f; (Eccl) Hostie f.

waffle ['wɒfl] n Waffel f; (col: empty talk) Geschwafel nt; vi (col) schwafeln.

waft [wɑ:ft] vti wehen.

wag [wæg] vt tail wedeln mit; vi (tail) wedeln; her tongue never stops —ging ihr Mund steht nie still.

wage [weɪdʒ] n (Arbeits)lohn m; vt führen; —s pl Lohn m; — claim Lohnforderung f; — earner Lohnempfänger(in f) m; — freeze Lohnstopp m.

wager ['weɪdʒə*] *n* Wette *f*; *vti* wetten.

waggle ['wægl] *vt tail* wedeln mit; *vi* wedeln.

wag(g)on ['wægən] *n (horse-drawn)* Fuhrwerk *nt*; *(US Aut)* Wagen *m*; *(Brit Rail)* Waggon *m*.

wail [weɪl] *n* Wehgeschrei *nt*; *vi* wehklagen, jammern.

waist [weɪst] *n* Taille *f*; **—coat** Weste *f*; **—line** Taille *f*.

wait [weɪt] *n* Wartezeit *f*; *vi* warten *(for* auf +*acc)*; **to —** *for* sb to do sth darauf warten, daß jd etw tut; **— and see!** abwarten!; **to —** *at* table servieren; **—er** Kellner *m*; *(as address)* Herr Ober *m*; **—ing list** Warteliste *f*; **—ing room** *(Med)* Wartezimmer *nt*; *(Rail)* Wartesaal *m*; **—ress** Kellnerin *f*; *(as address)* Fräulein *nt*.

waive [weɪv] *vt* verzichten auf (+*acc)*.

wake [weɪk] *irreg vt* wecken; *vi* aufwachen; **to — up** *to (fig)* sich bewußt werden *(of* +*gen)*; *n (Naut)* Kielwasser *nt*; *(for dead)* Totenwache *f*; **in the — of** unmittelbar nach; **—n** *vt* aufwecken.

walk [wɔːk] *n* Spaziergang *m*; *(way of walking)* Gang *m*; *(route)* Weg *m*; **—s of** life *pl* Sphären *pl*; **to take** sb *for* **a —** mit jdm einen Spaziergang machen; **a 10-minute —** 10 Minuten zu Fuß; *vi* gehen; *(stroll)* spazierengehen; *(longer)* wandern; **—er** Spaziergänger *m*; *(hiker)* Wanderer *m*; **—ie-talkie** tragbare(s) Sprechfunkgerät *nt*; **—ing** *n* Gehen *nt*; Spazieren-(gehen) *nt*; Wandern *nt*; **a Wander—**; **—ing stick** Spazierstock *m*; **—out** Streik *m*; **—over** *(col)* leichter Sieg *m*.

wall [wɔːl] *n (inside)* Wand *f*; *(outside)* Mauer *f*; **—ed** *a* von Mauern umgeben.

wallet ['wɒlɪt] *n* Brieftasche *f*.

wallow ['wɒləʊ] *vi* sich wälzen *or* suhlen.

wallpaper ['wɔːlpeɪpə*] *n* Tapete *f*.

walnut ['wɔːlnʌt] *n* Walnuß *f*; *(tree)* Walnußbaum *m*; *(wood)* Nußbaumholz *nt*.

walrus ['wɔːlrəs] *n* Walroß *nt*.

waltz [wɔːlts] *n* Walzer *m*; *vi* Walzer tanzen.

wan [wɒn] *a* bleich.

wand [wɒnd] *n* Stab *m*.

wander ['wɒndə*] *vi (roam)* (herum)wandern; *(fig)* abschweifen; **—er** Wanderer *m*; **—ing** *a* umherziehend; *thoughts* abschweifend.

wane [weɪn] *vi* abnehmen; *(fig)* schwinden.

want [wɒnt] *n (lack)* Mangel *m (of* an +*dat)*; *(need)* Bedürfnis *nt*; **for — of** aus Mangel an (+*dat)*; **—** *of* mangels (+*gen)*; *vt (need)* brauchen; *(desire)* wollen; *(lack)* nicht haben; **I — to go** ich will gehen; **he —s confidence** ihm fehlt das Selbstvertrauen.

wanton ['wɒntən] *a* mutwillig, zügellos.

war [wɔː*] *n* Krieg *m*.

ward [wɔːd] *n (in hospital)* Station *f*; *(child)* Mündel *nt*; *(of city)* Bezirk *m*; **to — off** abwenden, abwehren.

warden ['wɔːdən] *n (guard)* Wächter *m*, Aufseher *m*; *(in youth hostel)* Herbergsvater *m*; *(Univ)* Heimleiter *m*.

warder ['wɔːdə*] *n* Gefängniswärter *m*.

wardrobe ['wɔːdrəub] n Kleider-
schrank m; (clothes) Garderobe f.
ware [wɛə*] n Ware f; —house
Lagerhaus n.
warfare ['wɔːfɛə*] n Krieg m;
Kriegsführung f.
warhead ['wɔːhed] n Sprengkopf m.
warily ['wɛərɪlɪ] ad vorsichtig.
warlike ['wɔːlaɪk] a kriegerisch.
warm [wɔːm] a warm; welcome
herzlich; vti wärmen; — up vt aufwärmen; vi warm werden; —
hearted a warmherzig; —ly ad
warm; herzlich; —th Wärme f;
Herzlichkeit f.
warn [wɔːn] vt warnen (of, against
vor + dat); —ing Warnung f;
without —ing unerwartet; —ing
light Warnlicht nt.
warp [wɔːp] vt verziehen; —ed a
(lit) wellig; (fig) pervers.
warrant ['wɔrənt] n Haftbefehl m.
warranty ['wɔrəntɪ] n Garantie f.
warrior ['wɔrɪə*] n Krieger m.
warship ['wɔːʃɪp] n Kriegsschiff nt.
wart [wɔːt] n Warze f.
wartime ['wɔːtaɪm] n Kriegszeit f,
Krieg m.
wary ['wɛərɪ] a vorsichtig;
mißtrauisch.
was [wɒz, wəz] pt of be.
wash [wɒʃ] n Wäsche f; to give
sth a — etw waschen; to have a
— sich waschen; vt waschen;
dishes abwaschen; vi sich
waschen; (do washing) waschen;
— away vt abwaschen, wegspülen;
—able a waschbar; —basin Wasch-
becken nt; —er (Tech)
Dichtungsring m; (machine)
Wasch- or Spülmaschine f; —ing
Wäsche f; —ing machine Waschmaschine f; —ing powder Wasch-
pulver nt; —ing-up Abwasch m;

— leather Waschleder nt; —-out
(col) (event) Reinfall m; (person)
Niete f; —room Waschraum m.
wasn't ['wɒznt] = was not.
wasp [wɒsp] n Wespe f.
wastage ['weɪstɪdʒ] n Verlust m;
natural — Verschleiß m.
waste [weɪst] n (wasting) Verschwendung f; (what is wasted)
Abfall m; —s pl' Einöde f; a
(useless) überschüssig, Abfall-; vt
object verschwenden; time, life
vergeuden; vi: — away verfallen;
—ful a, —fully ad ver-
schwenderisch; process aufwendig; —land Ödland nt; —paper
basket Papierkorb m.
watch [wɒtʃ] n Wache f; (for
time) Uhr f; to be on the — (for
sth) (auf etw acc) aufpassen; vt
ansehen; (observe) beobachten;
(be careful of) aufpassen auf
(+ acc); (guard) bewachen; to —
TV fernsehen; to — sb doing sth
jdm bei etw zuschauen; — it! paß
bloß auf!; vi zusehen; (guard)
Wache halten; to — for sb/sth
nach jdm/etw Ausschau halten; —
out! paß auf!; —dog (lit)
Wachthund m; (fig) Wächter m;
—ful a wachsam; —maker
Uhrmacher m; —man (Nacht)-
wächter m; — strap Uhrarmband
nt.
water ['wɔːtə*] n Wasser nt; —s
pl Gewässer nt; vt (be)gießen;
(river) bewässern; horses tränken;
vi (eye) tränen; my mouth is —ing
mir läuft das Wasser im Mund
zusammen; — down vt ver-
wässern; — closet (Wasser)klosett
nt; —colour, (US) —color
(painting) Aquarell nt; (paint)
Wasserfarbe f; —cress
(Brunnen)kresse f; —fall Wasser-

fall *m*; — **hole** Wasserloch *nt*; —**ing can** Gießkanne *f*; — **level** Wasserstand *m*; —**lily** Seerose *f*; —**line** Wasserlinie *f*; —**logged** *a ground* voll Wasser; *wood* mit Wasser vollgesogen; —**melon** Wassermelone *f*; — **polo** Wasserball(spiel) *nt*; —**proof** *a* wasserdicht; —**shed** Wasserscheide *f*; —**skiing** Wasserschilaufen *nt*; **to go** —**skiing** wasserschilaufen gehen; —**tight** *a* wasserdicht; —**works** *pl* Wasserwerk *nt*; —**y** *a* wäss(e)rig.

watt [wɒt] *n* Watt *nt.*

wave [weɪv] *n* Welle *f*; (*with hand*) Winken *nt*; *vt* (*move to and fro*) schwenken; *hand, flag* winken mit; *hair* wellen; *vi* (*person*) winken; (*flag*) wehen; (*hair*) sich wellen; **to** — **to sb** jdm zuwinken; **to** — **sb goodbye** jdm zum Abschied winken; —**length** (*lit, fig*) Wellenlänge *f.*

waver ['weɪvə*] *vi* (*hesitate*) schwanken; (*flicker*) flackern.

wavy ['weɪvɪ] *a* wellig.

wax [wæks] *n* Wachs *nt*; (*sealing* —) Siegellack *m*; (*in ear*) Ohrenschmalz *nt*; *vt floor* (ein)wachsen; *vi* (*moon*) zunehmen; —**works** *pl* Wachsfigurenkabinett *nt.*

way [weɪ] *n* Weg *m*; (*road also*) Straße *f*; (*method*) Art und Weise *f*, Methode *f*; (*direction*) Richtung *f*; (*habit*) Eigenart *f*, Gewohnheit *f*; (*distance*) Entfernung *f*; (*condition*) Zustand *m*; **a long** — **away** *or* **off** weit weg; **to lose one's** — sich verirren; **to make** — **for sb/sth** jdm/etw Platz machen; **to be in a bad** — schlecht dransein; **do it this** — machen Sie es so; **give** — (*Aut*) Vorfahrt achten!; — **of thinking** Meinung *f*; **to get one's own** — seinen Willen bekommen;

one — **or another** irgendwie; **under** — **im** Gange; **in a** — in gewisser Weise; **in the** — im Wege; **by the** — übrigens; **by** — **of** (*via*) über (+*acc*); (*in order to*) um ... zu; (*instead of*) als; **'—in'** 'Eingang'; **'— out'** 'Ausgang'; —**lay** *vt irreg* auflauern (+*dat*); —**ward** *a* eigensinnig.

we [wiː] *pl pron* wir.

weak *a*, —**ly** *ad* [wiːk, -lɪ] schwach; —**en** *vt* schwächen, entkräften; *vi* schwächer werden; nachlassen; —**ling** Schwächling *m*; —**ness** Schwäche *f.*

wealth [welθ] *n* Reichtum *m*; (*abundance*) Fülle *f*; —**y** *a* reich.

wean [wiːn] *vt* entwöhnen.

weapon ['wepən] *n* Waffe *f.*

wear [wɛə*] *n* (*clothing*) Kleidung *f*; (*use*) Verschleiß *m*; *vt irreg* (*have on*) tragen; *smile etc* haben; (*use*) abnutzen; *vi* (*last*) halten; (*become old*) (sich) verschleißen; (*clothes*) sich abtragen; — **and tear** Abnutzung *f*, Verschleiß *m*; — **away** *vt* verbrauchen; *vi* schwinden; — **down** *vt people* zermürben; — **off** *vi* sich verlieren; — **out** *vt* verschleißen; *person* erschöpfen; —**er** Träger(in *f*) *m.*

wearily ['wɪərɪlɪ] *ad* müde.

weariness ['wɪərɪnəs] *n* Müdigkeit *f.*

weary ['wɪərɪ] *a* (*tired*) müde; (*tiring*) ermüden; *vt* ermüden; *vi* überdrüssig werden (*of gen*).

weasel ['wiːzl] *n* Wiesel *nt.*

weather ['weðə*] *n* Wetter *nt*; *vt* verwittern lassen; (*resist*) überstehen; —**beaten** *a* verwittert; *skin* wettergegerbt; —**cock** Wetterhahn *m*; — **forecast** Wettervorhersage *f.*

weave [wi:v] *vt irreg* weben; **to —**
one's way through sth sich durch
etw durchschlängeln; **—r** Weber(in
f) *m.*

weaving ['wi:vɪŋ] *n* Weben *nt*,
Weberei *f.*

web [web] *n* Netz *nt*; (*membrane*)
Schwimmhaut *f*; **—bed** *a*
Schwimm-, schwimmhäutig;
—bing Gewebe *nt.*

wed [wed] *vt' irreg* (*old*) heiraten.

we'd [wi:d] **= we had; we
would.**

wedding ['wedɪŋ] *n* Hochzeit *f*; **—
day** Hochzeitstag *m*; **— present**
Hochzeitsgeschenk *nt*; **— ring**
Trau- or Ehering *m.*

wedge [wedʒ] *n* Keil *m*; (*of cheese
etc*) Stück *nt*; *vt* (*fasten*)
festklemmen; (*pack tightly*)
einkeilen.

Wednesday ['wenzdeɪ] *n* Mittwoch
m.

wee [wi:] *a* (*esp Scot*) klein, winzig.

weed [wi:d] *n* Unkraut *nt*; *vt* jäten;
—killer Unkrautvertilgungsmittel
nt.

week [wi:k] *n* Woche *f*; **a — today**
heute in einer Woche; **—day**
Wochentag *m*; **—end** Wochenende
nt; **—ly** *a, ad* wöchentlich; *wages,
magazine* Wochen-.

weep [wi:p] *vi irreg* weinen.

weigh [weɪ] *vti* wiegen; **— down**
vt niederdrücken; **— up** *vt* prüfen,
abschätzen; **—bridge** Brücken-
waage *f.*

weight [weɪt] *n* Gewicht *nt*; **to
lose/put on —** abnehmen/
zunehmen; **—lessness** Schwere-
losigkeit *f*; **—lifter** Gewichtheber
m; **—y** *a* (*heavy*) gewichtig;
(*important*) schwerwiegend.

weir [wɪə*] *n* (Stau)wehr *nt.*

weird [wɪəd] *a* seltsam.

welcome ['welkəm] *n* Willkommen
nt, Empfang *m*; *vt* begrüßen.

welcoming ['welkəmɪŋ] *a*
Begrüßungs-; freundlich.

weld [weld] *n* Schweißnaht *f*; *vt*
schweißen; **—er** Schweißer *m*;
—ing Schweißen *nt.*

welfare ['welfɛə*] *n* Wohl *nt*;
(*social*) Fürsorge *f*; **— state** Wohl-
fahrtsstaat *m.*

well [wel] *n* Brunnen *m*; (*oil —*)
Quelle *f*; **a** (*in good health*)
gesund; **are you —?** geht es Ihnen
gut?; *interj* nun, na schön;
(*starting conversation*) nun, tja;
—, —! na, na!; *ad* gut; **— over**
40 weit über 40; **it may —** be es
kann wohl sein; **it would be (as)
— to ...** es wäre wohl gut, zu ...;
you did — (not) to ... Sie haben
gut daran getan, (nicht) zu ...;
very — (*O.K.*) nun gut.

we'll [wi:l] **= we will, we shall.**

well-behaved ['welbɪ'heɪvd] *a*
wohlerzogen.

well-being ['welbi:ɪŋ] *n* Wohl *nt*,
Wohlergehen *nt.*

well-built ['wel'bɪlt] *a* kräftig
gebaut.

well-developed ['weld'veləpt] *a* a
girl gut entwickelt; *economy*
hochentwickelt.

well-earned ['wel'ɜ:nd] *a rest*
wohlverdient.

well-heeled ['wel'hi:ld] *a* (*col:
wealthy*) gut gepolstert.

wellingtons ['welɪŋtənz] *npl*
Gummistiefel *pl.*

well-known ['wel'nəʊn] *a person*
weithin bekannt.

well-meaning ['wel'mi:nɪŋ] *a*
person wohlmeinend; *action*
gutgemeint.

well-off ['wel'ɒf] a gut situiert.
well-read ['wel'red] a (sehr) belesen.
well-to-do ['weltə'du:] a wohlhabend.
well-wisher ['welwɪʃə*] n wohlwollende(r) Freund m, Gönner m.
wench [wentʃ] n (old) Maid f, Dirne f.
went [went] pt of go.
were [wɜ:*] pt pl of be.
we're [wɪə*] = we are.
weren't [wɜ:nt] = were not.
west [west] n Westen m; a West-, westlich; ad westwärts, nach Westen; **—erly** a westlich; **—ern** a westlich, West-; n (Cine) Western m; **—ward(s)** ad westwärts.
wet [wet] a naß; **— blanket** (fig) Triefel m; **—ness** Nässe f, Feuchtigkeit f; '**— paint**' 'frisch gestrichen'.
we've [wi:v] = we have.
whack [wæk] n Schlag m; vt schlagen.
whale [weɪl] n Wal m.
wharf [wɔ:f] n Kai m.
what [wɒt] pron, interj was; a welche(r,s); **— a hat!** was für ein Hut!; **— money I had** das Geld, das ich hatte; **— about ...?** (suggestion) wie wär's mit ...?; **— about it?**, so —? na und?; **well, — about him?** was ist mit ihm?; and **— about me?** und ich?; **— for?** wozu?; **—ever** a: **—ever he says** egal, was er sagt; **no reason —ever** überhaupt kein Grund.
wheat [wi:t] n Weizen m.
wheel [wi:l] n Rad nt; (steering —) Lenkrad nt; (disc) Scheibe f; vt schieben; vi (revolve) sich drehen; **—barrow** Schubkarren m; **—chair** Rollstuhl m.

wheeze [wi:z] n Keuchen nt; vi keuchen.
when [wen] ad interrog. wann; ad,cj (with present-tense) wenn; (with past tense) als; (with indir question) wann; **—ever** ad wann immer; immer wenn.
where [wɛə*] ad (place) wo; (direction) wohin; **— from** woher; **—abouts** ['wɛərə'bauts] ad wo; n Aufenthalt m, Verbleib m; **—as** [wɛər'æz] cj während, wo ... doch; **—ever** [wɛər'evə*] ad wo (immer).
whet [wet] vt appetite anregen.
whether ['weðə*] cj ob.
which [wɪtʃ] a (from selection) welche(r,s); rel pron der/die/das; (rel: which fact) was; (interrog) welche(r,s); **—ever** (book) he takes welches (Buch) er auch nimmt.
whiff [wɪf] n Hauch m.
while [waɪl] n Weile f; cj während; **for a —** eine Zeitlang.
whim [wɪm] n Laune f.
whimper ['wɪmpə*] n Wimmern nt; vi wimmern.
whimsical ['wɪmzɪkəl] a launisch.
whine [waɪn] n Gewinsel nt, Gejammer nt; vi heulen, winseln.
whip [wɪp] n Peitsche f; (Parl) Einpeitscher m; vt (beat) peitschen; (snatch) reißen; **—round** (col) Geldsammlung f.
whirl [wɜ:l] n Wirbel m; vti (herum)wirbeln; **—pool** Wirbel m; **—wind** Wirbelwind m.
whirr [wɜ:*] vi schwirren, surren.
whisk [wɪsk] n Schneebesen m; vt cream etc schlagen.
whisker ['wɪskə*] n (of animal) Barthaare pl; **—s** pl (of man) Backenbart m.
whisk(e)y ['wɪski] n Whisky m.

whisper ['wɪspə*] n Flüstern nt; vi flüstern; (leaves) rascheln; vt flüstern, munkeln.

whist [wɪst] n Whist nt.

whistle ['wɪsl] n Pfiff m; (instrument) Pfeife f; vti pfeifen.

white [waɪt] n Weiß nt; (of egg) Eiweiß nt; (of eye) Weißes nt; a weiß; (with fear) blaß; **--collar worker** Angestellte(r) m; **-- lie** Notlüge f; **--ness** Weiß nt; **--wash** n (paint) Tünche f; (fig) Ehrenrettung f; vt weißen, tünchen; (fig) reinwaschen.

whiting ['waɪtɪŋ] n Weißfisch m.

Whitsun ['wɪtsn] n Pfingsten nt.

whittle ['wɪtl] vt: **-- away** or **down** stutzen, verringern.

whizz [wɪz] vi sausen, zischen, schwirren; **-- kid** (col) Kanone f.

who [huː] pron (interrog) wer; (rel) der/die/das; **--ever** [huː'evə*] pron wer immer; jeder, der/jede, die/jedes, das.

whole [həʊl] a ganz; (uninjured) heil; n Ganze(s) nt; **the -- of the year** das ganze Jahr; **on the --** im großen und ganzen; **--hearted** a rückhaltlos; **--heartedly** ad von ganzem Herzen; **--sale** Großhandel m; a trade Großhandels-; destruction vollkommen, Massen-; **--saler** Großhändler m; **--some** a bekömmlich, gesund.

wholly ['həʊlɪ] ad ganz, völlig.

whom [huːm] pron (interrog) wen; (rel) den/die/das/die pl.

whooping cough ['huːpɪŋkɒf] n Keuchhusten m.

whopper ['wɒpə*] n (col) Mordsding nt; faustdicke Lüge f.

whopping ['wɒpɪŋ] a (col) kolossal, Riesen-.

whore ['hɔː*] n Hure f.

whose [huːz] pron (interrog) wessen; (rel) dessen/deren/ dessen/deren pl.

why [waɪ] ad warum; interj nanu; **that's --** deshalb.

wick [wɪk] n Docht m.

wicked ['wɪkɪd] a böse; **--ness** Bosheit f, Schlechtigkeit f.

wicker ['wɪkə*] n Weidengeflecht nt, Korbgeflecht nt.

wicket ['wɪkɪt] n Tor nt, Dreistab m; (playing pitch) Spielfeld nt.

wide [waɪd] a breit; plain weit; (in firing) daneben; **-- of** weitab von; ad weit; daneben; **--angle a lens** Weitwinkel-; **--awake** a hellwach; **--ly** ad weit; known allgemein; **--n** vt erweitern; **--ness** Breite f, Ausdehnung f; **--open a** weit geöffnet; **--spread a** weitverbreitet.

widow ['wɪdəʊ] n Witwe f; **--ed** a verwitwet; **--er** Witwer m.

width [wɪdθ] n Breite f, Weite f.

wield [wiːld] vt schwingen, handhaben.

wife [waɪf] n (Ehe)frau f, Gattin f.

wig [wɪg] n Perücke f.

wiggle ['wɪgl] n Wackeln nt; vt wackeln mit; vi wackeln.

wigwam ['wɪgwæm] n Wigwam m, Indianerzelt nt.

wild [waɪld] a wild; (violent) heftig; plan, idea verrückt; **the --s** pl die Wildnis; **--erness** ['wɪldənəs] Wildnis f, Wüste f; **--goose chase** fruchtlose(s) Unternehmen nt; **--life** Tierwelt f; **--ly** ad wild, ungestüm; exaggerated irrsinnig.

wilful ['wɪlfʊl] a (intended) vorsätzlich; (obstinate) eigensinnig.

will [wɪl] v aux: **he -- come** er wird kommen; **I -- do it!** ich werde es tun; n (power to choose) Wille m;

(*wish*) Wunsch *m*, Bestreben *nt*; (*Jur*) Testament *nt*; *vt* wollen; —ing *a* gewillt, bereit; —ingly *ad* bereitwillig, gern; —ingness (Bereit)willigkeit *f*.

willow ['wɪləʊ] *n* Weide *f*.

will power ['wɪl'paʊə*] *n* Willenskraft *f*.

wilt [wɪlt] *vi* (ver)welken.

wily ['waɪlɪ] *a* gerissen.

win [wɪn] *n* Sieg *m*; *irreg vt* gewinnen; *vi* (*be successful*) siegen; to — sb over jdn gewinnen, jdn dazu bringen.

wince [wɪns] *n* Zusammenzucken *nt*; *vi* zusammenzucken, zurückfahren.

winch [wɪntʃ] *n* Winde *f*.

wind [waɪnd] *irreg vt rope* winden; *bandage* wickeln; to — one's way sich schlängeln; *vi* (*turn*) sich winden; (*change direction*) wenden; — up *vt clock* aufziehen; *debate* (ab)schließen.

wind ‚[wɪnd] *n* Wind *m*; (*Med*) Blähungen *pl*; —break Windschutz *m*; —fall unverhoffte(r) Glücksfall *m*.

winding ['waɪndɪŋ] *a road* gewunden, sich schlängelnd.

wind instrument ['wɪndɪnstrumənt] *n* Blasinstrument *nt*.

windmill ['wɪndmɪl] *n* Windmühle *f*.

window ['wɪndəʊ] *n* Fenster *nt*; — box Blumenkasten *m*; — cleaner Fensterputzer *m*; — ledge Fenstersims *m*; — pane Fensterscheibe *f*; —-shopping Schaufensterbummel *m*; —sill Fensterbank *f*.

windpipe ['wɪndpaɪp] *n* Luftröhre *f*.

windscreen ['wɪndskriːn], (*US*) **windshield** ['wɪndʃiːld] *n* Wind-

schutzscheibe *f*; — wiper Scheibenwischer *m*.

windswept ['wɪndswept] *a* vom Wind gepeitscht; *person* zersaust.

windy ['wɪndɪ] *a* windig.

wine [waɪn] *n* Wein *m*; —glass Weinglas *nt*; — list Weinkarte *f*; — merchant Weinhändler *m*; — tasting Weinprobe *f*; — waiter Weinkellner *m*.

wing [wɪŋ] *n* Flügel *m*; (*Mil*) Gruppe *f*; —s *pl* (*Theat*) Seitenkulisse *f*; —er (*Sport*) Flügelstürmer *m*.

wink [wɪŋk] *n* Zwinkern *nt*; *vi* zwinkern, blinzeln; to — at sb jdm zublinzeln; forty —s Nickerchen *nt*.

winner ['wɪnə*] *n* Gewinner *m*; (*Sport*) Sieger *m*.

winning ['wɪnɪŋ] *a team* siegreich, Sieger-; *goal* entscheidend; *n*: —s *pl* Gewinn *m*; — post Ziel *nt*.

winter ['wɪntə*] *n* Winter *m*; *a clothes* Winter-; *vi* überwintern; — sports *pl* Wintersport *m*.

wintry ['wɪntrɪ] *a* Winter-, winterlich.

wipe [waɪp] *n* Wischen *nt*; *vt* wischen, abwischen; — out *vt debt* löschen; (*destroy*) auslöschen.

wire ['waɪə*] *n* Draht *m*; (*telegram*) Telegramm *nt*; *vt* telegrafieren (*sb* jdm, *sth* etw); —less Radio(apparat *m*) *nt*.

wiry ['waɪərɪ] *a* drahtig.

wisdom ['wɪzdəm] *n* Weisheit *f*; (*of decision*) Klugheit *f*; — tooth Weisheitszahn *m*.

wise [waɪz] *a* klug, weise; —crack Witzelei *f*; —ly *ad* klug, weise.

wish [wɪʃ] *n* Wunsch *m*; *vt* wünschen; he —es us to do it er möchte, daß wir es tun; with best —es herzliche Grüße; to — sb goodbye jdn verabschieden; to —

to do sth etw tun wollen; **—ful**
thinking Wunschdenken *n*.

wisp [wɪsp] *n* (Haar)strähne *f*; (*of*
smoke) Wölkchen *nt*.

wistful ['wɪstful] *a* sehnsüchtig.

wit [wɪt] *n* (*also* **—s**) Verstand *m*
no pl; (*amusing ideas*) Witz *m*;
(*person*) Witzbold *m*; at one's **—s'**
end mit seinem Latein am Ende;
to have one's **—s** about one auf
dem Posten sein.

witch [wɪtʃ] *n* Hexe *f*; **—craft**
Hexerei *f*.

with [wɪð, wɪθ] *prep* mit; (*in spite
of*) trotz (+*gen or dat*); **—** him it's
... bei ihm ist es ...; to stay **—**
sb bei jdm wohnen; I have no
money **—** me ich habe kein Geld
bei mir; shaking **—** fright vor
Angst zitternd.

withdraw [wɪð'drɔ:] *irreg vt*
zurückziehen; *money* abheben;
remark zurücknehmen; *vi* sich
zurückziehen; **—al** Zurückziehung
f; Abheben *nt*; Zurücknahme *f*;
—al symptoms *pl* Entzugser-
scheinungen *pl*.

wither ['wɪðə*] *vi* (ver)welken;
—ed a verwelkt, welk.

withhold [wɪð'həʊld] *vt irreg*
vorenthalten (*from sb* jdm).

within [wɪð'ɪn] *prep* innerhalb
(+*gen*).

without [wɪð'aʊt] *prep ohne*; it
goes **—** saying es ist selbstverständlich.

withstand [wɪð'stænd] *vt irreg*
widerstehen (+*dat*).

witness ['wɪtnəs] *n* Zeuge *m*;
Zeugin *f*; *vt* (*see*) sehen, miter-
leben; (*sign document*)
beglaubigen; *vi* aussagen; **— box**,
(*US*) **— stand** Zeugenstand *m*.

witticism ['wɪtɪsɪzəm] *n* witzige
Bemerkung *f*.

witty *a*, **wittily** *ad* ['wɪtɪ, -lɪ]
witzig, geistreich.

wizard ['wɪzəd] *n* Zauberer *m*.

wobble ['wɒbl] *vi* wackeln.

woe [wəʊ] *n* Weh *nt*, Leid *nt*,
Kummer *m*.

wolf [wʊlf] *n* Wolf *m*.

woman ['wʊmən] *n*, *pl* **women**
Frau *f*; *a* **—in** *f*.

womb [wu:m] *n* Gebärmutter *f*.

women ['wɪmɪn] *npl of* **woman**.

wonder ['wʌndə*] *n* (*marvel*)
Wunder *nt*; (*surprise*) Staunen *nt*,
Verwunderung *f*; *vi* sich wundern;
I — whether ... ich frage mich, ob
...; **—ful** *a* wunderbar, herrlich;
—fully *ad* wunderbar.

won't [wəʊnt] = **will not**.

wood [wʊd] *n* Holz *nt*; (*forest*)
Wald *m*; **—** carving
Holzschnitzerei *f*; **—ed** bewaldet,
waldig, Wald-; **—en** a (*lit, fig*)
hölzern; **—pecker** Specht *m*;
—wind Blasinstrumente *pl*;
—work Holzwerk *nt*; (*craft*)
Holzarbeiten *pl*; **—worm**
Holzwurm *m*.

wool [wʊl] *n* Wolle *f*; **—len**, (*US*)
—en a Woll-; **—ly**, (*US*) **—y** a
wollig; (*fig*) schwammig.

word [wɜ:d] *n* Wort *nt*; (*news*)
Bescheid *m*; to have a **—** with sb
mit jdm reden; to have **—s** with
sb Worte wechseln mit jdm; by **—**
of mouth mündlich; *vt*
formulieren; **—ing** Wortlaut *m*,
Formulierung *f*.

work [wɜ:k] *n* Arbeit *f*; (*Art, Liter*)
Werk *nt*; *vi* arbeiten; *machine*
funktionieren; (*medicine*) wirken;
(*succeed*) klappen; **—s** (*factory*)
Fabrik *f*, Werk *nt*; (*of watch*) Werk
nt; **— off** *vt debt* abarbeiten; *anger*
abreagieren; **— on** *vi*
weiterarbeiten; *vt* (*be engaged in*)

arbeiten an (+dat); (influence) bearbeiten; — out vi (sum) aufgehen; (plan) klappen; vt problem lösen; plan ausarbeiten; — up to vt hinarbeiten auf (+acc); to get — ed up sich aufregen; —able a soil bearbeitbar; plan ausführbar; —er Arbeiter(in f) m; —ing class Arbeiterklasse f; —ing-class a Arbeiter-; —ing man Werktätige(r) m; —man Arbeiter m; —manship Arbeit f, Ausführung ·f; —shop Werkstatt f.

world [wɜːld] n Welt f; (animal etc) Reich nt; out of this — himmlisch; to come into the — auf die Welt kommen; to do sb/sth the — of good jdm/etw sehr gut tun; to be the — to sb jds ein und alles sein; to think the — of sb große Stücke auf jdn halten; —famous a weltberühmt; —ly a weltlich, irdisch; —wide a weltweit.

worm [wɜːm] n Wurm m.

worn [wɔːn] a clothes abgetragen; —out a object abgenutzt; person völlig erschöpft.

worried ['wʌrɪd] a besorgt, beunruhigt.

worrier ['wʌrɪə*] n: he is a — er macht sich (dat) ewig Sorgen.

worry ['wʌrɪ] n Sorge f, Kummer m; vt quälen, beunruhigen; vi (feel uneasy) sich sorgen, sich (dat) Gedanken machen; —ing a beunruhigend.

worse [wɜːs] a comp of bad schlechter, schlimmer; ad comp of badly schlimmer, ärger; n Schlimmere(s) nt, Schlechtere(s) nt; —n vt verschlimmern; vi sich verschlechtern.

worship ['wɜːʃɪp] n Anbetung f, Verehrung f; (religious service) Gottesdienst m; (title) Hoch-

würden m; vt anbeten; —per Gottesdienstbesucher(in f) m.

worst [wɜːst] a superl of bad schlimmste(r,s), schlechteste(r,s); ad. superl of badly am Schlimmsten, am ärgsten; n Schlimmste(s) nt, Ärgste(s) nt.

worsted ['wʊstɪd] n Kammgarn nt.

worth [wɜːθ] n Wert m; £10 — of food Essen für 10 £; a wert; —seeing sehenswert; it's — £10 es ist 10 £ wert; —less a wertlos; person nichtsnutzig; —while a lohnend, der Mühe wert; ad: it's not —while going es lohnt sich nicht, dahin zu gehen; —y ['wɜːðɪ] a (having worth) wertvoll; wert (of gen), würdig (of gen).

would [wʊd] v aux: she — come sie würde kommen; if you asked he — come wenn Sie ihn fragten, würde er kommen; — you like a drink? möchten Sie etwas trinken? —be a angeblich; —n't = — not.

wound [wuːnd] n (lit, fig) Wunde f; vt verwunden, verletzen (also fig).

wrangle ['ræŋgl] n Streit m; vi sich zanken.

wrap [ræp] n (stole) Umhang m, Schal m; vt (also — up) einwickeln; deal abschließen; —per Umschlag m, Schutzhülle f; —ping paper Einwickelpapier nt.

wreath [riːθ] n Kranz m.

wreck [rek] n Schiffbruch m; (ship) Wrack nt; (sth ruined) Ruine f, Trümmerhaufen m; a nervous — ein Nervenbündel nt; vt zerstören; —age Wrack nt, Trümmer pl.

wren [ren] n Zaunkönig m.

wrench [rentʃ] n (spanner) Schraubenschlüssel m; (twist)

Ruck *m*, heftige Drehung *f*; *vt* reißen, zerren.

wrestle ['resl] *vi* ringen.

wrestling ['reslɪŋ] *n* Ringen *nt*; **—** match Ringkampf *m*.

wretched ['retʃɪd] *a* hovel elend; (col) verflixt; I feel — mir ist elend.

wriggle ['rɪgl] *n* Schlängeln *nt*; *vi* sich winden.

wring [rɪŋ] *vt irreg* wringen.

wrinkle ['rɪŋkl] *n* Falte *f*, Runzel *f*; *vt* runzeln; *vi* sich runzeln; (material) knittern.

wrist [rɪst] *n* Handgelenk *nt*; —watch Armbanduhr *f*.

writ [rɪt] *n* gerichtliche(r) Befehl *m*.

write [raɪt] *vti irreg* schreiben, —down *vt* niederschreiben, aufschreiben; — off *vt* (dismiss) abschreiben; — out *vt* essay abschreiben; cheque ausstellen; — up *vt* schreiben; —off: it is a off das kann man abschreiben; —r

Verfasser *m*; (author) Schriftsteller *m*; **—up** Besprechung *f*.

writing ['raɪtɪŋ] *n* (act) Schreiben *nt*; (hand—) (Hand)schrift *f*; **—s** *pl* Schriften *pl*, Werke *pl*; **—paper** Schreibpapier.

wrong [rɒŋ] *a* (incorrect) falsch; (morally) unrecht; (out of order) nicht in Ordnung; he was — in doing that es war nicht recht von ihm, das zu tun; what's — with your leg? was ist mit deinem Bein los?; to go — (plan) schiefgehen; (person) einen Fehler machen; *n* Unrecht *nt*; *vt* Unrecht tun (+dat); —ful *a* unrechtmäßig; —ly *ad* falsch; accuse zu Unrecht.

wrought [rɔ:t] *a*: — iron Schmiedeeisen *nt*.

wry [raɪ] *a* schief, krumm; (ironical) trocken; to make a — face das Gesicht verziehen.

X

X, x [eks] *n* X *nt*, x *nt*.

Xmas ['eksməs] *n* (col) Weihnachten *nt*.

X-ray ['eks'reɪ] *n* Röntgenaufnahme *f*; *vt* röntgen.

xylophone ['zaɪləfəʊn] *n* Xylophon *nt*.

Y

Y, y [waɪ] *n* Y *nt*, y *nt*.

yacht [jɒt] *n* Jacht *f*; **—ing** (Sport)segeln *nt*; **—sman** Sportsegler *m*.

Yank [jæŋk] *n* (col) Ami *m*.

yap [jæp] *vi* (dog) kläffen; (people) quasseln.

yard [jɑ:d] *n* Hof *m*; (measure) (englische) Elle *f*, Yard *nt*, 0,91 *m*;

—stick (fig) Maßstab *m*.

yarn [jɑ:n] *n* (thread) Garn *nt*; (story) (Seemanns)garn *nt*.

yawn [jɔ:n] *n* Gähnen *nt*; *vi* gähnen.

year ['jɪə*] *n* Jahr *nt*; —ly *a*, *ad* jährlich.

yearn [j3:n] *vi* sich sehnen (for

nach); **—ing** Verlangen *nt,*
Sehnsucht *f.*

yeast [ji:st] *n* Hefe *f.*

yell [jel] *n* gellende(r) Schrei *m; vi*
laut schreien.

yellow ['jeləʊ] *a* gelb; *n* Gelb *nt;*
— fever Gelbfieber *nt.*

yelp [jelp] *n* Gekläff *nt; vi* kläffen.

yeoman ['jəʊmən] *n:* Y— **of the**
Guard Leibgardist *m.*

yes [jes] *ad* ja; *n* Ja *nt,* Jawort *nt;*
—man Jasager *m.*

yesterday ['jestədeɪ] *ad* gestern; *n*
Gestern *nt;* **the day before —**
vorgestern.

yet [jet] *ad* noch; (*in question*)
schon; (*up to now*) bis jetzt; *and*
— again und wieder *or* noch
einmal; **as — bis** jetzt; (*in past*)
bis dahin; *cf* doch, dennoch.

yew [ju:] *n* Eibe *f.*

Yiddish ['jɪdɪʃ] *n* Jiddisch *nt.*

yield [ji:ld] *n* Ertrag *m; vt* result,
crop hervorbringen; *interest, profit*
abwerfen; (*concede*) abtreten; *vi*
nachgeben; (*Mil*) sich ergeben.

yodel ['jəʊdl] *vi* jodeln.

yoga ['jəʊɡə] *n* Joga *m.*

yoghurt ['jɒɡət] *n* Joghurt *m.*

yoke [jəʊk] *n* (*lit, fig*) Joch *nt.*

yolk [jəʊk] *n* Eidotter *m,* Eigelb *nt.*

yonder ['jɒndə*] *ad* dort drüben,
da drüben; *a* jene(r, s) dort.

you [ju:] *pron* (*familiar*) (*sing*)
(*nom*) du; (*acc*) dich; (*dat*) dir;
(*pl*) (*nom*) ihr; (*acc, dat*) euch;
(*polite*) (*nom, acc*) Sie; (*dat*)
Ihnen; (*indef*) (*nom*) man; (*acc*)
einen; (*dat*) einem.

you'd [ju:d] **= you had; you
would.**

you'll [ju:l] **= you will, you
shall.**

young [jʌŋ] *a* jung; *npl* **die
Jungen;** **—ish** *a* ziemlich jung;
—ster Junge *m,* junge(r) Bursche
*m/*junge(s) Mädchen *nt.*

your ['jɔ:*] *poss a* (*familiar*) (*sing*)
dein; (*pl*) euer, eure *pl;* (*polite*) Ihr.

you're ['jʊə*] **= you are.**

yours ['jɔ:z] *poss pron* (*familiar*)
(*sing*) deine(r, s); (*pl*) eure(r, s);
(*polite*) Ihre(r, s).

yourself [jɔ:'self] *pron* (*emphatic*)
selbst; (*familiar*) (*sing*) (*acc*) dich
(selbst); (*dat*) dir (selbst); (*pl*)
euch (selbst); (*polite*) sich (selbst);
you're not **— mit dir/Ihnen ist**
etwas nicht in Ordnung.

youth [ju:θ] *n* Jugend *f;* (*young
man*) junge(r) Mann *m;* (*young
people*) Jugend *f;* **—ful** *a* jugendlich; **— hostel** Jugendherberge *f.*

you've [ju:v] **= you have.**

Z

Z, z [zed] *n* Z *nt,* z *nt.*

zany ['zeɪnɪ] *a* komisch.

zeal [zi:l] *n* Eifer *m;* **—ous** ['zeləs]
a eifrig.

zebra ['zi:brə] *n* Zebra *nt;* **— crossing** ['zi:brə'krɒsɪŋ] Zebrastreifen *m.*

zenith ['zenɪθ] *n* Zenit *m.*

zero ['zɪərəʊ] *n* Null *f;* (*on scale*)
Nullpunkt *m;* **— hour** die Stunde
X.

zest [zest] *n* Begeisterung *f.*

zigzag ['zɪgzæg] *n* Zickzack *m; vi*
im Zickzack laufen/fahren.

zinc [zɪŋk] n Zink nt.

Zionism ['zaɪənɪzəm] n Zionismus m.

zip [zɪp] n (also — fastener, —per) Reißverschluß m; vt (also — up) den Reißverschluß zumachen (+gen)

zither ['zɪðə*] n Zither f.

zodiac ['zəʊdɪæk] n Tierkreis m.

zombie ['zɒmbɪ] n Trantüte f.

zone [zəʊn] n Zone f; (area) Gebiet nt.

zoo [zu:] n Zoo m; —logical [zəʊə'lɒdʒɪkəl] a zoological; —logist [zu:'ɒlədʒɪst] Zoologe m; —logy [zu:'ɒlədʒɪ] Zoologie f.

zoom [zu:m] vi (engine) surren; (plane) aufsteigen; (move fast) brausen; (prices) hochschnellen; — lens Zoomobjektiv nt.

Countries, nationalities and languages

I am German/English/Albanian ich bin Deutscher/Engländer/Albaner

a German/an Englishman/an Albanian ein Deutscher/Engländer/Albaner;
a German (woman/girl)/an English woman/girl/an Albanian (woman/girl) eine Deutsche/Engländerin/Albanerin

do you speak German/English/Albanian? sprechen Sie Deutsch/ Englisch/Albanisch?

the Adriatic die Adria.
the Aegean die Ägäis.
Afghanistan Afghanistan nt; **Afghan** n Afghane m, Afghanin f; a afghanisch.
Africa Afrika nt; **African** n Afrikaner(in f) m; a afrikanisch.
Albania Albanien nt; **Albanian** n Albanier(in f) m; a albanisch.
Algeria Algerien nt; **Algerian** n Algerier(in f) m; a algerisch.
the Alps pl die Alpen pl.
America Amerika nt; **American** n Amerikaner(in f) m; a amerikanisch.
the Andes pl die Anden pl.
Angola Angola nt; **Angolan** n Angolaner(in f) m; a angolanisch.
the Antarctic die Antarktis; **Antarctic** a antarktisch.
Arabia Arabien nt; **Arab, Arabian** n Araber(in f) m; a arabisch.
the Arctic die Arktis; **Arctic** a arktisch.
Argentina, the Argentine Argentinien nt; **Argentinian** n Argentinier(in f) m; a argentinisch.
Asia Asien nt; **Asian** n Asiat(in f) m; a asiatisch.
Asia Minor Kleinasien nt.
Athens Athen nt.
the Atlantic (Ocean) der Atlantik, der Atlantische Ozean.
Australia Australien nt; **Australian** n Australier(in f) m; a australisch.
Austria Österreich nt; **Austrian** n Österreicher(in f) m; a österreichisch.
the Baltic die Ostsee.
Bavaria Bayern nt; **Bavarian** n Bayer(in f) m; a bay(e)risch.

the Bay of Biscay (der Golf von) Biskaya f.

Belgium Belgien nt; Belgian n Belgier(in f) m; a belgisch.

the Black Forest der Schwarzwald.

Bolivia Bolivien nt; Bolivian n Bolivianer(in f) m, Bolivier(in f) m; a boliv(ian)isch.

Brazil Brasilien nt; Brazilian n Brasilianer(in f) m; a brasilianisch.

Britain Großbritannien nt; Briton n Brite m, Britin f; British a britisch.

Brittany die Bretagne; Breton n Bretone m, Bretonin f; a bretonisch.

Brussels Brüssel nt.

Bulgaria Bulgarien nt; Bulgarian, Bulgar n Bulgare m, Bulgarin f; Bulgarian a bulgarisch.

Burma Birma nt; Burmese n Birmane m, Birmanin f; a birmanisch.

California Kalifornien nt; Californian n Kalifornier(in f) m; a kalifornisch.

Cambodia Kambodscha nt; Cambodian n Kambodschaner(in f) m; a kambodschanisch.

Canada Kanada nt; Canadian n Kanadier(in f) m; a kanadisch.

the Canary Islands pl die Kanarischen Inseln pl.

the Caribbean die Karibik; Caribbean a karibisch.

Central America Zentralamerika nt.

the Channel Islands pl die Kanalinseln pl, die Normannischen Inseln pl.

Chile Chile nt; Chilean n Chilene m, Chilenin f; a chilenisch.

China China nt; Chinese n Chinese m, Chinesin f; a chinesisch.

Cologne Köln nt.

Colombia Kolumbien nt; Colombian n Kolumbianer(in f) m, Kolumbier(in f) m; a kolumb(ian)isch.

Lake Constance der Bodensee.

Cornish a von/aus Cornwall.

Corsica Korsika nt; Corsican n Korse m, Korsin f; a korsisch.

Crete Kreta nt; Cretan n Kreter(in f) m; a kretisch.

Cuba Kuba nt; Cuban n Kubaner(in f) m; a kubanisch.

Cyprus Zypern nt; Cypriot n Zypriot(in f) m; a zypriotisch.

Czechoslovakia die Tschechoslowakei; Czech, Czechoslovak(ian) n Tscheche m, Tschechin f; a tschechisch.

Denmark Dänemark nt; Dane n Däne m, Dänin f; Danish a dänisch.

Dutch a see Holland.

East Germany Deutsche Demokratische Republik f; East German n Staatsbürger(in f) m der Deutschen Demokratischen Republik; he is an East German er ist aus der DDR; a der DDR; East German towns Städte (in) der DDR.

Ecuador Ecuador nt; Ecuadorian n Ecuadorianer(in f) m; a ecuadorianisch.

Egypt Ägypten nt; Egyptian n Ägypter(in f) m; a ägyptisch.

Eire ['eərə] (Republik f) Irland nt.

England England nt; Englishman/-woman n Engländer(in f) m; English a englisch.

the English Channel der Ärmelkanal.

Ethiopia Äthiopien nt; Ethiopian n Äthiopier(in f) m; a äthiopisch.

Europe Europa nt; European n Europäer(in f) m; a europäisch.

Fiji (Islands) pl die Fidschiinseln pl; Fijian n Fidschianer(in f) m; a fidschianisch.

Filipino n see the Philippines.

Finland Finnland nt; Finn n Finne m, Finnin f; Finnish a finnisch.

Flanders Flandern nt; Fleming n Flame m, Flämin f; Flemish a flämisch.

754

Florence Florenz *nt*; Florentine *n* Florentiner(in *f*) *m*; a florentinisch.
France Frankreich *nt*; Frenchman/-woman *n* Franzose *m*, Französin *f*; French a französisch.
Geneva Genf *nt*; Lake Geneva der Genfer See.
Germany Deutschland *nt*; German *n* Deutsche(r) *m*, Deutsche *f*; a deutsch.
Ghana Ghana *nt*; Ghanaian *n* Ghanaer(in *f*) *m*; a ghanaisch.
Great Britain Großbritannien *nt*.
Greece Griechenland *nt*; Greek *n* Grieche *m*, Griechin *f*; a griechisch.
the Hague Den Haag.
Haiti Haiti *nt*; Haitian *n* Haitianer(in *f*) *m*, Haitier(in *f*) *m*; a haitianisch, haitisch.
Hawaii Hawaii *nt*; Hawaiian *n* Hawaiier(in *f*) *m*; a hawaiisch.
the Hebrides *pl* die Hebriden *pl*.
the Himalayas *pl* der Himalaja.
Holland Holland *nt*; Dutchman/-woman *n* Holländer(in *f*) *m*; Dutch a holländisch, niederländisch.
Hungary Ungarn *nt*; Hungarian *n* Ungar(in *f*) *m*; a ungarisch.
Iceland Island *nt*; Icelander *n* Isländer(in *f*) *m*; Icelandic a isländisch.
India Indien *nt*; Indian *n* Inder(in *f*) *m*; a indisch.
Indonesia Indonesien *nt*; Indonesian *n* Indonesier(in *f*) *m*; a indonesisch.
Iran (der) Iran; Iranian *n* Iraner(in *f*) *m*; a iranisch.
Iraq (der) Irak; Iraqi *n* Iraker(in *f*) *m*; a irakisch.
Ireland Irland *nt*; Irishman/-woman *n* Ire *m*, Irin *f*; Irish a irisch.
Israel Israel *nt*; Israeli *n* Israeli *mf*; a israelisch.
Italy Italien *nt*; Italian *n* Italiener(in *f*) *m*; a italienisch.
Jamaica Jamaika *nt*; Jamaican *n* Jamaikaner(in *f*) *m*, Jamaiker(in *f*) *m*; a jamaikanisch, jamaikisch.
Japan Japan *nt*; Japanese *n* Japaner(in *f*) *m*; a japanisch.
Jordan (der) Jordan; Jordanian *n* Jordanier(in *f*) *m*; a jordanisch.
Kenya Kenia *nt*; Kenyan *n* Kenianer(in *f*) *m*; a kenianisch.
the Kiel Canal der Nord-Ostsee-Kanal.
Korea Korea *nt*; Korean *n* Koreaner(in *f*) *m*; a koreanisch.
Laos Laos *nt*; Laotian *n* Laote *m*, Laotin *f*; a laotisch.
Lapland Lappland *nt*; Lapp *n* Lappe *m*, Lappin *f*; a lappisch.
Latin America Lateinamerika *nt*.
Lebanon (der) Libanon; Lebanese *n* Libanese *m*, Libanesin *f*; a libanesisch.
Liberia Liberia *nt*; Liberian *n* Liberianer(in *f*) *m*; a liberianisch.
Libya Libyen *nt*; Libyan *n* Libyer(in *f*) *m*; a libysch.
Lisbon Lissabon *nt*.
London London *nt*; Londoner *n* Londoner(in *f*) *m*; London a Londoner *inv*.
Luxembourg Luxemburg *nt*; Luxembourger *n* Luxemburger(in *f*) *m*.
Majorca Mallorca *nt*; Majorcan *n* Bewohner(in *f*) *m* Mallorcas; a mallorkinisch.
Malaysia Malaysia *nt*; Malaysian *n* Malaysier(in *f*) *m*; a malaysisch.
Malta Malta *nt*; Maltese *n* Malteser(in *f*) *m*; a maltesisch.
the Mediterranean (Sea) das Mittelmeer.
Mexico Mexiko *nt*; Mexican *n* Mexikaner(in *f*) *m*; a mexikanisch.
Milan Mailand *nt*; Milanese *n* Mailänder(in *f*) *m*; a mailändisch.
Mongolia die Mongolei; Mongolian *n* Mongole *m*, Mongolin *f*; a mongolisch.
Morocco Marokko *nt*; Moroccan *n* Marokkaner(in *f*) *m*; a marrokkanisch.

Moscow Moskau *nt*; **Muscovite** *n* Moskauer(in *f*) *m*; a moskauisch.

Munich München *nt*.

Naples Neapel *nt*; **Neapolitan** *n* Neapolitaner(in *f*) *m*; a neapolitanisch.

the Netherlands *pl* die Niederlande *pl*.

New Zealand Neuseeland *nt*; **New Zealander** *n* Neuseeländer(in *f*) *m*; **New Zealand** a neuseeländisch.

Nigeria Nigeria *nt*; **Nigerian** *n* Nigerianer(in *f*) *m*; a nigerianisch.

Normandy die Normandie; **Norman** *n* Normanne *m*, Normannin *f*; a normannisch.

Northern Ireland Nordirland *nt*.

the North Sea die Nordsee.

Norway Norwegen *nt*; **Norwegian** *n* Norweger(in *f*) *m*; a norwegisch.

the Pacific (Ocean) der Pazifik, der Pazifische or Stille Ozean.

Pakistan Pakistan *nt*; **Pakistani** *n* Pakistaner(in *f*) *m*; a pakistanisch.

Palestine Palästina *nt*; **Palestinian** *n* Palästinenser(in *f*) *m*; a palästinensisch.

Paraguay Paraguay *nt*; **Paraguayan** *n* Paraguayer(in *f*) *m*; a paraguayisch.

Paris Paris *nt*; **Parisian** *n* Pariser(in *f*) *m*; a Pariser *inv*.

the People's Republic of China die Volksrepublik China.

Persia Persien *nt*; **Persian** *n* Perser(in *f*) *m*; a persisch.

Peru Peru *nt*; **Peruvian** *n* Peruaner(in *f*) *m*; a peruanisch.

the Philippines *pl* die Philippinen *pl*; **Filipino** *n* Philippiner(in *f*) *m*; a, **Philippine** a philippinisch.

Poland Polen *nt*; **Pole** *n* Pole *m*, Polin *f*; a polnisch.

Portugal Portugal *nt*; **Portuguese** *n* Portugiese *m*, Portugiesin *f*; a portugiesisch.

Puerto Rico Puerto Rico *nt*; **Puerto-Rican** *n* Puertoricaner(in *f*) *m*; a puertoricanisch.

the Pyrenees *pl* die Pyrenäen *pl*; **Pyrenean** a pyrenäisch.

the Red Sea das Rote Meer.

Rhodes Rhodos *nt*.

Rhodesia Rhodesien *nt*; **Rhodesian** *n* Rhodesier(in *f*) *m*; a rhodesisch.

Rome Rom *nt*; **Roman** *n* Römer(in *f*) *m*; a römisch.

Ro(u)mania Rumänien *nt*; **Ro(u)manian** *n* Rumäne *m*, Rumänin *f*; a rumänisch.

Russia Rußland *nt*; **Russian** *n* Russe *m*, Russin *f*; a russisch.

the Sahara die Sahara.

Sardinia Sardinien *nt*; **Sardinian** *n* Sarde *m*, Sardin *f*; a sardisch.

Saudi Arabia Saudi-Arabien *nt*; **Saudi (Arabian)** *n* Saudiaraber(in *f*) *m*; a saudiarabisch.

Scandinavia Skandinavien *nt*; **Scandinavian** *n* Skandinave *m*, Skandinavin *f*; a skandinavisch.

Scotland Schottland *nt*; **Scot, Scotsman/-woman** *n* Schotte *m*, Schottin *f*; **Scottish, Scots, Scotch** a schottisch.

Siberia Sibirien *nt*; **Siberian** *n* Sibirier(in *f*) *m*; a sibirisch.

Sicily Sizilien *nt*; **Sicilian** *n* Sizilianer(in *f*) *m*, Sizilier(in *f*) *m*; a sizilianisch, sizilisch.

South Africa Südafrika *nt*; **South African** *n* Südafrikaner(in *f*) *m*; a südafrikanisch.

the Soviet Union die Sowjetunion.

Spain Spanien *nt*; **Spaniard** *n* Spanier(in *f*) *m*; **Spanish** a spanisch.

Sri Lanka Sri Lanka *nt*; **Sri Lankan** *n* Ceylonese *m*, Ceylonesin *f*; a ceylonesisch.

the Sudan der Sudan; **Sudanese** *n* Sudanese *m*, Sudanesin *f*, Sudaner(in *f*) *m*; a sudanesisch.

the Suez Canal der Suez-Kanal.

Sweden Schweden *nt;* **Swede** *n* Schwede *m,* Schwedin *f;* **Swedish** *a* schwedisch.
Switzerland die Schweiz; **Swiss** *n* Schweizer(in *f*) *m;* *a* Schweizer *inv,* schweizerisch.
Syria Syrien *nt;* **Syrian** *n* Syrer(in *f*) *m,* Syrier(in *f*) *m;* *a* syrisch.
Tahiti Tahiti *nt;* **Tahitian** *n* Tahitianer(in *f*) *m;* *a* tahitianisch.
Taiwan Taiwan *nt;* **Taiwanese** *n* Taiwanese(r) *m,* Taiwanesin *f;* *a* taiwanesisch.
Tanzania Tansania *nt;* **Tanzanian** *n* Tansanier(in *f*) *m;* *a* tansanisch.
Tenerife Teneriffa *nt.*
Thailand Thailand *nt;* **Thai** *n* Thailänder(in *f*) *m;* *a* thailändisch.
the Thames die Themse.
the Tyrol Tirol *nt;* **Tyrolean** *n* Tiroler(in *f*) *m;* *a* Tiroler *inv.*
Tunisia Tunesien *nt;* **Tunisian** *n* Tunesier(in *f*) *m;* *a* tunesisch.
Turkey die Türkei; **Turk** *n* Türke *m,* Türkin *f;* **Turkish** *a* türkisch.
Uganda Uganda *nt;* **Ugandan** *n* Ugander(in *f*) *m;* *a* ugandisch.
the United Kingdom das Vereinigte Königreich.
the United States *pl* (of America) die Vereinigten Staaten *pl* (von Amerika).
Uruguay Uruguay *nt;* **Uruguayan** *n* Uruguayer(in *f*) *m;* *a* uruguayisch.
Venezuela Venezuela *nt;* **Venezuelan** *n* Venezolaner(in *f*) *m;* *a* venezolanisch.
Venice Venedig *nt;* **Venetian** *n* Venezianer(in *f*) *m;* *a* venezianisch.
Vienna Wien *nt;* **Viennese** *n* Wiener(in *f*) *m;* *a* wienerisch, Wiener *inv.*
Vietnam Vietnam *nt;* **Vietnamese** *n* Vietnamese(r) *m,* Vietnamesin *f;* *a* vietnamesisch.
Wales Wales *nt;* **Welshman/-woman** *n* Waliser(in *f*) *m;* **Welsh** *a* walisisch.
Warsaw Warschau *nt.*
West Germany die Bundesrepublik (Deutschland); **West German** *n* Bundesdeutsche(r) *m,* Bundesdeutsche *f;* *a* Bundes-, der Bundesrepublik.
the West Indies *pl* Westindien *nt;* **West Indian** *n* Westinder(in *f*) *m;* *a* westindisch.
the Yemen (der) Jemen; **Yemeni, Yemenite** *n* Jemenit(in *f*) *m;* *a* jemenitisch.
Yugoslavia Jugoslawien *nt;* **Yugoslav(ian)** *n* Jugoslawe *m,* Jugoslawin *f;* *a* jugoslawisch.
Zaire Zaire *nt.*
Zambia Sambia *nt;* **Zambian** *n* Sambier(in *f*) *m;* *a* sambisch.

English abbreviations

AD	after (the birth of) Christ *Anno Domini, nach Christi, A.D., n. Chr.*	
AGM	annual general meeting *Jahresvollversammlung*	
am	before midday (ante meridiem) *vormittags, vorm.;* 1.00am. *1.00 Uhr*	
arr	arrival, arrives *Ankunft, Ank.*	
asst	assistant *Assistent, Mitarbeiter*	
Ave	avenue *Straße, Str.*	
BA	Bachelor of Arts *Bakkalaureus der Philosophischen Fakultät*	
B and B	bed and breakfast *Zimmer mit Frühstück,* in catalogue: *Zi. m Fr.,* as sign: *Fremdenzimmer*	
BAOR	British Army of the Rhine *(britische) Rheinarmee*	
BC	before (the birth of) Christ *vor Christi Geburt, v. Chr.*	
BO	body odour *Körpergeruch*	

Bros	[brɔs] brothers *Gebrüder, Gebr.*
BSc	Bachelor of Science *Bakkalaureus der Naturwissenschaftlichen Fakultät*
Cantab	[ˈkæntæb] Cambridge University (Cantabrigiensis) *Cambridge*
CBI	Confederation of British Industry *Bundesverband der britischen Industrie*
cc	cubic centimetres *Kubikzentimeter, ccm.*
CD	Diplomatic Corps (French: Corps Diplomatique) *Diplomatisches Corps, CD*
CIA	Central Intelligence Agency *CIA*
CID	Criminal Investigation Department *Kriminalpolizei*
cif	cost insurance and freight *Kosten, Versicherung und Fracht einbegriffen*
C-in-C	Commander-in-Chief *Oberkommandierender*
cm	centimetre(s) *Zentimeter, cm*
c/o	care of *bei, c/o*
COD	cash on delivery *gegen Nachnahme*
C of E	Church of England *anglikanische Kirche*
cwt	hundredweight ≈ *Zentner, ztr.*
DA	(US) District Attorney *Bezirksstaatsanwalt*
dep	depart(s) *Abfahrt, Abf.*
dept	department *Abteilung, Abt.*
DJ	dinner jacket *Smoking*; disc jockey *Diskjockey*
ed	edited by *herausgegeben, hrsg.*; editor *Herausgeber, Hrsg.*
EEC	European Economic Community *Europäische Wirtschaftsgemeinschaft, EWG*
eg	for example (exempli gratia) *zum Beispiel, z.B.*
ESP	extrasensory perception *übersinnliche Wahrnehmung*
ETA	estimated time of arrival *voraussichtliche Ankunft*
etc	etcetera, and so on *und so weiter, usw., etc.*
FBI	Federal Bureau of Investigation *FBI*
fig	figure, illustration *Abbildung, Abb.*
fob	free on board *frei Schiff*
gbh	grievous bodily harm *schwere Körperverletzung*
GI	(government issue) private in the American Army *amerikanischer Soldat, GI*
govt	government *Regierung*
GP	General Practitioner *praktischer Arzt*
GPO	General Post Office *Britische Post; Hauptpostamt*
HM	His/Her Majesty *Seine/Ihre Majestät*
HMS	His/Her Majesty's Ship *Schiff der Königlichen Marine*
hp	(Brit) hire purchase *Abzahlungskauf*; horsepower *Pferdestärke, PS*
HQ	headquarters *Hauptquartier*
hr(s)	hour(s) *Stunde(n), Std.*
HRH	His/Her Royal Highness *Seine/Ihre Hoheit*
ID	identification *Ausweis*

i.e.	that is (id est) *das heißt, d.h.*
IOU	I owe you *Schuldschein*
JP	Justice of the Peace *Friedensrichter*
km	kilometre(s) *Kilometer, km*
kph	kilometres per hour *Stundenkilometer, km/h*
LA	Los Angeles
lb	pound (weight) *Pfund, Pfd.*
LP	long-playing (record), long-player *Langspielplatte, LP*
Ltd	limited (in names of businesses) *Gesellschaft mit beschränkter Haftung, GmbH*
MA	Master of Arts *Magister Artium, M.A.*
max	maximum *maximal, max*
MI5	department of British Intelligence Service (originally Military Intelligence) *Britischer Geheimdienst*
min	minimum *minimal*
MIT	Massachusetts Institute of Technology
mm	millimetre(s) *Millimeter, mm*
mod cons	[mɔdˈkɔnz] modern conveniences (cooker, lights, *etc*) *mit allem Komfort*
MOT	Ministry of Transport (used for the roadworthiness test of motor vehicles) *Technischer Überwachungsverein, TÜV*
MP	Member of Parliament *Abgeordneter*; military policeman *Militärpolizist, MP*
mpg	miles per gallon *Meilen pro Gallone, Benzinverbrauch*
mph	miles per hour *Meilen pro Stunde*
Mr	[mɪstə] Mister *Herr*
Mrs	[mɪsɪz] Mistress *Frau*
Ms	[maz] *Frau*
NAAFI	[næfɪ] (*Brit*) Navy, Army and Air Force Institutes (canteen services) *Kantine*
NATO	[neɪtəʊ] North Atlantic Treaty Organization *Nordatlantikpakt, NATO*
NB	note well (nota bene) *notabene, NB*
NCO	non-commissioned officer *Unteroffizier, Uffz.*
no(s)	number(s) *Nummer(n), Nr.*
o.n.o.	or nearest offer *oder höchstes Angebot*
Oxon	[ɔksɔn] Oxford University (Oxonia) *Oxford*
oz	ounce(s) (onza) *Unze*
p	page *Seite, S.*; (new) pence *Pence, p*
PA	public address (system) *Lautsprecheranlage*
pa	per year (per annum) *pro Jahr, jährlich, jhrl.*
PC	police constable *Polizeibeamter*; Privy Councillor *Mitglied des Geheimen Staatsrats*
PhD	Doctor of Philosophy *Doktor der Philosophie, Dr. phil.*
PM	Prime Minister *Premierminister*
pm	afternoon (post meridiem) *nachmittags, nachm.*; 10.00pm *22.00 Uhr*

pop	population *Einwohner, Einw.*
POW	prisoner of war *Kriegsgefangener*
pp	pages *Seiten, ff.,* pro persona, for *im Auftrag, i.A.*
PRO	public relations officer *PR-Chef*
PS	postscript *Nachschrift, PS*
pto	please turn over *bitte wenden, b.w.*
QC	Queen's Counsel *Anwalt der königlichen Anwaltskammer*
RADA	Royal Academy of Dramatic Art
RAF	Royal Air Force *britische Luftwaffe*
Rd	road *Straße, Str.*
Rev	Reverend *Herr Pfarrer*
RIP	rest in peace (requiescat in pace) *ruhe in Frieden, R.I.P.*
RSVP	please reply (written on invitations, French: répondez s'il vous plait) *um Antwort wird gebeten, u.A.w.g.*
Rt Hon	Right Honourable *Anrede für Grafen etc, Abgeordnete und Minister*
s.a.e.	stamped addressed envelope *vorfrankierter Umschlag*
SOS	(save our souls) *SOS*
Sq	square (in town) *Platz, Pl.*
ss	steamship *Dampfer*
St	saint *Sankt, St.;* street *Straße, Str.*
st	stone (weight) *6,35 kg*
STD	subscriber trunk dialling *Selbstwählfernverkehr*
TB	tuberculosis *Tuberkulose, TB*
Tel	telephone *Telefon, Tel.*
TUC	Trades Union Congress *Gewerkschaftsbund*
UFO	['ju:fəu] unidentified flying object *unbekanntes Flugobjekt, Ufo*
UK	United Kingdom *Vereinigtes Königreich*
UN	United Nations *Vereinte Nationen*
USA	United States of America *Vereinigte Staaten von Amerika, USA;* United States Army *Amerikanische Armee*
USAF	United States Air Force *Amerikanische Luftwaffe*
USN	United States Navy *Amerikanische Marine*
USSR	Union of Soviet Socialist Republics *Sowjetunion, UdSSR*
VAT	[also væt] value added tax *Mehrwertsteuer, Mehrw.St.*
VD	venereal disease *Geschlechtskrankheit*
VHF	very high frequency *Ultrakurzwelle, UKW*
VIP	very important person *wichtige Persönlichkeit, VIP*
viz	[vɪz] namely (videlicet) *nämlich*
VSO	voluntary service overseas *Entwicklungshilfe*
WASP	(US) White Anglo-Saxon Protestant
WC	water closet *Toilette, WC*
ZIP	[zɪp] (US) Zone Improvement Plan (postal code) *Postleitzahl, PLZ*

English irregular verbs

present	pt	ptp	present	pt	ptp
arise (arising)	arose	arisen	cut (cutting)	cut	cut
awake (awaking)	awoke	awaked	deal	dealt	dealt
			dig (digging)	dug	dug
be (am, is, are; being)	was, were	been	do (3rd person: he/she/it/does)	did	done
bear	bore	born(e)	draw	drew	drawn
beat	beat	beaten	dream	dreamed (also dreamt)	dreamed (also dreamt)
become (becoming)	became	become			
befall	befell	befallen	drink	drank	drunk
begin (beginning)	began	begun	drive (driving)	drove	driven
behold	beheld	beheld	dwell	dwelt	dwelt
bend	bent	bent	eat	ate	eaten
beseech	besought	besought	fall	fell	fallen
beset (besetting)	beset	beset	feed	fed	fed
			feel	felt	felt
bet (betting)	bet (also betted)	bet (also betted)	fight	fought	fought
			find	found	found
bid (bidding)	bid	bid	flee	fled	fled
bind	bound	bound	fling	flung	flung
bite (biting)	bit	bitten	fly (flies)	flew	flown
bleed	bled	bled	forbid (forbidding)	forbade	forbidden
blow	blew	blown	forecast	forecast	forecast
break	broke	broken	forego	forewent	foregone
breed	bred	bred	foresee	foresaw	foreseen
bring	brought	brought	foretell	foretold	foretold
build	built	built	forget (forgetting)	forgot	forgotten
burn	burnt or burned	burnt (also burned)	forgive (forgiving)	forgave	forgiven
burst	burst	burst	forsake (forsaking)	forsook	forsaken
buy	bought	bought			
can	could	(been able)	freeze (freezing)	froze	frozen
cast	cast	cast	get (getting)	got	got, (US) gotten
catch	caught	caught			
choose (choosing)	chose	chosen	give (giving)	gave	given
cling	clung	clung	go (goes)	went	gone
come (coming)	came	come	grind	ground	ground
cost	cost	cost	grow	grew	grown
creep	crept	crept	hang	hung (also hanged)	hung (also hanged)

present	pt	ptp	present	pt	ptp
have (has; having)	had	had	seek	sought	sought
hear	heard	heard	sell	sold	sold
hide (hiding)	hid	hidden	send	sent	sent
hit (hitting)	hit	hit	set (setting)	set	set
hold	held	held	shake (shaking)	shook	shaken
hurt	hurt	hurt	shall	should	——
keep	kept	kept	shear	sheared	shorn (also sheared)
kneel	knelt (also kneeled)	knelt (also kneeled)	shed (shedding)	shed	shed
know	knew	known	shine (shining)	shone	shone
lay	laid	laid	shoot	shot	shot
lead	led	led	show	showed	shown
lean	leant (also leaned)	leant (also leaned)	shrink	shrank	shrunk
leap	leapt (also leaped)	leapt (also leaped)	shut (shutting)	shut	shut
learn	learnt (also learned)	learnt (also learned)	sing	sang	sung
			sink	sank	sunk
leave (leaving)	left	left	sit (sitting)	sat	sat
lend	lent	lent	slay	slew	slain
let (letting)	let	let	sleep	slept	slept
lie (lying)	lay	lain	slide (sliding)	slid	slid
light	lit (also lighted)	lit (also lighted)	sling	slung	slung
lose (losing)	lost	lost	slit (slitting)	slit	slit
make (making)	made	made	smell	smelt (also smelled)	smelt (also smelled)
may	might	——	sow	sowed	sown (also sowed)
mean	meant	meant	speak	spoke	spoken
meet	met	met	speed	sped (also speeded)	sped (also speeded)
mistake (mistaking)	mistook	mistaken	spell	spelt (also spelled)	spelt (also spelled)
mow	mowed	mown (also mowed)	spend	spent	spent
must	(had to)	(had to)	spill	spilt (also spilled)	spilt (also spilled)
pay	paid	paid	spin (spinning)	spun	spun
put (putting)	put	put	spit (spitting)	spat	spat
quit (quitting)	quit (also quitted)	quit (also quitted)	split (splitting)	split	split
read	read	read	spoil	spoiled (also spoilt)	spoiled (also spoilt)
rend	rent	rent	spread	spread	spread
rid (ridding)	rid	rid	spring	sprang	sprung
ride (riding)	rode	ridden	stand	stood	stood
ring	rang	rung	steal	stole	stolen
rise (rising)	rose	risen	stick	stuck	stuck
run (running)	ran	run			
saw	sawed	sawn			
say	said	said			
see	saw	seen			

present	pt	ptp	present	pt	ptp
sting	stung	stung	throw	threw	thrown
stink	stank	stunk	thrust	thrust	thrust
stride (striding)	strode	strode	tread	trod	trodden
strike (striking)	struck	struck (also stricken)	wake (waking)	woke (also waked)	woken (also waked)
strive (striving)	strove	striven	waylay	waylaid	waylaid
swear	swore	sworn	wear	wore	worn
sweep	swept	swept	weave (weaving)	wove (also weaved)	woven (also weaved)
swell	swelled	swollen (also swelled)	wed (wedding)	wedded (also wed)	wedded (also wed)
swim (swimming)	swam	swum	weep	wept	wept
swing	swung	swung	win (winning)	won	won
take (taking)	took	taken	wind	wound	wound
teach	taught	taught	withdraw	withdrew	withdrawn
tear	tore	torn	withhold	withheld	withheld
tell	told	told	withstand	withstood	withstood
think	thought	thought	wring	wrung	wrung
			write (writing)	wrote	written